The Law
of
South Africa

Second Edition
Volume 9

The Law
of
South Africa

WA JOUBERT

SC MA LLB LLD LLD(hc)

FOUNDING EDITOR

JA FARIS

BA LLB LLM LLD

Attorney of the High Court of South Africa
Professor of Law, University of South Africa

PLANNING EDITOR

Editorial panel to this volume

The Hon LTC HARMS

BA LLB

Judge of the Supreme Court of Appeal of South Africa

JA FARIS

BA LLB LLM LLD

Attorney of the High Court of South Africa
Professor of Law, University of South Africa

Second Edition

Volume 9

LexisNexis Butterworths
Durban
2005

Members of the LexisNexis Group worldwide

South Africa	LexisNexis Butterworths **DURBAN** 215 North Ridge Road, Morningside, 4001 **JOHANNESBURG** Grayston 66, 2 Norwich Close, Sandton, 2196 **CAPE TOWN** Ground Floor, Waterford House, 2 Ring Road, Century City, 7441 **www.lexisnexis.co.za**
Argentina	LexisNexis Argentina, BUENOS AIRES
Australia	LexisNexis, CHATSWOOD, New South Wales
Austria	LexisNexis Verlag ARD Orac GmbH & Co KG, VIENNA
Canada	LexisNexis Butterworths, MARKHAM, Ontario
Chile	LexisNexis ChileLtda, SANTIAGO DE CHILE
Czech Republic	Nakladatelství Orac sro, PRAGUE
France	Editions du Juris-Classeur SA, PARIS
Hong Kong	LexisNexis Butterworths, HONG KONG
Hungary	HVG-Orac, BUDAPEST
India	LexisNexis Butterworths, NEW DELHI
Ireland	Butterworths (Ireland) Ltd, DUBLIN
Italy	Giuffrè Editore, MILAN
Malaysia	Malayan Law Journal Sdn Bhd, KUALA LUMPUR
New Zealand	LexisNexis Butterworths, WELLINGTON
Poland	Wydawnictwo Prawnicze LexisNexis, WARSAW
Singapore	LexisNexis Butterworths, SINGAPORE
Switzerland	Stämpfli Verlag AG, BERNE
United Kingdom	LexisNexis Butterworths Tolley, LONDON, WC2A
USA	LexisNexis, DAYTON, Ohio

© 2005

Reissue Volume 1996
ISSN 0 409 00448 0
ISBN 0 409 022 527

Managing Editor
MANDY KÜHNE
BA LLB LLM(Cantab)

Junior Editor
AGNIEZSKA STARZAK
BA(Hons)

Bibliographer
SARAH PUGSLEY
BCom LLB MPhil(Cantab)

Indexer
PAULA LOYNES
BA BBibl

Printed and bound by Interpak Books Pietermaritzburg

CONTRIBUTORS

The following authors have contributed the titles in this volume:

EMOTIONAL SHOCK | JM POTGIETER BIur LLB LLM
Professor of Law, University of South Africa

Updated by | L STEYNBERG BIur LLB LLM
Associate Professor, University of South Africa

ENERGY | R STEIN BA LLB LLM (London)
Visiting Professor of Law, Mandela Institute,
University of the Witwatersrand

KB OMIDIRE LLB LLM LLM MBA (Nigeria)

Assisted by | G ANKIAH BA(Hons) LLB LLM
Attorney of the High Court

ENRICHMENT | JG LOTZ BA LLB
Advocate of the High Court
Professor of Law, University of South Africa

Updated by | FDJ BRAND SC BA LLB LLM
Judge of the Supreme Court of Appeal

ENVIRONMENTAL
CONSERVATION | MA KIDD BCom LLB LLM PhD
Professor of Law, University of KwaZulu-Natal

Original text by | MA RABIE BA LLB LLD
Advocate of the High Court
Professor of Law, University of Stellenbosch

ESTATE AGENTS | JEANNIE VAN WYK BBibil LLB LLM LLD
Professor of Law, University of South Africa

Original text by | C SMITH BA LLB
Attorney of the High Court
Professor of Law, University of South Africa

ESTOPPEL | PJ RABIE SC MA PhD LLB

v

Former Judge of the Appellate Division of the Supreme Court

Updated by   H DANIELS SC BA LLB
Judge of the High Court

EVIDENCE   CWH SCHMIDT BA LLB LLD
Advocate of the High Court
Professor of Law, University of South Africa

DT ZEFFERTT BA LLB
Advocate of the High Court
Professor of Law, University of the Witwatersrand

Updated by   DP VAN DER MERWE BIur LLB LLD
Advocate of the High Court
Professor of Law, University of South Africa

The law stated in this volume is in general that in force on 31 January 2005

TABLE OF CONTENTS

EMOTIONAL SHOCK

by

JM POTGIETER

(*updated by L STEYNBERG*)

REFERENCES TO OTHER TITLES

SELECTED LITERATURE

Burchell "An Encouraging Prognosis for Claims for Damages for Negligently Inflicted Psychological Harm" 1999 *SALJ* 697

Burchell *Principles of Delict* 1994

McQuoid-Mason "Emotional Shock: Shades of Descartes?" 1975 *SALJ* 18

Neethling "Deliktuele Aanspreeklikheid Weens die Veroorsaking van Psigiese Letsels" 2000 *TSAR* 1

Neethling "Gedingsvatbaarheid van Senuskok Weens die Verneem van 'n Kind se Dood" 1998 *THRHR* 335

Neethling *Persoonlikheidsreg* 1998

Neethling and Potgieter "Bester v Commercial Union Versekeringsmpy van SA Bpk 1973 1 SA 769 (A)" 1973 *THRHR* 175

Neethling and Potgieter "Emosionele Skok, Juridiese Kousaliteit en Bydraeende Nalatigheid" 1997 *THRHR* 548

Neethling, Potgieter and Visser *Law of Delict* 2001

Potgieter "Delictual Liability for Intentional Infliction of Emotional Distress in SA Law?" 1976 *Codicillus* 11

Tager "Nervous Shock and Mental Illness" 1973 *SALJ* 123

Van der Vyver "Bester v Commercial Union Versekeringsmpy van SA Bpk 1973 1 SA 769 (A)" 1973 *THRHR* 169

Van der Walt and Midgley *Delict: Principles and Cases vol 1* 1997

INTRODUCTION[1]

1 Liability in delict An action in delict[2] may lie for patrimonial loss or sentimental damage caused by intentional[3] or negligent infliction of emotional shock.[4] An action for loss of support can also be instituted by the dependants of a breadwinner who died due to the infliction of severe shock.[5]

1 *Historical note* In stating the law with regard to emotional shock, frequent reference has been made to English decisions in this field. This was done because of the scantiness of Roman-Dutch authority with regard to emotional shock, the relatively few South African cases in this area and especially because of the extensive references made by South African courts to English cases. (See par 4 fns 11 and 12 post). It is not suggested that these English cases should be regarded as authoritative for South African law; they are quoted to serve as historical background and to provide illuminating factual examples.

2 *Actio legis Aquiliae, actio iniuriarum* and action for pain and suffering – see par 13 post.

3 In criminal law, intentional infliction of emotional shock as such is not regarded as an offence. However, conduct which causes emotional shock may conceivably constitute the offences of *crimen injuria*; cf *S v M* 1979 2 SA 25 (A) 27C–D. See title CRIMINAL LAW.

4 For the distinction between intentional and negligent infliction of emotional shock, see par 9 post.

5 *Masiba v Constantia Insurance Co Ltd* 1982 4 SA 333 (C) 343G–344A; Van der Walt 1983 *THRHR* 436 450.

2 Definition Emotional shock can be described as sudden, painful emotion or fright resulting from the realisation or perception of an unwelcome or disturbing event which involves an unpleasant mental condition such as fear, anxiety or grief.[1] The term "emotional shock" can, however, sometimes be confusing, since transient shock does not attract damages; it is rather the mental (psychological) and physical consequences which flow from it which may be compensable.[2] In *Barnard v Santam Bpk*,[3] Van Heerden DCJ opined that the term "senuskok" ("nervous shock") is not only an obsolete term without any specific psychiatric meaning, but it may also be misleading. The only relevant question should be whether the plaintiff sustained a recognisable psychological lesion ("psigiese letsel"). The existence of such a lesion should, as a rule, be proved by supporting psychiatric evidence.[4]

1 In *Jaensch v Coffey* (1984) 155 CLR 549 567 shock was defined as: "the sudden sensory perception – that is, by seeing, hearing or touching – of a person, thing or event, which is so distressing that the perception of the phenomenon affronts or insults the plaintiff's mind and causes a recognisable psychiatric illness." According to Mullany and Handford *Tort Liability for Psychiatric Damage* 26 mental distress usually consists of the following unpleasant emotions: fear of apprehension; horror; grief, sorrow and loneliness; shame, humiliation and embarrassment; anger, annoyance and vexation; disappointment and frustration; worry and anxiety.

2 According to Mullany and Handford 15 modern cases rest on the principle that the plaintiff must suffer legally recognised harm

– some recognisable psychiatric injury or illness resulting from the infliction of traumatic shock – rather than mere mental or emotional distress or suffering such as grief, sorrow, distress, worry, anxiety, disappointment, anger, outrage and the like. The genesis of contemporary thought can be traced to the leading expression by Lord Denning MR in *Hinz v Berry* [1970] 2 QB 40 42–43: "In English law no damages are rewarded for grief and sorrow caused by a person's death. No damages are to be given for the worry about the children, or for the financial strain or stress, or the difficulties of adjusting to a new life. Damages are however recoverable for nervous shock, or, to put it in medical terms, for any recognisable psychiatric illness caused by the breach of duty by the defendant." See in general

Neethling *Persoonlikheidsreg* 112–115.

3 [1999] 4 All SA 403 (SCA); 1999 1 SA 202 (SCA) 208J–209A. See also Burchell 1999

SALJ 697 697–698; Neethling, Potgieter and Visser *Law of Delict* 290–291.

4 *Barnard v Santam Bpk* supra 216E–F.

3 Causes and effects Emotional shock may, *inter alia*,[1] be caused by the prejudiced person's fear for his or her own safety[2] or the safety of another person,[3] or for the safety of his or her own property,[4] by observing a gruesome or disturbing accident,[5] or by learning of the death of a relative or loved one[6] or of other disturbing events.[7]

Emotional shock is usually of a trivial nature and relatively short duration with no significant detrimental effect on the plaintiff's physical or mental well-being.[8] On the other hand, it can cause more serious adverse physical or mental conditions.[9] It is only in the lastmentioned instances that a prejudiced person can claim damages in respect of emotional shock.[10]

1 The list of causes furnished here includes only those causes already expressly recognised by our courts. It is, however, not a *numerus clausus* and our courts may follow trends in other jurisdictions and recognise further causes. Breach of contract (eg breach of promise) is an example of a possible further cause for emotional shock to be recognised by our courts. See *Clinton-Parker v Administrator, Tvl; Dawkins v Administrator, Tvl* 1996 2 SA 37 (W) 39J–40E in which the plaintiffs based their claim on delict, alternatively breach of contract. See further Mullany and Handford *Tort Liability for Psychiatric Damage* 51–56 and Brooks 1977 *De Rebus* 14 14–16 for more examples.

2 As in *Hauman v Malmesbury Divisional Council* 1916 CPD 216; *Creydt-Ridgeway v Hoppert* 1930 TPD 664; *Victorian Railways Commissioners v James Coultas & Mary Coultas* (1888) 13 AC 222; *Dulieu v White & Sons* [1901] 2 KB 669. See also par 12 post.

3 As in *Bester v Commercial Union Versekeringsmpy van SA Bpk* 1973 1 SA 769 (A) (brother); *Masiba v Constantia Insurance Co Ltd* 1982 4 SA 333 (C) (wife and child); *Sueltz v Bolttler* 1914 EDL 176 and *Els E v Bruce, Els J v Bruce* 1922 EDL 295 (spouse); *Road Accident Fund v Sauls* 2002 2 SA 55 (SCA) (fiancée); *Hambrook v Stokes Bros* [1925] 1 KB 141; *King v Phillips* [1953] 1 QB 429; 1953 1 All ER 617 and *Boardman v Sanderson* 1964 1 WLR 1317 (children); *Dooley v Cammell Laird & Co Ltd* [1951] 1 Lloyd's rep 271 (co-workers).

4 As in *Masiba v Constantia Insurance Co Ltd* supra 343F. See par 11 post.

5 As in *Mulder v South British Insurance Co Ltd* 1957 2 SA 444 (W) (plaintiff seeing her little son's head being crushed by the wheel of a bus); *Lutzkie v SAR & H* 1974 4 SA 396 (W) (plaintiff witnessing death of co-passenger in bus accident); *Oelofsen v Cigna*

Insurance Co of SA Ltd 1991 1 SA 74 (T) (deceased was in a car hitting another car, shooting across the road, hitting a drum on the side of the road and turning through 180°); *Hinz v Berry* [1970] 1 All ER 1074 (CAC) (plaintiff seeing her husband's and children's gruesome mutilation in a car accident); *Mary T R Currie v William Wardrop* 1927 SC 538 and *Road Accident Fund v Sauls* supra (plaintiff's fiancé injured in car accident); *Hay or Bourhill v Young* [1943] AC 92 (plaintiff hearing collision between motorcycle and car and seeing victim's blood on road).

6 As in *Waring & Gillow Ltd v Sherborne* 1904 TS 340 (spouse); *Layton & Layton v Wilcox & Higginson* 1944 SR 48 and *Barnard v Santam Bpk* [1998] 4 All SA 403 (SCA); 1999 1 SA 202 (SCA) (child); *Schneider v Eisovitch, Same v Same* 1960 2 QB 430 (spouse).

7 As in *Els E v Bruce, Els J v Bruce* supra (defendant insulting plaintiff and threatening to harm her husband); *Boswell v Minister of Police* 1978 3 SA 268 (E) (defendant, knowing this information to be false, telling plaintiff that he (the defendant) had shot and killed plaintiff's nephew); *Masiba v Constantia Insurance Co Ltd* supra (the deceased was subjected to a sequence of stress-causing events, being himself assaulted, seeing his wife being hit by a car and witnessing his own car with occupants in it (including his child) being struck by another car, and all of this happening in a matter of minutes); *N v T* 1994 1 SA 862 (C) (plaintiff instituting a claim in her personal capacity and in her capacity as natural guardian of an eight year old child for emotional shock arising out of the rape of the child); *Creydt-Ridgeway v Hoppert* supra (plaintiff attacked by defendant's dog); *Wilkinson v Downton* [1897] 2 QB 57 (defendant, knowing this information to be false, telling plaintiff that her

husband was seriously injured in an accident); *Owens v Liverpool Corporation* [1939] 1 KB 394 (coffin in hearse toppling over as result of collision with tram); *Chadwick v British Railways Board* 1967 1 WLR 912 (observing victims of gruesome train accident); *Majiet v Santam Ltd* [1997] 4 All SA 555 (C) (plaintiff came across the dead body of her son in the street); *Clinton-Parker v Administrator, Tvl*; *Dawkins v Administrator, Tvl* supra (plaintiffs discovered two years later that their babies had been swapped at birth).

8 As in *Layton & Layton v Wilcox & Higginson* supra (plaintiff compelled to lie down and rest on the afternoon after her daughter's burial as a result of shock caused by learning of daughter's death); *Muzik v Canzone Del Mare* 1980 3 SA 470 (C) (plaintiff experienced discomfort after eating poisonous food in a restaurant, but failed to prove any mental or physical harm); and apparently in *Lutzkie v SAR&H* supra (plaintiff sustaining no "permanent consequences" as a result of shock suffered when witnessing death of boy in bus accident; but see McQuoid-Mason 1975 *SALJ* 18 19).

9 "Damage from emotional shock may be, in medical language, 'somatic' or 'psychic' and not infrequently it is a combination of both. These terms mean respectively 'organic' (ie physical) and 'mental' (ie non-physical). Organic sequelae of an emotional shock would include miscarriage, coronary thrombosis and cerebral haemorrhage ('stroke'). Psychic sequelae would include hysteria and various neuroses. It is important to note that psychic damage may give rise to physical symptoms; hence conversion hysteria (purely psychic damage) may give rise to paralysis of one or more limbs, a condition which would clearly rank as a physical illness for legal purposes" (Harvard 1956 *Modern LR* 478 479). See Mullany and Handford 14–42 for a thorough discussion on this matter. Examples of relatively serious physical or mental consequences caused by emotional shock are anxiety neuroses (cf *Bester v Commercial Union Versekeringsmpy van SA Bpk* supra;

Chadwick v British Railways Board supra); miscarriage (cf *Waring & Gillow Ltd v Sherborne* supra; *Sueltz v Bolttler* supra; *Dulieu v White & Sons* supra; *Hay or Bourhill v Young* supra); severe haemorrhage (cf *Hambrook v Stokes Bros* supra); neurodermatitis and depression (cf *Schneider v Eisovitch, Same v Same* supra); amnesia and impaired eyesight (cf *Victorian Railways Commissioners v James Coultas & Mary Coultas* supra); irritability, morbid depression and exhaustion (cf *Hinz v Berry* supra); acute depression (cf *Majiet v Santam Ltd* supra); mixed anxiety depressive disorder (cf *Clinton-Parker v Administrator, Tvl*; *Dawkins v Administrator, Tvl* supra); post-traumatic stress disorder (cf *Road Accident Fund v Sauls* supra); pain (cf *Dulieu v White & Sons* ("bodily pain")); *Waring & Gillow Ltd v Sherborne* ("mental pain"); *Els E v Bruce, Els J v Bruce* supra and *Hauman v Malmesbury Divisional Council* supra ("much pain"); *Layton & Layton v Wilcox & Higginson* supra ("pain, suffering and mental agony"); *Gibson v Berkowitz* [1997] 1 All SA 99 (W); 1996 4 SA 1029 (W) ("severe pain and discomfort")); impaired sleep (cf *Bester v Commercial Union Versekeringsmpy van SA Bpk* supra; *Creydt-Ridgeway v Hoppert* supra; *Chadwick v British Railways Board* supra; *Road Accident Fund v Sauls* supra); constipation (cf *Els E v Bruce, Els J v Bruce*); diarrhoea (cf *Creydt-Ridgeway v Hoppert* supra; *Chadwick v British Railways Board* supra ("his tummy appears to be upset" (917)); trembling (cf *Boswell v Minister of Police* supra; *Chadwick v British Railways Board* supra; *King v Phillips* supra); collapse (cf *Boswell v Minister of Police* supra; *Owens v Liverpool Corp Ltd* supra); high blood-pressure (cf *Boswell v Minister of Police* supra; *Creydt-Ridgeway v Hoppert* supra); piles (cf *Creydt-Ridgeway v Hoppert* supra); devastating emotional trauma (cf *N v T* supra and *Barnard v Santam Bpk* supra); and stroke leading to death (cf *Masiba v Constantia Insurance Co Ltd* supra; *Oelofsen v Cigna Insurance Co of SA Ltd* supra).

10 See Burchell 1999 *SALJ* 617 699 for criticism on this restriction.

4 Historical background In 1904[1] and 1914[2] two delictual claims based on negligent infliction of emotional shock were rejected by South African courts, the reason in both cases being that the damage was "too remote" because the plaintiffs had not feared for their personal safety.[3] The first successful claim was instituted in 1916[4] and others in 1922[5] and 1930.[6] Lack of a "duty of care" led to dismissals of claims on two later occasions.[7] The action based on emotional shock was established firmly in 1973 when in *Bester v Commercial Union Versekeringsmpy van SA Bpk*[8] the Appellate Division, basing its decision solidly on South African common law principles, granted patrimonial and sentimental damages for purely mental injury caused by negligent infliction of emotional shock after the court *a quo* rejected the claim on the ground that purely mental indispositions were not actionable.[9]

Prior to the Appellate Division's decision in 1973 in *Bester v Commercial Union Versekeringsmpy van SA Bpk*, South African law on delictual liability for infliction of emotional shock disclosed a lack of clear guidelines and well-grounded principles. Roman-Dutch authority in this field is scant.[10] Our courts have consistently sought guidance in English law[11] in which the action based on infliction of emotional shock was already firmly established early in this century.[12]

Various policy considerations and other factors have hindered the development of an action on the ground of the infliction of emotional shock to a greater or lesser extent.[13] Among these are the ideas that to allow actions for bodily injury caused by emotional shock places too heavy a burden upon the individual in the community,[14] that mental injuries cannot be measured in terms of money,[15] and are therefore not capable of redress,[16] the possibility that mental injuries may be simulated and the resultant fear of a profusion of illegitimate and fanciful claims.[17] Sometimes mental injuries have been confused with passing emotions such as fright, grief, fear and the like[18] for which recovery has always been refused.[19]

In the light of the appellate court's decision in the *Bester* case[20] it can now be safely stated that none of these factors will constitute a bar to recovery of damages caused by the infliction of emotional shock.

1   *Waring & Gillow Ltd v Sherborne* 1904 TS 340.
2   *Sueltz v Bolttler* 1914 EDL 176.
3   See Van der Merwe and Olivier *Die Onregmatige Daad in die SA Reg* 331; Boberg *Law of Delict vol I: Aquilian Liability* 175.
4   *Hauman v Malmesbury Divisional Council* 1916 CPD 216.
5   *Els E v Bruce, Els J v Bruce* 1922 EDL 295.
6   *Creydt-Ridgeway v Hoppert* 1930 TPD 664.
7   In 1944 in *Layton & Layton v Wilcox & Higginson* 1944 SR 48 and in 1957 in *Mulder v South British Insurance Co Ltd* 1957 2 SA 444 (W).
8   1973 1 SA 769 (A). See also *Lutzkie v SAR & H* 1974 4 SA 396 (W) and *Muzik v Canzone Del Mare* 1980 3 SA 470 (C), where a claim was refused *inter alia* because the plaintiff's injuries had not been serious enough, and *Boswell v Minister of Police* 1978 3 SA 268 (E), where the plaintiff's claim succeeded.
9   *Bester v Commercial Union Versekeringsmpy van SA Bpk* 1972 3 SA 68 (D).
10 In *Waring & Gillow Ltd v Sherborne* supra Innes CJ stated: "There is no authority for holding that the Roman-Dutch law allowed damages to be awarded for mental suffering unaccompanied by physical injury or illness in an action founded on negligence." See also the argument of the plaintiff's counsel in *Bester v Commercial Union Versekeringsmpy van*

SA Bpk 1973 1 SA 769 (A) 770F; McQuoid-Mason 1973 *THRHR* 115 130.
11 See eg *Waring & Gillow Ltd v Sherborne* supra 348 349; *Sueltz v Bolttler* supra 178 180 181; *Hauman v Malmesbury Divisional Council* supra 219; *Els E v Bruce, Els J v Bruce* supra 299; *Creydt-Ridgeway v Hoppert* supra 666; *Layton & Layton v Wilcox & Higginson* supra 50; *Mulder v South British Insurance Co Ltd* supra 445–449; *Bester v Commercial Union Versekeringsmpy van SA Bpk* 1973 1 SA 769 (A) 779 780; *Majiet v Santam Ltd* [1997] 4 All SA 555 (C) 560; *Barnard v Santam Bpk* [1998] 4 All SA 403 (SCA); 1999 1 SA 202 (SCA) 210F–212I; *Road Accident Fund v Sauls* 2002 2 SA 55 (SCA) 63D–H; but see *Bester v Commercial Union Versekeringsmpy van SA Bpk* 1972 3 SA 68 (D) 72A. See in general Boberg 175. In more recent cases reference is also made to Australian, American and Canadian case law (cf *Clinton-Parker v Administrator, Tvl*; *Dawkins v Administrator, Tvl* 1996 2 SA 37 (W) 65E–69A; *Majiet v Santam Ltd* supra 561c–g 567e; *Barnard v Santam Bpk* supra 211B–H).
12 See eg *Wilkinson v Downton* [1897] 2 QB 57; *Dulieu v White & Sons* [1901] 2 KB 669; *Hambrook v Stokes Bros* [1925] 1 KB 141.
13 Mullany and Handford *Tort Liability for Psychiatric Damage* 43–44 identify seven reasons why a claim for damages cannot be

instituted for "mere" mental or emotional distress or suffering: the law is unable to value such injury; problems of proof; remoteness of the damage; danger of false claims succeeding; it is something experienced by any normal person when someone they love is killed or injured; the rule acts as a deterrent to trivial claims; and emotional distress ranks lower down the list than physical harm caused by impact.

14 See *Sueltz v Bolttler* supra 180; *Union Government (Minister of Railways & Harbours) v Warneke* 1911 AD 657 667; *Bester v Commercial Union Versekeringsmpy van SA Bpk* 1972 3 SA 68 (D) 74D–E.

15 Cf *Bester v Commercial Union Versekeringsmpy van SA Bpk* 1972 3 SA 68 (D) 73G.

16 *Bester v Commercial Union Versekeringsmpy van SA Bpk* supra 73D–F. It is stated in *Hauman v Malmesbury Divisional Council* supra 220 that damages caused by infliction of emotional shock can, according to Roman-Dutch law, be recovered only if the shock impaired the plaintiff's "bodily health and strength". In the appeal from the *Bester* case

1973 1 SA 769 (A) 778H), Botha JA held the view that the use of the term "bodily health and strength" in the *Hauman* case is not necessarily a reference to a physical injury alone, but probably includes the plaintiff's mental state too.

17 See *Union Government (Minister of Railways & Harbours) v Warneke* supra 667; *Sueltz v Bolttler* supra 180. However, the retarding influence in this factor on the development of an action based on emotional shock in South African law seems to have been slight.

18 Cf *Bester v Commercial Union Versekeringsmpy van SA Bpk* 1972 3 SA 68 (D) 72. Mere emotional sorrow, sadness or grief (eg as a result of the death of a child) is not considered to be a psychiatric injury (cf *Barnard v Santam Bpk* supra 217). See also Burchell 1999 *SALJ* 697 702.

19 See *Union Government (Minister of Railways & Harbours) v Warneke* supra; *Pauw v African Guarantee & Indemnity Co Ltd* 1950 2 SA 132 (SWA).

20 1973 1 SA 769 (A).

REQUIREMENTS FOR LIABILITY

5 General The general requirements for delictual liability apply in an action based on the infliction of emotional shock.[1] At first our courts imposed a variety of additional requisites for liability. It was required, for example, that any mental disturbance must have originated from a physical injury, or that the emotional shock must have affected the physical constitution.[2] Damages on the ground of emotional shock were, moreover, recoverable only if the injured party had been in personal danger.[3] The Appellate Division's decision in *Bester v Commercial Union Versekeringsmpy van SA Bpk*[4] established that in our law the criterion of liability for injury caused by shock is the reasonable foreseeability of injury by shock. In the light of this decision any further requisites over and above the general requirements for delictual liability are not to be regarded as indispensable conditions for liability on the ground of emotional shock.[5] At most they should be seen as practical criteria to be applied as guidelines in determining whether the harm was reasonably foreseeable.[6] Even though there seems to be consensus in general on the fact that the criterion for liability in emotional shock cases is reasonable foreseeability, there are different points of view on whether this criterion forms part of the element of wrongfulness, negligence or legal causation.[7] For practical reasons reasonable foreseeability will in this text be discussed under legal causation.[8]

The requirements for delictual liability as applied in cases involving emotional shock will be stated in the proceeding paragraphs.

1 Cf *Bester v Commercial Union Versekeringsmpy van SA Bpk* 1973 1 SA 769 (A) 781G–H. See Van der Walt and Midgley *Delict: Principles and Cases vol I* 76. For the general requirements for delictual liability, see title DELICT.

2 See *Hauman v Malmesbury Divisional Council* 1916 CPD 216 220; *Bester v Commercial Union Versekeringsmpy van SA Bpk* 1972 3 SA 68 (D) 73D–F; Neethling, Potgieter and Visser *Law of Delict* 291. See par 11 post.

3 *Waring & Gillow Ltd v Sherborne* 1904 TS

340 349; *Sueltz v Bolttler* 1914 EDL 176 180 181; *Mulder v South British Insurance Co Ltd* 1957 2 SA 444 (W) 449H. See par 12 post.

4 1973 1 SA 769 (A) 777C–E; Boberg *Law of Delict vol I: Aquilian Liability* 176; Neethling, Potgieter and Visser 291–293; Van der Merwe and Olivier *Die Onregmatige Daad in die SA Reg* 330.

5 See Van der Merwe and Olivier 330–331; Boberg 176.

6 *Bester v Commercial Union Versekeringsmpy van SA Bpk* supra 781A–B; *Boswell v Minister of Police* 1978 3 SA 268 (E) 274F–H; Boberg 176 183; Van der Merwe and Olivier 331; *Masiba v Constantia Insurance Co Ltd* 1982 4 SA 333 (C) 343D–E.

7 *Bester v Commercial Union Versekeringsmpy* supra 777C (reasonable foreseeability is the test for liability for negligence). Boberg 178 states that it is a question of negligence, but because of the historical evolution of the subject and the fact that shock may also be caused intentionally, it will be more appropriate to treat it as an aspect of wrongfulness. Boberg (192) also criticises Berman AJ's application (in *Masiba v Constantia Insurance Co Ltd* supra 341–342) of the foreseeability criterion laid down in *Bester v Commercial Union Versekeringsmpy* supra. According to Boberg (in agreement with Burchell 1982 *Annual Survey of SA Law* 176 179) the learned judge erred in not adopting the relative negligence approach, but instead characterising the issue as one of remoteness of damage (causation). See Van der Walt 1983 *THRHR* 436 448 on the uncertainty in English law whether the criterion of the unforseeable plaintiff refers to the "duty to take care" test (negligence) or to "remoteness of damage" (legal causation). Neethling, Potgieter and Visser 292–293 consider reasonable foreseeability to fall within the ambit of either negligence or legal causation. According to Neethling, Potgieter and Visser the question of negligence arises where the shock or psychiatric injury is the only or at least (one of) the first harmful consequence(s) of the wrongdoer's conduct. However, where the emotional shock is a further (subsequent or more remote) consequence of the wrongdoer's already established negligent act, the question of legal causation is at hand. See also Neethling 2000 *TSAR* 1 5–6. In *Barnard v Santam Bpk* [1998] 4 All SA 403 (SCA); 1999 1 SA 202 (SCA) 215 the Supreme Court of Appeal held that even in the case of the reasonable foreseeability of remote psychological lesion one is still concerned with the question of negligence and not legal causation. However, Van Heerden DCJ remarked (at 210) that from a practical point of view, as far as the foreseeability of a psychological lesion is concerned, it does not make any difference whether the one or the other construction is preferred. Van der Walt *Huldigingsbundel vir WA Joubert* 257 states that the *Bester* test of reasonable foreseeability would be of value only if it could be applied as a policy consideration in the determination of wrongfulness. Van der Walt (257–260) gives a thorough and worthwhile explanation of how the flexible criterion of the *boni mores* can function as the principle for the development (or restriction) of delictual liability in cases of emotional shock in future. Midgley 1992 *THRHR* 441 444–445 agrees with this view and refers to Lord Olivier's comments in *Alcock v Chief Constable of the South Yorkshire Police* [1991] 4 All ER 907 (HL) 925g–h in support thereof. Midgley (444) suggests an approach similar to that of the English courts, where cases involving psychiatric injury are treated in the same way as pure economic loss cases, and made the following important statement (445): "There is no need to adhere to rigid categories for determining liability, especially when it makes no difference which element of liability is used. Courts should have flexible criteria at their disposal when attempting to resolve difficult issues and provided that the basic principles do not conflict, there appears to be no harm in choosing which of the two elements, wrongfulness or causation, is the more suitable tool for dealing with a particular issue." See also Van der Walt and Midgley 76 and Visser 1977 *DJ* 37 37–47.

8 See par 12 post.

6 The act For the purposes of infliction of emotional shock, the conditions of an act as an element of a delict are satisfied if the doer by his or her voluntary conduct creates circumstances which cause another to suffer emotional shock. Often the driving of a motor vehicle is the cause of the emotional distress suffered by the victim[1] but other acts may also cause it.[2]

1 See *Sueltz v Bolttler* 1914 EDL 176; *Mulder v South British Insurance Co Ltd* 1957 2 SA 444 (W); *Bester v Commercial Union Versekeringsmpy van SA Bpk* 1973 1 SA 769 (A); *Lutzkie v SAR & H* 1974 4 SA 396 (W); *Masiba v Constantia Insurance Co Ltd* 1982 4 SA 333 (C); *Oelofsen v Cigna Insurance Co of SA Ltd* 1991 1 SA 74 (T); *Majiet v Santam Ltd* [1997] 4 All SA 555 (C); *Barnard v Santam Bpk* [1998] 4 All SA 403 (SCA); 1999 1 SA 202 (SCA); *Road Accident Fund v Sauls* 2002 2 SA 55 (SCA).

2 Cf *Hauman v Malmesbury Divisional Council* 1916 CPD 216 (detonating dynamite); *Els E v Bruce, Els J v Bruce* 1922 EDL 295 (using threatening words); *Creydt-Ridgeway v Hoppert* 1930 TPD 664 (an attack by a dog); *Boswell v Minister of Police* 1978 3 SA 268 (E) (deliberately providing false, distressing information); *M v N* 1981 1 SA 136 (Tk) and *N v T* 1994 1 SA 862 (C) (rape); *Clinton-Parker v Administrator, Tvl; Dawkins v Administrator, Tvl* 1996 2 SA 37 (W) (swapping of babies at birth); *Gibson v Berkowitz* 1996 4 SA 1029 (W) (physical injury during medical procedure). Publication of a defamatory statement may, in an extreme case, lead to the plaintiff suffering emotional shock (see Burchell *Law of Defamation in SA* 306). See par 3 fn 1 ante on the possibility of breach of contract as an act that may cause emotional shock.

7 Factual causation A factual, causal *nexus* must exist between the act, the emotional shock and the harm suffered. Medical or psychiatric evidence may be an important factor in establishing a causal *nexus*, especially between the emotional shock and the harm suffered.[1] However, other evidence may also be used.[2]

1 Cf eg *Bester v Commercial Union Versekeringsmpy van SA Bpk* 1973 1 SA 769 (A) 775H–776D; *Boswell v Minister of Police* 1978 3 SA 268 (E) 271H–272F; *Masiba v Constantia Insurance Co Ltd* 1982 4 SA 333 (C) 340B–341H; *Oelofsen v Cigna Insurance Co of SA Ltd* 1991 1 SA 74 (T) 79B–81I; *N v T* 1994 1 SA 862 (C) 864C–F; *Clinton-Parker v Administrator, Tvl; Dawkins v Administrator, Tvl* 1996 2 SA 37 (W) 41H–42F 46G–51H; *Gibson v Berkowitz* [1997] 1 All SA 99 (W); 1996 4 SA 1029 (W) 1036C–1037H 1043E–1047F; *Majiet v Santam Limited* [1997] 4 All SA 555 (C) 564f–565h.

2 Eg the testimony of the plaintiff (cf *Clinton-Parker v Administrator, Tvl; Dawkins v Administrator, Tvl* supra 42F–46G or the testimony of family or friends of the victim (cf *Bester v Commercial Union Versekeringsmpy van SA Bpk* supra 775H (father); *Boswell v Minister of Police* supra 272D (friend) and *Majiet v Santam Ltd* supra 562g–564c (husband and friend)) or the testimony of lay-witnesses at the scene of an accident (cf *Oelofsen v Cigna Insurance Co of SA Ltd* supra 80I–J and *Majiet v Santam Ltd* supra 562e–g).

8 Wrongfulness The unlawfulness of conduct which induces emotional shock lies in the infringement of the victim's bodily integrity which is an aspect of his or her right to personality.[1]

The causing of even slight physical or mental injury by the infliction of emotional shock should in the absence of grounds of justification be regarded as a wrongful infringement of the victim's personality right to bodily integrity.[2] Liability will, however, only follow where the emotional shock has induced relatively serious physical or mental harm.[3] Non-liability because of the trivial nature of the harm suffered should be explained on the basis of *de minimis non curat lex*.[4]

A person who causes physical or mental injury through infliction of emotional shock should be entitled to the same grounds of justification as one who causes bodily injury by more direct means such as physical impact.[5]

1 Cf *Universiteit van Pretoria v Tommie Meyer Films (Edms) Bpk* 1977 4 SA 376 (T) 383A. Conduct causing emotional shock may also infringe other personality rights such as the right to dignity, as illustrated by the facts of *Els E v Bruce, Els J v Bruce* 1922 EDL 295. The victim's health was impaired as a result of the defendant's threatening and insulting language. Her dignity may also have been infringed by the insults. See also *M v N* 1981 1 SA 136 (Tk) 138D–E and *N v T* 1994 1 SA 862 (C) 864G.

2 Neethling *Persoonlikheidsreg* 32; Midgley 1992 *THRHR* 441 444.

3   *Bester v Commercial Union Versekeringsmpy van SA Bpk* 1973 1 SA 769 (A) 779H; *Muzik v Canzone Del Mare* 1980 3 SA 470 (C) 474D–H; Van der Walt *Huldigingsbundel vir WA Joubert* 249–251; Neethling, Potgieter and Visser *Law of Delict* 291–292; Boberg *Law of Delict vol I: Aquilian Liability* 176; and

see par 11 post.

4   Cf McQuoid-Mason 1973 *THRHR* 115 135, 1975 *SALJ* 18 19; Neethling and Potgieter 1973 *THRHR* 175 179 180; Neethling, Potgieter and Visser 292.

5   For grounds of justification, see title DELICT.

9 Fault The requirements of fault for liability on the grounds of infliction of emotional shock are no different from the fault criterion applicable to delictual liability generally.[1] Damages are recoverable for physical or mental injury arising from emotional shock, whether negligently[2] or intentionally[3] caused.

In most cases of negligent infliction of emotional shock, either negligence was not disputed by the defendant,[4] or the court found it unnecessary to decide upon it.[5] The duty of care doctrine of negligence was applied in three cases.[6] In two of these, in considering whether a duty of care existed, the courts applied the foreseeable plaintiff principle:[7] in *Layton and Layton v Wilcox and Higginson*[8] the court accepted the foreseeable plaintiff theory as formulated by Lord Wright in *Hay or Bourhill v Young*[9] and found that the defendants were possibly negligent towards the plaintiff's husband, but not towards the plaintiff. In *Mulder v South British Insurance Co Ltd*[10] the court found negligence to exist in respect of a child who was killed when a bus ran over him and crushed his head, but no duty of care existed to the child's mother who suffered emotional shock as a result of witnessing the accident.

In view of the fact that reasonable foreseeability and not direct consequences is employed in emotional shock cases as the criterion for legal causation or imputability of harm,[11] it should no longer be necessary to apply the foreseeable plaintiff norm in order to establish negligence.[12] Some writers[13] refer to the test of "relative negligence" in determining liability in emotional shock cases. This is a reference to the fusing of the foreseeability of *some* harm (the negligence issue) and the foreseeability of the general nature of the harm (the remoteness issue) into one test, or in other words, the foreseeability of the general nature of the harm.[14] This view is, however, not generally excepted.[15]

Intentional infliction of emotional shock should be regarded as *iniuria* actionable under the *actio iniuriarum*.[16] Unfortunately the principles of this action have as yet not been applied clearly and unequivocally in this type of case.[17] In *Waring and Gillow Ltd v Sherborne*[18] the court, after rejecting an action on the ground of *negligent* infliction of emotional shock, continued: "It would be different, under certain circumstances, in an *actio injuriam* based upon a wilful attack upon or violation of the feelings of another. In such a case it might be possible to award compensation for the outrage of the feelings or the insult to the honour". *Els E v Bruce, Els J v Bruce*[19] was the first case in South African law which dealt directly with intentional infliction of emotional shock. In this case the court held that the *actio iniuriarum* was the appropriate remedy where the defendant adversely affected the victim's health by addressing her in an insulting and threatening manner. At first sight it appears, however, as if Hutton AJP regarded negligence as an adequate degree of fault for the *actio iniuriarum* (for which intention is traditionally required). The judge stated: "in order to sustain such an action [the *actio iniuriarum*] the law provides that the defendant must either have intended the results which are complained of, or that he might reasonably have contemplated these results following upon his action . . . [T]he defendant could very reasonably have contemplated that the threat made use of by him to this woman . . . might result in her sustaining a shock, and that thereby her health would be seriously affected."[20] It is submitted that this statement should not be interpreted to mean that the court regarded negligence as sufficient to satisfy the requirements for the *actio iniuriarum*. Rather it would seem that the judge confused *dolus eventualis* with negligence. It appears that, having found that the defendant acted intentionally, he attempted to describe *dolus eventualis* as the relevant form of intent. This conclusion is somewhat strengthened by the court's later remark[21] that the principles which it had laid down (that is with regard to fault)[22] were in accordance with those enunciated in the cases cited by plaintiff's counsel. Counsel for the plaintiffs cited *inter alia Janvier v Sweeney*[23] and *Wilkinson v Downton*,[24] two well-known English cases concerning intentional infliction of emotional shock, declaring that they were "directly in point".[25] Therefore it is submitted that *Els E v Bruce, Els J v Bruce* constitutes authority for the viewpoint that interference with bodily integrity through intentional infliction of emotional shock should be regarded as an *iniuria* and actionable under the principles of the *actio iniuriarum*.

The defendant in *Boswell v Minister of Police*[26] clearly acted intentionally. The appropriate action for sentimental damages would thus have been the *actio iniuriarum*. However, as the plaintiff's particulars of claim were not framed to include damages intentionally caused,[27] the court awarded damages on the basis of the negligence actions.[28] It is, therefore, submitted that the principles of the *actio iniuriarum* are broad and flexible enough to accommodate cases of intentional infliction of emotional shock.[29]

Two much more complex and challenging issues regarding fault have not been addressed in our case law, namely the role of voluntary assumption of risk[30] and contributory negligence[31] in emotional shock claims. Judicial references to the assumption of risk doctrine in emotional shock cases are few and far between, though in *Dulieu v White & Sons*,[32] a case reported in 1901, Kennedy J suggested that there could be no question that a person who suffered nervous shock as a result of narrowly escaping being hit by a negligently driven vehicle was *volens* to such risk merely by using the streets.[33] This does not necessarily still hold true today. It is suggested that the general principles regarding voluntary assumption of risk be applied to cases of emotional shock.[34] The complex problem of contributory negligence can surface in two ways, either in cases where the emotional shock suffered by the plaintiff stems from fear for his or her own safety if an accident or near-accident results from the combined negligence of both defendant and plaintiff, or in cases where emotional shock results from an accident to someone else and the question arises whether the secondary victim's claim is affected by contributory negligence on the part of the primary victim.[35] In the firstmentioned cases the position in reported international case law is clear: the plaintiff's claim for emotional shock will be reduced proportionally in accordance to the plaintiff's own negligence.[36] The issue in the secondmentioned cases is, however, more complex and contains some anomalies in international case law.[37] Nonetheless it is submitted that the primary victim's contributory negligence should not reduce the damages of a secondary victim who has suffered resulting emotional shock.[38]

1 See title DELICT.
2 *Hauman v Malmesbury Divisional Council* 1916 CPD 216; *Bester v Commercial Union Versekeringsmpy van SA Bpk* 1973 1 SA 769 (A); *Masiba v Constantia Insurance Co Ltd* 1982 4 SA 333 (C). See Neethling 2000 *TSAR* 1 5.
3 *Waring & Gillow Ltd v Sherborne* 1904 TS 340 348; *Els E v Bruce, Els J v Bruce* 1922 EDL 295 298–299; *Boswell v Minister of Police* 1978 3 SA 268 (E) 273A–B; *M v N* 1981 1

SA 136 (Tk); *N v T* 1994 1 SA 862 (C). According to Parmanand 1984 *SALJ* 171 173 liability for emotional distress was in England at first only recognised when it was inflicted intentionally. Liability for negligent infliction of emotional distress came only later.
4 *Waring & Gillow Ltd v Sherborne supra* 343; *Bester v Commercial Union Versekeringsmpy van SA Bpk* 1972 3 SA 68 (D) (negligence

initially disputed but later acknowledged: 69H 70A); *Bester v Commercial Union Versekeringsmpy van SA Bpk* 1973 1 SA 769 (A) 776F; *Lutzkie v SAR & H* 1974 4 SA 396 (W) 397A; *Masiba v Constantia Insurance Co Ltd* supra 339G–H; *Clinton-Parker v Administrator, Tvl*; *Dawkins v Administrator, Tvl* 1996 2 SA 37 (W) 40D; *Gibson v Berkowitz* [1997] 1 All SA 99 (W); 1996 4 SA 1029 (W) 1032D; Van der Merwe and Olivier *Die Onregmatige Daad in die SA Reg* 245 fn 2 333 fn 6.

5 *Sueltz v Bolttler* 1914 EDL 176 180; *Oelofsen v Cigna Insurance Co of SA Ltd* 1991 1 SA 74 (T) 76B–E.

6 *Hauman v Malmesbury Divisional Council* supra; *Layton & Layton v Wilcox & Higginson* 1944 SR 48; *Mulder v South British Insurance Co Ltd* 1957 2 SA 444 (W).

7 *Layton & Layton v Wilcox & Higginson* supra; *Mulder v South British Insurance Co Ltd* supra. The foreseeable plaintiff principle was devised by the court in *Hay or Bourhill v Young* [1943] AC 92 in order to curb the growing trend towards extending liability in cases of emotional shock. This trend resulted from the application of the duty of care doctrine combined with the direct consequences criterion for legal causation or imputability of harm; cf *Hambrook v Stokes Bros* [1925] 1 KB 141; *Owens v Liverpool Corporation* [1939] 1 KB 394. The foreseeable plaintiff theory made it possible to hold that the defendant was negligent towards one person but not towards another because damage to the former was foreseeable but not towards the latter; cf *Hay or Bourhill v Young* supra 100 102 104 105 110 119. See also *Dooley v Cammell Laird & Co Ltd* 1951 1 Lloyd's Rep 271; *Schneider v Eisovitch, Same v Same* 1960 2 QB 430 441; *Boardman v Sanderson* 1964 1 WLR 1317; *Chadwick v British Railways Board* 1967 1 WLR 912 921; *King v Phillips* [1953] 1 QB 429 436; but see Denning J's judgment (439 440).

8 Supra 50.

9 [1942] 2 All ER 396 404.

10 Supra.

11 See *Bester v Commercial Union Versekeringsmpy van SA Bpk* 1973 1 SA 769 (A) 779H; *Clinton-Parker v Administrator, Tvl*; *Dawkins v Administrator, Tvl* supra 52F–G; *Road Accident Fund v Sauls* 2002 2 SA 55 (SCA) 60.

12 *Bester v Commercial Union Versekeringsmpy van SA Bpk* 1973 1 SA 769 (A) 777C 779H 780H 781A–B 781E–F; *Boswell v Minister of Police* supra 273H 274A–H.

13 Burchell 1982 *Annual Survey of SA Law* 176 179; Boberg *Law of Delict vol I: Aquilian Liability* 192; Burchell 1999 *SALJ* 697 700.

14 See *Road Accident Fund v Sauls* supra 60.

15 See Van der Walt *Huldigingsbundel vir WA Joubert* 253. See also *Gibson v Berkowitz* supra 1051C–1052G on the distinction between negligence and legal causation.

16 Cf Potgieter (1976) 1 *Codicillus* 11; Parmanand 1984 *SALJ* 171 176 states that it is immaterial whether this intention takes the form of *dolus directus*, *dolus indirectus* or *dolus eventualis*; Boberg 187; Burchell *Principles of Delict* 63; Neethling, Potgieter and Visser *Law of Delict* 291 fn 96.

17 In *M v N* supra and *N v T* supra the plaintiffs claimed damages arising out of rape. In both cases it can be accepted that the defendants acted with intent. It is, however, not clear from the judgments whether the claims were based on the Aquilian action, the action for pain and suffering or on the *actio iniuriarum*. The plaintiffs succeeded in their claims in both cases. Parmanand 1984 *SALJ* 171 178 refers to *Alsteen v Gehl* 21 Wis 2d 349 (1963), a valuable decision by the Wisconsin Supreme Court on intentional infliction of emotional distress. In that case (359–360) it was decided that the plaintiff would have to prove that (a) the defendant's conduct was intentional; (b) it would be regarded as extreme and outrageous by the average member of the community; (c) it was a factual cause of the emotional injury; and (d) the plaintiff suffered an extreme disabling emotional response to the defendant's conduct.

18 Supra 348.

19 Supra.

20 *Els E v Bruce, Els J v Bruce* supra 298–299.

21 *Els E v Bruce, Els J v Bruce* supra 299.

22 *Els E v Bruce, Els J v Bruce* supra 298 299.

23 [1919] 2 KB 316.

24 [1897] 2 QB 57.

25 *Els E v Bruce, Els J v Bruce* supra 297.

26 Supra 273H 274G–H 275A.

27 See *Boswell v Minister of Police* supra 275C–D.

28 Supra 275A–F.

29 See in general Boberg 187–188; Parmanand 1984 *SALJ* 171–179.

30 See Burchell 1999 *SALJ* 699 704 709–710.

31 See, however, *Gibson v Berkowitz* supra 1051C–1052F.

32 [1901] 2 KB 669 672.

33 Mullany and Handford *Tort Liability for Psychiatric Damage* 258.

34 For the general principles see Neethling, Potgieter and Visser 97–98 167–171. See also *Bassanese v Martin* (1982) 31 SASR 461; *Rootes v Shelton* (1967) 116 CLR 383; *Bondarenko v Sommers* (1968) 69 SR (NSW) 269.

35 Mullany and Handford 248–256.

36 See *Shotter v R & H Green & Silley Weir Ltd* [1951] 1 Lloyd's Rep 329; *Kwok v British Columbia Ferry Corp* (1987) 20 BCLR (2d) 318; *Regan v Harper* [1971] Qd R 191. In *Gibson v Berkowitz* supra 1051C–1052G it was held that only pre-delictual negligence could lead to a reduction in a claim for damages, while post-delictual negligence bore on legal causation and could be regarded as a *novus actus interveniens* which sufficiently interrupted the chain of causality to absolve the defendant from liability. See Neethling and Potgieter 1997 *THRHR* 548 for a discussion of the *Gibson* case.

37 The general principle in these cases is formulated by Lord Wright in *Hay or Bourhill v Young* supra as follows: "If,

however, the appellant has a cause of action it is because of a wrong to herself. She cannot build on a wrong to someone else. Her interest, which was in her own bodily security, was of a different order from the interest of the owner of the car" (108). However, in two major decisions this general principle was not followed, namely in *Dillon v Legg* (1968) 441 P 2d 912 and in *Alcock v Chief Constable of the South Yorkshire Police* [1992] 1 AC 310, where it was suggested that the contributory negligence of the primary victim should affect a secondary victim's claim.

38 Mullany and Handford 256 agree that *dicta* in leading cases contrary to this statement are influenced by outdated ideas of contributory negligence or unnecessary limits on the scope of psychiatric damage recovery, and cannot stand against the clear trend in negligence law away from the identification of one plaintiff with the want of care of another.

10 Liability without fault Where physical or mental harm arises out of circumstances which have traditionally led to liability without fault, redress will not be denied merely because the harm was caused through the infliction of emotional shock.[1]

1 Thus where a person sustains ill-health as a result of emotional shock suffered when attacked and bitten by a dog, liability will lie regardless of any fault on the part of the dog's owner; see *Creydt-Ridgeway v Hoppert*

1930 TPD 664; Boberg *Law of Delict vol I: Aquilian Liability* 183. With regard to delictual liability for damage caused by animals, see titles ANIMALS; DELICT.

11 Damage

(a) *General* Infliction of emotional shock can cause personality infringement[1] as well as patrimonial loss.[2]

(b) *Physical or mental injury* Compensation is recoverable for patrimonial and sentimental damage caused through the infliction of emotional shock if the emotional shock gave rise to physical or mental harm.[3] In delictual liability no distinction exists between physical and mental injury.[4]

Purely physical injury need not necessarily be present for liability to follow.[5] Compensation may be awarded for mental injury unaccompanied by physical harm.[6]

(c) *Serious injury* No recovery will be permitted for unpleasant emotions of a trivial nature and relatively short duration which have no significant adverse effect on the victim's physical or mental well-being.[7] Compensation will be awarded only for reasonably serious physical or mental injury which has a marked effect on the victim's health.[8]

(d) *Property* In the English decision of *Owens v Liverpool Corporation*[9] it was held that an action based on emotional shock should in principle not be restricted to instances where the shock flowed from a fear for human safety. In this case actions succeeded on the ground of emotional shock suffered when the plaintiffs saw a coffin topple over as a result of a collision between a tram and a hearse. In the South African case of *Masiba v Constantia Insurance Co Ltd*[10] Berman AJ indicated that even fear of damage to one's property may be sufficient to found an action for shock,[11] provided the other requirements of liability are satisfied.[12]

1 Infliction of emotional shock usually infringes the personality right to bodily integrity by inducing physical or mental harm; see par 3 ante.

2 Patrimonial loss usually comprises the expenses incurred in medical and psychiatric treatment of the victim (see *Sueltz v Bolttler* 1914 EDL 176 180; *Hauman v Malmesbury Divisional Council* 1916 CPD 216 217; *Creydt-Ridgeway v Hoppert* 1930 TPD 664 669; *Layton & Layton v Wilcox & Higginson* 1944 SR 48 49; *Mulder v South British Insurance Co Ltd* 1957 2 SA 444 (W) 445; *Lutzkie v SAR & H* 1974 4 SA 396 (W) 397; *Bester v Commercial Union Versekeringsmpy van SA Bpk* 1973 1 SA 769 (A) 775; *Clinton-Parker v Administrator, Tvl*; *Dawkins v Administrator, Tvl* 1996 2 SA 37 (W) 70; *Gibson v Berkowitz* [1997] 1 All SA 99 (W); 1996 4 SA 1029 (W) 1057; *Majiet v Santam Ltd* [1997] 4 All SA 555 (C) 569), but may also include an item such as loss of income (see *Hauman v Malmesbury Divisional Council* supra 217; *Mulder v South British Insurance Co Ltd* supra 445; *Gibson v Berkowitz* supra 1054D–F; *Majiet v Santam Ltd* supra 569–570; and cf *Els E v Bruce*, *Els J v Bruce* 1922 EDL 295 299) or loss of support (see *Masiba v Constantia Insurance Co Ltd* 1982 4 SA 333 (C) 343G–H). See also *Clinton-Parker v Administrator, Tvl*; *Dawkins v Administrator, Tvl* supra in which damages were awarded to two mothers for travelling expenses for the purpose of maintaining contact with their biological children.

3 *Bester v Commercial Union Versekeringsmpy van SA Bpk* 1973 1 SA 769 (A) 781H–782A.

4 In *Bester v Commercial Union Versekeringsmpy van SA Bpk* 1972 3 SA 68 (D) the court *a quo* distinguished between physical and mental harm for the purpose of delictual liability, holding that compensation will not be granted for mental injury in the absence of physical injury (73D–F). This distinction was, however, rejected by Botha JA on appeal: "Die senu- en breinstelsel is . . . net so 'n deel van die fisiese liggaam as wat 'n arm of been is, en 'n besering aan die senu- of breinstelsel is net so 'n besering van die fisiese organisme as wat 'n beseerde arm of been is" (779B–C). ("The nervous or brain system is . . . just as much part of the body

as an arm or a leg, and an injury to the nervous or brain system is just as much an injury to the physical organism as is an injured arm or leg"). In England the distinction between physical and mental injury probably played a role in the rejection of a claim on the ground of emotional shock in an early case: *Victorian Railways Commissioners v James Coultas & Mary Coultas* (1888) 13 AC 222. But already in *Dulieu v White & Sons* [1901] 2 KB 669 Kennedy J foresaw that physicians might regard mental injury as an impairment of the physical organism (677) and in *Hambrook v Stokes Bros* [1925] 1 KB 141 the distinction between physical and mental injury was rejected by Atkin J (153 154). See also *Hay or Bourhill v Young* [1943] AC 92 103; *Owens v Liverpool Corporation* [1939] 1 KB 394. But see Boberg *Law of Delict vol I: Aquilian Liability* 183–184 questioning whether the Appellate Division's decision in *Bester*'s case really swept away any distinction between physical and psychological injury. He asks a valid question: if there is indeed no distinction, "why should reasonable foreseeability of *injury by shock*, and not simply reasonable foreseeability of *any bodily injury*, be the touchstone of liability?"

5 The victim in the *Bester* case suffered purely mental, not physical, injury. The court *a quo* (1972 3 SA 68 (D)) concluded that according to the principles of the *actio legis Aquiliae* redress on the ground of emotional shock which gave rise to purely mental injury would be granted only in circumstances where the mental injury was caused by physical harm, or where the mental injury gave rise to an impairment of the physical organism or physical health (73D–F). Cf *N v T* 1994 1 SA 862 (C) 864H; *Hauman v Malmesbury Divisional Council* supra 220, but see *Bester v Commercial Union Versekeringsmpy van SA Bpk* 1973 1 SA 769 (A) 778D–779A and McQuoid-Mason 1973 *THRHR* 115 121. On appeal Botha JA held that compensation is recoverable for purely mental injury, irrespective of the presence of physical injury: "Om 'n benadeelde dus skadevergoeding of genoegdoening te ontsê bloot op grond van die feit dat die senuskok en gevolglike leed nie met 'n suiwer fisiese besering gepaard gaan nie, kan nouliks op

logiese gronde geregverdig word" (777G–H). ("To deny a victim patrimonial or sentimental damages merely on the grounds that the nervous shock and resulting harm do not involve a purely physical injury, can hardly be justified on logical grounds.") This principle has also been recognised in English law; see *Behrens v Bertram Mills Circus Ltd* [1957] 2 QB 1 28; *Chadwick v British Railways Board* 1967 1 WLR 912 917; *Hinz v Berry* [1970] 1 All ER 1074 (CAC) 1075f 1077b 1078d.

6 *Bester v Commercial Union Versekeringsmpy van SA Bpk* 1973 1 SA 769 (A) 777G–H 779H; *Masiba v Constantia Insurance Co Ltd* supra 343C–D; *N v T* supra 864H; *Clinton-Parker v Administrator, Tvl*; *Dawkins v Administrator, Tvl* supra 52G–H 54A–E; *Majiet v Santam Ltd* supra 557b–559f; *Barnard v Santam Bpk* [1998] 4 All SA 403 (SCA); 1999 1 SA 202 (SCA) 214D–215C; *Road Accident Fund v Sauls* 2002 2 SA 55 (SCA) 60A–61E 62F–G.

7 In setting out the circumstances in which damages will be awarded on the ground of emotional shock, Botha JA stated in *Bester v Commercial Union Versekeringsmpy van SA Bpk* 1973 1 SA 769 (A): "Ek verwys hier nie na niksbeduidende emosionele skok van kortstondige duur wat op die welsyn van die persoon geen wesenlike uitwerking het nie, en ten opsigte waarvan genoegdoening gewoonlik nie verhaalbaar sou wees nie" (779H). ("Here I am not referring to insignificant emotional shock of short duration which has no substantial effect on the person's well-being, and in respect of which sentimental damages would not normally be recoverable.") The principle that damages will not be awarded for trivial consequences of emotional shock has from the outset been recognised by our courts; see *Waring & Gillow Ltd v Sherborne* 1904 TS 340 348; *Steenkamp v Juriaanse* 1907 TS 980 986 987; *Union Government (Minister of Railways & Harbours) v Warneke* 1911 AD 657 667; *Creydt-Ridgeway v Hoppert* supra 666; *Pauw v African Guarantee & Indemnity Co Ltd* 1950 2 SA 132 (SWA); *Layton & Layton v Wilcox & Higginson* supra 51; *Lutzkie v SAR & H* supra 398; *Boswell v Minister of Police* 1978 3 SA 268 (E) 273F–G. The plaintiff in *Muzik v Canzone Del Mare* 1980 3 SA 470 (C) was denied recovery for anxiety resulting from food poisoning. Broeksma J held (474D–H) that, even if this amounted to nervous shock or psychiatric injury, it had been of short duration and had not caused the plaintiff

mental or physical impairment or affected his bodily well-being in any way. See also Boberg 177. Cf McQuoid-Mason 1973 *THRHR* 115 132, 1975 *SALJ* 18–19; Tager 1972 *SALJ* 435 438, 1973 *SALJ* 123 124; Boberg 176–177. Millner 1957 *SALJ* 263 265 stated the principle thus: "It is . . . only for serious nervous shock that the law accords a remedy – not simply transient feelings of fright, but physical illness which admits tangible proof." In English law Fleming *Torts* declares that "(m)ere anguish or fright will not do" (33) whilst in *Mrs Euphemia Hay or Bourhill v James Young* 1941 SC 395 Aitchison J required "an actual physical disorder of the nervous constitution of the body, producing in consciousness an intellectual or emotional stress, resulting, or capable of resulting in incapacity in varying degree" (432). See also *Barnard v Santam Bpk* supra 217; Burchell 1999 *SALJ* 697 702; *Majiet v Santam Ltd* supra 558g 567e–568g; Neethling 2000 *TSAR* 1 4–5.

8 The question whether a specific injury is serious enough to invoke liability will depend upon the circumstances of each particular case. In *Layton & Layton v Wilcox & Higginson* supra the plaintiff had to lie down and rest for an afternoon as a result of shock. This was regarded as too trivial to compensate (51). In *Lutzkie v SAR & H* supra a claim based on shock was dismissed on the ground that the plaintiff had suffered "no permanent consequences" as a result of the shock (398B–D). The effect of the shock was not described. It is highly doubtful whether the effects need to be "permanent" in order for a claim to succeed; cf McQuoid-Mason 1975 *SALJ* 18–19. In *Boswell v Minister of Police* supra the plaintiff collapsed and lost consciousness as a result of emotional shock. Furthermore she felt weak, had a headache and suffered from high blood pressure. She felt shaky for a month after the infliction of the shock. A physician testified that the shock would have "a substantial effect on her health" (272B). In the court *a quo* the magistrate rejected her claim on the ground that the effects which she suffered as a result of the emotional shock were of "a trivial and transitory nature" (273D: free translation). However, on appeal Kannemeyer J allowed the claim. He found that the "shock suffered by the plaintiff caused her health to be impaired", that it had "substantial effect on her health" and that the effects could "hardly be called trifling or

passing" (273D–H). In *N v T* supra the
mother of a then eight year old child
claimed for damages arising out of the rape
of the child. Williamson J held "that the
rape was a devastating emotional trauma for
the child and her innocent and carefree
growing-up has been fundamentally affected
. . . [T]he effects of the trauma . . . are likely
to remain for many years, if not forever"
(864D–F). In respect of the mother's claim
in her personal capacity Williamson J held
that "[s]he was very shocked by the whole
accident and has had the ongoing distress of
having to witness and handle on a daily basis
her daughter's trauma. Her suffering has
been and still is very real" (864F–G). In *Majiet v Santam Ltd* supra the mother of a nine-
year-old child sustained severe emotional
trauma because of what she saw and heard at
the accident scene where her son was struck
and killed by a motor-vehicle. "The difficulty about this case is of course the fact that
the plaintiff must have suffered bereavement
(which is not compensable) as a result of her
son's death, but that this bereavement has
not resolved itself with the result either that
the bereavement has resulted in a major depressive disorder or that the apprehension of
the aftermath of the accident by the plaintiff
has caused a major depressive disorder. Both
experts were agreed that the plaintiff is
not suffering simply from bereavement . . .

Ordinarily, and in the normal course the
depression resolves within two months"
(565d–g). In the *Majiet* case the two experts
agreed that some six years after the death of
her son the plaintiff still suffered from a major depression (565c–d). The fact that a
plaintiff had to undergo medical or psychiatric treatment as a result of the infliction of
emotional shock, and the fact that the consequences suffered as a result of the shock
lasted for a relatively long period, may be
important factors in finding that harm suffered was grave enough to be compensated.

9   Supra 396.
10 Supra 343F.
11 Contra Van der Walt *Huldigingsbundel vir
    WA Joubert* 254. Van der Walt (254–255
    260) is prepared to accept shock after the
    "mishandling of dead bodies" as a possible
    cause for liability, but he does not feel that
    shock in respect of damage to property or
    fear for the life of a loved animal such as was
    done in *Corso v Crawford Dog & Cat Hospital
    Inc* 415 NYS 182 (1979) and *Campbell v
    Animal Quarantine Station* 632 P 2d 1066
    (Hawaii 1981), to be actionable. See also
    Boberg 192; Burchell 1982 *Annual Survey of
    SA Law* 171 179; Mullany and Handford
    Tort Liability for Psychiatric Damage 49 fn 187.
12 Burchell 60; Mullany and Handford 208–
    212.

12 Legal causation (imputability of harm) Even though the courts in the past
have applied the reasonable foreseeability test to determine for which, if any, of the
harmful consequences caused by the wrongful and culpable infliction of emotional
shock a doer should be liable,[1] the new flexible approach to legal causation, as was
introduced in *S v Mokgethi*[2] and *International Shipping Co (Pty) Ltd v Bentley*,[3] should
now be applied. According to this flexible approach the overriding question to be
determined is whether there was a sufficiently close relationship between the wrongdoer's negligent act and the emotional shock that it may, in view of policy
considerations based on reasonableness, fairness and justice, be imputed to the wrongdoer.[4] The criterion of foreseeability now merely plays a subsidiary role, although a
very important role.[5] Factors which may be taken into consideration in determining
whether the harm was reasonably foreseeable[6] are for example that the emotional
shock resulted from conduct which also caused injury to the victim through physical
impact,[7] the fact that the doer through his or her conduct caused the victim to fear
personal injury,[8] the fact that the victim personally witnessed the events causing the
emotional shock,[9] the fact that the victim was a close relative or friend of a person
who was killed or injured in the incident causing the emotional shock,[10] and the fact
that the plaintiff was peculiarly susceptible to emotional shock.[11]

These factors will now be considered:

(a)   *Impact*   In addition to damages for pain, suffering, disfigurement, loss of amenities and so forth, the courts commonly award damages on the ground of emotional

shock where this stems from an injury caused by physical impact.[12] In these circumstances the harm is more foreseeable than that caused by the infliction of emotional shock through means other than physical impact. However, impact is not an indispensable condition for liability based on emotional shock.[13]

(b) *Personal danger* In early cases the courts adopted the view that a person who suffered harm through the infliction of emotional shock was not entitled to damages if the shock sustained by the person was not due to the person's fear of injury to him or herself.[14] Initially the "personal danger" requirement was connected with the concept of "remoteness of damage": harm resulting from emotional shock was considered to be "too remote" to be compensated if the victim did not fear for his or her own safety.[15] Later the absence of personal danger was found to contribute to the lack of a "duty of care" towards the victim: "Where there is no personal apprehension of danger there is not sufficiently close relationship between the negligence and the fright or shock for a finding to be justified that there was a duty of care in relation to the person suffering from the fright or shock."[16]

Fear by the victim for his or her personal safety as an essential for liability on the ground of emotional shock has been rejected by the Appellate Division.[17] However, the court conceded that harm resulting from emotional shock caused in circumstances where the victim feared personal injury will be more foreseeable than the harm suffered through emotional shock sustained as a result of witnessing or hearing of another's distress.[18]

(c) *Witnessing the events causing emotional shock* The law no longer requires that the victim of emotional shock must personally have perceived the events causing the emotional shock for delictual liability to be established.[19] The Appellate Division has indicated that harm resulting from emotional shock may also be reasonably foreseeable where the victim learns of distressing events after they occur.[20] However, the fact that the victim of emotional shock personally witnessed the disturbing events may be an important factor in deciding that the ensuing harm was reasonably foreseeable.[21]

(d) *Recovery by non-relatives* The question of the reasonable foreseeability of the emotional shock and resulting harm suffered by a plaintiff who was neither a relative of nor involved in a close relationship with the person killed, injured or endangered in the events giving rise to the emotional shock, has not yet been pertinently raised in the courts.[22] In all the cases based on emotional shock the plaintiffs have either themselves been involved in the distressing incidents[23] or been in a close relationship with those involved.[24]

The fact that the plaintiff was not a relative or close friend of the person endangered should not necessarily constitute a bar to recovery on the ground of emotional shock.[25] In formulating the reasonable foreseeability criterion as applicable to claims based on emotional shock, the Appellate Division did not restrict reasonable foreseeability of harm by emotional shock to relatives or close acquaintances of the person involved in the incident causing emotional shock.[26] Without requiring any special relationship between the person endangered and the plaintiff who suffered emotional shock, the court declared that the requirement of reasonable foreseeability might also be satisfied where the plaintiff suffered emotional shock and resulting harm as a result of having to witness or learn about another being exposed to danger.[27] The fact that the endangered person was a close relative or friend of the plaintiff who suffered emotional shock, and ensuing harm as a result of the incident should, however, be important factors in deciding that the emotional shock and resulting harm were reasonably foreseeable.[28]

(e) *Susceptibility to emotional shock* A defendant who causes physical or mental injury by inflicting emotional shock cannot escape liability by proving that the plaintiff was peculiarly susceptible to injury caused by the infliction of emotional shock.[29] Especially so if the wrongdoer acted with intent as was stated in *Boswell v Minister of Police*.[30] In *Masiba v Constantia Insurance Co Ltd*[31] Berman AJ affirmed a contention previously made by Boberg[32] that some actionable injury by shock must be foreseeable before the thin-skull rule can be applied to a shock case. In other words, the thin-skull rule does not entitle a person to whom no harm was foreseeable to sue: it entitles a person to whom some harm was foreseeable to compensation for the additional harm resulting from his or her pre-existing susceptibility.[33]

1 *Bester v Commercial Union Versekeringsmpy van SA Bpk* 1973 1 SA 769 (A) 777C–E 779H 781A–B 781E–G; *Boswell v Minister of Police* 1978 3 SA 268 (E) 273H 274F–H. In two early decisions the harm which flowed from the emotional shock was found to be "too remote" to be compensated on the ground that the victims had not feared for their personal safety: *Waring & Gillow Ltd v Sherborne* 1904 TS 340 348; *Sueltz v Bolttler* 1914 EDL 176 181; and cf par (c) below. On two later occasions an action was granted because the harm was found to be the "direct, natural or reasonable result" (*Hauman v Malmesbury Divisional Council* 1916 CPD 216 219) and the "natural and reasonable result" (*Creydt–Ridgeway v Hoppert* 1930 TPD 664 666) of the infliction of emotional shock. See also *Clinton-Parker v Administrator, Tvl; Dawkins v Administrator, Tvl* 1996 2 SA 37 (W).

2 1990 1 SA 32 (A).

3 1990 1 SA 680 (A).

4 *S v Mokgethi* supra 40–41; *International Shipping Co (Pty) Ltd v Bentley* supra 700–701; Neethling, Potgieter and Visser *Law of Delict* 292 fn 111; *Clinton-Parker v Administrator, Tvl; Dawkins v Administrator, Tvl* supra 57E–F; *Gibson v Berkowitz* [1997] 1 All SA 99 (W); 1996 4 SA 1029 (W) 1040H–I; *Road Accident Fund v Sauls* 2002 2 SA 55 (SCA) 61G; *Barnard v Santam Bpk* [1998] 4 All SA 403 (SCA); 1999 1 SA 202 (SCA) 215D–F.

5 "Having regard to *Bester's* case and subsequent Appellate Division cases, foreseeability may well be a factor to be considered in determining liability" (*Clinton-Parker v Administrator, Tvl; Dawkins v Administrator, Tvl* supra 57E–F). Cf *Road Accident Fund v Sauls* supra 61G ("The test to be applied is a flexible one in which factors such as reasonable foreseeability, directness, the absence or presence of a *novus actus interveniens*, legal policy, reasonableness, fairness and justice all play their part"). It is the general manner in which the harm will occur that must be reasonably foreseeable, though not necessarily the precise or exact manner in which the

harm will occur (cf *Road Accident Fund v Sauls* supra 60D; *Majiet v Santam Ltd* [1997] 4 All SA 555 (C) 568g–h).

6 Boberg *Law of Delict vol I: Aquilian Liability* 176 identifies the following factors to be taken into consideration: the relationship between the plaintiff and the person physically injured; the proximity of the plaintiff to the scene; and the defendant's knowledge of these circumstances.

7 See par (a) below.

8 See par (b) below.

9 See par (c) below.

10 See par (d) below.

11 See par (e) below.

12 *Bester v Commercial Union Versekeringsmpy van SA Bpk* supra 777F. Cf *Waring & Gillow Ltd v Sherborne* supra 348; *Creydt–Ridgeway v Hoppert* supra 666; *Pauw v African Guarantee & Indemnity Co Ltd* 1950 2 SA 132 (SWA) 136; *Gibson v Berkowitz* supra 1032G–I.

13 "Actual physical force or physical violence need not necessarily be the cause of the injury. In other words there need not be any actual physical impact": *Hauman v Malmesbury Divisional Council* supra 219. See *Creydt–Ridgeway v Hoppert* supra 665 666; *Bester v Commercial Union Versekeringsmpy van SA Bpk* supra 779G; *Majiet v Santam Ltd* supra 557b–c. Impact as a requirement for liability based on emotional shock was rejected in English law in *Dulieu v White & Sons* [1901] 2 KB 669 673 674.

14 *Waring & Gillow Ltd v Sherborne* supra 349; *Sueltz v Bolttler* supra 180 181. The "personal danger" requirement originated in a *dictum* by Kennedy J in *Dulieu v White & Sons* supra 675: "The shock, where it operates through the mind, must be a shock which arises from a reasonable fear of immediate personal injury to oneself." English courts rejected this requirement in 1925: *Hambrook v Stokes Bros* [1925] 1 KB 141 152 (per Banks J) 157 (per Atkin J). Cf also *Mary TR Currie v William Wardrop* 1927 SC 538; *Hay or Bourhill v Young* [1943] AC 92 99 105 111; *Dooley v Cammell Laird & Co Ltd* 1951 1 Lloyd's Rep 271; *Boardman v Sanderson*

1964 1 WLR 1317; *Chadwick v British Railways Board* 1967 1 WLR 912 919; *Hinz v Berry* [1970] 1 All ER 1074 (CAC).

15 *Waring & Gillow Ltd v Sherborne* supra 349; *Sueltz v Bolttler* supra 181. Cf *Tager* 1971 *SALJ* 435 436; Millner 1957 *SALJ* 263 264; McQuoid-Mason 1973 *THRHR* 115 120. In *Hauman v Malmesbury Divisional Council* supra too the validity of the "personal danger" requirement was apparently accepted (219). But see *Bester v Commercial Union Versekeringsmpy van SA Bpk* supra 780C–D.

16 *Mulder v South British Insurance Co Ltd* 1957 2 SA 444 (W) 449H; Boberg *Law of Delict vol I: Aquilian Liability* 176–177. But see *Bester v Commercial Union Versekeringsmpy van SA Bpk* supra 780G–H.

17 *Bester v Commercial Union Versekeringsmpy van SA Bpk* supra 781A–B.

18 *Bester v Commercial Union Versekeringsmpy van SA Bpk* supra 781A–B. See *Masiba v Constantia Insurance Co Ltd* 1982 4 SA 333 (C) 343D–E; *Barnard v Santam Bpk* supra 211I–212C 214D–I; Mullany and Handford *Tort Liability for Psychiatric Damage* 207–208. See *Majiet v Santam Ltd* supra 560h–561c; *Clinton-Parker v Administrator, Tvl; Dawkins v Administrator, Tvl* supra 53J–54B and Burchell 1999 *SALJ* 697 706 on the distinction between primary and secondary victims.

19 See *Majiet v Santam Ltd* supra 568g–j; *Barnard v Santam Bpk* supra 214F–I; cf *Bester v Commercial Union Versekeringsmpy* supra 780 781. It has been decided that a person will be liable if he or she causes emotional shock and resulting harm by informing the victim of disturbing events, knowing the information to be false, with the intention of inducing emotional shock: *Boswell v Minister of Police* supra. Cf *Wilkinson v Downton* 1897 2 QB 57. Similarly, a person ought to incur liability if he or she causes emotional shock by informing the victim of disturbing events in a reprehensible manner which the reasonable person would realise could harm the victim. The reasonable person would therefore exercise more discretion in informing the victim of the distressing incident. In *Alcock v Chief Constable of the South Yorkshire Police* [1991] 4 All ER 907 (HL) 915f–g it was decided that a television broadcast did not bring the plaintiff within the "proximity" of the event (Midgley 1992 *THRHR* 441 441–443). See Mullany and Handford 78–85 134–152 on the application of the "proximity" test in general and on means of communicating bad news (153–191). Cf

Winfield *Tort* 121 and Boberg 184.

20 *Bester v Commercial Union Versekeringsmpy van SA Bpk* supra 781A. Cf *Boswell v Minister of Police* supra.

21 Cf *Barnard v Santam Bpk* supra 214H–I.

22 In English law the action based on emotional shock is not restricted to a specific class of persons. Compensation has been granted, eg, to a person who suffered shock as a result of fearing for the life of his fellow-workers (*Dooley v Cammell Laird & Co Ltd* supra) and to a person who suffered shock after rendering assistance at the scene of a gruesome train accident (*Chadwick v British Railways Board* supra). Cf *Hambrook v Stokes Bros* supra 157 158. With regard to English law, Tager (436) concludes that "the range of potential plaintiffs is limited only by the criterion of foreseeability". In *Road Accident Fund v Sauls* supra the class of persons that could claim was extended beyond blood or legal relations to include a fiancée.

23 *Hauman v Malmesbury Divisional Council* supra; *Els E v Bruce, Els J v Bruce* 1922 EDL 295; *Creydt-Ridgeway v Hoppert* supra; *Bester v Commercial Union Versekeringsmpy van SA Bpk* 1972 3 SA 68 (D); 1973 1 SA 769 (A); *Lutzkie v SAR&H* 1974 4 SA 396 (W); *M v N* 1981 1 SA 136 (Tk); *Masiba v Constantia Insurance Co Ltd* supra; *Gibson v Berkowitz* supra; *Clinton-Parker v Administrator, Tvl; Dawkins v Administrator, Tvl* supra.

24 *Waring & Gillow Ltd v Sherborne* supra and *Sueltz v Bolttler* supra (spouse); *Layton & Layton v Wilcox & Higginson* 1944 SR 48 and *Mulder v South British Insurance Co Ltd* supra (child); *Bester v Commercial Union Versekeringsmpy van SA Bpk* 1972 3 SA 68 (D) and 1973 1 SA 769 (A) (brother); *Boswell v Minister of Police* supra (cousin); *N v T* 1994 1 SA 862 (C) (daughter); *Majiet v Santam Ltd* supra and *Barnard v Santam Bpk* supra (son); *Road Accident Fund v Sauls* supra (fiancée).

25 The House of Lords in *Alcock v Chief Constable of the South Yorkshire Police* [1991] 4 All ER 907 (HL) 919j saw no reason for limiting the class of persons to whom a duty is owed to close family relationships: plaintiffs who can prove a relationship "so close and intimate that their love and affection for the victim is comparable to that of the normal parent, spouse or child of the victim" can sue in respect of psychiatric injury (Midgley 1992 *THRHR* 441 442). In South African law a claim by a fiancée succeeded (*Road Accident Fund v Sauls* supra). See Mullany and Handford 106–133 for a complete

reference on relationships and emotional shock claims.

26 *Bester v Commercial Union Versekeringsmpy van SA Bpk* 1973 1 SA 769 (A) 780H–781A.

27 *Bester v Commercial Union Versekeringsmpy van SA Bpk* supra 780H–781A. According to Van der Walt *Huldigingsbundel vir WA Joubert* 260 such another person may include a fiancé(e) or a confidant.

28 In a case where the plaintiff did not personally witness the gruesome event, but only heard of it afterwards, "[i]t is quite possible and indeed, even probable, that plaintiff would not have been able to claim had she not had so close a relationship with her son" (*Majiet v Santam Ltd* supra 568f). Cf *Barnard v Santam Bpk* supra 215B–C.

29 The rule is stated thus in *Boswell v Minister of Police* supra 272F–G: "A defendant must take his victim as he finds him, and the fact that the plaintiff is peculiarly prone to more excessive injury is not relevant to a decision of a defendant's liability." See also *Majiet v Santam Ltd* supra 567b–e; *Gibson v Berkowitz* supra 1049A; *Clinton-Parker v Administrator, Tvl*; *Dawkins v Administrator, Tvl* supra 64I–65D; Neethling 2000 *TSAR* 1 10; Neethling and Potgieter 1997 *THRHR* 548 550–551; Parmanand 1984 *SALJ* 171 177–178; Burchell 1982 *Annual Survey of SA Law* 176 179.

30 Supra 274G–H.

31 Supra 342B–F. See also *Clinton-Parker v Administrator, Tvl*; *Dawkins v Administrator, Tvl* supra 65B–D.

32 1973 *Annual Survey of SA Law* 139; Boberg *Law of Delict vol I: Aquilian Liability* 183.

33 In the *Boswell* case the effects of the emotional shock may have been aggravated since the plaintiff was possibly suffering from high blood pressure (272F–G) and the same holds true for the deceased in the *Masiba* case (340D–341A). In many other cases involving the infliction of emotional shock, the effects of the shock may have been aggravated by the presence of a pre-existing mental or physical weakness on the part of the plaintiff. Eg the plaintiffs in *Waring & Gillow Ltd v Sherborne* supra and *Sueltz v Bolttler* supra were pregnant and the plaintiff in *Els E v Bruce, Els J v Bruce* supra was in a "delicate state of health". In *Creydt-Ridgeway v Hoppert* supra the plaintiff suffered ill-health due to change of life and feared hydrophobia. The same holds true in English law. The "thin skull" rule, which also applies to cases involving the causing of physical injury by direct impact or force (cf *Wilson v Birt (Pty) Ltd* 1963 2 SA 508 (D); *Potgieter v Rondalia Assurance Corporation of SA Ltd* 1970 1 SA 705 (N)), was formulated by Kennedy J in *Dulieu v White & Sons* supra 679 and expressed in the well-known phrase "a wrongdoer must take his victim as he finds him" by Lord Wright in *Hay or Bourhill v Young* supra 109–110. Cf *Owens v Liverpool Corporation* [1939] 1 KB 394; *Behrens v Bertram Mills Circus Ltd* [1957] 2 QB 1 26; Burchell 1982 *Annual Survey of SA Law* 176 179; Neethling and Potgieter 1973 *THRHR* 175 179–180; Neethling, Potgieter and Visser *Law of Delict* 295. See in general on the susceptible plaintiff Mullany and Handford 224–238.

REMEDIES

13 Damages and interdict[1] Patrimonial loss, whether intentionally or negligently caused, is recovered through the *actio legis Aquiliae*.[2]

The action for pain and suffering is instituted to recover a *solatium* for the infringement of physical or mental integrity through negligent infliction of emotional shock.[3]

The *actio iniuriarum* is available for the recovery of a *solatium* where the plaintiff suffered personality infringement through intentional infliction of emotional shock.[4]

An interdict to forbid the respondent from inflicting emotional shock upon the applicant may in particular circumstances be appropriate.[5]

1 For a general discussion of the delictual remedies, see title DELICT.

2 Cf *Bester v Commercial Union Versekeringsmpy van SA Bpk* 1973 1 SA 769 (A) 776D–E.

3 *Bester v Commercial Union Versekeringsmpy van*

SA Bpk supra 776D–E. However, in *Boswell v Minister of Police* 1978 3 SA 268 (E) the court held that the action for pain and suffering is appropriate even if the doer acted intentionally (273A–B). Traditionally the remedy for sentimental damage caused by the intentional infringement of a personality right is the *actio iniuriarum*. The action for pain and suffering is independent of the *actio legis Aquiliae* and the *actio iniuriarum*: *Hoffa v SA Mutual Fire & General Insurance Co Ltd* 1965 2 SA 944 (C). Consequently there should be no objection to instituting the action for pain and suffering to recover a *solatium* irrespective of whether the claimant also suffered patrimonial loss. In *Bester v Commercial Union Versekeringsmpy van SA Bpk* supra the victim, a minor, suffered only personality infringement and no patrimonial loss as a result of the negligent infliction of emotional shock. His father succeeded in recovering compensation on his behalf through the action for pain and suffering. The father suffered patrimonial loss which he recovered through the *actio legis Aquiliae* (776D). In *Boswell v Minister of Police* supra the plaintiff did not claim compensation for patrimonial loss (275B). She succeeded in a claim for general damages through the action for pain and suffering on the ground of intentional infliction of emotional shock (275A–G).

4   *Els E v Bruce, Els J v Bruce* 1922 EDL 295 298. Cf *Boswell v Minister of Police* supra 275C–D; *Waring & Gillow Ltd v Sherborne* 1904 TS 340 348. See Potgieter (1976) 1 *Codicillus* 11 11–16; Boberg *Law of Delict vol I: Aquilian Liability* 187; Burchell *Principles of Delict* 63; Neethling, Potgieter and Visser *Law of Delict* 291 fn 96; Neethling 2000 *TSAR* 1 2; Neethling *Persoonlikheidsreg* 114–115.

5   Eg where the respondent repeatedly threatens to kill or injure a relative of the applicant, thereby creating a danger of emotional shock to the applicant. Cf the facts of *Boswell v Minister of Police* supra.

ENERGY

by

R STEIN and KB OMIDIRE (*assisted by G ANKIAH*)

REFERENCES TO OTHER TITLES

INTRODUCTION

14 Introduction Energy law is a fast evolving and complex body of law. It spans many legal disciplines, including, but not limited to competition law, constitutional law, the law of contract, environmental, health and safety law. As challenging as harnessing energy on earth has always been to humankind, so too has the task of regulating the use of nature's forces to ensure sustained availability of energy to meet the needs of present and future generations.

Energy resources are generally divided into two categories – those which are considered to be renewable (for example, water) and those which are not (for example, coal which takes many millions of years to regenerate). A distinction is also made between primary and secondary sources of energy. Electricity is considered to be a secondary source as its generation is dependant on, for example, the burning of fossil fuels such as coal, gas or oil.[1]

In South Africa, many statutes have been and will be enacted to regulate the various sectors of the country's energy economy. Those statutes deal with a wide range of inter-related issues affecting human dignity, quality of life, environmental, health and safety issues, sustainable energy development, energy efficiency, service delivery, economic growth and development and the search for alternative renewable sources of energy. International trends have also changed and had an influence on South African energy policy.[2]

This chapter examines regulatory instruments governing the different sectors of South Africa's energy economy.

The title is divided as follows:

(a) the National Energy Regulator Act of 2004;[3]

(b) electricity: Electricity Act of 1987;[4] Eskom Conversion Act of 2001;[5]

(c) hydroelectric Power: the National Water Act of 1998;[6]

(d) gas: the Gas Act of 2001;[7]

(e) liquid fuels: the Mineral and Petroleum Resources Development Act of 2002;[8] Petroleum Products Act of 1977;[9] Petroleum Pipelines Act of 2003[10] and Petroleum Pipelines Levies Act of 2004;[11] Central Energy Fund Act;[12] and

(f) nuclear energy: the Nuclear Energy Act of 1999;[13] National Nuclear Regulator Act of 1999.[14][15]

---

1 The enormous reserve of coal in South Africa has for many years constituted the main source of its energy production. The country is also a world leader in the production of synthetic fuels, and a regional leader in petroleum refining. The African continent's first nuclear power plant was developed in South Africa. As a relatively arid country, the country has a large number of dams in its river systems to conserve water for its rural and for urban areas, with some of them generating hydroelectric power ("An Energy Overview of the Republic of SA"; a publication of the Fossil Energy International, US. Department of Energy, October 2003). These various sources of energy are subject to statutory regulation, placing them under the control of regulatory agencies established by law. The government department responsible for the overall supervision of the energy sector in South Africa is the Department of Minerals and Energy. The department is responsible for the initiation and co-ordination of government policy on energy, and it also oversees the activities of the various regulatory authorities established to control the different sub-sectors of energy.

The energy sector causes significant positive and negative environmental and resource impacts. With South Africa being dependent on coal for more than 75% of its energy needs, it is therefore not a surprise that the country is responsible for 1.6% of global greenhouse gas emissions. To address this problem, South Africa ratified the United Nations Framework Convention on Climate Change ("FCCC") in August 1997, which is being developed through protocols, the most important being the Kyoto Protocol.

2 Significant international shifts have occurred in post-oil-crisis energy policies. Perhaps the most important is the realisation that commercial energy will not become scarce in the short term. Energy security is now being achieved through greater diversification and flexibility of supply, including increased cross-boarder energy trade. Another trend is the increasing realisation by governments that they do not have to be the provider of services. Governments can achieve their national goals through ensuring that services are delivered rather than providing them themselves. Energy markets are being restructured to encourage greater competition, even in the grid-based electricity and natural gas industries, which have traditionally been regarded as natural monopolies. Heightened competition has necessitated the development of increasingly sophisticated regulatory regimes for the licensing of the industry.

The energy sector has significant environmental impacts and these have become an international issue. For example, the reduction of emissions is becoming increasingly important. Energy investments are subjected to greater environmental scrutiny and there is greater focus on energy end-uses, with policies for encouraging efficiency and demand-side management. The research and development of alternative and renewable energy sources is also being promoted. The energy sector is increasingly being funded with private finance.

3 40 of 2004.
4 41 of 1987.
5 13 of 2001.
6 36 of 1998.
7 48 of 2001.
8 28 of 2002.
9 120 of 1977.
10 60 of 2003.
11 28 of 2004.

12 38 of 1977.
13 46 of 1999.
14 47 of 1999.
15 The White Paper on the Energy Policy of South Africa Published in December 1988, by the Department of Minerals and Energy, and the White Paper on the Renewable Energy Policy of the Republic of South Africa (GN 513 of 2004), indicate the inter-relationships between the existing statutes regulating energy and the anticipated statutes, many of which are still in the form of bills, and others already enacted, but yet to attain commencement.

The thrust of the policy on energy is to be found in the 1998 White Paper on the Energy Policy of South Africa. Constitutional responsibility imposes an obligation on the state to develop efficient energy sources to cater for the needs of the nation, made available to the people at an affordable cost. Government's goal is to ensure that the energy sector makes a significant contribution to a successful and sustainable national growth and development strategy, and to realise this goal (pr 3.2.2. of the 1998 White Paper).

In the White Paper on the Renewable Energy Policy of the Republic of South Africa of 2004, sustainable development is defined as "the integration of social, economic and environmental factors into planning, implementation and decision-making so as to ensure that development serves present and future generations." Renewable energy that is produced from sustainable natural resources will contribute to sustainable resources White Paper on Renewable Energy Policy of 2004 par 7.1). Renewable energy resources provide approximately 10% of South Africa's primary energy. Biomass accounts for close to 10% of net energy use at the national level. Hydro-electric power contributes less than 1% of electricity generation. Other renewable energy sources make up a small amount of energy supply in the country (par 7.7). The development of government's renewable energy policy is guided by a rationale that South Africa disposes of very attractive renewable resources, particularly solar and wind, and that renewable applications are in fact the least cost energy service, more so, when social and environmental costs are taken into account.

15 Constitutional duty of the state The Constitution[1] imposes an obligation on the state to ensure that the right of citizens to a clean environment is not compromised. The section guarantees the right of everyone:

(a)   to an environment that is not harmful to their health or well-being; and

(b)   to have the environment protected, for the benefit of present and future generations, through reasonable legislative and other measures that:

(i) prevent pollution and ecological degradation;

(ii) promote conservation; and

(iii) secure ecologically sustainable development and use of natural resources while promoting justifiable economic and social development.[2]

1   Constitution of the Republic of SA 108 of 1996.

2   S 24. See further titles ENVIRONMENTAL LAW; CONSTITUTIONAL LAW.

NATIONAL ENERGY REGULATOR ACT

INTRODUCTION

16 Purpose of the Act The National Energy Regulator Act[1] was assented to by the president on 30 March 2005 and has not yet come into operation. The preamble to the Act indicates that it will have a far-reaching impact on the South African energy sector. More importantly, the Act appears to have sounded the final death knell for the long-pending Electricity Regulation Bill which has made extensive provisions for the regulation of electricity in the country. The new Act establishes a single regulator, the National Energy Regulator, to regulate the electricity, piped-gas and petroleum pipeline industries; and to provide for matters connected therewith.[2] The Act establishes the National Energy Regulator as a juristic person.[3]

The Act has implications for existing sector-specific regulators. Unlike the existing legislation regulating energy which makes provisions for the functions of the sector regulator, or as contained in the Bill, the functions of the regulator are to be deciphered by reference to the relevant sector-specific legislation. Thus, for the functions of the regulator in relation to gas, reference must be made to section 4 of the Gas Act;[4] for its functions in relation to liquid fuels and petroleum, reference must be made to section 4 of the Petroleum Pipelines Act;[5] and for electricity, reference must be made to section 4 of the Electricity Act.[6]

It is important to note that in taking over the regulation of gas and petroleum, the regulator is not limited as to time, implying that the functions of the regulator in relation to gas and petroleum are effective from the date of commencement of the National Energy Regulator Act;[7] whereas for electricity, the regulator's functions will only be effective "with effect from a date determined by the Minister by notice in the *Gazette*" which in event should not be earlier than 31 May 2005.[8]

1   40 of 2004.
2   Preamble to the Act; s 2.
3   S 3.
4   48 of 2001; see pars 65 et seq post.

5   60 of 2003; see pars 119 et seq post.
6   41 of 1987; see pars 30 et seq.
7   40 of 2004.
8   S 4(2); see par 19 post.

NATIONAL ENERGY REGULATOR

17 Functions The Energy Regulator must:

(a)   undertake the functions of the Gas Regulator as set out in section 4 of the Gas Act;[1]

(b)   undertake the functions of the Petroleum Pipelines Regulatory Authority as set out in section 4 of the Petroleum Pipelines Act;[2] and

(c)   with effect from a date determined by the Minister by notice in the *Gazette*, undertake the functions of the National Electricity Regulator as set out in section 4 of the Electricity Act.[3]

The date contemplated in (c) above must be after 31 May 2005.[4]

1 48 of 2001.	40 of 2004 s 4(1).
2 60 of 2003.	4 S 4(2).
3 41 of 1987: National Energy Regulator Act	

18 Composition The Energy Regulator consists of four full-time and five part-time members appointed by the minister.[1]

The minister must designate one of the part-time members as chairperson of the Energy Regulator and another part-time member as deputy chairperson.[2]

The minister must designate one of the full-time members as the Chief Executive Officer of the Energy Regulator.[3]

The minister must designate one of the other three full-time members to be primarily responsible for electricity regulation, another for piped-gas regulation and another for petroleum pipeline regulation.[4]

If the chairperson is for any reason unable to perform his or her functions, the deputy chairperson must perform them until the minister designates another chairperson.[5]

A part-time member of the Energy Regulator holds office for a period of four years. A full-time member of the Energy Regulator holds office for a period of five years. The minister may re-appoint a member of the Energy Regulator. If a vacancy occurs on the Energy Regulator the minister may fill the vacancy temporarily for a period of not more than 12 months by appointing a person without complying with section 6(7) of the National Energy Regulator Act.[6]

Members of the Energy Regulator must be paid for their services such remuneration and allowances as the minister may determine with the concurrence of the Minister of Finance.[7]

1 National Energy Regulator Act 40 of 2004	4 S 5(4).
s 5(1).	5 S 5(5).
2 S 5(2).	6 S 5(6).
3 S 5(3).	7 S 5(7).

19 Disqualifications and requirements for membership No person may be appointed as or remain a member of the Energy Regulator if that person:

(a)   is not a South African citizen or the holder of a permit as a permanent resident in the Republic;

(b)   is an unrehabilitated insolvent;

(c)   has, within a period of ten years immediately before the date of the proposed appointment, been convicted of an offence involving dishonesty or served a sentence of imprisonment without the option of a fine for any other offence; or

(d)   has, after appointment, been convicted of an offence involving dishonesty or been sentenced to imprisonment without the option of a fine for any other offence.[1]

The minister must appoint, as members of the Energy Regulator, persons who:

(a)   collectively have adequate legal, technical, business, economic or other experience relevant to the electricity, piped-gas and petroleum pipelines industries;

(b)   are collectively broadly representative of South African society as a whole;

(c)   are committed and available to fulfil their role as members of the Energy Regulator; and

(d)   demonstrate impartiality and objectivity in such a manner that a fair balance between continuity and capacity building is achieved.[2]

Upon appointment:

(a)   every full-time member must terminate any employment or consulting relationship he or she has with any person, firm, association or company engaged in the electricity, piped-gas and petroleum pipelines industries and may not take up any such employment or consulting arrangement during his or her period of membership of the Energy Regulator;

(b)   every full-time and part-time member must disclose to the minister and the Energy Regulator his or her pecuniary interest in any person, firm, association or company engaged in the electricity, piped-gas and petroleum pipeline industries; and

(c)   every full-time and part-time member must disclose to the minister and the Energy Regulator if his or her spouse, life partner or child is in the employ of or acts as a consultant to, or has any relationship with, any person, firm, association or company engaged in the electricity, piped-gas and petroleum pipelines industries, or has any pecuniary interest in any such person, firm, association or company.[3]

A member may not at any time be present during the discussion of or the making of a decision on, or take part in, any matter before the Energy Regulator in which that member or his or her spouse, life partner, child or associate has a direct or indirect pecuniary interest.[4]

If a member acquires such an interest, that member must immediately in writing declare that fact to the minister and the Energy Regulator.[5]

If the spouse, life partner or child of a member acquires an interest as contemplated above, such member must immediately in writing declare that fact to the minister and the Energy Regulator.[6]

Before appointing members to the Energy Regulator, the minister must by notice in the *Gazette* call for nominations from members of the public.[7]

The notice published before the commencement of the National Energy Regulator Act calling for nominations for the first appointments to the Energy Regulator must be regarded as having been validly published in terms of this section.[8]

1 National Energy Regulator Act 40 of 2004	5 S 6(5).
s 6(1).	6 S 6(6).
2 S 6(2).	7 S 6(7).
3 S 6(3).	8 S 6(8).
4 S 6(4).	

20 Vacation of office and termination of appointment of members A part-time or full-time member of the Energy Regulator must vacate his or her office if that member:

(a)   becomes of unsound mind;

(b)   has been absent from more than two consecutive meetings without leave of the chairperson for each absence;

(c) resigns by written notification to the minister;

(d) materially fails to perform any duty imposed on him or her in terms of the National Energy Regulator Act,[1] the Electricity Act,[2] the Gas Act[3] or the Petroleum Pipelines Act;[4] or

(e) becomes disqualified from being a member on any of the grounds referred to in section 6 (1) of National Energy Regulator Act.[5]

The minister may terminate the appointment of a member of the Energy Regulator if such member contravenes section 9.[6]

1 40 of 2004.	4 60 of 2003.
2 41 of 1987.	5 40 of 2004 s 7(1).
3 48 of 2001.	6 S 7(2); see par 22 post for s 9.

21 Meetings The Energy Regulator must meet at such times and places as may be determined by the chairperson. The chairperson must convene such meetings of the Energy Regulator as are necessary for the proper performance of its functions.[1]

The chairperson must, upon a written request of the Chief Executive Officer or two other members, convene a special meeting to be held within two weeks after the date of receipt of such request.[2]

If the chairperson is absent from a meeting of the Energy Regulator the deputy chairperson must chair the meeting.[3]

If both the chairperson and the deputy chairperson are absent from a meeting, the chairperson must designate another part-time member to chair that meeting.[4]

Unless other procedures are prescribed by the Energy Regulator, the chairperson of any meeting of the Energy Regulator must determine the procedures to be followed at such meeting.[5]

The quorum for any meeting of the Energy Regulator is a majority of its serving members or four members, whichever is the greater.[6]

A decision of the majority of the members present at a meeting constitutes a decision of the Energy Regulator. In the event of an equality of votes on any matter the person chairing the meeting has a casting vote in addition to his or her deliberative vote.[7]

No decision taken by the Energy Regulator is invalid merely because of a vacancy on the Energy Regulator or because any person not entitled to sit as a member sat as such at the time when the decision was taken if the rest of the members present at the meeting and entitled to sit as members at the meeting constituted a quorum and the decision was taken by a majority of those members present and entitled to vote.[8]

Any meeting of the Energy Regulator must be open to the public unless the quorate meeting passes a resolution to the effect that, for the part of the meeting concerned, the information to be discussed during that part of the meeting would create a record that would in turn oblige the Energy Regulator to refuse access to that information in terms of the Promotion of Access to Information Act.[9] If the Energy Regulator takes a decision in any other manner than at a formal meeting, such decision comes into effect after it has been reduced to writing and signed by a majority of the members and it must be submitted for noting at the first formal meeting of the Energy Regulator following the decision. The Energy Regulator must cause a record of all of its proceedings to be kept.[10]

The Energy Regulator may establish subcommittees of its members to perform such functions of the Energy Regulator as it may determine, including conducting hearings and inquiries and sitting as a tribunal. He or she must determine the composition of a subcommittee, and may at any time dissolve or reconstitute a subcommittee. The Energy Regulator must designate a member of a subcommittee as chairperson of that subcommittee. The Energy Regulator is not absolved from the performance of any function entrusted to a subcommittee.[11]

The Energy Regulator must make rules concerning the manner in which notice of meetings to be held and the business to be conducted thereat is brought to the attention of the public.[12]

1 National Energy Regulator Act 40 of 2004 s 8(1).	7 S 8(7).
	8 S 8(8).
2 S 8(2).	9 2 of 2000.
3 S 8(3).	10 National Energy Regulator Act 40 of 2004 s 8(9).
4 S 8(4).	
5 S 8(5).	11 S 8(10).
6 S 8(6).	12 S 8(11).

22 Duties of members Members of the Energy Regulator must:

(a) act in a justifiable and transparent manner whenever the exercise of their discretion is required;[1]

(b) at all times act in the interests of the Energy Regulator and not in their own or sectoral interests;[2]

(c) act independently of any undue influence or instruction;[3]

(d) recuse themselves from and refrain from voting on or discussing any matter, pending before the Energy Regulator, in which they have a direct or indirect pecuniary interest;[4]

(e) act in a manner that is required and expected from the holder of a public office;[5] and

(f) act in the public interest.[6]

1 National Energy Regulator Act 40 of 2004 s 9(a).	4 S 9(d).
	5 S 9(e).
2 S 9(b).	6 S 9(f).
3 S 9(c).	

23 Decisions of Energy Regulator Every decision of the Energy Regulator must be in writing and be:

(a) consistent with the Constitution[1] and all applicable laws;

(b) in the public interest;

(c) within the powers of the Energy Regulator, as set out in the National Energy Regulator Act,[2] the Electricity Act,[3] the Gas Act[4] and the Petroleum Pipelines Act;[5]

(d) taken within a procedurally fair process in which affected persons have the opportunity to submit their views and present relevant facts and evidence to the Energy Regulator;

(e) based on reasons, facts and evidence that must be summarised and recorded; and

(f) explained clearly as to its factual and legal basis and the reasons therefor.[6]

Any decision of the Energy Regulator and the reasons therefor must be available to the public except information that is protected in terms of the Promotion of Access to Information Act.[7]

Any person may institute proceedings in the High Court for the judicial review of an administrative action by the Energy Regulator in accordance with the Promotion of Administrative Justice Act.[8]

Any person affected by a decision of the Energy Regulator sitting as a tribunal may appeal to the High Court against such decision. The procedure applicable to an appeal from a decision of a magistrate's court in a civil matter applies, with the changes required by the context, to such an appeal.[9]

1　Constitution of the Republic of SA 108 of 1996.
2　40 of 2004.
3　41 of 1987.
4　48 of 2001.
5　60 of 2003.
6　National Energy Regulator Act 40 of 2004

s 10(1).
7　2 of 2000: National Energy Regulator Act 40 of 2004 s 10(2).
8　3 of 2000: National Energy Regulator Act 40 of 2004 s 10(3).
9　S 10(4).

24　Personnel　Subject to the directions of the Energy Regulator, the Chief Executive Officer is also responsible for:

(a)　the day-to-day management of the affairs of the Energy Regulator;

(b)　the appointment of other employees and contracting with persons to assist the Energy Regulator in the performance of its functions; and

(c)　administrative control over the employees of the Energy Regulator.[1]

The Energy Regulator must, on the recommendation of the Chief Executive Officer, from time to time determine the personnel and other resources to be made available to the full-time members contemplated in section 5(4) of the National Energy Regulator Act[2]

The employees of the Energy Regulator must be paid such remuneration, allowances, subsidies and other benefits as the Energy Regulator may determine with the approval of the minister and the Minister of Finance.[3]

Despite the above provisions, the minister may, where he or she determines a need exists, instruct the Energy Regulator to make use of persons employed by or contracted to the department or another licensing or regulatory authority falling under the minister's jurisdiction.[4]

Section 9 applies to every member of the personnel of the Energy Regulator, with the changes required by the context.[5]

1　National Energy Regulator Act 40 of 2004 s 11(1).
2　S 11(2); see par 18 ante.
3　S 11(3).
4　S 11(4).
5　S 11(5).

25　Funds　For the purpose of regulation of the piped-gas and petroleum pipelines industries, the funds of the Energy Regulator consist of:

(a)　money appropriated by Parliament;

(b)　levies imposed by or under separate legislation;

(c)　charges for dispute resolution and other services rendered in terms of the National Energy Regulator Act;[1] and

(d)　licence fees.[2]

For the purpose of regulation of the electricity industry, the funds of the Energy Regulator consist of:

(a)   money appropriated by Parliament;

(b)   funds collected under section 5B of the Electricity Act;[3] and

(c)   levies imposed by or under separate legislation.[4]

1   40 of 2004.
2   S 12(1).
3   41 of 1987; see par 31 post.

4   National Energy Regulator Act 40 of 2004
    s 12(2).

26 Accounting The Energy Regulator must perform its functions in accordance with the Public Finance Management Act.[1]

The Energy Regulator must keep separate accounts for the electricity, piped-gas and petroleum pipelines regulatory functions.[2]

The costs of the Energy Regulator must be shared between the electricity, piped-gas and petroleum pipeline regulatory functions in proportion to the costs incurred by the Energy Regulator in respect of each of those regulatory functions. Money appropriated by Parliament must be allocated to the separate accounts for the electricity, piped-gas and petroleum pipeline regulatory functions in proportion to the costs incurred by the Energy Regulator in respect of each of those functions unless Parliament determines otherwise. Money received by the Energy Regulator other than money appropriated by Parliament must be paid into the account that is kept for the industry from which such money was received, and must be used for the sole benefit of that industry.[3]

The Energy Regulator must open one or more accounts in its name with one or more financial institutions and deposit therein all money received from the sources contemplated in section 12 of the National Energy Regulator Act.[4]

The financial records of the Energy Regulator must be audited by the auditor-general.[5]

The financial year of the Energy Regulator starts on 1 April of one year and ends on 31 March of the following year.[6]

1   1 of 1999: National Energy Regulator Act
    40 of 2004 s 13(1).
2   S 13(2).
3   S 13(3).

4   S 13(4).
5   S 13(5).
6   S 13(6).

27 Reporting by Energy Regulator The annual report required of public entities in terms of the Public Finance Management Act[1] may include any matter that the Energy Regulator deems necessary but must, in respect of electricity, piped-gas and petroleum pipeline matters, include information on:

(a)   licences granted, amended or withdrawn;[2]

(b)   regulations made and directives issued by the minister;[3]

(c)   the envisaged strategies of the Energy Regulator;[4]

(d)   the existing position and envisaged commercial developments with respect to the electricity, piped-gas and petroleum pipeline industries;[5]

(e)   the position regarding health, safety and environmental matters;[6]

(f)   access to network infrastructure;[7] and

(g)   tariffs or tariff structures set or approved.[8]

1 1 of 1999.
2 National Energy Regulator Act 40 of 2004
    s 14(a).
3 S 14(b).
4 S 14(c).

5 S 14(d).
6 S 14(e).
7 S 14(f).
8 S 14(g).

GENERAL PROVISIONS

28 Transitional provisions As from the date of commencement of the National Energy Regulator Act:[1]

(a) the person who immediately before the commencement of the Act held the office of Chief Executive Officer of the National Electricity Regulator is deemed to be the Chief Executive Officer of the Energy Regulator;

(b) the persons who constituted the other personnel of the National Electricity Regulator immediately before the commencement of the Act are deemed to be the personnel of the Energy Regulator;

(c) the assets of the National Electricity Regulator vest in the Energy Regulator and the Energy Regulator takes over the liabilities of the National Electricity Regulator.[2]

Decisions of the National Electricity Regulator in force immediately before the date contemplated in section 4(1)(c)[3] remain in force until amended, replaced or repealed by the Energy Regulator.[4]

1 40 of 2004; date of commencement yet to be proclaimed.
2 S 16(1).
3 Ie the date, as determined by the minister by notice in the *Gazette*, when the National

Energy Regulator will undertake the functions of the National Electricity Regulator as set out in s 4 of the Electricity Act 41 of 1987.
4 National Energy Regulator Act 40 of 2004 s 16(2).

ELECTRICITY

GENERAL

29 Introduction Mindful of the challenges facing electricity utilities to meet new pressures resulting from global markets and the need to open up the local industry to foreign investors to fund power sector expansion and development, the government is committed to the optimisation of the operations of the energy sector in order to maximise its potential for adequate, reliable, and low cost electricity to serve the people and industries of South Africa.[1] The realisation of this objective is however premised on the recognition that the number of distributors of electricity has to be reduced to a much smaller manageable number, while a reform of both the generation and the transmission sectors will have to be undertaken in due course.[2] The Electricity Act[3] is the primary regulatory statute for electricity.[4] It is proposed that Eskom, which generates by far most of electricity in South Africa, will be restructured.[5] The new National Energy Regulator Act,[6] and the Electricity Distribution Industry Restructuring Bill,[7] are intended to facilitate the realisation of the policy objectives highlighted above. The Energy Regulation Act has replaced the Electricity Regulation Bill, which was intended to establish a National Electricity Regulatory Authority. However, the new Act establishes a regulator to deal with various kinds of energy, and, although it relates specifically to electricity, has been dealt with separately under a separate heading above.[8]

1 See par 7.1.1. of the 1998 White Paper.

2 Par 7.1.1.

3 41 of 1987.

4 Eskom is South Africa's dominant electricity facility and ranks among the world's top five facilities in terms of capacity. Eskom is reputed to be one of the lowest-cost producers of electricity in the world. It sells approximately 40% of its electricity to local authorities which re-sell it to end-users. It also sells electricity to neighbouring countries such as Lesotho, Swaziland, Botswana, Mozambique, Namibia and Zimbabwe, representing 2.4% of total sales. Eskom supplies more than 95% of South Africa's electricity. Of the electricity supplied, 90% is generated by fossil fuel fired stations, 7% by nuclear power, 1% by hydro stations and a small portion is imported.

5 Electricity generated by Eskom is transmitted over its national transmission network to distributors and consumers countrywide. Eskom is governed by a stakeholder-based Electricity Council, while municipal distributors are under the direct control of their elected local councils: par 7.1. of the White Paper.
The separation of Eskom into generation, transmission and distribution will result in more transparency and accountability in the electricity supply industry. Different generation companies will ensure that there is competition in the industry which should result in enhanced efficiency and effectiveness in this sector.

6 40 of 2004.

7 GN 1288 of 2003. The challenges militating against the effective distribution and supply of electricity include the fact that about 40% of all homes, and tens of thousands of schools and clinics are without access to electricity. The distribution sector is highly fragmented, with over 400 distributors, resulting in low efficiencies, high costs, disparities in tariffs, and financial viability problems of many distributors. There is a high degree of non-payment of tariffs, which constitute a burden for the municipalities given the fact that the municipal electricity departments are expected to contribute towards the funding of other municipal services (par 7.1.1).
Government is committed to the restructuring of the industry and the consolidation of the electricity distribution industry into the maximum number of financially viable independent regional electricity distributors (REDs) (par 7.1.3.3). In implementing the foregoing objectives, the Cabinet after the consideration of the Electricity Distribution Industry Restructuring Bill GN 1288 of 2003, has approved that the Bill be released for public comments.
The Bill provides that the minister may set standards or issue guidelines as to the form and substance of service delivery agreements between REDs and municipalities in the national interest. The guidelines are expected to advise municipalities, multi-jurisdictional municipal service districts, and REDs with respect to the form and content of service delivery agreements, and may provide for procedures for entering into such agreements, the review thereof, and for standard terms, conditions and provisions which may be contained in a service delivery agreement. A municipality may enter into a service delivery agreement with a RED as service provider of the services which the RED is licensed to provide, either directly or through a multi-jurisdictional municipal service district (s 36 of the Bill). The terms of a service delivery agreement are binding on the parties to it. The creation of RED's should result in better service delivery to customers and eventually to better prices (s 37).

8 See pars 16–28 ante.

ELECTRICITY ACT

30 Control of the supply of electricity The Electricity Control Board which was previously constituted under the Electricity Act of 1958,[1] continues to exist under the 1987 Electricity Act[2] as a juristic person known as the National Electricity Regulator.[3] The main objects of the regulator are to exercise control over the electricity supply industry so as to ensure order in the generation and efficient supply of electricity.[4]

1   40 of 1958 s 22.
2   41 of 1987.
3   Ss 2 2A.
4   S 3. The electricity regulations are contained

in *Government Gazette* GN R506, 25 March
1988 as amended: *Government Gazette* GN
R2665, 16 November 1990.

31 Composition of regulator   The regulator consists of not less than seven and not more than nine members appointed by the minister.[1] A member of the regulator[2] will be appointed on such conditions, including conditions relating to the payment of remuneration and allowances, as the minister may determine with the concurrence of the Minister of Finance.[3] The members of the regulator must as far as practicable include persons having sufficient knowledge of matters relating to electricity tariffs, cost accounting, legal aspects or electricity supply systems.[4]

The minister must appoint one of the members of the regulator as chairperson, provided that in the absence of the chairperson from a meeting of the regulator, the members present at that meeting may elect one of their number to preside at that meeting on condition that an acting chairperson has not been appointed by the minister.[5]

Any person will be disqualified from being appointed as a member of the regulator if he or she is of unsound mind or if he or she has at any time been convicted of an offence involving dishonesty, or has been sentenced for any other offence to a period of imprisonment without the option of a fine.[6]

A member of the regulator vacates office if:

(a)   he or she tenders his or her resignation in writing to the minister;

(b)   he or she becomes disqualified from being appointed as a member of the regulator;

(c)   he or she has been absent, without leave of the regulator, from more than two consecutive meetings of the regulator;

(d)   the minister withdraws his or her appointment on the ground that in the opinion of the minister he or she is incompetent or unfit to fulfil the duties.[7]

Provision is made for the appointment and functions of a Chief Executive Officer of the regulator,[8] the method of raising and utilising funds,[9] the keeping of accounts[10] and the furnishing of reports to the minister.[11]

1   Electricity Act 41 of 1987 s 5(1)(a). Not more than three members may be persons employed in the public service.
2   Excluding a member who is in the full-time employment of the state.
3   S 5(1)(b).
4   S 5(1)(c).
5   S 5(1)(d).
6   S 5(3).
7   S 5(4).
8   See s 5A.
9   See s 5B.
10   See s 5C.
11   See s 5D.

32 Functions of regulator   The regulator may:

(a)   issue licences for the generation, provision and, within the area determined by it, distribution of electricity;

(b)   determine the prices at and conditions on which electricity may be supplied by a licensee;

(c)   at the request of any licensee or its consumer, settle disputes between licensees among themselves or between licensees and their consumers or prospective consumers regarding:

(i)   the right to supply;

(ii)   the quality of such supply and the provision of services in connection therewith;

(iii) the conditions on and prices at which electricity is supplied;

(iv) the installation and functioning of meters;

(v) the suitability of the equipment of the licensee;

(vi) delays in or refusal of supply by a licensee;

(vii) any other matter in respect of which a licensee or its consumer requests the regulator to act as mediator;[1]

(d)   collect information which it deems necessary from undertakers or consumers;

(e)   perform inspections of the equipment of licensees;

(f)   exercise the other powers assigned to it by the Electricity Act.[2]

The regulator may advise the minister on any matter relating to the electricity supply industry and it may for this purpose carry out such investigations as it or the minister deems necessary.[3]

1 In terms of the Electricity Act 41 of 1987   2 S 4(1)(c)–(f).
   s 4(2), any decision of the regulator regarding   3 S 4(4).
   any such dispute will be binding on the parties.

33 Regulator's powers of entry and inspection and calling for returns The regulator or its authorised representative is empowered:

(a)   at all reasonable times to inspect plant and machinery as well as books of account on the premises of any licensee;

(b)   to call upon a licensee to furnish returns prescribed by the board or any other particulars the regulator may require.[1]

The regulator may require that the accuracy of the returns and particulars be verified on oath.[2]

Any person who refuses to allow any such inspection or fails to comply with any such demand, or who willingly obstructs or hinders the regulator or its representative in any such inspection commits an offence and is liable on conviction to a fine not exceeding the amount the minister prescribes by regulation for each day the failure or refusal continues and, in respect of such hindrance or obstruction, to a fine prescribed by the minister or imprisonment not exceeding six months or both such fine and imprisonment.[3]

If any person divulges information he or she has obtained by such inspection, except for the purpose of carrying out his or her duties under the Electricity Act or as a witness in court or at an arbitration under the principal Act, that person commits an offence and is liable on conviction to a fine not exceeding the amount which the minister may prescribe or to imprisonment for a period not exceeding six months or both such fine or imprisonment.[4]

1 Electricity Act 41 of 1987 s 22(1). Any   2 S 22(2).
   person authorised to conduct such an in-   3 S 22(3).
   spection must exhibit his or her authorisa-   4 S 22(4).
   tion to the person so affected: s 22(5).

34 Undertakings to be carried on under licence or permit Electricity may only be supplied or generated under the authority of a licence, provided that a licence will not be required by any person, excluding a local authority, who does not sell more than five gigawatt hours of electricity per annum.[1] The regulator may, with the approval of the minister, exempt any undertaker or withdraw any exemption so granted in respect of the licensing requirements.[2]

1 Electricity Act 41 of 1987 s 6(1). See s 1 for
   the meaning of the term "local authority".
2 S 6(2).

35 Application for and granting of licences An application for a licence may be made to the regulator in the manner prescribed by regulation.[1] The regulator may require an applicant to publish a notice which furnishes information regarding such application in a newspaper circulating in the area of the proposed undertaking.[2]

Any objection to the grant of a licence must be lodged with the regulator within 60 days after publication of the notice; objections may be heard at a public hearing arranged by the regulator; and notice of the hearing must be given to an objector and an applicant at least 14 days prior thereto.[3] The regulator must make its decision regarding the application known as soon as possible after the hearing.[4] These provisions are equally applicable to any application for an amendment of a licence.[5]

1 Electricity Act 41 of 1987 s 7(1). See s 1 for   3 S 7(3).
   the meaning of the term "licence".   4 S 7(4).
2 S 7(2).   5 S 7(5).

36 Form and conditions of licence Every licence must be in the prescribed form and contain a Schedule of approved tariffs chargeable by the licensee for the supply, provision or distribution of electricity to the different classes of consumers.[1]

The regulator may determine conditions relating to:

(a)   the maximum capacity of supply of the undertaking;

(b)   the area of supply of the undertaking;

(c)   the classes of consumers to which electricity may be supplied;

(d)   the conditions on which the licensee may supply electricity to its consumers;

(e)   the obligation of the licensee to supply electricity;

(f)   the period within which the provision of electricity will commence;

(g)   the quality of supply;

(h)   any other matter connected with the carrying on of the undertaking.[2]

The conditions under which a local authority supplies electricity outside its area of jurisdiction in terms of a duly issued licence must be the same as those applicable in respect of the supply within its area of jurisdiction.[3] Furthermore, a licensee may not cede or transfer his or her licence without the consent of the regulator.[4] The regulator may at any time after granting the licence impose in writing any addition to or amendment of the conditions of the licence.[5]

1 Electricity Act 41 of 1987 s 8(1).   is entitled to prescribe other conditions.
2 S 8(2).   4 S 8(4).
3 S 8(3). In terms of s 8(3) proviso, the regulator   5 S 8(5).

37 Duties of the licensee A statutory duty rests upon every licensee up to the limit, if any, of electricity which the licensee may generate or supply in terms of his or her licence to supply electricity within the area of supply mentioned in the licence to every applicant who is in a position to pay for the electricity.[1] In the case of undue delay or refusal on the part of the licensee to supply any applicant with electricity, that applicant may appeal to the regulator, which must decide whether the licensee must undertake the supply and determine the conditions on which it must be done.[2]

The licensee is not obliged to supply electricity to any premises having a separate supply unless the prospective consumer has agreed to pay or has given security for payment of a sum which would, in the opinion of the regulator, give the licensee an income which is sufficient to cover the expenses incurred by the licensee in meeting the demand for electricity.[3]

Except for reasons beyond his or her control, a licensee may not reduce or discontinue the supply of electricity unless the consumer is insolvent or has failed to pay the agreed charges or to comply with the conditions of supply and has failed to remedy the default within 14 days of receiving written notice to do so.[4]

1 Electricity Act 41 of 1987 s 10(1).	3 S 10(3).
2 S 10(2).	4 S 11.

38   Charges for supply of electricity, revision of prices and surplus profits   Prices chargeable by a licensee for the supply of electricity to consumers are specified in the Schedule contained in the licence.[1] The regulator may revise the Schedule of approved tariffs in a licence[2] and may also approve a deviation from a Schedule of approved tariffs.[3] The licensee may be required by the regulator at its discretion to publish an application for the revision of the Schedule.[4]

1 Electricity Act 41 of 1987 s 9(1).	*Government Gazette* GN 730, 5 April 1990.
2 S 9(2).	4 S 9(4). In such an instance, the provisions of
3 S 9(3). For the levy on electricity, see	s 7(2)–(4) will apply *mutatis mutandis*.

39   Expropriation of licensed undertakings   Whenever an undertaking is taken into possession[1] or there is a takeover of assets,[2] the undertaker or the transferee, as the case may be, must compensate the former undertaker for the nett value of the assets belonging to or used in connection with that undertaking.[3] Expropriation is subject to the condition that a value, fair at the time of expropriation, be paid to the undertaker.[4] In determining this amount, goodwill, prospective profits or the fact that the takeover is compulsory are not taken into account.[5] In the event of any dispute the amount payable is to be determined by arbitration.[6]

1 Electricity Act 41 of 1987 s 12.	5 S 14(3)(a). See also s 14(3)(b) for further
2 S 13.	details regarding the determination of such
3 S 14(1).	value.
4 S 14(2).	6 S 14(4).

40   Failure of licensee to meet obligations   If a licensee fails to comply with the terms and conditions of the licence duly granted under the Electricity Act,[1] the regulator may upon giving 30 days notice require the licensee to meet such obligations.[2] If the licensee does not comply with the requirements of the notice:

(a)   he or she will be guilty of an offence;[3]

(b)   the regulator may recommend to the minister to authorise the undertaker to take possession of the undertaking of the licensee; and

(c)   the regulator may also withdraw a licensee's licence at any time.[4]

In the event of the undertaker taking possession of the undertaking, the undertaker must for its own account carry on such undertaking or provide for the carrying on of the undertaking by another person.[5]

1 41 of 1987.	s 12(1)(b) or (c), see also s 12(2)–(3).
2 S 12(1).	5 S 12(4). S 12(4) proviso provides that
3 Upon conviction, this offence will be	whoever takes over the undertaking must
punishable in terms of the provisions of s 27.	also take over its assets.
4 S 12(1)(a)–(c). For the application of	

41 Standard units for the measurement of electricity and the mode of supplying electricity The minister may make regulations regarding the units or standard for the measurement of power, the frequency, type of current and pressure of electricity generated as well as the mode of supplying electricity.[1]

1 Electricity Act 41 of 1987 s 28(1)(g)–(i).

42 Requirements regarding generating plant Machinery for the generation of electricity should be erected in accordance with the regulations in respect of frequency, type of current or pressure, unless the plant is for the owner's own use and its rated capacity does not exceed 500kW or it is specially exempted by the regulator.[1] In the event of the rated capacity of a plant for an owner's own use exceeding 500kW, such a plant, if not exempted by the regulator, should comply with the regulations and requirements stipulated by the regulator.[2] Any person who wishes to erect a plant for his or her own use, must, prior to its erection, furnish the regulator with particulars of that plant.[3]

1 Electricity Act 41 of 1987 s 20(1)(a)–(b).
2 S 20(2)(a).
3 S 20(2)(b).

43 Acquisition of rights to water and land An undertaker, whether a riparian owner or not, must apply for permission to a water court established under the Water Act[1] to use or to store water from a public stream.[2] The water court is empowered to grant or refuse the application, to impose conditions *inter alia* with regard to the prevention of pollution, to assess the amount of compensation and determine the persons to whom and the manner in which compensation is to be paid.[3]

Expropriation is subject to the approval of and to the conditions imposed by the minister.[4] This approval will not be granted unless the minister is satisfied, after considering a report by the regulator, that the right to the land cannot be acquired on reasonable terms by agreement with the owner and that such right is reasonably required for the generation or supply of electricity.[5] The report of the regulator is furnished only after the matter has been determined at a public hearing of which the regulator has given the owner at least 14 days' notice and at which the owner has been able to raise any objection to the expropriation.[6] The regulator must also notify the owner and the undertaker of its findings.[7]

Where expropriation is to be effected in terms of an agreement with the owner of the land but he or she is not prepared to accept the compensation offered therefor, the parties may agree that compensation be payable in accordance with the Expropriation Act.[8] In such a case the application for compensation must be made to the appropriate court within six months of the agreement; failing this the compensation payable is that offered by the undertaker entitled to expropriate.[9]

1 54 of 1956 (now repealed and replaced by the National Water Act 36 of 1998). For the rights of an owner of land expropriated in terms of the Electricity Act 40 of 1958 s 43 (now the Electricity Act 41 of 1987 s 19), see *Elektrisiteitsvoorsieningskommissie v Fourie* 1988 2 SA 627 (T).
2 Electricity Act 41 of 1987 s 18(1).
3 S 18(2)
4 S 19(1).
5 S 19(2). In terms of s 19(2) proviso 1, neither the minister nor the regulator may make a finding regarding compensation payable to the owner. S 19(2) proviso 2 provides that if agreement cannot be reached under the provisions of s 19(2)(a) as to compensation, compensation must be determined in accordance with the provisions of the Expropriation Act 63 of 1975.
6 Electricity Act 41 of 1987 s 19(3)(a)–(b).

7 S 19(3)(c).
8 63 of 1975 ss 12 14–15.
9 Electricity Act 41 of 1987 s 19(5). See also

s 19(4) for the provisions that apply in the event of the minister approving such an acquisition.

44 Supply of electricity by local authorities Unless an authorised undertaking has acquired the right of supply within the area of jurisdiction of a local authority, the sale and distribution of electricity within the area is under the control of the local authority.[1] The minister may, if in his or her opinion it is in the national interest, direct the regulator to gather information in respect of the supply of electricity by a local authority and the minister may issue directives for the efficient utilisation of electricity after having consulted the parties involved.[2]

Whenever a local authority intends to establish a power station or to enlarge any existing power station to an extent exceeding within any period of 12 months 10 per cent of its existing rated generating capacity, it is obliged to apply to the regulator for its approval; the application must be supported by a full report by a professional engineer.[3] Before considering the application the regulator is obliged to call upon Eskom for a report on the proposals, and the local authority is under a duty to supply Eskom with such information as it may require for the purpose of drawing up the report.[4] Eskom is entitled to charge a fee for this report; the amount of such fee, if not agreed upon, is determined by the minister.[5] In its report to the regulator, Eskom must state what in its opinion is the best course for the local authority concerned to pursue, and in particular whether Eskom can itself provide a supply of electricity with advantage to the interests of the ratepayers and consumers; if so, it must submit its estimates and terms.[6]

Where the supply of electricity or the construction of distribution lines is to be undertaken by anyone other than the local authority within whose area of jurisdiction the intended supply or construction is to be effected, the consent of the local authority concerned must be obtained; this provision does not, however, apply where the electricity supply is to the South African Transport Services for traction purposes.[7]

If the consent of the relevant local authority is unreasonably withheld, the matter is referred to the regulator for decision after a public hearing of which the parties to the dispute have had at least 14 days' notice.[8]

1 Electricity Act 41 of 1987 s 15(1).
2 S 15(2).
3 S 16(1).
4 S 16(2).

5 S 16(4).
6 S 16(3).
7 S 17.
8 S 17 proviso.

45 Authorised undertaker's powers with regard to entry and inspection and breaking up of streets Lines, meters, fittings and other apparatus belonging to an undertaker and lawfully placed on premises not in the undertaker's possession, whether or not fixed to such premises, remain his or her property and may be removed by such undertaker; such lines, meters and the like are not subject to any landlord's hypothec nor are they to be taken in any process of law against the occupier of the premises. Adequate indication must be given on such premises that the undertaker is the actual owner of the fittings and other apparatus.[1]

Any person authorised thereto in writing by the undertaker may at all reasonable times enter the premises for inspection and removal of such lines, meters and other apparatus or for determining the electricity consumed or to cut off the supply.[2] All damage caused by such entry, inspection or removal must be made good by the authorised undertaker.[3]

An authorised undertaker is empowered within his area of supply to break up streets[4] for the construction of pipe and power lines.[5] Not less than 30 days' notice of the intention do this must be given to the authority concerned except in the case of an emergency.[6] The undertaker must furthermore carry out the necessary work under the supervision of the relevant authority, in accordance with a plan showing the route and specifications approved by the authority.[7] The undertaker is obliged to remove any rubble occasioned by the work and, while the street is broken up, provide for adequate fencing and lighting during the night.[8] Any cost reasonably and necessarily incurred by the authority exercising supervision must be borne by the undertaker.[9] The undertaker is also liable for loss or damage caused by his or her negligence in carrying out the work.[10]

1 Electricity Act 41 of 1987 s 24(1).
2 See s 23(1).
3 S 23(3).
4 For the purposes of s 25, "street" includes any road, square or open or enclosed public place: s 25(8).
5 S 25(1).
6 S 25(2).
7 S 25(3).
8 S 25(4).
9 S 25(6).
10 S 25(7).

46 Liability of undertaker for damage or injury In any civil proceedings against an undertaker arising out of damage or injury caused by induction or electrolysis or in any other manner by means of electricity generated or transmitted by or leaking from the plant or machinery of any undertaker, the damage or injury will be presumed to have been caused by the negligence of the undertaker, unless the contrary is proved.[1]

1 Electricity Act 41 of 1987 s 26.

47 Offences and penalties A person who carries on an undertaking in contravention of the provisions of the Electricity Act[1] or of the conditions of his or her licence is liable on conviction to a fine prescribed by the minister for every day on which the undertaking is so carried on.[2]

Anyone who knowingly abstracts, diverts or uses electricity unlawfully is liable on conviction to the penalties which may be imposed for theft.[3]

A fine prescribed by the minister and/or imprisonment for a period not exceeding 12 months is the penalty which may be imposed in an instance where any person cuts, damages or interferes with any apparatus for the generation or distribution of electricity.[4]

1 41 of 1987.
2 S 27(1).
3 S 27(2).
4 S 27(3).

48 Courts' attitude to payment for electricity Two important decisions on the subject of electricity have been handed down:

In *Senekal Inwonersvereniging v Plaaslike Oorgangsraad*[1] the first applicant was a body made up of residents of Senekal. The second applicant was also a resident of Senekal. The respondent was a local authority and a licensee in terms of the Electricity Act.[2] The first applicant decided that the electricity account rendered monthly by the respondent would be paid in full. However the amount levied by the respondent for services and rates would be kept back, pending instructions from the first applicant on how funds were to be handled. Respondent sent out a notice on 11 December 1997 stating that the electricity supply of anyone who had not paid their accounts in full would be disconnected.

The applicants obtained a rule *nisi* prohibiting the respondent from disconnecting the electricity supply to a consumer if that consumer had paid the full amount due in respect of the supply of electricity, regardless of whether he owed any other amount to the respondents for other services. On the return date of the rule *nisi*, the respondent submitted that formal decisions had been taken on two occasions that the electricity supply of all residents who had not paid all the accounts in respect of services and rates in full would be disconnected.

The Electricity Act, the Local Authority Ordinance Act of 1962 (Free State) and the Electricity Supply Regulations promulgated in terms of the Ordinance, all contained provisions regarding the disconnection of the supply of electricity. In terms of section 11(b) of the Act, the licensee could not discontinue the supply of electricity to a consumer unless the consumer failed to pay the agreed charges or to comply with the conditions of supply. In terms of regulation 11(1) of the Regulations, the respondent could disconnect the supply of electricity when "any levies for or in connection with the electricity supplied" were due to the council. The respondent submitted that this included levies in connection with the supply of electricity of whatever kind, and that the other levies were used for the payment of the indirect supply of electricity to consumers. It was thus argued that should the consumer fail to pay any of those other levies, he or she would also fail to pay a levy in respect of the supply of electricity. Therefore the supply to the consumer could be discontinued even though he or she had paid the electricity component of the account.

The court held that the respondent's contention regarding the wide meaning of the words in regulation 11(1) could not be accepted. Even though the words "in connection with" did not have a precise meaning, the words, taking into account the nature and intention of the regulations and the context of the words in the regulations as a whole, had to be given their ordinary literal meaning. The court held further that the reference to "levies for and in connection with electricity" in the regulations related to the supply to a consumer. The levies could only refer to electricity supply to or in connection with electricity supply to a consumer. According to the regulations, there could also be levies payable other than the levies for electricity supplied, for example for testing of electrical installations. The reference in regulation 11 related to such levy, which was not a levy for electricity supplied but a levy in connection with the supply of electricity.

The court held further that the first applicant and the second applicant had not failed to pay the levies or charges for the supply of electricity. Nor had they failed to comply with the condition of supply. In the light of the statutory provision applicable, the decision of the respondent to disconnect the electricity supply of residents who had not paid all accounts in respect of services and rates in full could not be valid. The court held accordingly, that the respondent's threat and decision to discontinue the electricity supply was unlawful and that the applicants were entitled to an interdict.

In *Hartzenberg v Nelson Mandela Metropolitan Municipality (Despatch Administrative Unit)*[3] the applicants were in unlawful occupation of houses in a particular township within the respondent's area of jurisdiction. The applicants continued to use water and electricity supplied to the properties by the respondent. Prepaid electricity metres were installed on the properties but the respondent continued to render accounts in respect of water consumed on the properties. The applicants had all run up substantial arrears on their water accounts. The respondent had been unable to restrict the water supplied to the properties because the applicants had refused the respondent's plumbers access to the properties. Because the applicants were in unlawful occupation, the registered owner of the properties had refused to accept responsibility for the arrears on the water account. Consequently the respondent discontinued the electricity supply to the properties, despite the fact that there were no arrears in respect of the consumption of electricity.

A rule *nisi* was issued ordering the respondent to restore the electricity supply pending the return date and was further called upon to show cause on the return date why it should not be ordered to reinstate the electricity supply with immediate effect. In its defence, the respondent raised section 19 of the Standard Electricity Supply By-law (Western Cape) and sections 96, 97(1)(g) and 102 of the Local Government: Municipal Systems Act,[4] as well as a resolution of the respondent's predecessor in title which had resolved to bar consumers who had prepaid electricity metres from the prepaid electrical system if they failed to pay for other municipal services.

The court held that section 10 (the right to dignity) and section 12(1)(d) (the right to freedom and security of the person) of the Constitution[5] were not of application to the present circumstances, as was contended by the applicants. The court held further that the only issue was whether the respondent was entitled to cut the electricity supply to relevant houses because of the failure by the applicants to pay their water accounts. The court held further that section 19 of the Standard Electricity By-law did not give the respondent the power to discontinue the electricity supply in the event of the payment in respect of the supply of any other service, apart from electricity, being in arrears. The by-law dealt specifically with electricity and, if the legislature had intended it to refer to the supply of any commodity other than electricity, it should specifically have said so.

The court held further that section 97(1)(g) of the Local Government: Municipal Systems Act[6] did not assist the respondent. It merely set out a debt collection policy to be adopted and did not provide the respondent with any powers. Section 102(1)(b) similarly did not assist the respondent. Furthermore, for several reasons, the resolution passed by the respondent's predecessor could not be raised in favour of the respondent, including the fact that it was not shown that the resolution had been published in the *Gazette* and therefore that it had become a by-law; and the fact that the resolution itself required that notice be given to the consumers and there was no proof that this had been done. The court held accordingly that the respondent was not entitled to discontinue the electricity supply because of the arrears on the applicants' water account.

1 1998 3 SA 719 (O).
2 41 of 1987.
3 2003 3 SA 633 (SE).
4 31 of 2000.
5 Constitution of the Republic of SA 108 of 1996.
6 32 of 2000.

ESKOM CONVERSION ACT

49 Conversion of Eskom to a public company The Eskom Conversion Act[1] repeals in its entirety the Eskom Act,[2] and the Eskom Amendment Acts of 1991 and 1995.[3][4] The object of the Eskom Conversion Act is to convert Eskom into a public company having a share capital as contemplated in section 19(1)(a) of the Companies Act,[5] with its entire share capital held by the state.[6] Consequently, with effect from a date determined by the minister, Eskom will be deemed to be a public company incorporated in terms of the Companies Act and be known as Eskom Holdings Limited.[7] The conversion of Eskom does not affect its continued corporate existence, or any of the rights, liabilities, and obligations acquired or incurred by Eskom at any time before its conversion. The terms and conditions of service of its employees will not be affected by the conversion.[8]

1   13 of 2001
2   40 of 1987.
3   15 of 1991 and 69 of 1995 respectively.
4   Eskom Conversion Act 13 of 2001 s 10, and
    Schedule to the Act.
5   61 of 1973.
6   Eskom Conversion Act 13 of 2001 s 2. The

provisions of ss 32, 44(1), 54(2), 59, 63(2), 64, 172 and 344 of the Companies Act 61 of 1973 will not apply to Eskom for as long as the state continues to hold the majority of its equity.

7   Eskom Conversion Act 13 of 2001 s 2.
8   S 4.

50   Powers and duties of Eskom Eskom may enter upon any land for the purpose of making plans and surveys thereof. If any damage is caused to such land in the course of such entry or survey, Eskom is liable to pay compensation. Irrespective of whether or not the owner of the land agrees, Eskom may transfer to its subsidiary companies any servitude or other similar rights in terms of which Eskom may have effected improvements on such land. Such transfer must be by way of a deed of cession attested by a notary, and the relevant registrar of deeds must make appropriate entries and endorsements to give effect to the transaction.[1]

1   Eskom Conversion Act 13 of 2001 s 5.

51   Corporate status of Eskom The Registrar of Companies must register the memorandum and articles of association of Eskom, the contents of which will determined by the minister. The minister must enter into a shareholder compact with Eskom Holdings Limited, mindful of the developmental role of Eskom Holdings Limited, and the promotion of universal access to affordable electricity, taking into account the cost of electricity, financial sustainability, and the competitiveness of Eskom.[1] All borrowings effected by Eskom and any interest accruing thereon will constitute a first charge against its revenues and assets, and on all moneys recovered or to be recovered by it, except otherwise agreed between Eskom and the lender. If any interest due in respect of security remains unpaid for three months after a written demand has been lodged with Eskom, the holder may apply to the High Court for the appointment of a receiver of its revenues and assets. The court may make such order or orders and give such directions as may be necessary to raise and pay the moneys due, and in particular may order that any prices for electricity supplied or to be supplied by Eskom be increased to meet the deficit.[2]

1   Eskom Conversion Act 13 of 2001 s 6.
2   S 7.

52   Taxation of Eskom and its subsidiaries Section 10(12)(cA) of the Income Tax Act[1] does not apply in respect of the receipts and accruals of Eskom and its subsidiaries. The Minister of Finance, after consultation with the Minister of Minerals and Energy, must determine the tax values of the capital assets owed by Eskom and any of its subsidiaries for the purpose of calculating capital allowance.[2]

1   58 of 1962.
2   Eskom Conversion Act 13 of 2001 s 8.

53   Miscellaneous The minister may by notice in the *Gazette* make regulations necessary for the achievement of the objects of the Eskom Conversion Act.[1] Notwithstanding repeal of the Eskom Act[2] by section 10 of the new Act, anything done in terms of that Act which may be done in terms of the new Act, continues to be valid with force and effect.[3]

1   13 of 2001 s 9.
2   40 of 1987.
3   Eskom Conversion Act 13 of 2001 s 11.

HYDROELECTRIC POWER

GENERAL

54 Introduction[1] There are two major river systems in South Africa – the Orange (including its main tributary, the Vaal river) and the Limpopo. There are other smaller rivers in the southern part of the country, flowing southward into either the Indian or Atlantic oceans. Many of the rivers have been dammed to conserve water for agricultural use and for use in the urban areas. A few of the rivers generate hydroelectric power, the largest of them being the 1,000 MWe Drakensberg facility. Licensing for dams for hydropower is a confusing maze because of the necessity of the regulation and management of water resources, and the scope of regulation existing for the generation of electricity. While the regulator of electricity utility hardly makes environmental consideration a critical element, the approval for a dam facility is ordinarily centred on the pillars of sustainable development, namely, social, economic, and environmental considerations.

Any project involving the construction of dams for the generation of electricity is subject to the provisions of two main statutes: the Electricity Act[2] in relation to licensing for the generation of electricity, and the National Water Act.[3]

1 Dams have made an important and significant contribution to human development in the area of water management, hydro power, irrigation, and other uses. However, in the consideration of dams and hydropower, there are issues of equity, governance, justice, power issues, as well as social and environmental concerns. Environmentalists consistently argue that the most serious negative consequences are often manifested in flooding, biodiversity problems, displacement of people, and destabilisation of ecosystems. To resolve these problems, the World Commission on Dams recommends that decision-making on water and energy development should reflect a comprehensive approach to integrate social, environmental and economic dimensions of development; create greater levels of transparency and certainty for all involved; and increase levels of confidence in the ability of nations and communities to meet their future water and energy needs: see *Dams and Development: A New Framework for Decision-making*, The Report of the World Commission on Dams November 2000, Earthscan Publications, London.

2 41 of 1987. This has been discussed in detail in pars 29–48 ante.

3 36 of 1998.

ELECTRICITY ACT

55 General The Electricity Act[1] has been discussed in detail above.[2] Its aim is to provide for the continued existence of the Electricity Control Regulator and for control of the generation and supply of electricity; and for matters connected therewith.

Of relevance to this section, in terms of the Act "distribution" means the furnishing of electricity to end-users, "Minister" means the Minister of Mineral and Energy Affairs, "supply" means the provision or distribution of electricity or both, and "consumer" means a person supplied with electricity. The Act defines "licence" as a licence granted to by the regulator under the Act for the generation and supply of electricity; a "licensee" as the holder of a licence; while "undertaking" means any undertaking for the supply of electricity within a defined area, with all the assets and liabilities appertaining thereto.

Licence fees and applications for licences have been discussed elsewhere.[3]

1 41 of 1987.
2 See pars 29–48 ante.
3 See pars 31 35 ante; ss 5(3)(b) 7 7(4).

NATIONAL WATER ACT

56 Purpose The preamble to the National Water Act[1] explains its purpose: upon recognising that water is a scarce and unevenly distributed national resource occurring in many different forms as part of a unitary, inter-dependent cycle, and the need for the integrated management of all aspects of water resources, the Act makes provision for a fundamental reform of the law relating to water resources, and for matters connected therewith. Chapter 12 of the Act makes provisions for the safety of dams. The reason for this chapter is the need to make provisions for measures aimed at improving the safety of new and existing dams with a safety risk, so as to reduce the potential for harm to the public, damage to property or to resource quality. The duties imposed on the owner of a dam under the Act are in addition to common law duties, and the Act imposes a statutory duty of care on the professional involved with dams. The duty is towards the state and the general public. Only dams which are classified as "dams with a safety risk" are subject to the provisions.[2]

1   36 of 1998.
2   See ch 12 preamble.

57 Critical definitions The following definitions contained in the National Water Act[1] are of importance:

(a)   "approved professional person" means a person registered in terms of the Engineering Profession of South Africa Act,[2] and approved by the minister after consultation with the Engineering Council of South Africa;

(b)   "dam with a safety risk" means any dam:

(i)   which can contain, store or dam more than 50 000 cubic metres of water, whether that water contains any substance or not, and which has a wall of a vertical height of more than five metres, measured as the vertical difference between the lowest downstream ground elevation on the outside of the dam wall and the non-overspill crest level or the general top level of the dam wall;

(ii)   belonging to the category of dams declared under section 118(2) of the National Water Act[3] to be dams with a safety risk; or

(iii)   declared under section 118(3)(a) to be a dam with a safety risk;

(c)   "task" includes a task relating to designing, constructing, altering, repairing, impounding water in, operating, evaluating the safety of, maintaining, monitoring or abandoning a dam with a safety risk;

(d)   "Minister", within the provision of section 1 of the Act, means the Minister of Water Affairs and Forestry.

1   36 of 1998 ch 12 s 117.
2   114 of 1990.
3   36 of 1998.

58 Licence for the use of water The National Water Act[1] requires that a person who is required or wishes to obtain a licence to use water must apply to the relevant responsible authority[2] for a licence.[3] A reasonable fee may be charged for the application by the authority. The application is to be made in the specified manner for the purpose and must contain information required by the authority. The applicant may be required to provide additional information, and an assessment by a competent person on the likely effect of the proposed licence on the resource quality, as well as an independent review of the said assessment by a person acceptable to the responsible authority. The authority may conduct its own investigations on the application and its effect on water resource, and may invite written comments from organs of state and other persons interested in the matter. The applicant must be afforded an opportunity to make representations on any aspect of the licence application. The authority may direct that any assessment required be compliant with the regulations made pursuant to the provisions of section 26 of the Environment Conservation Act.[4] Upon reaching a decision on the licence application, the responsible authority must promptly notify the applicant and any person who has objected to the application, and at the request of any of such persons, give written reasons for its decision.[5]

1 36 of 1998.

2 The Act assigns different functions to various persons, officers and committees for different classes of water usage.

3 S 40.

4 73 of 1989: National Water Act 36 of 1998 s 41. See further title ENVIRONMENTAL LAW.

5 S 42.

59 Control measures for dam with safety risk The owner of a dam must:

(a) within the specified period provide the minister with any information, drawing, specifications, design assumptions, calculations, documents and test results requested by the minister; or

(b) give any person authorised by the minister access to that dam, to enable the minister to determine whether:

(i) that dam is a dam with a safety risk;

(ii) that dam should be declared to be a dam with a safety risk;

(iii) a directive should be issued for specific repairs or alterations to that dam; or

(iv) the owner has complied with the provisions of the National Water Act[1] applicable to that dam.[2]

The minister may give written notice to the owner of a dam, declaring the dam to be a dam with a safety risk, and direct the owner of a dam with a safety risk to submit at the owner's cost, a report of an approved professional person regarding the safety of that dam. The owner of such dam may be directed to undertake specific repairs or alterations to the dam which are necessary to protect the public, property or the resource from the risk of failure of the dam. If the owner fails to comply with the directive, the minister may effect the repairs or alterations and recover the cost from the owner.[3]

1 36 of 1998.

2 S 118(1).

3 S 118(2).

60 Responsibilities of approved professional persons Regardless of how appointed, an approved professional person has a duty of care to the state and the general public. Such person must carry out his or her duty in accordance with sound engineering practices, compile and keep prescribed records, and issue a completion certificate on the action taken on the dam and that such action is in line with sound engineering practices, including the report on a safety evaluation of the dam.[1]

1 National Water Act 36 of 1998 s 119.

61 Registration of dam with a safety risk The owner of a dam with a safety risk must register the dam. The application must be made within 120 days of the dam becoming capable of containing, storing, or impounding water; or after the date on which an already completed dam is declared to be a dam with a safety risk; or after publication of a notice declaring a category of dams to be dams with a safety risk. In the event of a change of ownership of such dam, the successor in title must promptly inform the director-general of the succession, for the substitution of the name of the owner.[1]

1 National Water Act 36 of 1998 s 120.

62 Considerations for declaring dams with safety risk In declaring a dam or a category of dams to be a dam or category of dams with a safety risk, the minister must consider the need to protect the public, property and resource against potential hazards, the extent of potential harm involved, the cost of any prescribed measures and whether or not they are achievable, the socio-economic impact if the dam fails, and for each specific dam, particulars relating to its design, construction, repairs, alterations, status, the professionals involved, and the manner in which water is continued, stored, or impounded in the dam.[1] The minister may exempt owners of dams belonging to certain categories from the foregoing compliance provisions. Such exemptions must be in writing by notice in the *Gazette*, and may be with conditions imposed. The exemptions may be withdrawn at any time.[2]

1 National Water Act 36 of 1998 s 121.
2 S 122.

63 Regulations regarding dam safety The minister may make regulations for the establishment of a register of approved professional persons for dealing with dams with safety risk; approval procedure; fees payable for admission into different classes of approved professionals; obligations of dam owners; directives on the monitoring of dams; and the registration of dams with a safety risk. In making the regulations, the minister may not act arbitrarily. The minister must consult the Engineering Council of South Africa, and any appropriate statutory professional bodies.[1]

1 National Water Act 36 of 1998 s 123.

GAS

GENERAL

64 Introduction South Africa has relatively known gas resources of about 30 billion cubic metres off the south coast and some very small recent discoveries of about 3 billion cubic metres off the west coast. The potential natural gas resources have not yet been fully investigated. Potential gas development projects entail major capital investments, locked into immovable assets with long-term returns, hence, investors require stable policy conditions.[1] Gas has a number of characteristics from an energy policy perspective, and the development of its industry will stimulate inter-fuel competition, provide environmental benefits through lower emissions in contrast to oil and coal, provide greater options for industrial thermal applications, and increase the diversity of fuel supplies, and hence, improve South Africa's energy security.[2] The value chain associated with gas is complex, ranging from exploration, which includes geological surveys and seismic technology, to extraction, storage, transportation, as well as consumption. Hence, there is a need for a robust regulatory framework to address its different aspects.

1 Par 7.5.2 of the 1998 White Paper.
2 Par 7.5.3.

GAS ACT

INTRODUCTION

65 Objective of the Act The objects of the Gas Act[1] are to promote the efficient, effective, sustainable and orderly development and operation of gas transmissions, storage, distribution, liquefaction and re-gasification of gas and trading services; to facilitate investment in the gas industry; and ensure the safe, efficient, economic and environmentally responsible transmission, distribution, storage, liquefaction and re-gasification of gas. Other purposes of the Act include the facilitation of promotion of companies in the gas industry owned or controlled by historically disadvantaged South Africans by means of licence conditions to make them competitive; to ensure that gas transmission, storage, distribution, trading, liquefaction and re-gasification are provided on an equitable basis and that the interest and needs of all parties concerned are taken into consideration; while promoting skills and employment equity in the gas industry. The Act is also concerned with the development of competitive markets for gas and gas services; gas trade between South Africa and other countries; and the promotion of access to gas in an affordable and safe manner.[2]

1 48 of 2001; date of commencement yet to
  be proclaimed (s 37).
2 S 2.

NATIONAL GAS REGULATOR

66 National Gas Regulator The National Gas Regulator is a juristic person.[1] Its functions include the issuance of licences for the construction of gas transmission, storage, distribution, liquefaction and re-gasification facilities; conversion of infrastructure into transmission, storage, distribution, liquefaction and re-gasification facilities; operation of gas transmission, storage, distribution, liquefaction and re-gasification facilities; and trading in gas. It is to gather information relating to the production, transmission, storage, distribution, trading, liquefaction and re-gasification of gas. The National Gas Regulator is empowered to issue notices in terms of section 26(1) of the Gas Act in relation to contraventions of the Act and to take remedial action in terms of section 26(2), which includes imposing fines on defaulters. The regulator is authorised to undertake investigations and inquiries into the activities of licensees, and could consult with government departments and other institutions regarding any matter contemplated in the Act.

The National Gas Regulator is to consult with government departments and gas regulatory authorities of other countries in order to promote and facilitate the construction and development of gas transmission, storage, distribution, liquefaction and re-gasification facilities and services. Other functions include the regulation of prices; the monitoring, approval, and the regulation of transmission and storage tariffs. The Regulator is authorised to take appropriate action to ensure that tariffs are applied in a non-discriminatory manner as contemplated in section 22. It may expropriate land or any right in land as may be necessary for the performance of the functions of licensees, and may exercise such power or perform any duty conferred or imposed upon it under any law. The Regulator must promote competition, and the optimal use available gas resources. The decisions of the Regulator must be in accordance with published government policies.[2]

Decisions of the Regulator must be consistent with the Constitution[3] and the Gas Act; be in the public interest; and within the powers conferred upon it, taken within a procedurally fair process based on facts and evidence that must be summarised and recorded with the decision. The decision must be in writing and clearly explained, with the reasons therefor made available to the public. Any person adversely affected by the decision of the National Gas Regulator may bring such decision for a review by the High Court.[4]

The National Gas Regulator must prepare annual reports as required under the terms of the Public Finance Management Act.[5] Such reports must be accompanied by information on the licences granted, amended or withdrawn; regulations made and directives issued; future strategies; existing and envisaged commercial development with respect to the transmission, storage, distribution, liquefaction and re-gasification of gas and the gas trade; and the position regarding health and safety industry.[6] The auditor-general must audit the financial records of the Regulator.[7]

1 Gas Act 48 of 2001 s 3.	4 Gas Act 48 of 2001 s 10.
2 S 4.	5 1 of 1999.
3 Constitution of the Republic of SA 108 of	6 Gas Act 48 of 2001 s 14.
1996.	7 S 13(3).

GAS LICENCES AND REGISTRATION

67 Activities requiring licence A licence issued by the National Gas Regulator is required for the construction of gas transmission, storage, distribution, liquefaction and re-gasification facilities, or trading in gas. A person engaged in a Schedule 1[1] activity is not required to apply for, or hold a licence, though activities referred to in items 1 and 2 of Schedule 1 must be registered. The National Gas Regulator may determine whether a person is engaged in an activity requiring a licence; and may direct any person engaged in an activity requiring a licence, but without the necessary licence, to cease such an activity.[2] The owner of an operation involving the production or importation of gas; or an activity referred to in items 1 and 2 of Schedule 1 must register such operation with the Regulator.[3]

1 Schedule 1 activities involve the transmission of gas for a person's exclusive use, small biogas projects in rural communities and gas reticulation and trading related thereto, as well as LPG supplied from a bulk storage	tank or cylinder, piped at less than 2 bar gauge and crossing no more than 4 erf lines between separate property boundaries.
	2 Gas Act 48 of 2001 s 15.
	3 S 28.

68 Gas licensing and local authorities The effect of the licence provisions of the Gas Act[1] must be taken with caution in view of section 156(1)(a) of the Constitution[2] which provides that "a municipality has exclusive authority in respect of, and has the right to administer the local government matters listed in part B of Schedule 4". Gas reticulation is subject to the exclusive legislative competence of the local governments by virtue of Part B of Schedule 4. Pursuant to this provision, some local authorities have issued by-laws for the licensing of activities involving gas. An example is the Gas Licence By-laws[3] issued by the Greater Johannesburg Transitional Metropolitan Council.

1 48 of 2001.	1996.
2 Constitution of the Republic of SA 108 of	3 3326 of 2000.

69 Application for licence An application for a licence must be in the prescribed form and in accordance with prescribed procedure. Any application must include the name, company number (if any) and principal place of business of the applicant; particulars of the owners or shareholders of the applicant if the applicant is not a natural person; documents demonstrating the administrative, financial and technical abilities of the applicant; a description of the proposed facility to be constructed or operated, including maps and diagrams where appropriate; a general description of the type of customers to be served and the tariff policies to be applied; the plans and ability of the applicant to comply with all labour, health, safety and environmental legislation; and a detailed description of the gas that will be traded under the licence, and such other particulars as may be prescribed.[1] The applicant must publish a notice of the application in at least two newspapers circulating in the area of the proposed activity in any two official languages, one of which must be English, giving information on the name of the applicant; the object of the application; the place where the application will be made available for inspection; the period within which any objections to the issue of the licence may be lodged with the Regulator; the address of the National Gas Regulator where such objections may be lodged; and that the objections must be substantiated by an affidavit or solemn declaration.[2]

Before considering an application, if the National Gas Regulator is of the view that the proposed construction of gas facilities or provision of gas services should be altered to provide access to third parties, it must inform the applicant of this view and request the applicant to supply reasons as to why such a condition should not be imposed. The Regulator may also direct the applicant to alter the plans for the proposed construction of gas facilities or provision of gas services in order to comply with applicable health, safety or environmental legislation. The National Gas Regulator must furnish the applicant with all substantiated objections contemplated in section 17 of the Gas Act.[3]

Any person owning or operating gas facilities or trading in gas prior to the commencement of the Act must within six months after its commencement apply for a licence in terms of the Act.[4]

1 Gas Act 48 of 2001 s 16.   3 S 18.
2 S 17.   4 S 35.

70 Finalisation of application The Regulator must address issues relating to control or restrictions to guarantee compliance with applicable health, safety or environmental legislation, and may require such additional information as may be necessary to consider the application properly.[1] Decisions on an application must be made within 60 days if no objections have been received or after having received the response of the applicant to those objections. The minister may direct that the Regulator satisfies itself that such application meets specified criteria, reflecting the national interest, the promotion of regional growth, or any other social objective.[2] A copy of the decision showing the factors on which the decision was made must be delivered to the applicant.[3] Separate licences must be issued for the construction of gas transmission, storage, distribution, liquefaction and re-gasification facilities; and for the operation of gas transmission, storage or distribution facilities; and for trading in gas.[4]

1 Gas Act 48 of 2001 s 18.   3 S 19(3).
2 S 19(2).   4 S 19(4).

71 Conditions of licence The National Gas Regulator may impose licence conditions which may require a licensee to carry out the construction, operation or trading activities for which the licence is granted; and provide information regarding the participation of historically disadvantaged South Africans in the licensees activities. The conditions may require access to third parties on commercially reasonable terms to uncommitted capacity in transmission pipelines; that interested parties must be allowed to negotiate changes with transmission companies in the routing, size and capacity of proposed pipelines; and that a distributor will be granted the construction, operation and trading licence for its exclusive geographic area. An exclusive geographic area must be based on the distributor's ability to supply present and future potential customers at competitive prices; maximum prices for distributors, reticulators and all classes of consumers must be approved by the National Gas Regulator where there is inadequate competition as contemplated in chapters 2 and 3 of the Competition Act.[1] Licence conditions may require that an advisory service with regard to the safe and efficient use, handling and storage of gas must be provided to customers other than eligible customers, by the trading licensee; that licensees must maintain their facilities in a fully operative condition; that all customers in a licensed distribution area, except eligible customers and reticulators, must purchase their gas from the distribution company licensed for that area.[2] Any person aggrieved by a condition imposed, may apply to the National Gas Regulator to have the condition reviewed.[3]

1   89 of 1998.
2   Gas Act 48 of 2001 s 21(1).
3   S 21(2).

72   Term and amendment of licences   A license issued in terms of the Gas Act[1] is valid for a period of 25 years or such longer period as the National Gas Regulator may determine.[2] A licensee may apply to have his or her licence renewed.[3] An application for renewal must be granted, but the Regulator may set new or different licence conditions.[4] A licensee may not assign its licence to another party.[5]

The National Gas Regulator may vary, suspend or remove any of the licence conditions, or may include additional conditions on application by the licensee, with the permission of the licensee, upon non-compliance by a licensee with a licence condition, if it is necessary for the purposes of the Act, or on application by any affected party.[6]

1   48 of 2001.   4   S 23(3).
2   S 23(1).   5   S 23(4).
3   S 23(2).   6   S 24.

73   Revocation of licence on licensee's application   The National Gas Regulator may revoke a licence on the application of a licensee if the licensed facility or activity is no longer required, or is not economically justifiable, or another person is willing to assume the rights and obligation of the licensee and a new license is issued to such person.[1]

1   Gas Act 48 of 2001 s 25.

74   Contravention of licence   If a licensee contravenes or fails to comply with the condition of a licence or any provision of the Gas Act,[1] the National Gas Regulator may serve a notice on that licensee directing him or her to comply with the condition or the provision of the Act within a reasonable period.[2] If the licensee fails to comply with such notice, the Regulator may sit as a tribunal and, with due regard to section 10 of the Act, decide on the matter and may impose a fine not exceeding R2 000 000 per day for each day on which the contravention or failure to comply continues.[3] Any person adversely affected by a decision of the tribunal may bring such decision under appeal to the High Court.[4]

1   48 of 2001.   3   S 26(2).
2   S 26(1).   4   S 26(4).

75 Revocation of licence by the court The National Gas Regulator may apply to the High Court for an order suspending or revoking a licence if there exists any ground justifying such suspension or revocation, such as the failure of the licensee to carry out the construction, operation or trading activities for which the licence was granted.[1]

1 Gas Act 48 of 2001 s 27.

76 Non-discrimination and transparency Licensees may not discriminate between customers or classes of customers regarding access, tariffs, prices, conditions or service except for objectively justifiable differences regarding such matters as quantity, transmission distance, length of contract, load profile, interruptible supply or other distinguishing feature approved by the National Gas Regulator.[1]

Whenever a state-controlled entity that acquired a licence pursuant to the national interest, the promotion of regional growth, or any other social objective sells any of its shares or any of its assets to any privately controlled entity, it must do so by means of an open and transparent bidding procedure.[2]

1 Gas Act 48 of 2001 s 22.
2 S 20.

GENERAL PROVISIONS

77 Powers of the National Gas Regulator Any person authorised in writing by the National Gas Regulator may at all reasonable times enter any property on which a licensed activity is taking place and inspect any facility, equipment, machinery, book, account or other document found. The Regulator may require that the accuracy of this information or document given to it be verified on oath or by way of a solemn declaration.[1]

1 Gas Act 48 of 2001 s 29.

78 Resolution of disputes by the National Gas Regulator The National Gas Regulator may with the approval of the parties to a dispute, act as mediator or arbitrator in any matter concerning trading of gas or the rendering of services.[1] Any decision taken by the National Gas Regulator acting as arbitrator or by another arbitrator acting as such is binding on the parties to the dispute.[2] When acting as an arbitrator, the Regulator must issue a decision on the matter.[3] The National Gas Regulator may, on request of the parties involved, appoint another person suitable to act as that mediator or arbitrator.[4]

1 Gas Act 48 of 2001 s 30(2)(a).
2 S 30(3).
3 S 30(1)(b).
4 S 30(4).

79 Investigations by National Gas Regulator The National Gas Regulator must conduct investigations into complaints by customers relating to the supply of gas; unreasonable or excessive prices or tariffs imposed by a licensee; and unreasonable differences regarding the supply of gas or gas services by licensees.[1] The National Gas Regulator may not conduct investigations into disputes concerning breach of contract between a licensee and an eligible customer.[2]

1 Gas Act 48 of 2001 s 31(1).
2 S 31(2).

80 Expropriation of land by National Gas Regulator The National Gas Regulator may expropriate land or any right in land on behalf of the licensee for gas transmission, storage, distribution, liquefaction or re-gasification facilities in accordance with section 25 of the Constitution.[1] The Regulator may only exercise these powers if it is satisfied that a licensee is unable to acquire land or a right in land by agreement with the owner; and the land or right in land is reasonably required by a licensee for gas transmission, storage, distribution, liquefaction or re-gasification facilities which will enhance the Republic's gas infrastructure.[2]

1 Constitution of the Republic of SA 108 of
  1998: Gas Act 48 of 2001 s 32.
2 S 32(3).

81 Rights of licensee in respect of premises or land belonging to others and regulations and rules Subject to the approval of the relevant authorities, a licensee may lay and construct pipes for the distribution of gas under or over any street and may from time to time repair, alter or remove these pipes. The licensee is responsible for any restoration necessary as a result of such construction. Any person authorised in writing by a licensee may at all reasonable times enter any premises to which gas has been supplied in order to inspect, repair, replace or alter any pipe, metre, fitting, work and apparatus belonging to such licensee; to ascertain the quantity of gas consumed; or where a gas supply is no longer required, for the purpose of removing any pipe, metre, fitting, work and apparatus belonging to such licensee.[1]

The minister may by notice in the *Government Gazette* make regulations regarding fair administrative action by the National Gas Regulator; criteria for distribution; the rehabilitation of land used in connection with transmission, storage, distribution, liquefaction or re-gasification of gas or the trading therein; the requirements that must be met by a person in order to qualify as an eligible customer; the procedure to be followed during expropriation proceedings; the rendering of information to the National Gas Regulator; price regulation procedures and principles; and mechanisms to promote historically disadvantaged South Africans.[2] Before promulgating these regulations the minister must consult with the National Gas Regulator and invite public comments.[3]

The National Gas Regulator may make rules regarding the procedures to be followed at its meetings; the keeping of records by the National Gas Regulator; the form, manner and content of licence applications; the procedure to be followed in considering licence applications; the procedure to be followed in variation, extension, removal or revocation of license conditions; the form in which registration must be lodged; inspection of the construction and operation of any gas facility or any trading in gas; and consultation with interested and affected parties.[4]

1 Gas Act 48 of 2001 s 33.   3 S 34(2).
2 S 34(1).   4 S 34(3).

82 Mozambique Gas Pipeline Agreement The Mozambique Gas Pipeline Agreement was entered into between the minister, the Minister of Trade and Industry, and Sasol Limited, concerning the introduction of natural gas by pipelines from the Republic of Mozambique into South Africa.[1] The agreement binds the National Gas Regulator until ten years after natural gas is first received from Mozambique.[2] From the date of conclusion of the agreement, the terms of agreement relating to the exclusive rights and periods granted in respect of transmission and distribution of gas; third party access to the transmission pipeline from Mozambique and to certain of Sasol's pipelines; prices charged by Sasol for gas; Sasol's obligation to supply customers, distributors and reticulators with gas; and administration of the agreement constitute conditions of a licence within the terms of section 19 of the Gas Act.[3] The National Gas Regulator must formally issue licences to the entities contemplated in the agreement.[4]

1 Gas Act 48 of 2001 s 36(1).   3 S 36(3).
2 S 36(2).   4 S 36(4).

LIQUID FUELS

GENERAL

83 Introduction Crude oil is South Africa's single largest import item. Approximately 15 per cent of the country's primary energy consumption is currently met by imported crude oil.[1] The liquid fuels industry is largely characterised by a unique regulatory framework and a significant degree of government involvement. All rights to natural oil (including oil and gas) are vested in the state as enshrined in the Mining Rights Act,[2] and the right is retained as such in the Mineral and Petroleum Resources Development Act of 2002,[3] which provides that "mineral resources are the common heritage of all people of South Africa and the State is the custodian thereof for the benefit of all South Africans".[4] Minerals and petroleum are non-renewable natural resources. The state has an obligation to protect the environment for the benefit of present and future generations, to ensure ecologically sustainable development of mineral and petroleum resources and to promote economic and social development. There is a need to uplift the communities affected by mining. The state must bring about equitable access to South Africa's mineral and petroleum resources and must eradicate all forms of discriminatory practices in the mineral and petroleum industries. The Constitution[5] obliges the state to take legislative and other measures to redress the results of past racial discrimination. The state must guarantee security of tenure in respect of prospecting and mining operations.

The government believes that the desired attributes for the liquid fuels industry can best be met in an environment of minimum governmental intervention and regulation. Therefore, government will facilitate an environment within which the industry can conduct its business effectively and on a competitive basis.[6] Relevant statutes within the regulatory framework for liquid fuels in South Africa are the Petroleum Products Act,[7] the Petroleum Pipelines Act[8] and the Mineral and Petroleum Resources Development Act.[9]

1 White Paper par 7.4.1.   1996.
2 20 of 1967.   6 Par 7.4.2 of the White Paper.
3 28 of 2002.   7 120 of 1977.
4 S 3.   8 60 of 2003.
5 Constitution of the Republic of SA 108 of   9 28 of 2002.

MINERAL AND PETROLEUM RESOURCES DEVELOPMENT ACT

FUNDAMENTAL PRINCIPLES

84 Objects of the Act The Mineral and Petroleum Resources Development Act[1] recognises the state's right to exercise sovereignty over all the minerals and petroleum resources within the Republic; and that the state is the custodian of the nation's mineral and petroleum resources.

Minerals are dealt with elsewhere;[2] this title deals only with the provisions of the Act relating to petroleum.

The Act seeks to promote equitable access to the nation's petroleum resources; expand opportunities for historically disadvantaged persons to enter petroleum industries; promote economic growth and petroleum resources development; promote employment and the social and economic welfare of all South Africans. The Act will facilitate the provision of security of tenure in respect of exploration and production operations; give effect to section 24 of the Constitution[3] by ensuring that the nation's petroleum resources are developed in an orderly and ecologically sustainable manner while promoting social and economic development; and ensure that holders of production rights contribute towards the socio–economic development of the areas in which they are operating.[4] In interpreting the Act, where the common law is inconsistent with the Act, the Act will prevail.[5]

1   28 of 2002.
2   See title MINING AND MINERALS.
3   Constitution of the Republic of SA 108 of 1996.

4   Mineral and Petroleum Resources Development Act 28 of 2002 s 2.
5   S 4(2).

85 Rights over petroleum resources The state is the custodian of the petroleum resources of the Republic and these resources must be regulated for the benefit of all South Africans.[1] The state, acting through the minister, may grant, issue, refuse, control, administer and manage any reconnaissance permission, prospecting right, permission to remove, mining right, mining permit, retention permit, technical co-operation permit, reconnaissance permit, exploration right and production right; and may levy any fee in terms of relevant legislation.[2] The minister must ensure the sustainable development of South Africa's petroleum resources within the framework of national environmental policy while promoting economic and social development.[3]

1   Mineral and Petroleum Resources Development Act 28 of 2002 s 3(1).

2   S 3(2).
3   S 3(3).

86 Nature of rights under the Act The legal nature of a prospecting right, exploration right or production right is that they are limited real rights.[1] The holder thereof may enter the land to which such right relates and may bring onto that land any machinery or equipment and build upon any surface, underground or under sea infrastructure which may be required for the purposes of prospecting, mining, exploration or production; prospect, mine or explore that land for the mineral or petroleum for which such right has been granted; remove and dispose of any such mineral found during the course of prospecting, mining, exploration or production. The holder of such right may use water, subject to the National Water Act,[2] from any natural spring, lake, river or stream that is situated on or flowing through such land, or sink a well or borehole required for prospecting, mining, exploration or production on such land; and carry out any other activity incidental to prospecting, mining, exploration or production operations which do not contravene the provisions of the Mineral and Petroleum Resources Development Act.[3] No person may prospect for or mine any mineral or petroleum on any area without an approved environmental management programme; the relevant permit; and consulting with the land owner or lawful occupier of the land in question.[4]

1   Mineral and Petroleum Resources Development Act 28 of 2002 s 5(1).
2   36 of 1998.

3   28 of 2002 s 5(3).
4   S 5(4).

87 Principles of administrative justice Subject to the Promotion of Administrative Justice Act of 2000,[1] any administrative decision taken in terms of the Mineral and Petroleum Resources Development Act[2] must be conducted within a reasonable time and in accordance with the principles of lawfulness, reasonableness and procedural fairness. Any such decision must be in writing and accompanied by written reasons for such decision.[3] By this provision it is implied that such administrative action may be subject to judicial review, and to the extent that decisions must be accompanied with reasons, transparency in actions will be encouraged.

1   3 of 2000.
2   28 of 2002.
3   S 6.

88 Territorial waters, continental shelf, and exclusive economic zones For the purposes of the Mineral and Petroleum Resources Development Act,[1] the minister may by notice in the *Gazette* divide the Republic, territorial waters, continental shelf and exclusive economic zone into regions.[2] South Africa is a party to the 1958 Convention on the Continental Shelf, which recognises the right of coastal states to exercise sovereignty over the continental shelf for purposes of exploring and exploiting its natural resources, the sea-bed and subsoil. The country is also a signatory to the 1982 Law of the Sea Convention.[3]

1   28 of 2002.
2   S 7.
3   Fuggle and Rabie (eds) *Environmental*

Management in SA Juta & Co Cape Town 1992.

PETROLEUM EXPLORATION AND PRODUCTION

89 Designated agency The Mineral and Petroleum Resources Development Act[1] provides for the granting of exploration rights and production rights and the issuing of technical co-operation permits and reconnaissance permits.[2] The minister may designate an organ of state or a wholly owned and controlled agency or company belonging to the state to perform the functions referred to in this chapter of the Act.[3]

The designated agency must promote onshore and offshore exploration for and production of petroleum; receive and evaluate applications for reconnaissance permits, technical co-corporation permits, exploration rights and production rights, and make recommendations to the minister; monitor and report regularly to the minister in respect of compliance with such permits or rights; receive, interpret or disseminate geological information relating to petroleum; advise the minister on the need to carry out on behalf of the state reconnaissance operations in connection with petroleum; review and make recommendations to the minister with regard to the approval of environmental management plans or programmes; and perform any other function which the minister may determine.[4]

The designated agency is funded by money appropriated by Parliament.[5]

1   28 of 2002.   4   S 71.
2   S 69.   5   S 72
3   S 70.

90 Invitation for applications The minister may, by notice in the *Gazette*, invite applications for exploration and production rights.[1] The designated agency may otherwise directly receive applications for exploration and productions rights which are not subject to an invitation.[2] The designated agency must inform the minister of an application within seven days of receipt thereof.[3]

1   Mineral and Petroleum Resources Development Act 28 of 2002 s 73(1).   2   S 73(2).
3   S 73(3).

91 Application for reconnaissance permit An applicant for a reconnaissance permit must lodge the application at the office of the designated agency; in the prescribed manner; and together with the prescribed non-refundable application fee.[1]

The designated agency must accept an application if these requirements are met; and if no other person holds a technical co-operation permit, exploration right or production right for petroleum over any part of the area.[2] If the designated agency accepts the application, it must notify the applicant to submit an environmental management plan; and to consult with any affected party.[3]

1   Mineral and Petroleum Resources Development Act 28 of 2002 s 74(1).

2   S 74(2).

3   S 74(4).

92   Issuing and duration of reconnaissance permit

92   Issuing and duration of reconnaissance permit The minister must issue a reconnaissance permit if the applicant has access to financial resources and has the technical ability to conduct the proposed reconnaissance survey; the estimated expenditure is compatible with the intended reconnaissance operation; the reconnaissance will not result in unacceptable pollution, ecological degradation or damage to the environment; the applicant has the ability to comply with the relevant provisions of the Mine Health and Safety Act;[1] and the applicant is not in contravention of any relevant provision of the Mineral and Petroleum Resources Development Act.[2] The minister must refuse to issue a reconnaissance permit if the applicant does not meet the above requirements.[3] A reconnaissance permit issued is subject to prescribed terms and conditions; valid for a period not exceeding one year; not an exclusive right; not transferable; and not renewable.[4] The holder of the reconnaissance permit must actively conduct reconnaissance operations in respect of petroleum on the relevant area.[5]

1   29 of 1996.
2   28 of 2002 s 75(1).
3   S 75(2).

4   S 75(4).
5   S 75(5).

93   Application for technical co-operation permit

93   Application for technical co-operation permit An application for a technical co-operation permit must be lodged at the office of the designated agency; in the prescribed manner; and together with the prescribed non-refundable application fee.[1] The designated agency must accept an application if the above requirements are met; and if no other person holds a technical co-operation permit, exploration rights or production rights for petroleum over any part of the area.[2]

1   Mineral and Petroleum Resources Development Act 28 of 2002 s 76(1).

2   S 76(2).

94   Issuing and duration of technical co-operation permit

94   Issuing and duration of technical co-operation permit The minister must issue a technical co-operation permit if the applicant has access to financial resources and has the technical ability to conduct the proposed technical co-operation study; the estimated expenditure is compatible with the intended technical co-operation study; and the applicant has not contravened any relevant provision of the Mineral and Petroleum Resources Development Act.[1] The minister must refuse to issue a technical co-operation permit if the application does not meet these requirements.[2] A technical co-operation permit issued is subject to prescribed terms and conditions; valid for a period not exceeding one year; not transferable; and not renewable.[3]

1   28 of 2002 s 77(1).
2   S 77(2).
3   S 77(4).

95   Rights and obligations of holder of technical co-operation permit

95   Rights and obligations of holder of technical co-operation permit The holder of a technical co-operation permit has the exclusive right to apply for and be granted an exploration right in respect of the area to which the permit relates.[1] The holder of a technical co-operation permit must actively carry out the technical co-operation study; and comply with the terms and conditions of the technical co-operation permit.[2]

1 Mineral and Petroleum Resources Development Act 28 of 2002 s 78(1).
2 S 78(2).

96 Application for exploration right An application for an exploration right must be lodged at the office of the designated agency; in the prescribed manner; and together with the prescribed non-refundable application fee.[1] The designated agency must accept an application if these requirements are met; and if no other person holds a technical co-operation permit, exploration right or production right for petroleum over any part of the area.[2] If the designated agency accepts the application, it must notify the applicant to consult with any affected parties; and to submit an environmental management programme.[3] Any technical co-operation permit in respect of which an application for exploration right has been lodged will, notwithstanding its expiry date, remain in force until such application has been granted or refused.[4]

1 Mineral and Petroleum Resources Devel-   3 S 79(4).
  opment Act 28 of 2002 s 79(1).   4 S 79(5).
2 S 79(2).

97 Granting and duration of exploration right The minister must grant an exploration right if the applicant has access to financial resources and has the technical ability to conduct the proposed exploration operation optimally; the estimated expenditure is compatible with the intended exploration operation; the minister has approved the environmental management programme; the applicant has the ability to comply with the relevant provisions of the Mine Health and Safety Act;[1] the applicant is not in contravention of any relevant provision of the Mineral and Petroleum Resources Development Act;[2] the applicant has complied with the terms and conditions of the technical co-operation permit, if applicable; and the granting of such right will further the objects referred to in section 2(d) and (f).[3] The minister must refuse to grant an exploration right if the application does not meet with all these requirements.[4] An exploration right is valid for a period specified in the right, which may not exceed three years.[5]

1 29 of 1996.   4 S 80(3).
2 28 of 2002.   5 S 80(5).
3 S 80(1).

98 Application for renewal of exploration right An application for the renewal of an exploration right must be lodged at the office of the designated agency; in the prescribed manner; and together with the prescribed non-refundable application fee.[1] An application for renewal must state the reasons and period for which the renewal is required; include a detailed report reflecting the exploration results and the exploration expenditure incurred; include a report showing the extent of compliance with the environmental management programme, the rehabilitation to be completed and the estimated cost thereof; and include a detailed exploration work programme for the renewal period.[2] An exploration right may be renewed for a maximum of three periods not exceeding two years each.[3] An exploration right in respect of which an application for renewal has been lodged will, notwithstanding its expiry date, remain in force until such time as the application for renewal has been granted or refused.[4]

1 Mineral and Petroleum Resources Devel-   3 S 81(4).
   opment Act 28 of 2002 s 81(1).   4 S 81(5).
2 S 81(2).

99 Rights and obligations of holder of exploration right The holder of an
exploration right has the exclusive right to apply for and be granted a production right
in respect of the petroleum and the exploration area in question; has the exclusive
right to apply for and be granted a renewal of an exploration right; has the exclusive
right to remove and dispose of any petroleum samples found during the course of
exploration; and may only transfer and encumber the exploration right, subject to
section 11 of the Mineral and Petroleum Resources Development Act.[1] The holder of
an exploration right must register the right at the Mining Titles Office.[2]

1 28 of 2002.
2 S 82.

100 Application for production right An application for a production right
must be lodged at the office of the designated agency; in the prescribed manner; and
together with the prescribed non-refundable application fee.[1] The designated agency
must accept an application if these requirements are met; and if no other person holds
a technical co-operation permit, exploration right or production right for petroleum
over any part of the area.[2] If the designated agency accepts the application, it must
notify the applicant to consult with interested and affected parties; and conduct an
environmental impact assessment and submit an environmental management programme for approval.[3]

1 Mineral and Petroleum Resources Devel-   2 S 83(2).
   opment Act 28 of 2002 s 83(1).   3 S 83(4).

101 Granting and duration of production right The minister must grant a
production right if the applicant has access to financial resources and has the technical
ability to conduct the proposed production operation optimally; the estimated expenditure is compatible with the intended production operation; the production will not
result in unacceptable pollution, ecological degradation or damage to the environment; the applicant has the ability to comply with the relevant provisions of the Mine
Health and Safety Act;[1] the applicant is not in contravention of any relevant provision
of the Mineral and Petroleum Resources Development Act;[2] the applicant has complied with the terms of the exploration right, if applicable; the applicant has provided
financial and otherwise for a prescribed social and labour plan; the petroleum can be
produced optimally; the granting of such right will further the objects referred to in
section 2(d) and (f).[3] The minister must refuse to grant a production right if the
application does not meet these requirements.[4] A production right is valid for the
period specified in the right, which period may not exceed 30 years.[5] A production
right comes into effect on the date on which the environmental management programme is approved.[6]

1 29 of 1996.   4 S 84(2).
2 28 of 2002.   5 S 84(4).
3 S 84(1).   6 S 84(5).

102 Application for renewal of production right An application for renewal of
a production right must be lodged at the office of the designated agency; in the
prescribed manner; and together with the prescribed non-refundable application fee.[1]
An applicant for renewal must state the reasons and period for which the renewal is

required; include a detailed report reflecting the production results and the production expenditure incurred; include a report reflecting the extent of compliance with the approved environmental management programme, the rehabilitation to be completed and the estimated costs thereof; and include a detailed production work programme for the renewal period.[2] A production right may be renewed for further periods, each of which may not exceed 30 years at a time.[3] A production right in respect of which an application for renewal has been lodged, will despite its expiry date, remain in force until such time as such application has been granted or refused.[4]

1 Mineral and Petroleum Resources Development Act 28 of 2002 s 85(1).	3 S 85(4).
	4 S 85(5).
2 S 85(2).	

103 Rights and obligations of holder of production right The holder of a production right has the exclusive right to apply for and be granted renewal of the production right in respect of the petroleum area in question; has the exclusive right to remove and dispose of any petroleum found; and may only transfer and encumber the production right, subject to section 11 of the Mineral and Petroleum Resources Development Act.[1] The holder of a production right must register the right at the Mining Titles Office.[2]

1 28 of 2002.
2 S 86.

104 Development of petroleum reservoir as unit If an exploration right or a production right has been granted over an area which geologically forms part of the same petroleum reservoir to which any other exploration or production rights exist, the holders of such rights must prepare a scheme for the development of the petroleum reservoir as a unit. The holders must submit this scheme to the designated agency for approval by the minister.[1]

1 Mineral and Petroleum Resources Development Act 28 of 2002 s 87.

105 Information and data The holder of a permit or right who conducts reconnaissance operations, technical co-operation studies, exploration operations or production operations must submit such information or data to the designated agency.[1] Subject to the Promotion of Access to Information Act,[1] all information or data submitted must be kept confidential by the agency.[2] Neither the state nor any of its employees is liable for the *bona fide* or inadvertent release of information or data submitted.[3]

1 2 of 2000.	Development Act 28 of 2002 s 88(1).
2 Mineral and Petroleum Resources	3 S 88(2).

106 Financial guarantee In addition to section 5 of the Mineral and Petroleum Resources Development Act,[1] no exploration operation or production operation may commence unless the holder has provided for a financial provision guaranteeing the availability of sufficient funds for the due fulfilment of all exploration and production work programmes by the holder.[2]

1 28 of 2002; see par 86 ante.
2 S 89.

107 Minister's power to suspend or cancel permits or rights The minister
may cancel or suspend any reconnaissance permit, technical co-operation permit,
exploration right or production right in accordance with the procedure in section 47
of the Mineral and Petroleum Resources Development Act.[1]

  1 28 of 2002 s 90.

GENERAL AND MISCELLANEOUS PROVISIONS

108 Power to enter prospecting area, mining area or retention area The
minister may authorise any member of the board, the regional manager or any officer
to enter any reconnaissance, prospecting, mining, exploration, production or retention area or any place their prospecting operations or mining operations are being
conducted where he or she has reason to believe that a provision of the Mineral and
Petroleum Resources Development Act[1] has been, is being, or will be contravened.
The authorised person may direct the person in control of or employed at such area
to furnish any information that pertains to the investigation; and to render such
assistance as the authorised person requires. The authorised person may take samples
of any material or substance found in such area. The authorised person may also seize
any material, substance, book, record or other document which may be relevant to a
prosecution under the Act.[2]

  1 28 of 2002.
  2 S 91(a)–(f).

109 Routine inspections An authorised person may, without a warrant, enter any
reconnaissance, prospecting, mining production or exploration or retention area in
order to inspect any activities, process or operations; and require the holder or the
person in charge of such area to produce any book, record, statement or other document relating to matters dealt within the Mineral and Petroleum Resources Development Act[1] for inspection.[2]

  1 28 of 2002.
  2 S 92.

110 Orders, suspension and instructions If an authorised person finds that a
contravention or suspected contravention of any provision of the Mineral and Petroleum Resources Development Act[1] or a failure to comply with a term of condition of
any right, permit or permission has occurred or is occurring, or she may order the
holder or the person in charge of such area to take immediate rectifying steps; or
order that the operation be suspended or terminated.[2] The director-general must
confirm or set aside such an order.[3]

  1 28 of 2002.
  2 S 93(1).
  3 S 93(2).

111 Prohibitions No person may obstruct, hinder or oppose any authorised person
in the performance of his or her functions in terms of the Mineral and Petroleum
Resources Development Act.[1]

  The holder of a right, permit or permission may not subject his or her employees to
any occupational detriment on account of such employees disclosing information to
the minister, regarding the failure by such holder to comply with any provision of the
Act.[2] Occupational detriment means "occupational detriment" as defined in the
Protected Disclosures Act.[3]

1 28 of 2002 s 94.
2 S 95(1).
3 26 of 2000: Mineral and Petroleum

Resources Development Act 28 of 2002
s 95(2).

112 Internal appeal process and access to courts Any person whose rights or legitimate expectations have been materially and adversely affected or who is aggrieved by any administrative decision in terms of the Mineral and Petroleum Resources Development Act,[1] may appeal to the director-general or the minister.[2] An appeal does not suspend the administrative decision, unless it is suspended by the director-general or the minister, as the case may be.[3] No person may apply to the court for review until that person has exhausted his or her remedies in terms of this section.[4]

1 28 of 2002.   3 S 96(2).
2 S 96(1).   4 S 96(3).

113 Offences and penalties Any person is guilty of an offence if he or she contravenes any provision of the Mineral and Petroleum Resources Development Act;[1] submits inaccurate or misleading information required under the Act; or fails to provide a written notice or consult with the minister in terms of section 26(3).[2]

The Act provides for imposition of various fines and periods of imprisonment depending on the provision contravened.[3]

As far as criminal provisions are concerned, the Act binds the state.[4]

1 28 of 2002.   3 S 99.
2 S 98.   4 S 109.

114 Amendment of rights, permits, programmes and plans A permission, right, permit, work programme and environmental management programme or plan may not be amended or varied without the written consent of the minister.[1]

1 Mineral and Petroleum Resources Development Act 28 of 2002 s 102.

115 Delegation and assignment The minister may delegate any power conferred on him or her under the Mineral and Petroleum Resources Development Act,[1] except a power to make regulations or deal with any appeal, to the director-general, the regional manager or any officer.[2] The director-general, the regional manager or any officer may further delegate such power or duty to any other officer.[3] The minister, director-general, regional manager or officer is not divested of any power or exempted from any duty delegated by him or her.[4]

1 28 of 2002.   3 S 103(3).
2 S 103(1).   4 S 103(5).

116 Land owner or lawful occupier of land cannot be traced If the applicant for a right, permit or permission cannot trace the land owner or lawful occupier of the land to which the application relates, or the land owner or lawful occupier is deceased and no successor can be readily traced, the regional manager may grant consent to the applicant to enter such land.[1]

1 Mineral and Petroleum Resources Development Act 28 of 2002 s 105.

117 Exemption from certain provisions of the Act The minister may exempt any organ of state from certain provisions of the Mineral and Petroleum Resources Development Act.[1] Despite this exemption, the organ of state must submit an environmental management programme for approval.[2] A landowner of lawful occupier may, under certain circumstances, be exempted from certain provisions of the Act.[3]

1 28 of 2002 s 106(1).
2 S 106(2).
3 S 106(3).

118 Regulations The minister may by notice in the *Gazette* make regulations regarding the conservation of the environment in the vicinity of any mine; the management of the impact of any mining operation on the environment; the rehabilitation of disturbances of the surface of land; the prevention and control of pollution of the air, land, sea or other water, including ground water; the establishment of accounts for the carrying out of an environmental management programme; the assumption by the state of responsibility under certain circumstances; the exploitation, processing or disposal of any minerals; procedures in respect of appeals; fees payable in terms of the Mineral and Petroleum Resources Development Act;[1] the form of any application; the form, conditions, issuing, renewal, abandonment, suspension or cancellation of any environmental management programme, permit, licence, certificates or permissions; the prohibition on the disposal of any mineral; any matter which must be prescribed for in terms of the Act.[2]

No regulation relating to state revenue or expenditure may be made by the minister except with the concurrence of the Minister of Finance.[3]

1 28 of 2002.
2 S 107(1)(a)–(l).
3 S 107(2).

PETROLEUM PIPELINES ACT

GENERAL

119 Objects of Act The objects of the Petroleum Pipelines Act[1] are to promote competition in the construction and operation of petroleum pipelines, loading facilities and storage facilities; promote the efficient, effective, sustainable and orderly development, operation and use of petroleum pipelines, loading facilities and storage facilities; ensure the safe, efficient, economic and environmentally responsible transport, loading and storage of petroleum; promote equitable access to petroleum pipelines, loading facilities and storage facilities; facilitate investment in the petroleum pipeline industry; provide for the security of petroleum pipelines and related infrastructure; promote companies in the petroleum pipeline industry that are owned or controlled by historically disadvantaged South Africans by means of licence conditions to enable them to become competitive; promote the development of competitive markets for petroleum products; and promote access to affordable petroleum products.[2]

1 60 of 2003 (date of commencement to be
  proclaimed).
2 S 2.

AUTHORITY AND MEMBERS

120 Establishment and duties of Authority The Petroleum Pipelines National Electricity Regulatory Authority ("the Authority") is established as a juristic person.[1] The Authority must issue licences for the construction and conversion of petroleum pipelines, loading facilities and storage facilities; and the operation of petroleum pipelines, loading facilities and storage facilities; gather information relating to the construction, conversion and operation of petroleum pipelines, loading facilities and storage facilities; undertake investigations into the activities of licensees; act as mediator or arbitrator in accordance with the Petroleum Pipelines Act; consult, where necessary, with government departments and other bodies regarding any matter contemplated in the Act; set or approve tariffs; monitor and take appropriate action to ensure that access to petroleum pipelines, loading facilities and storage facilities is provided in a non–discriminatory, fair and transparent manner; promote competition in the petroleum pipeline industry; and take decisions that are not at variance with published government policy. The authority may expropriate land or any right in land necessary for the exercise of the licensee's rights; and perform any activity incidental to the performance of its duties.[2]

1 Petroleum Pipelines Act 60 of 2003 s 3.
2 S 4(a)–(m).

121 Constitution of Authority The Authority consists of five members appointed by the minister.[1] The minister must appoint the chairperson.[2] A member holds office for four years.[3] Members are paid such remuneration and allowances as the minister may approve, with the concurrence of the Minister of Finance.[4]

1 Petroleum Pipelines Act 60 of 2003 s 5(1).   3 S 5(4).
2 S 5(2).   4 S 5(5).

122 Disqualification and requirements regarding appointment of members to Authority A person may not be appointed or remain a member of the Authority if he or she is not a South African citizen or a permanent resident in South Africa; is an unrehabilitated insolvent; has been convicted of an offence involving dishonesty; or there is a probability of a material conflict of interest between the interests of that person as member of the board and his or her personal, professional or business interests.[1]

1 Petroleum Pipelines Act 60 of 2003 s 6.

123 Vacation of office and termination of appointment A member must vacate office if he or she becomes of unsound mind; has been absent from more than two consecutive meetings without leave of the chairperson; resigns; materially fails to perform any duty; or becomes disqualified from being a member in terms of section 6 of the Petroleum Pipelines Act.[1]

1 60 of 2003 s 7.

124 Meetings of Authority The chairperson must convene such meetings as are necessary for the proper performance of the Authority's functions.[1] The quorum for any meeting is a majority of its members.[2] The Authority must keep a record of all its proceedings.[3]

1 Petroleum Pipelines Act 60 of 2003 s 8(2).
2 S 8(4).
3 S 8(8).

125 Duties of members of Authority Members must act in a justifiable and transparent manner whenever the exercise of their discretion is required; act in the interest of the Authority and not in their own or sectoral interests; act independently of any undue influence or instructions; recuse themselves from and refrain from voting on or discussing any matter before the authority in which they have a direct or indirect interest; and act in a manner that is required and expected from the holder of a public office.[1]

1 Petroleum Pipelines Act 60 of 2003 s 9.

126 Decisions of Authority Any decision of the Authority must be consistent with the Constitution[1] and the Petroleum Pipelines Act;[2] in the public interest; taken within a procedurally fair process; based on facts and evidence that must be summarised and recorded with the decision; in writing and explained clearly as to its factual and legal basis.[3] Any decision and its reasons must be made available to the public.[4] Any person adversely affected by a decision of the Authority may bring such decision under review by the High Court.[5]

1 Constitution of the Republic of SA 108 of 1996.
2 60 of 2003.
3 S 10(1).
4 S 10(2).
5 S 10(3).

127 Personnel of Authority The Authority must appoint a Chief Executive Officer.[1] The Chief Executive Officer is responsible for the day-to-day management of the affairs of the Authority, and for administrative control over its employees.[2]

1 Petroleum Pipelines Act 60 of 2003 s 11(1).
2 S 11(2).

128 Funds, accounting and reporting The funds of the Authority consist of appropriation from the National Revenue Fund; levies imposed by separate legislation; charges for mediation, arbitration and other services rendered; and donations or contributions received from persons, institutions, government.[1]

The Authority must comply with the Public Finance Management Act.[2] The financial records of the Authority must be audited by the auditor-general.[3]

The Authority must submit an annual report to the minister. The report must include information on licence applications granted, amended or withdrawn; rules made and directives issued; the envisaged strategies of the Authority; existing and envisaged developments regarding construction and operation of petroleum pipelines, loading facilities and storage facilities; and heath, safety and environmental issues in the petroleum industry.[4]

1 Petroleum Pipelines Act 60 of 2003 s 12.
2 1 of 1999: Petroleum Pipelines Act 60 of 2003 s 13(1).
3 S 13(3).
4 S 14.

LICENCES

129 Activities requiring licence A person may not, without a licence, construct a petroleum pipeline, a loading facility or a storage facility; or operate a petroleum pipeline, loading facility or storage facility.[1] The Authority may determine whether a person is engaged in an activity requiring a licence; and may direct any person engaged in an activity requiring a licence who is not in possession of the necessary licence to cease such activity.[2]

1 Petroleum Pipelines Act 60 of 2003 s 15(1).
2 S 15(2).

130 Application for licence An application for a licence must be made in the prescribed form and procedure.[1] An application must include the name, company number (if any) and principle place of business of the applicant; particulars of the owners or shareholders of the applicant or if not a natural person; documents demonstrating the administrative, financial and technical abilities of the applicant; a description of the proposed pipeline, loading facility or storage facility to be constructed or operated; a description of the tariff and price policies to be applied; and the plans and ability of the applicant to comply with labour, health, safety, security and environmental legislation.[2] The applicant may request confidential treatment of commercially sensitive information.[3]

The applicant must publish a notice of the application in at least two newspapers circulating in the area of the proposed activity.[4] The advertisement must state in particular the period within which any objections to the issue of the licence may be lodged.[5]

1 Petroleum Pipelines Act 60 of 2003 s 16(1).
2 S 16(2).
3 S 16(3).
4 S 17(1).
5 S 17(2).

131 Particular information to be supplied by applicant Before considering an application for a licence, the Authority, if it is of the view that a proposed construction of the petroleum pipeline, loading facility or storage facility should be altered to provide access to third parties, must inform the applicant of that view and request the applicant to give reasons as to why the application should not be considered subject to the imposition of such conditions;[1] may direct the applicant to alter the plans for the proposed construction of petroleum facilities in order to comply with labour, health, safety, security and environmental legislation;[2] must furnish the applicant with all substantiated objections contemplated in section 17 of the Petroleum Pipelines Act;[3] and may request additional information as may be necessary to consider the application properly.[4]

1 Petroleum Pipelines Act 60 of 2003 s 18(a).
2 S 18(b).
3 S 18(c).
4 S 18(d).

132 Finalisation of application The Authority must decide on an application within 60 days after the expiration of the period contemplated in section 17 of the Petroleum Pipelines Act,[1] if no objections have been received; or after receiving the response of the applicant to those objections.[2] The Authority may issue separate or combined licenses for the construction of petroleum pipelines or pipeline systems, loading facilities and storage facilities; and the operation of petroleum pipelines or pipeline systems, loading facilities and storage facilities.[3]

1 60 of 2003.
2 S 19(1); see par 130 ante.
3 S 19(3).

133 Conditions of licence The Authority may impose licence conditions within the following framework of requirements and limitations: a licensee must carry out the construction or operations activities for which the licence is granted; licensees must provide the prescribed information to the Authority on the commercial arrangements regarding the participation of historically disadvantaged South Africans in the licensee's activities; the petroleum loading, pipeline and storage activities of vertically integrated companies may be required to be managed separately with no cross subsidisation; a petroleum pipeline may be licensed for either crude oil or petroleum products, but not both unless the Authority, in the case of an emergency, waives this condition; third parties must have access on commercially reasonable terms to un-committed capacity in petroleum pipelines that are controlled by private entities; third parties must have access on commercially reasonable terms to petroleum pipelines that are controlled by state entities but may have such access only under certain conditions; interested parties must be allowed to negotiate changes with pipeline licensees in the routing, size and capacity of proposed petroleum pipelines; licensees must allow interconnections with the facilities of other licensees, as long as the interconnection is technically feasible and the person requesting interconnection bears the increased costs; third parties must have access on commercially reasonable terms to uncommit-ted capacity in loading facilities; third parties must have access on commercially reasonable terms to uncommitted capacity in storage facilities; tariffs set by the Au-thority for petroleum pipelines; tariffs approved by authority for loading facilities and storage facilities; licensees must maintain their license loading facilities, petroleum pipelines or storage facilities in a fully operational condition; health, safety and envi-ronmental standards required by the Authority; and strategic security standards re-quired by the Authority.[1] Any person aggrieved by a condition imposed by the Authority may apply to the Authority to amend or delete the condition. If the ag-grieved person is not the licensee, the authority must inform the licensee of the application.[2]

1 Petroleum Pipelines Act 60 of 2003 s 20(1).
2 S 20(2).

134 Non-discrimination Licensees may not discriminate between customers or classes of customers regarding access, tariffs, prices, conditions or service except for objectively justifiable and identifiable grounds.[1]

1 Petroleum Pipelines Act 60 of 2003 s 21.

135 Term of licence Any licence issued in terms of the Petroleum Pipelines Act[1] is valid for 25 years.[2] A licensee may apply to have his or her licence renewed.[3] Every application for renewal must be granted if the licensee has complied with the licence conditions.[4] When renewing a licence, the Authority may impose different condi-tions.[5] A licensee may not sell or assign the licence.[6] Any person taking over the business of the licensee must apply for a licence in his or her own right.[7]

1	60 of 2003.	5	S 22(4).
2	S 22(1).	6	S 22(5).
3	S 22(2).	7	S 22(6).
4	S 22(3).		

136 Amendment of licence The Authority may vary, suspend or remove any of the licence conditions, or may include additional conditions on application by the licensee; with the permission of the licensee; upon non-compliance by a licensee with a licence condition; if it is necessary for the purposes of the Petroleum Pipelines Act;[1] on application by any affected party; and in the case of an emergency.[2]

1 60 of 2003.
2 S 23.

137 Revocation of licence on application The Authority may revoke a licence on the application of a licensee if the licensed facility or activity is no longer required or is not economically justifiable; or another person is willing and able to assume the rights and obligations of the licensee and a new licence is issued to such person.[1]

1 Petroleum Pipelines Act 60 of 2003 s 24.

138 Contraventions If a licensee contravenes or fails to comply with a condition of the licence or any provision of the Petroleum Pipelines Act,[1] the Authority may serve a notice on the licensee in which he/she is directed to comply with the condition or provision of the Act within a reasonable period.[2] If a licensee fails to comply, the Authority may sit as a tribunal and decide on the matter and may impose a penalty or a fine not exceeding R2 million per day for each day on which the contravention or failure to comply continues.[3] Any person adversely affected by a decision of the tribunal may appeal to the High Court.

1   60 of 2003.
2   S 25(1).
3   S 25(2).

139 Revocation of licence by court The Authority may apply to the High Court for an order suspending or revoking a licence.[1] The court may grant or refuse the application, and may make such order as to costs and maintaining the service of the licensee as it may deem fit.[2]

1   Petroleum Pipelines Act 60 of 2003 s 26(1).
2   S 26(2).

140 Health, safety, security and environment The Authority may require a licensee to submit a guarantee to ensure compliance with any condition relating to health, safety, security or the environment prior to, during or after the period of validity of the license.[1]

1   Petroleum Pipelines Act 60 of 2003 s 27.

141 Setting and approval of tariffs The Authority must set as a condition of a license the tariffs to be charged by a licensee in the operation of a petroleum pipeline.[1] A licensee may request the Authority to review its tariff from time to time.[2] A licensee may not charge any other tariff for the licensed activity than that approved by the Authority.[3]

1   Petroleum Pipelines Act 60 of 2003 s 28(1).
2   S 28(2).
3   S 28(3).

GENERAL PROVISIONS

142 Entry, inspection and gathering of information and investigations by Authority Any person authorised by the Authority may enter any property on which a licensed activity is taking place and inspect any facility, equipment, machinery, book, account or other document found there; and require any person to furnish the Authority with such information as may be necessary for the proper administration of the Petroleum Pipelines Act.[1] No information obtained by the Authority which is of a non-generic, confidential, personal, commercially sensitive or proprietary nature may be made public.[2]

The Authority must investigate complaints of discrimination regarding tariffs or conditions of access; and failure to obtain access to petroleum pipelines, loading facilities or storage facilities.[3]

1   60 of 2003 s 29(1).
2   S 29(4).
3   S 31.

143 Voluntary resolution of disputes by Authority The Authority may, with the approval of all parties to a dispute, act as mediator or arbitrator in any matter falling within the ambit of the Petroleum Pipelines Act.[1] Any decision taken by the Authority acting as arbitrator is binding on the parties to the dispute.[2]

1 60 of 2003 s 30(1).
2 S 30(3).

144 Expropriation by Authority In pursuit of the objects of the Petroleum Pipelines Act,[1] the Authority may expropriate land or any right in land on behalf of a licensee in accordance with section 25 of the Constitution.[2] The procedure must be prescribed by regulations. The Authority may exercise these powers only if it is satisfied that a licensee is unable to acquire land or a right in land by agreement with the owner; and the land or right in land is reasonably required by a licensee for facilities which will enhance the Republic's petroleum pipelines infrastructure.[3]

1 60 of 2003.
2 Constitution of the Republic of SA 108 of
   1996: Petroleum Pipelines Act 60 of 2003
   s 32(2).
3 S 32(3).

145 Regulations The minister may make regulations regarding ensuring fair administrative action by the Authority; the rehabilitation of land used in connection with petroleum pipelines, loading facilities and storage facilities, the provision of security for rehabilitation purposes; the procedure in mediation and arbitration proceedings; the procedure for expropriation proceedings; the rendering of information to the Authority; the methodology to be followed by the Authority in setting and approving tariffs and price regulation principles; mechanisms to promote historically disadvantaged South Africans; and any other matter that may be prescribed in terms of the Petroleum Pipelines Act.[1] Before promulgating regulations, the minister must consult with the Authority and invite public comment.[2]

1 60 of 2003 s 33(1).
2 S 33(2). See s 33(3) for the making of rules.

146 Prohibition of agreements contrary to Act An agreement may not contravene any provision of the Petroleum Pipelines Act,[1] licence, condition attached to a licence, regulation, rule or directive issued under the Act.[2] Any agreement in contravention of this provision is void.[3]

1 60 of 2003.
2 S 34(1).
3 S 34(2).

147 Transitional provisions Any person owning or operating petroleum pipelines, loading facilities or storage facilities prior to the commencement of the Petroleum Pipelines Act[1] must, within six months after commencement, submit to the Authority an application for a licence.[2] The Authority must grant a license unless it finds that the applicant is unable or unwilling to own or operate petroleum pipelines, loading facilities or storage facilities in a manner consistent with the objectives of the Act.[3]

1 60 of 2003.
2 S 35(1).
3 S 35(2).

PETROLEUM PIPELINES LEVIES ACT

148 Imposition of levies The Petroleum Pipelines Levies Act[1] has been promulgated, but has not yet come into operation. According to the Act, the Authority[2] may by notice in the *Gazette*:

(a) impose levies for the purpose of meeting the general administrative and other costs of the Authority and the functions performed by the Authority;

(b) specify the intervals and times in respect of payment of such levies;

(c) determine interest as contemplated in section 4; and

(d) vary levies.[3]

The levies imposed under the above provision must be:

(a) based on the amount of petroleum, measured in litres, delivered by importers, refiners and producers to inlet flanges of petroleum pipelines; and

(b) paid by the person holding the title to the petroleum immediately after it has entered the inlet flange.[4]

Before imposing levies, varying levies, or determining interest, the Authority must:

(a) publish the proposed levies, variation or determination in such a manner as it considers appropriate in order to bring the proposed levies, variation or determination to the attention of stakeholders in the petroleum pipelines industry, together with a statement explaining the reasons for the proposed imposition or variation of levies or determination of interest and an invitation for representations to be made to the Authority within a specified and reasonable time;

(b) have regard to any representation made to it in terms of paragraph (a);

(c) give the minister[5] notice in writing of the proposed imposition or variation of levies, or determination of interest, and specify the period for which such imposition, variation or determination is intended to be operational;

(d) provide the minister with reasons for the imposition or variation of levies or determination of interest;

(e) provide the minister with evidence of consultation with stakeholders or attempts to consult with stakeholders in the petroleum pipelines industry and of the degree of concurrence among such stakeholders with regard to the imposition or variation of levies or determination of interest.[6]

The minister must, with the concurrence of the Minister of Finance, within a period of 60 days after receiving a notice contemplated above, give the Authority written approval or disapproval of the proposed imposition, variation or determination and, in the event of disapproving that imposition, variation or determination, also give reasons for the disapproval thereof.[7]

After receipt of the notice the minister may, with the concurrence of the Minister of Finance, recommend an alternative levy or interest determination.[8]

The Authority may impose or vary levies or determine interest only after the levies or interest have been approved by the minister with the concurrence of the Minister of Finance.[9]

The Authority must publish the notice at least 30 days before the commencement of that imposition, variation or determination.[10]

The levies imposed, levies varied or interest determined under this section must be reviewed annually by the Authority.[11]

1   28 of 2004.
2   "Authority" means the Authority established
     by s 3 of the Petroleum Pipelines Act 60 of
     2003: Petroleum Pipelines Levies Act 28 of
     2004 s 1.
3   S 2(1).
4   S 2(2).
5   "Minister" means the Minister of Minerals

and Energy: s 1.
6   S 2(3).
7   S 2(4).
8   S 2(5).
9   S 2(6).
10   S 2(7).
11   S 2(8).

149 Disposal and management of levies

The levies imposed, levies varied and interest determined under section 2(1) of the Petroleum Pipelines Levies Act[1] form part of the funds of the Authority.[2]

The levies and interest collected by the Authority must be paid into a bank account designated for that purpose by the Authority and approved by the National Treasury in terms of section 7(2) of the Public Finance Management Act.[3]

At least six months before the start of the financial year of the Department of Minerals and Energy, or such other period as may be agreed upon between the minister and the Authority, the Authority must submit to the minister:

(a)   a budget of estimated revenue and expenditure for the next financial year of the Authority as required by section 53 of the Public Finance Management Act; and

(b)   a business plan in the format prescribed under section 54(1) of the Public Finance Management Act, covering the affairs of the Authority for the following three financial years.[4]

The budget and business plan must be submitted for the approval of the minister and the concurrence of the Minister of Finance.[5]

1   28 of 2004.
2   S 3(1).
3   1 of 1999: Petroleum Pipelines Levies Act

28 of 2004 s 3(2).
4   S 3(3)(a).
5   S 3(3)(b).

150 Non-payment of levies

Where a levy is not paid by the person holding the title to the petroleum immediately after it has entered the inlet flange[1] on the day such levy became due and payable, that person is, apart from payment of the levy, liable to interest calculated upon the unpaid amount of the levy from that date.[2]

The calculation of interest due and payable to the Authority must be based on the uniform interest rate contemplated in section 80(1)(b) of the Public Finance Management Act.[3][4]

Levies and interest due are deemed to be a debt due to the Authority and may be recovered by the Authority by judicial process in any competent court.[5]

1   See Petroleum Pipelines Levies Act 28 of
     2004 s 2(2)(b); par 148 ante.
2   1 of 1999: subject to s 4(2) and (3) of the
     Petroleum Pipelines Levies Act 28 of 2004.

3   S 4(1).
4   S 4(2).
5   S 4(3).

151 Levy imposition to lapse after five years

Any levy imposed in terms of section 2(1)(a) of the Petroleum Pipelines Levies Act[1] lapses five years after the day on which it was introduced.[2]

The minister must, at least three months but not more than 12 months before the day on which an imposition of such a levy would otherwise lapse, on written request of the Authority and with the concurrence of the Minister of Finance, give the Authority in writing approval or disapproval of a re-imposition of such levy and, in the event of disapproving the re-imposition, also give reasons for the disapproval thereof.[3]

Before approving a re-imposition, the minister must commission a review of the performance of the Authority.[4]

1 28 of 2004.	3 S 5(2).
2 S 5(1).	4 As contemplated in s 6: s 5(3).

152 Assessment of performance of Authority In terms of the Petroleum Pipelines Levies Act,[1] "performance" in relation to the Authority means all or any of the following matters:

(a) the efficiency, economy and effectiveness of the Authority's management of the financial resources at its disposal;

(b) the benefits deriving from the Authority's work to those who bear the levies and other charges imposed by the Authority; and

(c) any other matter determined by the minister in writing and with the concurrence of the Minister of Finance.[2]

The minister may, after consultation with the Authority, appoint any person to conduct an assessment of, and report to the minister and the Minister of Finance on the performance of the Authority if the minister is satisfied that:

(a) there is sufficient concern among stakeholders in the petroleum pipelines industry about the performance of the Authority to justify an assessment of that performance; or

(b) the performance of the Authority is inadequate.[3]

Nevertheless, the minister must commission an assessment of the performance of the Authority at least once every five years. The person appointed to conduct the assessment must report to the Minister and the Minister of Finance.[4]

1 28 of 2004.	3 S 6(2).
2 S 6(1).	4 S 6(3).

PETROLEUM PRODUCTS ACT

153 Definition and control "Petroleum product" is defined in the Petroleum Products Act[1] as petroleum fuel and any lubricant, whether used or unused, and includes any other substance which may be used for a purpose for which petroleum fuel or lubricant may be used.[2]

In order to conserve petroleum products, provision is made for control by regulation of the supply, use, storage, sale and transportation of such products. Regulations may be made to this end by the minister and the Controller of Petroleum Products.[3] The minister may prohibit the publication or disclosure of the source, manufacture, transportation, destination, storage, consumption, quantity or stock level of any petroleum product acquired or manufactured for or in the Republic. Provision is also made for an agreement to be entered into between the minister and any person to exempt such person from the abovementioned prohibitions.[4]

Provision is made for ministerial appointment of persons in the public service as controllers and inspectors with power to search premises, vehicles or vessels and seize and dispose of any petroleum product.[5] These inspectors, who must be in possession of a certificate of appointment, are subject to the direction and control of the minister,[6] who is, however, empowered to delegate any of his or her powers.[7] The minister is furthermore empowered to exempt persons from the provisions of the Act.[8]

Contravention of the provisions of the Act or the hindering of inspectors in the exercise of their functions may render the wrongdoer liable to a fine not exceeding R2 000 or imprisonment for two years or both. Further penalty by virtue of suspension or cancellation of drivers' or trading licences as well as confiscation of property is possible.[9] An employer or principal may be held vicariously liable in the commission of an offence under the Act. The onus is on the employer to prove that he or she did not connive at the offence and took reasonable steps to prevent its commission and that the act or commission did not fall within the scope of employment of the person concerned.[10]

1 120 of 1977. The Petroleum Products Act as amended is thought be to outdated and is no longer in line with the socio-political and economic dynamics of the South African liquid fuels industry, not meeting the present-day governance needs of the sector. The Petroleum Products Amendment Act 58 of 2003 when it comes into operation, will promote the transformation of the South African petroleum and liquid fuels industry, by giving effect to the "Charter for the South African Petroleum and Liquid Fuels Industry on Empowering Historically Disadvantaged South Africans in the Petroleum and Liquid Fuels Industry", and through licensing. The Act also creates a legislative framework for a system aimed at the regulation of the liquefied petroleum gas and paraffin for the promotion of access to affordable petroleum products by low-income consumers for household use.
New provisions are inserted into the 1977 Act to deal with: prohibition of certain activities; licensing; transformation of South African petroleum and liquid fuels industry; transitional licensing provisions; system for allocation of licenses; and system for allocation of licences for liquefied petroleum gas and paraffin.
The provisions in the 1977 Act dealing with the following subjects in the 1977 Act are reviewed in line with the objects highlighted in the memorandum of objects attached to the Act: the sections dealing with offences and penalties; appeal; arbitration; and regulations.

2 S 1.

3 See s 2. For the principal regulations in respect of petroleum products, see *Government Gazette* GN R2298, 11 October 1985, as amended by *Government Gazette* GN R275, 17 January 1992.

4 S 4A.

5 S 3(1) (4).

6 S 3(5)–(6).

7 S 6.

8 S 5.

9 See s 12.

10 S 7.

CENTRAL ENERGY FUND

154 Payment of certain monies into Central Energy Fund, utilisation and investment thereof, and management of affairs of CEF (Proprietary) Limited Money that accrues to the Central Energy Fund in terms of section 1A of the Central Energy Fund Act;[1] section 11 of the Petroleum Products Act;[2] any other law; and money that accrues to the fund from any other source, must be paid into the Central Energy Fund, controlled by CEF (Proprietary) Limited. Money paid into the Central Energy Fund must be utilised for the acquisition of coal, the exploitation of coal deposits, the manufacture of liquid fuel, oil and other products from coal, the marketing of these products; the acquisition, generation, manufacture, marketing or distribution of any other form of energy, and research connected to that; and any other object for which the funds may be applied which has been designated by the minister with the concurrence of the Minister of Finance. The affairs of CEF (Proprietary) Limited are controlled by a board of directors. A director will not be personally liable for any loss or damage arising out of, or in connection with, the performance of his or her duties as a director, unless the loss or damage is due to bad faith or gross negligence on his or her part, or to a failure by the director to comply with the Central Energy Fund Act.[3]

The chairperson of CEF (Proprietary) Limited is the accounting officer of CEF (Proprietary) Limited and SFF Association.[4]

1 38 of 1977.
2 120 of 1977.

3 38 of 1977 s 1.
4 S 1E.

155 Levy on fuel and the utilisation and investment thereof The Minister of Mineral and Energy Affairs may impose a levy for the benefit of the Equalisation Fund, controlled by CEF (Proprietary) Limited, on every litre of petrol, aviation spirit, kerosene, distillate fuel, residual fuel oil, naphtha, base oil, products of base oil for every kilogram of grease or liquefied petroleum gas which is manufactured, distributed or sold in the Republic, or imported into the Republic. The minister may impose a levy for the benefit of the Central Energy Fund on every litre of petrol, distillate fuel or residual fuel oil. A levy may differ according to the purpose for which the product is used. The minister may exempt any person from the payment of a levy. However, there is no exemption from the payment of a levy, except on such conditions as the minister may determine, in respect of petroleum products manufactured from raw materials produced in the Republic; petroleum products manufactured for use outside the Republic from raw materials produced outside the Republic; petroleum products on which customs or excise duty is payable; or such other petroleum products as the Minister may determine. Money paid into the Equalisation Fund, in addition to money raised by means of a levy, will be money that accrues in terms of section 11 of the Petroleum Products Act,[1] or any other law; money that may accrue from any other source; and money obtained by CEF (Proprietary) Limited or the SFF Association from the sale of crude oil, petroleum products and products determined by the Minister of Mineral and Energy Affairs; and money received by agreement from the government of a foreign State. The money paid into the Equalisation Fund must be utilised for the financing of any increase in the cost of purchasing crude oil or petroleum products; for the purchase, acquisition, distribution, sale, saving, conservation, storage or utilisation of crude oil or petroleum products; for the acquisition, generation, manufacture, marketing or distribution of any other form of energy; and for any other object relating to energy as approved by the Minister of Mineral and Energy Affairs.[2]

1 120 of 1977.
2 Central Energy Fund Act 38 of 1977 s 1A.

156 Offences and penalties Any person who fails to comply with section 1A of the Central Energy Fund Act;[1] without lawful reasons refuses or fails to comply with any reasonable demand for information made by a person responsible for the collection of any levy; resists or wilfully obstructs such person from the performance of his or her duties; or discloses to any unauthorised person information in respect of a levy imposed, will be guilty of an offence.[2]

1 38 of 1977.
2 S 1B.

157 Share Capital of CEF (Proprietary) Limited and SFF Association The share capital of CEF (Proprietary) Limited and SFF Association consists of amounts determined by the Minister of Mineral and Energy Affairs. Shares in CEF (Proprietary) Limited may be taken up by the state only. Shares in SFF Association may be taken up by CEF (Proprietary) Limited only. Shares in CEF (Proprietary) Limited and SFF Association are not transferable.[1]

1 Central Energy Fund Act 38 of 1977 s 1D.

NUCLEAR ENERGY

NUCLEAR ENERGY ACT

GENERAL[1]

158 Powers of minister The minister,[2] by notice in the *Government Gazette*, may declare any substance with a degree of purity as specified in the notice, to be restricted material[3] for the purposes of the Nuclear Energy Act.[4] The minister may declare any substance containing uranium or thorium with concentration and mass limits higher than those specified in the notice, to be source material[5] for the purposes of the Act,[6] and may declare any of the following with concentration and mass levels higher than those specified in the notice, to be special nuclear material:[7]

(a) plutonium-239;

(b) uranium-233;

(c) uranium enriched in its 235 or 233 isotope;

(d) transuranium elements; or

(e) any composition of any of the materials referred to in paragraphs (a), (b), (c) and (d), or any composition of those materials and any other substance or substances.[8]

The minister may also declare any facility, installation, plant or structure designed or adapted for or involved with any process within the nuclear fuel cycle involving radioactive material, to be a nuclear installation,[9] [10] exempt any radioactive material from the provisions of the Act;[11] declare equipment and material specially designed or prepared for the processing, use or production of nuclear material, to be nuclear-related equipment and material;[12] [13] and determine the levels of specific activity and total activity of radioactive material to which the provisions of the Act do not apply.[14]

1 Nuclear energy contributes about 3% of the national energy supply, and about 6% of South Africa's electricity. In terms of beneficial use, nuclear energy has the lowest adverse impact on the environment. It does not produce carbon emissions associated with coal in the generation of electricity. Eskom owns and operates the 1840 MW Koeberg nuclear power station outside Cape Town. There are concerns voiced by communities and environmental groups as to the safety of the installation and its operations. The Nuclear Energy Act 46 of 1998 and the National Nuclear Regulator Act 47 of 1999 have been enacted to provide a regulatory framework for the energy sector to address the problems.
South Africa is a party to the Convention on Nuclear Safety. The objective of the Convention is *inter alia* to achieve and maintain a high level of nuclear safety worldwide through the enhancement of national measures and international co-operation, including where appropriate, safety-related technical cooperation. Contracting parties are enjoined to prevent accidents with radiological consequences and to mitigate such

consequences should they occur. The Convention imposes an obligation on the contracting parties to establish and maintain a legislative and regulatory framework to govern the safety of nuclear installations (art 7).

2 S 50 of the Nuclear Energy Act 46 of 1999 vests the responsibility for the Republic's institutional nuclear obligations in the Minister of Minerals and Energy.[3]

3 "Restricted material" means beryllium and zirconium and any other substance declared under s 2(a) to be restricted material: Nuclear Energy Act s 1.

4 S 2(a).

5 "Source material" means any material declared under s 2(b) to be source material: s 1.

6 S 2(b).

7 "Special nuclear material" means any material declared under s 2(c) to be special nuclear material: s 1.

8 S 2(c).

9 "Nuclear installation" means a nuclear installation as defined in s 1 of the National Nuclear Regulator Act 47 of 1999.

10 Nuclear Energy Act 46 of 1999 s 2(d). The Nuclear Installation Licences Regulations have been published: GN R479 of 12 May

2001.
11 S 2(e).
12 "Nuclear–related equipment and material" means equipment and material declared

under s 2(f) to be nuclear-related equipment and material: s 1.
13 S 2(f).
14 S 2(g).

SOUTH AFRICAN NUCLEAR ENERGY CORPORATION, LIMITED

159 Establishment The South African Nuclear Energy Corporation Ltd, which is a juristic person, has been established.[1] It is a public company,[2] and its main objects are to perform the functions mentioned in section 13 of the Nuclear Energy Act.[3] The minister must take all the steps that are necessary for the formation and incorporation of the corporation as a public company with a share capital within the meaning of the Companies Act.[4] The state will be the only member and shareholder of this company upon its incorporation.[5] The minister, who represents the state, must sign the memorandum of association, articles of association and all other documents necessary in connection with the formation and incorporation of the company.[6] The Registrar of Companies must register the memorandum of association and articles of association as signed by the minister and incorporate the company as a public company under the name "The South African Nuclear Energy Corporation Limited", with the state as its only member and shareholder, and issue to the company a certificate to commence business with effect from the date of the company's incorporation.[7] The state's rights as member and shareholder of the corporation are to be exercised by the minister.[8] The relationship between the corporation and the minister representing the state as the only member and shareholder, may be more closely defined in an agreement entered into by the corporation and the minister for that purpose.[9]

The memorandum of association and articles of association of the corporation must be so drawn up that their contents are consistent with the Act.[10] An amendment of the memorandum of association or articles of association affecting any arrangement made by any provision of the Act will not be operative or have any legal force unless and until the relevant provision of the Act has been amended accordingly and that amendment has come into effect.[11] The provisions of the Companies Act, which are not in conflict with the Act, will apply to the corporation.[12] A provision of the Companies Act will not apply to the corporation in the following circumstances: where, because of any special or contrary arrangement made under the Nuclear Energy Act, such a provision is clearly inappropriate or incapable of being applied,[13] or the Minister of Trade and Industry has issued a declaration with regard to the provision.[14]

The minister, after consultation with the corporation, may from time to time, as and when considered necessary, request the Minister of Trade and Industry to declare any particular provision of the Companies Act not to be applicable to the corporation.[15] The request must be fully motivated, and the necessary particulars about the request, together with the related motivation, must be made known by the Registrar of Companies by notice in the *Government Gazette*. In that notice the registrar must also invite interested persons who may have any objections to such a declaration, to submit their objections and representations to a person named in the notice, or, if sent by post, to place that person in possession of their objections and representations, not later than 21 days after the date of the notice.[16] After having considered the objections and representations received within the prescribed period, the Minister of Trade and Industry may, by notice in the *Government Gazette*, declare the whole or any part of any provision of the Companies Act about which the abovementioned request was made, not to be applicable to the corporation with effect from a date stated in that notice, if satisfied on reasonable grounds that the non–application of that provision to the corporation will contribute to its efficiency or will reduce the corporation's operating costs,[17] and will not reduce or limit the corporation's accountability as a public institution or detract from the requirements of transparency as regards its functioning and operations,[18] and will not be prejudicial to the rights, interests or claims of the corporation's creditors or employees or to the rights or interests of any other interested parties.[19]

On a specified date, the corporation will be entitled to and have claim to any money which, immediately before that date, stood to the credit of the Atomic Energy Corporation Ltd.[20] On the specified date, the following will pass to and vest in the corporation:

(a)   all immovable property registered in the name of the Atomic Energy Corporation Ltd and consisting of land, and any servitudes or other real rights with regard to land;[21]

(b)   land and any servitudes or other real rights with regard to land (including any right to use land temporarily) acquired by the Atomic Energy Corporation Ltd[22] for the purposes of or in connection with the functions, business or operations of the Atomic Energy Corporation Ltd;[23]

(c)   any other assets of which the Atomic Energy Corporation Ltd is the owner, immediately before the specified date, for the purposes of or in terms of the previous Act;[24] and

(d)   any liabilities which were incurred by the Atomic Energy Corporation Ltd[25] or pursuant to its operations and activities thereunder, which are still outstanding immediately before the specified date. The registrar of deeds concerned must make the entries and endorsements that may be necessary to give effect to section 8(2) in or on any relevant register, title deed or any other document that is filed or on record in the deeds registry or has been submitted to that registrar, and no office fees or other money will be payable with regard to such an entry or endorsement.[26]

The minister may transfer so much of the state's shares in a subsidiary company[27] as the cabinet approves to such transferees in such manner and on such terms and conditions as the cabinet approves.[28] The proceeds of any transfer[29] may be used wholly or partially for such purpose as the cabinet approves, but all proceeds not so used within the period determined by the cabinet must be paid into the National Revenue Fund.[30] In exchange for the net value of the assets passing to and vesting in the corporation,[31] the state, by virtue of having been the sole shareholder in the Atomic Energy Corporation Ltd, will hold fully paid-up shares in the corporation for an amount equal to the net value of the assets so invested in the corporation[32] or for an amount equal to a percentage, specified in the agreement, of the net value of the assets so invested.[33] [34] If the amount for which shares in the corporation are to be held by the state[35] is less than the net value of the assets so passing to and vesting in the corporation, the corporation will be indebted to the state for an amount equal to the difference between the net value of those assets and the value of the shares to be so held; the amount of that difference will be regarded and treated as a loan granted to the corporation by the state.[36] The terms and conditions of that loan must be set out in the agreement mentioned in section 10(1): in that agreement provision may be made that the corporation issues the state with debentures for the whole or any part of the amount of the loan.[37] For the purposes of section 10, any reference to the net value of the assets invested in the corporation, however expressed, must be understood to mean all the money mentioned in section 8(1) plus the value of all the movable, immovable and other property passing to the corporation in terms of section 8(2)(a), (b) and (c), presenting the sum of all the liabilities passing to the corporation.[38] [39] Where the value of any assets consisting of immovable property is to be determined for the purposes of section

10, regard must be had to the criteria mentioned in section 12(1) and 12(5)(b) to (f) and (h) of the Expropriation Act.[40] [41] The corporation's financial year will be from 1 April in any year to 31 March in the following year, both days included. However, the first financial year will run from the specified date to 31 March in the following year, both days included.[42] Despite the provisions of any other law, the corporation may not be placed under judicial management or in liquidation except if authorised by an act of Parliament adopted specially for that purpose.[43]

1   Nuclear Energy Act 46 of 1999 s 3(1).
2   S 3(2), despite the provisions of the Companies Act 61 of 1973 or any other law and in accordance with s 4.
3   46 of 1999 s 3(3).
4   61 of 1973: Nuclear Energy Act 46 of 1999s 4(1), subject to ss 3, 4 and 5.
5   S 4(2).
6   S 4(3)(a), despite the provisions of the Companies Act 61 of 1973.
7   Nuclear Energy Act 46 of 1999 s 4(3)(b).
8   S 4(4)(a).
9   S 4(4)(b), subject to the principal Act.
10   S 5(1).
11   S 5(2), despite the Companies Act 61 of 1973.
12   Nuclear Energy Act 46 of 1999 s 6(1), subject to s 6(2).
13   S 6(2)(a).
14   S 6(2)(b), under s 7(3).
15   S 7(1).
16   S 7(2).
17   S 7(3)(a).
18   S 7(3)(b).
19   S 7(3)(c).
20   S 8(1).
21   S 8(2)(a).
22   In terms of the Nuclear Energy Act 131 of 1993.
23   Nuclear Energy Act 46 of 1999 s 8(2)(b).
24   S 8(2)(c).
25   In terms of the Nuclear Energy Act 131 of 1993.
26   Nuclear Energy Act 46 of 1999 s 8(2)(d) (3).
27   Contemplated in s 14(1)(a)(i).
28   S 9(1), despite any provisions of a law to the contrary.
29   In terms of s 9(1).
30   S 9(2).
31   In terms of s 8.
32   S 10(1)(a).
33   Subject to s 10(2).
34   S 10(1)(b).
35   In terms of s 10(1).
36   S 10(2)(a).
37   S 10(2)(b).
38   S 10(3).
39   In terms of s 8(2)(d).
40   63 of 1975.
41   Nuclear Energy Act 46 of 1999 s 10(4).
42   S 11.
43   S 12.

160 Functions The main functions of the corporation are:

(a)   to undertake and promote research and development in the field of nuclear energy and radiation sciences and technology and, subject to the Safeguards Agreement, to make these generally available;[1]

(b)   to process source material, special nuclear material and restricted material and to reprocess and enrich source material and nuclear material;[2] and

(c)   to co-operate with any person or institution in matters falling within these functions subject to the approval of the minister.[3]

In order to create and utilise viable business opportunities in commerce and industry, the corporation may:

(a)   produce and otherwise acquire reports, computer software and other intellectual property and dispose thereof;[4]

(b)   manufacture and sell instruments, equipment and similar products;[5]

(c)   process and sell minerals;[6]

(d)   produce and process metals, chemicals and related products; [7]

(e)   with the permission of the minister, and subject to the Nuclear Energy Act:

(i)   sell or otherwise commercially exploit those metals, chemicals and related products;[8] and

(ii) for reward render to any person or institution any service falling within the ambit of the corporation's functions.[9]

The corporation may, at the request or with the written permission of the minister, undertake the development, transfer or exploitation of nuclear technology or nuclear-related technology on behalf of or in collaboration with any person, or institution in, or any government or administration of, any other country or territory.[10]

The corporation may:

(a) provide collateral security, including guarantees, to a financial institution as defined in section 1 of the Financial Services Board Act,[11] in respect of a loan granted by the financial institution to any employee of the corporation in order to acquire, improve or enlarge immovable property for the purposes of occupation;[12]

(b) build, cause to be built, buy or hire dwelling houses, flats or flat buildings for occupation by the corporation's employees, and may sell or let such houses or flats to its employees or, if no longer reasonably required, otherwise alienate or let, or otherwise deal with, such houses, flats or flat buildings;[13]

(c) establish, erect, operate or carry on sports and recreational facilities, social clubs, social and health services, restaurants, hostels and study bursary schemes for the benefit of the corporation's employees, or any other similar undertakings or schemes which in the opinion of the chief executive officer may be beneficial to those employees.[14]

The corporation, with the written permission of the minister granted with the agreement of the Minister of Finance, may raise loans to finance any expenditure that may be incurred by the corporation during any financial year in connection with its functions, business and operations in terms of the Act.[15] The permission may be granted subject to any conditions determined by the minister acting with the agreement of the Minister of Finance.[16] The state, represented by the minister acting with the agreement of the Minister of Finance, may guarantee any loan raised by the corporation.[17] The corporation, with the agreement of the minister so acting, may issue debentures in respect of a loan so raised.[18]

1 Nuclear Energy Act 46 of 1999 s 13(a).
2 S 13(b).
3 S 13(c). For certain general provisions regarding ancillary powers and functions of the corporation, see s 14(1).
4 S 14(2)(a).
5 S 14(2)(b).
6 S 14(2)(c).
7 S 14(2)(d).
8 S 14(2)(e)(i).
9 S 14(2)(e)(ii).
10 S 14(3).
11 97 of 1990.
12 Nuclear Energy Act 46 of 1999 s 14(4)(a).
13 S 14(4)(b).
14 S 14(4)(c).
15 S 15(1).
16 S 15(2).
17 S 15(3).
18 S 15(4).

161 Control and management of affairs of corporation The corporation is governed and controlled, in accordance with the Nuclear Energy Act,[1] by a board of directors.[2] The board must ensure that the goals of the Act are actively pursued, and must exercise general control over the performance of the corporation's functions.[3] The board represents the corporation, and all acts performed by the board or on its authority will be the acts of the corporation.[4]

The minister may at any time discharge a director from office:

(a) if the director repeatedly has failed to perform the duties of that office efficiently;

(b)   if, because of any physical or mental illness or disability, the director has become incapable of performing the functions of that office or performing them efficiently; or

(c)   for misconduct.[5]

A director vacates office:

(a)   upon becoming disqualified in terms of section 16(3);

(b)   when discharged in terms of section 17(1);

(c)   upon having been absent from three consecutive meetings of the board without the chairperson's permission, unless the board has condoned the absence on good reasons advanced; and

(d)   when the person's resignation as a director takes effect.[6]

All meetings of the board are held at the times and places that the board determines.[7] The chairperson may at any time call a special meeting of the board to be held at a time and place as determined by the chairperson.[8] All directors must be notified in writing of any meeting.[9] A majority of the total number of directors forms a quorum at any meeting of the board.[10]

The board may from time to time appoint one or more committees to assist the board in performing its functions.[11] A committee may consist of one or more members, and may be a standing committee or an *ad hoc* committee appointed for a particular task and period only. A committee must at all times have at least one director as member.[12] If such a committee has two or more members, the board must designate one of them as the committee's chairperson, who must be a director of the board.[13] The corporation may pay a member of a committee who is not in the full-time service of the state or an employee of the corporation, the remuneration and allowances determined by the minister with the agreement of the Minister of Finance.[14] A member of a committee holds office at the board's pleasure.[15] The board may fill a vacancy in any committee.[16]

The board,[17] by special resolution, may delegate any of the powers and assign any of the functions or duties conferred or imposed on it by the operation of section 16(1) or conferred or imposed on it elsewhere by the Act, to its chairperson, any other appointed director, the Chief Executive Officer or any committee of the board.[18] However, the board will not be divested of any power nor be relieved of any function or duty it may have delegated or assigned.[19] The delegation or assignment:

(a)   may be made on and subject to any conditions determined by the board;

(b)   may be given together with the power to subdelegate or further assign, on and subject to any conditions so determined, if any;[20]

(c)   must be communicated to the delegatee or assignee in writing.[21] [22]

The board, by special resolution, may at any time:

(a)   amend or revoke a delegation or assignment made under section 21(1);

(b)   withdraw any decision made by the delegatee or assignee with regard to a delegated or assigned matter, and decide the matter itself; however, a decision made by a delegatee or assignee may not be withdrawn where it confers a right or entitlement on any third party.[23]

The minister, may by notice in the *Government Gazette*, from time to time:

(a)   prohibit the delegation by the board of any particular power or its assignment of any particular function or duty, whether generally or in the circumstances specified in the notice;

(b)   limit the circumstances in which any particular power, function or duty of the board may be delegated or assigned, as the case may be;

(c)   prescribe conditions for the delegation of any particular power or assignment of any particular function or duty;

(d)   in relation to any power, function or duty of the board specified in the notice, prohibit subdelegation or further assignment, as the case may be, in the event of the board's delegation of that power or assignment of that function or duty.[24]

1   46 of 1999.
2   S 16(1)(a).
3   S 16(1)(b).
4   S 16(1)(c). For the composition of the board and further general provisions, see s 16(2)–(9).
5   S 17(1)(a)–(c).
6   S 17(2)(a)–(d).
7   S 18(1).
8   S 18(2).
9   S 18(3).
10   S 18(4). For general provisions regarding meetings, see s 17(5)–(8).
11   S 19(1).
12   S 19(2).
13   S 19(3).
14   S 19(4).
15   S 19(5).
16   S 19(6). For general provisions regarding minutes that the board and committees have to keep, see s 20.
17   Subject to s 21(2), (3) and (4).
18   S 21(1)(a).
19   S 21(1)(b).
20   Subject to s 21(4).
21   The written communication must contain full particulars of the matters being delegated or assigned and of the conditions determined under s 21(1)(a), if any, and, where the power of subdelegation or further assignment is conferred, must state that fact as well as any conditions determined under s 21(1)(b), if any.
22   S 21(2)(a)–(c).
23   S 21(3)(a)–(b).
24   S 21(4)(a)–(d).

162   Chief Executive Officer   The minister must after consultation with the board appoint a suitable person as Chief Executive Officer of the corporation.[1] A person will be disqualified from being appointed or remaining a Chief Executive Officer if subject to any of the disqualifications mentioned in section 16(3)(a) to (f) of the Nuclear Energy Act.[2] The Chief Executive Officer holds office for a period specified in the letter of appointment but not exceeding three years, and may be re-appointed upon expiry of that term of office.[3] The minister may at any time remove the Chief Executive Officer from office:

(a)   if the Chief Executive Officer has repeatedly failed to perform the duties of office efficiently;

(b)   if, because of any physical or mental illness or disability, the Chief Executive Officer has become incapable of performing the functions of that office or performing them efficiently; or

(c)   for misconduct.[4]

The person who, immediately before the specified date was the Chief Executive Officer of the Atomic Energy Corporation Ltd by virtue of appointment in that office,[5] will from the specified date until the date on which the appointment of the corporation's first Chief Executive Officer[6] takes effect, act as, and perform the functions imposed by or in terms of the Act on, the corporation's Chief Executive Officer.[7] A person so acting is not precluded from being appointed as the corporation's Chief Executive Officer.[8]

1   Nuclear Energy Act 46 of 1999 s 22(1).
2   S 22(2).
3   S 22(3).
4   S 22(4)(a)–(c).
5   Under s 11 of the Nuclear Energy Act 131 of 1993.
6   Under the Nuclear Energy Act 46 of 1999 s 22(1).
7   S 22(5)(a).
8   S 22(5)(b).

163 General management of corporation The corporation's day-to-day business and operations are under the general management of the Chief Executive Officer, subject to the general or specific directions and instructions, if any, that the board may issue from time to time.[1] The Chief Executive Officer must:

(a) ensure that the functions of the corporation in terms of the Act are complied with;

(b) report to the board on the proper performance and functioning of the corporation;

(c) compile a report on the activities of the corporation for each financial year and submit the report to the board for approval;

(d) each financial year, after consulting the board, furnish the minister with a plan of action for the activities of the corporation.[2]

The Chief Executive Officer may delegate any of the powers, and assign any of the functions or duties attached to that office, to any employee of the corporation.[3][4]

Subject to the general or special directions of the board, if any, the Chief Executive Officer may appoint the staff for the corporation that may be necessary to perform the work arising from or connected with the corporation's functions, business and operations in terms of the Act.[5]

1 Nuclear Energy Act 46 of 1999 s 23(1).
2 S 23(2)(a)–(d). For general provisions regarding the duties of the Chief Executive Officer, see s 23(3)–(5).
3 S 21(1)(b), (2)(a) and (c)(3) and (4) will apply, reading in the changes necessary in the context, to any delegation or assignment in terms of s 24: s 24(2).
4 S 24(1).
5 S 25(1).

164 Finances of corporation The corporation is funded and provided with capital from:

(a) the capital invested in or lent to the corporation as contemplated in section 10 of the Nuclear Energy Act;[1]

(b) money appropriated by Parliament for that purpose;

(c) income derived from the sale or other commercial exploitation of its products, technology, services or expertise in terms of the Act;

(d) loans raised by the corporation in terms of section 15;

(e) the proceeds of any sale of assets authorised in terms of the Act;

(f) income or interest earned on the corporation's cash balances or on money invested by it; and

(g) money received by way of grant, contribution, donation or inheritance from any source inside or outside the Republic, but money from abroad may be received only with the minister's approval.[2]

Money that in terms of section 26(1) are the funds of the corporation, are utilised to meet the expenditure incurred by the corporation in connection with its functioning, business and operations.[3] This money may be so utilised only as provided for in a statement of the corporation's estimated income and expenditure contemplated in section 26(4), that has been approved by the minister.[4] Money received by way of grant, contribution, donation or inheritance in terms of section 26(1)(g), must be utilised in accordance with the conditions, if any, imposed by the grantor, contributor, donor or testator concerned.[5] The board must in each financial year, at a time determined by the minister, submit to the minister for approval a statement of the corporation's estimated income and expenditure for the next financial year. However, the board may at any time during the course of a financial year concerned, submit a supplementary statement of estimated income and expenditure of the corporation for that financial year, to the minister for approval.[6] The minister may grant the approval of the statement of estimated income and expenditure, with the agreement of the Minister of Finance.[7] The corporation may not incur any expenditure in excess of the total amount so approved.[8] The board may establish a reserve fund for any purpose that is connected with the corporation's functions and has been approved by the minister, and may allocate to the reserve fund the money that may be made available for that purpose in the statement of estimated income and expenditure (including any supplementary statement) so approved.[9] The Chief Executive Officer, subject to the conditions set by the board, must open an account in the name of the corporation with an institution registered as a bank in terms of the Banks Act,[10] and deposit therein all money contemplated in section 26(1).[11] The money of the corporation that is not required for immediate use or as a reasonable working balance, may be invested with the Corporation for Public Deposits established by section 2 of the Corporation for Public Deposits Act.[12][13] The corporation is deemed to be a listed entity as defined in the Reporting by Public Entities Act.[14][15]

1 46 of 1999.
2 S 26(1)(a)–(g).
3 S 26(2).
4 S 26(3)(a).
5 S 26(3)(b).
6 S 26(4)(a).
7 S 26(4)(b).
8 S 26(4)(c).
9 S 26(5).
10 94 of 1990.
11 Nuclear Energy Act 46 of 1999 s 26(6)(a).
12 46 of 1984.
13 Nuclear Energy Act 46 of 1999 s 26(6)(b).
14 93 of 1992 (now repealed) s 1.
15 Nuclear Energy Act 46 of 1999 s 27.

165 Rights to discoveries, inventions and improvements made by corporation's employees and certain other persons The rights in all discoveries, inventions and improvements made by employees of the corporation in the course of their work as its employees,[1] vest in the corporation which, with the minister's permission, may make any such discovery, invention or improvement available for use in the public interest, subject to any conditions and the payment of any fees and royalties that may be determined by the corporation and approved by the minister.[2] The corporation may, for such a discovery, invention or improvement, pay out of its funds to the employee concerned any bonus, reward or other financial benefit that the board may determine.[3] The Chief Executive Officer, on the instruction of the board, may apply on behalf of the corporation for a patent in terms of the Patents Act,[4] for any invention or improvement referred to in section 28(1) of the Nuclear Energy Act.[5] The Chief Executive Officer may direct the registrar of patents to keep secret any such invention and the manner in which it is to be applied.[6] The rights in respect of any discovery, invention or improvement made by employees of the corporation in the course of any work done by them as in that capacity on behalf of or for the benefit of another person or institution, vest in the corporation unless otherwise agreed between the corporation and the person or institution concerned.[7] The rights in respect of any discovery, invention or improvement made in the course of work or during a special investigation done or carried out by any other person or institution on behalf of or for the benefit of the corporation, vest in the corporation or in the other person or institution, or in the corporation, and the person or institution jointly, as may be agreed in writing by the parties beforehand, and the party or parties whom the rights in such an invention or improvement are vested, may apply for a patent for the invention or improvement.[8]

1 Nuclear Energy Act 46 of 1999, subject to the provisions of s 28(4)–(5).
2 S 28(1).
3 S 28(2).
4 57 of 1978.
5 Nuclear Energy Act 46 of 1999 s 28(3)(a).
6 S 28(3)(b).
7 S 28(4).
8 S 28(5).

166 Provisions with regard to security of corporation's installations, sites and premises The installations, sites, premises and land belonging to or under the control of the corporation, on which any of its business, operations and activities in terms of the Nuclear Energy Act[1] are conducted or performed or any records in connection therewith are kept, stored or to be found, are restricted areas.[2] Consequently, the corporation may make any arrangements it considers reasonably necessary for the proper protection of:

(a)   those installations, sites, premises and land (hereinafter called high security areas);

(b)   the persons employed or present at or in the high security areas;

(c)   all property of the corporation, whether of a physical or intellectual nature, at or in the high security areas; and

(d)   the records and information of the corporation that are kept, stored or to be found thereat or therein, irrespective of the manner in which or the medium on or by means of which the records and information are kept, stored or recorded.[3]

A person may not be allowed to enter or be present in a high security area unless the person has consented to any search that may be conducted.[4] Any person authorised in writing by the Chief Executive Officer, may:

(a)   search any person or vehicle about to enter or leave any high security area, and may open and inspect any container or parcel and inspect any object, device, article, item or thing (including any material or substance) which is in the possession of such a person or is on or in that vehicle;

(b)   search any person present or any vehicle found in the high security area if there are reasonable grounds to suspect that any person or anything in the person's possession or in or on the vehicle, constitutes a threat to or endangers the lives or physical integrity of persons or the physical safety of property;

(c)   seize or attach any object, device, article, item or thing (including any material or substance) in the possession of a person mentioned in (a) or (b) above, or found on or in such a vehicle:

(i)   if such an object, device, article, item or thing belongs to the corporation or is subject to its control and is not in the lawful possession of the person or lawfully being conveyed in or on the vehicle for the purpose of performing any function or work of the corporation; or

(ii)   if, in the opinion of the authorised person, it constitutes a threat or danger of the nature contemplated in (b) above, or may be used by the person from whom it was taken or any other person for the purposes of a threat or danger of that nature;

(d)   arrest any person found in unlawful possession of restricted matter or anything else contemplated in (c)(i) above, or any person mentioned in (b) above.[5]

1 46 of 1999.
2 S 29(1).
3 S 29(2)(a)–(d). For the regulations on the development surrounding any nuclear installation to ensure the effective implementation of any nuclear emergency plan, see *Government Gazette* 25217 GN 1054, 25 July 2003.
4 S 29(3), such search being conducted in terms of s 29(4)(a).
5 S 29(4)(a)–(d).

167 Exemption from duties and fees The corporation, but not its subsidiary companies, is exempt from the payment of any duty or fee which, were it not for the provisions of this section, would have been payable by it to the state in terms of any law,[1] in respect of an act or transaction to which the corporation is a party, or any document connected with such an act or transaction.[2]

1   Except the Customs and Excise Act 91 of   1991.
    1964 or the Value Added Tax Act 89 of   2   Nuclear Energy Act 46 of 1999 s 30.

168 Disclosure of confidential information concerning corporation's activities Information concerning any operation, transaction, project, work or activity of the corporation in connection with restricted matter or any restricted act or activity which is not yet public knowledge, may not be published or made known or be transmitted or otherwise disclosed,[1] except with the written permission of the Chief Executive Officer acting on the authority of the board, by any:

(a)   employee or former employee of the corporation or of a subsidiary company;

(b)   any person who is or was involved in the business, operations or activities of the corporation or subsidiary company in the capacity of agent, contractor or consultant or in any similar or related capacity, as well as the employee, partner or associate of such a person.[2]

This does not preclude the disclosure of information in so far as may be necessary for the exercise of any power or performance of any function or duty of the corporation in terms of the Nuclear Energy Act or for the performance of any work in this connection or on the order of a competent court of law.[3]

1   Nuclear Energy Act 46 of 1999, subject to   2   S 31(1)(a)–(b).
    s 31(2).   3   S 31(2)(a)–(b).

169 Minister may authorise performance of corporation's functions by other person or body in certain circumstances If, in any particular case, the corporation should fail, in relation to any matter or matters, to perform any function imposed on the corporation in circumstances where, in law, it is under a duty to perform that function, the minister, by notice in writing to the board, may order the corporation to perform the function concerned, which must be specified in the notice.[1] The board and the Chief Executive Officer must ensure that any lawful order is complied with.[2] If the corporation fails to comply with such an order, the minister, in writing, may authorise any person or other body that is competent and has the necessary capacity for that purpose, to perform that function in relation to the particular matter or matters, as the case may be.[3] The minister may recover from the corporation the costs of having such a function performed by a person or body so authorised.[4]

1   Nuclear Energy Act 46 of 1999 s 32(1).   3   S 32(3).
2   S 32(2), read with s 32(1).   4   S 32(4).

NUCLEAR NON-PROLIFERATION

170 Minister's responsibilities concerning Republic's international obligations The minister acts as the national authority of the Republic for the purposes of the implementation and application of the Safeguards Agreement and any additional protocols in order to timeously detect and identify nuclear material intended to be used for peaceful nuclear activities and deter the diversion of such nuclear material to the manufacture of nuclear weapons or other nuclear explosive devices or for use in connection with any other purpose that is unknown.[1]

In order to fulfil these responsibilities:

(a) the minister must liaise with the International Atomic Energy Agency on an ongoing basis as regards:

(i) negotiations on subsidiary arrangements under the Safeguards Agreement;

(ii) the furnishing and updating of information regarding the design of nuclear installations and sites;

(iii) the furnishing of reports required by or in terms of the Safeguards Agreement and the subsidiary arrangements thereunder;

(iv) requests for exemption from or termination of safeguards relating to nuclear material;

(v) the provision of facilities and support to the inspectors of the International Atomic Energy Agency;

(vi) the selection of inspectors nominated in respect of the Republic by the International Atomic Energy Agency;

(vii) the accompaniment of that agency's inspectors during inspections; and

(viii) the handling of importation into, and exportation from, the Republic of equipment and samples;[2]

Moreover, the minister may issue instructions:

(a) concerning the measuring methods and systems with regard to nuclear material;

(b) on the procedures for the handling of shipper-receiver differences in respect of nuclear material;

(c) requiring and otherwise relating to the undertaking of periodic physical stock-taking of nuclear material;

(d) on the operation of accounting systems in relation to any materials;

(e) relating to the keeping of records and reporting on nuclear material;

(f) relating to the furnishing of information regarding the design, and changes to the design of nuclear installations and sites;

(g) on the provision of information about the importation into, and exportation from, the Republic of nuclear material and nuclear-related equipment and material;

(h) about applications for the exemption from or termination of requirements or safeguards in relation to nuclear material;

(i) about the physical protection of nuclear material.[3]

Furthermore, the minister may:

(a) have the arrangement and verification undertaken of the physical inventory of any nuclear material in the Republic;

(b) have inspections and investigations undertaken in accordance with and subject to sections 37, 38 and 39 of the Nuclear Energy Act;

(c) cause the measuring methods and systems employed by any person or body with regard to nuclear material to be verified;

(d) have samples taken of and analysis undertaken of any product, article, object or thing subject to section 38;

(e) have independent measurements of nuclear material taken.[4]

The minister may also apply any measures he or she considers necessary for the containment and surveillance of nuclear material.[5] In addition, the minister must consult with the South African Council for the Non-Proliferation of Weapons of Mass Destruction, established by the Non-Proliferation of Weapons of Mass Destruction Act,[6] on any matter affecting the proliferation of weapons of mass destruction.[7]

Any person in possession of, using, handling or processing nuclear material must:

(a)   keep the prescribed records;

(b)   submit the prescribed reports to the minister at the times or intervals or on the occurrence of any event as prescribed;

(c)   perform the prescribed measurements on nuclear material and maintain the prescribed measuring control programmes;

(d)   in the prescribed manner provide the minister with information regarding the design of any nuclear installation and site concerned and all changes effected to the design thereof;

(e)   periodically undertake the physical stocktaking of nuclear material in the manner and at the times as prescribed;

(f)   in the prescribed manner give prior notice of the importation or exportation of nuclear material and nuclear-related equipment and material;

(g)   implement and maintain the prescribed physical protective measures in respect of nuclear material;

(h)   without delay report to the minister any loss of nuclear material in excess of the prescribed limits;

(i)   periodically, at the times and in the manner as prescribed, provide the minister with schedules of planned activities;

(j)   allow the designated officials of the International Atomic Energy Agency and any inspectors appointed under section 53 to carry out, without hindrance, inspections at any nuclear installation or site with a view to monitoring compliance with the provisions regarding nuclear non-proliferation.[8]

All information furnished or disclosed by any person in compliance or supposed compliance with these provisions, as well as all accompanying information contained in the communication or presentation of the firstmentioned information, is highly confidential and may not be published or otherwise made known or disclosed by the minister or any official of the state while serving as such except in so far as may be necessary for or in connection with the exercise of any power or performance of any function or duty of the minister, in terms of the Act, or for the performance of any work in connection therewith or on the order of a competent court of law.[9]

All fees that from time to time, are due to the International Atomic Energy Agency by the Republic, must be paid by the minister on behalf of the Republic.[10]

1   Nuclear Energy Act 46 of 1999 s 33(1).
2   S 33(2)(a)(i)–(viii).
3   S 33(2)(b)(i)–(ix).
4   S 33(2)(c)(i)–(v).
5   S 33(2)(d).
6   87 of 1993 s 4.
7   Nuclear Energy Act 46 of 1999 s 33(2)(e).
8   S 33(3)(a)–(j).
9   S 33(4)(a). "Accompanying information", for the purposes of s 33(4)(a), means any information whatsoever which does not have to be furnished or disclosed to the minister in terms of s 33, whether derived directly from any express statement made in the communication or presentation or indirectly, by implication or inference, having regard to the context of the communication or presentation and, *inter alia*, to surrounding facts or circumstances, particular personal knowledge, the manner or medium of communication or presentation: s 33(4)(b).
10   S 33(5).

171 Authorisations required for acquisition or possession of, and certain activities relating to, nuclear material, restricted material and nuclear-related equipment and material Except with the written authorisation of the minister, no person, institution, organisation or body may:

(a) be in possession of any source material, except where:

(i) the possession has resulted from prospecting, reclamation or mining operations lawfully undertaken by the person, institution, organisation or body; or

(ii) the possession is on behalf of anyone who had acquired possession of the source material in the manner mentioned in (i) above; or

(iii) the person, institution, organisation or body has lawfully acquired the source material in any other manner;[1]

(b) be in possession of the following:

(i) special nuclear material;

(ii) restricted material;

(iii) uranium hexafluoride (UF6);

(iv) nuclear fuel;

(v) nuclear-related equipment and material;[2]

(c) acquire, use or dispose of any source material;[3]

(d) import any source material into the Republic;[4]

(e) process, enrich or reprocess any source material;[5]

(f) acquire any special nuclear material;[6]

(g) import any special nuclear material into the Republic;[7]

(h) use or dispose of any special nuclear material;[8]

(i) process, enrich or reprocess any special nuclear material;[9]

(j) acquire any restricted material;[10]

(k) import any restricted material into the Republic;[11]

(l) use or dispose of any restricted material;[12]

(m) produce nuclear energy;[13]

(n) manufacture or otherwise produce or acquire, or dispose of, uranium hexafluoride (UF6);[14]

(o) import uranium hexafluoride (UF6) into the Republic;[15]

(p) manufacture, or acquire, or dispose of, nuclear fuel;[16]

(q) import nuclear fuel into the Republic;[17]

(r) manufacture or otherwise produce, import, acquire use or dispose of nuclear-related equipment and material;[18]

(s) dispose of, store or reprocess any radioactive waste or irradiated fuel (when the latter is external to the spent fuel pool);[19]

(t) transport any of the abovementioned materials;[20]

(u) dispose of any technology related to any of the abovementioned materials or equipment.[21]

The minister may, after consultation with the South African Council for the Non-Proliferation of Weapons of Mass Destruction on any matter affecting the proliferation of weapons of mass destruction, grant any such authorisation, after application made to the minister in the prescribed manner for that purpose.[22] The authorisation may be granted subject to any conditions, if any, that the minister may determine.[23]

Where an application for such an authorisation has been refused, the minister, in writing, must inform the applicant accordingly, stating the reasons for the refusal.[24]

1 Nuclear Energy Act 46 of 1999 s 34(1)(a)(i)–(iii).
2 S 34(1)(b)(i)–(v).
3 S 34(1)(c).
4 S 34(1)(d).
5 S 34(1)(e).
6 S 34(1)(f).
7 S 34(1)(g).
8 S 34(1)(h).
9 S 34(1)(i).
10 S 34(1)(j).
11 S 34(1)(k).
12 S 34(1)(l).
13 S 34(1)(m).
14 S 34(1)(n).
15 S 34(1)(o).
16 S 34(1)(p).
17 S 34(1)(q).
18 S 34(1)(r).
19 S 34(1)(s).
20 S 34(1)(t).
21 S 34(1)(u).
22 S 34(2)(a).
23 S 34(2)(b).
24 S 34(3).

172 Exportation of source, special nuclear or restricted material or nuclear-related equipment and material A person may not export any source material, special nuclear material or restricted material or any nuclear-related equipment and material from the Republic except with the written authorisation of the minister.[1] The minister, having consulted with the South African Council for the Non-Proliferation of Weapons of Mass Destruction on any matter affecting the proliferation of weapons of mass destruction and duly taken into account the provisions of the Nuclear Non-proliferation Treaty, the Safeguards Agreement and the Republic's obligations under any other treaty or international agreement with another state, may grant any authorisation after application made to the minister in the manner as prescribed for that purpose.[2]

The authorisation may be granted subject to any conditions, if any, that the minister may impose. However, where the source material, special nuclear material, restricted material or nuclear-related equipment and material is to be exported:

(a) to a nuclear weapons state, the authorisation at all times must be made subject to the condition that the material and equipment concerned may be used for peaceful purposes only;

(b) to a non-nuclear weapons state, the authorisation at all times must be made subject to the condition that the material and equipment concerned will be subject to comprehensive international safeguards at all times.[3]

Where an application for such an authorisation has been refused, the minister must in writing inform the applicant accordingly, stating the reason for the refusal.[4]

1 Nuclear Energy Act 46 of 1999 s 35(1).
2 S 35(2) read with s 35(1).
3 S 35(3)(a)–(b).
4 S 35(4).

173 Furnishing of information and reports The minister, in writing, may direct any person to whom authorisation was granted to furnish to the minister a return concerning:

(a) any source material, restricted material or special nuclear material acquired by, in the possession of, or under the control of that person;

(b) any nuclear-related equipment or material acquired by, in the possession of, or under the control of that person;

(c) any other information in that person's possession relating to any work carried out by, on behalf of or under the direction of that person in connection with the production, use, processing, enrichment or reprocessing of source material, restricted material, special nuclear material or nuclear energy, or in connection with research with regard to related matters.[1]

The return to be so furnished, must contain the particulars and be accompanied by the plans, drawings and other documents specified in the direction.[2]

1 Nuclear Energy Act 46 of 1999 s 36(1)(a)–
  (c), read with s 34 or s 35.
2 S 36(2).

174 Inspectors An inspector duly appointed may at any reasonable time, without a warrant, enter upon or enter any land, premises, place or means of conveyance at, on or in which restricted matter is kept or to be found or at, on, in, from where or by means of which any restricted act or activity is performed or carried out, with a view to performing thereat, thereon or therein, any inspection or investigation necessary or expedient for monitoring compliance with:

(a)   the terms of the minister's authorisation for possessing the restricted matter or performing or carrying out the restricted acts or activity, and compliance with the provisions of the Nuclear Energy Act[1] relating to restricted matter or restricted acts or activities;

(b)   the conditions imposed by the minister under sections 34 or 35, as the case may be, in respect of that authorisation;

(c)   any other relevant requirement imposed by or in terms of the Act with regard to restricted matter or restricted acts or activities.[2]

An inspector may not search the land, premises, place or means of conveyance except on the authority of a warrant.[3]

An inspector acting on the authority of a warrant, may enter upon or enter any land, premises, place or means of conveyance:

(a)   at, on or in which there is to be found or on reasonable grounds is expected to be found, any restricted matter the possession of which is unlawful in terms of section 34, or anything reasonably suspected of being such restricted matter;

(b)   at, on, in, from or by means of which, any restricted act or activity on reasonable grounds is suspected to be or to have been performed or carried out without the necessary authorisation in terms of sections 34 or 35, as the case may be,

and inspect and search the land, premises, place or means of conveyance and any person thereat, thereon or therein, for restricted matter or evidence relating to possession of restricted matter or a restricted act or activity, and for any other evidence relating to the contravention of section 34 or section 35 in relation to the restricted matter or restricted act or activity.[4]

For the purposes of entering and searching a means of conveyance, any inspector who is assisted by a police official may stop the means of conveyance, whether public or private, if necessary by force, wherever found. An inspector who has gained access to any land, premises, place or means of conveyance on the authority of a warrant, may:

(a)   take any steps that may be reasonably necessary to terminate the unlawful performance or carrying out of a restricted act or activity at, on, in, from or by means of the land, premises, place or means of conveyance and to prevent the recurrence of such an act or activity;

(b)   seize and detain, and, where applicable, remove for detention, restricted matter found at, on or in the land, premises, place or means of conveyance;

(c)   bar or restrict access to the land or premises, place or any part thereof, or seal off or seal the premises, place or means of conveyance;

(d)   seize and detain, and, where applicable, remove for detention, any tools or equipment used or suspected on reasonable grounds to have been used to perform or carry out a restricted act or activity;

(e)   in any manner reasonably appropriate, take samples of any mineral, material or substance found on, under, or in the land, premises, place or means of conveyance for the purpose of analysis or conducting any test or investigation in respect thereof, and remove, and retain without compensation, any sample so taken; and

(f)   question any person at, on or in the land, premises, place or means of conveyance who may furnish any information about restricted matter or a restricted act or activity, and demand and procure from that person any book, document, plan, sketch or other record of whatever nature that may be relevant to the acquisition or possession of the restricted matter, or to the performance or carrying out of the restricted act or activity, and make copies or extracts from such a book, document, plan, sketch or other record.[5]

An inspector who, without a warrant, has entered upon or entered any land, premises, place or means of conveyance and who, in the course of carrying out or conducting any inspection or investigation threat, thereon or therein in terms of that section:

(a)   is satisfied on reasonable grounds that an offence in terms of section 56, based on the unlawful possession of restricted matter or the performance or carrying out of any restricted act or activity without the minister's authorisation in terms of sections 34 or 35 or on the breach of any term of, or condition imposed in respect of, such an authorisation, has been committed at, on, in, from or by means of the land, premises, place or means of conveyance, may, in so far as may be appropriate and reasonably necessary in the circumstances, exercise any of the powers contemplated in section 38(2)(a) to (f), but excluding the power in terms of section 38(2)(e) to take a sample of any mineral, material or substance from below the surface of land. However, such a sample may be taken from below the surface of land:

(i)   with the consent of the owner or person in control of the land, premises or place concerned; or

(ii)   on the authority of a warrant;

(b)   suspects, on reasonable grounds, that such an offence has been committed at, on, in, from or by means of the land, premises, place or means of conveyance, may bar or restrict access to the land, premises or place or any part thereof, or seal off or seal the premises, place or means of conveyance pending the issuing of a warrant in terms of section 40 that authorises the inspector to search the land, premises, place or means of conveyance or any person thereat, thereon or therein. Upon the issue of the warrant, the inspector also may, in so far as may be appropriate and reasonably necessary in the circumstances, exercise any of the powers contemplated in section 38(2)(a) to (f) in accordance with the provisions of those paragraphs.[6]

Despite the preceding provisions, an inspector may, during the day and after having furnished proof of identity, without a warrant enter or enter upon any land, premises, place or means of conveyance and exercise thereat, thereon or therein the power of search, if the person who is competent to consent to the entry and to the search gives that consent.[7]

The powers conferred on an inspector may be exercised only if the inspector, when requesting that person for consent, informs that person of the nature and extent of the powers contemplated in those paragraphs.[8]

An answer given or statement made by any person to an inspector, if self-incriminating, will not be admissible as evidence against that person in criminal proceedings instituted in any court against that person, except in criminal proceedings where that person is tried for an offence,[9] and then only to the extent that such an answer or statement is relevant to those proceedings.[10]

Before carrying out or conducting any inspection or investigation or conducting any search, the inspector concerned must consult with a knowledgeable person employed or performing duties at or in connection with the land, premises or place, or any part thereof, where the inspection is to be carried out or the investigation or search is to be conducted, with a view to determining whether the carrying out or conducting of the inspection, investigation or search at the relevant venue will or is likely to endanger or be harmful to the health of a person or will or is likely to result in the injury of any person or damage to any property.[11] Where the inspector and the person so consulted, hold different views on the matter, the inspector may refer the matter to the minister for a decision.[12] In undertaking any inspection or investigation or any search, or exercising any prescribed power, an inspector who considers it necessary, may:

(a)   be accompanied and assisted by any person that the inspector regards suitable for that purpose;

(b)   bring onto or into the land, premises, place or means of conveyance on or in which:

(i) the inspection or investigation is to be carried out or conducted, any apparatus, equipment, machinery and tools required for the purposes of the inspection or investigation; or

(ii) the search is to be conducted, any apparatus, equipment, machinery and tools required for the purpose or for performing any act mentioned in section 38(2).[13]

Where the inspection, investigation or search is to be carried out or conducted on or in any land, premises or place, the vehicles necessary for the conveyance of the apparatus, equipment, machinery or tools concerned must, if required and where possible, be allowed onto or into the land, premises or place concerned.[14]

1   46 of 1999.
2   S 37(1)(a)–(c).
3   s 37(2), read with s 40.
4   S 38(1).
5   S 38(2)(a)–(f).
6   S 38(3)(a)–(b).
7   S 38(4)(a), read with s 38(1)(a)–(b) (2)(a)–(f) and subject to s 38(4)(b).
8   S 38(4)(b), read with s 38(2)(a)–(f).
9   In terms of s 56(1)(c)(iv).
10   S 38(5).
11   S 39(1)(a).
12   S 39(1)(b).
13   S 39(2)(a)–(b).
14   S 39(3).

175 Provisions regarding issuing and execution of warrants Any warrant may be issued in chambers by any judge of the High Court or by a magistrate who has jurisdiction in the area in which:

(a)   the land, premises or place where the search is to be undertaken, is situated;

(b)   the means of conveyance to be searched, is to be found; or

(c)   the land from under the surface of which a sample is to be taken, is situated.[1]

A warrant[2] will be issued only if it appears to the judge or magistrate from information on oath or affirmation that there are reasonable grounds for believing that:

(a)   restricted matter, the possession of which is unlawful in terms of section 34 of the Nuclear Energy Act, is to be found on or in the land, premises, place or means of conveyance for which the search warrant is required; or

(b)   a restricted act or activity is being, has been or is likely to be performed or carried out thereat, thereon, therein or therefrom; or

(c)   an offence in terms of section 56 based on the unlawful possession of restricted matter or the performance or carrying out of any restricted act or activity without the minister's authorisation, in terms of sections 34 or 35, is being or has been committed at, on, in, from or by means of the land, place, premises or means of conveyance concerned.[3]

The inspector applying for the warrant must indicate whether the search of any person will be or is likely to be necessary. No person may be searched unless it is expressly authorised in the warrant.[4] The entry upon or entry onto or into the land, premises, place or means of conveyance specified in a warrant[5] and, where authorised by that warrant, the search of any person thereat, thereon or therein, must be conducted with strict regard to decency and order, including the individual's right to respect for and protection of personal dignity, freedom and security of person and personal privacy.[6]

An inspector who, on the authority of a warrant,[7] may enter upon or enter, and search, any land, premises, place or means of conveyance and, where applicable, search any person thereat, thereon or therein, may use the force that may be reasonably necessary to overcome any resistance to the entry and search.[8] A warrant[9] will be issued only if it appears to the judge or magistrate from information on oath or affirmation that there are reasonable grounds for believing that:

(a)   an offence contemplated in section 40(2)(c) has been committed; and

(b)   the sample to be taken from under the surface of the land concerned is likely to afford or corroborate evidence relating to that offence.[10]

A warrant may be issued on any day and remains in force until the occurrence of any of the following events (whichever occurs first):

(a)   the warrant has been executed; or

(b)   it is cancelled by the judge or magistrate who issued it, or, if not available, by any other judge, or by any other magistrate with like authority, as the case may be; or

(c)   the expiry of three months from the day of its issue; or

(d)   the purpose for which the warrant was issued, no longer exists.[11]

A warrant so issued may be executed by day only, unless the person who has issued the warrant has authorised the execution thereof by night.[12] An inspector executing a warrant must immediately before commencing with its execution:

(a)   furnish proof of identity to the person in control of the land, premises, place or means of conveyance to be entered upon or entered, if that person is present, and hand to that person a copy of the warrant, or, if that person is not present, affix a copy of the warrant to a prominent spot at, on or to the land, premises, place or means of conveyance; and

(b)   at the request of that person, furnish to that person particulars regarding the inspector's authority to execute the warrant and production of the inspector's certificate of appointment.[13]

1 Nuclear Energy Act 46 of 1999 s 40(1).
2 Contemplated in s 38(1) or (3)(b).
3 S 40(2).
4 Such warrant being issued in terms of s 40(2).
5 S 40(3).
6 S 40(4).
7 Such warrant being issued under s 40(2).
8 S 40(5).
9 Contemplated in s 38(3)(a).
10 S 40(6).
11 S 40(7)(a)–(d).
12 S 40(8).
13 S 40(9)(a)–(b).

176 General Whenever, in exercising any power or performing any function under the Nuclear Energy Act[1] which affects or is likely to affect any person, or in proposing to do so, the minister is satisfied on reasonable grounds that disclosure of the reasons for exercising or performing the power or function or proposing to do so will endanger or be harmful to the security of the Republic, the minister need not disclose those reasons.[2] This does not preclude any High Court from inquiring into and deciding on the validity of any non–disclosure purporting to be so justified.[3] The court conducting such an inquiry may at any time on application by the minister or of its own accord, order that the proceedings before it be conducted *in camera* if the interests of the security of the state so require. For that purpose the court must assess the matters raised and the evidence, statements and addresses that have been or may be tendered, made or given, as well as other developments in the matter, on an ongoing basis for potential danger or harm to the security of the Republic.[4]

In the case of any civil or criminal proceedings before a court of law, or any proceedings before an arbitration tribunal, arising from the application or administration of the Act, the court or arbitral tribunal, as the case may be, may direct that the proceedings before it be held *in camera* if the interest of the security of the Republic so require.[5] For that purpose, the court or tribunal, as the case may be, must assess the matters raised and the evidence, statements and addresses that have been or may be tendered, made or given in the proceedings concerned, as well as other developments in the proceedings, on an ongoing basis for potential danger or harm to the security of the Republic.[6]

The minister must appoint suitably qualified persons who are fit and proper persons as inspectors.[7] A certificate of appointment must be issued to every person so appointed.[8] The qualifications of inspectors may be prescribed by the minister.[9]

The minister may make regulations not inconsistent with the Act, with regard to anything which in terms of the Act, may or must be prescribed or provided for or governed or otherwise dealt with by regulation.[10] In any regulations, provision may be made:

(a) that the contravention of or failure to comply with any particular provisions thereof, will be an offence; and

(b) that a person convicted of such an offence will be punishable with a term of imprisonment not longer than the period specified in the regulations or with a fine, but no term of imprisonment in excess of 12 months may be so specified.[11]

Before any regulations are made, the minister must by notice in the *Government Gazette*, invite the public to comment on the proposed regulations and consider that comment.[12]

The minister may delegate any power and assign any function conferred or imposed upon the minister in terms of the Act, except the power to make regulations, to the Director–General of the Department of Minerals and Energy, who may subdelegate or re–assign any delegated power or assigned function in the circumstances and manner as prescribed.[13]

1 46 of 1999.
2 S 51(1).
3 S 51(2)(a).
4 S 51(2)(b).
5 S 52(1).
6 S 52(2).
7 S 53(1).
8 S 53(2).
9 S 53(4).
10 S 54(1).
11 S 54(2). For the standing of the regulations under the Nuclear Energy Act 131 of 1993, see s 54(3) of the Nuclear Energy Act 46 of 1999.
12 S 54(4).
13 S 55(1). For further details, see s 55(2)–(5).

NATIONAL NUCLEAR REGULATOR ACT

177 Introduction[1] The National Nuclear Regulator Act[2] has been promulgated to provide for the establishment of a National Nuclear Regulator to regulate nuclear activities, for the objects and functions of the regulator, and the manner in which it is to be managed. The Act makes provisions for safety standards and regulatory practices for the protection of persons, property and the environment against nuclear damage.[3]

The Act provides that the following provisions of the Nuclear Energy Act of 1993[4] are repealed:

(a) chapters V and VI;

(b) section 1, in so far as it relates to anything in any of these chapters; and

(c) the provisions of chapter VII, in so far as they related to the Council for Nuclear Safety.[5]

In addition, on the specified date, anything done before such date in terms of any provision of the previous Act repealed by section 54(1) of the Nuclear Regulator Act, and which could be done in terms of the Nuclear Regulator Act, is regarded to have been done in terms of the Act, except where otherwise provided in the Act.[6]

---

1 Nuclear energy has a vital role to play in sustainable economic development because it is emission-free, and provides abundant, reliable, and reasonable affordable supply of electricity. The nuclear energy industry has followed comprehensive waste management practices since its beginning about 40 years ago. The Vienna Convention on Civil Liability for Nuclear Damage, 1963, for example, noted the desire of the contracting parties to establish minimum standards to provide financial protection against damage resulting from certain peaceful uses of nuclear energy. The Convention contains copious provisions for the determination of liability resulting from damage caused by nuclear installation and the determination of compensation payable to victims of such damages.

2 47 of 1999.

3 See preamble to the Act.

4 131 of 1993.

5 National Nuclear Regulator Act 47 of 1999 s 54(1).

6 S 54(2).

178 Definitions and application of Act For the purposes of the National Nuclear Regulator Act:[1]

"Action" means:

(a) the use, possession, production, storage, enrichment, processing, reprocessing, conveying or disposal of, or causing to be conveyed, radioactive material;

(b) any action, the performance of which may result in persons accumulating a radiation dose resulting from exposure to ionising radiation; or

(c) any other action involving radioactive materials.

"Nuclear accident" means:

(a) any unintended event at a nuclear installation, which causes off-site public exposure of the order of at least one-tenth of the prescribed limits;

(b) the spread of radioactive contamination on a site or exposure of a worker above the prescribed limits or a significant failure in safety provisions other than a nuclear accident.

"Nuclear installation" means:

(a) a facility, installation, plant or structure designed or adapted for or which may involve the carrying out of any process, other than the mining and processing of ore, within the nuclear fuel cycle involving radioactive material, including, but not limited to:

    (i) a uranium or thorium refinement or conversion facility;

    (ii) a uranium enrichment facility;

    (iii) a nuclear fuel fabrication facility;

    (iv) a nuclear reactor, including a nuclear fission reactor or any other facility intended to create nuclear fusion;

    (v) a spent nuclear fuel reprocessing facility;

    (vi) a spent nuclear fuel storage facility;

    (vii) an enriched uranium processing and storage facility; and

    (viii) a facility specifically designed to handle, treat, condition, temporarily store or permanently dispose of any radioactive material which is intended to be disposed of as waste material; or

(b) any facility, installation, plant or structure declared to be a nuclear installation in terms of section 2(3) of the National Nuclear Regulator Act.

"Radioactive material" means any substance consisting of or containing, any radioactive nuclide, whether natural or artificial, including, but not limited to, radioactive waste and spent nuclear fuel.

"Radioactive nuclide" means any unstable atomic nucleus, which decays spontaneously with the accompanying emission of ionising radiation.[2]

The Act applies to the siting, design, construction, operation, decontamination, decommissioning and closure of any nuclear installation. The Act also applies to vessels propelled by nuclear power or having radioactive material on board which is capable of causing nuclear damage and any action which is capable of causing nuclear damage.[3] The Act does not however apply to:

(a) exposure to cosmic radiation or to potassium-40 in the body or any other radioactive materials or actions not amenable to regulatory control as determined by the Minister of Minerals and Energy ("the minister"), after consultation with the board;

(b) subject to section 42(4), any action where the radioactivity concentrations of individual radioactive nuclides, or the total radioactivity content, are below the exclusion levels provided for in the safety standards contemplated in section 36;

(c) Group IV hazardous substances as defined in section 1 of the Hazardous Substances Act;[4] and

(d) exposure to ionising radiation emitted from equipment, declared to be a Group III hazardous substance in terms of section 2(1)(b) of the Hazardous Substances Act.[5]

Notwithstanding, the minister may, after consultation with the board and by notice in the *Government Gazette*, declare any facility, installation, plant or structure, including a mine or ore-processing facility, to be a nuclear installation.[6]

---

1 47 of 1999.
2 S 1.
3 S 2(1).
4 15 of 1973.

5 National Nuclear Regulator Act 47 of 1999 s 2(2).
6 S 2(3).

179 National Nuclear Regulator The National Nuclear Regulator Act[1] provides for the establishment of a juristic person to be known as the National Nuclear Regulator, comprising a board, a Chief Executive Officer and staff.[2] Chapter 2 of the Act provides for all matters incidental and connected with the establishment of such National Nuclear Regulator, including the objects of the regulator, the functions of the regulator, the control and management of affairs of the regulator, the meetings of the board, the Chief Executive Officer of the regulator, the funds of the regulator and the judicial management and liquidation of the regulator. Two functions of the regulator are the fulfilment of national obligations in respect of international legal instruments concerning nuclear safety, and to ensure that provisions for nuclear emergency planning are in place.[3] The regulator is exempt from the payment of any duty or fee which would have been payable by it to the state in terms of any law, except the Customs and Excise Act,[4] and the Value Added Tax Act,[5] in respect of any act or transaction or any document connected with that Act or transaction.

1 47 of 1999.	4 91 of 1964.
2 S 3.	5 89 of 1991.
3 S 5.	

180 Restriction on certain actions No person may site, construct, operate, decontaminate or decommission a nuclear installation, except under the authority of a nuclear installation licence.[1] In addition, no vessel which is propelled by nuclear power or which has on board any radioactive material capable of causing nuclear damage may anchor in the territorial waters of the Republic or enter any port of the Republic except under the authority of a nuclear vessel licence.[2] Furthermore, no person may engage in any action that may be capable of causing nuclear damage, except under the authority of a certificate of registration or a certificate of exemption.[3]

1 National Nuclear Regulator Act 47 of 1999	2 S 20(2).
s 20(1).	3 S 20(3).

181 Application for nuclear installation or vessel licence, and for registration certificate or exemption The National Nuclear Regulator Act[1] imposes a duty on anyone wishing to site, construct, operate, decontaminate or decommission a nuclear installation to apply in the prescribed form to the Chief Executive Officer for a nuclear installation licence, furnishing such information as the board requires. Third-party input and comments are allowed on the application prior to consideration and approval, and further debates may be arranged for hearings on health, safety and environmental issues as the board of the regulator may determine. Subject to the board's approval, the Chief Executive Officer may refuse to approve an application, though in such case, he or she must provide the applicant with the reasons for refusal; or the application may be granted subject to conditions.[2]

Any person wishing to engage in any action which is capable of causing nuclear damage, may apply in the prescribed form to the Chief Executive Officer for a certificate of registration or a certificate of exemption.[3] The format and the procedure for the application must comply with the provisions set out in section 22(2) and section 22(3) of the Nuclear Regulator Act.

1 47 of 1999.
2 S 20.
3 S 21.

182 Conditions relating to nuclear installation licence, nuclear vessel licence or certificate of registration The Chief Executive Officer may establish standard conditions applicable to one or more categories of certificates of registration.[1] The Chief Executive Officer may also impose any condition in a nuclear installation or vessel licence or certificate of registration which may be necessary to ensure the protection of persons, property and the environment against nuclear damage, or for the rehabilitation of the site.[2] The Chief Executive Officer has the power to amend any condition in a nuclear installation or vessel licence or certificate of registration.[3] The minister may, on the recommendation of the board and in consultation with the Minister of Finance and by notice in the *Government Gazette*, determine the fees payable to the regulator in respect of any application for the granting of a nuclear authorisation and an annual nuclear authorisation fee.

1 National Nuclear Regulator Act 47 of 1999   2 S 23(2).
  s 23(1).   3 S 23(3).

183 Special conditions relating to nuclear vessel licence

The Chief Executive Officer may, in terms of section 24 of the Nuclear Regulator Act[1] include in a nuclear vessel licence, certain conditions relating to liability for nuclear damage and security for nuclear damage.[2] In addition, any other conditions that the Chief Executive Officer considers necessary to ensure compliance with the safety standards contemplated in section 36 of the Act may be included. If the vessel in question is registered outside the Republic, the appropriate terms of any agreement between the government of the Republic and the government of the country in which the vessel is registered must be included in a nuclear vessel licence.[3] The conditions imposed on a nuclear vessel licence may be amended or repealed by the Chief Executive Officer.[4]

1 47 of 1999.   3 S 24(2).
2 S 24(1).   4 S 24(3).

184 Responsibilities of holders of nuclear authorisation

The holder of a nuclear authorisation must display copies of that authorisation at such places and in such languages determined by the Chief Executive Officer to ensure public access to the conditions specified in the authorisation.[1] The holder of a nuclear authorisation must implement an inspection programme to ensure compliance with all conditions of the nuclear authorisation.[2] Information or monthly returns must be provided on the nuclear authorisation licence to the Chief Executive Officer.[3] The holder must establish a public safety information forum to inform the persons living in the municipal area in respect of which an emergency plan has been established. If there is a potential of an accident occurring, the holder must enter into agreements with the relevant municipal and provincial authorities for the establishment of emergency plans, and obtain approval therefore.[4] The holder is to cover the cost of such establishment.[5]

The National Nuclear Regulator Act provides that a nuclear authorisation may not be transferred.[6]

1 National Nuclear Regulator Act 47 of 1999   4 S 26(4).
  s 26(1).   5 S 28.
2 S 26(2).   6 S 25.
3 S 26(3).

185 Revocation and surrender of nuclear authorisation

The Chief Executive Officer may, with the approval of the board, revoke a nuclear authorisation.[1] The holder of a nuclear authorisation may also surrender that authorisation.[2]

1 National Nuclear Regulator Act 47 of 1999   set out in s 27(3) and (4) must be complied
  s 27(1).   with.
2 S 27(2). In such circumstances, the provisions

186 Financial security by holder of nuclear installation licence

The minister must categorise the various nuclear installations in the Republic, based on the potential consequences of a nuclear accident.[1] In addition, the minister must determine:

(a)   the level of financial security to be provided by holders of nuclear installation licences in respect of each of those categories; and

(b)   the manner in which that financial security is to be provided;

in order for the holder of a nuclear installation licence to fulfil any liability which may be incurred in terms of section 30 of the National Nuclear Regulator Act.[2]

Furthermore, the minister may, after consultation with the board, for so long as the holder of a nuclear installation licence may be liable for nuclear damage:

(a)   increase or decrease the level of financial security to be provided by that holder; and

(b)   if financial security has not been required in terms section 29(2), require that holder to provide financial security;

(c)   discharge that holder from the requirement to provide financial security; and

(d)   amend the manner in which that holder must provide financial security.[3]

If nuclear damage occurs and compensation is claimed as a result thereof or if the minister is satisfied that such compensation is likely to be claimed, the minister may require the holder of the nuclear installation licence in question to give additional financial security in respect of those claims, to an amount which the minister determines. In addition, the holder of a nuclear installation licence must annually provide proof to the regulator that any claim for compensation to an amount contemplated in section 30(2) of the Act can be met.[4]

Article III Vienna Convention on Civil Liability for Nuclear Damage imposes an obligation on the operators of nuclear installations and facilities to provide such financial security or guarantees therefor.

1   National Nuclear Regulator Act 47 of 1999   3   S 29(3).
    s 29(1).   4   S 29(4).
2   S 29(2).

187 Strict liability of holder of nuclear licence for nuclear damage The National Nuclear Regulator Act[1] imposes a higher degree of liability than the Convention on Civil Liability for Nuclear Damage. While Article II of the Convention requires a proof of causation and damage, the Act imposes a strict liability on the holder in the event of an accident. The Act provides that the holder of a nuclear installation licence is, whether or not there is intent or negligence on his or her part, liable for all nuclear damage caused by or resulting from the relevant nuclear installation during the holder's period of responsibility:

(a)   by anything being present or which is done at or in the nuclear installation or by any radioactive material or material contaminated with radioactivity which has been discharged or released, in any form, from the nuclear installation; or

(b)   by any radioactive material or material contaminated with radioactivity which is subject to the nuclear installation licence, while in the possession or under the control of the holder of that licence during the conveyance thereof from the nuclear installation licence, to any other place in the Republic or in the territorial waters of the Republic from or to any place in or outside the Republic.[2]

The liability for nuclear damage by any holder of a nuclear installation licence is limited, for each nuclear accident, to the amount determined pursuant to section 29(2).[3]

A victim of a nuclear accident may claim benefits in terms of the Compensation for Occupational Injuries and Diseases Act,[4] or under the National Nuclear Regulator

Act, but such person may not benefit in terms of both the National Nuclear Regulator Act and the Compensation for Occupational Injuries and Diseases Act.[5]

The holder of a nuclear installation licence is not liable to any person for any nuclear damage to the extent to which such nuclear damage is attributable to the presence of that person or any property of that person at or in the nuclear installation or on the site in respect of which the nuclear installation licence has been granted, without the permission of the holder of that licence or of a person acting on behalf of that holder, or if that person intentionally caused, or intentionally contributed to, such damage.[6] The holder of a nuclear installation licence retains any contractual right of recourse or contribution which the holder has against any person in respect of any nuclear damage for which that holder is liable in terms of section 30(1) of the National Nuclear Regulator Act.[7] If the Chief Executive Officer has not determined any conditions for liability for nuclear damage for holder of a nuclear vessel licence, the provisions of section 30 apply with the changes required by the context.[8]

1 47 of 1999.
2 S 30(1).
3 S 30(2). For the purposes of s 30(1) of the National Nuclear Regulator Act 47 of 1999, radioactive material or material contaminated with radioactivity which has been conveyed on behalf of the holder of a nuclear installation licence is regarded as being in the possession or under the control of the holder of that licence: s 30(4).
4 130 of 1993.
5 National Nuclear Regulator Act 47 of 1999 s 30(5).
6 S 30(6).
7 S 30(7).
8 S 31.

188 Liability of holder of certificate of registration for nuclear damage The liability of a holder of a certificate of registration, for any nuclear damage caused by virtue of that certificate during his or her period of responsibility, is to be determined in accordance with the common law or the Compensation for Occupational Injuries and Diseases Act,[1] as the case may be.[2]

1 130 of 1993.
2 National Nuclear Regulator Act 47 of 1999 s 32.

189 Claims for compensation in excess of maximum liability If the total amount of claims for compensation against a holder of a nuclear installation licence or the total amount of claims for compensation against such holder plus the estimated amounts of claims for compensation likely to be required to be paid, exceeds the amount for which that holder has given security, the holder must immediately notify the board and the minister in writing.[1] The notice must include the particulars set out in section 33(2) of the National Nuclear Regulator Act. On receipt of such notice, the minister must table in Parliament a report on the nuclear damage in question, which recommends that Parliament appropriate funds for rendering financial assistance to the holder for the amount by which the claims exceed the security available, and by notice in the *Government Gazette*, suspend the obligation to pay the claims in respect of that nuclear damage until Parliament has decided on the recommendation.[2]

The liability of a person, who has provided or must provide financial security, is not affected by any appropriation If Parliament has, by resolution, decided that funds to an amount specified in the report by the minister be appropriated, no payment of any such claim for compensation arising out of the nuclear damage concerned may be made after the passing of such resolution without the approval of the minister or an order of court.[3]

1 National Nuclear Regulator Act 47 of 1999 s 33(1).
2 S 33(3).
3 S 33(5).

190 Prescription of actions An action for compensation in terms of section 30, 31 or 32 of the National Nuclear Regulator Act[1] may not be instituted after the expiration of a period of 30 years from the date of the occurrence which gave rise to the right to claim that compensation or the date of the last event in the course of that occurrence or succession of occurrences, if a continuing occurrence or a succession of occurrences, all attributable to a particular event or the carrying out of a particular operation, gave rise to that right.[2] If the claimant concerned became aware or, by exercising reasonable care, could have become aware of the identity of the holder of the nuclear authorisation concerned and the facts from which the right to claim compensation arose during the period of 30 years, an action for compensation in terms of section 30, 31 or 32 may not be instituted after the expiration of a period of two years from the date on which he or she so became aware or could have become aware.[3]

Article VI of the of the Vienna Convention on Civil Liability for Nuclear Damage fixes the limitation period for bringing an action for damages arising from nuclear accidents to ten years.

1   47 of 1999.
2   S 34(1).
3   S 34(2).

191 Compensation for injuries of regulator's employees If a person who is employed by the regulator, while so performing services, suffers a personal injury or contracts a disease attributable to ionising radiation, and in respect of which no liability can be established in terms of section 30, 31 or 32 of the National Nuclear Regulator Act,[1] the regulator must defray all reasonable expenses incurred by such person in respect of any medical treatment, including, but not limited to, the supply and maintenance of any artificial part of the body or other device, necessitated by such injury or disease, and pay compensation in respect of disablement or death caused by such injury or disease.[2]

It should be noted that nothing in section 35 precludes an employee of the regulator from claiming a benefit in terms of the Compensation for Occupational Injuries and Diseases Act,[3] but such employee may not benefit both in terms of the Nuclear National Regulator Act and the Compensation for Occupational Injuries and Diseases Act.[4] In addition, nothing in the section affects any right, which any person has in terms of any contract of employment, to benefits more favourable than those to which that person may be entitled in terms of this section.[5]

1   47 of 1999.
2   S 35(1).
3   130 of 1993.

4   National Nuclear Regulator Act 47 of 1999
    s 35(2).
5   S 35(3).

192 Safety standards and regulatory practices The minister must make regulations regarding safety standards and regulatory practices.[1] Before any regulations are made, the minister must invite the public to comment on the proposed regulations and consider that comment.[2]

1   National Nuclear Regulator Act 47 of 1999
    s 36(1).
2   S 36(2).

193 Duties regarding nuclear accidents and incidents If a nuclear accident occurs in connection with a nuclear installation, nuclear vessel or action, the holder of the nuclear authorisation in question must immediately report it to the regulator in accordance with the provisions set out in section 37(2) and section 37(3) of the National Nuclear Regulator Act.[1] If a nuclear incident occurs on site, the holder of the nuclear authorisation in question must report it to the regulator within the period stipulated in that authorisation.[2]

1   47 of 1999 s 37(1).
2   S 37(5).

194 Record of nuclear installations and accidents, and incidents and access thereto The regulator must keep a record of the particulars, a map showing the location and where applicable, diagrams showing the position and limits, of nuclear installations in respect of which a nuclear installation licence has been granted.[1] In addition, if the regulator believes that a risk of nuclear damage arising from anything done or being done or is present at or in any nuclear installation in respect of which a nuclear installation licence is no longer in force, it may remove the particulars in connection from that record.[2]

The regulator must keep and maintain a record of the details of every nuclear accident and nuclear incident, store that record safely, retain that record for 40 years from the date of the nuclear accident or nuclear incident, and on the request of any person, make that record available to that person.[3]

1   National Nuclear Regulator Act 47 of 1999   2   S 39(2).
    s 39(1).   3   S 40.

195 Appointment and powers of inspectors The Chief Executive Officer must appoint suitably qualified inspectors to enforce compliance with the objects of the regulator.[1] The Chief Executor Officer must issue to every person appointed, a certificate to the effect that such person has been so appointed and restricting such person to the actions in respect of which he or she may exercise the powers and perform the duties conferred on an inspector in terms of the National Nuclear Regulator Act.[2]

The regulator may make or cause to be made such arrangements for the proper protection or security of property, which belongs to the regulator or is on any premises on which activities of the regulator are performed.[3] In addition, no unauthorised persons may enter any premises which are under the control of the regulator and which the regulator has identified as premises where information relating to the security and safety of a nuclear installation is kept.[4]

1   National Nuclear Regulator Act 47 of 1999   are set out in s 41(4).
    s 41(1).   3   S 42(1).
2   S 41(2). The powers and duties conferred or   4   S 42(2).
    imposed on an inspector in terms of the Act

196 Appeal Any person adversely affected by any action or decision of an inspector may appeal to the Chief Executive Officer against that action or decision.[1]

Any person adversely affected by a decision of the Chief Executive Officer, may appeal against that decision to the board.[2]

Any person adversely affected by a decision of the board, either in terms of section 44(3) of the National Nuclear Regulator Act or in the exercise of any power in terms of the Act, may appeal against that decision to the minister.[3]

Any person adversely affected by a decision of the minister, either in terms of section 45(3) or in the exercise of any power in terms of the Act, may appeal against that decision to the High Court.[4]

1 National Nuclear Regulator Act 47 of 1997 s 43(1). The procedure of such an appeal is set out in s 43(2) and (3).

2 S 44(1). The procedures to be followed for such an appeal are set out in s 44(2) and (3).

3 S 45(1). The procedure to be followed for such an appeal is set out in s 45(2) and (3).

4 S 46(1). The procedure to be followed for such an appeal is set out in s 46(2) and (3).

197 Regulations The minister may, after consultation with the board and by notice in the *Government Gazette*, make regulations as to any matter required or permitted to be prescribed in terms of the National Nuclear Regulator Act[1] or necessary for the effective administration of the Act.[2] Any regulation made may provide that the contravention or failure to comply therewith is an offence, and a person convicted of that offence is punishable with a prescribed fine or a term of imprisonment not longer than the period so prescribed.[3] Before any regulations are made, the minister must, by notice in the *Gazette*, invite comment on the proposed regulations and consider that comment.[4]

The content for the application for a nuclear installation licence or certificate of registration must contain the following:

(a) an indication of whether the application is made for a nuclear installation licence or a certificate of registration;

(b) the full name of the applicant;

(c) if the applicant is a juristic person, a certified copy of the certificate of incorporation or founding document or any other establishing document and physical address of its head office or its *domicilium citandi* and *executandi*;

(d) if the applicant is a natural person, his or her identification number and date of birth;

(e) the physical address of the proposed installation (as or where the proposed action will be carried out);

(f) the postal address of the applicant;

(g) a description of the nuclear installation on the nature of the proposed action and any other relevant information which may be required by the Chief Executive Officer, and

(h) a signature by the applicant or, in the case of a juristic person, the signature of a duly authorised person and a certified copy of that authorisation.[5]

1 47 of 1999.

2 S 47(1).

3 S 47(2).

4 S 47(3).

5 See GN R479 of 12 May 2000; *Government Gazette* 23207 GN R295, 15 March 2002.

198 Delegations and assignment by minister The minister may delegate any power and assign any duty conferred or imposed upon the minister in terms of the National Nuclear Regulator Act[1] to the Director-General: Minerals and Energy.[2] Such a delegation or assignment must be in writing and may be subject to any conditions or limitations determined by the minister.[3] In addition, the minister is not divested of any power nor relieved of any duty by such delegation or assignment.[4]

1 47 of 1999.

2 S 48(1).

3 S 48(3).

4 S 48(4).

199 Disagreement between minister and board If the minister rejects a recommendation of the board, the minister and the board must endeavour to resolve their disagreement.[1] If the minister and the board fail to resolve their disagreement, the minister makes the final decision, in consultation with the relevant minister.[2]

1 National Nuclear Regulator Act 47 of 1999
  s 49(1).
2 S 49(2).

200 Disclosure of information "Information" includes anything purporting to be information or containing or providing information.[1] No person may disclose to any other person or publish any information which relates to any nuclear installation or site or vessel or action in respect of which a nuclear authorisation has been issued, if the disclosure of that information is likely to jeopardise the physical security arrangements in respect of such installation, site, vessel or action as required by the Regulator for the protection of persons or the security of the Republic. No person may be in the possession of any documents if not authorised and such possession is likely to jeopardise the physical security arrangements in respect of such installation, site, vessel or action as required by the Regulator for the protection of persons or the security of the Republic.

Furthermore, no person may receive any information knowing or having reasonable grounds to believe that it has been disclosed to him or her in contravention of the provisions of the section. A person must take reasonable steps to safeguard information, which he or she has in his or her possession or under his or her control. The provisions are subject to any national legislation contemplated in section 32(2) of the Constitution.[2]

Despite the provisions of any other law, no person is civilly or criminally liable or may be dismissed, disciplined, prejudiced or harassed on account of having disclosed any information if the person in good faith believed at the time of the disclosure that he or she was disclosing evidence of a health or safety risk or a failure to comply with a duty imposed by the Nuclear Regulator Act and the disclosure was made in accordance with section 51(5).[3]

Section 51(4) applies only if the person concerned:

(a)   disclosed the information concerned to: a committee of Parliament or a provincial legislature; the Public Protector; the Human Rights Commission; the auditor-general; the National Director of or a Director of Public Prosecutions; the minister; the Regulator; or more than one of the bodies or persons referred to above; or

(b)   disclosed the information concerned to one or more news medium and on clear and convincing grounds (of which he or she bears the burden of proof) believed at the time of the disclosure that the disclosure was necessary to avert an imminent and serious threat to the health and safety of an individual or the public or giving due weight to the importance of open, accountable and participatory administration, that the public interest in disclosure of the information clearly outweighed the need for non-disclosure; or

(c)   disclosed the information concerned substantially in accordance with any applicable external or internal procedure; or

(d)   disclosed information which, before the time of the disclosure of the information, had become available to the public, whether in the Republic or elsewhere.[4]

1 National Nuclear Regulator Act 47 of 1999   1999 s 51(2).
  s 51(1).   3 S 51(4).
2 Constitution of the Republic of SA 108 of   4 S 51(5).
  1996: National Nuclear Regulator Act 47 of

201 Offences and penalties Any person who contravenes or fails to comply with certain sections of the National Nuclear Regulator Act[1] is guilty of an offence.[2] In addition, any person who contravenes or fails to comply with any provision of the Act or any condition, notice, order, instruction, directive, prohibition, authorisation, permission, exemption, certificate or document determined, given, issued, promulgated or granted in terms of the Act is, if any such contravention or failure is not declared an offence in terms of section 52(1) of the Act, guilty of an offence.[3]

  1 47 of 1999.
  2 S 52(1).
  3 S 52(2).

202 Reproduction of documents by regulator The regulator may reproduce or cause to be reproduced documents in its possession or under its control and keep or cause to be kept the reproduction instead of the original document in question.[1]

  1 National Nuclear Regulator Act 47 of 1999
     s 53.

203 Legal succession to Council for Nuclear Safety The Regulator is substituted for the Council for Nuclear Safety in any contract or agreement entered into by the latter before the specified date, if the contract or agreement relates to any matter which, on the specified date, falls within the Regulator's competence in terms of the National Nuclear Regulator Act[1] and has not yet expired or any obligation has not been fulfilled, whichever is applicable.[2]

  1 47 of 1999.
  2 S 55.

CO-OPERATIVE AGREEMENTS

204 Time period for the conclusion of co-operative agreements The Regulator must, within six months of the regulations coming into effect, conclude a co-operative agreement in respect of the monitoring and control of radioactive material or exposure to ionising radiation with every relevant organ of state, including but not limited to: the Department of Health (Directorate Radiation Control), Department of Minerals and Energy (Chief Inspector of Mines; Deputy Director-General: Mineral Development; Deputy Director-General: Energy); Department of Environmental Affairs and Tourism, Department of Water Affairs and Forestry, Department of Labour, Department of Transport.[1]

  1 *Government Gazette* 23207 GN R295, 15
     March 2002 reg 2.

205 Procedures, including procedures for public participation The Regulator and each relevant organ of state must, within six months of the regulations coming into effect and, after consultation with any relevant statutory stakeholder body, produce a draft co-operative agreement in respect of each of the following: ensuring the effective monitoring and control of the nuclear hazard; co-ordinating the exercise of such functions; minimising the duplication of such functions and procedures regarding the exercise of such functions; and promoting consistency in the exercise of such functions. This draft co-operative agreement must be made available for public comment over a period of 30 days and the regulator must, in consultation with the relevant organ of state, consider such comments and finalise the agreement for submission to the Minister of Minerals and Energy for publication in the *Gazette*.[1]

  1 Reg 3.

206 Mechanisms for dispute resolution in respect of the conclusion of co-operative agreements and matters to be provided for in such agreements Any dispute between the regulator and another relevant organ of state that cannot be resolved by the parties must be referred to the Minister of Minerals and Energy for determination in consultation with the minister responsible for the other organ of state.[1]

Co-operative agreements must contain at least the following: the time period for the implementation of co-operative agreements, which must be within four months of it being concluded; a description of how the functions in respect of the monitoring and control of radioactive material or exposure to ionising radiation will be co-ordinated to avoid unnecessary duplication and omissions regarding safety requirements and the issuing of conflicting instructions; measures to resolve non-compliance with a co-operative agreement; a description of how any dispute in respect of the interpretation or application of co-operative agreements will be resolved; a description of the mechanisms and procedures for co-operation between the parties; a provision to use the same set of safety standards; a description of how the monitoring and compliance enforcement functions will be co-ordinated and allocated; a record of any delegations, assignments or agency arrangements; provision for expert assistance and support by one organ of state to another, as and when required; a description of how relevant information will be shared; a description of co-ordinated response to incidents or accidents and a description of the manner in which the co-operative agreement may be amended.[2]

1 Reg 4.
2 Reg 5.

ENRICHMENT

by

JG LOTZ
(*updated by FDJ BRAND*)

REFERENCES TO OTHER TITLES

SELECTED LITERATURE

De Vos *Verrykingsaanspreeklikheid in die SA Reg*
Eiselen "Herlewing van die Algemene Verrkingsaksie" 1992 *THRHR* 124
Van Zyl *Negotiorum Gestio in SA Law*

INTRODUCTION

207 Meaning of "enrichment" The term "enrichment" is used to describe the situation which occurs when one person's estate is increased at the expense of another without legal cause. From the fact of such increase an obligation arises in certain circumstances in terms of which the person whose estate has been increased has a duty to restore the increase to the person at whose expense the increase has taken place. Enrichment is therefore a source of a legal obligation.[1]

1 For the various sources of obligations, see
    title OBLIGATIONS.

208 Development and extent of liability for enrichment In Roman law there was no general liability for enrichment, although there are texts in the *Corpus Iuris Civilis* which appear to indicate the contrary.[1] Relief was, however, granted in specific circumstances.[2]

The enrichment actions of Roman law were received into Roman–Dutch law.[3] It remains a moot point whether classical Roman–Dutch law[4] reached the stage where a general enrichment action was available.[5] It has been demonstrated quite convincingly, however, that in the eighteenth century Dutch practice, the existence of a general enrichment action had come to be accepted.[6]

The enrichment actions of classical Roman–Dutch law are still available to a plaintiff in South African law. The courts have also repeatedly recognised liability for enrichment in circumstances where none of the old actions would lie. In some of these judgements statements were made that were understood by academic writers to support the existence of a general enrichment action.[7] Others were not so persuaded.[8] Eventually the Appellate Division availed itself of the opportunity, in *Nortje v Pool*[9], to conclude the debate. As far as our common law is concerned, the court accepted[10] the view widely held at the time[11] that there is no evidence of the evolvement of a general enrichment action in either Roman or Roman–Dutch law. With reference to South African authorities, the majority of the court sided with those who believed that such developments as there were did not amount to the recognition of a general enrichment action.[12] Moreover, so the court held, the recognition of a general action before the parameters and requirement of such action have been clearly defined, would only lead to uncertainty in our law. Consequently the majority of the court expressed its preference for an incremental development of these parameters and requirements over time, which might eventually lead to the recognition of a general enrichment action.[13] As to the manner in which such development should occur, the tenor of the majority judgment seemed to indicate that it would have to happen through the extension of existing enrichment actions to analogous situations.[14]

According to some authorities the time has now arrived for the recognition of a general enrichment action.[15] However, when the Appellate Division was pertinently invited to take this final step, it declined the invitation on the basis that such decision was not necessary for the purposes of that case.[16] At the same time, the court consistently confirmed its willingness to broaden the scope of enrichment liability by extending the limits of existing *condictiones*.[17] More recently it has been repeatedly indicated in *obiter dicta* that at least some judges of the Supreme Court of Appeal share the view that the law has reached the stage of development where the adoption of a general enrichment action should be considered.[18] At present a statement of the law of liability for enrichment must, however, still take the form of a discussion of old enrichment actions and of the ad hoc extensions that had taken place.

1 Cf *D* 12 6 14, 50 17 206. In these texts the prohibition against enrichment is so widely stated, however, that they could not possibly provide a basis for liability. If their terms were to be enforced, all commerce would be stultified. See also Zimmermann and Du Plessis 1992 *Acta Juridica* 60; DH van Zyl 1992 *Acta Juridica* 115.

2 Eg, in the circumstances covered by the various *condictiones sine causa*.

3 Largely with the same content and with retention of their Roman law appellations. The names of the actions had no procedural significance, serving merely as useful labels to identify specific sets of circumstances in which an action would lie.

4 This term, borrowed from De Vos *Verrykingsaanspreeklikheid*, is used here to mean the Roman-Dutch law of the seventeenth and eighteenth centuries.

5 There is a strong body of academic opinion which believes that Grotius *Inleiding* 3 10 18 demonstrates the acceptance of a general enrichment action: Scholtens 1966 *SALJ* 394–395; Feenstra in Schrage (ed) *Unjust Enrichment: The Comparative Legal History of the Law of Restitution* Vol 15 197; Van Zyl 1992 *Acta Juridica* 123–125. Others hold the view that Grotius in the paragraph referred to is discussing the *condictio sine causa specialis* and not a general enrichment action: De Vos 72–74. See also Botha JA in *Nortje v Pool* 1966 3 SA 96 (A) 135.

6 Cf Van Bynkershoek *Obs Tum* 277 303 2751 2754 and Pauw *Obs Tum Nov* 12 196 558. See also Scholtens 1966 *SALJ* 391 et seq; De Vos 110–119; Van Zyl 1992 *SALJ* 127–128.

7 See eg De Vos 304 and the authorities there cited.

8 See eg *Pucjlowski v Johnson's Executors* 1946 WLD 1 3; *Le Roux v Van Biljon* 1956 2 SA 17 (T) 20; John *'n Oorsig van Ongeregverdigde Verryking as 'n Gedingsoorsaak in die Suid-Afrikaanse Reg* 140.

9 Supra.

10 135–136.

11 The main reason why the decision of the Hooge Raad referred to in fn 6 supra had no influence on the views held at the time was that the compilations of these decisions by Van Bynkershoek and Pauw were only published in the 1960's whereas the researches by Prof de Vos upon which the court primarily relied in this regard, were published in the first edition of his work in 1958. See also Scholtens 1966 *SALJ* 391; De Vos 112.

12 Per Botha JA (Williamson and Wessels JJA concurring) 136–139.

13 139–140A. Cf the minority judgment of Rumpff JA who found that it was not necessary for him to comment on whether a general enrichment action formed part of South African Law, but nevertheless indicated that he was favourably disposed towards its recognition.

14 139H.

15 See eg *Blesbok Eiendomsagentskap v Cantamessa* 1991 2 SA 712 (T); Eiselen 1992 *THRHR* 124; Sonnekus 1992 *THRHR* 301; Visser 1991 *AS* 113; Van Zyl 1992 *Acta Juridica* 115; Visser *Southern Cross* 555.

16 *Kommissaris van Binnelandse Inkomste v Willers* 1994 3 SA 283 (A) 334.

17 *Willis Faber Enthoven (Pty) Ltd v Receiver of Revenue* 1992 4 SA 202 (A) 223G; *Kommissaris van Binnelandse Inkomste v Willers* supra 331B–333E; *Bowman, De Wet & Du Plessis v Fidelity Bank Ltd* [1997] 1 All SA 317 (A); 1997 2 SA 35 (A) 40A–B; *First National Bank of Southern Africa Ltd v Perry* [2001] 3 All SA 331 (SCA); 2001 3 SA 960 (SCA) 971. Accordingly the present state of the law has been described as follows by Schutz JA in *McCarthy Retail Ltd v Shortdistance Carriers CC* [2001] 3 All SA 236 (SCA); 2001 3 SA 482 (SCA) 487E–J: "Unlike other branches of our law, the rich Roman source material has not led to an unqualified judicial recognition (with a few exceptions) of a unified general principle of unjustified enrichment, from which solutions to particular instances may be derived. Rather there has been an augmentation of the old causes of action, from case to case, usually with reference to rules treated as being of general application. This has led to a more or less unified patchwork . . . And although there has been no unequivocal recognition of a general enrichment action, time and again unjustified enrichment principles have been treated as a source of obligations being the basis for creating a new class or subclass of liability in particular circumstances."

18 *McCarthy Retail Ltd v Shortdistance Carriers CC* supra 487–489; *First National Bank of*

Southern Africa Ltd v Perry supra 969–970. The argument for the acceptance of a general enrichment action appears to have been strengthened by the adoption of such a general action in related legal systems. See eg Zimmermann and Du Plessis *Acta Juridica* 57 et seq; Van Zyl 1992 *Acta Juridica* 128 et seq; Sonnekus 1992 *THRHR* 301. Cf the Scottish law of unjustified enrichment Hellwege 2000 *Stellenbosch LR* 50.

209 General requirements for liability for enrichment Although there is no general action based on enrichment in South African law,[1] there are nonetheless certain general requirements for any action based on enrichment.[2] These requirements are as follows:

(a) *The defendant must be enriched* Enrichment may be constituted by an increase in the defendant's assets which would not have taken place but for the enriching fact, by a non-decrease in his assets which would have taken place but for that fact,[3] by a decrease of liabilities which would not have taken place[4] or by a non-increase of liabilities which would have taken place. The total package of the defendant's assets and liabilities after the alleged enrichment occurred must be compared with what it was prior thereto.

Payment of money is itself *prima facie* proof of enrichment, but not conclusive proof. In assessing whether the defendant has been enriched by the payment, account must be taken of any performance rendered by the defendant which was juridically connected with the receipt of money.[5]

An enrichment claim has been recognised for recovery of the benefits derived from the use and occupation of property enjoyed by reason of a purported or inchoate lease.[6] Apart from this instance, the courts have, however, been reluctant to allow an enrichment action based merely on the use of another's property.[7]

Where the enrichment consists in an increase in the market value of property, an action will lie only where such increase is the result of tangible useful improvements which were effected to the property.[8]

In an enrichment action the defendant's liability is confined to the amount of his or her actual enrichment at the time of the commencement of the action.[9] This means that the defendant is not liable for benefits that he or she could have derived from the enriching fact but did not.[10] It also means that where the defendant's enrichment is diminished or lost before action is instituted, his or her liability is likewise reduced or extinguished,[11] subject to the following qualifications:

(i) From the moment that the defendant becomes aware or should have been aware that he or she has been enriched *sine causa* at the expense of another, the defendant's liability is reduced or extinguished only if the defendant is able to prove that the diminution or loss of his or her enrichment was not due to his or her fault.[12]

(ii) From the moment the defendant is in *mora* the rule *mora debitoris perpetuat obligationem* applies. From that moment the defendant's liability is reduced or extinguished only if he or she is able to prove that the event which diminished or extinguished his or her enrichment would also have operated against the plaintiff if performance had been made timeously.[13]

To what extent a person who has been enriched is entitled to reject or waive his or her enrichment will emerge from the discussions of the specific enrichment actions.

(b) *The plaintiff must be impoverished* The quantum of the plaintiff's claim is the amount by which the plaintiff has been impoverished or by which the defendant has been enriched, whichever is the lesser.[14] Every enrichment action must consequently embrace an inquiry not only into the defendant's enrichment, but also into the plaintiff's impoverishment. Impoverishment may be constituted by a decrease or non-increase in assets or an increase or non-decrease in liabilities. The rules that apply in the determination of the defendant's enrichment apply *mutatis mutandis* in the determination of the defendant's impoverishment. So, for example, expenses saved as a result of an unjustified alienation of property may reduce the plaintiff's actual impoverishment.[15]

(c) *The defendant's enrichment must be at the expense of the plaintiff*[16] It is not sufficient that the defendant has been enriched and the plaintiff impoverished; there must be a causal link between the enrichment and the impoverishment. The interpretation of this requirement has caused difficulty in cases of so-called "indirect enrichment", cases in which three or more parties are involved. For example, where A, in terms of a contract between himself and B, makes performance to B but the benefit of the performance accrues to C. In practice two types of situations arise. In situations of the first type A, for example, contracts with B to build a swimming-pool on land which belongs to C[17] or A contracts with B to repair C's car[18] or to take care of C's furniture.[19] In the type two situation C (the owner) contracts with B to perform certain work on C's property and B then enters into a subcontract with A to perform part of B's obligations in terms of the main contract.[20] In both situations the question is whether A has an enrichment action against C if B fails to carry out his contractual obligations towards A. In a situation of the first type the Transvaal High Court decided unequivocally in *Gouws v Jester Pools (Pty) Ltd*[21] that C is enriched at B's expense and not at the expense of A, and that consequently A does not have an enrichment claim against C. At the same time it was held, also in the type one situation, that where A is in lawfully acquired possession of C's property on the improvement or preservation of which he has expended his labour, money or material in terms of a contract with B, A may exercise an enrichment lien (*ius retentionis*) against C in order to procure the amount of C's enrichment.[22] In the result an indirect remedy was afforded where on the same facts a direct remedy was denied. The attempt by the Appellate Division in *Brooklyn House Furnishers (Pty) Ltd v Knoetze & Sons*[23] to reconcile this anomaly was found to be wrong in *Buzzard Electrical (Pty) Ltd v 158 Jan Smuts Avenue Investments (Pty) Ltd.*[24] Neither an action nor a lien can exist, so the court held in the *Buzzard* case, without an underlying liability for enrichment. Consequently, as far as the type one situation is concerned, either the *Brooklyn House Furnishers* line of cases or *Gouws* must go. They cannot exist side by side.[25] Since the *Buzzard Electrical* case concerned a type two (that is to say, a subcontractor) situation, the Appellate Division found it unnecessary to decide with reference to the type one situation whether it is *Gouws* or *Brooklyn House Furnishers* that has to give way.[26] In a case not involving a subcontractor (in other words, a type one case) decided subsequent to *Buzzard's* case,[27] the Cape High Court opted for the *Brooklyn House* line of cases. The decision in *Gouws*, so the court held, was unjust and inequitable in that it denied A an enrichment action against C when it was quite clear that A was impoverished and C enriched as a result of A's construction of a swimming-pool on C's property in circumstances where B's disappearance from the scene rendered any potential action against him valueless.[28] The *Brooklyn House Furnishers* approach also gained support in an *obiter* statement by a majority of the Supreme Court of Appeal.[29] Academic writers seem to be fairly equally divided in their respective views.[30] A third, novel, approach to the problem is that there is no single right or wrong answer applicable to all type one cases, but that the most satisfactory solution is to allow each particular factual situation to be judged in accordance with policy considerations that are relevant in that case.[31]

As to the type two situation (involving a subcontractor) it was pertinently decided in the *Buzzard* case that A has no enrichment claim, either directly or indirectly by way of an enrichment lien against the owner, C, for the work that the subcontractor

A, had done pursuant to his subcontract with B. In this type of situation, so the court held, the source of C's enrichment is not the work done by A but the main contract between C and B. In these circumstances, the court concluded, it cannot be said that C was enriched *at the expense* of C.[32] The proposition was also formulated on the alternative basis that, because C had got exactly what he bargained for with B in terms of the main contract, any enrichment on the part of C cannot be said to be unjustified or *sine causa*.[33] In view of this decision in the *Buzzard* case, those earlier cases where subcontractors were held to have an enrichment lien against the owner in the type one situation,[34] involving a subcontractor, can no longer be regarded as good law.

(d) *The enrichment must be unjustified (sine causa)* If the mere fact that one person was enriched at the expense of another were to give rise to an enrichment action, liability would be so wide as to put an end to all profit-taking. To restrict liability for enrichment it is consequently required that the enrichment must be unjustified (*sine causa*). This means that there must be no sufficient ground recognised by law (*causa*) to justify the transfer or retention[35] of value which has passed from the plaintiff's estate to that of the defendant.[36]

1 See par 208 ante.
2 For an endorsement of the four general requirements set out in this paragraph, see eg *McCarthy Retail Ltd v Shortdistance Carriers CC* [2001] 3 All SA 236 (SCA); 2001 3 SA 482 (SCA) 490 (per Schutz JA) 496 (per Harms JA). See also Eiselen and Pienaar *Unjustified Enrichment* 26; Visser *Wille's Principles* 631 et seq.
3 Cf *Brooklyn House Furnishers (Pty) Ltd v Knoetze & Sons* 1970 3 SA 264 (A) 271E–F.
4 Voet *Commentarius* 24 1 3; *Guarantee Investment Corporation Ltd v Shaw* 1953 4 SA 479 (SR) 481H–482A; *Nortje v Pool* 1966 3 SA 96 (A) 115.
5 *Govender v Standard Bank of SA Ltd* 1984 4 SA 392 (C) 404; *Wynland Construction (Pty) Ltd v Ashley-Smith* 1985 3 SA 798 (A); *B & H Engineering v First National Bank of SA Ltd* 1995 2 SA 279 (A) 294; *Nedcor Bank Ltd v ABSA Bank* 1995 4 SA 727 (W) 730.
6 *Lobo Properties (Pty) Ltd v Express Lift Co (SA) (Pty) Ltd* 1961 1 SA 704 (C); *Liebenberg v Liebenberg* 1971 1 SA 878 (C).
7 See eg *Greenhills Producers (Pty) Ltd (in Liquidation) v Benjamin* 1960 4 SA 188 (E); *Dugas v Kempster Sedgwick (Pty) Ltd* 1961 1 SA 784 (D). See, however, the *obiter dictum* by Jansen JA in *Hefer v Van Greuning* 1979 4 SA 952 (A) 959. See also De Vos *Verrykingsaanspreeklikheid* 268 330.
8 *Nortje v Pool* supra 130 133. Cf De Vos 329. In exceptional cases an action will lie also in the case of luxury improvements; see par 229 post.
9 Cf D 12 6 26 12, 12 6 65 8 dealing with the *condictio indebiti*.
10 Cf Grotius *Inleiding* 3 30 1, 3 30 3; Voet 12

1 5. It is suggested that the court's conclusion in *Krueger v Navratil* 1952 4 SA 405 (SWA) 409 that "a claim based on undue enrichment includes profit which the defendant may or could have derived from the use of the stolen property" was wrong; see *Dilmitis v Niland* 1965 3 SA 492 (SR); and see De Vos 331 332.
11 It is, however, not always easy to determine whether enrichment has actually fallen away or not. For example where the enrichment consists of the receipt of money (or other *res fungibiles*), it has been argued that the receiver must be regarded as being permanently enriched since the value of the received money is added to his or her estate. The old writers were divided on this question (see De Vos 201 et seq) but the courts have adopted the view that even where *res fungibiles* are involved, a defendant's liability is confined to the amount by which he or she is still enriched at the time of the action: *King v Cohen, Benjamin & Co* 1953 4 SA 641 (W) 650–651; *Weedon v Bawa* 1959 4 SA 735 (D); *African Diamond Exporters (Pty) Ltd v Barclays Bank International Ltd* 1978 3 SA 699 (A) 709; De Vos 205; Visser 1982 *Acta Juridica* 175. The onus of proving nonenrichment is on the defendant: *Le Riche v Hamman* 1946 AD 648; *African Diamond Exporters (Pty) Ltd v Barclays Bank International Ltd* supra 713–714; *Hosken Employee Benefits (Pty) Ltd v Slabe* 1992 4 SA 183 (W); *ABSA Bank Ltd v Standard Bank of SA Ltd* [1997] 4 All SA 673 (SCA); 1998 1 SA 242 (SCA) 252; *First National Bank of Southern Africa Ltd v Perry* [2001] 3 All SA 331 (SCA); 2001 3 SA 960 (SCA) 972.

12 See *D* 12 6 26 12; *D* 12 6 65 8; Voet 12 6 12; Van der Keessel *Prael ad Gr* 3 30 19 (with reference to the *contictio indebiti*). It appears, however, that the rule can be accepted as one of general application: see *Le Riche v Hamman* supra; *Tellurometer (Pty) Ltd v PDC (Pty) Ltd* 1978 3 SA 563 (C); *African Diamond Exporters (Pty) Ltd v Barclays Bank International Ltd* supra 711–713; *McCarthy Retail Ltd v Shortdistance Carriers CC* supra 491; De Vos 207–208 336; Visser *Wille's Principles* 633; Eiselen and Pienaar 40. The rule does not apply to minors which means that a minor's liability is always limited to the amount of his or her actual enrichment at the time that the action is instituted: *Edelstein v Edelstein* 1952 3 SA 1 (A) 12. Cf De Vos 219 et seq 336 fn 40.

13 De Vos 201. For a discussion of the effects of *mora debitoris*, see title CONTRACT. See also Van Zijl Steyn *Mora Debitoris* 90, De Wet and Van Wyk *Kontraktereg en Handelsreg* 5 ed Vol 1 163 351. Apparently minors are again exempted from this effect of *mora debitoris*; see De Vos 336–337; Visser *Wille's Principles* 633 fn 22.

14 This follows from the next requirement, ie that the defendant's enrichment must be at the plaintiff's expense. See *Fletcher & Fletcher v Bulawayo Waterworks Co Ltd, Bulawayo Waterworks Co Ltd v Fletcher & Fletcher* 1915 AD 636 649.

15 De Vos 339; Eiselen and Pienaar 62.

16 Cf *Fletcher & Fletcher v Bulawayo Waterworks Co Ltd, Bulawayo Waterworks Co Ltd v Fletcher & Fletcher* supra 649; *Skyword (Pvt) Ltd v Peter Scales (Pvt) Ltd* 1979 1 SA 570 (R).

17 *Gouws v Jester Pools (Pty) Ltd* 1968 3 SA 563 (T).

18 *New Club Garage v Milborrow & Son* 1931 GWL 86; *ABSA Bank Ltd t/a Bankfin v Stander t/a CAW Paneelkloppers* 1998 1 SA 939 (C); 1997 CLR 154 (C).

19 *Brooklyn House Furnishers (Pty) Ltd v Knoetze & Sons* supra.

20 *Frame v Palmer* 1950 3 SA 340 (C); *Knoll v SA Flooring Industries Ltd* 1951 1 SA 404 (T); *Wynland Construction (Pty) Ltd v Ashley-Smith* 1985 3 SA 798 (A); *Buzzard Electrical (Pty) Ltd v 158 Jan Smuts Avenue Investments (Pty) Ltd* [1996] 3 All SA 1 (A); 1996 4 SA 19 (A).

21 Supra.

22 *United Building Society v Smookler's Trustees & Golombick's Trustee* 1906 TS 623; *Land Bank v Mans* 1933 CPD 16; *Brooklyn House Furnishers (Pty) Ltd v Knoetze & Sons* supra. For a discussion of liens in general, see title LIEN. See also on liens in general and on enrichment and on enrichment liens in particular, *Goudini Chrome (Pty) Ltd v MCC Contracts (Pty) Ltd* 1993 1 SA 77 (A) 84J–85C.

23 Supra 275A–D.

24 Supra 26I–J.

25 See also *Singh v Santam Insurance Ltd* [1997] 1 All SA 525 (A); 1997 1 SA 291 (A) 297; *McCarthy Retail Ltd v Shortdistance Carriers CC* supra 493.

26 See *Buzzard Electrical (Pty) Ltd v 158 Jan Smuts Avenue Investments (Pty) Ltd* supra 27. The question whether *Brooklyn House Furnishers* had been correctly decided was also left open by the Appellate Division in *Standard Kredietkorporasie Bpk v JOT Motors (Edms) Bpk h/a Vaal Motors* 1986 1 SA 223 (A) 237.

27 Ie *ABSA Bank Ltd t/a Bankfin v Stander t/a CAW Paneelkloppers* supra.

28 Supra 952–953. See also *Hubby's Investments (Pty) Ltd v Lifetime Properties (Pty) Ltd* [1997] 3 All SA 202 (W); 1998 1 SA 295 (W).

29 In *McCarthy Retail Ltd v Shortdistance Carriers CC* supra 493B–F where Schutz JA *inter alia* expressed himself as follows: "The case before us does not require us to decide the question which line of approach [ie *Brooklyn House Furnishers* or *Gouws*] is to be accepted . . . For myself, I think there is much to be said for the justice of the lien [ie the *Brooklyn House Furnishers* line of] cases, an unsophisticated justice though it may be, but with which we have lived for a long time. A improves a car at the instance of B, wrongly believing him to be the owner. C claims the car by virtue of his ownership. Is he to get it scot-free? Or is he to first pay A his necessary and reasonable expenses . . . ? The question whether C is enriched at the expense of A or of B in the example given is in any event a matter of semantics . . . When A improves C's vehicle the ownership in the improvements passes at once to C's estate by accession and it seems to me to pass there directly from A's estate. Is it not a fiction that it passes through the estate of B, even though A owes a contractual obligation to him to effect the repairs?" (Although Olivier and Cameron JJA concurred in the whole of the judgment by Schutz JA, Smalberger ADCJ (495) and Harms JA (496–498) pertinently refrained from expressing any view in

this regard.)

30 So, eg, De Vos 1969 *SALJ* 227, 1970 *Acta Juridica* 236–241, *Verrykingsaanspreeklikheid* 343–346 350–351 and Sonnekus 1996 *TSAR* 583 et seq hold the view that *Gouws* was correctly decided whereas Honoré 1960 *Acta Juridica* 236; Scholtens 1968 *SALJ* 371; and Nathan 1974 *THRHR* 101 are in favour of *Brooklyn House Furnishers*. See also Eiselen and Pienaar 76–77 for a rendition of both views.

31 See Visser *The Quest for Justice: Essays in Honour of Michael McGregor Corbett* (Kahn ed) 358–361; Visser and Miller 2000 *SALJ* 594. This approach is favoured by Van Zyl J in *ABSA Bank Ltd t/a Bankfin v Stander t/a CAW Paneelkloppers* supra 953.

32 *Buzzard Electrical (Pty) Ltd v 158 Jan Smuts Avenue Investments (Pty) Ltd* supra 29F–G.

33 *Buzzard Electrical (Pty) Ltd v 158 Jan Smuts Avenue Investments (Pty) Ltd* supra 29G. For this requirement see sub-par (d) below.

34 Eg *Howes & Clover (Pty) Ltd v Ruskin* 1978 1 SA 99 (W).

35 Among academic writers there is a difference in emphasis of what appears to be opposite sides of the same coin. According to the formulation proposed by Visser *Wille's Principles* 634, *Condictio Indebiti* 217 et seq, the requirement is that there must be no *causa retendi*, ie no cause for *the retention* of the enrichment by the defendant. De Vos 353, on the other hand, puts the emphasis on the absence of a *causa dandi*, ie a ground for *transfer*. Though the two lines of approach seem, in most cases, to lead to the same practical result, Visser's formulation

appears to be well supported by authority. See also Eiselen and Pienaar 28.

36 See *Pretorius v Commercial Union Versekeringsmaatskappy van SA Bpk* 1995 3 SA 778 (O); *Wilkens v Bester* [1997] 2 All SA 386 (A); 1997 3 SA 347 (SCA); *McCarthy Retail Ltd v Shortdistance Carriers CC* supra 496–497; *First National Bank of Southern Africa Ltd v Perry* supra 969. Like the requirement referred to in (c), ie that the defendant's enrichment must be at the plaintiff's expense, the *sine causa* requirement has caused difficulty in the multi-party situations. As appears from the discussion under par (c) above, the issue has been resolved by the Supreme Court of Appeal in the so-called type two situations (involving a subcontractor), in *Buzzard Electrical (Pty) Ltd v 158 Jan Smuts Avenue Investments (Pty) Ltd* supra. In these situations, so the court held, the performance by the subcontractor, A, which caused the enrichment of the owner, C, was not *sine causa* since C was entitled to receive exactly that performance in terms of his contract with the main contractor, B. In situations not involving a subcontractor the question whether C's performance should be regarded as *cum causa* or *sine causa* was specifically left open by the Supreme Court of Appeal in the *Buzzard* case. In the meantime there is High Court authority for both points of view. See eg *Gouws v Jester Pools (Pty) Ltd* supra; *ABSA Bank Ltd t/a Bankfin v Stander t/a CAW Paneelkloppers* supra; *Hubby's Investments (Pty) Ltd v Lifetime Properties (Pty) Ltd* supra.

CONDICTIO

INTRODUCTION

210 Meaning of the term The term "condictio" is derived from the Roman law *legis actio per condictionem* which was a special form of process within the early Roman *legis actio* procedure. "Condictio", in turn, has its origin in the Latin verb "condicere" which means "to give notice". By the *legis actio per condictionem* a plaintiff claimed either a fixed sum of money (*certa pecunia*) or a specific thing (*certa res*) without specifying the cause of action.[1]

When the *legis actiones* were replaced by the formulary system of procedure, the name *condictio* continued to be used for those actions which had formerly been brought before a judge by way of a *legis actio per condictionem*. A *condictio* at this stage was a strictly personal action for a fixed sum or a specific thing which did not require a recital of the cause of action relied upon. As a result it could accommodate a variety of causes of action. In later Roman law a *condictio incerti* developed by which an *incertum* could be claimed.

Of the *condictiones* one group, the *condictiones ob causam (rem) dati*, were enrichment actions. They lay for the recovery of a thing which had been transferred in ownership and were granted in cases where the reason (*causa*) for the transfer of the thing did not justify its retention by the transferee. In the post-classical era certain fixed types of *condictio ob causam dati* developed. Of these the most important were the *condictio indebiti*, the *condictio ob turpem vel iniustam causam*, the *condictio causa data causa non secuta* and the *condictio sine causa (specialis)*.[2] These actions still form part of South African law, their object, in principle, is "the recovery of property in which ownership has been transferred pursuant to a juristic act which was *ab initio* unenforceable or has subsequently become inoperative".[3]

1 Gaius *Institutiones* 4 18 19.
2 On the Roman origins of the present day law of enrichment, see generally Schultz, *Classical Roman Law* 611 et seq, Thomas *Textbook of Roman Law* 326–328, Van Oven *Romeinsch Privaatrecht* 204 366; Kaser *Römisches Privaatrecht* 187–192; De Vos *Verryking-saanspreeklikheid* 7 et seq; Zimmermann *The Law of Obligations: Roman Foundations of the*

Civilian Tradition 834 et seq.
3 Per Van den Heever J in *Pucjlowski v Johnson's Executors* 1946 WLD 1 6. See also *McCarthy Retail Ltd v Shortdistance Carriers CC* [2001] 3 All SA 236 (SCA); 2001 3 SA 482 (SCA) 489; *First National Bank of Southern Africa Ltd v Perry* [2001] 3 All SA 331 (SCA); 2001 3 SA 960 (SCA) 970.

CONDICTIO INDEBITI

211 Object The object of the *condictio indebiti* is to recover money or other property transferred in intended payment or performance of a non-existent debt.[1]

1 Voet *Commentarius* 12 6 1; *Le Riche v Hamman* 1946 AD 648 656.

212 Requirements The requirements of the *condictio indebiti* are as follows[1]:

(a) Generally speaking the action is only available where ownership of money or other property had been transferred by the act (*negotium*) of the parties.[2] Even in Roman times, however, the action had been extended, in the form of the *condictio possesionis* to recover possession where a non-owner transferred the possession of a thing *indebite* to another.[3] There is, in addition, some authority for the proposition that the *condictio indebiti* also lies for the recovery of the value of a *factum*.[4] This authority is, however, doubtful and the generally accepted view appears to be that neither the *condictio indebiti* nor any other of the *condictiones sine causa* is available to recover the value of a *factum*.[5] That does not exclude the possibility that the *condictio indebiti* can now be extended to allow the claim for a *factum* performed *indebite* as well. Such extension would seem to be a fair and natural one.[6]

(b) The *condictio indebite* lies only against the *recipiens* of the *indebitum*. Of course, the person who physically received the money or property is not necessarily in law regarded as the *recipiens*. So, for example, the person who physically received the transfer could be a mere conduit or an agent of the *recipiens*. Such person can also be someone nominated by the *recipiens* as the one to whom payment should be made. On the other hand, one is not the *recipiens* of a payment merely because it was intended or happens in the result to benefit one. In every case the action lies against the true *recipiens*.[7]

(c) It is a general requirement that the plaintiff must be the one who is considered in law to have made the payment. Again, as in the case of the *recipiens*, this does not mean that the plaintiff must be the one who has physically paid the money.[8] Moreover, the *condictio indebiti* has been extended to entitle an underpaid creditor of a deceased estate to recover from overpaid heirs or legatees even though the payment had been made by the executor.[9] More recently the remedy has also been made available to an unpaid creditor of a dissolved company to claim an overpayment from a share holder who received more than he was entitled to from the liquidator of the company.[10]

(d) The transfer of money or property must have taken place *indebite* in the widest sense. It means that there must have been no legal or natural obligation to give it.[11] Even if the *causa* for the transfer subsequently proves to be unlawful, the *condictio indebiti* is still excluded.[12] Payment by the debtor of a debt after it had been extinguished by prescription is not regarded as *indebite* and therefore not recoverable with the *condictio indebiti*.[13] On the other hand it has been held that where payment was made to satisfy a debt subject to a suspensive condition in the mistaken belief that the condition had been fulfilled, the amount paid may be reclaimed with the *condictio indebiti*.[14] This seems to be an exception to the general principle in that although a conditional debt may not be *due* and *payable*, there is an existing debt.[15] Another exception to the general principle is made in the case of minors. A minor who performs in terms of an unauthorised contract may reclaim the performance even though such a contract created a natural obligation on the part of the minor.[16] This rule in favour of minors also applies to payments made *ultra vires* by persons in a representative capacity. Such payments can, in principle, also be reclaimed with the *condictio indebiti*.[17]

(e) The payment or transfer must have been effected *solvendi animo per errorem*, meaning, in the mistaken belief that the debt was due. Accordingly, a payment will as a general rule not be recoverable if the plaintiff knew that it was not due and even a doubt whether it is due or not would prevent recovery.[18] And exception to the error requirement is that the *condictio indebiti* does find application even where payment was made with the knowledge or belief that it is not owing, if it was made under protest.[19] Formerly it was required that the mistake be one of fact or at least one of mixed law and fact and not a pure error of law.[20] This distinction between errors of fact and errors of law was subjected to criticism over many years.[21] Eventually it was recognised by the Appellate Division in *Willis Faber Enthoven (Pty) Ltd v Receiver of Revenue*[22] that an error of law can also give rise to the *condictio indebiti*. As a result the distinction between errors of law and errors of fact which had sometimes been difficult to make,[23] was finally rendered irrelevant.

(f) For a mistake of fact or law to give rise to a *condictio indebiti* the mistake must be excusable; the ignorance must not be *supina aut affecta*.[24] There have been many attempts to lay down rules in order to define what would be an excusable error and what would not constitute an excuse.[25] However, "since one is concerned with the exercise of a value judgment, it seems inappropriate to refine the test of whether judicial exculpation is justified".[26] The general requirement that the mistake must not be inexcusable does not apply to someone, like an executor, who is acting for the benefit of others and who has paid the *indebitum* in that capacity.[27]

1 As was, however, pointed out by Harms JA in *Bowman, De Wet & Du Plessis v Fidelity Bank Ltd* [1997] 1 All SA 317 (A); 1997 2 SA 35 (A) 40, the principles underlying the *condictio indebiti* are not immutable. Accordingly the *condictio* can be extended to analogous factual situations which do not strictly comply with its stated requirements.

2 See *D* 12 6 33; Honoré 1958 *Acta Juridica* 135.

3 *D* 39 6 12; *D* 12 6 15 1; Voet *Commentarius*12 6 12; De Vos *Verrykingsaanspreeklikheid* 23–24 191–192.

4 Voet 12 6 12; *Frame v Palmer* 1950 3 SA 340 (C) where the *condictio indebiti* was considered available for payment of both work

done and material supplied. See also the minority judgment of Rumpff JA in *Nortje v Pool* 1966 3 SA 96 (A) 121. In the majority judgment (134E–G) the question was pertinently left open.

5   In *Gouws v Jester Pools (Pty) Ltd* 1968 3 SA 563 (T) 575A Jansen JA stated: "Moreover, the prevalent view appears to be that the value of a *factum* cannot be claimed by any of the *condictiones sine causa*."

6   See eg De Vos 199; Eiselen and Pienaar *Unjustified Enrichment* 108.

7   *Licences & General Insurance Co v Ismay* 1951 2 SA 456 (E); *Phillips v Hughes; Hughes v Maphumulo* 1979 1 SA 225 (N) 228–229; *Minister van Justisie v Jaffer* 1995 1 SA 273 (A) 280–281; 1995 1 SACR 292 (A); *Randcoal Services Ltd v Randgold & Exploration Co Ltd* 1998 4 SA 825 (SCA) 842–843.

8   Voet 12 6 8; Honoré 1958 *Acta Juridica* 135; *African Diamond Exporters (Pty) Ltd v Barclays Bank International Ltd* 1978 3 SA 699 (A) 713. A practical application of these principles is to be found, for example, in *Van Wijk's Trustee v African Banking Corporation* 1912 TPD 44, *Brand v Volkskas Bpk* 1959 1 SA 494 (T) and *Besselaar v Registrar, Durban & Coast Local Division* 2002 1 SA 191 (D).

9   See eg *Colonial Treasurer v Swart* 1910 TPD 552 555; *De Villiers v Bullbrand Fertilizers Ltd* 1941 TPD 131 133; *Prinsloo v Woolbrokers Federation Ltd* 1955 2 SA 298 (N) 299; *Roy Evans & Co (Pty) Ltd v Cramer* 1961 3 SA 857 (T); *Mosam v De Kamper* 1964 3 SA 794 (T); *Van Zyl v Serfontein* 1992 2 SA 450 (C). See also De Vos 172 et seq.

10   *Kommissaris van Binnelandse Inkomste v Willers* 1994 3 SA 283 (A), thereby overruling *Rapp & Maister Holdings Ltd v Ruflex Holdings (Pty) Ltd* 1972 3 SA 835 (T). See also *Bowman, De Wet & Du Plessis v Fidelity Bank Ltd* supra; Eiselen and Pienaar 155.

11   *Le Riche v Hamman* 1946 AD 648; *Rulten v Herald Industries (Pty) Ltd* 1982 3 SA 600 (D) 606; *Klein v SA Transport Services* 1992 3 SA 509 (W) 517. It follows that where payment of an existing debt was motivated by error, it is not *indebite* and therefore not recoverable by the *condictio indebiti*.

12   The plaintiff may, however, have an enrichment claim under the *condictio ob turpem causam*: *First National Bank of Southern Africa Ltd v Perry* [2001] 3 All SA 331 (SCA); 2001 3 SA 960 (SCA) 969. For the *condictio ob turpem vel iniustam causam* see pars 214 et seq post.

13   Prescription Act 68 of 1969 s 10(3).

14   *Wilkens v Bester* [1997] 2 All SA 386 (SCA); 1997 3 SA 347 (SCA) 358; *Bowman, De Wet & Du Plessis v Fidelity Bank Ltd* supra 44.

15   Therefore the appropriate action would appear to be the *condictio causa data causa non secuta* and not the *condictio indebiti*. See Eiselen and Pienaar 111. For the *condictio causa data causa non secuta* see generally par 217 post.

16   De Vos 24 184; Visser, *Wille's Principles* 637.

17   *Bowman, De Wet & Du Plessis v Fidelity Bank Ltd* supra 40 44.

18   See eg *Vergotinie v Ceres Municipality* (1904) 21 SC 28; *Commissioner for Inland Revenue v First National Industrial Bank Ltd* 1990 3 SA 641 (A); *ABSA Bank Ltd v De Klerk* [1998] 4 All SA 674 (W); 1999 1 SA 861 (W).

19   *Union Government (Minister of Finance) v Gowar* 1915 AD 426 433–434 (Innes CJ) 445–446 (De Villiers AJA); *Port Elizabeth Municipality v Uitenhage Municipality* 1971 1 SA 724 (A) 741–742; *Commissioner for Inland Revenue v First National Industrial Bank supra.*

20   *Rooth v S* (1888) 2 SAR 259; *Benning v Union Government (Minister of Finance)* 1914 AD 420; *Miller v Bellville Municipality* 1973 1 SA 914 (C).

21   See eg De Vos 182–183; Visser *Wille's Principle* 637.

22   1992 4 SA 202 (A). See also *Minister van Justisie v Jaffer* supra 279.

23   See eg *Barker v Bentley* 1978 4 SA 204 (N); *Salandia (Pty) Ltd v Vredenburg-Saldanha Municipality* 1985 3 SA 265 (C); *Vluvo Investments (Pty) Ltd v Bezri* 1985 4 SA 367 (T).

24   Despite strong criticism against this requirement (see eg De Vos 69–70 184–185; Visser *Condictio Indebiti* 171–182; *Wille's Principles* 637, Scholtens 1972 *AS* 126, 1977 *AS* 167; Eiselen and Pienaar 127) it has specifically been maintained by the Appellate Division in its most recent pronouncement on the matter in *Willis Faber Enthoven (Pty) Ltd v Receiver of Revenue* supra 223–224. See also *Rahim v Minister of Justice* 1964 4 SA 630 (A); *Bowman, De Wet & Du Plessis v Fidelity Bank Ltd* supra 44.

25   See eg *Barclays Bank International Ltd v African Diamond Exporters (Pty) Ltd* 1977 1 SA 298 (W) 305.

26   Per Harms JA in *Bowman, De Wet & Du Plessis v Fidelity Bank Ltd* supra 44E.

27   *Bowman, De Wet & Du Plessis v Fidelity Bank Ltd* supra 44G–45G.

213 Extent of defendant's liability In principle the defendant must restore the transferred thing itself or, in the case of *res fungibiles*, an equivalent quantity of the thing.[1] Where the thing itself is returned, its fruits (less production costs)[2] and accessions[3] must be returned with it. Interest which the defendant may have received on a sum of money paid to him or her *indebite* is apparently not regarded as fruit and need not be restored.[4] If the recipient is unable to restore either the thing or its equivalent, its surrogate[5] or value[6] can be recovered from the recipient.

As the *condictio indebiti* is an enrichment action, the defendant may tender the thing in the condition it is in at the time of action.[7] Where the defendant has lost or disposed of the thing, his or her liability is likewise restricted to the amount by which he or she is still enriched at the time of action, subject, of course, to the exceptions set out above.[8] Non-enrichment is consequently a good defence against a plaintiff's claim for the full value of the transferred property.[9] The onus to prove non-enrichment (or a diminution of enrichment) is on the defendant, and should the defendant fail to prove it, he or she remains liable for the full value of the property.[10]

The defendant (recipient) is entitled to compensation for his or her expenditure on the thing.[11] Where the defendant has rendered counter-performance, he or she is further entitled to the return of his or her performance or, where the plaintiff is no longer in possession of it, its value. The defendant may refuse to restore until the plaintiff tenders restoration on his or her side.[12]

1 *D* 12 6 7; Voet *Commentarius* 12 6 12 13. See also De Vos *Verrykingsaanspreeklikheid* 26.

2 See *D* 12 6 65 5; *C* 7 51 1. Cf also *D* 5 3 36 5.

3 *D* 12 6 15 et seq, 12 6 65 5.

4 See *Baliol Investment Co (Pty) Ltd v Jacobs* 1946 TPD 269 272–274. The issue of interest actually received by the defendant should not be confused with the question whether the defendant is liable for interest *a tempore morae*. The basis for the claim of *mora* interest is not enrichment but compensation paid to the plaintiff for the loss that the plaintiff suffered through being deprived of the use of his or her money. Accordingly, liability for *mora* interest is determined by the legal principles regarding *mora* interest in general and not by the law of enrichment. See *Commissioner for Inland Revenue v First National Industrial Bank Ltd* 1990 3 SA 641 (A); De Vos 199 et seq; Eiselen and Pienaar *Unjustified Enrichment* 43–44. Cf *Amalgamated Society of Woodworkers of SA v Die 1963 Ambagsaalvereniging* 1968 1 SA 283 (T).

5 If there is one. Thus where the recipient has sold the thing he or she is liable to restore the purchase price; cf Voet 12 6 12.

6 That is if the recipient remains enriched through his or her receipt of the thing at the time when the action is instituted; see *Le Riche v Hamman* 1946 AD 648; *King v Cohen Benjamin & Co* 1953 4 SA 641 (W). See also par 209 ante.

7 Cf Wessels *Contract* 3702.

8 Par 209 ante.

9 See Voet 12 6 12; Van der Keessel *Prael* 3 30 19; *Le Riche v Hamman* supra; *King v Cohen Benjamin & Co* supra; *African Diamond Exporters (Pty) Ltd v Barclays Bank International Ltd* 1978 3 SA 699 (A).

10 Cf *Le Riche v Hamman* supra; *King v Cohen Benjamin & Co* supra; *African Diamond Exporters (Pty) Ltd v Barclays Bank International Ltd* supra.

11 *D* 12 6 26 12, 12 6 65 5. It is not clear from these texts whether the recipient is entitled to compensation for all expenses or for *impensae necessariae* and *impensae utiles* only. De Vos 28 is of the view that the recipient is not entitled to compensation in respect of expenses from which the plaintiff (transferor) will derive no benefit when the thing is restored to him or her. This view seems to be in accordance with the underlying principles of enrichment liability. See also Visser *Wille's Principles* 632.

12 Cf *Wepener v Schraader* 1903 TS 629; *Van der Berg v Shaw* 1933 TPD 242; *Mattheus v Stratford* 1946 TPD 498; *Bushney v Joliffe* 1953 4 SA 273 (W). Although the claims in *Wepener v Schraader* supra; *Van der Berg v Shaw* supra and *Bushney v Joliffe* supra were for the ejectment of buyers under void contracts of sale and were consequently not *conditiones indebiti*, these cases nevertheless support the inference that the person against whom a *condictio indebiti* is brought can resist the

action until the plaintiff tenders to restore. See De Vos 196–198. Consistent application of the principle that the plaintiff must tender to restore whatever he or she has received, would mean, for example, that he or she would also have to tender compensation for the use of property. It appears, however, that our law of enrichment has not reached the stage of development where all the side effects of enrichment, positive and negative, are taken into account; De Vos 198 333–334; Visser 632 fn 17. See also *Dugas v Kempster Sedgwick (Pty) Ltd* 1961 1 SA 784 (D).

CONDICTIO OB TURPEM VEL INIUSTAM CAUSAM

214 Object Where money or other property has been transferred in terms of an illegal agreement, the *condictio ob turpem vel iniustam causam* lies to recover that which has been so transferred or the value thereof.[1]

1 Cf *D* 12 5, 27 3 5; *C* 4 7; Grotius *Inleiding* 3 30 17; Voet *Commentarius* 12 5; Van Leeuwen *Cens For* 1 4 14 8–15, *RHR* 4 14 4–6; De Vos *Verrykingsaanspreeklikheid* 20–23 66–68 160–171; *Jajbhay v Cassim* 1939 AD 537; *First National Bank of Southern Africa Ltd v Perry* [2001] 3 All SA 331 (SCA); 2001 3 SA 960 (SCA).

215 Requirements The requirements of the *condictio ob turpem vel iniustam causam* are as follows:

(a) The ownership of the property must have passed with the transfer.[1]

(b) The transfer must have taken place in terms of an illegal agreement,[2] an agreement, that is, the conclusion, performance or object of which is prohibited by law[3] or is contrary to good morals or public policy.[4]

(c) In both Roman and Roman-Dutch law it was a requirement that the plaintiff must have been free from *turpitudo*; if the plaintiff had acted dishonourably in making performance, the *condictio* was refused.[5] In South African practice, too, a *turpis* plaintiff was until 1939 consistently refused an action for restitution, usually with an appeal to the rule *in pari delicto potior est conditio defendentis (possidentis)*.[6] In 1939 the Appellate Division added a gloss to the *par delictum* rule to the effect that the rule may be relaxed "where it is necessary to prevent injustice or to promote public policy".[7] The rule is consequently no longer rigidly applied, and the fact that a plaintiff has him or herself been guilty of dishonourable conduct does not, today, operate as an absolute bar to a plaintiff's action for recovery of his or her performance.[8] The *par delictum* rule finds application only where the plaintiff's conduct has indeed been dishonourable. Where performance, even though prohibited, is not dishonourable, the plaintiff must succeed.[9]

1 This is the *datio* requirement discussed in par 212 ante. The value of a *factum* cannot be recovered.

2 It is not a requirement, however, that the defendant must have been aware of the illegality at the time of *transfer*. Even if the defendant *received* innocently the *condictio* is available against the defendant if he or she became aware of the illegality of the *causa* for the transfer while still in possession of the thing: *First National Bank of Southern Africa Ltd v Perry* [2001] 3 All SA 331 (SCA); 2001 3 SA 960 (SCA) 968–971. In the *Perry* case money obtained through fraud was paid into an account with the defendant bank. As a result of the rule that, once money is mixed with other money ownership in it passes by operation of law, the defendant bank became the owner of the money. Consequently, the remedy of a *rei indicatio* was not available to the owner. Although the defendant bank was unaware of the fraud when it took transfer of the money, the Supreme Court of Appeal held that the owner could recover the amount by which the bank had been enriched through the *condictio ob turpem vel iniustam causam* since the bank became aware of the illegality of the underlying transaction while the money was still in its possession. The court found authority for

this proposition primarily in *D* 12 5 6.

3 Agreements are sometimes prohibited by law but are nevertheless valid if concluded in contravention of the prohibition, the sanction attached to the contravention being something different such as a fine or other penalty. Whether the intention of the legislature was to render an agreement in contravention of the prohibition invalid, is dependent upon the proper interpretation of the statutory provision in question; cf *Standard Bank v Estate Van Rhyn* 1925 AD 266; *Pottie v Kotze* 1954 3 SA 719 (A); *Eland Boerdery (Edms) Bpk v Anderson* 1966 4 SA 400 (T); *Swart v Smuts* 1971 1 SA 819 (A); *Metro Western Cape (Pty) Ltd v Ross* 1986 3 SA 181 (A). If the conclusion is that the agreement is valid, despite the illegality, there can be no question of the condition of what has been performed in terms of the (valid) agreement. The *condictio ob turpem vel iniustam causam* finds application only in those cases where the agreement is void for illegality. From agreements that are void because they are illegal must be distinguished agreements that are void because of a failure to comply with the formalities prescribed for their conclusion – eg writing – in the case of an agreement which is void on formal grounds, the action is the *condictio indebiti*, not the *condictio ob turpem vel iniustam causam*.

4 As to when an agreement will be regarded as *contra bonos mores* or contrary to public policy: see eg *Magna Alloys & Research SA (Pty) Ltd v Ellis* 1984 4 SA 874 (A); *Sasfin (Pty) Ltd v Beukes* 1989 1 SA 1 (A); *Brisley v Drotsky* 2002 12 BCLR 1229 (SCA); 2002 4 SA 1 (SCA); *Afrox Healthcare Bpk v Strydom*

[2002] 4 All SA 125 (SCA); 2002 6 SA 21 (SCA); De Wet and Van Wyk *Kontraktereg en Handelsreg* 5 ed Vol 1 89; Lubbe and Murray *Contract* 270; Kerr *Law of Contract* 171; Christie *The Law of Contract* 398.

5 *D* 12 5 3, 8; *C* 4 7 2; Grotius *Inleiding* 3 1 43, 3 30 17; Van Leeuwen *RHR* 4 14 4, *Cens For* 1 4 14 8–10; Voet *Commentarius* 12 5 2; Schorer *ad Gr* 3 3 49 fn 315. In Roman law this rule was relaxed in certain circumstances; see *Jajbhay v Cassim* 1939 AD 537. In Roman-Dutch law, however, there was apparently no relaxation: see eg De Vos *Verrykingsaanspreeklikheid* 168.

6 Cf *Sandeman v Solomon* (1907) 28 NLR 140; *Levy v Katz* 1914 WLD 88; *Brandt v Bergstedt* 1917 CPD 344; *United Provident Assurance Association of SA Ltd v Vivian* 1930 CPD 364.

7 See *Jajbhay v Cassim* supra, particularly 544 550.

8 See eg *Petersen v Jajbhay* 1940 TPD 182; *Padayachey v Lebese* 1942 TPD 10; *Visser v Rousseau* 1990 1 SA 139 (A); *Maseko v Maseko* 1992 3 SA 190 (W). In the *Visser* case the question whether relative degrees of turpitude on the part of the plaintiff and the defendant, respectively, can play any role in the relaxation of the *par delictum* rule was left open by the Appellate Division. For an example where the *par delictum* rule was not relaxed, see *Henry v Branfield* 1996 1 SA 244 (D).

9 Cf *Wylock v Milford Investments (Pty) Ltd* 1962 4 SA 298 (C); *Minister van Justisie v Van Heerden* 1960 4 SA 377 (O); *First National Bank of Southern Africa Ltd v Perry* supra 969.

216 Extent of defendant's liability The defendant is liable to restore the transferred thing with its fruits[1] (less production costs) and accessions.[2] Where the thing has been lost or destroyed in the hands of the defendant, the defendant remains liable to restore its full value.[3] The latter proposition needs to be qualified at least to the extent that the defendant's liability is reduced or extinguished if the thing had been lost, destroyed or damaged at a time when the defendant was unaware of the illegality of the underlying transaction. It is only from the time that the defendant gains knowledge of the impoverished party's claim that he or she, "so to speak, hold for the benefit of the original owner".[4]

The defendant is probably entitled to compensation for his or her necessary and useful expenses on the thing.[5] It has been held that before a plaintiff can succeed, he or she must tender return of any counter-performance made by the defendant.[6] This rule can obviously apply only if the defendant would not be prevented by the *par delictum* rule from recovering from the plaintiff.[7]

1 As in the case of the *condictio indebiti*, interest on money is not regarded as fruits; see *C* 4 7 4.
2 This by analogy with *D* 12 6 15 et seq, 12 6

65 5 dealing with the *condictio indebiti* and *D* 12 4 7 1, 12 4 12 dealing with the *condictio causa data causa non secuta*.

3 The authority for this is Voet *Commentarius* 12 5 1 followed in *Minister van Justisie v Van Heerden* 1960 4 SA 377 (O) 382. Voet's reasoning that the recipient remains liable because the action "*ex quodam quasi maleficio descendat*" is not convincing when it is borne in mind that the *condictio ob turpem vel iniustam causam* is an enrichment action and not a delictual action. The reasoning in the *Van Heerden* case that the recipient remains liable because a *turpis* person is always in *mora* is likewise not convincing, bearing in mind that the defendant might be completely unaware of his or her duty to restore. See also De Vos *Verrykingsaanspreeklikheid* 171.

4 Per Schutz JA in *First National Bank of Southern Africa Ltd v Perry* [2001] 3 All SA 331 (SCA); 2001 3 SA 960 (SCA) 971H.

5 After analogy of *D* 12 6 26 12, 12 6 65 5 dealing with the *condictio indebiti*; see par 213 ante.

6 Cf *Albertyn v Kumalo* 1946 WLD 529. In this case the action was vindicatory but from the approach of the court it is clear that the rule would also apply to the *condictio ob turpem vel iniustam causam*. See also *MCC Bazaar v Harris & Jones (Pty) Ltd* 1954 3 SA 158 (T) 162. In *Dugas v Kempster Sedgwick (Pty) Ltd* 1961 1 SA 784 (D) 794 and *Lydenburg Voorspoed Ko-öperasie v Els* 1966 3 SA 34 (T) the rule was accepted in circumstances where the *condictio ob turpem vel iniustam causam* lay, although the court in each case assumed that the *condictio sine causa* (*specialis*) was involved.

The defendant should be able to refuse to give up his or her enrichment until the plaintiff restores on his or her side, but if the defendant gives up his or her enrichment without insisting on restoration by the plaintiff, he or she should, in turn, be entitled to bring the *condictio ob turpem vel iniustam causam* against the plaintiff, subject once again to the *par delictum* rule; see De Vos 163–167. See also par 213 fn 11 ante.

7 Cf the facts of *Minister van Justisie v Van Heerden* supra.

CONDICTIO CAUSA DATA CAUSA NON SECUTA

217 Circumstances in which action lies The *condictio causa data causa non secuta*, though still part of the law,[1] finds but restricted application.[2] It lies to recover (a) that which has been transferred[3] on the assumption that a particular event will take place in future[4] when that event does not take place; and (b) that which has been transferred subject to a modus that is disregarded or frustrated.[5]

1 See Wessels *Contract* pars 3721–3746 3760–3762; *Baliol Investment Co (Pty) Ltd v Jacobs* 1946 TPD 269; *Turnbull v Potchefstroom Town Council* 1950 1 SA 804 (T); *Gulamhussen & Co Ltd v Kenney* 1952 3 SA 366 (T); *Shell Co of SA Ltd v Gerrans Garage (Pty) Ltd* 1954 4 SA 752 (G). See also De Vos *Verrykingsaanspreeklikheid* 154 et seq; Visser *Wille's Principles* 635; Eiselen and Pienaar *Unjustified Enrichment* 157.

2 In Roman and Roman-Dutch law its application was wider; see De Vos 69 et seq 10 et seq. Although it has been suggested that this *condictio* is also available to recover money or property transferred in terms of a contract which was subsequently cancelled (see eg the authorities cited in De Vos 157 fn 19) the Appellate Division decided in *Baker v Probert* 1985 3 SA 429 (A) 438–439 that the claim for restitution of performance following upon cancellation is not a *condictio* but a distinct contractual remedy. See also *Tweedie v Park Travel Agency (Pty) Ltd t/a Park Tours* [1998] 3 All SA 57 (W); 1998 4 SA 802 (W) 809. Moreover, where a contract is avoided on the basis of misrepresentation, duress or undue influence the proper remedy is *restitutio in integrum* which is not an enrichment action either: *Davidson v Bonafede* 1981 2 SA 501 (C) 510; *Feinstein v Niggli* 1981 2 SA 684 (A) 700. See also De Vos 157–159; Eiselen and Pienaar 170.

3 This is once again the *datio* requirement discussed in par 212 ante. By "transferred" is therefore to be understood a transfer of ownership.

4 Transfer must, in other words, take place against a *causa futura*. Where the assumption relates to a fact of the past or present, the plaintiff's action is the *condictio sine causa specialis*; see par 219 post. Cf *Fourie v CDMO Homes (Pty) Ltd* 1982 1 SA 21 (A). There is considerable difference of opinion whether an assumption can indeed relate to future fact. De Vos 155, 1976 *TSAR* 79 and Van der Merwe and Van Huyssteen 1985

THRHR 469 are of the opinion that it can. De Wet and Van Wyk *Kontraktereg en Handelsreg* 5 ed Vol 1 154, on the other hand, hold the opinion that an assumption can only relate to past or present facts. Uncertainty as to future facts, so they contend, is a *condition* and not an *assumption*. In *Williams v Evans* 1978 1 SA 1170 (C) 1174 De Vos's view received the approval of a single judge. However, in *Hare's Brickfields Ltd v Cape Town City Council* 1985 1 SA 769 (C) 781 a full bench of the Cape Provincial Division overruled the decision in *Williams v Evans* supra on the basis that the views expressed by De Wet and Van Wyk are to be preferred. See also *Sonarep (SA) (Pty) Ltd v Motorcraft (Pty) Ltd* 1981 1 SA 889 (N) 901–902; *First National Bank of SA Ltd v Tvl Rugby Union* [1997] 1 All SA 743 (W); 1997

3 SA 851 (W) 864. It follows from this that if the view of De Wet and Yeats, that an assumption cannot relate to a future event is to be accepted, the field of application of the *contictio causa data causa non secuta* will be limited even further to the extent that it applies exclusively to the frustrated modus.

5 *Mackenzie v Mutual Life Insurance Co of New York & Bilbrough* 1906 TH 116; *Venter's Executor v Lombard* 1919 TPD 177; *African Realty Trust Ltd v Holmes* 1922 AD 389 400–402; *Gulamhussen & Co Ltd v Kenney* supra; *Shell Co of SA Ltd v Gerrans Garage (Pty) Ltd* supra; *Levin v Levin* 1960 4 SA 469 (W); cf *Benoni Town Council v Minister of Agricultural Credit & Land Tenure* 1978 1 SA 978 (T) and the comments on this decision by Eiselen and Pienaar 161–162.

218 Extent of defendant's liability The defendant must restore the transferred thing with its fruits (less production costs) and accessions.[1] Where the defendant is no longer in possession of the thing he or she must restore its value.[2] As the *condictio causa data causa non secuta* is an enrichment action, non-enrichment is a good defence.[3]

The defendant is probably entitled to compensation for all *impensae necessariae* on the thing and for *impensae utiles* to the extent to which the value of the thing has been enhanced thereby.[4]

1 See *D* 12 4 7 1, 12 4 12 and cf *D* 12 6 15 et seq, 12 6 65 5. Interest is not regarded as fruit and need therefore not be restored: *Baliol Investment Co (Pty) Ltd v Jacobs* 1946 TPD 269.

2 See *D* 12 4, 39 6 37 1.
3 Subject, of course, to the exceptions set out in par 209 ante.
4 After analogy of *D* 12 6 26 12 and 12 6 65 5 dealing with the *condictio indebiti*.

CONDICTIO SINE CAUSA

219 Introduction In Roman law there were apparently two *condictiones sine causa* – a *condictio sine causa generalis* and a *condictio sine causa specialis*.[1] The *condictio sine causa generalis* could take the place of any of the three *condictiones* discussed so far, namely the *condictio indebiti*, the *condictio ob turpem vel iniustam causam* and the *condictio causa data causa non secuta*. If any one of these *condictiones* lay, the *condictio sine causa generalis* could be used instead. If none of them was available, neither was the *condictio sine causa generalis*.[2] The *condictio sine causa specialis*, on the other hand, was available in certain circumstances where none of the other *condictiones* could be instituted. What is discussed in this section is the *condictio sine causa specialis*.

1 The terms are not themselves of Roman origin. They are the creation of later writers on Roman law; De Vos *Verrykinsaanspreeklikheid* 29. In Roman–Dutch law the term

condictio sine causa has the same double meaning; see Voet *Commentarius* 12 7 1.
2 See De Vos 30.

220 Circumstances in which the action lies It is difficult to determine the precise scope of the *condictio sine causa (specialis)* in Roman law since the *corpus iuris*, instead of stating principles, merely mentions examples from which it is difficult to extrapolate exact principles.[1] In Roman-Dutch law there was no greater clarity.[2] Even today there remains a lot of uncertainty about the field of application of this enrichment action. Though the existence of the _condictio sine causa_ has been repeatedly confirmed, the courts have thus far specifically refrained from attempting to define its ambit.[3] In the result the scope of the action can only be described by way of examples from which areas of application may be determined. According to these examples the _condictio sine causa specialis_ seems to be available in the following four areas of application:[4]

(a)   where money or property[5] has been transferred to the defendant in terms of a valid _causa_ which later falls away. In this form the _condictio sine causa_ is also known as the _condictio ob causam finitam_.[6] The _Digest_[7] presents the following example: A, a dry-cleaner, compensates a customer, B, for clothing which A has lost. If subsequently the clothing is found, A may reclaim his payment with the _condictio sine causa_. Another example in this category is where A transfers a thing to B in terms of a contract which is subsequently terminated by supervening impossibility of performance. A may recover his performance under the contract with the _condictio sine causa_;[8]

(b)   The _condictio sine causa_ lies against a defendant who has _bona fide_ disposed of or consumed the plaintiff's property if:

(i)   the defendant obtained possession of the property through a _negotium_ between him or herself and the plaintiff;[9] or

(ii)   the defendant obtained possession of the plaintiff's property consisting of money otherwise than through a _negotium_ with the plaintiff, gratuitously, that is to say, _ex causa lucrative_;[10]

(c)   The _condictio sine causa_ has been held to be the appropriate remedy where a bank seeks to recover the amount paid to the payee of a cheque after the cheque had been countermanded by the drawer;[11]

(d)   The _condictio sine causa (specialis)_ is available where the ownership of property is transferred _sine causa_ to the defendant but the circumstances are such that none of the other _condictiones sine causa_ would lie. The exact parameters of such liability have, however, not been established.[12] An example of such a case would be where a thing is transferred against a false assumption relating to a fact concerning the past or present.[13]

1 De Vos _Verrykingsaanspreeklikheid_ 30; _Rulten v Herald Industries (Pty) Ltd_ 1982 3 SA 600 (D) 606.

2 De Vos 71 et seq.

3 _Govender v Standard Bank of SA Ltd_ 1984 4 SA 392 (C) 396; _B&H Engineering v First National Bank of SA Ltd_ 1995 2 SA 279 (A) 285.

4 Eiselen and Pienaar _Unjustified Enrichment_ 170–171; Visser _Wille's Principles_ 638–639.

5 As in the case of the three _condictiones_ so far considered, the _condictio sine causa_ is not available to recover the value of a _factum_: De Vos 36 74.

6 De Vos 31; Visser 638.

7 _D_ 12 7 2. See also Voet _Commentarius_ 12 7 1; _Snyman v Pretoria Hypotheek Maatschappij_ 1916 OPD 263.

8 _Wiley v Mundinch & Co_ (1902) 19 SC 447 452; _Holtshausen v Minnaar_ (1905) 10 HCG 50; _Hughes v Levy_ 1907 TS 276; _Rulten v Herald Industries (Pty) Ltd_ supra 610. However, if a contract is cancelled by agreement or for breach or if it is avoided for fraudulent misrepresentation, duress or undue influence, the appropriate remedy to recover performance is not an enrichment action but a contractual remedy and _restitutio in integrum_, respectively: see par 217 fn 2 ante and the authorities there cited.

9 _D_ 12 18 2 18 1; _Union Government (Minister of Agriculture) v Lombard_ 1926 CPD 150; _Greenhills Producers (Pty) Ltd (In Liq) v Benjamin_ 1960 4 SA 188 (E); De Vos 210; Eiselen and Pienaar 183.

10 _Trahair v Webb & Co_ 1924 WLD 227; _Govender v Standard Bank of SA Ltd_ supra 405; _Commissioner of Customs & Excise v Bank of Lisbon International Ltd_ 1994 1 SA 205 (N) 214–215. In _Leal & Co v Williams_ 1906 TS 554 and _Van der Westhuizen v McDonald & Mundel_ 1907 TS 933 it was held that the English doctrine of conversion is not part of our law and consequently that no action lies where possession of someone else's property was received _bona fide_ and _ex causa onerosa_

and consumed or alienated in equal good faith. Where possession is received gratuitously but the property is something other than money, the position is doubtful, but see *Campbell v Blue Lime Association Ltd* 1918 TPD 309 312. It is suggested that where something other than money is received *ex causa lucrativa* the *condictio sine causa* should also lie. Where vindication of the property is still possible the condition is excluded since in that situation the defendant who alienated the property cannot be said to be enriched at the plaintiff's expense: *D* 7 9 12; *D* 12 1 23; *D* 24 1 5 8. Although the *condictio* is also available against the *mala fide* defendant the more appropriate remedy against such defendant would be in delict: De Vos 213.

11 *B&H Engineering v First National Bank of SA Ltd* supra 279 284. In *Natal Bank Ltd v Roorda* 1903 TH 298 the court suggested that the appropriate remedy is the *condictio indebiti*. However, in *Govender v Standard Bank of SA Ltd* supra 398 it was held that the remedy available to the bank was the *condictio sine causa* and not the *condictio indebiti*. In the *B&H Engineering* case the Appellate Division approved of the *Govender* case. The *ratio decidendi* appears from the following succinct

statement by Grosskopf JA (284G–I): "A *condictio indebiti* lies to recover a payment made in the mistaken belief that there is a debt owing. However, a bank paying a cheque knows that it owes no debt to the payee. Its mistake lies, not in a belief that it owes money to the payee, but in a belief that it has a mandate from the drawer to make the payment. In these circumstances the appropriate remedy is not the *condictio indebiti* but the *condictio sine causa*." See also eg *ABSA Bank Ltd v Standard Bank of SA Ltd* [1997] 4 All SA 673 (SCA); 1998 1 SA 242 (SCA); Pretorius 1995 *THRHR* 733; Malan 1995 *TSAR* 782; Van Zyl 1998 *TSAR* 177.

12 See also Visser 639; De Vos 33 et seq; Eiselen and Pienaar 171. Where there is no transfer of property involved the *condictio sine causa* is not the appropriate action; see *McCarthy Retail Ltd v Shortdistance Carriers CC* [2001] 3 All SA 236 (SCA); 2001 3 SA 482 (SCA) 489.

13 Cf *D* 12 7 5; Voet 12 7 2. Where the assumption relates to the future, the action is the *condictio causa data causa non secuta*; see par 217 ante.

221 Extent of defendant's liability Where the defendant consumed or disposed of property of which he or she had the possession but not the ownership, the plaintiff's claim is for the value of the property.[1] Where the defendant obtained the ownership of the property, he or she must restore the property itself with its fruits (less production costs) and accessions.[2] Where the defendant is no longer in possession of the property, he or she must restore its value.[3]

Since the *condictio sine causa* is an enrichment action the plaintiff must establish that the defendant has been enriched.[4] As in the case of the other *condictiones*, non-enrichment or decrease of enrichment is a good defence to the action.[5] The defendant is entitled to compensation for all *impensae necessariae* on the property and for *impensae utiles* to the extent to which the value of the property has been enhanced thereby.[6] Where the defendant has performed something on his or her side, he or she is entitled to the return of his or her performance, or where the plaintiff is no longer in possession of it, its value. The defendant may refuse to restore until the plaintiff tenders restoration on his or her side.[7]

1 Cf *D* 12 1 18 1; *Campbell v Blue Lime Association Ltd* 1918 TPD 309; *Union Government (Minister of Agriculture) v Lombard* 1926 CPD 150; *Trahair v Webb & Co* 1924 WLD 227. Where the property has been sold, it is suggested that the value must be accepted to equal the price for which it was sold; see *D* 12 1 23.

2 By analogy with *D* 12 4 7 1, 12 4 12 dealing with the *condictio causa data causa non secuta* and *D* 12 6 1 5 et seq, 12 6 65 5 dealing with the *condictio indebiti*. Interest is not

regarded as fruit and need not be restored. There is no direct authority for this statement, but it is submitted that the position must necessarily be the same as in the case of the other *condictiones*; see pars 209 216 fn 1 12 fn 1 ante.

3 This is the position as far as the other *condictiones sine causa* are concerned (see pars 213 216 218 ante) and must obviously be the position in the case of the *condictio sine causa specialis* as well.

4 So, for example, where the bank sought to

recover the amount paid to the payee on a cheque after the cheque had been counter-manded by the drawer, the bank's claim was dismissed on the basis that the payee had not been enriched since its receipt of the amount of the cheque was balanced by its loss of a claim against the drawer: *B&H Engineering v First National Bank of SA Ltd* 1995 2 SA 279 (A); *Govender v Standard Bank of SA Ltd* 1984 4 SA 392 (C). See also *Nedcor*

Bank Ltd v ABSA Bank Ltd 1995 4 SA 727 (W).
5 Subject once again to the exceptions set out in par 209 ante.
6 By analogy with *D* 12 6 26 12 and 12 6 65 5 dealing with the *conditio indebiti*.
7 Also by analogy with the *conditio indebiti*; see par 213 ante; *Dugas v Kempster Sedgwick (Pty) Ltd* 1961 1 SA 784 (D); *Lydenburg Voorspoed Ko-öperasie v Els* 1966 3 SA 34 (T).

ACTION OF THE NEGOTIORUM GESTOR

222 Introduction When one person (the *gestor*) voluntarily administers the affairs of another (the *dominus*) without the latter's authority, there is created between them the quasi-contractual relationship of *negotiorum gestio* in terms of which the *dominus* is bound to reimburse the *gestor* for expenses the latter may reasonably incur or for any loss the *gestor* may sustain in the administration of the affairs of the *dominus*.[1] The action of the *negotiorum gestor* is not an enrichment action,[2] save in the four instances discussed in the paragraph that follows.

1 See *D* 3 5, *C* 2 18. For a detailed discussion of *negotiorum gestio* (unauthorised administration), see Rubin *Unauthorized Administration*; De Villiers and Macintosh *The Law of Agency* 3 ed (by JM Silke) ch 5; title MANDATE AND NEGOTIORUM GESTIO.
2 Broadly stated, the *gestor* is entitled to claim all his or her necessary and useful expenses. The *gestor* is not limited to the enrichment of the *dominus*. See De Vos *Verrykingsaanspreeklikheid*

41 83 213; Van Zyl *Saakwaarnemingsaksie as Verrykingsaksie in die SA Reg* 1–10, *Negotiorum Gestio in SA Law* 84 et seq. Odendaal v Van Oudtshoorn 1968 3 SA 433 (T) 437; *Kunneke v Eerste Nasionale Bank van Suidelike Afrika Bpk* 1997 3 SA 300 (T); *ABSA Bank Ltd t/a Bankfin v Stander t/a CAW Paneelkloppers* 1998 1 SA 939 (C) 944; 1997 CLR 154 (C).

223 Circumstances in which *negotiorum gestio* gives rise to an enrichment action The four instances in which a *gestor's* claim is restricted to the amount by which the *dominus* has been enriched are the following:

(a)   where the *gestor* has administered the affairs of a minor;[1]

(b)   where the *gestor* has *mala fide* administered the affairs of another for his or her own benefit and not for that of the *dominus*;[2]

(c)   where the *gestor* has administered the affairs of another in the *bona fide* belief that they were his or her own;[3] and

(d)   where he or she has administered the affairs of another against the expressed wishes of the *dominus*.[4]

1 See *D* 3 5 5 2, 3 5 36; *C* 2 18(19) 2; Grotius *Inleiding* 1 8 5, 3 6 9; Voet *Commentarius* 26 8 2; Van Leeuwen *RHR* 4 2 3, *Cens For* 1 1 17 10; Van der Keessel *Prael* 1 8 5, 3 1 26, 3 30 3; De Vos *Verrykingsaanspreeklikheid* 42–43 84 214–215; Van Zyl *Saakwaarnemingsaksie as Verrykingsaksie in die SA Reg* 12–22 90–91 149–150. Eiselen and Pienaar *Unjustified Enrichment* 222.
2 See *D* 3 5 5 5; Voet 3 5 5, 3 5 9; Groenewegen *De Leg Abr ad D* 3 5; De Vos 42 84 215; Van Zyl 22-28 91–94 153–159;

Odendaal v Van Oudtshoorn 1968 3 SA 433 (T); *Blesbok Eiendomsagentskap v Cantamessa* 1991 2 SA 712 (T) 718.
3 See *D* 3 5 48; *Klug & Klug v Penkin* 1932 CPD 401; De Vos 84–85; Van Zyl 29–36 94–96 152–153. Cf also the position of a *bona fide* possessor or *bona fide* occupier who has preserved or improved the property of another: pars 227–235 post. In *ABSA Bank Ltd t/a Bankfin v Stander t/a CAW Paneelkloppers* 1998 1 SA 939 (C); 1997 CLR 154 (C) it was held that the enrichment action

under consideration was available to A who effected repairs to the motor vehicle of C on the instructions of B. However, in *McCarthy Retail Ltd v Shortdistance Carriers CC* [2001] 3 All SA 236 (SCA); 2001 3 SA 482 (SCA) 490 (per Schutz JA) 496 (per Harms JA) the appropriate enrichment action in similar circumstances was held to be the action of the *bona fide* occupier (see par 235 post. See also par 209 ante with regard to enrichment in multi-party situations in general).

4 See Groenewegen *De Leg Abr ad C* 2 19 (18) 24; Voet 3 5 11; *Colonial Government v Smith & Co* (1901) 18 SC 380 and in particular *Standard Bank Financial Services Ltd v Taylam (Pty) Ltd* 1979 2 SA 383 (C). This rule does not authorise an indiscriminate interference in the affairs of others or an unwarranted disregard of their wishes. Before an action will lie where the *gestor* has acted against the expressed wishes of the *dominus*, some just cause will have to be shown for disregarding those wishes: *Standard Bank Financial Services Ltd v Taylam (Pty) Ltd* supra 392–393 395. See also *Kunneke v Eerste Nasionale Bank van Suidelike Afrika Bpk* 1997 3 SA 300 (T) 313–314. It should be mentioned that there is also strong authority amongst the institutional writers for refusing an action to a *gestor* who has acted against the wishes of the *dominus*; see eg Van Leeuwen *Cens For* 1 4 26 1 and Van der Keessel *Prael* 3 3 30, 3 27 5. See further De Vos 84 214; Van Zyl 96–97 150–152.

224 Extent of the defendant's liability The *dominus* must reimburse the *gestor* for the necessary and useful expenses the latter has incurred and for any loss he or she has suffered.[1] The *gestor* is not entitled to remuneration for his or her labour but there is authority for the view that the *gestor* is entitled to compensation for the income he or she has lost by expending labour on managing the affairs of the *dominus*.[2] All this is subject to the limitation that the defendant is liable for no more than his or her actual enrichment. As the *gestor's* action is an enrichment action in the circumstances discussed in this section, non-enrichment of the *dominus* is, of course, a good defence to the action.

1 See *D* 3 5 2; Gaius *Institutiones* 3 27 1; Grotius *Inleiding* 3 27 5; Voet *Commentarius* 3 5 8; *New Club Garage v Milborrow & Son* 1931 GWL 86; *Williams' Estate v Molenschoot & Schep (Pty) Ltd* 1939 CPD 360; *ABSA Bank Ltd t/a Bankfin v Stander t/a CAW Paneelkloppers* 1997 CLR 154 (C); 1998 1 SA 939 (C).
2 See Van Leeuwen *Cens For* 1 4 26 4;

Vinnius *Commentarius ad Inst* 3 27 1; Voet 3 5 8; Huber *Hed. Rechts* 3 28 6; Van der Keessel *Praelectiones* 3 27 5. *Grant's Farming Co Ltd v Attwell* (1901) 9 HCG 91 95; *New Club Garage v Milborrow & Son* supra; *Williams' Estate v Molenschoot & Schep (Pty) Ltd* supra; *Nortje v Pool* 1966 3 SA 96 (A) 121 126.

ACTION AGAINST PERSONS HAVING LIMITED CAPACITY TO ACT

225 Introduction A minor or other person having limited capacity to act is not liable in terms of his or her unauthorised contract. Where such person has accepted performance from the other party, however, he or she may be liable on the ground of enrichment.[1]

1 See Grotius *Inleiding* 1 8 5, 1 11 5, 3 1 26, 3 6 9, 3 30 3, 3 30 11; Voet *Commentarius* 3 5 8, 4 4 22, 15 1 11, 23 2 43, 26 8 2; Van Leeuwen *RHR* 1 16 8, 4 2 3 *Cens For* 1 1 17 10, 1 4 3 2; Van der Keessel *Prael* 1 8 5, 1 11 5, 3 6 9, 3 30 3; *Edelstein v Edelstein* 1952 3 SA 1 (A); *Forster v Becker* 1914 EDL 193 196; *Karsten v Forster* 1914 CPD 919; *Gammon v McClure* 1925 CPD 137 139; *Oelofse v*

Grundling 1952 1 SA 338 (C); *Molyneux v Natal Land & Colonization Co Ltd* 1905 AC 555 (PC) 569; De Vos *Verrykinsaanspreeklikheid* 46–48 95–96 219 et seq; Boberg *Persons and the Family* 2 ed 799–809; Eiselen and Pienaar *Unjustified Enrichment* 187 193–194; Van der Vyver and Joubert *Personereg en Familiereg* 3 ed 165–166; Barnard, Cronje and Olivier *Persone- en Familiereg* 2 ed 88 et seq.

226 Extent of defendant's liability The defendant must restore what he or she received or, where that is no longer possible, the amount by which he or she is still enriched as a result of the plaintiff's performance.[1] As the plaintiff's action is an enrichment action, non-enrichment is a good defence.[2] Where the defendant has him or herself made performance in terms of the contract, the defendant will probably be entitled to refuse to restore until the return of his or her own performance is tendered to him or her.[3] Should the defendant satisfy the plaintiff's claim without insisting on the return of his or her own performance, he or she has, depending on the circumstances, a *rei vindicatio* or a *condictio* available to recover his or her performance or its value.[4]

1 See once again the authorities cited in par 225 fn 1 ante. Where the defendant was supplied with necessaries or where the defendant used what he or she received to procure necessaries he or she remains enriched, the enrichment in such cases taking the form of expenses saved; see De Vos *Verrykingsaanspreeklikheid* 46 95; Boberg *Persons and the Family* 2 ed 809–815; Van der Vyver and Joubert *Persone- en Familiereg* 3 ed 166–167.

2 Which defence in the case of a minor, whose enrichment is determined at *litis contestatio*, is not subject to the exceptions set out in par 209 ante. See *D* 3 5 36(37) et seq, 4 4 34 et seq; Voet *Commentarius* 3 5 8; De Vos 46 95–96 336 fn 40 337 fns 43–44.

3 By analogy with the position obtaining where one of the *conditiones sine causa* is instituted.

4 See par 216 fn 6 ante.

ACTIONS OF PERSONS WHO HAVE PRESERVED OR IMPROVED THE PROPERTY OF ANOTHER

GENERAL

227 Introduction There are many circumstances in which the possessor or occupier of another's property may expend his or her money, material or labour on the preservation or improvement of that property, and in some of those circumstances such expenditure may result in the enrichment of the owner of the property at the expense of the possessor or occupier. In both Roman and Roman-Dutch law certain categories of possessors and occupiers were in certain circumstances entitled to compensation for their expenses[1] and this right to compensation has been extended considerably in South African law.[2] Whether an action for compensation will lie in a particular case depends on the category to which the possessor or occupier who incurred the expenses belongs, and on the circumstances under which the expenses were incurred. In the discussion which follows it will consequently be necessary to distinguish between various categories of possessors and occupiers. Consideration will first be given to the rights of compensation that pertains to *bona fide* possessors. Thereafter the discussion will move on to an inquiry of how the position of other categories of possessors and occupiers either correspond to or differ from the position of the *bona fide* possessor.[3]

1 In Roman law the right to compensation was in the main enforceable only by means of an *exceptio doli* or a *ius retentionis*; in Roman-Dutch law it was enforceable by action; see De Vos *Verrykingsaanspreeklikheid* 48 et seq 96 et seq; Eiselen and Pienaar *Unjustified Enrichment* 246; *Nortje v Pool* 1966 3 SA 96 (A) 129.

2 Ie by the inclusion of further categories of occupiers; see De Vos 224 et seq.

3 For a discussion of the various categories of possessors and occupiers, see eg Van der Merwe *Sakereg* 2 ed 154; De Vos *Verrykingsaanspreeklikheid* 245–247; title THINGS. For present purposes a distinction will be drawn between *bona fide* possessors; *mala fide* possessors, lawful occupiers, *bona fide* occupiers and *mala fide* occupiers. Broadly speaking, these categories can be defined as follows: (a) A *bona fide* possessor is someone who

controls the moveable or immovable property of another *animo domini* under the *bona fide* but mistaken belief that he or she is the owner. (b) A *mala fide* possessor, on the other hand, possesses the property of another *animo domini* and behaves like the owner in all respects while knowing that he or she is not the owner. (c) An occupier, again, is a person who does not have the *animus domini* but who occupies the immovable property or holds the moveable property of another person. Lawful occupiers are those who are legally entitled to occupation. *Bona fide* occupiers believe that they are entitled to occupation though they are not. (d) *Mala fide* occupiers are those who occupy property as if they are entitled to do so while knowing that they are not.

BONA FIDE AND MALA FIDE POSSESSORS

Bona Fide Possessors

228 Action where immovable property has been preserved or improved A *bona fide* possessor who has expended his or her money or material[1] on the preservation or improvement of the immovable property of another, has a claim for compensation.[2] Generally speaking the action is against the person who is the owner of the property at the time the claim is made.[3] However, if it should transpire that it was the previous owner who had been enriched, the claim for compensation is against that person, despite the fact that the possessor's *ius retentionis*,[4] which is a real right, is enforceable against the present owner.[5]

1 But not the possessor's labour, save in so far as the expenditure of his or her labour has resulted in lost income; cf *Ras v Vermeulen* 1927 OPD 5; *Harrison v Marchant* 1941 WLD 16; *Nortje v Pool* 1966 3 SA 96 (A) 121 126; *Brooklyn House Furnishers (Pty) Ltd v Knoetze & Sons* 1970 3 SA 264 (A). See also De Vos *Verrykingsaanspreeklikheid* 230; Eiselen and Pienaar *Unjustified Enrichment* 242. On the analogous position of the *negotiorum gestor*, see Van Leeuwen *Cens For* 1 4 26 4, 3 27 5, Voet *Commentarius* 3 5 8; *New Club Garage v Milborrow & Son* 1931 GWL 86; *Williams' Estate v Molenschoot & Schep (Pty) Ltd* 1939 CPD 360. See also par 224 fn 2 ante.

2 In *Meyer's Trustee v Malan* 1911 TPD 559 there are *dicta* to the effect that a *bona fide* possessor cannot give up possession and sue for compensation when such possessor has not been molested and no demand has been made upon him or her to vacate the property. This view is clearly untenable (see De Vos 226–227) but was nevertheless followed on a number of occasions. It has since been rejected in *Nortje v Pool* supra 108 125 and *Rademeyer v Rademeyer* 1968 3 SA 1 (C) 12. The correct position can only be that the possessor may bring an action as soon as he or she becomes aware of the true position; cf *Schoon's Trustee v Schoon's Executors* 1915 CPD 786. See also De Vos 227; Van der Merwe *Sakereg* 2 ed 156.

3 *Compere v Coetzee* 1975 2 SA 430 (T); *Winterton v Estate Allhusen* 1925 CPD 190; *Badroodien v Van Lier* 1928 CPD 311.

4 See par 231 post.

5 *SA Association v Van Staden* (1892) 9 SC 95; *Corneilssen v Petersen* 1913 CPD 329; *Crous v Crous* 1937 CPD 250 257; De Vos 231; Van der Merwe *Sakereg* 156; Delport and Olivier *Sakereg* 128. See also *Van der Burgh v Van Dyk* 1993 3 SA 312 (O) 321–322.

229 Extent of the right to compensation Where the expenses were necessary for the preservation or protection of the property (called *impensae necessariae*) and the possessor's efforts to preserve or protect the property were successful, the possessor is entitled to reimbursement of all his or her expenses.[1] Since Roman times, the underlying theory has been that the owner would of necessity have incurred the same expenses. Consequently the owner has been enriched by the fact that his or her estate did not decrease by that amount. However, so the theory goes, if the possessor's efforts to preserve and protect the property were unsuccessful, then the owner did not save any expenses.[2] Where the possessor has effected useful improvements to the property (in other words, where the possessor incurred so-called *impensae utiles*),[3] he or she is entitled either to his or her expenses or to the amount by which the value of the property has been enhanced, whichever is the lesser.[4] In the case of luxury improvements (referred to as *impensae voluptuariae*)[5] no compensation is payable save, apparently, where the yield of the property has been increased or the owner intends selling the property and the price has been increased as a result of the improvements.[6] The value of any fruit gathered by the possessor before *litis contestatio*, less production costs, is set off against the expenses.[7] "Fruit" apparently includes the rent received where the possessor has leased out the property,[8] but not the use and enjoyment of the property[9] nor fruit yielded by the improvements themselves.[10]

1 See Voet *Commentarius* 6 1 36; *De Beers Consolidated Mines v London & SA Exploration Co* (1893) 10 SC 359; *Lechoana v Cloete* 1925 AD 536 547; *Nortje v Pool* 1966 3 SA 96 (A) 131.

2 See De Vos *Verrykingsaanspreeklikheid* 51; Visser *Wille' Principles* 640; Van der Merwe *Sakereg* 2 ed 156.

3 Ie tangible improvements to the property itself which improve the property and increase its market value and which are useful according to the economic and social views of the community; cf Voet 2 5 1 3; Schorer *ad Gr* 2 48 13 fn 244; *Lechoana v Cloete* supra 547; *Nortje v Pool* supra 130–131; *Brooklyn House Furnishers (Pty) Ltd v Knoetze & Sons* 1970 3 SA 264 (A) 270. It is suggested that the distinction drawn between *impensae utiles* and *impensae voluptuariae* in *United Building Society v Smookler's Trustees & Golombick's Trustee* 1906 TS 623 627 to the effect that "useful expenses" means expenses which increase the market value of the property while "luxury expenses" means expenses which neither preserve the property nor increase its market value but merely satisfy the caprice or fancy of a particular individual, is wrong. Expenses may be luxury expenses even though they increase the market value of the property. See also Van der Merwe 153; De Vos 228; Sonnekus en Neels *Sakereg* 2 ed 239. Cf *Quarrying Enterprises (Pvt) Ltd v John Viol (Pvt) Ltd* 1985 3 SA 575 (ZH) 578; Visser 641.

4 See *D* 6 1 38; Voet 6 1 36; Schorer fn 92 2 10 9(8); *Bellingham v Bloommetje* 1874 4 Buch 36; *De Beers Consolidated Mines v London & SA Exploration Co* supra; *Rubin v Botha* 1911 AD 568; *Fletcher & Fletcher v Bulawayo Waterworks Co Ltd, Bulawayo Waterworks Co Ltd v Fletcher & Fletcher* 1915 AD 636; *Lechoana v Cloete* supra; *Nortje v Pool* supra 106 124 133; *Rademeyer v Rademeyer* 1967 2 SA 702 (C) 706.

5 Ie all improvements of a luxurious nature,

whether or not the value of the property is increased thereby. See also fn 3 supra.

6 *Fletcher & Fletcher v Bulawayo Waterworks Co Ltd, Bulawayo Waterworks Co Ltd v Fletcher & Fletcher* supra 648; *Nortje v Pool* supra 106 124; De Vos 50–52 96–97 109 228–229; Van der Merwe 155.

7 Van Leeuwen *Cens For* 1 2 6 4, *RHR* 2 6 3; Voet 6 1 38, 41 1 32; *Fletcher & Fletcher v Bulawayo Waterworks Co Ltd, Bulawayo Waterworks Co Ltd v Fletcher & Fletcher* supra 650–651; *Rademeyer v Rademeyer* supra 707–708; *Boikhutsong Business Undertakings (Pty) Ltd v Grobler* 1988 2 SA 676 (BA) 683. Where land has been in the hands of a *bona fide* possessor, the owner of the land is restricted in his or her bid to obtain compensation for fruit gathered by the possessor before *litis contestatio* to deducting the value of such fruit from the possessor's claim for compensation. The owner is not granted an action to enforce a claim for compensation and since the possessor acquires ownership of the fruit, vindication is excluded; see, generally, Scholtens 1958 *SALJ* 282 and De Vos 97 224; Van der Merwe 266.

8 There is apparently no direct authority for this statement, but it is suggested that the contention by De Vos 53 fn 22 that "fruit" included rent received by the possessor, is a reasonable one, cf *Rademeyer v Rademeyer* supra 710–711.

9 See *Rademeyer v Rademeyer* supra 711–712; De Vos 53. The underlying reasoning appears to be that unlike the *bona fide* occupier who expects to be liable to pay for the use and occupation of the property, the *bona fide* possessor is under the impression that he or she is the owner and therefore does not contemplate that he or she must pay compensation; see *Rademeyer v Rademeyer* supra 711.

10 Voet 6 1 39, *Fletcher & Fletcher v Bulawayo Waterworks Co Ltd, Bulawayo Waterworks Co Ltd v Fletcher & Fletcher* supra 650; *Rademeyer v Rademeyer* supra 707.

230 The possessor's *ius tollendi* The right to compensation for useful expenses (*impensae utiles*) is not an absolute right. A wide discretion is given to the judge to bring about an equitable result. Where improvements can be removed without injury to the property, the owner of the property may be allowed to waive his or her enrichment in which case the possessor has to be satisfied with the removal of his or her material.[1] Alternatively the owner may be allowed to retain the attachment on payment to the possessor of the value the material would have after separation.[2] Save in the exceptional circumstances set out above,[3] no compensation is payable in respect of luxury expenses (*impensae voluptuariae*) and the possessor is restricted to recovering his or her material as far as removal can be effected without damaging the property. If the owner is prepared to pay the possessor the value which the material would have after separation, he or she is not entitled to remove it.[4]

1　See *D* 6 1 38; Voet *Commentarius* 6 1 36; *Fletcher & Fletcher v Bulawayo Waterworks Co Ltd, Bulawayo Waterworks Co Ltd v Fletcher & Fletcher* 1915 AD 636 648; *Willoughby's Consolidated Co Ltd v Copthall Stores Ltd* 1918 AD 1 20; *Meyer's Trustee v Malan* 1911 TPD 559; *Ras v Vermeulen* 1927 OPD 5; *Van der Merwe Sakereg* 2 ed 159; *De Vos Verrykingsaanspreeklikheid* 288–294.

2　*D* 6 1 38; Voet 6 1 36; and cf *Barnard v The Colonial Government* (1887) 5 SC 122 124–125; *Ras v Vermeulen* supra; Van der Merwe *Sakereg* 159

3　In par 229 ante.

4　See Grotius *Inleiding* 2 10 8; Voet 6 1 36; Vinnius *Selectarum Iuris Quaestionum* 1 24; De Vos 52 97.

231 The possessor's *ius retentionis* A *bona fide* possessor who is in possession of the property which he or she has preserved or improved has a *ius retentionis* (enrichment lien), effective against all the world, until his or her claim for compensation has been satisfied.[1]

1　See *United Building Society v Smookler's Trustees & Golombick's Trustee* 1906 TS 623; *Kommissaris van Binnelandse Inkomste v Anglo American (OFS) Housing Co Ltd* 1960 3 SA 642 (A); *D Glaser & Sons (Pty) Ltd v The Master* 1979 4 SA 780 (C); *Syfrets Participation Bond Managers Ltd v Estate & Co-op Wine Distributors (Pty) Ltd* 1989 1 SA 106 (W) 110; *Goudini Chrome (Pty) Ltd v MCC Contracts (Pty) Ltd* 1993 1 SA 77 (A) 85; Delport and Olivier *Sakereg* 2 ed 487 et seq; Van der Merwe *Sakereg* 158 711 et seq.

232 Movable property A *bona fide* possessor who has preserved or improved the movable property of another has the same right to compensation and the same *ius retentionis* as the *bona fide* possessor of immovable property.[1]

1　Cf Grotius *Inleiding* 2 10 4; Voet *Commentarius* 41 1 27; Van Leeuwen *Cens For* 1 2 5 8; *Colonial Government v Smith & Co* (1901) 18 SC 380; *Wipplinger v Wax* 1933 EDL 60; *Acton v Motau* 1909 TS 841; *McCarthy Retail Ltd v Shortdistance Carriers CC* [2001] 3 All SA 236 (SCA); 2001 3 SA 482 (SCA) 489. The suggestion in *Reed Bros v Ford* 1923 TPD 150 that a *bona fide* possessor who has improved another's movable property has no action for compensation but only a *ius retentionis* has been disapproved in *Rondalia Bank Bpk v Pieter Nel Motors (Edms) Bpk* 1979 4 SA 467 (T) and the court saw no reason why a *bona fide* possessor of a movable thing should not be able to claim compensation for improvements effected to it by him or her. See also in this regard *Van der Burgh v Van Dyk* 1993 3 SA 312 (O) 318 319; De Vos 1974 *THRHR* 308, *Verrykingsaanspreeklikheid* 97 233.

MALA FIDE POSSESSORS

233 *Mala fide* possessors With regard to *impensae necessariae* the position of the *mala fide* possessor is the same as that of the *bona fide* possessor, both as far as his or her claim for compensation and his or her *ius retentionis* are concerned.[1] The question whether the *mala fide* possessor is also entitled to claim compensation for *impensae utiles* has, however, not been finally resolved. According to the majority of Roman-Dutch writers the position of the *mala fide* possessor could also in this regard be likened to that of the *bona fide* possessor.[2] Even so there is an influential dissenting minority.[3] Our case law follows the same pattern. Although the majority of decisions, mostly *obiter*, support the view that as far as the *mala fide* possessor's entitlement to compensation is concerned his or her position is no different from that of the *bona fide* possessor,[4] there are also decisions to the contrary.[5] In its most recent pronouncement on the subject, the Appellate Division found it unnecessary to determine the position of the *mala fide* possessor for the purposes of that case.[6]

The question whether the *mala fide* possessor has a *retentionis* is even more uncertain. Some decisions tend to indicate that the *mala fide* possessor does have such a right[7] while others lend support to the view that he or she has not.[8]

1 Grotius *Inleiding* 2 10 8; *De Beers Consolidated Mines v London & SA Exploration Company* (1893) 10 SC 359 372; *Standard Kredietkorporasie Bpk v JOT Motors (Edms) Bpk h/a Vaal Motors* 1986 1 SA 223 (A) 235.

2 See eg Groenewegen *ad Inst* 2 1 30; Van Leeuwen *Cens For* 1 2 5 10; Voet *Commentarius* 5 3 21 23, 6 1 36.

3 Grotius *Inl* 2 10 8; Van der Keessel *Prael* 2 10 8. With regard to the disagreement among the old authorities, see in general also: *Spencer v Gostelow* 1920 AD 617 636; *JOT Motors (Edms) Bpk h/a Vaal Datsun v Standard Kredietkorporasie Bpk* 1984 2 SA 510 (T) 514; De Vos *Verrykingsaanspreeklikheid* 102, Van der Merwe *Sakereg* 2 ed 159.

4 See *Bellingham v Bloommetje* 1974 4 Buch 36; *Campbell v The Golden Crescent Gold Mining Co Ltd* (1890) 3 SAR 248; *Lechoana v Cloete* 1925 AD 536 547–548; *Banjo v Sungrown (Pty) Ltd* 1969 1 SA 401 (N); *Nortje v Pool* 1966 3 SA 96 (A) 129–130; *BK Tooling (Edms) Bpk v Scope Precision Engineering (Edms) Bpk* 1979 1 SA 391 (A); *JOT Motors (Edms) Bpk h/a Vaal Datsun v Standard Kredietkorporasie Bpk* supra.

5 *De Beers Consolidated Mines v London & SA Exploration Co* supra 372; *Currey v Stevens* (1903) 9 HCG 298; *Raba v Ngoma* 1913 EDL 469; *Quarrying Enterprises (Pvt) Ltd v John Viol (Pvt) Ltd* 1985 3 SA 575 (ZH) 581.

6 *Standard Kredietkorporasie Bpk v JOT Motors (Edms) Bpk h/a Vaal Motors* supra 235. See also De Vos 236; Delport and Olivier *Sakereg* 2 ed 126; Eiselen and Pienaar *Unjustified Enrichment* 283. The reference in *ABSA Bank Ltd t/a Bankfin v Stander t/a CAW Paneelkloppers* 1998 1 SA 939 (C) 950; 1997 CLR 154 (C) that in *JOT Motors* the Appellate Division confirmed the reasoning of the Court *a quo* as far as the position of the *mala fide* possessor is concerned, cannot be sustained.

7 See eg *Bellingham v Bloommetje* supra; *JOT Motors (Edms) Bpk h/a Vaal Datsun v Standard Kredietkorporasie Bpk* supra. In the same matter the question was, however, left open by the Appellate Division: *Standard Kredietkorporasie Bpk v JOT Motors (Edms) Bpk h/a Vaal Motors* supra. Cf also *Acton v Motau* 1909 TS 841. Those institutional writers who gave the *mala fide* possessor an action for compensation (see fn 2 supra) also gave the *mala fide* possessor a *ius retentionis*.

8 *De Beers Consolidated Mines v London & SA Exploration Co* supra 372; *United Building Society v Smookler's Trustees & Golombick's Trustee* 1906 TS 623 633; *Brooklyn House Furnishers (Pty) Ltd v Knoetze & Sons* 1970 3 SA 264 (A) 275. See also in general De Vos 237; Van der Merwe 160.

BONA FIDE, MALA FIDE AND LAWFUL OCCUPIERS

234 Introduction In classical Roman-Dutch law a *bona fide* occupier, unlike a *bona fide* possessor, was not entitled to compensation for improvements effected to the property of another,[1] but a right to compensation was granted to certain classes of lawful occupiers.[2] In South African law there have been ad hoc extensions of the *bona fide* possessor's action to *bona fide* occupiers and to lawful occupiers in general.[3]

1 See *Nortje v Pool* 1966 3 SA 96 (A) 128 129.

2 Cf eg Voet *Commentarius* 21 1 4 (buyers), 5 3 23, 6 3 52, 13 6 10 (borrowers); Grotius *Inleiding* 3 8 7, Voet 6 3 52 13 7 10 (pledgees); Grotius *Inleiding* 2 10 8 (lessees). See also generally De Vos *Verrykingsaanspreeklikheid*

107–110.

3 *Nortje v Pool* supra 129–130; *McCarthy Retail Ltd v Shortdistance Carriers CC* [2001] 3 All SA 236 (SCA); 2001 3 SA 482 (SCA) 489; and see pars 235–237 post.

235 Bona fide occupiers[1] A *bona fide* occupier who has expended his or her money or material on the preservation or improvement of another's property is today in the same position as a *bona fide* possessor,[2] save that in the case of a *bona fide* occupier, unlike that of a *bona fide* possessor, an equitable deduction may be made in respect of the occupier's use and possession of the land.[3]

1 For a discussion of the concept "*bona fide* occupier", see par 228 fn 3 ante and the authorities there cited.

2 *Bellingham v Bloommetje* 1874 4 Buch 36 (rather unsatisfactory because the court apparently regarded the *bona fide* occupier as a *bona fide* possessor); *Rubin v Botha* 1911 AD 568; *Fletcher & Fletcher v Bulawayo Waterworks Co Ltd, Bulawayo Waterworks Co Ltd v Fletcher & Fletcher* 1915 AD 636 647 655; *Nortje v Pool* 1966 3 SA 96 (A) 129–130. In *Earljay Holdings (Pty) Ltd v Moldenhauer* 1984 3 SA 354 (E) 358-359 it was held that a person who entered into a lease of land with a person who was not the owner was entitled to claim compensation from the owner for useful improvements effected by him or her.

See also *McCarthy Retail Ltd v Shortdistance Carriers CC* [2001] 3 All SA 236 (SCA); 2001 3 SA 482 (SCA) 496.

3 See *Rubin v Botha* supra 577; but see also Innes CJ's remarks on this aspect of the *Rubin* case in *Fletcher & Fletcher v Bulawayo Waterworks Co Ltd, Bulawayo Waterworks Co Ltd v Fletcher & Fletcher* supra 647. The underlying reason for the differentiation is that while the *bona fide* possessor, who thinks that he or she is the owner, does not envisage that he or she could be called upon to pay for occupation, the *bona fide* occupier generally must contemplate such possibility: *Rademeyer v Rademeyer* 1967 2 SA 702 (C) 711.

236 Mala fide occupiers[1] Whether a *mala fide* occupier who has expended his or her money or material on the preservation or improvement of another's property is entitled to compensation has not yet been decided.[2] It is suggested that in view of the extension of the *bona fide* possessor's action to a *bona fide* occupier, the *mala fide* occupier's position must by analogy be linked to that of the *mala fide* possessor. Subjected to the reservation that both the *mala fide* possessor and the *mala fide* occupier of moveable property will normally be a thief, the weight of academic opinion appears to be that both *mala fide* possessors and *mala fide* occupiers should be treated in the same way as *bona fide* possessors.[3]

1 For a discussion of the concept "*mala fide* occupier", see par 228 fn 3 ante and the authorities there cited.

2 Both *Acton v Motau* 1909 TS 841 and *Raba v Ngoma* 1913 EDL 469 were concerned with *mala fide* occupiers, but the courts regarded them as *mala fide* possessors.

3 See eg De Vos *Verrykingsaanspreeklikheid* 258; Van der Merwe *Sakereg* 2 ed 162; Visser *Wille's Principles* 642. Cf *Peens v Botha-Odendaal* 1980 2 SA 381 (O) 388; *Weilbach v Grobler* 1982 2 SA 15 (O) 29; *Quarrying Enterprises (Pvt) Ltd v John Viol (Pvt) Ltd* 1985 3 SA 575 (ZH) 581.

237 Lawful occupiers[1] The *bona fide* possessor's action for compensation and *ius retentionis* has also been extended to a lawful occupier,[2] but with the difference that, as in the case of a *bona fide* occupier, an equitable amount may be deducted in respect of the use and occupation of the land.[3][4]

1 Certain lawful occupiers, ie fiduciaries, usufructuaries, lessees and precarious occupiers are, however, in a different position. For

a discussion of the concept "lawful occupier", see par 228 fn 3 ante and the authorities there cited.

2 See *Salzer v Salzer* 1919 EDL 221; *Brown v Brown* 1929 NPD 41; *Harrison v Marchant* 1941 WLD 16; *De Jager v Harris & The Master* 1957 1 SA 171 (SWA); *Kommissaris van Binnelandse Inkomste v Anglo American (OFS) Housing Co Ltd* 1960 3 SA 642 (A); *De Kock v Van Schalkwyk* 1966 1 SA 696 (O); *Banjo v Sungrown (Pty) Ltd* 1969 1 SA 401 (N). Many of these cases have unsatisfactory aspects in that the lawful occupiers were regarded either as *bona fide* possessors or *bona fide* occupiers. There is no doubt that a lawful occupier does have an enrichment action and a *ius retentionis*; see *Nortje v Pool* 1966 3 SA 96 (A) 130.

3 *Brown v Brown* supra; *Von Wuldfling-Eybers v Soundprops 2587 Investments CC* 1994 4 SA 640 (C) 647.

4 See pars 238–242 post.

FIDUCIARIES, USUFRUCTUARIES, LESSEES AND PRECARIOUS OCCUPIERS

238 Introduction Fiduciaries, usufructuaries, lessees and precarious holders are all in lawful occupation of property. Their respective rights to compensation for improvements to the property are governed by special rules and consequently require separate treatment.

239 Fiduciaries[1] As far as compensation for improvements is concerned a fiduciary is treated as a *bona fide* possessor. A fiduciary is not, however, entitled to compensation for day-to-day repairs to the property and the value of the fruit that the fiduciary has had from the property can, for obvious reasons, not be set off against his or her claim for compensation.[2]

1 For a discussion of the concept "fiduciary", see titles SUCCESSION; THINGS.
2 See Voet *Commentarius* 36 1 61; *Du Plessis v Estate Meyer* 1913 CPD 1006; *Brunsdon's Estate v Brunsdon's Estate* 1920 CPD 159; *Engelbrecht v Mundell's Trustee* 1934 CPD 111; *Ex parte Boshoff* 1943 OPD 56; *Ex parte Boshoff (2)* 1943 OPD 170; *Ex parte Van Zyl* 1948 2 SA 210 (C); Joubert 1960 *THRHR* 11.

240 Usufructuaries[1] A usufructuary who is under a duty to maintain the property over which he or she has the usufruct,[2] is not, in the absence of special circumstances, entitled to any compensation in respect of expenses which he or she has incurred in maintaining or making improvements to the property.[3] What will constitute special circumstances entitling the usufructuary to compensation is not wholly clear, but permission by the owner for the usufructuary to incur expenses on improvements to the property will apparently constitute such a circumstance[4] and so, apparently, will the fact that the object of the expenses was the permanent preservation of the property as opposed to normal day-to-day maintenance.[5] In the case of a usufructuary, too, the value of the fruit that he or she has had from the property cannot be set off against the claim for compensation.[6]

1 For a discussion of the concept "usufructuary", see titles SUCCESSION; THINGS.
2 On the usufructuary's duty to maintain, see titles SUCCESSION; THINGS; Joubert 1958 *THRHR* 256.
3 *Brunsdon's Estate v Brunsdon's Estate* 1920 CPD 159; Van der Merwe 2 ed *Sakereg* 166.
4 Cf *Brunsdon's Estate v Brunsdon's Estate* supra.
5 See Grotius *Inleiding* 2 39 6; Schorer *ad Gr* 2 39 6; Van Leeuwen *RHR* 2 9 10, *Cens For* 1 2 15 8; Voet *Commentarius* 7 1 36.
6 See Joubert 1960 *THRHR* 11 14–15.

241 Lessees[1] In Roman-Dutch law all lessees were originally in exactly the same position as *bona fide* possessors as regards compensation for and removal of improvements made by them to the leased property during the currency of the lease.[2] Malpractices among lessees led, however, to legislation by the Estates of Holland which severely restricted the right to compensation of lessees of agricultural land.[3] This legislation was received into South African law[4] and still governs the position of lessees of rural tenements. The question whether the placaats apply to leases of urban tenements as well, is a controversial one.[5]

During the currency of the lease the lessee[6] may remove all structures, except necessary improvements, provided he or she does not leave the property in a worse condition than it was in when he or she received it.[7] The lessee may further remove everything that he or she has sown or planted, provided once again that he or she leaves the property in the state in which he or she received it.[8] Upon termination of the lease the owner of the property becomes owner of all materials attached to the property during the currency of the lease which were not removed before termination[9] and thereafter the lessee may no longer remove such attachments, nor may the lessee enter upon the property to harvest and remove crops.[10] The lessee has, however, a claim for compensation in respect of those attachments which have not been removed at the termination of the lease.[11] This claim is restricted to attachments that were made with the consent of the lessor[12] and is further restricted to the value of the bare material used.[13] The cost of labour cannot be recovered.[14] In terms of the placaats[15] the lessee also has a claim for compensation for ploughing, tilling and sowing, and the cost of seed.[16] For trees which he or she has planted the lessee is entitled to compensation only if he or she planted them on the lessor's instruction or command,[17] and the claim is restricted to their cost at the time of planting.[18]

The lessee's claim for compensation lies against the person who is the owner of the land at the time of termination of the lease.[19] It has been held that the lessor can escape liability by allowing the lessee to remove the attachments from the property.[20] The placaats, however, do not provide for such an election on the part of the lessor.[21] It has further been held that the placaats have no application in the case of necessary improvements.[22] While it is true that the placaats do not refer to necessary improvements by name, it is equally true that they do not distinguish between different kinds of improvements. They simply regulate the question of compensation for improvements in general, which therefore include necessary improvements.[23]

A lessee whose position is governed by the placaats does not have a *ius retentionis* to enforce a claim for compensation. The lessee has to vacate the property upon termination of the lease.[24]

---

1 For a discussion of the concept "lessee", see title LEASE.

2 Grotius *Inleiding* 2 10 8; Van der Keessel *Prael* 2 10 8; *Lessing v Steyn* 1953 4 SA 193 (O) 199. For a discussion of the *bona fide* possessor's position, see pars 228–231 ante.

3 *Placaet van de Staten van Hollandt, tegens de Pachters ende Bruyckers van de Landen* dated 26 September 1658 (2 GPB 2515) re-enacted in identical terms by the *Renovatie-Placaet, noopende de Eygenaers en Pachters van de Landen* dated 24 February 1696 (4 GPB 465).

4 See *Barnard v The Colonial Government* (1887) 5 SC 122 125; *De Beers Consolidated Mines v London & SA Exploration Co* (1893) 10 SC 359 368–370; *Oosthuizen v Estate Oosthuizen* 1903 TS 688 692; *Rubin v Botha* 1911 AD 568 575 579; *Van Wezel v Van Wezel's Trustee* 1924 AD 409 416; *Lessing v Steyn* supra 201; *Syfrets Participation Bond*

Managers Ltd v Estate & Co-op Wine Distributors (Pty) Ltd 1989 1 SA 106 (W) 111; Palabora Mining Co Ltd v Coetzer 1993 3 SA 306 (T) 308.

5 In *De Beers Consolidated Mines v London & SA Exploration Co* supra 369–370 there is an *obiter dictum* to the effect that the placaats apply to urban tenements too. This *dictum* was referred to with approval in *Rubin v Botha* supra 579 (obiter) and *Van Wezel v Van Wezel's Trustee* supra 416. More recently the same view received judicial confirmation in *Syfrets Participation Bond Managers Ltd v Estate & Co-op Wine Distributors (Pty) Ltd* supra 111–112; *Palabora Mining Co Ltd v Coetzer* supra 308. On the other hand, the majority of academic authors argue (persuasively) that the view expressed by the courts cannot be sustained and that the application of the placaats should be limited to lessees of rural

tenements. See eg Van der Merwe *Sakereg* 2ed 166; De Wet & Van Wyk *Kontraktereg en Handelsreg* 4 ed 319 fn 47; Cooper *Landlord and Tenant* 2 ed 335–336; Kerr *The Law of Sale and Lease* 2 ed 418, et seq. See also *The Trustees in Insolvency of Lyons & Stone v The London & SA Exploration Co* (1892) 6 HCG 217 223; *Burrows v McEvoy* 1921 CPD 229 234.

6 The lessee, ie, whose position is governed by the placaats. Lessees to whom the placaats do not apply are in the same position as *bona fide* possessors.

7 *De Beers Consolidated Mines v London & SA Exploration Co* supra 369; *Van Wezel v Van Wezel's Trustee* supra 416 and *Lessing v Steyn* supra 200.

8 *Houghton Estate Co v FS McHattie & WS Barrat* (1894) 1 OR 92 103; *Burrows v McEvoy* supra 236; *Lessing v Steyn* supra 200; *Nogama v Holtshauzen* 1985 2 SA 581 (W) 582–583.

9 Art 12 of the placaats; *De Beers Consolidated Mines v London & SA Exploration Co* supra 372; *Oosthuizen v Estate Oosthuizen* supra 692; *Van Wezel v Van Wezel's Trustee* supra 418; *Lechoana v Cloete* 1925 AD 536 549.

10 *Stollreither v Meintjes* 1907 ORC 6; *Medalie v Botha* 1913 TPD 774; *Du Toit v Vorster* 1928 TPD 385; *Pike v Kockott* 1934 EDL 160; *Lessing v Steyn* supra. Contra, and rejected in the later cases referred to in this footnote, *Hansen & Latelle v Crafford* (1909) 26 SC 426 429; *Japtha v Mills' Executors* 1910 EDL 150 156–157.

11 But not for improvements that are not attachments, such as the clearing of bush or the digging of furrows and wells: see *Von Holdt v Bruwer* 1918 CPD 163.

12 Art 10; Van der Keessel *Thes Sel* 213, *Prael* 2 10 8; *De Beers Consolidated Mines v London & SA Exploration Co* supra 369; *Gibson v Frost* (1896) 13 SC 169; *Von Holdt v Bruwer* supra.

13 Which material does not include sand or lime; see art 11. See further Van der Keessel *Thes Sel* 213, *Prael* 2 10 8; *De Beers Consolidated Mines v London & SA Exploration Co* supra 373; *Kama's Estate v Kreusch* 1910 EDL

53; *Von Holdt v Bruwer* supra 166; *Steinbach v Schmidt* 1930 SWA 8 12–14.

14 Art 11; Van der Keessel *Thes Sel* 213, *Prael* 2 10 8; *De Beers Consolidated Mines v London & SA Exploration Co* supra; *Kama's Estate v Kreusch* supra; *Von Holdt v Bruwer* supra; *Steinbach v Schmidt* supra.

15 Art 10.

16 See *Von Holdt v Bruwer* supra 167. In the case of these activities the lessor's consent is not required, the land being let for agricultural purposes: Cooper 333.

17 Art 13; *De Beers Consolidated Mines v London & SA Exploration Co* supra 369.

18 Art 13; *Oosthuizen v Estate Oosthuizen* supra 693.

19 *Scrooby v Gordon & Co* 1904 TS 937; *Winterton v Estate Allhusen* 1925 CPD 190; *Van der Westhuizen v Van Wyk* 1966 2 PH A93 (O). That it should be the owner of the land at the time of termination of the lease who is held liable, follows from the fact that ownership of the attached material passes only on termination of the lease. It is consequently the owner of the land at that time who becomes owner of the material at the expense of the lessee. It is therefore submitted that *Gibson v Frost* supra, in which the lessee recovered compensation from the first owner, was wrongly decided. See also De Vos *Verrykingsaanspreeklikheid* 238 fn 116; Cooper 333–334.

20 *Kumalo v Piet Retief Village Council* 1931 TPD 165.

21 See also De Vos 103; Cooper 333–334.

22 *De Beers Consolidated Mines v London & SA Exploration Co* supra 369.

23 De Wet and Van Wyk 319; De Vos 104; Van der Merwe 165; *Syfrets Participation Bond Managers Ltd v Estate & Co-op Wine Distributors (Pty) Ltd* supra 111.

24 Art 10; Van der Keessel *Thes Sel* 213, *Prael* 2 10 8; *De Beers Consolidated Mines v London & SA Exploration Co* supra 368; *Oosthuizen v Estate Oosthuizen* supra 692; *Kama's Estate v Kreusch* supra; *Mackenzie v Basha* 1950 1 SA 615 (N) 619.

242 The precarious occupier (*precario tenens*)[1] A precarious occupier probably had no right to compensation for improvements in either Roman or Roman-Dutch law.[2] In South African law, however, the precarious occupier probably has such a right.[3] From the fact that this has not been finally decided, it follows that it cannot have been decided what the extent of the right is. In principle, and having regard to the position of other possessors and occupiers,[4] the precarious occupier ought to be entitled to all his or her *impensae necessariae* and to his or her *impensae utiles* to the extent to which the value of the property was enhanced thereby. Against this claim should be set off the value of the fruit gathered by the occupier. The occupier should also be granted a *ius retentionis* until he or she is compensated.[5]

1 See title THINGS for a discussion of the concept "*precario tenens*". Broadly stated it can be accepted for present purposes that a *precario tenens* ("houer ter bede") is someone who occupies the property of another without any compensation but only until the owner's consent is withdrawn.
2 See De Vos *Verrykingsaanspreeklikheid* 271–272.
3 The matter cannot be said to have been settled but there are *dicta* to the effect that

the occupier does have a right to be compensated. See *Lechoana v Cloete* 1925 AD 536; *Auby & Pastellides (Pty) Ltd v Glen Anil Investments (Pty) Ltd* 1960 4 SA 865 (A) 871; *Lydenburg Properties Ltd v Minister of Community Development* 1963 1 SA 167 (T) 173; *Nortje v Pool* 1966 3 SA 96 (A) 130 137; Van der Merwe *Sakereg* 2 ed 167.
4 See pars 228–231 ante.
5 See De Vos 273–274; Van der Merwe 167.

COMPENSATION FOR WORK DONE OR SERVICES RENDERED

243 Introduction In many bilateral contracts the common intention of the parties, expressed or implied, is that there should be an exchange of performances or that the one party can only demand performance after he or she has performed or tendered performance of his or her own obligations in terms of the agreement. Where on a proper interpretation of the contract the plaintiff's performance is due prior to or simultaneous with that of the performance claimed from the defendant, the latter can raise a defence which has been known since the fourteenth century as the *exceptio non adempleti contractus* ("the *exceptio*"). A defendant who relies on the *exceptio* is not seeking to rescind the contract. It is a stalemate defence and not a remedy for breach of contract. Accordingly, the extent of the plaintiff's failure to perform is irrelevant. It matters not that the plaintiff's performance can be described as substantial or material. Unless the plaintiff's performance is precisely and fully in accordance with the contract, the *exceptio* is available to the defendant, subject, of course, to the *de minimis* rule.[1] An example of a contract where one of the parties is normally obliged to perform first and where the *exceptio* is therefore available to the other side, is *locatio conductio operis* whereunder the *conductor operis* is normally obliged to carry out the work which he or she is engaged to do before the contract money can be claimed.[2]

It is immediately apparent that the *exceptio* can give rise to an inequitable result where, for example, in the case of *locatio conductio operis* the defendant (*locotor operis*) accepts and utilises the plaintiff's defective or incomplete performance while raising the *exceptio* against the plaintiff's claim for payment of the contract price. In a trilogy of cases decided in 1914[3] the Appellate Division came to the aid of the contractor who rendered defective or incomplete performance by allowing him to claim the contract price reduced by the costs of curing his incomplete or defective performance. Unfortunately the judgments in the trilogy created some uncertainty regarding the basis for the defendant's liability in these circumstances. While using the language of unjustified enrichment, the defendant's liability was calculated on the basis of the contract price.[4] In *BK Tooling (Edms) Bpk v Scope Precision Engineering (Edms) Bpk*[5] the Appellate Division availed itself of the opportunity to re-appraise the 1914 trilogy and the popular conception of these judgments. Where the defendant raises the *exceptio*, the plaintiff's claim for the contract price less the cost to cure the incomplete or defective performance, so the court held, is a claim *ex contractu* and not a claim based on unjustified enrichment.[6] It is only where the defect in the plaintiff's performance is of such a nature that the defendant is entitled to cancel the agreement and does so, but is unable to restore the incomplete or defective performance, that an enrichment claim is available.[7]

1 For the principle of reciprocity and the *exceptio non adempleti contractus* in general, see eg: *BK Tooling (Edms) Bpk v Scope Precision Engineering (Edms) Bpk* 1979 1 SA 391 (A); *Motor Racing Enterprises (Pty) Ltd (In Liquidation) v NPS (Electronics) Ltd* [1996] 4 All SA 601 (A); 1996 4 SA 950 (A); *Thompson v Scholtz* [1998] 4 All SA 526 (SCA); 1999 1 SA 232 (SCA); *Grand Mines (Pty) Ltd v Giddey* 1999 1 SA 960 (SCA); Christie *The Law of Contract* 4 ed 488 et seq; title CONTRACT.

2 See eg *ESE Financial Services (Pty) Ltd v Cramer* 1973 2 SA 805 (C) 808–809.

3 *Hauman v Nortje* 1914 AD 293; *Breslin v Hichens* 1914 AD 312; *Van Rensburg v Straughan* 1914 AD 317.

4 See eg *Nortje v Pool* 1966 3 SA 96 (A) 137; De Wet and Van Wyk *Kontraktereg en Handelsreg* 5 ed Vol 1 201 et seq; De Vos *Verrykingsaanspreeklikheid* 274 et seq.

5 Supra.

6 *BK Tooling (Edms) Bpk v Scope Precision Engineering (Edms) Bpk* supra 424 436. In *Thompson v Scholtz* supra this contractual claim for a reduced contract price was held to be available not only to *locatio conductio operis* but also to other types of contracts as well. See also *Klopper v Engelbrecht* 1998 4 SA 788 (W) 799–800; Christie 495.

7 *BK Tooling (Edms) Bpk v Scope Precision Engineering (Edms) Bpk* supra 424 436.

244 Extent of liability In *BK Tooling (Edms) Bpk v Scope Precision Engineering (Edms) Bpk*[1] the Appellate Division did not indicate the criterion for calculating the extent of the defendant's enrichment derived from the contractor's defective performance. It can, however, be inferred with some confidence that the calculation is to proceed according to normal enrichment principles and that the benchmark is not the contract price.[2] Since the contract price will normally include a profit for the contractor, it should not play any part in determining the plaintiff's impoverishment or the defendant's enrichment.[3]

Locatio conductio operarum is also a reciprocal agreement whereby an employee agrees to render services to an employer under the control and supervision of the employer against payment of remuneration.[4] Consequently, an employee who has been dismissed for serious misconduct before he or she has completed his or her contract of service cannot succeed with a contractual claim against his or her employer for services rendered. Our law does not, however, leave the employee without a remedy. On the basis of enrichment the employee will normally receive a *pro rata* part of the wage stipulated in the contract.[5] In a case of this nature the reference to the contract price in calculating the extent of the employer's enrichment appears to be justified. The enrichment of the employer will usually take the form of expenses saved and the only practical way of determining the amount of expenses so saved will normally be by reference to the stipulated wage.[6]

1 1979 1 SA 391 (A).

2 See the reference by Jansen JA at 422F to *Hitchins v Breslin* 1913 TPD 677 685. See also De Vos *Verrykingsaanspreeklikheid* 283. Cf *Hauman v Nortje* 1914 AD 293 304; *Van Rensburg v Straughan* 1914 AD 317 333.

3 See eg De Vos 276–283; De Wet and Van Wyk *Kontraktereg en Handelsreg* 5 ed 202.

4 See eg *Prins v Universiteit van Pretoria* 1980 2 SA 171 (T); De Wet and Van Wyk *Kontraktereg en Handelsreg* 4 ed 338–339.

5 *Spencer v Gostelow* 1920 AD 617 631.

6 See eg De Vos 296; Eiselen and Pienaar *Unjustified Enrichment* 393. Cf De Wet and Van Wyk *Kontraktereg en Handelsreg* 5 ed Vol 1 208.

ENVIRONMENTAL CONSERVATION

by

MA KIDD

(original text by MA RABIE)

REFERENCES TO OTHER TITLES

SELECTED LITERATURE

Fuggle and Rabie (eds) *Environmental Management in SA*
Kidd, M *An Evaluation of the Law Relating to Urban Solid Waste Management in SA* 1995
Rabie "A New Deal for Environmental Conservation: Aspects of the Environment Conservation Act 73 of 1989" 1990 *THRHR* 2
Rabie *SA Environmental Legislation*

GENERAL INTRODUCTION

ENVIRONMENT AND ENVIRONMENTAL LAW

245 General The concept "environment" was virtually unknown in legal language before 1970, although many problems which in effect constituted environmental problems have been addressed by legislation during the past three centuries. However, during the past decades much attention has been focused on environmental law and many legislative provisions have been passed specifically to deal with environmental problems. There is nevertheless a considerable degree of uncertainty as to what exactly constitutes environmental law. This uncertainty is due mainly to a lack of clarity over two fundamental issues, namely:

(a) what is understood by the "environment"; and

(b) which legal rules pertaining to the environment constitute "environmental law".

246 The concept "environment" There is no general agreement on exactly what is understood under the concept environment. Its meaning is often simply taken for granted. It is obvious, nevertheless, that any meaningful classification and discussion of environmental problems, as well as any advocacy of the cause of environmental conservation, presuppose clarity over the pivotal concept of environment. Such clarity is required also for the demarcation and analysis of the field of environmental law, if environmental law is understood to be the law relating to the environment.

Until recently, practical environmental conservation was not unduly hampered by this uncertainty concerning the concept environment. Traditionally, individual components of the environment were identified and treated separately. However, as the need for a holistic approach to environmental problems becomes manifest, the initial focus of concern should centre on the concept of environment as a whole and not only on its individual components. It is especially the declaration of an environmental policy and the processes of integrated environmental management and environmental impact analysis which highlight the need for agreement on what is to be understood by environment.

It should be recognised that environment is a relational concept; it denotes an inter-relationship between humans and their surroundings. Depending upon how extensive the latter is conceived, different approaches may be identified, namely an extensive or a limited approach.[1] This issue is characterised by much controversy.[2]

What is to be considered as the environment, in the final instance, seems to be a policy question upon which opinions may differ. This implies that what is considered as environmental conservation and as environmental law may even differ from one country to another and from time to time. The parameters of the concept environment are obviously still evolving and it would be unwise to attempt to formulate a fixed definition of the concept. In other words, it must to some extent be regarded as open-ended. For the purposes of South African law, environment is defined comprehensively in the National Environmental Management Act[3] as the surroundings within which humans exist and that are made up of:

(a) the land, water and atmosphere of the earth;

(b) micro-organisms, plant and animal life;

(c)   any part or combination of (a) and (b) and the interrelationships among and between them; and

(d)   the physical, chemical, aesthetic and cultural properties and conditions of the foregoing that influence human health and well-being.

1 See generally Rabie 1991 *Stell LR* 202 203–   2 Ibid.
   214.   3 107 of 1998 s 1.

247 Scope of environmental law   Once the meaning of environment has been determined, the broad scope of environmental law is established: an environmental law norm is one which relates to the environment.

Not every legal norm relating to the environment is regarded as constituting environmental law. Environmental law presupposes that the norm in question is aimed at or is used for environmental conservation.

A question which arises is whether a legal norm would qualify as constituting environmental law merely on account of its relevance or even potential relevance for environmental management or whether there should be a more direct, specific connection. According to the general aim of legislation and the degree of environmental relevance of the norms in question, the following gradations may be identified:

(a)   legislation which is aimed exclusively at environmental management and which contains only environmentally specific norms, such as the National Parks Act[1] and the Atmospheric Pollution Prevention Act;[2]

(b)   legislation which is calculated to promote an environmental object and which predominantly contains environmentally specific norms, but which also contains other provisions, for instance the Mountain Catchment Areas Act;[3]

(c)   legislation which is not as such directed at environmental management, but which includes individual provisions that are aimed thereat, for example the Nuclear Energy Act[4] and the Sea-Shore Act;[5]

(d)   legislation which is not aimed at environmental management, but which includes provisions that are directly or potentially of environmental significance, such as land use planning legislation;

(e)   legislation which is not aimed at environmental management, but at environmental exploitation, for instance the older mining legislation; and

(f)   legislation with no environmental relevance.

In addition to legislation, account must be taken of common law norms that may be applied to effect environmental conservation. There seems to be no common law norm designed specifically to serve this purpose. It has been recognised, nevertheless, that common law provisions such as an interdict, the *actio legis Aquiliae*, a public servitude, a trust and judicial review of administrative actions, although not designed specifically for environmental conservation, may be employed for this purpose.

It is important to examine which of the above provisions would qualify as environmental law norms. To commence with the obvious, the environmentally specific norms of categories (a) and (b) undoubtedly constitute environmental law, while the last category would clearly fall outside the purview of environmental law. As far as category (c) is concerned, it is submitted that an environmentally specific norm retains its nature, even though it is encountered in legislation which generally seeks to further some other cause. Purely exploitive legislation (category (e)) would obviously not constitute environmental law, but if legislation governing environmental exploitation contains provisions which seek to minimise the harmful impact upon the environment, such provisions should be regarded as establishing environmental law. The minimisation of such impact is, after all, the tenor of all pollution control provisions.

The most controversial question would probably be whether the provisions included in category (d) should be regarded as environmental law norms. Their environmental significance is established only when they are actually employed to serve the cause of environmental conservation. In and of themselves they constitute neutral provisions. In fact, they may even be utilised for environmentally harmful purposes. The question nevertheless remains whether such norms may be viewed as amounting to environmental law if they are applied to serve the cause of environmental conservation. Opposing views have been expressed as regards this issue.

If the question is approached in a purely dogmatic fashion, one would be inclined to rule out the label of environmental law for category (d). On the other hand, it may be argued that in view of environmental law's constituting cross-divisional law, implying that it contains norms belonging also to other (traditional) fields of law, this category may be regarded as falling within the purview of environmental law. Perhaps one should refer to environmental law in a narrow and a wide sense. It is significant that while most commentators agree on the central core of environmental law, there is some difference of opinion as to peripheral areas, which demonstrates a degree of arbitrariness in the treatment of the subject matter.[6] Some thought has been given to the possible codification of environmental law.[7]

1 57 of 1976.
2 45 of 1965.
3 63 of 1970.
4 46 of 1999.
5 21 of 1935.

6 For a more detailed discussion of the above problem, see Rabie 1991 *Stell LR* 202 215–220.
7 Rabie 1983 *De Rebus* 235 and Van Reenen 1994 *Stell LR* 214 331.

248 Nature of environmental law Among the best known legislative provisions governing environmental conservation are those relating to the declaration of environmental policy, the establishment of conservation areas and the obligation to assess the potential environmental impact of proposed actions. Perhaps the most ubiquitous provisions consist of regulations and directives issued by administrative bodies to landowners and other persons in terms of empowering legislation, as well as of control through administrative authorisation, registration or licensing. In addition, many provisions establish and empower administrative bodies themselves to manage various aspects of the environment.

Control through the issuance of regulations or directives or through a licence system is of course not unique to environmental law. The declaration of policy, previously regarded as belonging in a white paper or being expressed through some other political medium, has lately become an increasingly popular legislative technique. It is not uniquely reserved for environmental law. Likewise, provision for the establishment of particular areas is not restricted to environmental law. Moreover, the requirement governing the submission of an environmental impact report may be likened to an environmental *audi alteram partem*. In essence it is an administrative procedural provision, which, like *audi alteram partem*, is designed to influence administrative decision-making through an increased awareness of its potential consequences. The increasing insistence by environmentalists on public participation in such decision-making is a phenomenon which is shared by many others. In other words, environmental law does not (yet) contain distinctive principles of its own.[1]

Thus far, it appears that the greater proportion of environmental law falls squarely within the domain of administrative law, most of it being administrative law.[2] This characteristic is shared by a number of other fields of law that have been identified, such as the law relating to housing, public health, food and drugs, agriculture and aviation. It seems that in none of these fields any distinctive principles have yet evolved. This, however, has not prevented their recognition as separate areas of law. Nor should it imply that the search for such principles should be abandoned.

What distinguishes environmental law further is that its norms are encountered in several other conventional branches of law. Mention has already been made of its important administrative law component. Criminal law is almost invariably involved in environmental provisions, because most of these provisions are buttressed by criminal sanctions. Moreover, because land use practices and planning are fundamental to environmental conservation, property law is relevant,[3] besides private law remedies generally, especially to combat environmental nuisances[4] and to obtain compensation for environmental damage.[5] The unsuitability and failure of claims for compensation, moreover, has led to the involvement of insurance law, through efforts to establish compulsory insurance in respect of certain types of environmental damage. Although private law plays a far less significant role than does public law,[6] liability for environmental damage may nevertheless assist in reducing pollution.[7] Constitutional law has become relevant particularly through the recognition of a fundamental right to environmental integrity.[8] Environmental concerns play an increasingly important role as far as jurisprudence is concerned.[9] Finally, the global nature and scale of some environmental problems underscore the involvement of international law.[10]

Environmental law thus consists of a collection of legal norms encountered in a number of conventional fields of law. It shares this feature with certain other recognised areas of legal regulation, such as medical law, labour law, press law, social welfare law and the law relating to consumer protection. This factor, accordingly, does not disqualify the recognition of environmental law as a separate area of law.

Environmental law thus practically serves a type of omnibus function, accommodating principles of traditional fields of law, which are united only by their common object in serving environmental conservation. It therefore lacks systematic unity and may be referred to as cross-divisional law. In spite of this it is submitted that environmental law has gradually established itself as an identifiable branch of law.

1 For a different perspective see Cowen 1989 *THRHR* 3.

2 Eg the issue of *locus standi* in respect of judicial review has attracted much attention in environmental law; see Rabie and Eckard 1976 *CILSA* 141; Bray 1989 *CILSA* 33, 1992 *SA Public Law* 329, 1994 *THRHR* 481 and Labuschagne 1994 *SA Public Law* 458.

3 Cf Cowen *New Patterns of Land Ownership: The Transformation of the Concept of Ownership as Plena in re Potestas* 1984; Rabie 1985 *Acta Juridica* 289; Van der Walt 1987 *SALJ* 469 and Rabie "The Influence of Environmental Conservation on Private Landownership" in Van der Walt (ed) *Land Reform and the Future of Landownership in SA* 81.

4 See title NUISANCE.

5 See titles DAMAGES; DELICT.

6 Fuggle and Rabie (eds) *Environmental Management in SA* 137–138.

7 Havenga 1995 *SA Mercantile Law Journal* 187 188.

8 Many recent contributions have addressed this question: Glavovic 1988 *CILSA* 52;

Glazewski 1991 *SAJHR* 167; Rabie 1991 *SAJHR* 208; Lyster 1992 *SALJ* 518; Glazewski 1993 *Journal of African Law* 177; Burns "Green Rights: Theory and Development" in *SA in Transition – Green Rights and an Environmental Management System* 6; Viljoen "Green Rights and the Interim Constitution" in *SA in Transition – Green Rights and an Environmental Management System* 23; Glazewski 1994 *Environmental Liability* 16; Glazewski 1994 *Consultus* 22 (1994 *SAJELP* 3); Williams 1995 *De Rebus* 42; Campanella 1995 *Juta's Business Law* 5; Winstanley 1995 *SAJELP* 99, *Entrenching Environmental Protection: An Analysis of Several Provisions of the Interim Constitution which affect Environmental Conservation and Some Proposals for a New Constitution* LLM Natal, Durban 1995.

9 Van Niekerk 1975 *SALJ* 78; Glavovic 1984 *CILSA* 144; Burger 1991 *SA Public Law* 1.

10 See Devine and Erasmus "International Environmental Law" in Fuggle and Rabie 155.

HISTORICAL DEVELOPMENT OF ENVIRONMENTAL LAW

249 First three centuries of South African law The most prominent environmental issues which were the subjects of legislative regulation during the first half century of white settlement at the Cape since 1652, were the control of drinking water pollution and especially the conservation of wild animals.[1] No less than eight successive statutes within the first 40 years addressed the steadily growing problem of a diminishing wildlife on account of illegal and excessive hunting.

Apart from legislation, common law remedies, mostly of a private law nature, have traditionally been available to individual victims of pollution. These remedies were introduced into South Africa with the adoption of the Roman-Dutch law system.

Except for the continued effort to conserve wild animals, the eighteenth century saw very little manifestation of an environmental awareness and concern on the part of the various authorities.

The latter part of the nineteenth century and the first decade of the twentieth century witnessed a substantial growth in legislation aimed at wildlife conservation. At the same time provisions were enacted to control problem animals and noxious weeds. The first conservation areas were also established towards the end of the nineteenth century. Finally, colonial legislation relating to the protection of public health provided for the control of nuisances, which concept encompassed several aspects of environmental pollution.

The period from Union to the Second World War was characterised by legislation which, although not aimed primarily at conservation, had important environmental implications, such as legislation pertaining to irrigation, forests, public health, and the seashore. The most important conservation statute of this period was the National Parks Act.[2]

1 See generally on the historical development of environmental law Rabie and Fuggle "The Rise of Environmental Concern" in   Fuggle and Rabie *Environmental Management in SA* 11.
2 56 of 1926.

250 1940 to 1969: Three decades of intensified environmental concern This period was heralded by the Sea Fisheries Act,[1] which was the first comprehensive national statute regulating sea fisheries.

A remarkable piece of legislation, the Advertising on Roads and Ribbon Development Act,[2] followed. It controlled the display of advertisements along roads in order to prevent visual disturbance of roadside environments (and has now been assigned to the provinces).

Official action on soil erosion, which had commenced in 1914, culminated in the first substantial legislation, namely the Forest Act.[3] A landmark statute, the Soil Conservation Act of 1946,[4] followed and was eventually replaced by the Soil Conservation Act of 1969.[5]

Nature conservation, both at provincial and national level, continued to grow. Most of the provincial legislation was consolidated in single nature conservation ordinances during the 1960s. The National Parks Act of 1926[6] was replaced by the National Parks Act of 1962.[7]

A new Forest Act[8] replaced the old 1941 Act, while the National Monuments Act of 1969[9] replaced the Natural and Historical Monuments, Relics and Antiques Act of 1934.[10]

The Water Act[11] was the first legislative enactment which dealt comprehensively with industrial water pollution at national level.

The first comprehensive legislation on air pollution control was promulgated in the form of the Atmospheric Pollution Prevention Act.[12]

The control of pesticides originated with the promulgation of the Fertilizers, Farm Feeds, Agricultural Remedies and Stock Remedies Act.[13]

Authorisation for control over radioactive material was initiated through the Atomic Energy Act of 1948,[14] which was replaced by the Atomic Energy Act of 1967.[15] Control over nuclear installations was provided for by the Nuclear Installations (Licensing and Security) Act.[16]

During 1964 and 1967, four statutes consolidating most pre-union legislation were passed which provided the legislative basis for almost all mining of precious stones, precious metals, base minerals, natural oil and source material. These were the Precious Stones Act,[17] the Mining Rights Act,[18] the Mining Titles Registration Act[19] and the Atomic Energy Act.[20]

First steps to centralise land-use planning, thus far left to provincial and local authorities, were taken with the promulgation of the Natural Resources Development Act of 1947,[21] which, after some 20 years was substituted by the Physical Planning Act of 1967.[22]

1 10 of 1940.	12 45 of 1965.
2 21 of 1940. Cf Rabie 1987 *SA Public Law*	13 36 of 1947.
215.	14 35 of 1948.
3 13 of 1941.	15 90 of 1967.
4 45 of 1946.	16 43 of 1963.
5 76 of 1969.	17 73 of 1964.
6 56 of 1926.	18 20 of 1967.
7 42 of 1962.	19 16 of 1967.
8 72 of 1968.	20 90 of 1967.
9 28 of 1969.	21 51 of 1947.
10 4 of 1934.	22 88 of 1967.
11 54 of 1956.	

251 Environmental law 1970 to 1994 The beginning of the seventies is considered to be an environmental watershed, both nationally and internationally.

With the advent of the environmental era, a variety of new legislation provided for environmental control of aspects that either were not previously subject to control or were not treated satisfactorily.

The promulgation of the Mountain Catchment Areas Act,[1] the first substantial legislation aimed at mountain conservation, heralded the environmental era as far as legislation is concerned.

Both the Cape and Transvaal Nature Conservation Ordinances[2] were substituted by new ordinances during 1974 and 1983, respectively. Natal passed its first comprehensive Nature Conservation Ordinance in 1974.[3]

The National Parks Act of 1976[4] replaced the 1962 Act while the 1968 Forest Act was replaced by the Forest Act of 1984.[5] A novel concept of "lake area" was introduced by the Lake Areas Development Act.[6]

The Sea Fisheries Act of 1940 was repealed by the Sea Fisheries Act of 1973,[7] which latter Act was itself substituted by the Sea Fishery Act of 1988.[8]

The control of soil erosion and of noxious weeds was consolidated and improved by the Conservation of Agricultural Resources Act,[9] which replaced the Soil Conservation Act of 1969 and the Weeds Act of 1937. The malpractice of the creation of uneconomic farming units with its concomitant adverse effects on soil conservation was eliminated by the Subdivision of Agricultural Land Act.[10]

The ecological importance of the coastal zone and sea has been given legislative recognition. Apart from traditional legislation pertaining to living marine resources, additional legislation has been enacted, such as the Sea Birds and Seals Protection Act.[11] Moreover, comprehensive provision for marine oil pollution control was initially made in the Prevention and Combating of Pollution of the Sea by Oil Act of 1971,[12] now substituted by the 1981 Act.[13] Control over marine dumping was authorised by the Dumping at Sea Control Act.[14] The first significant legislation since the Sea-Shore Act of 1935[15] to deal with the coastal zone was enacted during 1986 in the form of regulations under the Environment Conservation Act of 1982.[16]

The Physical Planning Act of 1967 was replaced by the Physical Planning Act of 1991.[17]

The provisions of the Factories, Machinery and Building Work Act[18] (substituted by the Machinery and Occupational Safety Act)[19] for the protection of employees in factories and similar situations, were formally implemented for the first time, as far as noise control is concerned, during 1974. Extensive noise control by-laws were promulgated by the local authorities of Johannesburg and Pretoria during 1978. The first comprehensive set of draft noise control regulations was passed under the 1982 Environment Conservation Act.[20] Extensive noise control provisions were passed under the Environment Conservation Act of 1989.[21]

During 1973, the legislative powers of provincial councils were extended to include control over litter, resulting in the Prohibition of the Dumping of Rubbish Ordinance (Orange Free State)[22] and the Prevention of Environmental Pollution Ordinance (Natal).[23] Littering and waste management have been provided for in the 1989 Environment Conservation Act. The Health Act of 1977[24] substituted the veteran legislation of 1919, and deals with various types of pollution from different sources.

Control over exposure of persons to ionising radiation from electronic products was provided for the first time during 1971, with an amendment to the Public Health Act of 1919. Control is now exercised in terms of the Hazardous Substances Act.[25] Apart from being relevant to radioactive material, the Hazardous Substances Act provides for control over a wide variety of declared hazardous substances belonging to any of certain defined groups, including pesticides and solid wastes.

The 1965 Atmospheric Pollution Prevention Act[26] remains the principal legislation controlling air pollution. Its scope has increased significantly since the 1970s, particularly in respect of smoke, vehicular emissions and industrial pollution from scheduled processes.

The most significant environmental legislation during this period was the Environment Conservation Act of 1989.[27] It replaced, and extended the ambit of, the 1982 Act.

1   63 of 1970.
2   Cape Ord 19 of 1974 and Tvl Ord 12 of 1983.
3   Natal Ord 15 of 1974.
4   57 of 1976.
5   122 of 1984.
6   39 of 1975.
7   58 of 1973.
8   12 of 1988.
9   43 of 1983.
10   70 of 1970.
11   46 of 1973.
12   67 of 1971.
13   6 of 1981.
14   73 of 1980.
15   21 of 1935.
16   100 of 1982.
17   125 of 1991.
18   22 of 1941.
19   6 of 1983.
20   100 of 1982.
21   73 of 1989.
22   8 of 1976.
23   21 of 1981.
24   63 of 1977.
25   15 of 1973.
26   45 of 1965.
27   73 of 1989.

252 Environmental law since 1994 There has been considerable legislative activity since 1994, which signalled the onset of the new constitutional era. Much of the legislation has been profoundly influenced by the so-called "environmental right" in the Constitution,[1] which provides that:

everyone has the right:

(a) to an environment that is not harmful to their health or well-being; and

(b) to have the environment protected, for the benefit of present and future generations, through reasonable legislative and other measures that:

(i) prevent pollution and ecological degradation;

(ii) promote conservation; and

(iii) secure ecologically sustainable development and use of natural resources while promoting justifiable economic and social development.

Much of the new legislation also has a strong theme of equitable access to resources, which was not the case under much of the pre-1994 legislation. Other influences include international conventions, several of which South Africa ratified only in the 1990s.

Probably the most important of the new enactments is the National Environmental Management Act,[2] which provides a framework for environmental management in the country, and, as such, is largely concerned with the regulation of government activities, although it does contain several important sections both regulating and empowering citizens. This Act has already been amended twice, fortifying the provisions relating to environmental authorisations and enforcement.

As far as environmental authorisations are concerned, regulations in terms of the Environment Conservation Act were promulgated in 1997 relating to activities identified as having a detrimental impact on the environment and the authorisation process to be followed for such activities. The law relating to environmental authorisations has been a central aspect of environmental management and law since the promulgation of these regulations.

Water resources were for many years regulated by the Water Act,[3] which provided for access to water resources in a manner that excluded many members of the population from equitable access. This Act, and the old water law regime, has been replaced by the innovative National Water Act.[4]

Another sector where access to resources has been widened is in forestry, where the National Forests Act[5] has replaced the Forest Act of 1984. Other significant environmental law enactments since 1994 are the National Environmental Management: Protected Areas Act;[6] the National Environmental Management: Biodiversity Act;[7] and the Marine Living Resources Act.[8]

From the perspective of minerals and energy matters, several new Acts with direct impact on environmental concerns have appeared since 1994, namely the Mineral and Petroleum Resources Development Act,[9] and legislation concerning the nuclear industry and nuclear safety: the Nuclear Energy Act[10] and the National Nuclear Regulator Act.[11]

South Africa's international responsibilities under the World Heritage Convention are provided for in the World Heritage Convention Act.[12]

1 Constitution of the Republic of SA 108 of 1996 s 24. Cf Kidd *Environmental Law: A South African Guide* ch 3; Glazewski *Environmental Law in SA* ch 3.

2 107 of 1998.
3 54 of 1956.
4 36 of 1998.
5 84 of 1998.

6 57 of 2003.
7 10 of 2004.
8 18 of 1998.
9 28 of 2002.

10 46 of 1999.
11 47 of 1999.
12 49 of 1999.

OFFICIAL ADMINISTRATION OF ENVIRONMENTAL AFFAIRS

253 General Although the government in the past has been concerned with the administration of a variety of pieces of environmental legislation, it demonstrated a serious general environmental concern only in January 1971, when a cabinet committee was appointed to investigate environmental pollution.[1] Pollution and environmental conservation were discussed in Parliament in March 1971. Subsequently, a pollution subsidiary committee of the Prime Minister's Planning Advisory Council was appointed to investigate and report on the matter. It subsequently produced a comprehensive report.

A non-statutory South African Committee on Environmental Conservation was in turn established to advise this cabinet committee. The committee, renamed the Council for the Environment in 1975, consisted of representatives from government departments and other administrative bodies concerned with environmental affairs. The council, which functioned until the early 1980s, was given broad terms of reference regarding environmental conservation generally. It was replaced by a statutory council in 1982.

Before 1973, priority and policy determination had been effected through the Planning Advisory Council, while the function of co-ordinating legislation relating to the control of pollution and the conservation of natural resources had been entrusted to the Department of Planning. In 1973 it became the Department of Planning and the Environment's function to meet this need. In 1975, the Physical Planning Act,[2] which had been administered by this department, was amended and renamed the Environment Planning Act,[3] to make provision for the consideration of environmental factors in land-use planning. In 1979 the department became the Department of Environmental Planning and Energy. As a result of the rationalisation process in the civil service in 1980, the amalgamated Department of Water Affairs, Forestry and Environmental Conservation was formed. This department's name was subsequently changed to the Department of Environment Affairs, water affairs having been excised from the department's jurisdiction. It acquired jurisdiction over a number of environmental statutes which had previously been administered by other departments. Its task is therefore no longer restricted – as was the task of its predecessor – to mainly co-ordinating the environmentally relevant actions of other administrative bodies; it now administers some of the most important environmental statutes. It was also concerned with the devolution of powers process, providing policy guidelines for the administration of legislation by other bodies, mainly the various provincial administrations. The department's title was once again changed in 1994; it is now the Department of Environmental Affairs and Tourism.

Although the Department of Environmental Affairs and Tourism is now undoubtedly the most important body which administers environmental affairs at national level, several other central government departments are involved in the implementation of environmental legislation. Among the most important are the Departments of Agriculture, Health, Mineral and Energy Affairs, Water Affairs and Forestry, Land Affairs, Labour, Transport and Education. In addition to the abovementioned departments themselves, a number of statutory bodies which operate under the auspices of such departments, also exercise environmental functions, for example the National Parks Board.

Since the process of the devolution of administrative powers was introduced towards the end of the 1980s, an increasing number of environmental functions has
been transferred to the respective provincial administrations. Traditionally, the only
noteworthy important environmental function exercised by provincial administrations
was nature conservation, in other words the conservation of wild animals, plants and
freshwater fish, although land-use planning and control over solid waste was also
partly undertaken by provincial administrations. Additional devolved functions were
extended to include executive powers in respect of the sea-shore, sea fisheries, islands
and the coastal zone in general, besides control over certain state forests, including
mountain catchment areas, wilderness areas and forest nature reserves, as well as
control over protected natural environments.

According to the Constitution[4] various environmental matters – environment; nature conservation, excluding national parks, botanical gardens and marine resources;
pollution control and soil conservation – fall within the legislative and administrative
competence of the various provinces, concurrently with national government.[5]

Also in terms of the Constitution, local authorities exercise a variety of environmental functions, *inter alia*, air pollution, water and sanitation services including
domestic waste-water and sewage disposal systems, cleansing, control of public nuisances, noise pollution, and refuse removal, refuse dumps and solid waste disposal.[6]

1 See generally on the administration of
environmental affairs Schwella and Muller
"Environmental Administration" in Fuggle
and Rabie (eds) *Environmental Management in
SA* 1992 64.

2 88 of 1967.

3 88 of 1967.

4 Constitution of the Republic of SA 108 of
1996.

5 S 104(1) read with Sch 4. In certain exceptional instances, listed in s 146, an Act of

Parliament, which may deal with these subjects, will override provincial legislation.
See, generally, title CONSTITUTIONAL LAW.

6 S 156(1) read with Schs 4 and 5. National
and provincial governments have the legislative and executive authority to see to the
effective performance by municipalities of
their functions in respect of these matters by
regulating the exercise by municipalities of
their executive authority (s 155(7)).

NATIONAL ENVIRONMENTAL MANAGEMENT ACT

254 Scope and purpose There has never been one all-embracing environmental
statute in South Africa – environmental conservation provisions are contained in an
extremely wide variety of parliamentary Acts, provincial land laws, local by-laws and
ministerial regulations. Probably the most important of these, from the perspective of
environmental conservation and management in general, is the National Environmental
Management Act.[1] The purpose of the Act is to provide for co-operative environmental governance by establishing principles for decision-making on matters affecting
the environment, institutions that promote co-operative governance and procedures
for co-ordinating environmental functions exercised by organs of state; to provide for
certain aspects of the administration and enforcement of other environmental management laws; and to provide for matters connected therewith.[2] The Act, as the long
title suggests, is primarily concerned with regulating the way that organs of state
interact in management of the environment (the Act does bind the state except in so
far as any criminal liability is concerned),[3] but there are several provisions that regulate
citizens directly. The Act does not directly address specific environmental issues such
as biodiversity conservation and pollution and waste management; these and other
environmental concerns are largely regulated by other instruments.

1 107 of 1998.
2 Long title, amended by the National
   Environmental Management Amendment

Act 46 of 2003 (not yet in operation).
3 National Environmental Management Act
   107 of 1998 s 48.

255 National environmental management principles The National Environmental Management Act[1] contains an extensive list of principles that apply throughout the Republic to the actions of all organs of state that may significantly affect the environment and must:

(a) apply alongside all other appropriate and relevant considerations, including the state's responsibility to respect, protect, promote and fulfil the social and economic rights in chapter 2 of the Constitution[2] and in particular the basic needs of categories of persons disadvantaged by unfair discrimination;

(b) serve as the general framework within which environmental management and implementation plans must be formulated;

(c) serve as guidelines by reference to which any organ of state must exercise any function when taking any decision in terms of the Act or any statutory provision concerning the protection of the environment;

(d) serve as principles by reference to which a conciliator appointed under the Act must make recommendations; and

(e) guide the interpretation, administration and implementation of the Act, and any other law concerned with the protection or management of the environment.[3]

The first two principles provide that environmental management must place people and their needs at the forefront of its concern, and serve their physical, psychological, developmental, cultural and social interests equitably;[4] and that development must be socially, environmentally and economically sustainable.[5] These are followed by 18 further principles, some of which are further subdivided:

(a) Sustainable development requires the consideration of all relevant factors including the following:

(i) that the disturbance of ecosystems and loss of biological diversity are avoided, or, where they cannot be altogether avoided, are minimised and remedied;

(ii) that pollution and degradation of the environment are avoided, or, where they cannot be altogether avoided, are minimised and remedied;

(iii) that the disturbance of landscapes and sites that constitute the nation's cultural heritage is avoided, or where it cannot be altogether avoided, is minimised and remedied;

(iv) that waste is avoided, or where it cannot be altogether avoided, minimised and re-used or recycled where possible and otherwise disposed of in a responsible manner;

(v) that the use and exploitation of non-renewable natural resources is responsible and equitable, and takes into account the consequences of the depletion of the resource;

(vi) that the development, use and exploitation of renewable resources and the ecosystems of which they are part do not exceed the level beyond which their integrity is jeopardised;

(vii) that a risk-averse and cautious approach is applied, which takes into account the limits of current knowledge about the consequences of decisions and actions; and

(viii) that negative impacts on the environment and on people's environmental rights be anticipated and prevented, and where they cannot be altogether prevented, are minimised and remedied.[6]

(b) Environmental management must be integrated, acknowledging that all elements of the environment are linked and interrelated, and it must take into account the effects of decisions on all aspects of the environment and all people in the environment by pursuing the selection of the best practicable environmental option.[7]

(c) Environmental justice must be pursued so that adverse environmental impacts are not distributed in such a manner as to unfairly discriminate against any person, particularly vulnerable and disadvantaged persons.[8]

(d) Equitable access to environmental resources, benefits and services to meet basic human needs and ensure human well-being must be pursued and special measures may be taken to ensure access thereto by categories of persons disadvantaged by unfair discrimination.[9]

(e) Responsibility for the environmental health and safety consequences of a policy, programme, project, product, process, service or activity exists throughout its life cycle.[10]

(f) The participation of all interested and affected parties in environmental governance must be promoted, and all people must have the opportunity to develop the understanding, skills and capacity necessary for achieving equitable and effective participation, and participation by vulnerable and disadvantaged persons must be ensured.[11]

(g) Decisions must take into account the interests, needs and values of all interested and affected parties, and this includes recognising all forms of knowledge, including traditional and ordinary knowledge.[12]

(h) Community well-being and empowerment must be promoted through environmental education, the raising of environmental awareness, the sharing of knowledge and experience and other appropriate means.[13]

(i) The social, economic and environmental impacts of activities, including disadvantages and benefits, must be considered, assessed and evaluated, and decisions must be appropriate in the light of such consideration and assessment.[14]

(j) The right of workers to refuse work that is harmful to human health or the environment and to be informed of dangers must be respected and protected.[15]

(k) Decisions must be taken in an open and transparent manner, and access to information must be provided in accordance with the law.[16]

(l) There must be inter-governmental co-ordination and harmonisation of policies, legislation and actions relating to the environment.[17]

(m) Actual or potential conflicts of interest between organs of state should be resolved through conflict resolution procedures.[18]

(n) Global and international responsibilities relating to the environment must be discharged in the national interest.[19]

(o) The environment is held in public trust for the people, the beneficial use of environmental resources must serve the public interest and the environment must be protected as the people's common heritage.[20]

(p) The costs of remedying pollution, environmental degradation and consequent adverse health effects and of preventing, controlling or minimising further pollution, environmental damage or adverse health effects must be paid for by those responsible for harming the environment.[21]

(q) The vital role of women and youth in environmental management and development must be recognised and their full participation therein must be promoted.[22]

(r) Sensitive, vulnerable, highly dynamic or stressed ecosystems, such as coastal shores, estuaries, wetlands, and similar systems require specific attention in management and planning procedures, especially where they are subject to significant human resource usage and development pressure.[23]

The Constitutional Court has assumed, without deciding, that the principles can be applicable in a dispute between members of the public and the government.[24]

1 107 of 1998.
2 Constitution of the Republic of SA 108 of 1996.
3 National Environmental Management Act 107 of 1998 s 2(1).
4 S 2(2).
5 S 2(3).
6 S 2(4)(a).
7 S 2(4)(b).
8 S 2(4)(c).
9 S 2(4)(d).
10 S 2(4)(e).
11 S 2(4)(f).
12 S 2(4)(g).
13 S 2(4)(h).
14 S 2(4)(i).
15 S 2(4)(j).

16 S 2(4)(k).
17 S 2(4)(l).
18 S 2(4)(m).
19 S 2(4)(n).
20 S 2(4)(o).
21 S 2(4)(p).
22 S 2(4)(q).
23 S 2(4)(r).
24 *Minister of Public Works v Kyalami Ridge Environmental Association (Mukhwevho intervening)* 2001 7 BCLR 652 (CC); 2001 3 SA 1151 (CC) 69. Cf *BP Southern Africa (Pty) Ltd v MEC for Agriculture, Conservation, Environment & Land Affairs* [2004] 3 All SA 201 (W); 2004 5 SA 124 (W); *Sasol Oil (Pty) Ltd v Metcalfe* 2004 5 SA 161 (W).

256 National Environmental Management Forum The objects of the National Environmental Management Forum, established by the National Environmental Management Act,[1] are to inform the minister of the views of stakeholders regarding the application of the national environmental management principles; and advise the minister on any matter concerning environmental management and governance and specifically the setting and achievement of objectives and priorities for environmental governance; and appropriate methods of monitoring compliance with the national environmental management principles.[2] The forum may, on its own initiative and after consultation with the director-general, draw the minister's attention to any matter concerning environmental management requiring attention, and the minister may refer matters for consideration by the forum.[3]

The forum consists of at least 12 but not more than 15 members appointed by the minister,[4] who will be appointed on the basis that they represent stakeholders, or have experience, expertise or skills necessary to enable the forum to carry out its functions, but the minister must take into account the desirability of appointing women, youth and persons disadvantaged by unfair discrimination and ensure representation of vulnerable and disadvantaged persons.[5] Before the members are appointed, the minister must invite nominations from organised labour, organised business, non-governmental organisations and community-based organisations in a manner that he or she may consider appropriate, and invite nominations from others by notice in the *Government Gazette*, at least two nationally distributed newspapers, appropriate local newspapers and on the radio, specifying a period within which nominations must be submitted. The notice must stipulate the procedure to be adopted regarding such nominations, and the minister must consult with the MECs, the committees of the National Assembly and the National Council of Provinces that scrutinise environmental affairs.[6] The minister appoints the chairperson of the forum.[7]

Each member holds office for a period of two years,[8] and may be appointed for one further term.[9] A member of the forum must vacate the office in certain circumstances.[10] Members of the forum and members of a committee of the forum may be paid such remuneration and allowances for their services as the minister may determine with the concurrence of the Minister of Finance.[11] The minister must lay down rules for the functioning of the forum, including a constitution for the forum; the manner and timing of reports by the forum; and consultation with the director-general;[12] and make available funds for the functioning of the forum for purposes other than the payment of remuneration, from money appropriated by Parliament for this purpose, and funds obtained from donations or grants.[13] The director-general is responsible for providing staff assistance to the forum.[14] The minister must present an annual report to Parliament on the work of the forum, including the work plan for the next year, information and recommendations submitted, and a financial report and budget.[15] The meetings of the forum must be open to the public and all documents considered or produced by the forum must be available for inspection by the public.[16]

1 107 of 1998 s 3(1).
2 S 3(2).
3 S 3(3).
4 S 4(1).
5 S 4(2).
6 S 4(3).
7 S 4(4).
8 S 5(1). Cf s 4(5) for provision for members' alternates and replacements.
9 S 5(2).
10 S 5(3).
11 S 5(4). Cf s 5(5) for recusal of members in the case of financial interest.
12 S 6(1)(a).
13 S 6(1)(b).
14 S 6(2).
15 S 6(3).
16 S 6(4).

257 Committee for Environmental Co-ordination The object of the Committee for Environmental Co-ordination, which is established by the National Environmental Management Act,[1] is to promote the integration and co-ordination of environmental functions by the relevant organs of state, and in particular to promote the achievement of the purpose and objectives of environmental implementation plans and environmental management plans.[2] The committee's functions include the following:[3]

(a) scrutinising, reporting and making recommendations on the environmental implementation plans submitted to it;

(b) investigating and making recommendations regarding the assignment and delegation of functions between organs of state under the Act or any other law affecting the environment and regarding the practical working arrangements, including memoranda of understanding between the organs of state represented by members and other organs of state;

(c) investigating and recommending the establishment of mechanisms in each province, with the concurrence of the MEC, for providing a single point in the province for the receipt of applications for authorisations, licences and similar permissions required for activities under legal provisions concerned with the protection of the environment where such authorisations, licences or permissions are required from more than one organ of state, and procedures for the co-ordinated consideration of such applications by the organs of state concerned;

(d) making recommendations to co-ordinate the application of integrated environmental management as contemplated in chapter 5 of the Act, including co-operation in environmental assessment procedures and requirements and making determinations regarding the prevention of duplication of efforts;

(e) making recommendations aimed at securing compliance with the national environmental management principles and national norms and standards contemplated in section 146(2)(b)(i) of the Constitution;[4]

(f) making recommendations regarding the harmonisation of the environmental functions of all relevant national departments and spheres of government;

(g)   advising the minister on providing guidelines for the preparation of environmental management plans and environmental implementation plans; and

(h)   endeavouring to ensure compliance with the national environmental management principles by making appropriate recommendations, requiring reports from its
members and advising government on law reform.

The committee consists of the Director-General: Environmental Affairs and Tourism (chairperson);[5] the director-generals of some nine other government departments;
the provincial heads of department; one representative of organised local government;
and any other director-general appointed by the minister with the concurrence of the
minister under whose portfolio that department falls.[6] The committee may co-opt
persons and invite persons to meetings in order to assist it in carrying out its functions.[7] Provision is made for meetings, subcommittees and working groups of the
committee.[8] The committee is required to report annually to the minister (copies of
such report being made available to the public on request)[9] on the following:[10]

(a)   the work of the committee and the work plan for the next year;

(b)   comments submitted to the director-general on the environmental implementation and environmental management plans received;

(c)   recommendations made in respect of environmental implementation and environmental management plans received;

(d)   recommendations made in order to secure compliance with the principles set
out in section 2 of the National Environmental Management Act and national norms
and standards;

(e)   law reform undertaken and proposed by organs of state represented on the
committee;

(f)   compliance with environmental implementation and management plans by
municipalities; and

(g)   any other matter relevant to the co-ordination of policies, plans and programmes that may affect the environment.

The minister must present an annual report to Parliament on the work of the committee.[11]

1   107 of 1998 s 7(1).
2   S 7(2). These plans are explained in par 258
     post.
3   S 7(3).
4   Constitution of the Republic of SA 108 of
     1996: these are norms and standards laid
     down in national legislation in order to deal
     with a matter that, to be dealt with effec-
     tively, requires uniformity across the nation
     which will be provided by national legisla-
     tion by establishing such norms and stan-
     dards: s 146(2)(b) of the Constitution.

5   National Environmental Management Act
     107 of 1998 s 8(1)(a).
6   S 8(1). Cf s 8(4) and (5) for provision for
     alternate members.
7   S 8(2). Cf s 8(3) which requires considera-
     tion to be given to local government repre-
     sentation.
8   S 9.
9   S 10(2).
10   S 10(1).
11   S 10(3).

258 Environmental implementation and management plans Every national
department listed in Schedule 1 of the National Environmental Management Act[1] as
exercising functions which may affect the environment and every province had to
prepare an environmental implementation plan within one year of the promulgation
of the Act and at least every four years thereafter.[2] Every national department listed in
Schedule 2[3] as exercising functions involving the management of the environment
must prepare an environmental management plan within one year of the promulgation of the Act and at least every four years thereafter. National departments listed in

both Schedule 1 and Schedule 2 may prepare consolidated environmental implementation and management plans,[4] and may consist of the assembly of information or plans compiled for other purposes and may form part of any other process or procedure.[5] Every organ of state required to prepare these plans must in their preparation, and before submitting such plans, take into consideration every other environmental implementation plan and environmental management plan already adopted with a view to achieving consistency among such plans.[6] The director-general must, at the request of a national department or province, assist with the preparation of an environmental implementation plan,[7] and the minister may issue guidelines to assist provinces and national departments in the preparation of environmental implementation and environmental management plans.[8]

The purpose of environmental implementation and management plans is to:

(a)   co-ordinate and harmonise the environmental policies, plans, programmes and decisions of the various national departments that exercise functions that may affect the environment or are entrusted with powers and duties aimed at the achievement, promotion and protection of a sustainable environment, and of provincial and local spheres of government, in order to:

(i) minimise the duplication of procedures and functions; and

(ii) promote consistency in the exercise of functions that may affect the environment;

(b)   give effect to the principle of co-operative government in chapter 3 of the Constitution;[9]

(c)   secure the protection of the environment across the country as a whole;

(d)   prevent unreasonable actions by provinces in respect of the environment that are prejudicial to the economic or health interests of other provinces or the country as a whole; and

(e)   enable the minister to monitor the achievement, promotion, and protection of a sustainable environment.[10]

1 107 of 1998: these departments are: Environmental Affairs and Tourism; Land Affairs; Agriculture; Housing; Trade and Industry; Water Affairs and Forestry; Transport; Defence: Sch 1.

2 The minister may by notice in the *Government Gazette* extend the date for the submission of any environmental implementation plans and environmental management plans for periods not exceeding 12 months, on application by any organ of state, or on his or her own initiative with the agreement of the relevant minister where it concerns a national department, and after consultation with the Committee of Environmental

Co-ordination, amend Schs 1 and 2: s 11(5).

3 These departments are: Environmental Affairs and Tourism; Water Affairs and Forestry; Minerals and Energy; Land Affairs; Health; Labour.

4 S 11(3).
5 S 11(7).
6 S 11(4).
7 S 11(6).
8 S 11(8).
9 Constitution of the Republic of SA 108 of 1996.
10 National Environmental Management Act 107 of 1998 s 12.

259 Content of plans Every environmental implementation plan must contain:

(a)   a description of policies, plans and programmes that may significantly affect the environment;

(b)   a description of the manner in which the relevant national department or province will ensure that these policies, plans and programmes will comply with the national environmental management principles as well as any national norms and standards as envisaged under section 146(2)(b)(i) of the Constitution[1] and set out by the minister, or by any other minister, which have as their objective the achievement, promotion, and protection of the environment;

(c) a description of the manner in which the relevant national department or province will ensure that its functions are exercised so as to ensure compliance with relevant legislative provisions; and

(d) recommendations for the promotion of the objectives and plans for the implementation of the procedures and regulations referred to in chapter 5 of the National Environmental Management Act.[2]

Every environmental management plan must contain:

(a) a description of the functions exercised by the relevant department in respect of the environment;

(b) a description of environmental norms and standards, including norms and standards contemplated in section 146(2)(b)(i) of the Constitution, set or applied by the relevant department;

(c) a description of the policies, plans and programmes of the relevant department that are designed to ensure compliance with its policies by other organs of state and persons;

(d) a description of priorities regarding compliance with the relevant department's policies by other organs of state and persons;

(e) a description of the extent of compliance with the relevant department's policies by other organs of state and persons;

(f) a description of arrangements for co-operation with other national departments and spheres of government, including any existing or proposed memoranda of understanding entered into, or delegation or assignment of powers to other organs of state, with a bearing on environmental management; and

(g) proposals for the promotion of the objectives and plans for the implementation of the procedures and regulations referred to in chapter 5 of the National Environmental Management Act.[3]

1 Constitution of the Republic of SA 108 of 1996.
2 107 of 1998 s 13. The minister may, after consultation with the committee, make regulations for the purpose of giving effect to s 13(1)(b) and (c): s 13(2); see par 303 post.
3 S 14.

260 Submission, scrutiny and adoption of plans Every environmental implementation plan and every environmental management plan must be submitted to the committee[1] by a date to be set by the minister.[2] The committee scrutinises every environmental implementation plan and either recommends adoption of such plan, or reports to the minister as well as every other minister responsible for a department which is represented on the committee and every provincial premier concerned on the extent to which the environmental implementation plan concerned fails to comply with the national environmental management principles; the purpose and objectives of environmental implementation plans; or any relevant environmental management plan; and specifies changes needed in the environmental implementation plan concerned.[3] If the committee recommends adoption of an environmental implementation plan, then the relevant organ of state must adopt and publish its plan in the relevant *Government Gazette* within 90 days of such approval and the plan becomes effective from the date of publication.[4]

A national department which has submitted an environmental management plan must adopt and publish its plan in the *Gazette* within 90 days of such submission and the plan becomes effective from the date of publication.[5] The exercise of functions by organs of state may not be delayed or postponed on account of:

(a)   the failure of any organ of state to submit an environmental implementation plan;

(b)   the scrutiny of any environmental implementation plan by the committee;

(c)   the amendment of any environmental implementation plan following scrutiny of the plan by the committee;

(d)   any difference or disagreement regarding any environmental implementation plan and the resolution of that difference or disagreement; or

(e)   the failure of any organ of state to adopt and publish its environmental implementation or management plan.[6]

1   "Committee" means the Committee for Environmental Co-ordination.
2   National Environmental Management Act 107 of 1998 s 15(1).
3   S 15(2)(a). Cf s 15(3) and (4) for resolution of disagreement between committee and national department and committee and province respectively.
4   S 15(2)(b).
5   S 15(5).
6   S 15(6).

261 Compliance with plans Every organ of state must exercise every function it may have,[1] and that may significantly affect the protection of the environment, substantially in accordance with the environmental implementation or management plan prepared, submitted and adopted by that organ of state in accordance with this chapter of the National Environmental Management Act.[2] However, any substantial deviation from a plan must be reported immediately to the director-general and the committee.[3] Every organ of state must report annually within four months of the end of its financial year on the implementation of its adopted environmental management or implementation plan to the director-general and the committee.[4] The minister may, after consultation with the committee, recommend to any organ of state which has not submitted and adopted an environmental implementation or management plan, that it comply with a specified provision of an adopted environmental implementation plan or submitted environmental management plan.[5]

The director-general monitors compliance with environmental implementation and management plans and may take any steps or make any inquiries he or she deems fit in order to determine if plans are being complied with by organs of state; and if, as a result of such monitoring, the director-general is of the opinion that a plan is not substantially being complied with, he or she may serve a written notice on the organ of state concerned, calling on it to take such specified steps as he or she considers necessary to remedy the failure of compliance.[6] Within 30 days of the receipt of such notice, an organ of state must respond to the notice in writing setting out any objections to the notice, steps that will be taken to remedy failures of compliance, or other information that the organ of state considers relevant to the notice.[7] After considering the representations from the organ of state and any other relevant information, the director-general must within 30 days of receiving a response issue a final notice confirming, amending or cancelling the original notice; and specify steps and a time period within which steps must be taken to remedy the failure of compliance.[8]

Each provincial government must ensure that the relevant provincial environmental implementation plan is complied with by each municipality within its province, and municipalities adhere to the relevant environmental implementation and that management plans, and the national environmental management principles in the preparation of any policy, programme or plan, including the establishment of integrated development plans and land development objectives.[9]

The director-general must keep a record of all environmental implementation plans and environmental management plans, relevant agreements between organs of state and any reports submitted, and such plans, reports and agreements must be available for inspection by the public.[10]

1 Including those powers delegated or assigned to it by or under any law.
2 107 of 1998.
3 S 16(1)(a).
4 S 16(1)(b).
5 S 16(1)(c).
6 S 16(2).
7 S 16(3)(a).

8 S 16(3)(b). Cf s 16(3)(c) and (d) for resolution of disputes between the director-general and organs of state concerning compliance with plans.
9 S 16(4). S 16(2) and (3) apply to compliance by municipalities with the necessary changes.
10 S 16(5).

262 Reference to conciliation and arbitration Any minister, member of the executive council ("MEC") or municipal council, where a difference or disagreement arises concerning the exercise of any of its functions which may significantly affect the environment, or before whom an appeal arising from a difference or disagreement regarding the protection of the environment is brought under any law, may, before reaching a decision, consider the desirability of first referring the matter to conciliation and must, if he, she or it considers conciliation appropriate either:

(a) refer the matter to the director-general for conciliation under the National Environmental Management Act;[1] or

(b) appoint a conciliator on the conditions, including time-limits, that he, she or it may determine; or

(c) where a conciliation or mediation process is provided for under any other relevant law administered by such minister, MEC or municipal council, refer the matter for mediation or conciliation under such other law. Alternatively, if he, she or it considers conciliation inappropriate or if conciliation has failed, he, she or it may make a decision.[2] Anyone may request the minister, an MEC or municipal council to appoint a facilitator to call and conduct meetings of interested and affected parties with the purpose of reaching agreement to refer a difference or disagreement to conciliation in terms of the Act, and the minister, MEC or municipal council may appoint a facilitator and determine the manner in which the facilitator must carry out his or her tasks, including time-limits.[3] A court or tribunal hearing a dispute regarding the protection of the environment may order the parties to submit the dispute to a conciliator appointed by the director-general in terms of the Act and suspend the proceedings pending the outcome of the conciliation.[4]

Where a matter has been referred to conciliation in terms of the Act, the director-general may, on the conditions, including time-limits, that he or she may determine, appoint a conciliator acceptable to the parties to assist in resolving a difference or disagreement, but if the parties to the difference or disagreement do not reach agreement on the person to be appointed, the director-general may appoint a person who has adequate experience in or knowledge of conciliation of environmental disputes.[5]

A conciliator appointed in terms of the Act must attempt to resolve the matter by obtaining such information, whether documentary or oral, as is relevant to the resolution of the difference or disagreement; by mediating the difference or disagreement; by making recommendations to the parties to the difference or disagreement; or in any other manner that he or she considers appropriate.[6] In carrying out his or her functions, a conciliator must take into account the national environmental management principles.[7] A conciliator may keep or cause to be kept, whether in writing or by mechanical or electronic means, a permanent record of all or part of the proceedings relating to the conciliation of a matter,[8] and where such record has been kept, any member of the public may obtain a readable copy of the record upon payment of a fee as approved by Treasury.[9] Where conciliation does not resolve the matter, a conciliator may inquire of the parties whether they wish to refer the matter to arbitration and may with their concurrence endeavour to draft terms of reference for such arbitration.[10] The conciliator must submit a report to the director-general, the parties and the person who referred the matter for conciliation, setting out the result of his or her conciliation, and indicating whether or not an agreement has been reached.[11] In the event of no agreement having been reached, the report may contain the conciliator's recommendations and reasons therefor.[12] Where relevant, the report must contain the conciliator's comments on the conduct of the parties.[13] The report and any agreement reached as a result of the conciliation must be available for inspection by the public and any member of the public may obtain a copy thereof upon payment of a fee as approved by Treasury.[14] The director-general may from time to time, with the concurrence of the Minister of Finance, appoint persons or organisations with relevant knowledge or expertise to provide conciliation and mediation services.[15]

A difference or disagreement regarding the protection of the environment may be referred to arbitration in terms of the Arbitration Act,[16] and where this happens the parties thereto may appoint as arbitrator a person from the panel of arbitrators established in terms of section 21.[17]

1 107 of 1998.
2 S 17(1), subject to a proviso regarding the Development Facilitation Act 67 of 1995.
3 National Environmental Management Act 107 of 1998 s 17(2), subject to s 22.
4 S 17(3).
5 S 18(1).
6 S 18(2).
7 S 18(3).
8 S 18(4).
9 S 18(5).
10 S 18(6).
11 S 18(7)(a).
12 S 18(7)(b).
13 S 18(7)(c).
14 S 18(7)(d).
15 S 18(8).
16 42 of 1965.
17 National Environmental Management Act 107 of 1998 s 19.

263 Investigation and conflict management The minister may at any time appoint one or more persons to assist either him or her or, after consultation with a municipal council or MEC or another national minister, to assist such council or MEC or other minister in the evaluation of a matter relating to the protection of the environment by obtaining such information, whether documentary or oral, as is relevant to such evaluation and to that end:

(a) the minister may by notice in the *Government Gazette* give such person or persons the powers of a commission of inquiry under the Commissions Act;[1]

(b) the minister may make rules by notice in the *Gazette* for the conduct of the inquiry, provided that the decision of the inquiry and the reasons therefore must be reduced to writing;

(c) the director-general must designate, subject to the provisions of the Public Service Act,[2] as many officers and employees of the department as may be necessary to assist such person, and any work may be performed by a person other than such officer or employee at the remuneration and allowances which the minister with the concurrence of the Minister of Finance may determine.[3]

The minister may determine remuneration and allowances, either in general or in any particular case, to be paid to any person or persons appointed in terms of the National Environmental Management Act to render facilitation, conciliation, arbitration or investigation services, who are not in the full-time employment of the state.[4] The minister may create a panel or panels of persons from which appointment of facilitators and arbitrators may be made, or contracts entered into, in terms of the Act.[5]

Decisions under the Act concerning the reference of a difference or disagreement to conciliation, the appointment of a conciliator, the appointment of a facilitator, the appointment of persons to conduct investigations, and the conditions of such appointment, must be made taking into account the desirability of resolving differences and disagreements speedily and cheaply; the desirability of giving indigent persons access to conflict resolution measures in the interest of the protection of the environment; the desirability of improving the quality of decision-making by giving interested and affected persons the opportunity to bring relevant information to the decision-making process; any representations made by persons interested in the matter; and such other considerations relating to the public interest as may be relevant.[6] The director-general must keep a record and prepare an annual report on environmental conflict management for submission to the committee and the forum, for the purpose of evaluating compliance and conflict management measures in respect of environmental laws.[7] The director-general must designate an officer to provide information to the public on appropriate dispute resolution mechanisms for referral of disputes and complaints.[8]

1 8 of 1947.
2 103 of 1994.
3 National Environmental Management Act 107 of 1998 s 20.
4 S 21(1). This is done with the concurrence of the Minister of Finance and the funds are taken from money appropriated by Parliament for that purpose.
5 S 21(2). The Minister may, pending the establishment of a panel or panels in terms of s 21(2), adopt the panel established in terms of s 31(1) of the Land Reform (Labour Tenants) Act 3 of 1996: National Environmental Management Act 107 of 1998 s 21(3).
6 S 22(1).
7 S 22(2)(a). See s 22(2)(b) for contents of this report; s 22(2)(d) provides for inspection by the public.
8 S 22(2)(c).

264 General objectives of integrated environmental management The purpose of chapter 5 of the National Environmental Management Act[1] is to promote the application of appropriate environmental management tools in order to ensure the integrated environmental management of activities.[2] The general objective of integrated environmental management is to:

(a) promote the integration of the national environmental management principles into the making of all decisions which may have a significant effect on the environment;

(b) identify, predict and evaluate the actual and potential impact on the environment, socio-economic conditions and cultural heritage, the risks and consequences and alternatives and options for mitigation of activities, with a view to minimising negative impacts, maximising benefits, and promoting compliance with the national environmental management principles;

(c) ensure that the effects of activities on the environment receive adequate consideration before actions are taken in connection with them;

(d) ensure adequate and appropriate opportunity for public participation in decisions that may affect the environment;

(e) ensure the consideration of environmental attributes in management and decision-making which may have a significant effect on the environment; and

(f) identify and employ the modes of environmental management best suited to ensuring that a particular activity is pursued in accordance with the national environmental management principles.[3]

1 107 of 1998.
2 S 23(1).
3 S 23(2).

265 Environmental authorisations In order to give effect to the general objectives of integrated environmental management, the potential impact on the environment of listed activities must be considered, investigated, assessed and reported on to the competent authority[1] charged by the National Environmental Management Act with granting the relevant environmental authorisation.[2] The minister, and every MEC with the concurrence of the minister, may identify activities which may not commence without environmental authorisation from the competent authority; geographical areas based on environmental attributes in which specified activities may not commence without environmental authorisation from the competent authority; geographical areas based on environmental attributes in which specified activities may be excluded from authorisation by the competent authority; individual or generic existing activities which may have a detrimental effect on the environment and in respect of which an application for an environmental authorisation must be made to the competent authority.[3]

Procedures for the investigation, assessment and communication of the potential impact of activities must ensure, as a minimum, with respect to every application for an environmental authorisation:

(a) investigation of the environment likely to be significantly affected by the proposed activity and alternatives thereto;

(b) investigation of the potential impact of the activity and its alternatives on the environment and assessment of the significance of that potential impact;

(c) investigation of mitigation measures to keep adverse impacts to a minimum, as well as the option of not implementing the activity;

(d) public information and participation which provide all interested and affected parties, including all organs of state in all spheres of government that may have jurisdiction over any aspect of the activity, with a reasonable opportunity to participate in such information and participation procedures;

(e) reporting on gaps in knowledge, the adequacy of predictive methods and underlying assumptions, and uncertainties encountered in compiling the required information;

(f) investigation and formulation of arrangements for the monitoring and management of impacts, and the assessment of the effectiveness of such arrangements after their implementation;

(g) co-ordination and co-operation between organs of state in the consideration of assessments where an activity falls under the jurisdiction of more than one organ of state;

(h) that the findings and recommendations flowing from such investigation, the general objectives of integrated environmental management and the national environmental management principles are taken into account in any decision made by an organ of state in relation to the proposed policy, programme, plan or project; and

(i) that environmental attributes identified in the compilation of information and maps are considered.[4]

The minister, and every MEC with the concurrence of the minister, may make regulations:

(a) laying down the procedure to be followed in applying for, the issuing of and monitoring compliance with environmental authorisations;

(b) laying down the procedure to be followed and the institutional arrangements in respect of:

(i) the efficient administration and processing of environmental authorisations;

(ii) fair decision-making and conflict management in the consideration and processing of applications for environmental authorisations;

(iii) the preparation and evaluation of environmental impact assessments, strategic environmental assessments, environmental management plans and any other relevant environmental management instruments that may be developed in time;

(iv) applications to the competent authority by any person to be exempted from the provisions of any regulation in respect of a specific activity;

(c) prescribing fees to be paid for the consideration and processing of environmental authorisations and the review of documents, processes and procedures by specialists on behalf of the competent authority;

(d) requiring the provision of financial or other security to cover the risks to the state and the environment of non-compliance with conditions attached to environmental authorisations;

(e) specifying that environmental impact assessments, or other specified tasks performed in connection with an application for an environmental authorisation, may only be performed by an environmental assessment practitioner registered in accordance with the prescribed procedures:

(f) requiring that competent authorities maintain a registry of applications for, and records of decisions in respect of, environmental authorisations;

(g) specifying that a contravention of a specified regulation is an offence and prescribing penalties for the contravention of that regulation;

(h) prescribing minimum criteria for the report content for each type of report and for each process that is contemplated in terms of the regulations in order to ensure a consistent quality and to facilitate efficient evaluation of reports;

(i) prescribing review mechanisms and procedures including criteria for and responsibilities of all parties in, the review process; and

(j) prescribing any other matter necessary for dealing with making and evaluating applications for environmental authorisations.[5]

Authorisations or permits obtained under any other law for an activity listed or specified in terms of the Act do not absolve the applicant from obtaining authorisation under the Act and any such other authorisations or permits may only be considered by the competent authority if adequate public participation has been ensured.[6]

Only the minister may make regulations stipulating the procedure to be followed and the report to be prepared in investigating, assessing and communicating potential impacts where the activity will affect more than one province or traverse international boundaries, or affect compliance with obligations resting on the Republic under customary international law or a convention.[7]

1 "Competent authority" means the organ of state charged by the National Environmental Management Act 107 of 1998 with evaluating the environmental impact of that activity and, where appropriate, with granting or refusing an environmental authorisation in respect of that activity: s 1.

2 S 24(1). The director-general must co-ordinate the activities of organs of state referred to in s 24(1) and assist them in giving effect to the objectives of the section, and

such assistance may include training, the publication of manuals and guidelines and the co-ordination of procedures: s 23(3).

3 S 24(2). provided that where an activity falls under the jurisdiction of another minister or MEC, a decision must be taken after consultation with such other minister or MEC. Cf s 24(3) for the powers to compile information and maps that specify the environmental attributes of specific geographical areas.

4 S 24(4). Cf s 24(7), which provides that

compliance with the procedure laid down in terms of s 24(4) does not remove the need to obtain an authorisation, other than an environmental authorisation, for that activity from any organ of state charged by law with authorising, permitting or otherwise allowing the implementation of the activity.

5 S 24(5). Cf s 24(6) which allows an MEC to make regulations only in respect of listed activities or areas in respect of which the MEC is the competent authority.
6 S 24(8).
7 S 24(9).

266 Listing and delisting activities and areas Before identifying any activity or area in terms of section 24(2) of the National Environmental Management Act,[1] the minister or MEC, as the case may be, must publish a notice in the relevant *Government Gazette* specifying, through description, a map or any other appropriate manner, the area or activity it is proposing to list; and inviting interested parties to submit written comments on the proposed listing within a period specified in the notice.[2] The minister may delist an activity or area identified by the minister, and an MEC may, with the concurrence of the minister, delist an activity identified by the MEC.[3] The minister or MEC, as the case may be, must publish in the relevant *Gazette* a notice listing activities and areas identified (together with competent authorities identified) and the date on which the list is to come into effect.[4]

1 107 of 1998.
2 S 24A.
3 S 24B. Cf s 24B(3) requiring the minister or MEC, in delisting, to follow the requirements

for listing in s 24A with the necessary changes.
4 S 24D.

267 Identifying the competent authority When listing activities the minister, or the MEC with the concurrence of the minister, must identify the competent authority responsible for granting environmental authorisations in respect of those activities.[1] The minister must be identified as the competent authority if the activity:

(a) has implications for national environmental policy or international environmental commitments or relations;

(b) will take place within geographical areas based on environmental attributes in which specified activities may not commence without environmental authorisation from the competent authority or geographical areas based on environmental attributes in which specified activities may be excluded from authorisation by the competent authority as a result of the obligations resting on the Republic in terms of any international environmental instrument, other than any area falling within the sea-shore, a conservancy, a protected natural environment, a proclaimed private nature reserve, a natural heritage site, or the buffer zone or transitional area of a biosphere reserve or world heritage site;

(c) will affect more than one province or traverse international boundaries;

(d) is undertaken, or is to be undertaken, by a national department; a provincial department responsible for environmental affairs, or a statutory body, excluding any municipality, performing an exclusive competence of the national sphere of government; or

(e) will take place within a national proclaimed protected area or other conservation area under the control of a national authority.[2]

The minister or MEC, as the case may be, must publish in the relevant *Gazette* a notice listing the competent authorities identified (together with the listed activities and areas) and the date on which the list is to come into effect.[3]

1 National Environmental Management Act 107 of 1998 s 24C(1).
2 S 24C(2). Cf s 24C(3) which allows the

minister and MEC to vary by agreement decisions made in terms of s 24C(2).
3 S 24D.

268 Minimum conditions attached to environmental authorisations Every environmental authorisation must as a minimum ensure that:

(a)   adequate provision is made for the ongoing management and monitoring of the impacts of the activity on the environment throughout the life cycle of the activity;

(b)   the property, site or area is specified; and

(c)   provision is made for the transfer of rights and obligations when there is a change of ownership in the property.[1]

1 National Environmental Management Act
  107 of 1998 s 24E.

269 Consequences of commencement or continuation of listed activity Notwithstanding the provisions of any other Act, no person may commence a listed activity unless the competent authority has granted an environmental authorisation for the activity, and no person may continue an existing listed activity if an application for an environmental authorisation is refused.[1] It is an offence to do so, and it is also an offence to contravene the conditions applicable to any environmental authorisation granted for a listed activity.[2]

On application by a person who has committed such an offence the minister or MEC, as the case may be, may direct the applicant to compile a report containing an assessment of the nature, extent, duration and significance of the impacts of the activity on the environment, including the cumulative effects; a description of mitigation measures undertaken or to be undertaken in respect of the impacts of the activity on the environment; a description of the public participation process followed during the course of compiling the report, including all comments received from interested and affected parties and an indication of how issues raised have been addressed; an environmental management plan; and provide such other information or undertake such further studies as the minister or MEC may deem necessary.[3] This report must be considered by the minister or MEC once the applicant has paid an administrative fine not exceeding R1 million as determined by the competent authority, and thereafter may either direct the person to cease the activity, either wholly or in part, and to rehabilitate the environment within such time and subject to such conditions as the minister or MEC may deem necessary; or issue an environmental authorisation to such person subject to such conditions as the minister or MEC may deem necessary.[4] A person who fails to comply with a directive of, or a condition set by, the minister or MEC, is guilty of an offence.[5]

1 National Environmental Management Act
  107 of 1998 s 24F(1).
2 S 24F(2). Cf s 24F(3) for a defence relating to emergency so as to protect human life, property or the environment. The maximum penalty for committing this offence is a fine not exceeding R5 million or imprisonment
for a period not exceeding ten years, or both (s 24F(4)).
3 S 24G(1).
4 S 24G(2).
5 S 24G(3). The penalty is as prescribed in s 24F(4).

270 Registration authorities An association proposing to register its members as environmental assessment practitioners may apply to the minister to be appointed as a registration authority in such manner as the minister may prescribe.[1] The minister may, after considering an application, and any other additional information that he or she may require, appoint the association as a registration authority; or refuse the application, giving reasons for the refusal.[2]

The minister may, for good cause and in writing addressed to the association, terminate the appointment of an association as a registration authority,[3] and he or she must maintain a register of all associations appointed as registration authorities in terms of this section of the National Environmental Management Act.[4]

1 National Environmental Management Act 107 of 1998 s 24H(1). Cf s 24H(2) for pre-scribed contents of the application.

2 S 24H(3).
3 S 24H(4).
4 S 24H(5).

271 Appointment of external specialist to review assessment The minister or MEC may appoint an external specialist reviewer in instances where the technical knowledge required to review any aspect of an assessment is not readily available within the competent authority; or a high level of objectivity is required which is not apparent in the documents submitted, in order to ascertain whether the information contained in the documents is adequate for decision-making or whether it requires amendment.[1]

1 National Environmental Management Act 107 of 1998 s 24I. The costs may be recov-ered from the applicant.

272 International environmental obligations and agreements Where the Republic is not yet bound by an international environmental instrument, the minister may make a recommendation to cabinet and Parliament regarding accession to and ratification of an international environmental instrument, which may deal with the following:

(a)   available resources to ensure implementation;

(b)   views of interested and affected parties;

(c)   benefits to the Republic;

(d)   disadvantages to the Republic;

(e)   the estimated date when the instrument is to come into effect;

(f)   the estimated date when the instrument will become binding on the Republic;

(g)   the minimum number of states required to sign the instrument in order for it to come into effect;

(h)   the respective responsibilities of all national departments involved;

(i)   the potential impact of accession on national parties;

(j)   reservations to be made, if any; and

(k)   any other matter which in the opinion of the minister is relevant.[1]

Where the Republic is a party to an international environmental instrument the minister, after compliance with the provisions of section 231(2) and (3) of the Consti-tution,[2] may publish the provisions of the international environmental instrument in the *Government Gazette* and any amendment or addition to such instrument.[3] The minister may introduce legislation in Parliament or make such regulations as may be necessary for giving effect to an international environmental instrument to which the Republic is a party, and such legislation and regulations may deal with *inter alia* the following:

(a)   the co-ordination of the implementation of the instrument;

(b)   the allocation of responsibilities in terms of the instrument, including those of other organs of state;

(c)   the gathering of information, including for the purposes of compiling and up-dating reports required in terms of the instrument and for submission to Parliament;

(d)   the dissemination of information related to the instrument and reports from international meetings;

(e)   initiatives and steps regarding research, education, training, awareness-raising and capacity-building;

(f)   ensuring public participation;

(g)   implementation of and compliance with the provisions of the instrument, including the creation of offences and the prescription of penalties where applicable; and

(h)   any other matter necessary to give effect to the instrument.[4]

The minister must report to Parliament once a year regarding international environmental instruments for which he or she is responsible and such report may include details on:

(a)   participation in international meetings concerning international environmental instruments;

(b)   progress in implementing international environmental instruments to which the Republic is a party;

(c)   preparations undertaken in respect of international instruments to which the Republic is likely to become a party;

(d)   initiatives and negotiations within the region of Southern Africa;

(e)   the efficacy of co-ordination mechanisms; and

(f)   legislative measures that have been taken and the time frames within which it is envisaged that their objectives will be achieved.[5]

The minister must initiate an Annual Performance Report on Sustainable Development to meet the government's commitment to Agenda 21, which must cover all relevant activities of all national departments and spheres of government.[6] The purpose of the report is to provide an audit and a report of the government's performance in respect of Agenda 21; review procedures for co-ordinating policies and budgets to meet the objectives of Agenda 21; and review progress on a public educational programme to support the objectives of Agenda 21.[7]

Chapter 6 of the National Environmental Management Act[8] applies to any international environmental instrument whether the Republic became a party to it before or after the coming into force of the Act.[9] The provisions of any international environmental instrument published in accordance with this section[10] are evidence of the contents of the international environmental instrument in any proceedings or matter in which the provisions of the instrument come into question.[11]

1   National Environmental Management Act 107 of 1998 s 25(1). Cf s 25(4) for publication of intention to make a recommendation in terms of s 25(1).
2   Constitution of the Republic of SA 108 of 1996. These sections require the approval of the National Assembly and National Council of Provinces before international agreements bind the Republic.
3   National Environmental Management Act 107 of 1998 s 25(2).
4   S 25(3).
5   S 26(1).
6   S 26(2). All organs of state must provide information for the report to the minister, who may appoint persons as a secretariat to prepare the report.
7   S 26(2)(d).
8   Ss 25–27.
9   S 27(1).
10   It would appear that this word in the Act should be "chapter" and not "section".
11   S 27(2).

273   Duty of care and remediation of environmental damage   Every person who causes, has caused or may cause significant pollution or degradation of the environment must take reasonable measures to prevent such pollution or degradation from occurring, continuing or recurring, or, in so far as such harm to the environment is authorised by law or cannot reasonably be avoided or stopped, to minimise and rectify such pollution or degradation of the environment.[1] Also required to take such measures are persons including an owner of land or premises, a person in control of land or premises or a person who has a right to use the land or premises on which or in which any activity or process is or was performed or undertaken, or any other situation exists, which causes, has caused or is likely to cause significant pollution or degradation of the environment.[2] The reasonable measures required may include measures to:

(a) investigate, assess and evaluate the impact on the environment;

(b) inform and educate employees about the environmental risks of their work and the manner in which their tasks must be performed in order to avoid causing significant pollution or degradation of the environment;

(c) cease, modify or control any act, activity or process causing the pollution or degradation;

(d) contain or prevent the movement of pollutants or the causant of degradation;

(e) eliminate any source of the pollution or degradation; or

(f) remedy the effects of the pollution or degradation.[3]

The director-general or a provincial head of department may direct any person who fails to take the required reasonable measures, to investigate, evaluate and assess the impact of specific activities and report thereon; commence taking specific reasonable measures before a given date; diligently continue with those measures; and complete them before a specified reasonable date.[4]

If a person required under the National Environmental Management Act to undertake rehabilitation or other remedial work on the land of another, reasonably requires access to, use of or a limitation on use of that land in order to effect rehabilitation or remedial work, but is unable to acquire it on reasonable terms, the minister may expropriate the necessary rights in respect of that land for the benefit of the person undertaking the rehabilitation or remedial work, who will then be vested with the expropriated rights; and recover from the person for whose benefit the expropriation was effected all costs incurred.[5]

Should the recipient of a directive fail to comply, or inadequately comply, with the directive, the director-general or provincial head of department may take reasonable measures to remedy the situation,[6] and the director-general or provincial head of department may recover all costs incurred as a result of it taking remedial measures from any or all of the following persons:

(a) any person who is or was responsible for, or who directly or indirectly contributed to, the pollution or degradation or the potential pollution or degradation;

(b) the owner of the land at the time when the pollution or degradation or the potential for pollution or degradation occurred, or that owner's successor in title;

(c) the person in control of the land or any person who has or had a right to use the land at the time when:

(i) the activity or the process is or was performed or undertaken; or

(ii) the situation came about; or

(d) any person who negligently failed to prevent:

(i) the activity or the process being performed or undertaken; or

(ii) the situation from coming about,

provided that such person failed to take the reasonable measures required of him or her under section 28(1).[7]

Any person may, after giving the director-general or provincial head of department 30 days' notice, apply to a competent court for an order directing the director-general or any provincial head of department to take any of the steps listed in section 28(4) if the director-general or provincial head of department fails to inform such person in writing that he or she has directed a person contemplated in section 28(8) to take one of those steps.[8]

1 National Environmental Management Act 107 of 1998 s 28(1). In *Hichange Investments (Pty) Ltd v Cape Produce Co (Pty) Ltd t/a Pelts Products* [2004] 1 All SA 636 (E); 2004 2 SA 393 (E), the court stated that "the threshold level of significance will not be particularly high" (415A).

2 S 28(2).

3 S 28(3).

4 S 28(4). The director-general or competent authority may only issue a directive after consultation with any other organ of state concerned and after having given adequate opportunity to affected persons to inform him or her of their relevant interests. Consultation may be postponed if urgent action is necessary for the protection of the environment. Cf s 28(5) for the considerations the director-general or competent authority must take into account in issuing a directive.

5 S 28(6).

6 S 28(7).

7 S 28(8). Cf s 28(9), which allows the director-general to claim costs proportionally from any other person who benefited from the remedial steps taken; s 28(10) which requires that the costs be reasonable and that they may include labour, administrative and overhead costs; and s 28(11) which requires apportionment of costs if there is more than one person liable, according to the degree to which each was responsible for the harm to the environment resulting from their respective failures to take the measures required.

8 S 28(12) – the provisions of s 32(2) and (3) apply to such proceedings with the necessary changes. Cf s 28(13) which requires a court considering such an application to take into account the factors set out in s 28(5).

274 Protection of workers refusing to do environmentally hazardous work Notwithstanding the provisions of any other law, no person is civilly or criminally liable or may be dismissed, disciplined, prejudiced or harassed on account of having refused to perform any work if the person in good faith and reasonably believed at the time of the refusal that the performance of the work would result in an imminent and serious threat to the environment.[1] An employee who has thus refused to perform work must as soon thereafter as is reasonably practicable notify the employer either personally or through a representative that he or she has refused to perform work and give the reason for the refusal.[2] No person may advantage or promise to advantage any person for not exercising his or her right in terms of this section,[3] and no person may threaten to take any action contemplated by section 29(1) of the National Environmental Management Act against a person because that person has exercised or intends to exercise such right.[4]

1 National Environmental Management Act 107 of 1998 s 29(1), which applies whether or not the person refusing to work has used or exhausted any other applicable external or internal procedure or otherwise remedied

the matter concerned: s 29(3).

2 S 29(2).

3 S 29(4).

4 S 29(5).

275 Control of emergency incidents The responsible person[1] or, where the incident[2] occurred in the course of that person's employment, his or her employer must:

(a) forthwith after knowledge of the incident, report through the most effective means reasonably available the nature of the incident; any risks posed by the incident to public health, safety and property; the toxicity of substances or by-products released by the incident; and any steps that should be taken in order to avoid or minimise the effects of the incident on public health and the environment to the director-general, the South African Police Services and the relevant fire prevention service, the relevant provincial head of department or municipality; and all persons whose health may be affected by the incident;[3]

(b) as soon as reasonably practicable after knowledge of the incident take all reasonable measures to contain and minimise the effects of the incident, including its effects on the environment and any risks posed by the incident to the health, safety and property of persons; undertake clean-up procedures; remedy the effects of the incident; assess the immediate and long-term effects of the incident on the environment and public health;[4]

(c) within 14 days of the incident, report to the director-general, provincial head of department and municipality such information as is available to enable an initial evaluation of the incident, including the nature of the incident; the substances involved and an estimation of the quantity released and their possible acute effect on persons and the environment and data needed to assess these effects; initial measures taken to minimise impacts; causes of the incident, whether direct or indirect, including equipment, technology, system, or management failure; and measures taken and to be taken to avoid a recurrence of such incident.[5]

A relevant authority[6] may direct the responsible person to undertake specific measures within a specific time to fulfil his or her obligations under this section, but the relevant authority must, when considering any such measure or time period, have regard to the national environmental management principles; the severity of any impact on the environment as a result of the incident and the costs of the measures being considered; any measures already taken or proposed by the person on whom measures are to be imposed, if applicable; the desirability of the state fulfilling its role as custodian holding the environment in public trust for the people; and any other relevant factors.[7]

Should the responsible person fail to comply, or inadequately comply with such a directive, or there is uncertainty as to who the responsible person is, or there is an immediate risk of serious danger to the public or potentially serious detriment to the environment, a relevant authority may take the measures it considers necessary to contain and minimise the effects of the incident; undertake clean-up procedures; and remedy the effects of the incident.[8] The reimbursement of the reasonable costs of such measures incurred by the authority may be claimed by it from every responsible person jointly and severally.[9] The authority which has taken such steps must, as soon as reasonably practicable, prepare comprehensive reports on the incident, which reports must be made available through the most effective means reasonably available to:

(a) the public;

(b) the director-general;

(c) the South African Police Services and the relevant fire prevention service;

(d) the relevant provincial head of department or municipality; and

(e) all persons who may be affected by the incident.[10]

1 "Responsible person" includes any person who is responsible for the incident; owns any hazardous substance involved in the incident; or was in control of any hazardous substance involved in the incident at the time of the incident: National Environmental Management Act 107 of 1998 s 30(1).

2 "Incident" means an unexpected sudden occurrence, including a major emission, fire

or explosion leading to serious danger to the public or potentially serious pollution of or detriment to the environment, whether immediate or delayed: s 30(1)(a).

3 S 30(3).

4 S 30(4).

5 S 30(5).

6 "Relevant authority" means:

    (a) a municipality with jurisdiction over the area in which an incident occurs;

    (b) a provincial head of department or any other provincial official designated for that purpose by the MEC in a province

in which an incident occurs;

    (c) the director-general;

    (d) any other director-general of a national department: s 30(1). Cf s 30(2) for the hierarchy of action for relevant authorities.

7 S 30(6). Cf s 30(7) which provides that a verbal directive must be confirmed in writing at the earliest opportunity, which must be within seven days.

8 S 30(8).

9 S 30(9).

10 S 30(10).

276 Access to environmental information and protection of whistle-blowers Every person is entitled to have access to information held by the state and organs of state which relates to the implementation of the National Environmental Management Act[1] and any other law affecting the environment, and to the state of the environment and actual and future threats to the environment, including any emissions to water, air or soil and the production, handling, transportation, treatment, storage and disposal of hazardous waste and substances.[2] Organs of state are entitled to have access to information relating to the state of the environment and actual and future threats to the environment, including any emissions to water, air or soil and the production, handling, transportation, treatment, storage and disposal of hazardous waste held by any person where that information is necessary to enable such organs of state to carry out their duties in terms of the provisions of the Act or any other law concerned with the protection of the environment or the use of natural resources.[3] A request for information can be refused only:

(a) if the request is manifestly unreasonable or formulated in too general a manner;

(b) if the public order or national security would be negatively affected by the supply of the information; or

(c) for the reasonable protection of commercially confidential information;

(d) if the granting of information endangers or further endangers the protection of the environment; and

(e) for the reasonable protection of personal privacy.[4]

The minister may make regulations regarding access by members of the public to privately held information relating to the implementation of the Act and any other law concerned with the protection of the environment and may to this end prescribe the manner in which such information must be kept. However, such regulations must be reasonable and justifiable in an open and democratic society based on human dignity, equality and freedom.[5] In making such regulations, the minister must take into account the national environmental management principles, the reasons provided for refusal of information,[6] the provisions of international law and foreign law, and any other relevant considerations.[7]

Notwithstanding the provisions of any other law, no person is civilly or criminally liable or may be dismissed, disciplined, prejudiced or harassed on account of having disclosed any information, if the person in good faith reasonably believed at the time of the disclosure that he or she was disclosing evidence of an environmental risk and the disclosure was made in accordance with the following requirements:

The person must have:

(a)   disclosed the information concerned to:

(i)   a committee of Parliament or of a provincial legislature;

(ii)   an organ of state responsible for protecting any aspect of the environment or emergency services;

(iii)   the Public Protector;

(iv)   the Human Rights Commission;

(v)   any attorney-general or his or her successor;

(vi)   more than one of the bodies or persons referred to above;

(b)   disclosed the information concerned to one or more news media and on clear and convincing grounds believed at the time of the disclosure:

(i)   that the disclosure was necessary to avert an imminent and serious threat to the environment, to ensure that the threat to the environment was properly and timeously investigated or to protect him or herself against serious or irreparable harm from reprisals; or

(ii)   giving due weight to the importance of open, accountable and participatory administration, that the public interest in disclosure of the information clearly out-weighed any need for non-disclosure;

(c)   disclosed the information concerned substantially in accordance with any other applicable external or internal procedure for reporting or otherwise remedying the matter concerned; or

(d)   disclosed information which, before the time of the disclosure of the information, had become available to the public, whether in the Republic or elsewhere.[8] This applies whether or not the person disclosing the information concerned has used or exhausted any other applicable external or internal procedure to report or otherwise remedy the matter concerned.[9] No person may advantage or promise to advantage any person for not exercising his or her right to disclose information,[10] or threaten to take any action contemplated by section 31(4) against a person because that person has exercised or intends to exercise such right.[11]

At the time of the promulgation of the Act, these provisions were intended to be applicable only until such time as an Act contemplated by section 33(2) of the Constitution[12] was enacted. This Act, the Promotion of Access to Information Act,[13] has been enacted, but it provides that nothing in the Act prevents the giving of access to a record of a public or private body in terms of any legislation appearing in Schedule 1 or 2 of that Act respectively.[14] Schedule 1 includes section 31(1) and Schedule 2 includes section 31(2) of the National Environmental Management Act.[15] This suggests that, despite the enactment of the Promotion of Access to Information Act, section 31 of the National Environmental Management Act remains in force.

1   107 of 1998.
2   S 31(1)(a)
3   S 31(1)(b).
4   S 31(1)(c).
5   S 31(2).
6   In s 31(1)(c).
7   S 31(3).
8   S 31(4) read with s 31(5).
9   S 31(6).
10   S 31(7).
11   S 31(8).
12   Constitution of the Republic of SA 108 of 1996.
13   2 of 2000.
14   S 6.
15   107 of 1998.

277   Application of part 2 of chapter 7 of the Act   Part 2 of chapter 7 of the National Environmental Management Act,[1] headed "Application and enforcement of Act and specific environmental management Acts", applies to the enforcement of the

National Environmental Management Act and also the specific environmental management Acts,[2] which are the National Environmental Management: Biodiversity Act[3] and the National Environmental Management: Protected Areas Act[4] and any regulations or other subordinate legislation made in terms of those Acts.[5] For the purposes of this part of the Act, Schedule 1 to the Criminal Procedure Act[6] is deemed to include an offence committed in terms of the Act or a specific environmental management Act.[7]

1 107 of 1998.
2 S 31A(1). S 31A–Q was inserted by the National Environmental Management Act 46 of 2003 (not yet in operation). Cf s 31A(2) for reconciliation of meanings of words and expressions between the Act and the specific national environmental management Acts.
3 10 of 2004.
4 57 of 2003.
5 National Environmental Management Act 107 of 1998 s 1.
6 51 of 1977.
7 National Environmental Management Act 107 of 1998 s 31A(3). Sch 1 offences are those for which certain powers in respect of arrest are applicable (see ss 40, 42 and 49 of the Criminal Procedure Act 51 of 1977).

278 Environmental management inspectors The minister may designate as an environmental management inspector, any staff member of the department or any other organ of state, and at any time withdraw such a designation.[1] An MEC may designate as an environmental management inspector, any staff member of the department responsible for environmental management in the province or any other provincial organ of state or any municipality in the province, and at any time withdraw such designation.[2]

When designating a person as an environmental management inspector, the minister or MEC must determine whether the person concerned is designated for the enforcement of the National Environmental Management Act, a specific environmental management Act, specific provisions of the Act or a specific environmental management Act, the Act and all specific environmental management Acts, or any combination of those Acts or provisions of those Acts.[3] A person designated as an environmental management inspector may exercise any of the powers given to environmental management inspectors in terms of the Act that are necessary for the inspector's mandate and that may be specified by the minister or MEC by notice in writing to the inspector.[4]

The minister may, after consultation with the minister responsible for safety and security, prescribe qualification criteria for environmental management inspectors, and training that must be completed by environmental management inspectors.[5] A prescribed identity card must be issued to each person designated as an environmental management inspector, which must be produced on demand by a member of public together with the notice setting out that inspector's mandate.[6]

1 National Environmental Management Act 107 of 1998 s 31B(1), provided that a designation of a staff member of another organ of state requires agreement with the relevant organ of state: s 31B(2).
2 S 31C(1), provided that a designation of a staff member of another provincial organ of state or municipality requires agreement with that institution: s 31C(2).
3 S 31D(1), provided that an MEC may designate a person as an environmental management inspector for the enforcement of only those provisions of the Act or any specific environmental management Act which are administered by the MEC or a provincial organ of state; or in respect of which the MEC or a provincial organ of state exercises or performs assigned or delegated powers or duties: s 31D(2).
4 S 31D(3).
5 S 31E.
6 S 31F.

279 Powers and functions of environmental management inspectors An environmental management inspector within his or her mandate:

(a)　must monitor and enforce compliance with a law for which he or she has been designated;

(b)　may investigate any act or omission in respect of which there is a reasonable suspicion that it might constitute an offence in terms of such law, a breach of such law, or a breach of a term or condition of a permit, authorisation or other instrument issued in terms of such law.[1] An environmental management inspector must carry out his or her duties and exercise his or her powers in accordance with any instructions issued by the minister or MEC, as the case may be, and subject to any limitations and in accordance with any procedures that may be prescribed.[2] He or she may be accompanied by an interpreter or any other person whose assistance may reasonably be required,[3] and the inspector must exercise his or her powers in a way that minimises any damage to loss or deterioration of any premises or thing.[4]

An environmental management inspector within his or her mandate may:

(a)　question a person about any act or omission in respect of which there is a reasonable suspicion that it might constitute:

　　(i)　an offence in terms of a law for which that inspector has been designated;

　　(ii)　a breach of such law; or

　　(iii)　a breach of a term or condition of a permit, authorisation or other instrument issued in terms of such law;

(b)　issue a written notice to a person who refuses to answer such questions, requiring that person to answer questions put to him or her;[5]

(c)　inspect, or question a person about, any document, book or record or any written or electronic information which may be relevant for the purpose of the inspector's questioning or to which the National Environmental Management Act or a specific environmental management Act relates;

(d)　copy, or make extracts from, any such document, book or record or any written or electronic information, or remove such document, book, record or written or electronic information in order to make copies or extracts;

(e)　require a person to produce or deliver to a place specified by the inspector, any such document, book or record or any written or electronic information for inspection;

(f)　inspect, question a person about, and if necessary remove any specimen, article, substance or other item which, on reasonable suspicion, may have been used in:

　　(i)　committing an offence in terms of the law for which that inspector has been designated;

　　(ii)　breaching such law; or

　　(iii)　breaching a term or condition of a permit, authorisation or other instrument issued in terms of such law;

(g)　take photographs or make audio–visual recordings of anything or any person that is relevant for the purposes of an investigation;

(h)　dig or bore into the soil;

(i)　take samples;

(j)　remove any waste or other matter deposited or discharged in contravention of the law for which that inspector has been designated or a term or condition of a permit, authorisation or other instrument issued in terms of such law; or

(k) carry out any other prescribed duty not inconsistent with the Act and any other duty that may be prescribed in terms of a specific environmental management Act.[6]

A person who receives a written notice in terms of section 31H(1)(b) of the National Environmental Management Act, must answer all questions put to him or her truthfully and to the best of his or her ability, notwithstanding that an answer might incriminate him or her, but any answer that incriminates such person may not be used against him or her in any subsequent criminal proceedings for an offence in terms of the Act or a specific environmental management Act.[7]

An environmental management inspector must provide a receipt for any document, book, record or written or electronic information or any specimen, article, substance or other item removed, and return anything removed within a reasonable period or at the conclusion of any relevant criminal proceedings.[8]

In addition to these powers, an environmental management inspector, within his or her mandate, has all the powers assigned in terms of chapters 2, 5, 7 and 8 of the Criminal Procedure Act[9] to a police official who is not a commissioned officer.[10]

1 National Environmental Management Act 107 of 1998 s 31G(1).
2 S 31G(2)(a).
3 S 31G(2)(b).
4 S 31G(2)(c).
5 Such notice must be in the prescribed format and must require a person to answer specified questions either orally or in writing, and either alone or in the presence of a witness, and may require that questions are answered under oath or affirmation: s 31H(2).

6 S 31H(1). These powers may be exercised on or in respect of a vehicle, vessel or aircraft contemplated in s 31J (s 31J(5)); and on business or residential premises or land contemplated in s 31K (s 31K(7)).
7 S 31H(3).
8 S 31H(4), subject to s 34D.
9 51 of 1977.
10 National Environmental Management Act 107 of 1998 s 31H(5).

280 Seizure of items The provisions of sections 30 to 34 of the Criminal Procedure Act[1] apply to the disposal of anything seized in terms of part 2 of chapter 7 of the National Environmental Management Act,[2] subject to such modifications as the context may require.[3] When an item is seized in terms of this part of the Act, the environmental management inspector may request the person who was in control of the item immediately before the seizure of the item, to take it to a place designated by the inspector, and if the person refuses to take the item to the designated place, the inspector may do so.[4] In order to safeguard a vehicle, vessel or aircraft that has been seized, the environmental management inspector may immobilise it by removing a part.[5] An item seized in terms of this section, including a part of a vehicle, vessel or aircraft, must be kept in such a way that it is secured against damage.[6]

An environmental management inspector may:

(a) in the case of a specimen of a threatened or protected species or alien species being imported into the Republic, at the port of entry, request the person responsible for the import or that person's agent, to produce the original copies of the import permit, together with such other documentation as may be required; and

(b) in the case of a specimen of a threatened or protected species, being exported or re-exported from the Republic, at the port of exit, request the person responsible for the export or re-export or that person's agent to produce the original copy of the export or re-export permit, together with such other documentation as may be required.[7]

1   51 of 1977.
2   107 of 1998.
3   S 31I(1).
4   S 31I(2).

5   S 31I(3).
6   S 31I(4).
7   S 31I(5).

281   Powers to stop, enter and search vehicles, vessels and aircraft An environmental management inspector, within his or her mandate, may, without a warrant, enter and search any vehicle, vessel[1] or aircraft,[2] or search any pack-animal, on reasonable suspicion that that vehicle, vessel, aircraft or pack-animal is being or has been used, or contains or conveys anything which is being or has been used, to commit an offence in terms of the law for which that inspector has been designated; or a breach of such law or a term or condition of a permit, authorisation or other instrument issued in terms of such law; or contains or conveys a thing which may serve as evidence of such offence or breach.[3] An environmental management inspector may, without a warrant, seize anything contained in or on any vehicle, vessel, aircraft or pack-animal that may be used as evidence in the prosecution of any person for an offence in terms of the National Environmental Management Act or a specific environmental management Act.[4]

An environmental management inspector may, for the purpose of carrying out a search, at any time, and without a warrant order the driver of a vehicle or vessel to stop, or the pilot of an aircraft to land, or if necessary and possible, force the driver or pilot to stop or land, as the case may be.[5]

An environmental management inspector may apply to the national or provincial commissioner of police for written authorisation[6] to establish a roadblock or a checkpoint.[7]

1   "Vessel" means any waterborne craft of any kind, whether self-propelled or not, but does not include any moored floating structure that is not used as a means of transporting anything by water: National Environmental Management Act 107 of 1998 s 1 (note that the National Environmental Management Amendment Act 46 of 2003 has not yet been put into operation).

2   "Aircraft" means an airborne craft of any type whatsoever, whether self-propelled or not, and includes a hovercraft: National Environmental Management Act 107 of 1998 s 1 (note that the National Environmental Management Amendment Act 46 of 2003

has not yet been put into operation).

3   National Environmental Management Act 107 of 1998 s 31J(1).

4   S 31J(2), subject to s 31I.

5   S 31J(4).

6   In terms of s 13(8) of the South African Police Service Act 68 of 1995.

7   National Environmental Management Act 107 of 1998 s 31J(6). In this regard, an environmental management inspector has, within his or her mandate, all the powers of a member of the South African Police Service in terms of s 13(8) of the South African Police Service Act 68 of 1995.

282   Routine inspections An environmental management inspector within his or her mandate, may, at any reasonable time, without a warrant, enter and inspect any building, land or premises for the purposes of ascertaining compliance with the legislation for which that inspector has been designated, or a term or condition of a permit, authorisation or other instrument issued in terms of such legislation.[1] An inspector may also, with a warrant enter and inspect any residential premises for the purposes of ascertaining such compliance.[2] A magistrate may issue a warrant only on written application by an environmental management inspector setting out under oath or affirmation that it is necessary to enter and inspect the specified residential premises for the purposes of ascertaining compliance with the Acts for which that inspector has been designated.[3] An environmental management inspector may enter and inspect any residential premises without a warrant, but only if the person in control of the premises consents to the entry and inspection; or there are reasonable grounds to believe that a warrant would on application be issued, but that the delay that may be caused by applying for a warrant would defeat the object of the entry or inspection.[4] While carrying out a routine inspection, an environmental management inspector may seize anything in or on any business or residential premises or land that may be used as evidence in the prosecution of any person for an offence in terms of the National Environmental Management Act or a specific environmental management Act.[5]

1 National Environmental Management Act 107 of 1998 s 31K(1).
2 S 31K(2).
3 S 31K(3).
4 S 31K(4).
5 S 31K(5). Cf s 31K(6) which makes s 31I applicable to anything seized in terms of this section.

283 Compliance notices An environmental management inspector, within his or her mandate, may issue a compliance notice in the prescribed form and following a prescribed procedure if there are reasonable grounds for believing that a person has not complied with a provision of the law for which that inspector has been designated, or with a term or condition of a permit, authorisation or other instrument issued in terms of such law.[1] A compliance notice must set out:

(a)   details of the conduct constituting non-compliance;

(b)   any steps the person must take and the period within which those steps must be taken;

(c)   any thing which the person may not do, and the period during which the person may not do it; and

(d)   the procedure to be followed in lodging an objection to the compliance notice with the minister or MEC, as the case may be.[2]

An environmental management inspector may, on good cause shown, vary a compliance notice and extend the period within which the person must comply with the notice.[3] A person who receives a compliance notice must comply with that notice within the time period stated in the notice unless the minister or MEC has agreed to suspend the operation of the compliance notice.[4] A person who receives a compliance notice and who wishes to lodge an objection in terms of section 31M may make representations to the minister or MEC, as the case may be, to suspend the operation of the compliance notice pending finalisation of the objection.[5]

Any person who receives a compliance notice may object to the notice by making representations, in writing, to the minister or MEC, as the case may be, within 30 days of receipt of the notice, or within such longer period as the minister or MEC may determine.[6] After considering any such representations and any other relevant information, the minister or MEC may confirm, modify or cancel a notice or any part of a notice, and must specify the period within which the person who received the notice must comply with any part of the notice that is confirmed or modified.[7]

A person who fails to comply with a compliance notice commits an offence.[8] If a person fails to comply with a compliance notice, the environmental management inspector must report the non -compliance to the minister or MEC, as the case may be, and the minister or MEC may revoke or vary the relevant permit, authorisation or other instrument which is the subject of the compliance notice, take any necessary steps and recover the costs of doing so from the person who failed to comply, and report the matter to a Director of Public Prosecutions.[9]

1 National Environmental Management Act 107 of 1998 s 31L(1).	5 S 31L(5).
2 S 31L(2).	6 S 31M(1).
3 S 31L(3).	7 S 31M(2).
4 S 31L(4).	8 S 31N(1).
	9 S 31N(2).

284 Powers of South African Police Service members A member of the South African Police Service has, in respect of an offence in terms of the National Environmental Management Act[1] or a specific environmental management Act, all the powers of an environmental management inspector excluding the power to conduct routine inspections and the power to issue and enforce compliance notices.[2]

1 107 of 1998.

2 S 31O(1). Cf s 31O(2), which provides for the minister or MEC, with the concurrence of the minister responsible for safety and se-

curity, by written notice to a member of the South African Police Service, to assign to that member all the powers contemplated in s 31K–O.

285 Duty to produce documents and confidentiality Any person to whom a permit, licence permission certificate, authorisation or any other document has been issued in terms of the National Environmental Management Act or a specific environmental management Act, must produce that document at the request of an environmental management inspector.[1]

It is an offence for any person to disclose information about any other person if that information was acquired while exercising or performing any power or duty in terms of the Act or a specific environmental management Act, except:

(a) if the information is disclosed in compliance with the provisions of any law;

(b) if the person is ordered to disclose the information by a court;

(c) if the information is disclosed to enable a person to perform a function in terms of the Act or a specific environmental management Act; or

(d) for the purposes of the administration of justice.[2]

1 National Environmental Management Act 107 of 1998 s 31P.

2 S 31Q(1). A person convicted of an offence in terms of this section is liable to a fine or

imprisonment for a period not exceeding one year or to both fine and imprisonment: s 31Q(2).

286 Legal standing to enforce environmental laws Any person or group of persons may seek appropriate relief in respect of any breach or threatened breach of any provision of the National Environmental Management Act,[1] including a national environmental management principle, or of any provision of a specific environmental management Act, or of any other statutory provision concerned with the protection of the environment or the use of natural resources:

(a) in that person's or group of person's own interest;

(b) in the interest of, or on behalf of, a person who is, for practical reasons, unable to institute such proceedings;

(c) in the interest of or on behalf of a group or class of persons whose interests are affected;

(d) in the public interest; and

(e) in the interest of protecting the environment.[2]

A court may decide not to award costs against a person who, or group of persons which, fails to secure the relief sought in respect of any breach or threatened breach of any provision of the Act, including a national environmental management principle, or of any provision of a specific environmental management Act, or of any other statutory provision concerned with the protection of the environment or the use of natural resources, if the court is of the opinion that the person or group of persons acted reasonably out of a concern for the public interest or in the interest of protecting the environment and had made due efforts to use other means reasonably available for obtaining the relief sought.[3]

Where a person or group of persons secures the relief sought in respect of any breach or threatened breach of any provision of the Act, or of any provision of a specific environmental management Act, or of any other statutory provision concerned with the protection of the environment, a court may on application:

(a)   award costs on an appropriate scale to any person or persons entitled to practise as advocate or attorney in the Republic who provided free legal assistance or representation to such person or group in the preparation for or conduct of the proceedings; and

(b)   order that the party against whom the relief is granted pay to the person or group concerned any reasonable costs incurred by such person or group in the investigation of the matter and its preparation for the proceedings.[4]

1   107 of 1998.
2   S 32(1).
3   S 32(2). See *Silvermine Valley Coalition v*

Sybrand van der Spuy Boerderye [2002] 1 All SA 10 (C); 2002 1 SA 478 (C).
4   S 32(3).

287   Private prosecution   Any person may in the public interest, or in the interest of the protection of the environment, institute and conduct a prosecution in respect of any breach or threatened breach of any duty, other than a public duty resting on an organ of state, in any national or provincial legislation or municipal by-law, or any regulation, licence, permission or authorisation issued in terms of such legislation, where that duty is concerned with the protection of the environment and the breach of that duty is an offence.[1] The provisions of the Criminal Procedure Act[2] applicable to a private prosecution instituted and conducted under that Act must apply to a prosecution instituted and conducted under the National Environmental Management Act, provided that if:

(a)   the person prosecuting privately does so through a person entitled to practise as an advocate or an attorney in the Republic;

(b)   the person prosecuting privately has given written notice to the appropriate public prosecutor that he or she intends to do so; and

(c)   the public prosecutor has not, within 28 days of receipt of such notice, stated in writing that he or she intends to prosecute the alleged offence,

(i) the person prosecuting privately will not be required to produce a certificate issued by the attorney-general stating that he or she has refused to prosecute the accused; and

(ii) the person prosecuting privately will not be required to provide security for such action.[3]

The court may order a person convicted upon a private prosecution brought to pay the costs and expenses of the prosecution, including the costs of any appeal against such conviction or any sentence.[4] The accused may be granted an order for costs against the person prosecuting privately, if the charge against the accused is dismissed or the accused is acquitted or a decision in favour of the accused is given on appeal, and the court finds either that the person instituting and conducting the private prosecution did not act out of a concern for the public interest or the protection of the environment, or that such prosecution was unfounded, trivial or vexatious.[5] When a private prosecution is instituted in accordance with the provisions of the Act, the attorney-general is barred from prosecuting except with the leave of the court concerned.[6]

1 National Environmental Management Act 107 of 1998 s 33(1).	107 of 1998 s 33(2).
2 51 of 1977: see ss 8–17.	4 S 33(3).
	5 S 33(4).
3 National Environmental Management Act	6 S 33(5).

288 Criminal proceedings Whenever any person is convicted of an offence under any provision listed in Schedule 3 of the National Environmental Management Act[1] and it appears that such person has by that offence caused loss or damage to any organ of state or other person, including the cost incurred or likely to be incurred by an organ of state in rehabilitating the environment or preventing damage to the environment, the court may in the same proceedings at the written request of the minister or other organ of state or other person concerned, and in the presence of the convicted person, inquire summarily and without pleadings into the amount of the loss or damage so caused.[2] Upon proof of such amount, the court may give judgment therefor in favour of the organ of state or other person concerned against the convicted person, and such judgment will be of the same force and effect and executable in the same manner as if it had been given in a civil action duly instituted before a competent court.[3]

Whenever any person is convicted of an offence under any provision listed in Schedule 3 the court convicting such person may:

(a)   summarily inquire into and assess the monetary value of any advantage gained or likely to be gained by such person in consequence of that offence, and, in addition to any other punishment imposed in respect of that offence, the court may order the award of damages or compensation or a fine equal to the amount so assessed;[4] and

(b)   upon application by the public prosecutor or another organ of state, order such person to pay the reasonable costs incurred by the public prosecutor and the organ of state concerned in the investigation and prosecution of the offence.[5]

Whenever any manager, agent or employee does or omits to do an act which it had been his or her task to do or to refrain from doing on behalf of the employer and which would be an offence under any provision listed in Schedule 3 for the employer to do or omit to do, and the act or omission of the manager, agent or employee occurred because the employer failed to take all reasonable steps to prevent the act or omission in question, then the employer will be guilty of the said offence and, save that no penalty other than a fine may be imposed if a conviction is based on section 34(5), liable on conviction to the penalty specified in the relevant law and proof of such act or omission by a manager, agent or employee will constitute *prima facie* evidence that the employer is guilty under section 34(5).[6]

Whenever any manager, agent or employee does or omits to do an act which it had been his or her task to do or to refrain from doing on behalf of the employer and which would be an offence under any provision listed in Schedule 3 for the employer to do or omit to do, he or she will be liable to be convicted and sentenced in respect thereof as if he or she were the employer.[7]

Any person who is or was a director[8] of a firm[9] at the time of the commission by that firm of an offence under any provision listed in Schedule 3 will him or herself be guilty of the said offence and liable on conviction to the penalty specified in the relevant law, if the offence in question resulted from the failure of the director to take all reasonable steps that were necessary under the circumstances to prevent the commission of the offence. However, proof of the said offence by the firm will constitute *prima facie* evidence that the director is guilty under section 34(7).[10] Any such manager, agent, employee or director may be so convicted and sentenced in addition to the employer or firm.[11]

1 107 of 1998.
2 S 34(1). Sch 3 contains a list of provisions in both national and provincial environmental legislation for which s 34 applies. The minister may amend part (a) of Sch 3 (containing national legislation) by regulation, and an MEC may amend part (b) of Sch 3 (containing provincial legislation) in respect of the province of his or her jurisdiction by regulation: s 34(10).
3 S 34(2).
4 S 34(3).
5 S 34(4).
6 S 34(5).
7 S 34(6).
8 "Director" means a member of the board, executive committee, or other managing body of a corporate body and, in the case of a close corporation, a member of that close corporation or in the case of a partnership, a member of that partnership: s 34(9).
9 "Firm'" means a body incorporated by or in terms of any law as well as a partnership: s 34(9).
10 S 34(7).
11 S 34(8).

289 Offences relating to environmental management inspectors

A person is guilty of an offence if that person:

(a)   hinders or interferes with an environmental management inspector in the execution of that inspector's official duties;

(b)   pretends to be an environmental management inspector, or the interpreter or assistant of such an inspector;

(c)   furnishes false or misleading information when complying with a request of an environmental management inspector; or

(d)   fails to comply with a request of an environmental management inspector.[1]

1 National Environmental Management Act 107 of 1998 s 34A(1). A person convicted of such an offence is liable to a fine or to imprisonment for a period not exceeding one year or to both such fine and imprisonment: s 34A(2). S 34A–G were inserted by the National Environmental Management Act 46 of 2003 (not yet in operation).

290 Award of part of fine recovered to informant

A court which imposes a fine for an offence in terms of the National Environmental Management Act[1] or a specific environmental management Act may order that a sum of not more than one-fourth of the fine be paid to the person whose evidence led to the conviction or who assisted in bringing the offender to justice.[2]

1 107 of 1998.
2 S 34B(1). A person in the service of an organ of state or engaged in the implementation of the Act or a specific environmental management Act is not entitled to such an award: s 34B(2).

291 Cancellation of permits

The court convicting a person of an offence in terms of the National Environmental Management Act[1] or a specific environmental management Act may:

(a)   withdraw any permit or other authorisation issued in terms of the Act or a specific environmental management Act to that person, if the rights conferred by the permit or authorisation were abused by that person;

(b) disqualify that person from obtaining a permit or other authorisation for a period not exceeding five years;

(c) issue an order that all competent authorities authorised to issue permits or other authorisations be notified of any such disqualification.[2]

1 107 of 1998.
2 S 34C.

292 Forfeiture of items The court convicting a person of an offence in terms of the National Environmental Management Act[1] may declare any item including but not limited to any specimen, container, vehicle, vessel, aircraft or document that was used for the purpose of or in connection with the commission of the offence and was seized under the provisions of this part of the Act, to be forfeited to the state.[2] The minister must ensure that any specimen forfeited to the state is:

(a) repatriated to the country of export or origin as appropriate, at the expense of the person convicted of the offence involving that specimen;

(b) deposited in an appropriate institution, collection or museum, if:

(i) the specimen is clearly marked as a seized specimen; and

(ii) the person convicted of the offence does not benefit or gain from such deposit; or

(c) otherwise disposed of in an appropriate manner.[3]

1 107 of 1998.
2 S 34D(1). Cf s 34D(2) which makes the provisions of s 35 of the Criminal Procedure Act 51 of 1977 applicable to such forfeiture, subject to such modifications as the context may require.
3 National Environmental Management Act 107 of 1998 s 34D(3).

293 Treatment of seized live specimens Pending the institution of any criminal proceedings in terms of the National Environmental Management Act[1] or a specific environmental management Act or the resolution of such proceedings, a live specimen that has been seized must be deposited with a suitable institution rescue centre or facility which is able and willing to house and properly care for it.[2]

1 107 of 1998.
2 S 34E.

294 Security for release of vehicles, vessels or aircraft If a vehicle, vessel or aircraft is seized and is kept for the purposes of criminal proceedings, the owner or agent of the owner may at any time apply to a court for the release of such item.[1] A court may order the release of the item on the provision of security determined by the court.[2] The amount of the security must at least be equal to the sum of:

(a) the market value of the vehicle, vessel or aircraft;

(b) the maximum fine that a court may impose for the alleged offence; and

(c) costs and expenses incurred or reasonably foreseen to be incurred by the state in connection with prosecuting the offence and recoverable in terms of the National Environmental Management Act.[3]

1 National Environmental Management Act 107 of 1998 s 34F(1).
2 S 34F(2).
3 S 34F(3). Cf s 34F(4) which allows the court to provide for security of a lesser amount if the court is satisfied that there are circumstances which warrant it.

295 Admission of guilt fines The minister may by regulation specify offences in terms of the National Environmental Management Act[1] or a specific environmental management Act in respect of which alleged offenders may pay a prescribed admission of guilt fine instead of being tried by a court for the offence.[2] An environmental management inspector who has reason to believe that a person has committed an offence so specified may issue to the alleged offender a written notice referred to in section 56 of the Criminal Procedure Act.[3] The amount of the fine stipulated in this notice may not exceed the amount prescribed for the offence, and which a court would presumably have imposed in the circumstances.[4]

1 107 of 1998.
2 S 34G(1).
3 S 34G(2).
4 S 34G(3). Cf s 34G(4) which provides that the provisions of ss 56, 57 and 57A of the Criminal Procedure Act 51 of 1977 apply

subject to such modifications as the context may require, to written notices and admission of guilt fines referred to in s 34G of the National Environmental Management Act 107 of 1998.

296 Environmental management co-operation agreements The minister and every MEC and municipality, may enter into environmental management co-operation agreements with any person or community for the purpose of promoting compliance with the principles laid down in the National Environmental Management Act.[1] Environmental management co-operation agreements must:

(a) only be entered into with the agreement of:

(i) every organ of state which has jurisdiction over any activity to which such environmental management co-operation agreement relates;

(ii) the minister and the MEC concerned;

(b) only be entered into after compliance with such procedures for public participation as may be prescribed by the minister; and

(c) comply with such regulations as may be prescribed under section 45.[2]

Environmental management co-operation agreements may contain:

(a) an undertaking by the person or community concerned to improve on the standards laid down by law for the protection of the environment which are applicable to the subject matter of the agreement;

(b) a set of measurable targets for fulfilling the undertaking in (a), including dates for the achievement of such targets; and

(c) provision for:

(i) periodic monitoring and reporting of performance against targets;

(ii) independent verification of reports;

(iii) regular independent monitoring and inspections;

(iv) verifiable indicators of compliance with any targets, norms and standards laid down in the agreement as well as any obligations laid down by law;

(d) the measures to be taken in the event of non-compliance with commitments in the agreement, including where appropriate penalties for non-compliance and the provision of incentives to the person or community.[3]

The minister may make regulations concerning:

(a) procedures for the conclusion of environmental management co-operation agreements, which must include procedures for public participation;

(b) the duration of agreements;

(c) requirements relating to the furnishing of information;

(d) general conditions and prohibitions;

(e) reporting procedures;

(f) monitoring and inspection.[4]

1 107 of 1998 s 35(1).
2 S 35(2).
3 S 35(3).
4 S 45(1). Cf s 45(2) concerning the powers of an MEC or municipal council to substitute its own regulations or by-laws for the regulations issued by the minister.

297 Expropriation and reservation The minister may purchase or, subject to compensation, expropriate any property for environmental or any other purpose under the National Environmental Management Act,[1] if that purpose is a public purpose or is in the public interest.[2] The amount of compensation and the time and manner of payment must be determined in accordance with section 25(3) of the Constitution,[3] and the owner of the property in question must be given a hearing before any property is expropriated.[4]

The minister may reserve state land with the consent of the minister authorised to dispose of the land, and after consultation with any other minister concerned, for environmental or other purposes in terms of the Act, if that purpose is a public purpose or is in the public interest.[5]

1 107 of 1998.
2 S 36(1). Cf s 36(2) for application of the Expropriation Act 63 of 1975.
3 Constitution of the Republic of SA 108 of 1996.
4 National Environmental Management Act 107 of 1998 s 36(3).
5 S 37.

298 Intervention in litigation The minister may intervene in litigation before a court in any matter under the National Environmental Management Act.[1]

1 107 of 1998 s 38.

299 Agreements The director-general may enter into agreements with organs of state in order to fulfil his or her responsibilities.[1]

1 National Environmental Management Act 107 of 1998 s 39.

300 Appointment of employees on contract The director-general may appoint employees on contract outside the provisions of the Public Service Act[1] when this is necessary to carry out the functions of the department.[2] The director-general must, from time to time, and after consultation with the Department of Public Service and Administration, determine the conditions of employment of such employees.[3] Such employees must be remunerated from money appropriated for that purpose by Parliament.[4]

1 103 of 1994.
2 National Environmental Management Act 107 of 1998 s 40(1).
3 S 40(2).
4 S 40(3).

301 Assignment and delegation of powers The minister must record all assignments[1] in a Schedule to the National Environmental Management Act and may amend that Schedule.[2]

The minister may delegate a power or duty vested in him or her in terms of the Act or a specific environmental management Act to:

(a)   the director-general;

(b)   an MEC, by agreement with the MEC;

(c)   the management authority of a protected area; or

(d)   any organ of state, by agreement with that organ of state.[3]

Such delegation:

(a)   must be in writing;

(b)   may be made subject to conditions;

(c)   does not prevent the exercise of the power or the performance of the duty by the minister him or herself;

(d)   may include the power to subdelegate; and

(e)   may be withdrawn by the minister.[4]

The minister may confirm, vary or revoke any decision taken in consequence of a delegation or subdelegation, subject to any rights that may have accrued to a person as a result of the decision.[5] The minister may not delegate a power or duty vested in the minister in terms of the Act or a specific environmental management Act:

(a)   to make regulations;

(b)   to publish notices in the *Gazette*;

(c)   to appoint a member of a board or committee; or

(d)   to expropriate private land.[6]

The director-general may delegate a power or duty vested in him or her by or under the Act or a specific environmental management Act to:

(a)   the holder of an office in the department; or

(b)   after consultation with a provincial head of department, an officer in a provincial government or municipality.[7]

The director-general may permit a person to whom a power or duty has been delegated by the director-general to delegate further that power or duty.[8] Such delegation and permission:

(a)   must be in writing;

(b)   may be subject to conditions;

(c)   does not prevent the exercise of the power or the performance of the duty by the director-general him or herself; and

(d)   may be withdrawn by the director-general.[9]

The MEC of a province may delegate a power or duty vested in or delegated to the MEC in terms of the Act or a specific environmental management Act to:

(a)   the head of that MEC's department;

(b)   the management authority of a provincial or local protected area;

(c)   a municipality, by agreement with the municipality; or

(d)   any provincial organ of state, by agreement with that organ of state .[10]

Such a delegation:

(a)   must be in writing:

(b)   may be made subject to conditions;

(c)   does not prevent the exercise of the power or the performance of the duty by the MEC personally;

(d)   may include the power to subdelegate; and

(e)   may be withdrawn by the MEC.[11]

The MEC may confirm, vary or revoke any decision taken in consequence of a delegation or subdelegation, subject to any rights that may have accrued to a person as a result of the decision.[12] The MEC may not delegate a power or duty vested in the MEC in terms of the Act or a specific environmental management Act:

(a)   to make regulations;

(b)   to publish notices in the *Gazette*;

(c)   to appoint a member of a board or committee; or

(d)   to expropriate private land.[13]

1   "Assignment" means an assignment as contemplated in s 99 of the Constitution of the Republic of SA 108 of 1996: National Environmental Management Act 107 of 1998 s 1.
2   S 41(2).
3   S 42(1).
4   S 42(2). Cf s 42(2A) which requires the minister to give notice in the *Gazette* of any delegation of a power or duty to an MEC, the management authority of a protected area or an organ of state.
5   S 42(2B).
6   S 42(2C).
7   S 42(3).
8   S 42(4).
9   S 42(5).
10   S 42A(1).
11   S 42A(2).
12   S 42A(3).
13   S 42A(4).

302 Appeal to minister Any affected person may appeal, in the manner prescribed, to the minister against a decision taken by any person acting under a power delegated by the minister under the National Environmental Management Act.[1]

1   107 of 1998 s 43.

303 Regulations and model environmental management by-laws The minister may make regulations dealing with any matter which under the National Environmental Management Act[1] must be dealt with by regulation, and generally, to carry out the purposes and the provisions of the Act.[2] The minister may make different regulations under the Act in respect of different activities, provinces, geographical areas and owners or classes of owners of land.[3] The minister may by regulation provide that infringements of certain regulations constitute criminal offences and prescribe penalties for such offences.[4]

The minister may make model by-laws aimed at establishing measures for the management of environmental impacts of any development within the jurisdiction of a municipality, which may be adopted by a municipality as municipal bylaws.[5] Any municipality may request the director-general to assist it with the preparation of by-laws on matters affecting the environment, and the director-general may not unreasonably refuse such a request.[6] The director-general may institute programmes to assist municipalities with the preparation of by-laws for the purposes of implementing the Act.[7] The purpose of the model by-laws must be to:

(a)   mitigate adverse environmental impacts;

(b)   facilitate the implementation of decisions taken, and conditions imposed as a result of the authorisation of new activities and developments, or through the setting of norms and standards in respect of existing activities and developments; and

(c)   ensure effective environmental management and conservation of resources and impacts within the jurisdiction of a municipality in co-operation with other organs of state.[8]

The model bylaws must include measures for environmental management, which may include auditing, monitoring and ensuring compliance, reporting requirements and the furnishing of information.[9]

Before making any regulations under the Act, a minister or MEC must publish a notice in the relevant *Gazette* setting out the draft regulations; inviting written comments to be submitted on the proposed regulations within a specified period mentioned in the notice; and consider all comments received.[10] The minister must, within 30 days after promulgating and publishing any regulations, table the regulations in the National Assembly and the National Council of Provinces, and an MEC must so table the regulations in the relevant provincial legislature or, if Parliament or the provincial legislature is not then in session, within 30 days after the beginning of the next ensuing session of Parliament or the provincial legislature.[11] In considering regulations:

(a)   tabled in the National Assembly, a committee of the National Assembly must consider and report to the National Assembly;

(b)   tabled in the National Council of Provinces, a committee of the National Council of Provinces must consider and report to the National Council of Provinces; and

(c)   tabled in a provincial legislature, a committee of that provincial legislature must consider and report to the provincial legislature, whether the regulations:

(i)   are consistent with the purposes of the Act;

(ii)   are within the powers conferred by the Act;

(iii)   are consistent with the Constitution;[12] and

(iv)   create offences and prescribe penalties for such offences that are appropriate and acceptable.[13]

The National Council of Provinces may by resolution reject the regulations within 30 days after they have been tabled in the National Council of Provinces, and such rejection must be referred to the National Assembly for consideration.[14] The National Assembly, after considering any rejection of a regulation by the National Council of Provinces, and the relevant provincial legislature, may by resolution within 60 days after they have been tabled disapprove of the regulations, and may suspend its disapproval for any period and on any conditions to allow the minister or MEC to correct a defect.[15] If the National Assembly or provincial legislature disapproves of any regulation, the regulation lapses, but without affecting the validity of anything done in terms of the regulation before it lapsed, or a right or privilege acquired or an obligation or liability incurred before it lapsed.[16]

1   107 of 1998.
2   S 44(1).
3   S 44(2).
4   S 44(3).
5   S 46(1).
6   S 46(2).
7   S 46(3).
8   S 46(4).
9   S 46(5).
10   S 47(1).
11   S 47(2).
12   Constitution of the Republic of SA 108 of 1996.
13   National Environmental Management Act 107 of 1998 s 47(3).
14   S 47(4).
15   S 47(5).
16   S 47(6).

304 Regulations, legal documents and steps valid under certain circumstances   A regulation or notice, or an authorisation, permit or other document, made or issued in terms of the National Environmental Management Act[1] or a specific environmental management Act:

(a)   but which does not comply with any procedural requirement of the relevant Act, is nevertheless valid if the non-compliance is not material and does not prejudice any person;

(b)   may be amended or replaced without following a procedural requirement of the relevant Act if:

(i)   the purpose is to correct an error; and

(ii)   the correction does not change the rights and duties of any person materially.[2]

The failure to take any steps in terms of the Act or a specific environmental management Act as a prerequisite for any decision or action does not invalidate the decision or action if the failure is not material; does not prejudice any person; and is not procedurally unfair.[3]

1   107 of 1998.
2   S 47A(1). S 47A–D was inserted by the National Environmental Management Act

46 of 2003 (not yet in operation).
3   S 47A(2).

305 Consultation   When in terms of the National Environmental Management Act[1] or a specific environmental management Act the minister or an MEC is required to consult any person or organ of state, such consultation is regarded as having been satisfied if a formal written notification of intention to act has been made to that person or organ of state and no response has been received within a reasonable time.[2]

1   107 of 1998.
2   S 47B.

306 Extension of time periods   The minister or an MEC may extend, or condone a failure by person to comply with, a period in terms of the National Environmental Management Act[1] or a specific environmental management Act, except a period which binds the minister or MEC.[2]

1   107 of 1998.
2   S 47C.

307 Delivery of documents   A notice or other document in terms of the National Environmental Management Act[1] or a specific environmental management Act may be issued to a person:

(a)   by delivering it by hand;

(b)   by sending it by registered mail:

(i)   to that person's business or residential address; or

(ii)   in the case of a juristic person, to its registered address or principal place of business; or

(c)   where an address is unknown despite reasonable inquiry, by publishing it once in the *Gazette* and once in a local newspaper circulating in the area of that person's last known residential or business address.[2]

1   107 of 1998.
2   S 47D(1). Cf s 47D(2) which provides that such a notice or other document must be

regarded as having come to the notice of the person, unless the contrary is proved.

308 State bound and limitation of liability The National Environmental Management Act[1] is binding on the state except in so far as any criminal liability is concerned.[2] Neither the state nor any other person is liable for any damage or loss caused by:

(a)   the exercise of any power or the performance of any duty under the Act or any specific environmental management Act; or

(b)   the failure to exercise any power, or perform any duty under the Act or any specific environmental management Act, unless the exercise of or failure to exercise the power, or performance of or failure to perform the duty was unlawful, negligent or in bad faith.[3]

1   107 of 1998.
2   S 48.
3   S 49.

309 Miscellaneous provisions The National Environmental Management Act[1] repeals several provisions of the Environment Conservation Act.[2] Anything done or deemed to have been done under a provision repealed by the National Environmental Management Act remains valid to the extent that it is consistent with the Act until anything done under the Act overrides it; and is considered to be an action under the corresponding provision of the Act.[3]

1   107 of 1998.
2   100   of   1982:   National   Environmental
Management Act 107 of 1998 s 50.
3   S 51.

ENVIRONMENT CONSERVATION ACT

310 Introduction A prominent feature of South African environmental legislation is its diffuse nature, with provisions being contained in an extremely wide variety of parliamentary acts, provincial laws, local by-laws and ministerial regulations. In other words, there is no single statutory instrument which comprehensively codifies environmental law, nor is its materialisation ever likely or even feasible. The first Environment Conservation Act of 1982,[1] in spite of its all-embracing title, in fact regulated only a few environmental aspects. The Environment Conservation Act of 1989[2] considerably extended the scope of the 1982 Act and could be considered the most important single environmental statute until many of its provisions were repealed by the National Environmental Management Act.[3] However, it in no way constituted a codification; the title accordingly remains misleading.

There are several important provisions in the Environment Conservation Act that have not been repealed by the National Environmental Management Act that will be discussed under this heading, as they do not conveniently fit under other headings in this chapter. Other provisions, for example those relating to waste, are discussed under appropriate headings.

1   100 of 1982.
2   73 of 1989. See generally on the Act Hoogervorst (1989) 15 *SA Journal of Aquatic Sciences* 250; Glazewski 1989 *De Rebus* 872; Glavovic
1990 *SALJ* 107; Rabie 1990 *THRHR* 2; Bray 1990 *SA Public Law* 101; Barnard 1990 *De Rebus* 832 and Rabie 1994 *SAJELP* 113.
3   107 of 1998.

311 Waste and litter Some aspects of waste management[1] and the control of litter[2] are addressed by the Environment Conservation Act.

1   Environment Conservation Act 73 of 1989 ss 20 24. See par 332 post.
2   Ss 19 19A 24A.

312 Noise, vibration and shock The Environment Conservation Act[1] authorises the Minister of Environmental Affairs and Tourism to make regulations with regard to several aspects relating to the control of noise, vibration and shock.[2]

1 73 of 1989.
2 S 25.

313 Identified activities and environmental authorisations The Environment Conservation Act[1] provides for the identification of activities which, in the opinion of the Minister of Environmental Affairs and Tourism, may have a substantial detrimental effect on the environment.[2] Such activities require authorisation before they can be carried out,[3] and the minister may make regulations prescribing the process to be followed.[4]

1 73 of 1989.   3 S 22.
2 S 21.   4 S 26.

314 Limited development areas A provincial premier may by notice in the *Official Gazette* declare any area defined by the premier, as a limited development area.[1] A limited development area may not be declared unless the premier:

(a) has given notice in the *Official Gazette* and in certain newspapers[2] of his or her intention to declare such area as a limited development area;

(b) has permitted not fewer than 60 days for the submission to the director-general of the provincial government concerned of comment on the proposed declaration;

(c) has considered all representations received in terms of such notice; and

(d) has consulted each minister charged with the administration of any law which in the opinion of the premier relates to a matter affecting the environment in that area, as well as the premier in question.[3]

No person may undertake in a limited development area any development or activity prohibited by the premier by notice in the *Official Gazette*, or cause such development or activity to be undertaken unless he or she has on application been authorised thereto by a local authority designated by the premier by notice in the *Official Gazette*, on the conditions contained in such authorisation.[4] Contravention of this provision, or failure to comply with the conditions of the authorisation, constitutes an offence.[5]

In considering an application for the above authorisation the premier, or the designated local authority, may request the person to submit a report as prescribed, concerning the influence of the proposed activity on the environment in the limited development area.[6] The minister or a premier, as the case may be, may make regulations in respect of any abovementioned prohibited activity regarding environmental impact reports.[7]

1 Environment Conservation Act 73 of 1989   4 S 23(2).
  s 23(1). "Administrator" is defined in s 1.   5 S 29(4).
2 Ie in not fewer than one English and one   6 S 23(3).
  Afrikaans newspaper circulating in the area   7 S 26. See the draft regulations in *Government*
  in question: s 23(4)(a).   *Gazette* 15529 GN 171, 4 March 1994.
3 S 23(4).

315 Delegation The Minister of Environmental Affairs and Tourism, the Minister of Water Affairs and Forestry, a premier, a local authority or a government institution may on such conditions as he, she or it may deem fit delegate or assign any power or duty conferred upon or assigned to him. her or it by or under the Environment

Conservation Act[1] (excluding certain powers),[2] to respectively, any officer or employee of the Department of Environmental Affairs and Tourism, the Department of Water Affairs and Forestry or the provincial government or local authority or government institution concerned.[3]

The Director-General: Environmental Affairs and Tourism may, on such conditions as he or she may deem fit, delegate or assign any power or duty conferred upon or assigned to him or her by or under the Act, to any officer or employee of the department.[4]

1 73 of 1989.
2 Ie any power referred to in ss 24, 25, 26, 27 and 28: s 33(1).
3 S 33(1).
4 S 33(2).

316 Publication of draft notice for comment If the Minister of Environmental Affairs and Tourism, the Minister of Water Affairs and Forestry, a premier or any local authority, as the case may be, intends to issue a regulation or a direction in terms of the Environment Conservation Act,[1] declare an area to be a protected natural environment[2] or declare a policy,[3] a draft notice must first be published in the *Government Gazette* or the *Official Gazette* in question, as the case may be.[4]

The draft notice must include:

(a) the text of the proposed regulation, direction, declaration, identification or determination of policy;

(b) a request that interested parties should submit comments in connection with the proposed regulation, direction, declaration, identification or determination of policy within the period stated in the notice, which period may not be fewer than 30 days after the date of publication of the notice; and

(c) the address to which such comments must be submitted.[5]

1 73 of 1989 s 32(1)(a).
2 S 32(1)(b).
3 S 32(1)(c).
4 S 32(1).
5 S 32(2). If the minister or local authority concerned thereafter determines on any alteration of the draft notice published as aforesaid, it is not necessary to publish such alteration before finally issuing the notice: s 32(3).

317 Exemptions Any person, local authority or government institution may in writing apply to the Minister of Environmental Affairs and Tourism, or a premier, as the case may be, with the furnishing of reasons, for exemption from the application of any provision of any regulation, notice or direction which has been promulgated or issued in terms of the Environment Conservation Act.[1] In order to enable him or her to make a decision on such an application, the minister or premier may call for further information from the applicant.[2] The minister or premier may, after considering an application, refuse to grant exemption or in writing grant exemption from compliance with any or all of the provisions of any regulation, notice or direction, subject to such conditions as he or she may deem fit.[3]

If any such condition is not complied with, the minister or premier may in writing withdraw the exemption concerned or at his or her discretion determine new conditions.[4] The minister or premier may from time to time review any exemption granted or condition determined, and if he or she deems it necessary, withdraw such exemption or delete or amend such condition.[5]

1 73 of 1989 s 28A(1). Cf also s 18(7).
2 S 28A(2).
3 S 28A(3).
4 S 28A(4).
5 S 28A(5).

318 Special powers where environment is endangered or damaged If, in the opinion of the Minister of Environmental Affairs and Tourism or the premier, local authority or government institution concerned, any person performs any activity or fails to perform any activity as a result of which the environment is or may be seriously damaged, endangered or detrimentally affected, the minister, premier, local authority or government institution, as the case may be, may in writing direct such person to cease such activity; or to take such steps as the minister, premier, local authority or government institution, as the case may be, may deem fit within a period specified in the direction, with a view to eliminating, reducing or preventing the damage, danger or detrimental effect.[1] Failure to comply with such direction constitutes an offence.[2]

The minister or the premier, local authority or government institution concerned may direct such person to perform any activity or function at his or her own expense with a view to rehabilitating any damage caused to the environment as a result of such activity or failure, to the satisfaction of the minister, premier, local authority or government institution, as the case may be.[3] Failure to perform the required activity or function constitutes an offence.[4] Moreover, such failure entitles the minister, premier, local authority or government institution to perform such activity or function as if he, she or it were that person and may authorise any person to take all steps required for that purpose.[5] Any expenditure incurred in the performance of any such function may be recovered from the person concerned.[6]

1 Environment Conservation Act 73 of 1989 s 31A(1). It has been held that no direction under s 31A of the may be issued without the persons liable to be affected thereby being given notice of intention to issue the direction and without being given an opportunity to answer or respond to views held by the issuing authority: *Evans v Llandudno/*

Hout Bay Transitional Metropolitan Substructure 2001 2 SA 342 (C).
2 S 29(3).
3 S 31A(2).
4 S 29(3).
5 S 31A(3).
6 S 31A(4).

319 Powers in case of default by local authority If in the opinion of the premier of the province in question, any local authority fails to perform any function assigned to it by or under the Environment Conservation Act,[1] that premier may, after affording that local authority an opportunity of making representations to him or her, in writing direct such local authority to perform such function within a period specified in the direction. If the local authority fails to comply with such direction, the premier may perform such function as if he or she were that local authority and may authorise any person to take all steps required for that purpose.[2] Any expenditure incurred by the premier in the performance of any such function, may be recovered from the local authority concerned.[3]

Whenever in the opinion of the Minister of Environmental Affairs and Tourism a local authority has failed to perform a function referred to above, the minister may request the premier in question to act in terms of the above provision, and if the premier fails within 90 days after the date of such request to act accordingly, the minister may do anything which the premier could have done, and the above provisions apply *mutatis mutandis* with reference to the minister and anything done by the minister or under his or her authority.[4]

1 73 of 1989.
2 S 31(1).
3 S 31(2).
4 S 31(3).

320 Criminal liability Several actions are criminalised in terms of the Environment Conservation Act.[1]

In the event of a conviction in terms of the Act, the court may order that any damage to the environment resulting from the offence be repaired by the person so convicted, to the satisfaction of the Minister of Environmental Affairs and Tourism, the premier concerned or the local authority concerned.[2] If within a period of 30 days after a conviction or such longer period as the court may determine at the time of the conviction, the above order is not being complied with, the minister, the premier concerned or local authority concerned may itself take the necessary steps to repair the damage and recover the cost thereof from the person so convicted.[3]

1 73 of 1989 s 29(1) (2) (3) (4). Punishment ranges between a fine not exceeding R2 000 or imprisonment for a period not exceeding six months (or both such fine and imprisonment) to a fine not exceeding R100 000 or imprisonment for a period not exceeding ten years (or both such fine and imprisonment). Provision is also made, in the case of persistent offenders, for punishment in respect of each day during which the offence continues to be committed: s 29(6). Moreover, upon conviction the court is authorised to order forfeiture: s 30. Cf also s 41A in respect of powers of entry upon land. A magistrate's court is competent to impose any penalty provided for in the Act: s 29(9).

2 S 29(7).

3 S 29(8).

321 Appeals The Environment Conservation Act[1] provides for appeals in the following circumstances: any person who feels aggrieved at a delegated decision[2] in respect of the provisions of the Act dealing with waste management,[3] may appeal against such decision to the Minister of Water Affairs and Forestry in the prescribed manner, within the prescribed period and upon payment of the prescribed fee.[4]

Any person who feels aggrieved at a decision of an officer or employee enforcing a provision of the Act in respect of a protected natural environment may appeal against such decision to the premier concerned, in the prescribed manner, within the prescribed period and upon payment of the prescribed fee.[5]

Subject to the above provisions, any person who feels aggrieved at a decision of an officer or employee exercising any power delegated to him or her in terms of the Act or conferred upon him or her by regulation, may appeal against such decision to the Minister of Environmental Affairs and Tourism or the premier, as the case may be, in the prescribed manner, within the prescribed period and upon payment of the prescribed fee.[6]

The Minister of Environmental Affairs and Tourism, the Minister of Water Affairs and Forestry, or a premier, as the case may be, may, after considering such an appeal, confirm, set aside or vary the decision of the officer or employee or make such order as he or she may deem fit, including an order that the prescribed fee paid by the applicant or such part thereof as the Minister of Environmental Affairs and Tourism or premier concerned may determine, be refunded to that person.[7] Reference is made to the board of investigation which the Minister of Environmental Affairs and Tourism may appoint to assist him or her in the evaluation of appeals.

1 73 of 1989.

2 In terms of s 33.

3 In terms of s 20.

4 S 35(1).

5 S 35(2).

6 S 35(3).

7 S 35(4).

322 Review by High Court In addition to appeals, the Environment Conservation Act[1] also provides for review. Any person whose interests are affected by a decision of an administrative body under the Act, may within 30 days after having become aware of such decision, request such body in writing to furnish reasons for the decision within 30 days after receiving the request.[2] Within 30 days after having been furnished with such reasons or after the expiration of the period within which reasons had to be so furnished by the administrative body, the person in question may apply to a High Court having jurisdiction, to review the decision.[3]

1   73 of 1989.
2   S 36(1).
3   S 36(2). In terms of s 3 of the Promotion

of Administrative Justice Act 3 of 2000, such person is entitled to procedurally fair administrative action.

323 Compensation for loss If in terms of the provisions of the Environment Conservation Act[1] limitations are placed on the purposes for which land may be used, or on activities which may be undertaken on the land, the owner of, and the holder of a real right in, such land have a right to recover compensation from the Minister of Environmental Affairs and Tourism or premier concerned in respect of actual loss suffered by them consequent upon the application of such limitations.[2] The amount so recoverable must be determined by agreement[3] entered into between such owner or holder of the real right and the minister or premier as the case may be, with the concurrence of the Minister of State Expenditure.[4]

1   73 of 1989.
2   S 34(1).
3   In the absence of such agreement the amount to be paid will be determined by a court referred to in s 14 of the Expropriation Act 63

of 1975, and the provisions of that section and s 15 of that Act apply *mutatis mutandis* in determining such amount: Environment Conservation Act 73 of 1989 s 34(3).
4   S 34(2).

IDENTIFIED ACTIVITIES AND ENVIRONMENTAL AUTHORISATIONS

324 Introduction It is now almost universal practice for the impact of activities on the environment to be assessed prior to those activities being carried out. The impacts are usually assessed in a process known as an environmental impact assessment or "EIA". Although South African legislation does not use this term, the legislation does provide for a process of environmental authorisation of activities potentially detrimental to the environment. This is currently regulated by means of provisions of the Environment Conservation Act[1] and regulations under that Act. The National Environmental Management Act,[2] however, also provides for an environmental authorisation process and repeals the Environment Conservation Act provisions relevant to environmental authorisations. This repeal takes effect from a date to be published by the minister in the *Gazette*, which date may not be earlier than the date on which regulations or notices on the topic made or issued under the National Environmental Management Act are promulgated and the minister is satisfied that the regulations and notices under the Environment Conservation Act have become redundant.[3] Draft regulations under the National Environmental Management Act have been published,[4] but at the time of writing the Environment Conservation Act regime still applies. This may change soon.

1   73 of 1989 ss 21 22 26.
2   107 of 1998 s 24.
3   S 50(2) of the National Environmental

Management Act.
4   *Government Gazette* 27163 GN 12, 14 January 2005.

325 Identification of activities In terms of the Environment Conservation Act,[1] the Minister of Environmental Affairs and Tourism may by notice in the *Government Gazette* identify those activities which in his or her opinion may have a substantial detrimental effect on the environment, whether in general or in respect of certain areas.[2] Such activities may include the following:

(a) land use and transformation;

(b) water use and disposal;

(c) resource removal, including natural living resources;

(d) resource renewal;

(e) agricultural processes;

(f) industrial processes;

(g) transportation;

(h) energy generation and distribution;

(i) waste and sewage disposal;

(j) chemical treatment;

(k) recreation.[3]

The minister identifies such an activity only after consultation with:

(i) the minister of each state department responsible for the execution, approval or control of the activity in question;

(ii) the Minister of State Expenditure;[4] and

(iii) the premier[5] of the province concerned.[6]

No person may undertake any abovementioned activity or cause such an activity to be undertaken except by virtue of a written authorisation issued by the minister or by a premier or local authority or an officer, which premier, authority or officer must be designated by the minister by notice in the *Government Gazette*.[7] Contravention of this provision amounts to an offence.[8] Such authorisation may be issued only after consideration of reports concerning the impact of the proposed activity and of alternative proposed activities on the environment, which must be compiled and submitted by such persons and in such manner as may be prescribed.[9] The minister or a premier, as the case may be, may make regulations with regard to any identified activity, concerning:

(a) the scope and content of environmental impact reports, which may include, but are not limited to:

(i) a description of the activity in question and of alternative activities;

(ii) the identification of the physical environment which may be affected by the activity in question and by the alternative activities;

(iii) an estimation of the nature and extent of the effect of the activity in question and of the alternative activities on the land, air, water, biota and other elements or features of the natural and man–made environments;

(iv) the identification of the economic and social interests which may be affected by the activity in question and by the alternative activities;

(v) an estimation of the nature and extent of the effect of the activity in question and the alternative activities on the social and economic interests;

(vi) a description of the design or management principles proposed for the reduction of adverse environmental effects; and

(vii) a concise summary of the finding of the environmental impact report;

(b) the drafting and evaluating of environmental impact reports and of the effect of the activity in question and of the alternative activities on the environment; and

(c)   the procedure to be followed in the course of and after the performance of the activity in question or the alternative activities in order to substantiate the estimations of the environmental impact report and to provide for preventative or additional actions if deemed necessary or desirable.[10]

The minister or a premier, or a local authority or officer referred to above, may at his, her or its discretion refuse or grant the authorisation for the proposed activity or an alternative proposed activity on such conditions, if any, as he, she or it may deem necessary.[11] If such a condition is not complied with, an offence is committed[12] and the minister, any premier or any local authority or officer may withdraw the authorisation in respect of which such condition was imposed, after at least 30 days' written notice has been given to the person concerned.[13]

1   73 of 1989.
2   S 21(1).
3   S 21(2).
4   Defined in s 1.
5   Defined in s 1.
6   S 21(3).
7   S 22(1).
8   S 29(4).

9   S 22(2). On the legal implications of environmental impact assessment see Rabie 1976 *THRHR* 40, 1986 *SA Public Law* 18; Barnard 1992 *THRHR* 35.
10   S 26.
11   S 22(3).
12   S 29(4).
13   S 22(4).

326 Identified activities In a notice in terms of the Environment Conservation Act,[1] the minister identified the following activities as those which may have a substantial detrimental effect on the environment:[2]

(a)   the construction or upgrading[3] of:

(i)   facilities for commercial electricity generation with an output of at least 10 megawatts and infrastructure for bulk supply;

(ii)   nuclear reactors and facilities for the production, enrichment, processing, reprocessing, storage or disposal of nuclear fuels and wastes;

(iii)   with regard to any substance which is dangerous or hazardous and is controlled by national legislation, infrastructure, excluding road and rail, for the transportation of any such substance and manufacturing, storage, handling, treatment or processing facilities for any such substance;[4]

(iv)   roads, railways, airfields and associated structures;

(v)   marinas, harbours and all structures below the high-water mark of the sea and marinas, harbours and associated structures on inland waters;

(vi)   above ground cableways and associated structures;

(vii)   structures associated with communication networks, including masts, towers and reflector dishes, marine telecommunication lines and cables and access roads leading to those structures, but not including above ground and underground telecommunications lines and cables and those reflector dishes used exclusively for domestic purposes;

(viii)   racing tracks for motor-powered vehicles and horse racing, but not including indoor tracks;

(ix)   canals and channels, including structures causing disturbances to the flow of water in a river bed, and water transfer schemes between water catchments and impoundments;

(x)   dams, levees and weirs affecting the flow of a river;

(xi)   reservoirs for public water supply;

(xii) schemes for the abstraction or utilisation of ground or surface water for bulk supply purposes;

(xiii) public and private resorts and associated infrastructure;

(xiv) sewage treatment plants and associated infrastructure; and

(xv) buildings and structures for industrial, commercial and military manufacturing and storage of explosives or ammunition or for testing or disposal of such explosives or ammunition;

(b) the change of land use from:

(i) agricultural or zoned undetermined use or an equivalent zoning, to any other land use;[5]

(ii) use for grazing to any other form of agricultural use; and

(iii) use for nature conservation or zoned open space to any other land use;

(c) the concentration of livestock, aquatic organisms, poultry and game in a confined structure for the purpose of commercial production, including aquaculture and mariculture;

(d) the intensive husbandry of, or importation of, any plant or animal that has been declared a weed or an invasive alien species;

(e) the release of any organism outside its natural area of distribution that is to be used for biological pest control;

(f) the genetic modification of any organism with the purpose of fundamentally changing the inherent characteristics of that organism;

(g) the reclamation of land, including wetlands, below the high-water mark of the sea and in inland waters

(h) the disposal of waste in terms of section 20 of the Environment Conservation Act, excluding domestic waste, but including the establishment, expansion, upgrading or closure of facilities for all waste, ashes and building rubble

(i) scheduled processes listed in the Second Schedule to the Atmospheric Pollution Prevention Act;[6]

(j) the cultivation or any other use of virgin ground.[7]

---

1 73 of 1989.
2 *Government Gazette* 18261 GN R1182, 5 September 1997.
3 "Upgrading" means the expansion beyond its existing size, volume or capacity of an existing facility, installation or other activity referred to in this Schedule, but does not include regular or routine maintenance and the replacement of inefficient or old plant, equipment or machinery where such does not have an increased detrimental effect on the environment: Sch 1.
4 Cf *BP Southern Africa (Pty) Ltd v MEC for*

Agriculture, Conservation, Environment & Land Affairs [2004] 3 All SA 201 (W); 2004 5 SA 124 (W); *Sasol Oil (Pty) Ltd v Metcalfe* 2004 5 SA 161 (W).
5 Cf *Silvermine Valley Coalition v Sybrand van der Spuy Boerderye* [2002] 1 All SA 10 (C); 2002 1 SA 478 (C).
6 45 of 1965.
7 "Virgin ground" means land which has at no time during the preceding ten years been cultivated: Environment Conservation Act 73 of 1989 Sch 1.

327 Environmental authorisation process In a notice in terms of the Environment Conservation Act,[1] the minister set out the following process to be followed for the authorisation of identified activities:[2] An applicant:

(a) must appoint an independent consultant who must on behalf of the applicant comply with these regulations;

(b)   is solely responsible for all costs incurred in connection with the employment of the consultant or any other person acting on the applicant's behalf to comply with these regulations;

(c)   must ensure that the consultant has no financial or other interest in the undertaking of the proposed activity, except with regard to the compliance with these regulations;

(d)   must ensure that the consultant, while complying with these regulations, has:

(i) expertise in the area of environmental concern being dealt with in the specific application;

(ii) the ability to perform all the relevant tasks contemplated in these regulations;

(iii) the ability to manage the required public participation process;

(iv) the ability to timeously produce thorough, readable and informative documents;

(v) adequate recording and reporting systems to ensure the preservation of all data gathered; and

(vi) a good working knowledge of all relevant policies, legislation, guidelines, norms and standards;

(e)   must ensure that the consultant provides to the relevant authority access to, and opportunity for review of, all procedures, underlying data, reports and interviews with interested parties, whether or not such information may be reflected in a report required in terms of these regulations;

(f)   is responsible for the public participation process to ensure that all interested parties, including government departments that may have jurisdiction over any aspect of the activity, are given the opportunity to participate in all the relevant procedures contemplated in these regulations; and

(g)   must indemnify the government of the Republic, the relevant authority and all its officers, agents and employees, from any liability arising out of the content of any report, any procedure or any action for which the applicant or consultant is responsible in terms of the regulations.[3]

The relevant authority must:

(a)   ensure that officers, agents or consultants employed by the relevant authority to evaluate any reports submitted in terms of these regulations have:

(i) expertise in the area of environmental concern being dealt with in the specific application;

(ii) the ability to perform the evaluation tasks contemplated in these regulations efficiently;

(iii) the ability to produce timeously thorough, readable, and informative documents; and

(iv) a good working knowledge of all relevant policies, legislation, guidelines, norms and standards;

(b)   ensure that the evaluation and decisions required in terms of these regulations are done or reached efficiently and within a reasonable time, and that the applicant is informed immediately of any delay and is provided with a written explanation for any delay that may occur;

(c)   provide the applicant with any guidelines, as well as access to any other information in the possession of the relevant authority, that may assist the applicant in fulfilling its obligations in terms of these regulations; and

(d) try to keep the inputs required from the applicant to the minimum that are necessary to make an informed decision on the application, without putting any limitation on the rights that interested parties may have in terms of these regulations.[4]

While working for any applicant in terms of these regulations, a consultant may not work for any relevant authority in terms of these regulations in respect of the same application.[5]

An applicant must apply on the prescribed form to the relevant provincial authority for consideration, except that the provincial authority must refer the application to the minister for consideration:

(a) where the activity concerned has direct implications for national environmental policy or international environmental commitments or relations;

(b) where the activity concerned will take place within an area that is demarcated as an area of national or international importance, but does not include the seashore, conservancies, protected natural environments, proclaimed private nature reserves, natural heritage sites, and the buffer zones and transitional areas of biosphere reserves and world heritage sites;

(c) where the minister and the provincial authority jointly decide that an application in respect of a specific activity should be considered by the minister;

(d) where a national government department, the relevant provincial authority or a statutory body other than a municipality is the applicant; or

(e) where the activity has the potential to affect the environment across the borders of two or more provinces.[6]

After considering the application, the relevant authority may request the applicant to submit a plan of study for scoping for the purposes of a scoping report; or in a suitable case, to submit such scoping report without a prior plan of study.[7] A plan of study for scoping must include:

(a) a brief description of the activity to be undertaken;

(b) a description of all tasks to be performed during scoping;

(c) a schedule setting out when these tasks will be completed;

(d) an indication of the stages at which the relevant authority will be consulted; and

(e) a description of the proposed method of identifying the environmental issues and alternatives.[8]

The relevant authority may, after receiving such plan of study and after considering it, request the applicant to provide additional information that the relevant authority requires to accept the plan of study for scoping.[9]

On being informed by the relevant authority that the plan of study submitted has been accepted or on receiving the request to submit a scoping report, as the case may be, the applicant must submit a scoping report to the relevant authority, which must include:

(a) a brief project description;

(b) a brief description of how the environment may be affected;

(c) a description of environmental issues identified;

(d) a description of all alternatives identified; and

(e) an appendix containing a description of the public participation process followed, including a list of interested parties and their comments.[10]

The relevant authority may, after receiving the scoping report and after considering it, request the applicant to make the amendments that the relevant authority requires to accept the scoping report.[11] After a scoping report has been accepted, the relevant authority may decide that the information contained in the scoping report is sufficient for the consideration of the application without further investigation; or that the information contained in the scoping report should be supplemented by an environmental impact assessment which focuses on the identified alternatives and environmental issues identified in the scoping report.[12]

In the event of a decision that the scoping report must be supplemented by an environmental impact assessment, the applicant must submit a plan of study for an environmental impact assessment, which must include:

(a) a description of the environmental issues identified during scoping that may require further investigation and assessment;

(b) a description of the feasible alternatives identified during scoping that may be further investigated;

(c) an indication of additional information required to determine the potential impacts of the proposed activity on the environment;

(d) a description of the proposed method of identifying these impacts; and

(e) a description of the proposed method of assessing the significance of these impacts.[13]

The relevant authority may, after receiving this plan of study and after considering it, request the applicant to make the amendments to the plan of study that the relevant authority requires to accept the plan.[14]

After the plan of study for the environmental impact assessment has been accepted, the applicant must submit an environmental impact report to the relevant authority, which must contain:

(a) a description of each alternative, including particulars on the extent and significance of each identified environmental impact, and the possibility for mitigation of each identified impact;

(b) a comparative assessment of all the alternatives; and

(c) appendices containing descriptions of the environment concerned; the activity to be undertaken; the public participation process followed, including a list of interested parties and their comments; any media coverage given to the proposed activity; and any other information included in the accepted plan of study.[15]

After the relevant authority has made a decision on the basis of the scoping report, or has received an environmental impact report that complies with the requirements of these regulations, as the case may be, the relevant authority must consider the application and may decide to issue an authorisation with or without conditions, or refuse the application.[16]

The relevant authority must issue a record of such decision, and on request to any other interested party.[17] The record of the decision must include:

(a) a brief description of the proposed activity, the extent or quantities and the surface areas involved, the infrastructural requirements and the implementation programme for which the authorisation is issued;

(b) the specific place where the activity is to be undertaken;

(c) the name, address and telephone number of the applicant;

(d)   the name, address and telephone number of any consultant involved;

(e)   the date of, and persons present at, site visits, if any;

(f)   the decision of the relevant authority;

(g)   the conditions of the authorisation (if any), including measures to mitigate, control or manage environmental impacts or to rehabilitate the environment;

(h)   the key factors that led to the decision;

(i)   the date of expiry or the duration of the authorisation;

(j)   the name of the person to whom an appeal may be directed;

(k)   the signature of a person who represents the relevant authority; and

(l)   the date of the decision.[18]

An appeal to the minister or provincial authority[19] must be done in writing within 30 days from the date on which the record of decision was issued, and must set out all the facts as well as the grounds of appeal, and must be accompanied by all relevant documents or copies of them which are certified as true by a commissioner of oaths.[20] After the record of the decision has been issued by the relevant authority, any report submitted for the purposes of these regulations becomes a public document, subject to the rights of the owner of it.[21]

It has been held that it is inappropriate to require the a person carrying out an identified activity to follow the environmental authorisation process in a case where the activity had already been carried out (without the necessary authorisation).[22] On the other hand, another court held that the process could still be followed where the activity in question had commenced but was not yet completed.[23]

1   73 of 1989.

2   *Government Gazette* 18261 GN R1183, 5 September 1997.

3   Reg 3(1). If any of these provisions is not complied with by the applicant and not immediately attended to, after having been made aware of it by the relevant authority, the application is regarded to have been withdrawn (reg 3(2)).

4   Reg 3(3). The minister and provincial authority may jointly decide that an application may be considered by the provincial authority, provided that where the interests of more than one province are affected, all provinces must be involved in the decision (reg 3(3A)).

5   Reg 3(4).

6   Reg 4. If a local authority has been designated by the minister in terms of s 22(1) of the Act to issue authorisation for an activity specified by the minister, the provincial authority must refer an application in respect of such activity to that local authority for consideration.

7   Reg 5(1).

8   Reg 5(2). "Alternative", in relation to an activity, means any other possible course of action, including the option not to act (reg 1).

9   Reg 5(3).

10   Reg 6(1).

11   Reg 6(2).

12   Reg 6(3).

13   Reg 7(1).

14   Reg 7(2).

15   Reg 8.

16   Reg 9. The relevant authority may, from time to time, on new information, review any condition, and if it deems it necessary, delete or amend such condition, or at its discretion, determine new conditions, in a manner that is lawful, reasonable and procedurally fair (reg 9(3)).

17   Reg 10(1). The record of decision must indicate the period within which, and the method how, the applicant must make the record of decision available to any interested party.

18   Reg 10(2).

19   In terms of s 35(3).

20   Reg 11.

21   Reg 12.

22   *Silvermine Valley Coalition v Sybrand van der Spuy Boerderye* [2002] 1 All SA 10 (C); 2002 1 SA 478 (C).

23   *Eagles Landing Body Corporate v Molewa* 2003 1 SA 412 (T).

SOIL CONSERVATION

HISTORICAL DEVELOPMENT

328 Official investigations Shortly after Union, in view of the disastrous effects and steadily increasing severity of annual droughts throughout most of the interior, and due to the fact that soil erosion, which inevitably accompanied these droughts, had increased to such an extent as to render useless large parts of the land and was threatening many other parts, the Senate appointed a select committee to inquire into and report on this problem.

The report of the Select Committee on Droughts, Rainfall and Soil Erosion,[1] submitted during 1914, was the first official attempt at investigating the causes of droughts and soil erosion in South Africa. The committee found that all available evidence went to prove that there had been no definite diminution in the rainfall of South Africa, and concluded that soil erosion was the real explanation for the desiccation of certain areas in the country. The committee pointed out that soil erosion was caused by man in that he gradually destroyed the vegetation which formed the natural protection of the soil. Natural vegetation was destroyed by veld-burning, over-grazing, cutting down of trees and bush, and injudicious road and railway construction.

Little or no positive action resulted from the committee's findings and the situation continued to cause alarm. After the severe drought of 1919, the Drought Investigation Commission was appointed. This commission was to investigate and report, *inter alia*, upon any improvements in farming conditions generally, such as the provision of more water, prevention of soil erosion and any other matters which had a bearing on the methods by which losses to farmers resulting from periodic droughts in the drier parts of the country could be prevented. The commission submitted its final report in 1923.[2] This report has come to be regarded as a classic in the field of soil conservation. The commission dealt mainly with shortcomings in stock farming. It investigated the factors which lead to drought losses and found that the same factors were also responsible for soil erosion. It came to the same conclusion as the Senate Select Committee that the available meteorological data was insufficient to suggest that the average rainfall in South Africa had changed much, and the commission concluded that drought losses were caused principally by faulty veld and stock management, for instance kraaling of stock, overstocking, and destruction of vegetation. These malpractices led to a diminution of the land surface's capacity to absorb water, with the result that the canals by which water reached the sea were multiplied and enlarged. Soil erosion could thus be held responsible for the drying up of rivers and waterholes, the lowering of the water table, and the increasingly disastrous effects of droughts and heavy rains which had given rise to the belief that the climate was changing.

The report of the Drought Investigation Commission, which aroused wide interest, constitutes the first official attempt at a systematic and co-ordinated analysis of the fundamental shortcomings in agricultural land use. It is a very comprehensive and enlightening document, particularly in view of the fact that this pioneering investigation was undertaken so long ago.

Since these pioneering investigations, many further official commissions and committees of inquiry, conferences, and symposia that have studied the phenomenon of soil erosion and made recommendations as to its control, have to a greater or lesser extent vindicated the findings and recommendations of both the Select Committee and the Drought Investigation Commission.[3]

1 Senate SC 2–1914. See generally on soil conservation Verster, Du Plessis, Schloms and Fuggle "Soil" in Fuggle and Rabie (eds) *Environmental Management in SA* 181 and

Rabie 1974 *CILSA* 255.
2 UG 49–23.
3 See Rabie *SA Environmental Legislation* 19–25.

329 Development of legislation Before 1941 there was no substantial legislation dealing with soil conservation. Only legislation which was indirectly related to soil conservation, such as provisions aimed at the control of grass-burning and at the conservation of trees, had been enacted.[1]

The Forest Act of 1941[2] was the first substantial legislation providing for the control of soil erosion and related problems.

However, the most important landmark in the struggle against soil erosion was the enactment, during 1946, of the Soil Conservation Act.[3] This Act replaced the Forest Act in so far as the latter dealt with soil erosion control, and the new Act was designed to remedy the shortcomings of that Act and to provide comprehensive control of action aimed at combating soil erosion. The Act, moreover, did not only relate to combating and preventing soil erosion, but also provided for the conservation of vegetation and water supplies, which is logical in view of the close relationship between soil, water and vegetation.

Sadly, however, the Act did not realise the high expectations that were hoped for at its introduction. In view of its failure, new legislation was introduced in the form of the Soil Conservation Act of 1969.[4] Unfortunately this Act, like its predecessor, failed to realise the expectations that were held when it was introduced, and after some 14 years yet further legislation was introduced. The new statute which was called the Conservation of Agricultural Resources Act,[5] encompassed both the Soil Conservation Act of 1969 and the Weeds Act,[6] albeit in amended form.

1 See eg Ord 5 of 1836, Ord 28 of 1846, Act 18 of 1859, Act 28 of 1888, Act 20 of 1902 and Act 20 of 1908 (Cape); Law 21 of 1865, Act 31 of 1895 and Act 18 of 1902 (Natal); Law 2 of 1870, Law 8 of 1870 and Law 15 of 1880 (Tvl); ch 125 OFS Law Book of 1891 and Act 32 of 1908 (Free State). See also the Forest Act 16 of 1913, as amended

by the Forest (Demarcation) Act 14 of 1917 and Forest Act, 1913, Amendment Act 28 of 1930.
2 13 of 1941.
3 45 of 1946.
4 76 of 1969.
5 43 of 1983.
6 42 of 1937.

PRINCIPAL SOIL CONSERVATION PROVISIONS

330 Conservation of Agricultural Resources Act The Conservation of Agricultural Resources Act[1] constitutes the principal legislation dealing with soil conservation. There is, nevertheless, a variety of other legislation which is also related to soil conservation. The objects of the Act are to provide for the conservation of the natural agricultural resources of South Africa (defined as the soil, water sources and vegetation, excluding weeds and invader plants)[2] by the maintenance of the production potential of land, the combating and prevention of erosion and weakening or destruction of the water sources, and the protection of the vegetation and the combating of weeds and invader plants.[3] The Act does not apply to any land which is situated within an urban area[4] or within a declared mountain catchment area.[5]

1 43 of 1983.
2 S 1.
3 S 3.
4 S 2(1)(a). The provisions of the Act relating

to weeds and invader plants do, nevertheless, apply within an urban area: s 2(2)(a). Cf s 1 for the definition of "urban area".
5 S 2(1)(c).

331 Control measures In order to achieve the objects of the Conservation of Agricultural Resources Act,[1] the Minister of Agriculture[2] may prescribe control measures which must be complied with by land users[3] to whom they apply.[4] Such control measures may relate to:

(a) the cultivation[5] of virgin soil;[6]

(b) the utilisation and protection of land which is cultivated;

(c) the irrigation of land;

(d) the prevention or control of waterlogging or salination of land;

(e) the utilisation and protection of vleis, marshes, water sponges, water courses[7] and water sources;

(f) the regulation of the flow pattern of run-off water,

(g) the utilisation and protection of the vegetation;

(h) the grazing capacity[8] of veld, expressed as an area of veld per large stock unit;[9]

(i) the maximum number and the kind of animals which may be kept on veld;

(j) the prevention and control of veld fires;

(k) the utilisation and protection of veld which has burned;

(l) the control of weeds[10] and invader plants;[11]

(m) the restoration or reclamation of eroded[12] land or land which is otherwise disturbed or denuded;

(n) the protection of water sources against pollution on account of farming practices;

(o) the construction, maintenance, alteration or removal of soil conservation works[13] or other structures on land; and

(p) any other matter which the minister may deem necessary or expedient in order that the objects of the Act may be achieved.[14]

A number of control measures have been prescribed by regulation.[15] These measures relate to the cultivation of virgin soil[16] and of land with a certain slope;[17] the protection of cultivated land against erosion through the action of water[18] and wind;[19] the prevention of waterlogging and salination of irrigated land;[20] the utilisation and protection of vleis, marshes, water sponges and water courses;[21] regulating the flow pattern of run-off water;[22] the utilisation and protection of veld;[23] the grazing capacity of veld;[24] the number of animals that may be kept on veld;[25] the prevention and control of veld fires;[26] and the restoration and reclamation of eroded,[27] disturbed or denuded land.[28]

Failure by a land user to comply with any such control measure renders the land user liable to an offence.[29] Moreover, the executive officer[30] may by means of a direction (published by notice in the *Government Gazette* or contained in a written notice)[31] order a land user to comply with a particular control measure which is binding on him or her, or if it is in the opinion of the executive officer essential in order to achieve the objects of the Act, to perform or not to perform any other specified act on or with regard to the land in question.[32] A direction is binding upon the land user as well as his or her successors in title.[33] Refusal by a land user to receive a direction served on him or her in the prescribed manner or refusal or failure to comply with a direction constitutes an offence.[34]

1 43 of 1983.
2 Who may not delegate this power: s 26.
3 Cf s 1 for the definition of "land user".
4 S 6(1).

5 "Cultivation", in relation to land, means any act by means of which the topsoil is disturbed mechanically : s 1.
6 "Virgin soil" means land which in the

opinion of the executive officer has at no time during the preceding ten years been cultivated : s 1.

7 "Water course" means a natural flow path in which run-off water is concentrated and along which it is carried away : s 1.

8 "Grazing capacity", in relation to veld, means the production capacity over the long term of that veld to meet and feed requirements of animals in such a manner that the natural vegetation thereon does not deteriorate or is not destroyed : s 1.

9 "Large stock unit" means a unit which consists of the prescribed kind, type, breed, age or sex, or which is in a prescribed phase of production or is of a prescribed approximate live mass : s 1.

10 "Weed" means any kind of plant which has been declared a weed in terms of the Act and includes the seed of such plant and any vegetative part of such plant which reproduces itself asexually : s 1.

11 "Invader plant" means a kind of plant which has been declared an invader plant in terms of the Act, and includes the seed of such plant and any vegetative part of such plant which reproduces itself asexually : s 1.

12 "Erosion" means the loss of soil through the action of water, wind, ice or other agents, including the subsidence of soil : s 1.

13 For the definition of "soil conservation work", see par 332 post.

14 S 6(2).

15 Part 1 *Government Gazette* 9238 GN R1048, 25 May 1984.

16 Reg 2. "Virgin soil" means land which in the opinion of the executive officer has at no time during the preceding ten years been cultivated: s 1.

17 Reg 3.

18 Reg 4.

19 Reg 5.

20 Reg 6.

21 Reg 7.

22 Reg 8.

23 Reg 9.

24 Reg 10.

25 Reg 11.

26 Reg 12.

27 Reg 13.

28 Reg 14.

29 Ss 6(5) and 23(1)(a).

30 Designated in terms of s 4(1).

31 S 7(3)(a) and (b) and part III of the regulations in *Government Gazette* 9238 GN R1048, 25 May 1984.

32 S 7(1).

33 S 7(4)(a).

34 Ss 7(6) and 23(1)(a) and (c).

332 Maintenance of soil conservation works

A soil conservation work[1] must (except where otherwise provided) be maintained by every land user and his or her successors in title at his or her own expense in a manner which, in the opinion of the executive officer, will ensure its continued efficacy.[2] Refusal or failure to comply with this provision exposes the land user to a repayment in respect of soil conservation works for which monetary assistance was rendered.[3] Moreover, if the executive officer becomes aware of any such refusal or failure, he or she may order the land user concerned to repair or reconstruct the soil conservation work in question.[4] Contravention of any of these provisions constitutes an offence.[5]

1 "Soil conservation work" means any work which is constructed on land for (a) the prevention of erosion or the conservation of land which is subject to erosion; (b) the conservation or improvement of the vegetation or the surface of the soil; (c) the drainage of superfluous surface or subterranean water; (d) the conservation or reclamation of any water source; or (e) the prevention of the silting of dams and the pollution of water, but not a work which is constructed on land in the course of prospecting or mining activities: Conservation of Agricultural Resources Act 43 of 1983 s 1.

2 S 12(1)(a).

3 S 12(2)(a).

4 S 12(3).

5 Ss 12(5) 23(1)(a).

333 Minister's own performance of soil conservation actions

In addition to the minister's power to prescribe control measures, applicable to land users, the minister may on his or her own perform or cause to be performed on or in respect of any land any act which may be the subject of a control measure and which the minister may deem necessary in order to achieve the objects of the Conservation of

Agricultural Resources Act.[1] The costs involved may be recovered from the land-owner concerned.[2] The minister may also, with the concurrence of the owner[3] of any land and subject to such conditions as may be agreed upon between them, perform any act on or in respect of the land of that owner for the purpose of public demonstration or for research on any matter relating to veld, soil or water conservation or the combating of weeds or invader plants.[4]

1 43 of 1983 s 11(1).
2 S 11(2)(a) and (b).
3 For the definition of "owner", see s 1.

4 S 11(4)(a). This is done at state expense: s 11(4)(b).

334 Schemes The minister[1] may by notice in the *Government Gazette*, establish a scheme in terms of which assistance may be granted to land users by means of the payment of subsidies in respect of:

(a) the construction of soil conservation works;

(b) the reparation of damage to the natural agricultural resources or soil conservation works which has been caused by a flood or any other disaster caused by natural forces;

(c) the reduction of the number of animals being kept on land in order to restrict the detrimental effect of a drought on that land;

(d) the restoration or reclamation of eroded, disturbed, denuded or damaged land;

(e) the planting and cultivation of particular crops which improve soil fertility or counteract the vulnerability of soil to erosion;

(f) the combating of weeds or invader plants;

(g) the performance or omission of anything else which the minister may deem necessary or expedient in order to achieve the objects of the Conservation of Agricultural Resources Act.[2]

Certain schemes have been established.[3] It is an offence for a person, whose participation in a scheme has been approved, to fail to comply with the provisions of a scheme or to satisfy the conditions on which assistance in terms of a scheme has been rendered.[4]

1 Who may not delegate this power: Conservation of Agricultural Resources Act 43 of 1983 s 26.
2 S 8(1).

3 Cf *Government Gazette* 9238 GN R1044, R1045, R1046 and R1047, 25 May 1984.
4 S 9(2).

335 Expropriation of land If the minister is of the opinion that it is necessary for the restoration or reclamation of the natural agricultural resources of any land in order to achieve the objects of the Conservation of Agricultural Resources Act,[1] he or she may expropriate that land.[2]

1 43 of 1983.
2 S 14(1).

336 Conservation committees Conservation committees for determined areas may be established by the minister.[1] The duties of a conservation committee are to promote the conservation of the natural agricultural resources in the area concerned in order to achieve the objects of the Conservation of Agricultural Resources Act; to advise the department on any matter as to the application of the Act or a scheme in the area concerned, or which it may deem necessary in order that the objects of the Act may be achieved; and to exercise such other functions as it may be granted by the minister.[2] The minister may also establish regional conservation committees in respect of determined regions.[3] Such committees advise conservation committees in their respective regions on matters regarding the conservation of the natural agricultural resources; advise the department and the Conservation Advisory Board on any matter arising from the application of the Act or a scheme in the region concerned, or which it may deem necessary in order that the objects of the Act may be achieved in that region; and perform such other duties as may be imposed upon it by the minister.[4]

1 Conservation of Agricultural resources Act 43 of 1983 s 15(1). Cf s 15(3) for the appointment of members. CF also part IV of the regulations in *Government Gazette* 9238 GN R1048, 25 May 1984.

2 S 15(2).
3 S 16(1). Cf s 16(3) for the appointment of members.
4 S 16(2).

337 Conservation advisory board A conservation advisory board is established by the Conservation of Agricultural Resources Act[1] to advise the minister on matters concerning the desirability of prescribing specific control measures with regard to a particular area; the desirability of establishing a specified scheme, and the provisions of such scheme; and any other matter arising from the application of the Act or a scheme, or which it may deem necessary in order to achieve the objects of the Act or which the minister may refer to it for advice.[2]

1 43 of 1983 s 17(1). Cf s 17(3) in respect of membership.
2 S 17(2).

338 Official powers In addition to the powers already referred to in other sections, particular powers of investigation are conferred upon a variety of officials and other bodies.[1] Apart from his or her other powers, certain discretionary powers in respect of schemes are conferred upon the executive officer.[2] Provision is also made for the minister to delegate some of his or her powers.[3]

No person, including the state, is liable in respect of anything done in good faith in the exercise of a power or the performance of a duty conferred or imposed upon him or her by virtue of the Conservation of Agricultural Resources Act or a scheme.[4]

The minister may make regulations *inter alia* as to the powers and duties of a conservation committee and generally with reference to any matter which he or she considers necessary or expedient to prescribe in order to achieve or to promote the objects of the Act.[5]

1 Conservation of Agricultural Resources Act 43 of 1983 s 18(1), (2) and (4).
2 S 20(1), (2) and (3).
3 S 26.
4 S 28.
5 S 29(1). Cf *S v Buys* 1988 3 SA 789 (N); 1990 1 SA 101 (A).

339 Appeals Any person who considers him or herself aggrieved by any decision or action in terms of the Conservation of Agricultural Resources Act[1] or a scheme by the executive officer or any other officer to whom powers have been delegated, may appeal to the minister against the decision or action concerned.[2] The minister, whose decision is final,[3] may confirm, set aside or alter the decision or action against which the appeal is brought.[4]

1 43 of 1983.
2 S 21(1). Cf part VI of the regulations in *Government Gazette* 9238 GN R1048, 25 May 1984.
3 S 21(1)(d).
4 S 21(5)(a).

340 Secrecy It is an offence for any person, except for the purpose of the perform-ance of his or her functions under the Conservation of Agricultural Resources Act[1] or a scheme or for the purpose of legal proceedings under the Act, or when required to do so by any court or under any law, to disclose to any other person any information acquired by the person in the performance of his or her functions under the Act or a scheme, and which relates to the business or affairs of any other person.[2]

1   43 of 1983.
2   Ss 22 23(1)(c).

OTHER RELEVANT LEGISLATION

341 General Although the Conservation of Agricultural Resources Act[1] constitutes by far the most important legislation in respect of soil erosion control, there are provisions contained in other legislation that are also relevant as far as soil conserva-tion is concerned.

1   43 of 1983.

342 Mountain catchment areas The close relationship between soil, vegetation and water conservation is again illustrated by the conservation of mountain catchment areas. Although provision for the protection of mountain catchment areas did exist in other Acts,[1] it was felt that these protection measures, as applied by the various gov-ernment departments under whose control mountain catchment areas fell, did not always promote co-ordinated action. For this reason, it was decided to centralise the task of the protection of mountain catchment areas and to entrust this matter to the then Department of Forestry.[2] The Mountain Catchment Areas Act[3] was accordingly promulgated to provide for this centralised control. The Act is now administered by the various provincial governments.

In terms of the Act, mountain catchment areas may be declared by the minister.[4] The minister has wide powers to declare directions to be applicable to any owner or occupier of land situated in such areas.[5] These directions may relate to the conserva-tion, use, management and control of such land, the prevention of soil erosion, or the protection and treatment of natural vegetation.[6] The Act also makes provision for fire protection plans and the establishment of fire protection committees.[7]

1   See generally the *Report of the Interdepartmen-tal Committee on the Conservation of Mountain Catchments in SA* (1961) 30 et seq.
2   *House of Assembly Debates* 9 September 1970, 3708.
3   63 of 1970.

4   S 2.
5   S 3.
6   S 3(1)(a)(i) and (ii). Compensation is payable in respect of patrimonial loss caused by complying with these directions: s 4.
7   Ss 7 8.

343 Nature conservation Since nature conservation legislation is also aimed at the conservation of land and its vegetation, particularly in national parks and in provincial, municipal and private nature reserves, such legislation plays an important role in effecting soil conservation in these areas.

344 Road construction The construction of roads can lead to soil erosion in the surrounding areas. The South African National Roads Agency Limited and National Roads Act[1] accordingly provides that the South African National Roads Agency Limited has the power to perform any work in connection with any road (whether a national road or a road of which that municipality or province is the road authority), including the planning, design and construction of such a road;[2] and to plant trees, shrubs, other plants or grass, and protect or promote any vegetation, alongside the roadways of national roads, and to take any other steps or perform any other work considered desirable for the convenience of users of a national road or the appearance of a national road or in order to prevent soil erosion on a national road or to prevent it arising as a result of the construction of a national road.[3]

1 7 of 1998. See title ROADS AND ROAD TRANSPORT.	2 S 26(a).
	3 S 26(i).

CONSERVATION OF BIODIVERSITY

345 Introduction Biological diversity, or biodiversity, is the variability among living organisms from all sources including terrestrial, marine and other aquatic eco-systems and the ecological complexes of which they are part, and includes diversity within species, between species, and of ecosystems.[1] Until recently, South Africa had no national legislation that addressed conservation on a direct and comprehensive basis. The conservation of biodiversity has historically been something regulated at provincial level.[2] The provincial legislation focuses primarily on the conservation of species,[3] with little attention given to the conservation of habitats and ecosystems. In 2000, the government embarked on a process of developing new legislation aimed at conserving biodiversity. One of the main impetuses behind this legislation is the Convention on Biological Diversity of 1992. The new legislation, the National Environmental Management: Biodiversity Act, was enacted in 2004.

1 National Environmental Management: Biodiversity Act 10 of 2004 s 1.	2 Provincial ordinances.
	3 See pars 389 et seq 427 et seq post.

346 National Environmental Management: Biodiversity Act The objectives of the National Environmental Management: Biodiversity Act[1] are:

(a) within the framework of the National Environmental Management Act,[2] to provide for the management and conservation of biological diversity within the Republic and of the components of such biological diversity; the use of indigenous biological resources[3] in a sustainable manner; and the fair and equitable sharing among stakeholders of benefits arising from bioprospecting[4] involving indigenous biological resources;

(b) to give effect to ratified international agreements relating to biodiversity which are binding on the Republic;

(c) to provide for co-operative governance in biodiversity management; and

(d) to provide for a South African National Biodiversity Institute to assist in achieving the objectives of the National Environmental Management: Biodiversity Act.[5]

In fulfilling the rights contained in section 24 of the Constitution[6] (the environmental rights), the state through its organs that manage legislation applicable to biodiversity, must manage, conserve and sustain South Africa's biodiversity and its components and genetic resources; and implement the Act to achieve the progressive realisation of those rights.[7] The Act applies in the Republic, including its territorial waters, exclusive economic zone and continental shelf; and the Prince Edward Islands; and to human activity affecting South Africa's biological diversity and its components.[8] The Act binds all organs of state in the national and local spheres of government; and in the provincial sphere of government, subject to section 146 of the

Constitution.[9] The Act gives effect to ratified international agreements affecting biodiversity to which South Africa is a party, and which bind the Republic.[10]

1 10 of 2004.
2 107 of 1998.
3 "Indigenous biological resource", when used in relation to bioprospecting, means any indigenous biological resource as defined in s 80(2) of the National Environmental Management: Biodiversity Act 10 of 2004; or when used in relation to any other matter, means any resource consisting of any living or dead animal, plant or other organism of an indigenous species; any derivative of such animal, plant or other organism; or any genetic material of such animal, plant or other organism: s 1.
4 "Bioprospecting" in relation to indigenous biological resources, means any research on, or development or application of, indigenous biological resources for commercial or industrial exploitation, and includes:
(a) the systematic search, collection or gathering of such resources or making extractions from such resources for purposes of such research, development or application;
(b) the utilisation for purposes of such

research or development of any information regarding any traditional uses of indigenous biological resources by indigenous communities; or
(c) research on, or the application, development or modification of, any such traditional uses, for commercial or industrial exploitation: s 1.
5 S 2.
6 Constitution of the Republic of SA 108 of 1996.
7 National Environmental Management: Biodiversity Act 10 of 2004 s 3.
8 S 4(1).
9 S 4(2). The Act must be read with the National Environmental Management Act 107 of 1998 and guided by the national environmental management principles in s 2 of that Act: National Environmental Management: Biodiversity Act 10 of 2004 ss 6 and 7). Conflict between the National Environmental Management: Biodiversity Act and other legislation is dealt with in s 8.
10 S 5.

347 Norms and standards relating to biodiversity conservation The minister may by notice in the *Gazette*:

(a) issue norms and standards for the achievement of any of the objectives of the National Environmental Management: Biodiversity Act,[1] including for the management and conservation of South Africa's biological diversity and its components, and restriction of activities which impact on biodiversity and its components;

(b) set indicators to measure compliance with those norms and standards; and

(c) amend any such notice.[2]

Norms and standards may apply nationwide, in a specific area only, or to a specific category of biodiversity only;[3] and different norms and standards may be issued for different areas or different categories of biodiversity.[4]

1 10 of 2004.
2 S 9(1). Such notice must be preceded by the necessary consultative process (see ss 99 100).
3 S 9(3).
4 S 9(4).

348 South African National Biodiversity Institute The National Environmental Management: Biodiversity Act[1] establishes the South African National Biodiversity Institute ("SANBI") as a juristic person.[2] SANBI's functions are that it:

(a) must monitor and report regularly to the minister on the status of the Republic's biodiversity, the conservation status of all listed threatened or protected species and listed ecosystems and the status of all listed invasive species;

(b) must monitor and report regularly to the minister on the impacts of any genetically modified organism that has been released into the environment, including the impact on non-target organisms and ecological processes, indigenous biological resources and the biological diversity of species used for agriculture;

(c)   may act as an advisory and consultative body on matters relating to biodiversity to organs of state and other biodiversity stakeholders;

(d)   must co-ordinate and promote the taxonomy of South Africa's biodiversity;

(e)   must manage, control and maintain all national botanical gardens;

(f)   may establish, manage, control and maintain herbaria, and collections of dead animals that may exist;

(g)   must establish facilities for horticulture display, environmental education, visitor amenities and research;

(h)   must establish, maintain. protect and preserve collections of plants in national botanical gardens and in herbaria;

(i)   may establish, maintain, protect and preserve collections of animals and micro-organisms in appropriate enclosures;

(j)   must collect, generate, process, co-ordinate and disseminate information about biodiversity and the sustainable use of indigenous biological resources, and establish and maintain databases in this regard;

(k)   may allow, regulate or prohibit access by the public to national botanical gardens, herbaria and other places under the control of the institute, and supply plants, information, meals or refreshments or render other services to visitors;

(l)   may undertake and promote research on indigenous biodiversity and the sustainable use of indigenous biological resources;

(m)   may co-ordinate and implement programmes for the rehabilitation of ecosystems, and the prevention, control or eradication of listed invasive species;

(n)   may co-ordinate programmes to involve civil society in the conservation and sustainable use of indigenous biological resources and the rehabilitation of ecosystems;

(o)   on the minister's request, must assist him or her in the performance of duties and the exercise of powers assigned to the minister in terms of the Act;

(p)   on the minister's request, must advise him or her on any matter regulated in terms of the Act, including the implementation of the Act and any international agreements; the identification of bioregions and the contents of any bioregional plans; other aspects of biodiversity planning; the management and conservation of biological diversity; and the sustainable use of indigenous biological resources;

(q)   on the minister's request, must advise him or her on the declaration and management of, and development in, national protected areas; and

(r)   must perform any other duties assigned to it in terms of the Act or as may be prescribed.[3]

SANBI is given various general powers such as the power to appoint staff and open and operate its own bank accounts.[4] The Act also provides for its governing board, and the composition and membership thereof;[5] operating procedures of the board;[6] its administration;[7] financial matters;[8] and general supervisory matters.[9]

1   10 of 2004.
2   S 10.
3   S 11. When the institute gives advice on a scientific matter, it may consult any appropriate organ of state or other institution which has expertise in that matter.
4   S 12.
5   Ss 13–22.
6   Ss 23–27.
7   Ss 28–29.
8   Ss 30–32.
9   Ss 35–36.

349 National botanical gardens The minister, acting with the approval of the cabinet member responsible for the administration of the land in question, may declare any state land described in the notice as a national botanical garden, or part of an existing national botanical garden.[1] He or she may make a similar declaration by acting in accordance with an agreement with the owner of the land described in that agreement.[2] The declaration of state land as a national botanical garden, or part of an existing national botanical garden, may not be withdrawn and a part of a national botanical garden on state land may not be excluded from it except by resolution of each House of Parliament.[3]

1 National Environmental Management: Biodiversity Act 10 of 2004 s 33(1). The relevant notice must assign a name to the national botanical garden (which may be amended (s 34(1)); and the sites described in Sch 1 to the Forest Act 122 of 1984 (repealed), must be regarded as having been declared as national botanical gardens in terms of this section.
2 National Environmental Management: Biodiversity Act 10 of 2004 s 33(2).
3 S 34(2), although the minister may withdraw a declaration of a botanical garden on privately owned land (s 34(1)).

350 Biodiversity planning and monitoring The minister must prepare and adopt, by notice in the *Gazette*, a national biodiversity framework within three years of the date on which the National Environmental Management: Biodiversity Act[1] takes effect; must monitor implementation of the framework; must review the framework at least every five years; and may, when necessary, amend the framework.[2] The national biodiversity framework must provide for an integrated, co-ordinated and uniform approach to biodiversity management by organs of state in all spheres of government, non-governmental organisations, the private sector, local communities, other stakeholders and the public. It must be consistent with the National Environmental Management: Biodiversity Act; the national environmental management principles; and any relevant international agreements binding on the Republic; must identify priority areas for conservation action and the establishment of protected areas; and reflect regional co-operation on issues concerning biodiversity management in Southern Africa.[3] The framework may determine norms and standards for provincial and municipal environmental conservation plans.[4]

The minister or the MEC for environmental affairs in a province may, by notice in the *Gazette*, determine a geographic region as a bioregion for the purposes of the Act if that region contains whole or several nested ecosystems and is characterised by its landforms, vegetation cover, human culture and history; and biodiversity in such region; and publish a plan for the management of biodiversity and the components of biodiversity in such region.[5] The minister may enter into an agreement with a neighbouring country to secure the effective implementation of the plan.[6] A bioregional plan must contain measures for the effective management of biodiversity and the components of biodiversity in the region, provide for monitoring of the plan, and be consistent with the Act, the national environmental management principles, the national biodiversity framework, and any relevant international agreements binding on the Republic.[7] The minister or the relevant MEC must review a bioregional plan at least every five years, and assess compliance with the plan and the extent to which its objectives are being met.[8]

Any person, organisation or organ of state desiring to contribute to biodiversity management may submit to the minister for his or her approval a draft management plan for:

(a) a listed ecosystem,[9] or which is not listed but which does warrant special conservation attention;

(b)   a listed indigenous species,[10] or which is not listed but which does warrant special conservation attention; or

(c)   a migratory species to give effect to the Republic's obligations in terms of an international agreement binding on the Republic.[11]

The minister must publish by notice in the *Gazette* a biodiversity management plan that he or she has approved, determine the manner of implementation of the plan, and assign responsibility for the implementation of the plan to a person, organisation or organ of state identified by the minister as willing to be responsible for the implementation of the plan.[12] The minister may enter into a biodiversity management agreement with such responsible person, organisation or organ of state, or any other suitable person, organisation or organ of state, regarding the implementation of a biodiversity management plan, or any aspect of it.[13]

A biodiversity management plan must be aimed at ensuring the long-term survival in nature of the species or ecosystem to which the plan relates and provide for the responsible person, organisation or organ of state to monitor and report on progress with implementation of the plan.[14] It must be consistent with the following documents: the National Environmental Management: Biodiversity Act; the national environmental management principles; the national biodiversity framework; any applicable bioregional plan; any plans issued in terms of chapter 3 of the National Environmental Management Act; any municipal integrated development plan; any other plans prepared in terms of national or provincial legislation that is affected; and any relevant international agreements binding on the Republic.[15] The minister must review a biodiversity management plan at least every five years, and assess compliance with the plan and the extent to which its objectives are being met, and may amend such a plan, either on his or her own initiative or on request by an interested person, organisation or organ of state.[16]

The national biodiversity framework, a bioregional plan and a biodiversity management plan may not be in conflict with any environmental implementation or environmental management plans prepared in terms of chapter 3 of the National Environmental Management Act; any integrated development plans adopted by municipalities in terms of the Local Government: Municipal Systems Act;[17] any spatial development frameworks in terms of legislation regulating land-use management, land development and spatial planning administered by the cabinet member responsible for land affairs; and any other plans prepared in terms of national or provincial legislation that are affected.[18] An organ of state that must prepare an environmental implementation or environmental management plan in terms of chapter 3 of the National Environmental Management Act, and a municipality that must adopt an integrated development plan in terms of the Local Government: Municipal Systems Act must align its plan with the national biodiversity framework and any applicable bioregional plan; incorporate into that plan those provisions of the national biodiversity framework or a bioregional plan that specifically apply to it; and demonstrate in its plan how the national biodiversity framework and any applicable bioregional plan may be implemented by that organ of state or municipality.[19]

The minister must for the purposes of the biodiversity planning and monitoring chapter of the National Environmental Management Act designate monitoring mechanisms and set indicators to determine the conservation status of various components of South Africa's biodiversity, and any negative and positive trends affecting the conservation status of the various components.[20]

The minister must promote research done by the institute and other institutions on biodiversity conservation, including the sustainable use, protection and conservation of indigenous biological resources. Research on biodiversity conservation may include:

(a) the collection and analysis of information about the conservation status of the various components of biodiversity, negative and positive trends affecting the conservation status of various components and threatening processes or activities likely to impact on biodiversity conservation;

(b) the assessment of strategies and techniques for biodiversity conservation;

(c) the determination of biodiversity conservation needs and priorities; and

(d) the sustainable use, protection and conservation of indigenous biological resources.[21]

1 10 of 2004.

2 S 38. The minister must follow the necessary consultation process: s 47.

3 S 39(1).

4 S 39(2).

5 S 40(1). The minister may determine a region as a bioregion and publish a bioregional plan for that region either on his or her own initiative but after consulting the MEC for Environmental Affairs in the relevant province; or at the request of a province or municipality (s 40(2)). The MEC for environmental affairs may determine a region as a bioregion and publish a bioregional plan for that region only with the concurrence of the minister (s 40(3)). Any person or organ of state may, on the request of the minister or MEC, assist in the preparation of a bioregional plan (s 40(4)).

6 S 40(5) – the agreement must be submitted to Parliament.

7 S 41. The minister or MEC may, when necessary, amend a bioregional plan or the boundaries of the bioregion (the MEC may do so only with the concurrence of the minister): s 42.

8 S 42(1).

9 Listed in terms of s 52 (discussed below).

10 Listed in terms of s 56 (discussed below).

11 S 43(1).

12 S 43(2) (3).

13 S 44.

14 S 45.

15 S 45(c).

16 S 46, which provides for the necessary consultation process for amendment (s 46(3)).

17 32 of 2000.

18 National Environmental Management: Biodiversity Act 10 of 2004 s 48(1).

19 S 48(2). The SA National Biodiversity institute may assist in the alignment and coordination of the plans mentioned in the section (s 48(3)). Such bodies must also take into account the need for the protection of listed ecosystems (s 54 – see below).

20 S 49. The minister may require any person, organisation or organ of state involved in monitoring to report regularly to the minister on the results of such monitoring measured against the predetermined indicators; and the minister must annually report to Parliament on the information submitted to the minister and make such information publicly available.

21 S 50.

351 Protection of ecosystems The minister may, by notice in the *Gazette*, publish a national list of ecosystems that are threatened and in need of protection, and an MEC for environmental affairs in a province may similarly publish a provincial list of such ecosystems.[1] The following categories of ecosystems may be listed:

(a) critically endangered ecosystems, being ecosystems that have undergone severe degradation of ecological structure, function or composition as a result of human intervention and are subject to an extremely high risk of irreversible transformation;

(b) endangered ecosystems, being ecosystems that have undergone degradation of ecological structure, function or composition as a result of human intervention, although they are not critically endangered ecosystems;

(c) vulnerable ecosystems, being ecosystems that have a high risk of undergoing significant degradation of ecological structure, function or composition as a result of human intervention, although they are not critically endangered ecosystems or endangered ecosystems; and

(d)   protected ecosystems, being ecosystems that are of high conservation value or of high national or provincial importance, although they are not listed under the three categories above.

The minister and the relevant MEC must at least every five years review any national or provincial list.[2]

The minister may identify any process or activity in a listed ecosystem as a threatening process. A threatening process must be regarded as a specified activity contemplated in section 24(2)(b) of National Environmental Management Act and a listed ecosystem must be regarded as an area identified for the purpose of that section, meaning that such activity may not commence without the appropriate authorisation.[3]

1 National Environmental Management: Biodiversity Act 10 of 2004 s 52. "Ecosystem" is defined in s 1 as a dynamic complex of animal, plant and micro-organism communities and their non-living environment interacting as a functional unit. The list must describe in sufficient detail the location of the ecosystems listed (s 52(3)). An MEC must act with the concurrence of the minister, and must follow the required consultation process (s 63).
2 S 52(4).
3 S 53; for consultation process see s 63.

352 Protection of species The minister may, by notice in the *Gazette*, publish a list of:

(a)   critically endangered species, being any indigenous species facing an extremely high risk of extinction in the wild in the immediate future;

(b)   endangered species, being any indigenous species facing a high risk of extinction in the wild in the near future, although they are not a critically endangered species;

(c)   vulnerable species, being any indigenous species facing an extremely high risk of extinction in the wild in the medium-term future, although they are not a critically endangered species or an endangered species; and

(d)   protected species, being any species which are of such high conservation value or national importance that they require national protection, although they are not listed in the above categories.[1]

A person may not carry out a restricted activity involving a specimen of a listed threatened or protected species without the necessary permit.[2] A "restricted activity" is:

(i) hunting, catching, capturing or killing any living specimen of a listed threatened or protected species by any means, method or device whatsoever, including searching, pursuing, driving, lying in wait, luring, alluring, discharging a missile or injuring with intent to hunt, catch, capture or kill any such specimen;

(ii) gathering, collecting or plucking any specimen of a listed threatened or protected species;

(iii) picking parts of, or cutting, chopping off, uprooting, damaging or destroying, any specimen of a listed threatened or protected species;

(iv) importing into the Republic, including introducing from the sea, any specimen of a listed threatened or protected species;

(v) exporting from the Republic, including re-exporting from the Republic, any specimen of a listed threatened or protected species;

(vi) having in possession or exercising physical control over any specimen of a listed threatened or protected species;

(vii) growing, breeding or in any other way propagating any specimen of a listed threatened or protected species, or causing it to multiply;

(viii) conveying, moving or otherwise translocating any specimen of a listed threatened or protected species;

(ix) selling or otherwise trading in, buying, receiving, giving, donating or accepting as a gift, or in any way acquiring or disposing of any specimen of a listed threatened or protected species; or

(x) any other prescribed activity which involves a specimen of a listed threatened or protected species.[3]

The minister may, by notice in the *Gazette*, prohibit the carrying out of any activity which is of a nature that may negatively impact on the survival of a listed threatened or protected species, and which is specified in the notice, or prohibit the carrying out of such activity without a permit.[4]

---

1 National Environmental Management: Biodiversity Act 10 of 2004 s 56. The minister must follow the required consultation process (s 63) and must review the lists at least every five years (s 56).

2 S 57(1). The minister must follow the required consultation process (s 63). "Listed threatened or protected species" means any of the species listed in terms of s 56. The prohibition in s 57(1) does not apply in respect of a specimen of a listed threatened or protected species conveyed from outside the Republic in transit through the Republic to a destination outside the Republic, provided that such transit through the Republic takes place under the control of an environmental management inspector (s 57(3)). The permit referred to is issued in terms of ch 7 of the Act.

3 S 1.

4 S 57(2).

353 Trade in listed threatened or protected species Part 3 of chapter 4 of the National Environmental Management: Biodiversity Act[1] deals with the Republic's obligations in terms of the Convention on International Trade in Endangered Species of Fauna and Flora ("CITES").[2] To this end, the minister:

(a) must monitor compliance with the restricted activities[3] in so far as trade in specimens of listed threatened or protected species is concerned; and compliance in the Republic with CITES;

(b) must consult the scientific authority on issues relating to trade in specimens of endangered species regulated by CITES;

(c) must prepare and submit reports and documents in accordance with the Republic's obligations in terms of CITES;

(d) may provide administrative and technical support services and advice to organs of state to ensure the effective implementation and enforcement in the Republic of CITES;

(e) may make information and documentation relating to CITES publicly available; and

(f) may prescribe a system for the registration of institutions, ranching operations, nurseries, captive breeding operations and other facilities.[4]

The minister must establish a scientific authority for purpose of assisting in regulating and restricting the trade in specimens of listed threatened or protected species.[5] The scientific authority's functions are that it must:

(a) monitor in the Republic the legal and illegal trade in specimens of listed threatened or protected species;

(b) advise the minister and any other interested organs of state on the matters that it monitors;

(c)   make recommendations to an issuing authority on applications for permits in respect of restricted activities;[6]

(d)   make non-detriment findings on the impact of actions relating to the international trade in specimens of listed threatened or protected species;

(e)   advise the minister on:

(i) the registration of ranching operations, nurseries, captive breeding operations and other facilities;

(ii) whether an operation or facility meets the criteria for producing species considered to be bred in captivity or artificially propagated;

(iii) the choice of a rescue centre or other facility for the disposal of forfeited specimens;

(iv) any amendments to a notice published in terms of section 56(1) or 57(2);

(v) the nomenclature of species; or

(vi) any other matter of a specialised nature;

(f)   assist the minister or an environmental management inspector in the identification of specimens for the purpose of enforcing the provisions of the Act;

(g)   issue certificates in which the identification of a specimen is verified as being taxonomically accurate;

(h)   perform any other function that may be prescribed; or delegated to it by the minister;

(i)   deal with any other matter necessary for, or reasonably incidental to, its powers and duties;[7] and

(j)   publish in the *Gazette* any annual non-detriment findings on trade in specimens of listed threatened or protected species in accordance with CITES.[8]

1   10 of 2004.
2   S 59 refers to "an international agreement regulating international trade in specimens of endangered species which is binding on the Republic".
3   In terms of s 57.
4   S 59.
5   S 60. The SA National Biodiversity Institute must provide logistical, administrative and financial support for the proper functioning of the scientific authority.
6   In terms of s 57.
7   S 61. In performing its duties, the scientific authority must base its findings, recommendations and advice on a scientific and professional review of available information; and consult, when necessary, organs of state, the private sector, non-governmental organisations, local communities and other stakeholders before making any findings or recommendations or giving any advice.
8   S 62.

354 Alien species A person may not carry out a restricted activity involving a specimen of an alien species without the necessary permit,[1] which may be issued only after a prescribed assessment of risks and potential impacts on biodiversity is carried out.[2] A restricted activity, in relation to a specimen of an alien or invasive species, means:

(i) importing into the Republic, including introducing from the sea, any specimen of an alien or listed invasive species;

(ii) having in possession or exercising physical control over any specimen of an alien or listed invasive species;

(iii) growing, breeding or in any other way propagating any specimen of an alien or listed invasive species, or causing it to multiply;

(iv) conveying, moving or otherwise translocating any specimen of an alien or listed invasive species;

(v) selling or otherwise trading in, buying, receiving, giving, donating or accepting as a gift, or in any way acquiring or disposing of any specimen of an alien or listed invasive species; or

(vi) any other prescribed activity which involves a specimen of an alien or listed invasive species.[3]

The minister may, by notice in the *Gazette*, exempt from these restrictions any alien species specified in the notice; or any alien species of a category specified in the notice, such that any person may carry out a restricted activity involving a specimen of an exempted alien species without a permit.[4] The minister may also, by notice in the *Gazette*, publish a list of those alien species in respect of which a permit may not be issued and a person may not carry out any restricted activity involving a specimen of such an alien species.[5]

A person authorised by permit[6] to carry out a restricted activity involving a specimen of an alien species must comply with the conditions under which the permit has been issued, and take all required steps to prevent or minimise harm to biodiversity.[7] A competent authority[8] may, in writing, direct any person who has failed to comply with this duty, or who has contravened section 65(1) or section 67(2) of the National Environmental Management: Biodiversity Act, to take such steps as may be necessary to remedy any harm to biodiversity caused by the actions of that person and as may be specified in the directive.[9] If that person fails to comply with such a directive the authority may implement the directive; and recover from that person all costs incurred by the competent authority in implementing the directive.[10] Should an alien species establish itself in nature as an invasive species because of the actions of a specific person, a competent authority may hold that person liable for any costs incurred in the control and eradication of that species.[11]

1 A permit issued in terms of ch 7 of the National Environmental Management: Biodiversity Act 10 of 2004.
2 S 65.
3 S 1.
4 S 66. The necessary consultative process must be followed (s 79).
5 S 67. The lists published in terms of ss 66 and 67 must be regularly reviewed. The necessary consultative process must be followed (s 79).
6 In terms of s 65(1).
7 S 69(1).
8 "Competent authority", in relation to the control of an alien or invasive species, means:
(a) the minister;
(b) an organ of state in the national, provincial or local sphere of government designated by regulation as a competent authority for the control of an alien species or a listed invasive species in terms of the Act; or
(c) any other organ of state (s 1).
9 S 69(2).
10 S 69(3).
11 S 69(3).

355 Invasive species The minister must within 24 months of the date on which section 70 of the National Environmental Management: Biodiversity Act[1] takes effect, by notice in the *Gazette*, publish a national list of invasive species in respect of which chapter 5 of the Act must be applied nationally.[2] The same applies to an MEC for environmental affairs in a province in respect of a provincial list. A person may not carry out a restricted activity involving a specimen of a listed invasive species without the necessary permit,[3] which may be issued only after a prescribed invasive species assessment of risks and potential impacts on biodiversity is carried out.[4]

A person authorised by permit to carry out a restricted activity involving a specimen of a listed invasive species must take all the required steps to prevent or minimise harm to biodiversity.[5] A person who is the owner of land on which a listed invasive species occurs must notify any relevant competent authority, in writing, of the listed invasive species occurring on that land; take steps to control and eradicate the listed invasive species and to prevent it from spreading; and take all the required steps to prevent or minimise harm to biodiversity.[6] A competent authority may, in writing, direct any person who has failed to comply with these duties, or who has contravened section 71(1), to take such steps as may be necessary to remedy any harm to biodiversity caused by the actions of that person, or the occurrence of the listed invasive species on land of which that person is the owner, and as may be specified in the directive.[7] If that person fails to comply with such directive, a competent authority may implement the directive and recover all costs reasonably incurred by a competent authority in implementing the directive from that person, or proportionally from that person and any other person who benefited from such implementation of the directive.[8] Any person may request a competent authority, in writing, to issue such a directive, to which the authority must reply, in writing, within 30 days of receipt of the request.[9] Should a competent authority fail to respond to the request within the stated period or refuses the request, the person who made the request may apply to a court for an order directing that competent authority to issue the directive.[10]

Control and eradication of a listed invasive species must be carried out by means or methods that are appropriate for the species concerned and the environment in which it occurs.[11] Any action taken to control and eradicate a listed invasive species must be executed with caution and in a manner that may cause the least possible harm to biodiversity and damage to the environment.[12] The methods employed to control and eradicate a listed invasive species must also be directed at the offspring, propagating material and re-growth of such invasive species in order to prevent such species from producing offspring, forming seed, regenerating or re-establishing itself in any manner.[13] The minister must ensure the co-ordination and implementation of programmes for the prevention, control or eradication of invasive species,[14] and may establish an entity consisting of public servants to co-ordinate and implement programmes for the prevention, control or eradication of invasive species.[15]

The management authority of a protected area preparing a management plan for the area in terms of the National Environmental Management: Protected Areas Act[16] must incorporate into the management plan an invasive species control and eradication strategy,[17] and must at regular intervals prepare and submit to the minister or the MEC for Environmental Affairs in the province a report on the status of any listed invasive species that occurs in that area.[18] A status report must include:

(a)   a detailed list and description of all listed invasive species that occur in the protected area;

(b)   a detailed description of the parts of the area that are infested with listed invasive species;

(c)   an assessment of the extent of such infestation; and

(d)   a report on the efficacy of previous control and eradication measures.[19]

All organs of state in all spheres of government must prepare an invasive species monitoring, control and eradication plan for land under their control, as part of their environmental plans in accordance with section 11 of the National Environmental Management Act,[20] and the invasive species monitoring, control and eradication plans of municipalities must be part of their integrated development plans.[21] An invasive species monitoring, control and eradication plan must include:

(a)   a detailed list and description of any listed invasive species occurring on the relevant land;

(b)   a description of the parts of that land that are infested with such listed invasive species;

(c)   an assessment of the extent of such infestation;

(d)   a status report on the efficacy of previous control and eradication measures;

(e)   the current measures to monitor, control and eradicate such invasive species;

(f)   measurable indicators of progress and success, and indications of when the control plan is to be completed.[22]

1   10 of 2004.
2   S 70(1). These lists must be regularly reviewed (s 70(2)). An MEC may only act in concurrence with the minister (s 70(3)), and the necessary consultative process must be followed (s 79).
3   S 71(1); permit issued in terms of ch 7.
4   S 71(2).
5   S 73(1).
6   S 73(2).
7   S 73(3).
8   S 73(4).
9   S 74(1) (2).
10 S 74(3).
11 S 75(1).
12 S 75(2).

13 S 75(3).
14 S 75(4).
15 S 75(5).
16 57 of 2003; see s 39.
17 National Environmental Management: Biodiversity Act 10 of 2004 s 76(1).
18 S 77(1).
19 S 77(2).
20 107 of 1998.
21 National Environmental Management: Biodiversity Act 10 of 2004 s 76(2); the minister may request the SA National Biodiversity Institute to assist municipalities in performing these duties (s 76(3)).
22 S 76(4).

356 Genetically modified organisms If the minister has reason to believe that the release of a genetically modified organism into the environment under a permit applied for in terms of the Genetically Modified Organisms Act,[1] may pose a threat to any indigenous species or the environment, no permit for such release may be issued in terms of that Act unless an environmental assessment has been conducted in accordance with chapter 5 of the National Environmental Management Act[2] as if such release were activity contemplated in that chapter.[3] The minister must convey his or her belief to the authority issuing permits in terms of the Genetically Modified Organisms Act before the application for the relevant permit is decided.[4]

1   15 of 1997.
2   107 of 1998.
3   National Environmental Management: Biodiversity Act 10 of 2004 s 78(1). For the purposes of this subsection, "release" means

trial release or general release as defined in s 1 of the Genetically Modified Organisms Act 15 of 1997.
4   National Environmental Management: Biodiversity Act 10 of 2004 s 78(2).

357 Bioprospecting, access and benefit-sharing No person may, without the necessary permit engage in bioprospecting[1] involving any indigenous biological resources,[2] or export from the Republic any indigenous biological resources for the purpose of bioprospecting or any other kind of research.[3] Before any application for such permit may be considered by a relevant issuing authority,[4] the applicant must at the request of the issuing authority, disclose to that authority all information concerning the proposed bioprospecting and the indigenous biological resources to be used for such bioprospecting that is relevant for a proper consideration of the application.[5] Before a permit is issued, the issuing authority must protect any interests any of the following stakeholders may have in the proposed bioprospecting project:

(a)   a person, including any organ of state or community, providing or giving access to the indigenous biological resources to which the application relates; and

(b)   an indigenous community[6] whose traditional uses of the indigenous biological resources to which the application relates have initiated or will contribute to or form part of the proposed bioprospecting or whose knowledge of or discoveries about the indigenous biological resources to which the application relates are to be used for the proposed bioprospecting.[7]

If a stakeholder is a person providing or giving access to indigenous biological resources, an issuing authority may issue a permit only if:

(a)   the applicant has disclosed all material information relating to the relevant bioprospecting to the stakeholder and on the basis of that disclosure has obtained the prior consent of the stakeholder for the provision of or access to such resources;

(b)   the applicant and the stakeholder have entered into a material transfer agreement that regulates the provision of or access to such resources, and a benefit-sharing agreement that provides for sharing by the stakeholder in any future benefits that may be derived from the relevant bioprospecting; and

(c)   the minister has approved such benefit-sharing and material transfer agreements.[8]

If a stakeholder is an indigenous community as contemplated above, an issuing authority may issue a permit only if:

(a)   the applicant has disclosed all material information relating to the relevant bioprospecting to the stakeholder and on the basis of that disclosure has obtained the prior consent of the stakeholder to use any of the stakeholder's knowledge of or discoveries about the indigenous biological resources for the proposed bioprospecting;

(b)   the applicant and the stakeholder have entered into a benefit-sharing agreement that provides for sharing by the stakeholder in any future benefits that may be derived from the relevant bioprospecting; and

(c)   the minister has approved such benefit-sharing agreement.[9]

An issuing authority:

(a)   may engage the applicant and stakeholder on the terms and conditions of a benefit-sharing or material transfer agreement;

(b)   may facilitate negotiations between the applicant and stakeholder and ensure that those negotiations are conducted on an equal footing;

(c)   on request by the minister, must ensure that any benefit-sharing arrangement agreed upon between the applicant and stakeholder is fair and equitable;

(d)   may make recommendations to the minister; and

(e)   must perform any other functions that may be prescribed.[10]

A benefit-sharing agreement must:

(a)   be in a prescribed format;

(b)   specify:

(i) the type of indigenous biological resources to which the relevant bioprospecting relates;

(ii) the area or source from which the indigenous biological resources are to be collected or obtained;

(iiii) the quantity of indigenous biological resources that is to be collected or obtained;

(iv) any traditional uses of the indigenous biological resources by an indigenous community; and

(v) the present potential uses of the indigenous biological resources;

(c)   name the parties to the benefit-sharing agreement;

(d)   set out the manner in which and the extent to which the indigenous biological resources are to be utilised or exploited for purposes of such bioprospecting;

(e)   set out the manner in which and the extent to which the stakeholder will share in any benefits that may arise from such bioprospecting;

(f)   provide for a regular review of the agreement by the parties as the bioprospecting progresses; and

(g)   comply with any other matters that may be prescribed.[11]

A benefit-sharing agreement or any amendment to such an agreement must be submitted to the minister for approval, and does not take effect unless approved by the minister.[12]

A material transfer agreement must:

(a)   be in a prescribed format;

(b)   specify:

(i)   particulars of the provider, and the exporter or recipient, of the indigenous biological resources;

(ii)   the type of indigenous biological resources to be provided or to be given access to;

(iii)   the area or source from which the indigenous biological resources are to be collected, obtained or provided;

(iv)   the quantity of indigenous biological resources that is to be provided, collected, obtained or exported;

(v)   the purpose for which such indigenous biological resources are to be exported;

(vi)   the present potential uses of the indigenous biological resources; and

(vii)   conditions under which the recipient may provide any such indigenous biological resources, or their progeny, to a third party.[13]

A material transfer agreement or any amendment to such an agreement must be submitted to the minister for approval, and does not take effect unless approved by the minister.[14]

The National Environmental Management: Biodiversity Act establishes a Bioprospecting Trust Fund into which all moneys arising from benefit-sharing agreements and material transfer agreements, and due to stakeholders, must be paid, and from which all payments to, or for the benefit of, stakeholders must be made.[15] The director-general must manage the fund in the prescribed manner, and is accountable for the money in the fund in terms of the Public Finance Management Act.[16]

The minister may by notice in the *Gazette* declare that chapter 6 of the Act does not apply to indigenous biological resources specified in the notice or to an activity relating to such indigenous biological resources.[17]

1   "Bioprospecting", in relation to indigenous biological resources, means any research on, or development or application of, indigenous biological resources for commercial or industrial exploitation, and includes:
(a) the systematic search, collection or gathering of such resources or making extractions from such resources for purposes of such research, development or application;
(b) the utilisation for purposes of such research or development of any information regarding any traditional uses of indigenous biological resources by indigenous communities; or
(c) research on, or the application, development or modification of, any such traditional uses, for commercial or industrial exploitation (National Environmental Management: Biodiversity Act 10 of 2004 s 1).

2   "Indigenous biological resources" includes:

(a) any indigenous biological resources (meaning any living or dead animal, plant or other organism of an indigenous species; any derivative of such animal, plant or other organism; or any genetic material of such animal, plant or other organism (s 1)), whether gathered from the wild or accessed from any other source, including any animals, plants or other organisms of an indigenous species cultivated, bred or kept in captivity or cultivated or altered in any way by means of biotechnology;

(b) any cultivar, variety, strain, derivative, hybrid or fertile version of any indigenous species or of any animals, plants or other organisms referred to above;

(c) any exotic animals, plants or other organisms, whether gathered from the wild or accessed from any other source which, through the use of biotechnology, have been altered with any genetic material or chemical compound found in any indigenous species or any animals, plants or other organisms referred to above; but excludes–

  (i) genetic material of human origin;

  (ii) any exotic animals, plants or other organisms, other than exotic animals, plants or other organisms referred to above; and

  (iii) indigenous biological resources listed in terms of the International Treaty on Plant Genetic Resources for Food and Agriculture (s 80).

3 S 81(1).

4 "Issuing authority" means the minister; or an organ of state in the national, provincial or local sphere of government designated by regulation in terms of s 97 as an issuing authority for permits of the kind in question (s 1).

5 S 81(2).

6 The term "indigenous community" is not defined in the Act.

7 S 82(1).

8 S 82(2).

9 S 82(3).

10 S 82(4).

11 S 83(1).

12 S 83(2).

13 S 84(1).

14 S 84(2).

15 S 85. All money paid into the bioprospecting trust fund is trust money within the meaning of s 13(l)(fl(ii) of the Public Finance Management Act 1 of 1999.

16 National Environmental Management: Biodiversity Act 10 of 2004 s 85(3).

17 S 86. Such notice must follow the required consultation process (s 86(2)) and may be amended or withdrawn.

358 Permits Chapter 7 of the National Environmental Management: Biodiversity Act[1] provides for the permitting system for restricted or prohibited activities involving specimens of listed threatened or protected species; alien species; or listed invasive species; bioprospecting involving indigenous biological resources; and the export of indigenous biological resources for bioprospecting or any other type of research. It deals with the application procedure;[1] the contents of permits;[2] integrated permits;[3] and the cancellation of permits.[4] Before issuing a permit, the issuing authority may in writing require the applicant to furnish it, at the applicant's expense, with such independent risk assessment or expert evidence as the issuing authority may determine.[5] As far as alien and invasive species are concerned, a permit may be issued only if:

(a) adequate procedures have been followed by the applicant to assess the risks and potential impacts associated with the restricted activity;

(b) the relevant species has been found to have negligible or no invasive potential;

(c) the benefits of allowing the activity are significantly greater than the costs associated with preventing or remedying any resultant damage to the environment; or

(d) it is satisfied that adequate measures have been taken by the applicant to prevent the escape and spread of the species.[6] An appeal against a permitting decision lies with the minister[7] or with an appeal panel established by the minister.[8]

1 National Environmental Management: Biodiversity Act 10 of 2004 s 88.

2 S 90.

3 S 92.

4 S 93.

5 S 89.

6 S 91.

7 S 94.

8 S 95.

359 Enforcement of the Act The National Environmental Management: Biodiversity Act[1] provides for regulatory powers;[2] and the required consultation and public participation processes.[3] Various offences are provided for, for example, carrying out restricted activities in respect of listed threatened or protected species or acting contrary to the terms of a permit.[4]

1   10 of 2004.
2   S 97.
3   Ss 99 100.

4   S 101. The maximum penalty is a fine, or imprisonment for a period not exceeding five years, or both: s 102.

PROTECTED AREAS

360 The concept of protected area A protected area may in general be described as an area set aside and managed to conserve indigenous flora, fauna, ecosystems, natural resources and other natural phenomena. South African law provides for the establishment of a wide variety of protected areas, until recently in terms of a number of different Acts. Some such areas, such as forest wilderness areas, forest nature reserves and mountain catchment areas, certain provincial nature reserves and marine sanctuaries serve, almost exclusively, a conservation purpose, although research and limited recreational functions also play a role. Other areas, such as national parks and certain provincial nature reserves, although set aside principally for conservation, accommodate a substantial measure of tourism, while tourism and recreation outweigh conservation in respect of public resorts. In yet other areas, such as protected environments, conservation is only one of a number of aims pursued simultaneously, while conservation is a secondary aim in areas such as botanic gardens.

Apart from areas that are formally established as some or other category of protected area, certain areas are managed as protected areas in spite of their not having been formally set aside as such; for instance, certain state forest areas are managed as mountain catchments, and islands are conserved as breeding stations for sea birds and seals, and utilised for the collection of guano. The sea-shore mainly serves the cause of public recreation and is for this purpose conserved to some extent, while conservation is a secondary objective in respect of general defence areas.

While historically many types of protected areas were seen as sacrosanct wildlife sanctuaries, thinking has changed recently so that the accommodation of the lifestyles, aspirations and needs of local communities as part of the overall conservation ethic has become a globally accepted principle. According to the National Environmental Management: Protected Areas Act,[1] the purposes of the declaration of areas as protected areas are to:

(a)   protect ecologically viable areas representative of South Africa's biological diversity and its natural landscapes and seascapes in a system of protected areas;

(b)   preserve the ecological integrity of those areas;

(c)   conserve biodiversity in those areas;

(d)   protect areas representative of all ecosystems, habitats and species naturally occurring in South Africa;

(e)   protect South Africa's threatened or rare species;

(f)   protect an area which is vulnerable or ecologically sensitive;

(g)   assist in ensuring the sustained supply of environmental goods and services;

(h)   provide for the sustainable use of natural and biological resources;

(i)   create or augment destinations for nature-based tourism;

(j)   manage the interrelationship between natural environmental biodiversity, human settlement and economic development;

(k)   generally, contribute to human, social, cultural, spiritual and economic development; or

(l)   rehabilitate and restore degraded ecosystems and promote the recovery of endangered and vulnerable species.[2]

1   57 of 2003.
2   S 17.

361 Historical development of protected areas It would appear that the first formal protected areas were demarcated forest reserves, established by virtue of the Cape Forest Act of 1888.[1] Next followed the establishment of the Pongola game reserve in 1894 (deproclaimed during 1921), while the Hluhluwe, Umfolosi and Mkusi game reserves were established in 1897, the Sabie game reserve (later to become part of the Kruger National Park) in 1898, and Giant's Castle in the Drakensberg during 1903.

Up to 1940 the only protected areas of note that had been established, were some national parks, Natal provincial nature reserves, forestry nature reserves, botanic gardens and rock-lobster sanctuaries.

Most provincial, local and private nature reserves have been established since the late 1960s, while mountain catchment areas, wilderness areas, lake areas, nature areas and general marine sanctuaries have been established since the late 1970s. The only protected areas that have been regularly and consistently established during the last part of the nineteenth century are KwaZulu Natal provincial nature reserves.

1   28 of 1888. See generally on protected areas Hanks and Glavovic "Protected Areas" in Fuggle and Rabie (eds) *Environmental Management in SA* 690; Lampaert *De Wetgeving betreffende de Natuurgebieden in Zuid-Afrika* LLM UPE 1982; Rabie 1985 *CILSA* 51; Gordon *The Management of Nature Areas declared in terms of section 4(1)(b) of the Physical Planning Act 88 of 1967* LLM Wits 1987; Glavovic 1985 *CILSA* 343, 1985 *SALJ* 162; Visser 1988 *SALJ* 249; Glavovic *Wilderness and the Law* PhD Natal, Durban 1992; Lyster 1994 *De Jure* 136.

362 Total extent and representative coverage Estimates of the total land surface utilised for protected areas vary considerably. The area is, in fact, constantly changing as new areas are added and existing ones, or, parts thereof, excluded, but the main reason for the varying estimates is that there is no general agreement as to which areas qualify to be considered as protected areas. The IUCN (World Conservation Union) has a generally-accepted classification of protected areas,[1] against which individual countries' protected area coverage is often measured.

According to the United Nations Environment Programme, in 2003, South Africa had 349 protected areas conforming to the IUCN classification, covering 6 724 984 ha, together with 975 975 ha in other protected areas (non-IUCN), altogether making 7 700 958 ha, a percentage of 6.3 of the total land area in the country.[2] Internationally a figure of 10 per cent of the total land area is set as the ideal.

The total extent of protected areas obviously does not convey a true picture of the conservation status of protected areas in South Africa. The respective sizes of the individual areas play an important role. Some surveys, in fact, include only areas in excess of 1 000 ha. Moreover, it is of great importance to relate protected areas to their location and especially to the coverage of ecosystems, habitats and vegetation types. In this respect there seems to exist a disproportionate distribution and representation of protected areas in relation to ecosystems, habitats and vegetation types.[3] This is demonstrated by the fact that close to half of the total conserved area is made up by two national parks where the range of vegetation types is limited to eastern lowveld and Kalahari dune types of vegetation.

1 IUCN *Guidelines for Protected Areas Management Categories* (1994). See Republic of South Africa *White Paper on the Conservation of South Africa's Biological Diversity* (1997) at p 1.3.

2 UNEP World Commission on Protected Areas database (2003): it is not clear whether this figure includes marine protected areas. Cf EarthTrends (2003), which sets the figure at 7 653 000 ha (6.2%) (including marine protected areas).

3 Cf *Report of the Planning Committee of the President's Council on Nature Conservation in SA* PC 2/1984 3.8.1, 3.8.3.

363 National Environmental Management: Protected Areas Act

The National Environmental Management: Protected Areas Act[1] is aimed at providing, within the framework of national legislation, including the National Environmental Management Act, for the declaration and management of protected areas; for co-operative governance in the declaration and management of protected areas; to effect a national system of protected areas in South Africa as part of a strategy to manage and conserve its biodiversity; to provide for a representative network of protected areas on state land, private land and communal land; to promote sustainable utilisation of protected areas for the benefit of people, in a manner that would preserve the ecological character of such areas; to promote participation of local communities in the management of protected areas, where appropriate; and to provide for the continued existence of South African National Parks.[2] The National Environmental Management: Protected Areas Act repeals the National Parks Act[3] and the Lake Areas Development Act,[4] and sections 16 and 17 of the Environment Conservation Act.[5]

The state through its organs implementing legislation applicable to protected areas is required to act as trustee of protected areas in the Republic and must implement the National Environmental Management: Protected Areas Act in partnership with the people to achieve the progressive realisation of those rights.[6] The Act binds all organs of state and applies to the Prince Edward Islands and the exclusive economic zone and continental shelf of the Republic.[7] The Act is regarded as one of the specific environmental management Acts[8] and must be interpreted and applied in accordance with the national environmental management principles and be read with the applicable provisions of the National Environmental Management Act.[9] The National Environmental Management: Protected Areas Act must, in relation to any protected area, be read, interpreted and applied in conjunction with the National Environmental Management: Biodiversity Act.[10] The National Environmental Management: Protected Areas Act also deals with the question of conflict with other legislation and the status of provincial legislation on provincial and local protected areas, and essentially provides, subject to section 146 of the Constitution[11] which deals with conflicts between national and provincial legislation, that the Act will prevail over other legislation if the conflict specifically concerns the management or development of protected areas.[12]

1 57 of 2003 s 2.
2 107 of 1998.
3 57 of 1976.
4 39 of 1975.
5 73 of 1989: National Environmental Management: Protected Areas Act 57 of 2003 s 90. The latter sections are repealed in a province with effect from the date of publication by the MEC of regulations prescribing matters covered by these sections.

6 S 3.
7 S 4.
8 See s 1 of the National Environmental Management Act 107 of 1998.
9 National Environmental Management: Protected Areas Act 57 of 2003 s 5, which also provides that ch 4 of the National Environmental Management Act applies to the resolution of conflicts arising from the implementation of the National Environmental

Management: Protected Areas Act. See par 255 ante for discussion of the environmental management principles.

10   10 of 2004: National Environmental Management: Protected Areas Act 57 of

2003 s 6.

11   Constitution of the Republic of SA 108 of 1996.

12   National Environmental Management: Protected Areas Act 57 of 2003 ss 7 8.

364 System of protected areas in South Africa The National Environmental Management: Protected Areas Act[1] classifies protected areas into the following categories:[2]

(a)   special nature reserves, national parks, nature reserves (including wilderness areas) and protected environments;

(b)   world heritage sites;

(c)   marine protected areas;

(d)   specially protected forest areas, forest nature reserves and forest wilderness areas declared in terms of the National Forests Act;[3] and

(e)   mountain catchment areas declared in terms of the Mountain Catchment Areas Act.[4]

The minister must maintain a register called the Register of Protected Areas, which must contain a list of all protected areas, indicate the kind of protected area in each case, and contain any other information determined by the minister.[5] The minister may prescribe norms and standards for the achievement of any of the objectives of the National Environmental Management: Protected Areas Act, including for the management and development of protected areas in the first three categories referred to above. The minister may also prescribe indicators to measure compliance with those norms and standards, and the requirement for the management authorities of those protected areas to report on these indicators to the minister.[6] Norms and standards may apply nationwide, in a specific protected area only, or to a specific management authority or category of management authorities only.[7] In addition, different norms and standards may be issued for different areas, or different management authorities or categories of management authorities.[8]

A protected area which immediately before the National Environmental Management: Protected Areas Act took effect was reserved or protected in terms of provincial legislation for any purpose for which an area could in terms of the Act be declared as a nature reserve or protected environment, must be regarded to be a nature reserve or protected environment for the purpose of the Act.[9] Chapters 1 and 2 of the Act apply to world heritage sites, specially protected forest areas, forest nature reserves or forest wilderness areas, marine protected areas and mountain catchment areas.[10]

1   57 of 2003.

2   S 9.

3   84 of 1998.

4   63 of 1970.

5   National Environmental Management: Protected Areas Act 57 of 2003 s 10. A protected area declared in terms of provincial legislation must be included in the register as a nature reserve or protected environment depending on the purpose for which it was declared, and the cabinet member responsible for the administration of the National Forests Act 84 of 1998 and the MEC must notify the minister of all areas declared as

protected areas in terms of that Act or provincial legislation, as the case may be.

6   National Environmental Management: Protected Areas Act 57 of 2003 s 11, which provides for consultation with the MEC of each province and local government where applicable.

7   S 11(3).

8   S 11(4).

9   S 12.

10   Ss 13, 14, 15 and 16. The other provisions of the Act do not apply to world heritage sites except where expressly or by necessary implication provided otherwise. The other

provisions of the Act do not apply to specially protected forest areas, forest nature reserves or forest wilderness areas, but if any such area has been declared as or included in a special nature reserve or nature reserve, such area must be managed as, or as part of, the special nature reserve or nature reserve in terms of the Act in accordance with an agreement concluded between the minister and the cabinet member responsible for forestry.

365 Declaration of special nature reserves The minister may declare an area to be a special nature reserve or part of a special nature reserve and such declaration may only be issued to protect highly sensitive, outstanding ecosystems, species or geological or physical features in the area, and to make the area primarily available for scientific research or environmental monitoring.[1] The declaration of an area as a special nature reserve, or as part of an existing special nature reserve, may not be withdrawn and no part of a special nature reserve may be excluded from the reserve except by resolution of the National Assembly.[2]

1 National Environmental Management: Protected Areas Act 57 of 2003 s 18. Private land may only be declared a special nature reserve if the owner has consented to the declaration by way of a written agreement with the minister; and an area which was a special nature reserve immediately before this section took effect must for purposes of this section be regarded as having been declared as such in terms of this section. There are consultation requirements for the declaration of a special nature reserve in s 34(1).
2 S 19.

366 Declaration of national parks The minister may declare an area as a national park, or as part of an existing national park, and assign a name to the national park.[1] Such declaration may be made to:

(a)   protect the area if the area is of national or international biodiversity importance or is or contains a viable, representative sample of South Africa's natural systems, scenic areas or cultural heritage sites, or the ecological integrity of one or more ecosystems in the area;

(b)   prevent exploitation or occupation inconsistent with the protection of the ecological integrity of the area;

(c)   provide spiritual, scientific, educational, recreational and tourism opportunities which are environmentally compatible; and

(d)   contribute to economic development, where feasible.[2]

The declaration of a national park may only be withdrawn by resolution of the National Assembly.[3]

The minister may designate any national park or part thereof as a wilderness area, and such designation may only be issued:

(a)   to protect and maintain the natural character of the environment, biodiversity, associated natural and cultural resources and the provision of environmental goods and services;

(b)   to provide outstanding opportunities for solitude;

(c)   to control access which, if allowed, may only be by non-mechanised means.[4]

1 National Environmental Management: Protected Areas Act 57 of 2003 s 20(1). There are consultation requirements for the declaration of a national park in s 34(1).
2 S 20(2). Private land may only be declared a national park if the owner has consented to the declaration by way of a written agreement with the minister or South African National Parks (s 20(3)); the minister must notify the relevant MEC of any declaration of an area as a national park (s 20(4)); and an area which was a national park when this

section took effect must for purposes of this section be regarded as having been declared as such in terms of this section (s 20(5)).

3 S 21. If there is an agreement between the minister or South African National Parks and the owner of private land, if any of the parties withdraws from such agreement, the minister must withdraw the declaration in terms of which the land in question was declared a national park or part of an existing national park (s 21(2)).

4 S 22. Before designating a national park as a wilderness area, the minister must consult the management authority of the park.

367 Declaration of nature reserves The minister or the MEC may declare an area as a nature reserve, or as part of an existing nature reserve, and assign a name to the nature reserve.[1] Such a declaration may only be issued:

(a)   to supplement the system of national parks in South Africa;

(b)   to protect the area if the area has significant natural features or biodiversity; is of scientific, cultural, historical or archaeological interest, or is in need of long-term protection for the maintenance of its biodiversity or for the provision of environmental goods and services;

(c)   to provide for a sustainable flow of natural products and services to meet the needs of a local community;

(d)   to enable the continuation of such traditional consumptive uses as are sustainable; or

(e)   to provide for nature-based recreation and tourism opportunities.[2]

A declaration of a nature reserve may only be withdrawn in the case of a declaration by the minister, by resolution of the National Assembly; or in the case of a declaration by an MEC, by resolution of the legislature of the relevant province.[3] The minister or the MEC may designate a nature reserve as a specific type of nature reserve in accordance with such uniform system of types as may be prescribed.[4] The minister or MEC may designate a nature reserve or part thereof as a wilderness area, for the same reasons and subject to the same consultation as for national parks.[5] An MEC who makes declarations in respect of nature reserves, must promptly forward to the minister a copy of each relevant notice issued.[6]

1 National Environmental Management: Protected Areas Act 57 of 2003 s 23. There are consultation requirements for the declaration of a nature reserve in s 34(2).

2 S 23(2). Private land may only be declared a nature reserve if the owner has consented to the declaration by way of a written agreement with the minister or the MEC (s 23(3)). No area which is or forms part of a special nature reserve or national park may be declared as a nature reserve or as part of an existing nature reserve (s 23(4)). An area which was a nature reserve immediately before this section took effect must for purposes of this section be regarded as having been declared as such in terms of this section (s 23(5)).

3 S 24. If there is an agreement between the minister or MEC and the owner of private land, if any of the parties withdraws from such agreement, the minister or MEC must withdraw the declaration in terms of which the land in question was declared a nature reserve or part of an existing nature reserve (s 24(2)).

4 S 25.

5 S 26.

6 S 27.

368 Declaration of protected environments The minister or the MEC may declare any area as a protected environment, or as part of an existing protected environment, and assign a name to the protected environment.[1] A protected environment may be declared only to:

(a)   regulate the area as a buffer zone for the protection of a special nature reserve, national park, world heritage site or nature reserve;

(b) enable owners of land to take collective action to conserve biodiversity on their land and to seek legal recognition therefor;

(c) protect the area if the area is sensitive to development due to its biological diversity, natural characteristics, scientific, cultural, historical, archeological or geological value, scenic and landscape value, or provision of environmental goods and services;

(d) protect a specific ecosystem outside of a special nature reserve, national park, world heritage site or nature reserve;

(e) ensure that the use of natural resources in the area is sustainable; or

(f) control change in land use in the area if the area is earmarked for declaration as, or inclusion in, a national park or nature reserve.[2]

An area ceases to be a protected environment if that area is declared as, or included in, a national park or nature reserve or part thereof.[3] The declaration of a protected environment may be withdrawn by the minister or the MEC.[4] An MEC who makes declarations in respect of protected environments, must promptly forward to the minister a copy of each relevant notice issued.[5]

1 National Environmental Management: Protected Areas Act 57 of 2003 s 28. If the area is declared as a protected environment for the purpose described in (f), the declaration lapses at the expiry of three years from the date of publication of the notice of declaration, but the minister or the MEC may by notice in the *Gazette* extend that period for not more than one year (s 28(5)). There are consultation requirements for the declaration of a protected environment in s 34(2).

2 S 28(2). Private land may only be declared a protected environment if the owner has requested or consented thereto and the minister or the MEC has given the owner notice in writing (s 28(3)). No area which is or forms part of a special nature reserve, national park or nature reserve may be declared as a protected environment or as part of an existing protected environment (s 28(4)). An area which was a protected environment immediately before this section took effect must for purposes of this section be regarded as having been declared as such in terms of this section (s 28(7)).

3 S 28(6).
4 S 29.
5 S 30.

369 Consultation and public participation in the declaration of protected areas The minister, when issuing notices relating to the declaration of protected areas, may follow such consultative process as may be appropriate in the circumstances, but must consult all national organs of state affected by the proposed notice, in accordance with the principles of co-operative government as set out in chapter 3 of the Constitution,[1] consult the MEC of the province concerned, and the municipality in which the area concerned is situated, in the prescribed manner, consult any lawful occupier with a right in land in any part of the area affected, and follow the required process of public participation (described below).[2] The same applies to the MEC, except that the MEC must also consult with all provincial organs of state affected by any proposed notice.[3] The public participation process required of the minister or MEC is that they must publish the intention to issue a notice relating to the declaration of protected areas in the *Gazette* and in at least two national newspapers distributed in the area in which the affected area is situated; and if it is proposed to declare any private land as a protected environment, send a copy of the proposed notice by registered post to the last known postal address of each owner of land within the area to be declared, and inform in an appropriate manner any other person whose rights in such land may materially and adversely be affected by such declaration.[4]

The declaration of private land as a protected area, or as part thereof, may be initiated either by the minister, or the MEC or the owners of that land acting individually or collectively, and any request received by the minister or an MEC from the owners of private land for their land to be declared must be considered by the minister or MEC.[5]

The minister or the MEC must in writing notify the Registrar of Deeds whenever an area is declared as a protected area in terms of the National Environmental Management: Protected Areas Act or whenever a declaration in respect thereof is withdrawn or altered, which notification must include a description of the land involved and the terms and conditions of any notarial deed.[6]

1 Constitution of the Republic of SA 108 of 1996.
2 National Environmental Management: Protected Areas Act 57 of 2003 s 31.
3 S 32.
4 S 33. The publication in the *Gazette* and newspapers must invite members of the public and the persons in the area, if applicable, to submit to the minister or MEC written representations on or objections to the proposed notice within 60 days from the date of publication; and must contain sufficient information to enable members of the public to submit meaningful representations or objections, and must include a clear indication of the area that will be affected by the declaration.
The minister or MEC may in appropriate circumstances allow any interested person to present oral representations or objections,

but such representations or objections must be allowed where the proposed notice will affect the rights or interests of a local community (s 33(3)). The minister or MEC must give due consideration to all representations or objections received or presented before publishing the relevant notice (s 33(4)).
5 S 35. The terms of any written agreement entered into between the minister or MEC and the owner of private land are binding on the successors in title of such owner; and must be recorded in a notarial deed and registered against the title deeds of the property.
6 S 36. On receipt of the notification, the Registrar of Deeds must record any such declaration, withdrawal or alteration in relevant registers and documents in terms of the Deeds Registries Act 47 of 1937.

370 Management of protected areas[1] The minister must assign the management of a special nature reserve or a nature reserve to a suitable person, organisation or organ of state; must assign the management of a national park to South African National Parks or another suitable person, organisation or organ of state; and may assign the management of a protected environment to a suitable person, organisation or organ of state.[2] The same applies when notice is given by a MEC, other than in respect of national parks. The person, organisation or organ of state to whom the management of a protected area has been assigned in terms of the National Environmental Management: Protected Areas Act is the management authority of the area for the purposes of the Act.[3] Marine and terrestrial protected areas with common boundaries must be managed as an integrated protected area by a single management authority.[4] The management authority must manage the area exclusively for the purpose for which it was declared; and in accordance with the management plan for the area, the National Environmental Management: Protected Areas Act, the National Environmental Management: Biodiversity Act,[5] the National Environmental Management Act[6] and any other applicable national legislation, any applicable provincial legislation, in the case of a provincial protected area, and any applicable municipal by-laws, in the case of a local protected area.[7]

The management authority must, within 12 months of its assignment, submit a management plan for the protected area to the minister or the MEC for approval.[8] When preparing a management plan for a protected area, the management authority concerned must consult municipalities, other organs of state, local communities and other affected parties which have an interest in the area.[9] A management plan must take into account any applicable aspects of the integrated development plan of the municipality in which the protected area is situated.[10] The object of a management plan is to ensure the protection, conservation and management of the protected area concerned in a manner which is consistent with the objectives of the National Environmental Management: Protected Areas Act and for the purpose it was declared, and must contain at least:

(a)   the terms and conditions of any applicable biodiversity management plan;

(b)   a co-ordinated policy framework;

(c)   such planning measures, controls and performance criteria as may be prescribed;

(d)   a programme for the implementation of the plan and its costing;

(e)   procedures for public participation, including participation by the owner (if applicable), any local community or other interested party;

(f)   where appropriate, the implementation of community-based natural resource management; and

(g)   a zoning of the area indicating what activities may take place in different sections of the area, and the conservation objectives of those sections.[11]
A management plan may contain:

(a)   development of economic opportunities within and adjacent to the protected area in terms of the integrated development plan framework;

(b)   development of local management capacity and knowledge exchange;

(c)   financial and other support to ensure effective administration and implementation of the co-management agreement; and

(d)   any other relevant matter.[12]

The management authority may enter into an agreement with another organ of state, a local community, an individual or other party for the co-management of the area by the parties, or the regulation of human activities that affect the environment in the area, but this may not lead to fragmentation or duplication of management functions.[13] A co-management agreement may provide for:

(a)   the delegation of powers by the management authority to the other party to the agreement;

(b)   the apportionment of any income generated from the management of the protected area or any other form of benefit sharing between the parties;

(c)   the use of biological resources in the area;

(d)   access to the area;

(e)   occupation of the protected area or portions thereof;

(f)   development of economic opportunities within and adjacent to the protected area;

(g)   development of local management capacity and knowledge exchange;

(h)   financial and other support to ensure effective administration and implementation of the co-management agreement; and

(i)   any other relevant matter.[14]

A co-management agreement must provide for the harmonisation and integration of the management of cultural heritage resources in the protected area by the management authority, and be consistent with the other provisions of the National Environmental Management: Protected Areas Act.[15]

The minister and MEC may establish indicators for monitoring performance with regard to the management of national protected areas and the management of provincial and local protected areas respectively and the conservation of biodiversity in those areas.[16] The management authority of a protected area must monitor the area against such indicators and annually report its findings to the minister or MEC.[17] If the management authority of a protected area is not performing its duties in terms of the management plan for the area, or is underperforming with regard to the management of the area or the biodiversity of the area, the minister or the MEC must notify the management authority in writing of the failure to perform its duties or of the underperformance, and direct the management authority to take corrective steps set out in the notice within a specified time.[18] If the management authority fails to take the required steps, the minister or MEC may terminate that management authority's mandate to manage the protected area; and assign another organ of state as the management authority of the area.[19]

1 National Environmental Management: Protected Areas Act 57 of 2003 s 37 provides that except where expressly stated otherwise in ch 4, which deals with management of protected areas, the chapter only applies to a protected area which is a special nature reserve, national park, nature reserve or protected environment, and the expressions "protected area", "national protected area", "provincial protected area", "local protected area" and "protected environment" must be construed accordingly in the chapter.

2 S 38; provided that the owner and lawful occupier of a protected environment have requested or consented to such assignment, and the minister has given the owner and lawful occupier notice in writing. Assignment can only be made with the concurrence of the prospective management authority (s 39(1)).

3 S 38(3).
4 S 38(4).
5 10 of 2004.
6 107 of 1998.
7 National Environmental Management: Protected Areas Act 57 of 2003 s 40.
8 S 39(2). The management authority may amend the management plan by agreement

with the minister or the MEC, as the case may be (s 40(2)).
9 S 39(3).
10 S 39(4).
11 S 41(2). Management plans may include subsidiary plans, and the minister or MEC may approve the management plan or any subsidiary plan in whole or in part.
12 S 41(3).
13 S 42(1). The minister or the MEC, as the case may be, may cancel a co-management agreement after giving reasonable notice to the parties if the agreement is not effective or is inhibiting the attainment of any of the management objectives of the protected area (s 42(4)).
14 S 42(2).
15 S 42(3).
16 S 43.
17 S 43(3). The minister or MEC may appoint external auditors to monitor a management authority's compliance with the overall objectives of the management plan (s 43(4)).
18 S 44(1). The minister implements this section in relation to national protected areas and the MEC implements the section in relation to provincial and local protected areas.
19 S 44(2).

371 Access to protected areas No person may enter a special nature reserve, reside in a special nature reserve, or perform any activity in a special nature reserve, except for an official of the department[1] or another organ of state designated by the minister to monitor the state of conservation of the reserve, or of the biodiversity in the reserve, or the implementation of the management plan and the National Environmental Management: Protected Areas Act;[2] any police, customs or excise officer entering the area in the performance of official duties; or a person acting in terms of an exemption.[3] The management authority of a special nature reserve may, in writing and on conditions determined by it after consulting the minister, grant such exemption to:

(a) a scientist to perform scientific work;

(b)   a person to perform an activity related to the conservation of the reserve or of the biodiversity in the reserve;

(c)   a person recording a news event that occurred in the reserve or an educational or scientific programme;

(d)   an official of the management authority to perform official duties; or

(e)   an official of an organ of state to perform official duties.[4]

Despite any other legislation, no person may without the written permission of the management authority of a national park, nature reserve or world heritage site enter or reside in the park, reserve or site. This prohibition does not apply to:

(a)   an official of the department or of another organ of state designated by the minister or MEC to monitor the state of conservation of the reserve or site or of the biodiversity in the park, reserve or site, or the implementation of the management plan and the National Environmental Management: Protected Areas Act;

(b)   an official of the management authority performing official duties in the park, reserve or site;

(c)   any police, customs or excise officer entering the park, reserve or site in the performance of official duties;

(d)   the holder of a vested right to enter the park, reserve or site; or

(e)   a person travelling through the park, reserve or site by rail, as long as that person stays on the train or within the precincts of any railway station.[5]

A special nature reserve, national park or world heritage site includes the air space above the park, reserve or site to a level of 2 500 feet above the highest point of the reserve or site.[6] No person may land or take off in an aircraft in a special nature reserve, national park or world heritage site, except on or from a landing field designated by the management authority of that reserve, park or site, and with the permission of, and on conditions determined by, the management authority.[7] No person may fly over a special nature reserve, national park or world heritage site at an altitude of less than 2 500 feet, except as may be necessary for the purpose of permitted taking off or landing.[8]

1   Department of Environmental Affairs and Tourism.
2   57 of 2003.
3   S 45.
4   S 45(3).
5   S 46. If the management authority of a national park, nature reserve or world heritage site refuses permission to an official of an organ of state to enter the park, reserve or site for the performance of official duties, the minister may reconsider the matter; and either confirm the refusal or grant the permission (s 46(3)).

6   S 47(1).
7   S 47(2). The prohibitions in this section do not apply in an emergency; or to a person acting on the instructions of the management authority (s 47(4)).
8   S 47(3). The minister, acting with the concurrence of the cabinet member responsible for civil aviation, may prescribe further reasonable restrictions on flying over protected areas (s 47(5)).

372 Restrictions in protected areas Despite other legislation, no person may conduct commercial prospecting or mining activities in a special nature reserve, national park or nature reserve, or in a protected environment without the written permission of the minister and the cabinet member responsible for minerals and energy affairs, or in world heritage sites, marine protected areas and specially protected forest areas, forest nature reserves and forest wilderness areas declared in terms of the National Forests Act.[1]

The minister, after consultation with the cabinet member responsible for mineral and energy affairs, may, in relation to lawful mining and prospecting activities,[2] prescribe conditions under which those activities may continue in order to reduce or eliminate the impact of those activities on the environment or for the environmental protection of the area concerned.[3]

In general, activities in protected areas may be regulated or restricted to the extent prescribed by regulations made under the National Environmental Management: Protected Areas Act; by-laws made by the relevant municipality, in the case of local protected areas; and internal rules made by the managing authority of the area.[4] The management authority of a national park, nature reserve and world heritage site may, subject to the management plan of the park, reserve or site, carry out or allow a commercial activity in the protected area, or an activity aimed at raising revenue, enter into a written agreement with a local community inside or adjacent to the park, reserve or site to allow members of the community to use in a sustainable manner biological resources in the reserve or site, and set norms and standards for any such activity.[5] Such activity may not negatively affect the survival of any species in or significantly disrupt the integrity of the ecological systems of the nature reserve or world heritage site.[6] The management authority of the park, reserve or site must establish systems to monitor the impact of such activities on the park, reserve or site and its biodiversity, and compliance with any agreement with the community, and any relevant norms and standards set.[7] No development, construction or farming may be permitted in a national park, nature reserve or world heritage site without the prior written approval of the management authority.[8]

The minister or the MEC may restrict or regulate in a protected environment under the jurisdiction of the minister or the MEC development that may be inappropriate for the area given the purpose for which the area was declared, and the carrying out of other activities that may impede such purpose.[9]

The management authority of a national park, nature reserve or world heritage site may, in accordance with prescribed norms and standards, make rules for the proper administration of the area. These rules must be consistent with the Act and the management plan for the area, bind all persons in the area, including visitors, and may, as a condition for entry, provide for the imposition of fines for breaches of the rules.[10]

The sections relating to restrictions may not be applied in a manner that would obstruct the resolution of issues relating to land rights dealt with in terms of the Restitution of Land Rights Act[11] and the provision of essential services and the acquisition of servitudes for that purpose.[12] A person may exercise a right that that person may have to water in a public stream in a protected area, but subject to such conditions as may be prescribed by the minister with the concurrence of the cabinet member responsible for water affairs.[13]

1 122 of 1984 (now repealed): National Environmental Management: Protected Areas Act 57 of 2003 s 48. The minister, after consultation with the cabinet member responsible for mineral and energy affairs, must review all mining activities which were lawfully conducted in these areas immediately before this section took effect. When applying the section, the minister must take into account the interests of local communities and the environmental principles referred to in s 2 of the National Environmental Management Act 107 of 1998.

2 Mining activities already being carried on when the section came into effect or before a protected are is proclaimed.

3 National Environmental Management: Protected Areas Act 57 of 2003 s 48(3).

4 S 49.

5 S 50(1).

6 S 50(2).

7 S 50(3).

8 S 50(5).
9 S 51.
10 S 52.
11 22 of 1994.

12 National Environmental Management: Protected Areas Act 57 of 1993 s 53(1).
13 S 53(2).

373 South African National Parks South African National Parks ("SANP") established by the National Parks Act,[1] continues to exist as a juristic person despite the repeal of that Act by the National Environmental Management: Protected Areas Act,[2] and functions in terms of the new Act.[3] Its functions are that it must:

(a) manage the national parks and other protected areas assigned to it in accordance with the National Environmental Management: Protected Areas Act;

(b) protect, conserve and control those national parks and other protected areas, including their biological diversity; and

(c) on the minister's request, advise the minister on any matter concerning the conservation and management of biodiversity, and proposed national parks and additions to or exclusions from existing national parks; and

(d) on the minister's request, act as the provisional managing authority of protected areas under investigation in terms of the National Environmental Management: Protected Areas Act.[4]

In its management of national parks, SANP may:

(a) manage breeding and cultivation programmes, and reserve areas in a park as breeding places and nurseries;

(b) sell, exchange or donate any animal, plant or other organism occurring in a park, or purchase, exchange or otherwise acquire any indigenous species which it may consider desirable to re-introduce into a specific park;

(c) undertake and promote research;

(d) control, remove or eradicate any species or specimens of species which it considers undesirable to protect and conserve in a park or that may negatively impact on the biodiversity of the park;

(e) carry out any development and construct or erect any works necessary for the management of a park, including roads, bridges, buildings, dams, fences, breakwaters, seawalls, boathouses, landing stages, mooring places, swimming pools, oceanariums and underwater tunnels;

(f) allow visitors to a park;

(g) take reasonable steps to ensure the security and well-being of visitors and staff;

(h) provide accommodation and facilities for visitors and staff, including the provision of food and household supplies;

(i) carry on any business or trade or provide other services for the convenience of visitors and staff, including the sale of liquor;

(j) determine and collect fees for entry to or stay in a park or any service provided by it;

(k) authorise any person, subject to such conditions and the payment of such fees as it may determine, to carry on any business or trade, or provide any service, which SANP may carry on or provide, and provide the infrastructure for such business, trade or service;

(l) by agreement with a municipality, provide any service in a park which that municipality may or must provide in terms of legislation, or by agreement with any other organ of state, perform a function in a park which that organ of state may or must perform in terms of legislation; or

(m) perform such other functions as may be prescribed.[5]

In addition, chapter 5 of the Act provides for SANP's general powers,[6] its governing board and membership,[7] operating procedures of the board,[8] administration,[9] financial matters,[10] and related matters. The performance of SANP is subject to scrutiny by the minister in that the latter must monitor the performance by SANP of its functions and may:

(a) determine norms and standards for the performance by SANP of its functions;

(b) issue directives to SANP on measures to achieve these norms and standards;

(c) determine limits on fees charged by SANP in the performance of its functions;

(d) identify land for new national parks and extensions to existing national parks.[11]

1 57 of 1976.
2 57 of 2003.
3 S 54.
4 S 55(1).
5 S 55(2), which applies also to other protected areas managed by SANP, and these powers may be exercised by it to the extent that they are consistent with the purpose for which any such area was declared as a protected area.
6 S 56.
7 Ss 57–66.

8 Ss 67–71.
9 Ss 72 73.
10 Ss 74–77.
11 S 78. SANP must perform its functions subject to the norms and standards, directives and determinations issued by the minister in terms of this section. Moreover, in the absence of a functional board, the functions of the board revert to the minister who, in such a case, must perform those functions until the board is functional again (s 79).

374 Acquisition of rights in or to land The minister and MEC may acquire land, or any right in or to land, which has been or is proposed to be declared as or included in a national protected area, by purchasing the land or right; exchanging the land or right for other land or rights; or expropriating the land or right if no agreement is reached with the owner of the land or the holder of the right in or to the land.[1] South African National Parks ("SANP") may acquire private land, or any right in or to private land, which has been or is proposed to be declared as or included in a national park by purchasing the land or right, or if the land or right is donated or bequeathed to it, by accepting the donation or bequest.[2] If the parties fail to agree on a purchase price for such land or right, the minister may on behalf of SANP or the state expropriate the land or right.[3] The minister, MEC and SANP are also given the power to cancel a servitude on state land, or a privately held right in or to state land, which has been or is proposed to be declared as or included in a national protected area or national park.[4] The financing of the purchase of private land for the purpose of declaration as protected areas is sourced from money appropriated for this purpose from Parliament, or from the funds of SANP or the National Parks Acquisition Fund.[5]

1 National Environmental Management: Protected Areas Act 57 of 2003 s 80 – the minister must act with the concurrence of the cabinet member responsible for land affairs and the MEC with the approval of the executive council of the province. Expropriation must be in accordance with the Expropriation Act 63 of 1975, and subject to s 25 of the Constitution of the Republic of SA 108 of 1996. A mineral right may only be acquired or cancelled by means of

expropriation with the concurrence of the cabinet member responsible for mineral affairs (National Environmental Management: Protected Areas Act 157 of 2003 s 84).
2 S 81. SANP must act with the approval of the minister acting with the concurrence of the cabinet member responsible for land affairs.
3 S 81(2).
4 Ss 82 83.
5 S 85.

375 Administration and enforcement The minister and MECs are given regulatory powers relating to protected areas.[1] There are various offences under the National Environmental Management: Protected Areas Act, including the unauthorised access to protected areas and hindering or interfering with the management authority of a protected area.[2]

1 National Environmental Management: Protected Areas Act 57 of 2003 ss 86–88.
2 S 89.

376 Forest nature reserves and forest wilderness areas Forest nature reserves and forest wilderness areas are established in terms of the National Forests Act.[1] The Minister of Water Affairs and Forestry may declare a state forest or a part of it; purchase or expropriate land and declare it; or at the request or with the consent of the registered owner of land outside a state forest, declare it, as a specially protected area in one of the following categories:

(a) a forest nature reserve;

(b) a forest wilderness area; or

(c) any other type of protected area which is recognised in international law or practice.[2]

The minister may declare such an area only if he or she is of the opinion that it is not already adequately protected in terms of other legislation.[3]

The decision to declare a protected area may not be revoked, nor may a protected area which is state forest be sold, nor may a servitude over a protected area be granted, without the minister following the same procedure as that required for declaring the protected area, and the approval by resolution of Parliament.[4]

No person may cut, disturb, damage or destroy any forest produce[5] in, or remove or receive any forest produce from, a protected area, except in terms of the rules made for the proper management of the area; in the course of the management of the protected area by the responsible organ of state or person; in terms of a right of servitude; in terms of the authority of a licence granted or an exemption under the Act; or in the case of a protected area on land outside a state forest, with the consent of the registered owner or by reason of another right which allows the person concerned to do so.[6]

The minister is responsible for the management of the protected area, and must manage the protected area in a manner which is consistent with the purpose for which it was established, and make rules for the management of the protected area so as to achieve the purpose for which the area has been protected, unless suitable rules already exist for the area.[7] A person who contravenes the prohibition on the cutting, disturbance, damage or destruction of forest produce in or the removal or receipt of forest produce from a protected area is guilty of a second category offence.[8] A person who contravenes the management rules for the protected area is guilty of a third category offence.[9]

1 84 of 1998.
2 S 8(1).
3 S 8(2). The procedure for establishing protected areas under the National Forests Act is contained in s 9.
4 S 10(2).
5 "Forest produce" is anything which appears or grows in a forest, including any living organism, and any product of it, in a forest; and inanimate objects of mineral, historical, anthropological or cultural value (s 1).
6 S 10(1). This prohibition is subject to s 7(1), which provides that no person may cut, disturb, damage or destroy any indigenous, living tree in, or remove or receive any such tree from, a natural forest (a group of

indigenous trees whose crowns are largely contiguous; or which have been declared by the minister to be a natural forest) (s 1).

7 S 11.

8 A person who is guilty of a second category offence may be sentenced on a first conviction for that offence to a fine or imprisonment for a period of up to two years, or to both a fine and such imprisonment (s 58(2)).

9 S 62(2). A person who is guilty of a third category offence may be sentenced on a first conviction for that offence to a fine or imprisonment for a period of up to one year, or to both a fine and such imprisonment (s 58(3)).

377 Mountain catchment areas Mountain catchment areas are established in terms of the Mountain Catchment Areas Act.[1] The competent provincial authority to whom the administration of the Act has under the Constitution[2] been assigned[3] may by notice in the *Provincial Gazette* define any area and declare that area to be a mountain catchment area.[4] He or she may by such notice also alter the boundaries of the area in question or withdraw any notice whereby a mountain catchment area was established.[5] Although state land is not declared as mountain catchment areas in terms of the Act, certain parts of state forests, including some nature reserves and wilderness areas, are in practice managed as mountain catchments in combination with declared mountain catchment areas on private land.

Mountain catchment areas are administered by the provincial governments, assisted by advisory committees[6] and fire protection committees[7] which they may appoint. The competent provincial authority may declare a direction to be applicable with reference to land within a mountain catchment area, relating to the conservation, use, management and control of such land, the prevention of soil erosion, the protection and treatment of the natural vegetation and the destruction of intruding vegetation and any other necessary or expedient matter.[8] A direction may also be declared to be applicable to land outside the mountain catchment area concerned, but within 5 km from the boundary thereof, relating to the destruction of intruding vegetation.[9]

Compensation is payable in respect of actual patrimonial loss caused to an owner or occupier of land if in terms of a direction limitations are placed on the purposes for which land may be used,[10] while any land situated within a mountain catchment area upon which in terms of any direction no farming may be carried on, is exempt from all taxes imposed by a local authority on the value of immovable property.[11]

Moreover, the director-general of the provincial government concerned may, after consultation with the advisory committee in question, declare a fire protection plan to be applicable to land in the mountain catchment area concerned.[12] This plan relates basically to the regulation or prohibition of veld burning, the prevention, control and extinguishing of veld and forest fires and the functions of the fire protection committee concerned.[13] Such plan, the particulars of which must be published by notice in the *Provincial Gazette*,[14] is binding upon every owner and occupier of land with reference to which it has been applied.[15]

Finally, the competent provincial authority may itself perform or cause to be performed any act which it deems necessary in order to achieve any object of the Act, including acts ordered in terms of a direction or of a fire protection plan.[16]

1 63 of 1970.
2 Constitution of the Republic of SA 200 of 1993 s 235(8).
3 *Government Gazette* 16346 GN R28, 7 April 1995.
4 Mountain Catchment Areas Act 63 of 1970 s 2.
5 Ibid.
6 S 6.
7 S 7.
8 S 3(1).
9 Ibid.
10 S 4.
11 S 5.

12   S 8(1).
13   S 8(2).
14   S 8(3).

15   S 8(4).
16   S 12.

378   Provincial nature reserves   Provincial nature reserves are established in terms of the various provincial nature conservation ordinances.[1] The nomenclature adopted by the Natal Ordinance is that of national park, game reserve or nature reserve – all denoting the same concept of provincial nature reserve.

The Cape Nature and Environmental Conservation Ordinance[2] as an example provides that the administrator (provincial premier) may by proclamation establish a provincial nature reserve on any land under his or her control or management[3] or, after consultation and the conclusion of an agreement with any state department, on land which is under the control or management of such state department.[4] For this purpose the premier may by agreement or expropriation acquire suitable land[5] and appoint staff.[6] The premier may by proclamation, after due public notification and consideration of any objections, abolish such reserve.[7]

The head of the Department of Environmental and Cultural Affairs must manage, control and develop provincial nature reserves with a view to the propagation, protection and preservation of fauna and flora and may in this process also provide facilities for public recreation.[8] Wide powers are granted to the head to exercise these functions.[9] Moreover, the premier may make regulations to control a wide range of activities in respect of provincial nature reserves.[10] Besides such control, there is a general criminal prohibition on any person, without a permit, hunting any wild animal or picking any flora in a provincial nature reserve.[11]

1   Ie the OFS Ord 8 of 1969, the Natal Ord 15 of 1974, the Cape Ord 19 of 1974 and the Tvl Ord 12 of 1983. These Ordinances remain applicable in most of the nine provinces.
2   19 of 1974.
3   S 6(1)(a).
4   S 6(1A)(a)(i).

5   S 6(2)(a).
6   S 6(2)(b).
7   S 6(1)(d) (1A)(a)(iv).
8   S 6(3).
9   S 6(4).
10   S 6(6).
11   S 14.

379   Provincial parks   The Eastern Cape has enacted an Act[1] which provides for "provincial parks". The Eastern Cape Provincial Parks Board Act deals with the establishment of such parks, the establishment of a provincial Parks Board, the management of biodiversity in parks, and matters such as access to and restricted activities within parks.

1   Eastern Cape Provincial Parks Board Act 12 of 2003.

380   Local nature reserves   The Cape Nature and Environmental Conservation Ordinance[1] is the only ordinance which makes provision for the establishment of local nature reserves by local authorities, although local authorities elsewhere have also established local nature reserves by virtue of local by-laws. A local authority in the Cape may with the approval of the premier and subject to such conditions as he or she may specify, establish a local nature reserve on land vested in it or under its control or management, and may for that purpose acquire land by agreement or expropriation[2] and appoint staff.[3] A local authority desiring to establish a local nature reserve must comply with certain requirements relating to publication of its intention, affording an opportunity to persons wishing to object to such establishment, to do so.[4] The premier may in his or her discretion refuse or grant the application subject to such conditions as he or she may deem necessary or desirable,[5] which decision must be published in the *Provincial Gazette.*[6]

A local authority may with the approval of the premier at any time alter the boundaries of the local nature reserve concerned, or, after complying with the same requirements mentioned above in respect of the establishment, abolish such reserve, which alteration or abolition must be announced in the *Provincial Gazette.*[7]

A local authority is obliged, subject to the directions of the premier, to manage, control and develop the local nature reserve with a view to the propagation, protection and preservation of fauna and flora, and may in this process also provide facilities for public recreation.[8] Wide powers are conferred on a local authority to exercise these functions.[9] Moreover, a local authority which has established a local nature reserve must appoint an advisory board for the purpose of advising and making recommendations to it in connection with the management, control and development of such reserve.[10] A provincial subsidy is payable in respect of local nature reserves.[11] The premier may make regulations to control a wide range of activities in respect of local nature reserves.[12] Besides such control, there is a general provision that no person may, without a permit, hunt any wild animal or pick any flora in a local nature reserve.[13]

Finally, provision is made for provincial control over the local authority itself: if the premier is of the opinion that any action by a local authority in connection with the management of a local nature reserve is or will be detrimental to such reserve or to the purposes for which it was established, the premier may, after consultation with such local authority, prohibit such action or permit it subject to such conditions as he or she may determine.[14]

1 19 of 1974.
2 S 7(1).
3 Ss 7(6) 6(2)(b).
4 S 7(2).
5 S 7(4).
6 S 7(5).
7 S 7(7).
8 Ss 7(6) 6(3).
9 Ss 7(6) 6(4).
10 Ss 8 9.
11 S 11.
12 Ss 7(6) 6(6).
13 S 14.
14 S 10.

381 Private nature reserves Private nature reserves are established in terms of the provincial nature conservation laws such as those of the Cape, KwaZulu-Natal and the Free State. The Natal Ordinance makes provision for two types of such reserves, namely private nature reserves and private wild-life reserves. Moreover, the Natal ordinance also provides for the licensing of commercial game reserves, where game is maintained for business purposes. The Transvaal ordinance does not provide specifically for private nature reserves, although many such reserves have in fact been established.[1]

The Cape Nature and Environmental Conservation Ordinance[2] provides, for example, that any owner of land may, with the approval of the premier[3] and subject to such conditions as he or she may specify, establish a private nature reserve on land of which he or she is the owner.[4]

Any person who has established a private nature reserve may at any time with the approval of the premier alter the boundaries or abolish such reserve.[5] Moreover, any such reserve may at any time be abolished by the premier on good cause shown and after consultation with the person who established it.[6] Any such alteration or abolition must be published in the *Provincial Gazette.*[7]

Subject to any conditions imposed by the premier upon the establishment of a private nature reserve, the owner must manage, control and develop such reserve with a view to the propagation, protection and preservation of fauna and flora.[8] Such owner is granted certain privileges with regard to the hunting and selling of wild animals and the picking of flora found in such reserve.[9]

1 See Cape Ord 19 of 1974; Natal Ord 15 of 1974; OFS Ord 8 of 1969; Tvl Ord 12 of 1983.	4 S 12(1). 5 S 12(5)(a). 6 S 12(5)(b).
2 19 of 1974.	7 S 12(5)(c).
3 Which must be published in the *Provincial Gazette*: s 12(4).	8 S 13. 9 Ibid.

382 Botanical gardens Since considerable areas of natural vegetation in some botanic gardens have been left undeveloped as reserves, botanic gardens may in a broad sense be regarded as protected areas. The same does not apply to zoological gardens and they are therefore not included in the discussion. National botanical gardens are declared in terms of the National Environmental Management: Biodiversity Act.[1]

Control over national botanic gardens is exercised by the South African National Biodiversity Institute.[2] The declaration of state land as a national botanical garden, or part of an existing national botanical garden, may not be withdrawn and a part of a national botanical garden on state land may not be excluded from it except by resolution of each House of Parliament.[3]

1 10 of 2004 s 33(1).
2 S 11(1)(e).
3 S 34(2).

383 World Heritage Sites South Africa has six World Heritage Sites (sites that have been identified in terms of the Convention concerning the Protection of the World Cultural and Natural Heritage, or the World Heritage Convention).[1] The Convention's aim is to encourage the identification, protection and preservation of cultural and natural heritage around the world considered to be of outstanding value to humanity. World Heritage Sites are therefore not necessarily concerned with environmental conservation, although many are. The Convention is given effect to in South Africa by the World Heritage Convention Act.[2]

The minister is responsible for the procedure relating to the nomination of World Heritage Sites in accordance with the Act, the Convention and the Operating Guidelines, and the Department of Environmental Affairs and Tourism or a body determined by the Minister must identify places of potential cultural or natural heritage and investigate the desirability of nominating such places for inclusion on the World Heritage List.[3] The Act also provides, *inter alia*, for authorities which manage the sites,[4] and for the establishment of integrated management plans for the sites.[5]

1 These are: The Greater St Lucia Wetland Park; Fossil hominid sites of Sterkfontein, Swartkrans, Kromdraai and environs; Robben Island; Ukhahlamba Drakensberg Park; Mapungubwe Cultural Landscape; and Cape	Floral Region Protected Areas. 2 49 of 1999. 3 S 6. 4 Ch 3. 5 Ch 4.

384 National heritage resources National heritage resources are established in terms of the National Heritage Resources Act,[1] which provides that those heritage resources of South Africa which are of cultural significance or other special value for the present community and for future generations must be considered part of the national estate and fall within the sphere of operations of heritage resources authorities.[2] These resources may include landscapes and natural features of cultural significance.[3]

The South African Heritage Resources Agency may, with the consent of the owner of an area, by notice in the *Gazette* designate as a protected area:

(a) such area of land surrounding a national heritage site as is reasonably necessary to ensure the protection and reasonable enjoyment of such site, or to protect the view of and from such site; or

(b) such area of land surrounding any wreck as is reasonably necessary to ensure its protection; or

(c) such area of land covered by a mine dump.[4]

A provincial heritage resources authority may, with the consent of the owner of an area, by notice in the *Provincial Gazette* designate as a protected area:

(a) such area of land surrounding a provincial heritage site as is reasonably necessary to ensure the protection and reasonable enjoyment of such site, or to protect the view of and from such site; or

(b) such area of land surrounding any archaeological or palaeontological site or meteorite as is reasonably necessary to ensure its protection.[5]

No person may damage, disfigure, alter, subdivide or in any other way develop any part of a protected area unless, at least 60 days prior to the initiation of such changes, he or she has consulted the Heritage Resources Authority which designated such area in accordance with a procedure prescribed by that authority.[6] A heritage resources authority may make regulations providing for specific protections for any protected area which it has designated, including the prohibition or control of specified activities by any person in the designated area.[7] A local authority may, with the agreement of the heritage resources authority which designated a protected area, make provision in its town–planning scheme or in by–laws for the management of such area.[8]

Conservation areas declared under the National Monuments Act,[9] repealed and replaced by the National Heritage Resources Act, are regarded by the new Act as heritage areas.[10] This is provided that where no provision has been made for the protection of such areas in by–laws under the previous Act or in a town or regional planning scheme, the sections in the new Act applicable to heritage areas and local authorities[11] automatically apply to such heritage areas; and the local or other planning authority concerned must provide for the protection of such area in accordance with the relevant provisions of the Act[12] within three years of the commencement of this Act.

1 25 of 1999. See title HISTORICAL MONUMENTS.
2 S 3(1).
3 S 3(2)(d).
4 S 28(1). With regard to an area of land covered by a mine dump, SAHRA must make regulations providing for the protection of such areas as are seen to be of national importance in consultation with the owner, the Minister of Minerals and Energy and interested and affected parties within the mining community.
5 S 28(2).
6 S 28(3).
7 S 28(5).
8 S 28(6).
9 28 of 1969 s 5(9).
10 National Heritage Resources Act 25 of 1999 s 58(11)(c).
11 S 31(7)(a)–(c).
12 S 31.

385 Defence areas The acquisition, control and development of land for defence purposes was previously governed by the Defence Act of 1957.[1] The Minister of Defence was given wide powers to do or cause to be done all things which in his or her opinion were necessary for the efficient defence and protection of the Republic or any part thereof.[2] The minister could prohibit or restrict the access of all persons to land which is subject to military control.[3] The new Defence Act[4] does not however contain corresponding provisions.

1 44 of 1957.
2 S 76 (repealed).
3 S 89 (repealed).
4 42 of 2002.

386 Marine reserves The Marine Living Resources Act[1] empowers the Minister of Environmental Affairs and Tourism by notice in the *Government Gazette* to declare an area to be a marine protected area for the protection of fauna and flora or a particular species of fauna or flora and the physical features on which they depend; to facilitate fishery management by protecting spawning stock, allowing stock recovery, enhancing stock abundance in adjacent areas, and providing pristine communities for research; or to diminish any conflict that may arise from competing uses in that area.[2] No person may in any marine protected area, without permission:

(a) fish or attempt to fish;

(b) take or destroy any fauna and flora other than fish;

(c) dredge, extract sand or gravel, discharge or deposit waste or any other polluting matter, or in any way disturb, alter or destroy the natural environment;

(d) construct or erect any building or other structure on or over any land or water within such a marine protected area; or

(e) carry on any activity which may adversely impact on the ecosystems of that area.[3]

The minister may, after consultation with the Consultative Advisory Forum for Marine Living Resources, give permission in writing that any activity prohibited in terms of this section may be undertaken, where such activity is required for the proper management of the marine protected area.[4]

Several marine protected areas have been declared, including Aliwal Shoal and Table Mountain National Park.[5] The substance of the regulations declaring the individual areas differ from one another, but they deal with matters such as objectives and boundaries, as well as zones within the boundaries (for example, sanctuary zones and controlled zones), prohibited activities, research and commercial use.

1 18 of 1998. See title FISHERIES AND FISHING.
2 S 43(1).
3 S 43(2).
4 S 43(3).
5 *Government Gazette* 26430 GN 694–697, 3–4 June 2004.

387 Seashore The seashore, that is the water and the land between the low-water mark and the high-water mark, may to some extent, and broadly speaking, be regarded as constituting a protected area. The seashore is regulated in terms of the Sea-Shore Act.[1] In Roman-Dutch law the seashore was regarded as *res publica*, in other words property destined for public use, while the president of the Republic is declared by the Act to be the owner of the seashore.[2] The seashore is not capable of being alienated or let except as provided by law, or with the approval, by resolution, of Parliament,[3] and it cannot be acquired by prescription.[4]

Control over the use of the seashore is exercised by the relevant provincial governments.[5] Local authorities may also be authorised by the minister to make regulations relating to the use of the seashore.[6] Finally, the admiralty reserve, some narrow strips of land adjoining and running parallel to the landward side of the high-water mark, may also serve as a protected area.[7]

1 21 of 1935. See title SEA AND SEASHORE.
2 S 2(1).
3 S 6(1).
4 S 2(3).
5 The administration of most of the provisions

of the Act has been assigned to the relevant provincial governments: *Government Gazette* 16346 GN R27, 7 April 1995.
6 S 10(1).
7 Glazewski 1986 *Acta Juridica* 193–201.

388 Islands Most islands around the South African coast are in effect protected areas. Islands are controlled in terms of the Sea Birds and Seals Protection Act.[1] The Minister of Environmental Affairs and Tourism is empowered, by notice in the *Government Gazette* to insert in or delete from the Schedule the name or description of any island.[2] These islands are controlled as sanctuaries and breeding stations for sea birds, while commercial exploitation of guano is simultaneously undertaken on some of the islands. Control is effected in that it is a crime for anyone to set foot on or remain upon an island or there to disturb, capture or kill any sea bird or seal, or to damage the eggs of any sea bird or to collect or remove any such eggs or feathers or guano, except in the performance of duties under the Act or under the authority and subject to the conditions of an exemption or a permit.[3] Further control can be exercised through regulations.[4]

1 46 of 1973 Sch 1. See also title FISHERIES
  AND FISHING.
2 S 14.

3 S 3.
4 S 11.

CONSERVATION OF WILD ANIMALS

INTRODUCTION

389 General The conservation of wild animals must be accomplished through legislation since such animals are classified as *res nullius*[1] in South African law. A *res nullius* is a thing which belongs to nobody, but which can become the property of anyone who assumes possession of it through effective physical control (*occupatio*). The fact that wild animals are regarded as *res nullius* means that, save in the exceptional case where someone has acquired ownership of them, there are no private law remedies available to citizens when wild animals are killed, captured or injured.[2] The common law crimes of theft and malicious damage to property are also not applicable. Consequently wild animals would be without any legal protection if it were not for specific legislation for their conservation.

The conservation of wild animals in South Africa has been effected mainly at provincial level. Apart from conservation under national protected areas legislation and certain municipal by-laws, wild animals are currently conserved in terms of provincial legislation, although the National Environmental Management: Biodiversity Act[3] provides for the conservation of wild animals through provisions that are reliant for their operation on lists that have not yet been drawn up.

Traditionally, nature conservation – which encompasses the conservation of indigenous wild animals, plants and freshwater fish – has been effected by virtue of the Orange Free State Nature Conservation Ordinance,[4] the Cape Nature and Environmental Conservation Ordinance,[5] the Natal Nature Conservation Ordinance[6] and the Transvaal Nature Conservation Ordinance.[7] Besides these ordinances, several of the former so-called TBVC states and self-governing territories enacted their own nature conservation legislation. The Constitution[8] also determines that nature conservation falls within the concurrent legislative competence of national Parliament and the provinces,[9] and Mpumalanga has produced a nature conservation Act.[10] Since there are now nine provinces, there may potentially be nine different statutes on nature conservation, although with the promulgation of the National Environmental Management: Biodiversity Act, fragmentation should be minimised. For the sake of the present discussion, in respect of both wild animals and plants, reliance is placed upon the above nature conservation ordinances, referred to by their original titles and which continue to apply in the areas in which they formerly applied, until amended or repealed.[11] Reference continues to be made in the ordinances to the concept of "administrator" although this now mostly refers to the competent provincial authority to whom the legislation in question has been assigned under the Constitution.[12] It should be realised that the legal position which is described is subject to considerable potential change.

1 Van der Merwe and Rabie 1974 *THRHR* 37. See generally on the conservation of wild animals, Bothma and Glavovic "Wild Animals" in Fuggle and Rabie (eds) *Environmental Management in SA* 250; Rabie 1973 *CILSA* 145 and Glavovic 1988 *SALJ* 519.

2 See title ANIMALS; and cf generally Rabie and Van der Merwe 1990 *Stell LR* 1.

3 10 of 2004.

4 8 of 1969.

5 19 of 1974.

6 15 of 1974.

7 12 of 1983.

8 Constitution of the Republic of SA 108 of 1996.

9 Sch 4.

10 Mpumalanga Nature Conservation Act 10 of 1998. This Act is almost identical to the Tvl Ord, with a few changes.

11 Van Wyk in Van Wyk, Dugard, De Villiers and Davis *Rights and Constitutionalism. The New SA Legal Order* 131 165.

12 Constitution of the Republic of SA 108 of 1996 Sch 6 item 14.

WILD ANIMALS WITHIN PROTECTED AREAS

390 General As far as a systematic discussion of the legislation is concerned, a distinction should be drawn between the conservation of wild animals within protected areas and conservation outside such areas. Extensive protection prevails in protected areas. Control is established by fencing these reserves and by appointing staff to administer them. A variety of actions that can be detrimental to wildlife conservation are usually declared to be criminal, for example entering or residing in a protected area without permission; conveying into a reserve, or being in possession of weapons, traps, or snares; and killing, injuring, capturing or disturbing any animal within the protected area.[1] All wild animals are protected in this way and no exceptions are made, as is the case with wild animals outside reserves.

Provincial ordinances also make provision for the establishment of nature reserves on land held in private ownership, the so-called private nature reserves. In the case of these reserves the protection afforded to wild animals is not as extensive as that enjoyed by wild animals in the abovementioned reserves. Private nature reserves must be fenced and hunting in such reserves is an offence,[2] but the landowner (and other persons who have the landowner's permission) may obtain a permit to hunt wild animals in his or her nature reserve.[3] The Cape Ordinance determines that a person who has established a private nature reserve, and anyone authorised by that person, may at any time by any means other than the use of fire or poison, hunt any wild animal and may keep such animals in captivity.[4]

1 Ss 15(1) and 23 of the Natal Ord 15 of 1974; s 19 of the Tvl Ord 12 of 1983; ss 35(3) and 40 of the OFS Ord 8 of 1969

and ss 6(6) and 14 of the Cape Ord 19 of 1974.

2 S 19 of the Tvl Ord; ss 36 and 40 of the

OFS Ord and ss 60, 61(1), 62 and 76 of the Natal Ord. There is no special provision, with the exception of s 13 of the Cape Ord, which applies to the owner, or someone authorised by the owner, in respect of hunting in private nature reserves.

3   S 19 of the Tvl Ord and s 61(1) of the Natal

Ord. In terms of s 36(3) of the OFS Ord the hunting of any wild animal in a private nature reserve is apparently permissible, provided the landowner (or a person authorised by him) gives permission.

4   S 13(a) and (b) of the Cape Ord.

WILD ANIMALS OUTSIDE PROTECTED AREAS

CLASSES OF WILD ANIMALS

391 General An important concept basic to all the provincial nature conservation ordinances is that of "wild animal". This is usually defined in varying wide terms to mean any vertebrate animal belonging to a non-domestic species; the definition includes birds and reptiles but not fish, which are usually defined separately. The statutory definition also includes the carcass, eggs and several parts of the body in the concept of wild animal.[1] The utilisation and conservation of fish resources – both marine and freshwater fish – are discussed in another title.[2]

Wild animals outside protected areas are divided by law into various classes.[3] The class in which a species is placed is most important as the measure of protection that it is afforded depends upon such placement. It will thus be useful to consider the legal classes of animals and to indicate which provisions apply to them.

1   The definition varies in the various ordinances. Cf s 1(lxii) of the Tvl Ord 12 of 1983; s 1 of the OFS Ord 8 of 1969 and s 2(lxxiii) of the Cape Ord 19 of 1974. Cf also *S v Gawaseb* 1980 4 SA 399 (SWA).

2   See title FISHERIES AND FISHING.

3   The Natal Ord 15 of 1974 does not define "wild animal" but s 1 defines "indigenous mammal", "wild bird", and "indigenous amphibian, invertebrate or reptile".

392 All wild animals Some provisions in the respective ordinances of the Cape, Transvaal and the Orange Free State apply to all wild animals, bearing in mind that the concept excludes invertebrates and exotic species. These general provisions relate to prohibited weapons and methods of hunting,[1] the export and import of wild animals,[2] and in the Cape and the Free State the keeping of wild animals in captivity.[3] There are also other provisions which apply to all wild animals, namely the provisions of the Cape Ordinance in respect of the donation and possession of a wild animal or its carcass and the sale of a carcass,[4] and the provisions relating to the sale, donation, purchase or acquisition in the Free State Ordinance.[5] It is necessary to keep in mind that the abovementioned provisions apply also to all the classes of wild animals that are distinguished below.

1   Ss 29 and 33 of the Cape Ord 19 of 1974; s 27 of the Tvl Ord 12 of 1983 and ss 7 and 9 of the OFS Ord 8 of 1969.

2   S 44(1)(a) and (b) of the Cape Ord, ss 41 and 42 of the Tvl Ord and ss 15(b) and 16(b) of the OFS Ord.

3   S 31 of the Cape Ord and s 14(1) of the OFS Ord. In the Cape, however, s 31(1) does not apply in respect of birds which do not qualify as endangered or protected wild animals.

4   Ss 42 44 46.

5   S 14(2).

393 Game "Game" is the collective term employed in the Transvaal, Orange Free State and Natal ordinances to encompass the various classes of animals distinguished in the respective ordinances,[1] namely ordinary and protected game as well as certain protected wild animals in the Transvaal and the Free State and open, ordinary, protected and specially protected game in Natal. Certain provisions of these ordinances apply to all classes of game, in other words, those dealing with prohibited weapons and methods of hunting[2] and the sale[3] and purchase[4] of game. Other provisions dealing with all game are: the Transvaal and the Free State provisions dealing with hunting at night[5] and the conveyance of game;[6] the Transvaal provisions dealing with the keeping in captivity and possession of game,[7] the catching,[8] poisoning[9] of game and hunting in a nature reserve;[10] the Free State and Natal provisions relating to trespass with a weapon upon land on which game is likely to be found;[11] and the Natal provisions in respect of export,[12] hunting on a public road or road reserve,[13] killing marauding dogs,[14] the possession or handling of game under suspicion that it was hunted illegally,[15] and the possession or conveyance of a loaded firearm on any road traversing land in a locality in which game is or is likely to be found.[16]

1 Cf s 1(xx) of the Tvl Ord 12 of 1983; s 1 of the OFS Ord 8 of 1969 and s 1 of the Natal Ord 15 of 1974. The latter provision defines game more extensively as meaning any of the mammals or birds, alive or dead, mentioned in the Schedules containing the various classes of game (Schs 1–4), and includes any meat, fat or blood thereof, whether fresh, preserved, processed or manufactured in any manner, and also any tooth, tusk, bone, head, horn, shell, claw, hoof, hide, skin, hair, egg, feather or other durable portion of any such mammal or bird, whether preserved, processed, manufactured or not, but does not include any trophy ("trophy" is separately defined).
2 S 21 of the Tvl Ord; s 8 of the OFS Ord and ss 44 and 48(1) and (2) of the Natal Ord.
3 Ss 32 and 35 of the Tvl Ord; s 11 of the OFS Ord and s 49(1) of the Natal Ord.
4 S 31 of the Tvl Ord and s 49(2) of the Natal Ord.
5 S 20 of the Tvl Ord and s 6 of the OFS Ord.
6 S 38 of the Tvl Ord and s 13 of the OFS Ord.
7 Ss 37 and 39.
8 S 25.
9 S 31.
10 S 19.
11 S 21 of the OFS Ord and s 42(2) of the Natal Ord.
12 S 51.
13 S 45(1).
14 S 43.
15 S 39(1).
16 S 46.

394 Ordinary game The wild species listed as ordinary game appear in Schedules to the Transvaal,[1] Orange Free State[2] and Natal[3] Ordinances.

The provisions of the ordinances relating to ordinary game pertain to licences, hunting during open and closed seasons, hunting without a licence by the landowner and his or her relatives, and obtaining the landowner's permission to hunt ordinary game on his or her land.[4] The Natal Ordinance also regulates keeping ordinary game in captivity.[5]

The Cape Ordinance[6] does not distinguish a category of ordinary game, although some of the species listed as protected wild animals are regarded as ordinary game in the other provinces. This is because the list of protected wild animals in the Cape is much more extensive than the lists of ordinary game in the other provinces. Moreover, the Cape provisions dealing with protected wild animals also relate to licences or permits, hunting during open and closed seasons, and hunting without a licence by the landowner or his or her relatives.[7] Other provisions deal with daily bag limits for protected wild animals[8] and with the sale, purchase, donation, receipt as a donation or possession of such animals.[9]

1 12 of 1983 Sch 3.
2 8 of 1969 Sch 2.
3 15 of 1974 Sch 1.
4 S 17 of the Tvl Ord; ss 4 and 5 of the OFS Ord and ss 33(1)(a) and (b), 34(1)(b), (c) and (d), 34(2)(a) and (b) and 34(3) of the Natal Ord.
5 S 38.
6 19 of 1974.
7 S 27.
8 S 28.
9 S 44(1)(e).

395 Open game The Natal Ordinance[1] is the only one in which a category of open game is distinguished. The only provision dealing with open game is that which requires the landowner's or occupier's permission before open game may be lawfully hunted.[2]

1 15 of 1974.
2 S 33(1)(b).

396 Protected game Categories of protected game are distinguished in Schedules to the ordinances of the Transvaal,[1] Orange Free State[2] and Natal.[3] Reference has already been made to the position of protected wild animals in the Cape Ordinance.[4] These are treated in very much the same way as is ordinary game in the other provinces. Protected game may be hunted only in terms of a permit.[5]

1 12 of 1983 Sch 2.
2 8 of 1969 Sch 1.
3 15 of 1974 Sch 2.
4 19 of 1974.

5 S 16 of the Tvl Ord; s 2(3) of the OFS Ord and ss 33(1)(a) and 35(1)(a) of the Natal Ord.

397 Specially protected game The Natal and Transvaal Ordinances distingush a category of specially protected game. The hunting, capture and keeping in captivity of specially protected game is strictly regulated.[1] Unlawful possession of a trophy derived from specially protected game is rendered a separate offence.[2]

1 S 37 of the Natal Ord 15 of 1974 and ss 16A and 19(3) of the Tvl Ord 12 of 1983.
2 S 50(1).

398 Endangered and rare species of animals Categories of endangered and rare species of members of the animal kingdom are distinguished in the Transvaal[1] and Free State[2] ordinances. These species correspond to those listed in appendices I and II to the Convention on International Trade in Endangered Species of Wild Fauna and Flora (Washington 1973). The only provisions applicable specifically to such endangered and rare species are those dealing with export and import.[3] The Natal Ordinance[4] distinguishes only a category of endangered mammals[5] which corresponds to the mammal species listed in the IUCN Red Data Book. The only provision dealing specifically with endangered mammals is that relating to the purchase, acquiring, possession, keeping in captivity, sale, exchange or other disposal of such mammals.[6] The Cape Ordinance[7] distinguishes a category of endangered wild animals,[8] which lists eight species. The provisions applicable to endangered wild animals relate to measures to ensure their survival,[9] their hunting,[10] sale, purchase, donation or receipt as a donation,[11] and to anything manufactured from the carcass,[12] as well as the treatment of the carcass for certain purposes.[13]

1 12 of 1983 ch VIII.
2 8 of 1969 s 1.
3 S 98 of the Tvl Ord and ss 15(a) and 16(a) of the OFS Ord.
4 15 of 1974.
5 Sch 6.
6 S 79.
7 19 of 1974.

8 Sch 1.
9 S 17.
10 S 26.
11 S 44(1)(c).
12 S 44(1)(e). Possession of live endangered wild animals is also regulated.
13 S 44(1)(d).

399 Certain separate categories of wild animals The Natal Nature Conservation Ordinance[1] distinguishes a number of separate categories of wild animals, most of which are included in the Schedules of the other provinces which deal with the abovementioned categories of wild animals. Unlike the other provinces the Natal Ordinance has, in addition to a chapter on game, separate chapters for mammals, baboons and monkeys, amphibians, invertebrates and reptiles, and wild birds. In the other ordinances most of these animals are dealt with as game or as protected wild animals.

1   15 of 1974.

400 Protected wild animals A separate category of protected wild animals, containing some five species, is distinguished in the Transvaal Ordinance.[1] These animals are the subject of provisions dealing with hunting with a permit[2] and hunting under certain special circumstances.[3]

1   12 of 1983 Sch 4.
2   S 18.
3   S 23.

401 Exotic animals and problem animals The provisions with respect to these animals are dealt with in subsequent paragraphs.[1]

1   See pars 420 et seq.

HUNTING

402 General The concept of hunting features prominently in conservation legislation, for example hunting of protected wild animals and of ordinary game, hunting in a wildlife sanctuary, hunting at night, during the closed season or on land of which one is not the owner, and hunting with prohibited methods and weapons. The definition of "hunt" in various ordinances and statutes is generally not restricted to killing, but includes a wide variety of actions, some of which are not necessarily associated with killing. Thus, in the Free State "hunt" means "(a) in any manner whatsoever to kill or capture or to attempt to kill or capture; (b) to shoot at; (c) to search for, follow or lie in wait with intent to kill, shoot at or capture; or (d) wilfully to disturb."[1] Other ordinances have similar definitions.[2]

The definition of "hunt" covers a wide variety of actions, including actions that may not even qualify as attempted killing. This is defensible on the ground that conservation of wild animals goes much further than merely conserving their physical existence.[3] Not only killing or capturing, but also shooting at, searching for, following, lying in wait for and wilful disturbance of wild animals can adversely interfere with the objects of wildlife conservation.

The various actions included in the definition of hunt must be considered independently of each other. Therefore, the wilful disturbance of wild animals, even without an intention to kill or capture the animals concerned, can amount to hunting.[4] Killing, therefore, does not establish a genus, and the other actions included in the definition of hunt are not in this respect bound by the *eiusdem generis* rule. Wilful disturbance which is not calculated to affect wildlife conservation adversely accordingly does not amount to hunting.[5]

The question whether searching for or lying in wait for wild animals without the intention of killing or capturing them can amount to hunting, was left open in *R v Carter*.[6] The words "to search or lie in wait for", in the definition of "hunt" in Natal[7] are not further qualified. The question whether such actions can amount to hunting thus seem to depend on whether they were undertaken with an object which would be detrimental to the cause of wildlife conservation or not. Searching, or lying in wait, for wild animals with a view to observing or photographing them would, therefore, not amount to hunting. In the Transvaal,[8] Free State[9] and Cape[10] Ordinances, however, these words are qualified by the words "with intent to kill, shoot or capture". Searching for or lying in wait for wild animals without this intention will accordingly not amount to hunting in terms of these ordinances.

Mens rea, in the sense of both *dolus* and *culpa*, seems to be an element of the various offences where the hunting of game is involved. It would, therefore, be no defence on a charge of unlawfully hunting a protected wild animal for the accused to say that he or she mistook the protected wild animal for an animal which qualifies as game, if the mistaken belief was due to the accused's negligence.[11] Likewise, hunting on land without the landowner's permission is not excused by the accused's belief that he or she was not trespassing, where this belief was due to the accused's negligence.[12]

1   OFS Ord 8 of 1969 s 1.
2   S 1(xxii) of the Tvl Ord 12 of 1983; s 2(xxxi) of the Cape Ord 19 of 1974 and s 1 of the Natal Ord 15 of 1974.
3   *S v Hellerle* 1969 1 SA 420 (N) 425.
4   See *S v Hellerle* supra.
5   *S v Hellerle* supra 425. In view of this, it is doubtful whether *R v Linde* 1954 4 SA 203 (O) was correctly decided.
6   1954 2 SA 317 (E).
7   S 1.
8   S 1(xxii).
9   S 1.
10   S 2(xxxi).
11   *R v Stainer* 1956 3 SA 498 (FC) and *S v Botes* 1967 2 SA 533 (N).
12   *S v Oosthuizen* 1971 2 SA 300 (R). In *R v Van der Linde* 1953 1 SA 588 (G) it was decided that *mens rea* is not an element of this offence, but from the court's remarks it would seem that the accused were in actual fact negligent. Cf generally also *S v Bailey* 1968 3 SA 267 (N); *S v Williams* 1968 4 SA 81 (SWA); *S v Le Roux* 1969 3 SA 725 (T) and *S v Venter* 1979 2 SA 752 (T) 756D.

403   The hunting licence system   As mentioned, a hunting licence is required before ordinary or protected game may be hunted. In addition, permission must be obtained from the owner of the land upon which the animal is hunted. The name and address of the hunter, the species, sex and number of game that may be hunted, the fee, the period of validity of the licence, and the conditions to which the licence is subject, are usually specified in the licence.

The Natal Ordinance[1] makes provision for an elaborate system of some nine different types of hunting licences,[2] while the Transvaal Ordinance[3] also provides for permits for professional hunters.[4] The owner of land enjoys a number of privileges with regard to wild animals on his or her land – *inter alia*, that in certain instances he or she does not require a hunting licence.

1   15 of 1974.
2   Ss 33–36.
3   12 of 1983.
4   Ch IV.

404   The position of the landowner   The owner of land[1] (and in some instances the occupier and certain relatives of the owner),[2] is in a privileged position with regard to the wild animals that happen to be on his or her land. The landowner's permission is required for anyone to hunt legally on his or her land.[3] The landowner does not require a licence to hunt ordinary game in the open season.[4] The landowner may even be granted a licence to hunt in the closed season,[5] and is granted extensive powers to hunt in his or her private nature[6] reserve or on his or her land if its fencing complies with certain requirements.[7] When hunting, the landowner may utilise some weapons and methods that are otherwise prohibited.[8] A landowner is even granted certain powers as regards protected animals that cause damage to his or her property.[9]

1 "Owner of land" is defined in the various ordinances: s 1(xxxviii) of the Tvl Ord 12 of 1983; s 1 of the OFS Ord 8 of 1969; s 2(xlvi) of the Cape Ord 19 of 1974 and s 1 of the Natal Ord 15 of 1974.

2 Among the many relatives included, eg under the Cape Ord, are the spouse, parent, step-parent, adoptive parent, son-in-law, child, step-child, adopted child, brother, sister or grandchild of the landowner (s 2(lx)).

3 Ss 16(1)(b), 18(1)(a)(ii), 24(1) and 28(1) of the Tvl Ord; ss 5(c), 18 and 21(1)(a) of the OFS Ord; ss 39 and 40 of the Cape Ord and ss 33(1)(b), 34(1)(c), 34(2)(b), 35(1)(b), 35(2)(b) and 42(1) of the Natal Ord.

4 S 17(1)(b) of the Tvl Ord; s 5(a) and (b) of the OFS Ord; s 27(2) of the Cape Ord and s 34(3) of the Natal Ord. S 34(3) of the Natal Ord even allows the landowner to hunt protected game without a licence.

5 S 17(1)(f) of the Tvl Ord and s 34(2)(a) of the Natal Ord.

6 S 19(1) of the Tvl Ord; s 36(3) of the OFS Ord; s 13(a) of the Cape Ord and s 61 of the Natal Ord.

7 S 47 of the Tvl Ord and s 36 of the Cape Ord.

8 Ss 21(1), 22(1), 23(1) and 27(1) of the Tvl Ord; ss 8(i) and 9(i) of the OFS Ord and s 48(3) of the Natal Ord.

9 S 18(1)(b) of the Tvl Ord; s 2(3) of the OFS Ord and s 47 of the Cape Ord.

405 Prohibited methods, contrivances and weapons used for hunting

Provisions exist in terms of which it is an offence to use, without a permit, certain methods, contrivances or weapons for hunting wild animals. The following are usually prohibited: using a motor vehicle, boat or aircraft to drive wild animals; firing at them from such vehicles; using a dog, fire, poison, snare, trap, gin, net, bird-lime, pitfall, holding pen, trap-cage, or bow and arrow; automatic reloading firearms, missiles containing explosives, and set guns.[1]

However these provisions do not always apply to all wild animals. Prohibited weapons and methods apply only to protected wild animals and ordinary game,[2] although the prohibition of the Cape Ordinance applies to all wild animals.[3] Moreover, the owner or occupier of land is excluded from some of the prohibitions.[4] The Natal Ordinance does not render it an offence for the owner or occupier to set a trap or snare or to lay poison if such owner or occupier satisfies the court that it was done for the preservation of his or her livestock, crops, produce, or against the depredations of vermin, or marauding dogs, or the like, and that he or she took all reasonable precautions against game being caught or destroyed thereby.[5]

1 Ss 21 and 23 of the Tvl Ord 12 of 1983; ss 7, 8, 9 and 40 of the OFS Ord 8 of 1969; ss 29, 30, 32 and 33 of the Cape Ord 19 of 1974 and ss 48(1) and 55 of the Natal Ord 15 of 1974.

2 S 21 of the Tvl Ord applies only to game, as do s 8 of the OFS Ord and s 48(1) of the Natal Ord, while s 29(i), (ii) and (iii) of the Cape Ord exempts certain animals from some of the provisions in regard to some of

the prohibited hunting methods and weapons.

3 S 29.

4 Ss 21(1) and 23(1) of the Tvl Ord; ss 8(i) and 9(i) of the OFS Ord. In terms of the Cape Ord the landowner (and certain other persons) who has established a private nature reserve or who holds a certificate of adequate enclosure may, in principle, use any means to hunt.

5 S 48(3).

406 Prohibited places of hunting

Hunting on any land without the owner's permission is an offence.[1] Sometimes hunting on or from any public road is expressly declared to be an offence.[2] Local authorities generally prohibit even the firing of a gun in areas under their control.[3] The prohibition on hunting in protected areas has already been dealt with.

1 Ss 39, 40 and 85 of the Cape Ord 19 of 1974; ss 5(c), 18, 21(1)(a) and 40 of the OFS Ord 8 of 1969 and ss 33(1)(b), 34(1)(c), 34(2)(b), 35(1)(b), 35(2)(b) and 42(1) of the Natal Ord 15 of 1974. Cf also *S v Venter*

1979 2 SA 752 (T).

2 Ss 29(c) and 85 of the Cape Ord and ss 45 and 55 of the Natal Ord.

3 Cf also s 29(f) of the Cape Ord.

407 Prohibited times of hunting Hunting at night constitutes an offence unless a permit to do so is obtained.[1] In terms of the Free State[2] and Transvaal[3] Ordinances hunting on a Sunday is an offence. These provisions apply only to game.[4] Ordinary game may be hunted only in the open season;[5] the landowner is again privileged in that he or she may, under certain circumstances, hunt ordinary game during the closed season.[6]

1 S 20 of the Tvl Ord 12 of 1983; ss 6(a) and 40 of the OFS Ord 8 of 1969; ss 29(e) and 85 of the Cape Ord 19 of 1974 and ss 48(1)(e), 55, 127(c) and 130 of the Natal Ord 15 of 1974.
2 Ss 6(b) and 40.
3 S 1(b) Law 28 of 1896 (T).
4 S 20 of the Tvl Ord; s 6 of the OFS Ord and s 48(1) of the Natal Ord apply only to game. S 29 of the Cape Ord applies basically to all wild animals, but some exceptions are listed. Ss 114 and 130 of the Natal Ord

apply basically to all wild birds, but some birds listed in Sch 8 are excluded.
5 Ss 4 and 40 of the OFS Ord; s 17(1)(b) and (d) of the Tvl Ord; ss 27(1)(a) and 85 of the Cape Ord and ss 31(2) and 55 of the Natal Ord.
6 S 17(1)(f) of the Tvl Ord; s 27(2) of the Cape Ord and s 4 of the OFS Ord. In Natal a special game licence entitles the holder thereof to hunt ordinary game during the closed season: s 34(1)(c).

OTHER RESTRICTIONS

408 Keeping wild animals in captivity The catching,[1] possession, control or keeping in captivity[2] of live wild animals without a permit or licence constitutes an offence.[3] This protection is afforded only to game,[4] exotic animals[5] and certain listed invertebrates,[6] but in terms of the Cape and the Orange Free State Ordinances the offence relates to all wild animals.[7] A licence or permit can stipulate the conditions under which wild animals may be kept in captivity, and can be cancelled if its conditions are not met, thus affording a reasonable measure of control.

1 Cf s 1(viii) of the Tvl Ord 12 of 1983.
2 Cf s 2(xii) of the Cape Ord 19 of 1974 and s 1 of the Natal Ord 15 of 1974.
3 Ss 25, 27, 28, 29 and 39 of the Tvl Ord; ss 14, 19(1)(b) and 49 of the OFS Ord 8 of 1969 (cf also s 20); ss 31 and 85 of the Cape Ord and ss 37(1), 38(1), 55, 79, 80, 86, 90, 102(1) (cf 102(2)), 109, 118(1) and 130 of the Natal Ord.
4 Ss 38(1) and 55 of the Natal Ord and ss 25 and 39 of the Tvl Ord.
5 S 44(1)(b) of the Tvl Ord and s 19(1)(b) of the OFS Ord.

6 S 45 of the Tvl Ord.
7 However, in the Cape Ord wild birds which do not qualify as endangered or protected wild animals are excluded from this protection: s 31(1). In Natal, in principle, protection relates to all wild birds: s 118(1). However, birds mentioned in Sch 8 are excluded. In the Cape an exception is made with respect to the prohibition in question in favour of the owner of a private nature reserve and the holder of a certificate of adequate enclosure: ss 13(b) and 36(b).

409 Conveyance of wild animals The conveyance of live or dead wild animals without a permit or licence is an offence.[1] This offence is restricted to game, certain specifically listed animals and exotic animals, although the Cape Ordinance relates to all wild animals.[2]

1 Ss 38, 39, 43, 44 and 45 of the Tvl Ord 12 of 1983; ss 13, 14, 19(1)(b) and 40 of the OFS Ord 8 of 1969 and s 44(1)(a) of the Cape Ord 19 of 1974. The Tvl Ord allows

regulations to be made in regard to the conveyance of any wild animal: s 98(1)(f).
2 S 44(1)(a).

410 Cruelty to wild animals According to the Performing Animals Protection Act,[1] the exhibition or training of animals without a licence is an offence. In terms of the Animals Protection Act,[2] actions amounting to cruelty to animals constitute an offence. These provisions relate to wild animals only when they are in captivity or under the control of a person.

Some of the provisions of the nature conservation ordinances amount to protecting wild animals from cruelty (the prohibition on the use of certain methods and contrivances for hunting, and control of keeping wild animals in captivity).[3]

1 24 of 1935.
2 71 of 1962. See title ANIMALS.

3 Cf also s 86 of the Natal Ord 15 of 1974.

411 Purchase and sale of wild animals The sale or purchase[1] of wild animals without a permit constitutes an offence.[2] Although it is not always clearly stated, this prohibition should, bearing in mind the definition of "wild animal",[3] apply to live and dead animals, and to all parts of such animals including their eggs.

Most of the ordinances apply only to game,[4] including exotic animals[5] in some instances, and certain other specially listed animals, which are alive.[6]

1 The definition of "sell" covers a relatively wide field of actions, including hawk, peddle, barter or change, or offer, advertise, expose or have in possession for the purpose of sale, hawking, peddling, bartering or exchanging: s 2(lxi) of the Cape Ord 19 of 1974. Cf also s 1(lii) of the Tvl Ord 12 of 1983; s 1 of the OFS Ord 8 of 1969 and s 1 of the Natal Ord 15 of 1974. Even the donation of some wild animals is prohibited under certain circumstances. Cf ss 12, 14(2), 19(1)(b) and 40 of the OFS Ord; ss 35, 43, 44 and 45 of the Tvl Ord and ss 41, 44(1)(c) and (e) and 85 of the Cape Ord.

2 Ss 49(1) and (2), 55, 79, 81, 115(1) and 130 of the Natal Ord; ss 11, 14(2), 19(1)(b) and 40 of the OFS Ord; ss 32, 34, 43, 44 and 45 of the Tvl Ord and ss 44(1)(c) and (e) and 85 of the Cape Ord. See also ss 45 and 46 of the Cape Ord. Certain exceptions exist to

this rule, eg where the landowner, or a butcher who has obtained a licence, sells game that has been lawfully killed. Cf s 32 of the Tvl Ord and s 11 of the OFS Ord.

3 See par 389 ante.

4 S 49(1) and (6) of the Natal Ord apply only to game, while s 115(1) applies, in principle, to all wild birds, although birds mentioned in schedule 8 are excepted. S 11 of the OFS Ord applies only to game; ss 32 and 34 of the Tvl Ord apply only to game and exotic animals, and s 44(1)(c) and (e) of the Cape Ord relates only to endangered or protected wild animals. However, ss 45 and 46 of the Cape Ord apply to all wild animals.

5 S 19(1)(b) of the OFS Ord and s 44 of the Tvl Ord.

6 S 14(2) of the OFS Ord and s 43 of the Tvl Ord. Cf s 44(1)(e) of the Cape Ord.

412 Export and import of wild animals The exportation and importation of wild animals without a permit is an offence[1] in terms of the Orange Free State,[2] the Cape,[3] the Transvaal[4] and Natal Ordinances.[5]

It is only when the export and import, without permits, of all wild animals (dead or alive, or any part of them) is prohibited internationally that protection will be entirely successful. Thus the convention on International Trade in Endangered Species of Wild Fauna and Flora, which was concluded in Washington DC in March 1973, is of great significance. In terms of this convention international co-operation is established for the protection of certain species of wild fauna and flora against over-exploitation through international trade. South Africa was among the 80 countries represented at the conference during which this convention was concluded, and became a party to the convention in 1975.

1 Ss 44(1)(a) (b) and 85 of the Cape Ord 19 of 1974; ss 51(1) (2), 52, 55, 93, 99, 104, 109, 123, 125(1) (2), 130 of the Natal Ord 15 of 1974; ss 15, 16 and 40 of the OFS Ord 8

of 1969 and ss 41, 42, 44, 45 and 98 of the Tvl Ord 12 of 1983. Some exceptions are provided, eg ss 15 and 16 of the OFS Ord.

2 Ss 15, 16 and 40.

3 S 44(1)(a) (b).
4 Ss 41 42, 44 45 98.
5 It covers baboons, monkeys, amphibians, invertebrates, reptiles and birds, but as regards other wild animals it encompasses only game and exotic mammals.

413 Possession of dead animals It is an offence in terms of the Transvaal Ordinance to possess dead game if the possessor knows that such game was not hunted or acquired lawfully.[1] In terms of the Cape Ordinance possession of the carcass of any wild animal can constitute an offence.[2] In addition, provisions exist in terms of which any person who is found in possession of dead game where there is reasonable suspicion that it has been hunted unlawfully, and who is unable to give a satisfactory account of such possession, is guilty of an offence.[3] A person is also guilty of an offence if he or she acquires any dead game without having reasonable cause for believing that such game has been lawfully hunted.[4]

1 12 of 1983 s 37.
2 19 of 1974 s 42.
3 S 37(1)(b) of the Tvl Ord; s 40(1)(g) of the

OFS Ord 8 of 1969 and s 39(1) of the Natal Ord 15 of 1974.
4 S 37(1)(c) of the Tvl Ord.

414 Prohibitions relating to contrivances capable of capturing or killing wild animals Apart from the fact that hunting with traps, snares, nets and the like is an offence, it is also an offence to *possess* such contrivances or to bring them on to land where wild animals are present or are likely to be found.[1]

This provision does not apply to the premises where a licensed dealer carries on business,[2] or to the owner or occupier of such premises[3] or to a person who obtained the owner's permission.[4] Similarly, the manufacture, purchase and sale of these contrivances is not controlled, and this has a predictably detrimental effect on enforcement.

1 S 22 of the Tvl Ord 12 of 1983; s 10 of the OFS Ord 8 of 1969 and ss 47, 48(2) and 55 of the Natal Ord 15 of 1974.
2 S 22(1)(ii)(cc) of the Tvl Ord.

3 S 22(1)(ii)(aa) of the Tvl Ord and s 10 of the OFS Ord.
4 S 22(1)(ii)(dd) of the Tvl Ord and s 10 of the OFS Ord.

415 Unlawful possession of firearms The possession of a firearm without a licence, permit or authorisation is an offence in terms of the Firearms Control Act,[1] while certain fierarms are classed as prohibited firearms which may not be possessed or licensed.[2] These measures could possibly have some preventive effect.

1 60 of 2000 s 3.
2 S 4.

416 Trespass Entering or being upon occupied or unoccupied land without lawful reason, or the permission of the owner or occupier, is a criminal offence in terms of the Trespass Act.[1] Before anyone can hunt on any land, the owner's permission must be obtained. In addition, some of the ordinances contain specific provisions making trespass an offence under certain circumstances. For example, without the owner or occupier's permission, or without lawful reason, no person may, while in possession of a weapon, enter or be on any land upon which any game is found or is likely to be found.[2] Failure to leave immediately after having been told to do so can constitute a further offence.[3]

1 6 of 1959.
2 Ss 42(2) and 55 of the Natal Ord 15 of 1974; ss 21(1)(a) and 40 of the OFS Ord 8

of 1969 and s 24 of the Tvl Ord 12 of 1983.
Cf *S v Venter* 1979 2 SA 752 (T).
3 S 42(3) of the Natal Ord.

HABITAT PROTECTION

417 General Conservation of wild animals without the protection of their habitat is of little value. Although not directly responsible for wildlife extermination, the destruction of habitat is nevertheless just as detrimental to wildlife as is direct killing. Habitat destruction probably constitutes the greatest threat to wildlife today.

418 Habitat protection within protected areas The various kinds of protected areas and the extensive protection afforded to wildlife in these areas are discussed in other sections.[1] Here it suffices to point out that as far as national, provincial and municipal conservation areas are concerned, the principle that wildlife cannot be adequately protected without protection of its habitat is accepted and implemented.

1 See pars 390 et seq ante.

419 Habitat protection outside protected areas Several indigenous plants, shrubs and trees are protected in terms of the various nature conservation ordinances. This protection is, however, of little consequence as far as the protection of the habitat is concerned. Apart from the fact that the landowner and some of his or her relatives are exempted from the provisions, protection relates only to individual species of plants and not to entire habitat.

There are a number of statutes aimed at habitat protection.[1] These statutes are, however, primarily designed for the benefit of humans and any protection afforded to wildlife is largely coincidental. The conservation of habitat in terms of some of these statutes is nevertheless substantial. The state, for example, manages large areas of land which are unsuitable or unavailable for afforestation, or which have been declared as mountain catchment areas, predominantly as protected areas and thereby affords a suitable habitat for wild animals.

1 See, amongst others, the Acts discussed in
   the section on protected areas: pars 360 et
   seq ante.

CONTROL OF PROBLEM ANIMALS

420 General Certain wild animals are considered problem animals (previously termed vermin) because of their potential for detrimental interference in farming activities. Provision has accordingly been made for the organised killing of such animals. Such killing of wild animals is the antithesis of nature conservation but it is discussed here since it drastically affects certain wild animals.

421 Declaration of problem animals The control of problem animals is regulated in terms of the Problem Animals Control Ordinances of Natal,[1] the Cape,[2] and the Free State,[3] and by virtue of the Transvaal Nature Conservation Ordinance.[4]

The premier of the province concerned may declare any species of wild animal to be a problem animal within the whole, or any part, of the province in question.[5] Nature reserves are excluded from the provisions dealing with problem animal extermination.[6]

1 14 of 1978.
2 26 of 1957.
3 11 of 1967.
4 12 of 1983.
5 S 3 of the Natal Ord 15 of 1974; s 2 of
   the Cape Ord 19 of 1974 read with the

Schedule; s 56(2) of the Tvl Ord 12 of 1983
read with Sch 8, and s 1(1) of the OFS Ord
8 of 1969 read with Sch 1.
6 S 2 of the Natal Ord and s 55 of the Tvl
   Ord.

422 Problem animal hunt clubs Problem animal hunt clubs may be established and registered for the purpose of hunting problem animals.[1] Where no hunt clubs are established the provincial government may be called upon to assist in the hunting of problem animals,[2] while a local authority may itself act as a club.[3]

Every occupier of land in a problem animal hunting area is eligible for membership of the hunt club.[4] Provision is even made for compulsory membership.[5] The problem animal hunt club is obliged to control problem animals on all land in its hunting area.[6] For this purpose such a club has wide powers. It may, *inter alia*, provide for membership subscriptions,[7] maintain a pack of hounds,[8] and enter and hunt problem animals on any land without the consent of the owner or occupier thereof.[9] These are exceptional powers which can cut across private attempts to conserve wild animals. For example, it is an offence to obstruct a problem animal hunt club in the exercise of its function.[10] It is also an offence to injure or kill any hound, horse or other animal used in a hunt,[11] or to damage or destroy any equipment or property used for a hunt,[12] or to fail to render reasonable assistance to a hunt club.[13] The failure of a member, without reasonable excuse, to attend a hunt or to render assistance may lead to a fine being imposed upon that member by the club.[14]

1 S 6 of the Natal Ord 15 of 1974; s 4 of the Cape Ord 19 of 1974; ss 57 et seq of the Tvl Ord 12 of 1983 and s 2(1) of the OFS Ord 8 of 1969. These clubs are corporate bodies: s 8 of the Natal Ord and s 2(1) of the OFS Ord.
2 S 62 of the Tvl Ord.
3 S 7 of the Cape Ord.
4 S 6(2) of the Natal Ord; s 5(1) of the Cape Ord (this provision refers only to owners of land and not to occupiers) and s 2(2)(a) of the OFS Ord.
5 S 7 of the Natal Ord, s 5(2) of the Cape Ord and s 60(1)(c) of the Tvl Ord.
6 S 12 of the Natal Ord and s 8 of the Cape Ord.
7 S 10(2)(b) of the Natal Ord; s 5(3) of the Cape Ord; s 60(2)(c) of the Tvl Ord and s 2(2)(a) of the OFS Ord. Cf *Gouws v Oranje-Vrystaatse Ongedierte Bestrydings- en Wildbeskermingsvereniging* 1970 1 SA 508 (A),

in which it was decided that the OFS Ord (s 2) is not *ultra vires*. Cf also *R v Steenkamp* 1956 4 SA 187 (C).
8 S 13 of the Natal Ord and s 9 of the Cape Ord.
9 S 14 of the Natal Ord; s 11 of the Cape Ord; s 61(2) of the Tvl Ord and s 4 of the OFS Ord.
10 S 15(a) of the Natal Ord; s 13(a) of the Cape Ord; s 66(1)(c) of the Tvl Ord and s 13(1)(c) of the OFS Ord.
11 S 15(b) of the Natal Ord; s 13(b) of the Cape Ord and s 13(1)(d) of the OFS Ord. Cf *S v Pretorius* 1963 2 SA 111 (E); *S v Marshall* 1967 1 SA 171 (O).
12 S 15(c) of the Natal Ord; s 13(c) of the Cape Ord and s 13(1)(e) of the OFS Ord.
13 S 15(d) of the Natal Ord; s 13(d) of the Cape Ord and s 13(1)(f) of the OFS Ord.
14 S 61(7) of the Tvl Ord.

423 Offences relating to problem animals It is an offence to possess a problem animal or to keep one in captivity.[1] It is also an offence to import[2] or export[3] such an animal. Anyone who, having killed a problem animal, fails forthwith to bury or effectively destroy the carcass, is also guilty of an offence.[4] There are also certain offences relating to laying poison for problem animals.[5]

1 S 21 of the Natal Ord 15 of 1974; s 21(1) of the Cape Ord 19 of 1974; s 55 of the Tvl Ord 12 of 1983 and s 9 of the OFS Ord 8 of 1969. Some exemptions are allowed in terms of these provisions.
2 S 2A of the Cape Ord and s 41 of the Tvl Ord.
3 S 2A of the Cape Ord and s 42 of the Tvl Ord.

4 S 24 of the Natal Ord; s 22 of the Cape Ord and ss 11 and 13(1)(a) of the OFS Ord.
5 S 20 of the Natal Ord and ss 7 and 8 of the OFS Ord. Cf, however, s 48(3) of the Natal Ord, which allows the owner or occupier of land to set a trap or snare or to lay poison on such land for the preservation of his or her livestock or crops or produce against the depredations of vermin. S 79(d) of the Cape

Ord empowers the administrator (provincial premier)to declare any species of wild animal which in his or her opinion is, by reason of its prevalence in any area or its mode of living or other characteristics, detrimental to other wild animals or to property, to be a problem wild animal. In such a case the provisions of s 29 relating to prohibited methods of hunting may be suspended.

424 Other provisions concerning problem animal control Provision is made in the Natal and the Cape Ordinances for the payment of rewards for the killing of vermin.[1] Provision is also made for recovery from an occupier of land, who is not a member of the club concerned, of reasonable expenses incurred in the hunting of problem animals on that land.[2] The premier of a province may also grant financial assistance to hunt clubs[3] and provision is made for the limitation of the civil and criminal liability of hunt clubs and their members.[4]

1 S 3 of the Natal Ord 15 of 1974 (cf also ss 22 and 23) and s 16 of the Cape Ord 19 of 1974.

2 S 16 of the Natal Ord; s 61(5) of the Tvl Ord 12 of 1983 and s 4A of the OFS Ord 8 of 1969. Such expenses can, however, be claimed only in respect of animals which are classified as vermin: *Malan v*

Die Oranje-Vrystaatse Ongedierte Bestrydings- en Wildbewaringsvereniging 1976 1 SA 830 (O).

3 S 18 of the Natal Ord; ss 14 and 20 of the Cape Ord; s 65 of the Tvl Ord and s 2(4) of the OFS Ord.

4 S 9 of the Natal Ord and s 12 of the Cape Ord.

425 Hunting animals which cause damage to property Apart from the fact that the *edictum de feris* is available to a plaintiff who has suffered damage caused by a wild animal, the various provincial nature conservation ordinances provide for the hunting of wild animals that cause damage to property.

(a) *Killing in terms of a permit or by an official body* In the Cape Ordinance provision is made for granting a permit authorising the owner of land to kill certain protected and other wild animals for the protection of crops or any other property.[1] Through the permit system some control can be exercised in that the permit may stipulate conditions under which the killing may be undertaken. Certain provisions entitle the premier of the province or the Director of the Department of Nature Conservation to allow the hunting (or capture or removal) of wild animals that cause damage to property.[2]

(b) *Killing without a permit* The Transvaal and Orange Free State Ordinances give the owner (or occupier) of land the right to kill certain wild animals that damage property. The relevant provisions authorise the owner or occupier to hunt certain protected animals, ordinary game and other animals under the abovementioned circumstances.[3] In respect of other wild animals the common law principles in regard to necessity apply. The Natal Ordinance authorises the holder of a professional hunting licence to shoot ordinary or protected game if this is necessary to defend his or her client's life or property.[4] It is also expressly provided that any protected indigenous reptile may be killed or captured without a permit in defence of human life or property.[5]

1 S 47(1) of the Cape Ord 19 of 1974.

2 S 30(1) of the Tvl Ord 12 of 1983; s 18(1) of the Cape Ord and ss 40(1) and 41(1) of the Natal Ord 15 of 1974.

3 Ss 2(3) and 4 of the OFS Ord 8 of 1969 and ss 17(1)(e), 18(1)(b) and 23(1) of the Tvl

Ord. Cf *R v Moresby-White* 1970 1 SA 325 (RA) and *R v Swart* 1961 2 SA 540 (T).

4 S 33(6)(a) of the Natal Ord.

5 S 101(2). The surrender of the reptile so killed or captured may be ordered.

426 Exotic wild animals Exotic wild animals introduced into South Africa constitute a potential threat to indigenous animals, and to agriculture generally. A number of provisions which concern nature conservation and the protection of agriculture consequently relate to control over such exotic animals.[1] It is an offence in terms of nature conservation ordinances to import exotic wild animals into the various provinces unless a permit has been obtained.[2] It is also an offence, without a permit, to keep such animals in captivity[3] or to release them from captivity,[4] or to hunt, catch, possess, sell, buy, donate, receive or convey them.[5] Exotic animals that, in the opinion of the premier concerned, are detrimental to the preservation of fauna and flora, or are likely to be dangerous to human life, or to cause damage to property or that should be hunted in the interest of nature conservation, may under certain circumstances be hunted.[6]

The Agricultural Pests Act[7] also contains provisions related to control over exotic animals.[8] No person may import into South Africa any exotic animal, except with a permit.[9] The Minister of Agriculture may also prescribe control measures relating to the notification, keeping, removal or combating of exotic animals.[10] Contravention of the import provision or failure to comply with the provisions of a control measure amounts to an offence.[11]

1 An exotic animal is any live vertebrate animal (including a bird and reptile but not a fish) belonging to a non-domestic species and the habitat of which is not in any part of SA, and includes the egg of such animal: s 1(xvi) of the Tvl Ord 12 of 1983; s 1 of the OFS Ord 8 of 1969 and s 1 of the Natal Ord 15 of 1974 ("exotic mammal"). The Cape Ord 19 of 1974 does not contain any specific reference to exotic animals. However, the provisions of the Ordinance dealing with wild animals would cover exotic animals since the definition of "wild animal" in s 2(lxxiii) is not restricted to indigenous animals as is the definition of "wild animal" in the Nature Conservation Ordinances of Tvl and the OFS and of "indigenous mammal" and "wild bird" of the Natal Ord.

2 S 44(1)(a) of the Tvl Ord; ss 16(b) and 40(1)(d) of the OFS Ord and ss 52 and 123 of the Natal Ord. S 44(1)(a) of the Cape Ord, which prohibits the importation of any wild animal, would also cover exotic wild animals.

3 S 44(1)(b) of the Tvl Ord; ss 19(1)(b) and 40 of the OFS Ord; s 80 (cf ss 86 and 87) of the Natal Ord. S 31 of the Cape Ord, which prohibits the keeping in captivity of wild animals, relates also to exotic animals.

4 S 44(1)(a) of the Tvl Ord; ss 19(1)(a) and 40 of the OFS Ord and ss 53 and 124 of the Natal Ord.

5 Ss 29 and 44(1)(b) of the Tvl Ord; ss 19(1)(b) and 40 of the OFS Ord and s 81 of the Natal Ord.

6 S 17(1) of the OFS Ord and s 30(1) of the Tvl Ord.

7 36 of 1983.

8 An "exotic animal" means any vertebrate member of the animal kingdom which is not indigenous to SA, and includes the eggs of such member, but does not include such a member which is an animal to which the Livestock Improvement Act 25 of 1977 (repealed by the Animal Improvement Act 62 of 1998) applies or which is a fish as defined in the Sea Fishery Act 12 of 1988: Agricultural Pests Act 36 of 1983 s 1.

9 S 3(1)(a). The Minister of Agriculture may, however, import any exotic animal if its importation is in his or her opinion desirable in order to combat the occurrence of plants, pathogens, insects or exotic animals of a specific kind or is otherwise in the interests of any branch of agriculture: s 3(5).

10 S 6(1).

11 S 13(1)(a) and (c).

CONSERVATION OF INDIGENOUS PLANTS

INTRODUCTION

427 General There are a number of statutes in terms of which plants, used in the wide sense denoting flora generally, are conserved.[1] The principal legislation consists of the various provincial nature conservation ordinances, and the National Environmental Management: Biodiversity Act,[2] in terms of which, as was the case with animals, plants may be conserved by means of a listing process that has not yet been carried out. However there are some other important Acts which are relevant, particularly the protected areas legislation discussed above, the Mountain Catchment Areas Act,[3] the Conservation of Agricultural Resources Act,[4] and the National Forests Act.[5] As in the case of wild animals, it is necessary to draw a distinction between the conservation of plants within a protected area and conservation outside such an area.

1 See generally on indigenous plants Cowling and Olivier "Indigenous Plants" in Fuggle and Rabie (eds) *Environmental Management in SA* 212 and Glavovic *Flora and the Law: A Review of Existing Laws that protect Wild Plant Species in the RSA*. See also title AGRICULTURE.
2 10 of 2004.
3 63 of 1970.
4 43 of 1983.
5 84 of 1998.

CONSERVATION OF PLANTS WITHIN PROTECTED AREAS

428 General Provision is made in the various provincial nature conservation ordinances for the prohibition of a variety of actions, such as the picking of plants, that are or may be detrimental to the flora in provincial nature reserves.[1] Although various local authorities have established a number of municipal nature reserves where flora is protected, only the Cape Ordinance makes explicit provision for the establishment of such reserves,[2] and accordingly makes the abovementioned prohibitions applicable also to local reserves.[3]

Apart from the fact that the establishment of a private nature reserve may be made subject to conditions[4] that include the conservation of flora, actions detrimental to flora within a private nature reserve are prohibited on pain of criminal punishment.[5] The owner of the reserve is in most respects exempted.[6]

Flora in forest nature reserves or forest wilderness areas is protected, since actions that can detrimentally affect forest produce, which includes trees and plants,[7] are prohibited. No person may cut, disturb, damage or destroy any forest produce in, or remove or receive any forest produce from, a protected area, except in terms of the rules made for the proper management of the area; in the course of the management of the protected area by the responsible organ of state or person; in terms of a right of servitude; in terms of the authority of a licence granted or an exemption under the National Forests Act; or in the case of a protected area on land outside a State forest, with the consent of the registered owner or by reason of another right which allows the person concerned to do so.[8]

1 S 88 of the Tvl Ord 12 of 1983, ss 15 and 23 of the Natal Ord 15 of 1974, ss 35(3) and 40 of the OFS Ord 8 of 1969 and ss 14 and 85 of the Cape Ord 19 of 1974.
2 Cape Ord s 7(1).
3 S 14.
4 S 36(1) of the OFS Ord; ss 67 and 68 of the Natal Ord and s 12(3) of the Cape Ord. Failure to observe the conditions may lead to revocation of the proclamation of the reserve: s 40(1)(d) of the OFS Ord; s 72(1) of the Natal Ord and s 85(g) of the Cape Ord.
5 S 88(1) and (2) of the Tvl Ord; ss 36(3) and 40 of the OFS Ord and ss 60 and 76 of the Natal Ord.
6 S 88(1) of the Tvl Ord; s 36(3) of the OFS Ord; and s 13 of the Cape Ord.
7 National Forests Act 84 of 1998 s 1.
8 S 10(1).

CONSERVATION OF PLANTS OUTSIDE PROTECTED AREAS

429 Introduction The most important legislative provisions in terms of which indigenous plants are protected are the various nature conservation ordinances, namely the Transvaal Nature Conservation Ordinance,[1] the Free State Nature Conservation Ordinance,[2] the Natal Nature Conservation Ordinance[3] and the Cape Nature and Environmental Conservation Ordinance.[4] The provisions of these ordinances will accordingly be set out in some detail, bearing in mind the previous remarks made in respect of such provincial legislation. There is a variety of further legislation in terms of which plants (not necessarily indigenous) can be protected, namely the National Forests Act,[5] National Heritage Resources Act,[6] the Conservation of Agricultural Resources Act,[7] the Mountain Catchment Areas Act,[8] and the Sea Fishery Act.[9]

1 12 of 1983.	6 25 of 1999.
2 8 of 1969.	7 43 of 1983.
3 15 of 1974.	8 63 of 1970.
4 19 of 1974.	9 12 of 1988.
5 84 of 1998.	

PROTECTED PLANTS

430 General Except for some endangered or rare species, only indigenous plants are protected in terms of the various provincial nature conservation ordinances. An indigenous plant is legally defined as being any species of plant, shrub or tree that is indigenous to South Africa (whether cultivated or not) and includes the flower, seed, fruit, bulb, tuber, stem or root or any other part of such plant, shrub or tree; but not a plant, shrub or tree declared in terms of law to be a weed.[1]

Not all plants enjoy comprehensive protection in terms of the provincial nature conservation ordinances. A classification of plants into various categories has been made and the scope of a plant's protection depends to a large degree upon its status. The following categories are distinguished in Schedules to ordinances: unprotected, protected, and specially protected indigenous plants (Natal Ordinance); protected, and specially protected plants, as well as endangered, and rare species (Transvaal Ordinance); protected plants, endangered, and scarce species (Free State Ordinance); protected, and endangered flora (Cape Ordinance). The premier may by notice in the *Provincial Gazette* include in or delete from some Schedules the name of any indigenous plant.[2]

1 S 1(xxvi) of the Tvl Ord 12 of 1983; s 1 of the OFS Ord 8 of 1969; s 1 of the Natal Ord 15 of 1974 and s 2(xxviii) and (xxxiii)	of the Cape Ord 19 of 1974. 2 S 86(2) of the Tvl Ord and s 30(2) of the OFS Ord.

431 All indigenous plants Certain provisions of the various nature conservation ordinances apply to all indigenous plants. In the Natal Ordinance[1] all plants indigenous to the Republic of South Africa are in principle included in the Schedule specifying protected indigenous plants. Only a few plants are listed as unprotected indigenous plants,[2] while specially protected indigenous plants are listed separately[3] and further provisions apply specially to them. These provisions thus apply in principle to all indigenous plants.

All indigenous plants are protected in all provinces on or along public roads,[4] and no indigenous plant may be picked without the permission of the landowner.[5] The Cape and Natal Ordinances also regulate the donation[6] and export[7] of all indigenous plants, while the Cape Ordinance has separate provisions dealing with the possession of such plants[8] and with the sale of unprotected indigenous plants.[9] The Natal Ordinance also regulates the purchase,[10] sale[11] and exchange[12] of indigenous plants.

It should be borne in mind that since the abovementioned provisions apply to all indigenous plants, they also apply to the categories of plants listed hereunder.

1. 15 of 1974 Sch 11.
2. Sch 10.
3. Sch 12.
4. S 89 of the Tvl Ord 12 of 1983; s 32 of the OFS Ord 8 of 1969; s 63(1)(b)(ii) of the Cape Ord 19 of 1974 and s 202 of the Natal Ord.
5. S 90 of the Tvl Ord; s 31 of the OFS Ord; s 63(1)(c) of the Cape Ord. Cf s 205 of the Natal Ord.
6. S 71 of the Cape Ord and s 197 of the Natal Ord.
7. S 70 of the Cape Ord and s 198 of the Natal Ord.
8. S 72.
9. Ss 68 69.
10. S 194.
11. S 195.
12. S 197.

432 Protected indigenous plants A category of protected plants (or flora) is distinguished in all the ordinances. The position in the Natal Ordinance[1] has been set out above.[2] As far as protected plants are concerned, the other ordinances all have provisions dealing with the picking,[3] sale[4] and purchase[5] of such plants. In addition the Transvaal and the Free State Ordinances have provisions in respect of the donation,[6] conveyance,[7] exportation[8] and importation[9] of such plants.

1. 15 of 1974.
2. See 227 ante.
3. S 87 of the Tvl Ord 12 of 1983; s 30(3) of the OFS Ord 8 of 1969 and s 63(1)(b)(i) of the Cape Ord 19 of 1974.
4. S 91 of the Tvl Ord; s 33(1)(b) of the OFS Ord and ss 64, 66 and 67 of the Cape Ord.
5. S 92 of the Tvl Ord; s 34 of the OFS Ord and s 64 of the Cape Ord.
6. S 91 of the Tvl Ord and s 33(1)(b) of the OFS Ord.
7. S 93 of the Tvl Ord and s 33(2) of the OFS Ord.
8. S 91 of the Tvl Ord and s 33(1)(b) of the OFS Ord.
9. S 93 of the Tvl Ord and s 33(1)(b) of the OFS Ord.

433 Specially protected indigenous plants The Transvaal and Natal Ordinances[1] identify yet a further category of protected plants, namely specially protected plants. In both these ordinances the sale,[2] importation[3] and picking (or gathering)[4] of such plants are regulated, while the Transvaal Ordinance also regulates the possession, purchase, donation and receipt as donation, conveyance, removal and exportation[5] of such plants.

1. 12 of 1983 and 15 of 1974.
2. S 96 of the Tvl Ord and s 196(1) of the Natal Ord.
3. S 96 of the Tvl Ord and s 199 of the Natal
Ord.
4. S 96 of the Tvl Ord and s 200 of the Natal Ord.
5. S 96.

434 Endangered and scarce plants A category of endangered and scarce or rare species of plants is distinguished in the ordinances of the Transvaal, Free State and Cape.[1] In these ordinances the importation and exportation[2] of such plants are regulated, while the Free State and Cape Ordinances also deal with the sale or donation[3] of such plants. The Cape Ordinance also regulates the purchase or receipt as a donation[4] and the picking[5] of endangered flora, and also prescribes special measures to ensure the survival of such flora.[6]

1. 12 of 1983; 8 of 1969 and 19 of 1974.
2. S 98 of the Tvl Ord; s 33(1)(a) of the OFS Ord and s 62(1) of the Cape Ord.
3. S 33(1)(a) of the OFS Ord and s 62(1) of the
Cape Ord.
4. S 62(1).
5. S 63(1)(b)(i).
6. S 17.

435 Picking protected and other indigenous plants It is an offence, without a permit, to pick a protected plant.[1] "Pick" or "gather" is defined in wide terms as including to cut, chop off, take, pluck, uproot, break, damage or destroy.[2] Exemptions are provided in favour of the owner of land and of some of the owner's relatives with regard to protected plants on his or her land.[3]

It is likewise an offence to pick protected and any other indigenous plants on land of which one is not the owner, without the written permission of the landowner.[4]

The picking of any indigenous plant on a public road or within a certain area on both sides of a public road, without a permit, is also an offence.[5] Exceptions are provided in favour of the landowner and some of his or her relatives,[6] and in respect of plants unavoidably destroyed in the course of lawful road development and maintenance.[7]

1 S 87 and 96 of the Tvl Ord 12 of 1983; ss 30(3) and 40 of the OFS Ord 8 of 1969; ss 200 and 208 of the Natal Ord 15 of 1974 and ss 62(1), 63(1)(b)(i) and 85 of the Cape Ord 19 of 1974. The Cape Ord also provides that it is an offence to uproot the plant in the process of (lawfully) picking any flora (s 63(1)(a)).

2 S 1(xxix) of the Tvl Ord ("pick"); s 1 of the OFS Ord ("pick"); s 1 of Natal Ord ("gather") and s 1(xlviii) of the Cape Ord ("pick").

3 S 87(1) of the Tvl Ord; s 30(3) of the OFS

Ord; s 200(2) of the Natal Ord and s 63(3) of the Cape Ord.

4 S 90 of the Tvl Ord; ss 31(1) and 40 of the OFS Ord; ss 200(1) (3) and 208 of the Natal Ord and ss 63(1)(c) (2) and 85 of the Cape Ord.

5 S 89 of the Tvl Ord; ss 32 and 40 of the OFS Ord; ss 202(1) and 208 of the Natal Ord and ss 63(1)(b)(ii) and 85 of the Cape Ord.

6 S 89 of the Tvl Ord; s 32 of the OFS Ord and s 63(3) of the Cape Ord.

7 S 202(2) of the Natal Ord.

436 Purchase and sale of protected plants It is an offence to buy or receive consequent upon a donation a protected plant except from a person lawfully selling or donating it.[1] It is likewise an offence, without a permit, to sell or donate a protected plant.[2] "Sell" includes "hawk, peddle, barter or exchange or offer, advertise, expose or have in possession for the purpose of sale, hawking, peddling, bartering or exchanging".[3] In the Cape Ordinance there are certain precepts relating to the place of sale or purchase of protected flora,[4] and even of unprotected flora.[5]

Special provision is made in the Cape Ordinance for the registration and licensing of persons as flora growers and flora sellers, authorising them to sell protected plants on the premises to which the certificate of registration relates.[6]

1 Ss 92 and 96 of the Tvl Ord 12 of 1983; s 34 of the OFS Ord 8 of 1969 and s 194 of the Natal Ord 15 of 1974. Cf s 62(1) of the Cape Ord 19 of 1974 which requires a permit for the sale or donation of endangered flora.

2 Ss 91 and 96 of the Tvl Ord; ss 33(1) and 40 of the OFS Ord; ss 195(1), 196(1) and 208 of the Natal Ord and ss 62(1) and 85 of the Cape Ord. Certain exceptions are allowed – ss 91(1), 94 and 101(b) of the Tvl Ord; s 33(1)(i) and (ii) of the OFS Ord and

s 195(2) of the Natal Ord.

3 S 2(lxi) of the Cape Ord. Cf the definitions of "sell" in s 1(lii) of the Tvl Ord; s 1 of the OFS Ord and s 1 of the Natal Ord.

4 Ss 64 66.

5 Ss 68 69.

6 S 65. Cf also s 94 of the Tvl Ord and s 33(3) of the OFS Ord, in terms of which owners of registered nurseries may be exempted from some of the provisions of the ordinances in question.

437 Export and import of protected plants It is an offence, without a permit, to export from or import into the province concerned any protected plant.[1] Following the precepts of the Convention on International Trade in Endangered Species of Wild Fauna and Flora (Washington 1973), these provisions have been extended to include endangered and rare species of flora.[2]

1 Ss 91, 93 and 96 of the Tvl Ord 12 of 1983; ss 33(1)(b) and 40 of the OFS Ord 8 of 1969; ss 198(1), 199(1) and 208 of the Natal Ord 15 of 1974 and ss 62(1), 70 and 85 of the Cape Ord 19 of 1974. Certain exceptions are allowed: ss 91 and 93 of the Tvl

Ord; s 33(3) of the OFS Ord and ss 198(2) and 199(2) of the Natal Ord.
2 S 98 of the Tvl Ord and s 33(1)(a) of the OFS Ord. The OFS provision also covers the sale or donation of such species.

438 Conveyance of protected plants

Conveyance of protected plants, by someone who is not the holder of a permit, constitutes an offence.[1]

1 S 93 of the Tvl Ord 12 of 1983 and ss 33(2) and 40 of the OFS Ord 8 of 1969. Exceptions

are allowed: s 93(1) of the Tvl Ord and s 33(2)(a)–(d) of the OFS Ord.

439 Possession of protected plants

The possession of protected plants, in certain circumstances, constitutes an offence.[1]

1 Ss 95 and 96 of the Tvl Ord 12 of 1983; ss 203 and 208 of the Natal Ord 15 of 1974 and ss 62(1), 72 and 85 of the Cape Ord 19

of 1974. Certain exceptions are allowed: s 203 of the Natal Ord and s 62(2) of the Cape Ord.

440 Protection of trees in terms of the National Forests Act

The National Forests Act[1] provides for protection of trees in various ways. No person may cut, disturb, damage or destroy any indigenous, living tree[2] in, or remove or receive any such tree from, a natural forest[3] except in terms of a licence issued under the Act or an exemption.[4] The minister may issue a licence to cut, damage or destroy any indigenous, living tree in, or remove or receive any such tree from, a natural forest.[5]

The minister may declare a particular tree, a particular group of trees, a particular woodland,[6] or trees belonging to a particular species, to be a protected tree, group of trees, woodland or species.[7] No person may cut, disturb, damage, destroy or remove any protected tree, or collect, remove, transport, export, purchase, sell, donate or in any other manner acquire or dispose of any protected tree, except under a licence granted by the minister.[8] A list of protected tress has been published.[9]

1 84 of 1998. See title FORESTRY.
2 "Tree" is defined as including any tree seedling, sapling, transplant or coppice shoot of any age and any root, branch or other part of it (s 1).
3 A "natural forest" is a group of indigenous trees whose crowns are largely contiguous; or which have been declared by the minister to be a natural forest under s 7(2) (s 1). In terms of s 7(2), the minister may declare to be a natural forest a group of indigenous trees whose crowns are not largely contiguous; or where there is doubt as to whether or not their crowns are largely contiguous if he or she is of the opinion, based on scientific advice, that the trees make up a forest which needs to be protected in terms of the Act.
4 S 7(1). The licence is provided in terms of ss 7(4) or 23.

5 S 7(4).
6 A "woodland" is a group of indigenous trees which are not a natural forest, but whose crowns cover more than five per cent of the area bounded by the trees forming the perimeter of the group (s 1).
7 S 12(1). The minister may make such a declaration only if he or she is of the opinion that the tree, group of trees, woodland or species is not already adequately protected in terms of other legislation. The procedure for making such a declaration is set out in s 13, which must be followed for revocation of such order as well (s 15(2)). In terms of s 14, a temporary protection order may be made in an emergency.
8 S 15(1).
9 *Government Gazette* 26731 GN 1012, 27 August 2004.

441 Natural vegetation in mountain catchment areas

The competent provincial authority may by notice in the *Government Gazette* or by written notice to the owner or occupier of land which is situated within a mountain catchment area, declare a direction to be applicable with reference to such land, relating to the protection and treatment of the natural vegetation.[1]

1 S 3(1)(a)(i)(bb) of the Mountain Catchment Areas Act 63 of 1970, read with *Government Gazette* 16346 GN R28, 7 April 1995 which regulates the assignment of the Act to the provinces. Failure to comply with the directions constitutes an offence: s 14(b).

442 Plants as national heritage resources The National Monuments Act[1] provided for any property of aesthetic, historical or scientific interest to be established as a national monument.[2] Certain oak and baobab trees and modjadji palms were declared national monuments. Certain areas containing vegetation, such as Table Mountain and Paarl mountain, certain urban parks, and a nature reserve (at the University of the Western Cape), were also declared national monuments. The National Monuments Act was repealed by the National Heritage Resources Act,[3] which provides that sites and objects which prior to the commencement of the new Act were protected by notices in the *Gazette* in terms of the previous Act, will, subject to the provisions of any provincial legislation for heritage resources conservation and any agreement in that regard, and without the need for the publication of notices in the *Gazette*, continue to be protected in terms of the new Act.[4]

1 28 of 1969. See title HISTORICAL MONU-
  MENTS.
2 S 10.
3 25 of 1999.
4 S 58(11).

443 Vegetation and soil conservation One of the objects of the Conservation of Agricultural Resources Act[1] is to make provision for the conservation of vegetation.[2] Since conservation of the soil and of vegetation and water supplies constitutes an integrated whole, the provisions of this Act, relevant to soil conservation, are also applicable to the conservation of vegetation.

1 43 of 1983.
2 S 3.

444 Aquatic plants The Marine Living Resources Act[1] does not explicitly provide for the conservation of aquatic plants, but the definition of "fish" in the Act[2] includes aquatic plants, which are defined as any kind of plant, algae or other plant organism found in the sea or in or on the seashore.[3]

The Sea Fishery Act[4] provides for control over aquatic plants which constitute any kind of plant, alga or other plant organism found in the sea or in or on the seashore.[5] Subject to any regulation which the Minister of Environmental Affairs and Tourism may make,[6] no person may collect and remove or cause to be collected and removed any aquatic plants from the sea or the seashore, except for his or her own use and in prescribed quantities, without being the holder of a permit issued by the minister and otherwise than in accordance with the conditions contained in the permit.[7] Contravention of this provision constitutes an offence.[8]

It is also an offence in terms of the Sea Fishery Act to pollute the sea with anything which is or may be injurious to aquatic plants or fish food (which may include plant material), or which may disturb or change the ecological balance in any area of the sea, or which may detrimentally affect the marketability of aquatic plants.[9] It is likewise an offence in terms of provincial nature conservation ordinances to pollute waters with anything which is or may be injurious to fish food.[10]

1 18 of 1998. See title FISHERIES AND FISHING.
2 S 1: "fish" means the marine living resources of the sea and the seashore, including any aquatic plant or animal.

3 S 1.
4 12 of 1988. This Act was largely repealed by
   s 84(1) of the Marine Living Resources Act
   18 of 1998, but among the sections not replaced are those relating to shells and aquatic
   plants.
5 Sea Fishery Act 12 of 1998 s 1.

6 In terms of s 45.
7 S 38(1).
8 S 47(1)(g).
9 S 47(1)(k).
10 S 84 of the Tvl Ord 12 of 1983; s 48 the
    Cape Ord 19 of 1974 and ss 152 and 183 of
    the Natal Ord 15 of 1974.

CONTROL OF NOXIOUS PLANTS

445 Weeds With the exception of the Jointed Cactus Eradication Act,[1] all legislation before the Weeds Act[2] dealing with noxious weeds was passed at provincial
level.[3] During 1935 the second Schedule to the then Financial Relations Act[4] was
amended by the deletion of noxious weeds from provincial legislative competence.[5]
The Jointed Cactus Eradication Act[6] was repealed by the Weeds Amendment Act[7] and
jointed cactus was dealt with under the Weeds Act.[8] The Weeds Act was replaced by
the Conservation of Agricultural Resources Act.[9] At the time of writing, the National
Environmental Management: Biodiversity Act[10] provides for alien and invader species,
but the lists of such species have yet to be declared. If the publication of such lists
creates conflict between the National Environmental Management: Biodiversity Act
and the Conservation of Agricultural Resources Act, the former will prevail.[11]

Weeds and invader plants, which include their seeds and vegetative parts which
reproduce themselves asexually, are thus controlled by virtue of the Conservation of
Agricultural Resources Act. A plant is subject to control once the Minister of Agriculture has declared it to be a weed or an invader plant,[12] either throughout South Africa
or in one or more areas of the country.[13] Principal control is effected through control
measures which the minister is authorised to prescribe in relation to the control of
weeds and invader plants.[14] Such measures must be complied with by the land users to
whom they apply, and failure to do so constitutes an offence.[15] A further offence is
committed if a land user should fail or refuse to comply with a direction by means of
which he or she was ordered to comply with a particular control measure.[16] The
minister may establish a scheme in terms of which subsidies may be paid to land users
in respect of the combating of weeds and invader plants.[17] Moreover, the minister may
perform or cause to be performed any act related to the control of weeds and invader
plants[18] and may recover the relevant costs from the landowner concerned.[19]

It is an offence for anyone:

(a) to sell, agree to sell or offer, advertise, keep, exhibit, transmit, send, convey or
deliver for sale, or exchange for anything or dispose of to any person in any manner
for a consideration, any weed; or

(b) in any other manner whatsoever to disperse or cause or permit the dispersal of
any weed from any place in South Africa to any other place in the country.[20]

If seed, grain, hay or any other agricultural product contains any weed, the executive officer may issue an order that the seed, grain, hay or other agricultural product
concerned:

(a) be returned to the place of origin thereof;

(b) be forwarded to a specified place in order to have the weed concerned removed therefrom; or

(c) be destroyed in such manner as he or she may determine.[21]

Finally, if any weed adheres to an animal which is driven on a public road, conveyed in a vehicle or offered for sale at a livestock auction, the executive officer may
issue an order that the weed concerned be removed from that animal.[22]

In addition to the Conservation of Agricultural Resources Act, the Transvaal and Free State Nature Conservation Ordinances make provision for the eradication of plants which may be harmful to indigenous plants.[23] These ordinances, as well as the Cape Nature and Environmental Conservation Ordinance, empower the respective authorities to take such measures as may be necessary or desirable for the protection of plants.[24] Although rather vague, these provisions could be invoked in the battle against noxious plants.

1 52 of 1934. See also title AGRICULTURE.
2 42 of 1937.
3 Cf the Schedule to the Weeds Act.
4 10 of 1913.
5 Cf s 4(a) of Provincial Subsidies and Taxation Powers Further Amendment Act 50 of 1935.
6 52 of 1934.
7 32 of 1964.
8 42 of 1937.
9 43 of 1983.
10 10 of 2004.
11 S 8.
12 Cf the definitions of "invader plant" and "weed" in s 1 of the Conservation of Agricultural Resources Act 43 of 1983 and *Government Gazette* 9238 GN R1048, 25 May 1984 Part II.
13 S 2(3).
14 S 6(2)(l).
15 S 6(5).
16 S 7(1) (6).
17 S 8(1)(a)(vi).
18 S 11(1) (4)(a).
19 S 11(2)(a).
20 S 5(1) (6).
21 S 5(2)(a).
22 S 5(3)(a).
23 S 101(g)(iii) and (h)(iii) of the Tvl Ord 12 of 1983 and s 38(1)(o) of the OFS Ord 8 of 1969.
24 S 101(g)(ii) of the Tvl Ord and ss 38(1)(h) and 16(1)(c)(iii) of the Cape Ord 19 of 1974.

446 Intruding vegetation The respective provincial nature conservation bodies are also involved to some extent in the eradication of noxious plants. The Mountain Catchment Areas Act[1] empowers the competent provincial authorities to require vegetation which is, in their opinion, intruding vegetation to be destroyed.[2] Failure to comply with such a direction is an offence.[3] The direction may be applicable to a declared mountain catchment area or to any area within 5km of a mountain catchment.

1 63 of 1970.
2 S 3(1).
3 S 14(b).

447 Agricultural pests The Agricultural Pests Act[1] provides for control over plants and plant diseases with a view to protecting plants that are agriculturally important. As such this Act is not of great significance to nature conservation, particularly in respect of indigenous plants, although it may indirectly or incidentally benefit such plants. Control is exercised over the importation of plants in that it is an offence to import any plant, pathogen or growth medium into South Africa except on the authority of a permit.[2] Extensive powers are conferred upon the Minister of Agriculture[3] and the executive officer[4] to prevent the spreading of agricultural pests.

1 36 of 1983. See also title AGRICULTURE.
2 S 3(1).
3 Ss 6 8.
4 Ss 4 7.

448 Noxious aquatic growths The Cape Nature and Environmental Conservation Ordinance[1] provides that no person may cultivate, possess, transport, sell,[2] donate, buy[3] or otherwise acquire or import into the province any noxious aquatic growth.[4] There is a separate provision[5] which prohibits the release of such growths into inland waters.[6] The ordinance also provides that if the head of the Department of Environmental and Cultural Affairs is of the opinion that any aquatic growth[7] found in any inland waters is injurious to any fish, aquatic growth, or the water in such inland waters, he or she may order the owner of such inland waters to take such measures as he or she may determine to destroy such growth, and may render assistance to such owner if requested to do so.[8] If the owner refuses, or within a period of 12 months fails to comply with the order, the director may cause the growth concerned to be destroyed and recover the costs from such owner.[9]

The Transvaal Nature Conservation Ordinance[10] provides that it is an offence for any person without a permit to possess, sell,[11] purchase, donate, receive as a donation, import, convey, cultivate or place in any waters[12] certain species of aquatic growth.[13] The Free State Nature Conservation Ordinance[14] contains a similar provision, although the placing of such aquatic growths[15] in waters is not covered by the prohibition.[16] Moreover, the premier may in respect of the Transvaal Nature Conservation Ordinance[17] take any measure which he or she deems necessary or expedient for the control of weeds, invader plants or aquatic growths.[18]

1   19 of 1974.
2   "Sell" includes hawk, peddle, barter or exchange or offer, advertise, expose or have in possession for the purpose of sale, hawking, peddling, bartering or exchanging: s 2(lxi).
3   "Buy" includes barter or exchange: s 2(xi).
4   S 60. Three species of such noxious aquatic growths are listed in Sch 5.
5   S 50.
6   "Inland waters" means all waters which do not permanently or at any time during the year form part of the sea and includes any tidal river other than a tidal river in respect of which a notice issued under the Sea Fishery Act 12 of 1988 is in force: s 2(xxxv).
7   "Aquatic growth" means any vegetation which grows or is able to grow in inland waters: s 2(v).
8   S 19(1).
9   S 19(2).
10   12 of 1983.
11   "Sell" means sell, barter, offer or expose for sale, display for sale or give or offer as a valuable consideration: s 1(lii).
12   "Waters" means the waters in rivers, streams, creeks, lakes, pans, vleis, dams, reservoirs, furrows, canals and ponds: s 1(lx).
13   S 85(1).
14   8 of 1969.
15   Ie those listed in Sch 5 to the Ordinance.
16   S 29(1) read with s 40(1)(d).
17   12 of 1983.
18   S 101(g)(iii).

CONTROL OF MINING

INTRODUCTION

449 Mineral policy and mining legislation Thus far the discussion has concerned the conservation of renewable natural resources. Minerals are regarded for practical purposes as constituting a non-renewable natural resource. Mining and minerals are treated exhaustively in another title.[1] In this section attention is given only to certain aspects of mining legislation which affect the terrestrial environment.

Mining is regulated by the Mineral and Petroleum Resources Development Act,[2] which repeals, inter alia, the Minerals Act,[3] which itself consolidated virtually all previous mining legislation. The preamble of the new Act affirms that the state's obligation is to protect the environment for the benefit of present and future generations, to ensure ecologically sustainable development of mineral and petroleum resources and to promote economic and social development. In addition to environmentally relevant provisions in mining legislation, relevant environmental provisions are also encountered in other statutes, most notably in legislation concerning water and air pollution, solid waste management, soil conservation and environmental impact assessment.

1 See title MINING AND MINERALS; and see
generally Wells, Van Meurs and Rabie
"Terrestrial Minerals"; Gurney, McLachlan,
Kirkley and Glazewski "Offshore Minerals"
in Fuggle and Rabie (eds) *Environmental*

Management in SA 337 380; Rabie 1991
THRHR 774.
2 28 of 2002.
3 50 of 1991.

ENVIRONMENTAL REGULATION IN THE MINERAL AND PETROLEUM RESOURCES ACT

450 Granting of rights Chapter 4 of the Mineral and Petroleum Resources Development Act[1] covers the process for the application and granting of reconnaissance, prospecting and mining rights. One of the prerequisites for the granting of a prospecting right by the Minister of Mineral and Energy Affairs is that the prospecting will not result in unacceptable pollution, ecological degradation or damage to the environment.[2] An applicant for a prospecting right must submit an environmental management plan.[3] The same prerequisite applies in respect of the granting of a mining right,[4] application for which must be accompanied by an environmental impact assessment and environmental management programme.[5]

An applicant for a mining permit is also required to submit an environmental management plan.[6]

1 28 of 2002.
2 S 17(1)(c).
3 S 16(4)(a). An "environmental management
plan" is a plan to manage and rehabilitate the
environmental impact as a result of prospecting, reconnaissance, exploration or mining
operations conducted under the authority of

a reconnaissance permission, prospecting
right, reconnaissance permit, exploration
right or mining permit, as the case may be
(s 1).
4 S 23(1)(d).
5 S 22(4)(a).
6 S 27(5).

451 Environmental management principles and integrated environmental management The national environmental management principles in the National Environmental Management Act[1] apply to all prospecting and mining operations and any matter relating to such operations, and serve as guidelines for the interpretation, administration and implementation of the environmental requirements of the Mineral and Petroleum Resources Act.[2] Any prospecting or mining operation must be conducted in accordance with generally accepted principles of sustainable development by integrating social, economic and environmental factors into the planning and implementation of prospecting and mining projects in order to ensure that exploitation of mineral resources serves present and future generations.[3]

The holder of a reconnaissance permission, prospecting right, mining right, mining permit or retention permit:

(a) must at all times give effect to the general objectives of integrated environmental management laid down in the National Environmental Management Act;[4]

(b) must consider, investigate, assess and communicate the impact of his or her prospecting or mining on the environment;

(c) must manage all environmental impacts in accordance with his or her environmental management plan or approved environmental management programme, where appropriate and as an integral part of the reconnaissance, prospecting or mining operation, unless the minister directs otherwise (and failure to do so is an offence);[5]

(d) must as far as it is reasonably practicable, rehabilitate the environment affected by the prospecting or mining operations to its natural or predetermined state or to a land use which conforms to the generally accepted principle of sustainable development; and

(e) is responsible for any environmental damage, pollution or ecological degradation as a result of his or her reconnaissance prospecting or mining operations and which may occur inside and outside the boundaries of the area to which such right, permit or permission relates.[6]

The directors of a company or members of a close corporation are jointly and severally liable for any unacceptable negative impact on the environment, including damage, degradation or pollution advertently or inadvertently caused by the company or close corporation which they represent or represented.[7]

1   107 of 1998 s 2.
2   S 28 of 2002 s 37(1).
3   S 37(2).
4   107 of 1998 ch 5.

5   Mineral and Petroleum Resources Development Act 28 of 2002 s 98(a)(iii).
6   S 38(1).
7   S 38(2).

452 Environmental management programme and environmental management plan Every person who has applied for a mining right must conduct an environmental impact assessment and submit an environmental management programme within 180 days of the date on which he or she is notified by the Regional Manager to do so.[1] Any person who applies for a reconnaissance permission, prospecting right or mining permit must submit an environmental management plan as prescribed.[2] An applicant who prepares an environmental management programme or an environmental management plan must:

(a) establish baseline information concerning the affected environment to determine protection, remedial measures and environmental management objectives;

(b) investigate, assess and evaluate the impact of his or her proposed prospecting or mining operations on the environment, the socio-economic conditions of any person who might be directly affected by the prospecting or mining operation, and any national estate referred to in the National Heritage Resources Act;[3]

(c) develop an environmental awareness plan describing the manner in which the applicant intends to inform his or her employees of any environmental risks which may result from their work and the manner in which the risks must be dealt with in order to avoid pollution or the degradation of the environment; and

(d) describe the manner in which he or she intends to modify, remedy, control or stop any action, activity or process which causes pollution or environmental degradation; contain or remedy the cause of pollution or degradation and migration of pollutants; and comply with any prescribed waste standard or management standards or practices.[4]

The minister must, within 120 days from the lodgment of the environmental management programme or the environmental management plan, approve the same, if it complies with the above requirements, the applicant has made the necessary financial provision for remediation of environmental damage, and the applicant has the capacity, or has provided for the capacity, to rehabilitate and manage negative impacts on the environment.[5] The minister may not approve the environmental management programme or the environmental management plan unless he or she has considered any recommendation by the Regional Mining Development and Environmental Committee, and the comments of any state department charged with the administration of any law which relates to matters affecting the environment.[6] The minister may call for additional information from the applicant and may direct that the environmental management programme or environmental management plan in question be adjusted in such way as the minister may require.[7] When considering an environmental management plan or environmental management programme, the minister must consult with any state department which administers any law relating to matters affecting the environment.[8]

No person may prospect for or remove, mine, conduct technical co-operation operations, reconnaissance operations, explore for and produce any mineral or petroleum or commence with any work incidental thereto on any area without an approved environmental management programme or approved environmental management plan, as the case may be.[9] On the date upon which the environmental management programme is approved, the prospecting[10] and mining[11] rights become effective. The holder of a prospecting right must comply with the requirements of the approved environmental management programme,[12] as must the holder of a mining right.[13]

Residue stockpiles and residue deposits must be managed in the prescribed manner on any site demarcated for that purpose in the environmental management plan or environmental management programme in question.[14] No person may temporarily or permanently deposit any residue stockpile or residue deposit on any site other than on such a site.[15] It is an offence not to comply with these residue management requirements.[16]

1 Mineral and Petroleum Resources Development Act 28 of 2002 s 39(1).
2 S 39(2).
3 25 of 1999 s 3(2) but excluding ss (3)(2)(i)(vi) and (vii).
4 Mineral and Petroleum Resources Development Act 28 of 2002 s 39(3). Applications for reconnaissance permissions, prospecting rights or mining permits do not require consideration of socio-economic conditions or development of an environmental awareness plan (s 39(7)).
5 S 39(4)(a).
6 S 39(4)(b).
7 S 39(5). An environmental management programme or plan may be amended after consultation with the holder of the right or permit in question (s 39(6)).
8 S 40. The minister must request the head of a department being consulted, in writing, to submit the comments of that department within 60 days from the date of the request.

9 S 5(4).
10 S 17(5).
11 S 23(5).
12 S 19(2)(e).
13 S 25(2)(e).
14 S 42(1). "Residue deposit" means any residue stockpile remaining at the termination, cancellation or expiry of a prospecting right, mining right, mining permit, exploration right or production right; and "residue stockpile" means any debris, discard, tailings, slimes, screening, slurry, waste rock, foundry sand, beneficiation plant waste, ash or any other product derived from or incidental to a mining operation and which is stockpiled, stored or accumulated for potential re-use, or which is disposed of, by the holder of a mining right, mining permit or production right (s 1).
15 S 42(2).
16 S 98(a)(iv).

453 Financial provision for remediation of environmental damage An applicant for a prospecting right, mining right or mining permit must, before the minister approves the environmental management plan or environmental management programme, make the prescribed financial provision for the rehabilitation or management of negative environmental impacts.[1] If the holder of a prospecting right, mining right or mining permit fails to rehabilitate or manage, or is unable to undertake such rehabilitation or to manage any negative impact on the environment, the minister may, upon written notice to the holder, use all or part of the financial provision to rehabilitate or manage the negative environmental impact in question.[2] The holder of a prospecting right, mining right or mining permit must annually assess his or her environmental liability and increase his or her financial provision to the satisfaction of the minister,[3] who, if he or she is not satisfied with the assessment and financial provision contemplated in this section, may appoint an independent assessor to conduct the assessment and determine the financial provision.[4] The requirement to maintain and retain the financial provision remains in force until the minister issues a closure certificate to the holder, but the minister may retain such portion of the financial provision as may be required to rehabilitate the closed mining or prospecting operation in respect of latent or residual environmental impacts.[5]

1 Mineral and Petroleum Resources Development Act 28 of 2002 s 41(1).	3 S 41(3).
	4 S 41(4).
2 S 41(2).	5 S 41(5).

454 Termination of mining operations Even where mining operations have been discontinued, environmental problems associated with mining frequently continue. Water emanating from an abandoned mine may, by reason of its acidity, continue to cause the pollution of both surface and groundwater. Dust from abandoned mine dumps, soil erosion, especially in the case of abandoned opencast mines, and the dumping or impounding of solid or liquid waste, constitute further environmental problems which continue after mining operations have ceased. Furthermore, abandoned shafts, pits and other excavations, as well as subsidences or cavities, hold considerable danger to public safety. In order to combat these problems effectively – especially in the long term – provision should be made for the rehabilitation of the affected surfaces, once mining operations finally cease.

The holder of a prospecting right, mining right, retention permit or mining permit remains responsible for any environmental liability, pollution or ecological degradation, and the management thereof, until the minister has issued a closure certificate to the holder concerned.[1] On written application by such holder in the prescribed manner, the minister may transfer such environmental liabilities and responsibilities as may be identified in the environmental management plan or the environmental management programme and any prescribed closure plan to a person with such qualifications as may be prescribed.[2] The right or permit holder or the latter mentioned person, as the case may be, must apply for a closure certificate upon:

(a)   the lapsing, abandonment or cancellation of the right or permit in question;

(b)   cessation of the prospecting or mining operation;

(c)   the relinquishment of any portion of the prospecting of the land to which a right, permit or permission relates; or

(d)   completion of the prescribed closing plan to which a right, permit or permission relates.[3]

An application for a closure certificate must be made to the Regional Manager in whose region the land in question is situated within 180 days of the occurrence of the lapsing, abandonment, cancellation, cessation, relinquishment or completion, and must be accompanied by the prescribed environmental risk report.[4] No closure certificate may be issued unless the Chief Inspector and the Department of Water Affairs and Forestry have confirmed in writing that the provisions pertaining to health and safety and management of potential pollution to water resources have been addressed.[5] When the minister issues a certificate he or she must return such portion of the financial provision as the minister may deem appropriate to the holder of the prospecting right, mining right, retention permit or mining permit in question, but may retain any portion of such financial provision for latent and/ or residual environmental impact which may become known in the future.[6]

When a prospecting right, mining right, retention permit or mining permit lapses, is cancelled or is abandoned, or when any prospecting or mining operation comes to an end, the holder of any such right or permit may not demolish or remove any building, structure or object:

(a) which may not be demolished or removed in terms of any other law;

(b) which has been identified in writing by the minister for purposes of this section; or

(c) which is to be retained in terms of an agreement between the holder and the owner or occupier of the land, which agreement has been approved by the minister in writing.[7]

This does not apply to *bona fide* mining equipment, which may be removed.[8] Demolition or removal contrary to these requirements is an offence.[9]

1 Mineral and Petroleum Resources Development Act 28 of 2002 s 43(1).	5 S 43(5).
	6 S 43(6).
2 S 43(2).	7 S 44(1).
3 S 43(3).	8 S 44(2).
4 S 43(4).	9 S 98(a)(v).

455 Remediation of environmental damage If any prospecting, mining, reconnaissance or production operations cause or result in ecological degradation, pollution or environmental damage which may be harmful to the health or well-being of anyone and requires urgent remedial measures, the minister may direct the holder of the relevant right, permit or permission to investigate, evaluate, assess and report on the impact of any pollution or ecological degradation; take such measures as may be specified in such directive; and complete such measures before a date specified in the directive.[1] If the holder fails to comply with the directive, the minister may take such measures as may be necessary to protect the health and well-being of any affected person or to remedy ecological degradation and to stop pollution of the environment.[2] Before the minister implements any measure, he or she must afford the holder an opportunity to make representations to him or her.[3] In order to implement such measures, the minister may by way of an *ex parte* application apply to the High Court for an order to seize and sell such property of the holder as may be necessary to cover the expenses of implementing such measures.[4] In addition to such application, the minister may use funds appropriated for that purpose by Parliament to fully implement such measures.[5] The minister may recover an amount equal to the funds necessary to fully implement the measures from the holder concerned.[6]

If the minister directs that such remedial measures must be taken to prevent pollution or ecological degradation of the environment or to rehabilitate dangerous occurrences, but establishes that the holder of the relevant right or permit, or his or her successor-in-title, is deceased or cannot be traced or, in the case of a juristic person, has ceased to exist, has been liquidated or cannot be traced, the minister may instruct the Regional Manager concerned to take the necessary measures to prevent further pollution or degradation, or to make the area safe.[7] This must be funded from the financial provision made by the holder, where appropriate, or if there is no such provision or if it is inadequate, from money appropriated by Parliament for that purpose.[8] Upon completion of such measures, the Regional Manager must apply to the registrar concerned that the title deed of the land in question be endorsed to the effect that such land has been remedied.[9]

1 Mineral and Petroleum Resources Development Act 28 of 2002 s 45(1).	3 S 45(2)(b).
	4 S 45(2)(c).
2 S 45(2)(a).	5 S 45(2)(d).

6 S 45(2)(e).

7 S 46(1).

8 S 46(2).

9 S 46(3)(a). The registrar concerned must, on receipt of such application, make such

endorsements as he or she may deem necessary so as to give effect to provisions of that paragraph, and no office fee or other charge is payable to the registrar in respect of such endorsement (s 46(3)(b)).

456 Environmental conservation regulations Various regulations regulating the environmental impact of mining were made under the Mines and Works Act,[1] which was repealed by the Minerals Act.[2] In terms of the Minerals Act, these regulations remained in force despite the repeal of the Act in terms of which they were originally made. When the Minerals Act was repealed and replaced by the Mineral and Petroleum Resources Development Act,[3] there was no explicit savings clause for these regulations. However, the Act does provide that any old order mining right in force immediately before the Act took effect continues in force for a period not exceeding five years from the date on which the Act took effect subject to the terms and conditions under which it was granted or issued or was deemed to have been granted or issued.[4] This can be interpreted to mean that the regulations in question do continue to apply to old order mining rights.[5] These regulations would not, however, apply to new mining operations.

Alternatively, in terms of the Mine Health and Safety Act,[6] any health or safety standard which, immediately prior to the commencement of the Act, was incorporated under the provisions of the Minerals Act or the regulations made under that Act is deemed to be a health and safety standard. This requires distinguishing between those provisions which would qualify as health and safety standards, which several environmental provisions would, and those which would not.

The status of these regulations, therefore, is somewhat vague. For the sake of completeness, however, those regulations relevant to environmental conservation are listed below. They deal with:

(a)   prohibition of damage or removal of mine rehabilitation measures;[7]

(b)   rehabilitation concerning the replacement and re-establishment of removed topsoil and vegetation;[8]

(c)   permitting sand to be extracted from the channel of a stream or river as well as from a dam, pan or lake, but only on condition that adequate precautions are taken to ensure that the stability of the banks[9] is not affected by such operations[10] and to prevent the scouring and erosion of the banks which may result from such operations or work incidental thereto;[11]

(d)   unless exemption in writing is obtained from the regional director, all topsoil[12] removed at any opencast mine[13] for the purpose of exposing, working or searching for a mineral deposit, must be deposited at a specially selected site for replacement as topsoil during rehabilitation of the disturbed surface;[14]

(e)   the re-establishment of vegetation;[15]

(f)   water which contains poisonous or injurious matter in suspension or solution must be fenced off and may not be permitted to escape without previously having been rendered innocuous;[16]

(g)   control over waste disposal;[17]

(h)   control over effluent from sewerage systems;[18]

(i)   effluent produced from sand extraction operations may not be returned to any stream, river, dam, pan or lake unless such effluent conforms to the purity standards laid down by the Department of Water Affairs and Forestry;[19]

(j)   no sand dump or slimes dam may be established on the bank of any stream, river, dam, pan or lake without the written permission of the regional director and upon such conditions as he or she may prescribe;[20]

(k)   during the prospecting for or recovery of oil, all reasonable measures must be taken, to the satisfaction of the regional director, to prevent the escape of oil into the surroundings, either on land or in the sea;[21]

(l)   every mine dump must be covered with sludge or soil or otherwise dealt with satisfactorily so as to prevent the dissemination of dust or sand therefrom;[22]

(m)   no dumping or impounding of rubble, litter, garbage, rubbish or discards of any description, whether solid or liquid, may take place elsewhere than at demarcated sites. Every such site must be limited to a minimum and every dump or dam must be so controlled to ensure that the environment is, as far as it is practicable, not polluted;[23]

(n)   wherever practicable, waste material from reduction works, beneficiation plants, coal preparation plants, screening and washing installations and generating stations at a mine must be disposed of in the workings of such mine.[24]

1   27 of 1956.
2   50 of 1991.
3   28 of 2002.
4   Schedule II s 7.
5   Defined as any mining lease, consent to mine, permission to mine, claim licence, mining authorisation or right listed in Table 2 to Sch II in force immediately before the date on which the Act took effect and in respect of which mining operations are being conducted (Sch II s 1).
6   29 of 1996.
7   *Government Gazette* 2741 GN R992, 26 June 1970 reg 3.14(c), issued by virtue of the Minerals Act 50 of 1991 (*Government Gazette* 16214 GN R31, 13 January 1995).
8   Regs 5.12.3 and 5.13.2, applicable by virtue of the Minerals Act (s 68(2)). "Topsoil", according to the Minerals Act s 1, means that layer of soil covering the earth and which provides a suitable environment for the germination of seed, allows the penetration of water, is a source of micro-organisms, plant nutrients and in some cases seed, and of a depth of 0,5 metre or any other depth as may be determined by the regional director for each mining area.
9   "Bank" is defined as follows: (a) in the case of a stream or river, the ground bordering upon and within the high flood zone of the stream or river, or 100 metres from either side of the channel (defined in reg 5.11(d)), whichever area is the wider; and (b) in the case of a dam, pan or lake, the ground bordering upon the high-water mark of the dam, pan or lake and all ground within 100 metres of such high-water mark in an outward direction : reg 5.11(a).
10   Reg 5.14.1(a).
11   Reg 5.14.1(b).
12   "Topsoil" is defined as all cultivable soil material that can be removed mechanically to a depth of one metre without blasting: reg 5.11(e). The Minerals Act 50 of 1991 s 1 defines "topsoil" as that layer of soil covering the earth and which provides a suitable environment for the germination of seed, allows the penetration of water, is a source of micro-organisms, plant nutrients and in some cases seed, and of a depth of 0,5 metre or any other depth as may be determined by the regional director for each mining area.
13   An "opencast mine" is a mine, including prospecting operations and any hole, trench or other excavation made in the course of prospecting operations, where a mineral deposit is or has been worked at or from the surface of the earth after removal of the overburden: reg 5.11(c).
14   Reg 5.12.3. Where rehabilitation of the surface is carried out concurrently with prospecting, mining or operations incidental thereto, the topsoil may be replaced directly: reg 5.12.3.
15   Reg 5.13.2.
16   Regs 5.9.1 and 5.9.2. Cf *Lascon Properties (Pty) Ltd v Wadeville Investment Co (Pty) Ltd* [1997] 3 All SA 433 (W); 1997 4 SA 578 (W).
17   Regs 5.13.1 and 5.13.4.
18   Reg 4.12.
19   Reg 5.14.1(c)
20   Reg 5.14.3.
21   Reg 5.15.
22   Reg 5.10.
23   Reg 5.13.1.
24   Reg 5.13.4.

WATER POLLUTION CONTROL

457 Introduction While the earliest legislative concerns with water pollution were directed mainly at biological pollution, the development of industry after the Second World War has focused concern on chemical water pollution. This is also demonstrated by the introduction in 1956 of the Water Act,[1] which was not primarily concerned – as its predecessor, the Irrigation and Conservation of Waters Act[2] had been – with water for agricultural use. The Water Act[3] was the first South African legislation under which industrial water pollution was extensively controlled at national level. In its replacement, the National Water Act,[4] industrial water pollution is not expressly addressed and the pollution regime under the new Act is consequently less complex than under the previous Act. In addition to the National Water Act there is a wide variety of other Acts, ordinances, regulations and by-laws related to the control of both fresh water and marine pollution. The relevant legislation can be conveniently grouped together in three categories: legislation affecting primarily the source of pollution or dealing with activities that produce pollution; legislation dealing primarily with the effect of pollution; and legislation relating primarily to a particular geographical area.

1 54 of 1956. On water pollution control generally, see Lusher and Ramsden "Water Pollution" in Fuggle and Rabie (eds) *Environmental Management in SA* 456; Rabie and Lusher 1986 *Acta Juridica* 161 and Wiseman and Glazewski *SA Law pertaining to the*

Causes and Effects of Pollution affecting Water Resources CPE 1.5/91 1991. See also title WATER.
2 8 of 1912.
3 54 of 1956.
4 36 of 1998.

458 General prohibition of water pollution It is an offence for any person to unlawfully and intentionally or negligently commit any act or omission which pollutes[1] or is likely to pollute a water resource;[2] or unlawfully and intentionally or negligently commit any act or omission which detrimentally affects or is likely to affect a water resource.[3]

1 In the National Water Act 36 of 1998, "pollution" means the direct or indirect alteration of the physical, chemical or biological properties of a water resource so as to make it less fit for any beneficial purpose for which it may reasonably be expected to be used; or harmful or potentially harmful to the welfare, health or safety of human beings; to any aquatic or non-aquatic organisms; to the resource quality; or to property (s 1). "Water resource" includes a watercourse (a river or spring; a natural channel in which water flows regularly or intermittently; a

wetland, lake or dam into which, or from which, water flows and any collection of water which the minister may declare to be a watercourse, and a reference to a watercourse includes, where relevant, its bed and banks); surface water, estuary or aquifer (s 1).
2 S 151(1)(i).
3 S 151(1)(j). The sentence for either of these offences is, for a first conviction, a fine or five years' imprisonment or both and, for a second or subsequent conviction, a fine or ten years' imprisonment or both (s 151(2)).

459 Prevention and remedying effects of pollution An owner of land, a person in control of land or a person who occupies or uses the land on which any activity or process is or was performed or undertaken, or any other situation exists, which causes, has caused or is likely to cause pollution of a water resource, must take all reasonable measures to prevent any such pollution from occurring, continuing or recurring.[1] Such measures may include measures to:

(a)   cease, modify or control any act or process causing the pollution;

(b)   comply with any prescribed waste standard or management practice;

(c)   contain or prevent the movement of pollutants;

(d)   eliminate any source of the pollution;

(e)   remedy the effects of the pollution; and

(f)   remedy the effects of any disturbance to the bed and banks of a watercourse.[2]

A catchment management agency may direct any person who fails to take the required measures to commence taking specific measures before a given date; diligently continue with those measures; and complete them before a given date.[3] Should a person fail to comply, or comply inadequately with such a directive, the catchment management agency may take the measures it considers necessary to remedy the situation.[4] A catchment management agency may recover all costs incurred as a result of it acting under section 19(4) of National Water Act jointly and severally from the following persons:

(a)   any person who is or was responsible for, or who directly or indirectly contributed to, the pollution or the potential pollution;

(b)   the owner of the land at the time when the pollution or the potential for pollution occurred, or that owner's successor-in-title;

(c)   the person in control of the land or any person who has a right to use the land at the time when the activity or the process is or was performed or undertaken, or the situation came about; or

(d)   any person who negligently failed to prevent the activity or the process being performed or undertaken, or the situation from coming about.[5]

The catchment management agency may also claim costs from any other person who, in the opinion of the catchment management agency, benefitted from the measures undertaken by it, to the extent of such benefit.[6] If more than one person is liable, the catchment management agency must, at the request of any of those persons, and after giving the others an opportunity to be heard, apportion the liability, but such apportionment does not relieve any of them of their joint and several liability for the full amount of the costs.[7]

1   National Water Act 36 of 1998 s 19(1).

2   S 19(2).

3   S 19(3).

4   S 19(4).

5   S 19(5).

6   S 19(6). The costs claimed must be reasonable and may include, without being limited to, labour, administrative and overhead costs (s 19(7)).

7   S 19(8).

460   Control of emergency incidents   The responsible person,[1] any other person involved in the incident or any other person with knowledge of the incident must, as soon as reasonably practicable after obtaining knowledge of the incident,[2] report to the Department of Water Affairs and Forestry; the South African Police Service or the relevant fire department, or the relevant catchment management agency.[3] A responsible person must:

(a)   take all reasonable measures to contain and minimise the effects of the incident;

(b)   undertake clean-up procedures;

(c)   remedy the effects of the incident; and

(d)   take such measures as the catchment management agency may either verbally or in writing direct within the time specified by such institution.[4]

Should the responsible person fail to comply, or inadequately comply with a directive, or if it is not be possible to give the directive to the responsible person timeously, the catchment management agency may take the measures it considers necessary to contain and minimise the effects of the incident; undertake clean-up procedures; and remedy the effects of the incident.[5] The catchment management agency may recover all reasonable costs incurred by it from every responsible person jointly and severally.[6] The costs claimed may include, without being limited to, labour, administration and overhead costs.[7] If more than one person is liable, the catchment management agency must, at the request of any of those persons, and after giving the others an opportunity to be heard, apportion the liability, but such apportionment does not relieve any of them of their joint and several liability for the full amount of the costs.[8]

1 "Responsible person" includes any person who is responsible for the incident; owns the substance involved in the incident; or was in control of the substance involved in the incident at the time of the incident (National Water Act 36 of 1998 s 20(2)).
2 "Incident'" includes any incident or accident in which a substance pollutes or has the potential to pollute a water resource; or has, or is likely to have, a detrimental effect on a water resource (s 20(1)).
3 S 20(3).
4 S 20(4). A verbal directive must be confirmed in writing within 14 days, failing which it will be deemed to have been withdrawn (s 20(5)).
5 S 20(6).
6 S 20(7).
7 S 20(8).
8 S 20(9).

461 Regulation of water use amounting to water pollution One of the central concepts in the National Water Act[1] is that of "water use", which is defined to include activities which amount to water pollution: discharging waste or water containing waste into a water resource through a pipe, canal, sewer, sea outfall or other conduit; disposing of waste in a manner which may detrimentally impact on a water resource; disposing in any manner of water which contains waste from, or which has been heated in, any industrial or power generation process.[2] A person may use water only with a licence,[3] subject to three exceptions:

(a) if the water use is permissible in terms of Schedule 1 of the Act;

(b) if the water use is permissible as a continuation of an existing lawful use; or

(c) if the water use is permissible in terms of a general authorisation.[4]

If the water use is a polluting activity and the use requires a licence, then the licence will provide for the conditions of such use, including, for example, the required standards with which waste or water containing waste should comply before being put into a water resource. The Act provides that the responsible authority may attach conditions to licences that, *inter alia*, relate to return flow and discharge or disposal of waste, by specifying a water resource to which it must be returned or other manner in which it must be disposed of; specifying permissible levels for some or all of its chemical and physical components; specifying treatment to which it must be subjected, before it is discharged; and specifying the volume which may be returned.[5]

1 36 of 1998.
2 S 21(f)–(h).
3 S 22(1).
4 In terms of s 39.
5 S 29(1)(c).

462 Discharge of industrial effluent No person may dispose of industrial effluent in any manner other than that approved by the water services provider nominated by the water services authority having jurisdiction in the area in question.[1]

Schedule 1 of the National Water Act[2] contains activities which are regarded as "permissible use of water" and one of these activities is directly relevant to water pollution: a person may, subject to the Act, discharge waste or water containing waste, or run-off water, including stormwater from any residential, recreational, commercial or industrial site, into a canal, sea outfall or other conduit controlled by another person authorised to undertake the purification, treatment or disposal of waste or water containing waste, subject to the approval of the person controlling the canal, sea outfall or other conduit.[3] In practice, most industrial effluent is discharged into municipal sewerage systems, which would fall under this Schedule 1 item. This means that the discharge of effluent into a sewerage system is permissible without a licence under the Act. Such activity would, however, require the approval of the person controlling the sewerage system. In most cases, such approval and the conditions of such approval would be governed by municipal by-laws, which would typically set down tariffs for the amount of effluent discharged and also set down standards with which the effluent would have to comply.[4] Industry discharging effluent into a sewer would, consequently, have to ensure that such effluent was in compliance with the required municipal standards, which would often require on-site purification before discharge.

In terms of a general authorisation issued under the National Water Act, discharge of waste or water containing waste into a water resource through a pipe, canal, sewer or other conduit, and disposing in any manner of water which contains waste from, or which has been heated in, any industrial or power generation process is authorised, such that the user does not require a water-use licence, subject to certain conditions.[5] The authorisation does not:

(a)   apply to a person who discharges wastewater through sea outfalls, or to an aquifer, or any other groundwater resource;

(b)   apply to any water use under Schedule 1 of the National Water Act;

(c)   replace any existing authorisation that is recognised under the National Water Act;

(d)   exempt a person from compliance with section 7(2) of the Water Services Act;[6] or

(d)   exempt a person who uses water from compliance with any other provision of the National Water Act unless stated otherwise in this notice, or any other applicable law, regulation, ordinance or by-law.[7] The authorisation applies throughout the Republic, except for areas specified in Table 3.1 of the regulations,[8] and the duration is five years.[9]

The authorisation provides that a person who owns or lawfully occupies property registered in the Deeds Office as at the date of the notice; or lawfully occupies or uses land that is not registered or surveyed, outside of the areas as excluded from the regulations, may on that property or land discharge up to 2 000 cubic metres of wastewater[10] on any given day into a water resource that is not a listed water resource,[11] provided the discharge complies with the General Limit Values;[12] the discharge does not alter the natural ambient water temperature of the receiving water resource by more than 3 degrees Celsius; and the discharge is not a Complex Industrial Wastewater.[13] The general limit values contain maximum limit values for substances and properties of the water, such as faecal coliforms and various minerals.

As far as the discharge into a listed water resource is concerned, the person in question may discharge up to 2 000 cubic metres of waste water on any given day into a listed water resource, provided the discharge complies with the Special Limit Values;[14] the discharge does not alter the natural ambient water temperature of the receiving water resource by more than 2 degrees Celsius; and the discharge is not a Complex Industrial Wastewater.[15] The special limit values relate to the same substances and properties included in the general limit values, but the limits are more strict.[16]

A person may discharge stormwater runoff from any premises, not containing waste or wastewater emanating from industrial activities and premises, into a water resource.[17] The person making use of this authorisation is required to register the use,[18] and carry out self-monitoring of the discharge and submit the results to the relevant authority.[19] Contravention of any of the regulations is an offence.[20]

1 Water Services Act 108 of 1997 s 7(2). A "water services authority" means any municipality, including a district or rural council as defined in the Local Government Transition Act 209 of 1993, responsible for ensuring access to water services; and a "water services provider" means any person who provides water services to consumers or to another water services institution, but does not include a water services intermediary (Water Services Act 108 of 1997 s 1).
2 36 of 1998.
3 Sch 1 item 1(f) of the National Water Act. An entitlement under this Schedule does not override any other law, ordinance, by-law or regulation, and is subject to any limitation or prohibition thereunder.
4 See, eg, Durban Transitional Metropolitan Council Sewage Disposal Bylaws MN 27 13 May 1999 and Pietermaritzburg-Msunduzi Transitional Local Council Industrial Effluent Bylaws MN 93 19 November 1998.
5 *Government Gazette* 20526 GN 1191, 8 October 1999.
6 108 of 1997.
7 Reg 3.2 and 3.3.
8 Reg 3.4.
9 Reg 3.5.
10 "Waste water" means water containing waste, or water that has been in contact with

waste material (reg 3.6).
11 Certain water resources are listed in Table 3.4 of the regulations. These water resources have been identified as more sensitive receiving bodies than other water resources and require more stringent standards.
12 The "general limit values" are set out in Table 3.2.
13 Reg 3.7(1)(a). "Complex industrial wastewater" means wastewater arising from industrial activities and premises, that contains a complex mixture of substances that are difficult or impractical to chemically characterise and quantify, or one or more substances, for which a Wastewater Limit Value has not been specified, and which may be harmful or potentially harmful to human health, or to the water resource.
14 The "special limit values" are set out in Table 3.2.
15 Reg 3.7(1)(b).
16 For example, the general limit value for chemical oxygen demand is 75 mg/l, and 30 mg/l for the special value.
17 Reg 3.7(2).
18 Reg 3.8.
19 Reg 3.9.
20 Reg 3.12.

463 Disposal of waste which may detrimentally impact on a water resource There is a general authorisation in terms of the National Water Act[1] which relates to wastewater storage and disposal.[2] The authorisation applies throughout the Republic except for subterranean government water control areas,[3] and the duration is five years.[4] A person who owns or lawfully occupies property registered in the Deeds Office as at the date of the notice, or lawfully occupies or uses land that is not registered or surveyed, may on that property or land store up to 5 000 cubic metres of domestic and/or biodegradable industrial wastewater[5] for the purpose of re-use.[6]

Such a person may on that property or land store domestic and/or biodegradable industrial wastewater for the purpose of disposal of up to 10 000 cubic metres per property or land, or up to 50 000 cubic metres in a wastewater pond system per property or land.[7] Such an owner may on that property or land dispose of up to 1 000 cubic metres of:

(a)   domestic and/or biodegradable industrial wastewater, on any given day into a wastewater pond system, or into an evaporation pond system;

(b)   domestic wastewater or biodegradable wastewater into a wastewater irrigation system;

(c)   wastewater to an on-site disposal facility for grey water[8] generated by a single household; up to one cubic metre of biodegradable industrial wastewater on any given day; and domestic wastewater to a communal septic tank serving no more than 50 households;

(d)   domestic wastewater generated by a single household not permanently linked to a central waste collection, treatment and disposal system, to an on-site disposal facility; and

(e)   stormwater runoff from any premises not containing waste or wastewater from industrial activities and premises.[9]

A person may dispose of mine residue into mine residue deposits provided the mine residue is not from a Category A mine,[10] and the disposal is in accordance with specified documents.[11]

A person who stores wastewater in terms of this authorisation must submit a registration form obtainable from the department, for registration of the water use before commencement of storage if more than 1 000 cubic metres are stored for disposal or if more than 500 cubic metres are stored for re-use.[12] A person who disposes of wastewater in terms of this authorisation must submit a registration form obtained from the department, for registration of the water use before the commencement of the disposal if more than 50 cubic metres of domestic wastewater or biodegradable industrial wastewater is disposed of on any given day.[13] The responsible local authority must submit a registration form obtained from the department, to register the water use for disposal of domestic wastewater in areas where more than 5 000 households are served by on-site disposal sites, areas where the density of on-site disposal sites exceeds 10 per hectare, or areas served by communal septic tanks.[14]

Wastewater storage dams and wastewater disposal sites must be located outside of a watercourse, above the 100 year flood line, or alternatively, more than 100 metres from the edge of a water resource or a borehole which is utilised for drinking water or stock watering, and on land that is not, or does not overlie, a major aquifer.[15] The user is required to carry out monitoring.[16] The registered user must follow acceptable construction, maintenance and operational practices to ensure the consistent, effective and safe performance of any wastewater disposal system or wastewater storage dam,[17] and all reasonable measures must be taken to prevent wastewater overflowing from any wastewater disposal system or wastewater storage dam.[18] All reasonable measures must be taken to provide for mechanical, electrical or operational failures and malfunctions of any wastewater disposal system or wastewater storage dam.[19] Sewage sludge must be removed from any wastewater and the resulting sludge disposed of according to the requirements of any relevant law and regulation.[20] Any person who contravenes any provision of this authorisation is guilty of an offence.[21]

1   36 of 1998.
2   *Government Gazette* 20526 GN 1191, 8 October 1999.
3   Reg 4.4. These areas are contained in Table 4.1.
4   Reg 4.5
5   "Domestic wastewater" is wastewater arising from domestic and commercial activities and premises, and may contain sewage; and "biodegradable industrial wastewater" means wastewater that contains predominantly organic waste arising from industrial activities and premises, including:
    (a) milk processing;
    (b) manufacture of fruit and vegetable products;
    (c) sugar mills;
    (d) manufacture and bottling of soft drinks;
    (e) water bottling;
    (f) production of alcohol and alcoholic beverages in breweries, wineries or malt houses;
    (g) manufacture of animal feed from plant or animal products;
    (h) manufacture of gelatine and glue from hides, skin and bones;
    (i) abattoirs;
    (j) fish processing; and
    (k) feedlots (reg 4.6).
6   Reg 4.7.

7 Reg 4.8.
8 "Grey water" is wastewater generated through domestic activities and premises, including washing, bathing and food preparation, but does not contain sewage (reg 4.6).
9 Reg 4.9.
10 "Category A mine" is any gold or coal mine; any mine with an extractive metallurgical process, including heap leaching; or any mine where sulphate producing or acid generating material occurs in the mineral deposit (reg 4.6).

11 Reg 4.10. The disposal must be in accordance with GN 704, 4 June 1999, and with SABS Code 0286.
12 Reg 4.11.
13 Reg 4.12(1).
14 Reg 4.12(2).
15 Reg 4.13.
16 Reg 4.14.
17 Reg 4.15(1).
18 Reg 4.15(2).
19 Reg 4.15(3).
20 Reg 4.15(4).
21 Reg 4.17.

464 Controlled activities The National Water Act[1] contains certain controlled activities which no person may undertake unless such person is authorised to do so by or under the Act.[2] Controlled activities include irrigation of any land with waste or water containing waste generated through any industrial activity or by a waterwork; and intentional recharging of an aquifer with any waste or water containing waste.[3] In the case of authorisation of a controlled activity, the licensing authority may impose conditions specifying the waste treatment, pollution control and monitoring equipment to be installed, maintained and operated, and specifying the management practices to be followed to prevent the pollution of any water resource.[4]

There is a general authorisation in terms of the Act which relates to irrigation of land with waste or water containing waste.[5] The authorisation applies throughout the Republic except for subterranean government water control areas,[6] and the duration is five years.[7] A person who owns or lawfully occupies property registered in the deeds office as at the date of this notice, or lawfully occupies or uses land that is not registered or surveyed, may on that property or land irrigate up to 500 cubic metres of domestic or biodegradable industrial wastewater on any given day, provided the wastewater meets prescribed standards.[8] Such person may irrigate up to 50 cubic metres of biodegradable industrial wastewater on any given day, provided the wastewater meets prescribed standards.[9] A person who irrigates with wastewater in terms of this authorisation must submit a registration form obtained from the department for registration of the water use before commencement of irrigation if more than 10 cubic metres of wastewater are irrigated on any given day.[10] Wastewater irrigation in terms of this authorisation is only permitted if the irrigation takes place above the 100 year flood line, or alternatively, more than 100 metres from the edge of a water resource or a borehole which is utilised for drinking water or stock watering, and on land that is not or does not overlie a major aquifer.[11] The user is required to monitor and keep records.[12] The registered user must follow acceptable construction, maintenance and operational practices to ensure the consistent, effective and safe performance of the wastewater irrigation system, including the prevention of:

(a) waterlogging of the soil and pooling of wastewater on the surface of the soil;

(b) nuisance conditions such as flies or mosquitoes, odour or secondary pollution;

(c) waste, or wastewater, entering any surface water resource;

(d) the unreasonable chemical or physical deterioration of, or any other damage to, the soil of the irrigation site; and

(e) the unauthorised use of the wastewater by members of the public.[13]

All reasonable measures must be taken for storage of the wastewater used for irrigation when irrigation cannot be undertaken.[14] Suspended solids must be removed from any wastewater, and the resulting sludge disposed of according to the requirements of any relevant law or regulation.[15] All reasonable measures must be taken to provide for mechanical, electrical, operational, or process failures and malfunctions of the wastewater irrigation system.[16] All reasonable measures must be taken to collect stormwater runoff containing waste or wastewater emanating from the area under irrigation and to retain it for disposal.[17] Any person who contravenes any provision of this authorisation is guilty of an offence.[18]

1   36 of 1998.
2   S 37(2).
3   S 37(1)(a) (d).
4   S 29(d).
5   *Government Gazette* 20526 GN 1191, 8 October 1999
6   Reg 2.4. These areas are contained in Table 2.1.
7   Reg 2.5
8   Reg 2.7(1). The standards include, eg, faecal coliforms not exceeding 100 000 per 100 ml.
9   Reg 2.7(2). The standards are much the same as in the previous reg, except a different chemical oxygen demand value.
10   Reg 2.8.
11   Reg 2.9.
12   Reg 2.10.
13   Reg 2.11(1).
14   Reg 2.11(2).
15   Reg 2.11(3).
16   Reg 2.11(4).
17   Reg 2.11(5).
18   Reg 2.13.

465 Pollution associated with mining operations Extensive regulations, aimed at the prevention of water pollution from the operation of mines and works, were promulgated[1] in terms of the Water Act.[2] Despite that Act's repeal by the National Water Act,[3] the regulations remain in force by virtue of the new Act's savings clause.[4] These regulations prescribe that the person who is in control of a mine or works and the person who intends to establish a mine or works, must furnish the Director-General: Environmental Affairs and Tourism with certain information relating to that mine or works.[5] A number of important obligations are laid upon the manager of a mine or works: he or she is responsible for the compilation of a plan which must depict all works constructed for the control of water on the surface of a mine or works and must contain a list of prescribed details.[6] The manager must, moreover, cause effective measures to be taken to prevent effluent, including water pumped from underground or which flows naturally from a mine or works, from flowing or seeping beyond the boundaries of the property on which the mine or works is situated.[7] The manager also has a number of specific duties to perform with regard to mineral tailings and waste rock dumps, slimes dams and other sources of pollution,[8] in respect of waterways, stormwater drains and dams,[9] and with regard to domestic effluent.[10] Contravention of any regulation is an offence.[11] However, the minister may grant exemption from compliance with the provisions of any of these regulations if he or she is of the opinion that such compliance will be unduly onerous.[12]

1   *Government Gazette* 4989 GN R287, 20 February 1976.
2   54 of 1956 s 26(c) (d).
3   36 of 1998.
4   S 163(4), which provides that any regulation made under a law repealed by the Act remains in force and is considered to have been made under the Act to the extent that it is not inconsistent with the Act; and until it is repealed by the minister under the Act.
5   Reg 2.
6   Reg 5.
7   Reg 6.1.
8   Regs 7, 8, 11.1, 12, 14, 16 and 21.
9   Regs 9 and 19.
10   Reg 18.
11   Reg 24 read with s 170(3). Provision is made for vicarious responsibility: reg 3.
12   S 26(d).

466 Pollution resulting from drilling boreholes or sinking wells In order to sink, enlarge, deepen or alter a borehole, well or spring lawfully in a subterranean water control area for the abstraction or use of subterranean water, or to abstract or use such water, a person requires a permit from the Minister of Water Affairs and Forestry.[1] Conditions in this permit may stipulate that boreholes or wells must be protected in such a manner as to prevent contamination or pollution.[2]

1 Reg 6(1) published in *Government Gazette* 589 GN R1324, 30 August 1963 issued in terms of the Water Act 54 of 1956 s 30(2), and still valid in terms of s 163(4) of the

National Water Act 36 of 1998.
2 Reg 7(vii). Contravention of the regulations constitutes an offence: reg 9.

467 Pollution associated with waterborne transport

Persons using waterborne transportation are responsible for any resultant pollution of both inland waters and the sea. Although there are some provisions relating to the control of pollution from boats on inland water,[1] most provisions refer to the pollution of harbour waters and to the sea generally. Thus regulations applicable by virtue of the Legal Succession to the South African Transport Services Act[2] provide for control over the dumping of rubbish, including oil, into the waters of harbours,[3] while the Merchant Shipping Act,[4] the Dumping at Sea Control Act,[5] the Marine Pollution (Control and Civil Liability) Act[6] and the Marine Traffic Act[7] deal with marine pollution. These Acts are discussed in other sections.

1 Cf eg art 30 of the Schedule to the International Health Regulations Act 28 of 1974 read with s 2 of the Act.
2 9 of 1989.
3 See *Government Gazette* 8124 GN R562, 26 March 1982. The regulations, *inter alia*, provide for liability for oil spills from ships in harbours. For other provisions dealing

with water pollution control in harbours see s 14(3) of the International Health Regulations Act 28 of 1974 and art 30 of the Schedule, read with s 2 of the Act.
4 57 of 1951.
5 73 of 1980.
6 6 of 1981.
7 2 of 1981.

468 Pollution caused by wrecks

When a ship, which means any vessel used for transportation or for any other purpose on or near the surface of the water,[1] is wrecked, stranded or in distress within the territorial waters[2] or on or near the coasts of the Republic, the Minister of Transport may direct the master or owner of such ship, or both master and owner, either orally or in writing, to move the ship to a place specified by the minister or to perform such an act in respect of such ship as may be specified by the minister.[3] If the master or owner of such ship fails to perform, within the time specified by the minister, any act which he or she has been required to perform, he or she is guilty of an offence.[4] Moreover, the minister may cause such act to be performed.[5]

The minister may, notwithstanding the abovementioned provisions, cause any wreck or any wrecked, stranded or abandoned ship or any part thereof to be raised, removed or destroyed or dealt with in such manner as he or she may deem fit.[6] A wreck includes flotsam, jetsam, lagan and derelict found in or on the shores of the sea or of any tidal waters of the Republic; any portion of a ship or aircraft lost, abandoned, stranded or in distress; any portion of the cargo, stores or equipment of such ship or aircraft; and any portion of the personal property on board such ship or aircraft when it was lost, abandoned, stranded or in distress and belonged to any person who was on board that ship or aircraft at that time.[7]

If the minister incurred any expenses in connection with the exercise of any power in terms of these provisions, he or she may recover such expenses from the owner of the wreck or ship in question or, in the case of an abandoned wreck or ship, from the person who was the owner thereof at the time of the abandonment.[8]

The minister may sell any wreck or ship in respect of which any power has been exercised in terms of the abovementioned provisions, any part of such wreck or ship and any goods removed from it, and apply the proceeds of the sale towards defraying any expenses incurred in connection with the exercise of such power; or he or she may cause any wreck, ship or goods to be detained until security has been given for the payment of such expenses.[9] These provisions of the Merchant Shipping Act are supplemented by the Marine Traffic Act.[10] The latter Act renders it a criminal offence for any person within the territorial waters[11] or internal waters[12] intentionally to sink, dump or dispose of or cause to be sunk, dumped or disposed of a ship,[13] wreck or hulk except with the permission of the Minister of Transport and within the areas and on the conditions prescribed by regulation,[14] or abandon a ship which is not in distress or a hulk or an object which may interfere with navigation.[15]

1 Merchant Shipping Act 57 of 1951 s 2(1).
2 Territorial Waters Act 87 of 1963 s 2 (see now s 15 of the Maritime Zones Act 15 of 1994).
3 Merchant Shipping Act 57 of 1951 s 304A(1)(a).
4 S 312.
5 S 304A(1)(b).
6 S 304A(2).
7 S 2(1).
8 S 304A(3). See also s 304A(4) which empowers the minister in such instances to cause any goods to be removed from such wreck or ship.
9 S 304A(5). The minister or any person acting under the authority of the minister is not liable in respect of anything done in good faith in terms of the abovementioned provisions: s 304A(7).
10 2 of 1981.

11 As defined in the Territorial Waters Act 87 of 1963 s 2, ie the sea within a distance of 12 nautical miles from low-water mark: Marine Traffic Act 2 of 1981 s 1.
12 "Internal waters" means the waters on the landward side of the normal baseline from which the territorial waters are determined, and includes any harbour, fishing harbour and Saldanha Bay, Hout Bay, False Bay, the Knysna Lagoon, the Bay of Natal and Richards Bay: Marine Traffic Act s 1.
13 "Ship" means a waterborne craft or structure of any type, irrespective of the manner of propulsion or movement thereof, including a non-displacement craft and submarine or other underwater vehicle, but does not include a vessel propelled by oars: s 1.
14 S 6(1)(a) (2). "Wreck" and "hulk" are not defined.
15 S 6(1)(b) (2).

469 Pollution through dumping of substances at sea

The dumping of substances in the sea is controlled in terms of the Dumping at Sea Control Act,[1] which is administered by the Minister and Department of Environmental Affairs and Tourism.[2] However, in relation to any matter affecting Transnet Ltd, the minister may act only with the concurrence of the Minister of Transport.[3] The Act is the outcome of the 1972 London Convention on the Prevention of Marine Pollution by Dumping of Wastes and other Matter. The Act applies to the South African territorial waters[4] and to the sea between the high- and low-water marks.[5] It also applies in respect of the Prince Edward Islands.[6] Certain provisions even apply in respect of South African vessels,[7] aircraft[8] or citizens on the high seas, including the fishing zone.[9]

The Act relates to the dumping at sea of various types of substances:

(a) substances mentioned in Schedule 1,[10] namely prohibited substances;

(b) substances mentioned in Schedule 2,[11] namely restricted substances; and

(c) any other substance.[12]

It deals, moreover, with the loading of substances mentioned under (b)[13] and (c)[14] onto any vessel,[15] aircraft,[16] platform or other man-made structure[17] for dumping. It also deals with the disposal of any vessel at sea.[18]

1 73 of 1980.
2 S 1(1)(iv).
3 S 1(2).

4 Territorial Waters Act 87 of 1963 s 2 (see now s 15 of the Maritime Zones Act 15 of 1994).

5 Dumping at Sea Control Act 73 of 1980 s 1(1)(vii).

6 S 11.

7 "South African vessel" means any vessel registered in the Republic in terms of the Merchant Shipping Act 57 of 1951, or deemed to be so registered: s 2(8) of the Dumping at Sea Control Act 73 of 1980.

8 "South African aircraft" means any aircraft in the Republic: s 2(8).

9 S 2(6). Cf also s 2(7).

10 S 2(1)(a). The prohibited substances included in this Schedule are: organohalogen compounds; mercury and its compounds; cadmium and its compounds; persistent plastics and other persistent synthetic materials; high-level radioactive waste or other high-level radioactive matter prescribed by regulation with the concurrence of the Minister of Mineral and Energy Affairs; and substances in whatever form produced for biological and chemical warfare.

11 S 2(1)(b)(i). The restricted substances included in this Schedule are: arsenic and its compounds; lead and its compounds; copper and its compounds; zinc and its compounds;

organosilicon compounds; cyanides; fluorides; pesticides and their by-products not included in Sch 1; beryllium and its compounds; chromium and its compounds; nickel and its compounds; vanadium and its compounds; containers, scrap metal and any substances or articles that by reason of their bulk may interfere with fishing or navigation; radioactive waste or other radioactive matter not included in Sch 1; and ammunition. The minister may by notice in the *Government Gazette* amend any Schedule to the Act: s 9.

12 S 2(1)(c)(i).

13 S 2(1)(b)(ii).

14 S 2(1)(c)(ii).

15 "Vessel" means waterborne craft of any type whatsoever, whether self-propelled or not: s 1(1)(ix).

16 "Aircraft" means airborne craft of any type whatsoever, whether self-propelled or not: s 1(1)(i).

17 "Platform" and "other man–made structure" are not defined.

18 S 2(1)(b)(iii).

470 Offences Certain activities amount to an offence in terms of the Dumping at Sea Control Act:[1]

(a) *Dumping* "Dump", in relation to any substance, means deliberately to dispose of at sea from any vessel, aircraft, platform or other man–made structure, by incinerating or depositing in the sea. It does not, however, include the disposal at sea of any substance incidental to or derived from normal operations. Nor does it include the lawful depositing at sea of any substance for a purpose other than its mere disposal.[2]

It is an offence to dump any substance mentioned in Schedule 1 of the Act.[3] No permit may be granted to authorise the dumping of such substance. It is also an offence to dump any substance mentioned in Schedule 2.[4] However, a special permit may be obtained to legalise such dumping.[5] It is also an offence to dump any other substance not mentioned in Schedule 1 or 2.[6] However, a general permit may be obtained to legalise such dumping.[7]

(b) *Loading for dumping* It is an offence to load any substance mentioned in Schedule 2 on to any vessel, aircraft, platform or other man–made structure at sea for dumping.[8] As has been mentioned, a special permit may be obtained to legalise such dumping. It is also an offence to load any substance other than those mentioned in Schedule 1 or 2.[9] But, as already stated, a general permit may be obtained which would legalise such dumping.

(c) *Disposal* The deliberate disposal[10] at sea of any vessel,[11] aircraft,[12] platform or other man–made structure is an offence.[13] However, a special permit may be obtained which would legalise such disposal.[14]

1 73 of 1980.

2 S 1(1)(ii).

3 S 2(1)(a).

4 S 2(1)(b)(i).

5 S 3(1)(a)(i).

6 S 2(1)(c)(i).

7 S 3(1)(b).

8 S 2(1)(b)(ii).

9   S 2(1)(c)(ii).
10   "Dispose" is not defined.
11   Defined in s 1(1)(ix).

12   Defined in s 1(1)(i).
13   S 2(1)(b)(iii).
14   S 3(1)(a)(ii).

471 Exemptions In addition to the actions specifically excluded from the definition of "dump" in the Dumping at Sea Control Act,[1] there are two other instances which would exempt someone from liability for the abovementioned prohibited activities:

A person may prove[2] that the substance in question was dumped for the purpose of saving human life or for securing the safety of the vessel, and that such dumping was necessary for such purpose or was a reasonable step to take in the circumstances.[3]

The other exemption relates to the granting of permits. The minister may grant either a special or a general permit.[4]

A special permit authorises:

(a) dumping, on such conditions as the Director-General: Environmental Affairs and Tourism may think fit to attach to such permit, of any substance mentioned in Schedule 2;[5] or

(b) disposal at sea, on such conditions as the director-general may think fit to attach to such permit, of any vessel, aircraft, platform or other man-made structure.[6]

A general permit authorises the dumping, on such conditions as the director-general may think fit to attach to such permit, of any substance other than those mentioned in Schedule 1 or 2.[7]

Conviction of an offence may lead to cancellation or amendment of the permit by restricting the dumping or disposal authorised by it.[8] Where dumping has taken place in pursuance of any of the abovementioned exemptions, the master of the vessel, the pilot of the aircraft or the person in charge of the platform or other man-made structure in question, must forthwith report such dumping to the director-general in such manner and furnish such information in that regard as may be prescribed by regulation.[9]

Within 30 days after the end of each calendar year the director-general must, as far as he or she is able to do so, furnish the minister with a report regarding such year as to the number of the abovementioned permits that were granted,[10] and the nature and quantities of all substances or articles authorised by such permits to be dumped or disposed of at sea,[11] the dumping of which was reported as mentioned above,[12] or dumped or disposed of in contravention of the abovementioned provisions.[13] The report must also refer to the location, time and method of the dumping or disposal in question.[14]

1   73 of 1980 s 1(1)(ii).
2   S 2(2).
3   S 2(1).
4   S 3. Cf also s 8(1)(a) and (b) as regards regulations.
5   S 3(1)(a)(i).
6   S 3(1)(a)(ii).
7   S 3(1)(b).
8   S 3(3).
9   S 2(5). It is not expressly stated that

contravention of this provision would amount to an offence, although s 6(1)(c) would seem to imply that contravention of s 2(5) does amount to an offence.
10   S 4(a).
11   S 4(b)(i).
12   S 4(b)(ii).
13   S 4(b)(iii).
14   S 4(b).

472 Marine oil pollution Apart from international conventions aimed at oil pollution control in international waters, South Africa has its own national legislation to control pollution along its coastline. The Marine Pollution (Control and Civil Liability)

Act,[1] which is administered jointly by the Departments of Transport and Environmental Affairs and Tourism, provides for the prevention and combating of pollution by oil, discharged from ships, tankers or off-shore installations into South Africa's territorial waters and that portion of the fishing zone, situated within a distance of 50 nautical miles from the low-water mark, and includes the sea between the high- and low-water marks as well as any tidal lagoon or tidal river and internal waters.

South Africa has also adopted the International Convention for the Prevention of Pollution from Ships of 1973/1978 in the Marine Pollution (Prevention of Pollution from Ships) Act.[2] Another relevant instance where a South African statute is modelled on a convention is the Marine Pollution (Intervention) Act,[3] which is based on the International Convention Relating to Intervention on the High Seas in Cases of Oil Pollution Casualties.

The principal features of the Marine Pollution (Control and Civil Liability) Act[4] are that it makes provision for the criminal and civil liability of the master and/or owner of a ship, tanker or offshore installation, besides placing certain duties on these persons and empowering the Minister of Transport to undertake a wide range of actions with a view to preventing oil pollution. The key phrases of the Act concern the "discharge" of "oil" from a "ship", "tanker", or "offshore installation" into the "prohibited area" and the liability of the "owner" and "master".

1 6 of 1981, which replaced the first Act 67 of 1971. This Act was previously called the Prevention and Combating of Pollution of the Sea by Oil Act (name changed by the Shipping General Amendment Act 23 of 1997). For a discussion of the 1971 Act see Rabie SA *Environmental Legislation* 139–41. The 1981 Act was enacted to remedy shortcomings in the 1971 Act and to implement provisions of the International Convention on Civil Liability for Oil Pollution Damage of 1969, to which SA had acceded since the enactment of the 1971 Act. See generally on marine oil pollution control Stewart 1986 *Sea Changes* 106; Hiscox *Some Aspects of Oil Pollution off the SA Coast* LLM UCT 1988; Molden (1989) 15 *SA Journal of Aquatic*

Sciences 209; Van Eeden *Some Aspects limiting Liability of Tanker Owners for Oil Pollution Damage on the SA Coast and Maritime Zones* LLM UCT 1990.

2 2 of 1986. This Act was previously called the International Convention for the Prevention of Pollution from Ships Act (name changed by the International Convention for the Prevention of Pollution from Ships Amendment Act 66 of 1996).

3 64 of 1987. This Act was previously called the International Convention Relating to Intervention on the High Seas in Cases of Oil Pollution Casualties Act (name changed by the Shipping General Amendment Act 23 of 1997).

4 6 of 1981.

473 Definitions "Discharge" includes any escaping, spilling, leaking, pumping or dumping of oil from a ship, tanker or offshore installation into the sea.[1] "Oil" means any kind of mineral oil and includes spirit produced from oil and a mixture of such oil and water or any other substance.[2]

"Ship" means any kind of vessel or other sea-borne object from which oil can be discharged, excluding a tanker, whether or not such vessel or object has been lost or abandoned, has stranded, is in distress, disabled or damaged, has been wrecked, has broken up or has sunk.[3] "Tanker" means any seagoing vessel of any type whatsoever, actually carrying oil in bulk as cargo and in respect of which the provisions of the Convention on Civil Liability for Oil Pollution Damage, 1969, are applicable.[4] "Offshore installation" means a facility situated wholly or partly within the prohibited area and which is used for the transfer of oil from a ship or a tanker to a point on land or from a point on land to a ship or tanker or from a bunkering vessel to a ship or a tanker, and includes any exploration or production platform situated within the prohibited area and used in prospecting for or the mining of natural oil.[5]

"Prohibited area" means the territorial waters[6] of the Republic and that portion of the fishing zone,[7] as defined in the Territorial Waters Act, situated within a distance of 50 nautical miles from the low-water mark,[8] and includes the sea[9] between the high[10]- and low-water marks as well as any tidal lagoon[11] or tidal river[12] as defined in the Sea-Shore Act and internal waters[13] as defined in the Marine Traffic Act.

"Owner", in relation to a ship or tanker, means the person or persons registered as the owner of such ship or tanker or, in the absence of registration, the person or persons to whom such ship or tanker belongs.[14] "Master", in relation to a ship or a tanker, means any person (other than a pilot) having charge or command of such ship or tanker and, in relation to an offshore installation, means the person in charge of it.[15]

1 Marine Pollution (Control and Civil Liability) Act 6 of 1981 s 1(1).

2 S 1(1). However, for the purposes of ss 9(1)(a) and 13(1), oil is defined in par 5 of art 1 of the Convention on Civil Liability for Oil Pollution Damage, Brussels 1969.

3 S 1(1).

4 S 1(1).

5 S 1(1).

6 The sea within a distance of 12 nautical miles from the low-water mark forms the territorial waters of the Republic: s 1(1) of the Marine Pollution (Control and Civil Liability) Act and s 2 of the Territorial Waters Act 87 of 1963.

7 Cf s 3.

8 "Low-water mark" means the lowest line to which the water of the sea recedes during periods of ordinary spring tides: s 1(1)(x) of the Marine Pollution (Control and Civil Liability) Act 6 of 1981.

9 "Sea" means the water and the bed of the sea and includes the land between the high- and low-water marks as well as any tidal lagoon or tidal river as defined in the Sea-Shore Act 21 of 1935: Marine Pollution (Control and Civil Liability) Act 6 of 1981 s 1(1).

10 "High-water mark" means the highest line reached by the water of the sea during ordinary storms occurring during the most stormy period of the year, excluding exceptional or abnormal floods: s 1(1).

11 A "tidal lagoon" is any lagoon in which a rise and fall of the water-level takes place as a result of the action of the tides: s 1(1) of the Marine Pollution (Control and Civil Liability) Act and s 1 of the Sea-Shore Act 21 of 1935.

12 A "tidal river" is that part of any river in which a rise and fall of the water-level takes place as a result of the action of the tides: s 1 of the Sea-Shore Act 21 of 1935.

13 "Internal waters" means the waters on the landward side of the normal baseline from which the territorial waters are determined, and includes: (a) any fishing harbour as defined in the Sea Fishery Act 12 of 1988; and (b) Saldanha Bay, Hout Bay, False Bay, the Knysna Lagoon, the Bay of Natal and Richards Bay: s 1(iv) of the Marine Traffic Act 2 of 1981.

14 Marine Pollution (Control and Civil Liability) Act 6 of 1981 s 1(1).

15 S 1(1).

474 Minister's powers The minister concerned enjoys far-reaching powers in respect of the prevention and combating of marine oil pollution. If any oil is being discharged or is in the opinion of the minister likely to be discharged from a ship or tanker, the minister may, with a view to preventing the pollution or further pollution of the sea by such oil, require the master and/or owner of such ship or tanker to undertake any of a wide variety of actions.[1] If, in the opinion of the minister, the master and owner of the ship or tanker in question are or would be incapable of complying with his or her requirements, or if they refuse or fail to perform a required act, the minister may personally cause the act to be performed.[2] Moreover, the minister is granted further powers to take independent action in preventing or removing marine oil pollution, where oil is discharged or is likely to be discharged from a ship or tanker.[3]

1 Marine Pollution (Control and Civil Liability) Act 6 of 1981 ss 4(1) 6.

2 Ss 4(2)(a) 22(1). Cf ss 4(3) and 22(2) in respect of expenses relating to the minister's action.

3 S 5. Cf also ss 7 and 8 with regard to inspections and the right of entry. See generally s 27.

475 Civil liability of owner The owner of a ship, tanker or offshore installation is liable for any loss or damage caused in the area of the Republic by pollution resulting from the discharge of oil from such ship, tanker or offshore installation.[1] Moreover, the owner is also liable for the costs of any measures taken by the minister to reduce or prevent the abovementioned loss or damage, even if such discharge does not in fact occur.[2] If the discharge occurred without the owner's fault or privity, his or her liability may be limited,[3] while it may be entirely excluded if the owner proves that the discharge resulted from war or hostilities or an exceptional, inevitable and irresistible natural phenomenon,[4] or was wholly caused by a person not being the owner or a servant or agent of the owner, with intent to do damage,[5] or was wholly caused by the negligence of an authority which is responsible for the maintenance of lights or other navigational aids, in the exercise of that function.[6] In order to ensure payment of the owner's liability for the abovementioned loss, damage or costs, provision is made for compulsory insurance by owners of tankers carrying more than 2 000 long tons of oil[7] and for a deposit or guarantee in respect of other tankers, ships and offshore installations.[8] Moreover, failure by an owner of a ship to pay the abovementioned costs or to make the deposit or to furnish the guarantee in question, enables the minister to cause the ship to be detained, seized and realised in satisfaction of those costs.[9]

1 Marine Pollution (Control and Civil Liability) Act 6 of 1981 s 9(1)(a).
2 S 9(1)(b). Cf also s 9(1)(c) and 9(2)(a) and (b). The owner's liability ensues only in terms of the Act (s 10(1)), while the owner's servants or agents are not held liable at all (s 10(2)). The provisions of s 9(1) do not apply in respect of any warship or in respect of any tanker which is used exclusively in the service of any state for other than commercial purposes : s 11(1).
3 S 9(5).
4 S 9(3)(a).
5 S 9(3)(b).
6 S 9(3)(c).
7 S 13(1). This provision is enforced in that a certificate stipulating such insurance is required before such tanker may enter or leave a South African port or arrive at or leave an offshore installation in South African territorial waters: s 13(1).
8 S 16.
9 S 19.

476 Criminal liability of master and owner Contravention of most provisions of the Marine Pollution (Control and Civil Liability) Act,[1] or failure by the master and owner to comply with the duties placed upon them either by the minister or by the provisions of the Act, constitute offences.[2] The most serious offences are those relating to a failure to comply with the minister's precepts in cases where oil is discharged from a ship or tanker and a contravention of the provisions relating to compulsory insurance.[3] In both these instances the criminal penalty is utilised only as an indirect sanction, reliance being placed in the first instance upon administrative control. Moreover, a separate offence being of the same serious nature is committed directly by the master and owner if any oil is discharged from a ship, tanker or offshore installation into the prohibited area.[4] However, the accused may evade liability by proving[5] that the oil was discharged for the purpose of securing the safety of or preventing damage to the ship, tanker or offshore installation in question, or of saving life, or that the oil escaped in consequence of damage to the ship, tanker or offshore installation and that all reasonable steps were taken for preventing, stopping or reducing the escape of oil, or that the oil escaped by reason of leakage, and neither such leakage nor any delay in discovering it was due to any lack of reasonable care, and all reasonable steps were taken for stopping or reducing it.[6]

1 6 of 1981.
2 Ss 3(4) 8(2) 13(6) (7) 24(5) 30. Cf *S v Peppas* 1977 2 SA 643 (A).
3 S 30(2)(d).
4 Ss 2(1) 30(2)(d). S 2 has been repealed by s 28 of the Shipping General Amendment

Act 23 of 1997, a provision which will be
put into operation by proclamation.
5   Marine   Pollution   (Control   and   Civil

Liability) Act 6 of 1981 s 2(2).
6   S 2(1)(a) (b) (c).

477 Exemptions The minister may exempt any ship or any class of ships or any tanker or any class of tankers or any offshore installation from any of or all the provisions of the Marine Pollution (Control and Civil Liability) Act.[1]

1   6 of 1981 s 25(1).

478 Defraying expenses Provision is made for certain moneys obtained by virtue of the Marine Pollution (Control and Civil Liability) Act[1] to be paid into the State Revenue Fund.[2] Expenses incurred for a variety of actions in terms of the Act, such as to undertake or promote relevant research or to defray expenditure incurred in preventing or removing marine oil pollution, must be defrayed out of money appropriated by Parliament for such purposes.[3]

1   6 of 1981.
2   S 26(1).
3   S 26(2).

479 Oil pollution from wrecks Where oil pollution results or may result from a ship which is wrecked or in distress within the territorial waters of or on or near the coast of the Republic, the Minister of Transport may also act in terms of the Merchant Shipping Act[1] in dealing with the problem.[2]

1   57 of 1951.
2   S 304A.

480 Jurisdiction Both the Departments of Transport and of Environmental Affairs and Tourism are involved in marine oil pollution control. The former administers the Merchant Shipping Act,[1] the International Convention for the Prevention of Pollution from Ships Act[2] and the International Convention Relating to Intervention on the High Seas in Cases of Oil Pollution Casualties Act.[3] The latter department administers the Marine Pollution (Control and Civil Liability) Act,[4] jointly with Transport, while it is also responsible for other statutes dealing with marine pollution, such as the Dumping at Sea Control Act[5] and the Sea Fishery Act.[6]

The practical dividing line between the respective jurisdictions of these two departments is that Transport is responsible for oil while it is on board, while Environmental Affairs and Tourism is responsible if and when oil is spilled in the sea, or reaches the coastline. In other words, prevention of oilspills is the responsibility of the Department of Transport, while the clean-up aspects are vested in the Department of Environmental Affairs and Tourism. This division of responsibility means that Transport is responsible for taking preventive action while oil is on board a vessel and the possibility of an oil leak exists, while Environmental Affairs is responsible for combating operations when oil reaches the sea or coastline.[7]

1   57 of 1951.
2   2 of 1986.
3   64 of 1987.
4   6 of 1981.

5   73 of 1980.
6   12 of 1988.
7   Cf *Government Gazette* 10377 GN 1646, 8 August 1986.

481 Pollution detrimental to the marine habitat and its resources Adequate conservation of the marine habitat and its resources is dependent to a considerable degree upon international co-operation. A number of conventions accordingly deal with this matter. Among the most important municipal provisions that have been discussed, are the Dumping at Sea Control Act[1] and the Marine Pollution (Control and Civil Liability) Act.[2] Furthermore, the Sea Fishery Act[3] renders it an offence for anyone to dump, or to allow to enter or to permit to be dumped or discharged into the sea,[4] anything that is or may be injurious to fish,[5] fish food or aquatic plants, or which may disturb or change the ecological balance in any area of the sea, or which may detrimentally affect the marketability of fish or seaweed, or which may hinder the catching of fish.[6]

The Cape and Natal Nature Conservation Ordinances also contain provisions aimed at preventing the pollution of the sea. It is an offence in terms of the Cape Nature and Environmental Conservation Ordinance[7] to deposit or cause to be deposited in any inland waters or in any place from where it is likely to percolate into or in any other manner enter any inland waters,[8] anything, whether solid, liquid or gaseous, which is or is likely to be injurious to any fish or fish food or which, if it were so deposited in large quantities or numbers, would be so injurious.[9]

The Natal Nature Conservation Ordinance[10] prohibits anyone from depositing or discharging or allowing to enter or percolate into any waters[11] any substance, matter or thing, whether solid, liquid or gaseous, that is injurious or is liable to become injurious to fish or fish food.[12]

1 73 of 1980.
2 6 of 1981.
3 12 of 1988.
4 "Sea" means the water and the bed of the sea, including the seashore and the water and beds of tidal rivers and tidal lagoons; "sea-shore" means the water and the land between the low-water mark and the high-water mark: s 1.
5 "Fish" means every species of sea animal, whether vertebrate or invertebrate, and includes the spawn or larvae of any such sea animal, but does not include any seal or sea bird: s 1.
6 S 47(1)(k). Provision is made for additional penalties (s 47(2)(a)) and for forfeiture and seizure of certain items (s 48(1)). It is no defence for an accused in a prosecution for this offence to aver that he or she had no knowledge of a certain fact or that he or she did not act willfully: s 50(5). If in any prosecution for the abovementioned offence it is proved that in any area in the sea, within the distance of 8 km from any factory, any fish or fish food has been or is being injured or has died or is dying or its marketability or that of seaweed has been or is being adversely affected, or the ecological balance has

been or is being disturbed or changed, it will be presumed, until the contrary is proved, that it has been or is being caused by something discharged from that factory into the sea: s 50(4).
7 19 of 1974.
8 Although "inland waters" refers basically to all waters which do not permanently or at any time during the year form part of the sea, it does include tidal rivers: s 23. "Tidal rivers" is not defined in the Cape Ord, but according to the Sea-Shore Act 21 of 1935 (s 1) and the Sea Fishery Act 12 of 1988 (s 1) the water and the bed of any tidal river form part of the sea. The abovementioned offence, although dealing principally with inland waters, accordingly also applies to the sea.
9 Sea Fishery Act of 1988 s 48 read with s 85(a) of the Cape Ord 19 of 1974.
10 15 of 1974 (chapter on coastal fishing).
11 "Waters", in respect of coastal fishing, is defined as the Indian Ocean and includes any semi-enclosed bay, estuary and that portion of any tidal river which lies downstream or seaward of a point of demarcation fixed in terms of regulations: s 1.
12 Ss 183 185(1)(a).

482 Pollution detrimental to other aquatic environments The provisions dealing with water pollution control that have been discussed all result in the conservation of aquatic habitats and their resources. Certain provisions, however, deal with water pollution control with the explicit aim of conserving aquatic resources. Certain provincial nature conservation ordinances make it an offence for anyone to pollute water with substances that are injurious, or are likely or liable to become injurious, to fish or fish food.[1]

1 Tvl Ord 12 of 1983 s 84; Natal Ord 15 of
  1974 ss 152 and 208(1)(b) and Cape Ord 19
  of 1974 ss 48 and 86(1)(d).

483 Pollution detrimental to public health Almost all water pollution control is aimed at protecting the health of people, but certain provisions relate specifically to the protection of public health. Among the functions entrusted to the Department of Health by the Health Act[1] is the promotion of a safe and healthy environment.[2] The Minister of Health may delegate this function to a provincial government, subject to such regulations and conditions as may be imposed, and the minister must refund the provincial government for the expenses incurred in performing this function.[3] If the minister is satisfied after consultation with the local authority that such local authority is able to perform this function, or if the local authority requests delegation of this function, it can be delegated to the local authority and the minister must refund to the local authority expenses incurred.[4] More particularly, every local authority must adopt all lawful, necessary and reasonably practicable measures to prevent the occurrence within its district of any nuisance, unhygienic condition, offensive condition, or other condition which will or could be harmful or dangerous to the health of any person within its district or the district of any other local authority, or, where a nuisance or condition has occurred, to abate, or cause to be abated, such nuisance, or remedy, or cause to be remedied, such condition, as the case may be.[5] A local authority must also prevent the pollution of any water intended for the use of the inhabitants of its district, irrespective of whether such water is obtained from sources within or outside its district, or purify water which has become so polluted.[6] An abatement notice procedure has been prescribed in cases where in the opinion of a local authority a condition has arisen in its district which is of such a nature as to be offensive or a danger to health unless immediately remedied.[7] Finally, the minister has extensive powers to make regulations for the control of water pollution.[8]

The Sea-Shore Act[9] makes specific provision for the protection of human health against pollution of the seashore or the sea. Notwithstanding the provisions of the Health Act, it empowers the Minister of Health by notice in the *Government Gazette* to declare that any local authority may exercise, in respect of the seashore and the sea situated within or adjoining its area of jurisdiction, any of the powers that are conferred by the Health Act on a local authority.[10]

Moreover, the Minister of Environmental Affairs and Tourism (whose powers in this respect may be delegated to the executive committee of a province)[11] may make regulations or by notice in the *Government Gazette* authorise a local authority to make regulations for the prevention or regulation of deposit or discharge upon the seashore or in the sea of offal, rubbish, or anything liable to be a nuisance or danger to health.[12]

The International Health Regulations Act,[13] which will be discussed in another section, also contains a number of provisions pertaining specifically to the protection of human health against water pollution. Furthermore, water can, as a "foodstuff", be controlled in terms of the Foodstuffs, Cosmetics and Disinfectants Act.[14] The Minister of Health may make regulations prescribing the nature and composition of a foodstuff or standards for the consumption, purity or quality of it.[15] The minister may also prescribe any foodstuff to be deemed harmful or injurious to human health.[16]

Finally, reference can also be made to the control over the dumping (and other forms of disposal) of certain hazardous substances, and of radioactive waste in terms of the Hazardous Substances Act.[17]

1 63 of 1977.
2 S 14(1)(c).
3 S 14(2).
4 S 20(2) (3) (4).
5 S 20(1)(b).
6 S 20(1)(c).
7 S 27.
8 Ss 34 36A 37 38 39.
9 21 of 1935.
10 S 7(1).
11 S 11(2).
12 S 10(1)(d).
13 28 of 1974.
14 54 of 1972. "Foodstuff" means any article or substance ordinarily eaten or drunk by man: s 1.
15 S 15(1)(a) read with ss 5(5) and 18.
16 S 15(1)(e) read with ss 5(5) and 18.
17 15 of 1973.

484 Pollution of harbours Regulations issued in terms of the repealed South African Transport Services Act,[1] now applicable by virtue of the Legal Succession to the South African Transport Services Act,[2] provide for control over waste, including oil, in the water of harbours.[3] It is an offence for anyone to throw or deposit into any harbour stones, gravel, ballast, carcasses, cargo, dirt, ashes, bottles, baskets, rubbish, objectionable or malodorous matter or any other article or substance of whatsoever nature, or to spill paint in any harbour or cause or allow oily or waxy effluent or oil of any description, whether or not such oil is of a mineral, animal or vegetable origin, to be discharged or to escape into a harbour.[4]

If oil of any description or flammable liquid, effluent or water from an uncleaned oil tank, fish-oil tank, bilge or hold which has contained oil, flammable liquid or cargo of any kind, is discharged or allowed to escape into a harbour from a ship, the master of such ship will be deemed to have committed a breach of this regulation and will be personally liable to punishment for the breach and, in addition, will be liable for any costs that may be incurred by Transnet Ltd.[5]

If any act that constitutes a contravention of this regulation results in the obstruction of any berth in the harbour, the owner or master of the ship responsible for the obstruction must forthwith cause the obstruction to be removed at his or her expense, failing which Transnet Ltd may remove the obstruction at the expense of the owner or master, and should any other ship sustain damage as a result of the obstruction, the said owner or master will be liable for such damage.[6]

The master of every ship that is berthed alongside a quay or jetty must cause all the discharge outlets of the ship facing the quay or jetty to be closed or provided with adequate covers to prevent any inadvertent discharge of water or effluent onto the quay or jetty surface, bollards, moorings, telephone cables, fenders or hose connections.[7]

The International Health Regulations Act[8] provides that every seaport or inland port must be provided with an effective system for the removal and safe disposal of excrement, refuse, waste water, condemned food, and other matter dangerous to health.[9] Moreover, a health authority is empowered to adopt all practicable measures to control the discharge from any ship of sewage and refuse which might contaminate the waters of a port, river or canal.[10] It is an offence for the master of a ship or person in charge of any other means of transport to cause or permit any ballast, or refuse of any kind, to be ejected from the ship or other means of transport and a duty is cast upon such persons to cause all such matters to be removed to a place set apart for that purpose, or otherwise to dispose of as the port health officer may direct.[11] Moreover, when a cattle ship is in a filthy condition, it must be cleaned in an area designated by the health officer.[12] The port health officer, after consultation with the port captain, may require the master of the ship to keep all water-closets and latrines on the ship closed while in port.[13] Contravention of any of these provisions is an offence.[14]

It should be noted that the Marine Pollution (Control and Civil Liability) Act[15] applies to any harbour under the jurisdiction of Transnet Ltd and to any fishing harbour.[16]

1 65 of 1981 s 73.
2 9 of 1989 s 21(2).
3 *Government Gazette* 8124 GN R562, 26 March 1982 reg 38.
4 Ibid.
5 Ibid.
6 Ibid.
7 Ibid.
8 28 of 1974.
9 Art 14(3) of the Schedule to the Act.
10 Art 30 of the Schedule to the Act.

11 *Government Gazette* 4878 GN R2001, 24 October 1975 reg 28(1).
12 Reg 28(2).
13 Reg 28(3).
14 Reg 34(1). Cf also reg 34(2) for the personal liability of the master of the ship.
15 6 of 1981.
16 Cf the definition of "prohibited area" in s 1(1) of the Act, read with the definition of "internal waters" in the Marine Traffic Act 2 of 1981 s 1.

AIR POLLUTION CONTROL

INTRODUCTION

485 Private law remedies Private law remedies such as an interdict and the *actio legis Aquiliae* have traditionally been available to victims of air pollution.[1] However, in spite of their value to affected individuals, these remedies are not geared towards protecting the public interest.[2] For the latter purpose, reliance must be placed upon legislation.

1 As regards an interdict, cf *Herrington v Johannesburg Municipality* 1909 TH 179; *Winshaw v Miller* 1916 CPD 439; *Graham v Dittman & Son* 1917 TPD 288 and *Wynberg*
Municipality v Dreyer 1920 AD 439.
2 Cf Fuggle and Rabie *Environmental Concerns in SA* 38–41.

486 Control legislation The Atmospheric Pollution Prevention Act[1] provides for the uniform and comprehensive control of almost all air pollution. The only other legislation which deals with limited aspects of air pollution control are the Health Act,[2] regulations in terms of the Minerals Act[3] and the National Road Traffic Act.[4] At the time of writing it seems likely that the Atmospheric Pollution Prevention Act will shortly be replaced by new legislation.

1 45 of 1965. On air pollution control generally see Petrie, Burns and Bray "Air Pollution" in Fuggle and Rabie *Environmental Management in SA* 417; Ashby 1987 *SA Public Law* 140.
2 63 of 1977. See par 496 post.
3 50 of 1991 (although this Act has been repealed, the regulations are still, arguably, in force: see par 456 ante. See par 525 post for discussion of regs.
4 93 of 1996. See par 520 post.

487 Administrative bodies The Atmospheric Pollution Prevention Act[1] has been administered by the Minister of Environmental Affairs and Tourism since April 1995, whereas previously it was administered by the Minister of Health. The official who is primarily responsible for the administration of the Act is the chief air pollution control officer,[2] who is assisted by inspectors.[3] Other officials may also be involved in the application of the Act,[4] while many provisions are administered by local authorities. The Act provides for a defence against the liability of the chief officer, inspector or local authority for state action in terms of the Act, which action allegedly caused damage to property or personal injury or which detrimentally affected the rights of any person: the defence is available if the body involved has used the best known or the only or most practicable methods and has acted without negligence in the exercise of his or her powers or the performance of his or her duties.[5]

The Act establishes the National Air Pollution Advisory Committee.[6] Its functions are to:

(a) advise the minister on all matters relating to the control, abatement and prevention of air pollution;

(b) study and report to the minister on measures taken outside the Republic for the control of air pollution;

(c) stimulate interest in the problem of air pollution and for that purpose arrange for the delivery of lectures and addresses, the holding of discussions and the display of pictures, cinematograph films or exhibitions relating to that problem; and

(d) advise the minister generally in regard to any matter relating to air pollution as to which the committee considers it necessary to advise the minister or which the minister may refer to the committee for its advice.[7]

Finally, provision is made for the establishment by the minister of the Air Pollution Appeal Board[8] and of regional appeal boards.[9]

1 45 of 1965.
2 S 6(1)(a).
3 S 6(1)(b). See s 7(1) for powers of the chief officers and inspectors.
4 S 6(2).
5 S 7(3). A certificate to this effect, signed by the director-general, must be accepted by the court as *prima facie* evidence: s 7(3).
6 S 2(1). It consists of not less than seven and not more than 11 persons, appointed by the minister. Subcommittees may also be established: s 4.
7 S 3.
8 S 5(1)(a). The board hears and determines appeals in terms of ss 13, 35 or 38, or from decisions of a regional appeal board: s 5(1)(a). See pars 514 524 534 post.
9 S 5(1)(b). A regional appeal board hears and determines appeals from the decisions of local authorities in terms of s 25: s 5(1)(b). Cf s 5(2) and (3) in respect of membership of the above bodies.

488 Classification of air pollution Air pollution may be classified in several ways,[1] but is subdivided in terms of the Atmospheric Pollution Prevention Act[2] into four different types, namely noxious or offensive gases, smoke, dust and vehicle emissions.[3]

1 Cf Fuggle and Rabie *Environmental Management in SA* 417–418.
2 45 of 1965.
3 Of these four types of air pollutants, the first three are defined in s 1(1), while vehicle emissions also relate to noxious or offensive gases.

489 Controlled areas The different types of air pollution can be controlled only in areas which have been declared by the Minister of Environmental Affairs and Tourism to be controlled areas.[1]

1 Atmospheric Pollution Prevention Act 45 of 1965 ss 8 14(1) 27(1) 36(1).

CONTROL OF NOXIOUS OR OFFENSIVE GASES

490 Scheduled processes A noxious or offensive gas[1] is subject to control only if it results from the operation of a scheduled process.[2]

1 Defined in Atmospheric Pollution Prevention Act 45 of 1965 s 1(1).
2 71 scheduled processes have so far been listed in Sch 2.

491 Controlled area The whole of South Africa has been declared a controlled area as far as the control of noxious or offensive gases is concerned.[1]

1 *Government Gazette* 2179 GN R1776, 4 October 1968 issued in terms of the Atmospheric Pollution Prevention Act 45 of 1965 s 8, which empowers the Minister of Health, after consideration of a report by the National Air Pollution Advisory Committee, and after consultation with the Minister of Economic Affairs, to establish controlled areas.

492 Control exercised by chief officer Control of noxious or offensive gases is undertaken by the Chief Air PollutionControl Officer (hereinafter referred to as the chief officer)[1] and his or her staff.

1 See Atmospheric Pollution Prevention Act 45 of 1965 ss 6–7 as to appointment and powers of the chief officer. Cf also the definition of "chief officer": s 1(1). The government mining engineer may be authorised to exercise, in consultation with the chief officer, the chief officer's function with reference to mines and works: s 6(2)(a). The chief inspector of explosives may, likewise, be authorised to exercise the chief officer's functions with regard to explosives factories: s 6(2)(b).

493 Registration certificates and provisional registration certificates Control of noxious or offensive gases is exercised in that no person may carry on a scheduled process in or on any premises[1] unless such person is the holder of a registration certificate.[2] Moreover, no erection, alteration or extension to any existing building or plant, which is intended to be used for the purpose of carrying on any scheduled process in or on any premises, may be effected unless the person in question is the holder of a provisional registration certificate.[3]

Application for registration certificates and provisional registration certificates must be lodged with the chief officer.[4] After consideration of any such application the chief officer must grant the application and issue a registration certificate or provisional registration certificate, as the case may be, if is satisfied that the best practicable means[5] are being adopted for preventing or reducing to a minimum the escape into the atmosphere of noxious or offensive gases produced or likely to be produced by the scheduled process in question.[6] If the chief officer is not satisfied, he or she must by written notice require the applicant to take the necessary steps within the specified period to effect the abovementioned prevention or reduction of air pollution.[7] An applicant who has undertaken these steps is entitled to the issue of a registration certificate or a provisional registration certificate, as the case may be.[8] However, this right, as well as the chief officer's consideration whether a provisional registration certificate should be granted,[9] are subject to an important proviso, namely that the chief officer must be satisfied that the scheduled process in question may reasonably be permitted to be carried on in the locality affected, having regard to the nature of that process, the character of the locality in question, the purposes for which other premises in such locality are used and any other considerations which in his or her opinion have a bearing on the matter, and that the operation of that process in or on the premises in question would not be in conflict with any town planning scheme in operation or in the course of preparation in respect of such locality.[10]

The period of validity of a provisional registration certificate is restricted.[11] After completion to the satisfaction of the chief officer of any building or plant in respect of which a provisional registration certificate has been issued, the chief officer must, on application by the holder of that certificate, issue to him or her a registration certificate.[12]

A registration certificate has no restricted period of validity, but is subject to the condition that all plant and apparatus used for the purpose of carrying on the particular scheduled process, and all air pollution prevention equipment must at all times be properly maintained and operated and that the holder of the certificate must ensure that all other necessary measures are taken to prevent the escape into the atmosphere of noxious or offensive gases.[13] Moreover, the chief officer may at any time by written notice require the holder of a registration certificate to take steps to ensure the more effective operation of the air pollution prevention appliances provided for in such certificate.[14] Furthermore, the chief officer may at any time by written notice require the holder of a registration certificate within a reasonable time to take such steps as may be reasonable – having regard to the cost involved – to ensure more effective air pollution prevention by means of some other or improved process or equipment specified in the notice.[15]

Failure by the holder of a registration certificate to comply with the conditions of the certificate or with any of the abovementioned notices, entitles the chief officer by yet another written notice to call upon such holder to comply with such conditions or notices within a reasonable time. Should the holder again fail to comply with the conditions or notices within the prescribed time, the chief officer may in his or her discretion cancel or suspend the registration certificate.[16]

Despite the enforcement provisions in the Atmospheric Pollution Prevention Act, including criminal offences,[17] the minister has seen fit on more than one occasion to apply to the High Court for an interdict requiring persons to cease operation of scheduled processes without the necessary registration certificate.[18]

1 "Premises" means any building or other structure together with the land on which it is situated (including adjoining land used in connection with any activities carried on in such building or structure) and includes any land without any buildings or other structures, and any locomotive, ship, boat or other vessel which operates or is present within the area of a local authority or the precincts of any harbour: Atmospheric Pollution Prevention Act 45 of 1965 s 1(1).

2 S 9(1)(a)(i). S 9(1)(a)(ii) requires a person who had been carrying on scheduled processes prior to *Government Gazette* 2179 GN R1776, 4 October 1968 to apply within three months after that date for a registration certificate.

3 S 9(1)(b). See also s 9(1)(c).

4 See par 492 ante.

5 The concept "best practicable means" is defined in s 1(1) to include the provision and maintenance of the appliances necessary to prevent air pollution, the effective care and operation of such appliances, and the adoption of any other methods which, having regard to local conditions and circumstances, the prevailing extent of technical knowledge and the cost likely to be involved, may be reasonably practicable and necessary for the protection of any section of

the public against air pollution. It is a flexible concept which is interpreted by the chief officer. The chief officer sees his or her task in interpreting this important concept as follows: "The task of the chief officer is to assess the problems of air cleaning associated with each type of process, of which there may be many examples in the country, and to decide what degree of air cleaning can be achieved, bearing in mind the different techniques available, the costs associated with their installation and operation and the effects which these costs will have on the ability of the firms concerned to operate without financial loss" (Boegman 1972 *Clean Air Journal* 1 (2) 9). It should be emphasised that the application of the best practicable means is prescribed with a view to the protection of the public against air pollution: s 1(1).

6 S 10(2)(a)(i) (2)(b)(i). For an illustration of the certification process, cf *Hichange Investments (Pty) Ltd v Cape Produce Co (Pty) Ltd t/a Pelts Products* [2004] 1 All SA 636 (E); 2004 2 SA 393 (E).

7 S 10(2)(a)(iii) (2)(b)(ii).

8 S 10(3).

9 See s 10(2)(b).

10 S 10(4).

11 S 11(1).

12 S 11(3).

13 S 12(1). Allowance is made for unavoidable pollution during the starting up, breakdown, shutting down or disturbance of the plant or apparatus; see s 12(1) proviso.

14 S 12(2).

15 S 12(3).

16 S 12(4).

17 S 9(2) read with s 46.

18 *Minister of Health & Welfare v Woodcarb (Pty) Ltd* 1996 3 SA 155 (N); *Minister of Health v Drums & Pails Reconditioning CC t/a Village Drums & Pails* 1997 3 SA 867 (N).

494 Appeals Anyone who is aggrieved by a decision of the chief officer refusing an application for a registration certificate or a provisional registration certificate or cancelling or suspending a registration certificate or provisional registration certificate[1] or imposing any requirements in terms of the abovementioned notices, may within one month appeal against such decision to the air pollution appeal board,[2] which may make such order as it may consider equitable and whose decision will be final.[3]

1 Atmospheric Pollution Prevention Act 45 of 1965 s 12(4) (cf s 12(1) to which s 13(1)(a) refers), does not mention a provisional registration certificate.

2 Established in terms of s 5(1)(a).

3 S 13(1)(a). Cf also s 13(1)(b) (2)–(3). Such an appeal board was established in 1973 to hear an appeal by Iscor against the chief officer's refusal of an application for the provisional registration certificate. See Rabie 1974 *THRHR* 186.

495 Offences It is an offence for any person to carry on a scheduled process in or on any premises if such person is not the holder of a registration certificate, or to effect the erection, alteration or extension of any building or plant which is intended to be used for the purpose of carrying on any scheduled process in or on any premises, if he or she is not the holder of a provisional registration certificate.[1]

1 Atmospheric Pollution Prevention Act 45 of 1965 s 9(2) read with s 46.

496 Gases causing nuisance Gases, vapours and smell may give rise to a nuisance in terms of the Health Act.[1]

1 63 of 1977 s 1(xxvii)(f) (g).

CONTROL OF SMOKE

497 Controlled areas Control of smoke[1] emanating from premises[2] can be effected only within a controlled area.[3] The first local authority had its area declared a controlled area in 1966. One year later there were 14 such controlled areas and today there are about 160.

1 "Smoke" includes soot, grit and gritty particles emitted in smoke: Atmospheric Pollution Prevention Act 45 of 1965 s 1(1).

2 See par 493 fn 1 ante.

3 The Minister of Health establishes a controlled area only after consultation with the Minister of Economic Affairs, and he or she does so by notice in the *Government Gazette*: s 14(1).

498 Control exercised by local authority Control of smoke emanating from premises is generally left in the hands of local authorities,[1] whose concurrence is therefore generally sought before an area is declared a controlled area.[2] However, where the local authority concerned so requests, the Minister of Environmental Affairs and Tourism,[3] or where a controlled area is not under the jurisdiction of a local authority,[4] the minister, may by notice in the *Government Gazette* direct that the control of smoke be exercised by the chief officer.[5] Moreover, where on account of a report submitted to him or her by the national air pollution advisory committee,[6] the minister is satisfied that smoke emanating from any premises is causing a nuisance, he or she may authorise the chief officer to apply the provisions of the Atmospheric Pollution Prevention Act relating to smoke control to the area where the premises in question are situated, even without the concurrence of the local authority concerned.[7] If in such an event the area in which the premises are situated is not a controlled area, the minister may by notice in the *Government Gazette* declare the area concerned a controlled area, even without the concurrence of the local authority concerned.[8]

1 "Local authority" is defined in the Atmospheric Pollution Prevention Act 45 of 1965 s 1(1).
2 S 14(2). Cf also s 14(3).
3 S 14(4).
4 S 14(5)(a).
5 Provision is also made in the lastmentioned instance for control by the local authority adjoining the controlled area in question: s 14(5)(b). Where the local authority concerned requests the minister that the powers relating to smoke control be exercised by

the chief officer, the costs incurred by the chief officer in the exercise of these powers may be recovered from the local authority in question: s 14(4).
6 Established in terms of s 2. Cf also ss 3–4.
7 S 14(6)(a).
8 S 14(6)(b). Any costs incurred by the chief officer in connection with the exercise of powers in terms of s 14(6)(a) or (b) may be recovered from the local authority concerned: s 14(6)(d).

499 Levels of control Depending upon the degree of air pollution and the sophistication of the local authority's control programme, different levels of smoke control may be distinguished. The first level consists of control over the installation and siting of fuel burning appliances and over the construction of chimneys,[1] as well as the procedure which is followed where smoke or other products of combustion cause a nuisance.[2] Use is also made of the power to enter upon premises for investigation purposes.[3] The second level of control is reached when regulations are promulgated by the local authority concerned.[4] A third level of control consists of an elaborate set of such regulations.[5] The fourth and most intensive level of control consists of the establishment of smoke control zones.[6]

1 Atmospheric Pollution Prevention Act 45 of 1965 ss 15–16.
2 S 17.
3 S 23.
4 S 18.
5 Ibid.
6 S 20.

500 Control of the installation and siting of fuel burning appliances and of the construction of chimneys There is a prohibition on the installation in or on any premises[1] of certain fuel burning appliances.[2] Moreover, even as regards those appliances which may be installed, prior written notice to the local authority concerned, or the chief officer, as the case may be, is required.[3] Provision is, however, made for certain exemptions.[4]

Local authorities may not approve plans which provide for the construction of chimneys or for the installation of fuel burning appliances, unless they are satisfied that the height of the chimney will as far as practicable be sufficient to prevent smoke or any other product of combustion from becoming prejudicial to health or a nuisance to occupiers of surrounding premises, and that the fuel burning appliance will be suitably sited in relation to other premises in the surrounding areas.[5]

1 See par 493 fn 1 ante.
2 "Fuel burning appliance" means any furnace, boiler or other appliance designed to

burn or capable of burning liquid fuel or gaseous fuel or wood, coal, anthracite or other solid fuel, or used to dispose of any material by burning or to subject solid fuel to any process involving the application of heat: Atmospheric Pollution Prevention Act 45 of 1965 s 1(1). Cf also s 15(4)(a).

3 S 15(2).

4 S 15(3). The installation of fuel burning appliances in dwelling-houses is exempted: s 15(3)(a). Exemption is also allowed in respect of fuel burning appliances if the installation thereof was commenced or any agreement for the acquisition thereof was entered into prior to the date on which the area in question became a declared area in terms of s 14(1): s 15(3)(b). Cf also s 15(5).

5 S 16.

501 Smoke constituting a nuisance A special abatement notice procedure is prescribed for the case where smoke causes a nuisance. If, as a result of representations made to it by any occupier[1] of premises,[2] a local authority is satisfied that smoke or any other product of combustion emanating from premises is a nuisance[3] to such occupier, the local authority will have a notice served[4] upon the person responsible[5] for such nuisance, calling upon that person to abate the nuisance within a specified period[6] and to take the necessary steps to prevent its recurrence.[7]

Failure to comply with such notice, apart from constituting an offence,[8] entitles the court to order the convicted person to take such steps as may be necessary to prevent a recurrence of the nuisance within a prescribed period.[9] Should the person within one month from conviction fail to take steps to the satisfaction of the local authority concerned, with a view to the abatement of the nuisance which gave rise to the conviction, the local authority concerned may itself execute works and install appliances and take such other steps as it may consider necessary to abate the nuisance; it may, moreover, recover the cost so incurred from the convicted person.[10]

1 "Occupier" means the occupier of those premises or of any particular part thereof: Atmospheric Pollution Prevention Act 45 of 1965 s 1(1).

2 See par 493 fn 1 ante.

3 A presumption is created in s 17(2) that smoke is deemed to be a nuisance if it is prejudicial to health or affects the reasonable comfort of the occupier(s) of adjoining or nearby premises, or affects the normal use of such premises.

4 See s 17(3) as to how the notice is to be served.

5 Cf s 17(3)(a)–(b).

6 As regards this period, consultation with the chief officer is prescribed: s 17(1).

7 Ibid.

8 See par 506 post.

9 S 17(4).

10 S 17(7). See also Health Act 63 of 1977 ss 20(1)(b) 27 39.

502 Smoke control regulations A local authority may make regulations ranging over a wide variety of issues relating to smoke control,[1] and it may provide for penalties for contraventions of these regulations.[2] However, such regulations will have effect only if they have been approved by the Minister of Environmental Affairs and Tourism on the recommendation of the national air pollution advisory committee, and have been promulgated by the minister through a notice in the *Government Gazette.*[3]

A special procedure, similar to the abatement notice procedure prescribed in relation to smoke causing a nuisance,[4] is provided in the event of contravention of such regulations. If smoke is emitted or emanates from any premises in contravention of any such regulation, the local authority concerned may cause to be served on the owner or occupier of such premises a written notice[5] calling upon him or her to bring about, within a prescribed period,[6] the cessation of the emission or emanation of smoke from the premises.[7] However, such notice may be served in respect of premises in or on which a scheduled process is being operated only after consultation with the chief officer.[8]

Failure to comply with this notice constitutes an offence.[9] Moreover, if within one month from the date of conviction for such an offence, steps have not been taken to the satisfaction of the local authority concerned to comply with the notice, the local authority may cause such works to be undertaken and such appliances to be installed and such other measures to be taken as it may consider necessary to bring about the cessation of the emission or emanation of the smoke which was the subject of the notice; it may, in addition, recover the cost incurred from the person upon whom the notice was served.[10]

With the consent of the premier concerned and the Ministers of Economic Affairs and of Health, a local authority may enter into contracts for the supply of fuel which will facilitate or render possible the application of or compliance with regulations made by the local authority with a view to smoke control, and may indemnify or guarantee any producer or supplier of fuel against loss, or itself act as dealer in such fuel or make a contribution towards the cost of producing such fuel or of establishing an industry for the production of such fuel.[11]

1 Atmospheric Pollution Prevention Act 45 of 1965 s 18(1).
2 S 18(4).
3 S 18(5).
4 See par 501 ante.
5 Cf s 19(2) as to the method of serving the notice.
6 Cf s 19(4).
7 S 19(1).
8 S 19(3).
9 S 19(5). Failure to comply with the regulations, which failure gave rise to the notice, may, of course, also constitute an offence, as has just been mentioned; cf s 18(4).
10 S 19(6)(a). Cf also s 19(6)(b).
11 S 21.

503 Establishment of smoke control zones Provision is made for a local authority to issue an order declaring the area within its jurisdiction,[1] or any part of that area, to be a smoke control zone, and prohibiting the emanation or emission from any premises in that zone of smoke which exceeds a certain degree of colour or density.[2] A condition for the exercise of this power is that it must be confirmed by the Minister of Environmental Affairs and Tourism after consultation with the national air pollution advisory committee, and promulgated by the minister through notice in the *Government Gazette*.[3] A further condition is that the local authority, before approaching the minister, must have followed the prescribed procedure whereby provision is made for objections to the proposed establishment of a smoke control zone to be accomodated.[4] Failure to comply with the local authority's order constitutes an offence.[5]

1 Cf Atmospheric Pollution Prevention Act 45 of 1965 s 20(2).
2 S 20(1). Cf also s 20(3) (9).
3 Ibid. Cf also s 20(6)–(8).
4 S 20(4)–(5).
5 S 20(11).

504 Appeals Any person upon whom an abatement notice[1] has been served is granted an opportunity to appeal against such notice. First of all, if this notice has been served by an officer or servant of a local authority by virtue of delegated powers,[2] the person concerned may within 14 days appeal to the local authority itself, which may confirm or withdraw the notice. Furthermore, if the person is aggrieved by this decision of the local authority, or, generally, if any person upon whom an abatement notice has been served, wishes to do so, he or she may within 30 days after the date on which such decision was given or the notice was served, appeal against the decision or notice to the regional appeal board,[3] which may confirm or set aside the decision or notice. The decision of the board is subject to a right of appeal to the air pollution appeal board.[4]

1   In terms of the Atmospheric Pollution Prevention Act 45 of 1965 s 17 or s 19.
2   Cf s 22(1)–(2).

3   Established in terms of s 5(1)(b).
4   S 25(1). Cf also s 25(2)–(3).

505 Expenditure Authority is given to a local authority to incur expenditure in connection with the exercise of its powers in terms of the Atmospheric Pollution Prevention Act.[1]

1   45 of 1965 s 26.

506 Offences There are a number of offences relating to smoke control provisions. Installation of fuel burning appliances contrary to the abovementioned provisions[1] amounts to an offence.[2] Failure to comply with an abatement notice, as explained above, is an offence.[3] Contravention of smoke control regulations may also amount to an offence.[4] Anyone who fails to comply with an order relating to a smoke control zone[5] is likewise guilty of an offence.[6] Finally, failure to supply the required information concerning control to a local authority, or knowingly furnishing false or misleading information in any material respect, amounts to an offence.[7]

1   Par 500 ante.
2   Atmospheric Pollution Prevention Act 45 of 1965 s 15(6) read with s 46.
3   Ss 17(4) and 19(5) read with s 46.

4   S 18(4).
5   Par 503 ante.
6   S 20(11) read with s 46.
7   S 24(2) read with s 46.

507 State not bound Although the Atmospheric Pollution Prevention Act[1] generally does bind the state, the state is not bound by the provisions dealing with smoke control.[2] There is, however, a prescribed procedure whereby some measure of control over excessive smoke[3] emanation from premises as a result of the operation of a fuel burning appliance controlled by the state, can be exercised.[4] Moreover, where a chimney is to be constructed or a fuel burning appliance[5] is to be installed in or on any premises which are under the control of the state, notice of the proposed action must be given to the local authority in whose area of jurisdiction the premises are situated.[6]

1   45 of 1965.
2   S 47(1).
3   Ie smoke in excess of the standards prescribed in terms of s 20(1)(b) or of any regulations made under the Act.
4   S 47(3)–(6). The local authority concerned can give notice of such excessive smoke emanation through the Minister of Environmental Affairs and Tourism to the minister whose department is concerned or to the premier concerned, who must cause such steps to be taken as may be necessary and practicable to prevent or minimise the emission of such smoke; he or she must also furnish a report to the Minister of Health with regard to any steps taken in pursuance of the notice. Where the department concerned is that of health, the notice must be given to the Minister of Health him or herself, who must then cause such steps to be taken as have been mentioned above: s 47(3). Should such smoke emanate from any premises as a

result of the operation of any fuel burning appliance controlled by Transnet, the local authority concerned may give notice of that smoke emission directly to the Minister of Transport who must cause such steps to be taken as may be necessary to prevent or minimise such smoke emission: s 47(4). The Minister of Transport must annually furnish a comprehensive report to the Minister of Environmental Affairs and Tourism containing details of any such complaints and a brief summary of the action taken in pursuance of each such complaint: s 47(5). The latter minister is obliged annually to table before the House of Assembly *inter alia* a copy of every notice sent to him or her by a local authority in terms of s 47(3) during the preceding calendar year (s 47(6)(a)(i)), a copy of every report submitted to him or her in terms of s 47(3) or (5) during such calendar year (s 47(6)(a)(ii)) and a statement concerning any complaints lodged with him or her during such calendar year, due to the actions of his or her own department, and concerning the steps taken in pursuance thereof (s 47(5)(a)(iii)). Likewise, a premier must annually lay before the provincial legislature concerned a copy of every notice sent to him or her by a local authority in terms of

s 47(3) during the preceding calendar year (s 47(6)(b)(i)) and a copy of every subsequent report sent to the Minister of Environmental Affairs and Tourism (s 47(6)(b)(ii)).

5 Par 500 ante.
6 S 47(2).

CONTROL OF DUST

508 Dust control areas Dust control areas may be established by the Minister of Environmental Affairs and Tourism.[1]

1 The minister does so by notice in the *Government Gazette* and only after consideration of a report by the national air pollution advisory committee and after consultation with the Minister of State Expenditure: Atmospheric Pollution Prevention Act 45 of

1965 s 27(1). See generally Reilly *A Critical Analysis of the Environmental Controls in force within the RSA with particular reference to Mine Dumps and the Legislation applicable thereto* LLM thesis University of the Witwatersrand 1993.

509 Dust causing a nuisance Any person who, in a dust control area, on account of certain specified actions[1] which produce dust,[2] causes a nuisance to persons residing or present in the vicinity, must take the prescribed steps or, where no steps have been prescribed, adopt the best practicable means[3] for the abatement of such nuisance.[4] Dust can also give rise to a nuisance in terms of the Health Act.[5]

1 Atmospheric Pollution Prevention Act 45 of 1965 ss 22 28(1)(a)–(b) 29(1).
2 "Dust" means any solid matter in a fine or disintegrated form which is capable of being dispersed or suspended in the atmosphere: s 1(1).
3 See ss 28(2) and 1(1) for a definition of "best practicable means".

4 Ss 28(1) 29(1). Cf s 30 for the procedure to be adopted where the provisions of s 28(1)(b) apply, but the person obliged to abate the nuisance is deceased or (in the case of a corporate body) has ceased to exist. The government mining engineer acts for the chief officer; cf s 6(2)(a).
5 63 of 1977 s 1(xxvii)(f).

510 Dust control levy account A dust control levy account, to be administered by the Director-General: Environmental Affairs and Tourism, may be established by the Minister of Environmental Affairs and Tourism if, after consultation with the Minister of Mineral and Energy Affairs, the Minister of State Expenditure and the national air pollution advisory committee, he or she is satisfied that special provision is necessary to meet wholly or in part any expenditure required to be incurred for the more effective prevention of air pollution by dust.[1]

1 Atmospheric Pollution Prevention Act 45 of 1965 s 31.

511 Disposal of assets by mine ceasing operations If the government mining engineer is of the opinion that in view of the known and disclosed ore reserves of any mine, that mine is likely to cease mining operations within a period of five years, he or she must in writing advise the Minister of Mineral and Energy Affairs and the owner of that mine accordingly and forward a copy of such advice to the Minister of Environmental Affairs and Tourism.[1] After the date of receipt of such advice, no owner of a mine may, without the consent of the Minister of Health,[2] dispose of any asset of that mine before he or she has obtained a certificate by the chief officer to the effect that the necessary steps have been taken or that adequate provision has been made to prevent air pollution by dust.[3]

1 Atmospheric Pollution Prevention Act 45 of
  1965 s 32(1).
2 After consultation with the Minister of

Mineral and Energy Affairs.
3 S 32(2).

512 Regulations The Minister of Environmental Affairs and Tourism may, after consideration of a report by the national air pollution advisory committee, make regulations in respect of a number of issues relating to dust control.[1]

1 Atmospheric Pollution Prevention Act 45 of
  1965 s 33. Cf also s 34.

513 Appeals Any person who is aggrieved by any notice served upon him or her in terms of provisions of the Atmospheric Pollution Prevention Act[1] relating to dust control, may within 30 days after the date on which such notice was served (or within such further period as the air pollution board may allow), lodge an appeal with the air pollution appeal board against the notice. The board, whose decision will be final, may confirm, modify or set aside such notice.[2]

1 45 of 1965.
2 S 35(1). Cf also s 35(2)–(3).

514 Offences Contravention of a number of provisions relating to dust control amounts to an offence. Thus, anyone failing to take the prescribed steps (or to adopt the best practicable means) to abate the nuisance created by dust, as has been set out above,[1] is guilty of an offence.[2] Any person who fails to pay his or her contribution to the dust control levy account[3] or to furnish the required particulars in connection with it, also commits an offence.[4] Disposal of assets of a mine in contravention of the provisions set out above[5] amounts to an offence.[6] Finally, failure to grant admission to the chief officer or any other authorised person to enter upon premises within a dust control area where in his or her opinion a nuisance exists or may exist, or obstruction or interference with such person in the performance of his or her functions relating to dust control, constitutes an offence.[7]

1 Par 509 ante.
2 Atmospheric Pollution Prevention Act 45 of
  1965 ss 28(3) 29(4) read with s 46.
3 Par 510 ante.

4 S 31(6) read with s 46.
5 Par 511 ante.
6 S 32(2) read with s 46.
7 S 34(4) read with s 46.

CONTROL OF VEHICLE EMISSIONS

515 Controlled areas The provisions of the Atmospheric Pollution Prevention Act[1] relating to control of vehicle emissions apply only in areas under the jurisdiction of local authorities in respect of which they have been declared to be applicable by the Minister of Environmental Affairs.[2]

1 45 of 1965.
2 S 36(1). The minister does this by notice in
  the *Government Gazette* after consultation

with the national air pollution advisory
committee and the premier of the province
in which such area is situated.

516 Control exercised by local authority In the first place the co-operation of the local authority is sought in that no area is declared a controlled area without the concurrence of the local authority having jurisdiction in that area.[1] Moreover, the powers granted by the Atmospheric Pollution Prevention Act with regard to vehicle emission control are in principle to be exercised by the local authority who has jurisdiction in the controlled area in question.[2] However, if after consideration of a report submitted to him or her by the national air pollution advisory committee the Minister of Environmental Affairs and Tourism is of the opinion that a local authority has not satisfactorily exercised these powers, he or she may, after consultation with the Minister of Finance and with the local authority concerned, by notice in the *Government Gazette* direct that such powers be exercised by the chief officer.[3]

1 Atmospheric Pollution Prevention Act 45 of 1965 s 36(2). As has been pointed out (par 498 ante) the same applies in principle to controlled areas as far as smoke control is concerned, except that in the case of smoke control, controlled areas may in exceptional instances be declared even without the concurrence of the local authority concerned: s 14(6)(b).

2 S 36(3).

3 S 36(4). The costs incurred by the chief officer in the exercise of these powers may be recovered from the local authority concerned: s 36(4).

517 Control procedure Any authorised person[1] may require the driver of any vehicle on a public road within a controlled area to stop such vehicle, and carry out the prescribed examination of that vehicle on such road. Alternatively the authorised person may serve or cause to be served upon the registered owner of such vehicle a written notice[2] calling upon the owner to submit that vehicle, within a prescribed period and at a specified place, to the prescribed examination.[3]

If the examination of the vehicle reveals to the satisfaction of the examiner that noxious or offensive gases[4] are being emitted from such vehicle contrary to the provisions of regulations,[5] the examiner must serve or cause to be served on the registered owner of that vehicle a written notice[6] calling upon him or her to take the necessary steps for the prevention of such air pollution and to submit the vehicle to a further examination.[7]

1 Cf Atmospheric Pollution Prevention Act 45 of 1965 s 40.

2 Cf s 37(3).

3 S 37(1).

4 Defined in s 1(1).

5 Promulgated in terms of s 39. This section empowers the Minister of Environmental Affairs and Tourism to prohibit the use on a public road within a controlled area of any vehicle from which noxious or offensive gases exceeding a certain degree are emitted: s 39(1)(a).

6 Cf s 37(3).

7 S 37(2).

518 Appeals Any person who is aggrieved by any notice served upon him or her to take the necessary steps aimed at air pollution prevention and to submit the vehicle for a further examination,[1] may within 14 days after the date on which such notice was served (or within an extended period allowed by the air pollution appeal board), lodge an appeal with the air pollution appeal board against the notice; the board, whose decision will be final, may confirm, modify or set aside such notice.[2]

1 In terms of the Atmospheric Pollution Prevention Act 45 of 1965 s 37(2).

2 S 38(1). Cf also s 38(2).

519 Offences Anyone who fails to comply with the provisions of a notice, as explained above, is guilty of an offence.[1] It is also an offence to fail to stop a vehicle on a public road when requested to do so by an authorised person, or to refuse admission to such vehicle to such authorised person or to obstruct or interfere with such person in the performance of his or her functions with regard to vehicle emission control.[2]

1 Atmospheric Pollution Prevention Act 45 of 1965 s 37(4). This section also renders failure to comply with any requirement of s 37 an offence.

2 S 40(4).

520 Control of vehicle emissions at provincial level The Minister of Transport may, after consultation with the MECs, issue regulations regarding the emission of exhaust gas, smoke, fuel, oil, visible vapour, sparks, ash or grit from any vehicle which is operated on a public road.[1] The National Road Traffic Regulations[2] provide that no person may operate on a public road a motor vehicle if the exhaust gas or smoke from the engine is so dense as to cause a nuisance to, or obstruct the vision of other road users.[3]

1 National Road Traffic Act 93 of 1996 s 75(1)(e). See also title ROADS AND ROAD TRANSPORT.

2 *Government Gazette* 20963 GN R225, 17 March 2000.
3 Reg 209(c).

MISCELLANEOUS PROVISIONS

521 Right of entry upon land The chief officer or a local authority (or their delegates)[1] may enter upon land[2] for the purpose of carrying out any functions in terms of the Atmospheric Pollution Prevention Act.[3]

1 Cf also Atmospheric Pollution Prevention Act 45 of 1965 s 43(3).
2 Except land which constitutes the explosives area of any explosives factory: s 43(1).

3 S 43(1). They may take with them the necessary assistants, workmen, vehicles, appliances, instruments and materials.

522 Occupier and owner of building works Where the consent of the owner is required for works which are reasonably necessary in or in connection with a building in order to enable the building to be used for any particular purpose without contravention of any of the provisions of the Atmospheric Pollution Prevention Act,[1] and the occupier is unable to obtain such consent, and if he or she considers that the whole or any portion of the cost required to carry out the works should be borne by such owner or some other person, he or she may apply to a court for the necessary order.[2]

1 45 of 1965.
2 S 42.

523 State contributions The state may contribute[1] towards the expenditure incurred by any person in connection with research aimed at combating air pollution[2] or by a local authority in connection with the acquisition of equipment used to combat air pollution.[3]

1 Contributions from funds made available by Parliament are made by the Minister of Environmental Affairs and Tourism in consultation with the Minister of Finance:

Atmospheric Pollution Prevention Act 45 of 1965 s 45A.
2 S 45A(a).
3 S 45A(b).

524 Disclosure of information No information relating to any manufacturing process or trade secret used in carrying on any undertaking which has been obtained in terms of the Atmospheric Pollution Prevention Act[1] may be disclosed without the consent of the person carrying on such undertaking. Exemptions are allowed if the disclosure was made in connection with the performance of functions in terms of the Act or for the purpose of legal proceedings arising out of the Act.[2] This provision is now subject to the interim Constitution's[3] determination concerning access to information held by the state and to the Promotion of Access to Information Act.[4]

1 45 of 1965.
2 S 41(1). Disclosure contrary to the provisions

of s 41(1) amounts to an offence: s 41(2) read with s 46.

3 Constitution of the Republic of SA 200 of
   1993 s 23. See title CONSTITUTIONAL LAW.

4 2 of 2000.

AIR POLLUTION CONTROL IN MINES AND IN THE WORKPLACE

525 Protection of persons in mines and works Protection of persons in mines and works[1] against the hazards of air pollution ensues in terms of regulations[2] issued under the Mines and Works Act,[3] the current status of which are discussed above.[4] These regulations are extensive[5] and provide *inter alia* that no person is allowed to enter or remain in any place in a mine or works if the air contains harmful smoke, gas, fumes or dust perceptible by sight, smell or other senses, unless such person is wearing effective apparatus to prevent the inhalation of such pollution.[6] Excessive concentration of such air pollution may be specifically decreed by the director-general. This implies that no person may work in a place where such a degree of air pollution is present.[7] Workmen have to be withdrawn if the workings of a mine are dangerously polluted by inflammable or noxious gas.[8] There are also provisions relating to adequate ventilation.[9] Specific air quality standards are prescribed with regard to the workings of mines.[10] Special provisions apply to the use of internal combustion engines underground in mines.[11] No dust, fumes or smoke from any dust or fume extraction system may be discharged into the atmosphere unless adequate provision has been made to ensure that such discharge is harmless and inoffensive.[12] The regulations also provide that every mine dump must be covered with soil or sludge or otherwise be dealt with in order to prevent the dissemination of any form of pollution such as dust, smoke or fumes.[13]

Finally, regulations[14] issued in terms of the Machinery and Occupational Safety Act[15] and now applicable by virtue of the Occupational Health and Safety Act,[16] relate to the health of persons in their workplace.

1 Cf the definitions of "mine" and "works" in the Minerals Act 50 of 1991 s 1 (now repealed) and "mine" in the Mineral and Petroleum Resources Development Act 28 of 2002.

2 *Government Gazette* 2741 GN R992, 26 June 1970.

3 27 of 1956.

4 Par 456 ante.

5 See, generally, ch 10.

6 *Government Gazette* 2741 GN R992, 26 June 1970 regs 10 1 1, 10 6 4.

7 Reg 10 1 2.

8 Reg 10 6 5.

9 Cf regs 10 3 1, 10 6 1–3.

10 Regs 10 6 6 et seq.

11 Regs 10 25 1 et seq.

12 Reg 10 4.

13 Reg 5 10.

14 *Government Gazette* 10988 GN R2281, 19 October 1987.

15 6 of 1983.

16 85 of 1993 s 43(5).

CONTROL OF RADIATION

NUCLEAR LEGISLATION

526 General During July 1991 South Africa acceded to the Nuclear Nonproliferation Treaty of 1968 and subsequently, during September 1991, entered into a comprehensive safeguards agreement with the International Atomic Energy Agency. New legislation was accordingly required to give effect to these developments. This was accomplished by the Nuclear Energy Act of 1993,[1] which replaced the Nuclear Energy Act of 1982.[2] Since then, the 1993 Act has been replaced by two new Acts: the (new) Nuclear Energy Act[3] and the National Nuclear Regulator Act.[4]

1 131 of 1993. See generally on radiation in environmental context Le Roux, Van As, Burns, De Beer and Van der Merwe "Radiation" in Fuggle and Rabie (eds) *Environmental Management in SA* 544. See also title ENERGY.

2 92 of 1982. This Act, in its turn, replaced the Nuclear Installations (Licensing and Security) Act 43 of 1963 and the Atomic Energy Act 90 of 1967, which latter Act substituted the original Atomic Energy Act 35 of 1948.

3 46 of 1999.

4 47 of 1999.

527 Nuclear Energy Act The Nuclear Energy Act[1] is, by and large, not directly relevant to issues relating to environmental conservation, but it establishes a framework within which the control of radiation is pursued, so it will not be discussed in detail in this Chapter. The objectives of the Act are to:

(a)   provide for the establishment of the South African Nuclear Energy Corporation Limited, a public company wholly owned by the state, to define the corporation's functions and powers and its financial and operational accountability, and provide for its governance and management by a board of directors and a chief executive officer;

(b)   provide for responsibilities for the implementation and application of the Safeguards Agreement and any additional protocols entered into by the Republic and the International Atomic Energy Agency in support of the Nuclear Non-Proliferation Treaty acceded to by the Republic;

(c)   regulate the acquisition and possession of nuclear fuel, certain nuclear and related material and certain related equipment, as well as the importation and exportation of, and certain other acts and activities relating to, that fuel, material and equipment in order to comply with the international obligations of the Republic; and

(d)   prescribe measures regarding the discarding of radioactive waste and the storage of irradiated nuclear fuel.[2]

1 46 of 1999; see title ENERGY.

3 Long title to the Act.

528 Control over radioactive waste Except with the written authorisation of the Minister of Mineral and Energy Affairs, no person, institution, organisation or body may dispose of, store or reprocess any radioactive waste[1] or irradiated fuel (when the latter is external to the spent fuel pool).[2] The Nuclear Energy Act also regulates (including the prohibition of the disposal of) nuclear material of various kinds, which could be environmentally harmful.[3] A person is guilty of an offence upon performing or carrying out any restricted act or activity without the necessary authorisation, or in contravention of the relevant authorisation or any condition imposed in respect thereof.[4]

The authority over the management and discarding of radioactive waste and the storage of irradiated nuclear fuel vests in the minister.[5] The minister, in consultation with the Minister of Environmental Affairs and Tourism and the Minister of Water Affairs and Forestry, may make regulations prescribing the manner of management, storage and discarding of radioactive waste and irradiated nuclear fuel.[6] The minister must perform that function with due regard to the provisions of the National Nuclear Regulator Act.[7] Except where authorised by a ministerial authority issued under the Hazardous Substances Act,[8] no person may, without the written permission of the minister, discard radioactive waste in any manner or cause it to be so discarded.[9] Except with the written permission of the minister, no person may store any irradiated nuclear fuel or cause it to be stored.[10] A permission may be granted subject to any conditions that the minister, in concurrence with the Minister of Environmental

Affairs and Tourism and the Minister of Water Affairs and Forestry, deems fit to impose.[11] The conditions so imposed will be additional to any conditions contained in a nuclear authorisation under the National Nuclear Regulator Act.[12]

1 "Radioactive waste" is any radioactive material destined to be disposed of as waste material (Nuclear Energy Act 46 of 1999 s 1).
2 S 34(1)(s).
3 Cf s 34.
4 S 56(1)(d). The maximum penalty is a fine or ten years' imprisonment (s 56(2)(c)).
5 S 45(1).
6 S 45(2).
7 47 of 1999: Nuclear Energy Act 46 of 1999 s 45(3).
8 15 of 1973.
9 Nuclear Energy Act 46 of 1999 s 46(1).
10 S 46(2).
11 S 46(3).
12 47 of 1999.

529 National Nuclear Regulator Act The National Nuclear Regulator Act[1] is aimed at establishing a National Nuclear Regulator, and is intended to provide for safety standards and regulatory practices for protection of persons, property and the environment against nuclear damage.[2] Chapter 2 of the Act deals with the establishment, and administrative, management and financial matters of the regulator. The objects of the regulator are to:

(a) provide for the protection of persons, property and the environment against nuclear damage through the establishment of safety standards and regulatory practices;

(b) exercise regulatory control related to safety over the siting, design, construction, operation, manufacture of component parts, and decontamination, decommissioning and closure of nuclear installations; and vessels propelled by nuclear power or having radioactive material on board which is capable of causing nuclear damage, through the granting of nuclear authorisations;

(c) exercise regulatory control over other actions, to which the Act applies, through the granting of nuclear authorisations;

(d) provide assurance of compliance with the conditions of nuclear authorisations through the implementation of a system of compliance inspections;

(e) fulfil national obligations in respect of international legal instruments concerning nuclear safety; and

(f) ensure that provisions for nuclear emergency planning are in place.[3]

1 47 of 1999; see title ENERGY.
2 Long title of the Act.
3 S 5.

530 Nuclear authorisations No person may site, construct, operate, decontaminate or decommission a nuclear installation, except under the authority of a nuclear installation licence.[1] No vessel which is propelled by nuclear power or which has on board any radioactive material capable of causing nuclear damage may anchor or sojourn in the territorial waters of the Republic, or enter any port of the Republic, except under the authority of a nuclear vessel licence.[2] No person may engage in any action capable of causing nuclear damage (other than under the authority of licences mentioned above) except under the authority of a certificate of registration or a certificate of exemption.[3] The National Nuclear Regulator Act provides a detailed procedure for applications for the relevant licences, including the right of persons to make representations, relating to health, safety and environmental issues connected with the application.[4]

The chief executive officer may establish standard conditions applicable to one or more categories of certificates of registration.[5] The chief executive officer may impose any condition in a nuclear installation or vessel licence or certificate of registration which is necessary to ensure the protection of persons, property and the environment against nuclear damage, or which provides for the rehabilitation of the site.[6] The chief executive officer may include in a nuclear vessel licence:

(a) conditions relating to liability for nuclear damage which may determine, limit or preclude liability, despite any provisions to the contrary in any other law, or security for nuclear damage and the manner of providing the security, as determined by the minister;

(b) any other conditions which the chief executive officer considers necessary to ensure compliance with the required safety standards;[7]

(c) if the vessel in question is registered outside the Republic, the appropriate terms of any agreement between the government of the Republic and the government of the country in which the vessel is registered.[8]

A nuclear vessel licence is valid for such period as is determined by the chief executive officer, and may from time to time be renewed for any further period.[9] The holder of a nuclear vessel licence is not, solely because of the expiry of that licence, relieved of liability for nuclear damage resulting from anything which occurred or which was done or omitted during the currency of that licence.[10]

One of the mandatory responsibilities of the holder of a nuclear installation licence is to establish a public safety information forum, as prescribed, in order to inform the persons living in the municipal area in respect of which an emergency plan has been established[11] on nuclear safety and radiation safety matters.[12]

In the event of revocation or surrendering of a nuclear authorisation, or at any time during the period of responsibility of the holder of that authorisation, the chief executive officer, in writing, may give any direction to the person liable for nuclear damage, which the chief executive officer believes is necessary to prevent nuclear damage which may be caused by anything which is being done, may be done or was done, or is or was present, at or in the relevant nuclear installation or site.[13]

1	National Nuclear Regulator Act 47 of 1999 s 20(1).	7	In terms of s 36.
2	S 20(2).	8	S 24(1).
3	S 20(3).	9	S 24(4).
4	S 21(4).	10	S 24(5).
5	S 23(1).	11	In terms of s 38(1).
6	S 23(2).	12	S 26(4).
		13	S 27(4).

531 Financial security and liability The minister must, on the recommendation of the board (of directors of the regulator) and by notice in the *Gazette*, categorise the various nuclear installations in the Republic, based on the potential consequences of a nuclear accident,[1] and must, on the recommendation of the board and in consultation with the Minister of Finance and by notice in the *Gazette*, determine the level of financial security to be provided by holders of nuclear installation licences in respect of each of those categories, and the manner in which that financial security is to be provided, in order for the holder of a nuclear installation licence to fulfil any liability which may be incurred.[2] If nuclear damage occurs and compensation is claimed as a result thereof, or the minister is satisfied that such compensation is likely to be so claimed, the minister may require the holder of the nuclear installation licence in question to give additional financial security in respect of those claims or possible claims, to an amount which the minister, after consultation with the board, determines.[3] The holder of a nuclear installation licence must annually provide proof to the regulator that any claim for compensation to an amount contemplated in the liability provision of the National Nuclear Regulator Act[4] can be met.[5]

Only a holder of a nuclear installation licence is, whether or not there is intent or negligence on the part of the holder, liable for all nuclear damage caused by or resulting from the relevant nuclear installation during the holder's period of responsibility:

(a)   by anything being present or which is done at or in the nuclear installation or by any radioactive material or material contaminated with radioactivity which has been discharged or released, in any form, from the nuclear installation; or

(b)   by any radioactive material or material contaminated with radioactivity which is subject to the nuclear installation licence, while in the possession or under the control of the holder of that licence during the conveyance thereof from the nuclear installation to any other place in the Republic, or in the territorial waters of the Republic from or to any place in or outside the Republic.[6]

The liability for nuclear damage by any holder of a nuclear installation licence is limited, for each nuclear accident, to the amounts determined by the levels of financial security determined.[7] Such liability ends upon the relevant material coming onto another site in respect of which a nuclear installation licence has been granted, or onto a site or into the possession or the control of any person authorised in terms of the Hazardous Substances Act,[8] where such material is a Group IV hazardous substance.[9] The holder of a nuclear installation licence is not liable to any person for any nuclear damage to the extent to which such nuclear damage is attributable to the presence of that person or any property of that person at or in the nuclear installation or on the site in respect of which the nuclear installation licence has been granted, without the permission of the holder of that licence or of a person acting on behalf of that holder, or if that person intentionally caused, or intentionally contributed to, such damage.[10] The holder of a nuclear installation licence retains any contractual right of recourse or contribution which the holder has against any person in respect of any nuclear damage for which that holder is liable.[11] Any person who, without a nuclear installation licence, carries out an action for which such a licence is required, is, whether or not there is intent or negligence on the part of that person, liable for all nuclear damage.[12] The liability of a holder of a certificate of registration, for any nuclear damage caused by or resulting from any action carried out by virtue of that certificate during his or her period of responsibility, must be determined in accordance with the common law, or the Compensation for Occupational Injuries and Diseases Act,[13] as the case may be.[14]

If the total amount of claims for compensation against a holder of a nuclear installation licence, or the total amount of claims for compensation against such holder plus the estimated amount of claims for compensation likely to be required to be paid, exceeds, or is likely to exceed, the amount for which that holder has given security, the holder must immediately notify the board and the minister thereof in writing.[15] If on receipt of that notice, the minister is satisfied that the total amount of claims for compensation against a holder of a nuclear installation licence that is unpaid, and of such claims as are likely to be made thereafter, will exceed the amount of security given by that holder in respect of such claims, the minister must table in Parliament a report on the nuclear damage in question, which recommends that Parliament appropriate funds for rendering financial assistance to the holder to the amount by which the claims exceed or are likely to exceed the security which is available, and by notice in the *Gazette* suspend the obligation to pay the claims in respect of that nuclear damage until Parliament has decided about the recommendation.[16] The liability of a person who has provided or must provide financial security, is not affected by any appropriation by Parliament.[17]

Despite anything to the contrary in any other law, an action for compensation in terms of the National Nuclear Regulator Act may not be instituted after the expiration of a period of 30 years from the date of the occurrence which gave rise to the right to claim that compensation, or the date of the last event in the course of that occurrence or succession of occurrences, if a continuing occurrence or a succession of occurrences, all attributable to a particular event or the carrying out of a particular operation, gave rise to that right.[18] If the claimant concerned became aware, or by exercising reasonable care could have become aware, of the identity of the holder of the nuclear authorisation concerned, and the facts from which the right to claim compensation arose, during the period of 30 years, an action for compensation in terms of the Act may not be instituted after the expiration of a period of two years from the date on which he or she so became aware or could have become aware.[19]

If a person who is employed in any capacity by or on behalf of the regulator, while so performing services, suffers a personal injury or contracts a disease attributable to ionising radiation from any radioactive material, or to the flammable, explosive, poisonous or special properties of radioactive material, or to the ionising radiation produced by any apparatus, and in respect of which no liability can be established in terms of the Act, the regulator must defray all reasonable expenses incurred by or on behalf of such person in respect of any medical treatment, including, but not limited to, the supply and maintenance of any artificial part of the body or other device, necessitated by such injury or disease, and pay compensation in respect of disablement or death caused by such injury or disease.[20]

1   National Nuclear Regulator Act 47 of 1999 s 29(1). "Nuclear accident" means any occurrence or succession of occurrences having the same origin which results in the release of radioactive material, or a radiation dose, which exceeds the safety standards contemplated in s 36, and is capable of causing nuclear damage (s 1).
2   S 29(2).
3   S 29(4).
4   S 30(2).
5   S 29(5).
6   S 30(1). Radioactive material or material contaminated with radioactivity which is being conveyed on behalf of the holder of a nuclear installation licence is regarded to be in the possession or under the control of the holder of that licence (s 30(4)). Nothing in this section precludes a person from claiming a benefit in terms of the Compensation for Occupational Injuries and Diseases Act 130 of 1993, but such person may not benefit both in terms of the National Nuclear Regulator Act and the Compensation for Occupational Injuries and Diseases Act (National Nuclear Regulator Act 47 of 1999 s 30(5)). Nothing in this section affects any right, which any person has in terms of any contract of employment, to benefits more favourable than those to which that person may be entitled in terms of this section (s 30(9)). The provisions of s 30 apply also to

liability of a holder of a nuclear vessel licence, if the chief executive officer has not determined conditions for liability (s 31).
7   S 30(2).
8   15 of 1973 s 3A.
9   National Nuclear Regulator Act 47 of 1999 s 30(3). "Group IV hazardous substance" is defined in s 1 of the Hazardous Substances Act 15 of 1973.
10   National Nuclear Regulator Act 47 of 1999 s 30(6).
11   S 30(7).
12   S 30(8).
13   130 of 1993.
14   National Nuclear Regulator Act 47 of 1999 s 32.
15   S 33(1). Such notice must include particulars of the total number and amount of all such claims received, and an estimate of the number and amount of any other claims which may have to be satisfied (s 33(2)).
16   S 33(3). If Parliament has by resolution decided that funds to an amount specified in the report by the minister be appropriated, no payment of any such claim for compensation arising out of the nuclear damage concerned may be made after the passing of such resolution without the approval of the minister or an order of court (s 33(5)).
17   S 33(4).
18   S 34(1).
19   S 34(2). The running of the period of two

years is suspended from the date negotiations regarding a settlement by or on behalf of the claimant and the relevant holder of the nuclear authorisation are commenced in writing until the date any party notifies the other party that the negotiations are terminated (s 34(3)).

20 S 35. Nothing in this section precludes an employee of the regulator from claiming a benefit in terms of the Compensation for Occupational Injuries and Diseases Act 130

of 1993, but such employee may not benefit both in terms of the National Nuclear Regulator Act and the Compensation for Occupational Injuries and Diseases Act (National Nuclear Regulator Act 47 of 1999 s 35(2)). Nothing in this section affects any right, which any person has in terms of any contract of employment, to benefits more favourable than those to which that person may be entitled in terms of this section (s 35(3)).

532 Safety and emergency measures The minister must, on the recommendation of the board, make regulations regarding safety standards and regulatory practices.[1] If a nuclear accident occurs in connection with a nuclear installation, nuclear vessel or action, the holder of the nuclear authorisation in question must immediately report it to the regulator and to any other person described in that nuclear authorisation.[2] When the occurrence of a nuclear accident is so reported to the regulator, it must:

(a) immediately investigate such accident and its causes, circumstances and effects;

(b) in such manner as it thinks fit, define particulars of the period during which and the area within which, in its opinion, the risk of nuclear damage connected with the accident exceeds the applicable safety standards and regulatory practices;

(c) direct the holder of the nuclear authorisation in question to obtain the names, addresses and identification numbers of all persons who were during that period within that area; and

(d) if, of the opinion that it has not been informed of all persons who could have been present during that period within that area, publish by notice in the *Gazette* and in two publications of the daily newspapers in circulation in that area, the fact that a nuclear accident has occurred during that period within that area.[3]

The regulator must, in the prescribed manner, keep a record of the names of all persons who, according to its information, were within the area so defined at any time during the period so defined, and of such particulars concerning them as may be prescribed.[4] If a nuclear incident occurs on a site, the holder of the nuclear authorisation in question must report it to the regulator within the period stipulated in that authorisation.[5]

Where the possibility exists that a nuclear accident affecting the public may occur, the regulator must direct the relevant holder of a nuclear authorisation, other than a holder of a certificate of exemption, to:

(a) enter into an agreement with the relevant municipalities and provincial authorities to establish an emergency plan within a period determined by the regulator;

(b) cover the costs for the establishment, implementation and management of such emergency plan in so far as it relates to the relevant nuclear installation or any action capable of causing nuclear damage; and

(c) submit such emergency plan for its approval.[6]

The regulator must ensure that such emergency plan is effective for the protection of persons should a nuclear accident occur.[7] When a nuclear accident occurs, the holder of a nuclear authorisation, other than a holder of a certificate of exemption, in question must implement the emergency plan as approved by the regulator.[8] The minister may, on recommendation of the board and in consultation with the relevant municipalities, make regulations on the development surrounding any nuclear installation to ensure the effective implementation of any applicable emergency plan.[9]

The regulator must keep a record of the particulars, a map showing the location, and where applicable, diagrams showing the position and limits, of nuclear installations in respect of which a nuclear installation licence has been granted.[10] If the regulator believes that a risk of nuclear damage arising from anything done or being done, or which has been or is present, at or in any nuclear installation in respect of which a nuclear installation licence is no longer in force, is within the safety standards, it may remove the particulars in connection therewith from that record.[11] The regulator must keep and maintain a record of the details of every nuclear accident and nuclear incident, store that record safely, retain that record for 40 years from the date of the nuclear accident or nuclear incident, and on the request of any person, make the record available to that person.[12]

1 National Nuclear Regulator Act 47 of 1999 s 36(1). Before any regulations are made in terms of subsection (1), the minister must, by notice in the *Gazette*, invite the public to comment on the proposed regulations and consider that comment (s 36(2)).
2 S 37(1).
3 S 37(2).
4 S 37(3)(a). For the purposes of the proof of claims for compensation for nuclear damage, any such record is on its mere production by any person in a court of law admissible in evidence, and is *prima facie* proof of the presence of the person in question within the area and during the period so defined

(s 37(3)(b) (4). The right of any person to claim compensation from a holder of a nuclear authorisation in terms of s 30 is not prejudiced by the defining of any area or period in terms of s 37(2)(b), or the failure to record the name of any person in terms of s 37(3) (s 37(4)).
5 S 37(5).
6 S 38(1).
7 S 38(2).
8 S 38(3).
9 S 38(4).
10 S 39(1).
11 S 39(2).
12 S 40.

533 Miscellaneous As far as enforcement is concerned, the National Nuclear Regulator Act[1] provides for the appointment and powers of inspectors.[2] The regulator may make or cause to be made such arrangements as it considers necessary for the proper protection or security of property which belongs to, or is under the control of the regulator, or is on any premises on which activities of the regulator are performed.[3] No unauthorised person may enter any premises which are under the control of the regulator, and the regulator has identified as premises where information relating to the safety and security of or on a nuclear installation is kept.[4]

1 47 of 1999.
2 S 41.
3 S 42(1).

4 S 42(2). Contravention of this prohibition is an offence attracting a maximum penalty of a fine or ten years' imprisonment (s 52).

HAZARDOUS SUBSTANCES ACT

534 Group IV hazardous substances General control over certain radioactive material, namely Group IV hazardous substances, is exercised by virtue of the Hazardous Substances Act.[1] A Group IV hazardous substance is defined as radioactive material which is outside a nuclear installation,[2] and is not a material which forms part of or is used or intended to be used in the nuclear fuel cycle, and:

(a) has an activity concentration of more than 100 becquerels per gram and a total activity of more than 4 000 becquerels; or

(b) has an activity concentration of 100 becquerels or less per gram or a total activity of 4 000 becquerels or less and which the Minister of Health has by notice in the *Government Gazette* declared to be a Group IV hazardous substance, and which is used or intended to be used for medical, scientific, agricultural, commercial or industrial purposes, and any radioactive waste arising from such radioactive material.[3]

No person may produce or otherwise acquire, or dispose of, or import into the Republic or export from there, or be in possession of, or use, or convey or cause to be conveyed, any Group IV hazardous substance, except in terms of a written authority by the Director-General: Health[4] and in accordance with the prescribed conditions and such further conditions which the director-general may determine.[5] The minister may by notice in the *Government Gazette*:

(a) determine that any of the above prohibitions does not apply in respect of any Group IV hazardous substance mentioned in the notice; or

(b) exempt any person or category of persons from any of these prohibitions.[6] This provision has been implemented.[7]

Regulations issued by virtue of the Hazardous Substances Act[8] concern various aspects of Group IV hazardous substances. The regulations govern applications for and the period of validity of authority for the purposes of the producing or otherwise acquiring of, or disposing of, or the importing, exporting, being in possession of, using or conveying of Group IV hazardous substances.[9] Moreover, in addition to any condition that the director-general may in each case determine with regard to a specific authority,[10] all activities with regard to that authority are subject to conditions relating to the following subjects:

(a) general responsibilities of the holder of an authority;

(b) radiation protection officers;

(c) internal rules;

(d) controlled areas;

(e) stock records;

(f) safekeeping of records and registers;

(g) monitoring;

(h) storage places;

(i) disposal;

(j) radiation workers;

(k) medical examinations and health monitoring; and

(l) accidents and incidents.[11]

Finally, safety standards and obligations of persons with regard to Group IV hazardous substances concern the following:

(a) transportation;

(b) manufacture, distribution or installation of equipment;

(c) notification by medical practitioners and other persons;

(d) employees;

(e) restriction of exposure to ionising radiation;

(f) dose limits and dosimetry;

(g) dosimetry service;

(h) assessment of hazardous and contingency plans;

(i) investigation into and notification of overexposure;

(j) duties of radiation protection officers;

(k) examinations;

(l) radiation protection advisers;

(m) medical exposure;

(n) duties of medical physicists;

(o) conduct in the event of death, sequestration or insolvency;

(p) safety and warning notices; and

(q) entering a controlled area.[12]

1   15 of 1973.

2   As defined in the Nuclear Energy Act 131 of 1993.

3   S 1 of the Hazardous Substances Act 15 of 1973, as substituted by s 84 of the Nuclear Energy Act 131 of 1993.

4   Granted in terms of s 3A(2) of the Hazardous Substances Act 15 of 1973.

5   S 3A(1). Contravention of this provision is an offence: s 3A(6). Cf s 3A(3) for the performance of activities in the course of his or her employment by an employee of a holder of an authority in respect of Group IV hazardous substances. S 3A(4) deals with the

validity of an authority under s 50 of the Nuclear Energy Act 92 of 1982.

6   Hazardous Substances Act 15 of 1973 s 3A(5).

7   *Government Gazette* 14596 GN R246, 26 February 1993.

8   S 29: *Government Gazette* 14596 GN R247, 26 February 1993.

9   Ch 2.

10   In terms of s 3A(2) of the Hazardous Substances Act.

11   Ch 3.

12   Ch 4.

535 Ionising radiation by electronic products: Group III hazardous substances The Hazardous Substances Act[1] authorises the Minister of Health to declare any electronic product to be a Group III hazardous substance.[2] The following electronic products have thus been declared Group III hazardous substances:[3]

(a) electronic products generating X-rays or other ionising beams, electrons, neutrons or other particle radiation;

(b) electronic products generating electromagnetic radiation in the ultraviolet region;

(c) electronic products emitting coherent electromagnetic radiation produced by stimulated emission (laser products);

(d) electronic products emitting electromagnetic radiation in the infra-red region;

(e) electronic products emitting microwaves, radio or low frequency electromagnetic radiation;

(f) electronic products emitting ultrasonic vibrations;

(g) electronic products used for medical, dental or veterinary applications employing radioactive nuclides;

(h) high risk electronic products used for medical, dental or veterinary applications, and

(i) medium risk electronic products used for medical, dental or veterinary applications.

A consequence of the declaration of an electronic product as a Group III hazardous substance is that no person may sell, let, use, operate or apply any such substance or install or keep installed such substance on any premises unless a licence has been obtained, and otherwise than subject to prescribed conditions.[4] Provision is made for the issue of licences for Group III hazardous substances by the Director-General: Health.[5] The director-general may not grant an application for a licence unless he or she is satisfied as to a number of factors.[6] If an application is refused, the unsuccessful applicant may appeal to the minister against such refusal.[7] A licence may be withdrawn or suspended if any condition to which such licence is subject has not been complied with.[8] Extensive provisions exist in regard to inspection of grouped hazardous substances.[9] Finally, the minister may by notice in the *Government Gazette* (a) determine that the above prohibition does not apply to any Group III hazardous substance mentioned in the notice;[10] or (b) exempt any person or category of persons from the prohibition.[11]

The first set of regulations relating to the control of electronic products was promulgated in terms of the Public Health Act of 1919.[12] These regulations are now deemed to have been made under the Hazardous Substances Act.[13] The regulations may be grouped together as follows:

(a) *Regulations relating to the licensing of electronic products capable of emitting ionising radiation and of the premises on which they are to be used* Before anyone can use, modify or dispose of any listed electronic product on any premises, such product, as well as the premises on which it is to be used, must be licensed. A heavy burden is imposed on the licensee who is vicariously liable for any act of any other person unless the licensee proves that he or she did not permit or connive at such act, that he or she took all reasonable measures to prevent the act in question, and that the act did not fall within the course of the work or the scope of the authority of the person concerned. The licensee is also liable for the entire scope of radiation protection with regard to an electronic product or premises for which he or she holds a licence. Extensive provisions exist to ensure that the licensee is a person with adequate knowledge and experience as regards radiation protection. Any licence may be suspended or cancelled if the licensee or any of his or her radiation workers contravenes any of the regulations, or, in a case of emergency, where it is in the public interest to do so.

(b) *Regulations relating to the protection of radiation workers* With a view to protecting radiation workers, every licensee is obliged to keep a health register of all personnel employed by him or her as radiation workers, and only registered workers may, with the licensee's approval, handle radiation sources under his or her control and be exposed to radiation while they are working with such sources. The licensee must satisfy him or herself that any person who is registered as a radiation worker is medically fit, has adequate knowledge and experience to handle, and is fully conversant with the health and safety measures and operating instructions applicable to, the radiation equipment under his or her control. A copy of this register must be filed with the Department of Health to provide a central register of radiation workers. The licensee must, moreover, arrange for registered radiation workers to be medically examined, and to be monitored in accordance with the requirements of the regulations.

(c) *Regulations relating to the protection of patients* A number of obligations are imposed upon a licensee in order to ensure that patients are protected against unnecessary radiation. The licensee must ascertain that there has been no previous radiological examination that would make further examination unnecessary, and must keep a record of every patient exposed to radiation from an electronic product for which he or she is the licensee.

Exposure of persons to a useful beam[14] for non-medical purposes is allowed only in exceptional circumstances.

Further regulations issued in terms of the Hazardous Substances Act[15] provide for the institution of a National Advisory Committee on Electronic Products.[16] Finally, other regulations deal with the licensing for the purpose of the sale of listed electronic products (namely declared Group III hazardous substances); records to be kept by approved dealers and provisions relating to a defect and non-compliance with an applicable standard; and repair and modification of listed electronic products.[17]

1 15 of 1973.
2 S 2(1)(b).
3 *Government Gazette* 13299 GN R1302, 14 June 1991.
4 S 3(1)(b) (c). Contravention of s 3(1) is an offence : s 3(3). In the event of a person having a Group III substance in his or her possession before its declaration as a hazardous substance, the person may still sell, lease, use, operate, apply or install the substance within a period of 180 days from the date of declaration, provided that he or she applies for a licence authorising the proposed activity before the expiry of the period mentioned: s 3(2).
5 S 4(1)(b) (c).
6 S 4(4).
7 S 4(6)(b).
8 S 7.
9 Ss 8 9.
10 S 3(1A)(a).
11 S 3(1A)(b).
12 36 of 1919 s 133A. See *Government Gazette* 3991 GN R1332, 3 August 1973.
13 15 of 1973 s 32(2).
14 A "useful beam" is defined as any ionising radiation from a listed electronic product that can be employed for the purpose for which such product is used.
15 S 19(1).
16 *Government Gazette* 6309 GN R326, 23 February 1979.
17 *Government Gazette* 11823 GN R690, 14 April 1989.

536 Non-ionising radiation The Minister of Health is authorised by the Hazardous Substances Act[1] to declare any electronic product to be a Group III hazardous substance.[2] The definitions of "electronic product" and of "electronic product radiation"[3] make it clear that electronic products which may cause non-ionising radiation may also be declared to be Group III hazardous substances. Indeed, the minister has included such products in the list of electronic products published by virtue of the Act.[4]

1 15 of 1973.
2 S 2(1)(b).
3 S 1.
4 *Government Gazette* 13299 GN R1302, 14 June 1991.

NOISE CONTROL

PRIVATE LAW REMEDIES

537 General The *actio legis Aquiliae* and the *actio iniuriarum* are available to the plaintiff who has suffered damage, or injury to his or her personality, as a result of noise caused by the defendant. An interdict is also available in these instances and can be granted if the defendant's conduct was unlawful or threatened to be unlawful.[1] The factors that are normally considered in determining whether the defendant's conduct was unlawful include the type of noise, the degree of its persistence, the locality involved and the times when the noise is heard.[2] No fixed standard is available to determine the unlawfulness of the defendant's conduct, the criterion being "not the individual reaction of a delicate or highly sensitive person who truthfully complains that he finds the noise to be intolerable is to be decisive, but the reaction of the 'reasonable man' – one who, according to ordinary standards of comfort and convenience, and without any peculiar sensitivity to the particular noise, would find it, if not quite intolerable, a serious impediment to the ordinary and reasonable enjoyment of his property".[3]

1 There are a number of cases in our law in which an interdict was granted on account of disturbing noise: *Holland v Scott* 1882 (2) EDC 307; *Blacker v Carter* 1905 (19) EDC 223; *Graham v Dittman & Son* 1917 TPD 288; *Leith v Port Elizabeth Museum Trustees* 1934 EDL 211; *Prinsloo v Shaw* 1938 AD 570; *Ferreira v Grant* 1941 WLD 186; *De*

Charmoy v Day Star Hatchery (Pty) Ltd 1967 4 SA 188 (D); *Gien v Gien* 1979 2 SA 1113 (T) and *Die Vereniging van Advokate (TPA) v Moskeeplein (Edms) Bpk* 1982 3 SA 159 (T). Cf Rabie 1982 *THRHR* 442.

2 *De Charmoy v Day Star Hatchery (Pty) Ltd* supra 192D–E. Cf also *Leith v Port Elizabeth Museum Trustees* supra 213–214.

3 *De Charmoy v Day Star Hatchery (Pty) Ltd* supra 192E–F. Cf also *Leith v Port Elizabeth Museum Trustees* supra 213.

NATIONAL LEGISLATION

538 Transportation noise The Aviation Act[1] authorises the Minister of Transport to make regulations relating to the prevention of nuisance arising out of air navigation or aircraft factories, airports or other aircraft establishment. This includes the prevention of nuisance due to noise or vibration from the operation of machinery in aircraft on or above airports and by the installation in aircraft, or on airports, of means for the prevention of such noise or vibration, or otherwise.[2]

Noise caused by vehicles is addressed through regulations under the National Road Traffic Act.[3] The minister is empowered to make regulations regarding excessive noise owing to the design or condition of any vehicle or the loading thereof, or to the design, condition or misuse of a silencer, or of a hooter, bell or other warning device, when any such vehicle is operated on a public road.[4] Regulations under the Act[5] prohibit a person from operating on a public road a motor vehicle which, when tested, exceeds the limits prescribed in code of practice SABS 0181: "[t]he measurement of noise emitted by road vehicles when stationary".[6]

1 74 of 1962. See generally on noise control Johnston "Noise" in Fuggle and Rabie (eds) *Environmental Management in SA* 569; Meij and Rabie 1974 *CILSA* 84; Schröder 1977 *CILSA* 67. See also titles AVIATION AND AIR TRANSPORT; ROADS AND ROAD TRANSPORT.

2 S 22(1) (5).
3 93 of 1996.
4 S 75(f).
5 *Government Gazette* 20963 GN R225, 17 March 2000.
6 Reg 209(d).

539 Occupational exposure Noise affecting persons at a workplace or in the course of their employment or in connection with the use of machinery is controlled in terms of regulations which are applicable by virtue of the Occupational Health and Safety Act.[1]

Noise related to mining is controlled through regulations applicable by virtue of the Minerals Act.[2]

1 85 of 1993: *Government Gazette* 10988 GN R2281, 16 October 1987. The regulations were originally issued by the then Minister of Manpower in terms of the Machinery and Occupational Safety Act 6 of 1983. See also titles LABOUR LAW; PUBLIC HEALTH.

2 50 of 1991 (now repealed): *Government Gazette* 11905 GN R1130, 2 June 1989. The regulations were originally issued under the Mines and Works Act 27 of 1956. See discussion in par 456 ante regarding the status of these regulations.

540 Standards The Standards Act[1] makes provision for the issuance of compulsory specifications for commodities or the manufacture thereof.[2] No person may sell[3] a commodity for which a compulsory specification is in force unless that commodity complies with or has been manufactured in accordance with the compulsory specification.[4] Compulsory specifications relating to noise have been issued in respect of certain motor vehicles.[5]

1 29 of 1993.
2 S 22.

3 Widely defined as including the display, offer or advertising for sale; the export from

the Republic for or in pursuance of a sale; and having in possession for the purpose of sale, trade, manufacture or export from the Republic: s 1.

4   S 23(1).

5   Eg *Government Gazette* 8200 GN 957,

14 May 1982 and *Government Gazette* 9256 GN 1187, 15 June 1984 in terms of the repealed Standards Act 30 of 1982. These regulations remain in force by virtue of s 42(2) of the Standards Act 29 of 1993.

541   Environment Conservation Act The most important and most comprehensive provisions for noise control are found in the Environment Conservation Act[1] which authorises the making of regulations. The Act empowers the Minister of Environmental Affairs and Tourism to make regulations with regard to the control of noise, vibration and shock, concerning:

(a)   the definition of noise, vibration and shock;

(b)   the prevention, reduction or elimination of noise, vibration and shock;

(c)   the levels of noise, vibration and shock which must not be exceeded, either in general or by specified apparatus or machinery or in specified instances or places;

(d)   the type of measuring instrument which can be used for the determination of the levels of noise, vibration and shock, and the utilisation and calibration thereof;

(e)   the powers of provincial governments and local authorities to control noise, vibration and shock; and

(f)   any other matter which the minister may deem necessary or expedient in connection with the effective control and combating of noise, vibration and shock.[2]

Although not aimed specifically at noise control, the provisions whereby the minister is empowered to identify and prohibit certain activities, *inter alia*, industrial processes, land use and transportation, may find a ready application to noise sources.[3]

1   73 of 1989.

2   S 25.

3   Ss 21 22.

PROVINCIAL LEGISLATION

542   General Prior to the promulgation of the Road Traffic Act,[1] motor vehicle noise was controlled by virtue of the various provincial Road Traffic Ordinances. These ordinances have been replaced by the Act, which, nevertheless, is still administered by the provinces. The Road Traffic Act has been replaced by the National Road Traffic Act.[2]

Noise control should be a factor to be considered in town planning. However, the Provincial Town Planning Ordinances are too vague with regard to noise to have any significant effect in practice.

Finally, it should be noted that the Environment Conservation Act[3] provides that the regulations which may be issued in terms of the Act in respect of noise control[4] may assign functions to a provincial government.[5]

1   29 of 1989.

2   93 of 1996.

3   73 of 1989.

4   S 25.

5   S 28(a).

LOCAL LEGISLATION

543   General Local authorities are authorised by various provincial legislation to legislate on a variety of subjects relating to noise control. Among the actions that local authorities may control are the following: playing musical instruments or singing in or on any public place; using loudspeakers or similar devices for the purpose of advertising on or adjacent to any public place and keeping animals and birds that constitute a nuisance to the inhabitants of the municipality. Furthermore, local authorities may generally prohibit or restrict any action by which the peace in the municipality or the comfort, convenience, peace or quiet of the public may be disturbed or hindered.

Legislation for noise control is enacted most extensively at local level. Most local authorities have by-laws dealing with noise control. However, the provisions relating to noise control have normally been included in a variety of by-laws — for example, those dealing with licences, parks and traffic. In most local authorities there have been no separate noise control by-laws. Moreover, most of these provisions are very difficult to enforce, since reliance is often placed on subjective factors where no objective standard for the measurement of noise is laid down, such as "shrieking", "raucous" or "offensive" noise. It can also be very difficult to ascertain when noise causes a disturbance of the public peace.

The Transvaal Local Government Amendment Ordinance[1] inserted a provision in the Local Government Ordinance[2] empowering local authorities to deal with noise control more effectively.[3] The municipalities of Pretoria and of Johannesburg were the first to draft specific noise control by-laws.[4] These by-laws were followed by almost identical by-laws of several other local authorities. Although these by-laws represented a major step forward, they were completely reactive. What was still lacking was a pro-active approach that aimed at preventing noise problems through proper planning. This need was met by the Environment Conservation Act.[5]

1 22 of 1977.
2 17 of 1939.
3 S 80(125B) of the Tvl Ord.
4 Pretoria Noise-Abatement By-laws AN 816,

21 June 1978 and the Johannesburg Noise Control By-laws AN 1784, 29 November 1978.
5 73 of 1989.

544 Regulations in terms of the Environment Conservation Act The most important legislation pertaining to noise control by local authorities is found in the noise control regulations issued in terms of the Environment Conservation Act.[1] The regulations were published for general information in 1986[2] and again in 1988,[3] in terms of the Environment Conservation Act of 1982.[4] They were again published for public information early in 1990,[5] after which they were finally promulgated, in amended form, late in 1990.[6] Although these regulations constitute by far the most comprehensive noise control legislation in South Africa, it is important to realise that in so far as they affected the activities of any local authority or government institution, they could initially have been promulgated only with the concurrence of such local authority or government institution.[7] In other words, they had the nature of model regulations. During the first two years the regulations were thus promulgated in the area of jurisdiction of some 35 local authorities. Meanwhile, however, the Act was amended during 1992 to the extent that the concurrence of local authorities is no longer required. New draft noise regulations, in the same form as the previous regulations, but which will be applicable to all local authorities, have been published.[8]

The regulations consist of several general prohibitions, besides prohibitions relating specifically to "disturbing noise" and to "noise nuisance". The general prohibitions concern the establishment of new townships without a lay-out plan indicating the existing and future noise sources, with concomitant dBA values;[9] the erection of certain buildings in an existing township within a controlled area, unaccompanied by acoustic screening measures;[10] effecting changes to existing facilities, uses of land or buildings or erecting new buildings, if they, in the opinion of the local authority, will house or cause activities which will cause a disturbing noise (unless satisfactory pre-cautionary measures have been undertaken);[11] the building of a road, the changing of an existing road or the alteration of the speed limit on a road, if it will, in the opinion of the local authority, cause an increase in noise in or near residential areas or certain buildings (unless noise control measures have been taken);[12] the situation of certain erven within a controlled area in a new township or an area which has been rezoned;[13] the staging of an organised open-air music festival or similar gathering without the prior consent of a local authority;[14] the operation of certain sound amplification devices which exceed 95 dBA without displaying a prescribed warning;[15] the use of power tools or power equipment for construction, earth drilling or demolition works in residential areas during certain times;[16] driving a vehicle or allowing it to be driven on a public road, if the sound level exceeds certain prescribed sound levels;[17] and failing to comply with directives issued by a local authority in terms of the regulations.[18]

The prohibition of disturbing noise simply renders it an offence for any person to make, produce or cause a disturbing noise, or to allow it to be made, produced or caused by any person, machine, device or apparatus or any combination thereof.[19] A "disturbing noise" means a noise level which exceeds the zone sound level (a derived dBA value determined indirectly by means of a series of measurements, calculations or table readings designated by a local authority for an area)[20] or, if no zone sound level has been designated, a noise level which exceeds the ambient sound level at the same measuring point by 7 dBA or more.[21]

Finally, a number of prohibitions are directed at noise nuisance. A "noise nuisance" means any sound which disturbs or impairs or may disturb or impair the convenience or peace of any person.[22] No person may:

(a) cause a noise nuisance, or allow it to be caused, by operating or playing certain devices which produce, reproduce or amplify sound;[23]

(b) offer any article for sale by shouting or ringing a bell or allowing it to be done, in a manner which may cause a noise nuisance;[24]

(c) allow an animal owned or controlled by him or her to cause a noise nuisance;[25]

(d) build, repair, rebuild, modify, operate or test a vehicle, vessel or aircraft on residential premises, or allow it to be done, if it may cause a noise nuisance;[26]

(e) use or discharge any explosive, firearm or similar device which emits impulsive sound, or allow it to be done, if it may cause a noise nuisance, except with the consent of the local authority concerned;[27]

(f) on a designated piece of land move about on or in a recreational vehicle or exercise control over a recreational vehicle,[28] or as owner or person in control of the piece of land concerned, allow these actions on that piece of land, or in the air-space above;[29]

(g) except in an emergency, emit a sound, or allow a sound to be emitted, by means of a bell, carillon, siren, hooter, static alarm, whistle, loudspeaker or similar device, if it may cause a noise nuisance;[30]

(h) operate any machinery, saw, sander, drill, grinder, lawnmower, power garden implement or similar device in a residential area, or allow it to be operated, if it may cause a noise nuisance;[31]

(i) load, unload, open, shut or in any other way handle a crate, box, container, building material, rubbish container or similar article, or allow such actions, if it may cause a noise nuisance;[32]

(j) drive a vehicle on a public road in such a manner that it may cause a noise nuisance.[33]

Contravention of any of the abovementioned regulations constitutes an offence, the penalty being a fine of R20 000 or imprisonment for a period not exceeding two years, or both such fine and imprisonment.[34]

Among the powers conferred upon a local authority are the following: if a noise emanating from a building, premises, vehicle, recreational vehicle or street is a disturbing noise or a noise nuisance, or may in the opinion of the local authority concerned be such a noise, the local authority may instruct the person causing such noise or who is responsible therefor, or the owner or occupant of the building or premises from which or from where the noise emanates or may emanate, or all such persons, to discontinue or cause to be discontinued such noise, or to take steps to lower the level of the noise to a level conforming to the requirements of the regulations within the period stipulated in the instruction.[35] Failure to comply with this instruction constitutes an offence.[36] If an animal is involved, it may be impounded.[37]

If excavation work, earthmoving work, pumping work, drilling work, construction work or demolition work or any similar activity, power generation or music causes a noise nuisance or a disturbing noise, a local authority may issue an instruction that such action be forthwith discontinued until such conditions as the local authority may deem necessary have been complied with.[38]

A local authority may require that noise impact assessments or tests be conducted to its satisfaction, before changes are made to existing facilities or existing uses of land or buildings, or before new buildings are erected.[39]

A local authority may designate a "controlled area"[40] in its area of jurisdiction and it may designate "zone sound levels"[41] for specific areas.[42]

A local authority is also authorised to attach a vehicle if the sound level of such vehicle exceeds the prescribed sound level by more than 5 dBA.[43]

Finally, the regulations provide for exemptions if the emission of sound is for the purpose of warning people of a dangerous situation or takes place during an emergency.[44] Moreover, application may be made by any person to the local authority concerned for exemption from any provision of the regulations.[45]

1   73 of 1989.
2   *Government Gazette* 10522 GN 2407, 21 November 1986.
3   *Government Gazette* 11442 GN 547, 5 August 1988.
4   100 of 1982.
5   *Government Gazette* 12435 GN 896, 27 April 1990.
6   *Government Gazette* 12816 GN R2544, 2 November 1990.
7   S 28(i) (iii).
8   *Government Gazette* 15423 GN R55, 14 January 1994. The intention apparently was to obtain comments also from those local authorities which failed to have the 1990 regulations made applicable to their respective areas of jurisdiction. In 2004, these draft regulations had not yet been made final.
9   Reg 3(a).
10   Reg 3(b).
11   Reg 3(c).
12   Reg 3(d).
13   Reg 3(e).
14   Reg 3(g).
15   Reg 3(h).
16   Reg 3(i).
17   Reg 3(j).
18   Reg 3(f).
19   Reg 4. See *Nelson Mandela Metropolitan Municipality v Greyvenouw CC* 2004 2 SA 81 (SE).
20   Reg 1.
21   Ibid.
22   Ibid.
23   Reg 5(a).
24   Reg 5(b).
25   Reg 5(c).
26   Reg 5(d).
27   Reg 5(e).
28   Defined in reg 1.

29   Reg 5(f).
30   Reg 5(g).
31   Reg 5(h).
32   Reg 5(i).
33   Reg 5(j).
34   Reg 9.
35   Reg 2(c).
36   Reg 3(f).
37   Reg 2(g).

38   Reg 2(e).
39   Reg 2(d).
40   Defined in reg 1.
41   Ibid.
42   Reg 2(m).
43   Reg 2(h).
44   Reg 7(1).
45   Reg 7(2).

CONTROL OF PESTICIDES

AGRICULTURAL AND STOCK REMEDIES

545 Registration The Fertilizers, Farm Feeds, Agricultural Remedies and Stock Remedies Act[1] makes provision for the designation of an officer of the Department of Agriculture as the registrar of fertilisers, farm feeds, agricultural remedies and stock remedies.[2] As far as the control of pesticides is concerned, only the registration of agricultural remedies,[3] stock remedies[4] and of pest control operators[5] is of importance, although the Act also makes provision for the registration of fertilisers, farm feeds and sterilising plants. Application for the registration of these remedies[6] or of pest control operators must be made to the registrar in the prescribed manner.[7] Registration will take place only if the registrar is satisfied that the remedy in question is suitable and sufficiently effective for the purpose for which it is intended, that it complies with such requirements as may be prescribed, that it is not contrary to the public interest[8] that it be registered, and that the establishment where it is manufactured is suitable for such manufacture.[9] The suitability and efficacy of an agricultural remedy stated in an application for the registration thereof must be proved by results of trials.[10] Moreover, a procedure is prescribed for the determination of the toxicity and potential hazards of agricultural remedies.[11] Registration must be made subject to the prescribed and any additional conditions as may be determined by the registrar[12] and is valid for such period as may be prescribed,[13] subject to renewal.[14] A certificate of registration is issued,[15] which must be available for inspection.[16] Provision is made for the annual furnishing of statistical sales information in respect of agricultural remedies by the person in whose favour such remedy is registered.[17]

The registrar may cancel the registration of any of these remedies if he or she is satisfied:

(a) that a person has in connection with the registration concerned contravened or failed to comply with a provision of the Act;

(b) that a person has contravened or failed to comply with a condition to which the registration concerned is subject;

(c) that such remedy is not of the composition and efficacy specified in the application for registration thereof, does not possess the chemical, physical and other properties so specified and does not comply with any requirements that may be prescribed;

(d) that the practices followed and facilities available at or in respect of the establishment (the premises where the particular remedy is manufactured, controlled, packed, marked or labelled for the purposes of sale)[18] or the operation of the undertaking at such establishment are not suitable for the manufacture of the remedy concerned;

(e) that the person managing such undertaking does not have sufficient knowledge of the relevant provisions of the Act or of the practices to be followed in the operation of such undertaking;

(f) that it is contrary to the public interest that such remedy remain registered; or

(g) that any incorrect or misleading advertisement is used in connection with such remedy.[19]

The registration of a number of pesticides was cancelled in 1970 in terms of the penultimate provision, while the use of certain others was restricted.[20] The registrar may cancel the registration of a pest control operator if he or she is satisfied that the operator has contravened or failed to comply with the provisions of the Act or a condition of his or her registration,[21] or if it is contrary to the public interest that the operator in question remain registered.[22] If an application for the registration is refused, or conditions are determined on registration or any registration is cancelled, the registrar must furnish written reasons for his or her decision.[23] Moreover, a person who feels aggrieved by any such decision, is granted an appeal against the decision.[24] A registration of these remedies may also lapse; this will be the case if the person to whom the certificate of registration has been issued, ceases to manufacture or sell the remedy in question,[25] or if the establishment in question is no longer used for the manufacture of such remedies.[26]

1 36 of 1947. See generally on pesticides Giliomee and Glavovic "Pesticides" in Fuggle and Rabie (eds) *Environmental Management in SA* 523; Glavovic 1985 *SALJ* 674–685; and see title AGRICULTURE.

2 S 2(1). The registrar may delegate any of his or her powers, duties or functions: s 2(2)(1).

3 "Agricultural remedy" means any chemical substance or biological remedy, or any mixture or combination of any substance or remedy intended or offered to be used: (a) for the destruction, control, repelling, attraction or prevention of any undesired microbe, alga, nematode, fungus, insect, plant, vertebrate, invertebrate, or any product thereof, but excluding any chemical substance, biological remedy or other remedy in so far as it is controlled under the Medicines and Related Substances Act 101 of 1965, or the Hazardous Substances Act 15 of 1973; or (b) as plant-growth regulator, defoliant, desiccant or legume inoculant, and anything else which the minister has by notice in the *Government Gazette* declared an agricultural remedy for the purposes of the Fertilizers, Farm Feeds, Agricultural Remedies and Stock Remedies Act 36 of 1947: s 1. Although reference is made to agricultural remedies, the definition is so wide as to embrace remedies used in the domestic and industrial environment as well as rodenticides, fumigants and aerosols for household pest control: s 1.

4 "Stock remedy" means a substance intended or offered to be used in connection with domestic animals, livestock, poultry, fish or wild animals (including wild birds), for the diagnosis, prevention, treatment or cure of any disease, infection or other unhealthy condition, or for the maintenance or improvement of health, growth, production or working capacity, but excluding any substance in so far as it is controlled under the Medicines and Related Substances Act 101 of 1965: Fertilizers, Farm Feeds, Agricultural Remedies and Stock Remedies Act 36 of 1947 s 1.

5 "Pest control operator" means a person who as, or in the course of, his trade or occupation administers agricultural remedies for the purposes for which they are intended: s 1.

6 The Minister of Agriculture may exclude, subject to such conditions as he or she may determine, any of these remedies from the operation of any or all the provisions of the Act: s 13.

7 S 3(1). The making of any false or misleading statement in connection with an application for the registration of these remedies is an offence: s 18(1)(g)(i). As far as agricultural remedies are concerned, see *Government Gazette* 7934 GN R2561, 27 November 1981 regs 2–6. For stock remedies cf *Government Gazette* 3121 GN R857, 28 May 1971.

8 "Public interest" is not defined, which means that a wide discretion is awarded to the registrar.

9 S 3(2)(a). "Establishment" is defined in s 1. Registration may be refused if any previous registration of the remedy in question has been cancelled: s 3(2) proviso.

10 *Government Gazette* 7934 GN R2561,

27 November 1981 reg 12(1).
11 *Government Gazette* 7934 GN R2561, 27 November 1981 reg 13(1).
12 S 3(3). Failure to comply with a condition is an offence: s 18(1)(c).
13 S 3(3); ie a maximum period of one year in the case of agricultural remedies, since registrations lapse annually at the end of March: *Government Gazette* 7934 GN R2561, 27 November 1981 reg 3(1).
14 S 3(4) and *Government Gazette* 7934 GN R2561, 27 November 1981 regs 3(3) 4.
15 S 13(3).
16 S 4A(1)(a). Contravention of this provision is an offence: s 18(1)(l).
17 *Government Gazette* 7934 GN R2561,

27 November 1981 reg 11.
18 Cf the definition of "establishment" in s 1.
19 S 4(1).
20 The pesticides affected are the following: DDT, TDE (Rhothane), BHC, CIC, Dieldrin and HHDN (Aldrin), Nendrin (Endrin) Arsenic, Phosphorus, Endosulfan (Thiodan), Gamma–BHC (Lindane), and mixtures of DDT and other insecticides.
21 S 4(3)(a) (b).
22 S 4(3)(c).
23 S 5.
24 S 6.
25 S 4A(2)(a).
26 S 4A(2)(b).

546 Manufacture and related actions Control is exercised over the manufacture of agricultural and stock remedies in that in considering an application for registration of such remedies the registrar must be satisfied that the establishment where these remedies are manufactured is suitable for such manufacture.[1] Moreover, as has been pointed out, the registrar may cancel the registration of any remedy if he or she is satisfied that the practices followed and facilities available at or in respect of the establishment or the operation of the undertaking at such establishment are not suitable for the manufacture of the remedy concerned,[2] or that the person managing such undertaking does not have sufficient knowledge of the relevant provisions of the Act or of the practices to be followed in the operation of such undertaking.[3] The registration of the abovementioned remedies may also lapse if the establishment in question is no longer used for the manufacture of the remedies concerned.[4]

Extensive control is exercised over establishments where agricultural remedies are manufactured, controlled, packed, marked or labelled for the purpose of sale, through the prescription of requirements for such establishments,[5] the maintenance and care of facilities and equipment,[6] the practices to be followed[7] and the keeping of records at such establishments.[8]

1 Fertilizers, Farm Feeds, Agricultural Remedies and Stock Remedies Act 36 of 1947 s 3(2)(a).
2 S 4(1)(c).
3 S 4(1)(d).
4 S 4A(2)(b).

5 *Government Gazette* 7934 GN R2561, 27 November 1981 reg 8.
6 Reg 9.
7 Reg 7.
8 Reg 10. Contravention of any of these regulations is an offence: reg 20(a) (b) (d).

547 Importation Farming requisites landed at or imported through any port or place in the Republic may be detained and samples may be made thereof.[1] If an examination, analysis or test of such samples shows that any such farming requisite does not comply with the requirements of the Fertilizers, Farm Feeds, Agricultural Remedies and Stock Remedies Act, the Minister of Agriculture may order such farming requisite to be destroyed without compensation,[2] or at the option of the importer to be removed from the Republic within a specified period,[3] or permit the removal thereof from the port or place of entry subject to such conditions as he or she may determine.[4]

1 Fertilizers, Farm Feeds, Agricultural Remedies and Stock Remedies Act 36 of 1947 s 16(1). Cf ss 16(2) 15.

2 S 16(4)(a)(i).
3 S 16(4)(a)(ii).
4 S 16(4)(b).

548 Containers Specifications are prescribed as to the nature of containers in which agricultural remedies may be sold[1] and as to the labelling and marking of containers of agricultural remedies.[2]

1 Fertilizers, Farm Feeds, Agricultural Remedies and Stock Remedies Act 36 of 1947 s 7(1)(c) and *Government Gazette* 7934 GN R2561, 27 November 1981 reg 14.

2 S 7(1)(c) and *Government Gazette* 7934 GN R2561, 27 November 1981 reg 15. Contravention of any of these provisions is an offence: s 18(1)(c) and reg 20(d).

549 Advertisements Advertisements relating to agricultural remedies must comply with certain prescriptions.[1] Moreover, as has been pointed out, the registration of any agricultural or stock remedy may be cancelled if the registrar is satisfied that any incorrect or misleading advertisement is used in connection with such remedy.[2]

1 *Government Gazette* 7934 GN R2561, 27 November 1981 reg 17. Failure to comply with this regulation is an offence: reg 20(d), while the Fertilizers, Farm Feeds, Agricultural Remedies and Stock Remedies

Act 36 of 1947 s 18(1)(g)(iii) renders criminal any false or misleading statements in advertisements.

2 S 4(1)(f).

550 Sale No agricultural or stock remedy may be sold[1] unless:

(a) it is registered under the name and mark under which it is sold;[2]

(b) it is packed in such manner and mass or volume as may be prescribed;[3]

(c) the container in which it is sold complies with the prescribed requirements and is sealed and labelled or marked in the prescribed manner or, if it is not sold in a container, it is accompanied by the required invoice;[4] and

(d) it is of the composition and efficacy specified in the application for registration, possesses all chemical, physical and other properties so specified and complies with the prescribed requirements.[5]

Moreover, the Minister of Agriculture may prohibit[6] the sale, acquisition or disposal of agricultural or stock remedies either totally[7] or subject to such conditions as he or she may specify.[8] Any such prohibition may apply throughout the Republic or in one or more specified areas,[9] or to persons belonging to, or not belonging to, a specified class or group,[10] or in respect of all or one or more classes or kinds of such remedies.[11] Such a total prohibition covering the whole of the country has been enacted as regards the acquisition, disposal or sale of any agricultural or stock remedy which contains certain prohibited substances,[12] and there has been a prohibition in specified areas of certain hormonal herbicides.[13]

1 "Sell" includes to agree to sell, or to offer, advertise, keep, expose, transmit, convey, deliver or manufacture for sale, or to exchange or to dispose of to any person in any manner for any consideration whatever, or to transmit, convey or deliver in pursuance of a sale, exchange or disposal: Fertilizers, Farm Feeds, Agricultural Remedies and Stock Remedies Act 36 of 1947 s 1.

2 S 7(1)(a). However, an agricultural or stock remedy in respect of which the period of validity of the registration has expired, the certificate of registration has been cancelled (in terms of s 4), or has lapsed (in terms of s 4A(2)), and which, before or on the date of such cancellation or lapse, was no longer

under the control of, or owned by the person to whom that certificate was issued, may subject to the provisions of s 7bis, be sold: s 7(1)(a) proviso.

3 S 7(1)(b).

4 S 7(1)(c). It is an offence to sell any remedy upon the container of which a false or misleading statement in connection with such contents is printed or written: s 18(1)(h).

5 S 7(1)(d). Contravention of any of the provisions of s 7 is an offence: s 18(1)(c).

6 By notice in the *Government Gazette*: s 7bis(1). Moreover, it is an offence to sell any remedy which is not of the kind, nature, composition, strength, potency or quality described or represented when so sold: s 18(1)(i).

7 S 7bis(1)(a).

8 S 7bis(1)(b).

9 S 7bis(2)(a).

10 S 7bis(2)(b).

11 S 7bis(2)(c). Contravention of the prohibition is an offence: s 18(1)(c)bis.

12 *Government Gazette* 7566 GN R928, 1 May 1981. The prohibited substances are the following: a mixture of different isomer of

BHC (excluding gamma–BHC with a purity grade of at least 99 per cent (Lindane); Dichlor–diphenyl–trichloroethane (DDT); Dieldrin or aldrin, with the exception of aldrin for use underneath buildings for the control of wood destructing termites.

13 *Government Gazette* 13536 GN R2370, 27 September 1991.

551 Use The same enabling provision of the Fertilizers, Farm Feeds, Agricultural Remedies and Stock Remedies Act[1] entitling the Minister of Agriculture to prohibit the sale, acquisition or disposal of agricultural or stock remedies, relates also to the use of such remedies. The following prohibition has been promulgated:[2] as from 1 January 1982 no person may use any agricultural or stock remedy the sale of which has been prohibited in terms of the same abovementioned enabling provision.[3] Moreover, no person may use any agricultural remedy which:

(a) contains any inorganic arsenic compound on vegetative material, except material derived from citrus; and

(b) contains any mercury compound on seed, bulbs, tubers, stalks or other vegetative matter, which are intended for consumption by people, domestic animals, livestock, poultry, fish or wild animals.[4]

Finally, no person may use any agricultural remedy or stock remedy which is not registered under the Act for the treatment of a plant or animal of which the material or products are intended for consumption by people, domestic animals, livestock, poultry, fish or wild animals.[5]

Provision is also made for control over the use of agricultural remedies by commercial pest control operators, in other words, persons who as, or in the course of, their trade or occupation administer agricultural remedies for the purposes for which they are intended.[6] As has been pointed out, pest control operators have to be registered in terms of the Act. Such operators may be registered if the registrar is satisfied that the pest control operator in respect of whom registration is applied for has the prescribed qualifications or is otherwise, to such extent as may be determined by the registrar, skilled in the use of agricultural remedies, and that it is not contrary to the public interest that such operator be registered.[7] The registrar may cancel the registration of a pest control operator if he or she is satisfied that the operator has contravened or failed to comply with a provision of the Act or a condition of his or her registration,[8] or that it is contrary to the public interest that he or she remain registered,[9] while the registration of a pest control operator will lapse if the registered person ceases to be a pest control operator.[10] Extensive regulations have been promulgated as to the registration and duties of pest control operators.[11]

If the registrar is of the opinion that any equipment used by a registered pest control operator for the administration of any particular agricultural remedy is so unsuited to the administration of such remedy that the purpose for which the remedy is administered may be defeated, he or she may order the registered pest control operator to discontinue the use of such equipment when administering the remedy in question.[12] Furthermore, no person may for reward or in the course of any industry, trade or business, use, or recommend the use of an agricultural or stock remedy for a purpose or in a manner which is not specified on the label or on a container thereof or described on such container.[13] In addition, any person who at the request of the owner or the person in control of a thing, administers for consideration an agricultural remedy to that thing, must, before such administration, notify the owner or other person of the purpose of such administration; the registered name and number of the remedy; the precautions to be taken before, during and after such administration; and the number of his or her certificate of registration, if he or she is a registered pest control operator.[14]

1　36 of 1947 s 7bis.
2　*Government Gazette* 7566 GN R928, 1 May 1981.
3　Ibid.
4　Ibid.
5　Ibid. The provisions of the above GN do not apply to use of the remedies concerned for experimental purposes approved by the registrar or by or on recommendation of the registrar.
6　S 1.
7　S 3(2)(c).
8　S 4(3)(a) (b).
9　S 4(3)(c).
10　S 4A(2B).
11　*Government Gazette* 8783 GN R1449, 1 July 1983.
12　S 6A. Failure to comply with such an order is an offence: s 18(1)(bB).
13　S 7(2)(a).
14　S 10(1).

552 Registrar's powers In addition to the powers already referred to, the registrar has a number of specific powers relating *inter alia* to entry upon and examination of places, premises or vehicles in respect of which agricultural or stock remedies are for example manufactured, processed, exhibited, sold, used,[1] examination of books and documents,[2] operations or processes,[3] seizure of,[4] and the taking of samples[5] of agricultural or stock remedies.

1　Fertilizers, Farm Feeds, Agricultural Remedies and Stock Remedies Act 36 of 1947 s 15(1)(a).
2　S 15(1)(b). Cf also s 15(1)(d) and (e).
3　S 15(1)(c).
4　S 15(1)(e).
5　S 15(1)(f).

553 Notifiable medical condition In terms of the Health Act,[1] poisoning from any agricultural or stock remedy registered in terms of the Fertilizers, Farm Feeds, Agricultural Remedies and Stock Remedies Act,[2] is a notifiable medical condition.[3]

1　63 of 1977.
2　36 of 1947.
3　Health Act 63 of 1977 s 45 and *Government Gazette* 6628 GN R1802, 24 August 1979.

554 Occupational health and safety in regard to pesticides Regulations under the Occupational Health and Safety Act[1] regulate occupational exposure to hazardous chemical substances, pesticides included.[2] The regulations provide for the duties of employers and employees, assessment of exposure, monitoring and medical surveillance and other control measures.

1　85 of 1993.
2　*Government Gazette* 16596 GN R1179, 25 August 1995.

HAZARDOUS SUBSTANCES

555 Sale of grouped hazardous substances Pesticides may also be controlled by virtue of the Hazardous Substances Act[1] in terms of which any substance or mixture of substances which, in the course of customary or reasonable handling or use, including ingestion, might, by reason of its toxic, corrosive, irritant, strongly sensitising or flammable nature, or because it generates pressure through decomposition, heat or other means, cause injury, ill-health or death to human beings, to be a Group I or a

Group II hazardous substance.[2] Certain pesticides have been included in the list of declared Group I hazardous substances.[3]

No person may sell[4] any Group I hazardous substance unless he or she is the holder of a licence and otherwise than subject to the conditions[5] determined by the Director-General: Health.[6] Contravention of this provision is an offence.[7] However, no person will be convicted of such an offence if that person proves that he or she sold the substance in question in the condition in which he or she acquired or imported it or, if it was acquired or imported by his or her employer or principal, that he or she at no relevant time had reason to suspect that it was in any other condition than that in which it was so acquired or imported.[8]

Application for a licence to carry on business as a supplier of Group I hazardous substances must be lodged with the director-general who may require the applicant to furnish him or her with information,[9] and who may conduct an investigation of the applicant.[10] The director-general may not grant an application for a licence unless he or she is satisfied that:

(a) the applicant is a suitable person to carry on, or be involved in, the activities authorised by the licence;

(b) an interest which any person has in the applicant concerned, is reconcilable with the provisions of the Act;

(c) the applicant will be able to exercise sufficient control over the activities authorised by the licence;

(d) the licence concerned has not been issued to a sufficient number of persons; and

(e) the issue of the licence will be in the public interest.[11]

A licence is valid for an indefinite or prescribed period, but may be renewed.[12] If the director-general refuses an application for a licence, he or she must in writing furnish the applicant concerned with the reasons for such refusal and notify such applicant of the right of appeal.[13] Any person aggrieved by a decision of the director-general or any condition imposed by the director-general, may appeal to the Minister of Health, who may in his or her discretion confirm, set aside, amend or replace such decision or condition.[14]

Provision is, finally, made for the suspension and cancellation of licences. If the holder of a licence:

(a) has in connection with an application for a licence or renewal of a licence furnished the director-general with any information which to the knowledge of such holder is untrue or misleading in any material respect;

(b) has contravened or failed to comply with a condition subject to which the licence was issued or with a provision of the Act;

(c) has at any time been convicted of any offence which is of such a nature that in the opinion of the director-general the holder is not a suitable person to carry on or be involved in the activities authorised by the licence; or

(d) has ceased to carry on such activities,

the director-general may[15] suspend[16] or withdraw[17] such licence.[18]

Regulations in respect of Group I hazardous substances have been promulgated in terms of the Hazardous Substances Act.[19] These regulations regulate the process of licensing,[20] the conditions of sale or supply,[21] the records to be kept by licensees,[22] the labelling[23] and disposal of empty containers,[24] and the duties of inspectors and analysts.[25]

1 15 of 1973.
2 S 2(1)(a).
3 *Government Gazette* 9533 GN R2777, 21 December 1984.
4 "Sell" includes to offer, advertise, keep, display, transmit, consign, convey or deliver for sale, or exchange, or dispose of to any person in any manner, whether for a consideration or otherwise, or manufacture or import for use in the Republic: s 1. "Advertise", "manufacture" and "import" are also defined in s 1.
5 The director-general may by written notice to the licensee cancel or vary any condition to which the licence is subject, or impose a further condition : s 4(7).
6 S 3(1)(a). Provision is made for certain exceptions to this rule: ss 3(1A) and 3(2). The director-general may in writing authorise any officer in the Department of Health to perform any function conferred upon the director-general in terms of the Act : s 26.
7 S 5(3). The Act provides for vicarious responsibility : s 16.
8 S 14(b).
9 S 4(2).
10 S 4(3).
11 S 4(4).
12 S 5.
13 S 4(6).
14 S 6(1). The operation of a decision of the director-general, or a condition imposed by him or her, will not be suspended pending the outcome of an appeal: s 6(2).
15 After, by way of notice in writing, calling upon the licensee to show cause, within a specified period of at least 20 days, why the licence should not be suspended or cancelled: s 7(1)(e).
16 While a licence is suspended, it is deemed never to have been issued: s 7(3).
17 The licence must be withdrawn upon request of a licensee: s 7(4).
18 S 7(1) (2). A licensee may, after his or her licence has been withdrawn, continue on such conditions as the director-general may determine, to carry on his or her business for a period of 30 days or such longer period as the director-general may determine: s 7(5).
19 *Government Gazette* 9533 GN R2778, 21 December 1984.
20 Regs 2 3.
21 Reg 4.
22 Regs 5 6.
23 Reg 8.
24 Reg 10.
25 Reg 9.

FOODSTUFFS

556 Substances in foodstuffs The Foodstuffs, Cosmetics and Disinfectants Act[1] contains provisions aimed at the prohibition of the sale,[2] manufacture[3] or importation[4] of any foodstuffs[5] which contain or have been treated[6] with a prohibited substance,[7] or which contain a particular substance in a greater measure than that permitted by regulation, or have been treated with a substance containing a particular substance in greater measure than that permitted by regulation.[8] Contravention of these provisions is an offence.[9] The Minister of Health may make regulations prescribing any foreign substance, or the nature of foreign substances, that may be considered as unavoidably present in any foodstuffs or cosmetic as a result of the process of its collection, manufacture or treatment, or the greatest measure in which any such substance or substances of such nature may be present in any foodstuffs or cosmetic.[10] Utilising this power, the minister has promulgated regulations concerning the maximum limits for pesticide residues that may be present in foodstuffs.[11]

1 54 of 1972. See title FOOD, DRUGS AND HAZARDOUS SUBSTANCES.
2 Cf s 1 for definition of "sell".
3 Cf s 1 for definition of "manufacture".
4 Cf s 1 for definition of "import".
5 Cf s 1 for definition of "foodstuffs".
6 Cf s 1 for definition of "treated".
7 S 2(1)(a)(i).
8 S 2(1)(a)(ii).
9 S 2(1) read with s 18.
10 S 15(1)(d). Contravention of the regulation may be an offence: s 15(5).
11 *Government Gazette* 15486 GN R246, 11 February 1994.

SOLID WASTE MANAGEMENT

INTRODUCTION

557 Definition of waste For the purposes of this section, the discussion is confined to solid waste on land, although it is acknowledged that water and air are also polluted by solid waste. The parameters of the subject are somewhat diffuse on account of the overlap with air pollution and especially with freshwater and marine pollution.

The concept of waste is usually described in legislation by the use of different nouns, such as "garbage", "refuse", "offal", "rubbish" and "rubble", which nouns are mostly not defined. The Environment Conservation Act,[1] nevertheless, now defines both the concepts of "litter" and of "waste". "Litter", the more restricted concept, and, in fact, a component of the broader concept of "waste", is defined as any object or matter discarded or left behind by the person in whose possession or control it was.[2] "Waste" means any matter, whether gaseous, liquid or solid or any combination thereof, which is from time to time designated by the Minister of Environmental Affairs and Tourism by notice in the *Government Gazette* as an undesirable or superfluous by-product, emission, residue or remainder of any process or activity.[3]

In pursuance of this power the minister has identified[4] as an undesirable or superfluous by-product, emission, residue or remainder of any process or activity, any matter, gaseous, liquid or solid or any combination thereof, originating from any residential, commercial or industrial area, which:

(a) is discarded by any person; or

(b) is accumulated and stored by any person with the purpose of eventually discarding it, with or without prior treatment connected with the discarding thereof; or

(c) is stored by any person with the purpose of recycling, re-using or extracting a usable product from such matter, excluding:

    (i) water used for industrial purposes or any effluent produced by or resulting from such use which is discharged in compliance with the provisions of the Water Act[5] or on the authority of an exemption granted under the Act;[6]

    (ii) any matter discharged into a septic tank or french drain sewerage system and any water or effluent contemplated by the Water Act;

    (iii) building rubble used for filling or levelling purposes;

    (iv) any radioactive substance discarded in compliance with the provisions of the Nuclear Energy Act;[7]

    (v) any minerals, tailings, waste-rock or slimes produced by or resulting from the activities at a mine or works as defined in the Mines and Works Act[8] (now repealed); and

    (vi) ash produced by or resulting from activities at an undertaking for the generation of electricity under the provisions of the Electricity Act.[9]

1 73 of 1989. See generally Botha *SA Urban Solid Waste Legislation and its Application: Proposals towards Reform* MA UCT 1988; Lombard, Botha and Rabie "Solid Waste" in Fuggle and Rabie (eds) *Environmental Management in SA* 493; Barrie 1990 *TSAR* 426; CSIR *The Situation of Waste Management and Pollution Control in SA* CPR 1/91 1991; Glazewski, Neville-Smyly and Tonkin in Noble (ed) *Hazardous Waste in SA* vol 4: *Legislative Options*; Glazewski 1993 *CILSA* 234; Peckham 1994 *SAJELP* 85; Kidd *An Evaluation of the Law relating to Urban Solid Waste Management in SA* LLM Natal, Durban 1995.

2 S 1.

3 S 1.

4 *Government Gazette* 12703 GN 1986,

24 August 1990.

5 54 of 1956 s 21(1); see now the National
   Water Act 36 of 1998.

6 S 21(4).

7 131 of 1993; see now the Nuclear Energy
   Act 46 of 1999.

8 27 of 1956.

9 41 of 1987.

558 Classification of waste Waste may be classified by source, form, inherent properties or by its effects. It is customary in South Africa to identify different categories such as mining and mineral waste,[1] power generation waste, industrial waste, urban solid waste and nuclear and other hazardous waste. This is essentially a classification by source. However, legislation is not in principle classified according to such categories.

1 Such waste constitutes approximately 75 per
   cent of the total mass of South Africa's solid

waste stream of between 280 and 300 million tons per year.

559 National waste management policy The first national policy on waste management was contained in the *White Paper on a National Policy regarding Environmental Conservation.*[1] The Environment Conservation Act[2] authorised the Minister of Environmental Affairs and Tourism by notice in the *Government Gazette* to determine the general policy to be applied with a view to the protection of the environment against disturbance, deterioration, defacement, poisoning, pollution or destruction as a result of man-made structures, installations, processes or products or human activities.[3]

The general environmental policy which was thus determined provides that, in the first instance, pollution, of whatever nature, should be prevented by formulation of an effective comprehensive policy, the promulgation of appropriate legislation, the establishment and maintenance of norms and standards, the application of the best practicable environmental options based on the most suitable available technology, the fostering of positive attitudes among industrialists and the public, and participation in international co-operation.

In 2000, the department produced the *White Paper on Integrated Pollution and Waste Management for South Africa.*[4] The White Paper emphasises waste minimisation and pollution prevention, and addresses greater co-operation in respect of waste management, which is identified as being fragmented. The goals identified in the White Paper are effective institutional framework and legislation; pollution prevention, waste minimisation, impact management and remediation; holistic and integrated planning; participation and partnerships in integrated pollution and waste management governance; empowerment and education in integrated pollution and waste management; information management; and international co-operation.

1 WP 0–1980 par 4.8.

2 73 of 1989.

3 S 2(1)(c). This section has been repealed by
   the National Environmental Management

Act 107 of 1998 s 50(1).

4 *Government Gazette* 20978 GN 227,
   17 March 2000.

560 Variety of legislation Solid waste has been controlled in terms of South African legislation in a haphazard and unco-ordinated manner. A variety of Acts, ordinances, by-laws and regulations deal with certain aspects of solid waste, there being no comprehensive treatment of the subject matter. In fact, the comprehensive report, *The situation of waste management and pollution control in South Africa,* prepared by the CSIR Programme for the Environment, for the Department of Environment Affairs during 1991, revealed that an assortment of provisions dealing with waste on land is to be found scattered among at least 37 Acts of Parliament, 16 provincial ordinances and numerous local by-laws. This legislation, which is administered by a variety of public bodies, encompasses a diversity of activities which generate waste and many different types of waste that are produced.

It is not practicable to compile a comprehensive list of all the legal provisions dealing with solid waste (even if confined only to solid waste on land), although reference will be made to the most important relevant legislation. As has been pointed out, waste control legislation is not characterised by homogeneity or by comprehensive regulation of the subject matter. Moreover, practically every local authority has promulgated legislation pertaining to waste control, if only in relation to the protection of public health.

In the past, solid waste legislation has dealt mainly with the prohibition of littering and with refuse removal, and has been administered mainly at local government level. It has become apparent that litter and refuse form only a relatively small – albeit conspicuous – part of the problem, and that the active involvement of the provincial and central governments is necessary if the problem is to be combated in a co-ordinated and effective manner. It does seem that a new direction, aimed at achieving a more comprehensive legislative treatment of solid waste control, is developing in the Environment Conservation Act.[1] The Act, as will be shown, provides for control over waste disposal sites and for extensive waste management regulations. However, its provisions do not supersede the numerous existing provisions in other legislation.

1 73 of 1989.

NATIONAL LEGISLATION

561 Waste management regulations The Minister of Environmental Affairs and Tourism may by virtue of the Environment Conservation Act[1] make regulations with regard to waste[2] management, concerning:

(a) the manner in which an application for a disposal permit[3] must be submitted;

(b) the submission[4] of statistics on the quantity and types of waste produced;

(c) the classification of different types of waste and the handling, storage, transport and disposal of such waste;

(d) the reduction of waste by:

(i) modifications in the design and marketing of products;

(ii) modifications in manufacturing processes; and

(iii) the use of alternative products;

(e) the utilisation of waste by way of recovery, re-use or processing of waste;

(f) the location, planning and design of disposal sites and sites used for waste disposal;

(g) control over the management of sites, installations and equipment used for waste disposal;

(h) the administrative arrangements for the effective disposal of waste;

(i) the dissemination of information to the public on effective waste disposal;

(j) control over the import and export of waste;

(k) any other matter which the minister may deem necessary or expedient in connection with the effective disposal of waste for the protection of the environment; and

(l) the imposition of compulsory charging, deposits or related financial measures on waste types or specified items in waste types with the concurrence of the Minister of Finance.[5]

The minister may also make regulations with regard to the prohibition, control, sale, distribution, import or export of products that may have a substantial detrimental effect on the environment or on human health.[6]

Regulations made under the Environment Conservation Act will be discussed under the appropriate headings below.

1   73 of 1989.

2   "Waste" means any matter, whether gaseous, liquid or solid or any combination thereof, which is from time to time designated by the minister by notice in the *Government Gazette* as an undesirable or superfluous by-product, emission, residue or remainder of any process or activity : s 1.

3   In terms of s 20(1).

4   Subject to the provisions of the Statistics Act 66 of 1976 (now the Statistics Act 6 of 1999).

5   Environment Conservation Act 73 of 1989 s 24. The procedure for making regulations is provided for in s 24C.

6   S 24B. Nevertheless, two sets of draft regulations were issued in terms of the Environment Conservation Act 100 of 1982: *Government Gazette* 9838 GN 1549, 12 July 1985; *Government Gazette* 11473 GN 591, 26 August 1988.

562 Disposal sites It is an offence to establish, provide or operate any disposal site[1] without a permit issued by the Minister of Environmental Affairs and Tourism or contrary to the conditions of such permit.[2] Particular provisions govern the application for a disposal site permit.[3] The minister may issue a permit subject to such conditions as he or she may deem fit; alter or cancel any permit or condition in a permit; or refuse to issue a permit.[4] The minister may, moreover, exempt any person or category of persons from obtaining a permit, subject to such conditions as he or she may deem fit.[5] Finally, the minister must maintain a register in which details of every disposal site for which a permit has been issued, must be recorded.[6] The issuing of a waste disposal site permit is subject to the concurrence of the Minister of Water Affairs and Forestry, and the inclusion therein of the conditions contained in a Record of Decision issued by that minister regarding any measures that the minister considers necessary to protect a water resource as defined in the National Water Act.[7]

The minister may, from time to time by notice in the *Government Gazette*, issue directions with regard to:

(a)   the control and management of disposal sites in general;

(b)   the control and management of certain disposal sites or disposal sites handling particular types of waste; and

(c)   the procedure to be followed before any disposal site may be withdrawn from use or utilised for another purpose.[8]

Contravention of such directions constitutes an offence.[9]

Subject to the provisions of any other law, it is an offence for any person to discard waste or dispose of it in any other manner, except:

(a)   at a disposal site for which a permit has been issued; or

(b)   in a manner or by means of a facility or method and subject to such conditions as the Minister of Environmental Affairs and Tourism may prescribe.[10]

1   "Disposal site" means a site used for the accumulation of waste with the purpose of disposing or treatment of such waste: Environment Conservation Act 73 of 1989 s 1.

2   Ss 20(1) 29(4).

3   S 20(2) and (3) and *Government Gazette* 15832 GN R1196, 8 July 1994 regulate the form and information required, as well as appeals.

4   S 20(3).

5   S 20(4).

6   S 20(7).

7   36 of 1998 s 1.

8   Environment Conservation Act 73 of 1989 s 20(5).

9   S 29(4).

10   Ss 20(6) 29(4).

563 Litter It is an offence in terms of the Environment Conservation Act[1] to discard, dump or leave any litter[2] on any land or water surface, street, road or site in or on any place to which the public has access, except in a container or at a place which has been specially indicated, provided or set apart for such purpose.[3]

Two duties – buttressed by criminal sanctions[4] – are imposed upon every person or authority in control of or responsible for the maintenance of any place to which the public has access. Such person or authority must:

(a) at all times ensure that containers or places are provided which will normally be adequate and suitable for the discarding of litter by the public;[5] and

(b) within a reasonable time after any litter has been discarded, dumped or left behind at such place (with the inclusion of any pavement adjacent to, or land situated between, such a place and a street, road or site used by the public to obtain access to such place) remove such litter or cause it to be removed.[6]

The premier[7] may make regulations with regard to the control of the dumping of litter, concerning:

(a) the nature, design, number, provision and placing of containers for the dumping of litter;

(b) the nature, design, number, provision and placing of notices in respect of the dumping of litter;

(c) the cleaning, clearing away and removal of litter and the emptying and maintenance of containers for the dumping of litter;

(d) any other facilities or methods to prevent the dumping of litter, as well as programmes for the clearing away of litter;

(e) the powers of provincial governments, local authorities or government institutions to control and prevent the dumping of litter; and

(f) any other matter which he or she deems necessary or desirable to control and prevent the dumping of litter.[8]

No such regulations have yet been made.

1 73 of 1989.
2 "Litter" means any object or matter discarded or left behind by the person in whose possession or control it was : s 1.
3 Ss 19(1) and 29(3).
4 S 29(3).
5 S 19(2).
6 S 19A.
7 Defined in s 1.
8 S 24A.

564 Regulation of plastic carrier bags Regulations[1] under the Environment Conservation Act[2] prohibit the manufacture, trade and commercial distribution of domestically produced and imported plastic carrier bags[3] and plastic flat bags,[4] for use within the Republic of South Africa, other than those which comply with the compulsory specification under the Standards Act.[5] Contravention of this prohibition is an offence.[6]

1 *Government Gazette* 24839 GN R625, 9 May 2003.
2 73 of 1989 s 24(d).
3 "Plastic carrier bag" means a bag, made of plastic film, with handles, with or without gussets, and which complies with pars 4 and 5 of the compulsory specification.
4 "Plastic flat bag" means a bag, made of plastic film, without handles, with or without gussets, and which complies with pars 4 and 5 of the compulsory specification.
5 29 of 1993: reg 2.
6 Reg 3.

565 Health-related wastes Most solid waste provisions are directly or indirectly related to the protection of public health. Among the more specific legislation is the

Health Act,[1] which provides for the control of nuisances[2] and the making of regulations.[3] Moreover, the International Health Regulations Act[4] provides that every port and airport must be provided with an effective system for the removal and safe disposal of refuse.[5]

Regulations in terms of the Abattoir Hygiene Act[6] deal with the disposal or removal of remains and refuse from an abattoir.[7] The Sea-Shore Act[8] makes provision for the regulation of deposition or discharge upon the sea-shore, or in the sea, of offal, rubbish or anything liable to be a nuisance or danger to health.[9] Finally, the Medicines and Related Substances Act[10] regulates the disposal of medicines and related substances.[11]

1 63 of 1977.
2 S 1 read with s 20(1)(b).
3 Ch V.
4 28 of 1974.
5 Art 14(3) of the Schedule to the Act, read with s 2.
6 121 of 1992 s 24(1)(g) (i). This Act has been repealed by the Meat Safety Act 40 of 2000,

but regulations under the repealed Act remain in force in terms of s 25(2) of the new Act.
7 S 38(1)(n).
8 21 of 1935.
9 S 10(1)(d).
10 101 of 1965.
11 Ss 23 35(1)(xxvA) (xxviA).

566 Wastes on roads Both the Advertising on Roads and Ribbon Development Act[1] and the South African National Roads Agency Limited and National Roads Act[2] prohibit the leaving of any disused vehicle or machine or any rubbish or other refuse on certain roads, or within a certain distance of such roads.[3] In addition to the criminal sanction, a procedure is created to deal with the removal of discarded objects. The authority in question may remove such objects, or may order that they be removed, and may recover the costs of removal from the person who deposited or left them on the road in question.[4] No time limits or formalities are prescribed in relation to the removal and disposal of the disused vehicles or machines.

1 21 of 1940.
2 7 of 1998.
3 S 8(1) of the Advertising on Roads and Ribbon Development Act 21 of 1940 and s 51(1) of the South African National Roads Agency Ltd and National Roads Act 7 of 1998. "Disused vehicle or machine",

"rubbish" and "refuse" are not defined.
4 S 8(3) of the Advertising on Roads and Ribbon Development Act 21 of 1940 and s 51(2) and (3) of the South African National Roads Agency Ltd and National Roads Act 7 of 1998.

567 Hazardous waste A comprehensive study on hazardous waste in South Africa[1] revealed that in 1992 there were more than 30 Acts of Parliament and numerous sets of regulations and guidelines by virtue of which hazardous waste (albeit not only of a solid nature) may be potentially controlled by some 13 government departments.

Control over the dumping[2] and other forms of disposal of certain hazardous substances[3] may be effected through regulations made in terms of the Hazardous Substances Act.[4] Such regulations have been issued[5] in respect of the disposal of empty containers[6] of any Group I hazardous substance.[7] Returnable containers of certain hazardous substances[8] must, before being returned, be securely closed.[9] After being cleaned, such a container may be used as a container only for the hazardous substance that it originally contained.[10] Every empty hazardous substance container, the label of which does not specify that it should be returned to the supplier, must be perforated and flattened and then buried in the ground, or disposed of in an alternative safe manner.[11] There are also provisions relating to containers of hazardous substances being used as containers for foodstuffs and vice versa.[12] Contravention of any of these provisions amounts to an offence.[13]

Further regulations govern the transportation of dangerous goods and substances by road.[14]

Radioactive wastes are controlled in terms of the Nuclear Energy Act.[15]

Several proposals have been made aimed at a reform of the current legislation and its administration.[16]

1 Noble (ed) *Hazardous Waste in SA* vol 4 *Legislative Options Department of Environment Affairs.*

2 "Dump" means deposit, discharge, spill, release or cause or permit to be deposited, discharged, spilled or released (whether or not the substance in question is enclosed in a container, in such a place, under such circumstances or for such a period that the person depositing, discharging, spilling or releasing or causing or permitting this action, may reasonably be assumed to have abandoned it: Hazardous Substances Act 15 of 1973 s 1.

3 Ie of any grouped hazardous substance. Cf s 2 of the Act.

4 S 29(1)(a)(vi).

5 *Government Gazette* 9533 GN R2778, 21 December 1985 reg 10.

6 "Container" means the receptacle or package in which a product is offered for sale, but does not include any outer wrapping or box that is not customarily displayed: reg 1(1)(a).

7 Cf the Schedule to *Government Gazette* 9533 GN 2777, 21 December 1984. Included in Category B are a number of pesticides.

8 Ie a Category B Group I hazardous substance.

9 Reg 10(1).

10 Reg 10(2).

11 Reg 10(3).

12 Reg 10(4) (5).

13 Reg 11 read with s 29(8) of the Act.

14 In terms of the National Road Traffic Act 93 of 1996; *Government Gazette* 20963 GN R225, 17 March 2000 ch VIII.

15 131 of 1993.

16 Noble 53 et seq.

PROVINCIAL LEGISLATION

568 Dumping of rubbish The powers of provincial councils were extended in 1976 to enable them to legislate for the control of environmental pollution, particularly of littering.[1] Utilising this power, the Free State has been the first province to exercise the abovementioned powers. In that province dumping of rubbish is controlled in terms of the Prohibition of the Dumping of Rubbish Ordinance[2] which provides that no person may without authority throw, dump or leave any rubbish[3] on public land or water, except in a container or at a place specially adapted and set apart for such purpose;[4] or on private property in a defined area[5] in such manner that it is visible from a public road or place, unless such act is performed in connection with farming activities or for the purpose of immediately burying or destroying such rubbish.[6] Contravention of this prohibition is an offence.[7] Moreover, where an accumulation of rubbish exists, or rubbish lies scattered in sight of a public road or place, an authorised officer[8] may order[9] the owner or occupier of the land to clean up or remove such rubbish within a certain period.[10] Failure to comply with this order constitutes an offence[11] and entitles the officer to clean up or remove the rubbish at the expense of the owner or occupier.[12]

The KwaZulu Natal Prevention of Environmental Pollution Ordinance[13] renders it an offence for any person in any manner whatsoever and whether wilfully or negligently to perform any act of littering or pollution on, in or into any land, whether public or private or the sea or inland waters.[14] Provision is made for several exceptions.[15] The ordinance also provides for the appointment of inspectors[16] and the making of regulations.[17] The provisions of the ordinance apply in addition to and not in substitution for, the provisions of any other ordinance, by-law or regulation.[18]

1 Cf par 24 of the second Schedule to the Financial Relations Act 65 of 1976.

2 8 of 1976.

3 "Rubbish" means refuse, garbage, rubble or

discarded article, fluid, matter, substance or thing: s 1.

4 S 2(1)(a).

5 "Defined area" means: (a) the road reserve of a public road and the land situated within 150 meters from the boundaries of such reserve in so far as such reserve or land is not situated within the area of jurisdiction of a local authority; (b) land which is in the possession or under the control of the provincial government; and (c) an area which has been declared a defined area by the premier by notice in the *Provincial Gazette*: s 1.

6 S 2(1)(b).

7 S 4(1)(a) read with s 4(1)(i). When in a prosecution in terms of the ordinance it is alleged that rubbish has been thrown out or dumped from a vehicle, there is a rebuttable presumption that such rubbish was dumped by the owner or driver of the vehicle: s 4(2).

8 Cf s 3.

9 Ie by written notice.

10 S 2(2).

11 S 4(1)(b) read with s 4(1)(ii).

12 S 2(2).

13 21 of 1981.

14 S 2(1) and (2), read with s 6.

15 S 2(1)(a)–(f).

16 S 3.

17 S 4.

18 S 5.

569 Wastes on roads The control of solid waste at provincial level has in the past been exercised mainly in respect of solid waste pollution along roads. The various road ordinances prohibit anyone from depositing or leaving waste[1] on roads.[2]

1 S 21(1)(b) of the OFS Roads Ord 4 of 1968 refers to rubbish, stones, boulders, ash-heaps, glass, wire, tins, nails, pieces of metal, timber, tree stumps or any other waste material or abandoned property; Natal Roads Ord 10 of 1968 and Tvl Roads Ord 22 of 1957 have been repealed; s 64(1)(d) and (e) of the Cape Ord 19 of 1976 refers to anything of whatsoever nature which is or is likely to be offensive, dangerous, harmful or injurious to traffic.

2 S 21(1)(b) of the OFS Ord; s 64(1)(d) and (e) of the Cape Ord.

570 Assignments of administrative functions to provincial governments The administration of certain provisions of Acts of Parliament that deal with solid waste has been assigned in terms of the Constitution[1] to the provincial governments concerned. Relevant Acts include the Sea-Shore Act[2] and the Environment Conservation Act.[3] Moreover, according to the latter Act it is envisaged that the regulations that may be issued in terms of the Act in respect of waste management[4] and of litter[5] may assign functions to a provincial government.[6]

1 Constitution of the Republic of SA 108 of 1996 Sch 6 item 14.

2 21 of 1935. Cf *Government Gazette* 16346 GN R27, 7 April 1995.

3 73 of 1989. Cf *Government Gazette* 16346

4 S 24.

5 S 24A.

6 S 28(a).

GN R29, 7 April 1995.

LOCAL LEGISLATION

571 General The most common control of solid waste by local authorities is exercised over the littering, for example, of public places, streets, private premises, streams and dams. Refuse or rubbish is usually not defined, although a number of items are usually enumerated. The provisions are generally enforced through a criminal sanction.[1] Another common method of refuse control is through the abatement notice procedure prescribed for dealing with nuisances. In terms of this procedure a notice is served on the author of the nuisance calling upon him or her to remove or abate it within a specific time. Failure to comply with the notice is an offence, and entitles the local authority concerned itself to remove or abate the nuisance and to recover the costs incurred from the author of the nuisance.[2]

Control of solid waste by local authorities is also exercised through prescriptions relating to the keeping of animals,[3] the disposal of dead animals and the regulation of offensive trades.[4]

A local authority may also control the abuse of land due to parking or because of the accumulation or placing of articles or substances on it in a manner that is unsightly or would interfere with the amenities of the neighbourhood.[5] The main functions of local authorities in connection with solid waste are their obligations in the course of providing sanitary services for the collection and disposal of refuse.[6] Some local authorities have subdivided refuse into a number of different categories such as "house refuse", "garden refuse", "builder's refuse", "business refuse", and so on. The object of this subdivision is to differentiate between different kinds of refuse as far as charges and procedures relating to the collection, removal, storage and disposal of these wastes are concerned. An exemplary set of such by-laws has been promulgated for the Johannesburg municipality.[7]

Finally, provincial governments may in terms of the Sea-Shore Act[8] authorise local authorities to make regulations for the prevention or the regulation of the depositing or the discharging upon the sea-shore (or in the sea) of offal, rubbish or anything liable to be a nuisance or a danger to health.[9]

1 The position in respect of the repealed Tvl Roads Ord 22 of 1957 is taken as an example. Cf eg s 79(1)(a) and s 80(4)(a), (b) and (c) of the Tvl Local Government Ord 17 of 1939 and ss 24 and 25 of the Refuse (Solid Waste) By-laws of Johannesburg AN 1037 of 18 June 1975.

2 S 27 of the Health Act 63 of 1977.

3 S 80(7) Tvl Ord 17 of 1939.

4 Ss 80(15) and 95 of the Local Government Ord Tvl Ord 17 of 1939.

5 S 79quin(1)(b).

6 Cf s 20 of the Health Act 63 of 1977 and ss 79(2)(a) and 80(3) of the Tvl Ord 17 of 1939.

7 Refuse (Solid Waste) by-laws AN 1037 of 18 June 1975.

8 21 of 1935. The administration of the Act has been assigned to the relevant provincial government. Cf *Government Gazette* 16346 GN R27, 7 April 1995.

9 S 10(1)(d).

572 Assignment of administrative functions to local authorities Reference should, finally, also be made to the provisions of the Environment Conservation Act,[1] according to which regulations may be issued in respect of waste management[2] and of litter[3] and functions may be assigned to a local authority.[4] Furthermore, if in the opinion of the premier of a province any local authority within the province in question fails to perform any function assigned to it, the premier may, after affording the local authority an opportunity of making representations to him or her, by written notice direct such local authority to perform such function within a specified period and, if the local authority fails to comply with the direction, the premier may perform the function as if he or she were the local authority and may authorise any person to take all steps required for that purpose.[5] The premier may, in addition, recover the expenditure involved from the local authority concerned.[6] As a final backup the Minister of Environmental Affairs and Tourism is granted the same powers as those which the premier enjoys, if the latter has not acted in terms of the abovementioned provision.[7]

1 73 of 1989.

2 S 24.

3 S 24A.

4 S 28(a).

5 S 31(1).

6 S 31(2).

7 S 31(3).

ESTATE AGENTS

by

JEANNIE VAN WYK

(original text by C SMITH)

REFERENCES TO OTHER TITLES

SELECTED LITERATURE

Delport *South African Property Practice and the Law* (revision 9, 2001)
Kerr *Law of Agency*

INTRODUCTION

573 Nature of estate agency under common law The contract between a principal and an estate agent is not a contract of employment,[1] nor is it the ordinary contract between principal and agent.[2] Although an estate agency contract bears many of the characteristics of agency[3] and involves many of its obligations, it is actually a contract for a special service.[4] The owner agrees to pay the estate agent a commission if the estate agent introduces a purchaser who is prepared to accept the terms either indicated in advance or then imposed.[5] The agent has no authority to conclude the contract of sale and the owner is under no obligation to sell.[6] The estate agent has no power to create contractual relations between his or her principal and the third party; the estate agent is under no obligation to conduct the actual negotiations or to see to the completion of the ultimate contract of sale.[7] In short, an estate agent is an agent authorised to negotiate the sale or purchase of immovable property.[8] The service expected of the estate agent is the introduction of a person who is able, both legally and financially, to purchase.[9]

An estate agent is in a different position from most other persons who render professional services: sometimes he or she acts for the buyer, sometimes for the seller.[10] Unlike most other professional persons, an estate agent has no professional rules which inhibit him or her from energetically inviting business from both buyer and seller.[11] An estate agent owes a duty to his or her principal to act in good faith and may owe a duty to third parties with whom he or she might deal but, unlike a person who has entered into a contract of employment, an estate agent does not receive remuneration for discharging certain specified duties or obligations; an estate agent is remunerated if he or she brings about a specified event which he or she is under no obligation whatever to bring about.[12] In the absence of any stipulation to the contrary, a principal who employs an estate agent to find a purchaser for a house retains the right of selling the house to a third party who has not been introduced by the agent, either direct or through another agent, at any time before a proper offer is made to the principal by the original estate agent.[13]

1 *Gluckman v Landau & Co* 1944 TPD 261 267. Murray J was quoting with approval from the English decision *Luxor (Eastbourne) Ltd v Cooper* 1941 AC 108. See *Low v Shedden* [2001] 2 All SA 171 (C) 180I–181C.
2 *Gluckman v Landau & Co* supra 280.
3 See title AGENCY AND REPRESENTATION.
4 *Mackenzie v Flight* 1922 TPD 407 409.
5 *Mackenzie v Flight* supra 409.
6 *Mackenzie v Flight* supra 409.
7 *Gluckman v Landau & Co* supra 267; *Van Zyl*

& *Seuns (Edms) Bpk v Nel* 1975 3 SA 983 (N).
8 *Gluckman v Landau & Co* supra 268.
9 *Gluckman v Landau & Co* supra 268.
10 *Low v Shedden* supra 181B.
11 *Bosch v Flower Box (Pty) Ltd* 1971 4 SA 640 (E) 643.
12 *John H Pritchard & Associates (Pty) Ltd v Thorny Park Estates (Pty) Ltd* 1967 2 SA 511 (D) 517.
13 *Boose v Zeederberg & Duncan* 1918 CPD 283; *Gluckman v Landau & Co* supra.

574 Estate agents under statutory law In the Estate Agency Affairs Act[1] the term "estate agent" is defined as:

(a) any person who for the acquisition of gain on his or her own account or in partnership,[2] in any manner holds him or herself out as a person who, or directly or indirectly advertises[3] that he or she, on the instructions of or on behalf of any other person:

(i) sells or purchases or publicly exhibits for sale immovable property or any business undertaking or negotiates in connection therewith or canvasses or undertakes or offers to canvass a seller or purchaser therefor;[4] or

(ii) lets or hires or publicly exhibits for hire immovable property or any business undertaking or negotiates in connection therewith or canvasses or undertakes or offers to canvass a lessee or lessor therefor;[5] or

(iii) collects or receives any moneys payable on account of a lease of immovable property or any business undertaking;[6] or

(iv) renders any such other services as the minister, on the recommendation of the board may specify from time to time by notice in the *Government Gazette*;[7]

(b) for the purpose of appointment to the board as a member of the estate agents' industry, any director of a company, or a member who is competent and entitled to take part in the running of the business and the management, or a manager who is an officer, of a close corporation, which is an estate agent as defined in paragraph (a) above;[8]

(c) any director of a company or a member who is competent and entitled to take part in the running of the business and the management, or a manager who is an officer, of a close corporation which is defined as an estate agent and any person who is employed by an estate agent and performs on his or her behalf any of the acts referred to in (a)(i) and (ii) above for the following purposes:[9]

(i) the objects of the board;

(ii) the powers of the board;

(iii) the funds of the board;

(iv) the establishment and control of the estate agents fidelity fund;

(v) contribution to the estate agents fidelity fund;

(vi) applications for and issue of fidelity fund certificates and registration certificates;

(vii) application of moneys in the estate agents fidelity fund;

(viii) claims against the board in respect of the estate agents fidelity fund;

(ix) transfer of rights and remedies to the estate agents board;

(x) prohibition of rendering of services in certain circumstances;

(xi) disqualifications relating to fidelity fund certificates;

(xii) conduct deserving of sanction by estate agents;

(xiii) the regulations made by the minister after consultation with the estate agents board;

(xiv) prohibition of completion of documents by certain estate agents;

(d) any person who is employed by an attorney or professional company otherwise than as an attorney or an articled clerk[10] and whose duties consist wholly or primarily of the performance of any act referred to in paragraphs (a)(i) and (a)(ii) above on behalf of such an attorney or professional company for the following purposes:[11]

(i) the objects of the board;

(ii) the prescribed levies paid to the board by estate agents;

(iii) applications for and issue of fidelity fund certificates and registration certificates;

(iv) prohibition of rendering services in certain circumstances;

(v) disqualifications relating to fidelity fund certificates;

(vi) withdrawal and lapse of fidelity fund certificates;

(vii) the regulations made by the minister after consultation with the estate agents board.

The term "estate agent" does not include an attorney who on his or her own account or as a partner in a firm of attorneys or as a member of a professional company as an articled clerk,[12] performs any act referred to in paragraph (a) above in the course of and in the name and from the premises of such attorneys or professional company's practice, except if such an act is performed by an attorney or articled clerk in partnership with any person other than a partner in the practice of the attorney concerned or through the medium of or as a director of a company other than such professional company;[13]

(e) any person who was an estate agent at the time he or she was guilty of any act or omission which allegedly constitutes conduct deserving of sanction for the following purposes:

(i) the bringing and investigation of any charge of conduct deserving of sanction against an estate agent by the board;

(ii) the withdrawal of fidelity fund certificates by the board on a conviction of conduct deserving of sanction;

(iii) the institution of proceedings under the Act against an estate agent after an acquittal or a conviction upon a criminal charge of such an agent by a court of law;

(iv) the acceptance of a certified copy of the record of an estate agent's trial and conviction as sufficient proof of commission of an offence by such estate agent;

(v) the regulations prescribing the manner in which a charge of conduct deserving of sanction against an estate agent must be brought and investigated.[14]

1 112 of 1976. For a full statement of this Act, see pars 586–619 post.
2 For an interpretation of the words "on his own account or in partnership" see *Estate Agents Board v Swart* [1998] 4 All SA 373 (T); 1999 1 SA 1097 (T).
3 "Advertise" does not include to advertise in compliance with the provisions of any law: s 1(a) proviso. For an interpretation of the words "holds himself out as a person who, or advertises", see *Rogut v Rogut* 1982 3 SA 928 (A).
4 S 1(a)(i). See *Ronstan Investments (Pty) Ltd v Littlewood* [2001] 3 All SA 127 (SCA); 2001
3 SA 555 (SCA).
5 S 1(a)(ii).
6 S 1(a)(iii).
7 S 1(a)(iv).
8 S 1(b).
9 S 1(c).
10 As defined in the Attorneys Act 53 of 1979 s 1.
11 Estate Agency Affairs Act 112 of 1976 s 1(cA).
12 As defined in the Attorneys Act 53 of 1979 s 1.
13 Estate Agency Affairs Act 112 of 1976 s 1(d).
14 S 1(e).

CONTRACT BETWEEN PRINCIPAL AND ESTATE AGENT

575 Express agreement The usual contract between the principal and the estate agent is that the estate agent is entitled to an agreed or customary commission if he or she succeeds in introducing to the principal a person who is able, both legally and financially, to purchase and who is willing to purchase; and if the introduction is the effective cause of the conclusion of the sale.[1] No obligation is imposed on the agent to do anything; the contract is merely a promise binding on the principal to pay a sum of money on the happening of a specified event, which involves the rendering of some service by the agent.[2]

The principal may enter into contracts with as many estate agents as he or she pleases to sell the same property and there is no implied revocation of the mandate to one estate agent by entrusting the same commission to another.[3] The principal retains the right to sell his or her property to a person not introduced by the estate agent at any time without any liability to the agent.[4] Moreover, the owner does not bind him or herself to deal with the person introduced by the agent. There is on the other hand no obligation on the agent to seek for purchasers and there is no authority for holding the agent liable in damages if the agent fails to produce a purchaser when he or she had the opportunity to do so.[5]

1   *Gluckman v Landau & Co* 1944 TPD 261 273; *Flashco (Pvt) Ltd v Fox & Carney (Pvt) Ltd* 1980 1 SA 235 (ZRA); *Van Heerden v Retief* 1981 1 SA 945 (A).
2   *Luxor (Eastbourne) Ltd v Cooper* 1941 AC 108 quoted with approval in *Gluckman v Landau & Co* supra.
3   *Mackenzie v Flight* 1922 TPD 407 409
4   *Gluckman v Landau & Co* supra; *Nel v Grobbelaar & Viljoen Agentskappe (Edms) Bpk* 1983 4 SA 436 (O); *Mendes v Ermelo Eiendomme en Verhuringsagente* 1995 4 SA 821 (T).
5   *Mackenzie v Flight* supra 410.

576   Implied or tacit contract   If there is no express agreement between principal and agent, an implied or tacit contract may be inferred under certain circumstances. It would seem that there are two conflicting tests for inferring the existence of a tacit or implied contract.[1]

The first test is the "no other reasonable interpretation" test.[2] This test is explained as follows: in order to establish a tacit consent it is necessary to show, by a preponderance of probabilities, unequivocal conduct which is capable of no other reasonable interpretation than that the parties intended to, and did in fact, contract on the terms alleged. It must be proved that there was in fact *consensus ad idem*.[3]

The second test is the "most plausible probable conclusion" test.[4] In such a case a tacit contract has been established where, by a process of inference, it concludes that the most plausible probable conclusion from all the relevant proved facts and circumstances is that a tacit contract has come into existence.[5]

1   *Muller v Pam Snyman Eiendomskonsultante (Pty) Ltd* [2000] 4 All SA 412 (C); 2001 1 SA 313 (C). See *Steer Property Services (Pty) Ltd t/a Steer & Co v Estate Agency Affairs Board* [2002] 3 All SA 103 (C).
2   *Standard Bank of SA Ltd v Ocean Commodities Inc* 1983 1 SA 276 (A). Cf *Gordon Lloyd Page & Associates v Rivera* [2000] 4 All SA 241 (SCA); 2001 1 SA 88 (SCA) 95H–96G.
3   *Standard Bank of SA Ltd v Ocean Commodities Inc* supra 292B–C.
4   *Joel Melamed & Hurwitz v Cleveland Estates (Pty) Ltd; Joel Melamed & Hurwitz v Vorner Investments* 1984 3 SA 155 (A).
5   *Joel Melamed & Hurwitz v Cleveland Estates (Pty) Ltd; Joel Melamed & Hurwitz v Vorner Investments* supra 165.

FIDUCIARY RELATIONSHIP BETWEEN PRINCIPAL AND ESTATE AGENT

577   Performance of mandate   An estate agent stands in a position of trust towards his or her principal[1] and is obliged to observe the utmost good faith.[2] The duty of good faith imposed on an estate agent involves two elements: the agent must not make a secret profit out of the transaction, nor must the agent allow his or her own interests to conflict with the interests of the principal. An estate agent is not obliged to try to find a purchaser,[3] but if an estate agent is given a mandate by his or her principal to sell property, the principal is entitled to claim an exact performance of the terms of the mandate.[4] However, should the agent fail to find a person who will purchase on the terms of the mandate but introduces a person who negotiates with the principal and the seller agrees to accept a lower price, the agent is entitled to commission even though he or she has not performed the original mandate.[5] A mandate to an estate agent to find a purchaser has as its object the conclusion of a deed of sale, but places the agent under no obligation to engage in negotiations him or herself for the sale and to see to the completion of a deed of sale or the execution thereof.[6]

1 *Robinson v Randfontein Estates Gold Mining Co Ltd* 1921 AD 168. The relationship between principal and agent is analogous to the relationship between guardian and ward, or attorney and client.

2 *Tvl Cold Storage Co Ltd v Palmer* 1904 TS 4.

3 See par 575 ante.

4 *Burt v Ryan* 1926 TPD 680 682.

5 *Burt v Ryan* supra 682. The principle applied, according to this case, is that either the seller must be taken to have tacitly novated the original mandate, or the agent must be regarded as having substantially

performed his or her mandate. Where the original mandate fixes the price and the seller after negotiating with the purchaser agrees to less than the price fixed, then, unless the principle is applied of a tacit novation or of substantial performance, the seller could by the slightest modification in the price defeat the agent's claim to commission. Cf *Metro-Goldwyn-Mayer (SA) (Pty) Ltd v Herman* 1938 TPD 226 232.

6 *Van Zyl & Seuns (Edms) Bpk v Nel* 1975 3 SA 983 (N).

578 Conflict of interests It is the duty of an estate agent to act solely for the benefit of his or her principal.[1] Where the agent has an interest that is adverse to the principal's interest, then the onus is on the agent to show that he or she has made a complete disclosure to his or her principal and also that the principal has acquiesced in the transaction.[2] An agent authorised to sell, cannot legally purchase property entrusted to him or her for sale.[3] It is a clear rule of our law that an agent for the purpose of sale cannot purchase his or her principal's property.[4] The rule prohibiting an agent from purchasing his or her principal's property, which he or she is employed to sell, is based on the consideration that such an agent stands in a fiduciary capacity towards the principal.[5] If the agent were permitted to become the purchaser, the agent's duty to his or her principal and his or her own interest would be in direct conflict with each other.[6] The fact that a reserve price has been fixed does not affect the rule of law that an agent cannot buy the property which the agent is employed to sell.[7] An agent who decides to purchase the property him or herself becomes a principal in the transaction and cannot claim commission as an agent.[8] If the agent wants the commission he or she must forego any idea of him or herself becoming the purchaser.[9]

It is the duty of all agents, including estate agents, to conduct the affairs of their principals in the interests of their principals and not for their own benefit.[10] There is, however, an exception to this rule: if the seller with the full knowledge of the facts elects to adopt the sale, it becomes binding on the seller.[11] Similarly, if the seller expressly authorises the agent to buy the property him or herself the transaction is binding on the seller and he or she cannot repudiate it afterwards.[12]

1 *Mallinson v Tanner* 1947 4 SA 681 (T) 684.

2 *Mallinson v Tanner* supra 684.

3 *Hargreaves v Anderson* 1915 AD 519 522.

4 *Forbes, Still & Co v Sutherland* (1856) 2 S 231; *Hargreaves v Anderson* supra.

5 *Hargreaves v Anderson* supra.

6 *Hargreaves v Anderson* supra. Solomon JA remarked that the seller of a property naturally desires to obtain as high a price for it as possible, whereas the purchaser desires to obtain it at as low a price as possible.

7 *Hargreaves v Anderson* supra.

8 *Hargreaves v Anderson* supra. In *Salomons v Pender* 12 LT 267 Martin B said that in his opinion an agent who takes upon hi or herself the position of a principal annihilates all the rights as agent.

9 *Hargreaves v Anderson* supra.

10 *R v Milne & Erleigh* (7) 1951 1 SA 791 (A) 828. In *Mallinson v Tanner* supra an estate agent received a mandate to sell his principal's house for R4 000. The agent knew of

an offer to purchase at that sum by a pro-spective purchaser and himself offered R3 600 to his principal, who accepted this offer. Within half an hour the agent resold the house to the prospective purchaser for R4 000 plus R100 commission. The court

decided that the agent was liable to account to his principal for the difference in the amount.
11 *Hargreaves v Anderson* supra 522.
12 *Hargreaves v Anderson* supra 524.

579 Secret benefit From the general principle that an estate agent is not allowed to act in a matter where the agent's duty to his or her principal conflicts with his or her own interest, it follows that any secret benefit given by one contracting party to the agent of another is not permissible.[1] A secret benefit given with the intention of influencing the agent's mind in favour of the donor is a bribe, which entitles the principal to certain remedies against the agent and the donor, irrespective of the donor's motive or the effect of the benefit on the mind of the agent.[2] Any agent, including an estate agent, cannot make a secret benefit out of anything which belongs to his or her principal and which the agent possesses merely in a fiduciary capacity.[3] One of the remedies available to the principal whose agent has been bribed, is that he or she may repudiate the contract.[4] The principal is not bound to repudiate the contract; the principal may also confirm it. If the principal wishes to confirm the contract and claim the resulting benefit, he or she must show that such benefit arises from transactions completely covered by the prohibitive operation of the relationship.[5] An agent cannot retain any profit or benefit acquired by the agent in transactions within the scope of the agency unless the agent has the consent of his or her principal given with full knowledge of the material facts and under circumstances which rebut any presumption of undue influence.[6] So an estate agent who is instructed to acquire property on behalf of his or her principal cannot without such consent of the principal acquire property on his or her own behalf and subsequently resell it to his or her principal at an enhanced price.[7] In such a case the principal can treat the property as originally acquired for him or her and the resale as nugatory, and may recover from the agent the difference between the price of the resale and the price of the original sale.[8]

1 *Davies v Donald* 1923 CPD 295.
2 *Davies v Donald* supra 299. In *Mangold Bros Ltd v Minnaar & Minnaar* 1936 TPD 48 59 De Wet J said: "Where, shortly after the conclusion of a transaction . . . a secret pay-ment is made by one of the contracting par-ties to the confidential agent of the other contracting party by way of reward for his services for bringing about the contract, it would, in my opinion, in the words of Scrutton, LJ, be a conclusion very dangerous to the commercial world and to commercial morality to hold that such payment is not a corrupt one, and is not in fraud of the inno-cent party."
3 *Jones v East Rand Extension Gold Mining Co*

Ltd 1903 TH 325 335.
4 *Davies v Donald* supra 300.
5 *Robinson v Randfontein Estates Gold Mining Co Ltd* 1921 AD 168 178. Cf *Tvl Cold Stor-age Co Ltd v Palmer* 1904 TS 4.
6 *Jacobus Marler Estates v Marlet* 114 LT 640 quoted with approval in *Robinson v Randfon-tein Estates Gold Mining Co Ltd* supra 229.
7 Ibid.
8 Ibid. Cf *Tvl Cold Storage Co Ltd v Palmer* supra; *African Claim & Land Co Ltd v WJ Langermann* 1905 TS 494 495; *De Jager v Oli-fants Tin "B" Syndicate* 1912 AD 505 509; *Mallinson v Tanner* 1947 4 SA 681 (T). See also par 578 ante.

COMMISSION

580 Payment of agent's commission Although it is possible that an estate agent will be entitled to commission merely on the introduction of a person offering to purchase, the general balance of probability is against an arrangement of this sort.[1]

Normally the principal contemplates an actual sale of the property as the event upon which the promise to pay commission must be fulfilled[2] and it is improbable that a principal would bind him or herself to pay commission merely on production of a person willing to buy.[3] Where the instruction given by the principal is "to find a purchaser" the completion of a valid sale is the event upon which the estate agent's commission is payable, unless additional considerations indicate the contrary or another construction.[4] The phrase "to find a purchaser" means what it says, namely a person who in fact becomes a purchaser. The first stage of finding a purchaser obviously consists of the procuring by the agent of a person who makes a binding offer on the principal's terms to purchase. However, this does not conclude the matter, for that person must be turned into a purchaser, not necessarily by virtue of any further activity on the agent's part, but by the fact of the conclusion of a contract of sale.[5] An estate agent who sues for commission can succeed only if he or she proves that an enforceable sale has been completed.[6] If the sale entered into is subject to a suspensive condition and that condition has not been performed, there is no enforceable sale and the estate agent is not entitled to commission.[7] An agreement in terms of which an owner is obliged to pay commission irrespective of whether a valid contract of sale has been concluded or not or that the purchaser is unable to carry out his or her obligations in terms of the contract, is not unthinkable, but is so in conflict with the probabilities and normal business usage that a court of law could only interpret such an agreement in the estate agent's favour if the parties had so expressed themselves in very clear language.[8] Where an estate agent has furnished the principal with a binding offer from a person able to purchase and if a sale to that person results, the agent has earned his or her commission and the principal cannot lawfully avoid paying that commission should the principal for any reason decide to cancel the sale.[9] If a written agreement between seller and purchaser provides for the payment of commission to an estate agent, the agreement, although not signed by the agent, is binding on the seller/principal.[10] The onus lies on the estate agent to satisfy the court that the event has occurred which contractually entitles the agent to claim commission from the principal.[11]

An estate agent's contractual right to commission cannot be altered by other parties without his or her consent.[12]

Where no rate of commission is agreed at the outset, then the principle is that the estate agent is entitled to a reasonable remuneration, which is the prevailing, or standard or customary rate of commission.[13]

1 *Gluckman v Landau & Co* 1944 TPD 261 268.

2 *Gluckman v Landau & Co* supra 268. Lord Russell of Killowen in the well-known case of *Luxor (Eastbourne) Ltd v Cooper* 1941 AC 108 129 expressed this principle thus: "It is possible that an owner may be willing to bind himself to pay a commission for the mere introduction of one who offers to purchase at the specified or minimum price; but such construction of the contract would in my opinion require clear and unequivocal language."

3 *Gluckman v Landau & Co* supra; *Isaacson v Commercial Services Corporation of SA Ltd* 1931 NPD 80.

4 *Brayshaw v Schoeman* 1960 1 SA 625 (A);

Oliver v Diamond 1955 1 PH A22 (O). The phrase "to find a purchaser" has been described by Viscount Simon in *Luxor (Eastbourne) Ltd v Cooper* supra as being "not without ambiguity". See *Wacks v Record* 1955 2 SA 234 (C) 238.

5 *Gluckman v Landau & Co* supra 282.

6 *Naidu v Naidoo* 1967 2 SA 223 (N) 227.

7 *Naidu v Naidoo* supra 227. In *Martin v Currie* 1921 TPD 50 59 De Waal J said: "The law on the subject, I think, is quite settled and is to this effect, that if the relation of buyer and seller is really brought about by the act of the agent he is entitled to commission." See however *Commercial Business Brokers v Hassen* 1985 3 SA 583 (N) where it was held that an agent is entitled to his or her commission

notwithstanding the non-fulfilment of a suspensive condition in an agreement of sale when the parties expressly and unambiguously agree that commission will be paid upon signature of the agreement. In *Munitz v Steer's Trust Co (Pty) Ltd* 1993 2 SA 369 (C) the court indicated that an agent would be entitled to commission on the sale of a property even though the agent did not personally overcome obstacles which had previously prevented the sale. See also *Admin Estate Agents (Pty) Ltd t/a Larry Lambrou v Brennan* 1997 2 SA 922 (E).

8 *Roux v Schreuder* 1968 3 SA 616 (O) 620; *Brayshaw v Schoeman* supra; *John H Pritchard & Associates (Pty) Ltd v Thorny Park Estates*

(Pty) Ltd 1967 2 SA 511 (D) 514.

9 *Gluckman v Landau & Co* supra; *Watson v Fintrust Properties (Pty) Ltd* 1987 2 SA 739 (C).

10 *Baker v Afrikaanse Nasionale Afslaers & Agentskap Mpy (Edms) Bpk* 1951 3 SA 371 (A).

11 *Wacks v Record* supra; *Flashco (Pvt) Ltd v Fox & Carney (Pvt) Ltd* 1980 1 SA 235 (ZRA); *Tony Morgan Estates v Pinto* 1982 4 SA 171 (W).

12 *Adenia Eiendomme (Edms) Bpk v LPD Ondernemings Bk* [1997] 3 All SA 85 (T).

13 *Muller v Pam Snyman Eiendomskonsultante (Pty) Ltd* [2000] 4 All SA 412 (C); 2001 1 SA 313 (C).

581 Willingness and ability of purchaser to buy An estate agent is under no obligation to conduct the actual negotiations or to attend to the completion of the ultimate contract of sale, much less to its subsequent performance.[1] The service expected of the estate agent is the introduction of a person who is able, both financially and legally, to purchase and who is willing to purchase, such willingness being shown by the making of a binding offer of purchase at not less than the price originally fixed, or subsequently reduced, by the principal.[2] The phrase "finding a purchaser", although general and ambiguous,[3] entails introducing to the principal a purchaser ready and willing to purchase in the sense of a purchaser able to purchase and able to complete as well.[4]

Ability does not depend on whether the purchaser has the money in hand, nor does it depend on whether the purchaser has a binding agreement in terms of which a third person is obliged to provide him or her with resources to carry out the contract.[5] The question of the ability of the purchaser to perform his or her obligations is one of fact.[6] Where that question is confined to an investigation of the purchaser's own assets or existing cash or contractual resources, the inquiry will as a rule be fairly straightforward.[7] On the other hand, where the estate agent avers that the purchaser could have obtained financial assistance from sources which were not legally obliged to assist the purchaser, the agent must establish something more definite than mere speculative possibility.[8] The ability of the purchaser to pay must be assessed as at the moment of signing the contract.[9] If at that moment the purchaser was able to pay, the fact that financial misfortunes subsequently diminished or destroyed the ability to pay, is irrelevant.[10]

In cases where the purchaser undertakes to pay commission to the estate agent, the purchaser must be assumed to know that he or she is able to pay the purchase price. Accordingly the term "if the purchaser is able to purchase" should be not implied as it is usually, where the seller is the party who must pay the commission.[11]

1 *Gluckman v Landau & Co* 1944 TPD 261 267; *Van Zyl & Seuns (Edms) Bpk v Nel* 1975 3 SA 983 (N).

2 *Gluckman v Landau & Co* supra.

3 *Midgley Estates Ltd v Hand* [1952] 1 All ER 1394 (CA) 1396 quoted with approval in *Wacks v Record* 1955 2 SA 234 (C) 238.

4 *James v Smith* 1931 2 KB 317 318; *Wacks v Record* supra; *Gluckman v Landau & Co* supra; *Eschini v Jones* 1929 CPD 18 23.

5 *James v Smith* supra.

6 *Wacks v Record* supra.

7 *Wacks v Record* supra.

8 *Wacks v Record* supra 239. Ogilvie Thompson J put it thus: "If the contention is that the purchaser could have raised money to finance the purchase on the security of his existing assets and/or on the security of the property purchased, satisfactory evidence in support of that contention should be placed

before the Court. Such matters are ordinarily susceptible of relatively easy proof . . .
the agent, if he relies upon potential assistance to the purchaser by the latter's friends
or relatives, must place before the Court
evidence to show that – on a balance of
probabilities – such assistance would in fact
have been rendered."

9 *Beckwith v Foundation Investment Co* 1961 4
SA 510 (A) 513.

10 *Beckwith v Foundation Investment Co* supra
513.

11 *Du Plessis v Du Plessis* 1970 1 SA 683 (O)
686. See *Aida Uitenhage CC v Singapi* 1992 4
SA 675 (E) for a discussion of the circumstances under which an estate agent can recover commission from a purchaser who
fails, as a result of a breach of a contract of
sale, to ensure the fulfilment of a suspensive
condition.

582 Substantial performance Where an agent is given a mandate by his or her
principal to sell property, the principal is entitled to claim an exact performance of the
terms of the mandate.[1] If the agent introduces a person who negotiates with the
principal and, because of the introduction and negotiations the seller agrees to accept a
lower price, the agent is nevertheless entitled to commission notwithstanding the
failure to carry out the original mandate.[2] In principle there is no reason why an estate
agent should not be as much entitled to commission where the seller agrees to accept
different terms from those contained in the mandate as where the seller agrees to a
reduction in the price as originally fixed.[3] The discrepancy, however, must not be so
great that substantially a different transaction has resulted.[4] The principle applied is that
either the seller must be taken to have tacitly novated the original mandate, or the
agent must be regarded as having substantially carried out the agreement between the
agent and his or her principal.[5] If a sale for cash were one of the conditions imposed
on the agent, it would appear that the fact that afterwards credit is given does not
disentitle the agent to commission.[6] Substantial performance as opposed to full and
complete performance in every detail will suffice to entitle the agent to commission,
but an agent who has introduced as a purchaser one who refuses to buy but enters
into another contract which differs in material respects from the transaction specified
in the mandate is not entitled to commission.[7] So the difference between voluntary
purchase and sale and expropriation is so material that it cannot be held that where
expropriation results from the efforts of the agent, the latter has substantially performed his or he mandate.[8] Many of the cases in which an agent has been held to have
earned his or her commission despite the fact that a contract resulted on terms different from those specified in the mandate, turned not so much on substantial performance of the terms of the mandate as on implied variation or novation of those terms.[9]
The question whether there has been substantial performance of a mandate is one of
fact to be decided on the circumstances of each case.[10]

1 *Burt v Ryan* 1926 TPD 680 682.
2 *Burt v Ryan* supra 682; *Metro-Goldwyn-Mayer*
(*SA*) (*Pty*) *Ltd v Herman* 1938 TPD 226 232;
Doyle v Gibbon 1919 TPD 220; *Sammel v
Jacobs & Co* 1928 AD 353 355. For a matter
in which commission had been fixed arbitrarily without reference to a tariff and without the commission being a percentage of
the purchase consideration, see *Press v Jofwall
Investments* (*Pty*) *Ltd* 1981 1 SA 261 (W).
3 *Burt v Ryan* supra.
4 *Sammel v Jacobs & Co* supra.
5 *Burt v Ryan* supra.
6 *Solomon v Stone* 1914 CPD 261 263.
7 *John Wilkinson & Partners* (*Pty*) *Ltd v Berea
Nursing Home* (*Pty*) *Ltd* (*in voluntary Liquidation*) 1966 1 SA 791 (D) 796. In this case an

estate agent who was given a mandate to sell
property was not entitled to commission
when the party he introduced to the seller as
a prospective purchaser did not purchase the
property but expropriated it.
8 *John Wilkinson & Partners* (*Pty*) *Ltd v Berea
Nursing Home* (*Pty*) *Ltd* (*in voluntary Liquidation*) supra 798.
9 *John Wilkinson & Partners* (*Pty*) *Ltd v Berea
Nursing Home* (*Pty*) *Ltd* (*in voluntary Liquidation*) supra 796; *Metro-Goldwyn-Mayer* (*SA*)
(*Pty*) *Ltd v Herman* supra.
10 *Metro-Goldwyn-Mayer* (*SA*) (*Pty*) *Ltd v
Herman* supra; *Sammel v Jacobs & Co* supra;
Baring Eiendomme Bpk v Roux [2001] 1 All
SA 399 (A).

583 Effective cause In order to entitle an estate agent to commission on the sale of property, the agent must show that but for his or her introduction of the property to the purchaser the sale would not have gone through, that the introduction was the direct and effective cause of the sale and that the purchaser was induced to buy as a result of the introduction.[1] It must be asked if the sale was effected through the agent; if it was, the agent is entitled to commission.[2] If it was not, the agent is not entitled to any commission, however much energy he or she might have exerted to bring the sale about.[3] The question whether the sale was effected through his or her agency must be decided as an inference from the facts.[4] An agent is entitled to the commission if he or she can show that he or she is the *causa causans* that brought the sale about. It is not sufficient to show that the introduction was a *causa sine qua non*. It is necessary to show that the introduction was an effective cause in bringing about the sale.[5] Accordingly, where a principal agreed to give an estate agent a commission in the event of the sale of certain premises and the agent introduced a purchaser but no sale resulted and the purchaser of his own accord subsequently introduced another purchaser who purchased the premises, the agent was not entitled to commission.[6] Should the agent prove that the introduction that he or she has given the principal has caused the result desired by the principal, the agent is entitled to commission and it is not necessary for the agent to prove that he or she has conducted the negotiations which led to the actual drawing up of the contract. The sale of the property must have substantially proceeded from the agent's act, not as the indirect effect of a casual conversation.[7] It must not be assumed that anyone who introduces a purchaser to a seller is entitled to commission; it must be clear either that there is an express undertaking to pay commission, or that the seller intends to utilise the services of the other person as an estate agent.[8] The mere fact that an estate agent is instrumental in introducing a person who eventually buys the property is not sufficient, for the agent must prove that he or she was employed in his or her capacity as agent to effect the sale.[9] If an introduction does not immediately result in a sale it may subsequently still be the effective cause of the sale.[10]

If a new factor intervenes, causing or contributing to the conclusion of the sale, and that factor is not of the making of the agent, the final decision as to whether the agent is entitled to commission depends on the answer to the question – did the new factor outweigh the effect of the introduction by being more conducive to the bringing about of the sale or was the introduction overridingly effective?[11]

The onus rests on the estate agent and remains on the estate agent throughout to establish that he or she was the effective cause of the sale.[12] This onus may be discharged more readily where the sale follows immediately after the introduction of a purchaser than where there has been a long interval of time between the introduction and the conclusion of a contract.[13]

Where an estate agent introduces a person who subsequently purchases, then the agent has earned the commission and it is immaterial that the first negotiations led to nothing and are afterwards renewed without further introduction.[14] There is nothing to stop the principal from negotiating direct with the seller and selling the property for a smaller amount, but the agent is nevertheless entitled to his or her commission.[15] The fact that the agent ceases to be actively concerned in the negotiations does not necessarily deprive the agent of a claim for commission as the agent's introduction might still be the overriding factor inducing the sale.[16]

The employment of an auctioneer does not give the auctioneer any authority except to sell by public auction and the agency of an auctioneer ends as soon as the auction is held.[17] If the auctioneer does not sell by auction, he or she cannot afterwards sell by private treaty.[18] In the absence of any proof that the agency was renewed after the auction had concluded, the agent is not entitled to commission.[19]

Where the seller's agent introduces a purchaser who in turn approaches another agent who concludes the sale between the principal and purchaser, the first agent cannot be deprived of his or her commission because the second agent is the agent of the purchaser and is not the agent acting for the seller.[20]

An agent whose authority to sell on commission has terminated, is entitled to commission for a sale which was effected after termination but through services rendered by the agent before termination.[21]

1 *Mackie v Whyte & Turpin Ltd* 1923 TPD 347 348. The courts may however reject the *sine qua non* test; see *Vanarthdoy (Edms) Bpk v Roos* 1979 4 SA 1 (A). Even if the property is known to the purchaser and indeed to the seller the actions of an estate agent may *nevertheless* be the effective cause of a sale: *Vanarthdoy (Edms) Bpk v Roos* supra. An estate agent is entitled to commission after he or she has fulfilled the mandate, even if the sale is subsequently cancelled: *Venter Agentskappe (Edms) Bpk v De Sousa* 1990 3 SA 103 (A); *Jurgens Eiendomsagente v Share* 1990 4 SA 664 (A).

2 *Machonochie's Executrix v Bidewell-Edwards* (1892) 9 SC 204.

3 *Machonochie's Executrix v Bidewell-Edwards* supra.

4 *Machonochie's Executrix v Bidewell-Edwards* supra; *Mackie v Whyte & Turpin Ltd* supra.

5 *Millar, Son & Co v Radford* (1903) 19 TLR 575 quoted with approval in *Goddard v Arnold* 1922 TPD 167 169; *Le Grange v Metter* 1925 OPD 76. See *Vanarthdoy (Edms) Bpk v Roos* supra; *Lieb v I Kuper & Co (Pty) Ltd* 1982 3 SA 708 (T). See also *Knight Frank SA (Pty) Ltd v Nach Investments (Pty) Ltd* 1999 3 SA 891 (W); *Nach Investments (Pty) Ltd v Knight Frank SA (Pty) Ltd* [2001] 3 All SA 295 (A); *Wynland Properties CC v Potgieter* [1999] 3 All SA 567 (C); 1999 4 SA 1265 (C).

6 *Goddard v Arnold* supra; *Martin v Currie* 1921 TPD 50 59; *Schollum & Co v Lloyd* 1916 TPD 291; *Doyle v Gibbon* 1919 TPD 220 223; *Aida Real Estate Ltd v Lipschitz* 1971 3 SA 871 (W). See also *Wynland Properties CC v Potgieter* supra where it was held that where a purchaser, introduced by the estate agent, loses interest in the property after having defects in the property drawn to her attention, and later renews her interest in the property only after intervention by a third party, the estate agent is not the effective cause of the sale and is not entitled to commission.

7 In *Goddard v Arnold* supra De Waal J quoted from the judgment of Pollock CB in *Gibson v Crick* (1862) 31 LJ Ex 304 who said: "If a broker gives to the principal the name of another person, who names another, who alludes to another, and so on, and the principal employs the last named, that the broker should have any claim on the principal in such a case is simply preposterous." Cf *Hubbard & Snyman v Kaplan* 1935 TPD 122.

8 *Martin v Currie* supra 54.

9 *Martin v Currie* supra 54.

10 *Lombard v Reed* 1948 1 SA 30 (T); *Le Grange v Metter* supra; *Vanarthdoy (Edms) Bpk v Roos* supra; *Basil Elk Estates (Pty) Ltd v Curzon* 1990 2 SA 1 (T); *Edwards v Wynberg Club* 1990 2 SA 249 (C).

11 *Aida Real Estate Ltd v Lipschitz* supra 874. The removal of financial obstacles may be found to be the effective cause of the sale. See *Van Aswegen v De Clercq* 1960 4 SA 875 (A) 880.

12 *Wakefield & Sons (Pty) Ltd v Anderson* 1965 4 SA 453 (N) 455; *Barnard & Parry Ltd v Strydom* 1946 AD 931; *Lombard v Reed* supra.

13 *Wakefield & Sons (Pty) Ltd v Anderson* supra 457.

14 *Schollum & Co v Lloyd* supra 293; *Doyle v Gibbon* supra; *Abel v Perks* 1923 EDL 285 289; *Aida Real Estate Ltd v Lipschitz* supra; *Vanarthdoy (Edms) Bpk v Roos* supra; *Basil Elk Estates (Pty) Ltd v Curzon* supra; *Edwards v Wynberg Club* supra.

15 *Doyle v Gibbon* supra 223. This principle is naturally so because, as pointed out by Wessels JP, otherwise all the owner has to do is to negotiate direct with the purchaser and so escape the payment of commission. Cf *Abel v Perks* supra 289; *Vanarthdoy (Edms) Bpk v Roos* supra; *Basil Elk Estates (Pty) Ltd v Curzon* supra; *Edwards v Wynberg Club* supra.

16 *Aida Real Estate Ltd v Lipschitz* supra 874; *Vanarthdoy (Edms) Bpk v Roos* supra; *Basil Elk Estates (Pty) Ltd v Curzon* supra; *Edwards v Wynberg Club* supra.

17 *Martin v Currie* supra 53.

18 *Martin v Currie* supra 53.

19 *Martin v Currie* supra 60.

20 *Fassbender v Coetzee* 1941 SWA 4; *Kreser v Rosen (Pty) Ltd* 1938 TPD 403.

21 *Steyn v Joubert* 1923 TPD 275.

584 Competing agents Where a property is listed with several agents and they compete in trying to conclude a sale by a principal to a particular third party, it is not necessarily the agent who first introduces the purchaser who is entitled to commission but the agent who is the effective cause of the transaction being completed.[1] Often, however, the first introduction of the seller's property to the purchaser is the decisive factor, particularly in the ordinary case where nothing intervenes between the time of the introduction and the time of the sale.[2] The cumulative importance of a number of causes attributable to one agent may be such that although each in itself might be described as a *causa sine qua non*, the sum of the causes may be said to be the effective cause of the sale.[3] Where the contract made by an agent with a prospective purchaser is broken off and after a long interval the same purchaser reopens negotiations through another agent, the interruption may justify the inference that a sale which eventuates after resumed negotiations arises out of a fresh intervening cause and is not due to the efforts of the first agent.[4] The only way in which an agent who finds the purchaser can succeed in proving that the finding of the purchaser was the effective cause of the sale, is by evidence that the purchaser was willing and able to buy on the seller's conditions and that the sale was bound to have gone through quite independently of any negotiations conducted by another agent.[5]

Agents who have been given separate mandates to find a purchaser for the same property and produce the same purchaser cannot join in one action to sue the principal on the allegation that the sale had resulted from their joint efforts.[6] Neither of the agents can frame his or her claim in the alternative.[7]

1 *Webranchek v LK Jacobs & Co Ltd* 1948 4 SA 671 (A); *Eschini v Jones* 1929 CPD 18 29; *Howard & Decker Witkoppen Agencies & Fourways Estates (Pty) Ltd v De Sousa* 1971 3 SA 937 (T) 941. See *Blom v Thomson-Moore* 1993 3 SA 535 (SE) for the effect of multi-listings on an agent's commission.

2 *Barnard & Parry Ltd v Strydom* 1946 AD 931

936; *Howard & Decker Witkoppen Agencies & Fourways Estates (Pty) Ltd v De Sousa* supra.

3 *Webranchek v LK Jacobs & Co Ltd* supra.

4 *Webranchek v LK Jacobs & Co Ltd* supra.

5 *Eschini v Jones* supra.

6 *Van Straaten v Harris* 1955 1 SA 73 (W).

7 *Van Straaten v Harris* supra.

585 Principal preventing agent from earning commission When an estate agent has done all in the agent's power to perform his or her mandate, but the principal through the principal's own wish or fault fails to take the benefit of the agent's services or refuses to allow the agent to complete them, the agent is nevertheless entitled to his or her commission.[1] Undoubtedly the general rule is that the agent must perform his or her mandate in its entirety before being entitled to commission, but where the agent has substantially performed his or her mandate and complete performance is prevented by the act or neglect of the principal, the agent is entitled to the commission.[2] If a sale results because of the efforts of the estate agent, commission has been earned and the principal cannot lawfully avoid payment of that commission should he or she for any reason decide to cancel the sale.[3] Where no actual sale results, however, the agent is not entitled to commission even though he or she has furnished the principal with a binding offer from a person willing and able to purchase.[4] So a principal is not deprived of the freedom to decline an offer at his or her own discretion without having to show reasonable cause or just excuse for such refusal and the agent is not entitled to commission.[5] The seller is however deprived of the rights to sell or to appoint anyone else to do so during the specified period for which the estate agent had been authorised by the words "sole irrevocable authority" to the exclusive right or power to effect the sale of the property.[6]

1 *Consolidated Estates & Trusts Ltd v Turnbull* 1924 TPD 1 6.

2 *Consolidated Estates & Trusts Ltd v Turnbull* supra 6.

3 *Gluckman v Landau & Co* 1944 TPD 261 273; the rule, well stated in *Levy v Phillips* 1915 AD 139, is that when an agent has executed his or her mandate by bringing about a binding agreement between the agent's principal and the purchaser and the principal fails to benefit from the agreement because he or she chooses voluntarily to release the third party from his or her obligations, the agent's right to commission, which accrued when the agreement was made, remains unaffected.

4 *Gluckman v Landau & Co* supra; *Watson v Fintrust Properties (Pty) Ltd* 1987 2 SA 739 (C).

5 *Gluckman v Landau & Co* supra 275. Cf *Boose v Zeederberg & Duncan* 1918 CPD 283; *Bundshuh v Finnegan* 1975 1 SA 376 (C).

6 *Firs Investment Ltd v Levy Bros Estates (Pty) Ltd* 1984 2 SA 881 (A). See however *Nel v Grobbelaar & Viljoen Agentskappe (Edms) Bpk* 1983 4 SA 436 (O) where it was held that even if the seller confers the "sole right to sell the property" as an estate agent, it does not mean that the seller cannot sell the property him or herself and such a provision can, at the most, be interpreted to mean that the estate agent, to the exclusion of all others except the seller, had the sole right to sell the property.

ESTATE AGENCY AFFAIRS ACT

ESTATE AGENCY AFFAIRS BOARD

586 Establishment of Estate Agency Affairs Board and its constitution In terms of the Estate Agency Affairs Act[1] an Estate Agency Affairs Board has been established. This board is a juristic person and is known as the Estate Agency Affairs Board.[2]

The board consists of 15 members appointed by the Minister of Trade and Industry.[3] The minister must appoint as members of the board five members from the estate agents' industry.[4] The Secretary for Commerce requests the associations or organisations in writing to submit a list of estate agents.[5] If, after the expiry of a period of three months from the date on which the request was made, the associations or organisations have failed to submit the list or have submitted a defective list to the secretary, the minister must appoint suitable estate agents as members of the board in the place of the estate agents he or she would have appointed if the associations or organisations had not failed to submit the list or had not submitted a defective list.[6]

The minister must appoint as members of the board, five members from civil society, representing consumer interest.[7]

The minister must also appoint five members from related professions and institutions such as the legal profession, financial institutions, property owners and developers.[8]

The board must from time to time elect from its members a chairperson and vice-chairperson who hold office for a period of one year, and if neither the chairperson nor the vice-chairperson is present at any meeting of the board, the members present must elect from among their number a person to preside at that meeting.[9] A member of the board holds office for such period (but not more than three years) and on such conditions as the minister may determine at the time of his or her appointment.[10] Any member is, on the expiry of his or her term of office, eligible for re-appointment.[11]

An unrehabilitated insolvent or a person who has failed or is unable to comply in full with a judgment or order (including an order as to costs) given against him or her by a court of law in civil proceedings, a person who has been convicted of an offence involving an element of dishonesty, or a person who is not a South African citizen permanently resident in the Republic, may not be appointed as a member of the board.[12]

A member of the board must vacate office if he or she becomes disqualified as set out in the immediately preceding paragraph, or becomes of unsound mind, or ceases to be an estate agent, or fails to comply with the conditions determined by the minister at the time of the member's appointment, or has been absent from more than two consecutive meetings of the board without the leave of the board.[13]

If any member of the board dies or resigns[14] or ceases to be a member of the board, the minister may appoint any person as successor to that member for the unexpired period of office of that member.[15]

1 112 of 1976 s 2. The definition of "board" includes, for the purposes of s 32(7)(a)(ii), any committee of inquiry.
2 Ibid.
3 S 3(1).
4 S 3(2)(a).
5 S 3(3).
6 Ibid.
7 S 3(2)(b).
8 S 3(2)(c).
9 S 3(4).
10 S 3(5).
11 S 3(5) proviso.
12 S 3(6).
13 S 3(7).
14 The resignation must be in the form of a written notice addressed to the minister: s 3(8).
15 Ibid.

587 Meetings of the board and remuneration of its members The board must meet for the first time at a time and place determined by the Minister of Trade and Industry and thereafter at least once in each financial year at such times and places as the chairperson or, in his or her absence, the vice-chairperson, may determine.[1]

The chairperson or, in his or her absence, the vice-chairperson, may at any time of his or her own accord or at the written request of not less than six members convene a special meeting of the board.[2] A notice convening a special meeting of the board must state the purpose of that meeting.[3]

Six members constitute a quorum for any meeting of the board.[4]

The decision of the majority of members of the board present at a meeting of the board constitutes the decision of the board.[5] In the event of an equality of votes on any matter, the person presiding at the meeting in question has a casting vote in addition to his or her deliberative vote.[6]

No decision taken by the board or act performed under the authority of the board is invalid merely by reason of a vacancy on the board, or of the fact that any person not entitled to sit as a member of the board, sat as a member of the board at the time the decision was taken or the act was authorised, if the decision was taken or the act was authorised by the majority of the members of the board present at the time and who were entitled to sit as members of the board.[7]

Any member of the board who is not in the full-time employ of the state must be paid out of the funds of the board such remuneration and allowances as may be determined from time to time generally, or in any particular case by the minister.[8]

1 Estate Agency Affairs Act 112 of 1976 s 4(1).
2 S 4(2).
3 S 4(3).
4 S 4(4).
5 S 4(5).
6 Ibid.
7 S 4(6).
8 S 5.

588 Staff of board and designation of inspectors The work incidental to the carrying out of the functions by the board must be performed under its directions and control by persons appointed by it on such conditions and at such remuneration as the board may determine.[1] The board may designate such persons and any other person it deems fit to perform the functions of an inspector under the Estate Agency Affairs Act.[2]

1 Estate Agency Affairs Act 112 of 1976 s 6(1).
2 S 6(2). The powers and functions of such inspectors are described in s 32A. See par 614 post.

589 Objects of board The objects of the Estate Agency Affairs Board are, with due regard to the public interest, to maintain and promote the standard of conduct of estate agents and to regulate the activities of estate agents.[1]

1 Estate Agency Affairs Act 112 of 1976 s 7;
Hanley v Estate Agents Board 1978 3 SA 281 (T) 286.

590 Powers of board The board, in addition to any other power conferred upon it by the Estate Agency Affairs Act,[1] has the power to:

(a) appoint committees of which persons other than members of the board may with the approval of the Minister of Trade and Industry be members, to advise the board on any matters in respect of which the board possesses any power;[2]

(b) frame and publish, with the approval of the minister, a code of conduct which must be complied with by estate agents and take such steps as may be necessary or expedient to ensure such compliance;[3]

(c) encourage and promote the improvement of the standard of training of and services rendered by estate agents;[4]

(d) receive any application for exemption from the provisions of the Act and submit that application to the minister;[5]

(e) in general, take such other steps and perform such other acts as may be necessary or expedient in order to achieve its object.[6]

1 112 of 1976.
2 S 8(a).
3 S 8(b). The code of conduct was published under GN R3415, 24 December 1992. See *Fairbrass v Estate Agents Board* 1999 4 SA 1052 (W).
4 S 8(c). Regulations relating to the standard of training of estate agents were published under GN R1409, 1 July 1983 as amended: GN's R1468, 29 June 1990; R1923, 15 October 1993 and GN R631 of 23 June 2000.
5 S 8(d).
6 S 8(e).

591 Executive committee of board The board may appoint an executive committee of three or more members to exercise all the powers and to perform the functions of the board during the period between the meetings of the board.[1] Except as the board may direct otherwise, the executive committee does not have the power to set aside or amend any decision of the board.[2] Any act performed or decision taken by the executive committee is of force and effect except in so far as it is set aside or amended by the board at its next ensuing meeting.[3]

1 Estate Agency Affairs Act 112 of 1976 s 8A(1).
2 S 8A(2).
3 S 8A(3).

592 Committees of inquiry The Estate Agency Affairs Board may appoint any number of committees of inquiry as it deeds fit, each consisting of at least three members, one of whom must be appointed on account of his or her knowledge of the law, from among its members or from the ranks of those having a knowledge of the law or experience in dispute resolution or such other knowledge as, in the opinion of the board, renders them suitable for appointment as members of a committee of inquiry.[1] A committee of inquiry may exercise or perform any power or function which is entrusted to it in terms of the Estate Agency Affairs Act.[2]

The decision of the majority of members of the board present at a meeting of the board constitutes the decision of the board. In the event of an equality of votes on any matter, the person presiding at the meeting in question has a casting vote in addition to his or her deliberative vote. No decision taken by the board or act performed under the authority of the board is invalid merely by reason of a vacancy on the board, or of the fact that any person not entitled to sit as a member of the board, sat as a member of the board at the time the decision was taken or the act was authorised, if the decision was taken or the act was authorised by the majority of the members of the board present at the time and who were entitled to sit as members of the board.[3]

The board may alter the constitution of any committee of inquiry before the committee has commenced with an investigation contemplated in section 30(2).[4]

If a vacancy occurs on a committee of inquiry after the committee has commenced with an investigation, the investigation may be proceeded with before at least two members of the committee, but if only two serving members remain, they may take any decision referred to in section 30(3), (7) or (8) only by unanimous vote.[5]

1 Estate Agency Affairs Act 112 of 1976 s 8B(1). The committee of inquiry was previously known as the disciplinary committee. See *Steer Property Services (Pty) Ltd t/a Steer & Co v Estate Agency Affairs Board* [2002] 3 All SA 103 (C).
2 S 8B(2). See *Fairbrass v Estate Agents Board* 1999 4 SA 1052 (W).
3 S 8B(3).
4 S 8B(4). See par 611 post for investigation by the committee of inquiry.
5 S 8B(5). See par 611 post for provisions of s 30(3), (7) and (8).

593 Appeal against decision of committee of inquiry Any person who feels aggrieved by any decision taken by a committee of inquiry in the exercise of its powers and the performance of its functions, may, within 30 days after the committee of inquiry has informed that person in writing of the decision and upon payment of the prescribed fee, request the committee of inquiry to furnish reasons, in writing, for the decision.[1] Any person who feels aggrieved by any decision taken by a committee of inquiry in the exercise of its powers and the performance of its functions, may, within 30 days after the committee of inquiry has furnished reasons for its decision and after notice to the committee of inquiry, appeal to the board against the decision in the manner prescribed.[2]

The board must hear the appeal against the decision of the committee of inquiry in the prescribed manner and may after considering the appeal confirm, amend or reverse the decision,[3] remit the matter for further hearing, with such instructions as regards the taking of further evidence or otherwise as the board may deem necessary,[4] confirm or suspend any penalty imposed,[5] set aside any penalty imposed and impose any other penalty[6] or make another order.[7]

If a committee of inquiry has found an estate agent not guilty on a charge of conduct deserving of sanction, any person who lodges an appeal against the decision to the board must pay to the board a deposit, in an amount determined by the board, to cover the costs of the board and the estate agent concerned in respect of the appeal.[8] This deposit must be refunded in full if the appeal is successful or partly successful.[9]

A court may, on application by the board, order that a decision of, or penalty imposed by, a committee of inquiry not be stayed or suspended pending an appeal to the board, if the court considers such an order to be in the public interest.[10]

1 Estate Agency Affairs Act 112 of 1976 8C(1)(a).
2 S 8C(1)(b). See *Steer Property Services (Pty) Ltd t/a Steer & Co v Estate Agency Affairs Board* [2002] 3 All SA 103 (C).
3 S 8C(2)(a). See *Steer Property Services (Pty) Ltd t/a Steer & Co v Estate Agency Affairs Board* supra.
4 S 8C(2)(b).

5 S 8C(2)(c).
6 S 8C(2)(d); penalty as contemplated in s 30(3). See also par 611 post.
7 S 8C(2)(e); order as contemplated in s 30(7)(a). See also par 611 post.
8 S 8C(3)(a).
9 S 8C(3)(b).
10 S 8C(4).

594 Funds of board The funds of the Estate Agency Affairs Board consist of:

(a) all prescribed levies paid to the board by estate agents;[1]

(b) all moneys derived from any investments;[2]

(c) all other moneys which may accrue to the board from any other source.[3]

The board must utilise its funds to defray the expenses incurred by it in the performance of its functions and the exercise of its powers under the Estate Agency Affairs Act.[4] However, any moneys or other property donated or bequeathed to the board must be utilised in accordance with the conditions of that donation or bequest.[5] However, if the board, after investigation, has found that an estate agent failed to comply with any duty imposed on him or her in terms of the Act, has incurred any liability to pay attorney and client costs in respect of any proceedings instituted by it in terms of the Act for the recovery from an estate agent of any amount which is payable by the agent to the board or the fund, or has incurred any liability to pay audit fees in respect of an audit done on the instructions of the board in a case where a specific audit[6] has not been done, the board may recover the costs of such investigation in so far as it relates to such duty or the taxed amount of such attorney and client costs or the amount of such audit fees, as the case may be, from the estate agent concerned.[7]

The board must deposit all moneys received by it under the Act in an account opened by it at any bank approved by the minister.[8] The board may invest any moneys received under the Act and not required for immediate use, with the public debt commissioners or in such other manner as may be determined by the minister in consultation with the Minister of Finance.[9]

1 Estate Agency Affairs Act 112 of 1976 S 9(1)(a).
2 S 9(1)(b).
3 S 9(1)(c).
4 S 9(2).
5 S 9(2)(a).

6 Contemplated in ss 29 and 32(4). See pars 610 613 post.
7 S 9(2)(b).
8 S 9(3).
9 S 9(4).

595 Records, financial statements and auditing The financial year of the Estate Agency Affairs Board ends in each year on the date determined by the board with the approval of the Minister of Trade and Industry.[1]

The board must cause to be kept in one of the official languages, at an address in the Republic approved by the minister, such accounting records as are necessary fairly to reflect and explain the state of affairs of all moneys received or expended by it in terms of the Estate Agency Affairs Act, of all its assets and liabilities and of all its financial transactions and the financial position of its business.[2] In addition, the board must cause, as soon as possible but not later than six months after the end of each finical year, annual financial statements to be prepared showing, with all appropriate particulars, the moneys received and the expenditure incurred by it and its assets and liabilities at the end of the financial year.[3]

The accounting records and financial statements must be audited by an auditor appointed by the board.[4]

1 Estate Agency Affairs Act 112 of 1976   3 S 10(2)(b).
   s 10(1).   4 S 10(3).
2 S 10(2)(a).

596 Report by board The Estate Agency Affairs Board must furnish the Minister of Trade and Industry with such information as he or she may desire from time to time in connection with its functions and financial position and must, in addition, submit to the minister an annual report including audited financial statements on its functions.[1] Every report must, as soon as practicable, be tabled before the National Assembly and the National Council of Provinces by the minister.[2]

1 Estate Agency Affairs Act 112 of 1976   2 S 11(2).
   s 11(1).

ESTATE AGENTS FIDELITY FUND

597 Establishment and control of estate agents fidelity fund A fund, to be known as the Estate Agents Fidelity Fund, is established in terms of the Estate Agency Affairs Act.[1] The following amounts must be paid into this fund:

(a) all moneys paid as annual contributions in accordance with the provisions of the Act to or on account of the fund;[2]

(b) income derived from the investment of moneys in the fund;[3]

(c) all moneys recovered by or on behalf of the fund in the exercise of any right of action conferred by the Act;[4]

(d) all moneys received on behalf of the fund from any insurance company;[5]

(e) interest paid to the fund on moneys deposited in a trust account and on moneys invested by the fund in a savings or other interest-bearing account in a bank, building society or similar institution;[6]

(f) any other moneys accruing to the fund from any source.[7]

The fund must be controlled and managed by the board, which must utilise the moneys in the fund in accordance with the provisions of the Act.[8] All moneys forming part of the fund must, until they are invested or spent in accordance with the provisions of the Act, be paid into a bank approved by the Minister of Trade and Industry, to the credit of an account to be called the Estate Agents Fidelity Fund Account.[9]

1 112 of 1976 s 12(1). See *Ronstan Investments*   6 S 12(1)(e).
   (Pty) Ltd v Littlewood [2001] 3 All SA 127   7 S 12(1)(f).
   (SCA); 2001 3 SA 555 (SCA).   8 S 12(2). See *Steer Property Services (Pty) Ltd*
2 S 12(1)(a).   *t/a Steer & Co v Estate Agency Affairs Board*
3 S 12(1)(b).   [2002] All SA 103 (C).
4 S 12(1)(c).   9 S 12(3).
5 S 12(1)(d).

598 Determination of liabilities of fund The board must after the end of each financial year of the fund, determine to what extent, if at all, the total income of the fund during that financial year exceeded the expenditure incurred by or accrued to the fund during that financial year and must, if the fund's income exceeded its liabilities, determine how much of the excess may be utilised during the next financial year for the purposes of grants and other payments.[1] Any moneys in the fund not immediately required for the purposes of the fund must be invested in the prescribed manner.[2]

1 Estate Agency Affairs Act 112 of 1976
  s 12A(1). See also par 599 post.
2 S 12A(2).

599 Grants and other payments from fund The board may, from the amount determined by it and subject to such terms and conditions as it may deem fit, make grants with regard to research in fields of activity relevant to the business of estate agents in general, the maintenance and promotion of the standard of conduct of estate agents in general, and the maintenance and promotion of the training standards of estate agents in general.[1] The board may also make grants to any association or society of estate agents for the purposes of enabling that association or society to further the practice of estate agency or to maintain and promote the interests of estate agents in general.[2] The board may pay an honorarium or compensation to any person or institution for services with the object of enhancing the standard of conduct of estate agents in general, rendered at the request of the board,[3] and it may utilise such amount as it may determine for the purposes of advertising and promoting the services and facilities offered by estate agents in general or promoting public awareness in respect of matters relating to the acquisition and disposal of immovable property.[4]

The board may at any time revoke any grant.[5]

1 Estate Agency Affairs Act 112 of 1976
  s 12B(1)(a). For origin of grants see par 598
  ante.
2 S 12B(1)(b).
3 S 12B(1)(c).
4 S 12B(1)(d).
5 S 12B(2).

600 Group insurance schemes The board may in the public interest arrange any group insurance scheme with any insurer registered or deemed to be registered under the Insurance Act,[1] for the provision of indemnity insurance to cover estate agents' liability to members of the public on the grounds of malpractice, up to an amount determined by the board.[2] Any premium payable in respect of the insurance must be paid from the fund.[3]

1 27 of 1943 (now repealed by the Taxation
  Laws Amendment Act 30 of 2002 s 1(1)).
2 Estate Agency Affairs Act 112 of 1976
  s 12C(1).
3 S 12C(2).

601 Payments out of fund Subject to the provisions of the Estate Agency Affairs Act[1] there must be paid out of the fund whenever it is required:

(a)   the amount of all claims, including costs, allowed or established against the fund;[2]

(b)   any contribution in the discretion of the board in respect of any expense incurred by any claimant in establishing his or her claim;[3]

(c)   all legal accounting and other expenses incurred in investigating and defending claims made against the fund or otherwise incurred in relation to the fund;[4]

(d)   all premiums payable in respect of contracts of insurance entered into by the board;[5]

(e)   the expenses involved in the control of the fund, including remuneration and allowances to members of the board in connection with the management of the fund;[6]

(f) interest on and redemption of loans negotiated by the board on behalf of the fund;[7]

(g) any other moneys which must or may be paid out of the fund in accordance with the Act.[8]

1 112 of 1976.   5 S 13(d).
2 S 13(a).   6 S 13(e).
3 S 13(b).   7 S 13(f).
4 S 13(c).   8 S 13(g).

602 Auditing of accounts of fund

602 Auditing of accounts of fund The board must cause to be kept in one of the official languages at an address in the Republic approved by the Minister of Trade and Industry such accounting records as are necessary fairly to reflect and explain the state of affairs of all moneys received or expended by or on behalf of the fund, of all the assets and liabilities of the fund, and of all the financial transactions of the fund and the financial position of its business.[1]

The board must as soon as possible, but not later than six months after the end of each financial year of the fund ending in each year on a date determined by the board with the approval of the minister, cause annual financial statements in respect of the fund to be prepared showing, with all appropriate particulars, the moneys received and expenditure incurred by the fund during, and its assets and liabilities at the end of the financial year of the fund.[2]

The board must cause the accounting records and financial statements of the fund to be audited by an auditor appointed by the board.[3] The board must submit to the minister the audited annual financial statements of the fund in respect of each financial year.[4]

1 Estate Agency Affairs Act 112 of 1976   3 S 14(c).
   s 14(a).   4 S 14(d).
2 S 14(b).

603 Contributions to the fund by estate agents Every estate agent must, on making application in any year for a fidelity fund certificate as set out in the immediately succeeding paragraph, in addition to the prescribed levy,[1] pay as an annual contribution to the fund such amount as may be prescribed.[2]

1 Levies are set out in par 594 ante.
2 Estate Agency Affairs Act 112 of 1976 s 15.

604 Fidelity fund certificates The Estate Agency Affairs Act[1] provides that every estate agent or prospective estate agent, excluding certain estate agents,[2] must, within the prescribed period and in the prescribed manner, apply to the board for a fidelity fund certificate and such an application must be accompanied by levies and contributions.[3] Those estate agents excluded in terms of this provision must, within the prescribed period and in the prescribed manner, apply to the board for a registration certificate (not a fidelity fund certificate) and the application must be accompanied by the levy.[4]

Prior to the enactment of the Act an estate agent did not require a fidelity fund certificate in order to enable the agent to conduct his or her business. On the commencement of the Act it became illegal for an estate agent, no matter how long such agent had been conducting business as such, to continue his or her business unless he or she obtained a fidelity fund certificate. The board is the only body that is empowered under the Act to issue such a certificate.[5]

An application for a fidelity fund certificate is tantamount to an application for permission to trade, for without such a certificate an estate agent cannot carry on an estate agency business.[6]

The application for the fidelity fund certificate must be accompanied by the levies and contribution.[7] If the board on receipt of any application and the levies and contribution is satisfied that the applicant is not disqualified[8] from being issued with a fidelity fund certificate, it must issue, in the prescribed form, to the applicant a fidelity fund certificate which is valid until 31 December of the year to which the application relates.[9]

No fidelity fund certificate may be issued unless and until the provisions of the Act are complied with and any fidelity fund certificate issued in contravention of the provisions of the Act is invalid and must be returned to the board at its request.[10]

An estate agent who applies to the board for a fidelity fund certificate or a registration certificate after the prescribed period or whose application is not accompanied by the levy or the contribution as the case may be, must pay to the board a prescribed penalty in addition to the levy or contribution, and no fidelity fund certificate or registration certificate may be issued to the estate agent until the penalty has been paid.[11]

1   112 of 1976.
2   Estate agents referred to in s 1(cA) are excluded; see par 574 ante.
3   S 16(1). Levies are dealt with in par 594 ante and contributions in par 603 ante.
4   S 16(2). Levies are dealt with in par 594 ante. For earlier interpretation of s 16 see *Hanley v Estate Agents Board* 1978 3 SA 281 (T) 285.
5   *Lek v Estate Agents Board* 1978 3 SA 160 (C)

170–171 which was confirmed on appeal in *Estate Agents Board v Lek* 1979 3 SA 1048 (A).
6   Ibid.
7   S 16(1).
8   In terms of s 27. See par 608 post.
9   S 16(3). See also *Estate Agents Board v Lek* supra.
10   S 16(4).
11   S 16(5).

605 Application of fund moneys The fund must be held and applied to reimburse persons who suffer pecuniary loss by reason of theft of trust money, committed after the commencement of the Estate Agency Affairs Act,[1] by an estate agent or the failure of an estate agent to have opened and operated a separate trust account.[2]

Every action against the board in respect of the fund may be brought in the court within whose jurisdiction the cause of action arose.[3]

No person has any claim against the board in respect of theft or an estate agent's failure to keep and operate a separate trust account unless:

(a)   the claimant has, within three months after becoming aware of that theft or such failure or by the exercise of reasonable care should have become aware of the theft or such failure, given notice in writing to the board of his or her claim;[4] and

(b)   the claimant has, within six months after a written demand was sent to him or her by the board, furnished to the board such proof as the board may reasonably require.[5]

If the board is satisfied that, having regard to all the circumstances, a claim was lodged or the proof required by it was furnished as soon as practicable, it may in its discretion extend any of the periods referred to.[6]

1   112 of 1976.
2   S 18(1). See *Estate Agents Board v Swart* [1998] 4 All SA 373 (T); 1999 1 SA 1097 (T) for liability to compensate third parties

with regard to trust account. For details as to trust accounts see par 619 post. See *Mahadeo v Estate Agents Board* 1989 4 SA 926 (D) for the circumstances under which the board

will be liable to make payment out of the
fund. For the *locus standi* of the board to apply for relief by way of interdict see *Estate
Agents Board v Louis Locke Estates (Pty) Ltd*
1984 1 SA 709 (W). See also *Moodley v*

Estate Agents Board 1982 4 SA 709 (W).
3 S 18(2).
4 S 18(3)(a).
5 S 18(3)(b).
6 S 18(3) proviso.

606 Claims against board in respect of fund The board may at any time after
the commission of any theft or an estate agent's failure to keep and operate a separate
trust account in respect of which a claim relating to the fund arose, receive and settle
that claim.[1] The fact that a person who suffers loss as a result of the theft by an estate
agent of trust moneys is compensated from the fidelity fund does not mitigate the
seriousness of the agent's offence.[2] However, no person may without the permission
of the board commence any action against the board unless and until the claimant has
exhausted all relevant rights of action and other legal remedies available against the
estate agent in respect of whom the claim arose and against all other persons liable in
respect of the loss suffered by the claimant.[3]

No person may recover from the board any amount larger than the difference between the amount of the loss suffered by the person and the amount or value of all
moneys or other benefits which he or she received or is entitled to receive out of any
other source in respect of that loss.[4]

The board may at its discretion pay interest on the amount of any judgment obtained or any claim admitted against the fund, subject to the proviso that such interest
will not run from a date earlier than the date on which the board received written
notice of the claim against it and that the rate of interest does not exceed the prevailing rate of prescribed interest.[5]

No right of action lies against the board in respect of any loss suffered by the spouse
of an estate agent by reason of any theft committed by such estate agent.[6] Similarly, no
right of action lies against the board in respect of any loss suffered by any estate agent
by reason of any theft committed:

(a)   by the estate agent's partner;[7]

(b)   if such estate agent is a company, by any director of such company;[8]

(c)   if the estate agent is a director of a company, by any co-director in that company;[9]

(d)   if such an estate agent is a close corporation, by any member of such corporation;[10]

(e)   if the estate agent is a member of a close corporation, by any co-member in
such a corporation;[11]

(f)   by any person employed by the estate agent as an estate agent.[12]

No right of action lies against the board in respect of any loss suffered by any person
as a result of theft, or as a result of any other act or omission in connection with trust
moneys held or received on account of any other person by any person who is employed by an attorney or professional company as defined in the Attorneys Act[13]
otherwise than as an attorney or articled clerk and whose duties consist wholly or
primarily of the performance of any act as specified.[14]

In any action against the board in respect of the fund, the board may raise any defence which could have been raised by the person against whom the claim arose.[15]

If the board settles in full or in part any claim, all the rights and remedies of the
claimant in respect of that claim against the estate agent concerned or any other
person or, if applicable, in the case of death, insolvency or other legal incapacity of

that estate agent or other person, against the estate of that estate agent or other person, pass to the board to the extent of the settlement.[16]

Only moneys in the fund are available for the satisfaction of any judgment obtained in relation to the fund or for the payment of any claim allowed by the board.[17] However, if at any time there are insufficient moneys in the fund to settle all judgments and claims they must, to the extent in which they are not settled, be charged against future accumulations of the fund.[18]

The board may in its discretion determine the order in which judgments and claims against the fund may be settled and may, if the moneys in the fund are insufficient to settle in full all such judgments and claims, settle any judgment or claim pro rata to the amount available in the fund.[19]

The board may in its discretion enter into a contract with an insurer who carries on an insurance business in the Republic whereby the board will be indemnified to the extent and in the manner provided by such contract, against liability to pay claims.[20] Any such contract must be entered into in respect of estate agents generally.[21]

No claimant having a claim against the board has:

(a) by virtue of any insurance contract entered into by the board with an insurer, any right of action against that insurer;[22] and

(b) any right or claim in respect of any money paid or payable to the board by that insurer, but that money must be paid into the fund and applied by the board in accordance with the provisions of the Estate Agency Affairs Act to settle any relevant claim.[23]

No provision of any law relating to insurance applies in respect of the fund.[24]

1 Estate Agency Affairs Act 112 of 1976 s 19(1).
2 *S v Rossouw* 1991 1 SACR 561 (C).
3 S 19(1) proviso. Cf *Estate Agents Board v Mahadeo* 1991 3 SA 49 (N).
4 S 19(2).
5 S 19(3).
6 S 19(4)(a).
7 S 19(4)(b)(i).
8 S 19(4)(b)(ii).
9 S 19(4)(b)(iii).
10 S 19(4)(b)(iiiA).
11 S 19(4)(b)(iiiB).
12 S 19(4)(b)(iv).
13 53 of 1979.
14 Estate Agency Affairs Act 112 of 1976 s 19(4)(c). See s 1(cA) for definition of "estate agent"; par 574 ante.
15 S 20.
16 S 21. See *Estate Agents Board v Swart* [1998] 4 All SA 373 (T); 1999 1 SA 1097 (T) for rights of recourse against the board.
17 S 22(1).
18 Ibid.
19 S 22(2).
20 S 23(1).
21 S 23(2).
22 S 24(a).
23 S 24(b).
24 S 25.

607 Prohibition of rendering of services No person may perform any act as an estate agent unless a valid fidelity fund certificate has been issued to him or her and to every person employed by him or her as an estate agent and, if that person is a company, to every director of the company, or a close corporation, to every member of such close corporation referred to in paragraph (b) of the definition of "estate agent."[1]

1 Estate Agency Affairs Act 112 of 1976 s 26; see par 574 ante for the definition of "estate agent" (s 1(cA)). Failure to comply with the requirements of s 26 does not invalidate the contract of mandate between a principle and an estate agent nor is an estate agent thereby deprived of the right to claim his or her commission: *Noragent (Edms) Bpk v De Wet* 1985 1 SA 267 (T). In *Maree v Botha* 1992 3 SA 230 (T) it was held that a person who is not an estate agent and who was instrumental in concluding a sale of property, was entitled to claim payment of moneys equivalent to an agent's commission even

though the person did not hold a fidelity fund certificate. In *Ronstan Investments (Pty) Ltd v Littlewood* [2001] 3 All SA 127 (SCA); 2001 3 SA 555 (SCA) it was held that the consequence of contravening this section is that the person concerned is not entitled to remuneration from the performance of the act and the person also commits an offence in terms of s 34. See par 616 post.

608 Disqualifications relating to fidelity fund certificates The Estate Agency Affairs Act[1] provides that no fidelity fund certificate may be issued to any estate agent who, or, if such estate agent is a company, any company of which any director or if such an agent is a close corporation any corporation of which any member referred to in paragraph (b) of the definition of "estate agent":[1]

(a)   has at any time by reason of improper conduct been dismissed from a position of trust;[2]

(b)   has at any time been convicted of an offence involving an element of dishonesty;[3]

(c)   is an unrehabilitated insolvent in respect of whom the trustee of the insolvent estate has not certified that the insolvent is a fit and proper person to assume a position of trust and to be issued with a fidelity fund certificate;[4]

(d)   is of unsound mind;[5]

(e)   has had his or her fidelity fund certificate withdrawn;[6]

(f)   does not comply with the prescribed standard of training;[7]

(g)   does not have the prescribed practical experience.[8]

Furthermore, no fidelity fund certificate may be issued to any estate agent who has failed, in respect of the financial year which has expired before the date on which application for a certificate is made, to comply with any provision of section 29(b) or section 32(3)(b),[9] or has at any time been guilty of any act or omission in respect of which any person had to be compensated pursuant to section 18 from the fund unless the estate agent has paid the relevant amount in full to the board or the board is of the opinion that satisfactory arrangements for settlement of the amount have been made and the board has confirmed such arrangements.[10]

No fidelity fund certificate may be issued to any estate agent referred to in the definition of "estate agent"[11] if such estate agent carries out or intends to carry out business as an estate agent under a trade name which is identical or confusingly similar to the trade name of an estate agent:

(a)   already issued with a fidelity fund certificate;[12] or

(b)   whose fidelity fund certificate is suspended or has lapsed or has been withdrawn in terms of the Act.[13]

No fidelity fund certificate may be issued to any estate agent who is a director of a company, or who is a member referred to in the definition of "estate agent",[14] of a close corporation:

(a)   of which the fidelity fund certificate was withdrawn by the board in terms of section 28 or 30;[15]

(b)   which was prohibited in terms of section 32(6) from operating in any way on its trust, savings or other interest-bearing account,[16]

or any estate agent who within a period of six months before or on the date on which such fidelity fund certificate was so withdrawn or such company or close corporation was so prohibited, was a director of such company or such a member of such corporation.[17]

However, if in respect of any person who is subject to any disqualification referred to in this section, the board is satisfied that, with due regard to all the relevant considerations, the issue of a fidelity fund certificate to such person will be in the interest of justice, the board may issue, on such conditions as it may determine, a fidelity fund certificate to such person when he or she applies for it.[18]

This section does not contain an unqualified prohibition against the issue of a certificate. It requires the board, when an application for a fidelity fund certificate is received by it, to consider, in relation to the specific person who applies for that certificate, firstly whether the person falls within any of the disqualifications mentioned, and secondly, if the person does, whether in all the circumstances the interest of justice does not require that the certificate should nevertheless be issued to the person. The proviso is cast in the widest possible terms.[19]

If an application is refused by the board in the exercise of the discretion which vests in it pursuant to the proviso to section 27, the unsuccessful applicant is entitled to be furnished with reasons. This section of the Act clearly postulates an inquiry by the estate agents board into matters of fact in relation to the particular person whose application it is required to consider. The decision taken by the board is one which may directly affect the rights of the estate agent and involve civil consequences to the estate agent. Accordingly the board, when it acts in terms of section 27, does not exercise a purely administrative discretion; it in fact acts in a quasi-judicial capacity.[20]

1   112 of 1976.
2   S 27(a)(i) read with the definition of "estate agent" in s 1(b); see par 574 ante.
3   S 27(a)(ii). Cf *Lek v Estate Agents Board* 1978 3 SA 160 (C).
4   S 27(a)(iii).
5   S 27(a)(iv).
6   S 27(a)(v).
7   S 27(a)(vi).
8   S 27(a)(vii).
9   S 27(aA)(i). See *Ronstan Investments (Pty) Ltd v Littlewood* [2001] 3 All SA 127 (SCA); 2001 3 SA 555 (SCA).
10   S 27(aA)(ii).
11   See par (a) of definition of "estate agent" in s 1. See also par 574 ante.
12   S 27(aB)(i).
13   S 27(aB)(ii).
14   See par (b) of definition of "estate agent" in s 1. See also par 574 ante.
15   For ss 28 and 30 see pars 609 and 611 post.
16   For s 32 see par 613 post.
17   S 27(b).
18   S 27 proviso.
19   See *Lek v Estate Agents Board* supra 171 where Friedman J, discussing the proviso, stated that it requires the board to have regard to all relevant considerations and to consider whether the issue of a certificate to the particular applicant will be in the interest of justice. For an interpretation of the words "in the interests of justice" see *Steyn v Estate Agents Board* 1980 2 SA 334 (T).

20   *Lek v Estate Agents Board* supra 171–173. When a statute confers quasi-judicial powers to affect prejudicially the rights of a person or property, there is a presumption, in the absence of an express provision or of a clear intention to the contrary, that the powers will be exercised in accordance with the fundamental principles of justice, one of which is that the person affected should be given an opportunity of being heard. In the case of a person who has been convicted of an offence involving dishonesty, the board should consider the precise nature of the offence, its seriousness, how much time has elapsed since its commission and the punishment imposed. It should also inquire into the length of time that the agent has carried on his or her estate agency business, the estate agent's manner of conducting him or herself and the reputation the estate agent enjoys. See also *Hanley v Estate Agents Board* 1978 3 SA 281 (T) 287 where Nicholas J said that the applicant should make a full disclosure of the facts relating to his or her conviction and sentence. The applicant should also show that he or she has genuinely reformed and will conduct him or herself as an estate agent honestly and honourably.

609 Withdrawal and lapse of fidelity fund certificates The board, the executive committee or a committee of inquiry may withdraw a fidelity fund certificate issued to any person:

(a) who had been summoned in the prescribed manner to appear before the board or any committee of inquiry if such person without just cause fails to comply with the summons and prior to the date of appearance stated in the summons, has not been excused in writing by the board or committee of inquiry, as the case may be, from so appearing;[1]

(b) if such person is a company or a close corporation, and the fidelity fund certificate of any director of the company or of any member of the corporation has lapsed;[2]

(c) if such person, or if such person is a company, any director of that company or if such a person is a close corporation, any member referred to in paragraph (b) of the definition of "estate agent", of such corporation becomes subject to any disqualification.[3]

Any person who has in his or her possession or under his or her control any fidelity fund certificate which has been withdrawn, must at the request of the board return the certificate to the board.[4] The court may upon good cause shown and on application by the board, or any other person, withdraw any fidelity fund certificate issued to any person, and thereupon that person or any other person having such certificate in his or her possession or under his or her control must immediately return it to the board.[5] If it appears to the court that a person in respect of whom the board intends making an application to withdraw a fidelity fund certificate or to appoint a curator *bonis*, has left the Republic and that the person probably does not intend to return and that his or her whereabouts are unknown, the court may order that service on that person of any process in connection with such application may be effected by publication of such process in an Afrikaans and an English newspaper circulating in the district in which the said person's last known address, as entered in the records of the board, is situated.[6]

A fidelity fund certificate issued to any person lapses immediately and is of no force and effect if that person becomes subject to certain disqualifications[7] or is a company or close corporation, and the company or close corporation is being wound up, whether provisionally or otherwise, or is deregistered, as the case may be.[8] Any person who is in possession or control of a fidelity fund certificate which has lapsed must immediately return that certificate to the board.[9]

No person whose fidelity fund certificate has been withdrawn or has lapsed may directly or indirectly participate in the management of any business carried on by an estate agent in his or her capacity as such, or participate in the carrying on of such business, or to be employed, directly or indirectly, in any capacity in such business, except with the written consent of the board and subject to such conditions as the board may determine.[10] No estate agent may, directly or indirectly, in any capacity whatsoever employ such a person or allow or permit such a person directly or indirectly to participate in any capacity in the management or the carrying on of his or her business as an estate agent, except with the written consent of the board, and subject to such conditions as the board may impose.[11]

1 Estate Agency Affairs Act 112 of 1976
  s 28(1)(a).
2 S 28(1)(b).
3 S 28(1)(c). See par 574 ante for definition of
  "estate agent".
4 S 28(2)
5 S 28(3).
6 S 28(4). See s 32(6) discussed in par 613

post.
7 S 28(5)(a). For the disqualifications see par
  608 ante.
8 S 28(5)(b).
9 S 28(6).
10 S 28(7).
11 S 28(8).

GENERAL

610 Accounting records Every estate agent must in respect of his or her activities as such:

(a)　keep in one of the official languages at an address in the Republic such accounting records as are necessary fairly to reflect and explain the state of affairs of all moneys received or expended by the estate agent, including moneys deposited to a trust account or invested in a savings or other interest-bearing account, of all the agent's assets and liabilities and of all the agent's financial transactions and the financial position of his or her business;[1]

(b)　cause the accounting records to be audited by an auditor within four months after the financial year of the agent, which final date must, after commencement of the Estate Agents Amendment Act of 1984[2] (namely 18 April 1984) not be altered without the written approval of the board.[3]

1 Estate Agency Affairs Act 112 of 1976 s 29(a). See *Ronstan Investments (Pty) Ltd v Littlewood* [2001] 3 All SA 127 (SCA); 2001 3 SA 555 (SCA).

2 51 of 1984 s 9.
3 Estate Agency Affairs Act 112 of 1976 s 29(b).

611 Conduct deserving of sanction The Estate Agency Affairs Act[1] provides that any estate agent is guilty of conduct deserving of sanction[2] if he or she:

(a)　receives any remuneration for any act performed by him or her as an estate agent from two or more than two persons whose interests are not in all respects identical in respect of the performance of such act, unless those persons agreed thereto in writing;[3]

(b)　fails in respect of any act performed by him or her as an estate agent to give proper explanation in writing, within 30 days of being called upon in writing to do so, to any person having a material interest in the performance of that act;[4]

(c)　fails to pay any moneys due by him or her to the board or in respect of the fund within one month after those moneys became due;[5]

(d)　fails to furnish in writing within such period as the board may determine such information as the board may request in writing and reasonably require in order to exercise its powers properly under the Act;[6]

(e)　contravenes or fails to comply with any provision of the code of conduct;[7]

(f)　fails to comply with the requirements of the Act regarding the employment of a person whose fidelity fund certificate has lapsed or been withdrawn, the keeping of records and trust moneys; or contravenes provisions relating to the prohibition of rendering of services, failure to comply with the request of an inspector, hindering or obstructing an inspector or unauthorised completion of documents;[8]

(g)　in his or her capacity as director of a company or a close corporation both of which conduct the affairs of an estate agent and which has failed to keep proper accounting records in terms of section 29 of the Act, or has not complied with the requirements of section 32 in relation to the keeping of trust accounts, has not taken reasonable steps to prevent such a failure.[9]

(h)　commits an offence involving an element of dishonesty.[10]

The board or a committee of inquiry may in the prescribed manner bring and investigate any charge of conduct deserving of sanction against any estate agent.[11]

When any estate agent is found guilty of conduct deserving of sanction by the board or a committee of inquiry, the board or committee of inquiry, as the case may be, may:

(a)　withdraw the fidelity fund certificate of the estate agent and:

(i)　if the estate agent is a company, of every director of the company;[12]

(ii)　if the estate agent is a director of a company which is an estate agent, of that company;[13]

(iii)　if he or she in partnership acts as an estate agent, of every partner in that partnership;[14]

(iv)　if the estate agent is a close corporation, every member referred to in paragraph (b) of the definition of "estate agent" of such corporation;[15]

(v)　if he or she is a member of a close corporation which is an estate agent, of such corporation;[16]

(b)　impose on the estate agent a fine not exceeding R25 000 or such higher amount as may be prescribed by the minister by notice in the *Government Gazette* in order to counter the effect of inflation, and which is payable to the board;[17]

(c)　reprimand the estate agent.[18]

However, a fine or any portion thereof or the withdrawal of a fidelity fund certificate may be suspended for a period not exceeding three years and on such further conditions as the board or committee of inquiry, as the case may be, may determine.[19]

An appeal lies against a decision of the board taken in the exercise of these powers.[20]

The acquittal or conviction of an estate agent by any court of law on any criminal charge is not a bar to proceedings against the estate agent under the Act on a charge of conduct deserving of sanction, notwithstanding the fact that the facts set out in the charge of conduct deserving of sanction would, if proved, constitute the offence set out in the criminal charge on which the agent was acquitted or convicted, or any other offence on which the agent might have been convicted at the trial on the criminal charge.[21]

If the conduct deserving of sanction with which the estate agent is charged amounts to an offence of which he or she has been convicted by a court of law, a certified copy of the record of the trial and conviction by the court constitutes, on the identification of the estate agent as the person referred to in the record as the accused, sufficient proof of the commission by the estate agent of the offence, unless the conviction has been set aside by a superior court.[22] The estate agent charged is entitled to adduce evidence to show that he or she was in fact wrongly convicted.[23]

If any fine is not paid in full to the board within one month after it has been imposed, or arrangements for payment are not made to the satisfaction of the board within that period, the fidelity fund certificate of the person on whom the fine has been imposed must be suspended immediately and will be of no force and effect until the fine has been paid or the arrangements have been made.[24]

The board or a committee of inquiry may, whenever a fine has been imposed on an estate agent, order that any portion of the fine, but not exceeding 80 per cent of such fine, be applied towards the payment of compensation to any person who suffered a pecuniary loss as a result of the conduct of the estate agent in question.[25] The board must, on receipt of the fine imposed on the estate agent in question, make the payment. However, no payment must be made until all appeals in respect of the imposition of the fine have lapsed or been finalised or been abandoned.[26] A person is not precluded from pursuing a civil remedy against the estate agent, but if an award is made by a court in favour of a person who has received payment from the board, the court must take the payment into account.[27] A committee of inquiry may exercise the same powers conferred on the board provided that at least one member is qualified to be admitted as an advocate,[28] or to be admitted as an attorney,[29] or to be appointed as a magistrate[30] and for an uninterrupted period of at least five years has practised as an advocate or attorney or occupied the post of magistrate, or for that period was involved in the tuition of law or rendered services as a legal consultant.[31]

If an estate agent who has been charged with conduct deserving of sanction has been found not guilty by the board or a committee of inquiry or has been found guilty by a committee of inquiry and the estate agent's appeal to the board against the decision or penalty is successful or partly successful, the board may, on recommendation of the committee of inquiry concerned (if applicable) make a contribution from the fund, in the amount determined by the board, towards the costs incurred by the estate agent in respect of the hearing before the board or the committee of inquiry and, if applicable, the appeal heard by the board.[32]

1 112 of 1976
2 In terms of the Estate Agents Amendment Act 90 of 1998 the term "improper conduct" was replaced by the term "conduct deserving of sanction". Regulations regarding conduct deserving of sanction have been published in GN 51 of 26 January 2001 as amended: GN R 745 of 17 August 2001. See further par 621 post.
3 Estate Agency Affairs Act 112 of 1976 s 30(1)(a).
4 S 30(1)(b).
5 S 30(1)(c). See *Steer Property Services (Pty) Ltd t/a Steer & Co v Estate Agency Affairs Board* [2002] 3 All SA 103 (C).
6 S 30(1)(d).
7 S 30(1)(e). The code of conduct was published in *Government Gazette* GN R3415, 24 December 1992. See *Fairbrass v Estate Agents Board* 1999 4 SA 1052 (W).
8 S 30(1)(g). See *Estate Agents Board v Louis Locke Estates (Pty) Ltd* 1984 1 SA 709 (W); *Ronstan Investments (Pty) Ltd v Littlewood* [2001] 3 All SA 127 (SCA); 2001 3 SA 555 (SCA).
9 S 30(1)(gA).
10 S 30(1)(h). See *Fairbrass v Estate Agents Board* supra.
11 S 30(2). See *Fairbrass v Estate Agents Board* supra.
12 S 30(3)(a)(i).
13 S 30(3)(a)(ii).
14 S 30(3)(a)(iii).
15 S 30(3)(a)(iv) read with definition of "estate agent" in s 1 par (b).
16 S 30(3)(a)(v).
17 S 30(3)(b).
18 S 30(3)(c).
19 S 30(3) proviso.
20 An appeal lies by virtue of s 31. Cf *Hanley v Estate Agents Board* 1978 3 SA 281 (T).
21 S 30(4). See *Fairbrass v Estate Agents Board* supra.
22 S 30(5).
23 S 30(5) proviso.
24 S 30(6).
25 S 30(7)(a).
26 S 30(7)(b).
27 S 30(7)(c).
28 In terms of the Admission of Advocates Act 74 of 1964.
29 In terms of the Attorneys Act 53 of 1979.
30 In terms of the Magistrates' Court Act 32 of 1944 read with s 10 of the Magistrates Act 90 of 1993.
31 Estate Agency Affairs Act 112 of 1976 s 30(7)(d).
32 S 30(8).

612 Appeal The word "appeal" as used in section 31 of the Estate Agency Affairs Act[1] connotes a hearing in the nature of a review.[2] The appeal should be brought before the court by way of notice of motion in which has been set out the nature of the relief sought and which is supported by affidavits setting out all the relevant facts known to the agent and including copies of all relevant documents.[3]

Any person who feels aggrieved by any decision[4] taken by the board in the exercise of certain of its powers[5] may at any time after the person became aware of such decision but not later than one month after the board:

(a)   has informed the person in writing of that decision and on payment of the prescribed fees, request the board in writing to furnish him or her in writing with its reasons for its decision;[6]

(b)   has furnished the person with its reasons for its decision and after notice to the board, appeal to the court against the decision, and the court may:

     (i) dismiss the appeal;[7]

     (ii) if it is of the opinion that the board has not acted in accordance with the relevant provisions of the Act, give an order opposite to the decision of the board or amending the decision of the board.[8] The court is therefore not entitled to make a fresh determination of merits but may reverse or amend the board's decision only on limited legal grounds;[9]

     (iii) refer the matter back to the board for further consideration.[10] This the court would do, for example, in a case in which the board has taken into account something which it should not have taken into account, or in which it has failed to take into account something which it should have taken into account;[11] or

     (iv) give such other order, including any order as to costs, as it may deem fit.[12]

A court may, on application by the board, order that a decision of, or penalty imposed by the board, not be stayed or suspended pending an appeal to the court under the provisions of this section, if the court considers such an order to be in the public interest.[13]

1   112 of 1976.
2   *Lek v Estate Agents Board* 1978 3 SA 160 (C); *Hanley v Estate Agents Board* 1978 3 SA 281 (T) 286; *Estate Agents Board v Lek* 1979 3 SA 1048 (A); *Steer Property Services (Pty) Ltd t/a Steer & Co v Estate Agency Affairs Board* [2002] 3 All SA 103 (C).
3   *Lek v Estate Agents Board* supra; *Hanley v Estate Agents Board* supra 286; *Estate Agents Board v Lek* supra; *Steer Property Services (Pty) Ltd t/a Steer & Co v Estate Agency Affairs Board* supra.
4   According to *Lek v Estate Agents Board* supra 161, a decision taken by a corporate or juristic person has no legal efficacy until such

time as it has been communicated to the person concerned. Cf *Estate Agents Board v Lek* supra.
5   Under ss 8B(6), 16, 27, 28 or 30.
6   S 31(1)(a).
7   S 31(1)(b)(i).
8   S 31(1)(b)(ii).
9   *Hanley v Estate Agents Board* supra. Cf *Estate Agents Board v Lek* supra.
10   S 31(1)(b)(iii). See *Steyn v Estate Agents Board* 1980 2 SA 334 (T).
11   *Hanley v Estate Agents Board* supra.
12   S 31(1)(b)(iv).
13   S 31(2).

613   Trust account and investment of trust moneys   Every estate agent must open and keep one or more separate trust accounts, which must contain a reference to the section in the Estate Agency Affairs Act,[1] with a bank and such estate agent or the employee of such estate agent, must deposit in the account all trust money held or received by or on behalf of such estate agent and the name of such bank as well as the number of each such trust account must be notified to the board forthwith.[2]

Despite these provisions, any estate agent may invest in a separate savings or interest-bearing account opened by him or her with any bank, building society or any institution or class of institution designated by notice in the *Government Gazette* by the Minister of Trade and Industry in consultation with the Minister of Finance, any moneys deposited in his or her trust account which are not immediately required for any particular purpose.[3] Trust money in an account invested in terms of this section or deposited in terms of section 32(1) must be retained by the estate agent in question in that account until the estate agent is lawfully entitled to it or instructed to make payment therefrom to any person.[4]

Any savings or other interest-bearing account must contain a reference to this subsection.[5] Interest on moneys deposited in a trust account and on moneys invested must, subject to the express terms of the mandate in question, which must be in writing, be paid to the fund by the estate agent concerned.[6] The board may in the prescribed circumstances refund to an estate agent a prescribed portion of the interest paid by such estate agent to the fund.[7]

Every estate agent must:

(a) keep separate accounting records of all moneys deposited by the estate agent in his or her trust account and of all moneys invested by the estate agent in any savings or other interest-bearing account;[8]

(b) balance his or her books and records relating to any account at intervals of not more than one month, and cause them to be audited by an auditor within four months after the final date of his or her financial year.[9]

(c) administer the accounts in the prescribed manner.[10]

Any auditor who does an audit must, immediately after completing the audit, send a report in the prescribed form in regard to his or her findings to the board, and a copy to the estate agent concerned.[11]

The board may on good cause shown at any time order any estate agent by notice in writing to submit to the board within a period stated in the notice, but not less than 30 days, an audited statement fully setting out the state of affairs in respect of the accounting records.[12]

The court may on good cause shown on application by the board or any other competent person, prohibit an estate agent from operating in any way on his or her trust, savings or other interest-bearing account and may appoint a curator *bonis* to control and administer such trust, savings or other interest-bearing account, with such rights, duties and powers as the court may deem fit.[13]

If:

(a) the board under the provisions of the Act refuses to issue a fidelity fund certificate to any estate agent who applied for it, or has withdrawn a fidelity fund certificate issued to any estate agent;[14]

(b) any estate agent ceases to act as such;[15]

(c) any estate agent becomes subject to any disqualification,[16]

the estate agent concerned must wind up his or her trust, savings or other interest-bearing account in the prescribed manner and pay out in the prescribed manner the amount standing to credit of any account to the persons entitled to it.[17] The amount standing to the credit of the trust, savings or other interest-bearing account of any estate agent does not form part of the assets of the estate agent or, if he or she was a natural person and has died or has become insolvent, of his or her deceased or insolvent estate.[18]

1 112 of 1976.
2 S 32(1). See *Estate Agents Board v Louis Locke Estates (Pty) Ltd* 1984 1 SA 709 (W); *Estate Agents Board v Swart* [1998] 4 All SA 373 (T); 1999 1 SA 1097 (T); *Ronstan Investments (Pty) Ltd v Littlewood* [2001] 3 All SA 127 (SCA); 2001 3 SA 555 (SCA); *Steer Property Services (Pty) Ltd t/a Steer & Co v Estate Agency Affairs Board* [2002] 3 All SA 103 (C).
3 S 32(2)(a).

4 S 32(2)(e).
5 S 32(2)(b).
6 S 32(2)(c); *Steer Property Services (Pty) Ltd t/a Steer & Co v Estate Agency Affairs Board* supra.
7 S 32(2)(d); *Steer Property Services (Pty) Ltd t/a Steer & Co v Estate Agency Affairs Board* supra.
8 S 32(3)(a).
9 S 32(3)(b).
10 S 32(3)(c).
11 S 32(4).

12 S 32(5). Accounting records are dealt with in s 29; see par 610 ante.

13 S 32(6).

14 S 32(7)(a).

15 S 32(7)(b).

16 S 32(7)(c). For the disqualifications see s 27; see par 608 ante.

17 S 32(7).

18 S 32(8).

614 Powers of inspectors Any inspector furnished with an inspection authority in writing by the board may conduct an investigation to determine whether the provisions of the Estate Agency Affairs Act[1] are being or have been complied with and may, for that purpose, without giving prior notice, at all reasonable times:

(a) enter any place in respect of which the inspector has reason to believe that:

(i) any person there is performing an act as an estate agent;

(ii) is connected with an act performed by an estate agent;

(iii) there are books, records or documents to which the provisions of the Act are applicable;[2]

(b) order any estate agent or the manager, employee or agent of any estate agent to:

(i) produce to the inspector the fidelity fund certificate of that estate agent;

(ii) produce to the inspector any book, record or other document in the possession or under the control of that estate agent, manager, employee or agent;

(iii) furnish the inspector, at such place and in such manner as he or she may reasonably specify, with such information in respect of that fidelity fund certificate, book, record or other document as he or she may desire;[3]

(c) examine or make extracts from of copies of such fidelity fund certificate, book, record or other document;[4]

(d) seize and retain any such fidelity fund certificate, book, record or other document to which any prosecution or charge of conduct deserving of sanction under the Act may relate. However, the person from whose possession or custody any fidelity fund certificate, book, record or other document was taken, must at his or her request be allowed to make, at his or her own expense and under the supervision of the inspector concerned, copies thereof or extracts therefrom.[5]

No person may fail on demand to place at the disposal of any inspector anything in that person's possession or under his or her control or on his or her premises which may relate to any inspection.[6] Neither may any person hinder or obstruct any inspector in the exercise of the inspector's powers,[7] or falsely hold him or herself out to be an inspector.[8]

Any inspector must issue a receipt to the owner or person in control of anything seized and retained.[9]

Any inspector who exercises any power must, at the request of any person affected by the exercise of that power, produce the inspection authority in writing furnished to him or her.[10]

The provisions of the section, excluding the examining or making extracts from or copies of the fidelity fund certificate, book, record or other document do not apply in respect of any attorney, member of a professional company or articled clerk,[11] or any employee of any such attorney, member or company,[12] any premises from which such attorney or company conducts his, her or its practice,[13] and any book, record or document on such premises or in the possession or under the control of any attorney, member of a professional company or articled clerk,[14] or any employee of any such attorney, member or company.[15]

1 112 of 1976.
2 S 32A(1)(a).
3 S 32A(1)(b).
4 S 32A(1)(c).
5 S 32A(1)(d).
6 S 32A(2)(a).
7 S 32A(2)(b).
8 S 32A(2)(c).
9 S 32A(3).
10 S 32A(4).

11 See definition in s 1 of the Attorneys Act 53 of 1979.
12 Estate Agency Affairs Act 112 of 1976 s 32A(5)(a).
13 S 32A(5)(b).
14 See definition in s 1 of the Attorneys Act 53 of 1979.
15 Estate Agency Affairs Act 112 of 1976 s 32A(5)(c).

615 Regulations The Minister of Trade and Industry may after consultation with the board make regulations:

(a) to regulate, control or prohibit any practice followed by estate agents;[1]

(b) prescribing the tariff of fees at which estate agents may act as such;[2]

(c) prescribing the levies payable to the board by estate agents;[3]

(d) prescribing the contributions payable to the fund by estate agents;[4]

(e) prescribing the period within and the manner in which application must be made for a fidelity fund certificate;[5]

(f) prescribing the penalty payable to the board in terms of section 16(5) of the Estate Agency Affairs Act;[6]

(g) prescribing the form of a fidelity fund certificate;[7]

(h) prescribing the manner in which money in the fund not needed for immediate use may be invested;[8]

(i) relating to the standard of training and practical experience of estate agents;[9]

(j) prescribing the manner in which a charge of conduct deserving of sanction against any estate agent must be brought and investigated and the manner in which a person must be summoned to appear before a committee of inquiry or the board;[10]

(k) prescribing the fees payable under section 31(a);[11]

(l) prescribing the portion of the interest as well as the circumstances in which such interest may be refunded to an estate agent;[12]

(m) prescribing the manner in which any account referred to in section 32(3)(c) must be administered;[13]

(n) prescribing the procedure to be followed in respect of an appeal to the board and the manner in which the appeal must be heard;[14]

(o) prescribing the manner in which any account referred to in section 32(7) must be wound up and the amount standing to the credit of that account must be paid out;[15]

(p) prescribing the conditions in terms whereof of any person may carry on business as an estate agent from any residential premises;[16]

(q) as to, generally, any matter considered necessary or expedient to prescribe in order to achieve the objects of the Act.[17]

Different regulations may be made in respect of different estate agents or categories of estate agents.[18]

The minister may, on such conditions as he or she may think fit and after consultation with the board, by regulation exempt any estate agent or category of estate agent from any or all the provisions of the Act.[19]

1 Estate Agency Affairs Act 112 of 1976 s 33(1)(a).

2 S 33(1)(b).

3 S 33(1)(c). Regulations relating to the levies payable by estate agents to the board have been published under *Government Gazette* GN R1798 of 29 August 1986; corrected by GN R2106 of 3 October 1986; amended by GN R1699 of 26 August 1988; GN R1526 of 14 July 1989; GN R2752 of 30 November 1990; GN R1506 of 31 August 1994; GN R1030 of 27 August 1999 and GN R807 of 31 August 2001.

4 S 33(1)(d).

5 S 33(1)(e).

6 S 33(1)(eA).

7 S 33(1)(f). Regulations relating to the issue of fidelity fund certificates have been published under *Government Gazette* GN R1798 of 29 August 1986; corrected by GN R2106, 3 October 1986; amended by GN R1699 of 26 August 1988; GN R1526 of 14 July 1989; GN R2752 of 30 November 1990; GN R1506 of 31 August 1994; GN R1030 of 27 August 1999 and GN R807 of 31 August 2001.

8 S 33(1)(g).

9 S 33(1)(gA). Regulations relating to the standard of training of estate agents have been published under GN R 1409 of 1 July 1983 amended by GN R1468 of 29 June 1990; GN R1923 of 15 October 1993; GN R631 of 23 June 2000 and GN R 51 of 26 January 2001.

10 S 33(1)(h). Regulations relating to the manner in which a charge of conduct deserving of sanction against an estate agent may be brought and investigated have been published under GN 51 of 26 January 2001 as amended: GN R745 of 17 August 2001. See also par 621 post.

11 S 33(1)(i). In *Estate Agents Board v Fred P Ackermans Properties (Pty) Ltd* 1979 2 SA 987 (C) it was held that this prohibition relates also to any money held or received by an estate agent on account of any person. This decision was however set aside on appeal in *Fred P Ackerman's Properties (Pty) Ltd v Estate Agents Board* 1980 3 SA 451 (C) where it was held that s 32(6) authorised a court to place a curator in charge of an estate agent's accounts specifically listed in that section only, ie a separate trust account or separate savings account or other interest-bearing account and not in charge of any accounts containing money held or received by an estate agent on account of any person.

12 S 33(1)(iB).

13 S 33(1)(jA). See also par 613 ante.

14 S 33(1)(jB). See also par 612 ante. Regulations relating to appeals have been published under GN 3433 of 17 December 2002 and promulgated under GN 1334 of 9 May 2003. See *Steer Property Services (Pty) Ltd t/a Steer & Co v Estate Agency Affairs Board* [2002] 3 All SA 103 (C).

15 S 33(1)(k). See also pars 613 ante 620 post. Regulations relating to the trust account of an estate agent and investment of trust moneys have been published under GN R1472 of 29 July 1977 amended by GN R604 of 23 March 1979; GN R2418 of 28 November 1980; GN R948 of 1 May 1981; GN R 1415 of 3 July 1981; GN R 2499 of 13 November 1981; GN R1157 of 30 May 1985.

16 S 33(1)(kA).

17 S 33(1)(l). Penalties payable have been published under GN 10734 of 10 September 1999.

18 S 33(1A)

19 S 33(2). Regulations relating to the activities of estate agents exempted from the prescribed standard of training have been published under *Government Gazette* GN R1469 of 29 June 1990 as amended by GN R1963 of 15 October 1993. See also GN R631 of 23 June 2000.

616 Offences and penalties Any person who contravenes or fails to comply with any provisions of the Estate Agency Affairs Act[1] or any order or request issued or addressed under the Act is guilty of an offence and liable on conviction to a fine not exceeding R5 000 or to imprisonment for a period not exceeding five years, or both such fine and imprisonment.[2]

1 112 of 1976.

2 S 34. In *Ronstan Investments (Pty) Ltd v Littlewood* [2001] 3 All SA 127 (SCA); 2001 3 SA 555 (SCA) it was held that any person who acts contrary to the provisions of s 26 will not be entitled to remuneration in respect of a transaction concluded by him or her as an estate agent while failing to comply with the provisions of s 26. Penalties payable have been published under GN 10734 of 10 September 1999.

617 Estate agent not entitled to remuneration in certain circumstances The Estate Agency Affairs Act[1] provides that no estate agent is entitled to any remuneration or other payment in respect of or arising from the performance of any act referred to in the definition of "estate agent",[2] unless at the time of the performance of the act a valid fidelity fund certificate has been issued to such estate agent,[3] and if such estate agent is a company, to every director of such company or, if such estate agent is a close corporation, to every member of such corporation.[4]

No person referred to in paragraph (c) of the definition of "estate agent"[5] and no estate agent who employs such person, is entitled to any remuneration or other payment in respect of or arising from the performance by such person of any act referred to in that paragraph, unless at the time of the performance of the act a valid fidelity fund certificate has been issued to such person.[6]

1 112 of 1976.
2 See par (a) (i), (ii), (iii) or (iv) of the definition of "estate agent" in s 1. See par 574 ante.
3 S 34A(1)(a). See *Ronstan Investments (Pty) Ltd*

v Littlewood [2001] 3 All SA 127 (SCA); 2001 3 SA 555 (SCA).
4 S 34A(1)(b).
5 See definition in s 1; par 574 ante.
6 S 34A(2).

618 Prohibition of completion of documents by certain estate agents The Estate Agency Affairs Act[1] provides that an estate agent who has not complied with the prescribed standard of training may not in his or her capacity as an estate agent draft or complete any document or clause in a document conferring any mandate on any estate agent to perform any act referred to in paragraph (a) of the definition of "estate agent"[2] or relating to the sale or lease of immovable property.[3]

Any estate agent who contravenes this section is not entitled to any payment, remuneration or damages in respect of or by reason of any such document or for bringing about the transaction or agreement embodied in that document.[4]

1 112 of 1976.
2 See par 574 ante.
3 S 34B. See *Ronstan Investments (Pty) Ltd v*

Littlewood [2001] 3 All SA 127 (SCA); 2001 3 SA 555 (SCA).
4 S 34B(2).

619 Delegation of powers The Minister of Trade and Industry may, on such conditions as he or she may deem fit, delegate to an official in the Department of Commerce any or all the powers conferred upon the minister by the Estate Agency Affairs Act,[1] save the power to make regulations. The minister may at any time in writing revoke any delegation and the delegation of any power under the Act does not prevent the exercise of that power by the minister him or herself.[2]

1 112 of 1976 s 35(1).
2 S 35(2).

620 Trust account of estate agent and investment of trust moneys The Minister of Economic Affairs, after consultation with the estate agents board, has made the following regulations in regard to the trust account of an estate agent and the investment of trust moneys.

The report to be submitted by an auditor to the board in terms of the Estate Agency Affairs Act[1] must be in the specified form.[2] If the auditor is unable to furnish an unqualified report, this fact and the reasons therefor must be fully set out in the report sent by the auditor in place of the report in the prescribed form.[3] Otherwise the auditor's report must be as far as possible in the prescribed form.[4] Every auditor who has commenced or carried out an audit[5] must without delay report directly to the board if it comes to his or her notice that at any date the aggregate of the amounts of the funds in an estate agent's trust account[6] together with any funds available in a separate savings or other interest-bearing account[7] and any trust moneys held according to the estate agent's books of account and accounting records as cash on hand, is less than the total of the trust balance shown in the trust account in the ledgers of the estate agent.[8] "Trust balance" means the balance standing to the credit of any person in the books and records of an estate agent representing amounts held or received on behalf of such person, less any amount paid out in terms of a mandate from such person and less any commission and collection fee due to such estate agent up to the date of balancing.[9] The auditor must without delay report directly to the board if any material queries concerning the accounting systems, accounting records, the books of account or entries therein or the trust account, savings account or interest-bearing account which the auditor has raised with the estate agent have not been fully and promptly dealt with to the auditor's satisfaction.[10]

If one of the following events has taken place, namely, the board has refused to issue a fidelity fund certificate to any estate agent who applied for such certificate, or has withdrawn a fidelity fund certificate issued to any estate agent, or any estate agent ceases to act as such or any estate agent becomes subject to any disqualification,[11] then:

(a)   no moneys may be withdrawn from or paid out of the trust account or savings or other interest-bearing account without the consent in writing of the board;[12]

(b)   the estate agent concerned must, if he or she has ceased to act as such, notify the board in writing immediately of his or her ceasing to act;[13]

(c)   the estate agent must as soon as practicable give written notice to the bank, building society or institution with which the estate agent keeps the trust account or savings or other interest-bearing account, of the occurrence of any such event.[14] The estate agent must also give notice that in future no moneys may be withdrawn from or paid out of that account without the written consent of the board;[15]

(d)   the board itself may at any time give such notice to the bank, building society or other insititution;[16]

(e)   the estate agent must as soon as practicable in writing furnish the board with the names of the persons entitled to any moneys in that account, the amount to which any such person is entitled and the reasons therefor;[17]

(f)   after the estate agent has complied with the requirements of the regulations and with the written consent of the board, he or she must pay to the persons entitled to any moneys and to such other persons who in the opinion of the board are entitled to any moneys in such accounts, out of such accounts the moneys to which they are entitled.[18]

If after payment as provided for a balance remains in any of the accounts in question, the board must publish in the *Government Gazette* and in two newspapers circulating in the district in which the estate agent acted as such a notice stating that there is a balance remaining and inviting persons to lodge within 30 days after the date of that notice, with the board, in writing, any claim which they may have to that balance or part thereof.[19]

If no person proves any claim to the balance in question or any part thereof the estate agent is entitled to the balance or, after payment of any part of the balance to any person who has proved that he or she is entitled thereto, the estate agent is entitled to the remainder.[20]

After all moneys in the accounts have been paid to the persons entitled thereto the estate agent must wind up the accounts and notify the board in writing of the winding-up.[21]

Any interest received by or credited to an estate agent in respect of any period ending on the last day of February in each year and payable to the fund[22] must be paid regularly and promptly, but in any event not later than the last day of May in that year, to the fund or its nominee.[23] The board may in the prescribed circumstances refund to an estate agent 50 per cent of the interest paid by such estate agent to the fund.[24]

For the purposes of balancing his or her books and records[25] an estate agent must at intervals of not more than one calendar month extract a list of the balances standing to the credit of any person on the last day of the calendar month and must keep the lists of trust balances for not less than three years from the date on which they were extracted.[26]

1 112 of 1976 s 32(4).
2 The form is specified in the Schedule to the regulations published under *Government Gazette* GN R604, 23 March 1979 reg 2.1.
3 Reg 2.2.
4 Ibid.
5 Reg 2.3. The audit is carried out in terms of ss 29(b) 32(3)(b).
6 The trust account must be kept in terms of s 32(1).
7 These accounts must be kept in terms of s 32(2)(a).
8 Reg 2.3.1.
9 Reg 1.
10 Reg 2.3.2.
11 See s 32(7).
12 Reg 3.1.1.
13 Reg 3.1.2.1.
14 Reg 3.1.2.2.
15 Ibid.
16 Reg 3.1.2.2 proviso.
17 Reg 3.1.2.3.
18 Reg 3.1.2.4.
19 Reg 3.2.
20 Reg 3.3.
21 Reg 3.4.
22 The interest is payable in terms of s 32(2)(c).
23 Reg 4.1. See *Steer Property Services (Pty) Ltd t/a Steer & Co v Estate Agency Affairs Board* [2002] 3 All SA 103 (C).
24 Reg 4.2 and s 32(2)(d).
25 In terms of s 32(3)(b).
26 Reg 5.

621 Conduct deserving of sanction The Minister of Trade and Industry has, after consultation with the Estate Agency Affairs Board, made regulations pertaining to conduct deserving of sanction.[1] Any person may lodge a complaint, in the prescribed form, with the board.[2] On receipt the board may request further information, carry out any investigation, notify the person concerned of the complaint, request comments and advise the person about whom the complaint has been received.[3] Comments on the complaint may be given to the board.[4] The complaint may be withdrawn.[5]

Mediation is possible.[6]

If there is sufficient evidence to substantiate a complaint and a reasonable likelihood that a committee will find that the complaint, if proved, constitutes conduct deserving of sanction, the board must bring a charge against the respondent.[7] A charge must be in the prescribed form and must be accompanied by the prescribed documents.[8] The charge may be withdrawn.[9] The charge must be delivered to the respondent.[10]

The board has specified powers and duties in respect of the inquiry.[11]

The respondent and any witnesses must be summoned by the board.[12] A summons must be in the specified form.[13] Witnesses present at the inquiry must be paid.[14] The board may require the respondent to deposit a sum of money to cover costs of preparing, service of summons and witnesses.[15]

Should the respondent plead guilty to the charge he or she may notify the committee and submit a statement setting out mitigating circiumstances.[16] If the committee is satisfied that an inquiry is unnecessary it must examine the complaint and the statement of mitigation[17] and notify the complainant and respondent accordingly.[18]

Specific procedures are required for the inquiry.[19]

In order to determine the amount to be paid out and to whom the amount must be paid the committee must follow certain procedures[20] and notify the complainant and respondent of the award.[21]

A conviction on a charge of conduct deserving of sanction may be published. Reasons for decisions must be provided.[22] No person who has been summoned to appear at an inquiry or who has been called as a witness may, without lawful excuse, fail to appear, produce any book or document or answer any question, and such person must remain present until discharged.[23] Proceedings may not be disrupted and must be open to the public.[24]

1 Estate Agency Affairs Act 112 of 1976 s 33(1)(h). Regulations were published under GN R 51 of 26 January 2000 as amended by GN R745 of 17 August 2001.
2 Reg 2.
3 Reg 3(1).
4 Reg 3(2).
5 Reg 3(3).
6 Reg 4.
7 Reg 5(1).
8 Reg 5(2).
9 Reg 5(3).
10 Reg 5(4).
11 Reg 7.
12 Reg 8(1).
13 Reg 8(2).
14 Reg 8(3).
15 Reg 8(4).
16 Reg 9(1).
17 Reg 9(2).
18 Reg 9(3).
19 Reg 10.
20 Reg 11(1).
21 Reg 11(2).
22 Reg 12(1).
23 Reg 12(2).
24 Reg 12(3).

ESTOPPEL

by

PJ RABIE

(updated by H DANIELS)

REFERENCES TO OTHER TITLES

for   estoppel in criminal law ....   *see*   CRIMINAL PROCEDURE

SELECTED LITERATURE

De Wet "*Estoppel by Representation*" in die SA Reg
Hoffmann and Zeffertt *SA Law of Evidence*
Rabie *The Law of Estoppel in SA*
Schmidt *Bewysreg*
Spencer Bower and Turner *Estoppel by Representation*

INTRODUCTION

622 Scope of the title This title deals with (a) the *exceptio rei iudicatae* and (b) estoppel by representation. The *exceptio rei iudicatae* is sometimes referred to as estoppel by judgment, or estoppel *per rem iudicatam*.[1] It is also, very rarely, referred to as estoppel by record.[2] The expression estoppel by representation, as used in this title, includes what is sometimes referred to as estoppel by conduct and estoppel by negligence.[3]

1 See eg Hoffmann and Zeffertt Evidence 4 ed 335 et seq; Schmidt *Bewysreg* 4 ed 7 593 594.
2 For cases in which this English law expression appears, see *Turk v Turk* 1954 3 SA 971 (W) 972C; *Shokkos v Lampert* 1963 3 SA 421 (W) 426A; *S v Delport alias Boucher* 1984 1 SA 511 (O) 514H 515G.
3 See par 653 post.

EXCEPTIO REI IUDICATAE

MEANING, NATURE AND BASIS OF EXCEPTIO REI IUDICATAE

623 Meaning of *res iudicata* The words "*res iudicata*" mean, literally, a matter adjudged, and according to a text in the *Digest*,[1] which is also referred to by Voet,[2] a *res iudicata* is a matter in which an end has been put to disputes by the decision of a judge.

1 D 42 1 1.
2 *Commentarius* 42 1 1: *Res iudicata est quae finem controversiarum pronunciatione accepit, absolutione vel condemnatione.* That is: "A *res iudicata* is a matter in which an end has been put to disputes in a declaration of a judge by absolution or adverse judgment" (Gane).

Absolutio as here used by Voet is not absolution in the sense of absolution from the instance as that expression is used in modern practice, but a declaration by the judge that "*actorem non iure agere*", ie "that the plaintiff is not suing rightfully" (Gane): *niet ontfankelyk in synen eysch ende conclusie* (Voet 42 1 5).

624 Meaning and nature of the *exceptio* The *exceptio rei iudicatae* is not an exception in the sense in which that word is used in the modern law of procedure, but a defence which has to be pleaded and proved by the party raising it.[1] The gist of the *exceptio* is that the matter or question which is being raised by one's adversary has previously been finally adjudicated upon in proceedings between the parties and that it cannot be raised again.

According to Voet[2] the *exceptio* lies when a dispute which has been brought to an end (*lis terminata*) is again set in motion between the same persons, about the same thing (*de eadem re*) and on the same cause for claiming (*ex eadem petendi causa*). Voet adds that if any of the three requisites mentioned by him — namely the same persons, the same thing and the same cause for claiming — is absent, the *exceptio* does not apply.[3] Grotius' statement of the law relating to the *exceptio* is to the same effect as that of Voet. He states that the *exceptio* lies when the same matter in respect of which a final judgment has been given is again raised by the same parties on the same cause of action (*uit de zelve oorzaecke*).[4] The courts in South Africa have followed and applied the law as stated by these writers.[5]

In an early decision the Appellate Division, in discussing the question whether a defendant was entitled to raise an earlier judgment as *res iudicata*, held that it was necessary to establish whether that judgment had been given in an action (a) with respect to the same subject matter; (b) based on the same ground; and (c) between the same parties.[6] This test, which is referred to in another decision of the Appellate Division as the ordinary threefold test of *res iudicata*,[7] has been applied by that court in subsequent decisions.[8] If, therefore, a cause of action has previously been finally litigated between the parties, a subsequent attempt by the one to proceed against the other on the same cause for the same relief can be met by the *exceptio rei iudicatae vel litis finitae*.[9] The object of this principle, it has been said, is to prevent the repetition of lawsuits, the harassment of a defendant by a multiplicity of actions and the possibility of conflicting decisions.[10]

1 Voet *Commentarius* 42 1 47; *Lamb v The Colonial Secretary & The Rand Mining Estates Ltd* 1902 TS 319; *Lowrey v Steedman* 1914 AD 532 539; *Hatfield Town Management Board v Mynfred Poultry Farm (Pvt) Ltd* 1963 1 SA 737 (SR) 739. If the defence is not pleaded it may be taken to have been waived: *Blaikie-Johnstone v P Hollingsworth (Pty) Ltd* 1974 3 SA 392 (D) 395C–D.

2 44 2 3.

3 See also Huber *THRHR* 5 38 4: "to justify the exception, it is necessary that the persons should be the same, the things the same and the causes of action the same. If any one of these things is different, then it is fair that a new action should be allowed, since it cannot be said that the same question has been previously disposed of" (Gane).

4 Grotius *Inleiding* 3 49 2, which is translated as follows in Maasdorp's edition of the work (694): "The *exceptio rei iudicatae vel litis finitae* holds whenever the same thing, with respect to which a judgement having the force of a final or definitive sentence has been given, is again demanded by the same plaintiff of the same defendant, and upon the same grounds."

5 See eg *Hiddingh v Denyssen* (1885) 3 SC 424 450; *Bertram v Wood* (1893) 10 SC 177 180–181; *Ferreira v Minister of Social Welfare* 1958 1 SA 93 (E) 95H; *African Farms & Townships Ltd v Cape Town Municipality* 1963 2 SA 555 (A) 562B 564C–D; *Custom Credit Corporation (Pty) Ltd v Shembe* 1972 3 SA 462 (A) 472A–C; *Goldfields Laboratories (Pty) Ltd v Pomate Engineering (Pty) Ltd* 1983 3 SA 197 (W); *Horowitz v Brock* 1988 2 SA 160 (A) 178H–I.

6 *Mitford's Executor v Ebden's Executors* 1917 AD 682 686.

7 *Kethel v Kethel's Estate* 1949 3 SA 598 (A) 605: "same subject matter, same cause of action, same parties."

8 See eg *African Farms & Townships Ltd v Cape Town Municipality* supra 562A–B (the majority decision – the minority decided the case on another basis); *Custom Credit Corporation (Pty) Ltd v Shembe* supra 472A–B; *Horowitz v Brock* supra 178H.

9 *Custom Credit Corporation (Pty) Ltd v Shembe* supra 472A–B.

10 *Evins v Shield Insurance Co Ltd* 1980 2 SA 814 (A) 835G.

625 Basis and origin of the *exceptio* It is laid down in the *Digest* as a rule of law that a matter once adjudged is accepted as the truth,[1] in other words it is presumed that the judgment upon any claim submitted to a competent court is correct.[2] The presumption is one *iuris et de iure*, excluding every proof to the contrary.[3] It has its origin in considerations of public policy, which requires that there should be a term set to litigation, and in the requirements of good faith, which does not permit of the same thing being demanded more than once.[4]

According to Voet the main reason for the introduction of the *exceptio rei iudicatae* was to avoid the inextricable difficulties (*inexplicabiles . . . difficultates*) which could arise if different courts gave different or perhaps even mutually contradictory decisions on the same question.[5]

The effect of the aforesaid rule that a judgment is irrebuttably presumed to be correct is that the judgment in effect constitutes judicially determined law between the parties.[6] From this it follows that, in determining whether the *exceptio rei iudicatae* can be raised, the question is not whether the judgment is right or wrong, but simply whether there is a judgment. This conclusion applies to both civil[7] and criminal[8] law.

1 *D* 50 17 207: *res iudicata pro veritate accipitur.*
See *Bertram v Wood* (1893) 10 SC 177 180; *African Farms & Townships Ltd v Cape Town Municipality* 1963 2 SA 555 (A) 564B–C; *Le Roux v Le Roux* 1967 1 SA 446 (A) 461H–462A; *Liley v Johannesburg Turf Club* 1983 4 SA 548 (W) 552G–H.

2 *Bertram v Wood* supra 180.

3 *Bertram v Wood* supra 180; *African Farms & Townships Ltd v Cape Town Municipality* supra 564D–E.

4 *Bertram v Wood* supra 180, citing Gaius (*D* 50 17 57): *Bona fides non patitur ut bis idem exigatur*, ie good faith does not permit of the same thing being demanded twice. See also *R v Manasewitz* 1933 AD 165 178; *African Farms & Townships Ltd v Cape Town Municipality* supra 564D–F; *Le Roux v Le Roux* supra 461H–462D; *Custom Credit Corporation (Pty) Ltd v Shembe* 1972 3 SA 462 (A) 472D–E.

5 Voet *Commentarius* 44 2 1, cited in *Custom Credit Corporation (Pty) Ltd v Shembe* supra 472B–C. See also *Amalgamated Engineering Union v Minister of Labour* 1949 3 SA 637 (A) 661; *Brink v Gain* 1958 3 SA 503 (C) 506B–F; *Evins v Shield Insurance Co Ltd* 1980 2 SA 814 (A) 835G.

6 *Makings v Makings* 1958 1 SA 338 (A)

349B–C. See also Scholtens 1958 *SALJ* 252.

7 *African Farms & Townships Ltd v Cape Town Municipality* supra 564C–D. It follows from this that a party's knowledge that a judgment is wrong does not expose him or her to a charge of bad faith cognisable in a court of law; nor will the party's reliance on a judgment obtained by perjured evidence do so, unless the party was him or herself a party to the perjury: 564F–565A.

8 *S v Ndou* 1971 1 SA 668 (A) 676C. In *R v Manasewitz* supra the Appellate Division would seem to have disregarded this rule. All the members of the court were of the opinion that the Tvl Provincial Division had rightly considered an earlier decision of the same court to constitute *res iudicata* between the state and the accused, but four of the five members of the court proceeded to hold that the first judgment of the Tvl Provincial Division was wrong and that the Appellate Division was not bound to allow it to serve as the basis of a plea of *res iudicata*. This view is difficult to understand and it has been the subject of comment and criticism; see *S v Gabriel* 1971 1 SA 646 (RA); Zeffertt 1971 *SALJ* 318–319; Hoffmann and Zeffertt *Evidence* 4 ed 337 fn 35.

626 Ratio of *exceptio* underlies pleas of *autrefois acquit* and *autrefois convict* In terms of the Criminal Procedure Act[1] it is open to an accused, when pleading to a charge, to plead that he or she has already been convicted of the offence with which he or she is charged, or that he or she has already been acquitted of such offence.[2] In practice the first of these pleas is commonly called a plea of *autrefois convict*, and the second a plea of *autrefois acquit*. A plea of *autrefois acquit*, it has been held in decisions of the Appellate Division, is, or is equivalent to, the *exceptio rei iudicatae* of the common law.[3] The same applies to the plea of *autrefois convict*, the basis of the plea being generally the same as that of a plea of *autrefois acquit*.[4]

1 51 of 1977.

2 See s 106(1)(c)–(d) and the identically worded s 169(2)(c)–(d) of the Criminal Procedure Act 56 of 1955.

3 *R v Manasewitz* 1933 AD 165 168: "A plea of *autrefois acquit* is in fact equivalent to a plea of the *exceptio rei judicatae* in our law" (per Wessels CJ); *S v Moodie* 1962 1 SA 587 (A) 595F: "The plea of *autrefois acquit* is the *exceptio rei judicatae* of our common law",

citing the above-quoted statement of Wessels CJ in *R v Manasewitz* supra. See also *S v Ndou* 1971 1 SA 668 (A) 675E–F' and cf *O'Neill v SAR & H* 1958 3 SA 269 (A) 275H: "*autrefois acquit* is one of the forms of *res judicata* in our law" (per Schreiner JA); *S v Delport alias Boucher* 1984 1 SA 511 (O) 514H–515A.

4 *S v Matukani* 1961 3 SA 798 (T) 802F–G.

ELEMENTS OF EXCEPTIO REI IUDICATAE

FINAL JUDGMENT

627 Judgment pleaded must be final or definitive decision In order to found the *exceptio rei iudicatae*, the judgment pleaded must be a final or definitive decision, in other words a decision which put an end to the dispute (*lis*) between the parties.[1]

1 Voet *Commentarius* 44 2 3 states that the *exceptio* lies when a party seeks to raise afresh a *lis terminata*, ie a dispute which has already been brought to an end. Grotius *Inleiding* 3 49 2 says that the *exceptio* holds "whenever the same thing, with respect to which a judgment having the force of a final or definitive sentence has been given, is again demanded by the same plaintiff of the same defendant, and upon the same grounds" (Maasdorp). See also *Verhagen v Abramowitz* 1960 4 SA 947 (C) 951A–D; *S v Moodie* 1962 1 SA 587 (A) 596E–F: "in our common law the *exceptio rei judicatae* cannot succeed unless it is based on a final judgment on the merits"; *Custom Credit Corporation (Pty) Ltd v Shembe* 1972 3 SA 462 (A) 472A–B: "if a cause of action has been finally litigated between the parties, then a subsequent attempt by one to proceed against the other on the same cause for the same relief can be met by an *exceptio rei judicatae vel litis finitae*"; *African Wanderers Football Club (Pty) Ltd v Wanderers Football Club* 1977 2 SA 38 (A) 45E–G; *Evins v Shield Insurance Co Ltd* 1980 2 SA 814 (A) 835F–H 836F–G; *Mba v Southern Insurance Association Ltd* 1981 1 SA 122 (TkSC) 127C–G; *Liley v Johannesburg Turf Club* 1983 4 SA 548 (W) 552F.

628 Judgment pleaded must be a judgment on the merits In order to qualify as a final or definitive judgment, the judgment must be on the merits of the cause of action which it is sought to litigate afresh.[1] It follows that a judgment which is merely interlocutory or provisional – meaning that it is not intended to settle the dispute between the parties with finality – cannot found a plea of *res iudicata*.[2] A judgment on exception that a claim discloses no cause of action can support a plea of *res iudicata*, but not a judgment which upheld an exception on a purely technical ground.[3] An order of absolution from the instance is ordinarily not decisive of the issue(s) raised, in other words it decides nothing for or against either party, and it is accordingly not a final judgment capable of sustaining a plea of *res iudicata*.[4] An order dismissing a plaintiff's claim is usually taken to be the equivalent of an order of absolution from the instance since it decides nothing, except that the plaintiff has been refused the relief he sought.[5] An order dismissing or refusing an application, when made on the merits, has the same effect as a decision in favour of the respondent, and can therefore found a plea of *res iudicata*.[6] An order to the effect that no order is made on an application, or that leave is given to apply again on the same papers, is equivalent to an order of absolution from the instance.[7]

1 See eg *S v Moodie* 1962 1 SA 587 (A) 595F–596F; *Custom Credit Corporation (Pty) Ltd v Shembe* 1972 3 SA 462 (A) 472A; *African Farms & Townships Ltd v Cape Town Municipality* 1963 2 SA 555 (A) 562C–D: "The rule appears to be that where a court has come to a decision on the merits of a question in issue, that question, at any rate as a *causa petendi* of the same thing between the same parties, cannot be resuscitated in subsequent proceedings."

2 See eg *African Wanderers Football Club (Pty) Ltd v Wanderers Football Club* 1977 2 SA 38 (A) 45D–H 47H (interdict granted *pendente lite*); *Van der Linde v Van Straaten* 1976 1 SA 369 (O): an order for provisional sentence on a mortgage bond, even when it has become final in terms of Uniform Rules of Court r 8(11) because of the defendant's failure to enter into the principal case, cannot found a plea of *res iudicata* in a subsequent action by the defendant to set aside the bond if the court, when granting provisional sentence, did not intend to give a final decision on the defendant's defence that he had been induced by a false representation to pass the bond in the plaintiff's favour. See *S v McCarthy* 1995 3 SA 731 (A) 749B–G; 1995 2 SACR 157 (A).

3 *Kruger v Schoombie* 1916 EDL 279; and cf *S v*

Moodie supra 595F 596E–F.

4 *African Farms & Townships Ltd v Cape Town Municipality* supra 563D–F; *Bonthuys v Visser's Garage* 1950 3 SA 130 (SWA) 133E 134B. In *Cohn v Rand Rietfontein Estates Ltd* 1939 TPD 319 – a case of so-called issue estoppel, as to which see par 647 post – it was held that where a court, in decreeing absolution from the instance, nevertheless made a definite finding regarding a fact in issue, that finding could be raised as *res iudicata* in a subsequent action between the parties. The facts of the case were: C succeeded in the Tvl Provincial Division in a claim for agent's commission in respect of the sale of certain fixed property. The Appellate Division held that the document on which C relied meant that he would be entitled to receive commission only if his services were the effective cause of the sale, and that he had on his own admission not been the effective cause of the sale. Instead of ordering that the trial court's order be altered to one of judgment in favour of the defendant company, however, the Appellate Division ordered it to be altered to one of absolution from the instance, since it thought it possible that C might be entitled to obtain relief in some other form of action than that brought by him in the court *a quo*: *Rand Rietfontein Estates Ltd v Cohn* 1937 AD 317. In a subsequent action brought by C one of the claims advanced by him was substantially the same as that which the Appellate Division had held to be unfounded. The trial court held that the Appellate Division's finding supported a plea of *res iudicata*. In *Umvovo v Umvovo* 1953 1 SA 195 (A) the Appellate Division raised the question, without deciding, whether any conclusion reached in proceedings in which absolution was ordered could be binding in subsequent proceedings. Magistrates court r 32(3) provides *inter alia* that "a decree of absolution from the instance shall not be a defence to any subsequent action".

5 *Municipality of Christiana v Victor* 1908 TS 1117; *Becker v Wertheim, Becker & Leveson* 1943 1 PH F34 (A); *Van Rensburg v Reid* 1958 2 SA 249 (E) 252B–C.

6 *Purchase v Purchase* 1960 3 SA 383 (D) 385A–B; *African Farms & Townships Ltd v Cape Town Municipality* supra 563E–F.

7 *African Farms & Townships Ltd v Cape Town Municipality* supra 563F; *Sewnarain v Budha* 1979 2 SA 353 (N) 356A–E.

629 Judgment pleaded need not have been given in contested proceedings

A judgment need not have been given in contested proceedings in order to render it capable of supporting a plea of *res iudicata*. A judgment granted by consent,[1] or by default,[2] can therefore sustain a plea of *res iudicata*.

1 *Atmore v Atmore* 1932 TPD 154 159.

2 *Boshoff v Union Government* 1932 TPD 345 351; *Turk v Turk* 1954 3 SA 971 (W) 973B–C. It has been said (*Mvaami (Pvt) Ltd v Standard Finance Ltd* 1977 1 SA 861 (R) 867G–868D) that since a default judgment may have been granted merely as the result of the negligence, ignorance or indifference of the defendant, it ought to be scrutinised with great care, and that it should not be allowed to found an estoppel save in respect of what must necessarily and with complete precision have been decided by it. It was held *inter alia* in this case (868H) that a default judment which had been granted on a summons in which two causes of action were advanced in the alternative could not found a plea of *res iudicata* since it was impossible to say on which cause of action the judgment was given. See also *Town Council of Cape Town v The SA Missionary Society* (1901) 18 SC 216 (order made after the publication of a rule *nisi* which was not opposed). As to when a judgment granted after the issue of a rule *nisi* can constitute an estoppel against a person not formally a party to the proceedings, see *Amalgamated Engineering Union v Minister of Labour* 1949 3 SA 637 (A) 651 653 660 662; *Kethel v Kethel's Estate* 1949 3 SA 598 (A) 609.

630 Judgment subject to variation as circumstances change cannot support *exceptio*

Orders which are, whether according to the common law or according to statutory provisions, subject to variation when circumstances change, cannot be pleaded as *res iudicata*.[1] Examples of such orders are orders relating to the custody of minor children, orders refusing the ejectment of a tenant from statutorily controlled premises, and maintenance orders which are subject to alteration if circumstances change.[2]

1 *Le Roux v Le Roux* 1967 1 SA 446 (A) 462H–463G.

2 *Le Roux v Le Roux* supra 463B–C; *Lawson & Kirk (Pty) Ltd v Phil Morkel Ltd* 1953 3 SA

324 (A) 334E–F (case concerned with Rents Act 43 of 1950 s 22(1)); *Owen-Smith v Owen-Smith* 1982 1 SA 511 (ZS) 513D–E.

631 Judgment can be pleaded as *res iudicata* until formally set aside: general rule and exceptions thereto

A judgment ordinarily remains of force, and is consequently capable of supporting a plea of *res iudicata*, until such time as it is set aside by an order of court, whether on appeal, on review, or in proceedings for *restitutio in integrum*.[1] A judgment which is incorrect can, therefore, unless formally set aside, validly be raised as *res iudicata*.[2] A judgment which is null and void can similarly not be attacked when it is set up as *res iudicata* unless it has been formally set aside, but there is authority to the effect that no such formal order is necessary in the following three cases, namely a judgment given by a court lacking jurisdiction, a judgment given against a person who was not duly cited to appear, and a judgment given in the absence of a mandate to sue.[3] A party against whom a judgment of any of the three kinds just mentioned is pleaded as *res iudicata* is entitled to prove its nullity in the same proceedings in which the judgment is set up as *res iudicata*.[4] Account should, of course, be taken of current statutory provisions relating to the rescission of judgments.[5]

1 Voet *Commentarius* 49 8 3; Schorer *ad Gr* 3 49 5; *Liley v Johannesburg Turf Club* 1983 4 SA 548 (W) 550H 552E–H. As to setting aside a judgment in proceedings for *restitutio in integrum*, see *Makings v Makings* 1958 1 SA 338 (A).

2 See par 625 ante. Schorer 3 49 5 says that if a judge gives a decision "so diametrically contrary to law as to be manifestly due to an error of law, eg, if he declares valid a testament made by a minor, it will not even be necessary for the unsuccessful party in my opinion to appeal, for a decision which contains a clear error of law is regarded as if never delivered" (Maasdorp). This view of the law is questionable.

3 Voet 49 8 3 states that in his day the prevailing view was that "decisions are never annulled under cover of nullity without appealing", but that there were exceptions "when the nullity arises from a lack of jurisdiction, or of summons or of an attorney's mandate" (Gane). Schorer 3 49 5 is to the same effect. He says: "a judgment though *ipso iure* null and void, is valid unless appealed against and has the effect of *res iudicata*, unless indeed its nullity is due to want of jurisdiction or of service of summons or

of power to sue" (Maasdorp). South African courts have frequently applied this view of the law: see eg *R v Ntoyaba* (1886) 4 SC 249; *Lewis & Marks v Middel* 1904 TS 291 303; *Sliom v Wallach's Printing & Publishing Co Ltd* 1925 TPD 650 656; *Minister of Agricultural Economics & Marketing v Virginia Cheese & Food Co (1941) (Pty) Ltd* 1961 4 SA 415 (T) 422F–424F; *SA Sentrale Kooperatiewe Graanmpy Bpk v Shifren & the Taxing Master* 1964 1 SA 162 (O) 164D–H; *Mkhize v Swemmer* 1967 1 SA 186 (D) 197C–E; *Dada v Dada* 1977 2 SA 287 (T) 288C–F.

4 See *Lewis & Marks v Middel* supra 303: "the authorities are quite clear that where legal proceedings are initiated against a party, and he is not cited to appear, they are null and void; and upon proof of invalidity the decision may be disregarded, in the same way as a decision given without jurisdiction, without the necessity of a formal order setting it aside."

5 Thus s 36 of the Magistrates' Courts Act 32 of 1944 provides that the court may, upon application by any person affected thereby, rescind or vary any judgment granted by it which was void *ab origine*.

632 Abandonment of judgment or part thereof

The Magistrates' Courts Act[1] provides that a party may abandon the whole or any part of a judgment granted in his or her favour; that judgment in respect of the part abandoned must be entered for the other side, and that a judgment so entered must have the same effect in all respects as if it had been the judgment originally pronounced by the court. Consequently, where a plaintiff has abandoned a judgment in terms of this section, a subsequent claim based on the same cause of action as in the orginal proceedings may be met by a plea of *res iudicata*.[2] It has been held that there may also be an abandonment outside the provisions of the section, and that it may be coupled with a waiver of the right to plead *res iudicata*.[3] The Uniform Rules of Court[4] allow for the abandonment of a decision or a judgment, either in whole or in part, and provide that a decision or judgment abandoned in part will have effect subject to such abandonment.

1 32 of 1944 s 86.
2 See *Burridge v Chodos* 1928 OPD 16, decided with reference to s 83 of the Magistrates' Courts Act 32 of 1917, the predecessor of s 86 of the present Act.
3 *Scrooby v Engelbrecht* 1940 TPD 100 105.
4 Uniform Rules of Court r 41(2).

COMPETENT COURT

633 Judgment of a competent court given in judicial proceedings As stated above,[1] the basis of the *exceptio rei iudicatae* is that a judicial decision is presumed to be correct. Roman law texts show that it was the judgment of a *iudex* which could be set up as *res iudicata*,[2] and it is clear from the writings of Roman–Dutch law authors that in Holland a defendant could – save in certain exceptional cases, provided for by statute[3] – plead as *res iudicata* a judgment which had been given in judicial proceedings.[4] This is also the law in South Africa, for, save in certain exceptional cases,[5] it is required that the judgment which is pleaded in defence must have been given in judicial proceedings by a competent court having jurisdicition over the parties and the matter in question.[6] A judgment given by a court not having the necessary jurisdiction is a nullity[7] and cannot support a plea of *res iudicata*.[8]

1 Par 625 ante.
2 Eg *D* 42 1 1; and see Van der Keessel *Dictata* 3 30 15: *si quis iudicis sententia absolutus et postea ex eadem causa ab eodem actore denuo conveniatur, potest se tueri exceptione rei iudicatae*; ie if someone has been absolved by the judgment of a judge and is thereafter sued afresh by the same plaintiff on the same cause, he or she can protect him or herself by the *exceptio rei iudicatae*.
3 As to this, see par 634 post.
4 See eg Voet *Commentarius* 42 1 1–4 (in 42 1 2 Voet speaks of the *sententia* of a *iudex competens*); Grotius *Inleiding* 3 49 2 and Schorer's note thereon.
5 As to which, see par 634 post.
6 See, generally, *Bertram v Wood* (1893) 10 SC 177; *Muller v Love* (1907) 24 SC 338 340; *Lewis & Marks v Middel* 1904 TS 291 303; *Estate Brownson v President & Members, Income Tax Special Court* 1933 WLD 116; *Cohn v Rand Rietfontein Estates Ltd* 1939 TPD 319 324; *African Farms & Townships Ltd v Cape Town Municipality* 1963 2 SA 555 (A) 564C–E; *Narshi v Ranchod* 1984 3 SA 926 (C) 934B–D.
7 See *Lewis & Marks v Middel* supra 303; *Minister of Agricultural Economics & Marketing v Virginia Cheese & Food Co (1941) (Pty) Ltd* 1961 4 SA 415 (T) 422F–424A and the authorities there cited.
8 *Willis v Cauvin* (1883) 4 NLR 97 98; *R v Ntoyaba* (1886) 4 SC 249; *Moresby-White v Moresby-White* 1972 3 SA 222 (RA).

634 Extension of operation of *exceptio* to *transactio*[1] and award of arbitrators Statutory rules introduced in the Dutch courts in the sixteenth centruy provided that the *exceptio litis finitae* should be regarded as applying also to the exception of *transactio* (*exceptie van transactie*), or compromise, and the exception of award of arbitrators (*exceptie van uytspraecke van arbiters*).[2] In South Africa it has been held that a *transactio*, if pleaded and proved, has the effect of *res iudicata*,[3] and that the award of arbitrators is equivalent to *lis finita*, rendering the dispute between the parties *res iudicata*.[4]

1 A *transactio* is an agreement between two or more persons which is intended to put an end to existing litigation, or to prevent or avoid litigation: see *Gollach & Gomperts (1967) (Pty) Ltd v Universal Mills & Produce Co (Pty) Ltd* 1978 1 SA 914 (A) 921C–D.

2 Voet *Commentarius* 44 2 1; *Steytler v Fitzgerald* 1911 AD 295 340.

3 *Cachalia v Harberer & Co* 1905 TS 457 464 ("A compromise whether embodied in a judgment of the court or extra-judicial has the effect of *res judicata*"); *Western Assurance Co v Caldwell's Trustee* 1918 AD 262 270; *Mothle v Mathole* 1951 1 SA 785 (T) 789A–C; *Van Zyl v Niemann* 1964 4 SA 661 (A) 669H–670A (a compromise has the same effect as *res iudicata* and consequently precludes an action on the original cause of action unless the agreement expressly or by

clear implication provides that if it is breached a party can fall back upon his or her original cause of action). See *Gollach & Gomperts (1967) (Pty) Ltd v Universal Mills & Produce Co (Pty) Ltd* supra 922 B–C; *Syfrets Mortgage Nominees Ltd v Cape St Francis Hotels (Pty) Ltd* 1991 3 SA 276 (SECL) 288E–G.

4 *Schoeman v Van Rensburg* 1942 TPD 175 177; *Verhagen v Abramowitz* 1960 4 SA 947 (C) 950 et seq. In *Boland Bank Bpk v Steele* 1994 1 SA 259 (T) 269B–C it is said that although *transactio* and *res iudicata* have the same effect, the two concepts are not the same in all respects. The question of issue estoppel, the court said, does not arise in the case of *transactio*. As to issue estoppel, see pars 647–650 post.

635 Extension of operation of *exceptio* to judgments of statutory bodies other than courts of law

Decisions of statutory bodies other than courts of law are sometimes given the effect of *res iudicata*. Thus it has been held by the Appellate Division that the *exceptio* applies to orders of the water court dividing water in a public stream between riparian owners. In coming to this conclusion the court held that although there was little similarity between an ordinary contested trial in a court of law and an apportionment suit in a water court, there were provisions in the relevant Act which stressed the final and definitive character of such orders and that, in order to ensure that riparian owners should not be in constant uncertainty as to their rights, public policy required that the principle of *res iudicata* should be applicable to such orders.[1] Considerations of public policy have also been held to justify the application of the *res iudicata* principle to proceedings under certain sections of the Extradition Act,[2] the functions of the magistrate concerned being regarded as quasi-judicial.[3]

Parliament, and also other legislative bodies if acting within their powers,[4] can of course accord the force of *res iudicata* to the decisions of bodies created by them.[5]

1 *Le Roux v Le Roux* 1967 1 SA 446 (A) 462A–D.

2 67 of 1962 ss 9–10.

3 *Minister of Justice v Bagattini* 1975 4 SA 252 (T) 259C–E. See also *S v McCarthy* 1995 3 SA 731 (A); 1995 2 SACR 157 (A).

4 Cf *Durban City Council v Standard-Vacuum Refining Co (Pty) Ltd* 1961 2 SA 682 (N) 686E–G.

5 It was eg expressly provided in s 11(6) of the Population Registration Act 30 of 1950 (repealed by Act 114 of 1991 s 1(1)) that the decision of the board constituted under s 11 (or by the court on appeal to it, the court's decision being deemed to be a decision of the board) as to a person's racial classification was final and binding upon all persons. On this point, see *Secretary for the Interior v Moosa*

1970 4 SA 445 (A) 465A–D. See also Income Tax Act 58 of 1962 s 91(1)(b) which provides that a statement by the Commissioner for Inland Revenue setting out the tax payable by a person has, when filed with the clerk or registrar of a competent court, all the effects of a civil judgment given in that court. As to such a judgment and the question of *res iudicata*, see *Kruger v Sekretaris van Binnelandse Inkomste* 1973 1 SA 394 (A) 410D–413D. See also *Lewis & Marks v Middel* 1904 TS 291, where it was held that a land commission which had been appointed in terms of Law 4 of 1875 (T) to determine the correctness of farm boundaries was to be regarded as a tribunal closely resembling a court (303).

SAME PERSONS

636 Same persons It is a requirement of the *exceptio rei iudicatae* that the judgment pleaded in defence must be a judgment that was given in earlier proceedings between the same persons.[1]

1 See par 624 ante.

637 Meaning of "same persons" The words "same persons" do not mean only the identical individuals who were parties to the proceedings in which the judgment which is raised as *res iudicata* was given, for they include persons who are in law identified with those who were parties to the proceedings. Voet[1] gives various examples of persons who are identified with one another for the purpose of the *exceptio rei iudicatae*. Some of the examples given are: a deceased and his heir; a principal and his agent; a person under curatorship and his curator; a pupil and his tutor; a creditor and debtor in respect of a pledged article if the debtor gave the article in pledge after losing a suit in which a third party claimed it. An examination of the examples given by Voet shows that the persons who are deemed to be the same as the persons who were engaged in the earlier proceedings in which the judgment was given all derive their interest in the later proceedings from the parties to the earlier proceedings.[2] An owner of land has for the purpose of the *exceptio* been held to be bound by a judgment affecting the water rights of his predecessor-in-title,[3] and a tenant has been identified with his landlord with regard to the latter's right to own and occupy fixed property.[4]

On the other hand, a judgment given in proceedings between a man and a woman declaring the man to be the father of the woman's child, has been held to be incapable of estopping the man from raising the issue of paternity in subsequent proceedings instituted by the state in order to compel the man to contribute to the maintenance of the child, the court holding that the minister concerned derived his right to claim a contribution order not from the mother of the child, but from an Act of Parliament.[5] A trustee in an insolvent estate may properly be identified with the insolvent as far as lawful dealings and dispositions by him or her are concerned, but the trustee cannot be identified with the insolvent in respect of a judgment which he or she fraudulently and to the prejudice of his or her creditors allowed to be taken against him or herself, the reason being that the trustee must in such circumstances act in terms of the provisions of the Insolvency Act.[6] An insolvent cannot be identified with his or her trustee for the purposes of the *exceptio rei iudicatae* and a judgment obtained against the trustee in the absence of the insolvent and without his or her consent cannot be set up as *res iudicata* against the trustee.[7]

The requirement that the persons in the earlier and later proceedings must be the same does not mean that the person who raises the *exceptio* must necessarily have been the defendant in the earlier proceedings, nor that the party against whom it is raised must have been the plaintiff in the earlier proceedings.[8]

1 *Commentarius* 44 2 5. See also *Amalgamated Engineering Union v Minister of Labour* 1949 3 SA 637 (A) 654; *Kethel v Kethel's Estate* 1949 3 SA 598 (A) 603; *Ferreira v Minister of Social Welfare* 1958 1 SA 93 (E) 95–96; *Cassim v The Master* 1960 2 SA 347 (D) 355A–B, where reference is made to Voet and the examples given by him.

2 *Ferreira v Minister of Social Welfare* supra 95–96A.

3 *Le Roux v Le Roux* 1967 1 SA 446 (A) 460G–463H.

4 *Koster Koöperatiewe Landboumpy Bpk v Wadee* 1960 3 SA 197 (T) 199F–G.

5 *Ferreira v Minister of Social Welfare* supra 95H–96E.

6   24 of 1936; *Shokkos v Lampert* 1963 3 SA
    421 (W); *Swadif (Pty) Ltd v Dyke* 1978 1 SA
    928 (A) 945B–D; and see *Scharf v Dempers &*
    Co 1955 3 SA 316 (SWA).
7   *Cassim v The Master* supra 354E–355D.
8   *Cook v Muller* 1973 2 SA 240 (N) 245E–H.
    See also *Wolff v Solomon* (1898) 15 SC 297

306 (a judgment given on a defendant's
counterclaim can be set up against the defendant as *res iudicata* when he or she subsequently advances a claim which is
substantially the same as his or her counterclaim in the earlier proceedings.)

638 *Exceptio* can operate between co-defendants in earlier proceedings The
exceptio rei iudicatae may be raised by a person against someone who was his or her co-
defendant in the earlier proceedings if there was a dispute between them which was
settled by the judgment.[1]

1   *Mitford's Executor v Ebden's Executors* 1917
    AD 682; *Brink v Gain* 1958 3 SA 503 (C)
    508C–D.

639 Acting in personal or representative capacity The requirement that the
persons must be the same entails that they must in the earlier proceedings have litigated in the same capacity as that in which they litigate in the subsequent proceedings
in which the *exceptio rei iudicatae* is raised.[1] A judgment given against a person in his or
her personal capacity cannot therefore be set up against the person as *res iudicata* when
he or she subsequently sues in a representative capacity.

1   Schorer *ad Gr* 3 49 says that the "qualifica-
    tion" of the parties must be the same. He
    cites *D* 44 2 12–14 where it is said (14) that
    the *conditio personarum* must be the same. See
    Shokkos v Lampert 1963 3 SA 421 (W) 426A:

"It is necessary . . . that the parties to the
litigation (or their privies) should have
claimed or defended 'in the same right' in
the former proceedings as they represent in
the later ones."

**640 Requirement of "same persons" has result that verdict in criminal case
cannot be *res iudicata* in civil case and vice versa** The requirement that the
persons in the earlier and later proceedings must be the same has the effect[1] that a
verdict in a criminal case cannot be set up as *res iudicata* in a civil case.[2] It also explains
why a judgment given in a civil case cannot be set up as *res iudicata* in a criminal case.
Thus, an order made on a person's divorce ordering him to pay maintenance for his
children cannot be set up as *res iudicata* against him so as to preclude him from raising
the issue of paternity when subsequently prosecuted for failing to pay the maintenance
he was ordered to pay at the time of his divorce;[3] and an order of ejectment made
against a person in a civil case affords no proof against the person when he or she is
subsequently prosecuted for trespass.[4]

1   It is not suggested that this is the only reason
    why a verdict in a criminal case cannot be
    res iudicata in a civil case, or vice versa. Fur-
    ther consideration of the question is, how-
    ever, not necessary.
2   See eg *Fischer v Genricks* (1885) 4 SC 31;
    *Hornby v Municipal Council of Roodepoort-
    Maraisburg* 1917 WLD 54; *R v Van
    der Merwe* 1952 1 SA 647 (O) 649D–E. The
    case of *Schlapilis v Missewitz* 1904 TS 174
    was an unusual one: a statute required
    the court, on convicting an employer of
    having unlawfully withheld wages from an

employee, to give judgment for such wages
in favour of the employee, and it was held
that the prosecutor acted ad hoc as the agent
of the complainant concering the question
of wages, with the result that the judgment
could be set up as *res iudicata* against the employee when he subsequently sued for such
wages as he considered to be actually due to
him. Cf *Gagela v Ganca* (1907) 3 BAC 102: a
statute empowered a court convicting a person to award "reasonable compensation" to
the person injured, and it was held that a
complainant who did not apply for such

compensation but who accepted half the fine imposed on the accused was not precluded from subsequently claiming such damages as

he could prove to have actually suffered.
3 *R v Van der Merwe* supra 649D–E.
4 *R v Lechudi* 1945 AD 796 801.

SAME THING

641 Requirement of *eadem res* One of the traditional requirements of the *exceptio rei iudicatae* of Roman-Dutch law is that the judgment pleaded as *res iudicata* must have been about the same thing (*eadem res*) as that which is demanded in the later action.[1] It was held in a recent decision of the Appellate Division, however, that it is not an immutable requirement of the *exceptio rei iudicatae* that the same thing must have been demanded in the earlier as in the later proceedings.[2]

1 Voet 44 2 3; Vinnius 4 13 5; Grotius 3 49 2; *Bertram v Wood* (1893) 10 SC 177 180: "By the law of England the requisites of such a defence are that the judgment relied upon must have been between the same parties, and that the same point must have been at issue as in the suit in which the defence is pleaded. Under our law, however, there is a third requisite, namely that the same thing must have been demanded"; *McCallum v Lubbe* 1908 EDC 58 61; *Hornby v Municipal Council of Roodepoort-Maraisburg* 1917 WLD 54 56; *African Farms & Townships Ltd v Cape Town Municipality* 1963 2 SA 555 (A) 562A;

Custom Credit Corporation (Pty) Ltd v Shembe 1972 3 SA 462 (A) 472A–B; *Horowitz v Brock* 1988 2 SA 160 (A) 178: "The requisites of a valid defence of *res judicata* in Roman-Dutch law are that the matter adjudicated upon, on which the defence relies, must have been for the same cause, between the same parties, and the same things must have been demanded"; *Boland Bank Bpk v Steele* 1994 1 SA 259 (T) 269G.
2 *Kommissaris van Binnelandse Inkomste v ABSA Bank Bpk* 1995 1 SA 653 (A). See pars 647–650 post.

642 Meaning of "the same thing" The thing claimed in the earlier and later proceedings need not be precisely the same, for the *exceptio* lies where the whole of a thing was first demanded and a part therof is thereafter claimed or, conversely, where a part of a thing was first demanded and the whole of it is thereafter claimed.[1] It makes no difference whether the thing in question is a bodily item (*corpus*) or a right (*ius*).[2] Voet[3] cites various examples of when things are considered to be the same for the purpose of the *exceptio rei iudicatae*, for example if a person first demanded two items and thereafter claims one or the other thereof; or if a person failed in his or her claim for a bodily item (*corpus*) and thereafter claims an accessory (*accessio*) thereof; or if somebody who failed in an action to vindicate a farm subsequently claims the fruits thereof.

1 *D* 44 2 7 et seq; Voet *Commentarius* 44 2 3; Huber *RHR* 5 38 12: "A thing is one and the same when we claim first a part and then the whole of it; or vice versa, first the whole

and afterwards a part" (Gane).
2 *D* 44 2 7.
3 Voet 44 2 3.

SAME CAUSE OF ACTION

643 Requirement of same cause of action It is a requisite of the *exceptio rei iudicatae* that the cause of action in the proceedings in which the defence is raised must be the same as that on which final judgment was given in earlier proceedings.[1] As to the meaning of the expression "cause of action",[2] Voet[3] states that the *exceptio rei iudicatae* lies when there is the same cause for claiming (*eadem causa petendi*) as there was in the earlier proceedings. South African courts, relying on the authority of Voet, have held that the cause of claiming,[4] or the ground of the demand,[5] or the cause of complaint,[6] must be the same. Sometimes, when it is sought to convey the same idea of *eadem petendi causa*, it is said that the same matter must be in issue.[7]

1 See par 624 ante.

2 The expression is often used by the courts. See eg *McCallum v Lubbe* 1908 EDC 58 61; *Kethel v Kethel's Estate* 1949 3 SA 598 (A) 605.

3 *Commentarius* 44 2 3, 44 2 4. Van der Keessel *Prael* 3 49 2, in discussing the requisites of the *exceptio rei iudicatae*, also uses the expression *eadem causa petendi*.

4 *Ferreira v Minister of Social Welfare* 1958 1 SA

93 (E) 95H.

5 *African Farms & Townships Ltd v Cape Town Municipality* 1963 2 SA 555 (A) 562A.

6 *Hiddingh v Denyssen* (1885) 3 SC 424 450.

7 *Bertram v Wood* (1893) 10 SC 177 180; *Wolfaardt v Colonial Government* (1899) 16 SC 250 253: "As pointed out by Voet (44 2 4), the cause of action is the same whenever the same matter is in issue."

644 When causes of action are the same It is not the form of the proceedings which determines the sameness of the *causa petendi*, but the identity of the question (*quaestio*) raised in the earlier and subsequent proceedings.[1] Voet[2] states that it is not so much the *actio* as the source of the claim (*origo petitionis*) which makes a cause the same. As an example of causes of action being the same because of their having the same *origo*, Voet,[3] referring to Roman law, states that if as a result of a defect in a thing bought a purchaser had both the *actio redhibitoria* and the *actio quanti minoris* available to him in such a way that the latter action also emcompassed the former and he thereafter proceeded to employ one of those actions in suing the seller, he could be met with a plea of *res iudicata* if he subsequently instituted the other action against the seller. Since it is not the form of the proceedings which determines the identity of the *causa petendi*, but the identity of the question raised in the earlier and subsequent proceedings, it follows that the *exceptio rei iudicatae* cannot be defeated by the fact that the proceedings in which the defence is raised differ in form from the earlier proceedings.[4] It follows, too, that the reason why a person may think that a cause of action is available to him or her is of no consequence.[5]

1 Voet *Commentarius* 44 2 4. In *African Farms & Townships Ltd v Cape Town Municipality* 1963 2 SA 555 (A) 562C–D *causa* and *quaestio* are used as being synonymous. See also *Wolfaardt v Colonial Government* (1899) 16 SC 250 253: "the cause of the action is the same whenever the same matter is in issue."

2 44 2 4.

3 44 2 4.

4 See eg *Wolfaardt v Colonial Government* supra. W claimed damages from the government on the ground of trespass, alleging that it had unlawfully sunk a well on his farm which

reduced the supply of other water available to him on his farm. The court found that the well did not reduce the supply of other water available to him and that W had suffered no damage. A subsequent claim by W for the value of the water which the government had used was defeated by a plea of *res iudicata*, the court holding that W could not by changing the form of his action make substantially the same claim as that advanced in the earlier action.

5 *African Farms & Townships v Cape Town Municipality* supra 562E.

645 Determination of real question in issue In order to determine whether the question which is pleaded as *res iudicata* has already been decided in an earlier case between the parties, one must have regard to the pleadings and judgment in the earlier case.[1] It has been said in several cases that one does not look at the evidence.[2] It is a function of pleadings to settle the issues between the parties, and the pleadings will ordinarily set out the issues raised by the parties. But all issues raised in the pleadings are not necessarily always litigated and adjudicated upon and one must consequently have regard to the judgment in order to establish which issues were in fact considered and decided by the court.[3] It may happen, also, that the pleadings do not contain all the issues that were in fact considered and decided by the court, for sometimes an issue, although not specifically raised in the pleadings, is nevertheless fully canvassed in evidence by both sides in the sense that the court is expected to pronounce upon it as an issue in the case.[4] In order to determine whether an issue so raised was decided upon by the court, one will have to have regard to the court's judgment. The rule that one should have regard to the pleadings in order to determine the issues raised by the parties can obviously not apply in cases where the rules of the court concerned do not provide for pleadings in the ordinary sense. In such cases one must have regard to the judgment in order to determine what questions were raised and decided.[5]

1 *R v Manasewitz* 1933 AD 165 187; *Van Niewenhuizen v Richards* 1959 2 SA 686 (T) 687F.
2 See eg *Wolfaardt v Colonial Government* (1899) 16 SC 250 252; *McCallum v Lubbe* 1908 EDC 58 61; *Marks & Kantor v Van Diggelen* 1935 TPD 29 33.
3 See the observation in *R v Bekker* 1926 CPD 410 416 that a judgment is "binding as to the matter actually decided".
4 *South British Insurance Co Ltd v Unicorn Shipping Lines (Pty) Ltd* 1976 1 SA 708 (A) 714F–G.
5 *Bantu Reformed Apostolic Church v Ninow & Michael* 1947 1 SA 187 (N) 189–190.

646 Effect of final judgment on party's cause of action
The effect of a final judgment on a claim is to render the claimant's cause of action *res iudicata*.[1] If therefore a party with a single cause of action giving rise to a single claim obtains a final judgment on part of the claim, the judgment puts an end to the party's whole cause of action,[2] with the result that a subsequent claim for the balance of what the cause of action entitled him or her to claim in the first instance can be met with a plea of *res iudicata*.[3] When a cause of action gives rise to more than one remedy, a plaintiff who pursues one of those remedies and obtains a judgment thereon can be met with a plea of *res iudicata* if he or she should subsequently seek to pursue one of the other remedies, the reason being that a final judgment on part of one's cause of action puts an end to the whole of such cause of action.[4] It has been said in this connection that it is a rule of law that a party with a single cause of action should claim in one and the same action whatever remedies the law allows the party upon such cause of action.[5] This rule, sometimes referred to as the "once and for all" rule, taken together with the principle of *res iudicata*, has the effect that "where a final judgment has been given by a competent court, then subsequent litigation between the same parties, or their privies, in regard to the same subject matter and based upon the same cause of action is not permissible and, if attempted by one of them, can be met by the *exceptio rei judicatae vel litis finitae*."[6]

1 *Van Zyl v Niemann* 1964 4 SA 661 (A) 669–670A; *Custom Credit Corporation (Pty) Ltd v Shembe* 1972 3 SA 462 (A) 472A–B.
2 Eg of what may constitute a single cause of action, see *Evins v Shield Insurance Co Ltd* 1980 2 SA 814 (A) 836E–837E.
3 *Blaikie-Johnstone v P Hollingsworth (Pty) Ltd* 1974 3 SA 392 (D). See also *Van der Heever v Van Rooyen* (1894) 11 SC 51 54. The decision in *Lawton v Rens* (1842) 3 M 483 is against principle and cannot be supported. The plaintiff suffered damages in an amount of £790 by reason of the defendant's fraud. He claimed only £600 and, after obtaining judgment for that amount, instituted a second action for the balance, alleging that he had in error failed to claim the full amount in his first action. The defendant pleaded *res iudicata*, but the court, while holding that the *exceptio* was well pleaded, nevertheless held that the plaintiff should, because of his error, be relieved from the operation of the judgment. The Magistrates' Courts Act 32 of 1944 s 40 contains the following provision with regard to the splitting of claims: "A substantive claim exceeding the jurisdiction may not be split with the object of recovering the same in more than one action if the parties to all such actions would be the same and the point at issue in all such actions would also be the same."
4 See *Green v Coetzer* 1958 2 SA 697 (W); *Schnellen v Rondalia Assurance Corporation of SA Ltd* 1969 1 SA 517 (W); *Custom Credit*

Corporation (Pty) Ltd v Shembe supra 472A: "The law requires a party with a single cause of action to claim in one and the same action whatever remedies the law accords him upon such cause." In *Alfred McAlpine & Son (Pty) Ltd v Tvl Provincial Administration* 1977 4 SA 310 (T) 338B–C the court raised the question whether this statement in *Shembe's* case was intended to be a statement of "a substantive rule of procedural practice."

5 *Custom Credit Corporation (Pty) Ltd v Shembe* supra 472A. See also *Cape Town Council v Jacobs* 1917 AD 615 620; *Oslo Land Co Ltd v The Union Government* 1938 AD 584 591; *Kantor v Welldone Upholsterers* 1944 CPD 388 391; *Casely v Minister of Defence* 1973 1 SA 630 (A) 630C–D.

6 *Evins v Shield Insurance Co Ltd* supra 835F–H; *Union Wine Ltd v E Snell & Co Ltd* 1990 2 SA 189 (C) 195E–196J.

Issue Estoppel[1]

647 The question of issue estoppel Several judgments given in provincial and local divisions of the supreme court (as it was previously called) are to the effect that where a court, in giving a final judgment on the cause litigated before it, has, or is to be taken to have, determined a particular issue involved in that cause of action in a certain way, such determination may be raised as an estoppel in a subsequent action between the same parties, even if the subsequent action is founded on a different cause of action, if the same issue is again involved and the right to recover depends on that issue.[2]

The rule of *res iudicata* as applied in these cases is commonly referred to as "issue estoppel"[3] to distinguish it from the traditional *exceptio rei iudicatae* of Roman-Dutch law. The rule first found acceptance in South African case law in *Boshoff v Union Government*,[4] which was decided in 1932. The facts of the case, briefly stated, were: the plaintiff sued the defendant for damages on the ground that he had hired certain property from the defendant but that the defendant wrongfully cancelled the contract and ejected him from the property. A magistrate's court had previously, in a judgment by default, ordered the plaintiff's ejectment from the property. The defendant raised a plea of *res iudicata*, saying that he had previously claimed the plaintiff's ejectment from the property and that his claim was granted. He stated that the cancellation of the contract was in issue between the parties in the first action. The supreme court held that the magistrate's court, in ordering the plaintiff's ejectment from the property, must necessarily have determined that the lease had been validly cancelled by the defendant, and that the plaintiff was accordingly estopped from claiming damages on the ground that there had been unlawful cancellation of the lease. The court accordingly upheld the plea of *res iudicata*.

In its judgment in *Boshoff's* case the court, in dealing with the *exceptio rei iudicatae*, referred to Vinnius and Voet. With regard to Vinnius the court merely said that in *Bertram v Wood* De Villiers CJ quoted a passage from Vinnius (4 13 5) "which is to the effect that this exception only applies if there is the same question between the same persons".[6] The court referred to Voet at greater length. "According to *Voet* (44.2.3)", the court said, "the rule is that the exception can only be employed when an action which has been once terminated is again set in motion by the same parties, about the same thing, and based on the same cause of action"; and, also: "It appears from *Voet* (44.2.4) that, to use his own words, 'where it is competent to employ both the redhibitory action and the action *quanti minoris* on account of the article purchased being tainted with such a defect that the buyer would for that reason not have purchased it' . . .then if one action is used, the subsequent action can be met by the pleading of *res iudicata*. Now the redhibitory action and the *quanti minoris* action are different causes of action and it appears to me, therefore, that Voet cannot be using the words 'cause of action' or *eadem petendi causa* in the narrow pleading sense that they are sometimes used in our Courts". Having said this, the court turned to what is said in Phipson[7] regarding the English law of estoppel by judgment and found that there was such similarity between certain expressions used by Voet and Phipson that "one can safely turn to the English law as a guide on a point that has not been specifically dealt with in our law".[8] Having come to this conclusion, the judge proceeded to quote a passage from the first edition of Spencer Bower's work on *Res Judicata*,[9] saying that it correctly laid down the rule (namely of *res iudicata*) and that he proposed to apply it to the case before the court. The passage reads: "Where the decision set up as *res iudicata* necessarily involves a judicial determination of some question of law or issue of fact, in the sense that the decision could not have been legitimately or rationally pronounced by the tribunal without at the same time, and in the same breath, so to speak, determining that question or issue in a particular way, such determination, though not declared on the face of the recorded decision, is deemed to constitute an integral part of it as effectively as if it had been made so in express terms; but, beyond these limits, there can be no such thing as a *res iudicata* by implication".

1 This section is devoted to the question of "issue estoppel" in so far as it relates to the civil law. As to the question of issue estoppel in criminal law, see title CRIMINAL PROCEDURE.

2 See eg *Boshoff v Union Government* 1932 TPD 345; *Cohn v Rand Rietfontein Estates Ltd* 1939 TPD 319; *Bantu Reformed Apostolic Church v Ninow & Michael* 1947 1 SA 187 (N); *Turk v Turk* 1954 3 SA 971 (W); *Naidoo v Narainsamy* 1956 3 SA 223 (N); *Van Niewenhuizen v Richards* 1959 2 SA 686 (T); *Durban City Council v Standard-Vacuum Refining Co (Pty) Ltd* 1961 2 SA 682 (N); *Liley v Johannesburg Turf Club* 1983 4 SA 548 (W); *Boland Bank Bpk v Steele* 1994 1 SA 259 (T).

3 The name is derived form English law: see eg *Boland Bank Bpk v Steele* supra 259 269G–H; Zeffertt 1971 *SALJ* 312; Hoffmann and Zeffertt *SA Law of Evidence* 4 ed 350.

4 Supra 345. In *Horowitz v Brock* 1988 2 SA 160 (A) 179 the court said: "The doctrine of issue estoppel . . . although not specifically referred to by the name which it is currently known, appears to have first found acceptance in our law in *Boshoff v Union Government* 1932 TPD 345". See also *Kommissaris van Binnelandse Inkomste v ABSA Bank Bpk* 1995 1 SA 653 (A): "Dit word allerweë aanvaar, tereg, dat hierdie saak beslag gegee het aan die gebruikmaking van geskilpuntestoppel op provinsiale vlak".

5 (1893) 10 SC 177.

6 Vinnius said more than this. He referred to the requirements of *inter alia idem corpus, eadem quantitas, idem ius*.

7 The court referred to Phipson *Evidence* 7 ed 399 403.

8 *Boshoff v Union Government* supra.

9 S 162.

648 Long-held view that the decision in *Boshoff v Union Government*[1] is in conflict with the *exceptio rei iudicatae* The rule applied in *Boshoff v Union Government*[2] and in cases following thereon in a number of decisions of provincial and local divisions of the Supreme Court[3] was for a long time, until the recent decision of the Appellate Division in *Kommissaris van Binnelandse Inkomste v ABSA Bank Bpk*[4] widely considered to have been a rule of the English doctrine of issue estoppel and to be in conflict with the *exceptio rei iudicatae* in not requiring that the same thing must be demanded in the two actions involved.

In *Bertram v Wood*[5] De Villiers CJ, after stating that in English law the requisites for a defence of *res iudicata* are that the judgment relied upon must have been between the same parties and that the same point must have been at issue in the suit in which the defence is pleaded, went on to say: "Under our law, however, there is a third requisite, namely that the same thing must have been demanded". He referred *inter alia* to Vinnius and Voet,[6] and to Grotius. Grotius is very clear on the point. He says that the *exceptio* applies when the same thing (*de zelve zaecke*) is demanded (*werd geeischt*) by the same person, from the same person, and on the same ground.[7] The law as stated in *Bertram v Wood* was adopted, or referred to with approval, in a number of subsequent cases,[8] and it may safely be said that it was widely accepted that it was a requirement of the *exceptio rei iudicatae* of Roman-Dutch law that the same thing must have been demanded in the two relevant actions. Recent evidence that it was generally so accepted appears from the following statement in the judgment of the Appellate Division in the case of *Horowitz v Brock*,[9] which was decided in 1987. The court said: "The requisites of a valid defence of *res judicata* in Roman-Dutch law are that the matter adjudicated upon, on which the defence relies, must have been for the same cause, between the same parties, and the same thing must have been demanded". It also said: "The doctrine of issue estoppel does not require for its application that the same thing must have been demanded, and it is the lack of this element which distinguishes it from *res judicata*".[10]

1 1932 TPD 345.
2 Supra.
3 See par 647 fn 2 ante.
4 1995 1 SA 653 (A).
5 (1893) 10 SC 177 180.
6 At 180 181.
7 *Inleiding* 3 49 2.
8 See eg *McCallum v Lubbe* 1908 EDC 58 61;

Hornby v Municipal Council of Roodepoort-Maraisburg 1917 WLD 54 56; *African Farms & Townships Ltd v Cape Town Municipality* 1963 2 SA 555 (A) 562A; *Custom Credit Corporation (Pty) Ltd v Shembe* 1972 3 SA 462 (A) 472A–B.
9 1988 2 SA 160 (A) 178H–I.
10 At 179A.

649 Not an immutable requirement of *res iudicata* that the same thing must have been demanded in both actions

In *Kommissaris van Binnelandse Inkomste v ABSA Bank Bpk*[1] the Appellate Division held that the court in *Boshoff v Union Government*[2] did not base its decision on English law;[3] that it did not import, or intend to import, English law into South African law; that it considered what is stated in the passage it quoted from Spencer Bower's *Res Judicata* to be in accordance with Roman-Dutch law, and that it used that passage merely as a guide on a point that had not been specifically dealt with before in South African law.[4] The Appellate Division held, too, that Voet's example (in 44 2 4) of a plea of *res iudicata* being possible in actions based on the *actio redhibitoria* and the *actio quanti minoris*, which are different causes of action, shows that it is not an immutable requirement of *res iudicata* that the thing claimed in the two relevant actions must necessarily and in all circumstances be the same.[5]

1 1995 1 SA 653 (A).
2 1932 TPD 345.
3 *Kommissaris van Binnelandse Inkomste v ABSA Bank Bpk* supra 667–668A 669C–I.
4 *Kommissaris van Binnelandse Inkomste v ABSA Bank Bpk* supra 668B–C.
5 *Kommissaris van Binnelandse Inkomste v ABSA Bank Bpk* supra 668D. The court said: what is claimed with the *actio redhibitoria* is

without doubt not the same as that which is claimed with the *actio quanti minoris*, and yet the *exceptio rei iudicatae* applies. Voet's example and the court's acceptance in *Boshoff v Union Government* supra of a wide rather than a narrow meaning of *petendi causa* both necessarily imply that it is not an immutable requirement that the thing that is claimed must be the same.

650 The question whether issue estoppel is part of South African law

In *Kommissaris van Binnelandse Inkomste v ABSA Bank Bpk*,[1] the most recent Appellate Division case on *res iudicata*, the court found it unnecessary to decide whether issue estoppel has become part of the law of South Africa. The question did not arise, the court said.[2]

The court said in the same case that the decision in *Boshoff v Union Government*[3] did not import the English law of *res iudicata* into South African law, although it was true that the learned judge who heard the case had regard to the passage he quoted from Spencer Bower's *Res Judicata* as a guide in the decision he had to make. The real importance of *Boshoff*'s case, the Appellate Division said, is that it shows that the strict common law requirements of the defence of *res iudicata* (particularly *eadem res* and *eadem petendi causa*) should not in all circumstances be literally understood as being immutable rules, since there is room for adaptation and development on the basis of the underlying requirement of *eadem quaestio* and the *ratio* of the defence.[4] When viewed in this light, the court said, there can be no objection to the approach followed in *Boshoff*'s case. The unacceptable alternative would be to cling to statements appearing in the old authorities which might hinder the development of the law to meet the requirements of new factual situations.

The court added at the same time, however, that it is unnecessary to use the expression "issue estoppel" in South African law, and that it may even be misleading to speak of a doctrine of "issue estoppel" in the law of South Africa. And yet, the court said, it would hardly be reasonable to object to the use of the expression merely because it is derived from English law. It has been in use for a long time, the court said, and it is a useful expression to describe those cases which do not, strictly speaking, conform to the traditional requirements of the *exceptio rei iudicatae* because the same relief is not claimed on the same cause of action, but in which the defence may nevertheless be successful.

1 1995 1 SA 653 (A).

2 At 669F. See, to the same effect, *Horowitz v Brock* 1988 2 SA 160 (A) 179E, where the court found it unnecessary to decide whether issue estoppel has become part of South African law and said: "the principle expressed therein has not yet been pronounced upon by this court. It remains a vexed question whether issue estoppel is part of our law."

3 1932 TPD 345 350; *Kommissaris van Binnelandse Inkomste v ABSA Bank Bpk* supra 666F–G 669B–C.

4 *Kommissaris van Binnelandse Inkomste v ABSA Bank Bpk* supra 669F–H.

JUDGMENTS IN REM

651 Distinguished from judgments *in personam* The discussion in the aforegoing paragraphs of judgments which can be raised in support of a plea of *res iudicata* is concerned with judgments which are binding on persons who were parties to the suit in which they were delivered, or persons who are in law identified with those who were parties to the suit. Judgments of this kind, which are sometimes referred to as judgments *in personam*, are to be distinguished from what are called judgments *in rem*. A judgment *in rem* is one which declares or determines the status of a person or thing, and it is binding on everyone, not only those who were parties to the suit in which it was delivered or who are in law identified with such parties.[1] Examples of judgments *in rem* referred to in decided cases in South Africa are: a judgment declaring whether persons are married or divorced;[2] a judgment declaring a marriage to be void *ab initio*;[3] a decree presuming a person's death;[4] a judgment declaring that the status of a company in terms of the now-repealed Group Areas Act[5] is such that it is not entitled to own certain fixed property.[6]

1 *Ex parte Welsh: In Re Estate Keegan* 1943 WLD 147 149; *Koster Koöperatiewe Landboumpy Bpk v Wadee* 1960 3 SA 197 (T) 199D–F; *Tshabalala v Johannesburg City Council* 1962 4 SA 367 (T) 368H–370A.

2 *Ex parte Welsh: in re Estate Keegan* supra 149; *Amalgamated Engineering Union v Minister of Labour* 1949 3 SA 637 (A) 651.

3 *Ex parte Oxton* 1948 1 SA 1011 (C) 1015.

4 *Ex parte Welsh: in re Estate Keegan* supra 149.

5 41 of 1950. (This Act was repealed by Act 77 of 1957 s 44.)

6 *Koster Ko-op Landboumpy Bpk v Wadee* supra 199D–F. In *Tshabalala v Johannesburg City Council* supra it was decided that a decision by a magistrate's court that a by-law was *ultra vires* could not operate as a judgment *in rem*, the court holding *inter alia* (370A) that "an untenable position would arise if a palpably *ultra vires* by-law, declared to be valid

by a magistrate, should preclude every other magistrate with jurisdiction in the area of the municipality and also the division of the supreme court of the Province from holding that the by-law is invalid. If such were the case the magistrate would in effect confer on the municipality legislative powers beyond the scope of the particular enabling ordinance". Cf *Peri-Urban Areas Health Board v Breet* 1958 3 SA 783 (T) 785A where the court accepted without question that an ordinance was invalid because it had been found to be invalid in *R v Mziza* 1946 TPD 654. In *Tshabalala's* case (369A) it is also said, wrongly, it is submitted, that the case

of *R v Kriel* 1939 CPD 221, where it was held that a judgment declaring the accused to be the father of a certain child precluded him from thereafter again raising the issue of paternity, was decided on the footing that the judgment was a judgment *in rem. R v Kriel* supra would seem to have been decided on the basis of issue estoppel. See also *Registrar General, Zimbabwe v Chinwa* 1993 4 SA 272 (ZS), where it was held that a judgment declaring a person to be a citizen of Zimbabwe was concerned with a matter of status and was accordingly a judgment *in rem.*

ESTOPPEL BY REPRESENTATION

GENERAL STATEMENT OF DOCTRINE OF ESTOPPEL BY REPRESENTATION

652 General statement of the doctrine Briefly stated, the doctrine of estoppel by representation consists in this, that a person is precluded, that is estopped, from denying the truth of a representation previously made by him or her to another person if the latter, believing in the truth of the representation, acted thereon to his or her prejudice.[1] Stated more fully, the doctrine as applied in the courts of South Africa may be said to amount to the following: namely, that where a person (the representor) has by his or her words or conduct made a representation to another person (the representee) and the latter, believing the representation to be true, acted thereon and would suffer prejudice if the representor were permitted to deny the truth of the representation made by him or her, the representator may be estopped, that is precluded, from denying the truth of the representation.[2] This statement is subject to the qualification that in certain cases an estoppel will arise only if there was fault, that is, *dolus* or *culpa*, on the part of the representor when he or she made the representation on which the plea of estoppel is based.[3]

The doctrine of estoppel by representation is based on considerations of fairness and justice, and is aimed at preventing prejudice and injustice.[4] It is a rule of substantive law,[5] and its function is to provide a defence to a claim, or to counter a defence to a claim. It has to be pleaded and proved by the party who raises it.[6] It is not a cause of action and cannot found a claim, but it can, in an indirect way, by defeating a defence to a claim, operate to secure the enforcement of a claim.[7]

The various elements of the doctrine are discussed below.[8]

1 This statement was referred to in *Aris Enterprises (Finance) (Pty) Ltd v Protea Assurance Co Ltd* 1981 3 SA 274 (A) 291D–E as setting out the essence of the doctrine of estoppel by representation and recently again referred to and applied in *Sodo v Chairman ANC, Umtata Region* [1998] 1 All SA 45 (Tk) 51. See also *NBS Bank Ltd v Cape Produce (Pty) Ltd* [2002] 2 All SA 262 (SCA); 2002 1 SA 396 (SCA) 411; *Eastern*

Metropolitan Substructure v Peter Klein Investments (Pty) Ltd [2002] 1 All SA 187 (W); 2001 4 BCLR 344 (W); 2001 4 SA 661 (W).

2 *Waterval Estate & Gold Mining Co Ltd v New Bullion Gold Mining Co Ltd* 1905 TS 717 722–723; *Baumann v Thomas* 1920 AD 428 434–436; *Union Government v National Bank of SA Ltd* 1921 AD 121; *Union Government v Vianini Ferro-Concrete Pipes (Pty) Ltd* 1941

AD 43 49; *Poort Sugar Planters (Pty) Ltd v Minister of Lands* 1963 3 SA 352 (A) 363D–365; *Hauptfleisch v Caledon Divisional Council* 1963 4 SA 53 (C) 56E–57F; *Connock's (SA) Motor Co Ltd v Sentraal Westelike Ko-operatiewe Mpy Bpk* 1964 2 SA 47 (T) 49A–53H; *Johaadien v Stanley Porter (Paarl) (Pty) Ltd* 1970 1 SA 394 (A); *Oakland Nominees (Pty) Ltd v Gelria Mining & Investment Co (Pty) Ltd* 1976 1 SA 441 (A) 452A–H. See *Stellenbosch Farmers' Winery Ltd v Vlachos t/a Liquor Den* [2001] 3 All SA 577 (SCA) 581i–j; 2001 3 SA 597 (SCA) where Nienaber JA added that proof be furnished that "the reliance was not actuated by some external influence or factor other than the defendant's misrepresentation". See also *Sodo v Chairman ANC, Umtata Region* supra 51 where it was

found that the evidence tendered was insuffient to support the claim that the applicants were prejudiced in any manner; Rabie and Sonnekus 2 ed *The Law of Estoppel in SA* 1–2.

3 As to the question of fault, see pars 656 666–671 post.

4 The doctrine has been described as "a principle of justice and equity": *Moorgate Mercantile Co Ltd v Twitchings* [1975] 3 All ER 314 (CAC) 326d–e (Lord Denning MR).

5 It has been said in certain cases that it is a rule of evidence, but this view is untenable. See par 672 post.

6 See par 672 post.

7 Ibid.

8 See pars 672 et seq.

653 What expression "estoppel by representation" includes The expression "estoppel by representation" is in South African law usually taken to include what is sometimes referred to as estoppel by negligence,[1] estoppel by conduct and estoppel by silence, the term "representation" being wide enough to cover a representation made by conduct, including silence.

1 See par 668 post.

INTRODUCTION OF ENGLISH DOCTRINE OF ESTOPPEL BY REPRESENTATION INTO SOUTH AFRICAN LAW

654 Introduction of English doctrine of estoppel by representation and the courts' justification therefor The term "estoppel" has been taken over from English law, and so has the expression "estoppel by representation".[1] In a decision of the Supreme Court of the Cape of Good Hope the chief justice of the time[2] used the words *obstringitur ne in suum factum veniat*, which means one is bound not to go against one's own act, as being the language employed in Roman law to give expression to the idea that a person cannot evade the consequences of his or her own act.[3] In a later case he stated that "[t]he equivalent of the civil law of estoppel, in its limited sense, is *obstrictio ne quis contra suum factum veniat*", and that instances of the expression are continually found in Voet's commentaries.[4] He added that the use of the English law term "estoppel" unfortunately at once leads to the belief that "the whole law of estoppel has been imported from England".[5] Dealing with the same subject in another case, the chief justice stated that "it is by no means clear that the principles of the English law relating to estoppel are applicable, without any modification, in the law of this Colony."[6]

The English law terms have remained in constant use, and there has been much discussion of the question of Roman or Roman-Dutch law foundations of the doctrine of estoppel, and of the extent to which the English law of estoppel by representation has been introduced into the law of South Africa. In 1904 it was said in a judgment of a full bench of the Transvaal Supreme Court that "the principle which underlies the doctrine of estoppel is, in its main incidents, recognized by the Roman-Dutch law".[7] In the following year a full bench of the same court had occasion to consider the same matter again. In its judgment the court said *inter alia* that the English doctrine of estoppel *in pais*,[8] although not known to the law of South Africa by that name, is analogous to what was known in Roman law as the *exceptio doli mali*, a special form of defence that was introduced by the praetor in order that a person should not, by reason of the subtlety of the civil law and contrary to the dictates of natural justice, derive advantage from his or her own bad faith (*ne cui dolus suus per occasionem juris civilis contra naturalem aequitatem prosit*: D 44 4 1). A consideration of the many instances given in D 44 4 in which this defence can be maintained shows, the court said, that the doctrine of estoppel *in pais* is merely an exended interpretation of the principles underlying the *exceptio doli mali*. The court said furthermore that the application of the Roman law maxim *nemo contra suum factum venire debet* would create the same legal consequences as estoppel in English law; that the maxim is practically the estoppel by conduct of the English law; that the term "estoppel" had been generally adopted in practice in South Africa as a more convenient expression of the defence known in Roman law as the *exceptio doli mali*; and that the principles of the English law of estoppel by conduct, as evolved by the English courts, could in appropriate cases be applied in the courts of South Africa.

The views of the Transvaal Supreme Court were adopted by the Appellate Division in a decision given in 1920.[9] With regard to the name "estoppel", the court said that it had been taken over from English law, but that it was freely used in South Africa; and, with regard to the doctrine of estoppel, it said that it was as much a part of the law of South Africa as it was of the law of England, but that "the subject . . . has been much more fully developed by the decisions of the English Courts than it has been in our own authorities, so that in practice we usually look for guidance to the former rather than to the latter".[10] In another judgment given by the Appelllate Division in the same year it was said that "the doctrine of estoppel is now well recognised in our law, and our Courts have acted upon the rules of estoppel as laid down in the English cases".[11] In a case decided in the Appellate Division in 1921 the doctrine of estoppel was once again said to be in accordance with the principles of the law of South Africa and to be as much a part of the law of South Africa as it is of the law of England.[12] In a decision given in the Appellate Division in 1941 in connection with a defence of estoppel, the court quoted the general principle of estoppel as stated in the first edition of Spencer Bower *Estoppel by Representation*,[13] and, after pointing out that the statement was a statement of the English law, proceeded to say that the Appellate Division had in several cases "accepted the doctrine of estoppel as part of our law".[14] Spencer Bower's statement reads as follows: ""Where one person ('representor') has made a representation to another person ('representee') in words, or by acts and conduct, or (being under a duty to the representee to speak or act) by silence or inaction, with the intention (actual or presumptive), and with the result, of inducing the representee on the faith of such representation to alter his position to his detriment, the representor, in any litigation which may afterwards take place between him and the representee, is estopped, as against the representee, from making, or attempting to establish by evidence, any averment sustantially at variance with his former representation, if the representee at the proper time and in the proper manner, objects thereto".[15]

The aforementioned views of the Transvaal Supreme Court, as adopted by the Apellate Division, namely that an extended interpretation of the principles underlying the *exceptio doli mali* covers the doctrine of estoppel, and that the application of the maxim *nemo contra suum factum venire debet* would create the same legal consequences as estoppel in English law, have been criticised, and it has been contended that neither the *exceptio doli mali* nor the maxim *nemo contra suum factum venire debet* provided the courts with a valid basis for introducing the English law of estoppel into the law of South Africa.[16] With reference to this criticisim, it was remarked in a judgment given in the Transvaal Provincial Division that the English doctrine of estoppel by representation migrated to South Africa on the authority of a passport that it approximated the *exceptio doli mali* of the Roman law, and that however doubtful the validity of that passport might originally have been, the doctrine had become naturalised and domiciled in this country as part of its law.[17]

1 See eg *Baumann v Thomas* 1920 AD 428 434; De Wet *Estoppel by Representation* 1 9.
2 De Villiers CJ.
3 *Smit v Smit's Executrix* (1897) 14 SC 142 147.
4 *In re Reynolds Vehicle & Harness Factory Ltd* (1906) 23 SC 703 712–713. The chief justice referred to Voet *Commentarius* 6 1 17, 14 3 6. In 6 1 17 Voet uses the expression *nemo contra suum venire debet*. The same expression, although slightly differently worded, is used in 6 1 19. In 14 3 6 Voet uses the words *obstrictus . . . ne contra suum veniat*. The word *obstrictio* is not used by Voet, and it does not appear in any of the standard Latin dictionaries. Nor does it appear in Heumann and Seckel *Handlexicon zu den Quellen des römischen Rechts*.
5 *In re Reynolds Vehicle & Harness Factory Ltd* supra 712.
6 *Van Blommenstein v Holliday* (1904) 21 SC 11 17: "But I am satisfied that neither under the Roman nor under the Dutch law would a person who, by his words or conduct, has wilfully or negligently induced another to alter his own position in the belief that a certain state of facts exists, have been allowed to assert a right against such other person inconsistent with such state of facts."
7 *United SA Association Ltd v Cohn* 1904 TS 733 740 (per Innes CJ).
8 Estoppel by representation is believed to have developed from estoppel *in pais*:

Halsbury's Laws of England 16 422. Contra De Wet 2–9 where it is contended that it developed from equity.
9 *Baumann v Thomas* supra.
10 *Baumann v Thomas* supra 435.
11 *Rossouw & Steenkamp v Dawson* 1920 AD 173 181.
12 *Union Government v National Bank of SA Ltd* 1921 AD 121 126–127 133–134.
13 Par 15.
14 *Union Government v Vianini Ferro-Concrete Pipes (Pty) Ltd* 1941 AD 43 49. See also *Connock's (SA) Motor Co Ltd v Sentraal Westelike Ko-operatiewe Mpy Bpk* 1964 2 SA 47 (T) 49B–D where Spencer Bower's statement of the doctrine is quoted and where it is said that the statement is "usually accepted as being correct for practical purposes" and referred to in *NBS Bank Ltd v Cape Produce (Pty) Ltd* [2002] 2 All SA 262 (SCA); 2002 1 SA 396 (SCA).
15 This statement of the doctrine is retained in the current (third) edition of Spencer Bower and Turner *Estoppel by Representation* par 3, where it is said that it was accepted as accurate by Sir Raymond Evershed MR in *Hopgood v Brown* [1955] 1 All ER 550 (CA) 559.
16 De Wet 10–15 83–92.
17 *Connock's (SA) Motor Co Ltd v Sentraal Westelike Ko-operatiewe Mpy Bpk* supra 49A–B (per Trollip J).

655 Criticism by Appellate Division of early views Much of what was said in earlier cases concerning the introduction of the English law of estoppel into South Africa was severely criticised in a case which came before the Appellate Division in 1964.[1] The chief justice,[2] who delivered the judgment of the court (by four of the five judges who sat in the appeal), stated that the research which had been done in the earlier cases did not justify the view – and that he was not prepared to hold – that the application of the principles to be found in South African law would always create the same legal consequences as those accepted in English law.

He rejected the view that South African law on the subject had for all practical purposes been supplanted by English law and that South African courts were accordingly obliged to follow English decisions on the subject, and stated that South African courts had in a number of cases in the past referred to the foundations on which the South African law of estoppel was thought to rest.[3] The chief justice stated, also, that while South African courts could with advantage consult the English system with a view to obtaining clarity as how best to apply, adapt or develop the principles of South African law, they were not entitled to approach English law as if it were a recognised source of South African law.[4] The fifth judge in the case said that South African courts had pointed out over and over again that, in matters of estoppel, it was proper and safe to look for guidance to the decisions of the English courts.[5]

The chief justice again adverted to this topic in a later case in which estoppel was pleaded as a defence against a vindicatory claim.[6] Delivering the judgment of the court (by four of the five judges who sat in the case), he said that although parts of the English law of estoppel which were in accordance with the principles of South African law, or not in conflict therewith, had admittedly been applied in South African law, it could nevertheless not be maintained that the whole of the English law of estoppel had been incorporated into South African law.[7] The fifth judge held that it must be accepted as an accomplished fact that the doctrine of estoppel was received into South African law from English law, but that this did not mean that it should be allowed to function in a manner that was in conflict with, or divorced from, the principles of South African law.[8]

1 *Trust Bank van Afrika Bpk v Eksteen* 1964 3 SA 402 (A).
2 Steyn CJ.
3 At 411A–C.
4 At 411C–E.
5 At 415E–F.
6 *Johaadien v Stanley Porter (Paarl) (Pty) Ltd* 1970 1 SA 394 (A).
7 At 401D–E.
8 At 409–410.

ELEMENTS OF ESTOPPEL BY REPRESENTATION

REPRESENTATION

656 How a representation may be made A representation in the law of estoppel is a communication made by one person (the representor) to another (the representee). It can be made in any of the ways in which one person conveys thoughts to, or creates an impression in the mind of, another, for instance in words, whether oral or in writing, or by acts or conduct, including silence or inaction.[1] Silence or inaction can constitute a representation in circumstances in which there is a legal duty to speak or act.[2] Generally speaking, and depending on the relationship between the parties involved, the duty to speak or act arises if it is considered reasonable in the circumstances that the person concerned should speak or act in order to avoid the other person's acting to his or her detriment.[3] The test as to when the duty arises would seem to correspond with the test applied in the case of a delictual omission.[4] A representation made by a person's duly authorised agent is considered to be the representation of the person him or herself.[5] A person may in certain circumstances be bound by a representation which the person did not make him or herself, but which he or she, acting negligently, enabled another person, acting fraudulently, to make to the person who was misled into acting thereon to his or her prejudice.[6]

1 *Service Motor Supplies (1956) (Pty) Ltd v Hyper Investments (Pty) Ltd* 1961 4 SA 842 (A); *Resisto Dairy (Pty) Ltd v Auto Protection Insurance Co Ltd* 1963 1 SA 632 (A) 642; *Universal Stores Ltd v OK Bazaars (1929) Ltd* 1973 4 SA 747 (A) 761B–C; *Alfred McAlpine & Son (Pty) Ltd v Tvl Provincial Administration* 1977 4 SA 310 (T) 335; *Aris Enterprises (Finance) (Pty) Ltd v Protea Assurance Co Ltd* 1981 3 SA 274 (A) 291E–F.
2 *Martin v De Kock* 1948 2 SA 719 (A) 735: "silence can only give rise to estoppel where there is a duty to speak"; *Restisto Dairy (Pty) Ltd v Auto Protection Insurance Co Ltd* supra: insurance company held to be estopped from repudiating a policy on the ground that its silence and inaction in circumstances in which it was its duty, if it wished to repudiate the policy, to inform the insured of its decision within a reasonable time, constituted a representation that it had accepted liability and was dealing with the insured's claim; *Ross v Barnard* 1951 1 SA 414 (T): owner of motorcar estopped from vindicating it in the hands of someone who had bought it in good faith from a garage on the ground of her silence and failure to act when she knew that the garage, into whose possession the car had come, intended selling it; *Parsons v Langemann* 1948 4 SA 258 (C) 262; *Saridakis t/a Auto Nest v Lamont* 1993 2 SA 164 (C) 172I; *Jones v Trust Bank of Africa Ltd*

1993 4 SA 415 (C) 425A–D.

3 *Universal Stores Ltd v OK Bazaars (1929) Ltd* supra 761G–H; *Saridakis t/a Auto Nest v Lamont* supra 172I–J.

4 *Universal Stores Ltd v OK Bazaars (1929) Ltd* supra 762B–C, referring to *Regal v African Superslate (Pty) Ltd* 1963 1 SA 102 (A); *Saridakis t/a Auto Nest v Lamont* supra 172I–173B.

5 *Harriram v Khan* 1950 2 SA 200 (N).

6 Ewart *Estoppel by Misrepresentation* par 110 refers to a representation made in this

manner as one of "assisted misrepresentation". *Kajee v HM Gough (Edms) Bpk* 1971 3 SA 99 (N), the facts of which are set out in par 665 post, affords an example of a representation so made. *Fawdon v Lelyveld* 1937 TPD 339 was also such a case. See also *Union Government v National Bank of SA Ltd* 1921 AD 121, where, however, it was held that the person who had enabled the misrepresentation to be made had not been negligent.

657 Representation must be one of fact It has been stated as a rule in several cases, following English decisions, that to found an estoppel by representation, the representation must be one of an existing fact and not one of intention or future intention.[1] It follows that a mere expression of opinion cannot form the basis of an estoppel. A representation as to a person's state of mind has been held to be a statement of fact and therefore capable of sustaining a plea of estoppel, even when it relates to his or her conduct in the future. Thus, where a defence of estoppel was raised against a landlord who sought to eject a tenant for late payment of rent after it had over a long period accepted late payments without protest, it was unsuccessfully contended that there could be no estoppel because there had been no representation of an existing fact, but at most a tacit representation as to future conduct. The court held that the landlord's long-continued receipt, without protest, of late payments of rent constituted a representation as to its state of mind with regard to such payments and that it induced in the tenant the belief that it would not, without prior warning, insist on punctual payment of rent in future.[2] A representation of law cannot found an estoppel.[3] The reason for the rule is that it is reasonable to suppose that each party is in as good a position as the other to satisfy him or herself as to what the law is.[4] A statement involving a conclusion of law can, however, be made in such a way as to amount to a statement of fact.[5] A representation of mixed fact and law, it has been held in England, is capable of founding an estoppel.[6] A statement by one contracting party to another to the effect that he or she puts a certain construction on a clause in their contract and that he or she will abide by that construction is a statement of fact, not of law, and the party who made it will be precluded by the *exceptio doli* from denying the correctness in law of his or her construction if the other party was induced to enter into the contract by that construction.[7]

1 See eg *Wege v Kemp* 1912 TPD 135 138; *Baumann v Thomas* 1920 AD 428 435–436; *Hauptfleisch v Caledon Divisional Council* 1963 4 SA 53 (C) 57A–B: "it may be emphasized that the representation must relate to a statement of an existing fact . . . and that a mere statement as to, for instance, a future intention will not found an estoppel." It was held in this case that a representation that the respondent would not disturb the appellant in his occupation of certain property was a representation of a "future intention" and consequently not capable of founding an estoppel. See also *Alfred McAlpine & Son (Pty) Ltd v Tvl Provincial Administration* 1977 4 SA 310 (T) 335A–B; *Simpson v Selfmed Medical Scheme* 1992 1 SA 855 (C) 866D.

2 *Garlick Ltd v Phillips* 1949 1 SA 121 (A). See also *United Provident Assurance Co v Young* 1928 CPD 295 298; *Hoole v McQuade* 1944 CPD 442. It has been contended that the rule that a representation cannot found an estoppel if it relates to intention is unsound; see De Wet *Estoppel by Representation* 79–82. The limitation on the operation of estoppel by reason of the requirement that a representation must relate to an existing fact has in England led to the development of the doctrine "promissory estoppel", as to which see Spencer Bower and Turner *Estoppel by Representation* 3 ed pars 341–356. See *Central London Property Trust Ltd v High Trees House Ltd* [1956] 1 All ER 256 (KB) 258G–H where Denning J said: "There has been a

series of decisions over the last fifty years which, although said to be cases of estoppel, are not really such. They are cases of promises which were intended to create legal relations and which, in the knowledge of the person making the promise, were going to be acted on by the party to whom the promise was made, and have in fact been acted on." Relevant English cases are discussed by Olivier 1971 *SALJ* 321–333, who submits that, as far as South African law is concerned, if a promise is made with the intention that it should be binding, the promissee can rely on the promise, and that there is no need to employ the doctrine of estoppel.

3 See *Sampson v Union & Rhodesia Wholesale Ltd (in liq)* 1929 AD 468 477–481; *London County Territorial & Auxiliary Forces Association v Nichols* 1948 2 All ER 432 (CA) 435G.

4 *Sampson v Union & Rhodesia Wholesale Ltd* supra 481; *Lyle-Meller v A Lewis & Co (Westminster) Ltd* [1956] 1 All ER 247 (CA) 253.

5 *Collen v AA Mutual Insurance Association Ltd* 1954 3 SA 625 (E).

6 *Lyle-Meller v A Lewis & Co (Westminster) Ltd* supra.

7 *Sampson v Union & Rhodesia Wholesale Ltd (in liq)* supra 468 479 481.

658 The question of intention on the part of the representor It has been said in certain cases that the representation on which an estoppel is founded must have been made with the intention that it should be acted upon, and, also, that the representation must have been acted upon in the manner intended by the representor.[1] These statements are, however, incorrect in so far as they suggest that there must in all cases of estoppel be an intention on the part of the representor that the representee should act on the representation made by him or her, or act thereon in the manner intended by the representor. It may be accepted, of course, that if A makes a representation to B with the intention that B should act thereon and B does so, A will be estopped from going back on his or her representation. This does not mean, however, that the representation on which an estoppel is founded must necessarily have been made with the intention that it should be acted upon. Proof that such an intention is not required in all cases of estoppel is furnished by cases of so-called "assisted misrepresentation", that is, cases where a person is held bound by a representation which the person did not make him or herself, but which he or she negligently enabled an intervening fraudulent party to make to the person who acted thereon.[2] In cases of estoppel by silence,[3] too, the person who negligently fails to speak when there is a duty on him or her to do so, is liable to an estoppel because of his or her negligence, and not because of a representation made by such person with the intention that it should be acted upon.

In the case of representations made by conduct, too, it is not required for the creation of an estoppel that there should have been an intention as aforesaid on the part of the representor. The law is to the effect that a person may be bound by a representation made by his or her conduct if he or she should reasonably have expected that the other party might be misled thereby,[4] and if, at the same time, the other party (the representee) acted reasonably in construing the representation in the sense that he or she did.[5] With reference to *Connock's (SA) Motor Co Ltd v Sentraal Westelike Ko-operatiewe Mpy Bpk*,[6] *Monzali v Smith*[7] and *Poort Sugar Planters (Pty) Ltd v Minister of Lands*,[8] the court in *NBS Bank Limited v Cape Produce (Pty) Ltd*[9] found that where an intention to mislead was lacking and a course of conduct is relied upon as constituting the representation, the conduct must be of such a kind as could reasonably have been expected by the person for it. The point was made that "A court will not hold a person bound by consequences which he could not reasonably expect and are therefore not the natural result of his conduct." On the facts the court found that they "created a façade of regularity and order that made it possible for Assante . . . to pursue his dishonest schemes . . . That representation was that Assante was authorised to agree to terms of deposit and take money deposited, even in non–routine transactions such as were concluded with Lapiner." The bank was accordingly held liable.

1 See eg *Harriram v Khan* 1950 2 SA 200 (N) 203: "it is of course elementary that it should be acted upon"; *Hauptfleisch v Caledon Divisional Council* 1963 4 SA 53 (C) 57A–C: "The representation may be made expressly or by conduct. It must be made with the intention that it should be acted upon or the conduct of the representor must be such as to lead a reasonable man to take the representation to be true and believe that it was meant that he should act upon it in that manner".

2 See par 656 ante. In *Kajee v HM Gough (Edms) Bpk* 1971 3 SA 99 (N), the facts of which are set out in par 665 post, the company that was held to be estopped from recovering its motorcar from the person who purchased it from a fraudulent third party never intended to make any representation to the purchaser. See also *Fawdon v Lelyveld* 1937 TPD 339.

3 See par 669 post.

4 See *Strachan v Blackbeard & Son* 1910 AD 282 288–289; *Monzali v Smith* 1929 AD 382 386; *Quinn & Co Ltd v Witwatersrand Military Institute* 1953 1 SA 155 (T) 159E–F;

Poort Sugar Planters (Pty) Ltd v Minister of Lands 1963 3 SA 352 (A) 364A–B F–G; *Connock's (SA) Motor Co Ltd v Sentraal Westelike Ko-operatiewe Mpy Bpk* 1964 2 SA 47 (T) 51A; *Union National South British Insurance Co Ltd v Padayachee* 1985 1 SA 551 (A) 561I–562A.

5 See *Service Motor Supplies (1956) (Pty) Ltd v Hyper Investments (Pty) Ltd* 1961 4 SA 842 (A) 848G–H; *Electrolux (Pty) Ltd v Khota* 1961 4 SA 244 (W) 246A–C; *Poort Sugar Planters (Pty) Ltd v Minister of Lands* supra 365A–C; *Van Rooyen v Minister van Openbare Werke & Gemeenskapsbou* 1978 2 SA 835 (A) 849D–G; *ABSA Bank Bpk v Ramakatane* [2002] 1 All SA 559 (O) 565 566 where it was found that the purchaser of the vehicle acted reasonably in construing the representation in the sense that it did.

6 Supra.

7 1929 AD 382 386.

8 Supra 364A–B.

9 [2002] 2 All SA 262 (SCA); 2002 1 SA 396 (SCA).

659 The rule that a representation must be precise and unambiguous

It is a rule of English law that a representation in words can be the basis of an estoppel only if it is precise and unambiguous. A submission to the effect that a representation made in words can found an estoppel if the construction which the representee put thereon was a reasonable one, was rejected by the Court of Appeal in *Woodhouse AC Israel Cocoa Ltd SA v Nigerian Produce Marketing Co Ltd*,[1] and this decision was approved of by the House of Lords.[2] In South African law the rule has been applied in cases dealing with representations in words.[3] With regard to representations made by conduct, the law is to the effect that a representation can found an estoppel if it can reasonably be construed in the sense contended for by the representee, and if, at the same time, the representor should reasonably have expected that his or her conduct could mislead the representee.[4] It follows from this that the rule that a representation must be precise and unambiguous if it is to be capable of founding an estoppel can in South African law at most be of application to representations made in words.

The rule that a representation must be precise and unambiguous is, even if it is limited to representations in words, not a very satisfactory one. It is conceivable that a representation in words can sometimes be such as to be reasonably capable of more than one construction, but according to the rule no estoppel could arise in such a case. If the rule applicable to representations by conduct, as set out above, were made applicable to representations made in words, an estoppel would arise if the representee reasonably understood the represenation made to the representee in the sense contended for by him or her, and if, at the same time, the representor should reasonably have expected that his or her conduct could mislead the representee.

1 1971 1 All ER 665 (CAC). Phillimore LJ said in the course of his judgment: "The overwhelming emphasis throughout the cases is that the words if they are to constitute an estoppel must be clear and unambiguous or unequivocal" (675d–e).

2 *Woodhouse AC Israel Cocoa Ltd SA v Nigerian Produce Marketing Co Ltd* [1972] 2 All ER 271 (HL).

3 See *Hartogh v National Bank* 1907 TS 1092 1104: "Now the rule of law is clear, and has often been acted upon, that the statement or document which is relied upon as creating an estoppel must be precise and unambiguous"; *Southern Life Association Ltd v Beyleveld* 1989 1 SA 496 (A). In *B & B Hardware Distributors (Pty) Ltd v Administrator, Cape* 1989 1 SA 957 (A) the court said, referring to an

alleged representation by conduct, that a representation on which an estoppel is founded must be precise and unambiguous. The court referred to the two cases mentioned immediately above in this footnote, but failed to note that in those cases the rule that a representation must be precise and unambiguous was mentioned in connection with representations made in words. In *Saflec Security Systems (Pty) Ltd v Group Five Building (East Cape) (Pty) Ltd* 1990 4 SA 626 (E) 634–635 the court, following what was said in the *B & B Hardware* case, applied the rule that a representation must be precise and unambiguous to a representation made by conduct.

4 See par 658 fn 4 ante and the cases there cited.

660 Representation must have been made to person invoking estoppel

A person can rely on a representation as founding an estoppel only if it was made to that person, or to someone representing him or her, a representation made to other persons being *res inter alios acta*.[1] This does not mean, however, that the person raising the estoppel must establish that the representor made the representation to him or her or his or her representative personally, or alone, for it may be sufficient, depending on the facts of the case, to show that the representation was made to the public of which the person misled is a member.[2]

1 *Fellner v Dönges* 1953 2 SA 517 (T) 523 A–G. An artificial person naturally has to act through its officials, or other persons, representing it. Consequently, when an artificial person raises a plea of estoppel, it has to show that the representation on which the plea is founded was made to such official(s) or other person(s) representing it, and that he, or they, acted thereon to the prejudice of the artificial person: *B & B Hardware*

Distributors (Pty) Ltd v Administrator, Cape 1989 1 SA 957 (A) 965C–E.

2 See eg *United SA Association Ltd v Cohn* 1904 TS 733 740: "by indorsing the scrip in blank, he represented to all who saw it that it was scrip intended to pass from hand to hand, and to which the holder for the time being could give a good title"; *Hartogh v National Bank* 1907 TS 1092 1102.

ACTION ON FAITH OF REPRESENTATION AND RESULTING PREJUDICE

661 Action on faith of representation

The person who pleads an estoppel has to establish that he or she acted on the faith of a representation made to him or her by the representor and that, in doing so, the person altered his or her position to his or her detriment.[1] In other words, the person has to show *inter alia* that he or she was misled by the representation.[2] The person has to show, too, that he or she acted reasonably in relying on the representation.[3] A person who knows, or who is in law deemed to know because knowledge is imputed to him or her, that the real facts are not as stated in the representation made to such person, cannot be heard to say that he or she was induced to act to his or her prejudice on the faith of the representation.[4] Where there is such knowledge, there is obviously an absence of the required nexus between the representation and the representee's acting thereon to his or her detriment. A person is taken to know that a representation is false if he or she consciously abstains from doing something which in the ordinary course of business such person would have done because he or she is afraid of finding out the truth.[5] If a person makes a false representation to another, intending to mislead the other person, he or she cannot be heard to say that the person should not have believed him or her.[6]

1 *Baumann v Thomas* 1920 AD 428 435–436; *Union Government v Vianini Ferro-Concrete Pipes (Pty) Ltd* 1941 AD 43 49; *Poort Sugar Planters (Pty) Ltd v Minister of Lands* 1963 3 SA 352 (A) 363E; *Hauptfleisch v Caledon Divisional Council* 1963 4 SA 53 (C) 57C–D.

2 *Strachan v Blackbeard & Son* 1910 AD 282 289; *Monzali v Smith* 1929 AD 382 386.

3 See eg *Monzali v Smith* supra389 390 391. See also *American Jurisprudence* vol 28 *Estoppel and Waiver* par 76, where it is said that only "reasonably justified reliance" on a representation can create an estoppel.

4 *Bird v Sumerville* 1961 3 SA 194 (A) 204E–F; *Hauptfleisch v Caledon Divisional Council* supra 57C–D; *Abrahamse v Connock's Pension Fund* 1963 2 SA 76 (W) 79G–H; *Van Rooyen v Minister van Openbare Werke & Gemeenskapsbou* 1978 2 SA 835 (A) 849G–H. Where the representor is a company, the knowledge of the relevant facts that is required is its actual or imputed, and not merely constructive, knowledge. See *Connock's (SA) Motor Co Ltd v Sentraal Westelike*

Ko-operatiewe Mpy Bpk 1964 2 SA 47 (T) 53G–H, where it is also stated when knowledge can be imputed to a company; *Universal Stores Ltd v OK Bazaars (1929) Ltd* 1973 4 SA 747 (A) 761F–G; *NBS Bank Ltd v Cape Produce Pty Ltd* [2002] 2 All SA 262 (SCA); 2002 1 SA 396 (SCA).

5 *Hartogh v National Bank Ltd* 1907 TH 207; *Angehrn & Piel v Federal Cold Storage Co Ltd* 1908 TS 761 789. In both these cases reference was made to *In re Building Estates Brickfields Co (Parbury's Case)* 1896 1 Ch 100 106 where it is said that in cases of estoppel a person must be taken to know that a representation is false if the person "consciously abstains from doing that which as a matter of business he would do, and abstains because he would rather not know the truth."

6 *Angehrn & Piel v Federal Cold Storage Co Ltd* supra 788–789: "If a man tells you a falsehood intending to deceive you, it is not for him to complain that you are too credulous. He intended that you should believe him, and he cannot grumble if you do."

662 Alteration of position by representee A person may alter his or her position as a result of a representation made to him or her, not only by taking some positive action which causes such person prejudice, but also by refraining from doing something which would have been beneficial.[1]

1 *In re The Contributories of the Rosemount Gold Mining Syndicate In Liquidation* 1905 TH 169 205: "It seems to me to make but little difference whether a man, relying on a false representation, does something which is injurious or refrains from doing something

which would have been benficial. And I think it clear that the law draws no such distinction" (per Bristowe J); *South British Insurance Co Ltd v Glisson* 1963 1 SA 289 (D) 293B–C; *Albatross Fishing Corporation (Pty) Ltd v Ramsay* 1968 2 SA 217 (C) 220G–H.

663 Requirement of prejudice As stated above,[1] the person who pleads an estoppel has to establish that he or she acted on the faith of a representation made to him or her and that in doing so the person altered his or her position to his or her prejudice.[2] The "prejudice" which has to be established has a wide connotation, not permitting of precise definition. Thus it has been held that prejudice is not limited to direct, instantaneous and palpable loss of money, but that it also includes less gross and easily calculable detriment.[3] The cases show that there is no clear test as to when prejudice is to be regarded as being sufficiently real to be capable of founding an estoppel. They show also, it is submitted, that to establish prejudice capable of sustaining an estoppel it is sufficient to show that there may be pecuniary loss if the estoppel pleaded is refused, and that it is not necessary to show that there will in fact be such loss if the plea is refused. Thus, the loss by an insured of the right to call upon an insurance company to take upon itself the defence of an action for damages instituted against the insured by a third party, has been held to constitute prejudice capable of founding an estoppel, the court not inquiring into the possible outcome of the litigation between the insured and the third party, in other words the question whether the insured was likely to be ordered to pay damages to the third party;[4] and, a plaintiff's loss of security for the payment of damages that might be awarded to the plaintiff in an action against A and B, has been thought to be sufficient prejudice to support an estoppel even though there was nothing to show that the plaintiff was likely to succeed in a claim for damages, or that, if the plaintiff succeeded, A and B would not be able to satisfy the judgment given against them;[5] and it has been said that parting with money, and being out of it for a certain period of time, coupled with the trouble and possible expense of establishing the legal right to get it back, may amount to an alteration of the payer's position sufficient to establish an estoppel.[6]

As appears from the aforegoing, the requirement that there must be proof of prejudice does not mean that loss, in the sense of diminution of one's patrimony, must actually have been suffered by the person raising the estoppel at the time when the estoppel is pleaded or when the action is heard. The function or purpose of estoppel is to prevent prejudice or loss arising, and what a person invoking estoppel is required to prove is, therefore, that there will be prejudice (in the sense stated above) if the estoppel raised by the person is denied.[7]

1 See par 661 ante.

2 See eg *Heyman & Napier v Rounthwaite* 1917 AD 456 459 462; *Baumann v Thomas* 1920 AD 428 435–436; *Union Government v Vianini Ferro-Concrete Pipes (Pty) Ltd* 1941 AD 43 49. The words "prejudice", "detriment" and "loss" are used synonymously in the cases. What a representee who has acted to his or her prejudice on the faith of a representation made to him or her would have done if the representation had been different from what it was, is irrelevant to the question of the representee's prejudice: *Harriram v Khan* 1950 2 SA 200 (N) 204.

3 See *Autolec Ltd v Du Plessis* 1965 2 SA 243 (O) 250H, where the court, adopting the views expressed in the 1923 edition of Spencer Bower *Estoppel by Representation* 138–140 said: "Although the change of position must involve the practical or business affairs of the representee and not merely affect him philosophically or in his religious or other sentimental values, the detriment is not limited to direct, instantaneous and palpable loss of money but also includes less gross and easily calculable detriment." See also *ABSA Bank Bpk v Ramakatane* [2002] 1 All SA 559 (O) 566e–h where the approach of Hofmeyer J at 250G–H in the *Autolec* judgment was applied. As to the reference to Spencer Bower, see now Spencer Bower and Turner *Estoppel by Representation* 3 ed par110 104. Spencer Bower's views on the point have also been referred to in other cases: *Peri-Urban Areas Health Board v Breet* 1958 3 SA 783 (T) 790E; *South British Insurance Co Ltd v Glisson* 1963 1 SA 289 (D)

293G–H; *Mthanti v Netherlands Insurance Co of SA Ltd* 1971 2 SA 305 (N) 312B. De Wet *Estoppel by Representation* 16 says that the prejudice must be of a patrimonial kind. It has been suggested in certain academic writings that prejudice need not be of a patrimonial nature. See Rabie and Sonnekus 2 ed *The Law of Estoppel in SA* 102 109–114; and see *Sodo v Chairman ANC, Umtata Region* [1998] 1 All SA 45 (Tk) 51h-j.

4 *Resisto Dairy (Pty) Ltd v Auto Protection Insurance Co Ltd* 1963 1 SA 632 (A).

5 *South British Insurance Co Ltd v Glisson* supra. This view was expressed *obiter*, but it would seem to be in accordance with the view of the Appellate Division in *Resisto Dairy (Pty) Ltd v Auto Protection Insurance Co Ltd* ante.

6 *Fawdon v Lelyveld* 1937 TPD 339 342, adopting a statement made in *Compania Naviera Vasconzada v Churchill & Sim* [1906] 1 KB 237 250.

7 Cf *Grundt v The Great Boulder Pty Gold Mines Ltd* (1938) 59 CLR 641, an Australian case cited by Spencer Bower and Turner *Estoppel by Representation* 3 ed par 114 in which it is said *inter alia* that the basic purpose of the doctrine of estoppel is "to avoid or prevent a detriment to the party asserting the estoppel by compelling the opposite party to adhere to the assumption upon which the former acted or abstained from acting". Spencer Bower and Turner say (par 114) in this regard that the detriment which the representee must be shown to have suffered is judged only "at the moment when the representor proposes to resile from his representation". In South African law there

has been no decision on the question whether the benefit to which a representee may become entitled by virtue of a successful plea of estoppel should be restricted to the extent of the prejudice actually suffered by the representee. The point was raised, but not decided in two cases, namely: *Durban Corporation Superannuation Fund v Campbell* 1949 3 SA 1057 (D) and *Thompson v Voges* 1988 1 SA 691 (A). In the first of these cases the court appeared to favour the view that the relief afforded by estoppel should not exceed the actual prejudice suffered by the representee. In the second case the court indicated that the approach of English law to the question differs from that of American law. In English law the view that estoppel by representation is a rule of evidence has the effect that the representor is precluded from averring facts contrary to the representation made by him or her, with the result that the relief afforded to a representee who has successfully raised a plea of estoppel may turn out to be greater than the prejudice suffered by the representee. See *Ogilvie v West Australian Mortgage & Agency Corporation* [1896] AC 257; *Greenwood v Martin's Bank Ltd* 1933 AC 51; *Avon County Council v Howlett* [1983] 1 All ER 1073 (CAC). The basic approach of American law appears to be that estoppel by representation is a measure which is intended to prevent injustice and not an instrument of gain, and that the operation of estoppel should, therefore, not extend beyond the prejudice suffered: see *Corpus Juris Secundum* vol 31 *Estoppel* par 148; *American Jurisprudence* vol 28 *Estoppel and Waiver* par 34.

CAUSATION

664 Causal connection between representation and representee's acting to his or her prejudice: proximate cause test To determine whether a person has acted to his or her prejudice in reliance on a representation made to that person, the test, as stated in a number of Appellate Division decisions, is whether the representation was "the proximate", or "the real and direct" cause of such person's having acted to his or her prejudice.[1] The expressions "the proximate cause" and "the real and direct cause" are used in the cases as having the same meaning.[2]

The proximate cause test was first discussed by the Appellate Division in *Union Government v National Bank of SA Ltd*,[3] and because this case has often been followed in cases concerned with the question of causation, and because it is also the leading case on what is sometimes referred to in the cases as "estoppel by negligence",[4] its facts are set out in some detail.

A postal agent and part-time government employee, say P, permitted S, whom he had known for many years and whom he had no reason to distrust, to work in his office – a room in P's own premises which had been set aside as a post office – on four or five Sundays, S having told him that he wanted a quiet place in which to work. While he was in P's office, S used the post office's offical date stamp, which P had neglected to keep under lock and key, to stamp a number of unused blank postal order forms which had been stolen from a post office in another town about three years before. Having, by stamping the order forms, given them the appearance of validity, S disposed of them to various persons. Some of these persons deposited the orders they had acquired with the bank (the respondent in the appeal). The bank presented the orders to the post office and was paid their face value. The government (appellant in the appeal), on discovering that the orders were not genuine, sought to recover under a *conditio indebiti* the amount the post office had paid to the bank. The bank set up a defence of "estoppel by negligence", alleging that P had been negligent in not keeping the date stamp under lock and key and allowing S access to the room in which the stamp was kept.

It was held by the Appellate Division, reversing the decision of the Transvaal Provincial Division, that the government was not estopped from claiming the money the post office had paid to the bank.

Innes CJ decided the case on the basis that there had been no negligence on the part of P *vis-à-vis* the bank and that the government was accordingly not estopped from asserting the invalidity of the postal orders.

Solomon JA held that, even if P had been negligent (a question on which the learned judge expressed no opinion), his negligence was not the proximate cause of the bank's having been misled into believing in the genuineness of the postal orders. The learned judge held, furthermore, that even if there had been negligence on the part of P in his custody of the date stamp, such negligence was only "very remotely"[5] connected with the payment by the bank to the depositors of the false postal orders, and that such payment was "not the necessary or ordinary or likely result"[6] of that negligence. Payment would never have been made by the bank, the learned judge said, but for the occurrence of "the very extraordinary event"[7] that S should have obtained possession of a number of postal order forms which had been stolen three years earlier. The "direct cause"[8] of the bank's loss, the learned judge held, was "the intervention of an act of wickedness" on the part of S which P could not have been expected to anticipate.[9]

The third member of the court, Juta JA, decided the case on two grounds: first, that P had not been negligent *vis-à-vis* the bank, and second, that even if there had been negligence on his part, that negligence was not the proximate cause of the bank's loss. As to the question of causation, he posed the question whether P's negligence, if any, was the proximate cause of *damnum* to the bank, or whether it was not "too remote", and then proceeded to hold that events which intervened between the negligence (namely P's failure to keep the date stamp under lock and key) and the cashing of the orders by the bank prevented that negligence from being the proximate cause of the loss of the bank.[10]

As appears from the *Union Government v National Bank of SA Ltd* case, the proximate cause test is not a pure test of causation since it has, incorporated in it, a test of liability. A reading of the judgments of Innes CJ and Solomon JA shows that virtually the same considerations which led Innes CJ to hold that P had not been negligent *vis-à-vis* the bank were relied on by Solomon JA as showing that P's conduct was not the proximate cause of the bank's loss. Solomon JA held that even if P had been negligent, the payment by the bank to the depositors of the false postal orders was not the necessary or ordinary or likely result of that negligence, but that the direct cause of the bank's loss was the "act of wickedness" of S, which P could not necessarily have foreseen.[11] In a recent judgment[12] the Supreme Court of Appeal once more considered the so-called "facilitation theory", and the "proximate cause" test in the context of an intervening fraud committed by a third party and the related matter of "causation". After pointing out that the "facilitation theory" has long been discredited in this country (as to which see the *Union Government v National Bank of SA Ltd* case and the *Grosvenor Motors (Potchefstroom) Ltd v Douglas* case), Nienaber JA went on to explain that: "In the second place, where the basis for holding someone liable for holding out something is the image he conjured up which prompted the other party to react to his prejudice (cf *Southern Life Association Ltd v Beyleveld NO* 1989 (1) SA 496 (A) at 505F–G); if, due to some new circumstance (here the fraud of Da Silva) a new image is superimposed on the old one and it is the new image to which the other party responds and on which he relies, the original party can no longer be held to it, even if he would otherwise have remained liable (Rabie and Sonnekus (op cit at 56))."[13] The point made is clearly that the fraud as opposed to the initial representation was the proximate cause of the prejudice.

As to causation the learned judge went on to explain: "Finally, there is the related and parallel matter of causation. Instances of this kind are typified by Rabie and

Sonnekus (op cit at 19, 122) as 'cases of assisted misrepresentation'. In a passage cited at 18 from Cross on *Evidence* 6th ed (1993) this phenomenon is described as 'a type of estoppel . . . in which the party in whose favour it operates is the victim of a fraud of some third person facilitated by the careless breach of duty of the other party'. Rabie and Sonnekus (op cit at 122) continue: 'In cases of this kind difficult questions can arise as to whether the fraud of the intervening party, or the negligence of the owner which facilitated the commission of the fraud, should be regarded as having caused the representee to act to his prejudice.' In such situations our Courts have chiefly but not exclusively employed the so-called 'proximate cause' test (cf *Grosvernor Motors (Potchefstroom) Ltd v Douglas* (supra); *Standard Bank of South Africa Ltd v Stama (Pty) Ltd* 1975 (1) SA 730 (A) and 1975 (4) SA 965 (A)) or the 'real cause' test (*Saambou-Nasionale Bouvereniging v Friedman* 1979 (3) SA 978 (A) at 1005E–H) or even the test of foreseeability (*Union Government v National Bank of South Africa Ltd* (supra at 129, 138); *Monzali v Smith* 1929 AD 382 at 387; *Konstanz Properties (Pty) Ltd v Wm Spilhaus en Kie (WP) Bpk* 1996 (3) SA 273 (A) at 288F–G) in order to resolve the problem of whether one party's misrepresentation caused another party to act thereon to his prejudice."[14]

These tests are to be considered and viewed not in isolation as previously but in the context of a broader picture to include also matters of policy and fairness.

1 See eg *Union Government v National Bank of SA Ltd* 1921 AD 121 130 ("the proximate cause"), 134 ("the proximate cause"), 138 ("the direct cause"); *Grosvenor Motors (Potchefstroom) Ltd v Douglas* 1956 3 SA 420 (A) 426A ("the real and direct cause").

2 See the cases referred to in fn 1 supra and *Standard Bank of SA Ltd v Stama (Pty) Ltd* 1975 1 SA 730 (A) 743B–D as inserted by *Standard Bank of SA Ltd v Stama (Pty) Ltd* 1975 4 SA 965 (A), where Holmes JA, after quoting from the plea of the defendant in that case, said: "For the plea of estoppel to be effective in law, the 'reliance' there averred must mean not only that the representation influenced the defendant but that it was also the proximate cause of the defendant's acting to its detriment. Various other expressions are sometimes used to denote that necessary causal *nexus*, such as 'direct', 'effective' or 'immediate' (see Spencer Bower and Turner *Estoppel by Representation* 3rd ed pars 77 109; cf De Wet *Estoppel by Representation* 30). But in *Union Government v National Bank of SA Ltd* 1921 AD 121, and *Grosvenor Motors (Potchefstroom) Ltd v Douglas* 1956 3 SA 420 (A) 426A, 'proximate' was used; and I shall also use it." In *Saambou-Nasionale Bouvereniging v Friedman* 1979 3 SA 978 (A) 1005F it was suggested that the expression "real cause" should be used instead of "proximate cause". The suggestion is not a new one. More than a century ago, in *Seton, Laing & Co v Lafone* 1887 19 QBD 68 71 74, two members of the court thought

that "real" would be a more appropriate term to use than "proximate", but the third doubted whether "real" was any more free form difficulty than "proximate". The courts have continued to use the term "proximate".

3 Supra.

4 As to which, see par 668 post.

5 *Union Government v National Bank of SA Ltd* supra 136.

6 *Union Government v National Bank of SA Ltd* supra 136.

7 *Union Government v National Bank of SA Ltd* supra 136.

8 *Union Government v National Bank of SA Ltd* supra 137.

9 *Union Government v National Bank of SA Ltd* supra 137. In the course of his judgment Solomon JA also held that the bank's case could not be advanced by the application of the *dictum* that it was "a broad general principle that, whenever one of two innocent parties must suffer by the acts of a third, he who has enabled such third person to occasion the loss must sustain it". The *dictum* quoted is that of Ashurst J in *Lickbarrow v Mason* (1787) 2 TR 63 70. The learned judge rejected it as being too widely stated and said that it needed to be so qualified as to require *inter alia* that the neglect complained of must be the proximate cause of the loss which has been sustained. Innes CJ was of the same view (131). The Appellate Division again rejected the *dictum* of Ashurst J in *Grosvenor Motors (Potchefstroom)*

Ltd v Douglas supra 425F–H. See also *Con-*
nock's (SA) Motor Co Ltd v Sentraal Westelike
Ko-operatiewe Mpy Bpk 1964 2 SA 47 (T)
48G–H; *OK Bazaars (1929) Ltd v Universal*
Stores Ltd 1973 2 SA 281 (C) 287 *in fine.*

10 *Union Government v National Bank of SA Ltd*
supra 152.

11 *Union Government v National Bank of SA Ltd*
supra 152. As to the test of forseeability in
the proximate cause test, see also *Broekman v*

TCD Motors (Pty) Ltd 1949 4 SA 418 (T);
OK Bazaars (1929) Ltd v Universal Stores Ltd
supra 288B; and, in English law, *Mercantile*
Credit Co Ltd v Hamblin [1964] 3 All ER
592 (CA) 605D–E.

12 *Stellenbosch Farmers' Winery Ltd v Vlachos t/a*
Liquor Den [2001] 3 All SA 577 (SCA); 2001
3 SA 597 (SCA).

13 At 586j–587a.

14 At 587b–f.

665 Application of proximate cause test The application of the proximate cause test may give rise to difficult questions in cases where there are not only two parties involved, namely the representor and the representee, but also a third, intervening person who practises a fraud on the representee, which fraud is made possible, or is facilitated, by the conduct of the representor, who is the person against whom a defence of estoppel is raised. Situations of this kind, it would seem to appear from reported decisions of the courts, arise most commonly in cases where an owner of movable property has, by permitting the property to be in the possession of another person (sometimes with accompanying documents relating to the title of the property or authority to deal therewith), provided the latter with the opportunity to represent fraudulently to an innocent person that he or she is the owner of the property or that he or she has the right to dispose of it. In such cases (depending, of course, on the facts of each case) problems may arise as to whether the fraud of the intervening party, or the conduct of the owner of the property which permitted, or facilitated, the fraud is to be considered to be the proximate, or real and direct, cause of the representee's acting to his or her prejudice.[1] It has been said that in cases of this kind the negligent conduct of the person against whom the estoppel is raised can never be the proximate cause of the representee's having acted to his or her detriment because there is always interposed the misrepresentation of some third person.[2] A reading of relevant reported cases shows, however, that the application of the test has not always resulted in a finding that the fraud of the intermediary was the proximate cause of the innocent representee having acted to his or her loss.[3] The facts of a reported case may be cited by way of illustration.[4] B, a salesman in the employ of G, a motorcar dealer in Pretoria, sold a motorcar to R for R3 200. It was a cash sale and an "order form", signed by B and R, indicated that R had paid the full purchase price. B accepted R's cheque, gave him possession of the car, and handed to him the completed "order form" and documents showing that the car was licensed in R's name. R's cheque was dishonoured. R sold the car to K in Durban for R2 850. R showed K the documents he had received from B and explained to K that he was prepared to sell the car for less than he had paid for it because he required ready cash in order to finance a transaction on which he anticipated making a bigger profit than the R350 he was losing on the sale of the car to K. K accepted this explanation and, believing that R was entitled to dispose of the car, purchased it from him. The court found that B was negligent in not foreseeing that R's cheque might not be met and that R might thereafter, by being in possession of the car and the documents with which he had been furnished, induce some prospective purchaser to believe that he had paid for the car and that he was entitled to sell it. As to what was the proximate cause of K's having been misled, the court found that it was clear that K had not been misled solely by B's negligence, since K had also received and accepted an assurance from R that he had paid for the car and that he was entitled to sell it, but that it was equally clear that K would not have bought the car solely upon that assurance, and that the "effective cause" of his accepting R's assurance was the fact that B had enabled R to have possession not only of the car, but also of the signed "order form" and the documents showing that the car had been registered in his name. B's negligence was accordingly held to have been the proximate cause of K's being misled.[5]

It was held in a decision of a provincial division in 1965 that, to establish a defence of estoppel, it is sufficient to prove that the representation that was made by the person whom it is sought to estop was *an* inducing cause of the representee's acting to his or her detriment, and that it need not be shown that it was *the* inducing cause.[6] The court made no reference to earlier judgments of the courts requiring that the representation on which a plea of estoppel is based must be shown to have been the proximate cause of the representee's acting to his or her prejudice.[7] Subsequent judgments, including judgments of the Appellate Division, have restated the requirement that the representation relied on must have been the proximate, or real and direct, cause of the representee's loss.[8]

1 See eg *Bold v Cooper* 1949 1 SA 1195 (W) 1201; *Broekman v TCD Motors (Pty) Ltd* 1949 4 SA 418 (T) 425; *Ross v Barnard* 1951 1 SA 414 (T) 420B–E; *Grosvenor Motors (Potchefstroom) Ltd v Douglas* 1956 3 SA 420 (A) 425H–426A; *Kajee v HM Gough (Edms) Bpk* 1971 3 SA 99 (N) 106A–F.

2 Ewart *Estoppel by Misrepresentation* 119 (cited in De Wet *Estoppel by Representation* 31 fn 6): "In cases of assisted misrepresentation the neglect can never be the proximate cause of the leading of the person into the mistake. There is always interposed the misrepresentation of some third person". See also *Ross v Barnard* supra 420B: "Ordinarily where the owner has entrusted property to another, or knows that another has his property with knowledge of his ownership, the only risk of disposal of his property to a *bona fide* purchaser is the likelihood of a dishonest act by the possessor. In such cases ordinarily the proximate cause of the prejudice to the *bona fide* purchaser is the dishonest act of the possessor."

3 See eg *Ross v Barnard* supra; *United Cape Fisheries (Pty) Ltd v Silverman* 1951 2 SA 612 (T); *Kajee v H M Gough (Edms) Bpk* supra; *Akojee v Sibanyoni* 1976 3 SA 440 (W).

4 *Kajee v H M Gough (Edms) Bpk* supra.

5 R's possession of the car and the documents would obviously not have deceived K if they had not been used by R for the purpose of deceiving him. In the circumstances it may be suggested that K's deception was due to a combination of causes, namely B's careless acts and R's fraud, and that the court might

have considered that B's conduct was a sufficiently effective contributory cause to found an estoppel. At the same time it must be said that it seems to be questionable whether the proximate cause test, which apparently requires that a particular cause be singled out as the proximate, or effective, cause, would allow the suggested approach to the matter.

6 *Autolec Ltd v Du Plessis* 1965 2 SA 243 (O) 248D–E. See also *Credit Corporation of SA Ltd v Botha* 1968 4 SA 837 (N) 850–851A.

7 The court's authority for its view was Spencer Bower *Actionable Misrepresentation* 2 ed par 120 at 132. See also Spencer Bower and Turner *Estoppel by Representation* 3 ed par 102.

8 See eg *Standard Bank of SA Ltd v Stama (Pty) Ltd* 1975 1 SA 730 (A) 743B–D as inserted by Appendix I 1975 4 SA 965; *Oakland Nominees (Pty) Ltd v Gelria Mining & Investment Co (Pty) Ltd* 1976 1 SA 441 (A) 458F–459A, referred to in *ABSA Bank Beperk v Ramakatane* [2002] 1 All SA 559 (O); *Big Dutchman (SA) (Pty) Ltd v Barclays National Bank Ltd* 1979 3 SA 267 (W) 282F 284A. See also *Barclays Bank International Ltd v African Diamond Exporters (Pty) Ltd* 1977 1 SA 298 (W) 311D–F where it is said that *Autolec Ltd v Du Plessis* supra is of "doubtful authority" on the point in issue. See *Stellenbosch Farmers' Winery Ltd v Vlachos t/a Liquor Den* [2001] 3 All SA 577 (SCA); 2001 3 SA 597 (SCA) where an intervening fraud and the effect thereof and the application of the various tests are discussed; and see par 664 ante.

FAULT

666 The question whether fault, namely *dolus* or *culpa*, is a requirement of estoppel: in general It is clear law that *dolus* is not an essential element of estoppel.[1] It is therefore not necessary to show that the person against whom estoppel is invoked acted with the intention to deceive. As to the question whether fault in the form of *culpa*, or negligence, is a prerequisite to the operation of estoppel, the law would appear not to be wholly settled, and it would seem that there is no simple answer to the question that would hold good in all situations and in all types of cases. In *Johaadien v Stanley Porter (Paarl) (Pty) Ltd*,[2] decided by the Appellate Division in 1970, the chief justice, with whose judgment three other members of the court agreed, held that it is necessary, save possibly in certain exceptional circumstances,[3] to prove negligence on the part of the person whom it is sought to estop from vindicating his or her property, but he went on to say that it does not follow that the law will require proof of negligence in all cases of estoppel. The decisions of the courts, both in England and in South Africa, he said, do not justify the view that estoppel has a uniform pattern which is applicable in all circumstances, nor that there ought to be such a pattern. Distinctions are drawn, he said, and not without reason, since there is room for differentiation in accordance with the principles and requirements of fairness governing different kinds of situations, and there would, therefore, be nothing incongruous in making *culpa* a requirement of estoppel in cases of *rei vindicatio*, even though it might not be a general requirement of estoppel.[4] The fifth member of the court was of the opinion that a requirement of negligence in the circumstances of the case before the court would place a heavier burden on the defendant than was demanded by the old authorities, and that it would, also, be in conflict with the interests of commerce. He expressed the view that estoppel could be invoked if an owner, in addition to giving up possession of his or her property to someone else (for instance a borrower), performed some other act which, together with the giving up of possession, could create the impression that the possessor was entitled to sell the property on behalf of the owner, and if a reasonable person would have foreseen that the additional act could create an impression that might induce a reasonable propective purchaser to buy.[5]

In the next few paragraphs it is indicated what the courts have said in connection with the question of negligence in various types of cases.[6]

1 De Wet *Estoppel by Representation* 38–39; *Connock's (SA) Motor Co Ltd v Sentraal Westelike Ko-operatiewe Mpy Bpk* 1964 2 SA 47 (T) 49F–H; *Sonday v Surrey Estate Modern Meat Market (Pty) Ltd* 1983 2 SA 521 (C) 523F.

2 1970 1 SA 394 (A).

3 *Johaadien v Stanley Porter (Paarl) Pty Ltd* supra 409E–G; and see par 667 post.

4 *Johaadien v Stanley Porter (Paarl) Pty Ltd* supra 402–403A. De Wet 41 43 61 contends that South African courts, including the Supreme Court of Appeal, require proof of *culpa* in cases of estoppel and that *culpa* is the only possible theoretical basis of estoppel. In Schmidt *Bewysreg* (1972 ed) 448 it is argued that because the requirement of fault (*skuld*) is so deeply rooted in Roman-Dutch law, and

because the Appellate Division stated in *Trust Bank van Afrika Bpk v Eksteen* 1964 3 SA 402 (A) 410–411 (as to which case, see par 655 fns 1–5 ante) that the principles of estoppel are to be sought in Roman-Dutch law, either *dolus* or *culpa* should be required to found a defence of estoppel. The learned author makes no mention of the above-stated view of the Appellate Division in *Johaadien's* case.

5 *Trust Bank van Afrika Bpk v Eksteen* supra 411E–F 412A–B. For a discussion of the views expressed in this case, see Scholtens and Petersen 1970 *Annual Survey* 207–210.

6 It is not suggested that the types of cases to be referred to are clearly defined classes of cases, nor that they relate to different divisions or classes of estoppel.

667 Rei vindicatio cases In cases of *rei vindicatio* regard should in the first place be had to certain rules of the common law on the subject. Briefly stated, these are to the effect that, save in the case of goods entrusted to an agent for sale or a factor, an owner can recover his or her property if the person to whom it was entrusted improperly alienated or pledged it,[1] but that an owner may lose the right to vindicate his or her property if *culpa* can be imputed to the owner, or if the interests of commerce so demand.[2] With regard to the question of estoppel, it was held by the Appellate Division in *Grosvenor Motors (Potchefstroom) Ltd v Douglas*[3] that an owner is not estopped from vindicating his or her poperty unless it is proved that there was negligence on the owner's part. In *Johaadien v Stanley Porter (Paarl) (Pty) Ltd*[4] the Appellate Division qualified the view expressed by it in *Grosvenor Motors (Potchefstroom) Ltd v Douglas*[5] to some extent by saying that it was conceivable that an owner could, on an extended application of the *exceptio doli* and by reason of compelling considerations of fairness, be estopped from asserting his or her rights even if there were no *culpa* on his or her part.[6] In *Oakland Nominees (Pty) Ltd v Gelria Mining and Investment Co (Pty) Ltd*,[7] where the plaintiff sought an order declaring it to be the owner of certain shares, the Appellate Division held that the law of estoppel relating to *rei vindicatio* also applies to company share certificates. It was held that such certificates, even when accompanied by blank transfer forms, are not negotiable instruments, and that there is therefore no basis in law for regarding them as being excepted from the principles relating to *rei vindicatio*.[8] The law as stated with regard to vindicatory actions applies to both movable and immovable property.[9]

It was said in a case decided in the Cape Provincial Division in 1983 that "it is really only in the sphere of vindicatory actions that negligence is regarded as a requisite for estoppel".[10] This is, however, incorrect, as will appear from what is said in the next few paragraphs.

1 *Morum Bros Ltd v Nepgen* 1916 CPD 392 397; *Grosvenor Motors (Potchefstroom) Ltd v Douglas* 1956 3 SA 420 (A) 426C–D; *Barclays Western Bank Ltd v Fourie* 1979 4 SA 157 (C) 161–162D.

2 See *Johaadien v Stanley Porter (Paarl) (Pty) Ltd* 1970 1 SA 394 (A) 407H–408A 411C–D and the reference in that case to Matthaeus *Paroemia* 7 17, where it is said to be a general rule that *rei vindicatio* must be allowed except when *culpa* can be imputed to the owner or when the interests (*utilitas*) of commerce are repugnant thereto. See also *Morum Bros Ltd v Nepgen* supra 398; *Saflec Security Systems (Pty) Ltd v Group Five Building (East Cape) (Pty) Ltd* 1990 4 SA 626 (E) 635C–G; *Jones v Trust Bank of Africa Ltd* 1993 4 SA 415 (C) 424H–J; *Quenty's Motors (Pty) Ltd v Standard Credit Corporation Ltd* 1994 3 SA 188 (A); and see *ABSA Bank Bpk v Ramakatane* [2002] 1 All SA 559 (O) where the *Quenty's Motors* judgment at 199G–200C was referred to and applied.

3 1956 3 SA 420 (A) 427B–E, in the judgment of Steyn JA, with which three other members of the court agreed.

4 Supra.

5 Supra.

6 *Johaadien v Stanley Porter (Paarl) (Pty) Ltd* supra 409E–G. The views expressed on the question of negligence in the minority judgment in this case appear from par 666 ante.

7 1976 1 SA 441 (A), referred to in *ABSA*

Bank Bpk v Ramakatane supra.

8 *Oakland Nominees (Pty) Ltd v Gelria Mining & Investment Co (Pty) Ltd* supra 52A–H, where the court, confirming the view expressed in *Johaadien v Stanley Porter (Paarl) (Pty) Ltd* supra 409E–G, stated that an owner may "possibly", despite the absence of *culpa* on his or her part, be precluded from asserting his or her rights by compelling considerations of fairness within the broad concept of the *exceptio doli*. Cf *United SA Association Ltd v Cohn* 1904 TS 733: scrip certificates, endorsed in blank, were entrusted by the plaintiff company to one of its clerks; he stole some of the certificates and sold them to the defendant, who bought them without notice and in good faith. The plaintiff was held to be estopped from disputing the defendant's title, the court founding the estoppel on the basis that the plaintiff, by endorsing the scrip in blank and entrusting it to the clerk, represented that it was scrip that was intended to pass from hand to hand and, futhermore, placed the clerk in a position where he could deal with the scrip as if he were the owner thereof. The court did not discuss the question of negligence on the part of the plaintiff. See also *West v Pollak & Freemantle* 1936 WLD 37; 1937 TPD 64 and *West v De Villiers* 1938 CPD 96, where the courts followed *Cohn's* case without discussing the question of negligence. It has been contended that

the loss by a shareholder of his or her rights in circumstances such as those of *Cohn's* case is not based on fault, but that it is rather "a question of finding suitable and equitable criteria for attributing responsibility for the loss, resulting from the appearance that the third party was entitled to dispose of the shares, to one of two or more innocent parties": Malan 1977 *SALJ* 245 254.

9 *Apostoliese Geloofsending van SA (Maitland Gemeente) v Capes* 1978 4 SA 48 (C) 63.

10 *Sonday v Surrey Estate Modern Meat Market (Pty) Ltd* 1983 2 SA 521 (C) 534C.

668 Cases of "estoppel by negligence" The expression "estoppel by negligence" is often encountered in the cases,[1] but it is not quite clear to what type of case it properly relates. One view[2] is that the term is used to signify estoppel which arises by reason of a person's silence or inaction in circumstances in which the person was under a duty to speak or act, but the cases do not show that its use is limited to situations of that kind.[3] Another view is that the expression is used in connection with that type of case in which the party in whose favour it operates was the victim of the fraud of some third person facilitated by the careless breach of duty of the other party.[4] *Union Government v National Bank of SA Ltd*,[5] decided by the Appellate Division in 1921, was a case of this type (although the estoppel pleaded was not upheld). In an estoppel of this kind, it has been said, there must be, on the part of the person whom it is sought to estop, a neglect of some duty owing to the party misled; the neglect must be "in the transaction itself", and it must be the proximate cause of the other party's having acted to his or her prejudice.[6]

1 See eg *Union Government v National Bank of SA Ltd* 1921 AD 121 126 132 142; *Sprinz v Rayton Diamonds Ltd* 1926 WLD 23; *Broekman v TCD Motors (Pty) Ltd* 1949 4 SA 418 (T); *OK Bazaars (1929) Ltd v Universal Stores Ltd* 1973 2 SA 281 (C) 286.

2 See Spencer Bower and Turner *Estoppel by Representation* 3 ed par 74.

3 See also De Wet *Estoppel by Representation* 29 fn 1.

4 See Cross *Evidence* 96.

5 Supra. For the facts of this case, see par 664 ante.

6 *Union Government v National Bank of SA Ltd* supra 131. The court had regard – see the judgments of Innes CJ and Juta JA 127 143 – to one of the four propositions concerning estoppel laid down by Brett J in *Carr v The London & North Western Railway Co* (1875) LR 10 CP 307. The relevant proposition – the fourth – reads as follows: "If in the transaction itself which is in dispute, one has led another into the belief of a certain state of facts by conduct of culpable negligence calculated to have that result, and such culpable negligence has been the proximate cause of leading and has led the other to act by mistake upon such belief to his prejudice, the second cannot be heard afterwards, as against the first, to shew that the state of facts referred to did not exist." See also *Broekman v TCD Motors (Pty) Ltd* supra 423–425. It is not clear what the expression "in the transaction itself" means. See De Wet 29 fn 4. For a discussion of the various tests and their applicability see *Stellenbosch Farmers' Winery Ltd v Vlachos t/a Liquor Den* [2001] 3 All SA 577 (SCA); 2001 3 SA 597 (SCA).

669 Estoppel by silence As stated above,[1] a representation can in certain circumstances be made by silence or inaction. The law is to the effect that a person may be held to have made a representation capable of founding an estoppel when such preson remained silent or failed to act in circumstances where there was a duty on him or her to speak or act. Such a duty arises when the person concerned should, in the light of such person's knowledge of the facts of the case and the relationship between him or herself and the person who raises the estoppel, have foreseen that the latter could draw a wrong inference from his or her silence or inaction and act on that inference to his or her prejudice.[2] Statements in certain English cases to the effect that silence on which it is sought to base an estoppel must have been deliberate and intended to produce the result it did,[3] are not in accordance with South African law. American law on the point seems to be to the same effect as South African law.[4]

1 Par 656 ante.
2 See eg *Glatthaar v Hussan* 1912 TPD 322
328–329: "an owner of a lease, who stands
by and sees the property sold over which he
has a lease, is negligent if he does not protest, and by his negligence he alters the position of an innocent third party . . . Your
negligence causes injury to a third party
whom it was your duty to warn"; *Ross v
Barnard* 1951 1 SA 414 (T) 419A–H; *Garlick
Ltd v Phillips* 1949 1 SA 121 (A) 132–133;
*Resisto Dairy (Pty) Ltd v Auto Protection Insur-
ance Co Ltd* 1963 1 SA 632 (A) 642; *Universal Stores Ltd v OK Bazaars (1929) Ltd* 1973
4 SA 747 (A) 761G–H; *Jones v Trust Bank of

Africa Ltd 1993 4 SA 415 (C) 425A–D; De
Wet *Estoppel by Representation* 54: "[D]ie plig
om te spreek bestaan wanneer die redelike
man sou gepraat het."
3 See eg *Greenwood v Martins Bank Ltd* [1932]
All ER Rep 318 (HL) 321D: "Mere silence
cannot amount to a representation, but
when there is a duty to disclose deliberate
silence may become significant and amount
to a representation."
4 See *Corpus Juris Secundum* vol 31 *Estoppel* par
87: "Silence may support an estoppel where
the failure to speak is intentional or negligent".

670 Agency (or authority) by estoppel In an early Appellate Division case,
Strachan v Blackbeard & Son,[1] where the issue was whether the defendant was by reason
of a course of dealing estopped from denying that a certain person was authorised to
borrow money in his name and on his behalf, the court held that for such conduct to
found an estoppel it had to be of such a nature that it could reasonably have been
expected to mislead.[2] In a later Appellate Division case, *Monzali v Smith*,[3] where the
question was whether the defendant was by his previous conduct estopped from
denying that someone was authorised to act as his agent, it was held, with reference to
the principle laid down in *Strachan's* case, that the conduct relied on must be of such a
nature that it could reasonably have been expected to mislead; that the expectation
referred to is that of the person sought to be bound; that it must be a reasonable
expectation, in other words conclusion of a reasonable person placed in that
position; and that a court of law would not hold a person bound by consequences
which such person could not reasonably have expected and which are, therefore, not
the natural result of the person's conduct.[4]

These views were applied by the Appellate Division in a subsequent case.[5] In *Connock's (SA) Motor Co Ltd v Sentraal Westelike Ko-öperatiewe Mpy Bpk*,[6] where the issue
was whether the defendant was by its previous conduct estopped from asserting that
one of its employees had not been authorised to make certain purchases on its behalf,
the court distinguished between estoppel founded on a representation by express and
unequivocal statements of fact, on the one hand, and estoppel founded on a representation by mere conduct (including silence or inaction), on the other.[7] In the second
type of case (referred to in the judgment as estoppel based upon unintentional conduct), the court said, the courts take into account the representor's knowledge or
ignorance of the facts that give his or her conduct the significance attached to it by
the representee, the principle being that a court of law will not hold a person bound
by consequences which he or she could not reasonably have expected and which are
not the natural result of his or her conduct.[8] In cases of the first type (namely estoppel
founded on a representation by express and unequivocal statements of fact), the court
said, different considerations may apply. Different considerations, the court also said,
may possibly also apply in the case of representations by express and unequivocal
statements of fact and conduct which are made with the specific intention of being so
acted upon.[9]

It should be observed that much of the terminology used in the cases referred to in
this paragraph – for example expressions such as "reasonable man", "reasonable
expectation", "natural result" – coincides with that used when questions of negligence
are considered, but that it is not stated in any of them that negligence is required in

order to found an estoppel.[10] In *Johaadien v Stanley Porter (Paarl) (Pty) Ltd*[11] the chief justice, delivering the judgment of the court, referrred to the requirement for the operation of estoppel mentioned in *Strachan v Blackbeard & Son*[12] and *Monzali v Smith*[13] and stated that it could scarcely be distinguished from negligence.[14] The dissenting judge was not prepared to go so far.[15]

1   1910 AD 282.
2   *Strachan v Blackbeard & Son* supra 289.
3   1929 AD 382.
4   *Monzali v Smith* supra 386; *Union National South British Insurance Co Ltd v Padayachee* 1985 1 SA 551 (A) 561I–562A.
5   *Poort Sugar Planters (Pty) Ltd v Minister of Lands* 1963 3 SA 352 (A) 364. See also *Quinn & Co Ltd v Witwatersrand Military Institute* 1953 1 SA 155 (T) 159E–F.
6   1964 2 SA 47 (T).
7   *Connock's (SA) Motor Co Ltd v Sentraal Westelike Ko-öperatiewe Mpy Bpk* supra 49–50A.
8   *Connock's (SA) Motor Co Ltd v Sentraal Westelike Ko-op Mpy Bpk* supra 50F–51D. For the application of the principle enunciated in the *Connock's (SA) Motor Co Ltd* judgment see *NBS Bank Limited v Cape Produce (Pty) Ltd* [2002] 2 All SA 262 (SCA); 2002 1 SA 396 (SCA) 412.
9   *Connock's (SA) Motor Co Ltd v Sentraal Westelike Ko-operatiewe Mpy Bpk* supra 51D–F. In this connection the court mentioned, without discussing, certain cases which are referred to in par 671 post.
10 See the observation to this effect in *Credit*

Corporation of SA Ltd v Botha 1968 4 SA 837 (N) 84H.
11 1970 1 SA 394 (A).
12 Supra.
13 Supra.
14 *Johaadien v Stanley Porter (Paarl) (Pty) Ltd* supra 402G–H ("kwalik van nalatigheid te onderskei") ("barely distinguishable from carelessness").
15 *Johaadien v Stanley Porter (Paarl) (Pty) Ltd* supra 412H–413C. In English law there is authority to the effect that to establish "ostensible authority" there must have been negligence on the part of the person whom it is sought to estop. See eg *Mercantile Credit Co Ltd v Hamblin* [1964] 3 All ER 592 (CA) 602A–B. American law seems to be different. In *Corpus Juris Secundum* vol 31 *Estoppel* par 104 it is said that when the owner of property allows another person to appear to be the owner of the property or to have the power to dispose of it, a third party who innocently purchases that property will be protected regardless of whether the owner was negligent in entrusting the property to the wrongdoer.

671 Cases in which negligence held not to be a requirement

The question whether proof of *culpa* is necessary to estop the person shown as "purchaser" on what appears to be, but which is in fact not, a proper hire-purchase agreement from asserting as against the *bona fide* cessionary of the "seller's" rights under the agreement that the document is not an accurate reflection of the true facts, has been the subject of several decisions by the courts.[1] It was held in all but one[2] of the cases that the "purchaser" could not be allowed to dispute the truth of what was stated in the document and that negligence was not required to found estoppel. As for the ratio of these decisions, it was said in the most recent of the cases that it is the intentional act of the party who enables the document to be put forth to an innocent third party which operates to debar him or her, as a matter of justice, from asserting that the statements contained in the document are untrue when they have been acted upon by the third party to that party's prejudice.[3]

1   *Coetzee v Van der Westhuizen* 1958 3 SA 847 (T); *Trust Bank of SA Ltd v Maharaj* 1961 2 SA 770 (N); *Trust Bank van Afrika Bpk v Du Toit* 1961 3 SA 36 (T); *Trust Bank van Afrika Bpk v Van der Walt* 1962 1 SA 174 (T); *Credit Corporation of SA Ltd v Botha* 1968 4 SA 837 (N). The Hire-Purchase Act 36 of 1942 was repealed by the Credit Agreements Act 75 of 1980 s 29.

2   *Trust Bank van Afrika Bpk v Van der Walt* supra. The court held that the case was distinguishable on the facts from the earlier cases. The grounds of distinction were questioned in the later case of *Credit Corp of SA Ltd v Botha* supra 850B–C.
3   *Credit Corporation of SA Ltd v Botha* supra 838C–D.

PLEADING OF ESTOPPEL

672 Pleading of estoppel and onus Estoppel has to be pleaded,[1] and the onus to establish it rests on the party who pleads it.[2] It is sometimes said that estoppel cannot found a cause of action,[3] and that it is a weapon of defence, not one of offence.[4] This means, as far as the question of pleading is concerned, that a plaintiff cannot, in formulating a claim, allege – to take a simple illustration – that the defendant is estopped from denying that X was his or her agent for the purchase of certain goods from the plaintiff and that the defendant is therefore liable for the purchase price. What the plaintiff should do, it is said, is to make the positive allegation when setting out the claim that X was the defendant's duly authorised agent, and then, if that allegation is denied by the defendant, meet the denial in the replication by pleading that the defendant is estopped from denying X's authority. By pleading in such a way, it is said,[5] estoppel is used as a weapon of defence, and not as an instrument of attack. Estoppel is, of course, clearly used as a "weapon of defence" when it is pleaded in answer to allegations made by the plaintiff in setting out his or her claim.

1 *Union Government v National Bank of SA Ltd* 1921 AD 121 128; *Union Government v Vianini Ferro-Concrete Pipes (Pty) Ltd* 1941 AD 43 49–50; *Bydawell v Chapman* 1953 3 SA 514 (A) 523–524A; *Arthur v Central News Agency Ltd* 1925 TPD 588 595. In *Union Government (Minister of Railways & Harbours) v Landau & Co* 1918 AD 388 391 it is said that there is no rule requiring the defence of estoppel to be specially pleaded in every instance, but that it is "often advisable and proper to do so". The history of that case would seem to demonstrate that estoppel should be pleaded; see *Union Government (Minister of Railways & Harbours) v Landau & Co* 1918 AD 108. See also *Blackie Swart Argitekte v Van Heerden* 1986 1 SA 249 (A) 260I–J.

2 See eg *Strachan v Blackbeard & Son* 1910 AD 282 288–289; *Baumann v Thomas* 1920 AD 428 436 437; *Quinn & Co Ltd v Witwatersrand Military Institute* 1953 1 SA 155 (T) 159E–F; *Grosvenor Motors (Potchefstroom) Ltd v Douglas* 1956 3 SA 420 (A) 427D–E; *Poort Sugar Planters (Pty) Ltd v Minister of Lands* 1963 3 SA 352 (A) 363D–E. See also *Stellenbosch Farmers' Winery Ltd v Vlachos t/a Liquor Den* [2001] 3 All SA 577 (SCA) 581h–i; 2001 3 SA 597 (SCA) where it was said that "Where a misrepresentation is relied upon the party relying thereon has to establish the misrepresentation and a reliance thereon by the plaintiff, which reliance was 'the cause of his acting to his detriment' (cf *Oakland Nominees (Pty) Ltd v Gelria Mining & Investment Co (Pty) Ltd* 1976 1 SA 441 (A) at 452G; *Quenty's Motors (Pty) Ltd v Standard Credit Corporation Ltd* 1994 3 SA 188 (A) at 198G–199G)." Nienaber JA who delivered

the judgment added that "Such proof would, in my opinion, include proof that the reliance was not actuated by some external influence or factor other than the defendant's misrepresentation".

3 Eg *Union Government v National Bank of SA Ltd* supra 128; *Sprinz v Rayton Diamonds Ltd* 1926 WLD 23 28; *Pandor's Trustee v Beatley & Co* 1935 TPD 358 363 364; *Biloden Properties (Pty) Ltd v Wilson* 1946 NPD 736 749–750; *Mann v Sydney Hunt Motors (Pty) Ltd* 1958 2 SA 102 (G) 107. See also *Sodo v Chairman ANC, Umtata Region* [1998] 1 All SA 45 (Tk) 51 where the *dictae* in *Union Government v National Bank of SA Ltd* supra and the *Pandor's Trustee* judgment to the effect that estoppel cannot be invoked to create a cause of action was again applied.

It has on occasion been said in South African cases that estoppel is a rule of evidence (eg *Sprinz v Rayton Diamonds Ltd* supra 28; *Arthur v Central News Agency Ltd* supra 595), but this view cannot be supported. It is difficult to see how a defence which has to be pleaded can be regarded as a rule of evidence, and how a doctrine which involves, as shown above, the making of a representation, action on the faith thereof and resulting detriment, and negligence on the part of the representor can be looked upon as anything but a rule of substantive law. In *Halsbury's Laws of England* 16 par 951 (4 ed Reissue) it is said that estoppel is "more correctly viewed as a substantive rule of law". In Spencer Bower and Turner *Estoppel by Representation* 3 ed par 7 it is submitted that, while estoppel may be correctly placed somewhere between the law of evidence and the various branches of substantive law, "its place is nearer the former than the latter". See De Wet *Estoppel by Representation* 99–107; Hoffmann and Zeffertt *Evidence* 4 ed 334–335; Schmidt *Bewysreg* 4 ed 8.

4   Eg *Pandor's Trustee v Beatley & Co* supra 364; *Mann v Sydney Hunt Motors (Pty) Ltd* supra 107D–E; *Adriatic Insurance Co v O'Mant* 1964 3 SA 292 (SR) 295B–C; *Barclays Western Bank Ltd v Fourie* 1979 4 SA 157 (C) 160F–G. A successful plea of estoppel can prevent a person from saying that he or she did not intend to enter into an agreement although he or she did not actually have such an intention (*Van Ryn Wine & Spirit Co v Chandos Bar* 1928 TPD 417; *Peri-Urban Areas Health Board v Breet* 1958 3 SA 783 (T)). But, being merely a defence, estoppel cannot logically create an agreement. (In *Saambou-Nasionale Bouvereniging v Friedman* 1979 3 SA 978 (A) the court left undecided the question whether the rule that a person may be held to have intended to assent to an agreement although he did not actually have such an intention rests on the principle of

estoppel or on the so-called objective theory of contract.) Similarly, being merely a defence, estoppel cannot by itself create ownership. (*Barclays Western Bank Ltd v Fourie* supra 160F–H 162A–D.) It has been suggested, however, that a successful defence of estoppel against a vindicatory claim should not only prevent the owner from recovering his or her property, but should also cause his or her ownership in the property to pass to the person who raised the defence of estoppel. See Van Heerden 1970 *THRHR* 19; Louw 1975 *THRHR* 218; Visser 1994 *THRHR* 633; McLennan 1995 *SALJ* 730; Van der Merwe *Sakereg* 373. See also Rabie and Sonnekus 2 ed *The Law of Estoppel in SA* 23–26.

5   See eg *Mann v Sydney Hunt Motors (Pty) Ltd* supra 107D–E, where it is said: "An estoppel pleaded by the plaintiff in his replication to meet allegations raised in the plea is not the same thing as an estoppel used in the declaration as an instrument of attack. In our law estoppel remains a weapon of defence."

LIMITATIONS ON THE OPERATION OF ESTOPPEL

673 Limitations on the operation of estoppel: general Estoppel is not allowed to operate in circumstances where it would have a result which is not permitted by law. A defence of estoppel will therefore not be upheld if its effect would be to render enforceable what the law, be it the common law or statute law, has in the public interest declared to be illegal or invalid. The rule is demonstrated in the next few paragraphs with reference to decisions given by the courts in various branches of the law.

674 Illegal or invalid acts A person's previous concurrence in an illegality, whether according to the common law or statute law, cannot be relied upon by way of estoppel in order to prevent the person from claiming a discontinuance of the illegality.[1] Thus it has been held that a person was not estopped from claiming an order prohibiting the club of which he was a member from illegally operating a totalisator even although he had previously acquiesced in the illegality.[2] The court will not uphold an estoppel which is based on an agreement which is prohibited by law. A defendant, resisting an owner's claim for the return of his or her property, cannot therefore justify possession and raise an estoppel on the ground that he or she purchased the property from someone who purported to be the owner's agent where the transaction concerned was illegal for being in conflict with the provisions of the Sunday Law.[3]

The lack of formalities required by law to render an agreement valid, for example the requirement of writing or notarial execution, cannot be remedied by estoppel, since the recognition of the defence of estoppel in such cases would be to give effect to what the legislature has in the public interest declared to be invalid.[4] Where a contention based on the *exceptio doli* was advanced in a case of this kind, the court held that this equitable defence cannot prevail in cases which fall within the rule that contracts required by law to be in writing or notarially executed cannot be varied save by writing or a notarial instrument.[5]

The question whether a party to an agreement which is by statute declared to be null and void can raise the invalidity of the agreement against the cessionary of the other party's rights, has been the subject of several decisions relating to the Hire-Purchase Act.[6] Where such agreement is invalid for want of compliance with the provisions of the Act, the cessionary of the seller's rights will be estopped from suing the purchaser for payment if such cessionary was aware of the non-compliance with the provisions of the Act when he or she took cession, but it has been held that the cessionary will not be so estopped if he or she was ignorant of that fact at the time, the reasoning being that if he or she was ignorant of the fact that the agreement was in conflict with the provisions of the Act, there are no considerations of public policy which operate against the recognition of estoppel.[7] In coming to this conclusion, the court adopted the approach that whenever the person whom it is sought to estop relies on a statutory illegality, it is the duty of the court to determine whether it is in the public interest that the representee should be allowed to plead estoppel, and that when doing so the court will have regard to the mischief which the statute seeks to remedy, on the one hand, and to the conduct of the parties, on the other hand.[8]

With regard to fictional, or simulated, hire-purchase agreements it has been held in several cases that the cessionary of the seller's rights can rely on estoppel to defeat the defence that the agreement is not what it purports to be, the reasoning being that, since there was no intention to conclude a hire-purchase agreement as provided for in the Act, the court would not by refusing to uphold a plea of estoppel give effect to an agreement that is rendered void by statute.[9] Where a seller discounted a number of invalid hire-purchase agreements with a finance company and at the same time stood surety for the fulfilment of the purchasers' obligations under the agreements, it was held by the Appellate Division that the company, which had no knowledge of any invalidity or irregularity attaching to the agreements, was not estopped from suing the seller on the suretyship agreement. The chief justice, with whose judgment three other members of the court agreed, held that the suretyship agreement was something separate and distinct from the hire-purchase agreements and that the recognition of estoppel could therefore not be said to frustrate the intention of the legislature by giving effect to agreements which the legislature declared to be of no force or effect. The fifth member of the court also held that a reliance on estoppel was not excluded, but he did so on another, more general, ground, namely that the doctrine of estoppel is an equitable one, developed in the public interest, and that whenever a representor relies on a statutory illegality it is the duty of the court to determine whether it is in the public interest that the representee should be allowed to plead estoppel. The court, the learned judge said, will have regard to the mischief sought to be remedied by the statute, on the one hand, and to the conduct of the parties, on the other hand. In the case in issue, he said, it was *dolus* on the part of the seller to deny in the action against him the very fact which he deliberately represented to be true, namely that there were valid hire-purchase agreements in terms of which the purchasers were bound to make payment.[10]

1 *Merriman v Williams* 1880 F 135 176.
2 *Brady v SA Turf Club* (1906) 23 SC 385.
3 28 of 1896. *Western Credit Ltd v Mike Kopping's Truck Centre (Pty) Ltd* 1966 2 SA 387 (T).
4 See eg *Fuls v Leslie Chrome (Pty) Ltd* 1962 4 SA 784 (W) 787, where the court said that

"estoppels cannot prevail if such would re-sult in the nullification of a statute" and adopted the following statement in *In re A Bankruptcy Notice* 1924 2 Ch 76 (CA) 97: "it is impossible in law for a person to allege any kind of principle which precludes him from alleging the invalidity of that which the statute has, on the grounds of general public policy, enacted shall be invalid"; *Strydom v Die Land- & Landboubank van SA* 1972 1 SA 801 (A) 815H, where the following passage in Spencer Bower and Turner *Estoppel by Representation* 2 ed par 140 is quoted as stating the same principle in English law: "Nor can the lack of such essential formalities as the consent of a Minister of the Crown or the making of a contract under seal or other particular formalities prescribed by statute, be remedied by estoppel, when the statute has made them the necessary conditions of entering into the transaction." (See now Spencer Bower and Turner 3 ed par 141 at 140); and see *Oceanair (Natal) (Pty) Ltd v Sher* 1980 1 SA 317 (D) 325G–326C; *Volker v Maree* 1981 4 SA 651 (N) 656F–H; *Plascon-Evans Paints (Tvl) Ltd v Virginia Glass Works (Pty) Ltd* 1983 1 SA 465 (O) 471F–G.

5 *Barkhuizen v Jackson* 1957 3 SA 57 (T) 59C–D.

6 36 of 1942. This Act was repealed by the Credit Agreements Act 75 of 1980 s 29.

7 *Credit Corporation of SA Ltd v Botha* 1968 4 SA 837 (N) 851G–852A.

8 This was the approach followed by Hoexter AJA in *Trust Bank van Afrika Bpk v Eksteen* 1964 3 SA 402 (A) 415–416C. See also *Prinsloo v Van Zyl* 1967 1 SA 581 (T) 585B–H; *Syfrets Mortgage Nominees Ltd v Cape St Francis Hotels (Pty) Ltd* 1991 3 SA 276 (SE) 289E–G.

9 *Trust Bank of Africa Ltd v Malan* 1961 1 PH A37 (T); *Trust Bank of SA Ltd v Maharaj* 1961 2 SA 770 (N); *Autolec Ltd v Du Plessis* 1965 2 SA 243 (O) 244E–245A; *Credit Corporation of SA Ltd v Botha* supra 848A–849F. See also the *dictum* in *Trust Bank van Afrika Bpk v Eksteen* supra 414A–B.

10 *Trust Bank van Afrika Bpk v Eksteen* supra. There has been criticism of this decision, and also of other decisions upholding pleas of estoppel in cases of invalid and fictional hire-purchase agreements. For a discussion of the matter, see Nienaber 1964 *THRHR* 262, 1966 *THRHR* 51; Selvan 1965 *THRHR* 231.

675 *Ultra vires* acts A statutory body has such powers and duties as are entrusted to or imposed upon it by statute, and it cannot be bound by estoppel to do something beyond its powers, or to refrain from doing something which it is its duty to do.[1] The same principle applies to individuals with regard to powers and duties given to or imposed upon them by law. Thus it has been held that where a town clerk in error, which meant without the authority of the municipal council, issued a certificate to trade on the strength of which a general dealer's licence was issued by the revenue authorities, he was not estopped from refusing to put the name of the person concerned on the list of general dealers for the area concerned, the reasoning being that he could not by his mistake be compelled to bring about a position which he had no power in law to create by his own free will.[2] It has been held – to cite a few more illustrations – that a town councillor who had voted in favour of a resolution which was *ultra vires* of the municipality was not estopped from subsequently challenging the validity of action taken in pursuance of the resolution;[3] that a pension fund organisation was not estopped from asserting that a contract entered into by it was *ultra vires* of the organisation;[4] that a group areas development board performing statutory duties could not by reason of an error committed by the valuators appointed under the relevant Act be bound by estoppel to pay a larger sum for property than it was by law authorised to pay;[5] that the Land Bank, after causing certain property to be sold by auction without complying with certain necessary formalities, was not estopped from saying that no contract had come into being;[6] and that a municipality which had erroneously, and in conflict with the provisions of an ordinance, undercharged a person for electricity supplied to him, thereby giving him a preference over other users of electricity, could not be estopped from claiming the amount it had undercharged him.[7]

The Constitution[8] has, however, altered the context in which the doctrine of estoppel by representation in terms of public law is to be viewed. There is now a constitutional imperative to ensure that the common law evolves within the framework of the Constitution consistent with the basic norms of the legal order that it establishes. It has been stated that instead of focusing solely upon the nature of the statutory duty, the court should be entitled to balance the competing interests at stake and take into account factors such as the prejudice to the party seeking to raise the estoppel. Instead of a blanket barrier to the raising of estoppel the common law should be developed to emphasise the equitable nature of the remedy, its function as a rule allocating the incidence of loss and flexibility in taking into account what is right, just and fair in all the circumstances.[9] The proper approach, consistent with section 39(2) of the Constitution, is that the court should balance the individual and public interests at stake and decide on that basis whether the operation of estoppel should be allowed in a specific case'.[10]

A distinction must be drawn between acts which are *ultra vires* of a statutory body and those which are within such body's powers if done after some internal formalities have been complied with. In the latter type of case persons dealing with the body may, in the absence of knowledge to the contrary, assume that all the necessary formalities have been complied with, and may plead an estoppel if the defence is raised that the necessary formalities were not complied with.[11]

1 *Hoisain v Wynberg Municipality* 1916 CPD 194 198; *Hauptfleisch v Caledon Divisional Council* 1963 4 SA 53 (C) 57E–F 59F–G.

2 *Hoisain v Wynberg Municipality* supra; *Hoisain v Town Clerk Wynberg* 1916 AD 236 240. Cf *Mossel Bay Municipality v Ebrahim* 1952 1 SA 567 (C), where a local authority was held to be estopped from setting aside a certificate to trade previously issued by it, the *ratio* being that its previous decision did not constitute a violation of any statutory provision or a dereliction of any statutory duty, but was merely in conflict with a long-established policy.

3 *Maberley v Woodstock Muncipality* (1901) 18 SC 443. See also *Neale v East London Municipality* 1913 EDL 297.

4 *Abrahamse v Connock's Pension Fund* 1963 2 SA 76 (W) 79H. See also *Trust Bank of Africa Ltd v Appletime Engineering (Pty) Ltd* 1981 1 SA 374 (D) 377E–F, where the court said with regard to a company: "It cannot be bound by estoppel to do anything beyond its legal capacity."

5 *Singh v Group Areas Development Board* 1964 4 SA 391 (D) 395D–E 397B–C. (The relevant Act (Group Areas Development Act 69 of 1955) was repealed by the Community Development Act 3 of 1966 s 52.) See also *Surveyor-General (Cape) v Estate De Villiers* 1923 AD 588 630; *Salisbury City Council v Donner* 1958 2 SA 368 (SR) 372B–E.

6 *Strydom v Die Land- & Landboubank van SA* 1972 1 SA 801 (A). It is said in this case (816A–B) that if a statutory body performed an *ultra vires* act, either because it exceeded its powers or because it failed to comply with the requirements for validity prescribed by the legislature, it is considered in law not to have acted at all. See also *De Villiers v The*

Pretoria Municipality 1912 TPD 626 645–646.

7 *Durban City Council v Glenore Supermarket & Café* 1981 1 SA 470 (D); *Bekker v Administrateur, Oranje Vrystaat* 1993 1 SA 829 (O) 831J–832B. It has recently been held that although there is no obligation on a local authority to sue every debtor, there is indeed a positive duty imposed by s 49(1) of the Local Government Ordinance, Ordinance 17 of 1939 to recover charges levied in respect of services rendered by the municipality to the owner/occupier of a building. To allow an estoppel to be raised against such municipality or statutory body, would be to allow an intereference with or hindering of a plaintiff municipality in the performance of its statutory obligations: *Eastern Metropolitan Substructure v Peter Klein Investments (Pty) Ltd* [2001] 1 All SA 187 (W); 2001 4 BCLR 344 (W); 2001 4 SA 661 (W) where it was said (680) that there is consequently, in such circumstances, a statutory barrier to the raising of estoppel.

8 Constitution of the Republic of SA 108 of 1996.

9 *Pharmaceutical Manufacturers Association of SA: In re Ex parte President of the Republic of SA* 2000 3 BCLR 241 (CC); 2000 2 SA 674 (CC).

10 *Eastern Metropolitan Substructure v Peter Klein Investments (Pty) Ltd* supra 680 681, referring to Cockrell 1993 *Acta Juridica* 227 239–40; Ferreira (1991) 54 *THRHR* 388; *Trust Bank van Afrika Bpk v Eksteen* 1964 3 SA 402 (A) 415H– 416C:

11 *Hoisain v Town Clerk Wynberg* supra 240; *Roodepoort Settlement Committee v Retief* 1951 1 SA 73 (O) 79–81.

676 Questions of status and legal capacity Estoppel cannot be used in such a way as to give effect to what is not permitted or recognised by law. A court will accordingly not entertain a plea of estoppel if its effect would be to confer on a person or thing a status, legal capacity or jurisdiction which the person or thing does not in law possess. Thus, in a case which was reported in 1955 it was held that where a woman, married in community of property, falsely represented herself to be a major spinster and passed a mortgage bond in favour of the plaintiff, she could not be estopped from asserting, when sued on the bond, that she was married in community of property and that she had no *locus standi in iudicio*.[1] It has been held, too, that a company which had not been incorporated and registered in terms of the Companies Act[2] at the time when it entered into a contract, could not be estopped from saying that it had no legal existence at the time and that it could accordingly not be bound by any representation made by itself or anyone else regarding its status.[3] With regard to questions of marriage and divorce, there are decisions which, while not specifically dealing with the question of estoppel, are to the effect that a person who knowingly contracted a bigamous marriage is not precluded from claiming an annulment of the marriage,[4] and that a person who was, at his instance, granted a decree of divorce, is not precluded from subsequently claiming a rescission of the decree on the ground that the court which granted it had no jurisdiction to do so.[5] In another case,[6] where a minor had entered into a marriage without her guardian's consent but had after attaining majority voluntarily continued to live with the other party as man and wife for a period of five years, during which period two children were born of the union, it was held on exception to a plea that, although the marriage was null and void (not merely voidable) for want of the consent of the minor's guardian, her claim for the annulment of the marriage could be met by a plea of estoppel.[7] In coming to this conclusion the court said that the plaintiff must have played a part in deceiving the marriage officials; that she voluntarily continued to live with the defendant for five years after attaining majority; that two children were born of the union and that, because of the rule that "eene moeder maakt geen bastaard" ("a mother makes no bastard"), she could not be permitted to bastardise her children by claiming that the marriage was invalid.[8] The essence of the estoppel found by the court was, it would seem, the fact that the plaintiff had by her conduct ratified the marriage[9] and that it would be contrary to public policy to permit the plaintiff to have the marriage annulled.[10] The case was clearly not one of estoppel by representation as known to South African law.

With regard to minors and their lack of contractual capacity, decisions are not unanimous on the question whether a minor who has falsely represented him or herself to be of age, or to be emancipated, and has thereby induced someone to enter into a contract with him or her, is precluded from saying that he or she has no contractual capacity and thus cannot be held liable *ex contractu*. The most recent case on the point, differing from some earlier decisions on the same question, is to the effect that, while such a minor may be liable *ex delicto* (on account of his fraud), or on the basis of enrichment, he or she cannot be sued on the contract.[11]

1 *Rand Wholesale Outfitters (Pty) Ltd v Cassels* 1955 2 SA 66 (W).
2 61 of 1973.
3 *Trust Bank of Africa Ltd v Appletime Engineering (Pty) Ltd* 1981 1 SA 374 (D) 377E–F.
4 *Locke v Locke* 1951 1 SA 132 (N); *Vlook v Vlook* 1953 1 SA 485 (W); *Morrison v Morrison* 1972 3 SA 185 (C). Cf *Ngobeni v Gibitwayo (Ngobeni)* 1946 2 PH B58 (W) where

the court was not inclined to grant such a claim, saying that the plaintiff did not come to court with "clean hands". In English law there are, apparently, decisions to the effect that a party to a bigamous marriage may, depending on the facts, be estopped from asserting that such a marriage is void; see *Bullock v Bullock* [1960] 2 All ER 307 (PDA) 309I: "it is not . . . the law that there can be

no estoppel where the marriage is void because of bigamy" (313F). This view, it is said
in Spencer Bower and Turner *Estoppel by
Representation* 3 ed par 340, runs counter to
the principle which prevents estoppel making that legal which Parliament has declared
illegal.

5 *Dhanapalan v Panjalay* 1959 1 SA 622 (N).

6 *Pretorius v Pretorius* 1948 4 SA 144 (O).

7 The court said (152 *in fine*) that in Roman–
Dutch law, otherwise than in English law,
estoppel can be invoked against a defence
that a marriage is invalid. As pointed out in
fn 4 supra, there would seem to be authority
in English law for the view that estoppel can
be invoked to preclude a plea that a marriage is void on the grounds of bigamy.

8 153–154.

9 According to what is said in the judgment,
ratification of the marriage by the plaintiff
was all that was pleaded by the defendant.
The plea was (translated): "That the plaintiff
attained majority on 12 September 1942 and
that the parties lived together as man and
wife from the date of the marriage until 26
September 1947." See also 153 lines 1–6 of
the report where the court characterised as
"estoppel" the findings of the court of Holland in a case decided in 1706 that the
brothers and sisters of a man could not
attack the validity of his marriage because
they had acquiesced in it for a period of 20
years.

10 Hence, it would seem, the statement in the
judgment that the plaintiff should not be
allowed to bastardise her children, and the
observation (153–154) that the plaintiff,
while entering into the marriage *sub hasta
reipublicae*, so to speak, played a part in deceiving the marriage officials. The defendant, who was presumably a party to the
deception of the officials, did not plead that
he was misled by the plaintiff's conduct at
the time of the marriage.

11 *Louw v MJ & H Trust (Pty) Ltd* 1975 4 SA
268 (T). It has been contended that the case
was wrongly decided: see De Wet and Van
Wyk *Kontraktereg en Handelsreg* (5 ed) 63–64.
As to English law on the point, Spencer
Bower and Turner 3 ed par 128 say that in
view of the various common law and statutory rules which protect a minor as regards
contracts made by such minor during his or
her minority, a representation made by a
minor "is not allowed to operate against him
as an estoppel, where such estoppel, if allowed, would have the effect of depriving
him of this protection against liability on his
contracts." They add, however, that it is
otherwise where the minor's representation
"can be put as fraud".

EVIDENCE

by

CWH SCHMIDT and DT ZEFFERTT
(updated by DP VAN DER MERWE)

SELECTED LITERATURE

Cross *Evidence*
Hoffmann *SA Law of Evidence*
Phipson *Evidence*
Schmidt *Bewysreg*
Wigmore *Evidence*

INTRODUCTION

SCOPE AND SOURCES OF THE LAW OF EVIDENCE

677 The law of evidence The law of evidence is part of adjective law or the law of procedure in its widest sense, in other words the law governing litigation. It regulates the proof of facts in a court of law. Whereas substantive law lays down what has to be proved in any given issue and by whom, the rules of evidence relate to the manner of its proof.[1]

It has been held that the burden of proof,[2] estoppel by representation,[3] estoppel *per rem iudicatam*[4] and the parol evidence rule,[5] though they are usually treated in works on evidence, fall within the purview of substantive law; and that, although it is a rule of evidence that a vicarious admission is admissible if an identity of interest exists between declarant and litigant, the question whether in fact such identity exists is determined by the substantive law.[6]

1 *Tregea v Godart* 1939 AD 16 30.
2 As well as presumptions affecting the burden: *Tregea v Godart* supra 30; *During v Boesak* 1990 3 SA 661 (A) 672; *Eskom v First National Bank of Southern Africa Ltd* 1995 2 SA 386 (A) 390.
3 *Trust Bank van Afrika Bpk v Eksteen* 1964 3 SA 402 (A) 410; *Johaadien v Stanley Porter (Paarl) (Pty) Ltd* 1970 1 SA 394 (A) 401.
4 By implication: it was stated in *S v Ndou* 1971 1 SA 668 (A) 680B that English decisions on *res iudicata* have only persuasive force. If *res iudicata* fell within the law of evidence, English decisions would be binding. Cf *S v Gabriel* 1971 1 SA 646 (RA) 652D; *S v Vermeulen* 1976 1 SA 623 (C) 631H. According to Schmidt *Bewysreg* 7 fn 29 the fact whether a prior binding decision exists is one of the primary *probanda*, which are always indicated by substantive

law.
5 *Slabbert, Verster & Malherbe (Bloemfontein) Bpk v De Wet* 1963 1 SA 835 (O) 839H; *Schroeder v Vakansieburo (Edms) Bpk* 1970 3 SA 240 (T) 242F–H. The majority of decisions, however, point the other way and normally English precedents are followed, eg *Avis v Verseput* 1943 AD 331 378; *Union Government v Vianini Ferro-Concrete Pipes (Pty) Ltd* 1941 AD 43 47; *Du Plessis v Van Deventer* 1960 2 SA 544 (A) 548F; *Von Ziegler v Superior Furniture Manufacturers (Pty) Ltd* 1962 3 SA 399 (T) 403D–E; *Venter v Birchholtz* 1972 1 SA 276 (A) 282D; *Aubrey-Smith v Hofmeyr* 1973 1 SA 655 (C) 661D 663A. See pars 741 742 post.
6 *Botes v Van Deventer* 1966 3 SA 182 (A) 197. See also *Knouwds v Administrateur, Kaap* 1981 1 SA 544 (C) 552 on privity of interest.

678 Evidence Although the law of evidence regulates the proof of facts generally and therefore covers a wider field than merely that of the adduction of evidence, the latter is its main concern. Evidence has been said to encompass all the information given in a legal investigation to establish the fact in question.[1]

Judicial notice, formal admissions and presumptions establish facts but do not take the form of information presented to court by the parties.[2] They dispense with evidence and therefore are not covered by the above definition. But evidence is a flexible term that may bear different meanings for different purposes. In the context of a statutory provision it may include a fact judicially noticed.[3]

1 The Concise Oxford Dictionary speaks of "information (for example given personally or drawn from documents etc) tending to establish fact; statements or proofs admissible as testimony in court". Referring to this

definition the court in *Starr v Ramnath* 1954 2 SA 249 (N) adopted the definition in the main text as the "ordinary legal meaning of the word". See Zeffertt *Evidence* 3–5, however, on the difficulty of defining evidence.

2 Most presumptions, however, only operate if some basic fact has first been proved, and they only operate provisionally in the sense that they are neutralised by rebutting evidence. That presumptions do not constitute evidence was affirmed in *S v AR Wholesalers (Pty) Ltd* 1975 1 SA 551 (NC) 556H; that formal admissions do not constitute evidence, was affirmed in *R v V* 1958 3 SA 474

(G) 479; *S v Nzuza* 1963 3 SA 631 (A); *S v Mokgeledi* 1968 4 SA 335 (A) 337H.

3 Eg s 88 of the Criminal Procedure Act 51 of 1977, which provides that a defective indictment "shall . . . be cured by evidence at the trial": *S v Mbatha* 1963 4 SA 476 (N) referring to the corresponding section (s 179bis) in the previous Criminal Procedure Act 56 of 1955.

679 Sources Being part of adjective law the common law of evidence in South Africa consists of English Law as it existed on 30 May 1961, except as amended by statute.[1]

A number of scattered statutory provisions govern various aspects of the law of evidence. Although there is no single code, there are two statutes which can be said to be the prime sources of the law in this field. These are the Criminal Procedure Act[2] and the Civil Proceedings Evidence Act.[3]

To these should be added the South African Constitution.[4] The provisions of the final constitution have considerable implications for the law of evidence. Thus, a mere two subsections of the Constitution, as shown in the footnotes below, affect areas such as confessions and admissions (even admissions during plea proceedings),[5] the burden of proof,[6] privilege,[7] presumptions[8] and hearsay.[9] The entrenchment of the right to a fair trial has the effect of extending the grounds on which a confession might be ruled as inadmissible in evidence. The emphasis falls on the issue of fairness rather than the compliance with rules and formalities such as those contained in the Criminal Procedure Act.[10]

The Criminal Procedure Act, which, as its title implies, is concerned mainly with criminal procedure in the narrow sense, also touches upon a large number of evidential matters in their application to criminal proceedings. These include amongst others the competency and privileges of witnesses, the admissibility of evidence, corroboration, the proof of previous convictions and of finger, palm and footprints. Where a topic is not dealt with by way of an exhaustive statement of specific rules, it is usually, though not invariably,[11] covered by a provision to the effect that the law relating thereto is that which was applicable on 30 May 1961 (the day when South Africa became a Republic). Thus it is stated that no witness in criminal proceedings may "except as provided by this Act or any other law" be compelled to answer any question which the witness would not on 30 May 1961 have been compelled to answer by reason that the answer may expose him or her to a criminal charge.[12] Other topics dealt with in this fashion are the impeachment or support of a witness's credibility;[13] privilege from disclosure on the ground of public policy or public interest;[14] the competence, compellability and privileges of witnesses;[15] the character of the accused or of a female victim of an indecent offence;[16] and the admissibility of evidence in general.[17] These references to the law applicable on 30 May 1961 are, in effect, references to the law in force in the supreme court of judicature in England on that day.[18]

The Civil Proceedings Evidence Act[19] similarly contains various provisions dealing with specific aspects of evidence in civil proceedings, as well as a residuary section[20] which provides that the law of evidence, including the law relating to the competency, compellability, examination and cross-examination of witnesses, which was in force in respect of civil proceedings on 30 May 1961, will apply in any case not provided for in that Act or any other law. On that date various provincial statutes[21] regulating evidence in civil proceedings were in force and these contained, in turn, residuary provisions incorporating, directly or indirectly,[22] English law for matters not specifically covered.

The effect of provisions making English law applicable in South Africa is that only those English statutes which were in force at the date of incorporation[23] form part of the South African law of evidence. On the other hand, English decisions reinterpreting and therefore effectively changing the common law between the date of incorporation and 30 May 1961, have to be followed by South African courts – although the Supreme Court of Appeal, being the highest court in the South African hierarchy, may overrule them if it is convinced that they do not correctly reflect English law.[24] Post 1961 English judgments are not binding upon South African courts, but they may have considerable persuasive force.[25]

In an exceptional case, where South African law or practice is obviously incompatible with an English evidentiary principle, that principle may be rejected;[26] and South African courts may develop a binding rule of practice which has no counterpart in English law or practice.[27]

Although it is possible that South African public policy could differ from that of England, such difference would not be a valid ground for deviating from an English policy-based rule where English law is applicable by virtue of one of the above statutory provisions.[28]

---

1 *S v Desai* [1997] 2 All SA 298 (W); 1997 1 SA 845 (W); 1997 1 SACR 38 (W) 43; and see below.
2 51 of 1977.
3 25 of 1965.
4 Constitution of the Republic of SA 108 of 1996. The interim Constitution (Constitution of the Republic of SA 200 of 1993) has now been repealed by the Constitution of the Republic of SA 108 of 1996 s 242 read with Sch. 7.
5 S 35(2): "Every person who is arrested for allegedly committing an offence, has the right . . . (c) not to be compelled to make any confession or admission that could be used in evidence against that person".
6 S 35(3): "Every accused person has a right to a fair trial, which includes the right– . . . (g) to have a legal practitioner assigned to the accused person by the state . . . and to be informed of this right; . . . (h) to be presumed innocent, to remain silent and not to testify during the proceedings". See *S v Ngwenya* 1999 3 BCLR 308 (W); 1998 2 SACR 503 (W).
7 S 35(3): "Every accused person has the right to a fair trial which includes the right– (a) to be informed of the charge with sufficient detail to answer to".
8 See fn 5 supra.
9 S 35(3): "Every person has the right to a fair trial, which includes the right . . . (i) to adduce and challenge evidence".
10 51 of 1977 – see also the next paragraph. On this point, see *S v Manuel* 1997 11 BCLR 1597 (C); 1997 2 SACR 505 (C); *S v Khan* 1997 2 SACR 611 (SCA).
11 Topics not covered by a general reference to 30 May 1961 are, *inter alia*, the burden of proof, presumptions, judicial notice, the examination of witnesses, and hearsay.
12 Criminal Procedure Act s 203.
13 S 190(1).
14 S 202.
15 S 206. Note that s 192, which states that every person not expressly excluded by the Act from giving evidence is competent and compellable, is rendered subject to s 206, ie subject to the law applicable on 30 May 1961. Cf *Ex parte Minister of Justice: In re R v Demingo* 1951 1 SA 36 (A) (with reference to the equivalent provision in the Criminal Procedure and Evidence Act 31 of 1917).
16 Criminal Procedure Act 51 of 1977 s 227(1); Criminal Law and the Criminal Procedure Act Amendment Act 39 of 1989 s 2.
17 Criminal Procedure Act 51 of 1977 s 252.
18 By virtue of the corresponding provisions of the preceding Criminal Procedure Act 56 of 1955 before their amendment by the Criminal Procedure Amendment Act 92 of 1963.
19 25 of 1965.
20 S 42.
21 Ord 72 of 1830 (Cape); Law 17 of 1859 (Natal); Ord 11 of 1902 (OFS); Proc 16 of 1902 (Tvl). These statutes were repealed by s 44 of the Civil Proceedings Evidence Act 25 of 1965.
22 In the OFS the residuary section incorporated the law of the Cape of Good Hope,

which in turn incorporated English law.

23 Ie the earliest date of incorporation (eg 1830 in the Cape). Subsequent re-enactments in consolidating statutes (eg the Criminal Procedure Act 56 of 1955 and 51 of 1977) have not made more recent English legislation applicable.

24 *Van der Linde v Calitz* 1967 2 SA 239 (A) 251E–F. *In casu* an older privy council exposition of the law relating to state privilege was preferred to a more recent House of Lords exposition. The main reason advanced for this preference, ie, that the privy council was at that time the highest court of appeal in the South African hierarchy, has been criticised; see Davids 1967 *SALJ* 245; Ellison

Kahn 1967 *SALJ* 327; Schmidt *Bewysreg* 17. Cf Zeffertt *Evidence* 10–11; Schwikkard *Principles of Evidence* 3.5.1.

25 *Van der Linde v Calitz* supra 244–245; *Papenfus v Tvl Board for the Development of Peri-Urban Areas* 1969 2 SA 66 (T) 69H; *Rusmarc (SA) (Pty) Ltd v Hemdon Enterprises (Pty) Ltd* 1975 4 SA 626 (W) 630E–F.

26 *Ex parte Minister of Justice: In re R v Pillay* 1945 AD 653; *Incorporated Law Society of Natal v Hassim (also known as Essack)* 1976 4 SA 332 (N); *A Sweidan & King (Pty) Ltd v Zim Israel Navigation Co Ltd* 1986 1 SA 515 (D) 518.

27 *S v Lwane* 1966 2 SA 433 (A).

28 *Smit v Van Niekerk* 1976 4 SA 293 (A).

ADMISSIBILITY

RELEVANCE

680 General rule In its negative aspect, the general rule is that no evidence as to any fact, matter or thing is admissible if it is immaterial or irrelevant;[1] in its positive aspect, all facts of sufficient probative force are relevant and admissible unless their reception is prohibited by an exclusionary rule.[2]

1 Civil Proceedings Evidence Act 25 of 1965 s 2; Criminal Procedure Act 51 of 1977 s 210. For the relevant principles relating to bail proceedings, see *S v Nyengane* 1996 2 SACR 520 (E).

2 See par 598 post. In *S v Boesman* 1990 2 SACR 389 (E) it was held that the court has

an overall discretion, based on public policy, to exclude evidence which would otherwise be admissible. See also *S v Jantjie* 1992 1 SACR 24 (SE); *Shell SA (Edms) Bpk v Voorsitter, Dorperaad van die OVS* 1992 1 SA 906 (O); *S v Aimes* 1998 1 SACR 343 (C).

681 Relevance and admissibility A fact will not be admissible merely because it is logically relevant: evidence which is inadmissible because it falls within the ambit of an exclusionary rule may be logically relevant but, despite any probative force that it may have, it is not received.[1] Again, evidence may be rejected although it is both logically relevant and untouched by an exclusionary rule when its probative force is insufficient to warrant its reception. It is thus not *legally relevant* because its *degree of relevance*, although conducive to rational persuasion, is not sufficient to countervail the disadvantages that its admission may cause.[2]

The Constitution[3] has also affected the question of discretionary admissibility of illegally obtained evidence. In *S v Melani*,[4] the court held that there were three different ways in which the Constitution could be interpreted as to the question of what the "appropriate relief" would be in terms of section 7(4)(a) in respect of non-compliance with a provision such as section 25(2)(a), dealing with the rights of an arrested person to be informed of his or her rights. The first was the rigidly inclusionary rule as followed by British law and our own common law, provided the evidence was relevant. The second was the rigidly exclusionary rule followed by the United States courts which required that all evidence acquired in an unauthorised manner be excluded. The third, of which Canada is an example, constituted a compromise approach in terms of which a discretion was given to the judge to exclude such evidence depending on the circumstances of the case. In the opinion of the court, the latter offered the best opportunity to find a proper balance between the legitimate interests of an accused and those of the community at large. It was therefore decided to admit the evidence, so as not to let the law fall into disrepute in the eyes of the public, particularly since the events took place before the interim Constitution had come into force. As the police officer had acted in good faith and in a manner which would have been justified before the coming into operation of the Constitution and the relevant non-compliance with the latter was, in the particular circumstances of the case, not of a particularly serious nature, the exclusion of the evidence as to the alleged pointing out would have brought the administration of justice into discredit and dishonour.

The view that relevance and admissibility are distinct concepts is artificial. To argue that relevancy depends on reasoning, while admissibility depends on law, would ignore the fact that irrelevant evidence is excluded as a matter of law.[5] Such a view rests also on the false inarticulate premise that the determination of relevancy in legal proceedings depends on rational considerations only, that is to say, on pure logic. It is true that evidence will be irrelevant if it is incapable of inducing rational persuasion[6] and that, in this aspect, legal relevance is purely a matter of reason; but to be legally relevant (in the sense outlined above) evidence has to be sufficiently relevant to warrant its reception, in the circumstances, despite any disadvantages that may arise from its admission.[7] Legal relevance is, therefore, a juridical concept that involves both rational and practical considerations.

1 "The general rule of evidence under common law is that any evidence which is relevant is admissible unless there is some other rule of evidence which excludes it": *R v Schaube-Kuffler* 1969 2 SA 40 (RA) 50. Thus evidence, eg, which is excluded by the hearsay rule may have a strong logical relevance to an issue; it may be the best available evidence, but it is inadmissible.

2 See pars 683–688 post.

3 Constitution of the Republic of SA 108 of 1996 s 35(2)(a).

4 1995 5 BCLR 632 (E); 1995 4 SA 412 (E); 1995 2 SACR 141 (E). See also *Nombewu v S* [1996] 4 All SA 621 (E); 1996 12 BCLR 1635 (E); 1996 2 SACR 396 (E).

5 In SA by Civil Proceedings Evidence Act 25 of 1965 s 2; Criminal Procedure Act 51 of 1977 s 210.

6 *R v Trupedo* 1920 AD 58.

7 See pars 699–704 post for a practical application of this theory to similar facts.

682 Weight and relevance Questions of the weight and the admissibility of evidence are distinct and should never be confused. This principle signifies, first, that a fact will not be excluded for irrelevance simply because it is inconclusive and, secondly, that the judicial officer has initially to decide whether evidence materially tends to prove, or disprove, a fact or thing in issue and whether it is affected by an exclusionary rule; it is only after the judicial officer has decided that evidence is admissible that he or she (with assessors, if applicable) may determine its weight, that is to say, the extent to which it fulfils its probative purpose.[1] This does not derogate from the fact that, to be relevant and admissible, evidence must have sufficient probative force. Evidence that has no (or very little) weight can have no probative value and must necessarily be irrelevant. Again, the judicial officer, when making the initial decision to receive (or not to receive) evidence, has a discretion to exclude any fact or thing the probative force of which is insufficient to warrant its reception in the light of the practical difficulties that would arise were it to be admitted.[2] To say this is not to confuse weight and admissibility; the former comes down to a further refining of the exact probative value of admitted evidence.

1 O'Dowd *Evidence* 7–8.

2 *Delew v Town Council of Springs* 1945 TPD 128. See pars 683 700–704 post. See further Hoffmann 1974 *SALJ* 237, 1975 *LQR* 193.

683 Legal relevance The word "relevance" does not mean the same thing to the lawyer and the logician.[1] To the lawyer, relevancy is based on a blend of logic and experience. The law starts with this practical or common sense relevancy and then adds material to it or, more usually, excludes material from it, the result being what is legally relevant and admissible.[2]

The first requisite of legal relevance is that evidence has to be conducive to rational persuasion. This means that evidence must have some "logical" relevance.[3] It is precisely because relevancy has to be looked at with the eye of a lawyer rather than a logician that few, if any, of the definitions of relevance that have been propounded by legal writers or the courts would satisfy the semanticist or the philosopher.[4] Thus, to the lawyer, a fact is logically relevant when inferences may properly be drawn from it as to the existence, or non-existence, of a fact in issue;[5] and it has been said that relevancy exists when any two facts are so closely related to each other that according to the common course of events one, either taken by itself, or in connection with other facts, proves or renders improbable the past, present or future existence, or non-existence, of the other.[6] It matters not that the logician may easily fault this definition: relevance, to the lawyer, is a state which is determined by common sense and experience[7] – taking into account prevailing standards of reason that vary in time and place.[8]

It is generally correct to say that the law affords no test of relevancy. This follows from the fact that relevancy exists, and can only exist, in the circumstances of a particular case. A decision on the relevancy of evidence in that particular case will depend, first, on whether the evidence is capable of inducing rational persuasion and, then, on whether there are any legal rules or considerations of policy that would lead to its rejection as being legally irrelevant. But the law, in certain instances, does provide a test of relevance: a decision that evidence is relevant may lay down criteria that can guide, or even be authoritative, in subsequent cases;[9] and the law may expressly declare that, in certain circumstances, evidence is presumed to be relevant.[10] Again, a legal rule may exclude certain categories of logically relevant evidence that it regards, for reasons of fundamental judicial policy, as being legally irrelevant.[11] Thus, for instance, evidence whose sole relevance is to show that an accused is a bad person and, therefore, likely to be guilty, is logically relevant to the question of the accused's guilt; but it is not legally relevant.[12]

To be legally relevant evidence must be *sufficiently relevant* to warrant its being received in the circumstances of a particular case. The concept involves the idea that *it has to be worthwhile to admit the evidence*. To determine whether evidence is relevant, in the sense that it is worthwhile to receive it, its value as evidence has to be considered. If its probative force is such that, despite any disadvantages that may attach to admitting it, it would be worthwhile to receive it, it is relevant; if the disadvantages outweigh its probative force, it is legally irrelevant even though it may be logically relevant. Thus evidence may be excluded as legally irrelevant, despite its being logically relevant in the sense that an inference might be drawn from it as to the existence of a fact in issue, when to admit it would by unduly prejudicial, or when it would create side issues that would unduly distract the trier of fact from the main issues, or where its proof and counterproof would take up an undue time, or where to admit it would take the other side by surprise.[13] Where the presence of one, or more, or all of these factors leads the court to conclude that, in the circumstances, and taking into account the strength of its probative force, it is not worthwhile to receive evidence, that evidence is irrelevant in law. In other words, although the evidence is such that it could ground an inference as to the existence, or non-existence, of a fact in issue, such an inference would not, in the legal sense, be properly drawn.

1 Hoffmann 1974 *SALJ* 237, 1975 *LQR* 193.

2 *R v Matthews* 1960 1 SA 752 (A) 758; *S v Letsoko* 1964 4 SA 768 (A) 775; *S v Gokool* 1965 3 SA 461 (N) 465 475.

3 *R v Trupedo* 1920 AD 58; *S v Gokool* supra 475.

4 See Schmidt *Bewysreg* 387 fn 89.

5 *R v Trupedo* supra; *S v Shabalala* 1986 4 SA 734 (A).

6 Stephen *Digest of Evidence* s 1.

7 *R v Matthews* supra.

8 *Director of Public Prosecutions v Boardman* 1975 AC 421 (HL) 444; *Boardman v Director of Public Prosecutions* [1974] 3 All ER 887 898, where Lord Wilberforce remarks: "As was said by Lord Simon of Glaisdale in *Kilbourne's* case (1973 AC 729 (HL) 756; 1973 1 All ER 440 461) in judging whether one fact is probative of another, experience plays as large a place as logic . . . And in matters of experience it is for the judge to keep close to current mores. What is striking in one age is normal in another: the perversions of yesterday may be the routine or the fashion of tomorrow."

9 The danger of stressing that there may be precedents is that it may blind the judge to the true inquiry, ie whether in the circumstances of the particular case evidence is relevant. Thus an application of the relevancy theory in *R v Trupedo* supra, where, in the circumstances, evidence about the behaviour of a dog was held to be irrelevant, has led to the conclusion that there is a rule that evidence of the instinctive behaviour of police dogs is irrelevant and inadmissible. See, eg, *S v Moya* 1968 1 PH H148 (G); Barrie 1967 *Codicillus* 2 44. But particular

situations can give rise to authoritative lines of decisions. Thus, for instance, it has been held that the birth of a coloured child is relevant and admissible to show that the father was white (*R v D* 1958 4 SA 364 (A); *R v P* 1957 3 SA 444 (A)) but that evidence of a resemblance between a child and an alleged parent is generally thought to be so unreliable a guide as to be virtually worthless (cf *Mountford v Mukukumidzi* 1969 2 SA 56 (RA)). Similarly, judicial experience has led to authoritative pronouncements that when the provisions of a contract between A and B are in issue, evidence of the provisions of a contract between B and C will be irrelevant where no custom of trade to make such contracts, and no connection between the latter contract and the one in question have been shown to exist (see *inter alia Hollingham v Head* (1858) 27 LJCP 241; 4 CB (NS) 388; 140 ER 1135; cf *Lamb v Protea Assurance Co Ltd* 1970 2 SA 539 (E)).

10 See pars 690 700 post.

11 *Delew v Town Council of Springs* 1945 TPD 128. See further *Hollingham v Head* supra; *Metropolitan Asylum District Managers v Hill* 47 LT 29 34; cf *Wilkinson v Clark* 1916 2 KB 636 with *Holcombe v Hewson* (1810) 2 Camp 391; 170 ER 1194. Where the evidence of the collateral facts has sufficient probative value to warrant its reception it will be received: *Folkes, Bart v Chadd* (1782) 3 Dough 157; 99 ER 589; *Gosschalk v Rossouw* 1966 2 SA 476 (C); and see par 700 post.

12 See par 701 post.

13 *Delew v Town Council of Springs* supra.

684 Procedural aspects Since the relevancy of evidence may often become apparent after other evidence has been led, evidence may be received even though its relevance is not manifest when it is tendered. If its relevance does not become apparent at a later stage, it can then be rejected. The legal advisers of the parties are, in practice, sometimes asked to indicate in advance what subsequent evidence will be led in order to enable the court to determine whether the evidence will ultimately be relevant; but a party who calls a witness is not obliged to indicate in advance the relevancy of the testimony that is to be given by the witness.[1]

1 Schmidt *Bewysreg* 390; *S v Wilkens* 1962 4 SA 382 (T).

685 Classification of relevant evidence Evidence may be relevant (a) as constituting a fact in issue; (b) as evidence from which the existence (or non-existence) of a fact in issue may properly be drawn; (c) as a requisite for the admissibility of other evidence; and (d) as regards the reliability of other evidence and the credibility of witnesses.

686 The facts in issue Direct evidence, that is to say, direct assertions that a fact in issue (a *factum probandum*) exists, or does not exist, is always relevant.

In civil proceedings, any fact that is alleged by a party in a pleading that has either been denied by the other party in his or her pleadings, or which the latter is deemed to have denied in terms of the rules relating to civil procedure, is a fact in issue.

When, in criminal proceedings, an accused pleads not guilty, he or she puts all the facts that have been alleged against him or her in issue. But the law relating to criminal procedure may have the effect of reducing the number of issues that are raised by a plea of not guilty. When an accused pleads not guilty at a summary trial, the court may ask the accused whether he or she wishes to make a statement indicating the nature of his or her defence.[1] Where the accused does not make such a statement, or when the accused does and it is not clear from the statement to what extent he or she denies the issues raised by the plea, the court is entitled to question the accused in order to establish which allegations are in dispute.[2] It is required to ask the accused whether an allegation which is not placed in issue by the plea of not guilty may be recorded as an admission by the accused, and if the accused consents, it constitutes a waiver of proof.[3] A similar procedure applies when a charge is put to an accused at the end of the evidence for the prosecution at a preparatory examination and the accused, who has not pleaded before, pleads not guilty;[4] and where an accused is asked to plead in the magistrate's court in a matter triable in the High Court.[5]

The whole procedure with regard to admissions made during the plea procedure has been given a new dimension in the light of the Constitution's guarantee to the accused that he or she has the right to remain silent during plea proceedings.[6] Even though the Constitutional Court in *S v Zuma*[7] dealt with confessions and the court specifically refused to comment on "the right to silence during trial"[8], certain inferences may be drawn from that decision. The court found that the "right to silence" contains a "disparate group of immunities", containing *inter alia* the privilege against self-incrimination as well as the right not to be a compellable witness against oneself. This is based on a 300-year old tradition which has become one of the values by which the Constitution has to be interpreted and which came about as a result of revulsion against the tortures practiced by England's Star Chamber.[9] Even though this is a fundamental right, according to the Canadian two-stage procedure approved of in *S v Zuma*,[10] it would still be open to the state to prove that it was necessary for the public's right to be infringed in a higher cause and that section 115 of the Criminal Procedure Act[11] must remain on the statute book.

More recent cases have shed further light on this vexed question of the constitutional right to silence. In *S v Brown*,[12] *Osman v Attorney-General, Transvaal*[13] and *S v Boesak*[14] the courts have decided that an accused who refuses to testify is not convicted on the basis of silence alone, but because of a strong *prima facie* case for the state which stands unrebutted. In recent works by leading authors on evidence this problem is discussed under disparate headings. Thus Schmidt deals with it in the chapter on criteria and weight of evidence.[15] Schwikkard deals with the matter under private privilege and the evaluation of evidence[16] and Zeffertt under the privilege against self-incrimination and the right of the accused to remain silent.[17] While similar principles are involved, it should always be borne in mind that only a *witness* may make use of the privilege against self-incrimination and that it only relates to one specific question at a time. On the other hand the right to remain silent applies to a person having been arrested or arraigned as the *accused* during a trial. In the present work these matters will be further clarified under the respective headings mentioned earlier in this paragraph.

Where an accused pleads guilty he or she in theory disposes of the facts in issue by admitting all the allegations against him or her. But, since the prosecutor is entitled, on the question of sentence, either in a summary trial or where the accused has been arraigned for sentence or trial, to lead, and the court to hear, evidence, there may still be facts in issue despite the plea.[18]

In both civil and criminal proceedings the number of facts in issue at the beginning of a case may be reduced by subsequent formal admissions.[19]

The essential quality of a fact in issue is that if it is not proved, the party who relies upon it will necessarily fail in his or her claim or defence.[20] Thus, although a disputed circumstantial fact (a fact from which the existence, or non-existence, of a fact in issue may be inferred) resembles a fact in issue because it may be proved by direct or circumstantial evidence, it differs from a fact in issue in its essential nature.

1 Criminal Procedure Act 51 of 1977 s 115(1).
2 S 115(2).
3 S 115(2)(b).
4 S 132(2).
5 S 122(1).
6 Constitution of the Republic of SA 108 of 1996 s 35(3)(h) and (j), which should be read with s 35(1)(a), (b) and (c), which deals with similar rights for arrested and detained persons. See also *S v Melani* 1995 4 SA 412 (E) with regard to the similar provisions in the interim Constitution (Constitution of the Republic of SA 200 of 1993).
7 1995 4 BCLR 401 (CC); 1995 2 SA 642 (CC); 1995 1 SACR 568 (CC).
8 Par 34.
9 Par 30.
10 Supra par 21.
11 51 of 1977.
12 [1996] 3 All SA 625 (NC); 1996 11 BCLR 1480 (NC); 1996 2 SACR 49 (NC).
13 1998 11 BCLR 1362 (CC); 1998 4 SA 1224 (CC); 1998 2 SACR 493 (CC).
14 2000 3 SA 381 (SCA); 2000 1 SACR 633 (SCA).
15 *Bewysreg* 112–116.
16 *Principles of Evidence* 10.2.32 and 30.9 respectively.
17 *The South African Law of Evidence* 522–542.
18 Ss 112(3) 114(4) 140(4); *Khumalo v S* 1978 4 SA 516 (N); *S v Balepile* 1979 1 SA 702 (NC). The OPD seems to be of the opinion that evidence which is relevant to the guilt of the accused may be led even after an accused has pleaded guilty: *S v Quinta* 1979 2 SA 326 (O).
19 See ss 115 220 for criminal proceedings.
20 Schmidt *Bewysreg* 361–362.

687 Circumstantial evidence A circumstantial fact is one from which an inference may properly be drawn as to the existence, or non-existence, of a fact in issue. Any fact which tends to prove that the existence of a fact in issue is more probable, or less probable, will be logically relevant as will any fact that tends to deny a reasonably probable alternative hypothesis to the existence, or non-existence, of a fact in issue.

To be admissible circumstantial evidence must be more than merely logically relevant: its probative force must be sufficient to afford a reasonable inference as to a fact in issue and to warrant its reception despite the disadvantages that may be caused by its reception.[1]

Since relevancy cannot exist in a vacuum, and since it is a variable standard, little purpose would be served by listing the many instances in which evidence has been held to be relevant or irrelevant. At best these decisions may constitute illustrations of the application of a general principle; at worst they may be erroneously regarded as having created categories of admissibility or inadmissibility and thus obfuscate the true inquiry, namely, whether a fact is sufficiently relevant to be admitted in the circumstances of the particular case before the judicial officer. A good practical example of a court dealing with circumstantial evidence is the case of *R v Blom*.[2]

A relevant circumstantial fact that has been tendered by one party may be disputed by the other, in which event it may itself be proved by direct or relevant circumstantial evidence.

1 See par 683 ante.
2 1939 AD 188.

688 The relative worth of direct and circumstantial evidence It is sterile to compare the intrinsic value of direct and circumstantial evidence: there is no principle that says that direct evidence is inherently more reliable than circumstantial evidence (or vice versa).[1] The cogency of direct and circumstantial evidence depends on its nature in the circumstances of each particular case and may vary from being of the highest to the lowest in value.[2] It is undesirable for a presiding officer to record his or her subjective observations as opposed to objectively determinable facts, and if the defence disagrees with such observations, these have no evidential value and should be ignored.[3]

1 Wills *Circumstantial Evidence* 26; Wigmore *Evidence* 1 par 26; Phipson *Evidence* par 4.
2 *S v Mthetwa* 1972 3 SA 766 (A); Phipson par 4.
3 *S v Mohase* 1998 1 SACR 185 (O).

CHARACTER

689 Introduction When, in everyday life, an assessment is made about a person's character, various factors are taken into account: personal opinion; general reputation; rumour and specific acts from which an inference may be drawn about disposition. Evidence as to character is admissible in South African law in criminal and civil proceedings if it were to have been admissible on 30 May 1961.[1] This, in effect, enjoins the courts to apply the English law as it was on that critical date.[2] According to the rules of English law, character evidence (in theory, at least) means evidence of general reputation.[3] When character evidence is admissible in evidence in chief it has to take the form of witness's testimony about another person's reputation, that is to say, that person's general character. The witness may not give a personal opinion. Nor may a witness refer to rumour or specific acts.[4] Of course, evidence of general reputation must necessarily rest on hearsay opinion; but this theoretical difficulty is disregarded. Again, in practice, it is not always possible to confine evidence of character to reputation.[5]

Just as the word "character" means different things in everyday speech, it is not always used to mean the same thing in the law of evidence. For instance, when the Criminal Procedure Act[6] refers to "evidence as to character" in section 227 it means evidence of general reputation; but when an accused's character is subject to attack in terms of the provisos to section 197, that accused may be cross-examined in specific instances of misconduct. And, since a witness's credibility is always relevant, the witness's "character" (unless he or she is the accused)[7] may, subject to the privilege against self-incrimination and the bounds of decency and propriety,[8] be attacked in cross-examination. When that happens, specific acts of misconduct may be put to the witness if they are relevant to his or her credibility and the witness may be asked whether he or she has a reputation for untruthfulness.[9] Again, evidence of specific acts, which tend to show that the accused is a bad man, may, despite this fact, be admissible in terms of the similar fact rule if they have a strong probative force bearing on an issue in the case.[10] Here, the evidence is not admitted as "character evidence" in the strict sense of that expression. According to generally accepted theory it is received precisely because it is not relevant solely by way of character.[11]

It is said that the character of a witness is indivisible. Accordingly, it has been said that where a character witness testifies to the accused's good character, the witness may be asked about the accused's previous convictions that have nothing to do with the charge that the accused is facing.[12] Some writers think this to be wrong.[13]

1 Criminal Procedure Act 51 of 1977 s 227(1); Criminal Law and the Criminal Procedure
Act Amendment Act 39 of 1989 s 2; Civil Proceedings Evidence Act 25 of 1965 s 42,

which came into effect on 30 June 1967: *Naidoo v Marine & Trade Insurance Co Ltd* 1978 3 SA 666 (A) 677.

2 See par 677 ante.

3 *R v James Rowton* (1865) Le & CA 520; 169 ER 1497 (CCA); *R v Butterwasser* 1948 1 KB 4; [1947] 2 All ER 415.

4 *R v James Rowton* supra; *Sutter v Brown* 1926 AD 155; *Joseph v Black* 1930 WLD 327. See further *Hobbs v Tinling (CT) & Co Ltd, Hobbs v Nottingham Journal Ltd* 1929 2 KB 1; 1929 All ER 33.

5 Phipson *Evidence* par 527. Eg, an accused may testify to his or her own good character, but cannot give evidence about how others regard his or her reputation (what others say about the accused in his or her absence) and therefore the accused's evidence has to take the form of statements such as that he or she has led a good life, has never been in trouble and has done a number of good acts: Cross *Evidence* 401, who cites Lord Denning in *Plato Films Ltd v Speidel* 1961 AC 1090 1143.

6 51 of 1977. S 227(2) (4) has been inserted to provide that evidence of the character of the complainant in regard to a sexual offence may in certain circumstances not be adduced: Criminal Law and the Criminal Procedure Act Amendment Act 39 of 1989 s 2. See further par 696 post.

7 See par 695 post.

8 See par 770 post.

9 See par 695 post.

10 See par 700 post.

11 Ibid.

12 *Dicta* in *R v Winfield* [1939] 4 All ER 164 (CCA), approved in *Stirland v Director of Public Prosecutions* 1944 AC 315 (HL); [1944] 2 All ER 13 (HL). *Winfield* was charged with indecent assault; a defence witness, who had been called to testify to his good behaviour with women had been cross-examined about the accused's previous conviction for a crime of dishonesty. The decision was set aside on appeal for different reasons, but Humphreys J approved of the cross-examination. See further Cross 403.

13 Schmidt *Bewysreg* 444–445; cf Zeffertt *Evidence* 228–229 and Schwikkard 57. Schmidt argues that there has be a connection between the evidence of character and the crime, both with regard to the original evidence of good character as well as with the counterattack with regard to poor character. This view has much to be said for it: if the character evidence is completely unrelated to the issues, it is irrelevant; but the case law, such as it is, is against it. See further Cross 403–404; Gooderson 1953 *Cam LJ* 377.

690 General rule Evidence of character, that is to say, of general reputation, is exceptionally admissible. Normally character evidence is irrelevant and therefore inadmissible. The mere fact that character evidence is logically relevant to an issue will not render it admissible: it is admissible only if the law regards it as relevant, that is to say, if it is legally relevant in the circumstances.[1]

1 Eg, the fact that the accused is a thief is logically relevant to the accused's being guilty of theft; but according to the law of evidence it is not permissible to adduce evidence for the purpose of showing that, because the accused is a thief, it is likely that he or she is guilty of theft: it is not legally relevant. See par 683 ante.

691 Evidence in chief by character witnesses in criminal proceedings The prosecution may not lead character evidence (evidence of general reputation), or evidence of particular acts of misconduct by the accused,[1] for the purpose of showing that the accused is of bad character and therefore likely to have committed the offence with which he or she has been charged. (Evidence may, however, be adduced by the prosecution, despite its tendency to show that the accused is of bad character, if it is admissible under the similar fact rule; evidence that the accused has previously been convicted of an offence is, necessarily, admissible if it is an essential part of the subsequent offence with which the accused is charged; and in cases of receiving stolen property, the accused's previous convictions may be proved at any stage of the proceedings, in certain circumstances.)[2]

The accused is entitled to lead evidence of his or her own good character either by calling witnesses to testify to it or by testifying to it him or herself.[3] A witness who testifies to the accused's good character may, in theory, speak only of the accused's reputation;[4] but when the accused testifies, he or she cannot give evidence relating to what others say about his or her reputation: the accused may only say that his or her own conduct has been good in certain respects.[5] Evidence of the accused's good character has been said to be mainly relevant to the accused's credibility; but it may be taken equally into account as being relevant to the likelihood of the accused's being guilty.[6]

If the accused attacks the character of the complainant (or any other prosecution witness), the prosecution is not entitled *to lead evidence* showing that the accused is of bad character;[7] but if the accused gives evidence in his or her own defence, his or her character may be attacked in cross-examination.[8] However, if the accused (or his or her witnesses) should testify as to the accused's good character, the prosecution may lead evidence in rebuttal.[9] This evidence is in theory confined to evidence of bad reputation;[10] but evidence of the accused's previous convictions may be received.[11] Where witnesses volunteer evidence that the accused is of good character, the accused's character is not put in issue.[12]

1 *John Makin & Sarah Makin v The Attorney-General for New South Wales* 1894 AC 57 (PC) 65. See further *R v Paluszak* 1938 TPD 427; *R v Butterwasser* 1948 1 KB 4; [1947] 2 All ER 415 (CCA); *S v Sithole* 1980 4 SA 148 (D).

2 See pars 700–705 post.

3 *R v Gimingham* 1946 ED 156; *R v Bellis* [1966] 1 All ER 552 (CCA); *Attwood v R* (1960) 102 CLR 353 (HC of Aust).

4 Theoretically character evidence has to refer to general reputation only (*R v James Rowton* (1865) Le & CA 520; 169 ER 1497), but, as O'Dowd *Evidence* 31 correctly remarks: "In practice, however, evidence is often received to the effect that the accused has been a good husband and father or a diligent employee, has a good war record and so forth."

5 See par 689 fn 5 ante.

6 *R v Stannard* (1837) 7 C & P 673. See further *R v Mary Broadhurst, Theresa Meanley & Herbert Bliss Hill* (1918) 13 CAR 125; *Attwood v R* supra 359: it may be used in disproof of guilt: *R v Richardson, R v Long-man* 1969 QB 299; *R v Longman, R v Richardson* [1968] 2 All ER 761 (CA).

7 *R v Paluszak* supra; *R v Butterwasser* supra; cf *Jones v Director of Public Prosecutions* 1962 AC 365 (HL); [1962] 1 All ER 569 (HL).

8 See par 693 post.

9 *R v Redd* 1923 1 KB 104; *R v James Rowton* supra; *R v Butterwasser* supra.

10 In *R v James Rowton* supra the accused's witnesses had testified to his good character. On appeal it was held that evidence, given by a witness in rebuttal (who could not testify to the accused's reputation ("the neighbourhood's opinion")) to the effect that, in the opinion of the witness and others, the accused was "a man capable of the grossest indecency and the most flagrant immorality", had been wrongly received.

11 There is a *dictum* to this effect in *R v Redd* supra. O'Dowd 32 argues that *Redd's* case is not applicable in SA because it is in conflict with s 300 of the Criminal Procedure Act 56 of 1955 (which corresponds with s 211 of the Criminal Procedure Act 51 of 1977). In *Redd's* case a passage in Archbold *Pleading, Evidence and Practice* 36 ed 382, which said that the prosecution could prove the prisoner's previous convictions, was approved. Cross *Evidence* 349 points out that Archbold was relying on *R v Gadbury* (1838) 8 C & P 676 and *R v James Shrimpton* (1851) 2 Den 319. These cases relate to the proof of previous convictions under the Previous Convictions Act 1836 6 & 7 Will 4 and s 116 of the Larceny Act 1861 (24 & 25 Vict); they do not have a general significance and relate only to the special procedure under those statutes. It is this special procedure which, in O'Dowd's view (above), conflicts with South African statue law. *R v Triganzie* (1888) 15 OR 294 (cited by Cross 349) is authority for the view that in Canada, before the introduction of s 573 of the Canadian Criminal Code, a conviction was inadmissible to rebut evidence of character at common law.

12 *R v Redd* supra; see further, Zeffertt *Evidence* 240 fn 95; O'Dowd 33.

692 Witnesses (other than the accused) A witness's bad character is relevant to his or her credibility and a witness (other than the accused) may be asked whether he or she has a general reputation for untruthfulness. If the witness denies that he or she has such reputation, contradictory evidence may be adduced by calling a witness to testify that he or she would not believe the witness on his or her oath.[1] The witness's reasons for having such a disbelief may not be given in evidence in chief; but he or she may be cross-examined on them.[2]

Since witnesses are initially presumed to be of good character, evidence to show that a witness is of good character may not be given in evidence in chief: it would be irrelevant. If, however, a witness should have his or her character impeached by evidence that he or she has a bad reputation, evidence of such witness's good character may be adduced to bolster his or her testimony; but evidence of good character may not be adduced merely because a witness has had his or her character attacked in cross-examination.[3]

A witness who has testified to another's bad character may, subject to the exigency that there has to be an end to testimony, be impeached by character evidence like any other witness.[4]

Because the credibility of witnesses is always a material consideration, a witness (other than the accused)[5] may, subject to the privilege against self-incrimination and the protection given by the court to witnesses against questions that tend unduly to degrade character,[6] be asked relevant questions tending to show that he or she is of bad character and, therefore, unworthy of credit. The fact that a witness has been charged, but not convicted, of an offence proves nothing and is irrelevant. *A fortiori*, evidence that a complaint has been laid against a witness is immaterial. A witness may not, therefore, be cross-examined on complaints or charges that have not resulted in a conviction.[7]

In general, a witness's answers to a question put to that witness in cross-examination is final if it relates, according to traditional theory, to "collateral facts". This lacks precision.[8] A more recent tendency is to distinguish between questions that are relevant to credibility and questions that are relevant to an issue. An answer to the former is final.[9] To this there are exceptions, of which the following would be germane in this context: if the witness denies having been convicted of an offence, his or her previous conviction may be proved;[10] and if the witness denies that he or she has a reputation for untruthfulness, evidence may be adduced to show that the witness has such a reputation.[11] It would, perhaps, be better to formulate the rule thus: evidence will be inadmissible in rebuttal if it can serve only to prove that a witness is the kind of person who should be regarded as being untrustworthy or not worthy of being believed because he or she lied to the court.[12]

A witness may be impeached by evidence showing that his or her physical or mental condition throws doubt on his or her truthfulness or reliability.[13]

1 *R v Brown & Hedley* (1867) LR 1 CCR 70; (1867) 10 Cox CC 453; *Mawson v Hartsink* (1802) 4 Esp 102; cf *R v James Watson* (1817) 2 Stark 116; 22 Digest (Repl) 456 4418; see the discussion of these cases in Cross *Evidence* 237–238, and see, further, O'Dowd *Evidence* 28; *Toohey v Metropolitan Police Commissioner* 1965 AC 595 (HL) 606. See further *R v Adamstein* 1937 CPD 331 334.

2 *R v Richardson, R v Longman* 1969 QB 299; *R v Longman, R v Richardson* [1968] 2 All ER 761 (CCA); Cross 319–321; O'Dowd 28.

3 *R v Moore* 1948 2 SA 227 (C); cf *R v Wood* [1951] 2 All ER 112; *R v Benjamin* 1914 TPD 27.

4 O'Dowd 28–29, who cites *R v Walter Whelan* (1881) 14 Cox CC 595.

5 See par 694 post.

6 See par 776 post.

7 See the analogous position relating to the accused who has put his or her character in issue and who testifies in his or her own defence: par 694 post.

8 Schmidt *Bewysreg* 420–1; *S v Sinkankanka* 1963 2 SA 531 (A) 539; *S v Damalis* 1984 2

SA 105 (T); *S v Zwane* 1993 3 SA 393 (W); 1993 1 SACR 748 (W).

9 Ibid; *S v ffrench-Beytagh (3)* 1971 4 SA 571 (T) 572.

10 By virtue of s 6 of the Criminal Procedure Act 1865 (28 & 29 Vict c 18) which is incorporated into South African criminal procedure.

11 *R v Brown & Hedley* supra; *R v Gunewardene* 1951 2 KB 600; [1951] 2 All ER 290 (CCA); *R v Richardson, R v Longman* supra; *R v Longman, R v Richardson* supra.

12 See Schmidt 448 and the authorities there cited and criticised.

13 *Toohey v Metropolitan Police Commissioner* supra; Andrews 1965 *Crime LR* 641.

693 Cross-examination of character witnesses in criminal proceedings In England it has been held that a witness who testifies that the accused is of good character may be asked in cross-examination about the accused's previous convictions.[1] The matter is open in South Africa;[2] but, when it falls to be decided, English precedent should not be followed.[3] There is some authority, of dubious correctness, for the proposition that a character witness may be cross-examined with regard to a rumour that the accused committed a similar offence.[4] In other respects a character witness may be cross-examined, in the same manner as any other witness, about his or her own credibility.

1 *R v Winfield* [1939] 4 All ER 164 (CCA); *R v Redd* 1923 1 KB 104.

2 *R v Roberts* 1916 TPD 495.

3 See par 691 ante; and see Zeffertt *Evidence* 230.

4 *R v Wood & Parker* (1841) 5 Jur 225 cited by Cross *Evidence* 332 who maintains that character in this context means disposition as well as reputation.

694 The accused as a witness In terms of section 197 of the Criminal Procedure Act[1] an accused who gives evidence cannot be asked or required to answer any question tending to show that he or she has committed or has been convicted of or has been charged with any offence other than the offence with which he or she has been charged or that the accused is of bad character, unless the accused (or his or her legal representative) asks any question of any witness with a view to establishing his or her own good character, or unless the nature and conduct of the defence is such as to involve imputation of the character of the complainant or any other witness for the prosecution;[2] or unless he or she gives evidence against any other person charged with the same offence or an offence in respect of the same facts;[3] or unless the proceedings are such as described in section 240 or section 241 of the Act;[4] or unless the proof that the accused has committed or has been convicted of such other offence is admissible evidence to show that he or she is guilty of the offence with which he or she has been charged.[5]

The section proscribes questions that have a mere tendency to expose the accused to character attack. The approach is objective: what is important is the *effect* of the question and not the motive for asking it.[6] "Tending to show" means "tending to make known" or "to reveal".[7]

The section, except in certain special cases, prohibits questions that are relevant only to the accused's bad character; it does not prohibit questions that are relevant to an issue.[8]

An accused gives evidence of his or her good character when the accused asserts, or elicits, that he or she is of good character independently of his or her giving an account of what happened: the accused must endeavour (by means of questions or his evidence) to refer to his or her good character independently of the facts, specifically in order to have it taken into account as something in his or her favour: a mere canvassing of the relevant facts is insufficient to penalise the accused even if the facts may incidentally show the accused's character in a good light.[9]

Where an accused puts his or her character in issue, such accused may be cross-examined on his or her general reputation, disposition and specific acts of misconduct like any witness called by the accused to prove good character.[10] Character is indivisible. There is some authority that, once his or her good character has been put in issue, the accused may be cross-examined on all aspects of it that may be relevant to the accused's credibility even if they are irrelevant to any issue.[11]

The accused does not incur the procedural penalty of being exposed to cross-examination relating to his or her bad character if he or she does no more than properly develop the merits of the case, that is to say, where what the accused does is relevant to the question of his or her guilt.[12] Although it has been held that the accused does not put his or her character in issue by an act which is "an essential portion of the proof that the conduct of the accused is not criminal",[13] the weight of South African judicial authority suggests that the matter should be formulated thus: the mere fact that the nature or conduct of the defence involves, expressly or by implication, a serious imputation on the character of the complainant (or any other witness for the prosecution) does not put the accused's character in issue (if the accused should testify as a witness in his or her own defence) when what was done by the accused (or his or her legal representative or witnesses) is relevant to the question of the accused's guilt; but where the attack on the character of a prosecution witness is relevant to that witness's credibility only, the accused will be exposed to such procedural penalisation.[14] South African law differs from the English law in this regard.[15]

An imputation on the character of a prosecution witness may sometimes not be regarded as sufficient to expose the accused to having his or her character attacked in cross-examination unless it is sufficiently an imputation of his or her veracity to warrant this drastic consequence.[16] In any event, the court has a discretion to exclude cross-examination, even if the accused has technically exposed him or herself to character attack under the proviso, where it would be unfair to the accused. The fact that the imputation was not of a serious nature would be a relevant factor in the exercise of such a discretion.[17]

The prosecutor should not by his or her questions tempt, or drive, the accused to do something which might put the accused's character in issue[18] and it is good practice to warn an accused (particularly if the accused is unrepresented or ineptly defended) against exposing him or herself to attack.[19] Where counsel who appears on behalf of a number of accused attacks the character of a prosecution witness, such counsel should make it clear, initially, on behalf of which of the accused he or she is making the imputation lest he or she puts the character of all the accused in jeopardy.[20]

When one co-accused cross-examines another, who is charged with the same offence or in respect of the same facts, on his or her character,[21] he or she exercises a right and therefore the co-accused is not the victim of a procedural penalty.[22] Consequently there is no judicial discretion to stop such a cross-examination.[23]

The fact that an accused's character is in issue because the accused has impugned the character of a witness for the prosecution, does not entitle the prosecution to adduce character evidence against him or her in evidence-in-chief.[24]

---

1   51 of 1977. The section is substantially the same as s 1(f) read with s 1(e) of the English Criminal Evidence Act 1898 (61 & 62 Vict c36); but there are slight, albeit significant, modifications, particularly in s 197(b).

2   Criminal Procedure Act 51 of 1977 s 197(a).

3   S 197(b).

4   S 197(c).

5   S 197(d).

6   *R v Du Preez* 1943 AD 562 574. For instance, the following questions have the proscribed tendency: one that suggests that the accused was loitering at a police station: *R v Simon* 1925 TPD 297; or that the accused has previously been searched by the police: *R v Lipschitz* 1921 AD 282 287. The

mere asking of such a forbidden question is irregular and the judicial officer has to stop prohibited questions even if the accused does not object: *R v W* 1947 2 SA 708 (A) 717.

7 *Jones v Director of Public Prosecutions* 1962 AC 365 (HL); [1962] 1 All ER 569 (HL); if the accused has already revealed something that shows him or her to be of bad character, the prohibition falls away; see further Cross *Evidence* 391–392 and Schmidt *Bewysreg* 308; but see Zeffertt *Evidence* 237–238..

8 *S v Mokoena* 1967 1 SA 440 (A); see further *R v Rorke* 1915 AD 145; *R v Lipschitz* supra, which indicates that s 197(d) is supererogatory: it is included *ex abundant cautela*. English law is different (*Jones v Director of Public Prosecutions* supra) and also Rhodesian law: *R v Malindi* 1963 4 SA 677 (FC); the position of SA is attributable, to some extent, to an accident of draftsmanship (Zeffertt 236). There are *dicta* in Australia (which Heydon *Evidence* 276–277 calls "obscure") that support the SA conclusion: *Attwood v R* (1960) 102 CLR 353 (HC of Aust); see further Cross 391; Schmidt 308.

9 *R v Malindi* 1966 4 SA 123 (PC); *Keiswe Malindi v R* 1967 AC 439; *R v Ellis* 1910 2 KB 746; cf *Orman v R* 1941 SWA 11; *R v Ferguson* (1909) 2 CAR 250; *R v Baker* (1912) 7 CAR 252; *R v Henry Beecham* 1921 3 KB 464; *R v Samuel Parker* (1924) 18 CAR 14; *R v Stanley Darley Coulman* (1927) 20 CAR 106; *R v Samuel* (1956) 40 CAR 8. See further Cross 399.

10 See par 689 ante.

11 An *obiter dictum* in *R v Winfield* (1939) 27 CAR 139 approved, possibly, in *Stirland v Director of Public Prosecutions* 1944 AC 315 (HL) 324; [1944] 2 All ER 13 (HL) 18; see Cross 403–404; contra: Schmidt 309 fn 432. See also par 689 ante.

12 *S v V* 1962 3 SA 365 (E). See further *R v Lipschitz* supra; *R v Du Preez* supra; *Spence v R* 1946 NPD 696; *R v Rouse* 1904 1 KB 184 189.

13 *R v Hendrickz* 1933 TPD 451 458.

14 See the authorities cited in fn 12 supra. Thus the accused will not be penalised in a rape case if his defence is that the complainant consented to intercourse: *R v James Turner* 1944 KB 463; [1944] 1 All ER 599 (CCA); *Selvey v Director of Public Prosecutions* 1970 AC 304; [1968] 2 All ER 497 (HL); or where the defence implies or suggests that the prosecution witness has committed perjury by implicating him: *R v Du Preez* supra; see further *R v Lipschitz* supra; *R v Hendrickz* supra; or where the evidence throws light on how, or why, trouble between the complainant arose and this is relevant to the accused's defence: *Spence v R* supra; or where a woman maintains that she is pregnant by an accused who is alleged to have had illegal intercourse with her and she is cross-examined, and evidence is led to show that she could have been made pregnant by other men: *S v V* supra. Cf *R v Jenkins* (1945) 114 LJKB 425; (1945) 31 CAR 1; *R v Morrison* (1911) 6 CAR 159.

15 Cf *Selvey v Director of Public Prosecutions* supra where the House of Lords regarded the equivalent English provision as being clear and unambiguous and gave effect to what was regarded as its literal, grammatical meaning whilst, anomalously, recognising that an exception (or apparent exception) exists in the case of a defence of consent in a rape case. The better view is that the proviso contains profound obscurities (see Stone 1935 *LQR* 443 466). A similar formulation to that of South African law is to be found in *Dawson v R* (1961) 106 CLR 1 (HC of Aust); and see *Curwood v R* (1944) 69 CLR 561 (HC of Aust) 588. See further Zeffertt 240–241; Heydon 294–301; Stone 369.

16 Cross 405 and the authorities there cited.

17 *R v Klisser & Rosenberg* 1949 3 SA 807 (W); *Selvey v Director of Public Prosecutions* supra; see further, Heydon 298.

18 *R v Eidenow* (1932) 23 CAR 145; Cross 358.

19 *R v Cook* 1959 2 QB 340; 1959 2 All ER 97.

20 *R v Heyne* (2) 1958 1 SA 612 (W).

21 *R v Heyne* (2) supra; and see *R v Myataza* 1932 EDL 108 for an illustration of the working of the proviso. The new s 197(b) is worded differently from s 228(b) of the Criminal Procedure Act 56 of 1955 which it replaces. The old provision was defectively drafted (it provided for joint trials where the accused were tried for the same offence only: Zeffertt 243). Now all joint trials are covered.

22 *R v Bagas* 1952 1 SA 437 (A) 440–441.

23 *Murdoch v Taylor* 1965 AC 574; 1965 1 All ER 406.

24 See par 691 ante.

695 The complainant Although an accused is entitled to adduce evidence that a witness would not believe the complainant, who gives evidence, on oath,[1] the complainant's character is, normally, irrelevant and the accused has in general no right to lead evidence that the complainant has a bad general character; and the complainant's good character is similarly irrelevant.[2] The accused may attack the complainant's character in cross-examination and when the accused does so, he or she is not, of course, confined to suggesting to the complainant that he or she has a bad general character: specific acts of misconduct may be put. The complainant who testifies is a witness like any other witness. It follows that the complainant's answers to questions in cross-examination that are solely relevant to credibility may, in general, not be rebutted.[3] As amended, the Criminal Procedure Act[4] in section 227(2) provides that evidence regarding sexual intercourse by, or any sexual experience of, any female against or in connection with whom any offence of a sexual nature is alleged to have been committed, may not be adduced, and such female may not be questioned regarding such sexual intercourse or sexual experience, except with the leave of the court, which leave will not be granted unless the court is satisfied that such evidence or questioning is relevant, provided that such evidence may be adduced and such female may be so questioned in respect of the offence which is being tried; section 227(3) provides that before an application for leave contemplated in section 227(2) is heard, the court must direct that any person whose presence is not necessary may not be present at the proceedings, and the court may direct that a female referred to in section 227(2) may not be present; in terms of section 227(4) the provisions of section 227(2) to (3) apply *mutatis mutandis* in respect of a male against or in connection with whom any offence of an indecent nature is alleged to have been committed.[5]

That the accused has had intercourse with the complainant on previous occasions is relevant to the issue of consent and, accordingly, testimony by the accused to this effect is not, strictly speaking, "character evidence": it constitutes a relevant and admissible circumstantial fact.[6]

Where the charge is criminal *iniuria*, the fact that the complainant lacks *dignitas* is a defence.[7] The complainant's character is, therefore, in issue and evidence may be adduced to show that the complainant has the reputation of lacking dignity.[8] It has been suggested that previous conduct showing that the complainant lacks dignity may be received.[9] As regards charges of criminal defamation, evidence that the complainant is generally reputed to lack *fama* should, in principal, be received.[10] Where the charge is common assault, the complainant's lack of dignity or *fama* would not be a defence and the complainant's reputation in these respects would be irrelevant and inadmissible:[11] if the accused were to set up self-defence, the complainant's general reputation for violence and depravity could be relevant;[12] where the charge is indecent assault, the complainant's reputation may be as relevant as in a rape case.[13]

1 This flows from the fact that the complainant, here, is a witness like any other witness; the impeaching witness cannot, in examination in chief, be allowed to give his or her reasons for this belief: see par 693 ante; *R v Richardson, R v Longman* 1969 QB 299.

2 The complainant is not a party. See *R v Wood* [1951] 2 All ER 112. But, of course, if the evidence in rebuttal has a relevance to an issue other than by way of character, it is admissible: *R v M* 1970 1 SA 323 (RA). Cf *R v Benjamin* 1914 TPD 27.

3 See par 692 ante.

4 51 of 1977.

5 Criminal Law and the Criminal Procedure Act Amendment Act 39 of 1989 s 2. See *S v M* 2003 1 SA 341 (SCA); 2002 2 SACR 411 (SCA) where the court found no authority to interpret this section as intended to "militate against offensive, hostile and irrelevant questioning of complainants". The court also took account of the difficulty of determining whether cross-examination is relevant either to the issues or credibility: See further Zeffertt *Evidence* 246–247.

6 *R v Riley* 1957 2 SA 407 (A).

7 See title CRIMINAL LAW.
8 *R v Van Tonder* 1932 TPD 90.
9 Zeffertt *Evidence* 247 cites the case of *R v Curtis* 1926 CPD 385 where it was held that two specific acts of bad behaviour destroyed the complainants *dignitas*. He comments that this type of case should be reconsidred in the light of what is now regarded as the infereneces that may properly be drawn from sexual conduct.
10 O'Dowd 30 argues that the complainant's

reputation is in issue in a criminal case whenever it would be in issue in civil proceedings. As regards the plaintiff's character in a defamation suit, see par 699 post.
11 O'Dowd 30. But would these factors not be relevant to whether the accused's acts were of a serious nature or not and, therefore, relevant to sentence?
12 As is the deceased's in homicide: par 697 post.
13 Zeffertt 244 equates the position to rape.

696 The deceased in homicide cases Evidence of the deceased's character may be given if it is relevant. Thus, where the accused's defence is that he or she acted in self-defence, evidence may be led of the deceased's reputation for violence or depravity. Similarly, the deceased's character may be relevant where the accused maintains that he or she was provoked.[1]

1 *R v Biggin* 1920 1 KB 213; 1918–1919 All ER 501; see further *R v Thomas Hopkins* (1866) 10 Cox CC 229 (Phipson *Evidence* par 542): previous assaults by the deceased have been received.

697 Charges of keeping a brothel The bad character of women who frequent premises is relevant to the use to which those premises are put. Accordingly, evidence may be led by the prosecution that such women have the general reputation of being prostitutes.[1]

1 Cross and Wilkins *Evidence* 201.

698 The plaintiff and the defendant The character of the parties to a civil suit is normally irrelevant. In a defamation action, however, where the defendant pleads justification, the plaintiff's reputation is not in issue but specific instances may be relevant to the issue whether the defamatory words were true.[1] Again, when the defendant pleads privilege and avers that he or she had an honest belief in what he or she said, the truth of the defamatory words, and hence specific acts, may be relevant.[2] Reputation, or character in the proper sense, is relevant in mitigation of damages;[3] evidence of specific instances is inadmissible for this purpose.[4] Although it is unnecessary for the defendant to plead that the plaintiff is of bad character when the defendant wishes to rely on it in mitigation of damages, it is preferable that the plaintiff should be given prior notice of the defendant's intention to lead such evidence lest he or she be taken by surprise.[5] If the plaintiff gives evidence, he or she may be cross-examined like any other witness and specific acts of misconduct may be put to the plaintiff if they are relevant to his or her credibiltiy.[6] The plaintiff's general character is an issue and admissible in cases of seduction,[7] breach of promise[8] and adultery.[9] The character of the defendant is normally irrelevant and inadmissible whether in the form of specific acts[10] or, in the true sense of the word, reputation.[11] The reputation of the defendant will, however, be relevant to damages in a divorce action based on adultery.[12]

1 *SA Associated Newspapers Ltd v Yutar* 1967 3 SA 454 (A); and see *Williams v Shaw* (1884) 4 EDC 105.
2 *Vengtas v Nydoo* (5) 1963 4 SA 358 (D).
3 *Black v Joseph* 1931 AD 132; *Senkge v Bredenkamp* 1948 1 SA 1145 (O); *Thole v*

Minister of Justice 1967 3 SA 531 (D); *Geyser v Pont* 1968 4 SA 67 (W).
4 See the authorities cited in fn 3 supra; and see further *Plato Films Ltd v Speidel* 1961 AC 1090; (1961) 2 WLR 470 476; *Sutter v Brown* 1926 AD 155; but see *Goody v*

Odhams Press Ltd 1967 1 QB 333 (CA); [1966] 3 All ER 369 (CA); and cf *Walton v Cohn* 1947 2 SA 225 (N). It is possible that specific facts may be relevant for this purpose when the factors that the defendant relies on to mitigate damages are to be found in the circumstances in which the defamatory statement was made or in the truth of the allegation: Schmidt *Bewysreg* 442.

5 *Klisser v SA Associated Newspapers Ltd* 1964 3 SA 308 (C); *Thole v Minister of Justice* supra.

6 See par 695 ante. See further *Hobbs v Tinling (CT) & Co Ltd, Hobbs v Nottingham Journal Ltd* 1929 2 KB 1; 1929 All ER 33.

7 *Gleeson v Durrheim* 1869 Buch 244; *Van Staden v Rudy* 1908 EDC 7.

8 Specific acts as well as reputation in mitigation of damages and as relevant to a defence: Schmidt 442 who cites *Foulkes v Sellway* (1800) 3 Esp 236; *Baddeley v Mortlock* (1816) Holt 151; *Jefferson v Paskell* 1916 1 KB 57 68.

9 Either where the plaintiff's adultery is raised as a defence (Schmidt 442) or where the plaintiff's character is relevant to the quantum of damages – the reputation of both the spouses and the co-respondent is relevant in the latter regard: Zeffertt *Evidence* 249; Phipson *Evidence* 541; *Viviers v Kilian* 1927 AD 449; *Doyle v Salgo (1)* 1958 1 SA 36 (FC).

10 *Groenewald v Germishuys* 1914 CPD 268.

11 Schmidt 443.

12 *Butterworth v Butterworth & Englefield, Collins v Collins & Harrison, Barratt v Barratt & Fox, Howell v Howell & Walker, Adams v Adams & Ward, Ellworthy v Ellworthy & Ledgard* 1920 P 126 142–144; and see *Viviers v Kilian* supra; *Doyle v Salgo (1)* supra: where the plaintiff alleges adultery against the co-respondent, his spouse's character is relevant whether she is a defendant or not.

SIMILAR FACT EVIDENCE

699 Introduction The same considerations apply to the reception or exclusion of similar fact evidence in criminal and civil cases except that, in civil proceedings, the courts have not been so wary of admitting such evidence.[1]

In essence, the criminal courts have been very careful not to admit similar fact evidence unless its value as proof warrants its reception in the interests of justice and its reception does not operate unfairly against the accused.[2]

Traditionally the similar fact rule, as applies to criminal cases, is expressed by the juxtaposition of two principles: similar fact evidence cannot be used to show that the accused is the kind of person likely to have committed the crime with which he or she is charged, but it may be used when it is relevant to an issue before the court provided that this is not a relevance that rests solely on character.[3] This means that similar facts can only be admissible as relevant to an issue once they have not been excluded because of being relevant solely by way of character.[4]

It is a chain of reasoning that is prohibited and not necessarily a statement of fact.[5] If evidence is adduced to further the conclusion, by a process of reasoning, that the accused is a bad person and, therefore, likely to have committed the offence, the evidence is excluded; if there is some relevant, probative purpose for it other than for the prohibited form of reasoning, it may be received but, when it is received, the trier of fact must eschew the forbidden reasoning.[6]

This traditional approach was formulated by Lord Hershell in *John Makin and Sarah Makin v The Attorney-General for New South Wales*.[7] His remarks in that decision, which is regarded as the leading case,[8] have been applied again and again and are considered to be of crystal clarity.[9] They explain satisfactorily the reception or rejection of similar evidence in many instances, but there are some instances where they do not.[10] At times an accused's criminal propensity itself becomes so highly relevant to the question of his or her guilt in the circumstances of a particular case that it would be absurd not to use it.[11] Put in another way, justice demands its reception because of its strong probative force. Thus, sometimes, an accused's abnormal propensity may be a means of identification.[12] It is specious casuistry to say, when such evidence is received, that it has a relevance going beyond a relevance based on propensity. Be that as it may, the courts are reluctant to say explicitly that they admit such evidence because propensity itself is, in the circumstances, of great probative force.[13] It has been suggested that, because of this factor, the tendency of late in South Africa has been to avoid the *Makin* formulation and rather to ask whether there is a nexus in time, or place, or circumstance between similar facts and the facts in issue.[14] This is unhelpful and "seems to be only another way of saying that similar fact evidence must be highly relevant to the issue of guilt" if it is to be received.[15]

To the *Makin* formulation is added a rider: even where similar fact evidence is technically admissible it may, as a matter of practice, be excluded when its potentiality to prejudice an accused outweighs its probative value.[16] Such a residual discretionary rule serves only to obfuscate matters. If evidence is of such a nature that it is not worthy of being admitted because its probative force is not so strong as to warrant its admission in the light of the disadvantages of admitting it, *it is not legally relevant*[17] and is, therefore, inadmissible. Such a discretionary rule might serve a purpose where there is a jury system (the court might feel that the evidence would have a probative value, *vis-à-vis* a lawyer, that outweighs its potentiality to prejudice an accused but that, *vis-à-vis* a layman, its potentiality to cause prejudice outweighs its probative value) but it is of no use in South Africa which has done away with juries.[18]

A proper formulation of the similar fact rule demands that a stress should be placed on the fact that the admissibility of such evidence depends upon its *degree* of relevance;[19] that in the determination of this much depends on the experience and common sense of the judge;[20] that relevance does not exist in a vacuum;[21] and that there is no closed list of areas in which similar fact evidence is admissible.[22]

1 Per Lord Denning MR in *Mood Music Publishing Co Ltd v De Wolfe Ltd* [1976] 1 All ER 763 (CA) 766. The test is one of relevance: *R v Troskie* 1920 AD 466; *R v Mpanza* 1915 AD 348 352; *R v Kalkiwich & Kruger* 1942 AD 79 87; *S v Green* 1962 3 SA 886 (A) 894; *S v R* 1972 4 SA 57 (NC); *Jones v S* 1970 2 PH H129 (A).

2 *Mood Music Publishing Co Ltd v De Wolfe Ltd* supra 766.

3 *John Makin & Sarah Makin v The Attorney-General for New South Wales* 1894 AC 57 (PC). For a discussion of this formulation, see Hoffmann 1975 *LQR* 193; Sklar 1977 *McGill LJ* 60; Zeffertt 1977 *SALJ* 399.

4 Hoffmann 197: "The two branches are mutually exclusive: the second branch is residuary and admits only such evidence as is not excluded by the terms of the first."

5 *Director of Public Prosecutions v Boardman* 1975 AC 421 (HL); *Boardman v Director of Public Prosecutions* [1974] 3 All ER 887 (HL).

6 *Director of Public Prosecutions v Boardman* supra.

7 1894 AC 57 (PC).

8 *R v Katz* 1946 AD 71 79. See further *R v Zawels* 1937 AD 342 351; *S v Green* supra 894; *S v R* supra 60–61.

9 *Director of Public Prosecutions v Boardman* supra 461; *Boardman v Director of Public Prosecutions* supra 912 per Lord Salmon, who went on to say: "I doubt whether the learned analyses and explanations of that passage to which it has been subjected so often in the last 80 years add very much to it."

10 See pars 699 700 post.

11 Ibid.

12 Ibid.

13 Ibid.

14 Zeffertt *Evidence* 258.

15 Ibid.

16 *Harris v Director of Public Prosecutions* 1952 AC 694 (HL); [1952] 1 All ER 1044 (HL); *Director of Public Prosecutions v Boardman* supra.

17 *S v Green* supra 893–894. For a discussion of legal relevance, see par 683 ante.

18 *R v Velekaze* 1947 1 SA 162 (W); *R v Solomons* 1959 2 SA 352 (A) 362; *R v Roets* 1954 3 SA 512 (A) 521.

19 See pars 700 701 post.

20 Ibid.

21 See pars 680–688 ante.

22 See par 701 post.

700 Criminal proceedings: general rule The admission of similar fact evidence in criminal proceedings is exceptional and requires a strong degree of probative force.[1] Its admissibility depends upon its degree of relevance[2] in the circumstances[3] and the determination of this much depends on the experience and common sense of the judicial officer.[4] The reception of similar facts has to be warranted by their having so strong a probative value, in the circumstances, that they should be received in the interests of justice despite any disadvantages that there may be in admitting them.[5] Thus if their probative value is not so great as to outweigh the prejudice they may cause the accused, they should be excluded because their reception would operate unfairly against the accused.[6] Although there is a plethora of authority for the proposition that similar fact evidence is inadmissible if its sole relevance is to show that the accused's character is such as to make his or her guilt likely,[7] there are instances where evidence of the accused's criminal propensity has been of so strong a probative value as to warrant its reception.[8]

1 *Director of Public Prosecutions v Boardman* 1975 AC 421 (HL); *Boardman v Director of Public Prosecutions* [1974] 3 All ER 887 (HL) applied in *S v R* 1977 1 SA 9 (T). See further *R v Troskie* 1920 AD 466; *R v Katz* 1946 AD 71; *R v Viljoen* 1947 2 SA 56 (A); *R v L* 1951 4 SA 614 (A). See further Hoffmann 1975 *LQR* 193 195; Zeffertt 1977 *SALJ* 399. See also *S v Banana* 2000 2 SACR 1 (ZS). The criminal courts have been very careful not to admit such evidence unless its probative value is so strong that it should be received in the interests of justice: *Mood Music Publishing Co Ltd v De Wolfe Ltd* [1976] 1 All ER 763 (CA) 766.

2 It "requires a strong degree of probative force": *Director of Public Prosecutions v Boardman* supra 444; *Boardman v Director of Public Prosecutions* supra 897 (italics supplied); *Harris v Director of Public Prosecutions* 1952 AC 694 (HL) 710; [1952] 1 All ER 1044 (HL) 1050. See further *R v Troskie* supra; *R v Katz* supra; Hoffmann 195; Zeffertt 399. The difference between irrelevant and relevant evidence rests on a distinction in degree and not in kind; see pars 680–689 ante. It is a flexible principle: Wigmore *Evidence* 2 par 302 201; Hoffmann 1974 *SALJ* 236.

3 Relevance is not a neutral concept with monolithic attributes; it does not exist in a vacuum. See pars 680–688 ante.

4 *Director of Public Prosecutions v Boardman* supra 444; *Boardman v Director of Public Prosecutions* supra 698; *Director of Public Prosecutions v Kilbourne* 1973 AC 729 (HL) 756; [1973] 1 All ER 440 (HL) 461. Lord Wilberforce remarked in *Director of Public Prosecutions v Boardman* supra 444: "And in matters of experience it is for the judge to keep close to current mores. What is striking in one age is normal in another: the perversions of yesterday may be

the routine or the fashion of tomorrow."

5 *Director of Public Prosecutions v Boardman* supra; *Mood Music Publishing Co Ltd v De Wolfe Ltd* supra. See further par 701 post.

6 In *Harris v Director of Public Prosecutions* supra it was said that the judge has a discretion to exclude admissible similar fact evidence whose probative value is outweighed by its potential to prejudice the accused. See further *Director of Public Prosecutions v Boardman* supra; while this may be of use in a jury system (see par 701 post), it would be otiose in SA where juries have been abolished. Evidence of this kind should be regarded as being legally irrelevant and therefore inadmissible. The test is not whether evidence is logically relevant but whether it is legally relevant: *S v Green* 1962 3 SA 886 (A) 893–894.

7 *John Makin & Sarah Makin v The Attorney-General of New South Wales* 1894 AC 57 (PC); and see eg among many other decisions, *R v Troskie* supra; *R v Davis* 1925 AD 30; *R v Viljoen* supra; *R v L* supra; *R v D* 1958 4 SA 364 (A); *S v Green* supra 894; *S v R* 1972 4 SA 57 (NC); *S v B* 1976 2 SA 54 (C). See further *R v Horwood* 1970 QB 133 (CA); *Director of Public Prosecutions v Kilbourne* supra.

8 Thus the accused's abnormal propensity was relevant, in the circumstances of *Thompson v R* 1918 AC 221 (HL); 1918–1919 All ER 521 and *R v Straffen* 1952 2 QB 911 (CCA); [1952] 2 All ER 657 (CCA) to the accused's identity; in *R v William Henry Ball, R v Edith Lilian Ball* 1911 AC 47 (HL) and *R v Sims* 1946 KB 531 (CCA); [1946] 1 All ER 697 (CCA) to show that equivocal acts were guilty acts; see further *S v R* 1977 1 SA 9 (T) and cf *R v Davis* supra; *R v D* supra. See Cowen and Carter *Evidence* 119; Heydon

Evidence 263–264; Zeffertt 399. See further par 701 post. (There may be a situation in which the presence or absence of a particular character trait is in issue. Here conduct on other occasions, from which an inference relating to that issue may properly be drawn, will of course be relevant: *SA Associated Newspapers Ltd v Yutar* 1967 3 SA 454 (A)).

701 Application of the general rule in criminal proceedings In deciding whether similar fact evidence is probative of an issue, experience plays as large a part as logic.[1] The judge has to take into account current mores: what is striking in one age is normal in another.[2] Evidence of other occurrences which merely tend to deepen suspicion does not go to prove guilt.[3] The evidence has to be of sufficient probative value, having regard to the purpose to which it is directed, to make it desirable in the interests of justice that it should be admitted.[4] Various tests of relevancy have been laid down: is there a nexus in time, in method or in circumstance?[5] Is there such an underlying unity between the evidence as to make coincidence an affront to common sense?[6] But these tests say nothing more than that the evidence must be highly relevant[7] and it is better to look at the circumstances of each case and then to decide whether the advantages of admitting the evidence outweigh, or do not outweigh, the disadvantages of excluding it.[8] It is an error to attempt to draw up a closed list of the sort of general application.[9] The danger of illustrating the application of the principle by the categorisation of instances is that it may lead to an erroneous approach in which categories of admissibility are regarded as exceptions.[10] Such an approach leads to casuistry, to insoluble metaphysical problems as to the confines of the categories, and to the error of thinking that, because evidence slots into a category, it will be admissible.[11] With this warning in mind the illustrations of the application of the principle, below, may be looked to. The list of examples cannot, by definition, be exhaustive.

Similar fact evidence has been admitted to prove the commission of the actus reus It will not usually be necessary for the prosecution to have to resort to similar fact evidence for this purpose: the nature of the act will appear clearly from a description of the act itself.[12] But, when an act is equivocal, similar fact evidence may resolve the ambiguity,[13] that is to say, show the true nature of the act done by the accused.[14] This has been taken by the Appellate Division to signify that evidence of the repetition of acts may not be used to prove *the commission of an act* in issue but only its *nature* once its commission has been proved by the other admissible evidence.[15] It has been said that, normally, similar conduct shows only propensity and is therefore inadmissible to prove the *actus reus* in question.[16] But this approach is unsound in principle.[17] There are other decisions of the Appellate Division, also, that are inconsistent with the view that similar fact evidence cannot be used to prove the *actus reus*.[18] The House of Lords has held that evidence that a brother and sister had an illicit relationship, was in the circumstances of a particular case, relevant to whether they had committed incest on a subsequent occasion.[19] In other words, their propensity to commit incest was highly relevant to whether the *actus reus*, incest, had taken place.[20] Evidence of similar facts, here, was used to show that equivocal conduct was guilty conduct.[21] These decisions indicate that if similar fact evidence is relevant, if it has sufficient probative force in the circumstances, it may be used to prove the *actus reus*.[22] Thus evidence of the accused's systematic conduct[23] and of the repetition of strikingly similar instances,[24] has been received as relevant to such an issue.

Similar fact evidence has been resorted to in order to prove identity, or to link the accused with the commission of the offence A person with a motive is more likely to commit an offence than a person without a motive and, accordingly, there are instances in which similar fact evidence has been admitted because of its probative force in this regard.[25] Similar fact evidence may also be relevant if it is sufficiently probative of means and opportunity,[26] preparation,[27] special skill and knowledge,[28] method,[29] plan,[30] system or design.[31]

It does not follow that such evidence will necessarily be admissible merely because it is probative of these matters: it will be admissible if, in the circumstances of the case, its probative force is sufficiently strong to warrant its reception despite any prejudice it may cause the accused.[32] It will be inadmissible if its use is merely to deepen suspicion.[33] Again, these are not the only ways in which similar fact evidence may be relevant to identity.[34]

When the perpetrator of an offence must have been someone with an aberrant or bizarre personality, the fact that the accused has such a personality is obviously a relevant factor to link the accused with the commission of the offence.[35] It is not that offences of this kind form a special category:[36] there is nothing "special", for instance, in perversion;[37] but, in the circumstances of a particular case, the fact that an accused has an aberrant disposition *may* be so highly relevant to the question of guilt as to warrant the admission of evidence of his or her aberrant personality despite the disadvantages that there may be in admitting it.[38] In other words, although the decisions invariably say that one cannot use similar fact evidence to show that an accused had character attributes that may make it likely that he or she committed the offence[39] it is inescapable that evidence of an accused's criminal propensity may sometimes, in the circumstances of a particular case, be so highly relevant to guilt as to permit its reception.

Similar fact evidence has been used to prove mens rea[40] The repetition of strikingly similar evidence has been received to show that the accused's conduct was designed and not accidental, or that the accused's possession of something was guilty and not innocent.[41] The basis for the reception of this kind of evidence has been explained as resting on the doctrine of chances: the repetition of instances makes an innocent construction of the accused's actions or possession statistically unlikely.[42] Again, where guilty knowledge has to be proved by the prosecution, similar fact evidence may be relevant to show that it is unlikely that the accused did not have such knowledge.[43] Here the admission of the evidence rests upon the theory that the happening of a previous event may serve as a warning to the accused of the need to be prescient about the nature of a subsequent event.[44]

Similar fact evidence has been used as corroboration when it is relevant to confirm testimony.[45]

When similar fact evidence is admitted to prove negligence it is received because it is relevant. It will be relevant where there is a nexus such as may arise because of an inference (or "presumption") of continuity.[46]

1 *Director of Public Prosecutions v Boardman* 1975 AC 421 (HL) 444; *Boardman v Director of Public Prosecutions* [1974] 3 All ER 887 (HL) 898. See further *Director of Public Prosecutions v Kilbourne* 1973 AC 729 (HL) 756; [1973] 1 All ER 440 (HL) 461.

2 *Director of Public Prosecutions v Boardman* supra 444; *Boardman v Director of Public Prosecutions* supra 898.

3 *Harris v Director of Public Prosecutions* 1952 AC 694 (HL) 708; [1952] 1 All ER 1044 (HL) 1048. See further *Noor Mohamed v R* 1949 AC 182 (PC); [1949] 1 All ER 365 (PC).

4 See par 700 ante.

5 *R v John Bond* 1906 2 KB 389 424; 1906 All ER 24; *S v Green* 1962 3 SA 886 (A) 894;

S v Letsoko 1964 4 SA 768 (A) 775; *S v Gokool* 1965 3 SA 461 (N) 476; *S v R* 1972 4 SA 57 (NC); *Jones v S* 1970 2 PH H129 (A). That this is merely an elaboration of the principle that similar fact evidence is admissible if it is properly relevant emerges clearly from the words of Ogilvie Thompson AJ in *S v Green* supra 894: "facts relevant to the issue may always be proved, and any facts are so relevant if from their existence inferences may properly be drawn, as to the existence of the fact in issue. In order to enable any such inferences so to be drawn, the facts of the case must reveal a sufficient link between that issue and the 'similar facts' tendered in evidence." See further *Ogg v His Majesty's Advocate* 1938 JC 152 160.

6 Lord Simon of Glaisdale in *Director of Public Prosecutions v Kilbourne* supra 759; 461; *Director of Public Prosecutions v Boardman* supra 453–454; *S v R* 1977 1 SA 9 (T) 14.

7 See par 700 ante.

8 Ibid.

9 *R v Katz* 1946 AD 71 79: "Since it has sometimes been contended that the illustrations of relevancy given by Lord Hershell constitute categories into which such evidence must be fitted before it can be regarded as admissible, but this is a mistaken interpretation of the words used by Lord Hershell." See further *Harris v Director of Public Prosecutions* supra 705 1046.

10 As happened, perhaps, in *R v D* 1958 4 SA 364 (A).

11 Hoffmann 1975 *LQR* 193 200; Sklar 1977 *McGill LJ* 60; Zeffertt 1977 *SALJ* 399.

12 Per Nicholas J in *S v R* 1977 1 SA 9 (T) 13–14.

13 Ibid. Thus in *R v Maharaj* 1947 2 SA 65 (A), where an accused was charged with the illegal sale of yeast, evidence of previous transactions between the same parties was admitted as relevant to what had been agreed upon on the occasion in respect of which the charge had been brought. See further *R v Alberts* 1922 TPD 225; *R v Morrison & Auret* 1930 TPD 419.

14 *R v Sims* 1946 KB 531 (CCA) 540; [1946] 1 All ER 697 (CC) 701; *S v R* supra.

15 *R v D* supra.

16 *R v D* supra 369. Cf *S v Gokool* supra; *S v B* 1976 2 SA 54 (C); *S v R* supra.

17 Because the true inquiry is whether the evidence has a strong probative force in the circumstances (and not whether it slots into a category), ie whether it is legally relevant (see above).

18 *R v Katz* supra; *R v Viljoen* 1947 2 SA 56 (A); *Jones v S* supra. See further the adverse criticism of *R v D* supra in *S v B* supra; *S v R* supra; Zeffertt *Evidence* 284–285; Zeffertt 399.

19 *R v William Henry Ball, R v Edith Lilian Ball* 1911 AC 47 (HL).

20 The evidence in *Ball's* case was admitted "to establish the guilty relations between the parties and the existence of a sexual passion between them as elements in proving that they had illicit connection in fact on or between the dates charged": per Lord Loreburen LC 71.

21 *R v William Henry Ball, R v Edith Lilian Ball* supra as explained in *S v R* supra.

22 For a discussion of this, see Zeffertt 399.

23 As in *R v Katz* supra; *R v Swart* 1950 1 SA 818 (T). See further *R v Viljoen* supra; *S v Green* supra (fraud); *R v G* 1959 4 SA 39 (T) 41; *S v Gokool* supra (extortion); *S v Radebe* 1962 4 SA 609 (D) 611 (robbery and murder); *R v Roets* 1954 3 SA 512 (A) (corruption). Similarly, the system may be used in a different context than the proof of the *actus reus* to prove a mode of interrogation: *S v Letsoko* supra; *Gosschalk v Rossouw* 1966 2 SA 476 (C); *S v Yengeni (1)* 1991 1 SACR 322 (C); *S v Yengeni (2)* 1991 1 SACR 329 (C).

24 As in *S v R* supra; *R v Sims* supra; *S v Lebogang* 1980 4 SA 236 (O).

25 *R v Rorke* 1915 AD 145; *R v Le Riche* 1924 OPD 209; *R v Kumalo & Nkosi* 1918 AD 500; *R v Aquadro* 1934 OPD 36; *R v Stolz* 1944 WLD 107; *R v Lee* 1949 1 SA 1134 (A) 1145; *R v Matthews* 1960 1 SA 752 (A).

26 *R v Christians* 1925 TPD 868; *R v Kalkiwich & Kruger* 1942 AD 79; *R v Malini* 1948 1 SA 522 (EDL); *R v E* 1960 2 SA 691 (FC); *R v Solomons* 1959 2 SA 352 (A); *R v Dhlamini* 1960 1 SA 880 (D). See further *R v Armstrong* 1922 2 KB 555; [1922] All ER 153; *R v Kurash* 1937 2 All ER 130. (Cf *R v Dhlamini* supra with *R v Solomons* supra.)

27 *R v Troskie* 1920 AD 466; *R v Hair* 1927 AD 391; *R v D* 1942 CPD 103.

28 *R v Le Riche* supra; *R v Kalkiwich & Kruger* supra.

29 Where the accused is known to use, or threatens to use, a peculiar method to commit a crime and that method has been used to commit a crime: *R v Mpanza* 1915 AD 348; see further *S v M* 1963 3 SA 183 (T); and cf *Harris v Director of Public Prosecutions* supra.

30 Where several crimes are connected together as part of one scheme or plot they may be given in evidence to show the process of motive and design in the individual case: *R v Sebeso* 1943 AD 196; *R v Zawels* 1937 AD 342. Cf *R v Katz* supra; *R v Viljoen* supra where "system" was relevant to the *actus reus*. See also *R v Butelezi* 1944 TPD 254 259. A systematic repetition of instances may be relevant, as well, to *mens rea*; see below.

31 Pars 699 700 ante.

32 Ibid.

33 Ibid.

34 They do not, by definition, constitute categories, but mere applications of a general principle.

35 "Abnormal propensity is a means of identification", per Slade J in *R v Straffen* 1952 2

QB 911 (CCA) 916–917; [1952] 2 All ER 657 (CCA) 662.

36 *Director of Public Prosecutions v Boardman* supra. In *R v L* 1951 4 SA 614 (A) Centlivres CJ remarked: "that to suggest that an unnatural sexual crime such as sodomy should be an exception to the exclusionary rule would be both novel and anomalous." See further *Director of Public Prosecutions v Boardman* supra; *S v R* 1977 1 SA 9 (T).

37 Thus in *Thompson v R* 1918 AC 221 (HL) the accused was charged with having committed acts of gross indecency with two boys on 16 March. According to them he had arranged to meet them subsequently on 19 March near a public lavatory; when he met them he told them to go away and gave them money. He was arrested. His defence to the charge of committing the crimes on the 16th was an alibi. Evidence was received that two powder-puffs were found on the accused and that a number of photographs of naked boys, all indecent in attitude, had been found in his room. *In the circumstances* his abnormal propensity was highly relevant to his identity. See further *R v Straffen* supra; *Director of Public Prosecutions v Boardman* supra; *S v R* supra; Heydon *Evidence* 263–264; Cowen and Carter *Evidence* 119. Cf *R v Davis* 1925 AD 30; *R v D* 1942 CPD 103 where there was no "nexus" between evidence that the accused had an aberrant personality and any issue that the court had to decide, ie where evidence of the accused's perversion was legally irrelevant because it would merely have deepened suspicion. See further Zeffertt *Evidence* 280.

38 See eg *R v Davis* supra; *R v D* supra. This must be the result whenever the *Makin* formulation (see pars 699 700 ante) is applied.

39 As in *R v William Henry Ball*, *R v Edith Lilian Ball* supra; *Thompson v R* supra; *R v Sims* supra; *R v Straffen* supra. See further *S v B* supra. Cf *R v Davis* supra.

40 Either in showing "intent" or "knowledge".

41 *John Makin & Sarah Makin v The Attorney-General for New South Wales* 1894 AC 57 (PC). See also *R v Geering* (1849) 18 LJMC 215; *R v Grills* (1954) 73 WN 303 (Court of Criminal Appeal NSW); *R v Smith* (1915) 84 LJKB 2153; 1915 All ER 262; (1915) 11

CAR 229; *R v De Melker* 1933 WLD 37; *R v Arthur Charles Mortimer* (1936) 25 CAR 150. Cf *Noor Mohamed v R* supra. The same principles govern the reception of evidence to show that an equivocal act was committed with guilty intent: *R v Pharenque* 1927 AD 57. See further *R v John Bond* supra; *Harris v R* 1927 NPD 330. Cf *R v Zawels* supra (which relates to the "system design or plan" situation). Cf *R v Malgas* 1943 CPD 528 with *R v John Bond* supra. See further *R v Janke & Janke* 1913 TPD 382; *R v Khan* 1954 2 SA 340 (A). Before an inference may be drawn as to intent, the instances must be similar. "Similarity" cannot be defined; whether two facts are sufficiently similar to induce rational persuasion must, necessarily, depend on the circumstances of each case. Nor can anything hard and fast be laid down as to how many instances have to be repeated. It depends on the circumstances and the probative force of the similar facts. See *Director of Public Prosecutions v Boardman* supra; pars 699 700 ante.

42 Wigmore *Evidence* 2 par 302 196; Glanville Williams *Proof of Guilt* 230 quotes Lord Maugham: "No reasonable man would believe it possible that Smith had successively married three women, persuaded them to make wills in his favour, bought three baths, placed them in rooms which could not be locked, taken each wife to a doctor and suggested to him that she suffered from epileptic fits, and then had been so unlucky that each of the three had some kind of fit in the bath and been drowned."

43 *R v Keller & Parker* 1915 AD 98. Cf *R v Lipsitch* 1913 TPD 652.

44 *R v Keller & Parker* supra: previous conduct that indicated that the accused knew the difference between glass and diamonds (they had previously attempted to sell glass as diamonds) was relevant to rebut their defence to a charge of theft by false pretenses that glass was diamonds, that they had believed glass to be diamonds.

45 *S v R* 1977 1 SA 9 (T). See further *R v D* 1942 CPD 103; *S v B* supra.

46 Cf *R v Mahametza* 1941 OPD 1 with *R v Pohl* 1939 EDL 5.

702 Different charges Evidence on one count is not relevant and admissible to an issue on another count unless it would have been relevant to that issue if the latter had been the only issue to be tried and there had been one count in the indictment or charge.[1] In other words, the similar fact rule applies.[2]

1 *R v Butelezi* 1944 TPD 254; *S v R* 1977 1
   SA 9 (T) 12.
2 *S v Gokool* 1965 3 SA 461 (N) 475. Cf *R v*

L 1951 4 SA 614 (A). See further Zeffertt
Evidence 284–285.

703 Statutory provisions Section 211 of the Criminal Procedure Act[1] provides
that, except where otherwise provided by the Act[2] or where the fact of a previous
conviction is an element of the offence with which an accused has been charged,[3]
evidence that the accused was previously convicted of any offence (whether in the
Republic or elsewhere), is not receivable. Nor may an accused, if called as a witness,
be asked whether he or she has been so convicted.[4]

This provision does not exclude the admission of evidence of the fact of an accused's previous conviction if it is relevant to an issue under the similar fact rule. The
effect of section 252 of the Criminal Procedure Act is to allow the proof of similar
facts (including the fact of a criminal conviction) according to the rules of English law,
as they were on 30 May 1961.[5] Again, in terms of section 197(d) the accused who
gives evidence may be asked questions tending to show that the accused has been
convicted of such other offence where "the proof that he has committed or been
convicted of such other offence is admissible evidence to show that he is guilty of the
offence with which he has been charged". The fact that the accused has been convicted of a criminal offence, when it is strongly probative of his or her guilt in respect
of the charge, would be admissible evidence to show that the accused is guilty.[6]

Previous convictions may be proved after an accused has been convicted but before
sentence has been passed.[7] In a murder charge they may not be proved, for the purpose of guiding the court as to whether the death sentence should be imposed, before
the court has decided whether there are extenuating circumstances.[8]

Where an accused is charged with receiving stolen property which the accused
knew to be stolen, then, if it is proved that such property was found in the accused's
possession, evidence may be led at any stage of the proceedings that he or she had
been convicted of an offence involving fraud or dishonesty within five years immediately preceding the date on which he or she first appeared in the magistrate's court in
respect of the receiving charge.[9] This evidence may be taken into account for the
purpose of proving that the accused knew the property to have been stolen.[10] Not less
than three days' notice in writing has to be given to the accused that the prosecution
intends to adduce such evidence.[11]

Evidence is also admissible, when the accused is charged with receiving stolen
property, that the accused has been, within the period of 12 months immediately
preceding the date on which he or she first appeared in a magistrate's court in respect
of the charge, found in possession of other stolen property.[12] Not less than three days'
notice in writing has to be given before evidence of this kind may be received.[13] The
evidence may be taken into consideration for the purpose of proving that the accused
knew that the property, which forms the subject of the charge, was stolen.[14]

1 51 of 1977.
2 A previous conviction may be mentioned in
   the charge if it forms part of the offence
   (s 89); it may be alluded to where the accused is cross-examined about the commission of another crime (s 197); in offences
   relating to receiving stolen property (ss 240–
   241 – see below); where similar fact evidence is admissible (see above); in the proof
   of previous convictions for the purpose of

sentence (ss 271–274). In *S v Hlongwa* 1979
4 SA 112 (D) the court decided that the
proceedings in a bail application are not
"criminal proceedings in respect of any offence" as envisaged by s 211, and evidence
of the previous convictions of the accused
may consequently be admitted when his application for bail is considered.
3 S 211.
4 Ibid.

5 Because s 252 expressly, albeit indirectly, incorporates the English principles in force on 30 May 1961. See further Hiemstra *Strafproses* 633.

6 *R v Lipschitz* 1921 AD 282 287; *S v Mokoena* 1967 1 SA 440 (A). See also *R v Rorke* 1915 AD 145.

7 Ss 271–273.

8 *R v Owen* 1957 1 SA 458 (A). In *S v Shabalala* 1966 2 SA 297 (A) 300 301 it was said, however, that previous convictions

may be a factor to be taken into account in rebuttal of averments made by the accused when he attempts to prove extenuating circumstances. This is an exceptional case. See further Hiemstra 686.

9 S 241.

10 Ibid.

11 Ibid.

12 S 240(1). See commentary in Hiemstra 624.

13 S 240(1).

14 S 240(2).

704 Similar facts in civil cases Similar fact evidence is admissible in civil proceedings if its probative value is strong enough to warrant its reception in the interests of justice and its admission will not operate unfairly against the other party or parties.[1] In other words, the principle is the same as that in criminal cases.[2] The courts, however, are less wary of receiving similar fact evidence in the civil context than they are in the criminal context.[3] Logically relevant similar fact evidence should be excluded if its reception would create side issues that would unduly distract the trier of fact from the main issue.[4] Unduly prejudicial similar fact evidence would also be excluded.[5] So should collateral facts whose proof and counterproof would take up undue time[6] or whose reception would take the other side by surprise.[7]

1 *Mood Music Publishing Co Ltd v De Wolfe Ltd* [1976] 1 All ER 763 (CA) 766.

2 *Mood Music Publishing co Ltd v De Wolfe Ltd* supra 766.

3 *Mood Music Publishing co Ltd v De Wolfe Ltd* supra 766. The following decisions, among many others, afford an illustration of the application of the principle: *Holcombe v Hewson* (1810) 2 Camp 391; *Hollingham v Head* (1858) 4 CB (NS) 388; 140 ER 1135; *Kennedy v Dodson* 1895 1 Ch 334 (CA); *Manchester Brewery Co Ltd v Coombs* (1) (1900) 82 LT 347; *Metropolitan Asylum District Managers v Hill* 47 LT 29; *Hales v Kerr* 1908 2 KB 601; *Wilkinson v Clark* 1916 2 KB 636; *Coetzee v Union Periodicals Ltd* 1931 WLD 37; *Delew v Town Council of Springs* 1945 TPD 128; *Meerholz v Meerholz* 1949 2 SA 479 (O); *Mecl v Polokowsky* 1946 WLD 539;

Sachs v Werkerspers Uitgewersmpy (Edms) Bpk 1952 2 SA 261 (W); *Stanley Motors Ltd v Administrator, Natal* 1959 1 SA 624 (D); *Valkin v Daggafontein Mines Ltd* 1960 2 SA 507 (W); *Administrator, Cape v Preston* 1961 3 SA 562 (A); *Gosschalk v Rossouw* 1966 2 SA 476 (C); *SA Associated Newspapers Ltd v Yutar* 1967 3 SA 454 (A); *Goldberg v Standard General Insurance Co Ltd* 1980 3 SA 200 (A).

4 *Delew v Town Council of Springs* supra; *Laubscher v National Foods Ltd* 1986 1 SA 553 (ZH).

5 *Delew v Town Council of Springs* supra; *Laubscher v National Foods Ltd* supra.

6 *Delew v Town Council of Springs* supra; *Laubscher v National Foods Ltd* supra.

7 *Delew v Town Council of Springs* supra; *Laubscher v National Foods Ltd* supra.

OPINION

705 Introduction That a person holds, or does not hold, an opinion may be a fact in issue and this may be proved like any other relevant fact.[1] Where the opinion of the community is in issue, evidence of "reputation" is receivable.[2] Here, a different aspect of opinion evidence is considered: the reception, or rejection, of a witness's opinion relating to the facts in issue or circumstantial facts. Traditionally, it is said that a witness must confine him or herself to the "facts", that a witness must not resort to, or state, inferences unless he or she is allowed to do so by some "exception" to the general rule such as the "exception" relating to expert evidence. This approach cannot stand analysis – it rests on the premise that a clear distinction exists between "fact" and "inference" when there is no clear distinction.[3] The true inquiry is to determine what inferential testimony is objectionable and what is unobjectionable.

1 Schmidt *Bewysreg* 457.
2 Ibid.
3 Stated "facts" are, in the main, a compound of inferences (*R v Ndhlovu* 1954 4 SA 482 (N) 484) and the formulation assumes a clear distinction between "fact" and "inference" that cannot, therefore, exist. As will be seen below, opinion evidence is admitted when relevant and traditionally minded writers (such as May *Evidence* s 445 and O'Dowd *Evidence*) fail to stress that the "exceptions" constitute illustrations of opinion that is received because it is relevant.

706 General rule Opinion evidence is admissible if it is relevant; inadmissible if it is irrelevant.[1] If a witness's perceptions would be of assistance to the court, and if the witness can only communicate these perceptions adequately by summarising his or her impressions by resorting to and stating inferences, such a summarisation will be relevant and admissible. Conversely, if the witness can adequately communicate his or her perceptions without summarising his or her impressions by resorting to and stating inferences, a summarisation will be irrelevant and inadmissible.[2] The true inquiry relates to the *extent* to which a witness may properly be allowed to summarise his or her impressions. In one context it may be permissible, for instance to say that X looked "upset" or "angry"; in another, where X's appearance is a material or disputed issue, it would be improper: the witness should be asked to list his or her impressions.[3] At times it may be impossible for a witness to say anything at all without summarising his or her impressions.[4] The evidence of experts (in the narrow sense) and laymen is received when it is relevant, in the sense of its being able materially to assist the court. It is rejected when it is supererogatory: when it cannot assist the court it is irrelevant and inadmissible.[5]

1 *R v Vilbro* 1957 3 SA 223 (A) 228–229; *Ruto Flour Mills Ltd v Adelson (1)* 1958 4 SA 235 (T) 237; *R v David* 1962 3 SA 305 (SR) 306; *S v Nangutuuala* 1974 2 SA 165 (SWA) 167; *Coopers (SA) (Pty) Ltd v Deutsche Gesellschaft für Schädlingsbekämpfung mbH* 1976 3 SA 352 (A) 372. See further *Hollington v F Hewthorn & Co Ltd* 1943 KB 587 (CA) 589; [1943] 2 All ER 35 (CA); Wigmore *Evidence* 7 par 1918 applied in *R v Vilbro & Cooper* supra; but see *Gentiruco AG v Firestone SA*
(*Pty*) *Ltd* 1972 1 SA 589 (A) 618D.
2 If witnesses were not to be allowed to summarise inferences, their testimony would be interminable or, at least, it would be inconvenient and time-wasting: *Herbst v R* 1925 SWA 77 80.
3 *R v Ndhlovu* 1954 4 SA 482 (N) 484.
4 Eg, when a lay witness gives his or her impression of the speed of a vehicle, or the value of a property; see par 715 post.
5 See pars 709–711 715 post.

707 Procedure In civil trials[1] and criminal proceedings opinion evidence has to be given *viva voce*.[2] There are instances where, in criminal proceedings, opinion may be received on affidavit or certificate, as *prima facie* evidence. Whenever any fact established by an examination or process requiring any skill in biology, chemistry, physics, astronomy, geography, anatomy, pathology, or the identification of finger or palmprints is relevant, an affidavit alleging that it has been made by a person in the service of the state, a provincial administration, the South African institute for medical research, a university in the Republic or of any other body designated by the president of the Repulic is, upon its mere production, *prima facie* proof of that fact.[3] Section 212(4)(a) of the Criminal Procedure Act has been amended to include any fact established by any examination or process requiring any skill in human behavioural science.[4] Section 212(5) has been amended to provide that whenever the question as to the existence and nature of a precious metal or any precious stone is at issue, the submission of an affidavit by a state appraiser of precious metals or stones constitutes *prima facie* proof that it is a precious metal or a precious stone of a particular kind and that the appearance and the mass or value of the precious metal or precious stone is as specified.[5] A certificate may be received *in lieu* of an affidavit in any case where skill is required in chemistry, anatomy or pathology.[6] Affidavits by appraisers of precious metals or stones, who are in the service of the state, also constitute, on their production, *prima facie* proof of the mass and value of precious metal or stones.[7] The court may require, before an affidavit or certificate is produced as *prima facie* proof, that the person who made the affidavit or issued the certificate give oral evidence or it may cause written interrogatories to be sent to that person. The interrogatories, and the purported replies to them, are also admissible.[8]

In civil proceedings, a party who wishes to call an expert[9] has to give notice to his or her opponent, at least 14 days before the hearing, of intention to do so.[10] Such party must also deliver a summary of the expert's conclusions and his or her reasons for reaching them.[11] The parties may consent to a witness's being called without these formalities and the court has power to grant leave to a party to call a witness in the absence of due compliance.

1 Not, obviously, in motion proceedings. See title CIVIL PROCEDURE.

2 *S v Masilela* 1968 2 SA 558 (A): an opinion on foreign law which has not been proved in evidence cannot be used in argument; see further *Ex parte Smith* 1970 4 SA 122 (O). An opinion may be proved from the bar by consent: *Government of the Republic of SA v Ngubane* 1972 2 SA 601 (A) 609. A witness may, by express or tacit consent, read out his or her opinion and hand in the document that he or she has read after confirming that it reflects his or her opinion: *R v Van Schalkwyk* 1948 2 SA 1000 (O); *R v K* 1951 3 SA 180 (SWA). Cf *R v Birch-Monchrieff* 1960 4 SA 425 (T); *S v Joubert* 1971 3 SA 924 (E). See also par 713 post.

3 Criminal Procedure Act 51 of 1977 s 212(4)(a).

4 Correctional Services and Supervision Matters Amendment Act 122 of 1991 s 40.

5 For the application of Criminal Procedure Act 51 of 1977 s 212(4)(a), see *S v Nkhahale* 1981 1 SA 320 (O).

6 Criminal Procedure Amendment Act 5 of 1991 s 11.

7 Criminal Procedure Act 51 of 1977 s 212(4)(a).

8 A lay person who is able to give relevant views relating to an issue may possibly fall within the ambit of the provision. It is, perhaps, arguable that *Coopers (SA) (Pty) Ltd v Deutsche Gesellschaft für Schädlingsbekämpfung mbH* 1976 3 SA 352 (A) 370G–H, in suggesting that *R v Vilbro* 1957 3 SA 223 (A) 228G–H was an instance of the reception of "expert" testimony that "could be of great assistance to the court", was saying just this – in the *Vilbro* case, the opinion of a lay witness was received for this reason.

9 Uniform Rules of Court r 36(9); Magistrates Court r 24(9).

10 Uniform Rules of Court r 36(9); *Klue v Provincial Administration, Cape* 1966 2 SA 561 (E); Magistrates Court r 24(9). See *Coopers (SA) (Pty) Ltd v Deutsche Gesellschaft für Schädlingsbekämpfung mbH* supra.

11 *Klue v Provincial Administration, Cape* supra; *Coopers (SA) (Pty) Ltd v Deutsche Gesellschaft für Schädlingsbekämpfung mbH* supra; Uniform Rules of Court r 24(9); Magistrates Court r 24(9).

708 Ultimate issues In principle there is no rule that a witness cannot give his or her opinion on an issue that the court has ultimately to decide. A witness may give an opinion on an ultimate issue if his or her opinion is relevant, that is to say, if it would be impossible for the witness to render assistance to the court without giving the opinion. It follows from the principle that opinion evidence is admissible if it is relevant that the theory that a witness cannot "usurp the function of the court" by testifying on an ultimate issue is untenable. The function of the court is not usurped by opinion on an ultimate issue, since the court is never bound by what a witness says and the true inquiry is to determine when it will be right, and when it will be wrong, to admit opinion on an ultimate inquiry. This inquiry will be determined by the view that the court takes of the relevance of the evidence – its ability to be of appreciable help to the court.[1] Opinion evidence on an ultimate issue will more readily tend to be relevant when the subject is one upon which the court is usually quite incapable of forming an unassisted conclusion.[2] And, in the nature of things, opinion evidence will less readily tend to be relevant on matters directly in issue than upon other relevant facts.

Many decisions, however, still speak in terms of inadmissible opinion that "usurps" the function of the court.[3] It is not experts (in the narrow sense) only who may give their opinions on ultimate issues[4] but, in practice, there is a strong tendency to regard the evidence of lay persons on ultimate issues as constituting *prima facie* evidence only, which, if unchallenged, may be of greater significance.

A witness is not allowed to give an opinion upon the *general* or legal merits of the case.[5]

1 *R v Vilbro* 1957 3 SA 223 (A); *Ruto Flour Mills Ltd v Adelson (1)* 1958 4 SA 235 (T) 237; *Gentiruco AG v Firestone SA (Pty) Ltd* 1972 1 SA 589 (A) 616–617; *Coopers (SA) (Pty) Ltd v Deutsche Gesellschaft für Schädlingsbekämpfung mbH* 1976 3 SA 352 (A) 370. Thus in *Ruto Flour Mills Ltd v Adelson (1)* supra evidence of an accountant was received because the court considered it to be relevant, but in *R v Herholdt (1)* 1956 2 SA 714 (W) the court did not admit an accountant's evidence because, although it might have been helpful, the court had no real need for such assistance. For an exposition of the circumstances in which opinion evidence will be relevant and admissible; see

Colgate Palmolive (Pty) Ltd v Elida-Gibbs (Pty) Ltd 1989 3 SA 759 (W).
2 *R v Thomas Mason* (1911) 7 CAR 67; *Ireland v Taylor* 1949 1 KB 300 (CA) 312; *R v Holmes* [1953] 2 All ER 324 (CCA); *Ruto Flour Mills Ltd v Adelson (1)* supra.
3 Eg *S v Haasbroek* 1969 2 SA 624 (A).
4 *R v Cele* 1943 AD 123. Cf *R v Van Tonder* 1929 TPD 365; *R v Louw* 1930 CPD 368; *R v Ndhlovu* 1954 4 SA 482 (N); *S v Gouws* 1967 4 SA 527 (E); *S v Govender* 1968 3 SA 14 (N).
5 See par 710 fn 2 post. See further Phipson *Evidence* par 1210 fn 69; *S v Chabagae* 1978 4 SA 807 (O).

709 Expert evidence The opinion of an expert is admissible if it is relevant. It will be relevant if the witness's skill, training or experience enable him or her materially to assist the court on matters in which the court itself does not usually have the necessary knowledge to decide.[1] Where the topic is one in which the ordinary judicial officer could be expected to be able, unassisted, to draw an inference, expert evidence is supererogatory;[2] and where a witness does not have the necessary qualifications to draw an inference, his or her inference has no probative value and is, therefore, irrelevant and inadmissible.[3]

1 See the authorities cited in par 711 post.
2 *R v Makeip* 1948 1 SA 947 (A); cf *S v Nkosiyani* 1970 2 PH H170 (T). Thus, expert testimony is inadmissible to prove South African law or international law which forms part of South African law: *South Atlantic Islands Development Corporation Ltd v Buchan* 1971 1 SA 234 (C). It is

improper to lead expert testimony that corporal punishment has been excessive as it would be for the court to decide that issue: *R v Van Schalkwyk* 1948 2 SA 1000 (O) 1002.
3 *S v Mjakuca* 1967 3 SA 352 (C) 354–355; *S v Januarie* 1980 2 SA 598 (C); *Starke v Schreiber* 2001 1 All SA 167 (C).

710 Qualification of an expert An expert must be qualified. This means that the expert must satisfy the court that he or she possesses sufficient skill, training or experience to assist it.[1] The concept of what constitutes adequate qualification is elastic. It is not generally a *sine qua non* that an expert must have had theoretical training or practical experience: the expert's qualifications must be measured against the evidence the expert has to give in order to determine whether they are sufficient to enable him or her to give relevant evidence.[2]

1 *Menday v Protea Assurance Co Ltd* 1976 1 SA 565 (E) 579; *Mahomed v Shaik* 1978 4 SA 523 (N).

2 Schmidt *Bewysreg* 438 (2 ed, this point is not expressly repeated in the 3 ed), approved and applied in *S v Nangutuuala* 1974 2 SA 165 (SWA) 167. See further *Bristow v Sequeville* (1850) 5 Ex 275; 155 Er 118; *R v Silverlock* 1894 2 QB 766; *United States Shipping Board v The Ship St Albans* 1931 AC 632; *S v Kimimbi* 1963 3 SA 250 (C) 252; *S v Bertrand* 1975 4 SA 142 (C) 149; *Menday v Protea Assurance Co Ltd* supra 569. Sometimes technical or professional training or practical experience has been regarded as a *sine qua non*, sometimes not. It all depends on practical considerations and the nature of

the evidence to be led. Thus the evidence of a chemist with inadequate practical experience was rejected in *Van Heerden v SA Pulp & Paper Industries Ltd* 1945 2 PH J14 (W). But the modern trend is to admit the opinion of foreign lawyers on foreign law, even where they are deficient in professional practice, if they are able to assist the court: *Cooper-King v Cooper-King* 1900 P 65; *Brailey v Rhodesia Consolidated Ltd* 1910 2 Ch 95 102–103; *Barford v Barford & McLeod* 1918 P 140; *Ex parte Hiddingh's Goods of Bonelli* 1875 1 P 69. See also *The Sussex Peerage* (1844) 11 C & F 85 117–132; 8 ER 1034 1047–1053; *Hulscher v Voorschotkas voor Zuid Africa* 1908 TS 542.

711 The subject matter of expert evidence There is no closed list of topics on which expert evidence is admissible. At a given moment in time there are some subjects upon which a court is usually quite incapable of forming an opinion unassisted, and other upon which it could come to some sort of independent conclusions, but the help of an expert would be useful.[1] It is impossible to list all the areas where a judicial officer is usually quite incapable of forming an unassisted conclusion, particularly if one bears in mind that the state of communal (and, therefore, judicial) knowledge changes with time. They include, for instance, fingerprints;[2] medicine, psychiatry, chemistry, mathematics and engineering and the proof of foreign law.[3] Expert opinion is, in general, required to explain the workings and reliability of mechanical devices;[4] but the stage may be reached when the reliability of an instrument has so frequently been demonstrated to the courts that judicial notice may be taken of its reliability.[5]

Where evidence would be useful, but not essential, to assist the judicial officer, it will be admitted or rejected according to the view that the court takes of its relevance.[6] Although laymen are often permitted, for instance, to estimate age, speed and value, such topics, when they are of great importance in a case, may demand evidence of greater moment and the circumstances may be such that the court is quite incapable of reaching a conclusion unassisted by an expert in the strict sense. Thus a layman may be permitted to estimate the speed of a vehicle,[7] but when it is necessary to prove that the accused has transgressed a speed limit and recourse is had to mechanical or electronic timing devices, then, in the absence of any statutory presumption to the contrary, expert testimony is essential.[8] Similarly lay witnesses may estimate age[9] but, where it is necessary to prove age in order to establish guilt, expert, direct or real evidence is essential.[10] Any witness may identify the handwriting of a person whose handwriting is familiar to the witnedd,[11] but only an expert may be permitted to compare the handwriting of persons unknown to him or her.[12] The owner of a thing may be permitted to estimate its value,[13] but where the estimate is challenged or where the circumstances are such that only an expert could assist the court, then, obviously, only an expert's testimony would carry weight.[14] Laymen may testify that a person was drunk,[15] but the circumstances may demand expert testimony.[16]

An expert may testify on an ultimate issue if his or her evidence would be relevant in the sense that it would be of real assistance to the court.[17] An expert cannot testify on the legal or general merits of the case.[18]

1 Per Wessels JA in *Coopers (SA) (Pty) Ltd v Deutsche Gesellschaft für Schädlingsbekämpfung mbH* 1976 3 SA 352 (A) 370, approving Hoffman *Evidence* 294–295. See also *Holtzhauzen v Roodt* [1997] 3 All SA 551 (W); 1997 4 SA 766 (W).

2 *R v Morela* 1947 3 SA 147 (A); *R v Smit* 1952 3 SA 447 (A); *R v Nksatlala* 1960 3 SA 543 (A); *S v Nala* 1965 4 SA 360 (A).

3 *Cooper-King v Cooper-King* 1900 P 65; *Levy v Levy* (1904) 18 EDC 164; *Brailey v Rhodesia Consolidated Ltd* 1910 2 Ch 95 102–103; *Barford v Barford & McLeod* 1918 P 140; *Ex parte Hiddingh's Estate* 1940 CPD 121. See also *Hulscher v Voorschotkas voor Zuid Africa* 1908 TS 542.

4 *S v Mutle* 1970 4 SA 535 (T).

5 *S v Mthimkulu* 1975 4 SA 759 (A); see par 821 post. Thus, unless there is a statutory presumption of a device's accuracy such as the one created under s 212(10)(a) of the Criminal Procedure Act 51 of 1977, expert evidence is still necessary in SA to prove the workings and reliability of speedtesting devices such as gatsometers (*S v Margolis* 1964 4 SA 579 (T); *S v Du Plessis* 1966 1 SA 607 (C); *R v Harvey* 1969 2 SA 193 (RA); *S v Dawson* 1966 1 SA 259 (N); *S v Sabotker* 1970 1 SA 206 (C); cf *S v Sneddon* 1970 4 SA 241 (T); *S v Hengst* 1975 2 SA 91 (SWA)), but the time may come when it may not be (*R v Harvey* supra 200–201). Today, an expert (in the narrow sense) may be required to explain a device; tomorrow a layman's testimony may be sufficient: note that the ministerial conditions and requirements with regard to velocity measuring instruments has been withdrawn by *Government Gazette* 7688 GN R1611, 31 July 1981; *S v Wells* 1990 (1) SA 816 (A). See also *S v Verwey* 1979 1 SA 923 (Tk) and *S v Murray* 1979 2 SA 677 (E).

6 Cf *Ruto Flour Mills Ltd v Adelson (1)* 1958 4 SA 235 (T) with *R v Herholdt (1)* 1956 2 SA 714 (W). The evidence of language experts as to the meaning of words in a statute,

although useful as a point of reference, is opinion evidence and generally not admissible: *Association of Amusement & Novelty Machine Operators v Minister of Justice* 1980 2 SA 636 (A).

7 *R v Frankel* 1940 TPD 159.

8 *S v Currin* 1961 4 SA 393 (O); the authorities cited in fn 5 supra; but see s 212(10)(a).

9 *R v Cox* 1898 1 QB 179.

10 *S v Mohlobane* 1969 1 SA 561 (A); *S v Tango* 1969 2 SA 648 (C); *S v Kamfer* 1969 4 SA 250 (C); *S v Manyololo* 1969 4 SA 356 (E); *S v Pofadder* 1970 2 PH H141 (NC); *S v Van Rooi* 1976 2 SA 580 (A).

11 *R v Malan* 1925 TPD 807; *Doe on the Demise of Mudd v Suckermore* 1836 AD & E 703 704; 111 ER 1331 1345; *R v McCartney & Hansen* (1928) 20 CAR 179.

12 *Lansdown v Wajar* 1973 4 SA 329 (T); and see par 714 post; cf s 228 of the Criminal Procedure Act 51 of 1977 and s 4 of the Civil Proceedings Evidence Act 25 of 1965. See further *S v Smith* 1978 3 SA 749 (A).

13 Wigmore *Evidence* 3 par 716; *R v Ethel Beckett* (1913) 8 CAR 204; (1913) 29 TLR 332; *Bondcrete (Pty) Ltd v City View Investments (Pty) Ltd* 1969 1 SA 134 (N) 136.

14 Cf *Heath v Le Grange* 1974 2 SA 262 (C).

15 See par 714 fn 3 post.

16 *R v Mathsilso* 1956 2 PH H258 (O); *S v Mhetoa* 1968 2 SA 773 (O) 774H–775A.

17 *R v Mathsilso* supra; *Ruto Flour Mills Ltd v Adelson (1)* supra 237; *Firestone (SA) (Pty) Ltd v Gentiruco AG* 1970 2 SA 782 (T); *Gentiruco AG v Firestone SA (Pty) Ltd* 1972 1 SA 589 (A) 616–618; *South Atlantic Islands Development Corporation Ltd v Buchan* 1971 1 SA 234 (C). Cf *Publication Control Board v Gallo (Africa) Ltd* 1975 3 SA 665 (A) 671–672 with *Publications Control Board v William Heinemann Ltd* 1965 4 SA 137 (A) 147. See further *William Seed v John Higgins* (1860) 8 HLC 550; 11 ER 544; *R v Richards* (1858) 1 F & F 87; 175 ER 638.

18 See pars 709 710 fn 2 ante.

712 The basis of the opinion The opinion of an expert may be given on facts within his or her personal knowledge or on hypothetical facts. It is essential for the court to know what facts have been relied on as the basis of the opinion. It follows that the court should be made aware of the expert's assumed premises and the facts within the expert's personal knowledge on which he or she is relying. Bald statements of opinion may have little, if any, value;[1] the weight to be attached to them will depend on the circumstances.

An expert may refer to data garnered from the experience of others, provided that he or she has the necessary qualifications to evaluate the data and to know where to find reliable sources of information.[2] It follows that an expert may refer to the writings of others (either to refresh his or her memory or to support the opinion) if he or she has sufficient personal knowledge of the subject to be able to express a relevant opinion.[3] It is only that part of the writing to which the witness refers that is in evidence and the court cannot have regard to other passages that have not been canvassed by the witness.[4] Expert evidence should be presented in such a way that the court itself is in a position to make the observations on which the expert has relied for his or her conclusion.[5]

Opinion evidence that is not linked to the facts is mere abstract theory.[6] An expert cannot base his or her opinion, for instance, on documents that are not before the court.[7] Although a witness may refer to experiments that have become part of the generally accepted body of scientific knowledge,[8] the hearsay rule would prevent the witness from relying on assertions made by others in individual cases.[9]

An expert may refresh his or her memory from a report that has been made by that expert when his or her recollection of the events that it records was fresh. The expert may hand in the report with the consent, express or tacit, of the other side. A party may insist that his or her opponent's witness testifies *viva voce* but, as a matter of convenience, reports of experts are often handed in by consent as an embodiment of the witness's testimony.[10] The opposite party may insist on their being reproduced in the form of *viva voce* evidence and on their not being handed in during the examination in chief.[11] If the witness does not confirm this report it is not evidence despite being handed in.[12]

It seems that a failure to motivate an opinion adequately goes to weight rather than admissibiltiy[13] but, although weight and admissibility should never be confused, testimony that has no probative value is irrelevant and therefore inadmissible.

---

1 *Barry v R* 1940 NPD 130; *R v Jacobs* 1940 TPD 142; *R v Theunissen* 1948 4 SA 43 (C); *R v Dembo* 1952 2 SA 244 (T) 249; *S v Kimimbi* 1963 3 SA 250 (C); *S v Gouws* 1967 4 SA 527 (E); *S v Mhetoa* 1968 2 SA 773 (O); *S v Govender* 1968 3 SA 14 (N); *S v Du Preez* 1972 2 SA 519 (SWA); *S v Mngomezulu* 1972 1 SA 797 (A); *Mahomed v Shaik* 1978 4 SA 523 (N).

2 *S v Kimimbi* supra 252; *Menday v Protea Assurance Co Ltd* 1976 1 SA 565 (E). See also *The Sussex Peerage* (1844) 11 C & F 85 115; 8 ER 1034 1046.

3 *Van Heerden v SA Pulp & Paper Industries Ltd* 1945 2 PH J14 (W); *Menday v Protea Assurance Co Ltd* supra.

4 *R v Mofokeng* 1928 AD 132; *R v Basson* 1946 CPD 479; *R v Phillips* 1949 2 SA 671 (O) 676; *S v Harris* 1965 2 SA 340 (A); *S v Henning* 1972 1 PH H42 (N).

5 *S v Nthati* 1996 2 SACR 90 (O).

6 *S v Mngomezulu* supra.

7 *S v Seedat* 1971 1 SA 789 (N) 792–793.

8 *East London Railway Co v Thames Conservators* (1904) 90 LT 347: the report of a deceased witness relating to the construction of a tunnel was received on proof that it was accepted to be accurate by engineers. (See Phipson *Evidence* par 1158).

9 O'Dowd *Evidence* 102.

10 *R v Smit* 1946 AD 862 867.

11 See, in general, *R v Manda* 1951 3 SA 158 (A) 161; *R v Mbongwe* 1954 3 SA 1016 (T); *R v Kannemeyer* 1958 3 SA 56 (C); *S v Heller* (1) 1964 1 SA 520 (W); cf *R v Van Schalkwyk* 1948 2 SA 1000 (O); *R v Mutch* 1948 3 SA 1053 (C); *R v Theunissen* supra; *R v K* 1951 3 SA 180 (SWA). See par 797 post.

12 *R v Birch-Monchrieff* 1960 4 SA 425 (T); *S v Joubert* 1971 3 SA 924 (E).

13 *R v Mbongwe* supra; *S v Williams* 1985 1 SA 750 (C).

713 The weight of expert evidence It is for the court ultimately to decide whether an expert's opinion is to be relied on or not and to determine what weight (if any) has to be given to it.[1] The court must not blindly accept expert testimony. It is obliged, even where expert evidence is so technical that the average judicial officer would not be able properly to reach an unassisted conclusion, still to decide whether it would be safe to accept the opinion or not.[2] This is so even in the case of the comparison of fingerprints.[3] The court must not play the role of an expert[4] and therefore when dealing with finger-print evidence it must, when scrutinising the points of identity, do so with the intention of determining whether the expert's opinion can be safely relied on; its inquiry is not made to satisfy itself that there are the requisite number of points of identity.[5] If an expert on foreign law refers to a foreign statute, the court is entitled to interpret it and reach its own conclusion.[6]

Certain kinds of expert evidence are regarded with more circumspection than others. Thus handwriting evidence has been treated with some, perhaps unwarranted, suspicion.[7] Footprint identification has been said not to differ from the requirements of fingerprint and palmprint identification.[8] Some courts have looked with unwarranted circumspection at ballistic and toolmark evidence.[9]

There has been some reluctance to convict an accused solely on the uncorroborated evidence of an expert,[10] but there is no rule that a court cannot make a finding solely on the evidence of an expert.[11]

When proof of the accused's guilt is dependent on the result of scientific analysis, such as DNA evidence, the testing process, including control measures applied, have to be executed and recorded with so much care that it can later be verified by any objective scientist, and *a fortiori* also by the trial court.[12]

1 *R v Jacobs* 1940 TPD 142; *Annama v Chetty* 1946 AD 142 145; *R v Mbongwe* 1954 3 SA 1016 (T) 1019; *R v Sibanda* 1963 4 SA 182 (SR) 190; *S v Gouws* 1967 4 SA 527 (E) 528; *S v Du Preez* 1972 2 SA 519 (SWA). See also *S v Loubscher* 1979 3 SA 47 (A); *Guardian Royal Exchange Assurance Rhodesia Ltd v Jeti* 1981 2 SA 102 (ZA); *S v Baleka (3)* 1986 4 SA 1005 (T); *S v Van As* 1991 2 SACR 74 (W); *Van Eck v SANTAM Insurance Co Ltd* 1996 4 SA 1226 (C). See *Motor Vehicle Assurance Fund v Kenny* 1984 4 SA 432 (E) where the court held that the evidence of an eye witness is to be preferred over that of an expert in collision cases. It is trite law that direct and credible evidence regarding what occurred during an accident carries greater weight than the opinion of an expert irrespective of his or her experience: *Vergoedingskommissaris v Multilaterale Motorvoertuigongelukkefonds* [1998] 3 All SA 155 (O). In *S v Armstrong* 1998 1 SACR 698 (SE) it was held that the court has to be satisfied from its own observations that the conclusions of the expert are correct. See also *Michael v Linksfield Park Clinic (Pty) Ltd* [2002] 1 All SA 384 (SCA); 2001 3 SA 1188 (SCA) for the general approach of courts to expert evidence.

2 *R v Morela* 1947 3 SA 147 (A). For the cross-examination of expert witnesses, see *Meintjies & Van der Walt* 2001 DR 21.

3 Ibid; *R v Smit* 1952 3 SA 447 (A); *R v Nksatlala* 1960 3 SA 543 (A); *S v Nala* 1965 4 SA 360 (A) 362; *S v Khumalo* 1969 1 PH H21 (T). See also *S v Blom* 1992 1 SACR 649 (E).

4 *R v Fourie* 1947 2 SA 972 (EDL) 974; *Stewarts & Lloyds of SA Ltd v Croydon Engineering & Mining Supplies (Pty) Ltd* 1979 1 SA 1018 (W).

5 *S v Nala* supra. Cf the approach to handwriting: *Annama v Chetty* supra; *S v Smith* 1978 3 SA 749 (A).

6 *Concha v Murrieta, De Mora v Concha* (1889) 40 Ch 543 544; *Phipson Evidence* par 1235; *Atlantic Harvesters of Namibia (Pty) Ltd v Unterweser Reederei GMBH of Bremen* 1986 4 SA 865 (C).

7 *R v Stevenson* 1934 EDL 43; *R v Hurwitz & Da Costa* 1940 WLD 149; *R v Fourie* supra; *R v Chidota* 1966 3 SA 428 (RA); and see *R v Morela* supra; *R v Smit* supra, where the difference in approach to fingerprint and handwriting evidence is indicated. Cf s 228 of the Criminal Procedure Act 51 of 1977 and s 4 of the Civil Proceedings Evidence Act 25 of 1965; and see *S v Smith* supra.

8 *R v Modesane* 1932 TPD 165; *R v Nkele*
   1933 TPD 36; *R v Mlanto* 1935 EDL 280;
   R v Makoni 1935 *Justice Circular* 458; *R v*
   Louw 1946 OPD 80; *S v Limekayo* 1969 1
   SA 540 (E). Evidence of footprints is admissible, and the court must be cautious of relying upon such evidence, especially where it
   is the only evidence against the accused: *S v*
   Mkhabela 1984 1 SA 556 (A).
9 Zeffertt *Evidence* 311, who dissaproves of
   older Zimbabwean cases such as *R v Sibanda*
   supra and *R v Nyamayaro* 1967 4 SA 263
   (RA), preferring the more modern approach

as followed in *S v Mkhize* 1999 1 SACR
256 (W) 263. According to the latter case
the approach to be adopted when evaluating
ballistic evidence is similar to that adopted
by the courts in relation to fingerprint evidence.
10 *R v Van der Westhuizen* (1896) 6 CTR 233;
   Keeton v R 1906 EDC 56; *R v Stevenson* supra; *R v Fourie* supra; *R v Chidota* supra.
11 *Annama v Chetty* supra 154; see further *R v*
   Chidota supra; *R v Nyamayaro* supra.
12 *S v Maqhina* 2001 1 SACR 241 (T).

714 Lay opinion The opinion of a layman is admissible if it is relevant.[1] It will be
relevant if it would be of material assistance to the court to allow the witness to resort
to and state inferences where the witness's perceptions would be of assistance to the
court and the witness could not conveniently and adequately convey his or her
perceptions without doings so.[2] It will be relevant also if the witness possesses some
attribute that would enable him or her materially to assist the court in reaching a
conclusion[3] (even on an ultimate issue if it would be of appreciable help to allow the
witness to do so) and if it would be impossible for the witness to render such assistance without giving his or her opinion.[4] There is a strong tendency in practice,
certainly in criminal proceedings, to regard lay opinion, when it is received, as constituting *prima facie* evidence only: its effect is often said to depend on whether or not it
has been challenged.[5]

1 *R v Vilbro* 1957 3 SA 223 (A). See also
   Colgate Palmolive (Pty) Ltd v Elida-Gibbs (Pty)
   Ltd 1989 3 SA 759 (W).
2 *Herbst v R* 1925 SWA 77 80; *R v Ndhlovu*
   1954 4 SA 482 (N). This happens frequently, eg, when a witness is allowed to
   give his or her total impression that a person
   or thing made upon him or her when identifying that person or thing, in the identification of handwriting, the estimation of the
   speed of a vehicle, the value or age of a
   thing, and so on. For estimation of speed,
   see *R v Frankel* 1940 TPD 159; *S v De Jongh*
   1965 2 SA 589 (T) 593; age: *R v Cox* 1898
   1 QB 179; handwriting: *R v Malan* 1925
   TPD 807; *R v Fourie* 1947 2 SA 972 (EDL);
   value: *R v Etherl Beckett* (1913) 8 CAR 204;
   (1913) 29 TLR 332; *Bondcrete (Pty) Ltd v*
   City View Investments (Pty) Ltd 1969 1 SA
   134 (N). As to when expert evidence will be
   necessary to prove age, speed, value, to
   identify handwriting, and so on, see par 712
   ante. On the approach to handwriting evidence, see also par 712 ante. A witness's
   identification of a person has to be carefully
   scrutinised because of the dangers inherent
   in such evidence. Although a general impression is admissible, it should be tested and
   the witness ought to refer to specific identifying features if able to: *R v Shekelele* 1953 1

SA 636 (T); *R v T* 1958 2 SA 676 (A); *R v*
Mputing 1960 1 SA 785 (T); *S v Mehlape*
1963 2 SA 29 (A); and see *S v M* 1972 4 SA
361 (T) (voice identification); see further
R v Gericke 1941 CPD 211; *R v Chitate* 1966
2 SA 690 (RA).
3 *R v Vilbro* supra; and see *R v Cele* 1943 AD
123; *S v Haasbroek* 1969 2 SA 624 (A). A
layman may testify that someone was drunk:
R v Brorson 1949 2 SA 819 (T); *R v Ismail*
1951 1 SA 370 (T); *R v Ntholeng* 1952 3 SA
396 (O); *Mathsilsov v R* 1956 2 PH H258
(O); *R v Mgotywa* 1958 1 SA 99 (E); *R v*
Radebe 1960 4 SA 131 (T); *S v Edley* 1970 2
SA 223 (N). In SA a layman may testify also
that a person was unfit to drive a vehicle:
R v Seaward 1950 2 SA 704 (N), although
the circumstances may be such as to require
expert evidence: *S v Mhetoa* 1968 2 SA 773
(O). *R v Viljoen* 1946 2 PH H268 (C) over-
states the desirability of lay testimony.
4 *R v Vilbro* supra. See the discussion of
ultimate issues in par 709 ante. What has
been said of the circumscription of expert
testimony on ultimate issues *a fortiori* applies
to laymen.
5 Thus in *S v Haasbroek* supra it was held that
the evidence of a witness that Yskor was a
bedryf and not a *fabriek* (the ultimate issue)
constituted *prima facie* evidence of that fact.

Since the evidence had not been challenged, it was of significance in the case. See also *R v Ebrahim & Heskiah* 1921 TPD 305; *Chaikin v R* 1940 NPD 133; *R v Cele* supra; *R v Modesa* 1948 1 SA 1157 (T); *R v Sita* 1950 3 SA 460 (T) 463; *Fani v Johannesburg City Council* 1952 3 SA 37 (T) 40; *R v Jacob* 1956 1 SA 216 (SR); *R v Mhlambiso* 1956 3 SA 379 (EDL) 381; *R v Radebe* supra 134; *S v Bareeleng* 1969 4 SA 208 (NC) 212; *S v Claassen* 1976 2 SA 281 (O). Cf *S v Malefane* 1974 4 SA 613 (O); *S v Bertrand* 1975 4 SA 142 (C); *S v Brumpton* 1976 3 SA 236 (T) 242.

715 The rule in *Hollington v Hewthorn* Evidence that a party has been convicted of a criminal offence is not evidence, not even *prima facie* evidence, in a subsequent contested civil suit; it is the irrelevant opinion of another court.[1] In uncontested civil proceedings the fact of the conviction constitutes *prima facie* proof.[2] The finding of a court in civil proceedings is inadmissible in subsequent criminal proceedings[3] and a conviction is not evidence in subsequent criminal proceedings against someone else.[4]

Now that the courts have been given a discretion by section 3(1)(c) of the Law of Evidence Amendment Act[5] to allow hearsay to be given in the interests of justice, that aspect of the decision in *Hollington v F Hewthorn & Co Ltd*[6] should no longer present an obstacle. The court could now allow the record of the evidence given in the previous case to be admitted and then decide for itself on that evidence what the true facts were. The opinion objection remains, however, until a statutory change.

1 *Hollington v F Hewthorn & Co Ltd* 1943 KB 587 (CA); [1943] 2 All ER 35 (CA); *Goody v Odhams Press Ltd* 1967 1 QB 333 (CA); *Yusaf v Bailey* 1964 4 SA 117 (W); *Birkett v Accident Fund* 1964 1 SA 561 (T). See also *Du Toit v Grobler* 1947 3 SA 213 (SWA), where no reference was made to *Hollington v F Hewthorn & Co Ltd* supra. Cf *Jorgensen v News Media (Auckland) Ltd* 1969 NZLR 961 (CA). On the peculiar position relating to the removal of an attorney from the roll, see *Hassim (also known as Essack) v Incorporated Law Society of Natal* 1977 2 SA 757 (A); and see *General Medical Council v Spackman* 1943 AC 627 (HL); *Incorporated Law Society of Natal v Hassim (also known as Essack)* 1978 2 SA 285 (N). *Hollington v F Hewthorn & Co Ltd* supra has been the subject of much criticism: Law Reform Committee 15th report *The Rule in Hollington v Hewthorn* 1967 cmnd 3391; Cowen and Carter *Evidence* essay 6; Zeffertt *Evidence* 315–319; Davids 1968 *SALJ* 74; but see Bower and Turner *Res*

Judicata 221–222; Zeffertt 1970 *SALJ* 325.
2 *Lawrence v Lawrence* (1898) 15 SC 251; *Botha v Van Rensburg* 1908 EDC 339; *Prinsloo v Prinsloo* 1910 TPD 630; *Christie v Christie* 1922 WLD 109; *Reynolds v Reynolds* 1922 CPD 530; *De Lange v De Lange* 1923 EDL 19; *Ruxton v Ruxton* 1925 WLD 234; *Nicholson v Nicholson* 1927 EDL 164; *Kleynhans v Kleynhans* 1933 OPD 110; *Dickason v Dickason* 1934 NPD 97; *Ex parte Snitcher* 1938 EDL 202; *Wellbeloved v Wellbeloved* 1940 EDL 314; *Cassell v Cassell* 1941 EDL 123; *Petersen v Petersen* 1943 GWL 1; *Montgomery v Montgomery* 1956 2 SA 282 (W); but see *Naude v Naude* 1930 CPD 367. See further Davids 74; Claassen 1945 *SALJ* 14.
3 *R v Lechudi* 1945 AD 796.
4 *R v Xaki* 1950 4 SA 332 (EDL); *R v Lee* 1952 2 SA 67 (T); and see *R v Markins Motors (Pty) Ltd* 1959 3 SA 508 (A).
5 45 of 1988.
6 Supra.

RES GESTAE

716 Introduction Not only the law with regard to hearsay was affected by the Law of Evidence Amendment Act,[1] but also the closely related area of *res gestae*.[2] This concept has been accused of confusing the rule relating to relevance and the rule against hearsay.[3] The statutory amendment, making hearsay admissible within the presiding officer's discretion, has led to two lines of thought with regard to its practical effect on the concept of *res gestae*. The first, embodied by Schmidt,[4] is that the hearsay objection has now been taken care of, or at least that the rules have changed to such an extent that the huge encrustation of case law surrounding *res gestae* has diminished in importance. What remains is relevance, and that is better taken care of in categories more accurate than *res gestae*.[5]

The second, embodied by Zeffertt,[6] has been to keep intact most of the distinctions which characterised the old doctrine of *res gestae* and to endeavour to apply the new statutory provisions to these.

The courts have thus far sat on the fence with regard to the new role to be played by *res gestae*. Thus a magistrate in the court of first instance in the case of *S v Mpofu*[7] refused even to consider this exception since he felt that the new Act had superseded the common law principles. Alexander J seemed skeptical about the magistrate's motivation, but did not feel it necessary to decide the issue: "He appears to have done so on the basis that facts forming part of the res gestae are necessarily hearsay. It is not necessary for the purpose of this judgment to decide whether this is correct or not, for what is in issue here is manifestly the admissibility of hearsay evidence as defined in s 3(4) of the Act."[8]

The case could probably have been brought under the category of spontaneous reactions, the facts being that a witness had, immediately after a hit and run accident, written down the registration number of the offending vehicle on a slip of paper torn from a beer carton.

1　45 of 1988.
2　Literally, "matters being waged", in other words, those matters which are closely connected to the main actions.
3　Wigmore, as quoted by Paizes in 1985 *SALJ* 258.
4　In *Bewysreg*.
5　Thus the section on *res gestae* in Schmidt's

Bewysreg 485 et seq has been scaled down considerably. He does maintain some of the old categories, however, such as spontaneous exclamations: "Die spontane verklaring staan op eie pote" (487).
6　In *Evidence* 411 et seq
7　1993 3 SA 864 (N) 871.
8　871.

717 Spontaneous statements Evidence of spontaneous statements, that is to say, evidence of the spontaneous indication by speech, writing or conduct of the "speaker's" state of mind in regard to a particular fact,[1] will probably be received as admissible hearsay in terms of section 3(1)(c) of the Law of Evidence Amendment Act.[2]

To be admissible, the original speaker must first be shown to be unavailable as a witness.[3] Secondly, there must have been an occurrence which could produce a stress or nervous excitement.[4] Thirdly, the statement must have been made when the stress was still so operative upon the speaker that his reflective powers may be assumed to have been in abeyance.[5] Fourthly, the statement must not amount to the reconstruction of a past event.[6]

The manner in which the statement was made may, obviously, be a factor to be considered when the judicial officer decides whether or not the statement was spontaneous.[7] The mere fact that a statement was induced by a question will not signify that it was not spontaneous.[8] The judge has a discretion to decide whether the speaker had time to devise a story or whether the story was made spontaneously at a time of stress or danger.[9] The declaration has to relate to the event that gave rise to it.[10]

1　*S v Tuge* 1966 4 SA 565 (A). The suggestion in *Tustin v Arnold & Sons* (1915) 84 LJKB 2214; 22 Digest (Repl) 87 642 (cited in *Kelly v SAR&H* 1928 TPD 671) that a written declaration cannot be receivable is too dogmatic: "The rapid scribbling on an urgent request . . . may still be a completely spontaneous act performed at a time of

stress" (*S v Tuge* supra 574). See also *S v Mpofu* 1993 3 SA 864 (N). Earlier decisions that rested on strict contemporaneity as a *sine qua non* to admissibility must be taken as wrong (*R v Foster* (1834) 6 C & P 325; 172 ER 1261; *R v Bedingfield* (1879) 14 Cox CC 341; 14 Digest (Repl) 451 4370; *Joubert v SAR & H* 1930 TPD 164 (per Krause J); *R v*

Nicholls 1931 NPD 557; *Pincus v Solomon (1)* 1942 WLD 237 240. See also *R v Taylor* 1961 3 SA 616 (N) (where the spontaneity test was adumbrated, but the decision rested on the time factor); *Mabizela v Yorkshire Insurance Co Ltd* 1961 3 SA 820 (N) and *S v Qolo* 1965 1 SA 174 (A) (where evidence was excluded because it failed to satisfy either the requirement of spontaneity or contemporaneity).
2 45 of 1988.
3 *S v Tuge* supra 573–574.
4 *S v Tuge* supra 573–574.

5 *S v Tuge* supra 573–574. Although the test is one of spontaneity the time factor may enter into the determination whether the declaration was spontaneous: *R v Le Roux* (1897) 14 SC 424.
6 *S v Tuge* supra.
7 *S v Tuge* supra.
8 *S v Tuge* supra.
9 *S v Tuge* supra. See further *R v Le Roux* supra; *R v Taylor* supra.
10 *Kelly v SAR & H* supra; *R v Gibson* (1887) 18 QB 537. Cf *S v Tuge* supra.

718 Statements relevant to bodily sensation A statement by a person who is unavailable as witness, that describes physical sensation, is receivable in evidence[1] if it was made contemporaneously with the sensation that it describes.[2] Since the purpose of receiving the evidence is to describe sensation, it follows that it cannot be used to establish the cause of the sensation.[3]

1 *Aveson v Lord Kinnaird* (1805) 6 East 188; 102 ER 1258; *R v Gloster* (1888) 16 Cox CC 471; *Gilbey v Great Western Railway Co* (1910) 102 LT 202; *Amys v Barton* 1912 1 KB 40 (CA); *Tickle v Tickle* [1968] 2 All ER 154 (Div); *R v Kaiser* 1927 WLD 278.

Cf *R v William Nicholas* (1846) 2 C & K 246; 175 ER 102.
2 *R v Gloster* supra; but see *R v Black* (1922) 16 Car 118 196.
3 *R v Gloster* supra; *R v Kaiser* supra.

719 Statements and acts relevant to a person's state of mind When a person's state of mind is in issue, anything which that person said or did at the time when there was no reason for the person to give a false impression by his or her acts or statements of what his or her state of mind was, is relevant and admissible to prove his or her state of mind.[1] A person's state of mind, therefore, may be proved by what the person said him or herself at the material time, or by what may be inferred from the person's conduct. Thus a contemporaneous statement may be received for the purpose of drawing an inference that a person had knowledge of something[2] or that an act was done with a particular intention.[3] There is some authority for the proposition that an express assertion of intention to do something can be used only against a party and not in his or her favour.[4] The correct approach should be to admit such statements if they are relevant[5] and if they were made naturally,[6] that is to say, in circumstances when there was no reason for the declarant to give a false impression by the statement.[7] It is controversial whether or not such evidence was admitted under an exception to the hearsay rule;[8] it would seem that the better view is that statements of intention are admitted not as evidence of the truth of what they assert but simply as evidence to show the probability of the intended acts having been committed.[9] It follows that, in determining whether the statement is relevant (that is to say, whether it has real bearing on the probability of the acts having been done), the nearness in point of time of the declaration to the time when the act is alleged to have been committed, will be an important consideration.[10]

Evidence of what was said by someone else, that could have had an influence upon another person at the material time, may be received if an inference may properly be drawn as to the latter's state of mind from having heard the statement.[11]

1 *Thomas v Connell* 4 M & W 267; 150 ER 1429; *Estate De Wet v De Wet* 1924 CPD 341 342; *Curtis Estate v Gronningsaeter* 1942

CPD 531; *Ruto Flour Mills (Pty) Ltd v Adelson (3)* 1958 4 SA 311 (T); *Jacobs v Auto Protection Insurance Co Ltd* 1964 3 SA 379 (W);

S v R 1965 2 SA 463 (W); *Vermaak v Parity Insurance Co Ltd (in liquidation)* 1966 2 SA 312 (W); *Da Mata v Otto* 1971 1 SA 763 (T). See further *Lloyd v Powell Duffryn Steam Coal Co Ltd* 1914 AC 733; *R v Gandfield* (1846) 2 Cox CC 43; *R v Kukubula* 1958 3 SA 698 (SR).

2 *Estate De Wet v De Wet* supra; *Jacobs v Auto Protection Insurance Co Ltd* supra. Cf *Maudsley v Maudsley's Trustees* 1940 WLD 166 168; *Langham v Milne* 1961 1 SA 811 (N) 815. See also *R v Hlope* 1947 2 SA 453 (N).

3 *Senior v Commissioner for Inland Revenue* 1960 1 SA 709 (A). See further *Curtis Estate v Gronningsaeter* supra; *Ex parte Currie & May* 1966 2 SA 184 (R); *R v Malgas* 1943 CPD 528.

4 *Albrecht v Newberry* 1974 4 SA 314 (E). See also *R v Hardy* (1794) 24 Howell's State Trials 1065 1093: Such statements "are evidence against a prisoner and not for him, because the presumption is . . . that no man would declare anything against himself unless it were true; but that every man if he were in a difficulty, would make declarations for himself"; *R v William Arnold Thomson* 1912 3 KB 19. But see Wigmore *Evidence* 6 par 1732.

5 *Sugden v Lord St Leonards* 1876 1 P 154 242. See further *R v James Buckley* (1873) 13 Cox CC 293; *De Lange v Rudman* 1928 EDL 439; *R v Foreman (1)* 1952 1 SA 423 (SR); *R v Basson* 1965 1 SA 697 (C). In *Gleneagles*

Farm Dairy v Schoombee 1947 4 SA 66 (E) evidence was received that A had said that he was going to buy certain cows as evidence to show that he had bought them (but only to corroborate other evidence). Statements of intention were not received in *R v William Arnold Thomson* supra; *Albrecht v Newberry* supra; *R v Henry Wainwright & Thomas George Wainwright* (1875) 13 Cox CC 171. It may well be, however, that *R v William Arnold Thomson* supra, albeit unsound in principle, is binding in SA if this is regarded as a matter of hearsay. If this is so, evidence of this kind will be inadmissible.

6 Wigmore par 1725. Wigmore, however, may not be reflecting the English law and hence the South African law which, possibly, would be constrained to follow the unsound *R v William Arnold Thomson* supra.

7 Ibid.

8 See Zeffertt 1974 *SALJ* 425 where the contention that evidence of this kind had been admitted as an exception to the hearsay rule was made too dogmatically.

9 *Sugden v Lord St Leonards* supra 242.

10 *Sugden v Lord St Leonards* supra 242. See further *Robson, Assignees of Blakey v Kemp* 4 Esp 233; 170 ER 703; *In re Fletcher, Reading v Fletcher* 1917 1 Ch 339 342.

11 *R v Lalla* 1945 EDL 156; *R v Vincent, Frost & Edwards* (1840) 9 C & P 275; 173 ER 833; *Subramaniam v Public Prosecutor* 1956 1 WLR 965; 22 Digest (Repl) 95 530.

HEARSAY

720 General rule Subject to the provisions of any other law, hearsay evidence may not be admitted as evidence at criminal or civil proceedings, unless:

(a) each party against whom the evidence is to be adduced agrees to the admission thereof as evidence at such proceedings;

(b) the person upon whose credibility the probative value of such evidence depends, him or herself testifies at such proceedings; or

(c) the court, having regard to:

(i) the nature of the proceedings;

(ii) the nature of the evidence;

(iii) the purpose for which the evidence is tendered;

(iv) the probative value of the evidence;

(v) the reason why the evidence is not given by the person upon whose credibility the probative value of such evidence depends;

(vi) any prejudice to a party which the admission of such evidence might entail; and

(vii) any other factor which should in the opinion of the court be taken into account, is of the opinion that such evidence should be admitted in the interests of justice.[1]

Hearsay evidence may be provisionally admitted under section 3(1) of the Law of Evidence Amendment Act of 1988 if the court is informed that the person upon whose credibility the probative value of such evidence depends, will him or herself testify in such proceedings. Should this person not testify, the hearsay evidence evidence must be left out of the account unless the hearsay evidence is admitted under section 3(1)(a) or (c).[2]

The court has decided in terms of section 3(1)(c) to admit hearsay evidence, even though certain of the factors mentioned in section 3(1)(c), such as the nature of the proceedings and of the evidence and its purpose favoured exclusion. Because the probative value of the evidence, the reason why hearsay evidence was given, possible prejudice and an "other factor", namely serious consequences if the evidence were to be refused, all favoured acceptance, the court exercised its discretion and accepted the evidence.[3]

In deciding this point, the fact that the evidence would historically have been received as an exception to the hearsay rule, is a strong factor in admitting it under the new legislation.[4]

An unrepresented accused is entitled to have the effect of section 3(1)(c) explained to him or her; the accused also has a right to be heard on the issue whether the section should be invoked.[5]

Courts have been aware of the risks of accepting untested hearsay examination, especially in criminal cases. It has been held, on the one hand, that the flexibility of the new approach should not be negated by introducing reliability as an overriding requirement, or by falling back upon the common law rule against hearsay, and that it would not be in accordance with the intention of the legislature to hold that section 3(1)(c) should be applied only sparingly, or reluctantly.[6] On the other hand, it has also been held that the court has to be satisfied that it could safely eliminate any risk of falsification or deliberate reconstruction[7] and that it should not lightly decide in favour of allowing hearsay on controversial issues on which conflicting evidence has already been given.[8]

1 Law of Evidence Amendment Act 45 of 1988 s 3(1). See *S v Aspeling* 1998 1 SACR 561 (C); *Elandsrand Gold Mining Co Ltd v NUM obo Silemala* [1998] 8 BALR 1073 (IMSSA); *S v Mbanjwa* 2000 2 SACR 100 (D). See also S v *Ndhlovu* 2002 2 SACR 325 (SCA) on the test for "the interests of justice".

2 S 3(3).

3 *Hlongwane v Rector, St Francis College* 1989 3 SA 318 (D). An interesting point is whether the court exercises a discretion in this regard, or applies a legal rule. Zeffertt *Evidence* 368–369 argues for the latter interpretation because it would give the accused better constitutional protection and because the grounds for appeal are wider. This was also the approach taken by the Supreme Court of Appeal in the recent cases of *McDonald's Corporation v Joburgers Drive-Inn Restaurant (Pty) Ltd, McDonald's Corporation v Dax Prop CC, McDonald's Corporation v Joburgers Drive-Inn Restaurant (Pty) Ltd* [1996] 4 All SA 1

(A); 1997 1 SA 1 (A) 27 and *Makhathini v Road Accident Fund* [2002] 1 All SA 413 (SCA), 2002 1 SA 511 (SCA) 521. See *S v Ramavhale* 1996 1 SACR 639 (A) where the court warned against admitting hearsay evidence provisionally in terms of the Law of Evidence Amendment Act 45 of 1988 s 3(1)(c) where such evidence is decisive in convicting the accused, unless there are compelling justifications. In *Chairperson Independent Electoral Commission v Die Krans Ontspanningsoord (Edms) Bpk* 1997 1 SA 244 (T) the defendant was not allowed to rely on inadmissible hearsay evidence in summary judgment proceedings.

4 *Mnyama v Gxalaba* 1990 1 SA 650 (C). See also the authority quoted in par 722 fn 2 post.

5 *S v Ngwani* 1990 1 SACR 449 (N).

6 *Hewan v Kourie* 1993 3 SA 233 (T). See also with regard to labour law matters *NUMSA obo Kemp v Baldwins Steel* 1997 7 BALR 800

(CCMA).
7   *S v Mpofu* 1993 2 SA SACR 109 (N).
8   *S v Cekiso* 1990 4 SA 20 (E); and see *Metedad v*

National Employers' General Insurance Co Ltd
1992 1 SA 494 (W) as well as *Makhatini v Road Accident Fund* supra.

721 The concept of hearsay For the purposes of the Law of Evidence Amendment Act[1] hearsay evidence means evidence, whether oral or in writing, the probative value of which depends on the credibility of any person other than the person giving such evidence.[2] This definition is obviously wider than the previous common law one, as expressed in *Estate De Wet v De Wet*,[3] thereby including as hearsay certain statements which were doubtful before, such as "hearsay by implication".[4] The statutory amendment deliberately attempted to move away from the intention with which a statement is tendered (the "declaration oriented" approach) as a distinguishing feature of hearsay evidence, towards emphasis on the creditworthiness of the person who made the statement (the "declarant oriented" approach), on grounds which are arguable.[5]

The fact that a statutory definition now exists, does not necessarily mean that it will always be easy to determine whether given evidence amounts to hearsay, or not. Since the Act reads "Subject to the provisions of any other law", older statutory provisions dealing with hearsay will somehow have to be reconciled with it. The most important of these are chapter VI of the Civil Proceedings Evidence Act[6] (read with section 222 of the Criminal Procedure Act)[7] and the Electronic Communications and Transactions Act.[8] The statutory definition also includes the phrase "evidence, whether oral or in writing", which is so wide as to obscure the difference between documentary evidence and written hearsay, which was easily made in the older (declaration-oriented) approach, by simply looking at the intention with which the evidence is tendered. The previous approach also used the expression "statement", instead of the much wider present term "evidence".[9] In the third place, the problem of distinguishing hearsay in certain grey border areas has not been removed by the new statutory definition, but simply moved to another area, namely, when would evidence *depend* upon the credibility of another witness? The problem is, of course, that the credibility of the witness (in court) and the non-witness (who made the original statement) may both be in issue. It has been suggested that a phrase such as "controlled or determined by" is preferable to phrases such as "rests upon to a slight extent" or "rests entirely on".[10] Even so, the test is likely to be problematical to apply in practical circumstances.[11]

In practice, the court has not jettisoned the importance of the intention with which a statement is being tendered in evidence, as a distinguishing feature of hearsay evidence (the declaration-oriented approach.) In a post-1988 case, *Mdani v Allianz Insurance Ltd*,[12] Van Heerden JA warned against confusing two different questions, "i.e. whether an extra-curial admission was made and whether its content is true": "If A testified that B made such an admission, A's evidence in itself is clearly not hearsay. Whether B in fact made the admission, depends upon B's credibility and can be tested by cross-examination. What is hearsay, is the content of the admission if it is to be used to establish the truth of what was said. And whether the content is true or not, depends entirely upon B's credibility . . . Accordingly . . . A's evidence as to the content of B's admission falls within the definition of 'hearsay evidence' in s 3(4) of the Act and may therefore be admitted in terms of s 3(1) of the Act."[13]

It is now established that hearsay evidence is admissible in bail proceedings.[14]

1   45 of 1988.
2   S 1. Regarding hearsay at an intenal discipli-
    nary hearing, see Whitear-Nel 2001 *JBL* 73.

3   1924 CPD 341.
4   As was the case in *S v Van Niekerk* 1964 1 SA
    729 (C). In editions of his handbook

published before the latest statutory amendments, Zeffertt *Evidence* considered implied assertions to be inadmissible hearsay, but admissible if made concerning the conduct of the maker of the statement him or herself (probably because it goes to show state of mind). Schmidt *Bewysreg*, on the other hand, in prior editions, considered implied assertions not to amount to inadmissible hearsay. The view against admissibility is probably based on the case of *George Wright v Doe dem Sandford Tatham* (1937) 7 A & E 313; 112 ER 489; affirmed (1838) 5 C & F 670; 7 ER 559. The English case might, however, also be based on the fact that the excluded hearsay evidence also amounted to opinion evidence. The *Van Niekerk* case was probably wrongly decided in that the excluded letters ought to have been regarded as relevant circumstantial evidence – in other words, it had been tendered "circumstantially" and not "testimonially".

5 The SA Law Commission was obviously influenced by the doctoral thesis of Paizes *The Concept of Hearsay with Particular Emphasis on Implied Assertions* (1983), and included ch 10 of the thesis as an annexure to their report and recommendations which presaged the amendments. Paizes was responsible for the distinction mentioned in the main text above, between declaration- and declarant-oriented approaches, the author favouring the latter. His principle example is of X saying: "I can speak", which is then tendered in court, in X's absence, with the object of proving that X can speak. According to Paizes, this exposes the weakness of the declaration-oriented approach which will have to declare the statement hearsay, since it is being tendered for the truth of its contents ("tendered testimonially"). Schutte 1991 *THRHR* 495 et seq, is also impressed with this argument. The truth of the matter is, however, that the fact of X speaking is actually being "tendered circumstantially" to prove the mere fact that he is able to speak, the contents of his statement being completely irrelevant – he may as well have said "I am a Chinaman", or "when does the next bus leave for Clapham?" For this reason it is not hearsay evidence – even according to the declaration-oriented approach – see Van der Merwe *Obiter* 64 72. Paizes also prefers the arguments of (with respect) lesser known luminaries in the field of Evidence, such as Tribe, Jones and Lempert and Saltzburg, in preference to the views of Phipson, Cross

and McCormick (1983 *SALJ* 71 89). His comparative research with regard to opinion polls and hearsay in the same article indicates that England, Canada, the United States and New Zealand all prefer the declaration-oriented approach, with SA being split 50/50 (this was, of course, before the amending legislation in 1988). Cross closes his argument in favour of the declaration-oriented approach as follows: "It is nevertheless contended that concentration upon the presence of an intention to assert provides the most defensible watershed between hearsay and non-hearsay both as a matter of logical coherence and of practical common-sense" (517).

6 25 of 1965. See also par 800 post.

7 51 of 1977.

8 25 of 2002.

9 A will, a contract, or the address on an envelope would, for instance, not have been hearsay, since it was not being tendered to prove the "truth" of its contents, although questions such as authenticity would have taken up the court's time (see Binder *Hearsay Handbook* (2 ed) 16 21; and see *US v Singer* (8th Cir 1982) 687 F2d 1135 1147 and *US v Arrington* (5th Cir 1980) 618 F2d 1119 1126). De Vos and Van der Merwe *Stell LR* 1993 1 1 19 fn 69 would probably classify this under "documentary evidence", which they define as "getuienis wat by wyse van 'n dokument aangebied word" in order to distinguish it from "written evidence", which they define as "die mededelings vervat in 'n beëdigde verklaring", and to which they confine the scope of the statutory definition of written hearsay. This seems to be unnecessarily restrictive, leaving open the problem of written statements which are tendered not to prove that the contents are true, but that they have in fact been written. They are therefore being "tendered circumstantially", to allow the court to draw its own conclusions from the circumstances of the statement. *Aliter* in the case of a written witness statement if it was "tendered testimonially", namely it was expected of the court to believe the truth of the "story" related by the written statement. See Van der Merwe *Obiter* vol 15 1 1994, *Mdani v Allianz Insurance Ltd* 1991 1 SA 184 (A); pars 787 et seq post.

10 Zeffertt *Evidence* 366 suggests a test of "depended suffiently upon" with regard to the credibility of someone other than the witness so as to create sufficiently great

potential for prejudice.

11 De Vos and Van der Merwe (1993) 1 *Stell LR* 13 et seq; and see *Hewan v Kourie* 1993 3 SA 233 (T) where the court conceded that "to an extent" a statement depended also on the credibility of the witness in court, but that this did not render the statement of her deceased husband anything other than hearsay. The court felt it unnecessary to decide the exact meaning of the words "depends upon" and contented itself with stating that "depends upon" clearly cannot mean "to

rest entirely upon" (236G). See also *Rosenthal v Mastroguiseppe* [2000] 4 All SA 295 (SCA).

12 Supra.

13 189–190. Both Schmidt *Bewysreg* 485 and De Vos and Van der Merwe (1993) 4 *Stellenbosch LR* 7 19 concede that the intention with which a statement is tendered will still play a role in determining whether the statement is hearsay or not.

14 *Nqumashe v S* [2001] 4 All SA 471 (NC); 2001 2 SACR 310 (NC).

722 Exceptions to the hearsay rule under the common law A great number of statutory exceptions existed to the inadmissibility of, especially, written hearsay. It is unlikely that many of the common law exceptions will be of great practical importance in future, especially in view of the admission of hearsay in terms of section 3(1)(c) of the Law of Evidence Amendment Act[1] and the new set of criteria set out therein. However, the court may, in deciding upon the admissibility of hearsay evidence, have regard to the common law. It has, in fact, been decided that a court should not lightly decide not to admit evidence which has traditionally been admissible.[2]

The admissibility of certain trade or business records remains relevant. It had been mooted as a possible solution for the admissibility of computer records in the report of the South African Law Commission in this regard, and has now, in fact, become part of the recent legislation.[3] At present trade or business records are admissible in criminal matters in terms of section 221 of the Criminal Procedure Act.[4]

1 45 of 1988.

2 Precedent has developed along two lines in this regard. The more "cautious" approach has been followed in *S v Cekiso* 1990 4 SA 20 (E) and *Aetiology Today CC t/a Somerset Schools v Van Aswegen* 1992 1 SA 807 (W). The more "enthusiastic" approach appears in *Mnyama v Gxalaba* 1990 1 SA 650 (C) 653; *Metedad v National Employers' General Insurance Co Ltd* 1992 1 SA 494 (W) and *Hewan v Kourie* 1993 3 SA 233 (T). The whole question of documentary hearsay in the new dispensation is discussed in the chapter on documentary evidence.

3 Working document 60, Project 95 of the SA Law Commission. S 15(4) of the Electronic Communications and Transcations Act 25 of 2002 now admits into evidence "a data message made by a person in the ordinary course of business". See also pars 723 801 post.

4 51 of 1977, which is, in turn, based upon s 1 of the English Criminal Evidence Act of 1965, which was passed as a result of the decisions in *Myers v Director of Public Prosecutions* 1965 AC 1001; *R v Myers* [1964] 1 All ER 877 (CCA).

723 Admissibility of certain trade or business records[1] In criminal proceedings, where direct oral evidence of a fact would be admissible, any statement contained in a document and tending to establish that fact is admissible as evidence of that fact if certain requirements are satisfied.[2] The document has to be (or must form part of) a record relating to any trade or business and must have been compiled, in the course of that trade or business, from information supplied, directly or indirectly, by persons who have (or who may be reasonably supposed to have) personal knowledge of the matters dealt with in the information they supply.[3] In addition, the person who supplied the information recorded in the statement must either be dead, outside the Republic, unfit by reason of his or her physical or mental condition to attend as a witness or the person must not be able, with reasonable diligence, to be identified or found or be reasonably expected, having regard to the time which has elapsed since he or she supplied the information as well as all the circumstances, to have any recollection of the matters dealt with in the information he suppled.[4]

For the purpose of deciding whether or not a statement is admissible, the court may draw any reasonable inference from the form or content of the document in which the statement is contained, and may, in deciding whether or not a person is fit to attend as a witness, act on a certificate purporting to be a certificate of a registered medical practitioner.[5]

In estimating the weight to be attached to a statement that has been received, regard has to be had to all the circumstances from which an inference might reasonably be drawn as to its accuracy or inaccuracy and, in particular, to the question whether or not the person who supplied the information that was recorded in it had done so contemporaneously with the occurrence or existence of the facts stated in it and to the question whether or not that person, or any person concerned with making or keeping the record containing the statement, had an incentive to conceal or misrepresent the facts.[6]

A "business" is defined as including any public transport, public utility or similar undertaking carried on by a local authority and the activities of the post office, and the railways administration.[7] Included in the definition of a "document" is any device by means of which information is recorded or stored.[8] Thus it would seem that a recording disc, a tape recording and a computer print-out are documents within the meaning of the section.[9]

A "statement" includes any representation of fact whether made in words or otherwise.[10]

These provisions do not affect the admissibility of any other evidence which would have been admissible but for their enactment.[11]

Even though the matter is more fully dealt with under the section on computer evidence, it should be mentioned at this stage that the admissibility of trade or business records was part of the solution espoused by the South African Law Commission as a replacement for the Computer Evidence Act.[12] The new Electronic Communications and Transactions Act has now included "in the ordinary course of business" as one of the grounds for admitting data messages as evidence.[13] The matter will be more fully discussed below.[14]

1 S 221 of the Criminal Procedure Act 51 of 1977, that relates to such records, is framed in the same terms as s 1 of the English Criminal Evidence Act of 1965 which was passed in consequence of the decision of *Myers v Director of Public Prosecutions* 1965 AC 1001; *R v Myers* [1964] 1 All ER 877 (CCA) (Cross *Evidence* 498).

2 Criminal Procedure Act 51 of 1977 s 221(1). A "record" (unlike a document) is not defined. *R v Gwilliam* [1968] 3 All ER 821 (CA) did not decide whether a consignment note was a "record". See also *R v Barend Christian Greyling van Vreden* (1973) 57 CAR 818 (CA).

3 S 221(1)(a).

4 S 221(1)(b).

5 S 221(2).

6 S 221(3).

7 S 221(5).

8 Ibid.

9 Cross 498–499. See *S v Harper* 1981 1 SA 88 (D), where it was held that a computer print-out was admissible in terms of s 221. See further *S v De Villiers* 1993 1 SACR 574 (Nm) and *Dareen Sithole v The State* (unreported decision of the NPD – case no AR 641/90 – appeal judgment given on 14/3/1991). The latter case expressed several points of criticism on the *Harper* decision. See also fn 13 infra.

10 S 221(5).

11 S 221(4).

12 57 of 1983, which has been repealed by the

Electronic Communications and Transactions Act 25 of 2002 s 92.
13 S 15(4) of the Electronic Communications and Transactions Act which not only makes

these data messages admissible but also rebuttable proof of the facts contained therein.
14 See par 606 post.

724 Former proceedings Ordinarily, at common law, the record of a witness's testimony in former proceedings is hearsay and, as such, it is not evidence of the truth of its contents.[1] It may, however, be otherwise relevant, for instance to show inconsistency of conduct. Thus, the record of a criminal trial cannot, generally, be received in subsequent civil proceedings to prove the truth of what was said; but the criminal record may be handed in as an exhibit and the witnesses may be cross-examined on their previous testimony.[2]

To this principle there are statutory and common law exceptions, the most obvious being that the parties may agree to the former proceedings constituting evidence of their content.[3]

An exception at common law is of particular importance in civil proceedings. Evidence of a witness in former proceedings is admissible in subsequent proceedings between the same parties (or their privies) that involve substantially the same issues,[4] provided that the witness is unavailable to testify[5] and the opposition has had an opportunity to cross-examine.[6]

The criminal position is governed by the Criminal Procedure Act.[7]

The record of preparatory examination may be proved by producing it[8] or by proof of a copy.[9] Where an accused has been arraigned for sentence under section 139(a), the preparatory examination record, upon being proved, becomes evidence against the accused and part of the record of the court in which he or she has been arraigned.[10] Again, when a accused is arraigned for trial, the preparatory examination record, on being proved, becomes part of the record of the trial court and evidence against the accused (any admission made by the accused will also stand) *if* he or she pleads guilty or *if* the parties agree.[11] The record of the evidence of a bail application brought by an accused is admissible against the accused at the subsequent trial.[12]

There are important provisions, one mandatory, the other discretionary, relating to missing witnesses. The evidence of a witness, that has been recorded either at a former trial or a preparatory examination, is admissible at the trial of the accused if it is proved to the satisfaction of the court that the witness is dead, incapable of giving evidence, too ill to attend, or kept away from the trial by the accused. The evidence has to have been duly recorded and it must appear from the record of the former trial or preparatory examination that the accused or the state (as the case may be) had a full opportunity to cross-examine.[13] Since it is a requirement that the state must have had an opportunity to cross-examine, it follows that the accused must have the right to prove such evidence.[14] The trial court has a discretion to receive a witness's evidence at a preparatory examination, or former trial, if the witness cannot, after diligent search, be found or if he or she cannot be compelled to attend. Again, the evidence has to have been duly recorded and it must either appear from the previous record, or be proved to the satisfaction of the court, that the accused (or the state) had a full opportunity of cross-examining the witness.[15] The court may exercise its discretion on the application of the accused.[16]

In both civil and criminal proceedings, a witness's evidence in former proceedings will be received to prove the truth of its contents if it is admissible under section 34 of the Civil Proceedings Evidence Act[17] (which applied to criminal proceedings by virtue of section 222 of the Criminal Procedure Act).[18]

1 *African Guarantee & Indemnity Co Ltd v Moni* 1916 AD 524.

2 *African Guarantee & Indemnity Co Ltd v Moni* supra; *Gua v Willock* 1916 EDL 371; *Botha v Tunbridge* 1933 EDL 95 104; *Hattingh v Le Roux* 1939 EDL 217; *Rand Cold Storage & Supply Co Ltd v Alligianes* 1968 2 SA 122 (T) 125.

3 *Fourie v Morley & Co* 1947 2 SA 218 (N) 222; *Langham v Milne* 1961 1 SA 811 (N) 816.

4 *Da Silva v Da Silva* 1946 SR 109.

5 Schmidt *Bewysreg* 273–274; Zeffertt *Evidence* 401.

6 *Lensvelt & Co Ltd v John Swift Ltd* 1920 WLD 112.

7 51 of 1977.

8 S 129(1).

9 S 235(1). Cf *S v Kimbani* 1979 3 SA 339 (E).

10 S 140(2)(a).

11 S 141(3).

12 *S v Adams* 1993 1 SACR 611 (C). See also *S v Dlamini* 1998 5 BCLR 552 (N); *S v Dlamini, S v Dladla, S v Joubert, S v Schietekat* 1999 7 BCLR 771 (CC); 1994 SA 623 (CC); 1999 2 SACR 51 (CC); *S v Snyman* 1999 8 BCLR 931 (C); 1999 2 SACR 169 (C); *S v Cloete* 1999 2 SACR 137 (C).

13 Ss 214(a) 215; *R v McDonald* 1927 AD 110;

R v Mkwanazi 1935 TPD 129; *R v Goliath* 1946 EDL 310; *R v Matyeni* 1958 2 SA 573 (E).

14 This has long been controversial. For the position under former enactments, see *R v Cele* 1960 1 SA 292 (C); *R v Mazibuko* 1961 3 SA 113 (N); *S v Kali* 1964 1 SA 237 (O); *S v Andrews* 1964 4 SA 805 (C).

15 Ss 214(b) 215. On the exercise of the discretion, see *R v Andrews* 1920 AD 290; *R v Stoltz* 1925 WLD 38; *R v Rasool* 1927 TPD 73; *R v Malan* 1948 2 SA 327 (T); *R v Stoffels* 1948 2 SA 809 (C); *R v Dladla (1)* 1961 3 SA 919 (D); *R v Cele* supra; *S v Ngubane* 1961 4 SA 377 (N). An appeal court will not interfere with the exercise of the discretion by the exercise of its own discretion: *R v Andrews* supra; but the discretion has to be exercised in the normal judicial manner: *R v Labson* 1968 4 SA 108 (R) 109.

16 See fn 13 supra.

17 25 of 1965. Cf. *Magwanyana v Standard General Insurance Co Ltd* 1996 1 SA 254 (D). See *United Tobacco Co Ltd v Goncalves* 1996 1 SA 209 (W) for the meaning of the word "interested" contained in the Civil Proceedings Evidence Act 25 of 1965 s 34(3).

18 51 of 1977. See par 726 post.

725 The hearsay rule and the Constitution The Constitution[1] bestows upon an accused in a criminal trial, the right to "adduce and challenge evidence", which seems to imply the right to confront his or her accusers . Failure to explain this right to an unrepresented accused has been held to be unconstitutional in Namibia.[2] The question now arises whether the decision of a South African presiding officer to allow hearsay evidence might not infringe the constitutional right of the accused to confront the person whose statement is now being admitted in that person's absence from court.

Based on a comparison with the position in the United States of America, De Vos and Van der Merwe[3] are of the opinion that, since this view has not been taken in the United States, which is roughly comparable to South Africa, it is unlikely to be adopted in South Africa. The American situation obtains because the hearsay exception has been held to be historically reconcilable with the right to a fair trial in the United States; there is no absolute overlap between the right to confrontation and the prohibition against hearsay, even though they "stem from the same roots"; and the right to confrontation did not intend to create a new rule of process, since the 6th amendment to the American Constitution was intended to consolidate and preserve the right to confrontation – "and not to broaden it or disturb the exceptions".[4]

1 Constitution of the Republic of SA 108 of 1996.

2 *S v Wellington* 1991 1 SACR 144 (Nm).

3 *Stell LR* 1993 1 1 34 et seq and the academic and judicial authority there quoted.

4 *Dutton v Evans* 400 US 74 86 (1970).

PRIOR CONSISTENT STATEMENTS

726 General rule The prior consistent statements of a witness, whether oral or in writing, whether testified to by the witness or someone else, are excluded[1] because they are irrelevant, of insufficient probative force and capable of being easily fabricated.[2] Although this would have been more logical, present South African law is constrained by the residuary clauses pertaining to 30 May 1961: a prior consistent statement will be admissible only if it falls within a recognised exception to the rule.[3] A prior consistent statement will be received if it is admissible as part of the *res gestae*;[4] if it satisfies the requirements of part VI of the Civil Proceedings Evidence Act[5] (as incorporated into criminal proceedings);[6] to rebut a suggestion of recent fabrication;[7] as a complaint in a sexual case;[8] for purposes of identification;[9] and, possibly, the accused's favourable statements made at the time of charge or when being found in possession of recently stolen property may be admitted.[10] Here, the latter four exceptions will be discussed. When prior consistent statements are received, such statements are not evidence of the truth of their contents: they are admitted as being relevant to consistency.[11]

When evidence of a prior consistent statement is proved, it is preferable that it is testified to by the person to whom it was made or, at least, that the latter should confirm what the witness said.[12]

1 *Corke v Corke & Cooke* 1958 P 93; [1958] 1 All ER 224 (CA). See further *R v Manyana* 1931 AD 386; *R v Rose* 1937 AD 467; *R v Stephen Jood* 1949 1 SA 298 (G); *Vengtas v Nydoo (3)* 1963 3 SA 441 (D); *R v Mack* 1969 4 SA 53 (R) 54; *S v Bergh* 1976 4 SA 857 (A). See also *Jones v South Eastern & Chatham Railway Co's Managing Committee* (1918) 87 LJKB 775; 118 LT 802; *Gillie v Posho Ltd* [1939] 2 All ER 196 (PC); *Fox v General Medical Council* [1960] 3 All ER 225 (PC); Gooderson 1968 *Cam LJ* 64; Criminal Procedure Act 51 of 1977 s 190(1).
2 *R v Rose* supra; *Fox v General Medical Council* supra 230. See further *R v Roberts* [1942] 1 All ER 187 (CCA); Cross *Evidence* 281–282; cf Schmidt *Bewysreg* 397–399.
3 Cf Zeffertt *Evidence* 403–404: "But English

decisions appear, as at 20 (sic) May 1961, to have erected it into a rigid rule, subject to a list of exceptions." This is notwithstanding a decision such as *Holtzhauzen v Roodt* [1997] 3 All SA 551 (W); 1997 4 SA 766 (W) 774 which argues that no *numerus clausus* exists. Cf also Schmidt 399 who similary argues against a *numerus clausus*.
4 See par 716 ante. See also Cross 288–290.
5 25 of 1965. See par 721 ante.
6 By s 222 of the Criminal Procedure Act 51 of 1977.
7 Par 727 post.
8 Par 728 post.
9 Par 729 post.
10 Par 730 post.
11 Pars 727–730 post.
12 *R v M* 1959 1 SA 434 (A) 439.

727 To rebut a suggestion of recent fabrication A prior consistent statement is admissible to rebut a suggestion to a witness that his or her testimony has been recently fabricated.[1] A general attack on a witness's evidence will not suffice: there has to be the suggestion that the witness's story is a concoction and not merely that he or she has been inconsistent.[2] The prior statement when proved (usually in re-examination)[3] is not evidence of the truth of its content and does not corroborate the witness: it is relevant to support the witness's credibility by showing that he or she is consistent.[4]

1 *Pincus v Solomon (1)* 1942 WLD 237; *R v Kizi* 1950 4 SA 532 (A); *R v Dart (2)* 1951 1 SA 483 (W); *S v Sitwayi* 1961 4 SA 538 (E); *S v Mkohle* 1990 1 SACR 95 (A); *S v Winnaar* 1997 2 SACR 352 (O). See also *R v Arthur Benjamin* (1913) 8 CAR 146; *R v*

Roberts [1942] 1 All ER 187 (CCA); *R v Charles Oyesiku* (1971) 56 CAR 240; *R v Oyesiku* 1972 Crim LR 179.
2 *Fox v General Medical Council* [1960] 3 All ER 225 (PC).
3 Cross *Evidence* 291; but see *R v M* 1959 1

SA 434 (A) 439, which suggests that it would be best to prove a prior consistent statement by the testimony of the person to whom it was made or, at least, to get him or

her to confirm the witness.
4 *R v Vlok* 1951 1 SA 26 (C); *R v Abrey* 1959 2 SA 76 (E).

728 Complaints in sexual cases Evidence of the fact that the victim of a sexual offence (including offences against males)[1] made a complaint shortly after its happening, together with the particulars of the complaint,[2] may be given both by the victim and the person to whom it was made.[3]

Originally, complaints were admitted in rape cases only,[4] but in modern practice they are received in charges of sodomy,[5] indecent assault,[6] incest,[7] illicit intercourse with girls under the age of 16,[8] indecent acts with young girls and boys,[9] and criminal *iniuria*.[10] It has been held that, for a complaint to be admissible, the offence has to involve both the elements of violence and indecency,[11] but this is no longer correct: the extension of the ambit of admissibility to offences in which there is no element of force or violence contradicts such a view.[12] What is now required is simply that the complainant has to be the *victim* of a sexual offence.[13] Thus the complaint of a willing, adult participant in sodomy, incest, or prostitution is not receivable; but the complaints of an *unwilling* participant in such offences would be.[14] The law protects certain persons and, if this protection is violated, the protected person may be regarded as a victim. Thus a complaint will be inadmissible on a charge of illicit intercourse across the colour line,[15] but admissible where a child has been a participant in a sexual offence,[16] or where a willing, mentally-defective woman is the victim (if she is competent to testify and does testify).[17] The sexual offence must, however, have a physical element: a complaint is inadmissible on charges of using obscene language[18] or incitement to commit a sexual offence;[19] but it would be admissible on a charge of common assault that involves an indecent act.[20] It is possible that a complaint will be admissible on a charge of attempting to commit a sexual offence if the attempt has gone far enough.[21] If a complaint is admissible on one charge, but inadmissible on another, it may still be received.[22] The line between admissibility and inadmissibility is drawn on historic grounds and should be regarded as the product of an anomalous exception to a sound general rule that should not be obliterated by too great an extension of the exception.[23]

To be admissible the complaint has to have been voluntarily made.[24] The mere fact that the complaint was made in response to questioning does not signify that the complaint was involuntary.[25] It would be otherwise if the complaint had been obtained as a result of intimidating interrogation.[26] The complaint must not be put into the mouth of the complainant by leading questions;[27] but it would be quite wrong to insist on the absence of leading questions as if the questioning were before a court of law in examination in chief.[28]

The complaint has to have been made at the earliest opportunity which, in the circumstances, could be reasonably expected, to the first person to whom the complainant could reasonably be expected to make it.[29] This is a flexible concept and the determination of what was the first reasonable opportunity will depend on the facts of each case: a child, in the nature of things, may be reasonably expected to take much longer to complain than an adult, married woman.[30] The complaint may even have been given at different stages.[31]

It is essential that the complainant should testify; if the complainant is an incompetent witness, the complaint may not be received.[32] Neither the fact of the complaint nor its content may be given.[33]

A complaint, when it is admitted, does not prove the truth of its contents. Nor does it constitute corroboration of the complainant. Its purpose is to show consistency in the complainant's conduct and to negative consent.[34] But it is not a requisite that consent be in issue.[35]

It is unclear whether complaints may be admitted in civil cases.[36]

1 *R v Camelleri* 1922 2 KB 122; *R v Burgess* 1927 TPD 14.

2 *R v Lillyman* 1896 2 QB 167.

3 See below.

4 Schmidt *Bewysreg* 406–407.

5 *R v Komsane* 1928 EDL 423; the complainant was a young child and hence a "victim" and not a willing, adult participant.

6 *R v Lillyman* supra; *Guttenberg v R* 1905 TS 207; *S v V* 1961 4 SA 201 (O).

7 *Lutchman v R* 1915 NPD 205. The complainant was unwilling and hence a "victim": see below and note the doubt expressed in *R v Bezuidenhout* 1946 CPD 190.

8 *R v Ellis* 1936 SWA 10; *R v Du Plessis* 1922 TPD 153.

9 *R v Burgess* supra; *R v Busse* 1932 SWA 16; *R v T* 1937 TPD 389.

10 *R v S* 1948 4 SA 419 (G).

11 *Guttenberg v R* supra; *Lutchman v R* supra.

12 Schmidt 407.

13 Ibid.

14 *R v Komsane* supra; *Lutchman v R* supra.

15 *R v Gloose* 1936 2 PH F155 (SWA).

16 *R v Gannon* 1906 TS 114.

17 Schmidt 407.

18 *Westermeyer v R* 1911 NPD 197.

19 *Guttenberg v R* supra.

20 *R v Dray* 1925 AD 553.

21 Schmidt 407 fn 60.

22 *R v S* supra.

23 Schmidt 407–408; *R v Ellis* supra; *R v Gloose* supra.

24 *S v T* 1963 1 SA 484 (A).

25 *R v C* 1955 4 SA 40 (N).

26 *R v William Henry Osborne* 1905 1 KB 551 556; *S v T* supra.

27 *R v William Henry Osborne* supra; *Gittleson v R* 1938 SR 161.

28 Schmidt 408–409.

29 *R v William Henry Osborne* supra; *R v S* supra; *R v C* supra.

30 *R v Gannon* supra; *R v C* supra; *S v T* supra; *R v P* 1967 2 SA 497 (R). Cf *R v Du Plessis* supra. Important factors are the age of the complainant, whether the complainant comprehended the indecency of the act, the presence (or absence) of a person to whom a complaint could reasonably be expected to have been made. An important question is whether the complainant, because of the lapse of time, could possibly have made an untrue complaint: *S v V* supra 206.

31 *R v Kautumundu* 1936 2 PH F154 (SWA): an immediate complaint to a sister and a later complaint on the same day to the parents.

32 *R v Smith Malete* 1907 TH 235; *R v Kgaladi* 1943 AD 255; *Billy Max Sparks v R* 1964 AC 964 (PC). In *S v R* 1965 2 SA 463 (W) the complainant gave evidence but could not testify as to the alleged rape. The complaint was received as relevant to her state of mind and to rebut a defence of consent. The correctness of the decision is doubtful; see Schmidt 410.

33 *R v Smith Malete* supra; *R v Kgaladi* supra; cf *R v Wallwork* (1958) 42 CAR 334.

34 *R v M* 1959 1 SA 352 (A) 355; *S v V* supra 205; *S v R* supra 465. The latter decision is probably incorrect on the facts since there was no evidence by the complainant with which the complaint could be consistent. See also the reasoning of Schmidt 412.

35 *R v William Henry Osborne* supra.

36 There is some authority for the extension of the rule to civil cases: *Jones v South Eastern & Chatham Rail Co's Managing Committee* (1918) 87 LJKB 775 778; *Fromhold v Fromhold* (1952) 1 TLR 1522 1526 1528. Cf *De B v De B* 1950 VLR 242; 1950 ALR 547 (Vict Sup Ct FC); but see *Anderson v Anderson* 3 1965 QWN 15 (Australian Digest 2d 27 par 38).

729 Identification of the accused The fact that a witness has identified the accused for the first time in court may have little value.[1] It follows that the evidence of a previous identification is relevant and a witness who identifies an accused may, therefore, be asked whether the witness identified the accused on a prior occasion.[2] Others may also testify to what the witness said.[3] It is the fact of prior identification[4] that is relevant and evidence is not receivable of what the witness said about the accused's identifying features or that he or she gave an accurate description.[5] Nor may evidence be received, under this exception, as to what the witness said about the accused's actions.[6] What is receivable is the mere fact of the physical identification coupled with the identifying words that formed part of it.[7] If the witness does not testify, the evidence of what the witness said will be hearsay and inadmissible[8] unless it is admitted in terms of section 3(1)(c) of the Law of Evidence Amendment Act;[9] if the witness does give evidence, but fails to mention the prior identification, it is moot whether it may be proved by another witness.[10] The purpose of such evidence, when it is received, is to show the witness's consistency.[11]

In *S v Zwayi*[12] it was held that evidence as the result of an identification parade cannot be excluded merely on the basis that the accused is not afforded an opportunity of legal representation during this procedure.

Prior identification of the accused under controlled circumstances is often proved by means of an identification parade. Since any possible infringement of the accused's rights at such a parade only goes to weight and not admissibility, there is no need for a trial within a trial to be held.[13]

1 *Rassool v R* 1932 NPD 112; *R v Velekaze* 1947 1 SA 162 (W); *R v Mputing* 1960 1 SA 785 (T) 788. Identification of the accused: a witness may be asked to describe the accused, but the inability of the witness to do so is not necessarily fatal to the witness's identification of the accused: *S v Pretorius* 1991 2 SACR 601 (A). A dock identification of an accused has so little value that it should be inadmissible: *S v Maradu* 1994 2 SACR 410 (W). For factors relevant to the assessment of identification evidence, see *S v Majiame* 1999 1 SACR 204 (O).
2 *Rassool v R* supra.
3 It is common practice for a policeman to testify that the witness pointed out the accused. The words that accompany the equivocal act of pointing out give meaning to it or are implied: *Rassool v R* supra 115; *R v Velekaze* supra 167. See *S v Daba* 1996 1 SACR 243 (E) for a judgment on the facts pertaining to evidence of circumstances under which an identification parade was held.
4 *R v Christie* 1914 AC 545 551: "But beyond the mere fact of such identification the examination ought not to have proceeded", per Viscount Haldane.
5 *R v M* 1959 1 SA 434 (A); *R v Mack* 1969 4 SA 53 (R).
6 Because it is only the fact of the identification that is admissible; see fn 4 supra.
7 See fns 3 6 supra.
8 Because there is no evidence for it to be consistent with and its reception would infringe the hearsay rule.
9 45 of 1988.

10 Cf Zeffertt *Evidence* 409 and Schmidt *Bewysreg* 402 fn 26. Cf also Lord Atkinson in *R v Christie* supra, who regarded such evidence as admissible, with Viscount Haldane and Lord Moulton who did not. See further *Rassool v R* supra (which favours the view of Lord Atkinson); *R v Velekaze* supra (which left the matter open). Schmidt's view rests on the contention that, since the person who is said to have made the prior identification gave evidence (albeit not of that fact) and is available for cross-examination, it is not hearsay. He loses sight of the purpose for which the evidence is received, namely, to confirm an identification in court. More cogent, therefore, is the contention that it is irrelevant who proves it: whether it is proved by the witness or another person it still shows consistency. Hearsay does not enter the picture. Cf *R v Kgaladi* 1943 AD 255. See, further, Cross *Evidence* 293 fn 2; Gooderson 1968 *Cam LJ* 64.
11 *R v Christie* supra 551.
12 1998 2 BCLR 242 (Ck); 1997 2 SACR 772 (Ck).
13 *S v Mokoena* 1998 2 SACR 642 (W). An accused has no right to refuse to participate in a legally constituted identification parade whether or not the accused has had the benefit of prior legal advice: *S v Mphala* 1999 4 BCLR 481 (W); 1998 1 SACR 654 (W). See *S v Monyane* 2001 1 SACR 115 (T) for the circumstances when a trial-within-a-trial will be held to determine the admissibility of an identification parade.

730 Statements by an accused on being taxed with incriminating facts It has been said of English practice that a favourable statement made by the accused to the police, when taxed with incriminating facts, is admissible because of its relevance in showing the reaction of the accused.[1] Again, what an accused says in explanation of having been found in possession of stolen property, may be relevant to show consistency if he or she tells the same story in court.[2] Since these exceptions appear to have been recognised at common law[3] they should apply in South Africa in the absence of a local practice to the contrary. The statement is not evidence of the truth of its content: its reception is for the purpose of proving consistency.[4]

1 Cross *Evidence* 294–295; Gooderson 1968 *Cam LJ* 64; *R v Storey* (1968) 52 CAR 334.
2 Cross 218–219; Gooderson 64.
3 See the authorities cited by Gooderson quoted by Cross 293 fn 20.
4 *R v Storey* supra.

ADMISSIONS AND CONFESSIONS

731 General An admission is a statement adverse to the party making it; a confession is a particular kind of admission made in relation to a criminal charge. An admission may be "formal" or "informal". A formal admission is made in the pleadings or orally in court with a view to shortening the proceedings by placing the admitted fact out of contention; it is not an item of evidence, but a procedural way of dispensing with evidence.[1] An informal admission is a statement, usually made out of court, and which is presented as an item of evidence bearing upon a fact in issue. An arrested person has the constitutional right "to remain silent" during plea proceedings,[2] "to be informed promptly of the right to remain silent",[3] of "the consequences of not remaining silent",[4] and especially "not to be compelled to make any confession or admission that could be used in evidence against that person".[5] Cases expounding on similar rights with regard to accused persons have often used the test for a "fair trial" and the guaranteed right "to be presumed innocent, to remain silent, and not to testify during the proceedings".[6]

1 Logically, therefore, formal admissions should not fall under the heading of admissibility. They are discussed below, in conjunction with informal admissions, purely for convenience.
2 Constitution of the Republic of SA 108 of 1996 s 35(1)(a).
3 S 35(1)(b).
4 S 35(1)(b).
5 S 35(1)(c).
6 S 35(1)(h); and see *Ferreira v Levin, Vryenhoek v Powell* 1996 1 BCLR 1 (CC); 1996 1 SA 984 (CC); *Key v Attorney-General, Cape Provincial Division* 1996 6 BCLR 788 (CC); 1996 4 SA 187 (CC); 1996 2 SACR 113 (CC); *S v Melani* [1996] 1 All SA 137 (E); 1996 2 BCLR 174 (E); 1996 1 SACR 335 (E); *S v Motloutsi* [1996] 1 All SA 27 (C); 1996 2 BCLR 220 (C); 1996 1 SA 584 (C); 1996 1 SACR 78 (C); *S v Mayekiso* [1996] 3 All SA 121 (C); 1996 9 BCLR 1168 (C); 1996 2 SACR 298 (C); *S v Nombewu* [1996] 4 All SA 621 (E); 1996 12 BCLR 1635 (E); 1996 2 SACR 396 (E); *S v Van der Merwe* [1997] 4 All SA 87 (O); 1997 10 BCLR 1470 (O); 1998 1 SACR 194 (O); *S v Malefo* [1998] 1 All SA 647 (W); 1998 2 BCLR 187 (W); 1998 1 SACR 127 (W); *S v Marx* 1996 2 SACR 140 (W); *S v Agnew* 1996 2 SACR 535 (C); *S v Shongwe* [1998] 3 All SA 549 (T); 1998 9 BCLR 1170 (T); 1998 2 SACR 321 (T).

732 Formal admissions in civil proceedings A fact is formally admitted in the pleadings or in the course of the trial by the party or his or her representative. Such an admission is usually made in express terms, but it can be made by implication. Because an admission has important and serious consequences for the party making it, it must appear clearly and unequivocally that the admission was made expressly or by necessary implication.[1]

The consequences of a formal admission are that it becomes unnecessary to prove the admitted fact; and that such fact may not be disproved.[2] This latter prohibition is so stringent that a court will decide an issue on the basis of an admitted fact even when it knows that the admission is untrue.[3] This does not, however, mean that a party who made an untrue or erroneous admission has no remedy: such party may apply to have the admission withdrawn. If it was made in the pleadings, an amendment of the pleadings will have to be sought,[4] and this will be granted, in an appropriate case, even after judgment.[5] An amendment is usually granted if there is a reasonable explanation why the admission was made and why its removal is now sought, and if the removal thereof will not cause prejudice to the other party which cannot be cured by an appropriate order as to costs.[6]

1 *AA Mutual Insurance Association Ltd v Biddulph* 1976 1 SA 725 (A) 735. See also *Van der Merwe v Erasmus* 1945 TPD 97; *Standard Bank of SA Ltd v Minister of Bantu Education* 1966 1 SA 229 (N) 242–243.

2 Civil Proceedings Evidence Act 25 of 1965 s 15: "It shall not be necessary for any party in any civil proceedings to prove nor shall it be competent for any such party to disprove any fact admitted on the record of such proceedings." See also *Gordon v Tarnow* 1947 3 SA 525 (A) 531.

3 *Dinath v Breedt* 1966 3 SA 712 (T) 717. See also *Gordon v Tarnow* supra; *Van Deventer v De Villiers* 1953 4 SA 72 (C) 75–76.

4 *Gordon v Tarnow* supra; *Dinath v Breedt* supra; *Moresby-White v Moresby-White* 1972 3 SA 222 (RA) 224.

5 *Wehmeyer v Williams Hunt & Brook Ltd* 1940 CPD 511.

6 *Frenkel, Wise & Co Ltd v Cuthbert, Cuthbert v Frenkel, Wise & Co Ltd* 1946 CPD 735; *Watersmeet (Pty) Ltd v De Kock* 1960 4 SA 734 (E) 736 738; *President Versekeringsmpy Bpk v Moodley* 1964 4 SA 109 (T) 110H.

733 Formal admissions in criminal proceedings An accused, his or her legal advisor, or the prosecutor may now in criminal proceedings admit any fact placed in issue and any such admission will be sufficient proof that fact.[1] If at any stage during the proceedings, it appears to the public prosecutor that a particular fact or facts which must be proved in a charge against an accused will not be placed in issue in criminal proceedings against that accused, he or she may forward or hand a notice to the accused or his or her legal adviser setting out that fact or those facts and stating that such fact or facts will be deemed to have been proved at the proceedings unless notice is given that any such fact will be placed in issue.[2] There is no corresponding provision for admissions by the state, but there appears to be no reason why such an admission would not, similarly, furnish "sufficient proof" of the fact admitted.[3]

If the accused pleads guilty to the charge, but this plea is subsequently corrected by the court to one of not guilty, then any fact admitted in clarification of the accused's original plea will stand as proof of the fact admitted.[4] If the accused after pleading not guilty makes a statement indicating the basis of his or her defence, the court may, if the accused consents thereto, record any admission made by the accused as a formal admission.[5] It has been held that the admission, in explanation of a plea of not guilty, of all the elements of the offence, amounts to a confession and that a statutory requirement of confirmation[6] must be met before the accused can be found guilty;[7] but this decision has now been overruled.[8] If the court is satisfied that the accused is guilty, he or she can be found guilty without such confirmation.

It is a basic requirement that a formal admission be made "formally" and with the intention that it serve as an admission (in other words that the admitted fact is no longer in dispute).[9] Consequently, though it is possible to make such an admission tacitly or by conduct, this will rarely occur.[10]

The presiding officer should establish and record exactly what is being admitted: the precise facts.[11] He or she should, therefore, not accept a blanket admission of an entire record or the entire evidence of a witness.[12]

When an accused is represented, the court expects any formal admissions to be made by the accused's representative rather than by the accused him or herself.[13] If the accused is not represented and tenders an admission, he or she should be informed of the consequences and this should be recorded with the admission.[14]

When the accused or his or her representative tenders an admission the state has the option of accepting or rejecting it. If the admission is accepted, it is accepted *in toto*; so that if it contains facts which are favourable to the accused the facts will also be placed beyond contention.[15]

1 Criminal Procedure Amendment Act 86 of 1996 s 12; see s 10 which inserted a new s 212B into the Criminal Procedure Act 51 of 1977.

2 The accused could hardly be placed in a less favourable position than the state in this regard. Cf *R v Podbrey* 1948 2 SA 181 (C) 184–185.

3 Under the provisions of s 112. See *S v Andrews* 1984 3 SA 306 (E) where it was held that, although a statement under s 112(1)(b) was not a formal admission, it formed part of the evidential material and it was competent for the court to found a verdict on it.

4 Ss 113 114(3)(b). Cf *S v Lukele* 1978 4 SA 450 (T). For a discussion of the legal position relating to the admissibility and probative value of the admission, see *S v Nkhabelani* 1990 2 SACR 497 (B); *S v Nongabe* 1990 2 SACR 522 (O).

5 S 115(b). The admission is then deemed to be an admission under s 220. Note that an admission made in explanation of a plea of not guilty is not evidence; nor is it a formal admission unless it is properly recorded with the accused's consent: *S v Mathogo* 1978 1 SA 425 (O) 427; *S v Mayedwa* 1978 1 SA 509 (E); *S v Moloyi* 1978 1 SA 516 (O); *S v Cobothi* 1978 2 SA 749 (N) 752H; *S v Selane* 1979 1 SA 318 (T); but it may be an informal admission, according to Hiemstra CJ in *S v Malebo* 1979 2 SA 636 (BH) 641. Cf *S v Thela* 1979 3 SA 1018 (T). The decision in *S v Malebo* supra was applied in *S v Ngobo* 1980 1 SA 579 (B). In *S v Dingoos* 1980 1 SA 595 (O) it was held on review that a magistrate should not inquire from an accused whether the accused is prepared to admit what he or she has said but must first

ascertain which of the state's allegations are not in dispute and which can be formally admitted.

6 In terms of s 209; see *S v Mjoli* 1980 3 SA 172 (D).

7 *S v Klaasen* 1978 1 SA 355 (C).

8 *S v Talie* 1979 2 SA 1003 (C). See also Bekker 1978 *THRHR* 207; Van Wyk 1978 *De Jure* 181. S 209 is applicable only to extracurial confessions: *S v Murray* 1979 2 SA 677 (E).

9 *R v Van der Merwe* 1952 1 SA 143 (SWA) 145D.

10 *R v De Meyer* 1949 3 SA 892 (O) 897; *R v K* 1951 3 SA 180 (SWA) 182–183; *S v Van Pittius* 1973 3 SA 814 (C) 818; *S v Magubane* 1975 3 SA 288 (N) 291H. See *S v Murray* 1979 2 SA 677 (E), where the court decided that the mere failure by the accused to contest a certain aspect of the state's case disallowed him in an appeal from relying on lack of proof of that aspect at the trial, and this notwithstanding that this "admission" had not been formally noted; see contra: *S v Van den Berg* 1979 3 SA 1027 (NC).

11 *S v W* 1963 3 SA 516 (A) 522; *S v D* 1967 2 SA 537 (N) 538; *S v Gelderblom* 1973 1 SA 589 (C).

12 *S v D* supra; *S v Serobe* 1968 4 SA 420 (A) 426; *S v Thomo* 1969 1 SA 385 (A) 388; *S v Langa* 1969 3 SA 40 (N) 42.

13 *R v Nzimba* 1955 1 SA 40 (T); but note that an admission made by the accused's representative in explanation of his or her plea of not guilty must be confirmed by the accused before it can operate as a formal admission: s 115(3). See also *S v Calitz* 1979 2 SA 576 (SWA).

14 *S v M* 1967 1 SA 70 (N); *S v D* supra 538B.

15 *S v Kuzwayo* 1964 3 SA 55 (N).

734 Informal admissions generally Provided the various requirements have been met, admissions are admissible against a party irrespective of whether the party elects to give evidence. The hearsay rule does not exclude evidence of an admission. The reason for its admissibility is that whatever a person says to his or her detriment is likely to be the truth.

If a statement is admissible as an admission, the whole statement is admissible, including elements which favour the maker. Consequently, a party may even enjoy the benefit of a self-serving statement which the party would not have been allowed him or herself to place before the court.[1] But, obviously, the self-serving part of a statement need not necessarily be given the same weight as the adverse part.[2]

Whether a statement is an admission is determined objectively: it is not necessary that the maker should have known that what he or she said was adverse or intended it to be adverse.[3]

An admission need not necessarily be made in express terms: it can be made tacitly or by conduct.[4]

1 *R v Valachia* 1945 AD 826 837; *Narotam v Madhav* 1965 4 SA 85 (W) 88; *S v Bruce* 1972 4 SA 547 (N); *S v Ostilly* 1977 2 SA 104 (D). For an example of an informal admission which was held to be admissible although it was hearsay evidence, see *Kroon v JL Clark Cotton Co (Pty) Ltd* 1983 2 SA 197 (E). See also *S v Cloete* 1994 1 SACR 420 (A).

2 *Lambrechts v African Guarantee & Indemnity Co Ltd* 1955 3 SA 459 (A); *R v Vather* 1961 1 SA 350 (A); *Narotam v Madhav* supra; *S v Ostilly* supra; *S v Tovakepi* 1973 1 SA 694 (RA).

3 *R v Barlin* 1926 AD 459. See also, eg, *Naik v Pillay's Trustee* 1923 AD 471 476: the books of an insolvent are *prima facie* evidence against the insolvent "as being admissions by him", although, in keeping his books, the insolvent has no intention of admitting anything to anybody. Where part of the evidence adduced against an accused consisted of a demonstration by him of the operation of various explosive devices (which revealed that he had good knowledge thereof from which an inference could be drawn as to his complicity in the crime of which he was charged), the court held that such demonstration was not an admission requiring proof that it was freely and voluntarily given but was no different in principle from evidence relating to a pointing out: *S v Shezi* 1985 3 SA 900 (A). See also *S v Mbatha* 1985 2 SA 26 (D) for a discussion on the court's general discretion to exclude from evidence an accused's statement which does not amount to a confession if its prejudicial nature exceeds its probative value.

4 *Jacobs v Henning* 1927 TPD 324; *Benefit Cycle Works v Atmore* 1927 TPD 524 530; *Ward v Steenberg* 1951 1 SA 395 (T); *S v Mathlare* 2000 2 SACR 515 (SCA). A pointing out may in certain circumstances amount to an admission by conduct: *S v Jili* 1989 4 SA 921 (N).

735 Admissibility The essential requirement for the admissibility of an informal admission in both civil and criminal proceedings is that it was made voluntarily.[1] Even where the accused chooses to have the question of admissibility decided at the end of the trial, the court does not have a discretion in this regard and must use the trial-within-a-trial procedure.[2] In criminal proceedings compliance with this requirement has to be proved by the prosecution.[3] Admissibility is a matter of law and if necessary a trial within a trial will be held to determine the issue. Direct evidence is not essential: proof can be furnished for example by inference from facts such as a reminder to a suspect that there is no need to answer a question, the nature of an interrogation, the time when the admission was made (before or after arrest).[4] The fact that the maker of the admission was intoxicated will not usually affect its admissibility but may affect its cogency.[5] The so–called judges' rules, which were issued in 1931 to regulate the questioning of a suspect by the police, are mere administrative directives and compliance is not essential.[6]

In criminal proceedings the courts tend to focus upon the question whether the admission was induced by any promise or threat by a person in authority.[7] An exhortation merely to tell the truth without any indication of what the interrogator regards as the truth and what he or she desires to hear is not regarded as an inducement or threat;[8] nor is a warning that the failure to give an explanation will probably lead to arrest.[9] The fact that the maker of the admission was compelled by statute to make a statement (so that the statement cannot be said to have been made voluntarily) will not of itself render the admission inadmissible;[10] and a statement made by the accused at an inquiry into the accused's mental condition to establish his or her possible fitness to stand trial or his or her criminal responsibility is admissible in subsequent criminal proceedings against such accused only to the extent that it may be relevant to determine his or her mental condition.[11]

An amendment to the Criminal Procedure Act facilitates the proof of admissions made to a magistrate and reduced to writing by the magistrate or confirmed and reduced to writing in the magistrate's presence. This admission is admissible in evidence upon its mere production and is presumed to have been made voluntarily if it appears from the document to have been made voluntarily.[12]

1 Criminal Procedure Act 51 of 1977 s 219A; *R v Barlin* 1926 AD 459 462; *S v Cele* 1965 1 SA 82 (A); *Felton v Secretary for the Interior* 1972 3 SA 886 (A) 892; *S v Mpetha* (2) 1982 2 SA 406 (C). With regard to the self-induced expectation of benefits, see *S v Ndika* 2002 1 SACR 250 (SCA).

2 *S v Mhlakaza* [1996] 2 All SA 130 (C); 1996 6 BCLR 814 (C); 1996 2 SACR 187 (C).

3 *S v Loate* 1962 1 SA 312 (A) 316. The standard is the normal proof beyond a reasonable doubt: *S v Mabona* 1973 2 SA 614 (A). See also *S v Nkosi* 1980 3 SA 829 (A).

4 *R v Barlin* supra 465; *R v Burton* 1946 AD 773 780; *R v Dhlamini* 1949 3 SA 976 (N) 978; *S v Kasikosa* 1971 3 SA 251 (RA); *S v Grove-Mitchell* 1975 3 SA 417 (A) 420. See

also *Malope v S* 1999 3 All SA 95 (T) on a trial-within-a-trial.

5 *R v Moiloa* 1956 4 SA 824 (A) 828; *R v Scott* 1959 2 SA 786 (C); *S v Grove-Mitchell* supra.

6 *R v Kuzwayo* 1949 3 SA 761 (A) 767.

7 *R v Barlin* supra. See *S v Schultz* 1989 1 SA 465 (T).

8 *R v Dhlamini* supra.

9 *R v Magoetie* 1959 2 SA 322 (A).

10 *R v Moiloa* supra.

11 S 79(7).

12 S 219A inserted by the Criminal Procedure Amendment Act 56 of 1979 s 14. For an interpretation of Criminal Procedure Act 51 of 1977 s 219A(1), see *S v Yolelo* 1981 1 SA 1002 (A); *S v Dhlamini* 1981 3 SA 1105 (W); *S v Mpetha* (2) 1982 2 SA 406 (C).

736 Statements of third persons: vicarious admissions In principle an admission is receivable only against the person making it. A statement by a person other than the litigant can therefore not be presented as an admission of the litigant, irrespective of whether such statement is to the disadvantage of the maker or the litigant.[1] There are, however, exceptions.

A statement by a third person is admissible against a litigant if the litigant expressly or by implication authorised the third person to speak on his or her behalf and such person then made a statement adverse to the litigant. The authorisation may, therefore, be explicit, but it may also be implied, for example from the litigant's reference to the third person as a source of information,[2] or merely from the relationship of the declarant and the litigant. Thus, the servant,[3] legal adviser[4] or any agent or representative[5] of the litigant may, depending upon the nature of the relationship, be held to have had the authority to make an admission to the litigant's disadvantage. However, it should be noted that confidential statements addressed to the litigant are excluded;[6] that the statement must have been made while the relationship existed;[7] and that the statement cannot be used as evidence of the relationship.[8]

In criminal proceedings against a corporate body, any record which was made or kept by a director, servant or agent of the corporate body within the scope of his or her activities as director, servant or agent, or any document which was at any time in the custody or under the control of any such director, servant or agent within the scope of his or her activities as director, servant or agent, is admissible in evidence against the accused.[9]

The statement of a third person is also admissible against a litigant if the litigant adopts it as his or her own, or ratifies it. Such adoption or ratification may be implied from the litigant's reaction (even the litigant's silence) when he or she hears or becomes aware of the statement,[10] but it does not follow that any statement made in the presence of the litigant is admissible against the litigant unless he or she repudiates it.[11] The circumstances of each such case will have to be carefully investigated to see whether adoption or ratification can be inferred.[12]

The statement of a third party is admissible against a litigant when they share a privity or identity of interest or obligation. This generally occurs either when they have successive interests in a thing or when they have concurrent interests or a shared liability. Thus, such identity could exist between successive owners of property,[13] partners,[14] and husband and wife married in community of property (in regard to their joint estate).[15] There is, however, no such privity of interest between the third party insurer and the insured,[16] the Attorney's Fidelity Fund and a defalcating attorney,[17] or between the principal debtor and a surety,[18] or between the managing director of a company and the company.[19]

Whereas the rules determining the admissibility of vicarious admissions appertain to the law of evidence (and are thus derived from English law), the question whether a privity or identity of interest exists is a matter of substantive (South African) law.[20]

1 *Simmons v Gilbert Hamer & Co Ltd* 1963 1 SA 897 (N) 911H 919D; *Mitchell v Mitchell* 1963 2 SA 505 (D). This is also true of confessions: Criminal Procedure Act 51 of 1977 s 219.

2 Eg in *Van Rooyen v Humphrey* 1953 3 SA 392 (A). Cf *Taljaard v Sentrale Raad vir Koöperatiewe Assuransie Bpk* 1973 1 SA 837 (O).

3 *Botes v Van Deventer* 1966 3 SA 182 (A) 207B (*obiter*). Note that an insolvent's books are admissible against the insolvent if the entries were made by the bookkeeper within the apparent scope of his or her authority: *Naik v Pillay's Trustee* 1923 AD 471; *R v Wingfield* 1958 3 SA 44 (SR) 45H.

4 Such admissions will, however, usually take the form of formal admissions: see *McNutt v Tyrell* 1944 SR 139; *Standard Bank of SA Ltd v Minister of Bantu Education* 1966 1 SA 229 (N); *S v Gouws* 1968 4 SA 354 (G). See also *S v Gope* 1993 2 SACR 92 (Ck).

5 *Kapeller v Rondalia Versekeringskorporasie van SA Bpk* 1964 4 SA 722 (T) 730; *Simmons v Gilbert Hamer & Co Ltd* supra 912 919.

6 *Myburgh, Krone & Kie Bpkt (in liquidation) v Standard Bank of SA Ltd, Myburgh, Krone & Kie Bpkt (in liquidation) v National Bank of SA Ltd* 1924 CPD 122 144. A statement by an agent, even if made in the course of his or her duty, is admissible against the agent's principal only if made to a third person and not if made to the principal him or herself or to another servant or agent: *Lipschitz v Landmark Consolidated (Pty) Ltd* 1979 2 SA 482 (W).

7 *Wood v Dersley* (1882) 2 EDC 200; *R v Wingfield* supra.

8 *R v Koro* 1950 3 SA 797 (O) 802.

9 Criminal Procedure Act 51 of 1977 s 332(3). See *S v Harper* 1981 1 SA 88 (D).

10 *Jacobs v Henning* 1927 TPD 324; *Maharaj v Parandaya* 1939 NPD 239; *Sun Radio & Furnishers v Republic Timber & Hardware (Pty) Ltd* 1969 4 SA 378 (T) 381. Cf *Botes v Van Deventer* supra 206–207.

11 *R v Christie* 1914 AC 545; *R v Abrey* 1959 2 SA 76 (E) 81; *R v B* 1960 2 SA 424 (T); *S v Qolo* 1965 1 SA 174 (A) 179. Although these authorities refer specifically to the position of the accused, the same principle should apply to statements made in the presence of litigants in civil proceedings – though it should be noted that the right to remain silent may be said to afford the accused an additional protection, particularly if he or she remains silent in the face of an accusation by a police officer. See *R v Mashelele* 1944 AD 571 583; *R v Patel* 1946 AD 903 908; *S v Maritz* 1974 1 SA 266 (NC); Hugo 1971 *THRHR* 403.

12 *R v Abrey* supra; *S v Qolo* supra. Cf *Benefit Cycle Works v Atmore* 1927 TPD 524 530.

13 *Woolway v Rowe* (1834) 1 A & E 114; 110 ER 1151; *Gleneagles Farm Dairy v Schoombee* 1949 1 SA 830 (A).

14 *Morum v Pieters* 1927 SWA 36; *Taylor v Budd* 1932 AD 326; *R v Jaspan* 1940 AD 9 13.

15 *Oelofse v Grundling* 1952 1 SA 338 (C). There is normally no identity of interest between spouses married without community

of property: *Taljaard v Sentrale Raad vir Koöperatiewe Assuransie Bpk* supra. See also *Knouwds v Administrateur, Kaap* 1981 1 SA 544 (C).

16 *Union & SWA Insurance Co Ltd v Quntana* 1977 4 SA 410 (A).

17 *Basson v Attorney Guarantee, Notaries &*

Conveyancers Fidelity Fund Board of Control 1957 3 SA 490 (C) 495–496.

18 Ibid. 496D–E (*obiter*).

19 *Lipschitz v Landmark Consolidated (Pty) Ltd* supra.

20 *Botes v Van Deventer* supra.

737 Confessions: nature of A confession is an unequivocal acknowledgment of guilt, the equivalent of a plea of guilty before a court of law.[1] It is therefore an admission of all the elements of the offence charged.[2] Consequently a statement by the accused that he or she took something or killed a person would not constitute a confession, where a statement that he or she stole something or murdered a person would do so.[3] It follows, also, that a statement which does not exclude a possible defence, such as the possession of a permit or licence, could be an admission, but would fall short of a confession.[4] Whether the statement does, in fact, exclude a possible defence, can be inferred from the surrounding circumstances;[5] but the surrounding circumstances cannot be invoked to supplement what the accused has said in order to bring his or her statement within the definition of a confession.[6]

Some decisions require an *animus confitendi* on the part of the maker of the statement;[7] but others would appear to view a confession objectively, without reference to the maker's state of mind.[8]

A statement which is not a confession to the main charge, but does amount to a confession to a minor charge of which the accused could properly be convicted on the indictment, is treated as a confession for purposes of admissibility.[9]

1 *R v Becker* 1929 AD 167. Where the state endeavours to prove a statement by the accused as an admission but the defence argues that the particular statement amounts to a confession and should be inadmissible in terms of s 217(1)(a) of the Criminal Procedure Act 51 of 1977, it is appropriate for the presiding officer to conduct a preliminary inquiry to determine the nature of the statement before a trial is held in respect of the further question whether the statement is freely or voluntarily made: *S v K* 1999 2 SACR 388 (C).

2 Note that a confession is an extracurial statement: *S v Zulu* 1971 2 SA 208 (N). (*S v Klaasen* 1978 1 SA 355 (C), wherein it was held that the admission of all the elements of an offence during an explanation of a plea of not guilty amounts to a confession, was held to be incorrect for this reason: *S v Talie* 1979 2 SA 1003 (C).)

3 Cf *R v Deacon* 1930 TPD 233; *R v Intombane* 1933 AD 321; *R v Blyth* 1940 AD 355. A prior expression of an intention by an accused to kill is admissible. *S v Holshausen*

1983 2 SA 699 (D). See also par 723 ante.

4 *R v Verster* 1952 3 SA 452 (O); *R v Xulu* 1956 2 SA 288 (A); *S v Henman* 1974 4 SA 277 (E); *S v Zwane* 1976 1 SA 53 (N). See also *S v Pietersen* 1979 2 SA 1009 (E); *S v Ndamase* 1979 3 SA 346 (N); *S v Nombeko* 1996 4 All SA 462 (E).

5 *R v Swart* 1937 TPD 168; *R v H* 1948 4 SA 154 (T); *S v Motloung* 1970 3 SA 547 (T).

6 *S v Motara* 1963 2 SA 579 (T) 584–585; *R v Xulu* supra 293; *S v Gumede* 1963 2 SA 349 (N) 350. Cf *S v Grove-Mitchell* 1975 3 SA 417 (A).

7 Eg in *R v Zola* 1944 EDL 137 139. *R v Hanger* 1928 AD 459 possibly supports this "subjective" approach.

8 Eg *R v Pakkies* 1956 2 SA 145 (EDL) 147B; and see *S v Motloba* 1992 2 SACR 634 (B).

9 *S v Gcaba* 1965 4 SA 325 (N). The Appellate Division (now called the Supreme Court of Appeal) has not, however, committed itself in this regard: *R v Debele* 1956 4 SA 570 (A) 572F. See *S v Swartz* 1964 3 SA 757 (O); *S v F* 1967 4 SA 639 (W).

738 Confessions: general requirements for admissibility The conditions governing the admissibility of a confession are more stringent than those for an admission. They are set out in the Criminal Procedure Act.[1] It is incumbent upon the state to prove beyond a reasonable doubt that these conditions were complied with.[2]

The Act provides that no confession made by any person will be admissible against any other person.[3]

A confession, whether it was made to a peace officer or to any other person, must be proved to have been freely and voluntarily made by the accused in his or her sound and sober senses and without having been unduly influenced thereto.[4] A statement extracted by threats or physical violence would therefore be excluded.[5] It is still a moot point whether a statement made under statutory compulsion to speak can be said to have been made freely and voluntarily,[6] though a literal interpretation of the words would indicate that it was not so made.[7] The requirement that the maker of the statement must have been in his or her sound and sober senses does not necessarily exclude a statement by a person suffering from some form of mental affliction or by a person who is to some extent intoxicated. If the person was sufficiently *compos mentis* to know and appreciate what he or she was saying, the statement will not be inadmissible on this ground.[8] Undue influence has been found to have been present where the maker of the statement was given the impression that he or she would not be prosecuted if he or she were to make a confession,[9] or that the maker of the statement's family would be cared for if he or she were to be found guilty and that he or she would afterwards be reinstated in his or her job;[10] but not where he or she was merely admonished or encouraged to speak the truth;[11] or promised that the statement would be kept secret[12]; or told that the police were in possession of damaging evidence.[13] Whether such attempts to influence the accused would amount to "undue" influence would, in each individual case, have to be measured against all the surrounding circumstances.[14]

The Constitution[15] contains a number of sections which have an effect on the admissibility of confessions.

---

1   51 of 1977 s 217. A confession tendered in terms of s 217 by means of a tape recording and the transcription thereof is not admissible: *S v Mogale* 1980 1 SA 457 (T); *S v Segone* 1981 1 SA 410 (T).

2   *R v Jacobs* 1954 2 SA 320 (A) 323; *S v W* 1963 3 SA 516 (A) 521. This right has become a constitutional right in terms of the Constitution of the Republic of SA 108 of 1996 s 35(3).

3   Criminal Procedure Act 51 of 1977 s 219. See *R v Baartman* 1960 3 SA 535 (A) 542.

4   S 217(1). For a confession made under undue influence, see *S v Robertson* 1981 1 SA 460 (C); for the requirement of a free or voluntary confession, see *S v Nyembe* 1982 1 SA 835 (A); *S v Christie* 1982 1 SA 464 (A); *S v Mpetha* (2) 1983 1 SA 576 (C). Where the question of admissibility of a confession is clearly raised, an accused has the right to have that question tried as a separate and distinct issue: *S v De Vries* 1989 1 SA 228 (A). The entrenchment of the right to a fair trial has the effect of extending the grounds on which a confession may be ruled as inadmissible in evidence. The emphasis falls on the issue of fairness rather than the compliance with rules and formalities such as those contained in the Criminal Procedure Act 51 of 1977: *S v Manuel* 1997 11 BCLR 1597 (C); 1997 2 SACR 505 (C). See also *S v Khan* 1997 2 SACR 611 (SCA). Confessions made after an unlawful arrest are admissible where the accused knew they were under no obligation to confess: *S v Shabalala* 1996 1 SACR 627 (A). In *S v Motloung* 1997 3 All SA 18 (B) the accused was not allowed to cross-examine on whether a confession had been made freely and voluntarily. See *S v Mark* 2001 1 SACR 572 (C) regarding the twofold inquiry in terms of the Constitution of the Republic of SA 108 of 1996 s 35(5) with regard to the admissiblity of evidence obtained illegally.

5   See eg *S v Ngirazi* 1975 4 SA 436 (RA); *S v Mathe* 1976 1 SA 233 (O) 234H.

6   Inadmissible: *R v Dhlamini* 1952 2 SA 693 (T) 696; *S v Ismail* (1) 1965 1 SA 446 (N). Admissible: *S v Hlekani* 1964 4 SA 429 (E). Left undecided: S *v Alexander* (1) 1965 2 SA 796 (A) 814. In an instance where an accused was detained under the provisions of the Terrorism Act 83 of 1967 s 6, it was held that there is a likelihood that the fear of continued detention in solitary confinement is a real cause or inducing factor in making a statement and this amounts to undue influence: *S v Mpetha* (2) 1983 1 SA 576 (C).

7 See Schmidt *Bewysreg* 489.

8 *R v Ramsamy* 1954 2 SA 491 (A); *R v Mtabela* 1958 1 SA 264 (A); *S v Masia* 1962 2 SA 541 (A) 544H.

9 *S v Madiki* 1961 4 SA 101 (E); *R v Baartman* supra 540.

10 *R v Michael* 1962 3 SA 355 (SR).

11 *R v Afrika* 1949 3 SA 627 (O).

12 *S v Kearney* 1964 2 SA 495 (A) 500F.

13 *S v Zulu* 1965 3 SA 802 (N). Allowing one accused to hear what another accused is telling the police does not constitute undue influence: *S v Williams* 1991 1 SACR 1 (C).

14 *R v Masinyana* 1958 1 SA 616 (A). See also,

in connection with confessions induced by trickery, *R v Mthlongo* 1949 2 SA 552 (A) 557; *R v Kuzwayo* 1949 3 SA 761 (A) 769; *S v Biko* 1972 4 SA 492 (O) 499F–H; *S v Joone* 1973 1 SA 841 (C) 847–848. Confronting a suspect with another's statement in order to induce or trick the suspect into making a confession may amount to "undue influence": *S v Sampson* 1989 3 SA 239 (A).

15 Constitution of the Republic of SA 108 of 1996; and see par 731 ante as well as the cases cited in fn 3 supra. See also Zeffertt *Evidence* 448–462.

739 Confession made to a peace officer The Criminal Procedure Act[1] provides that a confession made to a peace officer other than a magistrate or justice of the peace, or, in the case of a peace officer referred to in section 334,[2] a confession made to such peace officer which relates to an offence with reference to which such peace officer is authorised to exercise any power conferred upon him or her under that section, will not be admissible in evidence unless confirmed and reduced to writing in the presence of a magistrate or justice of the peace. The right of an accused to legal representation should be communicated to the accused before his or her confession is taken down.[3]

A police officer or other peace officer who opens a letter (containing a confession) addressed to a justice, or who acts as interpreter when a confession is made to a justice, is not the person to whom the confession is made for the purposes of the above provision.[4] The presence of a police officer at the time when a confession is made does not necessarily mean that it is made to the police officer.[5]

Although certain police officers are at the same time justices of the peace and can, therefore, in terms of the above provision confirm a confession, it is preferable that confirmation takes place before a magistrate.[6]

When the confession is reduced to writing the person recording the confession should not act as editor, but should attempt to set down the *ipsissima verba* of the confessor.[7]

The Act further provides that where a confession is made to a magistrate and reduced to writing by the magistrate or is confirmed and reduced to writing in the presence of a magistrate, it will, upon the mere production thereof, be admissible in evidence against the maker if it appears from the document in which the confession is contained that it was made by a person whose name corresponds to that of the maker.[8] In *S v Zuma*[9] the Constitutional Court decided that section 217(1)(b)(ii) of the Criminal Procedure Act was unconstitutional since, by placing an onus on the accused to prove that his or her confession was not voluntary, this infringed upon the fundamental right of the accused to remain silent after arrest, not to be compelled to make a confession and not to be a compellable witness against him or herself. These were all connected with the presumption of innocence, which means that a conviction should not follow in spite of a reasonable doubt. Kentridge AJ applied the so-called "two stage" Canadian approach, firstly finding that a fundamental right of the accused had been infringed, and secondly that this could not be justified in terms of section 33 of the Constitution.[10] The court made it clear, however, that it was not pronouncing upon all statutory presumptions in criminal cases and that these would have to be considered individually.

The whole confession becomes admissible, when an accused referred to it directly, or by way of cross-examination.[11] The question whether a whole admission, made informally during explanation of plea in terms of section 115 of the Criminal Procedure Act, becomes admissible when reference is made to part of it, was addressed in *S v Cloete*.[12] The court preferred the approach in *R v Valachia*[13] to that followed in *S v Sesetse*[14] and found that there was no reason why a court should be entitled to have regard to the incriminating parts of such statements, while ignoring the exculpatory parts.

1 51 of 1977.
2 The section provides that the Minister of Justice may declare certain persons to be peace officers for certain purposes.
3 *S v Marx* 1996 2 SACR 140 (W). See also *S v Alcock* [2002] 3 All SA 644 (E) regarding the requirement of a prior police warning.
4 In *R v Blyth* 1940 AD 355 362 a letter containing a confession was addressed to a justice but received and opened by a police constable; it was held that the confession was made to the justice. Cf *S v Lotter* 1964 1 SA 229 (O). As to interpreters, see *R v Tshetaundzi* 1960 4 SA 569 (A) 573; *S v Mahlala* 1967 2 SA 401 (W) 405; *S v Lebea* 1975 4 SA 337 (W).
5 *R v De Souza* 1955 1 SA 32 (T).
6 *S v Mofokeng* 1968 4 SA 852 (W). Cf *R v De Waal* 1958 2 SA 109 (G); *S v Dhlamini* 1971 1 SA 807 (A); *S v Mdluli* 1972 2 SA 839 (A); *S v Biko* 1972 4 SA 492 (O); *S v Mazibuko* 1978 4 SA 563 (A).
7 *R v Ndoyana* 1958 2 SA 562 (E). Cf *S v Cele* 1965 1 SA 82 (A); *R v Schaube-Kuffler* 1969 2 SA 40 (RA).
8 S 217(1)(b)(i). See *Zulu v S* [1997] 4 All SA 515 (SCA); 1998 1 SACR 7 (SCA).
9 1995 4 BCLR 401 (CC); 1995 2 SA 642 (CC); 1995 1 SACR 568 (CC).
10 See now s 36 of the Constitution of the Republic of SA 108 of 1996. In *S v Mvelase* 1996 8 BCLR 1055 (N); 1997 2 SACR 445 (N), where the admissibility of a confession established in a trial within a trial held before the interim Constitution (Constitution of the Republic of SA 200 of 1993) had come into operation led to the setting aside of a conviction and sentence handed down after the commencement of the interim Constituion, the court found the admission of the confession was incorrect in that the onus had been incorrectly placed on the appellant causing an irregularity of such a serious and fundamental nature that it vitiated the proceedings.
11 S 217(3) of the Criminal Procedure Act 51 of 1977, which was specifically inserted to counter the effect of *R v Perkins* 1920 AD 307 – see Hiemstra 579–580. For an example of a confession being held to be admissible, see *S v Mvambo* 1995 1 SACR 180 (W). See also *S v Xaba* 1997 1 SACR 194 (W) for the requirements of the admissibility of a confession elicited by the cross-examination of an unrepresented accused.
12 1994 1 SACR 420 (A).
13 1945 AD 826. Here reference was made to extra-curial admissions, but since the court in *S v Cloete* supra found that the evidential value of admissions in terms of the plea procedures derived from the common law of evidence, there was no principle to distinguish between the two types of admission.
14 1981 3 SA 353 (A).

740 Facts discovered in consequence of inadmissible confession or admission The situation which obtained after the case of *S v Sheehama*,[1] (which decided that pointings out following upon a confession were also admissions and also had to be voluntary, while retaining the theory of confirmation by subsequent fact) was first discussed in *S v Jordaan*,[2] which approved of the latter exception, and in *S v January, Prokureur-Generaal, Natal v Khumalo*,[3] which decided that this exception no longer applies. Thus the train of development set in motion by the *Sheehama* case has now been completed. It is submitted that this is more in line with recent constitutional developments with regard to the fundamental rights of the accused to a fair trial.

In *S v Melani*[4] the court held that it had a discretion with regard to evidence obtained after one of the accused's fundamental rights had been ignored. The accused had been warned that he did not have to make a pointing out but not expressly of the consequences arising from such pointing out. The court found that since the exclusion of the evidence thus obtained would discredit and dishonour the administration of justice, the evidence could be admitted by means of the court's discretion.

1　1991 2 SA 860 (A).
2　1992 2 SACR 498 (A).
3　1994 2 BCLR 42 (D); 1995 1 SA 425 (D); 1994 2 SACR 801 (A). See also *S v Shangase* 1994 2 SACR 659 (D).
4　1995 5 BCLR 632 (E); 1995 4 SA 412 (E); 1995 2 SACR 141 (E). See also *S v Hoho* 1999 2 SACR 159 (C); *Ntzweli v S* [2001] 2 All SA 184 (C); 2001 2 SACR 361 (C); *S v R* 2000 1 SACR 33 (W); Schutte (2000) 13 *SACJ* 57. In order to discharge its onus in regard to an accused's sobriety, the state must be placed in a position to tender all relevant evidence which includes evidence of the accused's conduct at the time of pointing out: *S v Post* [2001] 2 All SA 339 (W); 2001 1 SACR 326 (W). Only when evidence is discovered as a consequence of violation of a fundamental right, renders the trial unfair or is otherwise detrimental to the administration of justice, is it to be excluded: *S v Lottering* 1999 12 BCLR 1478 (N). An intention to violate the rights of the accused may also play a role: *Mkhize v S* [2000] 1 All SA 572 (W); 1999 2 SACR 632 (W).

EXTRINSIC EVIDENCE

741　Inadmissibility of extrinsic or parol evidence　When a jural act is incorporated in a document, it is not generally permissible to adduce extrinsic evidence of its terms.[1] Thus, when a transaction has been reduced to writing, the writing is regarded as the exclusive memorial of the transaction and no evidence may be given to contradict, alter, add to or vary its terms.[2]

Although this is a rule of substantive law inasmuch as it determines the nature and scope of a jural act, its expression in the form of an exclusionary rule of evidence has resulted in the adoption of English law. English precedents are followed.[3]

The rule has been applied, not only to written contracts, but also to court judgments,[4] wills[5] and negotiable instruments.[6] In principle it is, as stated above, applicable to any jural act couched in documentary form.

The evidence excluded is usually parol, namely, oral, but it may also be other documentary evidence.[7] The term "parol evidence rule" when used in the present context is therefore, strictly speaking, a misnomer.

The application of the rule is governed by the intention of the party or parties to the legal act: the rule does not necessarily govern the whole act (for instance the entire contract), but only so much as the parties intended to express in written form.[8] The rule governs not only what is expressly written, but also what is implied – even if it is implied *ex lege*.[9] However, it does not govern matters incidentally included within the document and which do not form an integral part of the document.[10]

A statutory requirement that a jural act must be in writing to be valid has much the same effect as the parol evidence rule (in that oral evidence is excluded), but is in fact an entirely separate requirement.[11]

It is sometimes stated that the parol evidence rule does not operate against third parties (who are not parties to the jural act expressed in writing), but it does bind third parties who rely upon a written contract in order to prove the terms actually enforceable by the contracting parties – because as a matter of substantive law the document determines what those terms are.[12]

1　The following passage from Wigmore *Evidence* par 2425 has often been quoted with approval: "When a jural act is embodied in a single memorial, all other utterances of the parties on that topic are legally immaterial for the purpose of determining what are the terms of their act." See, generally, in addition to the standard textbooks on evidence, Kerr *Contract* 2 ed 192 et seq. See also Lamprecht and Van der Heever 1990 *The Magistrate* 3.
2　*Union Government v Vianini Ferro-Concrete Pipes (Pty) Ltd* 1941 AD 43 47; *National Board (Pretoria) (Pty) Ltd v Estate Swanepoel*

1975 3 SA 16 (A) 26A; *Rielly v Seligson &*
Clare Ltd 1977 1 SA 626 (A) 637D.

3 Eg in *Avis v Verseput* 1943 AD 331 378;
Union Government v Vianini Ferro-Concrete
Pipes (Pty) Ltd supra; *Du Plessis v Van De-*
venter 1960 2 SA 544 (A) 548; *Venter v*
Birchholtz 1972 1 SA 276 (A) 282; *Aubrey-*
Smith v Hofmeyr 1973 1 SA 655 (C); *Mosko-*
witz v The Master 1976 1 SA 22 (C) 24–25.

4 Eg *Postmasburg Motors (Edms) Bpk v Peens*
1970 2 SA 35 (NC) 39. As to an arbitration
award, see *Pretoria City Council v Buchanan*
1952 1 SA 236 (T) 243.

5 Eg *Moskowitz v The Master* supra (wherein
parol evidence was held to be admissible to
prove the true date of a will); *Radley v Stop-*
forth 1976 1 SA 378 (T).

6 Eg *Stiglingh v Theron* 1907 TS 998; *Cassiem v*

Standard Bank of SA Ltd 1930 AD 366.

7 *Strydom v Coach Motors (Edms) Bpk* 1975 4
SA 838 (T) 840E.

8 *Du Plessis v Nel* 1952 1 SA 513 (A) 539G;
Avis v Verseput supra 380. Cf *Pizani v First*
Consolidated Holdings (Pty) Ltd 1979 1 SA 69
(A).

9 *Aymard v Webster* 1910 TPD 123.

10 Eg *Du Plessis v Van Deventer* supra (parol
evidence to contradict a receipt incorporated
in a document); *Moskowitz v The Master* supra (parol evidence about the date of a will).
See the discussion of the "exception" rule
relating to memoranda, and so on, in par
763 post.

11 *Muller v Pienaar* 1968 3 SA 195 (A) 204H.

12 *Schroeder v Vakansieburo (Edms) Bpk* 1970 3
SA 240 (T) 242.

742 Rectification The parol evidence rule is tempered by a rule that a document which fails to reflect the common intention of the parties can be rectified to reflect such intention, and that extrinsic evidence is admissible to prove the intention as well as the reasons for the error or omission.[1] Although rectification is usually requested when the mistake in the document results from bad draftsmanship or an error in transcription or typing, it can also be granted when a document is drawn up in accordance with the wishes of the parties but fails to reflect their common intention, for example, because the parties themselves misconceived its legal effect.[2] It will operate not only to alter what is written, but also, if necessary, to insert what was omitted.[3]

Even where writing is a statutory requirement for validity, a document can be rectified to accord with the common intention of the parties.[4] Although the rectification of a will (as opposed to a contract) poses certain problems,[5] it is generally accepted that a will can be rectified; but is has been held that such rectification cannot go so far as to include the insertion of an omission.[6] However, the better view appears to be that there is no difference in principle between rectification by deletion or alteration and rectification by insertion.[7] In allowing an insertion in order to give effect to the true intention of the testator, the court will naturally act with circumspection and with awareness of the dangers of fraud.[8]

An agreement in written form which is invalid on the face of it can be rectified to validate it if the underlying agreement (as distinct from the document) is valid – provided it is not an agreement which is required by statute to be in writing.[9] If there is such a statutory requirement (for instance in the case of the sale of a fixed property) there must therefore be a valid written document before rectification can be contemplated: one cannot rectify a nullity.[10] However, an invalid clause can be rectified to validate it, even if there is such a statutory requirement, provided the document as a whole is otherwise valid. The valid document then serves as a platform to rectify the invalid clause.[11]

Before rectification can be contemplated, it must be requested in the pleadings.[12]

1 The underlying reason is that the parties should not, by reason of error or fraud, be placed in a legal relationship which they had not contemplated or intended: *Van Aswegen v Fourie* 1964 3 SA 94 (O) 100. A court cannot rectify an "error" which is not mutual; a contract cannot be altered to include a clause which was not mutually agreed upon: *Trust Bank of Africa Ltd v Frysch* 1976 2 SA 337 (C). But a unilateral error induced by the fraudulent conduct of the other party can be rectified: *Rosettenville*

Motor Exchange v Grootenboer 1956 2 SA 624 (T) 630.

2 *Mouton v Hanekom* 1959 3 SA 35 (A); *Rosenfeld v Teakland Sawmills (Pvt) Ltd* 1962 3 SA 919 (FC); *Otto v Heymans* 1971 4 SA 148 (T).

3 *Venter v Liebenberg* 1954 3 SA 333 (T); *Mouton v Hanekom* supra.

4 *Weinerlein v Goch Buildings Ltd* 1925 AD 282 294.

5 See the discussion in *Aubrey-Smith v Hofmeyr* 1973 1 SA 655 (C) 663 and the counter-arguments advanced in *Botha v The Master* 1976 3 SA 597 (E) 603H.

6 *Aubrey-Smith v Hofmeyr* supra.

7 *Ex parte Van der Spuy* 1966 3 SA 169 (T); *Botha v The Master* supra 603.

8 *Botha v The Master* supra 604.

9 *Spiller v Lawrence* 1976 1 SA 307 (N); *Magwaza v Heenan* 1979 2 SA 1019 (A).

10 *Wilken v Kohler* 1913 AD 135 141; *Dowdle's Estate v Dowdle* 1947 3 SA 340 (T) 354; *Kourie v Bean* 1949 2 SA 567 (T); *Rand vir Rand (Edms) Bpk v Boswell* 1978 4 SA 468 (W) 471; *Magwaza v Heenan* supra.

11 *Vogel v Volkersz* 1977 1 SA 537 (T).

12 *Strydom v Coach Motors (Edms) Bpk* 1975 4 SA 838 (T); *Levin v Zoutendijk* 1979 3 SA 1145 (W). See also *Townsend Productions (Pty) Ltd v Leech* [2001] 2 All SA 255 (C) 264; 2001 4 SA 33 (C); *Offit Enterprises (Pty) Ltd v Knysna Development Co (Pty) Ltd* 1987 4 SA 24 (C).

743 Validity The parol evidence rule does not preclude a party from attacking the validity of a jural act incorporated in a document. Despite what may be contained in the document, it would, therefore, be possible to adduce evidence of, for example, its illegality[1] or of fraud,[2] misrepresentation,[3] or lack of consensus.[4]

1 *Noffke v Credit Corporation of SA Ltd* 1964 3 SA 451 (T).

2 *Dawson v Cape Times Ltd* 1926 CPD 144.

3 *Janowski v Fourie* 1978 3 SA 16 (O).

4 *Munnik & Munnik v Sydney Clow & Co Ltd* 1965 4 SA 312 (T) 315. See also, eg

Williams v Evans 1978 1 SA 1170 (C): a contract entered into on the basis of a common assumption as to a future state of affairs (the granting of an overdraft) which did not materialise. See also *Kok v Osborne* 1993 4 SA 788 (SE).

744 True nature Where a contract is clothed in a form that disguises its true nature, it is permissible to lead parol evidence disclosing what, in fact, was agreed between the parties. The rationale for this "exception" is that the parol evidence rule applies only to a jural act incorporated in a document: here the jural act lies behind the document and may, therefore, be exposed.[1] Thus, where a contract is in the form of the hire of a number of mules, it is possible to give evidence that it was in fact a loan for which the mules would serve as security.[2]

1 *Beaton v Baldachin Bros* 1920 AD 312 315.

2 *Theron v Krige* 1926 CPD 51. See also *Roberts v Currie* 1911 TPD 336; *Cohen v*

Commissioner for Inland Revenue 1948 4 SA 616 (T); *Moodley v Moodley* 1991 1 SA 858 (D).

745 Receipt, memorandum It has already been stated that the parol evidence rule is applicable, in principle, only to jural acts incorporated in documents. It follows that a document which does not contain a jural act, but is merely, for instance, a memorandum or a receipt, is not subject to the rule. Thus, a statement made to a police officer at the scene of an accident, even if it was written down, may be proved by oral evidence;[1] and a letter containing the recollections of a party to an agreement does not exclude oral evidence of the agreement.[2]

Even if the document does incorporate a jural act and is subject to the parol evidence rule, a part thereof, such as the date,[3] or a receipt added to the substance of what is written,[4] may fall outside the ambit of the rule, and may thus be proved to be wrong by extrinsic evidence.

1 Cf *Botes v Van Deventer* 1966 3 SA 182 (A) 196G–H. In this case the best evidence rule was invoked and rejected, but, though the

judgment does not deal directly with parol evidence, it does confirm that in such a case the writing is not "the exclusive memorial" of what was recorded.

2 *Weintraub v Oxford Brick Works (Pty) Ltd* 1948 1 SA 1090 (T).

3 *Otto v Heymans* 1971 4 SA 148 (T) 154A;

Moskowitz v The Master 1976 1 SA 22 (C).

4 *Du Plessis v Van Deventer* 1960 2 SA 544 (A). Cf *Slabbert, Verster & Malherbe (Bloemfontein) Bpk v De Wet* 1963 1 SA 835 (O).

746 Suspensive conditions It is permissible to adduce evidence of a condition precedent which serves to suspend the operation of a written agreement. In this instance, it is said, the written agreement is not varied: its terms still stand, but its operation is suspended.[1] However, it is not permissible to adduce extrinsic evidence of a suspensive condition which forms an integral part of the agreement which it suspends;[2] nor of a suspensive condition which would merely suspend a part of an existing and operative written agreement.[3]

1 *Stiglingh v Theron* 1907 TS 998 1003; *Aymard v Webster* 1910 TPD 123 129; *Estate Max v McComb* 1937 TPD 195. See also *Medelowitz* 1978 *SALJ* 32.

2 *Thiart v Kraukamp* 1967 3 SA 219 (T).

3 *Slabbert, Verster & Malherbe (Bloemfontein) Bpk v De Wet* 1963 1 SA 835 (O) 839.

747 Collateral agreements Because the parol evidence rule applies only to that which the parties *intended* to express in writing, there is nothing to prevent the parties from validly expressing a part of their agreement collaterally in either written or oral form – and parol evidence of the collateral or parallel agreement is then admissible. If there is a conflict between the two agreements and both are in writing, it has to be resolved by interpretation; if there is a conflict between a written and an oral agreement, the written agreement must prevail – because, obviously, the oral agreement is not then truly collateral and the parol evidence rule applies.

Thus, a collateral agreement is an agreement which is not in conflict with the main written agreement. Although this principle is clear, difficulties occur in its application. In a leading case it has been held that an oral agreement for a servitude of right of passage over a portion of land sold may not be proved where the deed of sale is silent about such right, the reason being that the deed promised unqualified possession to the purchaser.[1] On the other hand, it has also been held that an oral undertaking to pay a quarter of the profits during two years following the dissolution of a partnership may be proved where the deed of dissolution contains no reference to such undertaking;[2] and, similarly, oral evidence limiting the duration of a written power of attorney has been permitted;[3] as well as oral evidence to the effect that a sum of money, payable by virtue of a written agreement, would have to be paid only if the creditor would provide free lodging for the debtor's children.[4] It would appear that the criterion for determining whether an oral agreement is collateral to a written contract which is silent as to the subject matter of the oral agreement, is whether the parties in fact intended it to be collateral.[5] In order to decide this issue, the court is entitled to examine all the circumstances surrounding the transaction, including the prior negotiations between the parties.[6]

1 *Du Plessis v Nel* 1952 1 SA 513 (A).

2 *Avis v Verseput* 1943 AD 331.

3 *National Board (Pretoria) (Pty) Ltd v Estate Swanepoel* 1975 3 SA 16 (A).

4 *Lambrechts v Burger* 1955 1 SA 476 (T).

5 *National Board (Pretoria) (Pty) Ltd v Estate Swanepoel* supra 26H.

6 *Capital Building Society v De Jager, De Jager v Capital Building Society* 1963 3 SA 381 (T); *Slabbert, Verster & Malherbe (Bloemfontein) Bpk v De Wet* 1963 1 SA 835 (O) 837C; *National Board (Pretoria) (Pty) Ltd v Estate Swanepoel* supra 26H.

748 Subsequent variation or rescission Where a transaction is reduced to writing at the instance of the parties, a subsequent verbal agreement to vary or rescind the written contract may be proved unless there is a clause in the written contract to the effect that any amendment thereof must be in writing.[1]

Where a contract is required by law to be in writing, however, any subsequent variation thereof must also be in writing,[2] but an agreement to cancel it entirely need not be in writing.[3]

1 *Kuper v Bolleurs* 1913 TPD 334; *Louw v Central Motors (Vivgrey) (Pty) Ltd* 1951 3 SA 461 (T) 465H; *Barkhuizen v Jackson* 1957 3 SA 57 (T) 58H; *Schoeman v Botha* 1968 1 SA 637 (T); *Phillips v Miller (1)* 1976 4 SA 84 (T); *Pelser v Smith* 1979 3 SA 687 (T); but cf *Hawken v Olympic Pools (Pty) Ltd* 1979 3 SA 224 (T). In *De Klerk v Old Mutual Insurance Co Ltd* 1990 3 SA 34 (E) it was confirmed that a subsequent verbal agreement which varied or rescinded the written contract, may be proved.

2 *Venter v Birchholtz* 1972 1 SA 276 (A). See, however, the qualification of this rule by virtue of estoppel in *Phillips v Miller (2)* 1976 4 SA 88 (W) 93.

3 *Le Grange v Pretorius* 1943 TPD 223; *Lombard v Van der Westhuizen* 1953 4 SA 84 (C); *Van der Walt v Minnaar* 1954 3 SA 932 (O); *Gouws v Montesse Township & Investment Corporation (Pty) Ltd, Montesse Township & Investment Corporation (Pty) Ltd v Standard Bank of SA Ltd* 1964 3 SA 221 (T).

749 The *exceptio doli* Despite some adverse comment,[1] it appears to be settled law that the *exceptio doli* can operate to allow extrinsic evidence of a document, even when rectification is not available as a remedy.[2] The *exceptio* does not, however, confer a general power on the courts to interfere with contractual rights and obligations on equitable grounds, for example, because one of the parties has driven a hard or harsh bargain, or because the court judges that the contract is "unfair" to one of the parties.[3] Although the precise limits of this application of the *exceptio* have not been defined, it has been authoritatively stated that it applies only where the enforcement of a contractual obligation would cause some great inequity and would amount to unconscionable conduct by the party claiming its enforcement.[4] It would, for instance, be unconscionable (and be regarded as fraudulent) to rely on your *summum ius* when you know full well that your claim is founded on mutual error.[5]

The *exceptio* is not available when writing is required by law and the claim for relief is based upon an oral representation or agreement, and rectification is not possible.[6]

1 Eg by Coetzee J in *Aris Enterprises (Finance) (Pty) Ltd v Waterberg Koelkamers (Pty) Ltd* 1977 2 SA 436 (T) 437–438.

2 See eg *Senekal v Home Sites (Pty) Ltd* 1950 1 SA 139 (W).

3 *North Vaal Mineral Co Ltd v Lovasz* 1961 3 SA 604 (T); *Rashid v Durban City Council* 1975 3 SA 920 (D) 927; *Paddock Motors (Pty) Ltd v Igesund* 1976 3 SA 16 (A) 28.

4 *Zuurbekom Ltd v Union Corporation Ltd* 1947 1 SA 514 (A) 537; *Rand Bank Ltd v Rubenstein* 1979 2 SA 848 (W).

5 *Weinerlein v Goch Buildings Ltd* 1925 AD 282.

6 *Barkhuizen v Jackson* 1957 3 SA 57 (T) 59C–D; *Da Mata v Otto* 1971 1 SA 763 (T) 772–773; *Venter v Birchholtz* 1972 1 SA 276 (A) 287A.

750 Evidence in aid of interpretation Although the basic canon of interpretation is that a document must be given the meaning intended by the author or authors, *which meaning can only be derived from the language used in the document itself,*[1] it is possible in exceptional cases to lead extrinsic evidence in aid of interpretation. These cases do not constitute exceptions to the parol evidence rule discussed above because there is no addition to, or variation of, the document. The purpose is rather to clarify what the document says.

Although words are usually given their customary or commonly accepted meaning,[2] it is always possible to adduce evidence showing that they were used in a specialised or technical sense.[3] It is also possible to adduce evidence to identify the persons and objects referred to in the document;[4] and generally to place the interpreter of the document "in the armchair of the author" by evidence of the facts of which the author was aware.[5] These aids to interpretation, though subject to the basic requirement of relevance, are not, it would appear, dependent upon the existence of an ambiguity.[6]

If an ambiguity does exist, it is permissible to lead extrinsic evidence of the surrounding circumstances until a sufficient degree of certainty as to the correct meaning is attained.[7]

The negotiations and the statements of the parties preceding the conclusion of a written contract are inadmissible.[8] The statements of a testator about his or her intentions are also inadmissible − except in the case of equivocation, which arises when the terms of a document apply with sufficient certainty to more than one person or object. This latter form of evidence, is however, admissible only if the equivocation cannot be resolved by recourse to the text or surrounding circumstances.[9]

It is not permissible, even in the case of a demonstrable omission, to add to a document on the basis of extrinsic evidence[10] − though there is authority to the effect that an omission in a document, even though it is required by law to be in writing, can be supplied by textual interpretation.[11] The parol evidence rule does not preclude extrinsic evidence which shows that the written contract should not take effect except in a certain contingency, but does prevent the alteration of the recorded terms of the contract.[12]

1 *Worman v Hughes* 1948 3 SA 495 (A) 505; *Ex parte Froy: In re Estate Brodie* 1954 2 SA 366 (C) 370; *Aubrey-Smith v Hofmeyr* 1973 1 SA 655 (C) 657; *Oatorian Properties (Pty) Ltd v Maroun* 1973 3 SA 779 (A); *Shoprite Checkers Ltd v Blue Route Property Managers (Pty) Ltd* 1994 2 SA 172 (C).

2 See eg *Jonnes v Anglo-African Shipping Co (1936) Ltd* 1972 2 SA 827 (A) 834E; *Sassoon Confirming & Acceptance Co (Pty) Ltd v Barclays National Bank Ltd* 1974 1 SA 641 (A) 646B.

3 *Richter v Bloemfontein Town Council* 1922 AD 57 70; *Gentiruco AG v Firestone SA (Pty) Ltd* 1972 1 SA 589 (A) 647; *Sassoon Confirming & Acceptance Co (Pty) Ltd v Barclays National Bank Ltd* supra.

4 *Richter v Bloemfontein Town Council* supra 59; *Delmas Milling Co Ltd v Du Plessis* 1955 3 SA 447 (A) 454; *Ex parte Eksekuteure Boedel Malherbe* 1957 4 SA 704 (C) 710; *Trust Bank of Africa Ltd v Frysch* 1977 3 SA 562 (A) 586; *Van der Merwe v Kenkes (Edms) Bpk* 1983 3 SA 909 (T).

5 *Ex parte Froy: In re Estate Brodie* supra 370; *Delmas Milling Co Ltd v Du Plessis* supra 454; *Ex parte Rossouw* 1960 1 SA 403 (G) 408; *Aubrey-Smith v Hofmeyr* supra; *1820 Settlers National Monument Foundation v Van Aardt* 1977 2 SA 368 (E) 371; *Sassoon Confirming & Acceptance Co (Pty) Ltd v Barclays National Bank Ltd* supra 648.

6 The authorities are not consistent according

to discussion in former editions of Schmidt *Bewysreg*. The fourth edition of *Bewysreg* (2000) no longer discusses the parol evidence rule and the exceptions thereto, viewing these provisions as part of substantive law: see *Bewysreg* 353. See, however, Zeffertt *Evidence* 321–356. for an extensive treatment of this rule.

7 *Delmas Milling Co Ltd v Du Plessis* supra 455; *Haviland Estates (Pty) Ltd v McMaster* 1969 2 SA 312 (A) 337; *Van Rensburg v Taute* 1975 1 SA 279 (A) 303; *Jacobsz v Fall* 1981 2 SA 863 (C).

8 *Delmas Milling Co Ltd v Du Plessis* supra 454; *Levin v Drieprok Properties (Pty) Ltd* 1975 2 SA 397 (A) 408. Cf *Mondorp Eiendomsagentskap (Edms) Bpk v Kemp & De Beer* 1979 4 SA 74 (A), in which case the majority judges of appeal decided that extrinsic evidence in aid of interpretation is permissible only when it is clear that a contract exists at all.

9 *Ex parte Von Broembsen* 1948 3 SA 1040 (O); *Ex parte Eksekuteure Boedel Malherbe* supra; *Ex parte Rossouw* supra; *Allen v Estate Bloch* 1970 2 SA 376 (C); *Ex parte Smith* 1970 4 SA 122 (O).

10 *Estate Gouws v Estate Marais* (1906) 23 SC 72. Cf *Miller & Miller v Dickinson* 1971 3 SA 581 (A) 589.

11 *Aubrey-Smith v Hofmeyr* supra. This treatment may, however, be looked upon as rectification rather than interpretation: see *Ex parte Van der Spuy* 1965 4 SA 336 (T); *Ex*

parte Dison 1968 3 SA 368 (W). As to the insertion of an omission by means of rectification, see par 742 ante.

12 *Philmatt (Pty) Ltd v Mosselbank Developments (CC)* [1996] 1 All SA 296 (A); 1996 2 SA 15 (A).

PRIVILEGE

PRIVATE PRIVILEGE

751 Introduction Private privilege is a right that is vested in a natural or juristic person (including the state) to prevent the disclosure of admissible evidence. It has to be claimed by the person in whom it vests.[1] The privilege against self-incrimination,[2] marital privilege[3] and, possibly in KwaZulu-Natal in civil actions, against questions tending to show that a witness has been guilty of adultery or other *stuprum*,[4] is available to the witness only; but professional privilege has a wider ambit: a party with a right to such a privilege may not only claim it when such party testifies, but the party may prevent his or her legal adviser or agent (but not an independent third party) from making disclosure.[5] A claim to privilege is not confined to the time of trial, but obtains also when discovery has to be made.[6] It does not entitle a witness to refuse to testify.[7] The witness (or, in the case of professional privilege, the party) must claim the privilege, at the appropriate time, during his or her testimony. An adverse inference may not be drawn against a party because he or she, or one of his or her witnesses, has exercised a privilege.[8] If another person obtains knowledge of a privileged communication or a copy of a privileged document, the privilege may be defeated: the communication or the copy may be proved in evidence;[9] but, in a criminal case, the judge or magistrate has a discretion to uphold the privilege if disclosure would operate unfairly against an accused.[10] When private privilege is claimed in respect of a document, the court has a right to inspect it in order to determine whether or not to uphold the claim.[11] It is an essential characteristic of private privilege that, while it is for the judge or magistrate to determine whether a valid claim has been made,[12] since the privilege is a personal right, it may be waived.[13] A claim to privilege may also be made before an administrative tribunal or official.[14] Although privileged documents may be seized in terms of chapter II of the Criminal Procedure Act,[15] the privilege has been said not to be consequently defeated.[16]

Statements that have been expressly or impliedly made "without prejudice" are not, strictly speaking, excluded because of private privilege: a person has a right to make an inadmissible admission in a "without prejudice" statement; it is not a right to prevent the disclosure of admissible evidence. They will, however, for the sake of convenience, be dealt with here. The privilege created by section 4(1) of the Income Tax Act[17] may properly be regarded as a private one and other statutory privileges will also be mentioned. The so-called "privileges" of an accused when giving evidence have nothing to do with a personal right to prevent the disclosure of otherwise admissible evidence and are dealt with elsewhere.[18] Evidence which is excluded because of the dictates of the public interest or the security of the state is dealt with below.[19]

1 *Schneider v Leigh* 1955 2 QB 195; [1955] 2 All ER 173 (CA). See further *His Majesty's Advocate v H D* 1953 SC (JC) 65; *R v Kweyi* 1957 3 SA 663 (EDL); *S v Lwane* 1966 2 SA 433 (A); *S v Van Vreden* 1969 2 SA 524 (N) 529. Cf *S v Moseli (2)* 1969 1 SA 650 (O). The privilege has been allowed even although a claim has not been made (*Estate* Bliden *v Sarif* 1933 CPD 271), but this is wrong in principle. *S v Lwane* supra makes it clear that in SA there is a general rule of practice in terms of which a judicial officer has a duty to warn a witness in criminal proceedings that the witness is not obliged to incriminate him or herself: if a witness has not been warned, the witness's answer may

not be admissible against him or her in subsequent criminal proceedings. See also Schmidt *Bewysreg* 571 who expresses doubt as to whether one can speak of a binding legal rule concerning a practice which does not even apply in England. Nonetheless he feels that this rule is a welcome development.

2 Par 752 post.

3 Par 753 post.

4 Par 757 post.

5 Par 754 post.

6 On the distinction between privilege and discovery see *International Tobacco Co (SA) Ltd v United Tobacco Cos. (South) Ltd (2)* 1953 3 SA 879 (W); *International Tobacco Co (SA) Ltd v United Tobacco Cos (South) Ltd (3)* 1953 4 SA 251 (W) 253–254.

7 *Waddell v Eyles & Welsh* 1939 TPD 198; *Andresen v Minister of Justice* 1954 2 SA 473 (W); *S v Govender* 1967 2 SA 121 (N).

8 *International Tobacco Co (SA) Ltd v United Tobacco Co (South) Ltd (1)* 1955 2 SA 1 (W) 10–11; but see the position in KwaZulu-Natal if the privilege relating to questions pertaining to adultery still applies.

9 *Williams v Shaw* (1884) 4 EDC 105; *Calcraft v Guest* 1898 1 QB 759; *Hurley & Seymour v WH Muller & Co* 1924 NPD 121; *Rumping v Director of Public Prosecutions* 1964 AC 814 (HL); [1962] 3 All ER 256 (HL); *S v Mushimba* 1977 2 SA 829 (A) 840.

10 *Rumping v Director of Public Prosecutions* supra; *S v Mushimba* supra 840.

11 *Pillay v New Zealand Insurance Co Ltd* 1957 1 SA 17 (N) 19; *Lenz Township Co (Pty) Ltd v Munnick* 1959 4 SA 567 (T). Support for this view is given by the fact that, at common law, the court had a residual right to inspect documents *in camera* where an objection had been taken that disclosure would adversely affect the public interest: *Van der Linde v Calitz* 1967 2 SA 239 (A).

12 *R v Fouche* 1953 1 SA 440 (W) 441.

13 *Waterhouse v Shields* 1924 CPD 155; *His Majesty's Advocate v HD* supra; *R v Ntshangela* 1961 4 SA 592 (A); *Ex parte Minister van Justisie: In re S v Wagner* 1965 4 SA 507 (A) 514.

14 *Waddell v Eyles & Welsh* supra; *R v Diedericks* 1957 3 SA 661 (EDL); *H Heiman, Maasdorp & Barker v Secretary for Inland Revenue* 1968 4 SA 160 (W) 163.

15 51 of 1977.

16 *Andresen v Minister of Justice* supra. Zeffertt *Evidence* 587–588 argues that this "privilege" has now been conflated with the fundamental rights of a suspect in terms of the Constitution of the Republic of SA 108 of 1996, and that this right should not easily be nullified.

17 58 of 1962.

18 Par 695 ante.

19 Pars 759–761 post.

752 Self-incrimination The privilege against self-incrimination is intended to encourage witnesses to testify by removing their fear that, if they were to enter the witness box, they might incriminate themselves.[1] In civil proceedings, the effect of section 14 read with section 42 of the Civil Proceedings Evidence Act,[2] read with previous provincial legislation, is to apply the English law as at 30 May 1961. The position in criminal law is governed by section 203 of the Criminal Procedure Act[3] which provides that no witness in criminal proceedings may, except as provided by that Act or any other law, be compelled to answer any question which he or she would not, on 30 May 1961, have been compelled to answer because the answer might expose him or her to a criminal charge. The law that applied in this regard was, by virtue of previous legislation, the English law; but the South African privilege would seem to be more limited than that previously applicable: section 203 confines the privilege to answers to questions that might expose a witness to a criminal charge, whilst in the past it extended to a penalty or a forfeiture as well.[4] Thus, it would appear that the privilege would not apply where a witness's answer would merely expose the witness to an administrative penalty such as a "banning" order.[5] The privilege may be claimed, however, when a magistrate takes evidence under section 205 of the Criminal Procedure Act[6] from any person likely to give material or relevant information as to any alleged offence and, usually, in administrative and quasi-judicial proceedings.[7] Most recently, the Constitution[8] has required that statutory provisions which infringe upon constitutional rights, such as the privilege against self-incrimination, have to pass the test as to whether such limitation is "reasonable and justifiable in an open and democratic society based on human dignity, equality and freedom."

The privilege has to be claimed by the witness in respect of each question[9] which implies that the witness has to be aware of his or her right to refuse to answer. But this is tempered by the fact that there is a general rule of practice in South Africa in terms of which a judicial officer has a duty to warn a witness in criminal proceedings that the witness is not obliged to give evidence that might have a tendency to expose him or her to a criminal charge. The requirement that the accused must be warned is applicable only to *viva voce* evidence before a judicial tribunal; the absence of a warning before the making of a written statement does not render the statement inadmissible in subsequent criminal proceedings against the deponent.[10] The duty arises whenever it appears that the witness might well be about to give such evidence, whether or not a specific question has been asked.[11] It is the duty of a prosecutor to warn the court that he or she intends to put an incriminating question.[12] Thus, where a prosecution witness made a confession at a previous trial, and it appeared that he had not been aware of his right to claim privilege, it was held that his confession was inadmissible against him at his subsequent trial.[13] It would seem that there is nothing in principle to confine this rule of practice to criminal proceedings.[14] A witness's reply will also be inadmissible in subsequent criminal proceedings if, after standing on the right not to incriminate him or herself, the witness was wrongly made to answer an incriminating question.[15] The privilege remains that of the witness and, once the witness is aware of his or her rights, it is for the witness to decide whether or not to anwer.[16] It is for the judicial officer to decide whether or not a question is incriminating and the judicial officer is not bound by the fact that a witness has said, under oath, that his or her answer would be incriminating: the court is entitled to inquire cautiously into the matter and to infer from the circumstances whether or not the answer would have such a tendency.[17] If a witness's previous testimony indicates that the witness could not incriminate him or herself if he or she were to answer, the claim to privilege will be dismissed unless possibly, the witness states that his or her previous testimony was false.[18] Some questions may obviously be incriminating; others, seemingly bland and innocuous, may nevertheless constitute a link in a chain of incriminating circumstances. Such questions are also to be regarded as incriminating.[19] There must always be, however, a genuine and reasonable danger that the questions may expose the witness to a criminal charge.[20] It is uncertain whether a witness may be protected against answering a question that would expose the witness to a criminal charge in a foreign country.[21] Once a witness has already incriminated him or herself, the privilege in that regard falls away.[22]

A witness cannot refuse to testify by virtue of his or her having claim to the privilege – as has been said, objection has to be taken to specific questions.[23] The scope of the privilege itself is modified in criminal proceedings by section 204 of the Criminal Procedure Act.[24] Whenever the prosecutor informs the court that any witness called on behalf of the prosecution will be required by the prosecution to answer questions which may incriminate the witness with regard to an offence specified by the prosecutor,[25] the court, if satisfied that the witness is a competent witness, must tell him or her that he or she is obliged to give evidence, that questions might be put to him or her which might incriminate him or her in regard to the specified offence, that the witness will be obliged to answer any question that may be put to him or her (whether by the prosecution, the accused or the court) despite the fact that the answer might incriminate him or her in respect of the specified offence (or of any other offence for which he witness could be found guilty on a charge relating to the specified offence), and that, if the witness answers frankly and honestly all questions put to him or her, he or she will be discharged from prosecution in respect of the specified offence (or from any other offence for which he or she could be found guilty on being charged with it).[26] The witness is then obliged to give evidence and cannot refuse to answer any question that might incriminate him or her on the specified charge or any other charge in respect of which a verdict of guilty would be competent.[27] A witness who, in the opinion of the court, answers frankly and honestly, will be discharged from prosecution;[28] but discharge from prosecution will be of no force and effect if it is given at a preparatory examination and the witness does not answer questions honestly and frankly at the ensuing trial.[29] Even if the witness is not discharged from prosecution, his or her incriminating answers in respect of the specified offence (or in respect of any other offence for which he or she could be found guilty on being charged with it), will, except on a charge of perjury or statutory perjury, be inadmissible.[30]

A person who, in a manner other than that envisaged by section 204, is freed from the risk of prosecution, is also not entitled to the protection of the privilege as regards the offence in respect of which the person has been indemnified.[31]

No one may be compelled to answer any question or give any evidence that his wife (or her husband) would not be compelled to answer if she (or he) were to give evidence.[32] A witness may, therefore, refuse to answer a question if the answer would incriminate his spouse except, possibly, if the one were to be a compellable witness against the other.[33]

A witness, either in criminal or civil proceedings, may not refuse to answer a question merely on the ground that the answer might show that the witness is liable to a civil claim or that he or she owes a debt.[34] Nor may an accused who gives evidence in his or her own defence refuse to answer a question that tends to incriminate the accused as regards the offence with which he or she has been charged.[35]

Some statutes, however, expressly exclude the privilege against self-incrimination.[36]

1 *S v Lwane* 1966 2 SA 433 (A) 438.
2 25 of 1965.
3 51 of 1977.
4 Cf the former provisions in s 234 of the Criminal Procedure Act 56 of 1955.
5 This question, which was left open in *S v Carneson* 1962 3 SA 437 (T), is now more easily answered since s 203 of the Criminal Procedure Act 51 of 1977 does not, as did s 234 of the Criminal Procedure Act 56 of 1955, give a witness the right to refuse to answer a question because, to do so, might expose the witness to a "penalty".
6 51 of 1977.
7 See, generally, *Waddell v Eyles & Welsh* 1939 TPD 198; *R v Diedericks* 1957 3 SA 661 (EDL); cf *S v Bosman, S v Kleinschmidt* 1980 1 SA 852 (A).
8 Constitution of the Republic of SA 108 of 1996 s 39(2). See also Zeffertt *Evidence* 526–529 and *Ferreira v Levin, Vryenhoek v Powell* 1996 1 BCLR 1 (CC); 1996 1 SA 984 (CC); *S v Kheswa* 1997 2 SACR 638 (D); *Mahomed v Attorney-General (Natal)* [1997] 4 All SA 599 (N); 1998 1 SACR 73 (N). Failure to advise an accused of his or her rights

before the accused takes a procedural step by which he or she might incriminate him or herself does not mean that evidence about that step is inadmissible merely because such advice is not given: *S v Shaba* 1998 1 SACR 16 (T); 1998 2 BCLR 220 (T).
9 *R v Kweyi* 1957 3 SA 663 (EDL) (which has in certain aspects been overruled by *S v Lwane* supra); see further *R v Heard* 1937 CPD 401; *Magmoed v Janse van Rensburg* 1993 1 SA 777 (A); 1993 1 SACR 67 (A). See Terblanche 1994 *SACJ* 177.
10 *S v Lwane* supra 444. There may be exceptions, however: 440 444F. See *S v Van Schoor* 1993 1 SACR 202 (E) with regard to a warning before the making of a written statement.
11 *S v Lwane* supra 444.
12 *S v Lwane* supra 440–441.
13 *S v Lwane* supra. The position is different in English law which the court had to apply. It did not. In following a South African practice that differed from English law the court, possibly acting in error, reached a satisfactory solution. This rule applies also to evidence given at an inquest: *S v Gqozo (1)* 1994 1

BCLR 1 (Ck); 1994 2 SACR 228 (Ck).

14 Zeffertt *Evidence* 526, *Ferreira v Levin*; *Vryenhoek v Powell* supra.

15 Zeffertt 526, who cites a number of cases including the *Ferreira* case, as well as *Magmoed v Janse van Rensburg* supra (inquest proceedings); and in terms of the Companies Act 61 of 1973, *Parbhoo v Getz* 1997 4 SA 1095 (CC).

16 *R v Ntshangela* 1961 4 SA 592 (A).

17 *R v Diedericks* supra; and see *Triplex Safety Glass Co Ltd v Lancegaye Safety Glass (1934) Ltd* 1939 2 KB 395; *S v Pogrund* 1961 3 SA 868 (T); *Masokanye v Additional Magistrate, Stellenbosch* 1994 2 SA 308 (C); 1994 1 SACR 21 (C).

18 *Rademeyer v Attorney-General* 1955 1 SA 444 (T) 446 448.

19 *S v Heyman* 1966 4 SA 598 (A) 608; *Magmoed v Janse van Rensburg* 1991 1 SACR 185 (C).

20 *Rex v Kuyper* 1915 TPD 308; *S v Carneson* supra 439 442. See further *R v Boyes* (1861) 1 B & S 311; 121 ER 730.

21 Cross *Evidence* 246. Cf *The King of the Two Sicilies v Willcocks* (1851) 1 Sim (NS) 301; 22 Digest (Reissue) 440 4373; *In re Atherton* 1912 2 KB 251 255 with *United States of America v McRae* (1868) LR 3 Ch A 79.

22 *S v Pogrund* supra 871.

23 *S v Bosman* 1978 3 SA 903 (O).

24 51 of 1977.

25 S 204(1). If a question would incriminate an accused in respect of an unspecified offence, he or she may refuse to answer it: *R v Ndabeni* 1959 2 SA 630 (E); *S v Bosman* supra. This procedure may also be followed in an inquiry under s 205 of the Act: *S v Bosman, S v Kleinschmidt* supra. See further *S v Waite* 1978 3 SA 896 (O) 897.

26 S 204(1)(a).

27 S 204(1)(b).

28 S 204(2). See *S v Lubbe* 1981 2 SA 854 (C).

29 S 204(3).

30 S 204(8).

31 *R v Kuyper* supra.

32 Criminal Procedure Act 51 of 1977 s 199; Civil Proceedings Evidence Act 25 of 1965 s 12.

33 Zeffertt 444.

34 Criminal Procedure Act 51 of 1977 s 200; Civil Proceedings Evidence Act 25 of 1965 s 14.

35 Criminal Procedure Act 51 of 1977 s 197.

36 See Insolvency Act 24 of 1936 s 65(2); Companies Act 61 of 1973 s 415(3).

753 Marital privilege A husband may not be compelled to disclose a communication that may have been made to him by his wife during their marriage and, similarly, no wife may be compelled to disclose what her husband may have communicated to her.[1] This will also apply to a communication made during the subsistence of a marriage or a putative marriage which has been dissolved or annulled by a competent court.[2] Any customary marriage or customary union, concluded under the indigenous laws and custom of any of the indigenous peoples of the Republic of South Africa or any marriage concluded under any system of religious laws, will be regarded as a valid marriage for purposes of the law of evidence.[3] Section 198(1) of the Criminal Procedure Act[4] is to the same effect. None of the provisions mention that a husband or wife is not compellable to disclose what he or she may have said to his or her spouse. That situation is dealt with in both enactments in an indirect and cumbersome manner: no one may be compelled to answer any question or give any evidence that his wife (or her husband) would not be bound to disclose if she (or he) were to give evidence.[5] The logical consequence is that communications of this kind are also privileged.

A person married in accordance with African law and custom (despite the registration or other recognition under any law of validity of the marriage) is deemed to be married "for purposes of the law of evidence".[6] It follows that communications made between spouses married under African law are also privileged. The Civil Proceedings Evidence Act is silent on the question but it seems that the result would be the same. It has also been held that where persons were married according to Hindu rites in circumstances where the particular marriage has all the attributes of a Christian marriage, one spouse is not a compellable witness where the other is charged with an offence.[7] By analogy, it is possible that communications between such spouses may be privileged. In *S v Johardien*[8] the court held that a witness who is not the *de jure* wife of the accused (or the *de jure* husband of the accused) is not entitled to invoke the privilege relating to marital communications set forth in section 198(1) of the Criminal Procedure Act;[9] the judgment in *S v Vengetsamy*[10] was not approved and not followed.

The Criminal Procedure Act provides that a person whose marriage has been dissolved or annulled by a *competent court* cannot be compelled to give evidence as to any fact, matter or thing which occurred during the subsistence of the marriage or putative marriage if he (or she) could not be compelled to do so were the marriage still subsisting. These provisions will also apply to a communication made during the subsistence of a marriage or putative marriage which has been dissolved or annulled by a competent court.[11] It may be inferred, therefore, that if the marriage were to have been dissolved by death, the privilege would fall away. Since death dissolves marriage, it is possible that the wording is wide enough to include a widower or widow as a person who could not be compelled to disclose what was communicated during the subsistence of the marriage; but the better view is that civil and criminal proceedings should be equated in this regard.[12]

In criminal cases one spouse is only exceptionally competent and compellable to give evidence for the prosecution against the other, but, even where the one is competent to testify against the other, the privilege may still hold.[13] However, the privilege has to be claimed by the person to whom the communication was made (or by whom it was made) and, if one spouse is a competent witness against the other, he (or she) is entitled to disclose that which had been communicated to him or her by the other spouse;[14] the spouse could also disclose that which he (or she) has communicated to the other spouse – the enactments merely imply that he (or she) cannot be compelled to do so.

The privilege rests on consideration of policy: it would offend public opinion if one spouse were to be forced to disclose what the other had said to him or her[15] and, according to some, the privilege is intended to foster matrimonial confidence. When communication has come to the attention of a third party, such considerations lose their cogency and the third party may testify about what he or she heard or, if the communication was in writing, the party may prove it[16] or give secondary evidence of its content.[17] In criminal proceedings the court has a discretion to exclude such evidence if its disclosure would operate unfairly against an accused.[18] Although it is for the witness to claim the privilege, judicial officers have a duty to inform witnesses of their rights.[19]

1 Civil Proceedings Evidence Act 25 of 1965 s 10(1).
2 S 10(2).
3 Justice Laws Rationalisation Act 18 of 1996 s 4 read with Sch 4.
4 51 of 1977.
5 Civil Proceedings Evidence Act 25 of 1965 s 12; Criminal Procedure Act 51 of 1977 s 199.
6 S 195(2).
7 *S v Vengetsamy* 1972 4 SA 351 (D).
8 1990 1 SA 1026 (C).
9 51 of 1977 s 198(1)–(2).
10 Supra.
11 *S v Taylor* 1991 2 SACR 69 (C).
12 There should not be a difference between criminal and civil proceedings; and the consideration that it would affront public

opinion if one spouse were to testify against the other (see below) does not apply.
13 Schmidt *Bewysreg* 567 considers that it does. The learned author cites no authority and gives no reasons for this conclusion; others, however, suggest that the privilege may be impliedly excluded when one spouse is compellable against the other: Zeffertt *Evidence* 620.
14 Zeffertt 619 who cites *His Majesty's Advocate v H D* 1953 SC (JC) 65.
15 Zeffertt 620; Schmidt 566.
16 *Rumping v Director of Public Prosecutions* 1964 AC 814 (HL); [1962] 3 All ER 256 (HL).
17 See in general par 790 post..
18 *Rumping v Director of Public Prosecutions* supra.
19 *Van Lill v S* (1969) (2) PH H219 (T).

754 Professional privilege Legal professional privilege is a right necessary for the proper functioning of the adversarial system and can be claimed not only in actual litigation but also to prevent seizure by warrant; the provisions of the Prevention of Organized Crime Act[1] do not override such privilege. This privilege, which rests on what Wigmore calls "the necessity of *providing subjectively for the client's freedom of apprehension* in consulting his legal adviser"[2] is based on the rationale that it is in the public interest to aid the ends of litigation. It is in the public interest to regard communications between a professional legal adviser and his or her client as being, in certain circumstances, inviolate;[3] similarly, the privilege extends to communications between third parties and lawyers if the communications were made in confidence for the primary purpose of being laid before the adviser at a time when litigation was pending or contemplated whether or not there are other purposes; it need not be the sole dominant purpose[4] since it is in the public interest to facilitate the obtaining and preparation of evidence. Professional privilege is a substantive rule of law and not merely a rule of evidence; privileged documents may not be seized in terms of a search warrant.[5]

As a corollary to the proposition that privilege is conceived as an aid to litigation and in the interests of the public, the privilege is the client's and not the lawyer's.[6]

No privilege attaches to communications that have been made to a doctor,[7] a clergyman,[8] an accountant,[9] a journalist,[10] a banker (except in a limited way, by virtue of statute),[11] an insurer,[12] or, for that matter, to anyone other than a lawyer.

Once a communication is privileged, it remains privileged: the privilege is for the benefit of the client and it does not matter what the nature of the subsequent proceedings may be.[13] The right to resist disclosure, in other words, serves to prevent the legal representative from betraying a confidential communication in a subsequent trial even if a different lawyer were to be employed. It may also pertain to the client's successor-in-title.[14]

If a third party (including a potential witness) overhears or reads what has been said, that party may testify to what he or she has heard or read.[15] The party cannot be stopped by the client or his or her legal representative.[16] There is, however, a suggestion of dubious value, that if a document should be duly obtained under a search warrant, the privilege is retained.[17] The better approach would be to say that, in criminal proceedings, the court has a discretion to prevent the disclosure of evidence if it would be unjust to the accused not to do so; it is doubtful whether such a discretion exists in civil proceedings.[18]

The law of professional privilege is the English law as it was on 30 May 1961.[19] The Criminal Procedure Act[20] states that a legal adviser is incompetent to give evidence against his or her client if he or she could not have done so on that date. It does not cover the whole field of the privilege: it does not deal with the situation where the client is not a party to litigation or with communication by the client him or herself or by agents of the client and the legal adviser. But there can be no doubt that the section does not replace the common law. The Civil Proceedings Evidence Act[21] does not deal specifically with the privilege, but the effect of section 42 is to apply the English law indirectly by freezing the position as it was on 30 May 1961 when the Act came into force on 30 June 1967. Various old colonial laws applied the English law.[22]

(a) *Communication between a legal adviser and his or her client*

The mere fact that a person is an advocate or an attorney does not give rise to the conclusion that everything that such person might say, or that might be said to him or her, for the purpose of obtaining his or her advice will be privileged.[23] For privilege to obtain, the person must be an adviser in a professional capacity.[24] This is a question of fact.[25] What it means is that the advice must not have been sought, or given, on a friendly basis only. But when is a lawyer a professional lawyer? Clearly, when he or she is acting in the course of independent practice. But many qualified lawyers are, today, employed as full-time, salaried legal advisers by corporations or statutory bodies. Whether they may be regarded as acting in their professional capacities must be considered to be an open question.[26]

The communication has to have been made in confidence[27] Thus, a client's instructions to an attorney to act on his or her behalf and to obtain a specific settlement, is not privileged: it lacks the element of confidentiality precisely because it was intended to be disclosed to the client's opponent[28] Similarly, where an attorney acts on behalf of both parties, this element may be absent.[29]

It has to be made either for the purpose of advice or litigation[30] Thus, if a lawyer hears a confession when he or she consults with a possible witness in a case, the communication will not be privileged at a subsequent trial of the witness because the witness had not sought legal advice when he or she had made it.[31] Again, a written statement made at a time when the obtaining of legal advice was not contemplated, will not be privileged.[32]

When a party gives evidence and, in so doing, testifies to facts that were put to that party's opponent's witnesses, the party may be asked whether he or she gave his or her version of the facts to his or her legal representatives: the party is not being asked what he or she told the legal adviser or to disclose the nature of the communication to the legal adviser.[33] It is the state of the legal representative's knowledge that is being tested.[34] On the other hand, the privilege extends not only to prevent the disclosure of the nature of what was said to the legal representative in confidence, but also to prevent the disclosure of what was not said.[35]

If a document is not privileged, privilege cannot be created merely by handing it, in a confidential manner, to the legal adviser: it will not be a communication for the purpose of obtaining legal advice.[36]

The privilege, which is a right of the client, has to be claimed[37] either by the client, the client's agent, or the client's legal representative on his or her behalf. If the client wishes to make disclosure, neither his or her representative nor the court is entitled to frustrate him or her: a judicial officer may inform the client of his or her rights (and indeed should do so particularly when the client is unrepresented), but cannot *mero motu* prevent disclosure.[38] As regards the legal adviser, it is his or her duty to claim the privilege; but when the legal adviser does so (or when he or she waives the privilege) he or she is acting for the client and not in his or her own right.[39] Privilege may be waived expressly or by implication.[40] The client's intention to waive the privilege may be inferred when, for instance, he or she relies on what was communicated as a defence,[41] or when there is an element of publication that warrants an inference that a privileged person no longer regards the contents of a communication as secret.[42]

The privilege does not apply if the client sought advice for the purpose of committing a crime or fraud even if the legal adviser is unaware of the client's intention.[43] In civil cases where fraud is alleged, the privilege may be defeated only once there is at least *prima facie* evidence that the client intended to obtain advice to facilitate the dishonest purpose.[44]

In civil proceedings there is no requirement that litigation has to have been contemplated: it suffices if legal advice was sought in confidence.[45]

Special rules apply to criminal proceedings A legal practitioner is competent and compellable to give evidence as to any fact, matter or thing which relates to, or is connected with, the commission of any offence with which his or her client is charged if such a fact, matter or thing came to the practitioner's knowledge before he or she had been professionally employed or consulted "with reference to the defence of the person concerned".[46]

(b) *Agents*

The privilege extends to communication with, or from agents; but there are additional requirements: the communication must have been made with the sole, or at least the primary, purpose of being brought to the attention of the legal adviser so that the legal adviser may give his or her advice on it;[47] and it must have been made at a time when litigation had commenced or, at least, when it was contemplated, that is to say, when litigation was likely or probable – the mere possibility of litigation is not enough.[48] In determining in a particular case whether litigation is contemplated, a litigant should not be prejudiced because he or she is astute to see the likelihood of litigation.[49]

There is no requirement that the statement has actually to be laid before the legal adviser: it suffices if there was an intention to do so.[50] Again, if the primary purpose was to lay it before the legal adviser, it matters not that there was also some other purpose in making the communication.[51] Each case has to be judged on its own facts.[52] Normally, for instance, a report by an insured to his or her insurer that he or she had been involved in an accident will not be privileged because it will not have been made at a time when it would be said that the occurrence was considered and the report made because litigation was then contemplated.[53] Information obtained by an agent for the purpose of being laid before the legal adviser will also be privileged; but information obtained by the agent at the client's behest will not be privileged if, at the time it was obtained, there was no intention to lay it before the legal adviser.[54] It is the litigant him or herself who must have contemplated the litigation or, in the case of a juristic person, a relevant official.[55]

The client may prevent the agent from disclosing a privileged communcation.[56]

(c) *Independent witnesses*

A statement by a potential independent witness is privileged if it is obtained for the purpose of contemplated litigation, that is to say, at a time when litigation was likely or probable.[57] It matters not that it was obtained by the client, the legal adviser or the agent of either of them. The ambit of the privilege is narrower than that of a privileged communication that was made by an agent:[58] the client cannot prevent an independent witness from disclosing what he or she said, or what had been said to him or her, when he or she made the statement; he may be asked what he or she said or did, or what was shown to him or her (other than a document which is itself privileged) at any consultation or interview with the client's legal adviser or representative.[59] It is not a requirement that a third party should have contemplated litigation.[60]

(d) *Witnesses' statements and "police docket privilege"*

A litigant is entitled to refuse to discover a privileged document. Professional privilege, therefore, is a ground, indeed the most usual ground, for such a refusal. A litigant may, therefore, refuse to disclose a privileged statement by a witness when he or she is called upon to make discovery.

Information as to the manner in which the statement was taken, that is to say, the questions that were asked and what was said to the witness, is also protected.[61]

The privilege is not confined only to the final statement, but includes everything called into existence for incorporation in the communication in its completed form.[62] When a party has been legally represented, his or her refusal to discover a document will normally be based on professional privilege. A litigant who conducts his or her case in person, however, may also refuse to disclose a statement by a witness. Although the matter is mixed up with public privilege in the shape of police privilege, especially with regard to the identity of informers, the privilege of witnesses in criminal trials with regard to their statements (the so-called "docket privilege") which existed since 1954[63] has now come to an end. This was effected by the Constitutional Court in its decision in *Shabalala v Attorney-General of the Tvl*[64] wherein Mahomed J decided that this privilege was not consistent with the accused's constitutional right to a fair trial.[65] The accused therefore has the right to access to these statements but the state can refuse to disclose these, if disclosure is not necessary for a fair trial. This depends upon several factors, such as: "The simplicity of the case, either on the law or on the facts or both; the degree of particularity furnished in the indictment or the summary of substantial facts in terms of section 144 of the Criminal Procedure Act; the particulars furnished pursuant to section 87 of the Criminal Procedure Act;[66] the details of the charge read with such particulars in the Regional and District Courts, might be such as to justify the denial of such access. The accused may, however, be entitled to have access to the relevant parts of the police docket even in cases where the particularity furnished might be sufficient to enable the accused to understand the charge against him or her but, in the special circumstances of a particular case, it might not enable the defence to prepare its own case sufficiently, or to properly exercise its right to adduce and challenge evidence;[67] or to identify witnesses able to contradict the assertions made by the State witnesses; or to obtain evidence which might sufficiently impact upon the credibility and motives of the State witnesses during cross-examination; or to properly instruct expert witnesses to adduce evidence which might similarly detract from the probability and the veracity of the version to be deposed to by the State witnesses; or to focus properly on significant matters omitted by the State witnesses in their depositions; or to properly deal with the significance of matters deposed to by such witnesses in one statement and not in another or deposed to in a statement and not repeated in evidence; or to hesitations, contradictions and uncertainties manifest in a police statement but overtaken by confidence and dogmatism in *viva voce* testimony."[68]

It was also decided that the accused does not have the right to consult with state witnesses if they themselves object, or if the state can prove that it has reasonable grounds to believe such consultation might lead to the intimidation of the witness or a tampering with the witness's evidence, or that it might lead to the disclosure of state secrets or the identity of informers, or that it might otherwise prejudice the proper ends of justice. Even then the court can still exercise a discretion to permit consultation.[69]

The Constitution[70] has affirmed the right of an accused to relevant information held by the state.[71] This right has been given further definition by the Promotion of Access to Information Act.[72] A number of cases have expounded upon what Zeffertt calls "the collision between the fundamental rights embodied within the privilege and the right that every person has of access to any information held by the state".[73]

Although a witness's statement is privileged (at least in civil cases), and although the client, the legal adviser or their agents are not obliged to answer questions about what an independent witness may have said, such a witness may be cross-examined as to what he or she said. And, if the independent witness wishes to disclose what he or she said, or what was said to him or her, the client cannot stop this.[74]

(e) *Minors*

It is possible that special rules may apply to communications about the whereabouts of minors of whom the court is upper guardian.[75]

1 121 of 1998. See *Bogoshi v Van Vuuren, Bogoshi v Director, Office for Serious Economic Offences* 1996 1 SA 785 (A). See also *SA Rugby Football Union v President of the Republic of SA* 1998 10 BCLR 1256 (T); 1998 4 SA 296 (T) for a discussion of the court's power to inspect documents in respect of which legal professional privilege is claimed.

2 Wigmore *Evidence* par 2290. See *Bogoshi v Van Vuuren, Bogoshi v Director, Office for Serious Economic Offences* 1993 2 SACR 98 (T); 1993 3 SA 953 (T).

3 See Zeffertt *Evidence* 556–590 and Cross *Evidence* 428–452 for a general discussion of the privilege.

4 *Wheeler v Le Marchant* (1881) 17 Ch 675 (CA). For South African practice, see *General Accident, Fire & Life Assurance Corporation Ltd v Goldberg* 1912 TPD 494; *Saven v AA Mutual Insurance Association Co Ltd* 1952 1 SA 110 (C); *United Tobacco Cos (South) Ltd v International Tobacco Co of SA Ltd* 1953 1 SA 66 (T) 68–70; *Potter v South British Insurance Co Ltd* 1963 3 SA 5 (W); *Boyce v Ocean Accident & Guarantee Corporation Ltd* 1966 1 SA 544 (SR). If the definite purpose of a document was submission to a legal adviser, it suffices for privilege to exist, whether or not there are other purposes; it need not be the sole or dominant purpose: *A Sweidan & King (Pty) Ltd v Zim Israel Navigation Co Ltd* 1986 1 SA 515 (D).

5 Wigmore par 2301; Law Reform Committee 16th Report *Privilege in Civil Proceedings* 1967 Cmnd 3472 par 20; *Sasol III (Edms) Bpk v Minister van Wet & Orde* 1991 3 SA 766 (T).

6 *Wright v Mayer* (1801) 6 Ves Jun 280; 31 ER 1051; *S v Green* 1962 3 SA 899 (D) 899–900; *S v Van Vreden* 1969 2 SA 524 (N); *S v Moseli (2)* 1969 1 SA 650 (O) 652–653; Wigmore par 2290 fn 8.

7 *Kingston's (Duchess) Case* (1776) 20 Howell's State Trials 355; *Wilson v Rastall* (1792) 4 TR 753 760; 100 ER 1283 1287; *R v Elizabeth Gibbons* (1823) 1 C & P 97; 171 ER 1117; *Wheeler v Le Marchant* supra; *Parkes v Parkes* 1916 CPD 702; *Botha v Botha* 1972 2 SA 559 (N). See further *Attorney-General v Mulholland, Attorney-General v Foster* 1963 2 QB 447 (CA) 489; [1963] 1 All Er 767 (CA) 771. Cf *S v Forbes* 1970 2 SA 594 (C), distinguished in *S v Webb (1)* 1971 2 SA 340 (T).

8 *Smit v Van Niekerk* 1976 4 SA 293 (A); Van der Vyver 1977 *THRHR* 217. It is submitted that *Wissekerke v C Wissekerke & L Wissekerke* 1923 1 PH F5 (T) was wrongly decided.

9 *Chantrey Martin & Co v Martin* 1953 2 QB 286 (CA); [1953] 2 All ER 691 (CA).

10 *R v Heard* 1937 CPD 401; *S v Pogrund* 1961 3 SA 868 (T); *Attorney-General v Mulholland, Attorney-General v Foster* supra; *Hitchcock v Germishuis* 1967 4 SA 279 (W); *R v Parker* 1965 4 SA 47 (SRA).

11 In SA bankers have a limited privilege. The Criminal Procedure Act 51 of 1977 s 236(4) has been amended and now provides that no bank may be compelled to produce any accounting record referred to in s 236(1) at criminal proceedings unless the court concerned orders that such record be produced.

12 *Howe v Mabuya* 1961 2 SA 635 (D).

13 *Estate Bliden v Sarif* 1933 CPD 271 274. See also *Euroshipping Corporation of Monrovia v Minister of Agricultural Economics & Marketing* 1979 1 SA 637 (C); *Jonas v Minister of Law & Order* 1993 2 SACR 692 (E). In *Mazele v Minister of Law & Order* 1994 1 SACR 406 (E); 1994 3 SA 380 (E) it was held that, in order to avoid unfairness in a civil case following a criminal case, the police docket should not be privileged beyond the date upon which the criminal proceedings were terminated.

14 *Calcraft v Guest* 1898 1 QB 759; 22 Digest (Reissue) 236 2032.

15 *Williams v Shaw* (1884) 4 EDC 105; *Hurley & Seymour v WH Muller & Co* 1924 NPD 121; *Schuster v Guether* 1933 SWA 108 118; *S v Mushimba* 1977 2 SA 829 (A) 840 (obiter). Cf *Rumping v Director of Public Prosecutions* 1964 AC 814 (HL); [1962] 3 All ER 256 (HL). The events recorded in *S v Mushimba* supra are unique in South African legal history. Privilege was completely eliminated both before and throughout the trial because an informer had penetrated the offices of the accused's attorneys. The grossness of the irregularity led to a failure of justice. The court did not have to deal with a situation where a single privileged document or statement had come to the attention of the representatives of the state.

16 See fn 14 supra.

17 *Andresen v Minister of Justice* 1954 2 SA 473 (W) (obiter). If secondary evidence may be given of an unfairly obtained (even illegally obtained) communication, then, *a fortiori* in the case where it is legally obtained. See the authorities cited in fn 14 supra.

18 *S v Mushimba* supra 840; *Rumping v Director of Public Prosecutions* supra; *Botha v Botha* supra.

19 As at 30 May 1961 the law that applied in

terms of s 201 in its original form was that which applied in similar proceedings pending in the supreme court of judicature in England, ie the English law on that date: see par 679 ante.

20 51 of 1977 s 201.

21 25 of 1965.

22 S 25 of Ord 72 of 1830 (Cape); s 1(a) of Law 17 of 1859 (Natal); s 16 of Proc 16 of 1902 (Tvl); s 6 of Proc 11 of 1902 (OFS). See *Naidoo v Marine & Trade Insurance Co Ltd* 1978 3 SA 666 (A) 677; *Gentiruco AG v Firestone SA (Pty) Ltd* 1972 1 SA 589 (A) 617.

23 *Minter v Priest* 1930 AC 558 569; 1930 All ER 431 434.

24 *R v Fouche* 1953 1 SA 440 (W).

25 *R v Fouche* supra. The charging of a fee would be a strong indication that he or she was not acting merely on a friendly basis; the failure to charge a fee would not, on the other hand, of itself indicate that the relationship was not a professional one.

26 Lord Denning in *Alfred Crompton Amusement Machines Ltd v Commissioners of Customs & Excise (No 2)* 1972 2 QB 102 (CA); [1972] 2 All ER 353 (QB), was of the opinion that because a salaried legal adviser, whether a barrister or solicitor, who is employed by a government department or a commercial concern has the same duties as a lawyer in private practice, professional privilege, within defined limits, attaches to confidential communications between the salaried adviser and his or her client. The court of appeal's view on this point was not challenged by the appellants in the House of Lords: *Alfred Crompton Amusement Machines Ltd v Commissioners of Customs & Excise (No 2)* [1973] 2 All ER 1169 (HL) 1182.

27 *Giovagnoli v Di Meo* 1960 3 SA 393 (D); *Resisto Dairy (Pty) Ltd v Auto Protection Insurance Co Ltd* 1962 2 SA 408 (C); *Euroshipping Corporation of Monrovia v Minister of Agricultural Economics & Marketing* supra; *H Heiman, Maasdorp & Barker v Secretary for Inland Revenue* 1968 4 SA 160 (W) stressed that it has to be made in confidence for the purpose of obtaining legal advice; and see *Nathan v Anderson & the Attorney-General of the Tvl* 1939 WLD 13.

28 *Giovagnoli v Di Meo* supra.

29 *Middeldorf v Zipper* 1947 1 SA 545 (SR); cf *Harris v Harris* 1931 P 10; *S v Van Vreden* supra. Cf *Kelly v Pickering (1)* 1980 2 SA 753 (R).

30 *Nathan v Anderson & the Attorney-General of the Tvl* supra; *R v Davies* 1956 3 SA 52 (A) (a doctor and a nurse where charged with culpable homicide and abortion. The nurse testified that certain documents had been kept recording information about patients. They were not privileged *inter alia*, because they had been completed at the time when treatment had been given, ie, there could be no question that they had been made for the purpose of obtaining legal advice); *S v Green* 1962 3 SA 899 (D) 900; *S v Kearney* 1964 2 SA 495 (A); *H Heiman, Maasdorp & Barker v Secretary for Inland Revenue* supra.

31 *S v Kearney* supra.

32 *R v Davies* supra; see the facts set out in fn 30 supra.

33 *S v Green* supra.

34 Schmidt *Bewysreg* 560

35 *S v Moseli (2)* supra 652.

36 *H Heiman, Maasdorp & Barker v Secretary for Inland Revenue* supra 164.

37 See fn 5 supra. See further *Schneider v Leigh* 1955 2 QB 195 (CA); [1955] 2 All ER 173 (CA).

38 *Schlosberg v The Attorney-General of the Tvl & the Additional Magistrate Johannesburg: In re R v Sandig* 1936 WLD 59; *Ditz v Attorney-General* 1936 NPD 345; *Schneider v Leigh* supra; *S v Moseli (2)* supra 652; but see *Estate Bliden v Sarif* supra which was, it is submitted, wrongly decided.

39 *Schlosberg v The Attorney-General of the Tvl & the Additional Magistrate Johannesburg: in re R v Sandig* supra; *Ditz v Attorney-General* supra.

40 *Waterhouse v Shields* 1924 CPD 155; *Ex parte Minister van Justisie: In re S v Wagner* 1965 4 SA 507 (A) 515; *Msimang v Durban City Council* 1972 4 SA 333 (D) wherein it was pointed out that two elements are predicated in every tacit waiver: fairness and consistence and, although on the facts a waiver had not been intended, considerations of fairness demanded the conclusion that privilege had been waived; see *S v Fourie* 1972 1 SA 341 (T). See also *Burnell v British Transport Commission* 1956 1 QB 187; [1955] 3 All ER 822 (CA); Wigmore par 2327. For an implied waiver of privilege, see *Bank of Lisbon & SA Ltd v Tandrien Beleggings (Pty) Ltd (2)* 1983 2 SA 626 (W). Where a client has disclosed a part of a privileged statement, the elements of fairness and consistency require the whole of the statement to be disclosed subject to the qualification that the whole statement need not be disclosed should it deal with separate matters; the issue as to whether a document deals with a single subject matter or spare subject matters should be settled by the presiding officer and

not the prosecution: *S v Nhlapo* 1988 3 SA 481 (T). In an instance where a diagram forming part of the plaintiff's privileged statement to his attorney was disclosed to the defendant on request in a spirit of co-operation, it was held that the privilege with regard to the statement remained intact: *Peacock v SA Eagle Insurance Co Ltd* 1991 1 SA 589 (C); *Harksen v Attorney-General of the Province of the Cape of Good Hope* 1998 2 SACR 681 (C).

41 *Waterhouse v Shields* supra.

42 *Ex parte Minister van Justisie: In re S v Wagner* supra; *S v Fourie* supra provides a good illustration. *AA Mutual Insurance Association Ltd v Blom* 1979 1 SA 491 (E); *Bowes v Friedlander* 1982 2 SA 504 (C). In an instance where the accused elected to give evidence concerning instructions given by them to their former counsel and sought to withdraw admissions made to counsel on the ground that counsel acted contrary to instructions in making the admissions, the court held that although the accused had waived the privilege attached to instructions given to their counsel, it was in general undesirable to compel an attorney or counsel to give evidence against his or her client, and refused an application by the state to call the counsel as a witness: *S v Boesman* 1990 2 SACR 389 (E).

43 *R v Cox & Railton* (1884) 14 QB 153; 1884 All ER 68; *Schlosberg v The Attorney-General of the Tvl & the Additional Magistrate Johannesburg: In re R v Sandig* supra; *R v Davies* supra; *Botes v Daly* 1976 2 SA 215 (N). See further *Re Arnott* 60 LT (NS) 109; *Harksen v Attorney-General of the Province of the Cape of Good Hope* supra.

44 Cross *Evidence* 254, citing *O'Rourke v Darbishire* 1920 AC 581; 1920 All ER 1; *Bullivant v A–G for Victoria* 1901 AC 196; 1901 All ER 812. He goes on to say that fraud "in this context does not extend to every act or scheme which is unlawful such, eg, as an inducement of breach of contract".

45 *Savides v Varsamopoulos* 1942 WLD 49.

46 A proviso to s 201 of the Criminal Procedure Act 51 of 1977.

47 *General Accident, Fire & Life Assurance Corporation Ltd v Goldberg* supra.

48 *General Accident, Fire & Life Assurance Corporation Ltd v Goldberg* supra; *Saven v AA Mutual Insurance Association Co Ltd* supra; *United Tobacco Cos (South) Ltd v International Tobacco Co of SA Ltd* supra; *Potter v South British Insurance Co Ltd* supra; *Boyce v Ocean Accident & Guarantee Corporation Ltd* supra; *Bagwandeen v City of Pietermaritzburg* 1977 3

SA 727 (N). Cf *Dingana v Bay Passenger Transport* 1971 1 SA 540 (E).

49 *United Tobacco Cos (South) Ltd v International Tobacco Co of SA Ltd* supra; *Bagwandeen v City of Pietermaritzburg* supra.

50 *Resisto Dairy (Pty) Ltd v Auto Protection Insurance Co Ltd* supra 409.

51 *United Tobacco Cos (South) Ltd v International Tobacco Co of SA Ltd* supra 73.

52 *Potter v South British Insurance Co Ltd* supra; *Bagwandeen v City of Pietermaritzburg* supra.

53 See, eg, *Saven v AA Mutual Insurance Association Co Ltd* supra; *Potter v South British Insurance Co Ltd* supra; *Boyce v Ocean Accident & Guarantee Corporation Ltd* supra; cf *Bagwandeen v City of Pietermaritzburg* supra. Nor will it usually be intended to be laid before the legal adviser for advice.

54 *United Tobacco Cos (South) Ltd v International Tobacco Co of SA Ltd* supra 70.

55 Ibid 72; *Bagwandeen v City of Pietermaritzburg* supra.

56 *International Tobacco Co (SA) Ltd v United Tobacco Cos (South) Ltd (3)* 1953 4 SA 251 (W).

57 *Potter v South British Insurance Co Ltd* supra 7; Zeffertt *Evidence* 593 who cites *Wheeler v Le Marchant* supra; *Dickie v Colonial Government* (1909) 26 SC 347; *Moffat v SA Breweries Ltd* 1912 WLD 104.

58 See fn 55 supra.

59 *International Tobacco Co (SA) Ltd v United Tobacco Cos (South) Ltd (2)* 1953 3 SA 879 (W); but cf *Vengtas v Nydoo* 1963 2 SA 504 (D).

60 Cross 251.

61 *International Tobacco Co (SA) Ltd v United Tobacco Cos (South) Ltd (3)* supra 255–256; *Resisto Dairy (Pty) Ltd v Auto Protection Insurance Co Ltd* supra 410; *S v Alexander (1)* 1965 2 SA 796 (A) 812.

62 *International Tobacco Co (SA) Ltd v United Tobacco Cos (South) Ltd (3)* supra.

63 In *R v Steyn* 1954 1 SA 324 (A), Greenberg AJ decided that, aside from legal professional privilege, witnesses had privilege on their witness statements, up to, and including the trial.

64 [1996] 1 All SA 64 (CC); 1995 12 BCLR 1593 (CC); 1996 1 SA 725 (CC); 1995 2 SACR 761 (CC).

65 As embodied in s 25(3) of the (interim) Constitution of the Republic of SA 200 of 1993 which has been repealed: Constitution of the Republic of SA 108 of 1996 s 242 read with Sch 7: see now s 35(3) of the 1996 Constitution. Although s 23 of the interim Constitution was also mooted in argument

against the privilege, the court felt that this did not take the matter any further, and decided the case entirely on the basis of s 25(3), specifically with the accused's right to be properly informed, so that a fair trial could result. The Investigation of Serious Economic Offences Act 117 of 1991 has also been repealed: National Prosecuting Authority Act 32 of 1998 s 44 read with the Schedule.

66 The application of the law pertaining to the adequacy of the particulars furnished might have to be re-examined having regard to the "spirit, purport and objects" of the Constitution.

67 S 25(3)(d).

68 Pars 36 and 37 of the judgment.

69 Par 72 of the judgment.

70 Constitution of the Republic of SA 108 of 1996.

71 S 32.

72 2 of 2000.

73 Zeffertt *Evidence* 576–577. See also *Jeeva v Receiver of Revenue, Port Elizabeth* 1995 2 SA 433 (SE); *Van Niekerk v City Council of Pretoria* [1997] 1 All SA 305 (T); 1997 3 SA 839 (T); *Le Roux v Direkteur-Generaal van Handel & Nywerheid* [1997] 2 All SA 636 (T); 1997 8 BCLR 1048 (T); 1997 4 SA 174 (T), *Klein v Attorney-General, Witwatersrand Local Division* 1995 3 SA 848 (W); 1995 2 SACR 210 (W); *Harksen v Attorney-General of the Province of the Cape of Good Hope* supra.

74 See fn 58 supra.

75 *Botes v Daly* supra: the legal adviser may be compelled to disclose the address of a minor, where it was given to the legala adviser in confidence, if it relates to a ward of court (*Ramsbotham v Senior* (1869) LR 8 Eq 575) and, "[i]n a broad sense . . . the power exercised by the courts in the Republic as upper guardians of minors is substantially in accordance with the powers assumed by the courts in England" (222).

755 Statements "without prejudice" The rationale for the "privilege"[1] that renders "without prejudice" communications inadmissible is that public policy demands that parties to disputes should be encouraged to avoid litigation and all the expenses, delays, hostility and inconvenience that it usually entails, by resolving their differences amicably in full and frank discussion without fear that, if the negotiations fail, any admissions made by them during these discussions will be used against them in ensuing litigation.[2] The law by virtue of the Civil Proceedings Evidence Act,[3] applies the law that was in force on 30 May 1961, although the Act only came into operation on 30 June 1967,[4] that is to say, the English law as at 30 May 1961.[5] A statement that has been expressly or impliedly made without prejudice in *bona fide* negotiations to settle a dispute is inadmissible without the consent of both parties.[6] Since the rule relating to "without prejudice" statements does not really appertain to a privilege, but is a right to make inadmissible admissions, it follows that, because the right vests in the parties only, a third party who overhears a "without prejudice" conversation cannot give evidence of its contents.[7] The usual procedure is to attack the words "without prejudice" (or similar words to the same effect) on a document, but the inclusion or exclusion of the words is not what counts and without prejudice communications may be oral as well as in writing. What really matters is whether the communication was intended to form part of a *bona fide* attempt to settle a dispute.[8] The purpose for which a party wishes to adduce such communication is all-important, for in exceptional circumstances it may be admitted, despite the general rule, to prove for example that it contains a threat, an act of insolvency, or possibly other matters that would be contrary to public policy to protect from being admissible.[9] Where an offer to settle is linked to a threat, the offer will not be admissible unless the threat constituted an offence of a delict that is in issue and the communication is tendered to prove that threat.[10] There is ordinarily no reason why the rule should not cover innocent misrepresentations if no settlement is reached.[11] Indeed, it has been held that although a communication has to be *bona fide* in order to be "privileged", the fact that it contains criminal or fraudulent statements does not make it *ipso facto* admissible unless the criminal or fraudulent element itself is in issue.[12] Where the *bona fides* of a communication is in issue, the inclusion of criminal or fraudulent elements in it may have a real relevance to that issue. If an offer of settlement necessarily would lead to an offence being committed if it were accepted, the privilege would not hold if the offer was tendered to prove that the offence had been committed; but the fact that it may be relevant to the maker's credibility will not defeat the privilege if further evidence would be required to determine whether an offence has been committed.[13] The court is entitled to see a document that is claimed to be inadmissible in order to determine whether or not it should be protected.[14]

The ambit of the rule extends to oral or written matter that flows from the communication even if it is not expressly said to be without prejudice.[15]

It is clear that admissions *that are quite unconnected with or irrelevant to* the settlement negotiations are not covered by the rule and are admissible in evidence.[16] The presence or absence of such a connection is a question of fact in which the intention of the party making the admission, as *objectively manifested*, may be of importance.[17] The better view is that the ambit of the rule extends to the exclusion of *matter not wholly unconnected with the negotiations* but irrelevant to the subsequent case then proceeding.[18] This liberal construction, although inconsistent with the narrower practice in some Commonwealth countries,[19] where it is required that the admission has to be reasonably incidental to the settlement negotiations, is more consistent with the less restrictive policy of English law and should, therefore, be the South African rule.[20] The matter has not, however, been resolved by the Supreme Court of Appeal.[21]

If the negotiations lead to a settlement, it is obvious that the terms of the settlement may be proved by the statements on which it was reached.[22] When negotiations result in a settlement, evidence about the settlement and the negotiations leading to it become admissible because the whole basis for non-disclosure has fallen away;[23] but "without prejudice" statements that have been made in the course of negotiations to settle a previous dispute are inadmissible in a later suit that involves issues not wholly unconnected with the earlier ones although they may be irrelevant to the subsequent negotiations.[24]

---

1   It is not really a privilege; see par 751 ante.

2   Per Trollip JA in *Naidoo v Marine & Trade Insurance Co Ltd* 1978 3 SA 666 (A) 677. See further *Kapeller v Rondalia Versekeringskorporasie van SA Bpk* 1964 4 SA 722 (T) 728; *Waste-Tech (Pty) Ltd v Van Zyl & Glanville* 2002 1 SA 841 (E).

3   25 of 1965 s 42. See also *Waste-Tech (Pty) Ltd v Van Zyl & Glanville* supra.

4   *Naidoo v Marine & Trade Insurance Co Ltd* supra 677; *Gentiruco AG v Firestone SA (Pty) Ltd* 1972 1 SA 589 (A) 617.

5   *Naidoo v Marine & Trade Insurance Co Ltd* supra 667.

6   *De Beers Consolidated Mines Ltd v Ettling* 1906 TS 418.

7   *Theodoropoulas v Theodoropoulas* 1964 P 311; [1963] 2 All ER 772 (A); *Pais v Pais* 1971 P 119; [1970] 3 All ER 491 (Div) 493.

8   *In re Daintry: Ex parte Holt* 1893 2 QB 116; *Ullman Bros Ltd v Kroonstad Produce Co* 1923 AD 449; *Merry v Machin* 1926 NPD 236; *Brauer v Markow* 1946 TPD 344; *Millward v Glaser* 1950 3 SA 547 (W) 554; *Mole v Mole* 1951 P 21; [1950] 2 All ER 328 (CA);

Henley v Henley 1955 P 202; [1955] 1 All ER 590 (Div).

9   *Naidoo v Marine & Trade Insurance Co Ltd* supra 681. As regards acts of insolvency, see *In re Daintry: ex parte Holt* supra as explained in *Coetzee v Union Government* 1941 TPD 1. For threats, see *Kurtz & Co v Spence & Sons* (1887) 57 LJ Ch 238; 22 Digest (Reissue) 407 4085; *Hoffend v Elgeti* 1949 3 SA 91 (A) 108–109. See further *Davenport v Davenport* 1930 WLD 202, which *Brauer v Markow* supra considered to be misleading to the extent that it regarded the fact that a threat accompanying an offer of settlement rendered the offer admissible, and *Hoffend v Elgeti* supra 108–109 states that a threat does not *ipso facto* have that effect.

10   *Hoffend v Elgeti* supra 108–109. Obviously a warning that litigation will be resorted to if there is no settlement is not a "threat" in this context.

11   *Naidoo v Marine & Trade Insurance Co Ltd* supra.

12   *Coetzee v Union Government* supra; *Brauer v Markow* supra.

13 Schmidt *Bewysreg* 570, commenting on *Brauer v Markow* supra.

14 *Brauer v Markow* supra 348; *Pillay v New Zealand Insurance Co Ltd* 1957 1 SA 17 (N) 19.

15 *Hoffend v Elgeti* supra 108.

16 *Naidoo v Marine & Trade Insurance Co Ltd* supra 678. See further *Waldridge v Kennison* (1794) 1 Esp 143; 170 ER 306; *Kapeller v Rondalia Versekeringskorporasie van SA Bpk* supra.

17 *Naidoo v Marine & Trade Insurance Co Ltd* supra 678–679. Cf *Ward v Steenberg* 1951 1 SA 395 (T) with *Cramer v Tothill* (2) 1945 TPD 368; *Botha v Van Niekerk* 1947 1 SA 699 (T).

18 *P Patlansky v J & B Patlansky* (2) 1917 WLD 10; cf *Wemyss v Stuart* 1961 3 SA 889 (D) 891.

19 Eg *Field v Commissioner for Railways for New South Wales* (1957) 99 CLR 285.

20 See the doubt expressed by Trollip JA in *Naidoo v Marine & Trade Insurance Co Ltd* supra 680 and the authorities there cited.

21 It was left open in *Naidoo v Marine & Trade Insurance Co Ltd* supra.

22 *Adkins & Hunter v MJ Crosbie & FW Crosbie & MM Crosbie's Executors* 1916 EDL 357 361.

23 *Gcabashe v Nene* 1975 3 SA 912 (D).

24 *P Patlansky v J & B Patlansky* (2) supra; see above as to the correctness of this approach.

756 Income tax and miscellaneous statutes Every person employed in carrying out the provisions of the Income Tax Act[1] is obliged to aid in preserving secrecy in regard to all matters that may come to the person's knowledge in the performance of his or her duties. Such person is not permitted to communicate any such matter to anyone other than the taxpayer concerned (or his or her legal representative); nor may the person suffer or permit anyone to have access to any records in the possession or custody of the secretary except in the performance of his or her duties under the Act or by order of a competent court.[2]

The interests that are protected are those of the taxpayer who is able to dispense with the protection when it would be in his or her interest to do so.[3] Although it has been held that the secrecy has, as a general rule, to be preserved in prosecutions against the taxpayer for offences other than those arising out of the Income Tax Act because it is more important to the state that persons taking part in illicit transactions should be encouraged, by an assurance of immunity against prosecution for the illegality, to disclose their profits under those transactions than that they should be prosecuted for them,[4] the immunity is excluded from prosecutions under the Income Tax Act.[5] The courts do not readily grant orders, against the will of the taxpayer, for the disclosure of information falling within the terms of the prohibition.[6] Even the use in court by representatives of the secretary of unreported judgments of the special income tax court, without the consent of the taxpayer, is prevented.[7] It is only a defined class of persons (those employed in carrying out the provisions of the Act) who are prevented from making disclosure, and documents in the possession of the taxpayer (or his or her representative) are not priviliged.[8] The state is bound by the privilege and it may not make use of protected matter, for example, to obtain a sequestration order.[9]

Information in the population register and identity documents may not be published or communicated except in certain cases, in terms of the Identification Act.[10] No entry made by the "competent person" who is "concerned" with making it under the Statistics Act[11] in any form, questionnaire, return, notice, book, register or other document may be admitted except in criminal prosecutions under the Income Tax Act.[12]

1 58 of 1962.

2 S 4(1).

3 *Margau v De Kok* 1947 4 SA 318 (W) (*obiter*); the taxpayer may agree to dispense with the protection: *Estate Dempers v Secretary for*

Inland Revenue 1977 3 SA 410 (A). Cf *Silver v Silver* 1937 NPD 129.

4 *In re Joseph Hargreaves Ltd* 1900 1 Ch 347 (CA) 350; *Silver v Silver* supra 134–135; *Greenspan v R* 1944 SR 149 155–156; *R v*

    Kassim 1950 4 SA 522 (A) 527 (*obiter*).

5   Greenspan *v* R supra; *R v Kassim* supra 527 (*obiter*).

6   Estate Dempers *v* Secretary for Inland Revenue supra 420.

7   Estate Dempers *v* Secretary for Inland Revenue supra 420. Usually a substantive application has to be made: *Union Government v Shiu* 1955 1 SA 298 (T) 301.

8   Crane *v* Johannesburg Stock Exchange Committee 1949 4 SA 835 (A); *Marais v Lombard*

    1958 4 SA 224 (E); *H Heiman, Maasdorp & Barker v Secretary for Inland Revenue* 1968 4 SA 160 (W).

9   Union Government *v* Shiu supra, where the information was not, however, within the ambit of the privilege; *Estate Dempers v Secretary for Inland Revenue* supra.

10 68 of 1997 s 21.

11 6 of 1999 s 17(4).

12 58 of 1962.

757 Adultery or *stuprum* Before the Civil Proceedings Evidence Act,[1] when it came into operation on 30 June 1967, repealed section 3 of the Natal Law to Amend the Law of Evidence,[2] a witness was not liable, except in certain instances, against his or her wish to be asked, or to be bound to answer any question tending to show that he or she was guilty of adultery or other *stuprum*.[3] It has been suggested[4] that, despite its repeal, section 3 probably continues to exist because section 42 of the Civil Proceedings Evidence Act retains the law, as it was on 30 May 1961, in any case not provided for in the Act, and the Act made no other provision in this regard.[5] If the provision is still operative, an unfavourable inference may sometimes be drawn against a party who relies on the privilege and deliberately refrains from giving evidence relating to a charge of adultery.[6]

1 25 of 1965.

2 5 of 1870; it did not apply where a woman was seeking to affiliate a child of hers or when a witness had already given evidence in the proceedings in proof of adultery or *stuprum*.

3 S 3. See *Thomson v Thomson* 1949 1 SA 445 (A).

4 Zeffertt *Evidence* 621.

5 Ibid. The provision is in the Schedule of repealed statutes. In *Thomson v Thomson* supra the plaintiff sued for an order of restitution

of conjugal rights and the defendant relied in her defence *inter alia* on six charges of adultery against the plaintiff. He gave evidence on the desertion but claimed the privilege against giving evidence on the adultery charges. The plaintiff's failure to testify, it was held, might operate generally to render it more probable that he had, at some time or place, committed adultery. (*Thomson's* case is discussed in *Galante v Dickinson* 1950 2 SA 460 (A) 464–465.)

6 *Thomson v Thomson* supra.

PUBLIC POLICY

758 Introduction In this section the so-called "privileges", by means of which public policy and the public interest are protected, will be discussed.

Except as provided by the Criminal Procedure Act[1] or any other law, no witness in criminal proceedings is compellable or permitted to give evidence as to any fact, matter or thing or as to any communication made to or by the witness if he or she would not have been compelled or permitted to do so on 30 May 1961 on the ground of the public policy or with regard to the public interest.[2] This has the effect of applying the rules of the English law of evidence (to the extent that they have not been altered by any South African law) as they were on 30 May 1961.[3] The same effect has been achieved by virtue of section 42 of the Civil Proceedings Evidence Act.[4]

These privileges differ from private privilege in that secondary evidence is not generally admissible to prove matter that is protected.[5] Again, the court may, in a proper case, enforce such a privilege *mero motu*.[6] This is quite different from the position as regards private privilege.[7]

The existence of a judicial discretion to exclude illegally or unfairly obtained evidence will also be examined.

1 51 of 1977 s 202.
2 For the meaning of the rather unclear provisos to the section, see Hiemstra *Strafproses* 502–505.
3 Hiemstra 505.
4 25 of 1965.
5 *Nyangeni v Minister of Bantu Administration &*

Development 1961 1 SA 547 (E); *Redelinghuys v Geidel* 1963 2 SA 274 (W); *Minister of Community Development v Saloojee* 1963 4 SA 65 (T); cf *S v Naicker* 1965 2 SA 919 (N).
6 See par 759 post.
7 See pars 751–757 ante.

759 Privilege arising out of the interests of the state and the need to protect its safety A great number of security statutes which characterised the "old" South Africa have now been repealed[1] and only the Internal Security Act of the previous dispensation, although much modified, still affects the privilege relating to the interests of the state.

This statutory provision approximates to the position at common law when the safety of the state and its citizens could be threatened by disclosure. At common law the position might well have been that, in cases involving the safety of the state, its international relations and very important executive documents, the court would be obliged either to exclude evidence *mero motu* or to accept a properly tendered objection without further inquiry.[2]

Where the production of evidence would affect the security to the state, the court may *mero motu* prevent its disclosure.[3] The principles of the common law deal with an objection which is taken to the production or reception of evidence on the basis that it would adversely affect the interests (rather than the security) of the state to allow its disclosure. An example would be the case of a document which belongs to a class, which has to be withheld from production *as a class*, on the grounds of the public interest.[4] The rules applicable are those of the English law of evidence as they were in force on 30 May 1961. This is the effect of section 202 of the Criminal Procedure Act[5] and section 42 of the Civil Proceedings Evidence Act.[6]

The court thus retains its common law power to overrule a properly tendered objection, in connection with any matter other than one affecting the security of the state, if it feels that it would be in the interests of justice to do so.[7] And the court's power to scrutinise the evidence in private remains inherent in this power.[8] It will be in rare instances only that an objection will be overruled. The residual power is one that has to be exercised with strict circumspection and will be used only where the court is satisfied that the objection is unjustifiable or that it cannot be sustained on reasonable grounds.[9] Furthermore, the court has to be on its guard against requiring an explanation that would cause precisely the injury that the right to withhold evidence is calculated to avoid.[10]

Secondary evidence is inadmissible to prove the content of a document that has been excluded because its disclosure would adversely affect the safety of the state or the interests of the state and the public.[11] Circumstantial evidence, from which the content of a privileged statement may be inferred, is inadmissible.[12]

A court should only exercise its residual right to scrutinise a document (that is to say, its right to do so when an objection has been taken other than on the basis that the state's security would be adversely affected by disclosure) once it has been decided not to accept, at face value, a possible ministerial objection to its diclosure.[13]

Waiver of state privilege is possible.[14]

As is the case with the police,[15] all prior court cases in this regard would have to be read in terms of the Constitution.[16] On the other hand, the rights of suspected criminals are not unlimited and may be legally curtailed, taking into account all relevant factors.[17]

1 By the Safety Matters Rationalisation Act 90 of 1996 s 1 read with Sch 1.

2 *Van der Linde v Calitz* 1967 2 SA 239 (A) 260; *Minister van Justisie v Alexander* 1975 4 SA 530 (A). See further *Conway v Rimmer* 1968 AC 910 (HL) 952; [1968] 1 All ER 874 (HL): "if the Minister's reasons are of a character which judicial experience is not competent to weigh, then the Minister's view must prevail", as per Lord Reid; see *Geldenhuys v Pretorius* 1971 2 SA 277 (O). In *Minister van Polisie v Marais* 1970 2 SA 467 (C) the court inspected a document that related to the security of the state, but did so with the minister's consent. Typical cases of this kind are *Duncan v Cammell, Laird & Co Ltd* 1942 AC 624; [1942] 1 All ER 587 (HL); *Nyangeni v Minister of Bantu Administration & Development* 1961 1 SA 547 (E).

3 *Van der Linde v Calitz* supra 260; *Conway v Rimmer* supra 950; 887; see further *Nyangeni v Minister of Bantu Administration & Development* supra 555.

4 A document such as those in *Van der Linde v Calitz* supra and *Conway v Rimmer* supra.

5 51 of 1977.

6 25 of 1965.

7 *Van der Linde v Calitz* supra.

8 *Robinson v State of South Australia* (2) 1931 AC 704 (PC); 1931 All ER 333; *Van der Linde v Calitz* supra; *Conway v Rimmer* supra.

9 *Van der Linde v Calitz* supra; *Geldenhuys v Pretorius* supra.

10 *Van der Linde v Calitz* supra.

11 *Nyangeni v Minister of Bantu Administration & Development* supra 557; *Redelinghuys v Geidel* 1963 2 SA 274 (W) 275–276.

12 *Minister of Community Development v Saloojee* 1963 4 SA 65 (T); but see *S v Naicker* 1965 2 SA 919 (N). Cf *Cape Town Municipality v Bethnal Investments (Pty) Ltd* 1972 4 SA 153 (C) 169–171.

13 See the dissenting judgment of Corbett JA in *Minister van Justisie v Alexander* supra 552.

14 *Nyangeni v Minister of Bantu Administration & Development* supra 574; presumably not if it would be against the public interest.

15 See par 760 post.

16 Constitution of the Republic of SA 108 of 1996.

17 S 36.

760 The police It has been correctly said that the whole business of crime is conducted in secret and devious ways against the interests of the state and that the work of defeating the operations of criminals has to be conducted by similar methods.[1] This may give rise to the conclusion that methods used by the police to detect crimes may be protected from disclosure. Thus, reports to a detective from his subordinates have been kept secret[2] and, where the police made use of a tape recorder to record a conversation, cross-examination relating to the manner in which the recording was obtained, was disallowed although the recording was received in evidence.[3]

In the light of the protection of the individual's rights against the state by the Constitution,[4] a careful weighing up of interests would now have to take place. All prior court cases would have to be read in terms of the Constitution. On the other hand, as was the case with state privilege, the rights of suspected criminals are not borderless and may be limited, taking into account all relevant factors.[5]

1 *R v Abelson* 1933 TPD 227 231.

2 *R v Abelson* supra 231.

3 *S v Peake* 1962 4 SA 288 (C).

4 Constitution of the Republic of SA 108 of

1996, particularly s 14 which deals with privacy. See generally title CONSTITUTIONAL LAW.

5 S 36.

761 The identity of informers The privilege that leads, generally, to the prevention of the identity of informers and the content of their information being disclosed, rests on the foundation that communications that have been made by them ought to receive encouragement and that the confidence that will lead to such communications being made can be created only by preventing the disclosure of their identity.[1] Public policy, then, demands that the identity of an informer and the content of the information given by the informer should be kept a secret; but this exclusionary privilege operates only when public policy requires that the name of the informer, or his or her information, should be kept secret because the informer's information relates to matters in respect of which persons might not inform if they were not protected, or for the reason that the candour and completeness of the informer's communication might be prejudiced if he or she were not protected, or for some other good reason.[2] The privilege, therefore, is not intended only to protect informers against the revenge of the criminals that they may implicate. An informer's identity is also protected so as to enable the state to combat crime. It follows that the informer cannot waive the privilege if public policy demands secrecy: it is not the informer's privilege but one that is conceived in the interests of the public.[3] Ever since South Africa became a constitutional democracy, the right to privacy, as guaranteed by the Constitution,[4] will also play a role in this regard.

An informer, in this context, is one who gives information of a kind predjudical to others whose enmity he or she might provoke by doing so. In addition, the information has to be of a kind which is, or might be, the cause of a criminal prosecution and it must have been given to officers of justice.[5]

It would be impossible to give a comprehensive definition that would include all cases in which a person acts as an informer.[6] The rule against disclosure of the identity of informers does not apply to every person who makes a statement to the police in connection with a prosecution, but only to informers properly so called whose identity is kept secret in the public interest.[7] The following instances of persons who would not be informers may profitably be given. A complainant who avers that an offence has been committed against his or her person or property is not an informer;[8] nor is a person who, having been involved in an accident, makes a statement about it.[9] The identity of a witness who observes an offence and who makes a statement to the police about it will not ordinarily be protected by the privilege. Thus a person who by chance happens to see an accident and who gives the police a statement relating to it cannot ordinarily be regarded as an informer.[10] A police officer who makes a statement about his or her observations does not fall within this ambit of the privilege because the police do not have to be encouraged to set the law in motion by keeping their identity secret.[11] But this would certainly be the case if the police officer had been acting secretly in disguise in order to bring criminals to justice and where the detection of further crime requires the police officer to continue to act in a covert fashion.

The rule that keeps an informer's identity secret is relaxed, that is to say, an informer's identity may be revealed when public policy demands disclosure. In the leading case on the subject the Appellate Division gave three examples where the rule preventing the disclosure of informers is relaxed: (a) when it is material to the ends of justice; (b) if it is necessary or right to do so in order to show the prisoner's innocence; and (c) when the reason for secrecy no longer exists.[12] These examples are not, however, exhaustive.[13] In all cases the fundamental inquiry is whether it can properly be said that it appears, from the circumstances, that the public policy requires the name of the informer to be kept secret.[14] Thus the court may order the privilege to fall away *in favorem innocentiae*;[15] and it does not apply where the identity of the informer is admitted or known.[16] It would appear, however, that the mere fact that a civil claim has been brought against a person, in which it is averred that he or she made a false statement to the police, will not lead to the privilege being defeated.[17]

The privilege is not confined to the person who sets the law in motion by reporting the occurrence of an offence: a person who identifies an offender after the commission of an offence has already become known, may also be an informer.[18]

The rules of English practice lack relevance to the South African situation because virtually all prosecutions here, unlike those in England, are at the public instance. Therefore, although section 202 of the Criminal Procedure Act[19] enjoins us to apply the English Law, English principles relating to the definition of an informer cannot be usefully adopted here and South African law has developed independently in a manner that is appropriate to local conditions.[20]

It would seem that the proviso to section 202 of the Criminal Procedure Act, which lays down that any person may in criminal proceedings adduce evidence of any communication alleging the commission of an offence if the making of that communication *prima facie* constitutes an offence, relates to informers.[21] The only offences to which the proviso can apply are criminal defamation, perjury, treason and a contravention of certain provisions of the Internal Security Act.[22] Thus, when the state requires the evidence of an informer to prove that such a criminal communication had been made, an informer cannot rely on the privilege against the disclosure of his or her identity.[23]

1 Wigmore *Evidence* par 2374, approved and applied in *Suliman v Hansa* 1971 4 SA 69 (D). This privilege has been qualified considerably by the judgment of *Shabalala v Attorney-General of the Tvl* [1996] 1 All SA 64 (CC); 1995 12 BCLR 1593 (CC); 1996 1 SA 725 (CC); 1995 2 SACR 761 (CC). See par 759 ante.

2 Per Watermeyer CJ in *Ex parte Minister of Justice: In re R v Pillay* 1945 AD 653 668. See further *Suliman v Hansa* supra.

3 *Olifant v R* 1937 2 PH H191 (T); but see *Harris v R* 1927 NPD 330 345, where Tatham J failed to realise that the public interest might debar an informer from making disclosure. Cf *Suliman v Hansa* supra where the informer acknowledged that he had been one and his identity had already been revealed. And it has been held that state privilege may be waived; see par 777 post.

4 Constitution of the Republic of SA 108 of 1996 s 14, and see *Swanepoel v Minister van Veiligheid & Sekuriteit* [1999] 3 All SA 285 (T); 1999 4 SA 549 (T); 1999 2 SACR 284 (T).

5 *R v Van Schalkwyk* 1938 AD 543 548. See also the text to fn 22 infra.

6 *Ex parte Minister of Justice: In re R v Pillay* supra 668.

7 *Scheepers v S* 1971 2 PH H101 (NC).

8 *Naylor v Wheeler* 1947 2 SA 681 (D) 685.

9 *Pechey v Lutchman* 1963 4 SA 112 (N) 115–116.

10 *R v Makaula* 1949 1 SA 40 (EDL) 46.

11 *Suliman v Hansa* 1971 2 SA 437 (D).

12 *Ex parte Minister of Justice: In re R v Pillay* supra. The entrenchment of the right to information has not abolished the informer privilege: *Els v Minister of Safety & Security* 1998 4 BCLR 434 (NC); 1998 2 SACR 93 (NC).

13 *Suliman v Hansa* 1971 4 SA 69 (D).

14 *Suliman v Hansa* supra.

15 *Tranter v Attorney-General & the First Criminal Magistrate of Johannesburg* 1907 TS 415; *S v Rossouw* 1973 4 SA 608 (SWA) 609.

16 *R v Van Schalkwyk* supra 549; *Ex parte Minister of Justice: In re R v Pillay* supra 666; *S v Rossouw* supra 609; *Suliman v Hansa* 1971 4 SA 69 (D) 72.

17 *Marais v Lombard* 1958 4 SA 224 (E) 230; *Suliman v Hansa* 1971 2 SA 437 (D) 440; cf *Lederman v Moharal Investments (Pty) Ltd* 1968 3 SA 372 (W), where the identity of the informer was known. Hiemstra *Strafproses* 503 submits that only an unusually valuable source of information would be protected despite the fact that false information led to an unwarranted and baseless prosecution.

18 *R v Makaula* supra.

19 51 of 1977.

20 Since *R v Van Schalkwyk* supra and *Ex parte Minister of Justice: In re R v Pillay* supra.

21 Hiemstra 505.

22 74 of 1982.

23 *R v Makaula* supra (*obiter*). See Hiemstra 496 for what has to be made out in order to defeat the privilege and the fact that the court has to make the final decision.

762 Judicial officers A judge or magistrate is a competent and compellable witness: magistrates frequently testify, for instance, about confessions that have been reduced to writing and confirmed in their presence. In practice, however, judges are protected against having to give evidence relating to proceedings that have been held before them. Judges cannot be expected to justify their decisions in the witness box and the law does not countenance such a procedure: it is contrary to public policy to allow a judge to be examined and cross-examined with reference not to facts but to the performance of his or her judicial duties.[1] It has been held that a court should not allow a subpoena to be issued against a judge so that the judge might answer an allegation that his or her notes reflected an inaccurate version of the evidence that he or she had heard.[2] The same privilege should extend to magistrates.[3]

Although a judge may give evidence as to "facts", it is undesirable that he or she should do so. Thus it has been held that a judge should not testify as regards perjury that may have been committed before himor her; the registrar should be called.[4] Magistrates, however, are often called to prove a charge of perjury when they have themselves kept the record which becomes, therefore, the best evidence of the accused's alleged perjury.[5]

1 *Ex parte Wolpert* 1917 WLD 98 99.
2 *Ex parte Wolpert* supra 99.
3 Schmidt *Bewysreg* 586.

4 *R v Ross* 1910 WLD 50.
5 *R v Manteti* 1920 EDL 297.

763 Arbitrators An arbitrator may testify about the factors that he or she took into account in reaching conclusions and in order to determine whether the arbitrator misdirected him or herself on the facts.[1] The arbitrator's evidence or, for that matter, the evidence of anyone else, however, is inadmissible to vary or explain his or her written award because of the prohibition of extrinsic evidence relating to a document.[2]

1 *Pretoria City Council v Buchanan* 1952 1 SA
236 (T) 243.

2 The exclusion of such evidence therefore has nothing to do with privilege.

764 Advocate and attorney Legal practitioners are competent and compellable witnesses but it is undesirable for them to give evidence about what happened in proceedings in which they may have been employed. It is preferable, where possible, to call others to testify. In any event, the client's private privilege will obtain.[1] Advocates are usually permitted to make unsworn statements from the bar; but, if one of the parties insists, they will be required to testify in the normal way.

1 See pars 751–757 ante; *S v Boesman* 1990 2
SACR 389 (E).

765 Illegally or unfairly obtained evidence Traditionally all relevant evidence (if not excluded by an exclusionary rule) was admissible and South African courts were not concerned with how it was obtained. In criminal cases the judicial officer had a discretion to disallow evidence if the strict rules of admissibility would operate unfairly against an accused,[1] for instance if it was obtained by a trick. It is most unlikely that the same position obtained in civil proceedings.[2]

This situation has changed dramatically as a result of the South African Constitution.[3] Now, evidence obtained through a breach of fundamental rights can only be admitted if it is justifiable in terms of the limitation clause of the Bill of Rights contained in in the Constitution.[4] In a number of criminal cases, unfairly obtained evidence has been held to be inadmissible.[5] It has been held that a civil court also has the discretion to exclude unfairly obtained evidence because the Constitution requires courts to promote the spirit, purport and objects of the Bill or Rights, but that a fundamental difference exists between criminal and civil courts in this regard.[6] Sometimes fairness may require unconstitutionally obtained evidence to be admissible,[7] but where evidence is obtained through a deliberate and conscious violation of constitutional rights, such evidence should be excluded.[8] For example, to admit evidence provided by the accused against him or herself without his or her knowledge as the result of the illegal monitoring of conversations with someone else, offends against the ideas of basic fairness and violates the accused's right against self-incrimination.[9] The provisions of section 35(5) of the Constitution are not limited to situations where there is a causal connection between the infraction of the constitutional right and the obtaining of the evidence, but includes all evidence coming into being through an act of a detainee subsequent to the violation of his or her constitutional rights.[10]

1 *Noor Mohamed v R* 1949 AC 182 (PC); [1949] 1 All ER 365 (PC); *Harris v Director of Public Prosecutions* 1952 AC 694 (HL); [1952] 1 All ER 1044 (HL); *Kuruma, Son of Kaniu v R* 1955 AC 197 (PC) 203; [1955] 1 All ER 236 (PC) 239; *Rumping v Director of Public Prosecutions* 1964 AC 814 (HL), [1962] 3 All ER 256 (HL); *S v Forbes* 1970 2 SA 594 (C) (distinguished in *S v Webb* (1) 1971 2 SA 340 (T)); *S v Mushimba* 1977 2 SA 829 (A) 840. See further *R v Lubela* 1923 TPD 229; *R v Lizzie* 1926 WLD 224; *R v Noorbhai* 1945 AD 58 78; *R v Bosch* 1949 1 SA 548 (A); *Ex parte Minister of Justice: In re R v Demingo* 1951 1 SA 36 (A); *R v Roets* 1954 3 SA 512 (A) 521, where Schreiner JA indicated that the rule of practice by which the court, in a proper case, should secure by intimation to the prosecution the exclusion of evidence the effect of which would be out of proportion to its probative value is, perhaps, more appropriate to a jury system. See further *King v R* 1969 1 AC 304 (PC); [1968] 2 All ER 610 (PC); cf *R v Wray* (1970) 11 DLR 3d 673; and see Heydon *Evidence* 230–254. See now *R v Sang* [1979] 2 All ER 1222 (HL) in which the question of a judicial officer's discretion to refuse to admit otherwise admissible evidence was once again in issue. Both in the court of appeal (*R v Sang, R v Mangan* 1979 2 All ER 46 (CA) and in the House of Lords, the *dictum* in *Kuruma, Son of Kaniu v R* supra, that evidence obtained by trickery could be excluded, was severely restricted, if not discounted: *S v Molautsi* 1980 3 SA 1041 (B).

2 In *Botha v Botha* 1972 2 SA 559 (N) Leon J doubted whether he had a discretion in the circumstances in which he was concerned and, in any event if there was a residual discretion, he considered it best that the evidence should be given. See also *S v Desai* [1997] 2 All SA 298 (W); 1997 1 SA 845 (W); 1997 1 SACR 38 (W).

3 Constitution of the Republic of SA 108 of 1996.

4 S 36.

5 See, eg, *S v Hammer* 1994 2 SACR 496 (C); *S v Motloutsi* [1996] 1 All SA 27 (C); 1996 2 BCLR 220 (C); 1996 1 SA 584 (C); 1996 1 SACR 78 (C). It was held in *S v Melani* 1995 4 SA 412 (E); [1996] 1 All SA 137 (E); 1996 2 BCLR 174 (E); 1996 1 SACR 335 (E) that the court's discretion to exclude evidence obtained in breach of the fundamental right contained in the (interim) Constitution of the Republic of SA 200 of 1993 s 25(2), is "appropriate relief" in terms of s 7(4) of the interim Constitution.

6 The accused in a criminal case enjoys constitutional protection in the shape of the privilege against self-incrimination and the right to silence. On the other hand the accued's defence does not have to be disclosed, whereas the civil litigant has the burden of full discovery: see *Fedics Group v Matus*; *Fedics Group v Murphy* 1998 2 SA 617 (C), [1997] 4 All SA 14 (C); 1997 9 BCLR 1199 (C); *Protea Technology Ltd v Wainer* 1997 9 BCLR 1225 (W); [1997] 3 All SA 594 (W).

7 *Key v Attorney-General, Cape Provincial Division* 1996 6 BCLR 788 (CC); 1996 4 SA 187 (CC); 1996 2 SACR 113 (CC).

8 *S v Mayekiso* [1996] 3 All SA 121 (C); 1996 9 BCLR 1168 (C); 1996 2 SACR 298 (C).

9 *S v Naidoo* [1998] 1 All SA 189 (D); 1998 1 BCLR 46 (D); 1998 1 SACR 479 (D). See also *S v Shongwe* [1998] 3 All SA 549 (T); 1998 9 BCLR 1170 (T); 1998 2 SACR 321 (T); *S v Madiba* 1998 1 BCLR 38 (D); *S v Malefo* [1998] 1 All SA 647 (W); 1998 2 BCLR 187 (W); 1998 1 SACR 127 (W).

10 *S v Soci* [1998] 2 All SA 18 (E); 1998 2 SACR 275 (E); 1998 3 BCLR 376 (E); and see *S v Ngcobo* 1998 10 BCLR 1248 (N) for the factors considered by the court in the exercise of its discretion to allow evidence following a failure to observe the pre-trial constitutional rights of the accused.

MEANS OF PROOF

WITNESSES

766 Competence and compellability generally In both civil and criminal proceedings the general rule is that every person is competent and compellable to give evidence.[1] The exceptions are dealt with below.

In criminal proceedings any question concerning the competence or compellability of a witness is decided by the court in which the proceedings are conducted.[2] This means that the parties cannot agree to the admission of evidence by an incompetent witness.[3] A question of competence is decided in the same way as a question of admissibility by the judge alone (though the assessors will normally be allowed to remain present); and if necessary, a "trial within a trial" may have to be held to decide the issue.[4]

The failure to attend as a witness, the refusal to be sworn, and the refusal, without just excuse, to answer questions or produce documents, are punishable offences.[5][6]

1 Civil Proceedings Evidence Act 25 of 1965 s 8 read with s 42; Criminal Procedure Act 51 of 1977 s 192 read with s 206. S 192 stipulates that every person "not expressly excluded by this Act" is both competent and compellable. Where the relevant residuary section (s 206) in effect refers to English law exceptions to the general principle of competence, such reference constitutes an "express exclusion" for the purposes of s 192: *Ex parte Minister of Justice: In re R v Demingo* 1951 1 SA 36 (A). As to sources generally, see par 779 ante.

2 S 193.

3 *S v Kumalo* 1962 4 SA 432 (N) 435D; *S v Thurston* 1968 3 SA 284 (A) 291D–C. If a witness is competent to give evidence for the state on one charge but incompetent on another, then cross-examination by the accused in respect of the charge on which the witness is incompetent does not make his or her evidence admissible: *S v Khanyapa* 1979 1 SA 824 (A). See also par 776 fn 26 post.

4 *R v Creinhold* 1926 OPD 151 154; *S v Thurston* supra 291B. For a judgment on the facts, see *S v Louw* 1996 2 SACR 563 (W).

5 Supreme Court Act 59 of 1959 ss 30–31; Magistrates' Courts Act 32 of 1944 s 51; Criminal Procedure Act 51 of 1977 ss 188–189. As to the meaning of "just excuse", see *S v Pogrund* 1961 3 SA 868 (T); *S v Weinberg* 1966 3 SA 272 (T); *S v Cameson* 1962 3 SA 437 (T); *S v Govender* 1967 2 SA 121 (N); *S v Molobi* 1976 2 SA 301 (W); *S v Maduna* 1978 2 SA 777 (D); *S v Waite* 1978 3 SA 896 (O); *S v Bosman* 1978 3 SA 903 (O); *S v Mthenjane* 1979 2 SA 105 (A). For a discussion of the principles involved in the duty to testify, see *Mattheys v Coetzee* [1997] 3 All SA 675 (W).

6 The Witness Protection Act 112 of 1998, except for ss 6 and 20, came into operation on 31 March 2000: Proc R16 of 31 March 2000. For the anonimity of witnesses, see *S v Ntoae* 2000 1 SACR 17 (W).

767 Disability and immaturity A person appearing or proved to be afflicted with mental illness or to be labouring under any imbecility of mind due to intoxication or drugs or the like, and who is thereby deprived of the proper use of his or her reason, is not competent to give evidence.[1] It should be noted that incompetence attaches to the person only if the disability or affliction deprives the person "of the proper use of his reason";[2] and it lasts only as long as the disability or affliction lasts, so that a drunken witness regains competence when sober.[3]

A deaf and dumb person is not incompetent to give evidence, provided that he or she can communicate with the court – if need be through an interpreter.[4]

There is no statutory provision governing a child's capacity to give evidence and there is no recognised age limit for a witness, but a child who is so immature that he or she cannot communicate intelligibly with the court or, even if he or she can, is unable to appreciate the duty to speak the truth, must obviously be disqualified.[5]

If a witness incurs a disability in the course of his or her testimony, rendering the witness incompetent, for instance through supervening illness, then the evidence already given will remain on record – at least in so far as cross-examination has taken place and such evidence has not been contested.[6]

1 Criminal Procedure Act 51 of 1977 s 194. See also the Civil Proceedings Evidence Act 25 of 1965 s 9.
2 Under the preceding Criminal Procedure Acts there was some dispute on the question whether the words "thereby deprived of the proper use of his reason" are applicable to the mentally ill as well as to the other category of incompetent witnesses (those affected by intoxication, drugs, and so on). The better view appears to be that they do apply to the mentally ill. This is supported by an *obiter dictum* in *S v Thurston* 1968 3 SA 284 (A) 290 as well as by the fact that no comma appears after "mentally ill", whereas one did appear after "insanity" in the preceding Criminal Procedure Act.
3 *R v Creinhold* 1926 OPD 151.
4 *R v Ranikolo* 1954 3 SA 255 (O).
5 *S v T* 1973 3 SA 794 (A). See also *Chaimowitz v Chaimowitz (1)* 1960 4 SA 818 (C) 822.
6 *R v Vilbro* 1957 3 SA 223 (A) 226.

768 Husband or wife In civil proceedings the husband or wife of a party is both competent and compellable to give evidence either for or against the party.

In criminal proceedings the husband or wife of the accused is a competent and compellable witness for the defence.[1] The wife or husband of an accused is competent, but not compellable, to give evidence for the prosecution in criminal proceedings, but is competent and compellable to give evidence for the prosecution at such proceedings where the accused is charged with:[2]

(a) any offence committed against the person of either of them[3] or of a child of either of them;

(b) any offence under certain sections of the Child Care Act,[4] committed in respect of any child of either of them;

(c) any contravention of any provision of section 11(1) of the Maintenance Act,[5] or of such provision as applied by any other law;

(d) bigamy;

(e) incest;

(f) abduction;

(g) any contravention of any provision of sections 2, 8, 9, 10, 11, 12, 12A, 13, 17 or 20 of the Sexual Offences Act;[6]

(h) perjury committed in connection with or for the purpose of any judicial proceedings instituted or to be instituted or contemplated by the one of them against the other, or in connection with or for the purpose of criminal proceedings in respect of any offence included in this subsection;

(i) the statutory offence of making a false statement in any affidavit or any affirmed, solemn or attested declaration if it is made in connection with or for the purpose of any such proceedings as are mentioned in paragraph (h) above.

1 Criminal Procedure Act 51 of 1977 s 196. The husband or wife can be called as a witness only upon the application of the accused and not, eg upon the application of the court: s 196(1)(b); *R v Jamba* 1947 4 SA 228 (C).
2 S 195.
3 As to the meaning of "offence against the person", see *S v Dhlamini* 1966 4 SA 149 (N) 152. Cf *R v Bakira* 1946 SR 92; *R v Hunda* 1956 3 SA 695 (SR).
4 74 of 1983 ss 50 50A 51–52.
5 99 of 1998.
6 23 of 1957.

769 The accused and the co-accused The accused is a competent witness for the defence at every stage of criminal proceedings, whether or not the accused is charged jointly with any other person, and will not be called as a witness except upon his or her own application.[1] Neither the prosecution, the court, nor the co-accused can therefore call the accused as a witness: the decision to give evidence is his or her own.[2] The court may, however, recall an accused person who has given evidence, but its discretion in this respect is limited and it cannot recall the accused to supply a deficiency in the state's case.[3]

It follows from the above that a co-accused can elect to give evidence in his or her own defence, but cannot be compelled to give evidence for any other accused or for the state. If, in giving evidence in his or her own defence, the co-accused furthers the cause of the other accused or of the state, such evidence is admissible, whatever its effect.[4] Even if he or she would be incompetent to give evidence for the state were he or she not an accused person, the evidence given upon his or her own application would be admissible against the co-accused. If he or she does elect to give evidence, both the state and the other accused can cross-examine him or her.[5]

If the state wishes to call a co-accused it can only do so by ensuring that the co-accused is no longer an accused in the case – for example by withdrawing the charge against him or her, by accepting his or her plea of guilty (in which case it would be preferable to have such co-accused sentenced before using him or her as a witness)[6] or by effecting a separation of trials.[7]

1 Criminal Procedure Act 51 of 1977 s 196(1).
2 It is an irregularity for the court to persuade the accused to give evidence when his or her original inclination was not to do so because this interferes with free choice: *S v Klumalo* 1972 4 SA 500 (O).
3 S 186; and cf *Sparrow v R* 1941 SR 24; *R v Naran* 1954 1 SA 509 (SR).

4 S 196(2), and see *S v Radloff* 1978 4 SA 66 (A).
5 *S v Langa* 1963 4 SA 941 (N); *S v Ntuli* 1978 2 SA 69 (A) 74A.
6 *Ex parte Minister of Justice: In re R v Demingo* 1951 1 SA 36 (A).
7 *R v Roberts* 1932 CPD 87; *S v Kumalo* 1962 4 SA 432 (N); *S v Hendrix* 1979 3 SA 816 (D).

770 Officers of the court A judge or magistrate is not competent to give evidence in a case over which he or she presides.[1] If the judge or magistrate has personal knowledge of a fact in issue and it is not capable of being judicially noticed, he or she should recuse him or herself and may then give evidence.[2] No subpoena may, however, be issued against a judge out of any court without the consent of that court – except that, if the court is an inferior court, the consent has to be given by the provincial division having appellate jurisdiction.[3]

Other officers of the court, such as advocates,[4] attorneys,[5] prosecutors[6] and interpreters[7] are competent witnesses, but their participation as witnesses in cases in which they are professionally involved should, if possible, be avoided.[8]

1 *Ex parte Minister of Justice: In re R v Demingo* 1951 1 SA 36 (A) 43G.
2 Phipson *Evidence* par 48. *S v Malgas* 1978 1 SA 313 (NC) provides an example of a magistrate recusing himself and then testifying before another magistrate about occurences at the trial where he had presided.
3 Supreme Court Act 59 of 1959 s 25. See *Ex parte Wolpert* 1917 WLD 98.

4 *R v Becker* 1929 AD 167; *Ganie v Parekh* 1962 4 SA 618 (N) 620B.
5 *R v Becker* supra.
6 Eg *Middeldorf v Zipper* 1947 1 SA 545 (SR) 548; *Hendricks v Davidoff* 1955 2 SA 369 (C); *Elgin Engineering Co (Pty) Ltd v Hillview Motor Transport* 1961 4 SA 450 (D) 454.
7 *R v Craig* (1904) 25 NLR 153.
8 Authoritites in fns 4–7 supra.

771 The president, members of Parliament, diplomats There is no statutory provision dealing with the compellabilty of the president of the Republic.

Members of Parliament cannot be required to give evidence in civil proceedings while in attendance on Parliament, unless the court holds its sittings at the seat of Parliament.[1]

Heads of state, diplomatic agents and various other persons connected with diplomatic missions or public international organisations and institutions are immune from the civil and criminal jurisdiction of the courts.[2] This immunity includes immunity from complusion to attend as a witness.

These provisions have also been extended to the United Nations, its specialised agencies and other international organisations.[3]

1 Powers and Privileges of Parliament Act 91 of 1963 s 7(1).
2 Diplomatic Immunities and Privileges Act 37
of 2001 s 4. See also title INTERNATIONAL LAW.
3 Diplomatic Immunities and Privileges Act s 4.

772 Attendance in court A party to civil proceedings attends court voluntarily if he or she wishes to give evidence. Witnesses in both civil and criminal proceedings may agree to attend voluntarily; and they may be compelled to attend by service of a subpoena.[1] If a witness is required to produce a book, paper or document, he or she can be compelled to do so by means of a subpoena (called a subpoena *duces tecum*) containing the necessary details,[2] or, in criminal proceedings in an inferior court, by a written notice handed to the witness by a police official.[3]

In criminal proceedings the court may at any stage subpoena a person as a witness, or cause a person to be subpoenaed as a witness; and it *shall* so subpoena or cause to be subpoenaed any person whose evidence appears to it essential for a just decision of the case.[4]

1 Supreme Court Act 59 of 1959 s 30 (r 38(1)); Magistrates' Courts Act 32 of 1944 s 51 (r 26); Criminal Procedure Act 51 of 1977 s 179(1)(a). See also titles CIVIL PROCEDURE; CRIMINAL PROCEDURE.
2 Ibid.
3 S 179(1)(b).
4 S 186; *S v B* 1980 2 SA 946 (A). See further title CRIMINAL PROCEDURE.

773 The sequence of evidence In civil proceedings the plaintiff, if he or she bears the burden of proof, first adduces his or her evidence, calling all the witnesses available to the plaintiff. The plaintiff then closes his or her case and, unless absolution from the instance is decreed, the defendant then adduces his or her evidence. If, on the other hand, the burden of proof is on the defendant, the defendant commences and the plaintiff follows. Where the burden[1] rests upon the plaintiff in respect of any one or more of the issues and upon the defendant in respect of any others, the plaintiff begins and the defendant follows, but the plaintiff has the right to call rebutting evidence on any issues in respect of which the onus was on the defendant.[2] Third parties or defendants in reconvention who are not plaintiffs in the action, adduce their evidence after the plaintiff and the defendant.[3]

In criminal proceedings the state adduces evidence[4] and, unless application for the discharge of the accused succeeds, the accused then leads his or her evidence.[5]

If, in criminal proceedings, the accused elects to give evidence, he or she is required (except where the court on good cause shown allows otherwise) to give evidence before other defence witnesses are called. If the accused elects not to give evidence but changes his or her mind after other defence witnesses have been called, he or she will be allowed to testify, but the court may then draw such inference from the accused's conduct as may be reasonable in the circumstances.[6]

1 "Onus of adducing evidence" in Uniform Rules of Court r 39(13); "burden of proving one or more of the issues" in Magistrates Court r 28(9)(a). See also par 842 post.
2 Uniform Rules of Court r 39(5)–(14); Magistrates Court r 28(7)–(9).
3 Uniform Rules of Court r 39(12).
4 Criminal Procedure Act 51 of 1977 s 150(2). Note the accused's explanation of his or her plea by virtue of s 115 is not evidence. As to the effect of such explanation, see title CRIMINAL PROCEDURE.

5 S 151. For the order in which several accused should present their cases to the court, see *S v Ngobeni* 1981 1 SA 506 (B).
6 S 151(1)(b). The convenience of witnesses may allow a court to alter the normal sequence of evidence in terms of s 151(1)(b): *S v Nene (1)* 1979 2 SA 520 (D). See *S v Lukhandile* 1999 1 SACR 568 (C) regarding the consequences of not allowing evidence from a witness who had been sitting in court during the case.

774 Evidence to be given *viva voce*; and exceptions The general rule in both civil and criminal proceedings is that evidence is given *viva voce*[1] in open court[2] by sworn witnesses.[3]

The *viva voce* rule does not necessarily mean that the witness should speak. What is required is that the witness should appear in person and communicate with the court. The rule is satisfied if a person who is unable to speak communicates by sign language through an interpreter or writes down his or her answers, which are then read out. In terms of the Criminal Procedure Act,[4] the expression *viva voce* will, in the case of a witness under the age of 18 years, be deemed to include demonstrations, gestures or any other form of non-verbal expression.[5] A witness is not allowed to prepare his or her evidence in written form and to read it out in court[6] or to hand in the writing as a transcript of his or her evidence. This latter rule is, however, subject to an exception in favour of expert medical witnesses: they are allowed to hand in a written report provided that they confirm it in the witness box.[7]

Affidavits Because *viva voce* evidence is time-consuming, there is a tendency to increase the areas where written evidence in the form of an affidavit is permitted to replace oral evidence. An affidavit is a written statement sworn to or confirmed before a commissioner of oaths.[8] It is mainly used in legal proceedings for non-contentious or formal evidence, or where the issues are such that the demeanour of a witness or his or her replies in cross-examination are not considered essential.

The Criminal Procedure Act contains a number of provisions permitting evidence to be given on affidavit, the affidavit supplying *prima facie* proof of the matter in question. These provisions deal with: testimony abouts acts, transactions or occurrences stated not to have taken place in any particular department or sub-department of the state or of a provincial administration or in any court of law or any bank;[9] information or documents stated not to have been furnished to an officer in the service of the state or a provincial administration;[10] the registration or recording of any matter, fact or transaction under any law;[11] also facts established by any examination or process requiring skill: (i) in biology, chemistry, physics, astronomy, geography or geology; (ii) in mathematics, applied mathematics or mathematical statistics or in the analysis of statistics; (iii) in computer science or in any discipline of engineering; (iv) in anatomy or in human behavioural sciences; (v) in biochemisty, in metallurgy, in microscopy, in any branch of pathology or toxicology; or (vi) in ballistics, in the identification of fingerprints or palm-prints or in the examination of disputed documents;[12] (with the proviso that if such affidavit or certificate contains an opinion, this affidavit or certificate will be *prima facie* proof of that opinion if: (i) the expertise of the declarant; and (ii) the grounds on which the opinion is based, can be determined from the affidavit or certificate);[13] the mass or value of precious stones or precious metal;[14] the finding of or action taken in connection with fingerprints or palmprints;[15] the physical condition or identity of any deceased person or dead body;[16] the receipt, custody, packing, marking, delivery or dispatch of any fingerprint, palmprint, article of clothing, specimen, tissue "or any object of whatever nature";[17] the details of any consignment of goods delivered to the railways administration for conveyance to a specified consignee;[18] compliance with the conditions and requirements prescribed for certain measuring instruments (compliance being required before any reading of such instrument may be accepted as proof in criminal proceedings);[19] and the sealing of and endorsement on a syringe intended for the drawing of blood or receptacle intended for the storing of blood.[20]

None of these provisions has a counterpart in civil proceedings, save only that relating to testimony about facts established by an examination or process requiring skill in bacteriology, biology, chemistry, physics, astronomy, anatomy or pathology. Such testimony may be given in affidavit form by certain designated categories of deponents – and the court may, upon application, order the deponent to give oral evidence or to reply to written interrogatories.[21]

The Electronic Communications and Transactions Act[22] provides a new solution for the admissibility of "data messages",[23] and does away with many of the traditional documentary requirements which were designed around "hard copy" and which made electronic evidence inadmissible.

Affidavit evidence is used considerably more often in civil procedure than in criminal procedure, particularly in application proceedings. The court has the power in such proceedings to order evidence to be given *viva voce* (which power it may exercise where there is a genuine dispute of fact that cannot be resolved without hearing witnesses). Although proceedings initiated by way of summons usually require *viva voce* evidence, summary judgment and provisional sentence proceedings are determined by affidavit; and the court has a general discretion to permit affidavit evidence *in lieu* of oral evidence in illiquid summons proceedings (usually exercised where the evidence is of a formal nature or where it would be extremely difficult or expensive for the witness to attend court).[24]

Commissions A commission may be issued in criminal proceedings where it appears to the court that the examination of a witness is necessary in the interests of justice and that attendance of the witness cannot be obtained without undue delay, expense or inconvenience, or that the witness is resident outside the Republic and his or her attendance cannot be obtained.[25] A magistrate (or, if the witness is outside the Republic, any competent person) is appointed to administer the oath or affirmation and to record the evidence, which is subscribed by the witness and the commissioner and then returned to the court which issued the commission. Any party to proceedings in which a commission is issued is entitled to transmit interrrogatories in writing or to examine the witness in person or through a representative. Whenever criminal proceedings are pending before any court and it appears to the court on application made before it that the examination of any witness who is resident in the Republic is necessary in the interests of justice and that the attandance of such witness cannot be obtained without undue delay, expense or inconvenience, the court may dispense with such attendance and issue a commission to any magistrate. The magistrate to whom the commission is issued, must proceed to the place where the witness is or must summon the witness before him or her, and take down the evidence in the prescribed manner. The witness must give his or her evidence upon oath or by affirmation, and such evidence must be recorded and read over to the witness, and if he or she adheres thereto, be subscribed by him or her and the magistrate. Any party to the proceedings in which a commission is issued in terms of these provisions, may:

(a)   transmit interrogatories in writing which the court issuing the commission may think relevant to the issue, and the magistrate to whom the commission is issued, must examine the witness upon such interrogatories; or

(b)   appear before such magistrate, either by a legal representative or in the case of an accused who is not in custody or in the case of a private prosecutor, in person, and examine the witness. Section 173 of the Criminal Procedure Act provides that the magistrate must return the evidence in question to the court which issued the commission, and such evidence must be open to the inspection of the parties to the proceedings and must, in so far as it is admissible as evidence in such proceedings, form part of the record of such court.

Provision has also been made in the Criminal Procedure Act[26] for intermediaries. Whenever criminal proceedings are pending before any court and it appears to such court that it would expose any witness under the age of 18 years to undue mental stress or suffering if the witness testifies at such proceedings, the court may appoint a competent person as an intermediary in order to enable such witness to give his or her evidence through that intermediary. No examination, cross-examination or re-examination of any witness in respect of whom a court has appointed an intermediary, except examination by the court, must take place in any manner other than through that intermediary. The said intermediary may, unless the court directs otherwise, convey the general purport of any question to the relevant witness.

If a court appoints an intermediary under these provisions, it may direct that the relevant witness must give evidence at any place:

(a)   which is informally arranged to set that witness at ease;

(b)   which is so situated that any person whose presence may upset that witness, is outside the sight and hearing of that witness; and

(c)   which enables the court and any person whose presence is necessary to the relevant proceedings to see and hear, either directly or through the medium of any electronic or other devices, that intermediary as well as that witness during his or her testimony. The minister may by notice in the *Government Gazette* determine the persons or the category or class of persons who are competent to be appointed as intermediaries. An intermediary who is not in the full-time employment of the state will be paid such travelling and subsistence and other allowances in respect of the services rendered by him or her as the minister, with the concurrence of the Minister of Finance, may determine.[27]

Recent amendments[28] provide that no oath affirmation or admonition which has been administered through an intermediary in terms of section 165 will be invalid and no evidence which has been presented through an intermediary will be inadmissible solely on account of the fact that such intermediary was not competent to be appointed as an intermediary in terms of a regulation referred to in section 170A(4)(a), at the time when such oath, affirmation or admonition was administered or such evidence was presented. In terms of section 170A(5)(b), if in any proceedings it appears to the court that an oath, affirmation or admonition was administered or that evidence has been presented through an intermediary who was appointed in good faith but, at the time of such appointment, was not qualified to be appointed as an intermediary in terms of a regulation referred to in section 170A(4)(a), the court must make a finding as to the validity of that oath, affirmation or admonition or the admissibility of that evidence, as the case may be, with due regard to:

(i)   the reason why the intermediary concerned was not qualified to be appointed as an intermediary, and the likelihood that the reason concerned will affect the reliability of the evidence so presented adversely;

(ii) the mental stress or suffering which the witness, in respect of whom that intermediary was appointed, will be exposed to if that evidence is to be presented anew, whether by the witness in person or through another intermediary; and

(iii) the likelihood that real and substantial justice will be impaired if that evidence is admitted. Section 170A(7)(a) provides that section 170A(5) does not prevent the prosecution from presenting anew any evidence which was presented through an intermediary referred to in the subsection. Furthermore, in terms of section 170A(6)(b), the provisions of section 170A(5) will be applicable also in respect of all cases where an intermediary referred to in that subsection has been appointed, and in respect of which, at the time of the commencement of that subsection the trial court of the court considering an appeal or review, has not delivered judgment.

The power to issue a commission is sparingly exercised, and it is usually exercised only if it can be shown that the evidence will be of a formal nature.[29]

In civil proceedings the court is given a discretion to issue a commission "where it appears convenient or necessary for the purposes of justice".[30] The parties have the right to submit interrogatories or to examine the witness. If the witness cannot be compelled to attend court, for example because he or she is seriously ill,[31] is detained under legislation prohibiting his or her appearance,[32] or is outside the Republic, the court will usually issue a commission (provided the evidence is sufficiently material) since the purposes of justice are better served by having the evidence on paper than by having no evidence at all.[33] Although materiality is required (the court will not appoint a commission for unimportant evidence) it is at the same time a favourable factor if the evidence is of a formal nature.[34]

Any provincial or local division of the High Court may, on application, issue an order for the examination of a witness within its jurisdiction where his or her evidence is required for civil or criminal proceedings pending before a foreign court. Such order will not, however, be granted if the evidence is required for criminal proceedings of a political character or if the witness is an accused person. If it is required for criminal proceedings the commissioner must be a magistrate.[35]

Interrogatories Courts of provincial and local divisions as well as magistrates' courts are empowered to order that the evidence of a person who is outside the court's jurisdiction be taken by means of interrogatories. In addition to the interrogatories (specific question) the appointed commissioner may put any other question calculated to obtain full and true answers to the interrogatories. The evidence so obtained is then certified as correct and returned to the court that issued the order.[36]

Preserving testimony Any person who will, upon the happening of a future event, become entitled to any interest in any asset the right or claim to which cannot be brought to trial by him or her before the happening of such event, may apply to the High Court for an order allowing evidence which could be material in establishing the right or claim to be taken on commission. Such evidence would then be admissible in future proceedings; but if the person who gave the evidence is then available the person presiding at such proceedings may refuse to accept the preserved testimony.[37]

Evidence in former proceedings Under the common law, testimony given by a witness in civil or criminal proceedings is admissible in subsequent proceedings between the same parties or their privies if the same issues are involved,[38] if there has been a full opportunitiy to cross-examine the witness and if the witness is incapable of being called.[39] Former testimony can also be admitted by consent in subsequent civil proceedings.[40] In addition, such testimony could be admissible under the provisions of part VI of the Civil Proceedings Evidence Act,[41] which is now applicable to both civil and criminal proceedings.[42]

There are various provisions in the Criminal Procedure Act[43] that govern the position when proceedings instituted before one court are continued before another. The normal rule is that the record of the former proceedings becomes incorporated into the record of the subsequent proceedings.[44] However, it is expressly stipulated that where an accused is arraigned for trial after a preparatory examination, the evidence will not form part of the record unless the accused pleads guilty at the trial or the parties agree to its admission.[45] On the other hand, it is further stipulated that such evidence *shall* be admissible at the trial if it is proved that the witness is dead, is incapable of giving evidence, is too ill to attend the trial or is kept away from the trial by the means and contrivance of the accused, and the accused or, as the case may be, the state, had a full opportunity to cross-examine the witness;[46] and that such evidence *may* be admissible if the witness cannot, after a diligent search, be found or cannot be compelled to attend the trial, and the accused or, as the case may be, the state, had a full opportunity to cross-examine the witness.[47]

A further provision stipulates that the evidence of a witness given at a former trial (as opposed to a preparatory examination) may be admitted in evidence at any later trial of the same person upon the same charge if the conditions set out above are satisfied.[48]

Finally, any evidence given at a meeting of the creditiors of an insolvent estate is admissible in any proceedings subsequently instituted against the person who gave the evidence.[49]

Any incriminating answer or information directly obtained, or incriminating evidence directly derived from, an interrogation with regard to an insolvent company will not be admissible as evidence in criminal proceedings in a court of law against the person concerned or the body corporate of which he or she is or was an officer, except in criminal proceedings where the person concerned is charged with an offence relating to:

(a) the administering or taking of an oath or the administering or making of an affirmation;

(b) the giving of false evidence;

(c) the making of a false statement; or

(d) a failure to answer lawful questions fully or satisfactorily.[50]

Criminal proceedings: proof of written statements by consent In criminal proceedings a written statement by any person other than the accused is admissible *in lieu* of oral evidence, provided that certain qualifications are met.[51] The statement must purport to be signed by the declarant, who must also declare that it is true to the best of his or her knowledge and belief and that he or she made the statement knowing that, if it were tendered in evidence, he or she would be liable to prosecution if he or she wilfully stated in it anything which he or she knew to be false or anything which he or she did not believe to be true.[52] If it then contains any statement which, if sworn, would amount to perjury, the declarant is deemed to have committed perjury and subject to the penalties prescribed for the crime of perjury.[53]

1 Criminal Procedure Act 51 of 1977 s 161. The requirement of *viva voce* evidence appeared in the Magistrates' Courts Act 32 of 1944 s 5(4), but this subsection was repealed by the Lower Courts Amendment Act 91 of 1977 s 1(b). So far as civil proceedings in general are concerned, the requirement stems from the Civil Proceedings Evidence Act 25 of 1965 s 42.

2 Criminal Procedure Act 51 of 1977 s 152; Magistrates' Courts Act 32 of 1944 s 5.

3 Instead of taking the prescribed oath, a witness can make an affirmation; and if he or she is unable to understand the nature of the oath or affirmation, he or she can be admonished to speak the truth: Criminal Procedure Act 51 of 1977 ss 162–164; Civil Proceedings Evidence Act 25 of 1965

ss 39–41. The testimony of a witness not properly placed under oath, affirmation or admonition to speak the truth in terms of the Criminal Procedure Act 51 of 1977 s 162 read with ss 163–164, lacks the status of evidence and cannot support a conviction in a criminal trial: *Henderson v S* [1997] 1 All SA 594 (C). See also *S v Malinga* 2002 1 SACR 615 (N).

4   51 of 1977.

5   *R v R* 1953 4 SA 364 (N).

6   *R v Elijah* 1963 3 SA 86 (SR) 89F.

7   This is treated as a procedural concession to a medical witness who refreshes his or her memory from a report made at the time of the medical examination: it goes no further. See *R v Birch-Monchrieff* 1960 4 SA 425 (T) 427; *S v Joubert* 1971 3 SA 924 (E); par 797 post.

8   The Justices of the Peace and Commissioners of Oaths Act 16 of 1963 governs the appointment and powers of justices of the peace and provides that the penalty for a false statement will be the same as that for perjury. Cf also *Dawood v Mahomed* 1979 2 SA 361 (D); *Enslin v Slabbert, Verster & Malherbe (Noord-Oos Kaap) (Edms) Bpk* 1979 2 SA 983 (O); *Lohrman v Vaal Ontwikkelingsmpy (Edms) Bpk* 1979 3 SA 391 (T).

9   Criminal Procedure Act 51 of 1977 s 212(1).

10 S 212(2). For the meaning of "prima facie evidence" in s 212(2) see *S v Veldhuizen* 1982 3 SA 413 (A).

11 S 212(3).

12 S 212(4). In any case in which skill is required in chemistry, anatomy or pathology, a certificate may be issued *in lieu* of an affidavit. Cf *S v Rantsane* 1979 4 SA 864 (O). See also *S v Van der Sandt* [1997] 3 All SA 139 (W); 1997 2 SACR 116 (W) for the requirements for compliance of the certificate.

13 Criminal Procedure Amendment Act 86 of 1996 s 9.

14 Criminal Procedure Act 51 of 1977 s 212(5).

15 S 212(6).

16 S 212(7).

17 S 212(8). In any case relating to an article of clothing, specimen or tissue, a certificate may be issued *in lieu* of an affidavit. The affidavit must comply strictly with the requirements in s 212(8): *S v Van der Westhuizen* 1989 1 SA 468 (T). It is not necessary for the certificate to allege custody and delivery of the sample where solely the receipt thereof was relevant to the issue before the court: *S v Abel* 1990 2 SACR 367 (C). See

also *S v Jantjies* 1990 2 SACR 660 (C).

18 S 212(9).

19 S 212(10).

20 S 212(11).

21 Civil Proceedings Evidence Act 25 of 1965 s 22.

22 25 of 2002.

23 S 1 defines a "data message" as "data generated, sent, received or stored by electronic means and includes – (a) voice, where voice is used in an automated transaction; and (b) a stored record."

24 Ss 13–19. See also Zeffertt *Evidence* 699–702; title INFORMATION TECHNOLOGY.

25 Criminal Procedure Act 51 of 1977 ss 171–173. For the application of s 171, see *S v Mzinyathi* 1982 4 SA 118 (T). The Republic has acceded to the convention on the taking of evidence abroad on civil or commercial matters, concluded at the Hague, 18 March 1970; GN R1271 of 3 October 1997. In *S v Lofty-Eaton* 1997 1 SACR 115 (NmH) it was held that the terms "any court" in the Criminal Procedure Act 51 of 1977 s 171, includes a court in Namibia before and after independence. See also *S v Basson* [2000] 3 All SA 393 (T); 2000 4 SA 479 (T); 2000 2 SACR 188 (T). For facts to be taken into account in terms of the International Cooperation in Criminal Matters Act 75 of 1996, see *S v Basson* supra.

26 1 of 1977 s 170A.

27 S 170A(4).

28 S 170A(5)–(7).

29 For the considerations influencing the grant or refusal of a commission, see *S v ffrench-Beytagh (2)* 1971 4 SA 426 (T); *S v Hassim* 1972 2 SA 448 (N); *S v Nyamayevu* 1978 2 SA 684 (R); *S v Hoare* 1982 3 SA 306 (N).

30 Unifrom Rules of Court r 38(3). See also Magistrates Court r 53(1), which states that a commission *de bene esse* may be issued "where it may be expedient and consistent with the ends of justice". See *Fernandes v Fittinghoff & Fihrer* CC 1993 2 SA 704 (W).

31 *Lloyd v Finnemore* 1917 EDL 270; *Estate Goosen v Estate Kellerman* 1920 CPD 588; *Gray v Gray* 1923 OPD 111; *Shield Insurance Co Ltd v Deysel* 1978 2 SA 164 (SE).

32 *Nxasana v Minister of Justice* 1976 3 SA 745 (D).

33 *Grant v Grant* 1949 1 SA 22 (C). Cf *S v ffrench-Beytagh (2)* supra.

34 For the various factors influencing the court's decision, see, in addition to the above, *Robinson v Randfontein Estates Gold Mining Co Ltd* 1918 TPD 420 423; *Hespel v*

Hespel 1948 3 SA 257 (EDL); *Smitham v De Luca* 1977 2 SA 582 (W).

35 Foreign Courts Evidence Act 80 of 1962. See also Supreme Court Act 59 of 1959 s 33, which now applies only to civil proceedings, for the manner of dealing with commissions *rogatoire* and letters of request. For the applicability of rules of evidence in proceedings before a commission constituted to obtain evidence required by a foreign court, see *Cline v Magistrate, Witbank* 1985 4 SA 605 (T). For the purpose of such a letter of request, see *Saunders v Minister of Justice* 1997 3 SA 1090 (C); 1997 1 SACR 689 (C).

36 S 32; Magistrates' Courts Act 32 of 1944 s 52 (r 26).

37 Civil Proceedings Evidence Act 25 of 1965 s 23.

38 *Da Silva v Da Silva* 1946 SR 109.

39 *Lensvelt & Co Ltd v John Swift Ltd* 1920 WLD 112. See, generally, Phipson *Evidence* par 1423.

40 *Langham v Milne* 1961 1 SA 811 (N); *Rand Cold Storage & Supply Co Ltd v Alligianes* 1968 2 SA 122 (T); *Ruthenberg v Otto* 1974 2 SA 268 (C). In the latter case an agreement that evidence adduced in previous criminal proceedings should be admitted as evidence in a later civil trial, subject to certain reservations, was held to be "curious" and to introduce "a procedure not to be recommended".

41 25 of 1965.

42 For a discussion of these provisions, see pars 799–803 post.

43 51 of 1977.

44 See s 116(2) (committal for sentence by regional court after trial in magistrate's court); s 121(5) (committal for sentence after plea of guilty in magistrate's court); s 122(4) (arraignment for trial after plea of not guilty in magistrate's court); s 124 (conversion of trial into preparataory examination); 140(2) (arraignment for sentence after preparatory

examination). See also ss 115A 122C(3) D(3) as further examples that the record in former proceedings becomes incorporated into the record of the subsequent proceedings. The former proceedings must have been regular in order that the record of those proceedings may become part of the record of subsequent proceedings: *S v Muzikayifani* 1979 2 SA 516 (D).

45 Criminal Procedure Act s 141(3).

46 S 214(a). See *R v Goliath* 1946 EDL 310; *R v Matyeni* 1958 2 SA 573 (E). The fact that the accused "or, as the case may be, the state" must have had the opportunity to cross-examine, shows that the section is available to both the state and the accused. Previous corresponding legislation only required that the accused should have had the opportunity to cross-examine and this led to doubt whether the provision was also available to the state.

47 S 214(b). See *R v Andrews* 1920 AD 290 293; *R v Stoltz* 1925 WLD 38; *R v Malan* 1948 2 SA 327 (T); *R v Stoffels* 1948 2 SA 809 (C); *R v Cele* 1960 1 SA 292 (C); *R v Dladla (1)* 1961 3 SA 919 (D); *S v Ngubane* 1961 4 SA 377 (N); *S v Sexwale (2)* 1978 3 SA 788 (T).

48 S 215; *S v Johannes* 1984 3 SA 274 (SWA).

49 Insolvency Act 24 of 1936 s 65(5). See *R v Jaspan* 1940 AD 9; *R v Segal* 1949 3 SA 67 (C); *S v Isaacs* 1968 2 SA 187 (D).

50 Companies Act 61 of 1973 s 415(5); *Fisheries Development Corporation of SA Ltd v Jorgensen, Fisheries Development Corporation of SA Ltd v AWJ Investments (Pty) Ltd* 1980 4 SA 156 (W).

51 Criminal Procedure Act 51 of 1977 s 213(1). An affidavit by a state witness tendered in terms of s 213 is inadmissible if the witness is called to give *viva voce* evidence: *S v Serapelo* 1979 4 SA 567 (B).

52 Criminal Procedure Act 51 of 1977 s 213(2).

53 S 213(6).

775 Evidence in chief A witness is first examined by the party calling him or her or by such party's legal representative. At this stage leading questions, namely questions which suggest the answer, may not as a rule be put to the witness. Such questions may, however, be put with reference to introductory or undisputed matters.

The examiner is not permittted to impeach the credibility of his or her own witness. The examiner may, therefore, not cross-examine the witness nor put questions (nor subsequently adduce evidence) to prove his or her bias, mendacity or weak character.[1] On the other hand there is nothing to prevent the examiner from subsequently calling other persons to contradict what his or her own witness said,[2] and the examiner may also prove an inconsistent statement previously made by the witness.[3]

It is only when a witness has been expressly declared by the court to be hostile to the party calling him or her that the latter may cross-examine that witness.[4]

1 Zeffertt *Evidence* 749–750; Schmidt *Bewysreg* 296.
2 *Moothoosamy v Murugan* 1919 NPD 402 404; *S v Maduna* 1978 1 SA 143 (D).
3 Civil Proceedings Evidence Act 25 of 1965 s 7; Criminal Procedure Act 51 of 1977 s 190(2). See *S v Muhlaba* 1973 3 SA 141 (R); *S v Dolo* 1975 1 SA 641 (Tk) 643. The

practical effect of the proof of such previous contradictory statements is almost invariably that the witness is discredited and his or her evidence is disregarded: *R v Nyede* 1951 3 SA 151 (T); *R v Loofer* 1952 3 SA 798 (C); *S v Dolo* supra 643–644; *Jabaar v SAR&H* 1982 4 SA 552 (C).
4 See par 776 post.

776 Cross-examination[1] After the examination in chief the witness is cross-examined by all the parties to the proceedings other than the party who called the witness and they have this right regardless of whether the witness's evidence in chief was favourable or adverse to their cause.[2] If the witness was called or recalled by the court, he or she can be cross-examined only by leave of the court.[3]

Every person sworn in as a witness is subject to cross-examination, including a witness who was only called to produce and identify a document[4] and a witness who, for some or other reason, was not examined in chief.[5]

It has already been seen that proof of a previous inconsistent statement made by the witness does not itself confer upon the party who called the witness the right to cross-examine him or her. Before a party can cross-examine his or her own witness, the court has to declare that the witness is hostile. In considering whether to make such a declaration the court will take into account all the facts and circumstances relative to the witness, including his or her demeanour. The fact that the witness made an inconsistent statement will, then, also be taken into account.[6]

Cross-examination differs from examination in chief in that leading questions may be put to the witness. If the witness happens to favour the cross-examiner then the answers to such questions will, however, carry little weight.[7] The questions need not bear only upon issues raised in the examination in chief. They do not necessarily have to be directly relevant to the issues, but may be relevant only to credibility.[8] They may not, however, be completely irrelevant, and the court should prevent "fishing expeditions" and aimless questioning intended only to tire, humiliate or anger the witness in the hope that he or she may make a damaging statement.[9]

The cross-examiner is not required to indicate in advance the relevance of his or her questions.[10]

Repetitive questioning is permissible, within reasonable bounds, because it is a means of testing consistency.[11] It is also permissible to put to the witness a statement that has been made or will be made by another witness;[12] or an inconsistent statement that the witness him or herself has made.[13]

Inadmissible evidence, such as an inadmissible confession,[14] hearsay evidence,[15] a document that has not been properly identified[16] or a privileged statement[17] may not be put to the witness; nor may inadmissible evidence be elicited from the witness.[18] There is no rule that a document which has not yet been proved by an accused (or a defendant) cannot not be put to a state witness (or a witness for the plaintiff) provided the document is proved in the course of the accused's (or defendant's) case.[19] Having attempted to introduce a new version of events into evidence, a litigant cannot simply revert to an older version once the new one has been rejected by the court.[20]

The court has a duty to explain the purpose and manner of cross-examination to an unrepresented accused.[21]

If a party elicits inadmissible evidence unfavourable to him or herself, or even if the party fails to object to inadmissible evidence elicited by the other party, he or she may, in civil proceedings, be held to have consented to its admission.[22] In criminal proceedings the matter is complicated by express statutory provisions protecting the accused from certain forms of damaging evidence. In general, the failure of the accused to object to inadmissible evidence does not render that evidence admissible.[23] It has been held that an accused cannot waive the statutory prohibition on hearsay evidence and on improperly obtained confessions by putting questions eliciting such evidence.[24] There are, however, certain important qualifications to this rule. If the accused inadvertently elicits an answer containing inadmissible evidence,[25] the anwer will remain on the record and the accused cannot then complain of an irregularity;[26] and there is now a statutory provision to the effect that an inadmissible confession will become admissible against the accused if he or she adduces evidence, either directly or in cross-examination, of any statement made by him or her either as part of or in connection with such confession, and the evidence is, in the opinion of the judge or presiding officer, favourable to the accused.[27]

Evidence elicited by the accused from a state witness who, in respect of that evidence, would be incompetent to testify for the state, does not thereby become admissible: the consent of the accused does not make a competent witness of a person who has been declared by statute to be incompetent.[28]

In terms of a provision of the Criminal Procedure Act[29] an accused who gives evidence may not be asked or required to answer any questions tending to show that he or she has committed or has been convicted of or has been charged with any offence other than the offence with which he or she is charged, or that he or she is of bad character.[30] There are four exceptions. Such questions may be asked, and must be answered, if the accused or his or her representative has questioned a witness or given evidence with a view to establishing his or her own good character, or the nature or conduct of the defence is such as to involve imputation of the character of the complainant or any other witness for the prosecution;[31] if the accused gives evidence against any other person charged with the same offence or an offence in respect of the same facts;[32] if the proceedings against him or her are such as are described in section 240 or 241 of the Criminal Procedure Act and the notice under those sections has been given to him or her;[33] or if the proof that the accused has committed or has been convicted of such other offence is admissible evidence to show that the accused is guilty of the offence with which he or she is charged.[34]

The failure to cross-examine a witness on any fact may have the effect that such fact cannot be contested.[35] In criminal proceedings it will usually have that effect if the prosecution fails to cross-examine; and usually not if an unrepresented accused fails to do so. The accused's case must be put to the state witnesses; a failure to do so can in an appropriate case justify an inference being drawn against the accused.[36]

---

1 See also title CRIMINAL PROCEDURE.
2 *R v Milne & Erleigh* (7) 1951 1 SA 791 (A) 818; *R v Ndawo* 1961 1 SA 16 (N) 17H; *S v Langa* 1963 4 SA 941 (N) 950–951. In civil proceedings (and possibly in criminal proceedings; see *R v Ismail* 1943 CPD 418) the court has a discretion to deviate from this rule. In *Novick v Comair Holdings Ltd* 1978 3 SA 333 (W) the court in exercising its discretion granted the right to ask leading questions only to counsel representing interests truly adverse to those of the litigants who called the witness.
3 *R v Kumalo* 1952 3 SA 223 (T).
4 *Waterhouse v Shields* 1924 CPD 155 157.
5 *R v Zawels* 1937 AD 342 349–350; *R v Ndawo* supra.
6 *R v Loofer* 1952 3 SA 798 (C) 804. *City Panel Beaters v Bhana & Sons* 1985 2 SA 155 (D); *S v Steyn* 1987 1 SA 353 (W). In *S v Dolo* 1975 1 SA 641 (Tk) 644 Munnik CJ (differing in this respect from Herbstein J in

Loofer's case) held that the mere fact of a previous inconsistent statement, if not satisfactorily explained, can be sufficient reason for declaring a witness to be hostile.

7 *R v Milne & Erleigh* (7) supra 817–818.

8 *Miller v Proos* 1935 OPD 183 188; *R v Ntshangela* 1961 4 SA 592 (A) 598G.

9 *Bagley v Cole Ltd* 1915 CPD 776; *R v Sacks* 1931 TPD 188; *S v Booi* 1964 1 SA 224 (E) 227H; *S v Cele* 1965 1 SA 82 (A) 91H; *S v Azov* 1974 1 SA 808 (T). See *Africa Solar (Pty) Ltd v Divwatt (Pty) Ltd* [2002] 3 All SA 369 (SCA); 2002 4 SA 681 (SCA); *S v Pietersen* [2002] 2 All SA 286 (C); 2002 1 SACR 330 (C).

10 *R v Amod* 1958 2 SA 658 (N) 661; *S v Cele* supra 91F; *S v Nkomo* 1975 3 SA 598 (N).

11 *R v De Bruyn* 1957 4 SA 408 (C) 412; *R v Amod* supra 661; *S v Makaula* 1961 4 SA 600 (E) 603; *S v Green* 1962 3 SA 886 (A) 888; *S v Nkomo* supra 600H; *S v Mngogula* 1979 1 SA 525 (T).

12 *Carroll v Carroll* 1947 4 SA 37 (D). See also *S v Tshabalala* 1999 1 SACR 163 (T).

13 *De Wet v President Versekeringsmpy Bpk* 1978 3 SA 495 (C) 498.

14 *R v Gibixegu* 1959 4 SA 266 (EDL); *S v Nkwanyana* 1978 3 SA 404 (N) 406.

15 *R v A* 1959 3 SA 498 (FC) 502.

16 *Howard & Decker Witkoppen Agencies & Fourways Estates (Pty) Ltd v De Sousa* 1971 3 SA 937 (T) 940.

17 *Israelsohn v Power & Ruskin* (1) 1953 2 SA 499 (W). Cf *S v Van Vreden* 1969 2 SA 524 (N); *Mlamla v Marine & Trade Insurance Co* 1978 1 SA 401 (E); *S v Mbata* 1977 1 SA 379 (O).

18 *R v Van Tonder* 1929 TPD 365 368 (inadmissible opinion).

19 *Van Tonder v Kilian* 1992 1 SA 67 (T); 1991 2 SACR 579 (T).

20 *Johnson v Road Accident Fund* [2000] 4 All SA 363 (C); 2000 1 SA 307 (C).

21 *S v Lekhetho* 2002 2 SACR 13 (O).

22 *R v Perkins* 1920 AD 307 (*obiter*); *De Klerk v*

Zagorie 1943 EDL 44.

23 *R v Chabane* 1948 1 SA 272 (O) 276; cf *R v De Meyer* 1949 3 SA 892 (O) 897.

24 *R v Perkins* supra; *R v Black* 1923 AD 388.

25 And the evidence elicited forms a natural part of the answer: *R v Bosch* 1949 1 SA 548 (A).

26 *R v Bosch* supra.

27 Criminal Procedure Act 51 of 1977 s 217(3) and see the discussion of s 217(3) in Hiemstra *Evidence* 556.

28 *S v Khanyapa* 1979 1 SA 824 (A), overruling *S v Batyi* 1964 4 SA 427 (E).

29 S 197. See also s 211, which specifically prohibits evidence and questions about previous convictions.

30 See *R v W* 1947 2 SA 708 (A) 717; *S v V* 1962 3 SA 365 (E); *S v Mokoena* 1967 1 SA 440 (A) 444–445. Cf *R v Malindi* 1963 4 SA 677 (FC) 681–682; *R v Malindi* 1966 4 SA 123 (PC).

31 S 197(a). See *R v Hendrickz* 1933 TPD 451; *Orman v R* 1941 SWA 11; *R v Klisser & Rosenberg* 1949 3 SA 807 (W) 826; *S v V* supra; *R v Heyne* (2) 1958 1 SA 612 (W).

32 S 197(b). See *R v Myataza* 1932 EDL 108; *R v Bagas* 1952 1 SA 437 (A).

33 S 197(c). The two sections are concerned with receiving stolen property knowing it to be stolen. Under s 197(c) it is possible to question the accused or to lead evidence about possession of other stolen property (s 240) or about a conviction of an offence involving fraud or dishonesty, subject to certain conditions.

34 *R v Lipschitz* 1921 AD 282; *R v Hair* 1927 AD 391; *R v Solomons* 1959 2 SA 352 (A); *S v R* 1972 4 SA 57 (NC) 62–63. See also *S v Katamba* 2000 1 SACR 162 (NmS).

35 *R v Jawke* 1957 2 SA 187 (EDL); *R v Ngema* 1960 2 SA 263 (T); *S v Becker* 1968 1 SA 18 (C) 27; *S v P* 1974 1 SA 581 (RA); *S v Gobozi* 1975 3 SA 88 (E).

36 *S v Van As* 1991 2 SACR 74 (W).

777 Re-examination Re-examination is conducted by the party who called the witness and is subject to the same rules as examination in chief. The witness may not be cross-examined (no leading questions may be put to the witness) and his or her credibility may not be impeached. The purpose is to restore perspective and perhaps credibility afer the cross-examination. New ground may not be covered without leave of the court – and if it is granted, the other party or parties will be given the opportunity to cross-examine on the fresh evidence.[1]

1 See, generally, Zeffertt *Evidence* 763–764; Schmidt *Bewysreg* 314–315; Phipson *Evidence* par 1562.

778 Examination by court Although the court can question a witness at any stage of the proceedings (and not infrequently does intervene in the course of a party's examination in order to clarify a point) any lengthy examination by the court should stand over until the parties have completed their examination.[1] The purpose of the court's examination should be to elucidate any points that may still be obscure after examination by the parties;[2] but the court should not "descend into the arena".[3] It should not cross-examine a witness.[4] It must remain impartial and this should be evident from the nature and scope to the examination.[5] The admonition that the judge or presiding officer should not enter the arena is even more important in civil proceedings than in criminal proceedings;[6] in criminal proceedings the court will, if it is necessary in order that justice be done, come to the aid of the accused who is represented by inexperienced counsel.

1 *R v H* 1962 1 SA 197 (A) 205–206.
2 *R v Kumalo* 1947 4 SA 156 (N); *R v H* supra 205.
3 *R v Roopsingh* 1956 4 SA 509 (A); *S v Watson* 1977 3 SA 1110 (E).
4 *R v Ngcobo* 1925 AD 561 564; *R v Laubscher* 1926 AD 276 281; *R v Solomons* 1959 2 SA 352 (A) 363; *R v Baartman* 1960 3 SA 535

(A) 541.
5 *S v Wood* 1964 3 SA 103 (O); *Greenfield Manufacturers (Temba) (Pty) Ltd v Royton Electrical Engineering (Pty) Ltd* 1976 2 SA 565 (A); *S v Rousseau* 1979 3 SA 895 (T).
6 *Hamman v Moolman* 1968 4 SA 340 (A) 344G.

779 Refreshing memory A witnes is allowed to refresh his or her memory from a document made at a time when his or her recollection of the events recorded was still clear.[1] It is not essential that the witness should have made the document. It is sufficient if some other person recorded the events on the witness's instructions or if the witness read the document at a time when his or her memory was fresh and the contents coincided with his or her own recollection.[2] The witness is permitted to refer to the document in the witness box. The witness can be cross-examined on the document, which may be inspected by the cross-examiner and the court.[3] Any privilege which the witness may claim for the document is forfeited when he or she makes use of it.[4] The document does not, normally, become evidence in the case and cannot serve to corroborate the witness;[5] but in certain circumstances the document may be handed in by the witness as a convenient version of his or her oral evidence.[6]

1 *R v Isaacs* 1916 TPD 390; *R v Ndhlovu* 1950 4 SA 574 (N) 577.
2 *Rex v Varachia* 1947 4 SA 266 (T) 270; *R v O'Linn* 1960 1 SA 545 (N); *R v Mawena* 1961 3 SA 362 (SR) 366–367; *S v Van Tonder* 1971 1 SA 310 (T); *S v Smuts* 1972 4 SA 358 (T).
3 *R v Grieve* 1947 2 SA 264 (T); *S v Bergh* 1976 4 SA 857 (A) 864. Only the relevant part of the document becomes material for cross-examination: *Michael v Additional Magistrate of Johannesburg & Attorney-General* 1926 TPD 331; *R v Scoble* 1958 3 SA 667 (N) 669.
4 *Macduff & Co (In Liquidation) v Johannesburg*

Consolidated Investment Co Ltd 1923 TPD 318. Cf *Ex parte Minister van Justisie: In re S v Wagner* 1965 4 SA 507 (A) 513–514.
5 *S v Bergh* supra. In certain circumstances it could become evidence under ss 33–38 of the Civil Proceedings Evidence Act 25 of 1965 or s 222 of the Criminal Procedure Act 51 of 1977. See par 787 et seq post.
6 *Rex v Theunissen* 1948 4 SA 43 (C); *R v Mbongwe* 1954 3 SA 1016 (T); *R v Kannemeyer* 1958 3 SA 56 (C); *R v Birch-Monchrieff* 1960 4 SA 425 (T); *S v Ngwenya* 1966 1 SA 668 (N). Cf *S v Heller (1)* 1964 1 SA 520 (W).

780 Impeaching the credit of an opponent's witness Because cross-examination may range wider than evidence in chief, covering also factual issues which are relevant only to the credibility of the particular witness, difficulties arise when a party wishes to call evidence intended to show that a witness was untruthful or mistaken in replying to questions put by the cross-examiner. The general rule is that a witness may always be contradicted by other evidence if such evidence is relevant to one of the issues before the court, but that the witness may not be contradicted by other evidence on a purely collateral matter. Thus, if the sole purpose of the other evidence is to show that a witness lied (and it is not otherwise relevant), such evidence will be disallowed.[1]

1 *S v Sinkankanka* 1963 2 SA 531 (A); *S v ffrench-Beytagh* (*3*) 1971 4 SA 571 (T); *S v Cooper* 1976 1 SA 932 (T); *S v Maduna* 1978 1 SA 143 (D). See also title CRIMINAL PROCEDURE; par 776 ante.

REAL EVIDENCE

781 Nature of real evidence Real evidence is presented when a material object is produced for inspection by the court. The term is usually applied to exhibits such as clothing, a knife or a fingerprint, but it has also been extended to cover a document presented as a chattel (as opposed to a statement) or a person in so far as his or her appearance or demeanour is to be observed.

782 Presentation of real evidence Real evidence, in its normal sense of an object or chattel, is adduced through a witness who can identify the object.[1] The witness may be required to give opinion evidence about the object to establish its relevance.[2] There are, however, other ways of presenting real evidence. A person may be viewed by the court to establish, for instance, the person's race or age, without calling him or her or another person as a witness.[3] The court may also adjourn to the scene of an event for an inspection *in loco* – in which case the scene viewed by the court becomes real evidence.[4]

1 The object is inventoried and labelled or otherwise marked: Criminal Procedure Act 51 of 1977 s 136. See also *Miya v R* 1941 NPD 36; *Arthur v Bezuidenhout & Mieny* 1962 2 SA 566 (A) 571. In terms of s 232 of the Act the court may permit a party to criminal proceedings to produce a photograph of any article other than a document as evidence *in lieu* of such article.
2 *R v Vilbro* 1957 3 SA 223 (A) 228; *Arthur v Bezuidenhout & Mieny* supra.
3 See par 786 post.
4 See par 785 post. See also *S v Dippenaar* 1990 1 SACR 208 (T).

783 Finger, palm and footprints Prints are used to connect the accused with the crime. The court is informed that the accused's prints were taken[1] and that they are identical with those found at the scene of the crime or found on some object with which the case is concerned.[2] The comparison of finger-prints and palmprints should be made by an expert, who may give his or her evidence either *viva voce* or by affidavit.[3] If the court is satisfied that the witness or deponenet is indeed an expert and that he or she may be relied upon, it must accept his or her opinion.[4] Footprints, on the other hand, do not require analysis and explanation by an expert, and the court is not bound by the witness's opinion.[5]

Evidence of a fingerprint expert that the accused's fingerprints which the expert him or herself had taken on the morning of the trial and identified in relation to a set of fingerprints bearing the accused's name (which the expert had previously received), is admissible and it has to be accepted *prima facie* that the expert had done all that was necessary.[6] The state does not discharge its onus of proving identity beyond a reasonable doubt, if the photocopies of the SAP 76 form are of such poor quality that the court cannot assess the expert's evidence.[7]

1 The prints of the accused can be taken with his or her co-operation or, if the accused refuses to co-operate, under the provisions of s 37 of the Criminal Procedure Act 51 of 1977. The taking of fingerprints in terms of the s 37(1) does not constitute evidence given by the accused and consequently does not violate the rights contained in s 35 of the Constitution of the Republic of SA 108 of 1996 (previously s 25(2)(c) or s 25(3)(d) of the Constitution of the Republic of SA 200 of 1993): see *S v Maphumulo* 1996 2 BCLR 167 (N); 1996 2 SACR 84 (N). For considerations applicable to DNA-evidence, see Kirby and Downing (1999) 20 *Obiter* 307. See also Meintjes-van der Walt (2001) 14 *SACJ* 378.

2 In *R v Smit* 1952 3 SA 447 (A) it was held that it was not a requisite for the admissibility of fingerprint evidence that the object on which the print was found (a bottle) or the impression (or a photograph thereof) must be presented in evidence. In *Levack v Regional Magistrate, Wynberg* [1999] 3 All SA 374 (C); 1999 4 SA 747 (C); 1999 2 SACR 151 (C) the court held that a voice sample does amount to a "mark, characteristic or distinguishing feature" as in s 37(1)(c).

3 S 212(4). See also s 212(6) (8). For the necessity of placing comparative fingerprints before the court, see *S v Segai* 1981 4 SA 906 (O); for the placing of comparative charts before the court, see *S v Van Wyk* 1982 2 SA 148 (NC); *S v Phetshwa* 1982 3 SA 404 (E); *S v Gumede* 1982 4 SA 561 (T).

4 *R v Nksatlala* 1960 3 SA 543 (A); *S v Nala* 1965 4 SA 360 (A); *S v Malindi* 1983 4 SA 99 (T); *S v Khanyile* 1984 3 SA 756 (N).

5 *R v Makeip* 1948 1 SA 947 (A); *R v Debati* 1951 1 SA 421 (T); *S v Mkhabela* 1984 1 SA 556 (A).

6 *S v Nyathe* 1988 2 SA 211 (O).

7 *S v Miya* 1996 1 SACR 449 (N).

784 Handwriting Comparison of a disputed writing with any writing proved to be genuine may be made by a witness, and such writings and the evidence of any witness with respect thereto may be submitted as proof of genuineness or otherwise of the writing in dispute.[1] The writing so submitted for comparison is real evidence. Although a handwriting expert will usually be called upon to give evidence, a layman or the court itself can compare the writing; and the court is not bound by an expert's opinion.[2]

1 Criminal Procedure Act 51 of 1977 s 228; Civil Proceedings Evidence Act 25 of 1965 s 4. The writing is "proved to be genuine" if it is proved to be that of the person alleged to have written it: *S v Smith* 1978 3 SA 749 (A) 755–756. See *S v Duna* 1984 2 SA 591 (Ck) where it was held that, on a proper interpretation of ss 217 and 218, it is permissible for the state to have recourse to a handwritten statement constituting an inadmissible confession for the purpose of extracting words therefrom for analysis by a handwriting expert.

2 *Annama v Chetty* 1946 AD 142; *R v Fourie* 1947 2 SA 972 (EDL); *R v Smit* 1952 3 SA 447 (A).

785 Inspection *in loco* In both civil and criminal proceedings the court, whether it is an inferior or superior court, a court of first instance or a court of appeal, may, if it deems it necessary or expedient, adjourn to a place other than the place where the court is sitting in order to inspect an object that cannot conveniently be brought to court, or to view the *locus in quo*.[1] The decision to hold an inspection lies within the discretion of the court; a court of appeal will be most reluctant to hold that such decision was wrongly taken.[2]

It is preferable to hold the inspection in the presence of all the parties concerned. To hold it in the presence of one of the parties but not the other would constitute an irregularity;[3] but the court may, it seems, hold it in the absence of both parties.[4]

Though witnesses may attend the inspection and make statements, pointing out objects for example, whatever a witness has to say only becomes evidence if it is confirmed during examination under oath.[5] The court must place its observations on record and give the parties an opportunity of agreeing with them or challenging them and, if they wish, of leading evidence to correct them.[6]

1   Criminal Procedure Act 51 of 1977 s 169; Magistrates Court r 30(1)(d); Uniform Rules of Court r 39(16)(d). "Inspections *in loco* have become a recognized part of our legal system both in civil and criminal cases": per Hathorn AJA in *Kruger v Ludick* 1947 3 SA 23 (A) 31.

2   *R v Roberson* 1958 1 SA 676 (A) 679; *R v Sewpaul* 1949 4 SA 978 (N).

3   *Hansen v R* 1924 NPD 318; *Norwitz v Magistrate of Fauresmith & Bane* 1928 OPD 109.

4   *R v Magadla* 1924 EDL 21; *Hansen v R* supra; *Akoon v R* 1926 NPD 306; *R v Mouton* 1934 TPD 101; *Thubela v Pretorius* 1961 4 SA 506 (T).

5   *R v Van der Merwe* 1950 4 SA 17 (O) 20.

6   *R v Trotsky* 1947 1 SA 612 (SWA) 614; *Kruger v Ludick* supra 31; *R v Du Plessis* 1950 1 SA 297 (O); *R v Barnardo* 1960 3 SA 552 (A); *S v Bera* 1965 4 SA 411 (N).

786   Appearance of a person   The appearance of a person, whether the person is a witness or not, is real evidence if it is observed and noted by the court to establish a relevant fact. This can occur where, for example, identity is in issue,[1] the nature and extent of an injury,[2] race,[3] and age.[4] The court should record its views and apprise the parties thereof.[5]

It is probably correct to say that a witness's demeanour, in so far as it reflects upon his or her credibility, also constitutes real evidence.[6]

1   In *R v Nara Sammy* 1956 4 SA 629 (T) 630 the court of appeal wished to observe the accused's appearance to compare it with the evidence of identity, but was unable to compel him to be present when his counsel objected.

2   Eg *R v M* 1959 1 SA 434 (A) 436–437; *Buys v Lennox Residential Hotel* 1978 3 SA 1037 (C) 1039B.

3   Eg *R v S* 1954 3 SA 522 (A); *R v Vilbro* 1957 3 SA 223 (A); *S v D* 1976 3 SA 675 (E) 676–678.

4   In terms of s 337 of the Criminal Procedure Act 51 of 1977 the court can estimate the age of a person in criminal proceedings if no or insufficient evidence is available at the proceedings. For the application of this section (or its predecessor), see *S v Seleke* 1976 1 SA 675 (T) 688; *S v Fredericks* 1976 4 SA 234 (C); *S v Moeketsi* 1976 4 SA 838 (O) 840; *S v Swato* 1977 3 SA 992 (O); *S v Naude* 1978 1 SA 566 (T); *S v Nyathi* 1978 2 SA 20 (B). For the determination of attainment of the age of 18 years by an accused charged with murder, see *S v Ngoma* 1984 3 SA 666 (A). With regard to polygraph evidence, see Tredoux and Pooley 2001 *ILJ* 819; Collier 2001 *DR* 24.

5   *S v D* supra 676E–H.

6   As to demeanour generally, see par 847 post.

DOCUMENTARY AND RELATED EVIDENCE

787   Proof of a document: general principles   The definition of "document" is discussed in the next paragraph, but there also seems to be some confusion concerning the concept of "documentary evidence". A common sense definition would seem to be "evidence by means of document", but this is by no means universally accepted. It is suggested that greater clarity will obtain if a few distinctions are borne in mind.

In the first place, some documents (type one) are created to express the statement of *intention* of the creator. For instance, many documents (in the form of contracts) are created to archive the consensus obtained between two parties; a will (as the name indicates) serves to archive the expression of will of the testator, and so on.[1] As opposed to this, other documents (type two) are created to express a statement of *fact*, to relate a sequence of events, and so on. If this type of document is tendered to a court simply to prove that the statement of fact has in fact been made, it is being tendered circumstantially and will not be inadmissible as constituting hearsay evidence.[2] If it is tendered in an attempt to prove that its contents are true, it is being tendered testimonially, this will constitute hearsay, and the evidence will therefore be inadmissible.[3]

The above distinction is quite likely to survive the hearsay dispensation brought into being by the Law of Evidence Amendment Act of 1988,[4] but the statutory change has caused some confusion in the world of documentary evidence. This is because of the phrase: "evidence, whether oral *or in writing*"[5] in the statutory definition contained in section 1 of the Act. De Vos and Van der Merwe[6] criticise Schmidt for confusing written and documentary hearsay and for assuming that the Act would also be applicable to "documentary evidence", which they define as "nie getuienis vervat in skrif nie, maar getuienis, meesal mondeling, wat oor die inhoud van 'n dokument handel". They contrast this with "written evidence", defining it as: "die gepaste begrip om na die mededelings vervat in 'n beëdigde verklaring te verwys."

It is submitted that most affidavits used during litigation would constitute the "type two" document described above, since they are statements of fact, tendered to prove the truth of their contents, and would obviously also be hearsay evidence. Statements of fact not tendered to prove the truth of their contents and statements of intention (the "type one" document described in the previous paragraph) still constitute documentary evidence however, although not considered to be hearsay, simply because they are not being tendered testimonially, in other words to prove the "truth" of their contents. Thus the prohibition against documentary hearsay potentially applies to all documents, but its operation has always been limited by the purpose with which the document is tendered. "Documentary evidence" simply means "evidence by means of document", which should include affidavits.[7]

Leaving aside the question of hearsay, according to *Zeffertt*,[8] all documents have to comply with three conditions before the court will accept them. These relate to the "Best Evidence" rule, the document's authenticity and whether the Stamp Duties Act of 1968[9] has been complied with. The author re-emphasises that "type two" documents additionally have to pass the hearsay test.

1 Author's own terminology. Eg, in *S v Holshausen* 1983 2 SA 699 (D) a tape recording was admitted of a statement by the accused expressing the intent to commit the crime. This was not hearsay evidence and was therefore admitted by the court.

2 Author's own terminology. Eg. In *R v Miller* 1939 AD 106; *S v Holshausen* 1984 4 SA 852 (A); *Weintraub v Oxford Brick Works (Pty) Ltd* 1948 1 SA 1090 (T); *Knouwds v Administrateur, Kaap* 1981 1 SA 544 (C); *Selero (Pty) Ltd v Chauvier* 1982 2 SA 208 (T); Schmidt *Bewysreg* 352–353; Hiemstra *Strafprosesreg* 615; Van der Merwe 1994 *Obiter* 64 65. Neither would the "type one" document be considered hearsay evidence, since no statement of fact is being made. The very idea of a will constituting hearsay evidence, proves the untenability of such an argument.

3 Unless admitted in terms of s 3 of the Law of Evidence Amendment Act 45 of 1988.

4 Hiemstra 557 and De Vos and Van der Merwe 1993 *Stell LR* 1 20. See also par 721 ante.

5 Author's emphasis.

6 1993 *Stell LR* 1 19 fn 69.

7 Judicial definitions of "document" as in *R v Daye* 1908 2 KB 333 and *Seccombe v Attorney-General* 1919 TPD 270 are wide enough to include affidavits and many of the sections of the Criminal Procedure Act 51 of 1977 which provide for the admissibility of affidavits speak of "documents" specifically – ie ss 212 and 221, to mention but two examples.

8 *Evidence* 685 et seq: "These three rules will be discussed in more detail, but it must be emphasised at the outset that they deal only with the circumstances in which the court will receive evidence to prove what a document contains. They are not concerned with whether statements of fact in a document can be used to prove that those facts are true."

9 77 of 1968.

788 Proof of authenticity Statutory exceptions apart,[1] the usual method of proving a document which has not been discovered or admitted by the opponent is through a witness who can testify to its authenticity.[2] A document is authentic if it is what it is alleged to be by the party tendering it. Proof of authenticity is usually supplied by the author, executor or signatory of the document;[3] by a person who witnessed the making or signing of the document;[4] or by a person who can identify the handwriting or signature of the author.[5] In certain circumstances it will be sufficient to call a person who found the document in the opponent's possession or custody.[6]

"Ancient" documents (which are more than 20 years old) do not require proof of authenticity if they are produced from proper custody.[7]

Although foreign documents may be proved to be authentic in the ordinary way, they may be admitted upon mere production if authenticated abroad in accordance with certain rules of the High Court.[8]

A document that has not been authenticated where authentication is necesary, is inadmissible, and may not be used for purposes of cross-examination.[9]

1 Special statutory provisions are dealt with in par 791 post.

2 Eg *S v Mvulha* 1965 4 SA 113 (O). A document which is otherwise admissible can be used in cross-examination in spite of its authenticity being denied by the opposing party. It is only after the state or the plaintiff, as the case may be, has closed its case that the accused or the defendant has the opportunity to place his or her case before the court and tender evidence on the authenticity of documents: *S v Swanepoel* 1980 1 SA 144 (NC).

3 Eg *Policansky Bros Ltd v L & H Policansky* 1935 AD 89 90–91. See *Buyers Guide (Pty) Ltd v Dada Motors (Mafikeng) (Pty) Ltd* 1990 4 SA 55 (B).

4 In the case of wills or other testamentary writings it is necessary to call one of the attesting witnesses, unless all the witnesses are dead, incompetent to testify, outside the jurisdiction or unable to be traced. In the latter event, evidence of handwriting or of a non-attesting witness will suffice. The evidence of an attesting witness is no longer required for any other form of document: Civil Proceedings Evidence Act 25 of 1965 s 36; Criminal Procedure Act 51 of 1977 s 222.

5 Comparison of the disputed writing with writing which has been proved to be genuine is permissible only when neither the author nor a witness is available to give evidence: *Policansky Bros Ltd v L & H Policansky* supra; *CRC Engineering (Pty) Ltd v JC Dunbar & Sons (Pty) Ltd* 1977 1 SA 710 (W). As to this method of proof, see *Annama v Chetty* 1946 AD 142.

6 *R v Knight* 1934 EDL 274 285; *Howard & Decker Witkoppen Agencies & Fourways Estates (Pty) Ltd v De Sousa* 1971 3 SA 937 (T) 940F.

7 *Nolan v Povall* 1953 2 SA 202 (SR) 210; *Smith v Strydom* 1953 2 SA 799 (T) 805 read with s 5 of the Civil Proceedings Evidence Act 25 of 1965.

8 Uniform Rules of Court r 63. See also *Kaplan v Kaplan* 1936 WLD 51; *Ex parte Melcer* 1948 4 SA 395 (W); *Stift v Stift* 1952 4 SA 215 (O); *Friend v Friend* 1962 4 SA 115 (E); *Chopra v Sparks Cinemas (Pty) Ltd* 1973 2 SA 352 (D).

9 *Israelsohn v Power & Ruskin (1)* 1953 2 SA 499 (W); *Howard & Decker Witkoppen Agencies & Fourways Estates (Pty) Ltd v De Sousa* supra.

789 Stamp duty No instrument which is required to be stamped in terms of the Stamp Duties Act[1] can be produced or given in evidence or made available in any court of law unless it is duly stamped. This prohibition does not apply to criminal proceedings or to any proceedings by or on behalf of the state for the recovery of any duty on the instrument or of any penalty alleged to have been incurred under the Act in respect of such instrument.[2] The court before which an unstamped instrument is tendered may, however, admit it in evidence on condition that the instrument be stamped and any penalty that may have been incurred be paid.[3]

1 77 of 1968.

2 S 12. The exception in regard to criminal proceedings is repeated in s 251 of the Criminal Procedure Act 51 of 1977.

3 Stamp Duties Act 77 of 1978 s 12 proviso. See, in regard to the proviso, *Badat v Corondimas* 1947 2 SA 170 (D) 176; *Gleneagles Farm Dairy v Schoombee* 1947 4 SA 66 (EDL) 71; *De Meyer v Bam* 1951 4 SA 68 (N) 72; *Mullan v Vladislavich* 1961 1 SA 364 (T) 369. See also *Buyers Guide (Pty) Ltd v Dada Motors (Mafikeng) (Pty) Ltd* 1990 4 SA 55 (B).

790 Secondary evidence Secondary evidence of the contents of a document is evidence other than the original document itself.[1] The original document is primary evidence. There are no degrees of secondary evidence. Generally (there are, as will be seen, many statutory exceptions), if secondary evidence is inadmissible, then all forms of secondary evidence are inadmissible; and, conversely, if secondary evidence is admissible, then any form of secondary evidence is admissible.

The general rule is that secondary evidence is inadmissible. Thus the holder of a licence or certificate and the terms thereof can only be proved by producing the licence or certificate itself (or one of the copies specifically authorised by statute);[2] and proof of ownership in immovable property can only be proved by producing the title deeds or the register of the registrar of deeds (or an extract or affidavit authorised by statute).[3] There are many examples of the applciation of this rule.[4]

The rule applies only where the contents of the document are directly in issue: it does not apply where the contents of the document merely serve to prove some fact which is capable of proof by means other than the document itself. Thus the sale of goods in excess of a maximum price can be proved by oral evidence and without producing the relevant invoice.[5] The rule does not apply where the fact in issue is the existence of the document (as opposed to its contents) or the existence of a relationship or status derived from the document.[6]

Where the contents of the document are admitted by the opposite party it is unneccesary to produce the original. At civil proceedings the failure to object to secondary evidence is usually construed as an admission; at criminal proceedings, though an admssion can also be made by conduct, the courts will be less inclined to treat silence as an admission.[7]

Secondary evidence is admissible where the original document has been destroyed or cannot be found after proper search;[8] where it would be impossible or highly inconvenient to bring the original to court;[9] or where the original is in the possession of the opposite party[10] or a third party who refuses to produce it.[11]

There are numerous statutory exceptions to the rule prohibiting secondary evidence of a document.[12]

1 There may be more than one original. This will be the case when reproductions of a signed original are signed or initialled and are intended to serve as duplicate originals: *Forbes v Samuel* 1913 3 KB 706 722; *Lynes v International Trade Developer Inc* 1922 NPD 301; *Kiddie v Murray & Co* 1924 CPD 229; *Da Mata v Otto* 1972 3 SA 858 (A) 880 881; *Herstigte Nasionale Party van SA v Sekretaris van Binnelandse Sake & Immigrasie* 1979 4 SA 274 (T). With regard to documents which are stored on computer the electronic version will be considered the original – see par 809 post.

2 *R v Hulett* 1948 1 SA 808 (N); *R v De Meyer* 1949 3 SA 892 (O); *R v Koro* 1950 3 SA 797 (O); *R v Sonday* 1954 3 SA 641 (C); *S v Van Pittius* 1973 3 SA 814 (C).

3 *R v Nhlanhla* 1960 3 SA 568 (T); *R v Mabindla* 1960 4 SA 307 (E); *Gemeenskapsontwikkelingsraad v Williams (1)* 1977 2 SA 692 (W).

4 Eg also *R v Pelunsky* 1914 AD 360; *Ex parte Roche et uxor* 1947 3 SA 678 (D); *R v Van der Merwe* 1952 1 SA 143 (SWA); *S v Omega Bearing Works (Edms) Bpk* 1977 3 SA 978 (O); *Barclays Western Bank Ltd v Creser* 1982 2 SA 104 (T).

5 *R v Amod & Co (Pty) Ltd* 1947 3 SA 32 (A) 37. See also *Howe v Mabuya* 1961 2 SA 635 (D); *Botes v Van Deventer* 1966 3 SA 182 (A) 196H.

6 *R v Murway* 1918 NPD 29; *R v Lombard* 1957 2 SA 42 (T) 46; *Gemeenskapsontwikkelingsraad*

v Williams (1) supra 698E.

7 *R v De Meyer* supra; *R v Sonday* supra 644; *R v Nhlanhla* supra 571; *Gemeenskapsontwik-kelingsraad v Williams (1)* supra 701; *S v Omega Bearing Works (Edms) Bpk* supra 982–983; *S v Makoba* 1980 1 SA 99 (N).

8 *R v Amod & Co (Pty) Ltd* supra 40; *Ex parte Ntuli* 1970 2 SA 278 (W); *S v Tshabalala* 1980 3 SA 99 (A); *Singh v Govender Bros Construction* 1986 3 SA 613 (N).

9 Eg where the writing is inscribed on an immovable object or the document is

secured to something that cannot be transported into the court-room: *Watts & Darlow v R* 1919 NPD 108; or where it would be illegal to remove the document: *R v Zungu* 1953 4 SA 660 (N).

10 *R v Southall* 1921 TPD 403; *S v Miles* 1978 3 SA 407 (N).

11 *Boon v Vaughan & Co Ltd* 1919 TPD 77; *Standard Merchant Bank Ltd v Rowe* 1982 4 SA 671 (W).

12 Discussed in the next and subsequent paragraphs.

791 Statutory provisions Documentary evidence is extensively regulated by statute. Enactments permitting the statements of witnesses to be submitted in documentary form (usually by way of affidavit or certificate) instead of orally in the witness box, have been dealt with above.[1] The following paragraphs refer only to provisions allowing or facilitating the proof of documents as items of evidence.[2]

1 See par 787 ante.

2 Only the more significant provisions of the Civil Proceedings Evidence Act 25 of 1965 and the Criminal Procedure Act 51 of 1977 are referred to below. There are numerous and scattered other statutory regulations of

documentary evidence and these are dealt with, where appropriate, under the relevant titles. Documentary exceptions to the hearsay rule are discussed under hearsay evidence above; see pars 720 et seq ante.

792 The Documentary Evidence from Countries in Africa Act The Documentary Evidence from Countries in Africa Act[1] provides that, despite anything to the contrary in any rules of court made or in force under section 6 of the Rules Board for Courts of Law Act,[2] or any other law, but subject to the provisions of section 3, any document purporting to have been prepared, attested, certified, compiled or executed in a designated country[3] will, for the purposes of its admissibility as evidence in any civil or criminal proceedings in the Republic, be deemed to have been prepared, attested, certified, compiled or executed in the Republic.[4]

If under any law a document is admissible in evidence in civil or criminal proceedings if it has been prepared, attested, certified, compiled or executed by a particular institution or by a person holding a particular office, possessing a particular qualification, performing a particular function or engaged in a particular activity, a similar document emanating from a designated country will, for the purposes of such law and subject to the provisions of section 4, be admissible only if it appears on the face thereof to have been prepared, attested, certified, compiled or executed by an institution in the designated country in question or by a person in such country holding an office, possessing a qualification, performing a function or engaged in an activity equivalent to the corresponding institution in the Republic or to the office, qualification, function or activity of the corresponding person in the Republic, contemplated in such law.[5]

The minister may declare that a particular institution, office, qualification, function or activity in a designated country is equivalent to an institution, office, qualification, function or activity in the Republic mentioned in such notice.[6]

1 62 of 1993.

2 107 of 1985.

3 Ie a country in Africa designated by the minister in terms of the Documentary Evidence from Countries in Africa Act 62 of

1993 s 4(a): s 1.

4 S 2.

5 S 3.

6 S 4(b).

793 Proof of signature of public officer Any document purporting to bear the signature of a public officer and bearing a seal or stamp of the department, office or institution to which such officer is attached is, on its mere production, *prima facie* proof that the officer signed the document.[1]

1 Civil Proceedings Evidence Act 25 of 1965 s 6; Criminal Procedure Act 51 of 1977 s 231. See *S v Karolia* 1966 1 SA 343 (T): if there is no proper proof of the designation of the signatory in terms of these provisions the party tendering the document is not saved by the presumption of regularity – the document is inadmissible.

794 Proof of judicial proceedings Judicial proceedings may be proved by a certified copy of the original record. Proof of authenticity of the certification is not required.[1]

1 Civil proceedings: Civil Proceedings Evidence Act 25 of 1965 s 17; Supreme Court Act 59 of 1959 s 18; Magistrates Court r 61. Criminal Proceedings: Criminal Procedure Act 51 of 1977 s 235. For proof of previous conviction, see par 703 ante.

795 Public documents A distinction is drawn in common law between public and private documents. A public document is a document made by a public officer in the execution of a public duty; it is intended for public use; and the public has a right of access.[1] Such documents are admissible to prove the truth of the facts stated therein[2] and they are received in evidence upon their mere production from proper custody, without further proof of authenticity.[3]

Although various statutes deal with specific categories of documents that would be classed as public under the above definition, there are two provisions (the one relating to civil proceedings[4] and the other to criminal proceedings)[5] which provide in general terms that if a document (including a book) is of such a public nature as to be admissible in evidence upon its mere production from proper custody, any copy thereof or extract therefrom will be admissilbe if is is proved to be an examined copy or extract, or if it purports to be signed and certified as a true copy or extract by the officer to whose custody the original is entrusted.[6]

1 *Northern Mounted Rifles v O'Callaghan* 1909 TS 174 177. See also *Rex v Hoffman* 1941 OPD 65 71; *R v De Villiers* 1944 AD 493; *Hassim v Naik* 1952 3 SA 331 (A) 339; *S v Karge* 1971 3 SA 470 (T) 473; *Gemeenskapsontwikkelingsraad v Williams* (1) 1977 2 SA 692 (W) 696–697.
2 As an exception to the hearsay rule; see par 787 ante.
3 *S v Karge* supra 473G.
4 Civil Proceedings Evidence Act 25 of 1965 s 18. See *Tselentis Mining (Pty) Ltd v Mdlalose* [1997] 3 All SA 657 (N); 1998 1 BCLR 104 (N); 1998 1 SA 411 (N) for an exposition of the requirements of a photograph regarded as a public document in terms of s 18.
5 Criminal Procedure Act 51 of 1977 s 233.
6 See, in addition to the cases cited above, *S v Tsapo* 1970 2 SA 256 (T); *S v Nhlapo* 1970 2 SA 261 (T).

796 Official documents An official document is a document kept in the custody or under the control of a state official.[1] It therefore may or may not be a public document.

An original document can at civil proceedings be produced only upon the order of the head of the department in whose custody or under whose control the document is or of any officer in the service of the state authorised by such head, and at criminal proceedings only upon the order of the atttorney general. If the original is produced it is not necessary for the head of the department to appear in person: it may, at civil proceedings, be produced by any person authorised by the person ordering the production thereof and, at criminal proceedings, by any person authorised by the head of the department concerned.[2] It is, however, more usual to make use of a copy of the original or an extract therefrom. Such copy or extract is admissible *in lieu* of the original if it is certified as a true copy or extract by the head of the department concerned or by any state official authorised thereto by such head.[3]

1 Civil Proceedings Evidence Act 25 of 1965 s 19(1); Criminal Procedure Act 51 of 1977 s 234(1). See *S v Mvulha* 1965 4 SA 113 (O). In future it is likely that s 32 of the Constitution of the Republic of SA 108 of 1996, as well as the Promotion of Access to Information Act 2 of 2000, dealing with the right to information, will have an important bearing on access to public documents. See also *Tselentis Mining (Pty) Ltd v Mdlalose* [1997] 3 All SA 657 (N); 1998 1 BCLR 104 (N); 1998 1 SA 411 (N).

2 Civil Proceedings Evidence Act 25 of 1965

s 19; Criminal Procedure Act 51 of 1977 s 234(2). It would appear that some documents which are in the custody or under the control of state officials are not covered by these provisions. It could not be the intention that a police sketch and report in an accident case should be admissible without the express authorisation of a departmental head: *Cremer v Afdelingsraad, Vryburg* 1974 3 SA 252 (NC).

3 Civil Proceedings Evidence Act 25 of 1965 s 20; Criminal Procedure Act 51 of 1977 s 234(1).

797 Death of soldier: official report as evidence At any proceedings in which application is made for an order that the death of a soldier be presumed, any official report is, on its mere production by any person, admissible proof of the facts stated therein, provided such report is accompanied by an affidavit by the Chief of the National Defence Force. The affidavit must certify that the allegedly deceased person was at the time a soldier on active service; that the report was received through normal official channels and that the allegations of fact were made in the course of official duty; that the person has been posted as "missing"; and that no information is available in the records of the South African National Defence Force tending to show that the person is still alive.[1]

1 Civil Proceedings Evidence Act 25 of 1965
s 25.

798 Times of sunrise and sunset The times of sunrise and sunset on particular days at particular places in the Republic may be proved by means of tables prepared at an official observatory on mere production thereof by any party at both civil and criminal proceedings. Only tables approved from time to time in the *Government Gazette* by the Minister of Justice qualify under this provision.[1]

1 Civil Proceedings Evidence Act 25 of 1965
s 26; Criminal Procedure Act 51 of 1977
s 229.

799 Entries in bankers' books At criminal proceedings the entries in the accounting records (including any ledger, day-book or cash-book) of a bank[1] are *prima facie* proof of their contents upon the mere production of an affidavit in which it is stated that the deponent is in the service of the bank in question; that the accounting records are or have been the ordinary accounting records of the bank; that the documents or entries have been made in the usual and ordinary course of business; and that the accounting records are in the custody or under the control of the bank.[2] The entries in the accounting records of a bank, and any document which is in the possession of the bank and which refers to the said entries or to any business transaction of the bank, will, upon the mere production at criminal proceedings of an affidavit made by a person in the service of the bank and complying with certain conditions, be *prima facie* proof at such proceedings of the matters, transactions and accounts recorded in such accounting records or document.[3] In the light of the lack of constitutionality of section 217(1)(b)(ii) of the Criminal Procedure Act, there might be some doubt as to the constitutionality of the above provision. The decision which dealt with section 217, *S v Zuma*,[4] made it clear, however, that "a less Draconian presumption might pass muster". *In lieu* of the original accounting records, a copy of a document or entry may be proved upon the mere production of an affidavit in which it is stated that the deponent is in the service of the bank, that he or she has examined the document or entry and the accounting record in question and that a copy of the document or entry set out in the affidavit or in an annexure thereto is a correct copy thereof.[5] No bank can be compelled to produce its accounting records except by order of the court concerned.[6]

Any party against whom evidence is adduced in terms of the above provisions, or against whom it is intended to adduce such evidence, may, upon the order of the court before which the proceedings are pending, inspect the original of the entry in question and any account book in which such entry appears or of which such entry forms part, and may make copies thereof. The proceedings will be adjourned for the purpose of such inspection or the making of such copies upon the application of the party concerned.[7] The Criminal Procedure Act[8] has been inserted to provide that the term "document" will include a recording or transcribed computer printout produced by any mechanical or electronic device and any device by means of which information is recorded or stored.[9] There is a similar provision for the admission as *prima facie* evidence at civil proceedings of the entries in bankers' books,[10] as well as for the admission of examined copies *in lieu* of the original entries.[11] The party proposing to adduce the evidence has to give the other party at least ten days' notice in writing (or such other notice as may be ordered by the person presiding at the proceedings) of his or her intention to do so;[12] and the party receiving the notice may apply for an order permitting him or her to inspect the books and to make copies.[13]

The above provisions do not apply to any civil proceedings to which any bank whose books are required to be produced in evidence is a party.[14]

1 Criminal Procedure Act 51 of 1977 s 1(1). A "bank" means a bank as defined in the Banks Act 94 of 1990 s 1 and includes the Land and Agricultural Bank of SA referred to in s 3 of the Land Bank Act 13 of 1944, and a building society as defined in the Mutual Banks Act 124 of 1993 s 1. The Land Bank Act 13 of 1944 has been repealed and replaced: Land and Agricultural Development Bank Act 15 of 2002 s 53.
2 Criminal Procedure Act 51 of 1977 s 236(1).
3 S 236(2).
4 1995 4 BCLR 401 (CC); 1995 2 SA 642 (CC); 1995 1 SACR 568 (CC) 708G.
5 S 236(2).
6 S 236(4).
7 S 236(3). The provisions of s 236 have to be strictly complied with and a failure to object

to non-compliance will not be taken as consent thereto: *R v Pieterse* 1950 4 SA 21 (O); *Grubb v Mouton* 1958 1 SA 463 (T); *R v Bhoola* 1960 4 SA 895 (T); *S v Smit* 1966 1 SA 638 (O) – refering to s 265(1) of the previous Criminal Procedure Act 56 of 1955, which required ten days' notice to be given; General Law Third Amendment Act 129 of 1993 s 45.
8 51 of 1977.
9 See s 1 for definition of "document"; and see s 221.
10 Civil Proceedings Evidence Act 25 of 1965 s 28.
11 S 29.
12 S 30(1).
13 S 30(2).
14 S 32.

800 Documentary evidence under part VI of the Civil Proceedings Evidence Act The main purpose of the various sections incorporated under part VI of the Civil Proceedings Evidence Act,[1] and subsequently made applicable to criminal proceedings as well as civil proceedings,[2] is to render admissible documentary evidence that would otherwise be inadmissible by virtue of the hearsay rule. Apart from the hearsay aspect, which is dealt with elsewhere,[3] it should be noted that proof of authenticity is secured by the provision that a statement in a document must not for the purposes of the operative section be deemed to have been made by a person unless the document or the material part thereof was written, made or produced by the person or otherwise recognised by him or her in writing as one for accuracy of which he or she is responsible;[4] and that the court is empowered to admit a copy of the original document or of the material part thereof proved to be a true copy if it is satisfied that undue delay or expense would otherwise be caused.[5]

1 25 of 1965 ss 33–38.
2 By s 222 of the Criminal Procedure Act 51 of 1977.
3 See pars 721 et seq ante.
4 Civil Proceedings Evidence Act 25 of 1965 s 34(4). A thumbprint is a signature for the purposes of this subsection: *Putter v Provincial Insurance Co Ltd* 1963 3 SA 145 (W).

5 S 34(2)(b); see *Rawoot v Marine & Trade Insurance Co Ltd* 1980 1 SA 260 (C). A corresponding provision in an English statute has been interpreted to mean that a copy can only be admitted if the original is still in existence and not if the original has been lost or destroyed.

801 Trade or business records Statements contained in documents forming part of the trade or business records are admissible at criminal proceedings upon their mere production if the document was compiled from information supplied by persons having personal knowledge of that information and who are dead, absent, missing, incapacitated or cannot reasonably be expected to have any recollection of the matters dealt with in the information supplied.[1] This provision constitutes an exception to the hearsay rule.[2] The authenticity of the document cannot be evidenced by the document itself.[3] The original has to be produced.

This exception to the hearsay rule has been offered as a solution with regard to the admissibility of computer data in court as part of the new legislation to cope with the products of modern technology.[4]

1 Criminal Procedure Act 51 of 1977 s 221.
2 See par 723 ante, which deals with the section in greater detail.
3 S 221(2).

4 See the Electronic Communications and Transcations Act 25 of 2002 s 15(4), which creates a reverse onus. See also par 809 post.

802 Presumptions relating to certain documents There are four statutory[1] presumptions arising from documents (including any book, pamphlet, letter, circular letter, list, record, placard or poster), proved[2] to have been at any time on premises occupied by any association of persons, incorporated or unicorporated, or in the possession or under the control of any office-bearer, officer or member of such association. These presumptions apply only at criminal proceedings.

All statutory presumptions in criminal cases will now have to be read subject to the remarks in *S v Zuma*.[3] If it appears on the face of the document that a person of a name corresponding to that of an accused person is a member or an office-bearer of such association, the document will, upon its mere production by the prosecution, be *prima facie* proof that the accused is a member or an office-bearer of the association, as the case may be.[4] If it appears on the face of the document that a person of a name corresponding to that of an accused person who is or was a member of the association, is the author of the document, the document will, upon its mere production by the prosecution, be *prima facie* proof that the accused is the author thereof.[5] If the document appears on the face of it to be the minutes or a copy of or an extract from the minutes of a meeting by the association or of any committee thereof, it will, upon its mere production by the prosecution, be *prima facie* proof of the holding of such meeting and of the proceedings thereat.[6] If the document on the face of it discloses any object of the association, the document will, upon its mere production by the prosecution, be *prima facie* proof that such object is an object of the association.[7]

Evidence of a standard office practice in despatching documents via Docex is admissible to prove on a balance of probabilities that a document and its attachments have been sent.[8]

1　Criminal Procedure Act 51 of 1977 s 246.

2　See *S v Naidoo* 1966 4 SA 519 (N) 522.

3　1995 4 BCLR 401 (CC); 1995 2 SA 642 (CC); 1995 1 SACR 568 (CC).

4　S 246(a). See *S v Nkosi* 1961 4 SA 320 (T) 322 for a case in which this subsection was applied. See also *S v Twala* 1979 3 SA 864 (T).

5　S 246(b). The name need not be identical, but only similar: *S v Mothopeng* 1965 4 SA 484 (T).

6　S 246(c). See *R v Segale* 1959 1 SA 589 (T) 591–592 for a case in which this and s 246(d) were applied.

7　S 246(d); *R v Segale* supra.

8　*John v The Road Accident Fund* [1999] 4 All SA 355 (T); 2000 1 SA 459 (T).

803　Presumptions relating to absence from the Republic　If it appears *ex facie* a document (including any newspaper, periodical, book, pamphlet, letter, circular letter, list, record, placard or poster) that an accused person has been outside the Republic or has made any statement outside the Republic, then the document will upon its mere production by the prosecution at criminal proceedings be *prima facie* proof of such fact, provided that the document is accompanied by a certificate purporting to have been signed by the Secretary of Foreign Affairs to the effect that he or she is satisfied that the document is of foreign origin.[1]

1　Criminal Procedure Act 51 of 1977 s 247.

APPLIANCES AND DEVICES

804　Product of appliances and devices – evidential principles　The argument has been mooted[1] that the law of evidence should no longer endeavour to force the products of modern technology into the limited categories of either real or documentary evidence. This seems to have been the case with videotapes where different provincial divisions of the Supreme Court (now called the High Court) have variously applied the rules of documentary[2] and real[3] evidence to this form of evidence. Schmidt makes the point that the present rules of discovery, reliability and authenticity have all developed around traditional paper documents, with occasional patchwork in an effort to accomodate the products of photograhy, cinematography, audio and video magnetic tapes, mechanical data recording devices and finally, the computer.

The computer has placed the law of evidence under greater strain than any of its technological predecessors since it no longer works with analogue data, but with data in a digital form, which makes it very susceptible to manipulation. The new form of data has also led to a dramatic overhaul of telecommunications,[4] broadcasting and even publishing. The law of evidence has not yet been able to deal convincingly with even relatively dated technical phenomena such as Electronic Data Interchange (EDI).[5] Thus the optical storage of documents[6] or documents obtained from worldwide networks such as the Internet[7] are likely to present a much bigger legal headache. The following chapters will endeavour to find the present legal position, but since this field changes so rapidly, will also endeavour to give some guidance with regard to likely future developments.

1 Schmidt *Bewysreg* 358.
2 *S v Ramgobin* 1986 4 SA 117 (N).
3 *S v Mpumlo* 1986 3 SA 485 (E) and *S v Baleka (1)* 1986 4 SA 192 (T).
4 See Reed 1989 *Modern Law Review* 649 650.

5 See Eiselen 1992 *THRHR* 204 et seq and Van der Merwe 1994 *Obiter* 64 et seq.
6 Van der Merwe 68.
7 These implications are searchingly explored by Katsch in *Law in a Digital World* (1995).

805 Photographs Photographs may sometimes constitute real evidence, where the physical photograph itself is the "centre of attraction", either because it contains fingerprints on its surface (the subject of the photograph being immaterial), or because it is a very rare historical photograph which is the *corpus delicti* in a theft from a museum, or because it has been adjudged to be pornographic and someone possessed it in contravention of some statutory measure.[1]

The situation is arguably[2] quite different when the photograph is simply used to represent some situation and that situation is the subject matter of the particular court case. It now serves a documentary function and both the dictionary and judicial definitions of "document" are wide enough to include a photograph.[3] The wording of rules 35(1) and 36(4) of the Uniform Rules of Court also seems to lead, by necessary implication, to the fact that a photograph may be considered to be a document.[4]

The fact that the subject of a photograph is subject to human interpretation by the photographer by making use of telephoto lenses, lighting and the like, should go to weight rather than to admissibility.[5]

1 See Schmidt *Bewysreg* 361 et seq. The difference may perhaps be explained at the hand of a case like *S v W* 1975 3 SA 841 (T), where the photographs and video were used almost as an inspection *in loco*. See, however, the implied criticism of this case in *Bewysreg* 362: "Wanneer 'n foto egter aangebied word om dit wat deur die kamera afgeneem wor te bewys kom dit nader aan 'n dokument. Die 'inhoud' van die foto, net soos die inhoud van 'n dokument is hier die probans." It must be conceded that once one steps off this vital distinction it becomes almost impossible to distinguish between a photograph as real evidence and a photograph as documentary evidence. *S v Ramgobin* 1986 4 SA 117 (N) supports *S v W* supra to the extent that "photographs and films must be identified as true representations of the objects and persons which they purport to represent, before they can be said to be real evidence". It would seem that the courts find it handy to shuttle between defining this type of evidence as real, or documentary, depending on the specific exigencies of each case. For this reason the present author supports Schmidt's new third category of *sui generis* evidence.
2 See the argument in the previous footnote.
3 *R v Daye* 1908 2 KB 333 340; *Seccombe v Attorney-General* 1919 TPD 270 277 and *Sneech v Hill Kaplan Scott & Partners* 1981 3 SA 332 (A) 338.
4 *Protea Assurance Co Ltd v Waverley Agencies CC* 1994 3 SA 247 (C).
5 *S v W* supra 843.

806 Cinematographic film One is constrained to agree with the *obiter* judgment in *S v Mpumlo*[1] that a cine film is akin to a photograph since "A cine film is a series of images which can be visually observed by the naked eye, although the detail thereon would normally require enlarged reproduction, either as prints of individual frames or as a moving picture on a screen."

Although the learned judge found this type of medium "difficult to categorize", it is submitted that, like photographs, it should be considered to be documentary evidence, if the subject matter is what is really in issue. In practice, its importance is likely to diminish with the increasing use of magnetic videotape over developed film.

1 1986 3 SA 485 (E) 489.

807 Microfilm Like the two preceding categories of evidence, microfilm is "readable" by the human eye, even though the detail might require enlargement. It is usually submitted for its contents rather than to allow the court to inspect its surface, for example. This means that it also constitutes documentary evidence, although, in practice, it is usually submitted as secondary evidence of the original document, when this is permitted.[1]

Many statutes have been specifically amended to provide for the admissibility of microfilm instead of the original document. These amendments presumably take care of objections on the ground of lack of authenticity, best evidence as well as hearsay.

1 As in *Barclays Western Bank Ltd v Creser* 1982
  2 SA 104 (T) 106.

808 Audio- and videotape These differ from the previous categories in that they are not decipherable by the human eye in their native state and have to be "translated" by a tape player which converts the magnetic particles into sound or light impulses. They differ from computer magnetic[1] media in that the latter stores the data in a digital form, which is even more susceptible to manipulation than analogue data. Evidence in the form of tapes therefore has to be scrutinised with great care.

Schmidt[2] remarks upon the fact that a more liberal attitude was taken towards videotapes in *S v Mpumlo*[3] and *S v Baleka(1)*[4] than was adopted in *S v Singh*[5] and *S v Ramgobin*.[6] In the former two cases videotapes were considered to constitute real evidence and not documentary evidence, and therefore it was decided that the tapes did not have to comply with the (stricter) requirements of documentary evidence. At any rate it was felt that any possible deficiencies should go to weight rather than admissibility.

In *S v Singh*[7] and *S v Ramgobin*[8] a more conservative approach was adopted. Here it was felt that both audio- and videotapes should comply with documentary requirements with regard to originality and authenticity before they could even be admitted as evidence.

A tape recording of a conversation between a suspect and accused, made at the instigation of the suspect, would under the circumstances not be inadmissible because of the provisions of the Interception and Monitoring Prohibition Act;[9] obtaining the evidence does not infringe the accused's right of privacy.[10]

1 Although a major shift to optical media in the shape of compact and CD-ROM discs, Digital Audio Tape (DAT) and Digital Video Disc (DVD) is taking place.
2 *Bewysreg* 364–366.
3 1986 3 SA 485 (E).
4 1986 4 SA 192 (T).
5 1975 1 SA 330 (N).
6 1986 4 SA 117 (N).
7 Supra.
8 Supra.
9 127 of 1992.
10 *S v Kidson* 1999 1 SACR 338 (W); *Diablo Trade 28 (Pty) Ltd v Madiba Air (Pty) Ltd* [1999] 3 All SA 305 (W). See also *SATAWU obo Assegai v Autopax* [2002] 2 BALR 171 (AMSSA) for the use of videotapes in labour matters.

809 Computer evidence Computers should be distinguished from simple "counting machines" and calculators since the latter can be isolated from human intervention and interpretation and their working may be demonstrated to the court fairly easily. In this way, it has been possible to avoid hearsay objections by categorising evidence as real and getting it admitted in that way, for instance a radar trace of the movements of a ship, which was working without human intervention.[1] Hearsay objections would be unfounded, since recording is automatic and the only human mind through which the information had passed was that of witnesses to its operation, and these were present in court and subject to cross-examination.[2] Evidence of what appeared on the visual display of a breath-testing device has been accepted as being real evidence.[3] By analogy, the same argument should apply to a speed measuring device. Matters were thrown into confusion, however, when a court refused to accept computer print-outs with regard to the serial numbers of stolen British banknotes, holding that no personal knowledge had been proven.[4] Even academics, such as Smith,[5] have adopted the real evidence argument: "Hearsay invariably relates to information which has passed through a human mind. Thus (*sic*) information never did so."

The programmable nature of a computer and the digital[6] nature of its data, which allows its workings and its output to be constantly modified by human intervention, strains the analogy with real evidence, however. Countries have either passed special legislation to make computer-generated evidence admissible,[7] or have amended general civil and criminal procedure Acts to also make provision for this type of evidence, usually with analogy to documents. Schmidt's[8] call for a third category of evidence, namely that produced by appliances and devices, would seem to accord well with the first solution.

After lengthy investigations by the South African Law Commission and the Department of Communications, South Africa has led the way for Africa with its new Electronic Communications and Transactions Act. A signature may now be performed electronically and be admissible as part of a data message.[9] If it complies with certain technical requirements it constitutes an "advanced electronic signature" and is presumed to be valid until the contrary is proved.[10] The requirement of originality can also be met by a data message and it may not be excluded from evidence simply because of its format or the fact that it is no longer in its original form.[11] In assessing the evidential weight of such data message the court may have regard to various factors,[12] but if made in the ordinary course of business it will be admissible in evidence as rebuttable proof of any fact contained in it.[13] A "data message" now means data generated, sent, received or stored by electronic means and includes: (a) voice, where the voice is used in an automated transaction; and (b) a stored record.[14]

The new Act has repealed the Computer Evidence Act,[15] since it did not seem to work at all in practice. It is assumed that documentary evidence need not in future be handed up in hard-copy paper format – hopefully judges and magistrates will be equipped with electronic terminals or computers so as to be able to deal with these cases.

1 *The Statue of Liberty, Owners of Motorship Sappord Maru v Owners of Steam Tanker Statue of Liberty* [1968] 2 All ER 195 (CA). See also *R v Wood* (1983) Cr App R23 and *R v Ewing* [1983] 2 All ER 645.

2 Cross *Evidence* 50.

3 *Owen v Chesters* [1985] RTR 191 and *Gunn v Brown* 1986 SCCR 179 183. In *East West Transport Ltd v DPP* (reported in Nov 1995 *Criminal Law Review* 843) however, it was decided that since a computer generated weigh tickets at a sophisticated weight bridge, these constituted computer documents, and evidence was needed that the computer was operating properly, in order to comply with the provisions of s 69 of the UK Police and Criminal Evidence Act 1984.

Obiter, the court found that the printouts produced by a sophisticated "intoximeter" also constituted documents and the same procedure in terms of s 69 had to be followed. In the abovementioned issue of *Criminal Law Review* a commentator remarked that the only exception to the requirement of s 69 would be where an actual entry in the record was in issue (like a debit or a credit in a bank account) but not where it was being tendered "as evidence of any fact stated therein." Thus it would seem that in the UK the "tendering testimonially" and "tendering circumstantially" classification still makes the difference between admissibility or not. It also seems that when a computer comes upon the scene, the traditionally difficult distinction between real and documentary evidence becomes almost impossible. For this reason, the third category of evidence, namely that produced by appliances and devices, is becoming ever more important.

4 *R v Pettigrew* (1980) 71 Cr App Rep 39, although it should be mentioned that the computer concerned here was both recording information and performing an automated task. Cross 636 comments as follows on the case: "In fact it seems that proof of the commission of the automated task has been tendered in the same way as proof of operation of other scientific devices any problem would have been avoided."

5 1981 *Criminal Law Review* 387 391. Cf however, 1982 *Melbourne University Law Review* 617 623.

6 Digital (or binary) data, means that the data is no longer analogue, in that it causes light or sound waves, but simply consists of a series of one's and zero's, from which the computer fashions the most amazing creations.

7 Eg, SA, with the Electronic Communications and Transactions Act 25 of 2002.

8 *Bewysreg* (2000); and see par 804 ante.

9 S 13(2) (3) (5).

10 S 13(1) (4).

11 Ss 14 15(1).

12 S 15(2) (3).

13 S 15(4).

14 S 1. The definition is noteworthy for the fact that even electronic records now fall under the definition of "data message".

15 In *S v Mashiyi* 2002 2 SACR 387 (Tk) the court refused to allow documents, the contents of which had been processed and generated by computer. It should be borne in mind that this case was still decided in terms of the repealed Computer Evidence Act 57 of 1983.

PRESUMPTIONS

810 Nature and classification A presumption is a method of reasoning[1] or a legal device[2] whereby the existence of a fact is assumed. It usually, but not invariably, comes into operation upon proof of a basic fact giving rise to the assumption.

Presumptions have traditionally been classified as irrebuttable presumptions of law, rebuttable presumptions of law and (rebuttable) presumptions of fact. This terminology and classification is still recognised in South African decisions.

Irrebuttable presumptions of law are generally considered to fall outside the law of evidence. They are, in fact, rules of substantive law clothed in the form of rules of evidence.[3] Rebuttable presumptions of law are rules of law (within the law of evidence) compelling the provisional assumption of a fact. They are provisional in the sense that the assumption will stand unless it is destroyed by countervailing evidence. Presumptions of fact, on the other hand, are not rules of law, but are ordinary inferences drawn by the courts from the facts presented to them. It follows that they are also provisional in the sense referred to above.

In the following paragraphs some of the more important rebuttable presumptions (of law and of fact) are discussed.

1 In the case of presumption of fact.

2 In the case of presumption of law.

3 Consequently Roman-Dutch law and not English law determines their existence and operation: *S v Gabriel* 1971 1 SA 646 (RA) 665; cf *S v Gabriel* 1970 3 SA 442 (R).

Examples are the presumptions that a child under the age of seven years is *doli* and *culpae incapax*. See also Dlamini 2001 *THRHR* 544, 2002 *THRHR* 3 and 147 for a general review of presumptions in SA.

811 Legitimacy There is a presumption of law that a child is legitimate, in other words that the father and mother were married at the time of conception: *pater est quem nuptiae demonstrant.*[1] The party contesting this presumption bears the burden of proof,[2] which may be discharged, *inter alia*, by evidence showing that intercourse between husband and wife could not have taken place at the time of conception,[3] by evidence of negative blood tests and, possibly, by evidence of the use of contraceptives.[4]

Where the wife has remarried and the child could conceivably be that of either the first or the second husband, it is presumed that the second husband is the father.[5]

1 Grotius *Inleiding* 1 12 3; Voet *Commentarius* 1 6 6.

2 The burden is discharged on a balance of probabilities, but with recognition of the general improbability of adulterous conception: *Van Lutterveld v Engels* 1959 2 SA 699 (A) 702; *Mitchell v Mitchell* 1963 2 SA 505 (D) 508.

3 Expert evidence is sometimes adduced to prove the possible period of conception, but the court could also, in a suitable instance, take judicial notice thereof: *Mitchell v Mitchell* supra 507; cf *R v Sewgoolam* 1961 3

SA 79 (N) and *S v Sambo* 1962 4 SA 93 (E). In England, and also therefore in SA, evidence that the husband did not have access to his wife at the time of conception was, at one stage, inadmissible (*Russell v Russell* 1924 AC 687), but this impediment was removed by legislation: currently, so far as SA is concerned, by s 3 of the Civil Proceedings Evidence Act 25 of 1965.

4 This sort of evidence would, however, carry little, if any, weight: *R v Van der Merwe* 1952 1 SA 647 (O) 653F.

5 Voet 1 6 9.

812 Paternity When a woman accuses a man of being the father of her child, she normally has to prove paternity;[1] but if the man admits having had intercourse with her, whether at the time of conception or at any other time, then he is presumed to be the father.[2] This is a presumption of law and the onus lies upon the defendant (the man) to rebut it. Whether the presumption would also operate upon evidence, rather than an admission, of intercourse, is still uncertain. It is also uncertain whether the presumption becomes inoperative upon evidence that the woman has had intercourse with other men near the probable time of conception.[3]

The presumption can be rebutted, *inter alia,* by evidence that intercourse did not take place at the time of conception[4] and by blood tests.[5] Such evidence must prove on a balance of probabilities that the defendant could not possibly be the father (and not merely that he is probably not the father).[6]

1 *R v Swanepoel* 1954 4 SA 31 (O) 40; *S v Swart* 1965 3 SA 454 (A).

2 *R v Swanepoel* supra 40; *S v Swart* supra. See also *Holloway v Stander* 1969 3 SA 291 (A).

3 See the discussion of the *exceptio plurium concubentium* by Scholtens 1955 *SALJ* 144.

4 Such evidence is, however, of little value: *S v Sambo* 1962 4 SA 93 (E) 94E.

5 See generally *E v E* 1940 TPD 333; *Ranjith v Sheela* 1965 3 SA 103 (D); *Van der Harst v Viljoen* 1977 1 SA 795 (C).

6 *Mahomed v Shaik* 1978 4 SA 523 (N) 526D.

813 Marriage Several presumptions regulate the proof of marriage. When evidence is adduced of the celebration of a marriage ceremony, both the formal validity and the essential validity of the marriage are presumed.[1] These are rebuttable presumptions of law, and the onus lies upon the party contesting the marriage.[2]

If there is evidence to the effect that a man and a woman lived together as husband and wife and were generally regarded as such, it is presumed that they were, in fact, legally married.[3] This would appear to be a presumption of fact.

It is provided by statute that a marriage certificate will in all courts of law be *prima facie* evidence of the particulars set forth therein.[4]

There are also statutory provisions creating presumptive or *prima facie* proof of marriage in criminal proceedings for bigamy and incest upon proof of a marriage ceremony,[5] production of an extract from a marriage register[6] or evidence of cohabitation.[7]

1 *Fitzgerald v Green* 1911 EDL 432 449; *Ex parte Abrahams* 1937 EDL 107; *Ochberg v Ochberg's*

Estate 1941 CPD 15; *Ex parte L (also known as A)* 1947 3 SA 50 (C). This presumptive evidence is usually accepted only if no better evidence (a marriage certificate) is available: *Wittekind v Wittekind* 1948 1 SA 826 (W); contra: *R v Mbonambe* 1949 3 SA 558 (N).

2 *Ochberg v Ochberg's Estate* supra 33. Cf *Chikosi v Chikosi* 1975 2 SA 644 (R) 646.

3 *Fitzgerald v Green* supra. This presumption is considerably strengthened if there is also evidence of a marriage ceremony: *Ex parte L (also known as A)* supra 56.

4 See eg *W v W* 1976 2 SA 308 (W). As to foreign marriage certificates, see *Booysen v Booysen* 1958 3 SA 734 (O); *Saadien-Raad v Saadien-Raad* 1978 2 SA 271 (C). Cf *Chikosi v Chikosi* supra.

5 This provision is applicable only to a marriage ceremony within the Republic: Criminal Procedure Act 51 of 1977 ss 237(1) 238(2).

6 Such extract must be certified. If it is an extract from a foreign register, the signature on the certificate must be duly authenticated: ss 237(2) 238(2).

7 Mere evidence of cohabitiation is not, however, sufficient. There must also be evidence that the accused had participated in a marriage ceremony with the alleged spouse and had treated and recognised him or her as a spouse: ss 237(3) 238(2).

814 Capacity There appears to be a general presumption that a person has the capacity to perform a legal act. Thus any natural person is presumed to be capable of making a will,[1] entering into a marriage, concluding a contract or being a party to litigation – though contractual capacity[2] and the capacity to litigate[3] are *not* presumed in the case of a married woman.

There would also appear to be a general presumption of criminal and delictual capacity[4] – but this is subject to two exceptions: an *infans* (a child under the age of seven years) is irrebuttably presumed to lack both criminal and delictural capacity;[5] and an *impubes* (over seven but under 14 years) is rebuttably presumed to lack criminal capacity.[6]

1 *Kunz v Swart* 1924 AD 618; *Tregea v Godart* 1939 AD 16; *Kirsten v Bailey* 1976 4 SA 108 (C).

2 *Kent v Salmon* 1910 TPD 637 640; *Katzen v Mguno* 1954 1 SA 277 (T).

3 *Njobe v Njobe & Dube* 1950 4 SA 545 (C) 550; *Neseman & Neseman v Stratford* 1957 2 SA 363 (W); *Natalse Landboukoöperasie Bpk v Jordaan* 1961 2 SA 583 (N); *Rich v Lagerwey* 1973 1 SA 485 (W).

4 Thus, the party relying upon incapacity would have to put it in issue – though that party would not also necessarily bear the burden of proof: see eg *S v Mahlinza* 1967 1 SA 408 (A) 419; *S v Trickett* 1973 3 SA 526 (T); and a discussion of the latter by Schmidt 1973 *SALJ* 329. The fact that the accused bears the onus of proving insanity under common law is usually attributed to a presumption of sanity, which should be seen as a species of generic presumption of capacity.

5 *R v Lourie* (1892) 9 SC 432; *De Bruyn v Minister Van Vervoer* 1960 3 SA 820 (O) 825; *Van Oudtshoorn v Northern Assurance Co Ltd* 1963 2 SA 642 (A) 648H.

6 *R v K* 1956 3 SA 353 (A); *R v Tsutso* 1962 2 SA 666 (SR); *Jones v SANTAM Bpk* 1965 2 SA 542 (A); *Neuhaus v Bastion Insurance Co Ltd* 1968 1 SA 398 (A); *Roxa v Mtshayi* 1975 3 SA 761 (A); *S v M* 1978 3 SA 557 (TkSC). Evidence may now be adduced in legal proceedings where the question is in issue whether a boy under the age of 14 years has had sexual intercourse with any female, that such sexual intercourse has taken place, and no presumption or rule of law to the effect that such a boy is incapable of sexual intercourse will come into operation: Law of Evidence and the Criminal Procedure Act Amendment Act 103 of 1987 s 1.

815 Defamation A number of presumptions may become operative in a defamation suit (or any suit based upon the *actio iniuriarum*). The plaintiff, who bears the burden of proving publication of the defamatory (or injurious) statement, may be aided by a presumption that persons within earshot heard the statement.[1] Similarly, the plaintiff may be aided by a presumption that a defamatory statement on a postcard or in a telegram would have been read by a person or persons other than the addressee.[2] No such presumption, however, arises when a sealed letter has been sent to an individual; but it does arise in respect of a letter sent to a firm or company – unless it was addressed to an individual and marked private or confidential.[3] These are obviously presumptions of fact, namely, circumstantial evidence giving rise to inferences: their applicability will depend upon the particular facts of each case and only an evidential burden, or burden of rebuttal, is transferred to the defendant.

Once publication has been established two further presumptions, which may or may not be presumptions of law, become operative. The first is a presumption that the statement was published *animo iniuriandi* (the *animus* encompassing also knowledge of unlawfulness);[4] and the second that the publication was unlawful, namely that there was no justification such as a privileged occasion, fair comment, or truth and public benefit. The second presumption would appear to place the full burden of proof upon the defendant.[5] Whether the first has the same effect is unclear.[6]

It has been held that once justification has been established, the burden shifts back to the plaintiff to prove express malice on the part of the defendant. The scientific explantation of this shift is, it has been suggested,[7] that proof of malice is one way of establishing unlawfulness as it shows that the defendant exceeded the bounds of justification.

1 *Holdt v Meisel* 1927 SWA 45; *Whittington v Bowles* 1934 EDL 142.

2 *Pretorius v Niehaus* 1960 3 SA 109 (O) 112B–C.

3 *Pretorius v Niehaus* supra. See also *Trimble v Central News Agency Ltd* 1933 WLD 88 96 in regard to possible publication in a magazine or journal exhibited for sale in a bookshop.

4 *SA Uitsaaikorporasie v O'Malley* 1977 3 SA 394 (A) 405G–H.

5 *Maskowitz v Pienaar* 1957 4 SA 195 (A) 200D, with reference to a defence of privilege; *Craig v Voortrekkerpers Bpk* 1963 1 SA 149 (A) 157H; *Wentzel v SA Yster & Staalbedryfsvereniging, Wentzel v Blanke Motorwerkersvereniging* 1967

3 SA 91 (T) 98–99. Contra: *Groenewald v Minister van Justisie* 1973 2 SA 480 (O) 482. Cf *S v Marangarire* 1977 4 SA 237 (R) 239A: these presumptions are not applicable in criminal cases, ie the burden remains on the state.

6 See *Craig v Voortrekkerpers Bpk* supra 156–157; *Nydoo v Vengtas* 1965 1 SA 1 (A) 20F–H; *Moaki v Reckitt & Colman (Africa) Ltd* 1968 3 SA 98 (A) 105H; *Groenewald v Minister van Justisie* supra; *SA Uitsaaikorporasie v O'Malley* supra 403B 409C–F. Cf *S v Marangarire* supra.

7 By Joubert and Van der Walt 1967 *THRHR* 375 377. See further title DEFAMATION.

816 Regularity There is a general presumption that acts or events which occur regularly or routinely have followed a regular or routine course: *omnia praesumuntur rite esse acta*. It is based upon the statistical probability of regularity in an organised community. The presumption is usually one of fact, though in certain manifestations it appears to have hardened into one of law. There are too many varieties for a complete classification, but obviously it will only operate in circumstances where regularity is normally encountered.

One of the most fertile fields of application is that of official acts. It is presumed that any condition precedent to the validity of an official act has been complied with[1] and, more particularly, that the official (or body of officials) was qualified to perform the act in question[2] and complied with the necessary formalities.[3] This presumption does not, however, go so far as to permit the broad assumption that whatever any official does is lawful.[4]

When an official letter is written and a copy filed, it can be presumed that the letter was dispatched and that it was received by the addressee.[5] In the case of a letter from a private (non-government) source, the courts will usually require some evidence of a routine from which posting can be inferred.[6] It has been stressed that whether the inference can be drawn in a given case will depend upon all the circumstances and the applicable standard of proof.[7] This is a presumption of fact and the onus of proof is not affected.

Although machinery is often presumed to have functioned normally (as a presumption of fact), the existence of such a presumption has seldom been recognised in this field. In cases where the possible malfunction of, for example, trapping devices, traffic lights, and weighing scales has been put in issue, the courts have tended rather to approach the matter without any *a priori* bias towards regularity.[8]

1 *R v Magana* 1961 2 SA 654 (T) 656H. See also *Byers v Chinn* 1928 AD 322 333–334; *R v Naran Samy* 1945 AD 618 622; *R v Sacks* 1959 1 SA 788 (T) 792A; *R v Hotz* 1959 1 SA 795 (T) 799A; *R v Podbrey* 1948 2 SA 181 (C) 190; *Pretoria Stadsraad v Administrateur, Tvl* 1962 4 SA 467 (T); *Tikly v Johannes* 1963 2 SA 588 (T) 594G.

2 *R v Suliman* 1923 AD 659; *R v Mathlala* 1951 1 SA 49 (T); *R v Dumezweni* 1961 2 SA 751 (A) 755; *Bhendili v Attorney-General, Tvl* 1961 3 SA 232 (T).

3 *R v De Necker* 1921 CPD 567; *Schierhout v Union Government* 1927 AD 94 100; *R v Zondo* 1954 1 SA 209 (N) 211.

4 The presumption was considered, but not applied, in *R v Joffe* 1950 3 SA 251 (T); *R v Henkins* 1954 3 SA 560 (C); *Brand v Minister of Justice* 1959 4 SA 712 (A) 714; *S v Mcunu* 1962 1 SA 375 (N); *Attorney-General, Tvl v Manelis* 1964 3 SA 720 (T) 726; *S v Karge* 1971 3 SA 470 (T) 474; *Natal Estates Ltd v Secretary for Inland Revenue* 1975 4 SA 177 (A) 208; *Engineering Requisites (Pty) Ltd v Adam* 1977 2 SA 175 (O). The maxim *omnia praesumuntur rite esse acta* does not apply where the question in issue is whether an oath was administered by a commissioner of oaths who attested a document which bore the heading "affidavit": *Nkondo v Minister of Police* 1980 2 SA 362 (O).

5 *Cape Coast Exploration Ltd v Scholtz* 1933 AD 56 76; *R v Botha* 1960 4 SA 6 (T).

6 *Abdurahman v SA Medical Council* 1943 CPD 268; *Ebrahim v Excelsior Shopfitters & Furnishers (Pty) Ltd (2)* 1946 TPD 226; *Steyn's Estate v SA Mutual Life Assurance Society* 1948 1 SA 359 (C) 371; *S v Shepard* 1966 4 SA 530 (W) 532–533; *Micor Shipping (Pty) Ltd v Treger Gold & Sports (Pty) Ltd* 1977 2 SA 709 (W) 715B. See also *Mathobanyane v Vrystaatse Drankraad* [2000] 3 All SA 524 (O); 2000 4 SA 342 (O).

7 *Goldfields Confectionery & Bakery (Pty) Ltd v Norman Adam (Pty) Ltd* 1950 2 SA 763 (T) 768. See also *Vengatsamy v Scheepers* 1946 NPD 84; *Odendaalsrus Municipality v Odendaalsrus Gold, General Investment & Extensions Ltd* 1959 1 SA 374 (A) 382–383; *HK Outfitters (Pty) Ltd v Legal & General Assurance Society Ltd* 1975 1 SA 55 (T) 59.

8 *S v Margolis* 1964 4 SA 579 (T); *S v Curnick* 1974 3 SA 667 (E); *S v Bornman* 1975 1 SA 658 (T); *S v Pennels* 1977 1 SA 809 (N); *S v Brown* 1977 1 SA 907 (T).

817 Negligence The maxim *res ipsa loquitur* is often invoked where negligence is in issue. It means that "the facts speak for themselves" and is usually applied in negligence cases where the only known facts relating to the alleged negligent act consist of the occurrence itself.[1]

This is purely a presumption of fact and the burden of proof is not transferred to the party against whom the maxim is invoked.[2] It is applicable to criminal cases as well as civil cases, though in the former the inference can obviously only be drawn if the more stringent standard of proof for criminal cases is satisfied.[3]

1 *Sardi v Standard & General Insurance Co Ltd* 1977 3 SA 776 (A) 780D. See also *Hamilton v Mackinnon* 1935 AD 114; *Naude v Tvl Boot & Shoe Manufacturing Co* 1938 AD 379; *Administrator, Natal v Stanley Motors Ltd* 1960 1 SA 690 (A) 700; *Arthur v Bezuidenhout & Mieny* 1962 2 SA 566 (A); *Groenewald v Conradie, Groenewald v Auto Protection Insurance Co Ltd* 1965 1 SA 184 (A) 187F; *Rocky Lodge (Pvt) Ltd v Livie* 1977 3 SA 231 (RA) 232; *Dalion Materials (Pty) Ltd v Cintrust (Pty) Ltd* 1978 3 SA 599 (W) 605D.

2 *Arthur v Bezuidenhout & Mieny* supra; *Coleman v Mabuza* 1963 2 SA 498 (T); *Rankisson & Son v Springfield Omnibus Services (Pty) Ltd* 1964 1 SA 609 (D) 615–616; *Sardi v Standard & General Insurance Co Ltd* supra 780; *Goode v SA Mutual Fire & General Insurance Co Ltd* 1979 4 SA 301 (W).

3 *R v Whiley* 1935 CPD 466; *R v Girdlestone* 1948 4 SA 95 (SR).

818 Intention At one time it was thought that evidence of a criminal act would give rise to a presumption of law that the act was done intentionally[1] and that the natural and probable consequences of the act were contemplated and intended.[2] This presumption would then cast the burden of disproving intention upon the accused.[3] The existence of such a presumption is now denied;[4] but intention (encompassing the natural and probable consequences) can still often be inferred from the act. This would then be a presumption of fact and the burden of proof would not be affected.[5]

1 Eg *R v Butelezi* 1925 AD 160 169.
2 Eg *R v Jolly* 1923 AD 176 188.
3 Eg *R v Butelezi* supra.
4 Eg in *S v Mnyandu* 1973 4 SA 603 (N) 606.
5 *R v Taylor* 1949 4 SA 702 (A) 713; *S v*

Nkombani 1963 4 SA 877 (A) 883; *S v Kola* 1966 4 SA 322 (A) 327–328; *S v De Bruyn* 1968 4 SA 498 (A) 501H; *S v Singh* 1975 1 SA 330 (N) 335–336.

819 Continuance The existence of a fact will often give rise to a presumption of its continued existence. This is a presumption of fact: whether it can be invoked will depend upon the circumstances of each particular case.[1] Only when the continuance of a domicile is presumed is it possible to speak of the application of a presumption of law.

1 *R v Fourie* 1937 AD 31; *Lewin v Lewin* 1949 4 SA 241 (T) 277–278; *American Cotton Products Corporation v Felt & Tweeds Ltd* 1953 2 SA 753 (N); *Smith v Strydom* 1953 2 SA 799 (T) 803–804; *R v Ngotyana* 1956 4 SA 550 (A) 564; *Vulcan Rubber Works (Pty) Ltd v SAR & H* 1958 3 SA 285 (A) 290; *S v Steyn*

1963 1 SA 797 (W) 799H; *S v Lincey & Watson (Pty) Ltd* 1965 1 SA 572 (C) 574H; *Van den Bergh v Parity Insurance Co Ltd* 1966 2 SA 621 (W) 623; *Salisbury Bottling Co (Pvt) Ltd v Arista Bakery (Pvt) Ltd* 1973 3 SA 132 (RA).

820 Other presumptions In addition to the above, the following presumptions have been applied in South African cases:[1] that a spinster is a virgin;[2] that the possessor of a movable is the owner thereof;[3] that the possessor of stolen property stole it, or that the possessor received it knowing it to be stolen;[4] and that a person who gave money or property to another did not do so gratuitously.[5]

The so-called presumption of innocence is probably not a presumption in the usual (procedural) sense, but merely an expression of the principle that a person should not be convicted of a crimnal offence unless the state has proved his or her guilt beyond reasonable doubt.[6]

There is no presumption of law governing the sequence of death where a number of persons have died in a single accident.[7]

1 Because any inference can be classed as a presumption of fact it would not, however, be possible to compile a complete list. There is, indeed, no *numerus clausus*. In any event a multitude of presumptions are to be found in various legislative enactments, the most important of which are dealt with under other titles dealing with the related substantive law.
2 *Cranfield v Hoey* 1932 CPD 265; *Claassen v Van der Watt* 1969 3 SA 68 (T). Cf *Bull v Taylor* 1965 4 SA 29 (A) 33H.
3 *Zandberg v Van Zyl* 1910 AD 302; *Gleneagles Farm Dairy v Schoombee* 1949 1 SA 830 (A) 836; *K & D Motors v Wessels* 1949 1 SA 1

(A) 11–13; *Ruskin v Thiergen* 1962 3 SA 737 (A) 745. Cf *Ebrahim v Deputy Sheriff, Durban* 1961 4 SA 265 (D); *Geoghegan v Pestana* 1977 4 SA 31 (T) 35 et seq.
4 This is a presumption of fact, and may be rebutted by the possessor furnishing a reasonable explanation of his or her possession. See, generally, *R v Du Plessis* 1924 TPD 103; *R v Kumalo* 1930 AD 193; *R v Chetty* 1943 AD 514; *R v Nzimande* 1948 1 SA 1106 (N); *R v Charlston* 1955 3 SA 168 (T); *R v Morgan* 1961 2 SA 377 (T); *S v Rama* 1966 2 SA 395 (A); *S v Screech* 1967 2 SA 407 (E); *S v Nkomo* 1966 1 SA 831 (A); *S v Siswana* 1968 4 SA 251 (E); *S v Parrow* 1973

1 SA 603 (A); *S v Jantjies* 1999 1 SACR 32 (C).

5 *Timoney & King v King* 1920 AD 133 139; *Smith's Trustee v Smith* 1927 AD 482 487; *Stern v Kuper* 1941 WLD 223 228; *Avis v Verseput* 1943 AD 331 345 377; *Kannemeyer v Gloriosa* 1953 1 SA 580 (W) 585–586; *Thornycroft v Vas* 1957 3 SA 754 (FC) 756–757; *Twigger v Stanweave (Pty) Ltd* 1969 4 SA 369 (N).

6 *R v Benjamin* (1883) 3 EDC 337; *R v Britz* 1949 3 SA 293 (A) 302; *S v Belosevic* 1973 4 SA 347 (T). The presumption of innocence has on a few rare occasions been applied as a true presumption in civil proceedings; see eg *McKenzie v Van der Merwe* 1917 AD 41 45; *Van Breda v Victoria Falls & Tvl Power Co Ltd* 1916 AD 325; *Nkosi v Parity Insurance Co Ltd (In Liquidation)* 1966 1 SA 138 (T) 142; *Schoeman v Nieuwoudt* 1971 4 SA 161 (O) 162–163. The Constitutional Court has found the presumption of innocence to be

of value in the criminal case of *S v Zuma* 1995 4 BCLR 401 (CC); 1995 2 SA 642 (CC); 1995 1 SACR 568 (CC). For an example of a statutory presumption which is in breach of the presumption of innocence, and therefore invalid, see *S v Mbatha*, *S v Prinsloo* 1996 3 BCLR 293 (CC); 1996 2 SA 464 (CC); 1996 1 SACR 371 (CC).

7 *Nepgen v Van Dyk* 1940 EDL 123; *Ex parte Martienssen* 1944 CPD 139; *Ex parte Chodos* 1948 4 SA 221 (N); *Ex parte Graham* 1963 4 SA 145 (D); *Greyling v Greyling* 1978 2 SA 114 (T). When a court issues an order presuming the death of a person, it is not applying a procedural presumption (though a presumption of fact may give rise to the order). The order is a provisional decree that the consequence of death may follow. See *Ex parte Stoter* [1996] 4 All SA 329 (E); 1996 4 SA 1299 (E) for the factors to be taken into account when a presumption of death has to be determined.

JUDICIAL NOTICE

821 Principle of judicial notice When a court takes into account a fact which has not been proved in evidence, and has not been formally admitted or presumed, it is said to have taken judicial notice thereof.

It is a well-established principle that a court should decide a factual issue solely on the evidence placed before it. A trier of fact should, therefore, not rely on his or her personal knowledge;[1] indeed, personal knowledge of a fact in issue could be a ground for demanding the trier's recusal.[2] However, by way of exception, and in order to forestall needless litigation, a court may take judicial notice of any fact which is so commonly known or so easily and reliably ascertainable that it is virtually incontestable. In addition, it must take judicial notice of any point of domestic law applicable to the issues before it.

1 *R v Tager* 1944 AD 339 344. See *S v Mantini* 1990 2 SACR 236 (E). For a general review regarding judicial notice, see Dlamini 2001 *De Jure* 49.

2 *Kriel v McDonald* 1930 SWA 53; *R v Steenkamp* 1947 1 SA 714 (SWA) 718; *S v Bailey* 1962 4 SA 514 (E) 517. Cf *S v Essa* 1964 3 SA 13 (N).

822 Notorious facts A fact can be judicially noticed only if it is so well known as to be incapable of dispute among reasonably informed and educated people.[1] It is impossible to define more exactly where the line should be drawn; and, in any event, the courts appear to have a fairly wide discretion.

Courts have generally been reluctant to take notice of special characteristics or habits sometimes ascribed to members of the different racial groups in the country.[2] Trade practices in common usage are judicially noticed.[3] Although the courts sometimes accept the reliability of instruments known to be usually reliable,[4] as a general rule they require evidence that a particular instrument was performing properly where the accuracy of the instrument is an important factor in the case.[5]

Judicial notice has been taken of the fact that it is dangerous to travel through a town at 80km/h;[6] that a national road is a public road;[7] that when the traffic lights on the one side of an intersection are red, the lights on the intersecting side are green, provided that the proper functioning of the lights is not disputed;[8] that no fingerprints are identical;[9] that a certain product is imported;[10] and that billiards, table tennis and chess are games of skill and not of chance.[11] Courts have refused to take judicial notice of the contents of a milk shake;[12] the distance the sound of a pistol–shot will travel;[13] the nature of the game "poker";[14] the nature of a "bucket-shop";[15] and the age at which a girl reaches puberty.[16]

1 Zeffertt *Evidence* 717.

2 Eg in *R v Tusini* 1953 4 SA 406 (A) 411–412 (better eyesight in the dark than Europeans); *R v Maboko* 1956 3 SA 144 (G) 145D (capacity to absorb corporal punishment); *R v Sitimela* 1962 4 SA 60 (SR) (ability to identify a spoor); *S v Imene* 1979 2 SA 710 (A) ("men of the bush" means "terrorists").

3 Eg payment by cheque: *Schneider & London v Chapman* 1917 TPD 497; use of bank guarantee in sale of immovable property: *Breytenbach v Van Wijk* 1923 AD 541 547.

4 Watches and thermometers are said to be classic examples in *R v Harvey* 1969 2 SA 193 (RA) 200D–E.

5 *S v Margolis* 1964 4 SA 579 (T); *S v Du Plessis* 1966 1 SA 607 (C); *R v Harvey* supra; *S v Hengst* 1975 2 SA 91 (SWA) 97H; *S v Brown* 1977 1 SA 907 (T).

6 *R v Van der Merwe* 1943 CPD 25.

7 *R v Bikitsha* 1960 4 SA 181 (E).

8 *Van Wyk v S* [1997] 3 All SA 75 (E).

9 *Rex v Morela* 1947 3 SA 147 (A) 151.

10 *Rex v Parker* (1909) 26 SC 654 659.

11 *Ex parte Minister van Justisie: In re S v Concalves* 1976 3 SA 629 (A) 639.

12 *R v Tager* 1944 AD 339.

13 *R v Dhlumayo* 1948 2 SA 677 (A) 692.

14 *R v Shub* 1951 3 SA 23 (A).

15 *Joseph v Hein* 1975 3 SA 175 (W) 178.

16 *S v M* 1967 1 SA 70 (N). In *S v Steenberg* 1979 3 SA 513 (B) the court refused to take notice that the "duikers" referred to in evidence were "blue duikers". A court may not take judicial notice of a specific occurrence or incident: *S v Mkhwanazi* 1989 2 SA 802 (T). In *S v Ratte* 1998 1 SACR 323 (T) the court took judicial notice of the fact that an AK47 rifle is capable of being set to operate as a machine gun.

823 Locally known facts Judicial notice may be taken of facts which, though not generally known, are known to reasonably informed people in the area where the court sits.[1] Such facts would include (if sufficiently notorious) the name or character of a street,[2] the size and condition of a town,[3] the approximate distance between two points within a town[4] or between one town and another,[5] and the prevalance of crime within the court's area of jurisdiction.[6]

Although there are exceptions, courts have generally refused to take notice of the fact that a place falls within its jurisdiction or within the field of operation of a legal provision.[7]

1 It has been suggested that the true criterion is not the knowledge of the local man in the street, but the knowledge of a court sitting within the area of jurisdiction: Schmidt *Bewysreg* 192–193.

2 *R v De Necker* 1921 CPD 567 (*obiter*); *R v Van der Merwe* 1943 CPD 25; *R v Adkins* 1955 4 SA 242 (G).

3 *R v Van der Merwe* supra; *R v Levitt* 1933 CPD 411.

4 *Mahomed v R* 1946 Justice Circular 146, referred to in *R v Mbili* 1951 1 SA 110 (N).

5 Courts are, however, disinclined to take cognisance of precise distances: *R v Fanaroff* 1940

OPD 270; *R v Kruger* 1951 4 SA 37 (N).

6 *R v Ford* 1939 AD 559; *R v Stali* 1961 3 SA 1 (E); *S v Rakoti* 1970 3 SA 54 (O) 56. Cf *S v Malinga* 1962 1 SA 439 (T) 440. In *S v Mkhwanazi* 1989 2 SA 802 (T) the court refused to take judicial notice of statistics, compiled by an agricultural organisation, in regard to the prevalence of a specific crime within the court's area of jurisdiction.

7 *R v Cooper* 1920 EDL 374; *R v Levin* 1932 CPD 23; *R v Luwani* 1945 EDL 147; *S v Mbili* supra; *S v Mchunu* 1976 1 SA 320 (N) 321–322; *S v Koekemoer* 1978 2 SA 405 (O) 408.

824 Facts readily ascertainable To a limited extent[1] judicial notice is taken of facts which, though perhaps not generally known, are ascertainable from sources of indisputable accuracy. Thus a court can make use of an authoritative map to determine the location of a place or the boundaries of a geographical area;[2] of calendars to determine dates;[3] and tables (prepared at an official observatory) to determine the times of sunrise and sunset.[4]

Although it is not, generally, permissible for a court to refer to textbooks in order to establish technical or scientific facts, courts frequently use dictionaries to establish the meanings of words and (less frequently) history books to establish historical facts.[5]

1 There is no general rule that a fact which is reliably ascertainable can be judicially noticed. Notice is taken of such facts only in certain areas established by precedent.

2 *R v Pretoria Timber Co (Pty) Ltd* 1950 3 SA 163 (A) 172. See also *General Life Assurance Co v Moyle* 1919 AD 1 10; *R v Molo* 1953 2 SA 129 (EDL); *R v Hem* 1958 1 SA 741 (E); *S v Mosala* 1968 3 SA 523 (T).

3 There appears to be no reference to this practice in South African cases; but see Schmidt *Bewysreg* 194; Zeffertt *Evidence* 721

723. See also *S v Mpharu* 1981 2 SA 464 (NC) for an instance where judicial notice was taken of a calendar of the phases of the moon. In *S v Sibuyi* 1988 4 SA 879 (T) the court refused to take judicial notice of information contained in a diary (or calendar) of the phases of the moon.

4 Criminal Procedure Act 51 of 1977 s 229; Civil Proceedings Evidence Act 25 of 1965 s 26.

5 *Consolidated Diamond Mines of SWA Ltd v Administrator SWA* 1958 4 SA 572 (A) 610A.

825 Political and constitutional matters Judicial notice has been taken of various political and constitutional matters, such as the existence of a state of war,[1] the constitutional status and history of South Africa[2] and the origins of the League of Nations and the United Nations.[3] Such examples appear to fall under either cognisance of law or of notorious facts. Where the relationship between South Africa and another state is in issue, the courts will usually decline to take judicial notice, but will rely solely upon a certificate signed by the appropriate minister of state.[4]

Courts have, on occasion, made use of textbooks or other similar sources to establish facts about foreign states.[5]

1 There are numerous examples in English law: see Phipson *Evidence* par 52. It may be presumed that South African courts will adopt the same approach. See *S v Imene* 1979 2 SA 710 (A); *S v Twala* 1979 3 SA 864 (T).

2 *Green v Minister of the Interior* 1967 4 SA 503 (T) 506–507; *Harris v Minister of the Interior* 1952 2 SA 428 (A) 457; *Nasopie (Edms) Bpk v Minister van Justisie* 1979 3 SA 1228 (NC).

3 *R v Christian* 1924 AD 101.

4 *Hassim v Naik* 1952 3 SA 331 (A); *S v Devoy* 1971 3 SA 899 (A); *S v Oosthuizen* 1977 1 SA 823 (N). Cf *Madzimbamuto v Lardner-Burke, Baron v Ayre* 1968 2 SA 284 (RA) 309.

5 *Grgin v Grgin* 1961 2 SA 84 (W) 88; *Smith v Smith* 1970 1 SA 146 (R) 147H. See also the *obiter dictum* by Fagan CJ in *Consolidated Diamond Mines of SWA Ltd v Administrator SWA* 1958 4 SA 572 (A) 610A (for SWA/Namibia constititutional history).

826 Legal matters Subject to what is said below, it is not permissible to lead expert evidence on a point of law. The court notices it, not because it is a matter of common knowledge, but because the court is *the* organ of state entrusted with the fucntions of declaring and applying the law. It will take notice of both statute law and common law, but may hear evidence on the existence and scope of custom having legal effect.[1] By virtue of legislation, a court will also take judicial cognisance of anything published in the *Government Gazette* or the *Official Gazette* of any province,[2] and of the privileges, immunities and powers of Parliament or officers of Parliament.[3]

Courts not infrequently refer to foreign law for comparative purposes, citing for instance law reports, statutes, codes, and academic literature;[4] but where foreign law is actually applicable in a case (as can happen when a conflict of laws situation occurs) the foreign law has to be proved by an expert witness.[5] Where there is doubt about the content of foreign law, the court is aided by a presumption that it coincides with South African law.[6] English law has been held to be foreign law and therefore also has to be proved by an expert.[7]

International customary law is considered to be incorporated in South African law. It should be judicially noticed, and expert evidence to prove it is, in fact, inadmissible.[8]

Indigenous African law and custom are judicially noticed by the courts instituted to deal with suits involving only blacks, including those within the appellate hierarchy – though it is also possible for such courts to hear evidence on an obscure point of law or custom.[9] Indigenous law has been placed on the same footing as the law of a foreign state; a court may also take judicial notice of indigenous law in so far as such a law can readily be ascertained but nothing precludes the parties from adducing evidence of the substance of such a rule, subject to the following:

(a)   that such indigenous law may not be contrary to the principles of public policy or natural justice; and

(b)   that it will not be lawful for any court to declare that the custom of *lobola* or *bogadi* or any other similar custom is repugnant to such principles.[10]

1   Eg in *Van Breda v Jacobs* 1921 AD 330. For an instance where judicial notice was taken of a decision of court, see *Shell Zimbabwe (Pvt) Ltd v Webb* 1981 4 SA 749 (Z).

2   Criminal Procedure Act 51 of 1977 s 224; Civil Proceedings Evidence Act 25 of 1965 s 5; see *S v Hoosen* 1963 2 SA 340 (N) 341; *S v Di Stefano* 1977 1 SA 770 (C); *S v Koekemoer* 1978 2 SA 405 (O). Subordinate legislation not published in a government or provincial *Government Gazette* cannot be judicially noticed: *Serobe v Koppies Bantu Community School Board* 1958 2 SA 265 (O); *S v Van Rensburg* 1973 2 SA 543 (T) 544H. See, as to the scope of the maxim *iura novit curia*, Baxter 1979 *SALJ* 531.

3   Powers and Privileges of Parliament Act 91 of 1963 s 37.

4   An opinion on foreign law for comparative purposes should either be woven into counsel's address to the court or be proved by an expert witness; it cannot be handed in from the bar: *S v Masilela* 1968 2 SA 558 (A) 567.

5   *Schnaider v Jaffe* 1916 CPD 696; *Anderson v The Master* 1949 4 SA 660 (EDL); *G & P v Commissioner of Taxes* 1960 4 SA 163 (SR) 166F; *Yorigami Maritime Construction Co Ltd v Nissho-Iwai Co Ltd* 1977 4 SA 682 (C). A court may take judicial notice of the law of a foreign state in so far as such law can with sufficient certainty be readily ascertained,

although there is nothing which precludes any party from adducing evidence of the substance of a foreign legal rule which is in issue: Law of Evidence Amendment Act 45 of 1988 s 1(1)–(2). For the interpretation of this provision, see *Harnischfeger Corporation v Appleton* 1993 4 SA 479 (W).

6   *Rogaly v General Imports (Pty) Ltd* 1948 1 SA 1216 (C); *Estate H v Estate H* 1952 4 SA 168 (C); *Bank of Lisbon v Optichem Kunsmis (Edms) Bpk* 1970 1 SA 447 (W); *Ex parte Van Dam* 1973 2 SA 182 (W).

7   *Schlesinger v CIR* 1964 3 SA 389 (A) 396; *S v Dolman* 1970 4 SA 467 (T) 471.

8   *De Howorth v The SS "India"* (1), *Mann, George & Co (Delagoa) Ltd v The SS "India"* (2) 1921 CPD 451; *Ex parte Schumann* 1940 NPD 251 254; *South Atlantic Islands Development Corporation Ltd v Buchan* 1971 1 SA 234 (C) 238.

9   *Rowe v Assistant Magistrate Pretoria* 1925 TPD 361; *Ex parte Minister of Native Affairs: In re Yako v Beyi* 1948 1 SA 388 (A); *R v Dumezweni* 1961 2 SA 751 (A) 757; *S v Ngidi* 1969 1 SA 411 (N). See, however, an article by Bekker 1976 *THRHR* 359 for the contention that African law and custom should now be (and in practice is) considered as domestic law and not foreign law.

10   Law of Evidence Amendment Act 45 of 1988 s 1(1)–(2).

SUFFICIENCY

CORROBORATION AND CAUTIONARY RULES

827 Introduction A distinction is drawn between a rule requiring corroboration and a cautionary rule. The former (which has always been of statutory origin) demands that the evidence to be corroborated be supported in some material respect by evidence from another source; the latter (which is not statutory, but developed as a *usus fori*) may merely require that the particular evidence be treated with due caution.[1]

The present Criminal Procedure Act[2] conforms to the movement away from formalistic proof in that it contains only one requirement of formal corroboration, that pertaining to a confession,[3] whereas its predecessors contained various such provisions.[4] There is no statutory provision requiring corroboration in civil cases.

1 The means by which these requirements may be met are dealt with more fully in par 829 post. Corroboration may consist of circumstantial evidence: *Khumalo v S* [1998] 2 All SA 294 (N); 1998 1 SACR 672 (N). See also *S v M* 2000 1 SACR 484 (W) with regard to a general discretionary cautionary approach.

2 51 of 1977.
3 S 209. See par 828 post.
4 The previous Criminal Procedure Act 56 of 1955 contained specific corroboration provisions for perjury (s 256), treason (s 256), accomplice evidence (s 257), a plea of guilty in an inferior court (s 258(1)) and a confession (s 258(2)).

828 Formal corroboration: confessions The Criminal Procedure Act,[1] like its predecessors, permits the conviction of an accused person on the single evidence of a confession[2] that the accused committed the offence, provided that it is confirmed in a material respect or, if not so confirmed, that the commission of the offence be proved by evidence other than a confession. Confirmation has been found to exist, on a charge of murder, in the presence of arsenic in the body of the deceased;[3] on a charge of unlawfully entering an urban area, in the accused's presence within that area;[4] and on a charge of stock theft, in the fact that stock was missing from an enclosed paddock.[5] Confirmation may also be furnished by statements (other than the confession) made by the accused in or out of court.[6]

Whereas confirmation of the confession can be furnished by any evidentiary matter, including therefore formal admissions of the accused, proof *aliunde* of the commission of the offence can only be supplied by "evidence, other than such confession", which excludes formal admissions.[7] Proof *aliunde* of the offence can be furnished by the evidence of an accomplice.[8]

If an accused pleads not guilty and then in clarification of his or her plea in effect confesses to the crime, the abovementioned provision is not applicable; the accused may be found guilty on his or her uncorroborated statement.[9]

1 51 of 1977 s 209. Although the wording differs to some extent from that of the corresponding provision (s 258(2)) of the Criminal Procedure Act 56 of 1955, the meaning is essentially the same. Previous case law is therefore still relevant.
2 A confession is an unequivocal admission of all the elements of the offence, equivalent to a plea of guilty: see par 737 ante. A plea of guilty, however, is not a confession: *R v Mutimba* 1944 AD 23; *R v Fouche* 1958 3 SA 767 (T) 775D. And "confession" in the

context of the Criminal Procedure Act 51 of 1977 refers only to an extra-judicial statement. For the approach to be followed and where the accused made later statements in conflict with his confession, see *S v Mkize* 1992 2 SACR 347 (A).
3 *R v Blyth* 1940 AD 355.
4 *R v Lamunu* 1948 1 SA 712 (C).
5 *R v Mataung* 1949 2 SA 414 (O) 419–420, distinguished in *S v Irion* 1976 1 SA 551 (C).
6 *S v Mbambo* 1975 2 SA 549 (A) 553E.
7 *R v V* 1958 3 SA 474 (G) 479; *S v Nzuza*

1963 3 SA 631 (A); *S v Mokgeledi* 1968 4 SA 335 (A). See also with regard to labour law matters, *SACCAWU obo Dlabantu v OK Bazaars* [1999] 7 BALR 833 (CCMA).

8 *Peterson v R* 1910 TPD 859 863; cf *Rex v*

Geshen & Miller 1933 AD 137. This is *a fortiori* the position today, when the accomplice's evidence itself does not, in turn, require confirmation.

9 *S v Talie* 1979 2 SA 1003 (C).

829 Cautionary rules: nature of

Although it would be dangerous to generalise about the ways in which the various cautionary rules may be satisfied, it can be stated that such rules do not necessarily require corroboration in the sense of extraneous confirmatory evidence.[1] Features which point to the satisfaction or otherwise of a cautionary rule are the mendacity,[2] bias (or absence thereof)[3] and opportunities for observation of the witness or the opposing witnesses,[4] and the admissions[5] or failure to give or lead evidence[6] of the opposite party, as well as the general probabilities of the case.[7] These features are, however, not exhaustive. In essence, the requirement is that the trier of fact should warn him or herself of the danger of relying on the evidence which is subject to the cautionary rule, and should not do so unless there is some feature which renders it trustworty.[8] The feature or features that the court will consider to be important will largely depend upon the reason for caution in each particular instance.

The courts have been careful not to elevate the cautionary rules to rigid rules of law requiring formal compliance and have emphasised that "the exercise of caution should not be allowed to displace the exercise of common sense".[9] Ultimately, the question is still whether the requisite standard of proof (in criminal cases proof beyond a reasonable doubt) has been satisfied.[10] Nevertheless, it has been contended that at least some of the cautionary rules are, in fact, rules of law because they carry the sanction of nullity in the event of non-compliance.[11]

1 *R v Mpompotshe* 1958 4 SA 471 (A) 476E–F. See also *S v Wilmot* 2002 2 SACR 145 (SCA) regarding the proclivity of a witness to give false evidence.

2 *R v Ncanana* 1948 4 SA 399 (A) 405; *S v Letsedi* 1963 2 SA 471 (A) 473H; *S v Ganie* 1967 4 SA 203 (N) 206G; *S v Snyman* 1968 2 SA 582 (A) 585E; *S v B* 1976 2 SA 54 (C) 59B–C. See *S v Wilmot* supra on the proclivity of a witness to give false evidence.

3 Some of the cautionary rules, eg that relate to accomplice evidence, are based on the fact that the witness may have a motive to implicate the accused: *R v Ncanana* supra 405; *S v Letsedi* supra 473G–H; and it has been suggested that the evidence of any person who has such a motive should be treated with caution: *R v Dikant* 1948 1 SA 693 (O) 700. Consequently, the absence of such motive – eg, if an accomplice is already sentenced and convicted – would to a large extent remove the suspicion attached to his or her evidence: *R v Gumede* 1949 3 SA 749 (A) 755–756. As to an interest or bias adverse to the accused in the case of a single witness, see *R v Mokoena* 1932 OPD 79 80.

See also *S v Webber* 1971 3 SA 754 (A) 759D; *S v Bester* 1990 2 SACR 325 (A).

4 *R v Mokoena* supra 80.

5 *S v B* supra.

6 *R v Ncanana* supra; *R v Gumede* supra; *S v Letsedi* supra; *S v Snyman* supra; *S v B* supra. That the need for caution is reduced in paternity and seduction cases where the allegations are not denied under oath, was confirmed in *Mohamed Hoosain v Principal Immigration Officer* 1927 CPD 437 and *Strydom v Claase* 1943 WLD 112.

7 *S v Ganie* supra.

8 *R v Ncanana* supra; *R v Mbonambi* 1957 3 SA 232 (A) 235B. Cf *R v Mpompotshe* supra. See *S v F* 1989 3 SA 847 (A) for a discussion of the correct manner in which the cautionary rules should be applied.

9 *R v J* 1966 1 SA 88 (SRA) 90; *S v Snyman* supra 585G–H; *S v Artman* 1968 3 SA 339 (A) 341C.

10 *S v Letsedi* supra 474–475; *S v Kearney* 1964 2 SA 495 (A) 501H; *S v Snyman* supra 585F; *S v Artman* supra 341B.

11 Schmidt *Bewysreg* 122 fn 20, with reference to *R v Mbonambi* supra 235B.

830 Single witness In both civil and criminal cases the court may base its finding on the single evidence of a competent and credible witness.[1] There is under present law no statutory requirement of formal corroboration.[2] However, the courts will naturally treat the evidence of a single witness with more caution than that of a number of witnesses who corroborate eachother;[3] and it has been stated that the single witness should, in a criminal case, be relied upon only if his or her evidence is clear and satisfactory in every material respect.[4] The court will usually not rely upon such evidence if, for example, the witness has an interest or bias adverse to the accused; where the witness has made a previous inconsistent statement; where the witness contradicts him or herself; where the witness has been found guilty of an offence involving dishonesty; and where he or she has not had a proper opportunity for observation.[5] These factors are obviously not exhaustive, nor does their presence inevitably lead to a rejection of the witness's evidence: for instance, before rejecting the witness's evidence on the ground of bias, the court should investigate the intensity of the bias.[6] Ultimately, the relevant standard of proof will determine whether it would be correct to rely on the evidence of the single witness.[7]

The cautionary rule, which would appear to apply only to criminal cases, is not confined to those cases in which only one witness is called by the state: it is also applicable to the situation where a single witness testifies on one of several counts (though obviously he or she can then be corroborated by a witness testifying on another count);[8] where a single witness is called to prove a confession though there are other witnesses in the case;[9] where a single witness implicates the accused though several can testify that the crime was committted;[10] and even where two witnesses testify about the same subject matter but appear to be in collusion.[11]

1 Civil Proceedings Evidence Act 25 of 1965 s 16; Criminal Procedure Act 51 of 1977 s 208 which, unlike its predecessor, does not formally require that the witness be credible, though credibility must obviously flow from the standard of proof that must ultimately be met.
2 The predecessors of the present Criminal Procedure Act 51 of 1977 required more than one witness for certain aspects on charges of perjury and high treason: see Criminal Procedure Act 56 of 1955 s 256(a)–(b).
3 See the remarks of Fagan JA in *R v Mokoena* 1956 3 SA 81 (A) 86F.
4 *R v Mokoena* 1932 OPD 79 80 per De Villiers JP. See the criticism of this statement by Broome JP in *R v Abdoorham* 1954 3 SA
163 (N) 165 and the reply thereto by Fagan JA in *R v Mokoena* 1956 3 SA 81 (A) 86. Cf *S v Abrahams* 1979 1 SA 203 (A); *S v Kelly* 1980 3 SA 301 (A); *S v Sauls* 1981 3 SA 172 (A).
5 *R v Mokoena* 1932 OPD 79 80.
6 *S v Webber* 1971 3 SA 754 (A) 759D.
7 *R v Abdoorham* supra; *S v Artman* 1968 3 SA 339 (A) 341C; *S v Dladla* 1974 2 SA 689 (N) 692C; *Olifant v Shield Insurance Co* 1980 1 SA 903 (C).
8 *S v B* 1976 2 SA 54 (C); *S v R* 1977 1 SA 9 (T) 11H.
9 *S v Letsedi* 1963 2 SA 471 (A).
10 *R v Mokoena* 1956 3 SA 81 (A) 85G; *S v Teixeira* 1980 3 SA 755 (A).
11 *R v Vlok & Vlok* 1954 1 SA 203 (SWA).

831 Accomplices Under the statutes preceding the Criminal Procedure Act of 1977,[1] the evidence of an accomplice had to be supported by confirmation of such evidence or proof *aliunde* that the offence had actually been committed.[2] Because the requirement of proof *aliunde* failed to meet the danger inherent in accomplice evidence,[3] the courts developed a cautionary rule which has survived the repeal of the statutory requirement. In terms of this rule the triers of fact should warn themselves of the special danger of convicting on the evidence of an accomplice.[4] The most satisfactory way of meeting this danger is by corroboration implicating the accused;[5] but it will also be reduced if, for instance, the accused proves to be a lying witness or if he or she does not give evidence to contradict or explain that of the accomplice,[6] or if he or she implicates, in addition to the accused, someone near and dear to him or her and against whom he or she has no ground for rancour.[7][8] Even in the absence of such features a conviction will still be possible if the merits of the accomplice as a witness and the demerits of the accused are beyond question.[9]

It is possible for one accomplice to corroborate another in satisfaction of the cautionary rule,[10] although in that case the evidence of both accomplices should be treated with caution.[11] If the accomplice is also a single witness, the two cautionary rules are fused: no additional caution is required.[12]

The cautionary rule is applicable to the evidence of an accessory after the fact,[13] and also to that of any co-accused who implicates the accused when giving evidence in his or her own defence;[14] and it has been suggested that it should apply to the evidence of any witness who has a motive for implicating the accused,[15] though this may be too sweeping a statement.[16]

The fact that an accomplice has been sentenced lessens the suspicion attaching to the accomplice's evidence, but does not place the accomplice outside the ambit of the cautionary rule.[17]

1 51 of 1977.
2 Criminal Procedure and Evidence Act 31 of 1917 s 285; Criminal Procedure Act 51 of 1977 s 257.
3 The danger is not that no crime was committed (if there is an accomplice there must be a crime), but that the accomplice will implicate an innocent person. See *R v Ncanana* 1948 4 SA 399 (A) 405; *R v Mpompotshe* 1958 4 SA 471 (A) 476; *S v Malepane* 1979 1 SA 1009 (W). The cautionary rule is applicable where co-accused are accomplices; it does not only apply where accomplices testify for the state: *S v Johannes* 1980 1 SA 531 (A).
4 *R v Ncanana* supra 405. See also *S v Chouhan* 1987 2 SA 315 (ZS). The cautionary rule was restated in *S v Bester* 1990 2 SACR 325 (A).
5 Ibid.
6 Ibid. See also *R v John* 1943 TPD 295; *S v W* 1963 3 SA 516 (A) 523H.
7 *R v Gumede* 1949 3 SA 749 (A) 758. Cf *S v Masuku* 1969 2 SA 375 (N) 377B.
8 These features are not a *numerus clausus*.
9 *R v Ncanana* supra; *R v Mpompotshe* supra. This does not, however, mean that the accomplice's evidence must be completely without blemish: *R v Nqamtweni* 1959 1 SA 894 (A) 898H; *R v Kristusamy* 1945 AD 549

556; *R v Gumede* supra. It is not necessarily expected that the accomplice's evidence should be wholly consistent and wholly reliable or even wholly truthful; the ultimate test, after cautiously considering the accomplice's evidence, is whether the court is satisfied beyond reasonable doubt that in its essential features the story he or she tells is a true one: *S v Francis* 1991 1 SACR 198 (A).
10 *S v Hlapezula* 1965 4 SA 439 (A); *S v Hassim* 1973 3 SA 443 (A) 461.
11 *S v Ismail (2)* 1965 1 SA 452 (N) 456B; *S v Masuku* supra 377D; *S v Van Vreden* 1969 2 SA 524 (N) 532C.
12 *R v P* 1957 3 SA 444 (A); *S v Gokool* 1965 3 SA 461 (N) 472A.
13 *R v Nhleko* 1960 4 SA 712 (A) 722.
14 *S v Radloff* 1978 4 SA 66 (A); *S v Dladla* 1980 1 SA 526 (A).
15 *R v Dikant* 1948 1 SA 693 (O) 700; *S v Hlongwa* 1991 1 SACR 583 (A).
16 See generally, on the possible extension of the accomplice rule to other interested or biased witnesses, *R v George* 1953 1 SA 382 (A) 390; *S v Letsedi* 1963 2 SA 471 (A); *S v Zitha* 1965 1 SA 166 (E) 169; *S v Xoswa* 1965 1 SA 267 (C) 269.
17 *R v Gumede* supra; *R v Mbonambi* 1957 3 SA 232 (A) 235–236.

832 Children Although there is no statutory requirement that a child's evidence be corroborated, such evidence, if not corroborated, will only be accepted with great caution. The reason for this rule of practice, which is similar to that applied to the evidence of accomplices[1] and the victims of sexual offences,[2] is primarily (but not solely) based upon the imaginativeness and suggestibility of children.[3] The rule is to the effect that the trial court should fully appreciate the dangers inherent in the acceptance of such evidence,[4] but it does not attempt to enumerate the various factors that can lessen the danger – nor does it attempt to define the classes of children to whom it is applicable. Age is obviously one factor that must be taken into account,[5] but so, for example, is the nature of the evidence given,[6] the character and intelligence of the child,[7] the likelihood of a false identification,[8] and the presence or absence of a motive to conceal the truth.[9] Thus all the circumstances are taken into account to determine the extent of the danger and the need, if at all, for corroboration or caution.[10]

1 See par 831 ante.
2 See par 833 post. It quite often happens that both rules are applicable, ie when the child is the victim of a sexual offence: eg *R v W* 1949 3 SA 772 (A); *R v J* 1966 1 SA 88 (SRA); *S v R* 1977 1 SA 9 (T); *S v V* 1991 1 SACR 59 (T).
3 *R v Manda* 1951 3 SA 158 (A) 163C–D.
4 *R v Manda* supra 163E. A cautionary rule similar to that applied in criminal cases should be applied in civil cases: *Woji v SANTAM Insurance Co Ltd* 1980 2 SA 971 (SE).
5 *R v Manda* supra 62–163.
6 *R v Manda* supra 163B.
7 *R v Manda* supra 163A–C.
8 *R v J* supra 94–95.
9 *R v J* supra 94–95.

10 *R v S* 1948 4 SA 419 (G) 422; *R v Sikurlite* 1964 3 SA 151 (SR). See Hollely and Müller (1999) 20 *Obiter* 368 regarding the need for court preparation in the case of a child witness. See also Struwig 2001 *THRHR* 596 on a "commonsense approach" in evaluating the evidence of a child witness. For the general principles with regard to the use of intermediaries for child witnesses in terms of the Criminal Procedure Act 51 of 1977 s 170A(1) see S v *Stefaans* [1999] 1 All SA 191 (C); 1999 1 SACR 182 (C). The Criminal Procedure Act 51 of 1977 s 170A makes provision for an intermediary if direct testimony would expose a child witness to undue mental stress or suffering; proof on a balance of probabilities is required: *S v F* 1999 1 SACR 571 (C).

833 Sexual crimes The accusations of the victim of a sexual offence are viewed with suspicion mainly because the victim is usually emotionally affected,[1] but also for other reasons such as the possibility that an innocent person may be blamed because of the person's financial standing[2] or that consent to intercourse may be concealed, when the fact of intercourse is discovered, by pretending that it was forced.[3] The trial court has to warn itself of the danger of convicting on the uncorroborated evidence of the complainant.[4] Evidence that the complainant was indeed the victim of a sexual offence will usually be sufficient, but if there is a possible motive to implicate the wrong person it may be necessary to find evidence showing the accused's involvement.[5] However, like the cautionary rules for accomplices and children, this rule does not necessarily require corroboration in the above sense.[6] It can be satisfied by other factors such as the accused's failure to testify;[7] and ultimately it is the applicable standard of proof that determines whether the court should convict.[8]

Where there are a number of complainants the possibility that they may have influenced each other should be borne in mind.[9]

The general cautionary rule in offences of a sexual nature that complainants in sexual cases are more untruthful than complainants in other cases has been abolished.[10]

1 *R v Rautenbach* 1949 1 SA 135 (A) 143; *R v J* 1966 1 SA 88 (SRA) 92. In *S v D* 1992 1 SA 513 (Nm) the Namibian High Court held that the cautionary rule in sexual offences discriminates against women complainants and that it has no rational basis for its existence; only one rule applies, namely, whether the accused's guilt has been proved beyond reasonable doubt.

2 *R v W* 1949 3 SA 772 (A) 780.
3 *R v J* supra 93E. See also *S v F* 1989 3 SA 847 (A).
4 *R v Rautenbach* supra; *R v W* supra. See *S v S* 1990 1 SACR 5 (A). See also Illsey (2002) 15 *SACJ* 225, *S v M* 2002 2 SACR 411 (SCA) and *Myeni v S* [2002] 3 All SA 599 (A); 2002 2 SACR 411 (SCA) on sexual history evidence.

5 *R v W* supra. See also *S v Van der Ross* 2002 2 SACR 362 (C).

6 *R v J* supra.

7 *S v Snyman* 1968 2 SA 582 (A) 588–589. But see also *R v W* supra 781 per Watermeyer CJ: "No doubt . . . it is permissible for a court to convict in these sexual cases even where there is no corroboration of the complainant and even where the accused has given evidence and has not been proved to be a lying witness."

8 *S v Snyman* supra.

9 *S v R* 1977 1 SA 9 (T) 15G.

10 *J v S* [1998] 2 All SA 267 (SCA); 1998 2 SA 984 (SCA); *S v J* 1998 4 BCLR 424 (SCA); 1998 2 SA 984 (SCA). See also *S v Jackson* 1998 4 BCLR 424 (SCA); 1998 1 SACR 470 (SCA); *S v M* 1999 2 SACR 548 (SCA); *S v K* 2000 4 BCLR 405 (NmS).

834 Civil cases involving sexual misconduct In both seduction and paternity cases it has been held that the fact of sexual intercourse with the defendant cannot be proved by the uncorroborated evidence of the plaintiff.[1] It has also been stated in regard to paternity cases that the corroboration must take the form of some evidence in addition to the woman's which, in some degree, is consistent with her story and inconsistent with the innocence of the defendant,[2] but the latter requirement may set too high a standard.[3] Be that as it may, "corroboration" has been found in an offer of settlement;[4] a false denial, or false statement by the defendant about one of the surrounding facts;[5] and in his reaction when accused of paternity.[6] The above rule is applicable only when the defendant denies his misconduct under oath.[7]

The rule does not imply that a higher standard is to be applied than the usual standard of proof on a balance of probabilities.[8]

Where adultery is in issue corroboration is also usually sought, though this appears not to be an absolute requirement.[9] The modern approach is rather that, though there are moral and legal sanctions against adultery, so that a court will not easily be convinced that it has taken place, it can be inferred from the facts in the same way as other *facta probanda*.[10]

1 *Scholtemeyer v Potgieter* 1916 TPD 188 190; *Wiehman v Simon* 1938 AD 447 450; *Maharaj v Parandaya* 1939 NPD 239 241; *Davel v Swanepoel* 1954 1 SA 383 (A) 388–389; *Perumal v Naidoo* 1975 3 SA 901 (N) 902. Cf *R v W* 1949 3 SA 772 (A) 780. The courts should no longer, as a matter of *law*, insist upon corroboration of the evidence of complainants in paternity or seduction cases. As a rule of *practice* the trial court should always warn itself of the inherent danger of acting upon the testimony of the complainant: *Mayer v Williams* 1981 3 SA 348 (A).

2 *Mackay v Ballot* 1921 TPD 430 432; *Wiehman v Simon* supra.

3 See the comments in *R v W* supra 779; *Davel v Swanepoel* supra 388H; *S v Snyman* 1968 2 SA 582 (A) 589E.

4 *Van der Berg v Elzbeth* (1884) 3 SC 36.

5 *De Klerk v Drake* 1920 CPD 511; *Van der Merwe v Nel* 1929 TPD 551 558.

6 *Jacobs v Henning* 1927 TPD 324. For an exposition on these and other precedents, see *Davel v Swanepoel* supra 389.

7 *Blesse v Brock* 1948 2 SA 756 (N) 758.

8 *Moodley v Gramani* 1967 1 SA 118 (N) 120; *Mountford v Mukukumidzi* 1969 2 SA 56 (RA).

9 See eg *Welthagen v Welthagen* 1921 WLD 79; *Manser-Henrey v Manser-Henrey* 1927 WLD 28; *Mans v Mans* 1946 WLD 167; *Miles v Miles* 1949 2 SA 360 (D); *Towert v Towert* 1956 1 SA 429 (W) 432; *Manser v Manser* 1958 1 SA 399 (SR).

10 See generally the approach to this factual issue by the Appellate Division in *Smit v Arthur* 1976 3 SA 378 (A) 384.

835 Police traps and private detectives A trap, like an accomplice,[1] is, because of his or her involvement in the offence, in a strong position to provide damaging evidence. A trap's possible motive for misusing this advantage, however, differs from that of the accomplice: it lies in the fact that a trap is expected, and sometimes paid, to provide evidence for the state.[2] A trap is not a neutral witness. Consequently his or her evidence is viewed with suspicion.[3]

Material corroboration is usually,[4] though not, it would appear, invariably,[5] required. The danger implicit in a trap's evidence can, for example, be sufficiently reduced if he or she is observed by another witness[6] or if marked money is used,[7] but there are no fixed rules that have to be complied with. Each case has to be judged on its merits.[8]

Because a private detective has a similar interest in procuring damaging evidence, his or her evidence is also viewed with a measure of suspicion. Formal corroboration is not required, but the evidence is treated with caution.[9]

The Law Commission has recommended in a report that the trapping system be retained in South Africa but subjected to greater judicial control. The American defence of entrapment should not be incorporated into our law, but the system should be controlled by the acceptance of an exclusionary rule. The following factors must be considered when deciding whether evidence is improperly obtained:

(a)   whether any fundamental right in respect of the accused is infringed;

(b)   whether the accused is incited, instigated or persuaded to commit the offence;

(c)   any unlawful conduct relating to the setting of the trap on the part of any person involved in the trap;

(d)   whether at the time of the setting of the trap there is a reasonable suspicion that the accused has engaged in the kind of conduct at which he or she is intended to be caught;

(e)   whether there is manipulation of the accused's personal, economic or professional circumstances in order to increase the probability of an offence being committed;

(f)   any other factor which in the opinion of the court ought to be taken into account.[10]

1   Although a trap, in a sense, participates in the offence, he or she is not an accomplice: *R v Ndimangele* 1913 CPD 708; *S v Ganie* 1967 4 SA 203 (N) 211F; *S v Tsochlas* 1974 1 SA 565 (A) 574C.

2   *R v Littlejohn* 1912 TPD 781 783; *R v Sassin* 1919 AD 485; *R v Maharaj* 1947 2 SA 65 (A) 69; *R v Vlok & Vlok* 1954 1 SA 203 (SWA). Other possible motives are mentioned in *S v Chesane* 1975 3 SA 172 (T); *S v Mabaso* 1978 3 SA 5 (O) 10.

3   Though only if the trap induced or enticed the accused to commit the alleged offence: *S v Azov* 1974 1 SA 808 (T); cf *S v Pallis* 1976 1 SA 235 (RA) 237E.

4   *R v Kinsella* 1919 EDL 78.

5   *R v Boyd* 1947 3 SA 43 (C) 48; *R v Omar* 1948 1 SA 76 (T); *S v Mabaso* supra.

6   *R v Littlejohn* supra. The courts will, however, take into account that it is not always possible to keep a trap under observation: *R v Horwitz* 1913 EDL 277 280.

7   *Myers & Misnum v R* 1907 TS 760; *R v Oosthuizen* 1922 EDL 341; *S v Mabaso* supra.

8   *R v Omar* supra; *R v Katz* 1959 3 SA 408 (C) 413F; *S v Chesane* supra 173F–G.

9   *Van Vuuren v Van Vuuren* 1931 GWL 42; *Preen v Preen* 1935 NPD 138. See also *S v Dube* [2000] 1 All SA 41 (N); 2000 6 BCLR 685 (N); 2000 2 SA 583 (N); 2000 1 SACR 53 (N).

10   In *S v Nortje* [1996] 4 All SA 449 (C); 1996 SACR 308 (C) it was held that the cautionary rule applicable to police traps and informers has to be applied and that where the police act improperly, a balance has to be struck between the protection of society and the protection of the individual by excluding evidence which brings the administration of justice into disrepute.

836 Entrapment The setting of traps and undercover operations is regulated, as well as the determination of whether evidence so obtained will be admissible.

Any law enforcement officer, official of the state or any other person so authorised for such purpose (hereinafter referred to as an official or his or her agent) may make use of a trap or engage in an undercover operation in order to detect, investigate or uncover the commission of an offence, or to prevent the commission of any offence, and the evidence so obtained will be admissible if that conduct does not go beyond providing an opportunity to commit an offence.[1] However where the conduct goes beyond providing an opportunity to commit an offence, a court may admit evidence so obtained.[2][3]

In considering whether the conduct goes beyond providing an opportunity to commit an offence, the court must consider the following factors:

(a) whether prior to the setting of the trap or the use of an undercover operation, approval, if it was required, was obtained for the attorney-general to engage such investigative methods and the extent to which the instructions or guidelines issued by the attorney-general were adhered to;[4]

(b) the nature of the offence under investigation, including:

(i) whether the security of the state, the safety of the public, the maintenance of public order or the national economy is seriously threatened thereby;

(ii) the prevalence of the offence in the area concerned; and

(iii) the seriousness of the offence;[5]

(c) the availability of other techniques for the detection, investigation or uncovering of the commission of the offence or its prevention in the particular circumstances of the case and of the area concerned;[6]

(d) whether an average person who was in the position of the accused would have been induced into the commission of the offence by the kind of conduct employed by the official or his or her agent concerned;[7]

(e) the degree of persistence and number of attempts made by the official or his or her agent before the accused succumbed and committed the offence;[8]

(f) the type of inducement used, including the degree of deceit, trickery, misrepresentation or reward;[9]

(g) the timing of the conduct, in particular whether the official or his or her agent instigated the commission of the offence or became involved in an existing unlawful activity;[10]

(h) whether the conduct involved an exploitation of human characteristics such as emotions, sympathy or friendship or an exploitation of the accused's personal, professional or economic circumstances in order to increase the probability of the commission of the offence;[11]

(i) whether the official or his or her agent has exploited a particular vulnerability of the accused such as a mental handicap or a substance addiction;[12]

(j) the proportionality between the involvement of the official or his or her agent as compared to that of the accused, including an assessment of the extent of the harm caused or risked by the official or his or her agent as compared to that of the accused, and the commission of any illegal acts by the official or his or her agent;[13]

(k) any threats, implied or expressed, by the official or his or her agent against the accused;[14]

(l) whether, before the trap was set or the undercover operation was used, there existed any suspicion, entertained upon reasonable grounds, that the accused had committed an offence similar to that to which the charge relates;[15]

(m) whether by the official or his or her agent acted in good or bad faith;[16]

(n) any other factor which in the opinion of the court has a bearing on the question.[17]

If a court in any criminal proceedings finds that in the setting of a trap or the engaging of an undercover operation the conduct goes beyond providing an opportunity to commit an offence, the court may refuse to allow such evidence to be tendered or may refuse to allow such evidence already tendered, to stand, if the evidence was obtained in an improper or unfair manner and if the admission of such evidence would render the trial unfair or would otherwise be detrimental to the administration of justice.[18] When considering the admissibility of the evidence the court must weight up the public interest against the personal interest of the accused, having regard to the following factors, if applicable:

(a)   the nature and seriousness of the offence, including:

(i)   whether it is of such a nature and of such an extent that the security of the state, the safety of the public, the maintenance of public order or the national economy is seriously threatened thereby;[19]

(ii)   whether, in the absence of the use of a trap or an undercover operation, it would be difficult to detect, investigate or uncover it or to prevent its commission;[20]

(iii)   whether it is so frequently committed that special measures are required to detect, investigate or uncover it or to prevent its commission;[21] or

(iv)   whether it is so indecent or serious that the setting of a trap or the engaging of an undercover operation was justified;[22]

(b)   the extent of the effect of the trap or undercover operation upon the interests of the accused, if regard is had to:

(i)   the deliberate disregard, if at all, of the accused's rights or any applicable legal or statutory requirements;[23]

(ii)   the facility, or otherwise, with which such requirements could have been complied with, having regard to the circumstances in which the offence was committed;[24]

(iii)   the prejudice to the accused resulting from any improper or unfair conduct;[25]

(c)   the nature and seriousness of any infringement of any fundamental right contained in the Constitution;[26]

(d)   whether in the setting of a trap or the engagement of an undercover operation the means used were proportional to the seriousness of the offence;[27] and

(e)   any other factor which in the opinion of the court ought to be taken into account.[28]

A Director of Public Prosecutions may issue general or specific guidelines regarding the supervision and control of traps and undercover operations, and may require any official or his or her agent to obtain his or her written approval in order to set a trap or to engage in an undercover operation at any place within his or her area of jurisdiction, and in connection therewith to comply with his or her instructions, written or otherwise.[29]

An official or his or her agent who sets or participates in a trap or an undercover operation to detect, investigate or uncover or to obtain evidence of or to prevent the commission of an offence, must not be criminally liable in respect of any act which constitutes an offence and which relates to the trap or undercover operation if it was performed in good faith.[30] No prosecution for such an offence will be instituted against an official or his or her agent without the written authority of the attorney-general.[31]

If at any stage of the proceedings the question is raised whether evidence should be excluded in terms of section 252A(3) of the Criminal Procedure Act, the burden of proof to show, on a balance of probabilities, that the evidence is admissible, will rest upon the prosecution.[32] However, the accused must furnish the grounds on which the admissibility of the evidence is challenged.[33] Moreover, if the accused is not represented, the court must raise the question of the admissibility of the evidence.[34] The question whether evidence should be excluded in terms of section 252A(3) may, on application by the accused or the prosecution, or by order of the court of its own accord, be adjudicated as a separate issue in dispute.[35]

1 Criminal Procedure Act 51 of 1977 s 252A(1).
2 Subject to the provisions of s 252A(3).
3 S 252A(1) proviso.
4 S 252A(2)(a).
5 S 252A(2)(b).
6 S 252A(2)(c).
7 S 252A(2)(d).
8 S 252A(2)(e).
9 S 252A(2)(f).
10 S 252A(2)(g).
11 S 252A(2)(h).
12 S 252A(2)(i).
13 S 252A(2)(j).
14 S 252A(2)(k).
15 S 252A(2)(l).
16 S 252A(2)(m).
17 S 252A(2)(n).
18 S 252A(3)(a).
19 S 252A(3)(b)(i)(aa).
20 S 252A(3)(b)(i)(bb).
21 S 252A(3)(b)(i)(cc).
22 S 252A(3)(b)(i)(dd).
23 S 252A(3)(b)(ii)(aa).
24 S 252A(3)(b)(ii)(bb).
25 S 252A(3)(b)(ii)(cc).
26 Constitution of the Republic of SA 108 of 1996: Criminal Procedure Act 51 of 1977 s 252A(3)(b)(iii). See Naude 2001 *SACJ* 38 on the constitutionality of evidence relating to police traps.
27 S 252A(3)(b)(iv).
28 S 252A(3)(b)(v).
29 S 252A(4).
30 S 252A(5)(a).
31 S 252A(5)(b).
32 S 252A(6).
33 S 252A(6) proviso 1.
34 S 252A(6) proviso 2.
35 S 252A(7).

837 Identification Judicial experience has shown that evidence of identity should, particularly in criminal cases, be treated with great care. Even an honest witness is capable of identifying the wrong person with confidence.[1] Consequently, the witness should be thoroughly examined about the factors influencing his or her identification, such as the build, features, colouring and clothing of the person identified.[2] An early identification before the trial (which is admissible as an exception to the rule prohibiting previous consistent statements)[3] lends credibility to the evidence.[4] Particular care should be taken if the only evidence connecting the accused with the crime is that of a single identifying witness; then the cautionary rule relating to single witnesses should also be taken into account.[5]

1 *R v Masemang* 1950 2 SA 488 (A) 493; *R v Shekelele* 1953 1 SA 636 (T) 638. *S v Jochems* 1991 1 SACR 208 (A); *S v Zitha* 1993 1 SACR 718 (A); *Thebus v S* [2002] 3 All SA 781 (SCA); 2002 2 SACR 566 (SCA); *Ketani v S* [2002] 3 All SA 15 (C).
2 *R v Shekelele* supra. The type of questions that should be asked may vary, depending upon the circumstances of each case: *S v Mehlape* 1963 2 SA 29 (A) 32H. See also, generally, *R v Dladla* 1962 1 SA 307 (A) 310; *S v Sibanda* 1969 2 SA 345 (T) 349; *S v Mthetwa* 1972 3 SA 766 (A) 768.

3 See Zeffertt *Evidence* 403 et seq and Schmidt *Bewysreg* 397 et seq on this concept.
4 *R v Y* 1959 2 SA 116 (W) 119. It stands to reason that the questioning should then focus on the earlier identification: *S v Mehlape* supra. For a discussion of the reliability of an identification made from a photograph, see *S v Shandu* 1990 1 SACR 80 (N). Regarding the weight of an identification made in court, see *Matwa v S* [2002] 3 All SA 715 (E); *S v Matwa* 2002 2 SACR 350 (E).
5 *R v T* 1958 2 SA 676 (A).

838 Claims against deceased estates Claims against deceased estates are treated with caution because the estate is usually unable to confirm or deny the authenticity of the claim. However, the requirement is no higher than that applied in any case where interested evidence is given against somebody who is not in a position to answer it.[1]

1 *Wood v Estate Thompson* 1949 1 SA 607 (D) 614; *Borcherds v Estate Naidoo* 1955 3 SA 78 (A); *Cassel & Benedick v Rheeder & Cohen* 1991 2 SA 846 (A).

BURDEN OF PROOF

839 Distinction between burden of proof and evidential burden The burden or onus of proof determines the result if at the end of the trial the evidence is so evenly balanced that the court is unable to come to a definite conclusion. In order to convict, the evidence must establish the guilt of the accused beyond a reasonable doubt, which will be so only if there is no reasonable possibility that an innocent explanation, which has been put forward, might be true; this test must be established upon a consideration of all the evidence.[1] The party bearing the burden on any particular issue then fails to establish its claim or defence, as the case may be. This burden, which is a matter of substantive law and is determined by the pleadings, must be distinguished from the purely evidential burden of combating the opponent's evidence. The former is fixed at the commencement of the trial as soon as the issues are determined and is not shifted during the course of the trial: the latter arises as soon as the evidence casts on a litigant the risk of failure and may shift in the course of the trial as the risk shifts from one party to the other.[2]

A court does not base its decision whether to convict or acquit on only a portion of the evidence; the decision has to take into account all the evidence.[3]

1 *Vengatsamy v Scheepers* 1946 NPD 84 85; *Van Aswegen v De Clercq* 1960 4 SA 875 (A) 882E; *Twigger v Starweave (Pty) Ltd* 1969 4 SA 369 (N) 372B–C; *S v Van der Meyden* 1999 2 SA 79 (W); 1999 1 SACR 447 (W); *S v Sithole* 1999 1 SACR 585 (W).

2 *Tregea v Godart* 1939 AD 16 28; *Klaassen v Benjamin* 1941 TPD 80 85; *Pillay v Krishna* 1946 AD 946 952. See also *Woerman & Schutte v Masondo* [2002] 2 All SA 53 (SCA); 2002 1 SA 811 (SCA).

3 *S v Van Aswegen* 2001 2 SACR 97 (SCA).

840 Burden of proof of issues Where there are several issues in a case, there are separate burdens in relation to such issues and these will not necessarily rest upon the same party. The burden of any particular issue does not shift, but it is possible that the one burden will not arise until the other has been discharged.[1] In the case of mutually exclusive versions given in evidence, the plaintiff will only succeed if he or she satisfies the court on a preponderance of probabilities that the version is true and accurate and therefore acceptable and the other version is false and mistaken and falls to be rejected, taking into account the general probabilities.[2]

1 *Klaassen v Benjamin* 1941 TPD 80 85; *Pillay v Krishna* 1946 AD 946 952; *Heneke v Royal Insurance Co Ltd* 1954 4 SA 606 (A) 611.

2 *Baring Eiendomme Bpk v Roux* [2001] 1 All SA 399 (A).

841 Burden of proof on appeal In an appeal on a factual issue the court of appeal is at a disadvantage in that, unlike the trial court, it is unable to see and hear the witnesses and is not steeped in the atmosphere of the trial. Consequently, in the absence of a misdirection on fact by the trial judge, the presumption is that his or her conclusion is correct. The appellate court will only reverse the conclusion if it is convinced that it is wrong, and in this sense it may be said that there is an onus on the appellant.[1]

Where the court *a quo* has reached no finding at all on the credibility of witnesses to vitally important incidents, the appellate tribunal has to do its best on such material as it has before it. If the tribunal is unable to come to a definite decision on this material, the ordinary burden of proof becomes decisive.[2]

Similarly, when there has been a misdirection by the court *a quo*, the appellate tribunal is at large to disregard the reasons affected by the misdirection and to come to its own conclusion on the evidence (and credibility findings) unaffected by the misdirection;[3] if it is unable to arrive at a definite conclusion, it must apply the burden of proof.[4]

1 *Rex v Haefele* 1938 2 PH F180 (SWA); *Annama v Chetty* 1946 AD 142 149; *R v Dhlumayo* 1948 2 SA 677 (A); *R v Mtembu* 1950 1 SA 670 (A) 688; *Protea Assurance Co Ltd v Casey* 1970 2 SA 643 (A) 648D–E.

2 *Van Aswegen v De Clercq* 1960 4 SA 875 (A) 881–882; *Rautenbach v Fourie* 1977 4 SA 276 (T) 281; *Blysaag (Edms) Bpk v Theron* 1978 2 SA 624 (A) 627.

3 *R v Dhlumayo* supra and *R v Parker* 1958 2 SA 639 (A) 645 read with *S v Tuge* 1966 4 SA 565 (A) 568 and *S v Yusuf* 1968 2 SA 52

(A) 57; and see *Twigger v Stanveave (Pty) Ltd* 1969 4 SA 369 (N) 372–373. If a trial court misdirects itself as to where the onus lies, the court of appeal must nonetheless have regard to the court *a quo*'s findings regarding credibility in so far as these findings are not affected by its view of the onus in order to determine whether the party who actually bore the onus has discharged it: *S v Tshoko* 1988 1 SA 139 (A).

4 *Twigger v Stanveave (Pty) Ltd* supra.

842 Right to begin The burden of proof determines the sequence of evidence. The general rule in civil proceedings is that the party bearing the burden on the pleadings first adduces evidence, followed by his or her opponent. It would, however, probably be more accurate to speak in this connection of the party bearing the evidential burden.[1]

In criminal proceedings the state always begins.

The sequence of evidence is dealt with more fully above.[2]

1 *Mobil Oil Southern Africa (Pty) Ltd v Mechin* 1965 2 SA 706 (A) 710F. See also *Smith's Trustee v Smith* 1927 AD 482 487; *Munsamy (also known as Naidu) v Gengemma* 1954 4 SA

468 (N); *Groenewald v Minister van Justisie* 1972 3 SA 596 (O).

2 Par 773 ante.

843 Incidence in civil trials The basic rule is that the person who asserts must prove – because if one person claims something from another in a court of law, he or she has to satisfy the court that he or she is entitled to it.[1] Therefore the plaintiff normally bears the burden of proof in a civil trial. But it also not infrequently occurs that in respect of some of the issues, or even the sole issue, before the court, the defendant avers and the plaintiff denies. Then the defendant bears the burden of proving such issue(s).[2] The rule is therefore sometimes stated in the form that the person who makes the *positive* assertion (whether the plaintiff or defendant) must prove the facts so asserted. However, this basic rule is not invariably applied: where a negative assertion can be said to be an essential element of a party's claim or defence, that party will have the burden of proving it.[3]

When the defendant raises a special defence, in other words when the defendant does not deny the plaintiff's allegations but raises a fresh issue (when he or she confesses and avoids), then *quoad* that defence the defendant bears the burden of proof.[4] Thus when the plaintiff sues upon a promissory note payable on demand which is on the face of it unconditional and the defendant sets up a condition precedent that the note was only to become payable upon failure by him or her to fulfill certain obligations, the onus of proving the existence of the condition lies on the defendant.[5]

While the burden of proof is often cast upon the party against whom a presumption of law operates,[6] a presumption of fact can only affect the evidential burden.[7]

When a party has peculiar knowledge of a fact he or she is not for that reason saddled with the burden of proving that fact: peculiar knowledge affects the quantum of evidence expected from the party but does not affect the incidence of the burden of proof.[8] If such party fails to adduce evidence, in other words to transmit his or her knowledge to the court, the inference which is the least favourable to the party's cause may be drawn from the proven facts.[9]

In the final analysis the rules determining the incidence of the burden of proof rest "for their ultimate basis upon broad and undefined reasons of experience and fairness".[10]

1 *Pillay v Krishna* 1946 AD 946. Thus the person who impeaches a will must prove its invalidity: *Kunz v Swart* 1924 AD 618; *Tregea v Godart* 1939 AD 16; *Smith v Strydom* 1953 2 SA 799 (T) 803A. The person who relies on a contract must prove its existence and its terms: *Dave v Birrell* 1936 TPD 192; *Myers v Lesch* 1954 2 SA 487 (C) 490A; *Stewart v Zagreb Properties (Pvt) Ltd* 1970 4 SA 542 (R). And the onus rests on the party who avers that there was negligence (*Administrator, Natal v Stanley Motors Ltd* 1960 1 SA 690 (A) 701); that someone was mentally defective (*Pheasant v Warne* 1922 AD 481; *Ken Barnard Motor & Bandediens (Edms) Bpk v Pretorius* 1970 4 SA 712 (T)); that the court lacks jurisdiction (*Durban City Council v Kadir* 1971 1 SA 364 (N)); that a condition in a title deed should be deleted (*Swiss Hotels (Pty) Ltd v Pedersen* 1966 1 SA 197 (C); *Kleyn v Theron* 1966 3 SA 264 (T)); that a sum of money has been paid (*Pillay v Krishna* supra); that novation has taken place (*Desai v Inman & Co* 1971 1 SA 43 (N)); that it has duly performed its obligations under a contract (*Electra Home Appliances (Pty) Ltd v Five Star Transport (Pty) Ltd* 1972 3 SA 583 (W)), and so on. See *Vasco Dry Cleaners v Twycross* 1979 1 SA 603 (A), where the burden of proof rested throughout on the plaintiff to prove the terms of the contract, but where there rested an evidential burden on the defendant to rebut a *prima facie* case raised by the production of the contract admittedly signed by the parties. See also *Stocks & Stocks (Pty) Ltd v TJ Daly & Sons (Pty) Ltd* 1979 3 SA 754 (A).

2 Eg in *Pheasant v Warne* supra; *Durban City Council v Kadir* supra; *Pillay v Krishna* supra.

3 *Kriegler v Minitzer* 1949 4 SA 821 (A) 828; *Wessels v Wessels* 1950 3 SA 852 (O) 857C–D; *Pretorius v Van der Merwe* 1968 2 SA 259 (N); *Stocks & Stocks (Pty) Ltd v TJ Daly & Sons (Pty) Ltd* supra.

4 *Pillay v Krishna* supra 951–952.

5 *Pillay v Krishna* supra. Thus the defendant who admits the existence of a hire-purchase contract, but states that he or she had no knowledge that it was ceded by the other party to the plaintiff, must prove this statement (*Trust Bank van Afrika Bpk v Oosthuizen* 1962 2 SA 307 (T)); and the burden rests on the defendant who admits that a lease has, on the face of it, expired, but alleges that it was extended (*De Villiers v Pyott* 1947 1 SA 381 (C)); or that he or she has exercised an option to purchase (*Smith v Singandi* 1972 4 SA 439 (R)); who admits a contract of insurance, but alleges that the claimant (plaintiff) committed a breach of warranty (*Gangat v (1) The Licences & General Insurance Co Ltd, (2) SA National Trust & Assurance Co Ltd (2)* 1933 NPD 261; *Merchandise Exchange (Pty) Ltd v Eagle Star Insurance Co Ltd* 1962 3 SA 113 (C)); who admits a breach of contract and resultant damages, but alleges that the plaintiff failed to take reasonable steps to limit the damages (*Hazis v Tvl & Delagoa Bay Investment Co Ltd* 1939 AD 372 388; *Dykes v Gavanne Investments (Pty) Ltd* 1962 1 SA 16 (T)); or who states that a claim had become prescribed (*Groenewald v Minister van Justisie* 1972 3 SA 596 (O)). But when the defendant pleads that the plaintiff agreed to repair the defendant's motor-car without charge (*Dave v Birrell* supra) – or that the building which the plaintiff erected had to include a balcony and a staircase (*Kriegler v Minitzer* supra) – then the defnedant is not raising a special defence but traversing the plaintiff's cause of action in that he or she disputes the terms of the contract upon which the plaintiff relies. See also *Nel v Nelspruit Motors (Edms) Bpk* 1961 1 SA 582 (A); *Eaton & Louw v Arcade Properties (Pty) Ltd* 1961 4 SA 233 (T); *Bowden v Fouche* 1969 4 SA 201 (NC); *Pretorius v Van der Merwe* supra; *Topaz Kitchens (Pty) Ltd v*

Naboom Spa (Edms) Bpk 1976 3 SA 470 (A) 474; *Stocks & Stocks (Pty) Ltd v TJ Daly & Sons (Pty) Ltd* supra.

6 Thus the onus lies upon the party who seeks to rebut the presumption of ownership arising from the possession of a thing (*Zandberg v Van Zyl* 1910 AD 302; cf *Ruskin v Thiergen* 1962 3 SA 737 (A)); or the presumption that a will which is regular on the face of it, is valid (*Kunz v Swart* supra; *Sterban v Dixon* 1968 1 SA 322 (C)); or the presumption that a spinster is a virgin (*Cranfield v Hoey* 1932 CPD 265); or that every person is sane (*Pheasant v Warne* supra; *R v Kennedy* 1951 4 SA 431 (A)). However, it will still be a moot question whether a presumption of law necessarily determines the incidence of the burden of proof. The question was left undecided in *Tregea v Godart* supra 32–33 and *Nydoo v Vengtas* 1965 1 SA 1 (A) 21H. In *Myers v Lesch* supra it was held that the presumption against a donation does not transfer to the defendant the onus of finally satisfying the court about the nature of the transaction, where the defendant claims that it was in fact a donation. *Vasco Dry Cleaners v Twycross* supra; *Stocks & Stocks (Pty) Ltd v TJ Daly & Sons (Pty) Ltd* supra.

7 Eg the presumption of fact which arises when *res ipsa loquitur. Arthur v Bezuidenhout & Mieny* 1962 2 SA 566 (A); *Groenewald v*

Conradie, Groenewald v Auto Protection Insurance Co Ltd 1965 1 SA 184 (A); *Sardi v Standard & General Insurance Co Ltd* 1977 3 SA 776 (A) 780D.

8 *Abrath v The North Eastern Railway Co* (1883) 11 QB 440; *Union Government (Minister of Railways) v Sykes* 1913 AD 156; *Molteno Bros v SA Railways* 1936 AD 321 333; *Naude v Tvl Boot & Shoe Manufacturing Co* 1938 AD 379 392; *Durban City Council v SA Board Mills Ltd* 1961 3 SA 397 (A) 405A; *Gericke v Sack* 1978 1 SA 821 (A) 827E. The same rule applies in criminal cases: *R v Cohen* 1933 TPD 128; *Rex v Hoffman* 1941 OPD 65; *S v Theron* 1968 4 SA 61 (T) 63; *S v Langeveldt* 1969 1 SA 577 (T) 581H; *S v Witbooi* 1971 4 SA 138 (NC) 140–141.

9 *Galante v Dickinson* 1950 2 SA 460 (A) 465; *Botes v Van Deventer* 1966 3 SA 182 (A) 1888; *Henry v SANTAM Insurance Co Ltd* 1971 1 SA 468 (C) 472–473.

10 Wigmore *Evidence* par 2486, quoted with approval in *Pillay v Krishna* supra 954 and *Nydoo v Vengtas* supra 21H. In *Malahe v Minister of Safety & Security* [1998] 4 All SA 246 (SCA); 1999 1 SA 528 (SCA) the court held that the question whether a party has discharged the onus depends firstly on whether or not that party's version is more probable that that of the other party.

844 Incidence in criminal trials The basic principle that the person who avers must prove, as well as the presumption of innocence,[1] cast on the state the burden of proving every element of the crime including the act,[2] the unlawfulness thereof,[3] the accused's criminal capacity[4] and the accused's intention.[5] Statutory provisions apart, the only exception recognised under common law was that of a defence of "insanity": the accused would have to prove his or her own insanity on a balance of probability.[6] With the introduction of an administrative rather than a judicial inquiry procedure by the Criminal Procedure Act[7] for the determination of mental illness or mental defect in relation to both criminal capacity and the capacity to stand trial, this exception will probably no longer apply because the courts tend to avoid the device of a formal onus in administrative and related proceedings.

Although the state has the burden of disproving a defence such as necessity or automatism not caused by a mental defect, the burden does not operate until the defence has been put in issue.[8]

The general rule that the state bears the burden of proof applies only to the issue of the accused's guilt or innocence; the accused has to prove extenuating circumstances.[9]

1 *R v Benjamin* (1883) 3 EDC 337.

2 This includes the fact that it was the accused who committed the crime and that, eg the accused's alibi was fictitious: *R v Biya* 1952 4 SA 514 (A); *R v Hlongwane* 1959 3 SA 337 (A) 340–341. In *R v Motomane* 1961 4 SA

569 (W) it was stated that the accused has to establish any interruptions of the causal chain relied upon by him or her, but this *dictum* was criticised in *R v Mabole* 1968 4 SA 811 (R) 815. For the application of the maxim *res ipsa loquitur*, see *S v Mudoti* 1986 4

SA 278 (ZS).

3 Thus the state must prove the absence of justifiable self-defence (*R v Kaukakani* 1947 2 SA 807 (A) 814; *R v Zikalala* 1953 2 SA 568 (A); *R v Patel* 1959 3 SA 121 (A); *Ex parte die Minister van Justisie: In re S v Van Wyk* 1967 1 SA 488 (A); *S v Motleleni* 1976 1 SA 403 (A)); of necessity (*R v Britz* 1949 3 SA 293 (A) 302), of compulsion (*R v Samuel* 1960 4 SA 702 (SR); *S v Mtwetwa* 1977 3 SA 628 (E)) and of consent (*S v D* 1963 3 SA 263 (E)).

4 Thus the state must prove the absence of provocation (*R v Kaukakani* supra 814; *R v Thibani* 1949 4 SA 720 (A); *R v Kennedy* 1951 4 SA 431 (A) 438; *R v Krull* 1959 3 SA 392 (A); *S v Mangondo* 1963 4 SA 160 (A)); or that the accused had capacity despite his or her youth (*R v K* 1956 3 SA 353 (A); *S v M* 1978 3 SA 557 (TkSC)); or must negative a defence of drunkenness (*R v Taylor* 1949 4 SA 702 (A); *R v Huebsch* 1953 2 SA 561 (A); *R v Pethla* 1956 4 SA 605 (A)). Cf *S v M* 1979 4 SA 564 (B), where despite the prosecution's failure to prove criminal capacity in an accused less than 14 years of age, the court was entitled to look at the evidence as a whole to decide whether the presumption of incapacity had been rebutted.

5 *R v Ndhlovu* 1945 AD 369; *R v Mkize* 1951 3 SA 28 (A); *R v Horn* 1958 3 SA 457 (A); *S v Ndhlela* 1964 4 SA 703 (N) 706E; *S v Marshall* 1967 1 SA 171 (O) 175A.

6 *R v Ndhlovu* supra; *R v Kaukakani* supra; *R v*

Kennedy supra; *R v Von Zell* 1953 3 SA 303 (A). Where a defence of automatism or irresistible impulse is raised, the onus would probably be on the accused only if the automatism or impulse could be said to result from insanity; cf *R v Ahmed* 1959 3 SA 776 (W); *R v Rossouw* 1960 3 SA 326 (T); *R v H* 1962 1 SA 197 (A); *S v Van Zyl* 1964 2 SA 113 (A); *S v Bezuidenhout* 1964 2 SA 651 (A); *S v Piccione* 1967 2 SA 334 (N); *S v Trickett* 1973 3 SA 526 (T); *S v Burger* 1975 2 SA 601 (C) 609A. Where the state relies upon insanity, the state has the burden of proof: *R v Holliday* 1924 AD 250. Where the accused's insanity is investigated to determine his or her ability to stand trial, the burden would also rest upon the state under common law: *S v Ebrahim* 1973 1 SA 868 (A).

7 51 of 1977. In *Ellish v Prokureur-Generaal, Witwatersrandse Plaaslike Afdeling* 1994 5 BCLR 1 (W); 1994 4 SA 835 (W); 1994 2 SACR 579 (W) 259 the majority of the court decided since the Constitution had invested the presiding officer with a discretion with regard to bail: "in the interests of justice", this required a value judgment and there could be no question of a burden of proof.

8 *R v Thibani* supra (provocation); *S v Trickett* supra (sane automatism).

9 *R v Lembete* 1947 2 SA 603 (A); *S v Mdletshe* 1978 4 SA 75 (A); *S v Mienies* 1978 4 SA 560 (A) 563.

845 Statutory provisions There are numerous statutory provisions which expressly or by implication affect the incidence of the burden of proof.

An enactment to the effect that a fact is presumed unless the contrary is proved casts the onus in respect of that fact on the party against whom the presumption operates; but a presumption operating "in the absence of *evidence* to the contrary" only requires evidence, not proof, to counteract the presumption.[1] The latter effect is also achieved by a provision stipulating that evidence of one fact constitutes *prima facie* evidence or *prima facie* proof of another fact.[2]

A deeming provision, like an irrebuttable presumption, is usually a matter of substantive law: the fact that is deemed to exist cannot be refuted;[3] but some deeming provisions – those which stipulate that a fact must be deemed to exists unless the contrary is proved – have the same effect as a rebuttable presumption casting the burden on the party seeking to establish the contrary.[4]

In criminal proceedings the accused has to put in issue and prove any statutory "exception, exemption, proviso, excuse or qualification" which would exonerate him or her from criminal liability.[5] In addition, any person charged with an offence based upon the fact that that person carried on any occupation or business, performed any act, owned or had in his or her possession or custody or used any article or was present at or entered any place, has the burden of proving that he or she had the required authority in the form of a licence, permit, permission or other authority or qualification.[6]

When the state prosecutes a person for the commission of a statutory offence, it discharges its burden when the evidence brings the case *prima facie* within the terms of the enactment, and it then lies upon the accused to prove any other fact which would render the accused not guilty,[7] except that the state will have to prove *mens rea* where it is an ingredient of the offence.[8]

1   *R v Epstein* 1951 1 SA 278 (O).

2   *R v Epstein* supra 285. See also *Ex parte the Minister of Justice: In re R v Jacobson & Levy* 1931 AD 466; *R v Abel* 1948 1 SA 654 (A); *R v Ismail* 1952 1 SA 204 (A) 208H; *R v Jones* 1956 3 SA 208 (G); *R v Chizah* 1960 1 SA 435 (A) 442; *W v W* 1976 2 SA 308 (W) 315; *S v Ngoala* 1979 2 SA 212 (T). For a different interpretation (of s 28(1) of the Bills of Exchange Act 34 of 1964, which states that every party whose signature appears on a bill is *prima facie* deemed to have become a party thereto for value), see *Nelson v Marich* 1952 3 SA 140 (A). For the requirements of a referral to the Constitutional Court in the case of a reverse onus provision, see *S v Friedland* 1996 8 BCLR 1049 (W); 1996 1 SACR 114 (W). There is no rule of positive law that gives a statement of account any status in law since it does not constitute *prima facie* proof of the contents: *Van Rhyn v Telkom SA Bpk* [1996] 4 All SA 273 (T).

3   See eg *R v Van der Merwe* 1960 1 SA 565 (C) 567–568; *Pinkey v Race Classification Board* 1968 4 SA 628 (A) 637.

4   See eg *S v Mkize* 1975 1 SA 517 (A) 520; *S v Ngwenya* 1979 2 SA 96 (A).

5   Criminal Procedure Act 51 of 1977 s 90. As to what is an exception, exemption, proviso, excuse or qualification, see *R v Kula* 1954 1 SA 157 (A); *R v Shangase* 1960 1 SA 734 (A); *S v Gumede* 1969 3 SA 616 (T); *S v Ndomase* 1976 2 SA 47 (C) 48. S 90 is also likely to come under constitutional scrutiny following the decision in *S v Zuma* 1995 4 BCLR 401 (CC); 1995 2 SA 642 (CC); 1995 1 SACR 568 (CC), although the court confined its remarks to s 217(1)(b)(ii) of the Criminal Procedure Act 51 of 1977.

6   S 250 of the Criminal Procedure Act. See also Schmidt *Bewysreg* 68–69.

7   *R v Tolson* (1889) 23 QB 168 175; *R v Wallendorf* 1920 AD 383 401; *R v H* 1944 AD 121; *R v Britz* 1949 3 SA 293 (A); *R v Canestra* 1951 2 SA 317 (A); *R v Tsotsi* 1956 2 SA 782 (A); *R v H* 1962 1 SA 197 (A).

8   As regards *culpa*: *S v Fouche* 1974 1 SA 96 (A) 101 102; as regards *dolus*: *S v De Blom* 1977 3 SA 513 (A) 532 (though there may be some room for doubt whether *S v De Blom* supra went so far as to state a general principle, thereby overruling contrary older decisions). See also *S v Mohapi* 1977 4 SA 796 (O).

846 Standards of proof Where the plaintiff first adduces evidence the defendant may at the close of the plaintiff's case apply for absolution from the instance and this is granted if there is not sufficient evidence upon which a reasonable person could find for the plaintiff.[1] If absolution is to be averted, the plaintiff's evidence would therefore have to carry the potential for finding in the plaintiff's favour. This would not be the case if his or her evidence, though covering all the issues, were an utter fabrication[2] or too vague and contradictory to serve as proof.[3]

Similarly, at the close of the state's case in a criminal trial the accused may apply for his or her discharge on the ground that there is no evidence that he or she committed the offence referred to in the charge or any offence of which he or she may be convicted on the charge.[4] It has been held that the court may refuse to discharge the accused if it considers it possible that the case for the state may be strengthened by evidence adduced by the defence.[5]

At the close of the trial a different standard is applied. The question then is not what a reasonable court *could* or *might* find on the evidence, but what it *ought* to find.[6] The exact measure depends upon whether the court is concerned with civil or criminal proceedings. In civil proceedings proof is furnished upon a preponderance of probability;[7] and this is the case even when allegations of criminal or immoral conduct are to be proved.[8] However, in certain applications, for example for a temporary interdict[9] or for an attachment *ad fundandum iurisdictionem*,[10] the applicant only has to establish a *prima facie* case. In criminal proceedings, on the other hand, the state has to prove its allegations beyond reasonable doubt. This means that the accused is entitled to an acquittal if there is a reasonable possibility that the accused's version of the facts, if it would establish his or her innocence, is true.[11] But where the accused, and not the state, bears the burden of proof, the accused merely has to prove his or her case on a preponderance of probability; this means that the accused's version of the facts has to be more probable than that of the state.[12]

1 *Gascoyne v Paul & Hunter* 1917 TPD 170 173; *Gafoor v Unie Versekeringsadviseurs (Edms) Bpk* 1961 1 SA 335 (A) 340; *Supreme Service Station (1969) (Pvt) Ltd v Fox & Goodridge (Pvt) Ltd* 1971 4 SA 90 (RA); *Claude Neon Lights (SA) Ltd v Daniel* 1976 4 SA 403 (A) 409H. See also *S v V* 2000 1 SACR 453 (SCA).

2 *Katz v Bloomfield & Keith* 1914 TPD 379 381; *Theron v Behr* 1918 CPD 443; *Hodgkinson v Fourie* 1930 TPD 740 745; *Ruto Flour Mills (Pty) Ltd v Adelson (2)* 1958 4 SA 307 (T) 309.

3 *Ruto Flour Mills (Pty) Ltd v Adelson (2)* supra 309 with reference to *Shenker Bros v Bester* 1952 3 SA 664 (A) (the latter case was, however, concerned with the assessment of evidence at the close of the trial).

4 A successful application leads to a finding of not guilty: s 174 of the Criminal Procedure Act 51 of 1977. The discharge of the accused under this section can so result from the initiative of the prosecutor or the court itself: *R v Mkize* 1960 1 SA 276 (N), referring to the equivalent section in the preceding Criminal Procedure Act 56 of 1955. See generally *S v Heller (2)* 1964 1 SA 524 (W) 541; *S v Ngcube* 1976 1 SA 341 (N) 343; *S v Cooper* 1976 2 SA 875 (T) 890; *S v Ostilly* 1977 2 SA 104 (D) 106.

5 *R v Kritzinger* 1952 2 SA 401 (W); *Ruto Flour Mills (Pty) Ltd v Adelson (2)* supra 310. Sed quaere: *R v Herholdt (3)* 1956 2 SA 722 (W); *R v Mall (1)* 1960 2 SA 340 (N); *S v Heller (2)* supra; *S v Bouwer* 1964 3 SA 800 (O).

6 See the cases cited in fn 1 supra and *Ruto Flour Mills (Pty) Ltd v Adelson (2)* supra 309.

7 *Wildebeest v Geldenhuis* 1911 TPD 1050; *West Rand Estates Ltd v New Zealand Insurance Co Ltd* 1925 AD 245 262–263; *International Tobacco Co (SA) Ltd v United Tobacco Co (South) Ltd (1)* 1955 2 SA 1 (W) 13–14. See *National Employers' General Insurance Co Ltd v Jagers* 1984 4 SA 437 (E). Note that the expression "balance of probability (probabilities)" is also used.

8 Although it has been said that in such cases clear and satisfactory evidence must be adduced, there is no variation in the standard of proof required: "The requirement is still proof sufficient to carry conviction to a reasonable mind, but the reasonable mind is not so easily convinced in such cases because in a civilized community there are moral and legal sanctions against immoral and criminal conduct": *Gates v Gates* 1939 AD 150 155. See also *Cape Coast Exploration Ltd v Scholtz* 1933 AD 56; *Mine Workers' Union v Brodrick* 1948 4 SA 959 (A) 980; *Senior v Commissioner for Inland Revenue* 1960 1 SA 709 (A); *Ebrahim (Pty) Ltd v Mahomed* 1962 1 SA 90 (D); *Hepner v Roodepoort-Maraisburg Town Council* 1962 4 SA 772 (A); *Van Deventer v Van Deventer* 1962 3 SA 969 (N) 971–972; *Tvl & OFS Chamber of Mines v Hukki* 1964 2 SA 518 (T); *Yassen v Yassen* 1965 1 SA 438 (N) 442; *Moodley v Gramani* 1967 1 SA 118 (N) 120A; *Pretorius v Smith* 1971 4 SA 459 (T) 461A; *Olivier v Die Kaapse Balieraad* 1972 3 SA 485 (A) 496; *Kudo v Cape Law Society* 1977 4 SA 659 (A) 676. See *Maritime & General Insurance Co v Sky Unit Engineering (Pty) Ltd* 1989 1 SA 867 (T).

9 *Webster v Mitchell* 1948 1 SA 1186 (W) 1189 read with *Gool v Minister of Justice* 1955 2 SA 682 (C) 688E. See also *Sing & Co (Pty) Ltd v Pietermaritzburg Local Road Transportation Board* 1959 3 SA 822 (N); *Barnett v Cape Town Foreshore Board* 1960 4 SA 439 (C) 444–445; *Freinkel v Garment Workers Union of SA* 1961 1 SA 507 (W) 509; *Meyer v Netherlands Bank of SA Ltd* 1961 1 SA 578 (G) 581; *Epsom Motors (Pty) Ltd v Estate Winson* 1961 1 SA 687 (E) 693; *Selected Products Ltd v Enterprise Bakeries (Pty) Ltd* 1963 1 SA 237 (C) 240; *Wezel v Kimberley Municipality* 1963 1 SA 363 (G) 370; *Van Wyk v Steyn* 1963 4 SA 814 (G) 823; *Gosschalk v Rossouw* 1966 2 SA 476 (C) 489. However, if the application

is for a final interdict, the facts should be es-
tablished upon a preponderance of probabil-
ity: *Fourie v Uys* 1957 2 SA 125 (C); *Cape
Tex Engineering Works (Pty) Ltd v SAB Lines
(Pty) Ltd* 1968 2 SA 528 (C); *De Villiers v
Soetsane* 1975 1 SA 360 (E) 362; *Beukes v
Crous* 1975 4 SA 215 (NC).

10 *Bradbury Gretorex Co (Colonial) Ltd v
Standard Trading Co (Pty) Ltd* 1953 3 SA 529
(W) read with *Cochran v Miller* 1965 1 SA
162 (D) 163; *Yorigami Maritime Construction
Co Ltd v Nissho-Iwai Co Ltd* 1977 4 SA 682

(C) 687.

11 *R v Difford* 1937 AD 370 373; *R v Ndhlovu*
1945 AD 369 386; *R v M* 1946 AD 1023
1027; *S v Glegg* 1973 1 SA 34 (A) 38–39.
The standard does not vary according to the
seriousness of the crime: *S v Sinkankanka*
1963 2 SA 531 (A) 541. See *S v Ntele* 1998
2 SACR 178 (SCA).

12 *Ex parte Minister of Justice: In Re Rex v Bolon*
1941 AD 345; *Rex v Kaukakani* 1947 2 SA
807 (A); *S v Mdingi* 1979 1 SA 309 (A).

ASSESSMENT OF EVIDENCE

847 Circumstantial evidence The assessment of circumstantial or presumptive
evidence, namely evidence from which inferences are drawn about facts in issue, is in
a criminal case governed by two rules which flow logically from the standard of proof
applicable to such cases. These are: (a) the inference sought to be drawn must be
consistent with all the proved facts; (b) the proved facts should be such that they
exclude every reasonable inference from them save the one to be drawn.[1] In applying
these rules, however, it is necessary to look at the totality of the evidence adduced in
support of an inference: it is not each proved fact which must exclude all other inferences, but the facts as a whole.[2]

When an inference is drawn from circumstantial evidence in a civil case, the first
rule mentioned above is applicable (the inference must be consistent with all the
proved facts), but the second rule is not. The conclusion need not be the only reasonable one: it is sufficient if it is the more natural or plausible conclusion from amongst
several conceivable ones.[3]

1 *R v Blom* 1939 AD 188 202–203. See also
R v Magatuse 1941 AD 201; *Van Duyker v
District Court Martial* 1948 4 SA 691 (A) (applied to conviction by court martial); *S v
Dlodlo* 1966 2 SA 401 (A). See *S v Mtsweni*
1985 1 SA 590 (A) where the court pronounced a cautionary note against attaching
too much weight to untruthful evidence
when drawing an inference regarding an accused's guilt; untruthful evidence or a false
statement does not always justify an inference that the accused is guilty; the weight
given to such untruths must be related to the
circumstances of each case.

2 *R v De Villiers* 1944 AD 493; *R v Mtembu* 1950
1 SA 670 (A) 679; *R v Sacco* 1958 2 SA 349
(N); *R v Hlongwane* 1959 3 SA 337 (A) 340;
S v Shepard 1967 4 SA 170 (W); *S v Snyman*
1968 2 SA 582 (A) 589; *S v De Bruyn* 1968

4 SA 498 (A) 507. The requirement that the
court should look at the totality of the evidence and not employ a "piecemeal" process
of reasoning is also applicable to civil proceedings: *Grobbelaar v Havenga* 1964 3 SA
522 (N) and the cases cited (527). See also
S v Mashiane 1998 2 SACR 664 (NC); *S v
Mokgiba* 1999 1 SACR 534 (O).

3 *Govan v Skidmore* 1952 1 SA 732 (N) 734;
Ex parte Holden 1954 4 SA 128 (N); *Mer-
chand v Butler's Furniture Factory* 1963 1 SA
885 (N); *Ocean Accident & Guarantee Corp
Ltd v Koch* 1963 4 SA 147 (A) 159; *SAR &
H v Dhlamini* 1967 2 SA 203 (D); *Smit v Ar-
thur* 1976 3 SA 378 (A) 386; *AA Onderlinge
Assuransie-Assosiasie Bpk v De Beer* 1982 2 SA
603 (A); *Maritime & General Insurance Co v
Sky Unit Engineering (Pty) Ltd* 1989 1 SA 867
(T); *S v Van As* 1991 2 SACR 74 (W).

848 Demeanour The demeanour of a witness when the witness delivers his or her
evidence is an important factor in assessing the credibility of the witness.[1] But its
importance should not be exaggerated and it should always be considered in conjunction with the surrounding circumstances, inferences and other factors affecting the

probabilities.[2] Its usefulness as a guide to credibility diminishes when the witness is a member of another race,[3] is masked[4] or gives evidence through an interpreter.[5]

1 It can be the determining factor: *R v Abels* 1948 1 SA 706 (O) 708. Consequently a court of appeal will rarely upset a finding on credibility by a trial court: *R v Dhlumayo* 1948 2 SA 677 (A) 696 et seq; *Merchand v Butler's Furniture Factory* 1963 1 SA 885 (N) 890. Cf pars 781 786 ante. Over-emphasis of the advantages which the trial court enjoyed in assessing the credibility of a witness must be avoided: *Munster Estates (Pty) Ltd v Killarney Hills (Pty) Ltd* 1979 1 SA 621 (A).

2 *Estate Kaluza v Braeuer* 1926 AD 243

266–267; *R v Abels* supra 708. See also *R v Masemang* 1950 2 SA 488 (A) 495; *S v Dladla* 1974 2 SA 689 (N) 690–691; *Germani v Herf* 1975 4 SA 887 (A) 903; *S v Van Tellingen* 1992 2 SACR 104 (C); *Body Corporate of Dumbarton Oaks v Faiga* [1999] 1 All SA 229 (SCA); 1999 1 SA 975 (SCA).

3 Cf *Patel v Patel* 1946 CPD 46.

4 *S v Mgengwana* 1964 2 SA 149 (C).

5 *R v Kohlinfila Qwabe* 1939 AD 255 264; *S v Gandu* 1981 1 SA 997 (Tk).

849 False evidence The fact that a witness has told a lie does not mean that his or her evidence will inevitably be rejected *in toto*. All the circumstances have to be taken into account because it is possible that there may be some innocent reason for the untruth or that the remainder of the witness's evidence may not be tainted.[1] And it does not necessarily mean that the contrary of what the witness has said is the truth.[2] But if the accused in a criminal trial takes the risk of giving false evidence, he or she may forego the opportunity of establishing a defence or a mitigating factor which would otherwise be open to him or her.[3]

In certain circumstances a lie, whether told in or out of court, may be a fact from which a fact in issue can be inferred; it is often indicative of a guilty state of mind.[4] But the court should always be on its guard against the intrusion of any idea that a party should lose its case as a penalty for perjury.[5]

1 *R v Nel* 1937 CPD 327 330; *Maharaj v Parandaya* 1939 NPD 239 243; *R v Du Plessis* 1944 AD 314 323; *S v Letsoko* 1964 4 SA 768 (A) 776; *S v Oosthuizen* 1982 3 SA 571 (T); *S v Ndlovu* 1983 4 SA 507 (ZS); *S v Mkohle* 1990 1 SACR 95 (A).

2 *R v Weinberg* 1939 AD 71 80.

3 *R v Mlambo* 1957 4 SA 727 (A) 738C; *S v Nkomo* 1966 1 SA 831 (A) 833; *S v Rama* 1966 2 SA 395 (A) 400–401; *S v Mnguni* 1966 3 SA 776 (T) 778.

4 *Nolte v Rowe* 1926 TPD 615; *R v Simon*

1929 TPD 328; *Van der Merwe v Nel* 1929 TPD 551; *Poggenpoel v Morris* 1938 CPD 90; *Maharaj v Parandaya* supra 251; *R v Blom* 1939 AD 188. The fact that a false statement has been made is, however, normally used only as corroborative evidence, or as "makeweight", which can, in addition to other evidence, serve to tip the scales against the party who made the false statement: *R v Gani* 1958 1 SA 102 (A) 113; *R v T* 1958 2 SA 676 (A) 677E.

5 *Goodrich v Goodrich* 1946 AD 390 396.

850 Failure to give or lead evidence Where there is direct evidence in a criminal trial that the accused committed the crime, the accused's failure to testify (whatever the reason) in general *ipso facto* tends to strengthen the state case, since there is no testimony to contradict it and therefore less occasion or material for doubting it;[1] but it must also be borne in mind that uncontradicted evidence is not necessarily acceptable evidence – a principle which applies in both civil[2] and criminal cases,[3] but is of greater importance in criminal cases where the failure to testify is that of the accused.

Before the interim Constitution[4] came into being, the failure to testify may have led the court to draw an inference of guilt. The 1996 Constitution[5] now guarantees the right to a fair trial, which includes the fundamental right of the accused to remain silent after arrest, not to be compelled to make a confession and not to be a compellable witness against him or herself. In *S v Zuma*[6] these were all connected with the presumption of innocence, which means that a conviction should not follow in spite of a reasonable doubt. Kentridge AJ applied the so-called "two stage" Canadian approach, first finding that a fundamental right of the accused had been infringed, and secondly that this could not be justified in terms of section 33 of the Constitution. This presumption of innocence probably entails that no inference of guilt may be drawn from the silence of the accused alone. The fact that the state evidence stands uncontroverted, as explained in the previous paragraph, is probably not covered by the presumption of innocence, but any inference from the silence of the accused should not be added to the fact of uncontroverted evidence to strengthen the state's case even further.

In civil cases the failure to adduce or give evidence is usually looked upon as a strong indication that such evidence would be to the detriment of the party concerned.[7] Consequently it would entitle the court to select from alternative inferences that which favours the opposite party.[8] But this principle does not apply when the inference sought to be drawn is less probable than the other;[9] or when the opposite party's case is so weak that it does not call for a reply;[10] or when other evidence has been given which would lead the party to believe that what he or she has offered would suffice.[11] If both parties could have been expected to call a witness and refrained from doing so, the inference can be drawn against both of them though it may be stronger against the one than the other.[12]

The failure to testify can only be a factor in the case if the opposing party has adduced evidence calling for a reply. The accused's omission to enter the witness box cannot, for instance, serve to supply a deficiency in the case for the state.[13]

1 *S v Nkombani* 1963 4 SA 877 (A) 893G; *S v Snyman* 1968 2 SA 582 (A) 588G; *S v Mthetwa* 1972 3 SA 766 (A) 769. Cf the inference disadvantageous to an accused which may be drawn from the accused's failure to explain the basis of his or her defence in terms of the Criminal Procedure Act 51 of 1977 s 115; *S v M* 1979 4 SA 1044 (B); 1979 *THRHR* 214.

2 *Nelson v Marich* 1952 3 SA 140 (A) 149; *Shenker Bros v Bester* 1952 3 SA 664 (A) 670; *Sigournay v Gillbanks* 1960 2 SA 552 (A) 558; *Minister of Justice v Seametso* 1963 3 SA 530 (A) 534–535; *Da Mata v Otto* 1972 3 SA 858 (A) 869.

3 *S v Gokool* 1965 3 SA 461 (N) 469F; *S v Francis* 1991 1 SACR 198 (A).

4 Consitution of the Republic of SA 200 of 1993 s 242; now see ss 35(3) and 36 of the Constitution of the Republic of SA 108 of 1996.

5 S 35(3) of the 1996 Constitution.

6 1995 4 BCLR 401 (CC); 1995 2 SA 642 (CC); 1995 1 SACR 568 (CC).

7 *Sampson v Pim* 1918 AD 657 662; *Elgin Fireclays Ltd v Webb* 1947 4 SA 744 (A) 750; *Hairman v Wessels* 1949 1 SA 431 (O) 438; *Gleneagles Farm Dairy v Schoombee* 1949 1 SA 830 (A) 840; *Durban City Council v SA Board Mills Ltd* 1961 3 SA 397 (A) 405; *Kock v SKF Laboratories (Pty) Ltd* 1962 3 SA 764 (E); Rosseau v Viljoen 1970 3 SA 413 (C) 416.

8 *Galante v Dickinson* 1950 2 SA 460 (A) 465.

See also *Minister of Justice v Seametso* supra 535H; *Henry v SANTAM Insurance Co Ltd* 1971 1 SA 468 (C) 472–473; *Marine & Trade Insurance Co Ltd v Van der Schyff* 1972 1 SA 26 (A); *Roxa v Mtshayi* 1975 3 SA 761 (A) 769A.

9 *Labuschagne v Stadsraad van Johannesburg* 1967 4 SA 99 (W) 104; *Sampies v Bay Passenger Transport Ltd* 1971 3 SA 577 (A) 580.

10 *Putter v Provincial Insurance Co Ltd* 1963 3 SA 145 (W) 150; *Labuschagne v Stadsraad van Johannesburg* supra 103–104; *Tshabalala v Southern Insurance Association Ltd* 1976 2 SA 381 (C) 383; *Munster Estates (Pty) Ltd v Killarney Hills (Pty) Ltd* 1979 1 SA 621 (A); *Mpapeea v Rondalia Versekeringskorporasie van SA Bpk* 1979 2 SA 967 (O).

11 *Rand Cold Storage & Supply Co Ltd v Alligianes* 1968 2 SA 122 (T) 124E; *Shield Insurance Co Ltd v Theron* 1973 3 SA 515 (A) 517E–F.

12 *Webranchek v LK Jacobs & Co Ltd* 1948 4 SA 671 (A) 682; *Gleneagles Farm Dairy v Schoombee* supra 840; *Brand v Minister of Justice* 1959 4 SA 712 (A) 715H; *Lederman v Moharal Investments (Pty) Ltd* 1969 1 SA 190 (A) 200. See also *Botes v Van Deventer* 1966 3 SA 182 (A) 186H 187A 188D–G; *Rosseau v Viljoen* supra 416D; *Magagula v Senator Insurance Co Ltd* 1980 1 SA 717 (N).

13 *S v Masia* 1962 2 SA 541 (A) 546; *S v Miles* 1978 3 SA 407 (N) 413.

BIBLIOGRAPHY

Abbreviations

Acta Juridica	–	Cape Town Juta 1958–
Annual Survey	–	*Annual Survey of South African Law* Cape Town Juta 1948–
Camb LJ	–	*The Cambridge Law Journal* London Stevens & Sons 1921–
Clean Air Journal	–	Pretoria National Association for Clean Air 1973–
Codicillus	–	Pretoria Faculty of Law University of South Africa 1960–
CILSA	–	*Comparative and International Law Journal of Southern Africa* Pretoria Institute of Foreign and Comparative Law University of South Africa 1968–
Consultus	–	*Consultus: South African Bar Journal* Pretoria General Council of the Bar of South Africa 1988–
De Jure	–	Pretoria Fakulteit Regsgeleerdheid Universiteit van Pretoria 1968–
De Rebus	–	Pretoria The South African Attorneys' Journal Association of Law Societies of the Republic of South Africa 1979–
ILJ		*Industrial Law Journal* Cape Town Juta 1980–
Journal of African Law	–	London University of London School of Oriental and African Studies 1957–
JBL	–	*Juta's Business Law* Cape Town Juta 1993–
The Law Quarterly Review	–	London Stevens 1885–
The Magistrate	–	Johannesburg Magistrate's Association of South Africa 1965–
McGill Law Journal	–	Montreal Students of the Faculty of Law of McGill University 1952–
Modern Law Review	–	London Stevens 1937–
SAJELP	–	*South African Journal of Environmental Law and Policy* Pietermaritzburg School of Law University of Natal 1994–
SAJHR	–	*South African Journal on Human Rights* Cape Town Juta 1985–
SALJ	–	*South African Law Journal* Cape Town Juta 1901–
SA Merc LJ	–	*South African Mercantile Law Journal* Cape Town Juta 1989–
SAPL	–	*South African Public Law* Durban Butterworths 1986–
Stell LR	–	*Stellenbosch Law Review* Cape Town Juta 1990–
THRHR	–	*Tydskrif vir Hedendaagse Romeins-Hollandse Reg* Durban Butterworths 1937–

American Jurisprudence Vol 28 Estoppel and Waiver 2 ed Rochester NY The Lawyers Co-operative Publishing Company 1966

Arhchbold, JF *Pleading, Evidence and Practice in Criminal Cases* 44 ed Richardson, Thomas London Sweet & Maxwell

Ashby, KP "Acid Rain: Solution or Dissolution?" 1987 *SAPL* 140

Barnard, CE "Regsmaatstawwe by die Beoordeling van Projekte wat die Omgewing kan Benadeel" (1992) 55 *THRHR* 35

Barnard, D "Die Toepassing van die 1989-Omgewingsbewaringswet" 1990 *De Rebus* 832

Barrie, GN "International Law and the Safe Transport of Hazardous Material" 1990 *TSAR* 426

Barrie, GN "'n Geloofwaardige Getuie?" 1967 *Codicillus* 44

Baxter, LG "Civil Litigation and Jura Novit Curia" (1979) 96 *SALJ* 531

Bekker, JC "Judisiële Kennisname van Bantoereg en -gewoonte" (1976) 39 *THRHR* 359

Bekker, PM "S v Klaasen 1978 1 SA 355 (K)" (1978) 41 *THRHR* 207

Binder, DF *Hearsay Handbook* 2 ed New York Mcgraw-Hill 1983

Boberg, PQR *Law of Delict Vol 1 Aquilian Liability* Cape Town Juta 1984

Boberg, PQR "Liability for Nervous Shock" 1973 *Annual Survey* 136

Boberg, PQR *The Law of Persons and the Family* Cape Town Juta 1977

Boegman, N "Progress in the Application of Part II of the Atmospheric Pollution Prevention Act" 1972 *Clean Air Journal* 9

Botha, L *South African Urban Solid Waste Legislation and its Application: Proposals Towards Reform* MA Thesis Cape Town University of Cape Town 1988

Bothma, J du P and Glavovic, PD "Wild Animals" In Fuggle, RF and Rabie, MA (eds) *Environmental Management in South Africa* Cape Town Juta 1992

Bower, GS *The Law of Actionable Misrepresentation* 3 ed Turner London Butterworths 1974

Bower, GS *The Law Relating to Estoppel by Representation* 3 ed London Butterworths 1977

Bray, E "Fragmentation of the Environment: Another Opportunity Lost for a Nationally Coordinated Approach?" 1995 *SAPL* 173

Bray, E "Jacobs v Waks from an Environmental Angle" 1992 *SAPL* 329

Bray, E "The Liberation of Locus Standi in the Interim Constitution: an Environmental Angle" (1994) 57 *THRHR* 481

Bray, E "The New Environment Conservation Act versus the Demands of Environmental Realities" 1990 *SAPL* 101

Bray, W "Locus Standi in Environmental Law" (1989) 22 *CILSA* 33

Brooks, PEJ "Negligent Behaviour by Attorneys and Damages for Psychological Shock" 1977 *De Rebus* 14

Building the Foundation for Sustainable Development in South Africa Pretoria CSIR Department of Environment Affairs 1992

Burchell, JM "Nervous or Emotional Shock" 1982 *Annual Survey* 176

Burchell, JM *Principles of Delict* Cape Town Juta 1993

Burchell, JM *The Law of Defamation in South Africa* Cape Town Juta 1985

Burger, JC "Die Wysgerige Grondslae van Omgewingsbewaring" 1991 *SAPL* 1

Burns, Y "Green Rights: Theory and Development in South Africa" in *South Africa in Transition: Green Rights and an Environmental Management System* Pretoria University of South Africa 1993

Burns, Y and Bray, E "Die Presidentsraadsverslag oor 'n Nasionale Omgewingsbestuurstelsel" 1992 *SAPL* 127

Campanella, J "Environmental Rights and the New Constitution" 1995 *JBL* 5

Christinaeus, P *Practicarum Quaestionum Rerumque in Supremis Belgarum Curiis Actarum et Observatorum Decisiones* Antwerpen 1626

Claasen, CL "The Admissibility of Evidence of Criminal Convictions in Adultery Cases" (1945) 62 *SALJ* 14

Cooper, WE *Landlord and Tenant* 2 ed Cape Town Juta 1994

Corbett, MM and Buchanan, JL *The Quantum of Damages in Bodily and Fatal Injury Cases* 2 ed Cape Town Juta 1964

Corbett, MM and Buchanan, JL *The Quantum of Damages in Bodily and Fatal Injury Cases: General Principles* 3 ed Gauntlett, J Cape Town Juta 1985

Corpus Juris Secundum Vol 31 Estoppel St Paul Minn West Publishing Company 1936

Cowen, DV *New Patterns of Land Ownership: The Transformation of the Concept of Ownership as Plena in re Potestas* Johannesburg DV Cowen 1984

Cowen, DV "Toward Distinctive Principles of South African Environmental Law: Some Jurisprudential Perspectives and a Role for Legislation" (1989) 52 *THRHR* 3

Cowen, Z and Carter, PB *Essays on the Law of Evidence* Westport Conn Greenwood Press 1973

Cowling, RM and Olivier, NJJ " Indigenous Plants" in Fuggle, RF and Rabie, MA (eds) Environmental Management in South Africa Cape Town Juta 1992

Cross, Sir R and Tapper, C *Cross on Evidence* 7 ed London Butterworth 1990

Cross, Sir R and Wilkins, N *Cross and Wilkins: Outline of the Law of Evidence* 6 ed London Butterworths 1986

Davel, T "Aanspreeklikheid vir Suiwer Finansiële Verlies" (1979) 42 *THRHR* 214

Davel, T "Greenfield Engineering Works (Pty) Ltd v NKR Construction (Pty) Ltd 1978 4 SA 901 (N)" (1979) 42 *THRHR* 214

Davids, J "Judgments as Evidence" (1968) 85 *SALJ* 74

Davids, J "State Privilege and Precedent in the Law of Evidence" (1967) 84 *SALJ* 245

De Groot, H *Inleidinge tot de Hollandsche Rechtsgeleerdheid* 2 ed Dovering Fischer Meijers Leiden Universitaire Pers 1965

De Groot, H *Inleydinge met Aenmerkingen van S Groenewegen van der Made met Latijnsche Aanteekingen door W Schorer* Middelburg Gillissen 1767

De Groot, H *Introduction to Dutch Jurisprudence, with an appendix containing selections from the notes of W Schorer translated by AFS Maasdorp* 3 ed Cape Town Juta 1903

De Villiers, JE *see also* Silke, J

De Villiers, JE and Macintosh, JC *The Law of Agency in South Africa* 2 ed Knight Cape Town Juta 1956

De Vos, W "No Enrichment Action for Improvements to Movables" (1974) 37 *THRHR* 308

De Vos, W *Verrykingsaanspreeklikheid in die Suid-Afrikaanse Reg* 3 ed Cape Town Juta 1987

De Vos, WLeR and Van der Merwe, SE "Hoorsê: Verlede, Hede en 'n Handves" (1993) 4 *Stell LR* 7

De Wet, JC *"Estoppel by Representation" in die Suid-Afrikaanse Reg* LLD Thesis Stellenbosch University of Stellenbosch 1939

De Wet, JC and Van Wyk, AH *Die Suid-Afrikaanse Kontrakereg en Handelsreg Vol 1 Kontraktereg* 5 ed Durban Butterworths 1992

Devine, DJ and Erasmus MG "International Environmental Law" in Fuggle, RF and Rabie, MA (eds) *Environmental Management in South Africa* Cape Town Juta 1992

Dlamini, CRM "Judicial Notice in the South African Law of Evidence" (2001) 34 *De Jure* 49

Dlamini, CRM "Presumptions in the South African Law of Evidence (1)" (2001) 64 *THRHR* 3

Dlamini, CRM "Presumptions in the South African Law of Evidence (2)" (2001) 64 *THRHR* 147

Dlamini, CRM "Presumptions in the South African Law of Evidence (3)" (2001) 64 *THRHR* 544

Eiselen, GTS "Elektroniese Datawerwisseling (EDV) en die Bewysreg" (1992) 55 *THRHR* 204

Eiselen, GTS "Herlewing van die Algemene Verrykingsaksie" (1992) 55 *THRHR* 124

Environmental Liability Andover Sweet & Maxwell 1993-

Ewart, K "Estoppel by Misrepresentation" in De Wet, JC *"Estoppel by Representation" in die Suid-Afrikaanse Reg* LLD Thesis Stellenbosch University of Stellenbosch 1939

First Report on the Situation of Waste Management and Pollution Control in South Africa Pretoria CSIR Department of Environment Affairs 1991

Fuggle, RF and Rabie, MA (eds) *Environmental Concerns in South Africa: Technical and Legal Perspectives* Cape Town Juta 1983

Fuggle, RF and Rabie, MA (eds) *Environmental Management in South Africa* Cape Town Juta 1992

Gaius *Institutiones: the Institutes of Gaius* Oxford Clarendon Press (2 Vols) 1958–1963

Gibson, JTR *South African Mercantile and Company Law* 6 ed Cape Town Juta 1988

Giliomee, JH and Glavovic, PD "Pesticides" in Fuggle, RF and Rabie, MA (eds) *Environmental Management in South Africa* Cape Town Juta 1992

Glavovic, PD "An Introduction to Wildlife Law" (1988) 105 *SALJ* 519

Glavovic, PD *Flora and the Law: A Review of Existing Laws that Protect Wild Plant Species in the Republic of South Africa* Kirstenbosch Claremont Botanical Society 1993

Glavovic, PD "Human Rights and Environmental Law: the Case for a Conservation Bill of Rights" (1988) 21 *CILSA* 53

Glavovic, PD "Persistent Pesticides: Elixirs of Death or Boon to Mankind?" (1985) 102 *SALJ* 674

Glavovic, PD "Some Thoughts of an Environmental Lawyer on the Implications of the Environmental Conservation Act 73 of 1989: A Case of Missed Opportunities" (1990) 107 *SALJ* 107

Glavovic, PD "The Legal Status of Wilderness: Aspects of the 1984 Forest Act" (1985) 102 *SALJ* 162

Glavovic, PD "The Need for Legislative Adoption of a Conservation Ethic" (1984) 17 *CILSA* 144

Glavovic, PD *Wilderness and the Law* PhD Thesis University of Natal Durban 1992

Glavovic, PD "Wilderness: Source or Resource? A Suggested Wilderness Act for South Africa" (1985) 18 *CILSA* 343

Glazewski, JI "A New Environment Conservation Act: An Awakening of Environmental Law?" 1989 *De Rebus* 872

Glazewski, JI "Admiralty – Historical Anachronism or a Bonus for Conservation in the Coastal Zone" 1986 *Acta Juridica* 193

Glazewski, JI "Environmental Law and a New South African Constitution Dispensation" 1994 *Environmental Liability* 16

Glazewski, JI "Environmental Provisions in a New South African Bill of Rights" 1993 *Journal of African Law* 177

Glazewski, JI "Regulating Transboundary Movement of Hazardous Waste: International Developments and Implications for South Africa" (1993) 26 *CILSA* 234

Glazewski, JI "The Environment and the Interim Constitution" 1994 *Consultus* 22

Glazewski, JI "The Environment and the New Interim Constitution" 1994 *SAJELP* 3

Glazewski, JI "The Environment, Human Rights and a New South African Constitution" (1991) 7 *SAJHR* 167

Gluck, CF *Ausführliche Erlauterung der Pandecten nach Hellfeld: ein Commentar* Erlangen Palm (43 Vols) 1797–1843

Gooderson, RN "Is the Prisoner's Character Indivisible?" 1953 *Camb LJ* 377

Gooderson, RN "Previous Consistent Statements" 1968 *Camb LJ* 64

Gordon, S *The Management of Nature Areas Declared in terms of Section 4(1)(b) of the Physical Planning Act 88 of 1967* LLM Thesis Johannesburg University of the Witwatersrand 1987

Groenewegen van der Made, S a De *De Legibus Abrogatis et Inusitatis in Hollandia Vicinisque Regionibus* Leiden 1649

Grotius *see* De Groot, H

Gurney, JJ McLachlan, IR Kirkley, MB and Glazewski, JI "Offshore Minerals" in Fuggle, RF and Rabie, MA (eds) *Environmental Management in South Africa* Cape Town Juta 1992

Hanks, J and Glavovic, PD "Protected Areas" in Fuggle, RF and Rabie, MA (eds) *Environmental Management in South Africa* Cape Town Juta 1992

Harvard, J "Reasonable Foresight of Nervous Shock" 1956 *Modern Law Review* 478

Havenga, P "Liability for Environmental Damage" 1995 *SA Merc LJ* 187

Hazardous Waste in South Africa see Noble, RG (ed)

Heumann, HG and Seckel, von E *Handlexicon zu den Quellen des romischen Rechts* Jena Fischer 1907

Heydon, JD *Cases and Material on Evidence* London Butterworth 1975

Hiemstra, VG *Suid-Afrikaanse Strafproses* 5 ed Durban Butterworths 1993

Hoffmann, LH *see* Zeffertt, D

Hoffmann, LH "In Memorium: The Hon Heinrich de Villiers" (1974) 91 *SALJ* 236

Hoffmann, LH "Similar Facts after Boardman" 1975 *Law Quarterly Review* 193

Hoogervorst, A "A Personal Perspective on the Environmental Conservation Act no 73 of 1989" 1989 *South African Journal of Aquatic Sciences* 250

Huber, U *Heedendaegse Rechtsgeleertheyt* 4 ed Amsterdam Johannes Rotterdam 1742

Hugo, JH "Hearsay: Statements made in the Presence of the Accused" (1971) 34 *THRHR* 403

Huldigingsbundel vir WA Joubert see Strauss, SA (ed)

Johnston, CJ "Noise" in Fuggle, RF and Rabie, MA (eds) *Environmental Management in South Africa* Cape Town Juta 1992

Joubert, CP "Die Fiduciarius se Verpligting om Verbetering aan te bring" (1960) 23 *THRHR* 11

Joubert, WA and Van der Walt, JC "Wentzel v SA Yster en Staalbedryfsvereniging en andere Wentzel v Blanke Motorwerkingsvereniging en 'n ander 1967 (3) SA 91 (T)" (1967) 30 *THRHR* 375

Justinian I, *Emperor of the East The Institutes of Justinian* 7 ed Sandars London Longmans Green 1903

Kahn, E "The Rules of Precedent Applied in South African Courts" (cont) (1967) 84 *SALJ* 43

Kahn, E "The Rules of Precedent Applied in South African Courts" (cont) (1967) 84 *SALJ* 175

Kahn, E "The Rules of Precedent Applied in South African Courts" (1967) 84 *SALJ* 308

Kaser, M *Das Romische Privatrecht* Beck 1955–1959

Katsch, ME *Law in a Digital World* Oxford Oxford University Press

Kerr, AJ *The Principles of the Law of Contract* 3 ed Durban Butterworths 1989

Kerr, AJ *The Law of Agency* 3 ed Durban Butterworths 1991

Kidd, M *An Evaluation of the Law Relating to Urban Solid Waste Management in South Africa* LLM Thesis University of Natal Durban 1995

Labuschagne, JMT "Actio Popularis, Omgewingsreg en Regte van die Natuur" 1994 *SAPL* 458

Lampaert, LJEM-C, *De Wetgeving Betreffende de Natuurgebieden in Zuid-Afrika* LLM Thesis University of Port Elizabeth 1982

Lamprecht, CM and Van Den Heever, M "'n Praktiese Benadering tot die Wet op Rekenaargetuienis 57 van 1983" (1990) 25 *The Magistrate* 3

Le Roux, PR, van As, D, Burns, YM, De Beer, GP and van der Merwe, MG "Radiation" in Fuggle, RF and Rabie, MA (eds) *Environmental Management in South Africa* Cape Town Juta 1992

Liefsting, FBC *Algemeene Beginselen van de Leer der Rechtsgeldigheid van Verbintenissen uit Overeenkomst* Den Haag 1890

Lombard, R, Botha, L and Rabie, MA "Solid Waste" in Fuggle, RF and Rabie, MA (eds) *Environmental Management in South Africa* Cape Town Juta 1992

Lotz, J and Visser, D "Wouter de Vos – A Tribute" 1992 *Acta Juridica* Preface

Louw, JW "Estoppel en die Rei Vindicatio" (1975) 38 *THRHR* 218

Lusher, JA and Ramsden, HT "Water Pollution" in Fuggle, RF and Rabie, MA (eds) *Environmental Management in South Africa* Cape Town Juta 1992

Lyster, R "A Critical Analysis of the Proposed National Environmental Management System" (1995) 28 *CILSA* 228

Lyster, R "'Protected Natural Environments': Difficulties with Environmental Land Use Regulation and Some Thoughts on the Property Clause" (1994) 27 *De Jure* 136

Lyster, R "The Protection of Environmental Rights" (1992) 109 *SALJ* 518

May, HJ *South African Cases and Statutes on Evidence* 4 ed Cape Town Juta 1962

Mayr, R von *see* von Mayr, R

McQuoid-Mason, DJ "Emotional Shock: Shades of Descartes?" (1975) 92 *SALJ* 18

McQuoid-Mason, DJ "Emotional Shock – Why the Cartesian Distinction?" (1973) 36 *THRHR* 115

Meij, GV and Rabie, MA "Noise Control and the Law" (1974) 7 *CILSA* 84

Meintjies-Van der Walt, L "Cross-Examination of Expert Witnesses" 2001 *De Rebus* 22

Meintjies-Van der Walt, L "Dealing with DNA-Evidence: S v Maqhina 2001 (1) SACR 241 (T)" (2001) 14 *SACJ* 378

Mendelowitz, M "The 'Parol Evidence Rule' and Suspensive Conditions in Contract" (1978) 95 *SALJ* 32

Midgley, JR "The Role of Foreseeability in Psychiatric Injury Cases" (1992) 55 *THRHR* 441

Millin, P and Wille, G *Wille and Millin's Mercantile Law of South Africa* 18 ed Coaker and Zeffertt (eds) Johannesburg Hortors 1984

Millner, MA "Liability for Emotional Shock" (1975) 92 *SALJ* 263

Mullany, NJ and Handford, PR *Tort Liability for Psychiatric Damage: The Law of "Nervous Shock"* North Ryde NSW Law Book Company Sweet & Maxwell 1993

Nagel, CJ and Roesteoff, M "Verrykingsaanspraak van Bankier na Betaling van Afgelaste Tjek" (1993) 56 *THRHR* 486

Neethling, J *Persoonlikheidsreg* 3 ed Durban Butterworths 1991

Neethling, J and Potgieter, JM "Bester v Commercial Union Versekeringsmaatskappy van SA BPK 1973 I SA 769 (A)" (1973) 36 *THRHR* 175

Neethling, J, Potgieter, JM and Visser, PJ *The Law of Delict* 2 ed Durban Butterworths 1994

Nienaber, PM "Iets oor Verdiskontering, Estoppel en Borgtog" (1964) 27 *THRHR* 262

Nienaber, PM "Nogmaals Verdiskontering en Estoppel" (1966) 29 *THRHR* 51

Noble, RG (ed) *Hazardous Waste in South Africa* (5 Vols) Pretoria Department of Environment Affairs 1992

O'Dowd, AP *The Law of Evidence in South Africa* Cape Town Juta 1963

Olivier, PJJ "Promissory Estoppel in English and South African Law" (1971) 88 *SALJ* 321

Paizes, A "Public Opinion Polls and the Borders of Hearsay" (1983) 100 *SALJ* 71

Paizes, A *The Concept of Hearsay with Particular Emphasis on Implied Assertions* PhD Thesis Johannesburg University of the Witwatersrand 1983

Paizes, AP "Statements of Future Intention and the Res Gestae" (1985) 102 *SALJ* 258

Parmanand, SK "International Infliction of Emotional Distress – A Neglected Delict" (1984) 104 *SALJ* 171

Pauw, W *Observationes Tumultuariae Novae* Fischer et al (3 Vols) Haarlem Willink 1964–1972

Peckham, B "Some Thoughts on the Regulation of Hazardous Waste Disposal in South Africa" 1994 *SAJELP* 85

Peckius, P *Opera Omnia* Antwerpen 1666

Pengilley, PA "Machine Information: Is It Hearsay?" (1982) 13 *Melbourne University Law Review* 617

Petrie, JG, Burns, YM and Bray, W "Air Pollution" in Fuggle, RF and Rabie, MA (eds) *Environmental Management in South Africa* Cape Town Juta 1992

Phipson, SL *Phipson on Evidence* 12 ed Buzzard, May, Howard London Sweet & Maxwell 1976

Potgieter, JM "Delictual Liability for Intentional Infliction of Emotional Distress in South African Law" 1976 *Codicillus* I 11

Rabie, A "A Constitutional Right to Environmental Integrity: a German Perspective" (1991) 7 *SAJHR* 208

Rabie, A "A New Deal for Environmental Conservation: Aspects of the Environment Conservation Act 73 of 1989" (1990) 53 *THRHR* 2

Rabie, A "Codification of Environmental Law and the Environment Conservation Act" 1983 *De Rebus* 235

Rabie, A "Die Vereniging van Advokate (TPA) v Moskeeplein (Edms) Bpk 1982 3 SA 159 (T)" (1982) 45 *THRHR* 442

Rabie, A "Environmental Law in Search of an Identity" (1991) 2 *Stell LR* 202

Rabie, A "Legislation for the Rehabilitation of Mining Surfaces" (1991) 54 *THRHR* 774

Rabie, A "Report by the President's Council on a National Environmental Management System" (1992) 3 *Stell LR* 77

Rabie, A "South African Law Relating to Conservation Areas" (1985) 18 *CILSA* 51

Rabie, A "Strategies for the Implementation of Environmental Impact Assessment in South Africa" 1986 *SAPL* 18

Rabie, A "The Control of Advertisements Along Roads – An Environmental Perspective" 1987 *SAPL* 215

Rabie, A "The Environment Conservation Act and its Implementation" 1994 *SAJELP* 113

Rabie, MA "Appel deur Yskor Ingevolge die Wet op Voorkoming van Lugbesoedeling" (1974) 37 *THRHR* 186

Rabie, MA "Disclosure and Evaluation of Potential Environmental Impact of Proposed Governmental Administrative Action" (1976) 39 *THRHR* 40

Rabie, MA *South African Environmental Legislation* Pretoria Institute of Foreign and Comparative Law University of South Africa 1976

Rabie, MA "The Impact of Environmental Conservation on Land Ownership" 1985 *Acta Juridica* 289

Rabie, MA "The Influence of Environmental Conservation on Private Landownership" in Van der Walt, AJ (ed) *Land Reform and the Future of Landownership in South Africa* Cape Town Juta 1991

Rabie, MA "Wildlife Conservation and the Law" (1973) 6 *CILSA* 145

Rabie, MA and Fuggle, RF "The Rise of Environmental Concern" in Fuggle, RF and Rabie, MA (eds) *Environmental Management in South Africa* Cape Town Juta 1992

Rabie, MA and Lusher, JA "South African Marine Pollution Control Legislation" 1986 *Acta Juridica* 161

Rabie, MA and Van der Merwe, CG "Wildboerdery in Regsperspektief – Enkele Knelpunte" (1990) 1 *Stell LR* 112

Rabie, PJ *The Law of Estoppel in South Africa* Durban Butterworths 1992

Raney, SG "More Deficiencies in White Paper on the Environment" 1993 *De Rebus* 544

Reed, C "Authenticating Electronic Mail Messages – Some Evidential Problems" 1989 *Modern Law Review* 649

Reilly, AP *A Critical Analysis of the Environmental Controls in Force within the RSA with particular reference to Mine Dumps and the Legislation Applicable Thereto* LLM thesis Johannesburg University of Witwatersrand 1993

Report of the Planning Committee of the President's Council on Nature Conservation in South Africa Cape Town Government Printer 1984

Report of the Planning Committee of the President's Council on Priorities Between Conservation and Development Cape Town Government Printer 1984

Report of the Three Committees of the President's Council on a National Environmental Management System Cape Town Government Printer 1991

Schmidt, CWH *Bewysreg* 3 ed Durban Butterworths 1989

Schmidt, CWH "Laying the Foundation for a Defence of Sane Automatism" (1973) 90 *SALJ* 329

Scholtens, JE "Maintenance of Illegitimate Children and the Exceptio Pluriam Concubentium" (1955) 72 *SALJ* 144

Schorer, W *Aantekeninge op die Inleiding van De Groot* Middelburg 1784

Schroder, HHE "Noise Control Legislation" (1977) 10 *CILSA* 67

Schutte, F "Uitsluiting van Getuienis Ingevolge Artikel 35(5) van die Grondwet" (2000) 13 *SACJ* 57

Schutte, PJW "Aspekte van die Hoorsê Reël eooe Gewysig deur die Wysigingswet op die Bewysreg 45 van 1988" (1991) 54 *THRHR* 495

Schwella, E and Muller, JJ "Environmental Administration" in Fuggle, RF and Rabie, MA (eds) *Environmental Management in South Africa* Cape Town Juta 1992

Sher, H "Payments Made Under Mistake of Law" 1993 *JBL* 26

Silke, J *The Law of Agency in South Africa* 3 ed De Villiers Cape Town Juta 1981

Sklar, RB "Similar Fact Evidence – Catchwords and Cartwheels" 1977 *McGill Law Journal* 60

Smith, JC "The Admissibility of Statements by Computer" 1981 *Criminal Law Review* 387

Sonnekus, JC "Spolie van Waterverskaffing en die Passiwiteitsbeginsel" (1992) 55 *THRHR* 325

South Africa in Transition: Green Rights and an Environmental Management System: a collection of papers delivered and workshop held at a conference in Pretoria on 15 October 1993 Pretoria University of South Africa 1993

Stephen, Sir JF *A Digest of the Law of Evidence* 12 ed London MacMillan 1936

Stone, J "Cross-Examination by the Prosecution at Common Law and under the Criminal Evidence Act, 1898: a Commentary on Maxwell v Director of Public Prosecutions" 1935 *Law Quarterly Review* 443

Strauss, SA (ed) *Huldingsbundel vir WA Joubert: aan hom Aangebied by Geleentheid van sy Sewentigste Verjaarsdag op 27 Oktober 1988* Durban Butterworths 1988

Struwig, PJD "Evaluating the Evidence of the Child Witness – A Common Sense Approach" (2001) 64 *THRHR* 596

Tager, L "Nervous Shock and Mental Illness" (1973) 90 *SALJ* 123

Tager, L "Nervous Shock in South African Law" (1972) 89 *SALJ* 435

Terblanche, S "Privilegie teen Selfinkriminasie: 'n Tyd om weer te dink" (1994) 7 *SACJ* 177

The Situation of Waste Management and Pollution Control in South Africa Pretoria CSIR 1991

Tredoux, C and Pooley, S "Polygraph Based Testing of Deception and Truthfulness: An Evaluation and Commentary" 2001 *ILJ* 819

Van Bynkershoek, C *Observationes Tumultuariae* Meijers, De Blecourt, Bodenstein (4 Vols) Haarlem Tjeenk Willink 1926–1962

Van der Keessel, DG *Dictata ad Justiniani Institutionum* Beinart, Hijmans, Van Warmelo (2 Vols) Amsterdam Balkema 1965

Van der Keessel, DG *Praelectiones Iuris Hodierni ad Grotii* Van Warmelo, Coertze, Gonin, Pont Cape Town Balkema 1961–1967

Van der Keessel, DG *Theses Selectae Iuris Hollandici et Zelandici* Leiden Luchtmans 1800

Van der Linden, J *Rechtsgeleerd, Practicaal en Koopmans Handboek* Amsterdam Allart 1806

Van der Merwe, CG *Sakereg* Durban Butterworths 1979

Van der Merwe, CG and Rabie, MA "Eiendom van Wilde Diere" (1974) 37 *THRHR* 38

Van der Merwe, DP "Ontwikkelinge op die Raakvlak tussen Rekenaars en die Reg" (1991) 54 *THRHR* 95

Van der Merwe, S "The Constitutional Passive Defence Right of an Accused versus Prosecutorial and Judicial Comment on Silence: Must We Follow Griffin v California?" (1994) 15 *Obiter* 1

Van der Vyver, JD "Bester v Commercial Union Versekeringsmaatskappy van SA Bpk 1973 1 SA 769 (A)" (1973) 36 *THRHR* 169

Van der Vyver, JD "Die Swygreg van Kerkleraars" (1977) 40 *THRHR* 217

Van der Walt, AJ "The Effect of Environmental Conservation Measures on the Concept of Landownership" (1987) 104 *SALJ* 469

Van der Walt, AJ (ed) *Land Reform and the Future of Landownership in South Africa* Cape Town Juta 1991

Van der Walt, CFC "Hoe is die Aksie van Afhanklikes Afhanklik?" (1983) 46 *THRHR* 436

Van der Walt, JC "Die Condictio Indebiti as Verrykingsaksie" (1966) 29 *THRHR* 220

Van Heerden, HJO "Estoppel: 'n Wyse van Eiendomsverkryging?" (1970) 33 *THRHR* 19

Van Leeuwen, S *Censura Forensis, theoretico-practica* Leiden 1662

Van Leeuwen, S *Het Rooms-Hollandsch Recht* Rotterdam 1664

Van Niekerk, BJ "The Ecological Norm in Law or the Jurisprudence of the Fight Against Pollution" (1975) 92 *SALJ* 78

Van Niekerk, PJ "Metodologiese Probleme van die Regswetenskap as Voorvrae vir Regsvergelyking" (1991) 54 *THRHR* 485

Van Oven, JC *Leerboek van Romeinsch Privaatrecht* 3 ed Leiden E J Brill 1948

Van Reenen, TP "Environmental Policy-making and Effective Environmental Administration" 1994 *SAJELP* 35

Van Reenen, TP "Reflections on the Codification of South African Environmental Law (1) General Considerations" (1994) 5 *Stell LR* 214

Van Reenen, TP "Reflections on the Codification of South African Environmental Law (2) (1994) 5 *Stell LR* 331

Van Wyk, AJ "S v Klaasen 1978 (1) SA 355 (K)" (1978) 11 *De Jure* 181

Van Wyk, D (ed) *Rights and Constitutionalism: the New South African Legal Order* Cape Town Juta 1994

Van Zyl, DH *Die Saakwaarnemingsaksie in die Suid-Afrikaans Reg* PhD Thesis Leiden Rijksuniversiteit 1970

Van Zyl, DH *Negotiorum Gestio in South African Law: An Historical Comparative Analysis* PhD Thesis University of Cape Town 1983

Van Zyl, DH "The General Enrichment Action is Alive and Well" 1992 *Acta Juridica* 115

Verster, E, Du Plessis, W, Schloms, BHA and Fuggle RF "Soil" in Fuggle, RF and Rabie, MA (eds) *Environmental Management in South Africa* Cape Town Juta 1992

Viljoen, AJ "Green Rights and the Interim Constitution" in *South Africa in Transition: Green Rights and an Environmental Management System* Pretoria University of South Africa 1993

Vinnius, A *Commentarius in IV Libros Institutionum Imperialum* Leiden 1642

Vinnius, A *Selectarum Iuris Quaestionum Libri Duo* Leiden 1748

Visser, DP "Error of Law and Mistaken Payments: A Milestone" (1992) 109 *SALJ* 177

Visser, DP "Responsibility to Return Enrichment" 1992 *Acta Juridica* 175

Visser, DP "Unjustified Enrichment" 1991 *Annual Survey* 113

Visser, F "Nature Area Legislation in South Africa" (1988) 105 *SALJ* 249

Visser, PJ "Aanspreklikheid vir Senuskok na Ontvangs van 'n Nuusberig" 1977 *De Jure* 37

Visser, PJ "Estoppel en die Verkryging van die Eiendomsreg in Roerende Eiendom" (1994) 57 *THRHR* 633

Voet, J *Commentarius ad Pandectas* Den Haag De Hondt 1698–1704

Von Mayr, R *Die Condictio des Romischen Privatsrechtes* Liepzig Dunker & Humblot 1900

Wells, JD, van Meurs, LH and Rabie, MA "Terrestrial Minerals" in Fuggle, RF and Rabie, MA (eds) *Environmental Management in South Africa* Cape Town Juta 1992

Wessels, JW *The Law of Contract in South Africa* 2 ed Roberts Durban Butterworth 1951

Wigmore, JH *A Treatise on the Anglo-American System of Evidence in Trials in Common Law; including the Statutes and Judicial Decisions of all Jurisdictions of the United States and Canada* 3 ed Boston Little Brown and Co (10 Vols) 1940

Wigmore, JH *Evidence in Trials at Common Law* 4 ed Boston Little Brown (11 Vols) 1961–1988

Wille, G *Principles of South African Law* 8 ed Cape Town Juta 1991

Wille and Millin's Mercantile Law of South Africa see Millin, P and Wille, G

Williams, D "Green Rights: Section 29 of the Constitution" 1995 *De Rebus* 42

Williams, GL *The Proof of Guilt: A Study of the English Criminal Trial* 3 ed London Stevens 1963

Windscheid, B *Lehrbuch des Pandektenrechts* 9 Aulf Kipp Frankfurt am Main Rutten & Loening 1906

Winfield, PH *Winfield on Tort* 8 ed Jolowicz, Lewis London Sweet & Maxwell 1967

Winstanley, T *Entrenching Environmental Protection: An Analysis of Several Provisions of the Interim Constitution which affect Environmental Conservation and Some Proposals for a New Constitution* LLM Thesis University of Natal Durban 1995

Winstanley, T "Entrenching Environmental Protection in the New Constitution" 1995 *SAJELP* 85

Wiseman, K and Glazewski, JI *South African Law pertaining to the Causes and Effects of Pollution affecting Water Resources* Pretoria CSIR 1991

Zeffertt, D *Hoffmann and Zeffertt's The South African Law of Evidence* 4 ed Durban Butterworths 1988

Zeffertt, D "Issue Estoppel in South Africa" (1971) 88 *SALJ* 312

Zeffertt, D "Similar-fact Evidence in Criminal Proceedings" (1977) 94 *SALJ* 399

Zeffertt, D "Statements of Intention" (1974) 91 *SALJ* 425

Zeffert, D "The Rule in Hollington v Hewthorn Revisited" (1970) 87 *SALJ* 325

TABLE OF STATUTES

This table of statutes is arranged alphabetically under the short titles of the statutes.
References to pre-Union Acts, provincial Acts, provincial ordinances and foreign Acts follow after the
alphabetical table and are set out in chronological order. Rules of court follow at the end of the table.

TABLE OF CASES

H

PAR

INDEX

Emotional Shock

Energy

References are to paragraph numbers

References are to paragraph numbers

References are to paragraph numbers

References are to paragraph numbers

Enrichment

References are to paragraph numbers

Environmental Conservation

References are to paragraph numbers

References are to paragraph numbers

Environmental conservation
  access to information *see* Information
  atmosphere *see* Air pollution
  biodiversity protection *see* Biodiversity
    endangered ecosystems: treatment 255(r)
    protected species *see* Protected species
  constitutional requirement 252
  control of pesticides *see* Pesticides
  duty of care 273
  education regarding 255(h)
  expropriation for 297
  fauna *see* Wild animals
  flora *see* Indigenous plants
  for workers *see* Workplace environment
  harm done *see* Environmental damage
  hazardous substance control *see* Hazardous
    substances
    radioactive material *see* Radiation control
  in mining operations *see* Mining
  law *see* Environmental law
  noise pollution *see* Noise
  planning *see* Environmental management
  protected areas *see* Protected areas
  public health concerns *see* Public health
  soil conservation *see* Soil conservation
  territorial waters *see* Marine pollution
  threat from GMOs 356
  wastes *see* Waste management
  water *see* Water pollution

Environmental damage
  costs of remedying:
    awarded by court 288
    principle 255(p)
  criminal liability 320
  emergency incidents: control 275
  financial security against risk 265
    radiation damage 531
  from mining operations:
    financial provision 453
    remediation 455
    responsibility of rights holder 454
  nuclear damage *see* Radiation control
  prevention *see* Environmental management
  refusal to cause: workers' right 274
  remediation measures 273
    directions given for 318

Environmental impact assessment (EIA)
  purpose 255(i) 264(b)
  assessment practitioners: registration 270
  for activities requiring authorisation 264
    activities *see* Environmental management
    authorisation *see* Environmental authorisation
    report to competent authority 265 fn 1
  of mining operations 452
  review of assessment 271
  scope of assessment 265
  where damage has occurred 273(a)

Environmental justice
  meaning 255(c)
  equitable access to resources 255(d)

Environmental justice *continued*
  indigenous biological resource: benefit sharing
    357
  participation of affected parties 255(f)
  polluter pays principle 255(p)
  public interest cases *see* Legal proceedings

Environmental law
  generally 245
  administration of legislation 253
    co-ordinating body 257
    inter-governmental co-ordination 255(l)
      255(m)
    public servants contracted out for 300
    to be open and transparent 255(k)
  enforcement:
    admission of guilt fines 295
    by police 284
    management inspection *see* Inspectors
    through courts *see* Legal proceedings
    validity of irregular documents 304
  environment: *meaning* 246
  historical development:
    before 1940 249
    from 1940 to 1969 250
    from 1970 to 1994 251
    since 1994 252
  international *see* International conventions
  nature 248
  scope 247
  statutory measures:
    diverse nature 310
    partially repealed *see* Environment
      Conservation Act
    sustainable development 254 277

Environmental management
  administration:
    generally see Environmental law
    delivery of documents 307
    extension of time periods 306
    required consultation 305
    validity of notices 304
  agreements:
    department with organs of state 299
    management cooperation 296
  appeals to minister 302
  conflict management:
    inquiries and investigations 262
    intra-governmental disagreements 262
  harmful occurrences *see* Environmental damage
  integrated management:
    meaning 255(b)
    activities requiring authorisation 265
    notice listing or delisting activities 266
    objectives 264
  management and implementation plans:
    adoption and publication 260
    compliance monitoring 261
    content 259
    period for submission 258 fn 2
    preparation by organs of state 258
    submission to Committee 260

References are to paragraph numbers

References are to paragraph numbers

References are to paragraph numbers

References are to paragraph numbers

References are to paragraph numbers

Estate Agents

Estoppel

References are to paragraph numbers

References are to paragraph numbers

Evidence

References are to paragraph numbers

References are to paragraph numbers

References are to paragraph numbers

References are to paragraph numbers